CORNELL STUDIES IN CIVIL LIBERTY

First Amendment Freedoms

SELECTED CASES ON FREEDOM OF
RELIGION, SPEECH, PRESS, ASSEMBLY

BOOKS BY MILTON R. KONVITZ

On the Nature of Value

The Alien and the Asiatic in American Law

The Constitution and Civil Rights

Civil Rights in Immigration

Fundamental Liberties of a Free People

A Century of Civil Rights
(with Theodore Leskes)

EDITOR OF

Freedom and Experience
(with Sidney Hook)

Essays in Political Theory
(with Arthur E. Murphy)

Law and Social Action
by Alexander H. Pekelis

Education for Freedom and Responsibility
by Edmund Ezra Day

Liberian Code of Laws

Liberian Law Reports

Aspects of Liberty
(with Clinton Rossiter)

Bill of Rights Reader:
Leading Constitutional Cases

The American Pragmatists
(with Gail Kennedy)

Emerson: A Collection of Critical Essays
(with Stephen E. Whicher)

First Amendment Freedoms:
Selected Cases on Freedom of Religion,
Speech, Press, Assembly

First Amendment
FREEDOMS

Selected Cases on Freedom of Religion,
Speech, Press, Assembly

MILTON R. KONVITZ

★

Cornell University Press

ITHACA, NEW YORK

© 1963 by Cornell University

CORNELL UNIVERSITY PRESS

This book is based in part on the author's
Bill of Rights Reader: Leading Constitutional Cases,
first and second editions, copyrighted in 1954 and 1960.

First published 1963

JK
1726
.K677

Library of Congress Catalog Card Number: 63-18091

PRINTED IN THE UNITED STATES OF AMERICA

For my Mother

For everything there is a substitute
except the mother of one's youth.

Alma College Library
Alma, Michigan

Preface

THE first edition of my *Bill of Rights Reader: Leading Constitutional Cases* (1954) was a book slightly under six hundred pages. The second edition (1960), which omitted two cases from the first edition and included twenty-five new ones, grew to 850 pages. In the spring of 1963, when the third edition was being prepared, it soon became apparent that the book would reach the monstrous figure of fifteen hundred pages. This would have been out of the question, as to both bulk and price, for a serviceable textbook. The number of pages now needed for the First Amendment cases alone is substantially more than the whole of the second edition. In the face of this problem the publisher and the author decided that the time had come to divide the material into at least two separate books, planned so that each could stand independently of the other. This is the first book. The second will be devoted to cases on civil and political rights. There may be a third book, dealing with personal security and presenting cases such as now appear in Parts II and IX of the *Bill of Rights Reader*.

All this artifice in editing and publishing has been made necessary by one of the most significant developments in American political, moral, and social life, namely, the concentration in the United States Supreme Court—and in other courts also, but to a lesser degree—of cases dealing with the meaning and scope of the Bill of Rights. The stone which the builders of the original constitutional structure had disregarded has become the cornerstone, and that branch of the Federal Government which had been thought to be least important has come into a life that is full of vitality and drama. An appointment to the Supreme Court can no longer be thought of as a shelter from the wind: it requires men who have in their hearts the courage of entire battalions of soldiers.

The change in our estimate of the Bill of Rights derives from many causes, some of them objective and three-dimensional. This is not the place to discuss such a complex matter, but I would like to mention one generating factor of immeasurable importance: the dynamic and creative work of organizations like the American Civil Liberties Union, the National Association for the Advancement of Colored People, the American Jewish Congress, the American Jewish Committee, and the Workers Defense League. They have been moving forces in the judicial proceedings. One day the scholars who will write our political, social, and intellectual histories will find it necessary to devote many pages to the work of these agencies—to their lawyers and executive officers as well as to the lay leaders who give moral and financial support— and these pages will be among the most interesting and gratifying in the histories.

I have permitted myself to name these organizations here because I am ever aware of my personal debt to them; every American should feel equally indebted to them.

M. R. K.

Cornell University
June 18, 1963

Contents

Table of Cases

First Amendment Freedoms

SELECTED CASES ON FREEDOM OF
RELIGION, SPEECH, PRESS, ASSEMBLY

Freedom of Religion

1. *Freedom to Believe and Freedom to Act*

REYNOLDS *v.* UNITED STATES

98 US 145 (1878)

[The Constitution permits unlimited freedom of religious belief. There may be few absolutes in constitutional law, but freedom of religious belief is such an absolute.

[When it comes, however, to acting out one's belief, religious belief will not always exempt one from the provisions of the criminal law. The state may punish a person who handles a live copperhead snake even if he does this in the course of a religious or church service. *Bunn* v. *North Carolina*, 336 US 942 (1949), dismissing appeal of *State* v. *Massey*, 229 NC 734.

[For Mormons, polygamous marriages were at one time a religious duty. When Utah was a Territory, Congress enacted a statute making polygamy a criminal offense. This led to the *Reynolds Case* in the Supreme Court, which at once became a leading case. The opinion of Chief Justice Waite has often been cited and quoted. His opinion is notable also for his quotation from Jefferson's famous wall-of-separation letter, which was used effectively by the Court some seventy years later in the *Everson Case*, which is given later in this chapter.]

Mr. Chief Justice Waite delivered the opinion of the Court:

This is an indictment for bigamy under Section 5352, Revised Statutes, which, omitting its exceptions, is as follows: "Every person having a husband or wife living, who marries another, whether married or single, in a Territory, or other place over which the United States have exclusive jurisdiction, is guilty of bigamy, and shall be punished by a fine of not more than $500, and by imprisonment for a term of not more than five years." . . .

On the trial, the plaintiff in error, the accused, proved that at the time of his alleged second marriage he was, and for many years before had been, a member of the Church of Jesus Christ of Latter-Day Saints, commonly called the Mormon Church, and a believer in its doctrines; that it was an accepted doctrine of that church "That it was the duty of male members of said Church, circumstances permitting, to practice polygamy: . . . that this duty was enjoined by different books which the members of said Church believed to be of divine origin, and among others the Holy Bible, and also that the members of the Church believed that the practice of polygamy was directly enjoined upon the male members thereof by the Almighty God, in a revelation to Joseph Smith, the founder and prophet of said Church; that the failing or refusing to practice polygamy by such male members of said Church, when circumstances would admit, would be punished, and that the penalty for such failure and refusal would be damnation in the life to come." He also proved "That he had received permission from the recognized authorities in said Church to enter into polygamous marriage; . . . that Daniel H. Wells, one having authority in said Church to perform the marriage ceremony, married the said defendant on or about the time the crime is alleged to have been committed, to some woman by the name of Schofield, and that such marriage ceremony was performed under and pursuant to the doctrines of said Church."

Upon this proof he asked the court to instruct the jury that if they found from the evidence that he "was married as charged (if he was married) in pursuance of and in conformity with what he believed at the time to be religious duty, that the verdict must be 'not guilty.'" This request was refused, and the court did charge "That there must have been a criminal intent, but that if the defendant, under the influence of a religious belief that it was right—under an inspiration, if you please, that it was right—deliberately married a second time, having a first wife living, the want of consciousness of evil intent, the want of understanding on his part that he was committing a crime, did not excuse him; but the law inexorably in such case implies the criminal intent."

Upon this charge and refusal to charge the question is raised, whether religious belief can be accepted as a justification of an overt act made criminal by the law of the land. The inquiry is not as to the power of Congress to prescribe criminal laws for the Territories, but as to the guilt of one who knowingly violates a law which has been properly enacted, if he entertains a religious belief that the law is wrong.

Congress cannot pass a law for the government of the Territories which shall prohibit the free exercise of religion. The first amendment to the Constitution expressly forbids such legislation. Religious freedom is guarantied everywhere throughout the United States, so far as congressional interference is concerned. The question to be determined is, whether the law now under consideration comes within this prohibition.

The word "religion" is not defined in the Constitution. We must go elsewhere, therefore, to ascertain its meaning, and nowhere more appropriately, we think, than to the history of the times in the midst of which the provision was adopted. The precise point of the inquiry is, what is the religious freedom which has been guarantied?

Before the adoption of the Constitution, attempts were made in some of the Colonies and States to legislate not only in respect to the establishment of religion, but in respect to its doctrines and precepts as well. The people were taxed, against their will, for the support of religion, and sometimes for the support of particular sects to whose tenets they could not and did not subscribe. Punishments were prescribed for a failure to attend upon public worship, and sometimes for entertaining heretical opinions. The controversy upon this general subject was animated in many of the States, but seemed at last to culminate in Virginia. In 1784, the House of Delegates of that State having under consideration "A bill establishing provision for teachers of the Christian religion," postponed it until the next session, and directed that the bill should be published and distributed, and that the People be requested "to signify their opinion respecting the adoption of such a bill at the next session of Assembly."

This brought out a determined opposition. Amongst others, Mr. Madison prepared a "Memorial and Remonstrance," which was widely circulated and signed, and in which he demonstrated "that religion, or the duty we owe the Creator," was not within the cognizance of civil government. At the next session the proposed bill was not only defeated, but another, "for establishing religious freedom," drafted by Mr. Jefferson, was passed. In the preamble of this Act religious freedom is defined; and after a recital "That to suffer the civil magistrate to intrude his powers into the field of opinion, and to restrain the profession or propagation of principles on supposition of their ill tendency, is a dangerous fallacy which at once destroys all religious liberty," it is declared "that it is time enough for the rightful purposes of civil government for its officers to interfere when principles break out into overt acts against peace and good order." In these two sentences is found the true distinction between what properly belongs to the Church and what to the State.

In a little more than a year after the passage of this statute the convention met which prepared the Constitution of the United States. Of this convention Mr. Jefferson was not a member, he being then absent as minister to France. As soon as he saw the draft of the Constitution proposed for adoption, he, in a letter to a friend, expressed his disappointment at the absence of an express declaration insuring the freedom of religion, but was willing to accept it as it was, trusting that the good sense and honest intentions of the people would bring about the necessary alterations. Five of the States, while adopting the Constitution, proposed amendments. Three, New Hampshire, New York and Virginia, included in one form or another a declaration of religious freedom in the changes they desired to have made, as did also North Carolina, where the convention at first declined to ratify the Constitution until the proposed amendments were acted upon. Accordingly, at the first session of the first Congress the amendment now under consideration was proposed with others by Mr. Madison. It met the views of the advocates of religious freedom, and was adopted. Mr. Jefferson afterwards, in reply to an address to him by a committee of the Danbury Baptist Association, took occasion to say: "Believing with you that religion is a matter which lies solely between man and his God; that he owes account to none other for his faith or his worship; that the legislative powers of the Government reach actions only, and not opinions, I contemplate with sovereign reverence that act of the whole American people which declared that their Legislature should 'make no law respecting an establishment of religion or prohibiting the free exercise thereof,' thus building a wall of separation between Church and State. Adhering to this expression of the Supreme will of the Nation in behalf of the rights of conscience, I shall see, with sincere satisfaction, the progress of those sentiments which tend to restore man to all his natural rights, convinced he has no natural right in opposition to his social duties." Coming as this does from an acknowledged leader of the advocates of the measure, it may be accepted almost as an authoritative declaration of the scope and effect of the amendment thus secured. Congress was deprived of all legislative power over mere opinion, but was left free to reach actions which were in violation of social duties or subversive of good order.

Polygamy has always been odious among the Northern and Western Nations of Europe and, until the establishment of the Mormon Church, was almost exclusively a feature of the life of Asiatic and African people. At common law, the second marriage was always void, and from the earliest history of England polygamy has been treated as an offense against society. After the establishment of the ecclesiastical courts, and until the time of James I., it was punished through the instrumentality of those tribunals, not merely because ecclesiastical rights had been violated, but because upon the separation of the ecclesiastical courts from the civil, the ecclesiastical were supposed to be the most appropriate for the trial of matrimonial causes and offenses against the rights of marriage; just as they were for testamentary causes and the settlement of the estates of deceased persons.

By the Statute of 1 James I., ch. 11, the offense, if committed in England or Wales, was made punishable in the civil courts, and the penalty was death. As this statute was limited in its operation to England and Wales, it was at a very early period re-enacted, generally with some modifications, in all the Colonies. In connection with the case we are now considering, it is a significant fact that on the 8th of December, 1788, after the passage of the Act establishing religious freedom, and after the convention of Virginia had recommended as an amendment to the Constitution of the United States the declaration in a Bill of Rights that "All men have an equal, natural and unalienable right to the free exercise of religion, according to the dictates of conscience," the Legislature of that State substantially enacted the Statute of James I., death penalty included, because as recited in the preamble, "It hath been doubted whether bigamy or polygamy be punishable by the laws of this Commonwealth." From that day to this we think it may safely be said there never has been a time in any State of the Union when polygamy has not been an offense against society, cognizable by the civil courts and punishable with more or less severity. In the face of all this evidence, it is impossible to believe that the constitutional guaranty of religious freedom was intended to prohibit legislation in respect to this most important feature of social life. Marriage, while from its very nature a sacred obligation, is, nevertheless, in most civilized nations, a civil contract, and usually regulated by law. . . . There cannot be a doubt that, unless restricted by some form of constitution, it is within the legitimate scope of the power of every civil government to determine whether polygamy or monogamy shall be the law of social life under its dominion.

In our opinion the statute immediately under consideration is within the legislative power of Congress. It is constitutional and valid as prescribing a rule of action for all those residing in the Territories, and in places over which the United States have exclusive control. This being so, the only question which remains is, whether those who make polygamy a part of their religion are excepted from the operation of the statute. If they are, then those who do not make polygamy a part of their religious belief may be found guilty and punished, while those who do must be acquitted and go free. This would be introducing a new element into criminal law. Laws are made for the government of actions, and while they cannot interfere with mere religious belief and opinions, they may with practices. Suppose one believed that human sacrifices were a necessary part of religious worship, would it be seriously contended that the civil government under which he lived could not interfere to prevent a sacrifice? Or if a wife religiously believed it was her duty to burn herself upon the funeral pile of her dead husband, would it be beyond the power of the civil government to prevent her carrying her belief into practice?

So here, as a law of the organization of society under the exclusive dominion of the United States, it is provided that plural marriages shall not be allowed. Can a man excuse his practices to the contrary because of his religious belief? To permit this would be to make the professed doctrines of religious belief superior to the law of the land, and in effect to permit every citizen to become a law unto himself. Government could exist only in name under such circumstances.

A criminal intent is generally an element of crime, but every man is presumed to intend the necessary and legitimate consequences of what he knowingly does. Here the accused knew he had been once married, and that his first wife was living. He also knew that his second marriage was forbidden by law. When, therefore, he married the second time, he is presumed to have intended to break the law. And the breaking of the law is the crime. Every act necessary to constitute the crime was knowingly done, and the crime was, therefore, knowingly committed. Ignorance of a fact may sometimes be taken as evidence of a want of criminal intent, but not ignorance of the law. The only defense of the accused in this case is his belief that the law ought not to have been enacted. It matters not that his belief was a part of his professed religion; it was still belief, and belief only.

In *Regina* v. *Wagstaffe,* 10 Cox, Cr. Cas., 531, the parents of a sick child, who omitted to call in medical attendance because of their religious belief that what they did for its cure would be effective, were held not to be guilty of manslaughter, while it was said the contrary would have been the result if the child had actually been starved to death by the parents, under the notion that it was their religious duty to abstain from giving it food. But when the offense consists of a positive act which is knowingly done, it would be dangerous to hold that the offender might escape punishment because he religiously believed the law which he had broken ought never to have been made. No case, we believe, can be found that has gone so far. . . .

[Judgment of conviction affirmed.]

2. *Wall of Separation between Church and State*

a. Bus Fares for Parochial School Pupils

EVERSON *v.* BOARD OF EDUCATION OF TOWNSHIP OF
EWING

330 US 1 (1947)

[In the preceding case, *Reynolds* v. *United States,* the Supreme Court quoted from Jefferson's wall-of-separation letter, but this was done only in passing. In the *Everson Case,* however, the Supreme Court for the first time spelled out the doctrine of the separation of church and state and held that the First Amendment clause against an establishment of religion was intended to erect, in Jefferson's words, "a wall of separation between Church and State." The Court also held that this meaning and intention of the First Amendment apply to both the Federal Government and the states.

[With respect to these issues there was unanimity in the Court; four Justices, however—Jackson, Frankfurter, Rutledge, and Burton—held that the majority of the Court were in error when they decided that the wall of separation had not been breached when tax money was used to reimburse parents for the transportation by bus of their children to and from Roman Catholic parochial schools. Such use of public money, said the dissenting Justices, is a violation by the state of the provision of the First Amendment that no law shall be made "respecting an establishment of religion."

[This decision was sharply attacked by the Roman Catholic bishops of the United States in a public statement published on November 21, 1948. The statement argued that Jefferson's "metaphor" specifies only that there shall be no "established Church," no state religion; that the First Amendment means only that the Federal Government may not prefer one religion over another; that this amendment is no limitation on the powers of the states; that the decision pointed up the "impending danger of a judicial 'establishment of secularism' that would ban God from public life."

[Much use has been made of the decision of the Court and of the attacks on the decision in the controversy over congressional bills to use federal funds to aid elementary and secondary education—a controversy that has often agitated and divided the American people.]

Mr. Justice Black delivered the opinion of the Court:

A New Jersey statute authorizes its local school districts to make rules and contracts for the transportation of children to and from schools. The appellee, a township board of education, acting pursuant to this statute, authorized reimbursement to parents of money expended by them for the bus transportation of their children on regular busses operated by the public transportation system. Part of this money was for the payment of transportation of some children in the community to Catholic parochial schools. These church schools give their students, in addition to secular education, regular religious instruction conforming to the religious tenets and modes of worship of the Catholic faith. The superintendent of these schools is a Catholic priest.

The appellant, in his capacity as a district taxpayer, filed suit in a State court challenging the right of the Board to reimburse parents of parochial school students. . . .

The only contention here is that the State statute and the resolution, insofar as they authorized reimbursement to parents of children attending parochial schools, violate the Federal Constitution. . . .

The New Jersey statute is challenged as a "law respecting the establishment of religion." The First Amendment, as made applicable to the states by the Fourteenth, . . . commands that a state "shall make no law respecting an establishment of religion, or prohibiting the free exercise thereof." . . . These words of the First Amendment reflected in the minds of early Americans a vivid mental picture of conditions and practices which they fervently wished to stamp out in order to preserve liberty for themselves and for their posterity. Doubtless their goal has not been entirely reached; but so far has the Nation moved toward it that the expression, "law respecting the establishment of religion," probably does not so vividly remind present-day Americans of the evils, fears, and political problems that caused that expression to be written into our Bill of Rights. Whether this New Jersey law is one respecting an "establishment of religion" requires an understanding of the meaning of that language, particularly with respect to the imposition of taxes. Once again, therefore, it is not inappropriate briefly to review the background and environment of the period in which that constitutional language was fashioned and adopted.

A large proportion of the early settlers of this country came here from Europe to escape the bondage of laws which compelled them to support and attend government favored churches. The centuries immediately before and contemporaneous with the colonization of America had been filled with turmoil, civil strife, and persecutions, generated in large part by established sects determined to maintain their absolute political and religious supremacy. With the power of government supporting them, at various times and places, Catholics had persecuted Protestants, Protestants had persecuted Catholics, Protestant sects had persecuted other Protestant sects, Catholics of one shade of belief had persecuted Catholics of another shade of belief, and all of these had from time to time persecuted Jews. In efforts to force loyalty to whatever religious group happened to be on top and in league with the government of a particular time and place, men and women had been fined, cast in jail, cruelly tortured, and killed. Among the offenses for which these punishments had been inflicted were such things as speaking disrespectfully of the views of ministers of government-established churches, non-attendance at those churches, expressions of non-belief in their doctrine, and failure to pay taxes and tithes to support them.

These practices of the old world were transplanted to and began to thrive in the soil of the new America. The very charters granted by the English Crown to the individuals and companies designated to make the laws which would control the destinies of the colonials authorized these individuals and companies to erect religious establishments which all, whether believers or nonbelievers, would be required to support and attend. An exercise of this authority was accompanied by a repetition of many of the old-world practices and persecutions. Catholics found themselves hounded and proscribed because of their faith; Quakers who followed their conscience went to jail; Baptists were peculiarly obnoxious to certain dominant Protestant sects; men and women of varied faiths who happened to be in a minority in a particular locality were persecuted because they steadfastly persisted in worshipping God only as their own consciences dictated. And all of these dissenters were compelled to pay tithes and taxes to support government-sponsored churches whose ministers preached inflammatory sermons designed to strengthen and consolidate the established faith by generating a burning hatred against dissenters.

These practices became so commonplace as to shock the freedom-loving colonials into a feeling of abhorrence. The imposition of taxes to pay ministers' salaries and to build and maintain churches and church property aroused their indignation. It was these feelings which found expression in the First Amendment. No one locality and no one group throughout the Colonies can rightly be given entire credit for having aroused the sentiment that culminated in adoption of the Bill of Rights' provisions embracing religious liberty. But Virginia, where the established church had achieved a dominant influence in political affairs and where many excesses attracted wide public attention, provided a great stimulus and able leadership for the movement. The

people there, as elsewhere, reached the conviction that individual religious liberty could be achieved best under a government which was
stripped of all power to tax, to support, or otherwise to assist any or
all religions, or to interfere with the beliefs of any religious individual
or group.

The movement toward this end reached its dramatic climax in Virginia in 1785-86 when the Virginia legislative body was about to renew
Virginia's tax levy for the support of the established church. Thomas
Jefferson and James Madison led the fight against this tax. Madison
wrote his great Memorial and Remonstrance against the law. In it, he
eloquently argued that a true religion did not need the support of law;
that no person, either believer or non-believer, should be taxed to
support a religious institution of any kind; that the best interest of a
society required that the minds of men always be wholly free; and that
cruel persecutions were the inevitable result of government-established
religions. Madison's Remonstrance received strong support throughout
Virginia, and the Assembly postponed consideration of the proposed
tax measure until its next session. When the proposal came up for consideration at that session, it not only died in committee, but the Assembly enacted the famous "Virginia Bill for Religious Liberty" originally
written by Thomas Jefferson. The preamble to that Bill stated among
other things that

Almighty God hath created the mind free; that all attempts to influence it by
temporal punishments or burthens, or by civil incapacitations, tend only to
beget habits of hypocrisy and meanness, and are a departure from the plan
of the Holy author of our religion, who being Lord both of body and mind,
yet chose not to propagate it by coercions on either . . . ; that to compel
a man to furnish contributions of money for the propagation of opinions which
he disbelieves, is sinful and tyrannical; that even the forcing him to support
this or that teacher of his own religious persuasion, is depriving him of the
comfortable liberty of giving his contributions to the particular pastor, whose
morals he would make his pattern. . . .

And the statute itself enacted

That no man shall be compelled to frequent or support any religious worship, place, or ministry whatsoever, nor shall be enforced, restrained, molested,
or burthened in his body or goods, nor shall otherwise suffer on account of his
religious opinions or belief. . . .

This Court has previously recognized that the provisions of the
First Amendment, in the drafting and adoption of which Madison and
Jefferson played such leading roles, had the same objective and were
intended to provide the same protection against governmental intrusion on religious liberty as the Virginia statute. . . . Prior to the

adoption of the Fourteenth Amendment, the First Amendment did not apply as a restraint against the states. Most of them did soon provide similar constitutional protections for religious liberty. But some states persisted for about half a century in imposing restraints upon the free exercise of religion and in discriminating against particular religious group[s]. In recent years, so far as the provision against the establishment of a religion is concerned, the question has most frequently arisen in connection with proposed state aid to church schools and efforts to carry on religious teachings in the public schools in accordance with the tenets of a particular sect. Some churches have either sought or accepted state financial support for their schools. Here again the efforts to obtain state aid or acceptance of it have not been limited to any one particular faith. The state courts, in the main, have remained faithful to the language of their own constitutional provisions designed to protect religious freedom and to separate religions and governments. Their decisions, however, show the difficulty in drawing the line between tax legislation which provides funds for the welfare of the general public and that which is designed to support institutions which teach religion.

The meaning and scope of the First Amendment, preventing establishment of religion or prohibiting the free exercise thereof, in the light of its history and the evils it was designed forever to suppress, have been several times elaborated by the decisions of this Court prior to the application of the First Amendment to the states by the Fourteenth. The broad meaning given the Amendment by these earlier cases has been accepted by this Court in its decisions concerning an individual's religious fredom rendered since the Fourteenth Amendment was interpreted to make the prohibitions of the First applicable to state action abridging religious freedom. There is every reason to give the same application and broad interpretation to the "establishment of religion" clause. . . .

The "establishment of religion" clause of the First Amendment means at least this: Neither a state nor the Federal Government can set up a church. Neither can pass laws which aid one religion, aid all religions, or prefer one religion over another. Neither can force nor influence a person to go to or to remain away from church against his will or force him to profess a belief or disbelief in any religion. No person can be punished for entertaining or professing religious beliefs or disbeliefs, for church attendance or non-attendance. No tax in any amount, large or small, can be levied to support any religious activities or institutions, whatever they may be called, or whatever form they may adopt to teach or practice religion. Neither a state nor the Federal Government can, openly or secretly, participate in the affairs of any religious organizations or groups and vice versa. In the words of Jefferson, the clause against establishment of religion by law was intended to erect "a wall of separation between Church and State." . . .

We must consider the New Jersey statute in accordance with the foregoing limitations imposed by the First Amendment. But we must not strike that state statute down if it is within the State's constitutional power even though it approaches the verge of that power. . . . New Jersey cannot consistently with the "establishment of religion" clause of the First Amendment contribute tax-raised funds to the support of an institution which teaches the tenets and faith of any church. On the other hand, other language of the amendment commands that New Jersey cannot hamper its citizens in the free exercise of their own religion. Consequently, it cannot exclude individual Catholics, Lutherans, Mohammedans, Baptists, Jews, Methodists, Non-believers, Presbyterians, or the members of any other faith, *because of their faith, or lack of it,* from receiving the benefits of public welfare legislation. While we do not mean to intimate that a state could not provide transportation only to children attending public schools, we must be careful, in protecting the citizens of New Jersey against state-established churches, to be sure that we do not inadvertently prohibit New Jersey from extending its general state law benefits to all its citizens without regard to their religious belief.

Measured by these standards, we cannot say that the First Amendment prohibits New Jersey from spending tax-raised funds to pay the bus fares of parochial school pupils as a part of a general program under which it pays the fares of pupils attending public and other schools. It is undoubtedly true that children are helped to get to church schools. There is even a possibility that some of the children might not be sent to the church schools if the parents were compelled to pay [for] their children going to and from church [schools out of their own] pockets when transportation to a public school would have been paid for by the State. The same possibility exists where the state requires a local transit company to provide reduced fares to school children including those attending parochial schools, or where a municipally owned transportation system undertakes to carry all school children free of charge. Moreover, state-paid policemen, detailed to protect children going to and from church schools from the very real hazards of traffic, would serve much the same purpose and accomplish much the same result as state provisions intended to guarantee free transportation of a kind which the state deems to be best for the school children's welfare. And parents might refuse to risk their children to the serious danger of traffic accidents going to and from parochial schools, the approaches to which were not protected by policemen.

Similarly, parents might be reluctant to permit their children to attend schools which the state had cut off from such general government services as ordinary police and fire protection, connections for sewage disposal, public highways and sidewalks. Of course, cutting off church schools from these services, so separate and so indisputably marked off from the religious function, would make it far more difficult for the schools to operate. But such is obviously not the purpose of the First Amendment. That Amendment requires the state to be a neutral in its relations with groups of religious believers and non-believers; it does not require the state to be their adversary. State power is no more to be used so as to handicap religions than it is to favor them.

This Court has said that parents may, in the discharge of their duty under state compulsory education laws, send their children to a religious rather than a public school if the school meets the secular educational requirements which the state has power to impose. . . . It appears that these parochial schools meet New Jersey's requirements. The State contributes no money to the schools. It does not support them. Its legislation, as applied, does no more than provide a general program to help parents get their children, regardless of their religion, safely and expeditiously to and from accredited schools.

The First Amendment has erected a wall between church and state. That wall must be kept high and impregnable. We could not approve the slightest breach. New Jersey has not breached it here.

Affirmed.

Mr. Justice Jackson, dissenting:

I find myself, contrary to first impressions, unable to join in this decision. I have a sympathy, though it is not ideological, with Catholic citizens who are compelled by law to pay taxes for public schools, and also feel constrained by conscience and discipline to support other schools for their own children. Such relief to them as this case involves is not in itself a serious burden to taxpayers and I had assumed it to be as little serious in principle. Study of this case convinces me otherwise. The Court's opinion marshals every argument in favor of state aid and puts the case in its most favorable light, but much of its reasoning confirms my conclusions that there are no good grounds upon which to support the present legislation. In fact, the undertones of the opinion, advocating complete and uncompromising separation of Church from State, seem utterly discordant with its conclusion yielding support to their commingling in educational matters. The case which irresistibly comes to mind as the most fitting precedent is that of Julia who, according to Byron's reports, "whispering 'I will ne'er consent,'—consented."

The Township of Ewing is not furnishing transportation to the children in any form; it is not operating school busses itself or contracting for their operation; and it is not performing any public service of any kind with this taxpayer's money. All school children are left to ride as ordinary paying passengers on the regular busses operated by the public transportation system. What the Township does, and what the taxpayer complains of, is at stated intervals to reimburse parents for the fares paid, provided the children attend either public schools or Catholic Church schools. This expenditure of tax funds has no possible effect on the child's safety or expedition in transit. As passengers on the public busses they travel as fast and no faster, and are as safe and no safer, since their parents are reimbursed as before. . . .

Whether the taxpayer constitutionally can be made to contribute aid to parents of students because of their attendance at parochial schools depends upon the nature of those schools and their relation to the Church. The Constitution says nothing of education. It lays no obligation on the states to provide schools and does not undertake to regulate state systems of education if they see fit to maintain them. But they cannot, through school policy any more than through other means, invade rights secured to citizens by the Constitution of the United States. . . . One of our basic rights is to be free of taxation to support a transgression of the constitutional command that the authorities "shall make no law respecting an establishment of religion, or prohibiting the free exercise thereof." . . .

The function of the Church school is a subject on which this record is meager. It shows only that the schools are under superintendence of a priest and that "religion is taught as part of the curriculum." But we know that such schools are parochial only in name—they, in fact, represent a world-wide and age-old policy of the Roman Catholic Church. Under the rubric "Catholic Schools," the Canon Law of the Church, by which all Catholics are bound, provides:

1215. Catholic children are to be educated in schools where not only nothing contrary to Catholic faith and morals is taught, but rather in schools where religious and moral training occupy the first place. . . .

1216. In every elementary school the children must, according to their age, be instructed in Christian doctrine.

The young people who attend the higher schools are to receive a deeper religious knowledge, and the bishops shall appoint priests qualified for such work by their learning and piety.

1217. Catholic children shall not attend non-Catholic, indifferent, schools that are mixed, that is to say, schools open to Catholics and non-Catholics alike. The bishop of the diocese only has the right, in harmony with the instructions of the Holy See, to decide under what circumstances, and with what safeguards to prevent loss of faith, it may be tolerated that Catholic children go to such schools.

1224. The religious teaching of youth in any school is subject to the authority and inspection of the Church.

The local Ordinaries have the right and duty to watch that nothing is taught contrary to faith or good morals, in any of the schools of their territory.

They, moreover, have the right to approve the books of Christian doctrine and the teachers of religion, and to demand, for the sake of safeguarding religion and morals, the removal of teachers and books. . . .

It is no exaggeration to say that the whole historic conflict in temporal policy between the Catholic Church and non-Catholics comes to a focus in their respective school policies. The Roman Catholic Church, counseled by experience in many ages and many lands and with all sorts and conditions of men, takes what, from the viewpoint of its own progress and the success of its mission, is a wise estimate of the importance of education to religion. It does not leave the individual to pick up religion by chance. It relies on early and indelible indoctrination in the faith and order of the Church by the word and example of persons consecrated to the task.

Our public school, if not a product of Protestantism, at least is more consistent with it than with the Catholic culture and scheme of values. It is a relatively recent development dating from about 1840. It is organized on the premises that secular education can be isolated from all religious teaching so that the school can inculcate all needed temporal knowledge and also maintain a strict and lofty neutrality as to religion. The assumption is that after the individual has been instructed in worldly wisdom he will be better fitted to choose his religion. Whether such a disjunction is possible, and if possible whether it is wise, are questions I need not try to answer.

I should be surprised if any Catholic would deny that the parochial school is a vital, if not the most vital, part of the Roman Catholic Church. If put to the choice, that venerable institution, I should expect, would forego its whole service for mature persons before it would give up education of the young, and it would be a wise choice. Its growth and cohesion, discipline and loyalty, spring from its schools. Catholic education is the rock on which the whole structure rests, and to render tax aid to its Church school is indistinguishable to me from rendering the same aid to the Church itself.

It is of no importance in this situation whether the beneficiary of this expenditure of tax-raised funds is primarily the parochial school and incidentally the pupil, or whether the aid is directly bestowed on the pupil with indirect benefits to the school. The state cannot maintain a Church and it can no more tax its citizens to furnish free carriage to those who attend a Church. The prohibition against establishment of religion cannot be circumvented by a subsidy, bonus or reimbursement of expense to individuals for receiving religious instruction and indoctrination.

The Court, however, compares this to other subsidies and loans to individuals and says, "Nor does it follow that a law has a private rather than a public purpose because it provides that tax-raised funds will be paid to reimburse individuals on account of money spent by them in a way which furthers a public program. . . ." Of course, the state may pay out tax-raised funds to relieve pauperism, but it may not under our Constitution do so to induce or reward piety. It may spend funds to secure old age against want, but it may not spend funds to secure religion against skepticism. It may compensate

individuals for loss of employment, but it cannot compensate them for adherence to a creed.

It seems to me that the basic fallacy in the Court's reasoning, which accounts for its failure to apply the principles it avows, is in ignoring the essentially religious test by which beneficiaries of this expenditure are selected.
A policeman protects a Catholic, of course—but not because he is a Catholic;
it is because he is a man and a member of our society. The fireman protects
the Church school—but not because it is a Church school; it is because it is
property, part of the assets of our society. Neither the fireman nor the policeman has to ask before he renders aid "Is this man or building identified with
the Catholic Church?" But before these school authorities draw a check to
reimburse for a student's fare they must ask just that question, and if the
school is a Catholic one they may render aid because it is such, while if
it is of any other faith or is run for profit, the help must be withheld. To
consider the converse of the Court's reasoning will best disclose its fallacy.
That there is no parallel between police and fire protection and this plan of
reimbursement is apparent from the incongruity of the limitation of this Act
if applied to police and fire service. Could we sustain an Act that said the
police shall protect pupils on the way to or from public schools and Catholic
schools but not while going to and coming from other schools, and firemen
shall extinguish a blaze in public or Catholic school buildings but shall not
put out a blaze in Protestant Church schools or private schools operated for
profit? That is the true analogy to the case we have before us and I should
think it pretty plain that such a scheme would not be valid. . . .

There is no answer to the proposition, more fully expounded by Mr. Justice
Rutledge, that the effect of the religious freedom Amendment to our Constitution was to take every form of propagation of religion out of the realm
of things which could directly or indirectly be made public business and
thereby be supported in whole or in part at taxpayers' expense. That is a
difference which the Constitution sets up between religion and almost every
other subject matter of legislation, a difference which goes to the very root
of religious freedom and which the Court is overlooking today. This freedom
was first in the Bill of Rights because it was first in the forefathers' minds;
it was set forth in absolute terms, and its strength is its rigidity. It was intended not only to keep the states' hands out of religion, but to keep religion's
hands off the state, and, above all, to keep bitter religious controversy out
of public life by denying to every denomination any advantage from getting
control of public policy or the public purse. Those great ends I cannot but
think are immeasurably compromised by today's decision.

This policy of our Federal Constitution has never been wholly pleasing
to most religious groups. They all are quick to invoke its protections; they
all are irked when they feel its restraints. . . .

I cannot read the history of the struggle to separate political from ecclesiastical affairs, well summarized in the opinion of Mr. Justice Rutledge in
which I generally concur, without a conviction that the Court today is unconsciously giving the clock's hands a backward turn.

Mr. Justice Frankfurter joins in this opinion.

Mr. Justice Rutledge, with whom Mr. Justice Frankfurter, Mr. Justice Jackson and Mr. Justice Burton agree, dissenting:

Congress shall make no law respecting an establishment of religion, or prohibiting the free exercise thereof. . . ." US Const, Am Art 1.

Well aware that Almighty God hath created the mind free; . . . that to compel a man to furnish contributions of money for the propagation of opinions which he disbelieves, is sinful and tyrannical . . .

We, the General Assembly, do enact, That no man shall be compelled to frequent or support any religious worship, place, or ministry whatsoever, nor shall be enforced, restrained, molested, or burthened in his body or goods, nor shall otherwise suffer, on account of his religious opinions or belief. . . .

I cannot believe that the great author of those words [Jefferson], or the men who made them law, could have joined in this decision. Neither so high nor so impregnable today as yesterday is the wall raised between church and state by Virginia's great statute of religious freedom and the First Amendment, now made applicable to all the states by the Fourteenth. New Jersey's statute sustained is the first, if indeed it is not the second breach to be made by this Court's action. That a third, and a fourth, and still others will be attempted, we may be sure. . . .

This case forces us to determine squarely for the first time what was "an establishment of religion" in the First Amendment's conception; and by that measure to decide whether New Jersey's action violates its command. . . .

I.

Not simply an established church, but any law respecting an establishment of religion is forbidden. The Amendment was broadly but not loosely phrased. It is the compact and exact summation of its author's views formed during his long struggle for religious freedom. In Madison's own words characterizing Jefferson's Bill for Establishing Religious Freedom, the guaranty he put in our national charter, like the bill he piloted through the Virginia Assembly, was "a Model of technical precision, and perspicuous brevity." Madison could not have confused "church" and "religion," or "an established church" and "an establishment of religion."

The Amendment's purpose was not to strike merely at the official establishment of a single sect, creed or religion, outlawing only a formal relation such as had prevailed in England and some of the colonies. Necessarily it was to uproot all such relationships. But the object was broader than separating church and state in this narrow sense. It was to create a complete and permanent separation of the spheres of religious activity and civil authority by comprehensively forbidding every form of public aid or support for religion. In proof the Amendment's wording and history unite with this Court's consistent utterances whenever attention has been fixed directly upon the question.

"Religion" appears only once in the Amendment. But the word governs two prohibitions and governs them alike. It does not have two meanings, one narrow to forbid "an establishment" and another, much broader, for securing "the free exercise thereof." "Thereof" brings down "religion" with its entire and exact content, no more and no less, from the first into the second guaranty, so that Congress and now the states are as broadly restricted concerning the one as they are regarding the other.

No one would claim today that the Amendment is constricted, in "prohibiting the free exercise" of religion, to securing the free exercise of some formal or creedal observance, of one sect or of many. It secures all forms of religious expression, creedal, sectarian or nonsectarian, wherever and however taking place, except conduct which trenches upon the like freedoms of others or clearly and presently endangers the community's good order and security. For the protective purposes of this phase of the basic freedom, street preaching, oral or by distribution of literature, has been given "the same high estate under the First Amendment as . . . worship in the churches and preaching from the pulpits." And on this basis parents have been held entitled to send their children to private, religious schools. . . . Accordingly, daily religious education commingled with secular is "religion" within the guaranty's comprehensive scope. So are religious training and teaching in whatever form. The word connotes the broadest content, determined not by the form or formality of the teaching or where it occurs, but by its essential nature regardless of those details.

"Religion" has the same broad significance in the twin prohibition concerning "an establishment." The Amendment was not duplicitous. "Religion" and "establishment" were not used in any formal or technical sense. The prohibition broadly forbids state support, financial or other, of religion in any guise, form or degree. It outlaws all use of public funds for religious purposes.

II.

No provision of the Constitution is more closely tied to or given content by its generating history than the religious clause of the First Amendment. It is at once the refined product and the terse summation of that history. The history includes not only Madison's authorship and the proceedings before the First Congress, but also the long and intensive struggle for religious freedom in America, more especially in Virginia, of which the Amendment was the direct culmination. In the documents of the times, particularly of Madison, who was leader in the Virginia struggle before he became the Amendment's sponsor, but also in the writings of Jefferson and others and in the issues which engendered them is to be found irrefutable confirmation of the Amendment's sweeping content.

For Madison, as also for Jefferson, religious freedom was the crux of the struggle for freedom in general. . . . Madison was coauthor with George Mason of the religious clause in Virginia's great Declaration of Rights of 1776. He is credited with changing it from a mere statement of the principle of tolerance to the first official legislative pronouncement that freedom of conscience and religion are inherent rights of the individual. He sought also to have the Declaration expressly condemn the existing Virginia establishment. But the forces supporting it were then too strong.

Accordingly Madison yielded on this phase but not for long. At once he resumed the fight, continuing it before succeeding legislative sessions. As a member of the General Assembly in 1779 he threw his full weight behind Jefferson's historic Bill for Establishing Religious Freedom. That bill was a prime phase of Jefferson's broad program of democratic reform undertaken on his return from the Continental Congress in 1776 and submitted for the General Assembly's consideration in 1779 as his proposed revised Virginia code. With Jefferson's departure for Europe in 1784, Madison became the Bill's prime sponsor. Enactment failed in successive legislatures from its introduction in June, 1779, until its adoption in January, 1786. But during all this time the fight for religious freedom moved forward in Virginia on various fronts with growing intensity. Madison led throughout, against Patrick Henry's powerful opposing leadership until Henry was elected governor in November, 1784.

The climax came in the legislative struggle of 1784–1785 over the Assessment Bill. . . . This was nothing more nor less than a taxing measure for the support of religion, designed to revive the payment of tithes suspended since 1777. So long as it singled out a particular sect for preference it incurred the active and general hostility of dissentient groups. It was broadened to include them, with the result that some subsided temporarily in their opposition. As altered, the bill gave to each taxpayer the privilege of designating which church should receive his share of the tax. In default of designation the legislature applied it to pious uses. But what is of the utmost significance here, "in its final form the bill left the taxpayer the option of giving his tax to education."

Madison was unyielding at all times, opposing with all his vigor the general and nondiscriminatory as he had the earlier particular and discriminatory assessments proposed. The modified Assessment Bill passed second reading in December, 1784, and was all but enacted. Madison and his followers, however, maneuvered deferment of final consideration until November, 1785. And before the Assembly reconvened in the fall he issued his historic Memorial and Remonstrance.

This is Madison's complete, though not his only, interpretation of religious liberty. It is a broadside attack upon all forms of "establishment" of religion, both general and particular, nondiscriminatory or selective. Reflecting not only the many legislative conflicts over the Assessment Bill and the Bill for Establishing Religious Freedom but also, for example, the struggles for religious incorporations and the continued maintenance of the glebes, the Remonstrance is at once the most concise and the most accurate statement of the views of the First Amendment's author concerning what is "an establishment of religion." . . .

The Remonstrance, stirring up a storm of popular protest, killed the Assessment Bill. It collapsed in committee shortly before Christmas, 1785. With this, the way was cleared at last for enactment of Jefferson's bill for Establishing Religious Freedom. Madison promptly drove it through in January of 1786, seven years from the time it was first introduced. This dual victory substantially ended the fight over establishments, settling the issue against them. . . .

The next year Madison became a member of the Constitutional Convention. Its work done, he fought valiantly to secure the ratification of its great product in Virginia as elsewhere, and nowhere else more effectively. Madison was certain in his own mind that under the Constitution "there is not a shadow of right in the general government to intermeddle with religion" and that "this subject is, for the honor of America, perfectly free and unshackled. The government has no jurisdiction over it. . . ." Nevertheless he pledged that he would work for a Bill of Rights, including a specific guaranty of religious freedom, and Virginia, with other states, ratified the Constitution on this assurance.

Ratification thus accomplished, Madison was sent to the first Congress. There he went at once about performing his pledge to establish freedom for the nation as he had done in Virginia. Within a little more than three years from his lgislative victory at home he had proposed and secured the submission and ratification of the First Amendment as the first article of our Bill of Rights.

All the great instruments of the Virginia struggle for religious liberty thus became warp and woof of our constitutional tradition, not simply by the course of history, but by the common unifying force of Madison's life, thought and sponsorship. He epitomized the whole of that tradition in the Amendment's compact, but nonetheless comprehensive, phrasing.

As the Remonstrance discloses throughout, Madison opposed every form and degree of official relation between religion and civil authority. For him religion was a wholly private matter beyond the scope of civil power either to restrain or to support. Denial or abridgment of religious freedom was a violation of rights both of conscience and of natural equality. State aid was no less obnoxious or destructive to freedom and to religion itself than other forms of state interference. "Establishment" and "free exercise" were correlative and coextensive ideas, representing only different facets of the single great and fundamental freedom. The Remonstrance, following the Virginia statute's example, referred to the history of religious conflict and the effects of all sorts of establishments, current and historical, to suppress religion's free exercise. With Jefferson, Madison believed that to tolerate any fragment of establishment would be by so much to perpetuate restraint upon that freedom. Hence he sought to tear out the institution not partially but root and branch, and to bar its return forever.

In no phase was he more unrelentingly absolute than in opposing state support or aid by taxation. Not even "three pence" contribution was thus to be exacted from any citizen for such a purpose. Remonstrance, ¶ 3. Tithes had been the lifeblood of establishment before and after other compulsions disappeared. Madison and his coworkers made no exceptions or abridgments to the complete separation they created. Their objection was not to small tithes. It was to any tithes whatsoever. "If it were lawful to impose a small tax for religion, the admission would pave the way for oppressive levies." Not the amount but "the principle of assessment was wrong." And the principle was as much to prevent "the interference of law in religion" as to restrain religious intervention in political matters. In this field the authors of our freedom would not tolerate "the first experiment on our liberties" or "wait till usurped power had strengthened itself by exercise, and entangled the question in precedents." Remonstrance, ¶ 3. Nor should we.

In view of this history no further proof is needed that the Amendment forbids any appropriation, large or small, from public funds to aid or support any and all religious exercises. But if more were called for, the debates in the First Congress and this Court's consistent expressions, whenever it has touched on the matter directly, supply it.

By contrast with the Virginia history, the congressional debates on consideration of the Amendment reveal only sparse discussion, reflecting the fact that the essential issues had been settled. Indeed the matter had become so well understood as to have been taken for granted in all but formal phrasing. Hence, the only enlightening reference shows concern, not to preserve any power to use public funds in aid of religion, but to prevent the Amendment from outlawing private gifts inadvertently by virtue of the breadth of its wording. . . .

III.

Compulsory attendance upon religious exercises went out early in the process of separating church and state, together with forced observance of religious forms and ceremonies. Test oaths and religious qualification for office followed later. These things none devoted to our great tradition of religious liberty would think of bringing back. Hence today, apart from efforts to inject religious training or exercises and sectarian issues into the public schools, the only serious surviving threat to maintaining that complete and permanent separation of religion and civil power which the First Amendment commands is through use of the taxing power to support religion, religious establishments, or establishments having a religious foundation whatever their form or special religious function.

Does New Jersey's action furnish support for religion by use of the taxing power? Certainly it does, if the test remains undiluted as Jefferson and Madison made it, that money taken by taxation from one is not to be used or given to support another's religious training or belief, or indeed one's own. Today as then the furnishing of "contributions of money for the propagation of opinions which he disbelieves" is the forbidden exaction; and the prohibition is absolute for whatever measure brings that consequence and whatever amount may be sought or given to that end.

The funds used here were raised by taxation. The Court does not dispute, nor could it, that their use does in fact give aid and encouragement to religious instruction. It only concludes that this aid is not "support" in law. But Madison and Jefferson were concerned with aid and support in fact, not as a legal conclusion "entangled in precedents." . . . Here parents pay money to send their children to parochial schools and funds raised by taxation are used to reimburse them. This not only helps the children to get to school and the parents to send them. It aids them in a substantial way to get the very thing which they are sent to the particular school to secure, namely, religious training and teaching.

Believers of all faiths, and others who do not express their feeling toward ultimate issues of existence in any creedal form, pay the New Jersey tax. When the money so raised is used to pay for transportation to religious schools, the Catholic taxpayer to the extent of his proportionate share pays for the transportation of Lutheran, Jewish and otherwise religiously affiliated children to receive their non-Catholic religious instruction. Their parents likewise pay proportionately for the transportation of Catholic children to receive Catholic instruction. Each thus contributes to "the propagation of opinions which he disbelieves" in so far as their religions differ, as do others who accept no creed without regard to those differences. Each thus pays taxes also to support the teaching of his own religion, an exaction equally forbidden since it denies "the comfortable liberty" of giving one's contribution to the particular agency of instruction he approves.

New Jersey's action therefore exactly fits the type of exaction and the kind of evil at which Madison and Jefferson struck. Under the test they framed it cannot be said that the cost of transportation is no part of the cost of education or of the religious instruction given. That it is a substantial and a necessary element is shown most plainly by the continuing and increasing demand for the state to assume it. Nor is there pretense that it relates only to the secular instruction given in religious schools or that any attempt is or could be made toward allocating proportional shares as between the secular and the religious instruction. It is precisely because the instruction is religious and relates to a particular faith, whether one or another, that parents send their children to religious schools. . . . And the very purpose of the state's contribution is to defray the cost of conveying the pupil to the place where he will receive not simply secular, but also and primarily religious, teaching and guidance.

Indeed the view is sincerely avowed by many of various faiths, that the basic purpose of all education is or should be religious, that the secular cannot be and should not be separated from the religious phase and emphasis. Hence, the inadequacy of public or secular education and the necessity for sending the child to a school where religion is taught. But whatever may be the philosophy or its justification, there is undeniably an admixture of religious with secular teaching in all such institutions. That is the very reason for their being. Certainly for purposes of constitutionality we cannot contradict the whole basis of the ethical and educational convictions of people who believe in religious schooling.

Yet this very admixture is what was disestablished when the First Amendment forbade "an establishment of religion." Commingling the religious with the secular teaching does not divest the whole of its religious permeation and emphasis or make them of minor part, if proportion were material. Indeed, on any other view, the constitutional prohibition always could be brought to naught by adding a modicum of the secular.

An appropriation from the public treasury to pay the cost of transportation to Sunday school, to weekday special classes at the church or parish house, or to the meetings of various young people's religious societies, such as the Y.M.C.A., the Y.W.C.A., the Y.M.H.A., the Epworth League, could not withstand the constitutional attack. This would be true, whether or not secular activities were mixed with the religious. If such an appropriation could not stand, then it is hard to see how one becomes valid for the same thing upon the more extended scale of daily instruction. Surely constitutionality does not turn on where or how often the mixed teaching occurs.

Finally, transportation, where it is needed, is as essential to education as any other element. Its cost is as much a part of the total expense, except at times in amount, as the cost of textbooks, of school lunches, of athletic equipment, of writing and other materials; indeed of all other items composing the total burden. Now as always the core of the educational process is the teacher-pupil relationship. Without this the richest equipment and facilities would go for naught. . . . Without buildings, without equipment, without library, textbooks and other materials, and without transportation to bring teacher and pupil together in such an effective teaching environment, there can be not even the skeleton of what our times require. Hardly can it be maintained that transportation is the least essential of these items, or that it does not in fact aid, encourage, sustain and support, just as they do, the very process which is its purpose to accomplish. No less essential is it, or the payment of its cost, than the very teaching in the classroom or payment of the teacher's sustenance. Many types of equipment, now considered essential, better could be done without.

For me, therefore, the feat is impossible to select so indispensable an item from the composite of total costs, and characterize it as not aiding, contributing to, promoting or sustaining the propagation of beliefs which it is the very end of all to bring about. Unless this can be maintained, and the Court does not maintain it, the aid thus given is outlawed. Payment of transportation is no more, nor is it any the less essential to education, whether religious or secular, than payment for tuitions, for teachers' salaries, for buildings, equipment and necessary materials. Nor is it any the less directly related, in a school giving religious instruction, to the primary religious objective all those essential items of cost are intended to achieve. No rational line can be drawn between payment for such larger, but not more necessary, items and payment for transportation. The only line that can be so drawn is one between more dollars and less. Certainly in this realm such a line can be no valid constitutional measure. . . . Now, as in Madison's time, not the amount but the principle of assessment is wrong. . . .

IV.

. . . To say that New Jersey's appropriation and her use of the power of taxation for raising the funds appropriated are not for public purposes but are for private ends, is to say that they are for the support of religion and religious teaching. Conversely, to say that they are for public purposes is to say that they are not for religious ones.

This is precisely for the reason that education which includes religious training and teaching, and its support, have been made matters of private right and function, not public, by the very terms of the First Amendment. That is the effect not only in its guaranty of religion's free exercise, but also in the prohibition of establishments. It was on this basis of the private character of the function of religious education that this Court held parents entitled to send their children to private, religious schools. . . . Now it declares in effect that the appropriation of public funds to defray part of the cost of attending those schools is for a public purpose. If so, I do not understand why the state cannot go farther or why this case approaches the verge of its power.

In truth this view contradicts the whole purpose and effect of the First Amendment as heretofore conceived. The "public function"—"public welfare"—"social legislation" argument seeks, in Madison's words, to "employ Religion [that is, here, religious education] as an engine of Civil policy." Remonstrance, ¶ 5. It is of one piece with the Assessment Bill's preamble, although with the vital difference that it wholly ignores what that preamble explicitly states.

Our constitutional policy is exactly the opposite. It does not deny the value or the necessity for religious training, teaching or observance. Rather it secures their free exercise. But to that end it does deny that the state can undertake or sustain them in any form or degree. For this reason the sphere of religious activity, as distinguished from the secular intellectual liberties, has been given the twofold protection and, as the state cannot forbid, neither can it perform or aid in performing the religious function. The dual prohibition makes that function altogether private. It cannot be made a public one by legislative act. This was the very heart of Madison's Remonstrance, as it is of the Amendment itself.

It is not because religious teaching does not promote the public or the individual's welfare, but because neither is furthered when the state promotes religious education, that the Constitution forbids it to do so. Both legislatures and courts are bound by that distinction. In failure to observe it lies the fallacy of the "public function"—"social legislation" argument, a fallacy facilitated by easy transference of the argument's basing from due process unrelated to any religious aspect to the First Amendment.

By no declaration that a gift of public money to religious uses will promote the general or individual welfare, or the cause of education generally, can legislative bodies overcome the Amendment's bar. Nor may the courts sustain their attempts to do so by finding such consequences for appropriations which in fact give aid to or promote religious uses. . . . Legislatures are free to make, and courts to sustain, appropriations only when it can be found that in fact they do not aid, promote, encourage or sustain religious teaching or observances, be the amount large or small. No such finding has been or could be made in this case. The Amendment has removed this form of promoting the public welfare from legislative and judicial competence to make a public function. It is exclusively a private affair.

The reasons underlying the Amendment's policy have not vanished with time or diminished in force. Now as when it was adopted the price of religious freedom is double. It is that the church and religion shall live both within and upon that freedom. There cannot be freedom of religion, safeguarded by the state, and intervention by the church or its agencies in the state's domain or dependency on its largesse. . . . The great condition of religious liberty is that it be maintained free from sustenance, as also from other interferences, by the state. For when it comes to rest upon that secular foundation it vanishes with the resting. . . . Public money devoted to payment of religious costs, educational or other, brings the quest for more. It brings too the struggle of sect against sect for the larger share or for any. Here one by numbers alone will benefit most, there another. That is precisely the history of societies which have had an established religion and dissident groups. . . . It is the very thing Jefferson and Madison experienced and sought to guard against, whether in its blunt or in its more screened forms. The end of such strife cannot be other than to destroy the cherished liberty. The dominating group will achieve the dominant benefit; or all will embroil the state in their dissensions. . . .

Exactly such conflicts have centered of late around providing transportation to religious schools from public funds. The issue and the dissension work typically, in Madison's phrase, to "destroy that moderation and harmony which the forbearance of our laws to intermeddle with Religion, has produced amongst its several sects." . . . This occurs, as he well knew, over measures at the very threshold of departure from the principle. . . .

In these conflicts wherever success has been obtained it has been upon the contention that by providing the transportation the general cause of education, the general welfare, and the welfare of the individual will be forwarded; hence that the matter lies within the realm of public function, for legislative determination. State courts have divided upon the issue, some taking the view that only the individual, others that the institution receives the benefit. A few have recognized that this dichotomy is false, that both in fact are aided.

The majority here does not accept in terms any of those views. But neither does it deny that the individual or the school, or indeed both, are benefited directly and substantially. To do so would cut the ground from under the public function—social legislation thesis. On the contrary, the opinion concedes that the children are aided by being helped to get to the religious schooling. By converse necessary implication as well as by the absence of express denial, it must be taken to concede also that the school is helped to reach the child with its religious teaching. The religious enterprise is common to both, as is the interest in having transportation for its religious purposes provided.

Notwithstanding the recognition that this two-way aid is given and the absence of any denial that religious teaching is thus furthered, the Court concludes that the aid so given is not "support" of religion. It is rather only support of education as such, without reference to its religious content, and thus becomes public welfare legislation. To this elision of the religious element from the case is added gloss in two respects, one that the aid extended partakes of the nature of a safety measure, the other that failure to provide it would make the state unneutral in religious matters, discriminating against or hampering such children concerning public benefits all others receive.

As will be noted, the one gloss is contradicted by the facts of record and the other is of whole cloth with the "public function" argument's excision of the religious factor. But most important is that this approach, if valid, supplies a ready method for nullifying the Amendment's guaranty, not only for this case and others involving small grants in aid for religious education, but equally for larger ones. The only thing needed will be for the Court again to transplant the "public welfare—public function" view from its proper nonreligious due process bearing to First Amendment application, holding that religious education is not "supported" though it may be aided by the appropriation, and that the cause of education generally is furthered by helping the pupil to secure that type of training.

This is not therefore just a little case over bus fares. In paraphrase of Madison, distant as it may be in its present form from a complete establishment of religion, it differs from it only in degree; and is the first step in that direction. . . . Today as in his time "the same authority which can force a citizen to contribute three pence only . . . for the support of any one [religious] establishment, may force him" to pay more; or "to conform to any other establishment in all cases whatsoever." And now, as then, "either . . . we must say, that the will of the Legislature is the only measure of their authority; and that in the plentitude of this authority, they may sweep away all our fundamental rights; or, that they are bound to leave this particular right untouched and sacred." Remonstrance, ¶ 15.

The realm of religious training and belief remains, as the Amendment made it, the kingdom of the individual man and his God. It should be kept inviolately private, not "entangled . . . in precedents" or confounded with what legislatures legitimately may take over into the public domain.

V.

No one conscious of religious values can be unsympathetic toward the burden which our constitutional separation puts on parents who desire religious instruction mixed with secular for their children. They pay taxes for others' children's education, at the same time the added cost of instruction for their own. Nor can one happily see benefits denied to children which others receive, because in conscience they or their parents for them desire a different kind of training others do not demand.

But if those feelings should prevail, there would be an end to our historic constitutional policy and command. No more unjust or discriminatory in fact is it to deny attendants at religious schools the cost of their transportation than it is to deny them tuitions, sustenance for their teachers, or any other educational expense which others receive at public cost. Hardship in fact there is which none can blink. But, for assuring to those who undergo it the greater, the most comprehensive freedom, it is one written by design and firm intent into our basic law.

Of course discrimination in the legal sense does not exist. The child attending the religious school has the same right as any other to attend the public school. But he foregoes exercising it because the same guaranty which assures this freedom forbids the public school or any agency of the state to give or aid him in securing the religious instruction he seeks.

Were he to accept the common school, he would be the first to protest the teaching there of any creed or faith not his own. And it is precisely for the reason that their atmosphere is wholly secular that children are not sent to public schools. . . . But that is a constitutional necessity, because we have staked the very existence of our country on the faith that complete separation between the state and religion is best for the state and best for religion. Remonstrance, ¶¶ 8, 12.

That policy necessarily entails hardship upon persons who forego the right to educational advantages the state can supply in order to secure others it is precluded from giving. Indeed this may hamper the parent and the child forced by conscience to that choice. But it does not make the state unneutral to withhold what the Constitution forbids it to give. On the contrary it is only by observing the prohibition rigidly that the state can maintain its neutrality and avoid partisanship in the dissensions inevitable when sect opposes sect over demands for public moneys to further religious education, teaching or training in any form or degree, directly or indirectly. Like St. Paul's freedom, religious liberty with a great price must be bought. And for those who exercise it most fully, by insisting upon religious education for their children mixed with secular, by the terms of our Constitution the price is greater than for others.

The problem then cannot be cast in terms of legal discrimination or its absence. This would be true, even though the state in giving aid should treat all religious instruction alike. Thus, if the present statute and its application were shown to apply equally to all religious schools of whatever faith, yet in the light of our tradition it could not stand. For then the adherent of one creed still would pay for the support of another, the childless taxpayer with others more fortunate. Then too there would seem to be no bar to making appropriations for transportation and other expenses of children attending public or other secular schools, after hours in separate places and classes for their exclusively religious instruction. The person who embraces no creed also would be forced to pay for teaching what he does not believe. Again, it was the furnishing of "contributions of money for the propagation of opinions which he disbelieves" that the fathers outlawed. That consequence and effect are not removed by multiplying to all-inclusiveness the sects for which support is exacted. The Constitution requires, not comprehensive identification of state with religion, but complete separation. . . .

Two great drives are constantly in motion to abridge, in the name of education, the complete division of religion and civil authority which our forefathers made. One is to introduce religious education and observances into the public schools. The other, to obtain public funds for the aid and support of various private religious schools. . . . In my opinion both avenues were closed by the Constitution. Neither should be opened by this

Court. The matter is not one of quantity, to be measured by the amount of money expended. Now as in Madison's day it is one of principle, to keep separate the separate spheres as the First Amendment drew them; to prevent the first experiment upon our liberties; and to keep the question from becoming entangled in corrosive precedents. We should not be less strict to keep strong and untarnished the one side of the shield of religious freedom than we have been of the other.

The judgment should be reversed.

b. Released Time

McCOLLUM v. BOARD OF EDUCATION

333 US 203 (1948)

[The question considered in this case was whether there was a breach in the wall of separation between church and state when, under a "released time" arrangement, religious instruction classes were conducted during regular school time within a public school building by denominational teachers. Eight Justices held that this arrangement violated the First Amendment as made applicable to the states by the Fourteenth Amendment. They reaffirmed the broad principles that were formulated the previous year in the *Everson Case,* only this time they found that the constitutional guaranty had been violated.

[Justice Reed alone dissented—not, however, with respect to the broad principles involved, but with respect to their application to the facts in the case. He dissented on the ground that the "released time" arrangements constituted no violation of the provisions of the First Amendment.]

Mr. Justice Black delivered the opinion of the Court:

This case relates to the power of a state to utilize its tax-supported public school system in aid of religious instruction insofar as that power may be restricted by the First and Fourteenth Amendments to the Federal Constitution.

The appellant, Vashti McCollum, began this action for mandamus against the Champaign Board of Education in the Circuit Court of Champaign County, Illinois. Her asserted interest was that of a resident and taxpayer of Champaign and of a parent whose child was then enrolled in the Champaign public schools. Illinois has a compulsory education law which, with exceptions, requires parents to send their children, aged seven to sixteen, to its tax-supported public schools where the children are to remain in attendance during the hours when the schools are regularly in session. Parents who violate this law commit a misdemeanor punishable by fine unless the children attend private

or parochial schools which meet educational standards fixed by the
State. District boards of education are given general supervisory powers over the use of the public school buildings within the school district. . . .

Appellant's petition for mandamus alleged that religious teachers,
employed by private religious groups, were permitted to come weekly
into the school buildings during the regular hours set apart for secular
teaching, and then and there for a period of thirty minutes substitute
their religious teaching for the secular education provided under the
compulsory education law. The petitioner charged that this joint
public-school religious-group program violated the First and Fourteenth Amendments to the United States Constitution. The prayer of
her petition was that the Board of Education be ordered to "adopt and
enforce rules and regulations prohibiting all instruction in and teaching
of religious education in all public schools in Champaign School
District Number 71, . . . and in all public school houses and buildings
in said district when occupied by public schools." . . .

Although there are disputes between the parties as to various inferences that may or may not properly be drawn from the evidence concerning the religious program, the following facts are shown by the
record without dispute. In 1940 interested members of the Jewish,
Roman Catholic, and a few of the Protestant faiths formed a voluntary
association called the Champaign Council on Religious Education.
They obtained permission from the Board of Education to offer classes
in religious instruction to public school pupils in grades four to nine
inclusive. Classes were made up of pupils whose parents signed printed
cards requesting that their children be permitted to attend; they were
held weekly, thirty minutes for the lower grades, forty-five minutes for
the higher. The council employed the religious teachers at no expense
to the school authorities, but the instructors were subject to the approval and supervision of the superintendent of schools. The classes
were taught in three separate religious groups by Protestant teachers,
Catholic priests, and a Jewish Rabbi, although for the past several
years there have apparently been no classes instructed in the Jewish
religion. Classes were conducted in the regular classrooms of the
school building. Students who did not choose to take the religious instruction were not released from public school duties; they were required to leave their classrooms and go to some other place in the
school building for pursuit of their secular studies. On the other hand,
students who were released from secular study for the religious instructions were required to be present at the religious classes. Reports
of their presence or absence were to be made to their secular teachers.

The foregoing facts, without reference to others that appear in the record, show the use of tax-supported property for religious instruction and the close cooperation between the school authorities and the religious council in promoting religious education. The operation of the state's compulsory education system thus assists and is integrated with the program of religious instruction carried on by separate religious sects. Pupils compelled by law to go to school for secular education are released in part from their legal duty upon the condition that they attend the religious classes. This is beyond all question a utilization of the tax-established and tax-supported public school system to aid religious groups to spread their faith. And it falls squarely under the ban of the First Amendment (made applicable to the States by the Fourteenth) as we interpreted it in *Everson* v. *Board of Education*. . . . The majority in the *Everson Case*, and the minority . . . , agreed that the First Amendment's language, properly interpreted, had erected a wall of separation between Church and State. They disagreed as to the facts shown by the record and as to the proper application of the First Amendment's language to those facts.

Recognizing that the Illinois program is barred by the First and Fourteenth Amendments if we adhere to the views expressed both by the majority and the minority in the *Everson Case*, counsel for the respondents challenge those views as *dicta* and urge that we reconsider and repudiate them. They argue that historically the First Amendment was intended to forbid only government preference of one religion over another, not an impartial governmental assistance of all religions. In addition they ask that we distinguish or overrule our holding in the *Everson Case* that the Fourteenth Amendment made the "establishment of religion" clause of the First Amendment applicable as a prohibition against the States. After giving full consideration to the arguments presented we are unable to accept either of these contentions.

To hold that a state cannot consistently with the First and Fourteenth Amendments utilize its public school system to aid any or all religious faiths or sects in the dissemination of their doctrines and ideals does not, as counsel urge, manifest a governmental hostility to religion or religious teachings. A manifestation of such hostility would be at war with our national tradition as embodied in the First Amendment's guaranty of the free exercise of religion. For the First Amendment rests upon the premise that both religion and government can best work to achieve their lofty aims if each is left free from the other within its respective sphere. Or, as we said in the *Everson Case*, the First Amendment has erected a wall between Church and State which must be kept high and impregnable.

Here not only are the state's tax-supported public school buildings used for the dissemination of religious doctrines. The State also affords sectarian groups an invaluable aid in that it helps to provide pupils for their religious classes through use of the state's compulsory public school machinery. This is not separation of Church and State. . . . Reversed, . . .

Mr. Justice Frankfurter delivered the following opinion, in which Mr. Justice Jackson, Mr. Justice Rutledge and Mr. Justice Burton join:

We dissented in *Everson* v. *Board of Education,* . . . because in our view the Constitutional principle requiring separation of Church and State compelled invalidation of the ordinance sustained by the majority. Illinois has here authorized the commingling of sectarian with secular instruction in the public schools. The Constitution of the United States forbids this.

This case, in the light of the *Everson* decision, demonstrates anew that the mere formulation of a relevant Constitutional principle is the beginning of the solution of a problem, not its answer. This is so because the meaning of a spacious conception like that of the separation of Church from State is unfolded as appeal is made to the principle from case to case. We are all agreed that the First and the Fourteenth Amendments have a secular reach far more penetrating in the conduct of Government than merely to forbid an "established church." But agreement, in the abstract, that the First Amendment was designed to erect a "wall of separation between Church and State," does not preclude a clash of views as to what the wall separates. Involved is not only the Constitutional principle but the implications of judicial review in its enforcement. Accommodation of legislative freedom and Constitutional limitations upon that freedom cannot be achieved by a mere phrase. We cannot illuminatingly apply the "wall-of-separation" metaphor until we have considered the relevant history of religious education in America, the place of the "released time" movement in that history, and its precise manifestation in the case before us.

To understand the particular program now before us as a conscientious attempt to accommodate the allowable functions of Government and the special concerns of the Church within the framework of our Constitution and with due regard to the kind of society for which it was designed, we must put this Champaign program of 1940 in its historic setting. Traditionally, organized education in the Western world was Church education. It could hardly be otherwise when the education of children was primarily study of the Word and the ways of God. Even in the Protestant countries, where there was a less close identification of Church and State, the basis of education was largely the Bible, and its chief purpose inculcation of piety. To the extent that the State intervened, it used its authority to further aims of the Church.

The emigrants who came to these shores brought this view of education with them. Colonial schools certainly started with a religious orientation. When the common problems of the early settlers of the Massachusetts Bay

Colony revealed the need for common schools, the object was the defeat of "one chief project of that old deluder Satan, to keep men from the knowledge of the Scriptures." . . .

The evolution of colonial education, largely in the service of religion, into the public school system of today is the story of changing conceptions regarding the American democratic society, of the functions of State-maintained education in such a society and of the role therein of the free exercise of religion by the people. The modern public school derived from a philosophy of freedom reflected in the First Amendment. It is appropriate to recall that the Remonstrance of James Madison, an event basic in the history of religious liberty, was called forth by a proposal which involved support to religious education. . . . As the momentum for popular education increased and in turn evoked strong claims for State support of religious education, contests not unlike that which in Virginia had produced Madison's Remonstrance appeared in various forms in other States. New York and Massachusetts provide famous chapters in the history that established dissociation of religious teaching from State-maintained schools. In New York, the rise of the common schools led, despite fierce sectarian opposition, to the barring of tax funds to church schools, and later to any school in which sectarian doctrine was taught. In Massachusetts, largely through the efforts of Horace Mann, all sectarian teachings were barred from the common school to save it from being rent by denominational conflict. The upshot of these controversies, often long and fierce, is fairly summarized by saying that long before the Fourteenth Amendment subjected the States to new limitations, the prohibition of furtherance by the State of religious instruction became the guiding principle, in law and feeling, of the American people. In sustaining Stephen Girard's will, this Court referred to the inevitable conflicts engendered by matters "connected with religious polity" and particularly "in a country composed of such a variety of religious sects as our country." . . . That was more than one hundred years ago.

Separation in the field of education, then, was not imposed upon unwilling States by force of superior law. In this respect the Fourteenth Amendment merely reflected a principle then dominant in our national life. To the extent that the Constitution thus made it binding upon the States, the basis of the restriction is the whole experience of our people. Zealous watchfulness against fusion of secular and religious activities by Government itself, through any of its instruments but especially through its educational agencies, was the democratic response of the American community to the particular needs of a young and growing nation, unique in the composition of its people. A totally different situation elsewhere, as illustrated for instance by the English provisions for religious education in State-maintained schools, only serves to illustrate that free societies are not cast in one mould. . . . Different institutions evolve from different historic circumstances.

It is pertinent to remind that the establishment of this principle of Separation in the field of education was not due to any decline in the religious beliefs of the people. Horace Mann was a devout Christian, and the deep religious feeling of James Madison is stamped upon the Remonstrance. The secular public school did not imply indifference to the basic role of religion in the life of the people, nor rejection of religious education as a means of fostering it. The claims of religion were not minimized by refusing to make the public schools agencies for their assertion. The non-sectarian or secular public school was the means of reconciling freedom in general with religious freedom. The sharp confinement of the public schools to secular education was a recognition of the need of a democratic society to educate its children, insofar as the State undertook to do so, in an atmosphere free from pressures in a realm in which pressures are most resisted and where conflicts are most easily and most bitterly engendered. Designed to serve as perhaps the most powerful agency for promoting cohesion among a heterogeneous democratic people, the public school must keep scrupulously free from entanglement in the strife of sects. The preservation of the community from divisive conflicts, of Government from irreconcilable pressures by religious groups, of religion from censorship and coercion however subtly exercised, requires strict confinement of the State to instruction other than religious, leaving to the individual's church and home, indoctrination in the faith of his choice. This development of the public school as a symbol of our secular unity was not a sudden achievement nor attained without violent conflict. While in small communities of comparatively homogeneous religious beliefs, the need for absolute separation presented no urgencies, elsewhere the growth of the secular school encountered the resistance of feeling strongly engaged against it. But the inevitability of such attempts is the very reason for Constitutional provisions primarily concerned with the protection of minority groups. And such sects are shifting groups, varying from time to time, and place to place, thus representing in their totality the common interest of the nation.

Enough has been said to indicate that we are dealing not with a full-blown principle, nor one having the definiteness of a surveyor's metes and bounds. But by 1875 the separation of public education from Church entanglements, of the State from the teaching of religion, was firmly established in the consciousness of the nation. In that year President Grant made his famous remarks to the Convention of the Army of the Tennessee:

> Encourage free schools and resolve that not one dollar appropriated for their support shall be appropriated to the support of any sectarian schools. Resolve that neither the state nor nation, nor both combined, shall support institutions of learning other than those sufficient to afford every child growing up in the land the opportunity of a good common school education, unmixed with sectarian, pagan, or atheistical dogmas. Leave the matter of religion to the family altar, the church and the private school, supported entirely by private contributions. Keep the church and the state forever separate. . . .

So strong was this conviction, that rather than rest on the comprehensive prohibitions of the First and Fourteenth Amendments, President Grant urged that there be written into the United States Constitution particular elaborations, including a specific prohibition against the use of public funds for sectarian education, such as had been written into many State constitutions.

By 1894, in urging the adoption of such a provision in the New York Constitution, Elihu Root was able to summarize a century of the nation's history: "It is not a question of religion, or of creed, or of party; it is a question of declaring and maintaining the great American principle of eternal separation between Church and State." . . . The extent to which this principle was deemed a presupposition of our Constitutional system is strikingly illustrated by the fact that every State admitted into the Union since 1876 was compelled by Congress to write into its constitution a requirement that it maintain a school system "free from sectarian control."

Prohibition of the commingling of sectarian and secular instruction in the public school is of course only half the story. A religious people was naturally concerned about the part of the child's education entrusted "to the family altar, the church, and the private school." The promotion of religious education took many forms. Laboring under financial difficulties and exercising only persuasive authority, various denominations felt handicapped in their task of religious education. Abortive attempts were therefore frequently made to obtain public funds for religious schools. But the major efforts of religious inculcation were a recognition of the principle of Separation by the establishment of church schools privately supported. Parochial schools were maintained by various denominations. These, however, were often beset by serious handicaps, financial and otherwise, so that the religious aims which they represented found other directions. There were experiments with vacation schools, with Saturday as well as Sunday schools. They all fell short of their purpose. It was urged that by appearing to make religion a one-day-a-week matter, the Sunday school, which acquired national acceptance, tended to relegate the child's religious education, and thereby his religion, to a minor role not unlike the enforced piano lesson.

Out of these inadequate efforts evolved the week-day church school, held on one or more afternoons a week after the close of the public school. But children continued to be children; they wanted to play when school was out, particularly when other children were free to do so. Church leaders decided that if the week-day church school was to succeed, a way had to be found to give the child his religious education during what the child conceived to be his "business hours."

The initiation of the movement may fairly be attributed to Dr. George U. Wenner. The underlying assumption of his proposal, made at the Interfaith Conference on Federation held in New York City in 1905, was that the public school unduly monopolized the child's time and that the churches were entitled to their share of it. This, the schools should "release." Accordingly, the Federation, citing the example of the Third Republic of France, urged that upon the request of their parents children be excused from public school on Wednesday afternoon, so that the churches could provide "Sunday school on Wednesday." This was to be carried out on church premises under church authority. Those not desiring to attend church schools would continue their normal classes. Lest these public school classes unfairly compete with the church education, it was requested that the school authorities refrain from scheduling courses or activities of compelling interest or importance.

The proposal aroused considerable opposition and it took another decade for a "released time" scheme to become part of a public school system. Gary, Indiana, inaugurated the movement. At a time when industrial expansion strained the communal facilities of the city, Superintendent of Schools Wirt suggested a fuller use of the school buildings. Building on theories which had become more or less current, he also urged that education was more than instruction in a classroom. The school was only one of several educational agencies. The library, the playground, the home, the church, all have their function in the child's proper unfolding. Accordingly, Wirt's plan sought to rotate the schedules of the children during the school-day so that some were in class, others were in the library, still others in the playground. And some, he suggested to the leading ministers of the City, might be released to attend religious classes if the churches of the City cooperated and provided them. They did, in 1914, and thus was "released time" begun. The religious teaching was held on church premises and the public schools had no hand in the conduct of these church schools. They did not supervise the choice of instructors or the subject matter taught. Nor did they assume responsibility for the attendance, conduct or achievement of the child in a church school; and he received no credit for it. The period of attendance in the religious schools would otherwise have been a play period for the child, with the result that the arrangement did not cut into public school instruction or truly affect the activities or feelings of the children who did not attend the church schools.

From such a beginning "released time" has attained substantial proportions. In 1914–15, under the Gary program, 619 pupils left the public schools for the church schools during one period a week. According to responsible figures almost 2,000,000 in some 2,200 communities participated in "released time" programs during 1947. A movement of such scope indicates the importance of the problem to which the "released time" programs are directed. But to the extent that aspects of these programs are open to Constitutional objection, the more extensively the movement operates, the more ominous the breaches in the wall of separation.

Of course, "released time" as a generalized conception, undefined by differentiating particularities, is not an issue for Constitutional adjudication. Local programs differ from each other in many and crucial respects. Some "released time" classes are under separate denominational auspices, others are conducted jointly by several denominations, often embracing all the religious affiliations of a community. Some classes in religion teach a limited sectarianism; others emphasize democracy, unity and spiritual values not anchored in a particular creed. Insofar as these are manifestations merely of the free exercise of religion, they are quite outside the scope of judicial concern, except insofar as the Court may be called upon to protect the right of religious freedom. It is only when challenge is made to the share that the public schools have in the execution of a particular "released time" program that close judicial scrutiny is demanded of the exact relation between the religious instruction and the public educational system in the specific situation before the Court.

The substantial differences among arrangements lumped together as "released time" emphasize the importance of detailed analysis of the facts to which the Constitutional test of Separation is to be applied. How does "released time" operate in Champaign? Public school teachers distribute to their pupils cards supplied by church groups, so that the parents may indicate whether they desire religious instruction for their children. For those desiring it, religious classes are conducted in the regular classrooms of the public schools by teachers of religion paid by the churches and appointed by them, but, as the State court found, "subject to the approval and supervision of the Superintendent." The courses do not profess to give secular instruction in subjects concerning religion. Their candid purpose is sectarian teaching. While a child can go to any of the religious classes offered, a particular sect wishing a teacher for its devotees requires the permission of the school superintendent "who in turn will determine whether or not it is practical for said group to teach in said school system." If no provision is made for religious instruction in the particular faith of a child, or if for other reasons the child is not enrolled in any of the offered classes, he is required to attend a regular school class, or a study period during which he is often left to his own devices. Reports of attendance in the religious classes are submitted by the religious instructor to the school authorities, and the child who fails to attend is presumably deemed a truant.

Religious education so conducted on school time and property is patently woven into the working scheme of the school. The Champaign arrangement thus presents powerful elements of inherent pressure by the school system in the interest of religious sects. The fact that this power has not been used to discriminate is beside the point. Separation is a requirement to abstain from fusing functions of Government and of religious sects, not merely to treat them all equally. That a child is offered an alternative may reduce the constraint; it does not eliminate the operation of influence by the school in matters sacred to conscience and outside the school's domain. The law of imitation operates, and non-conformity is not an outstanding characteristic of children. The result is an obvious pressure upon children to attend. Again, while the Champaign school population represents only a fraction of the more than two hundred and fifty sects of the nation, not even all the practicing sects in Champaign are willing or able to provide religious instruction. The children belonging to these non-participating sects will thus have inculcated in them a feeling of separatism when the school should be the training ground for habits of community, or they will have religious instruction in a faith which is not that of their parents. As a result, the public school system of Champaign actively furthers inculcation in the religious tenets of some faiths, and in the process sharpens the consciousness of religious differences at least among some of the children committed to its care. These are consequences not amenable to statistics. But they are precisely the consequences against which the Constitution was directed when it prohibited the Government common to all from becoming embroiled, however innocently, in the destructive religious conflicts of which the history of even this country records some dark pages.

Mention should not be omitted that the integration of religious instruction within the school system as practiced in Champaign is supported by arguments drawn from educational theories as diverse as those derived from Catholic conceptions and from the writings of John Dewey. Movements like "released time" are seldom single in origin or aim. Nor can the intrusion of religious instruction into the public school system of Champaign be minimized by saying that it absorbs less than an hour a week; in fact, that affords evidence of a design constitutionally objectionable. If it were merely a question of enabling a child to obtain religious instruction with a receptive mind the thirty or forty-five minutes could readily be found on Saturday or Sunday. If that were all, Champaign might have drawn upon the French system, known in its American manifestation as "dismissed time," whereby one school day is shortened to allow all children to go where they please, leaving those who so desire to go to a religious school. The momentum of the whole school atmosphere and school planning is presumably put behind religious instruction, as given in Champaign, precisely in order to secure for the religious instruction such momentum and planning. To speak of "released time" as being only half or three quarters of an hour is to draw a thread from a fabric.

We do not consider, as indeed we could not, school programs not before us which, though colloquially characterized as "released time," present situations differing in aspects that may well be constitutionally crucial. Different forms which "released time" has taken during more than thirty years of growth include programs which, like that before us, could not withstand the test of the Constitution; others may be found unexceptionable. We do not now attempt to weigh in the Constitutional scale every separate detail or various combination of factors which may establish a valid "released time" program. We find that the basic Constitutional principle of absolute Separation was violated when the State of Illinois, speaking through its Supreme Court, sustained the school authorities of Champaign in sponsoring and effectively furthering religious beliefs by its educational arrangement.

Separation means separation, not something less. Jefferson's metaphor in describing the relation between Church and State speaks of a "wall of separation," not of a fine line easily overstepped. The public school is at once the symbol of our democracy and the most pervasive means for promoting our common destiny. In no activity of the State is it more vital to keep out divisive forces than in its schools, to avoid confusing, not to say fusing, what the Constitution sought to keep strictly apart. "The great American principle of eternal separation"—Elihu Root's phrase bears repetition—is one of the vital reliances of our Constitutional system for assuring unities among our people stronger than our diversities. It is the Court's duty to enforce this principle in its full integrity.

We renew our conviction that "we have staked the very existence of our country on the faith that complete separation between the state and religion is best for the state and best for religion." *Everson* v. *Board of Education*.

If nowhere else, in the relation between Church and State, "good fences make good neighbors."

Mr. Justice Jackson, concurring:

I join the opinion of Mr. Justice Frankfurter, and concur in the result reached by the Court, but with these reservations: I think . . . that we should place some bounds on the demands for interference with local schools that we are empowered or willing to entertain. I make these reservations a matter of record in view of the number of litigations likely to be started as a result of this decision. . . .

To me, the sweep and detail of these complaints is a danger signal which warns of the kind of local controversy we will be required to arbitrate if we do not place appropriate limitation on our decision and exact strict compliance with jurisdictional requirements. Authorities list 256 separate and substantial religious bodies to exist in the continental United States. Each of them, through the suit of some discontented but unpenalized and untaxed representative, has as good a right as this plaintiff to demand that the courts compel the schools to sift out of their teaching everything inconsistent with its doctrines. If we are to eliminate everything that is objectionable to any of these warring sects or inconsistent with any of their doctrines, we will leave public education in shreds. Nothing but educational confusion and a discrediting of the public school system can result from subjecting it to constant law suits.

While we may and should end such formal and explicit instruction as the Champaign plan and can at all times prohibit teaching of creed and catechism and ceremonial and can forbid forthright proselyting in the schools, I think it remains to be demonstrated whether it is possible, even if desirable, to comply with such demands as plaintiff's completely to isolate and cast out of secular education all that some people may reasonably regard as religious instruction. Perhaps subjects such as mathematics, physics or chemistry are, or can be, completely secularized. But it would not seem practical to teach either practice or appreciation of the arts if we are to forbid exposure of youth to any religious influences. Music without sacred music, architecture minus the cathedral, or painting without the scriptural themes would be eccentric and incomplete, even from a secular point of view. Yet the inspirational appeal of religion in these guises is often stronger than in forthright sermon. Even such a "science" as biology raises the issue between evolution and creation as an explanation of our presence on this planet. Certainly a course in English literature that omitted the Bible and other powerful uses of our mother tongue for religious ends would be pretty barren. And I should suppose it is a proper, if not an indispensable, part of preparation for a worldly life to know the roles that religion and religions have played in the tragic story of mankind. The fact is that, for good or for ill, nearly everything in our culture worth transmitting, everything which gives meaning to life, is saturated with religious influences, derived from paganism, Judaism, Christianity—both Catholic and Protestant—and other faiths accepted by a large part of the world's peoples. One can hardly respect a system of education that would leave the student wholly ignorant of the currents of religious thought that move the world society for a part in which he is being prepared.

But how one can teach, with satisfaction or even with justice to all faiths, such subjects as the story of the Reformation, the Inquisition, or even the New England effort to found "a Church without a Bishop and a State without a King," is more than I know. It is too much to expect that mortals will teach subjects about which their contemporaries have passionate controversies with the detachment they may summon to teaching about remote subjects such as Confucius or Mohammed. When instruction turns to proselyting and imparting knowledge becomes evangelism is, except in the crudest cases, a subtle inquiry.

The opinions in this case show that public educational authorities have evolved a considerable variety of practices in dealing with the religious problem. Neighborhoods differ in racial, religious and cultural compositions. It must be expected that they will adopt different customs which will give emphasis to different values and will induce different experiments. And it must be expected that, no matter what practice prevails, there will be many discontented and possibly belligerent minorities. We must leave some flexibility to meet local conditions, some chance to progress by trial and error. While I agree that the religious classes involved here go beyond permissible limits, I also think the complaint demands more than plaintiff is entitled to have granted. So far as I can see this Court does not tell the State court where it may stop, nor does it set up any standards by which the State court may determine that question for itself.

The task of separating the secular from the religious in education is one of magnitude, intricacy and delicacy. To lay down a sweeping constitutional doctrine as demanded by complainant and apparently approved by the Court, applicable alike to all school boards of the nation, "to immediately adopt and enforce rules and regulations prohibiting all instruction in and teaching of religious education in all public schools," is to decree a uniform, rigid and, if we are consistent, an unchanging standard for countless school boards representing and serving highly localized groups which not only differ from each other but which themselves from time to time change attitudes. It seems to me that to do so is to allow zeal for our own ideas of what is good in public instruction to induce us to accept the role of a super board of education for every school district in the nation.

It is idle to pretend that this task is one for which we can find in the Constitution one word to help us as judges to decide where the secular ends and the sectarian begins in education. Nor can we find guidance in any other legal source. It is a matter on which we can find no law but our own prepossessions. If with no surer legal guidance we are to take up and decide every variation of this controversy, raised by persons not subject to penalty or tax but who are dissatisfied with the way schools are dealing with the problem, we are likely to have much business of the sort. And, more importantly, we are likely to make the legal "wall of separation between church and state" as winding as the famous serpentine wall designed by Mr. Jefferson for the University he founded.

Mr. Justice Reed, dissenting: . . .

The phrase "an establishment of religion" may have been intended by Congress to be aimed only at a state church. When the First Amendment was pending in Congress in substantially its present form, "Mr. Madison said, he apprehended the meaning of the words to be, that Congress should not establish a religion, and enforce the legal observation of it by law, nor compel men to worship God in any manner contrary to their conscience." Passing years, however, have brought about the acceptance of a broader meaning, although never until today, I believe, has this Court widened its interpretation to any such degree as holding that recognition of the interest of our nation in religion, through the granting, to qualified representatives of the principal faiths, of opportunity to present religion as an optional, extracurricular subject during released school time in public school buildings, was equivalent to an establishment of religion. A reading of the general statements of eminent statesmen of former days, referred to in the opinions in this case and in *Everson* v. *Board of Education,* will show that circumstances such as those in this case were far from the minds of the authors. The words and spirit of those statements may be wholeheartedly accepted without in the least impugning the judgment of the State of Illinois.

Mr. Jefferson, as one of the founders of the University of Virginia, a school which from its establishment in 1819 has been wholly governed, managed and controlled by the State of Virginia, was faced with the same problem that is before this Court today: the question of the constitutional limitation upon religious education in public schools. In his annual report as Rector, to the President and Directors of the Literary Fund, dated October 7, 1822, approved by the Visitors of the University of whom Mr. Madison was one, Mr. Jefferson set forth his views at some length. These suggestions of Mr. Jefferson were adopted and . . . the Regulations of the University of October 4, 1824, provided that:

> Should the religious sects of this State, or any of them, according to the invitation held out to them, establish within, or adjacent to, the precincts of the University, schools for instruction in the religion of their sect, the students of the University will be free, and expected to attend religious worship at the establishment of their respective sects, in the morning, and in time to meet their school in the University at its stated hour.

Thus, the "wall of separation between church and state" that Mr. Jefferson built at the University which he founded did not exclude religious education from that school. The difference between the generality of his statements on the separation of church and state and the specificity of his conclusions on education are considerable. A rule of law should not be drawn from a figure of speech.

Mr. Madison's Memorial and Remonstrance against Religious Assessments relied upon by the dissenting Justices in *Everson* is not applicable here. . . . Throughout the Remonstrance, Mr. Madison speaks of the "establishment" sought to be effected by the act. It is clear from its historical setting and its language that the Remonstrance was a protest against an effort by Virginia to support Christian sects by taxation. Issues similar to those raised by the instant case were not discussed. Thus, Mr. Madison's approval of Mr. Jefferson's report as Rector gives, in my opinion, a clearer indication of his views on the constitutionality of religious education in public schools than his general statements on a different subject.

This Court summarized the amendment's accepted reach into the religious field, as I understood its scope, in *Everson* v. *Board of Education*. . . . I agree . . . that none of our governmental entities can "set up a church." I agree that they cannot "aid" all or any religions or prefer one "over another." But "aid" must be understood as a purposeful assistance directly to the church itself or to some religious group or organization doing religious work of such a character that it may fairly be said to be performing ecclesiastical functions. "Prefer" must give an advantage to one "over another." I agree that pupils cannot "be released in part from their legal duty" of school attendance upon condition that they attend religious classes. But as Illinois has held that it is within the discretion of the School Board to permit absence from school for religious instruction no legal duty of school attendance is violated. . . . If the sentence in the Court's opinion, concerning the pupils' release from legal duty, is intended to mean that the Constitution forbids a school to excuse a pupil from secular control during school hours to attend voluntarily a class in religious education, whether in or out of school buildings, I disagree. Of course, no tax can be levied to support organizations intended "to teach or practice religion." I agree too that the state cannot influence one toward religion against his will or punish him for his beliefs. Champaign's religious education course does none of these things.

It seems clear to me that the "aid" referred to by the Court in the *Everson Case* could not have been those incidental advantages that religious bodies, with other groups similarly situated, obtain as a by-product of organized society. This explains the well-known fact that all churches receive "aid" from government in the form of freedom from taxation. The *Everson* decision itself justified the transportation of children to church schools by New Jersey for safety reasons. It accords with *Cochran* v. *Louisiana State Bd. of Edu.*, 281 US 370, where this Court upheld a free textbook statute of Louisiana against a charge that it aided private schools on the ground that the books were for the education of the children, not to aid religious schools. Likewise the National School Lunch Act aids all school children attending tax exempt schools. In *Bradfield* v. *Roberts*, 175 US 291, this Court held proper the payment of money by the Federal Government to build an addition to a hospital, chartered by individuals who were members of a Roman Catholic sisterhood, and operated under the auspices of the Roman Catholic Church. This was done over the objection that it aided the establishment of religion. While obviously in these instances the respective churches, in a certain sense, were aided, this Court has never held that such "aid" was in violation of the First or Fourteenth Amendment.

Well-recognized and long-established practices support the validity of the Illinois statute here in question. That statute, as construed in this case, is comparable to those in many states. All differ to some extent. New York may be taken as a fair example. In many states the program is under the supervision of a religious council composed of delegates who are themselves communicants of various faiths. As is shown by *Bradfield* v. *Roberts,* the fact that the members of the council have religious affiliations is not significant. In some, instruction is given outside of the school buildings; in others, within these buildings. Metropolitan centers like New York usually would have available quarters convenient to schools. Unless smaller cities and rural communities use the school buildings at times that do not interfere with recitations, they may be compelled to give up religious education. I understand that pupils not taking religious education usually are given other work of a secular nature within the schools. Since all these states use the facilities of the schools to aid the religious education to some extent, their desire to permit religious education to school children is thwarted by this Court's judgment. Under it, as I understand its language, children cannot be released or dismissed from school to attend classes in religion while other children must remain to pursue secular education. Teachers cannot keep the records as to which pupils are to be dismissed and which retained. To do so is said to be an "aid" in establishing religion; the use of public money for religion.

Cases running into the scores have been in the state courts of last resort that involved religion and the schools. Except where the exercises with religious significance partook of the ceremonial practice of sects or groups, their constitutionality has been generally upheld. Illinois itself promptly struck down as violative of its own constitution required exercises partaking of a religious ceremony. *Ring* v. *Board of Education,* 245 Ill. 334. In that case compulsory religious exercises—a reading from the King James Bible, the Lord's Prayer and the singing of hymns—were forbidden as "worship services." In this case, the Supreme Court of Illinois pointed out that in the *Ring Case,* the activities in the school were ceremonial and compulsory; in this, voluntary and educational. . . .

The practices of the federal government offer many examples of this kind of "aid" by the state to religion. The Congress of the United States has a chaplain for each House who daily invokes divine blessings and guidance for the proceedings. The armed forces have commissioned chaplains from early days. They conduct the public services in accordance with the liturgical requirements of their respective faiths, ashore and afloat, employing for the purpose property belonging to the United States and dedicated to the services of religion. Under the Servicemen's Readjustment Act of 1944, eligible veterans may receive training at government expense for the ministry in denominational schools. The schools of the District of Columbia have opening exercises which "include a reading from the Bible without note or comment, and the Lord's prayer."

In the United States Naval Academy and the United States Military Academy, schools wholly supported and completely controlled by the federal government, there are a number of religious activities. Chaplains are attached to both schools. Attendance at church services on Sunday is compulsory at both the Military and Naval Academies. At West Point the Protestant services are held in the Cadet Chapel, the Catholic in the Catholic Chapel, and the Jewish in the Old Cadet Chapel; at Annapolis only Protestant services are held on the reservation, midshipmen of other religious persuasions attend the churches of the city of Annapolis. These facts indicate that both schools since their earliest beginnings have maintained and enforced a pattern of participation in formal worship.

With the general statements in the opinions concerning the constitutional requirement that the nation and the states, by virtue of the First and Fourteenth Amendments, may "make no law respecting an establishment of religion," I am in agreement. But, in the light of the meaning given to those words by the precedents, customs, and practices which I have detailed above, I cannot agree with the Court's conclusion that when pupils compelled by law to go to school for secular education are released from school so as to attend the religious classes, churches are unconstitutionally aided. Whatever may be the wisdom of the arrangement as to the use of the school buildings made with The Champaign Council of Religious Education, it is clear to me that past practice shows such cooperation between the schools and a non-ecclesiastical body is not forbidden by the First Amendment. When actual church services have always been permitted on government property, the mere use of the school buildings by a non-sectarian group for religious education ought not to be condemned as an establishment of religion. For a non-sectarian organization to give the type of instruction here offered cannot be said to violate our rule as to the establishment of religion by the state. The prohibition of enactments respecting the establishment of religion do not bar every friendly gesture between church and state. It is not an absolute prohibition against every conceivable situation where the two may work together, any more than the other provisions of the First Amendment—free speech, free press—are absolutes. If abuses occur such as the use of the instruction hour for sectarian purposes, I have no doubt, in view of the *Ring Case*, that Illinois will promptly correct them. If they are of a kind that tend to the establishment of a church or interfere with the free exercise of religion, this Court is open for a review of an erroneous decision. This Court cannot be too cautious in upsetting practices embedded in our society by many years of experience. A state is entitled to have great leeway in its legislation when dealing with the important social problems of its population. A definite violation of legislative limits must be established. . . . Devotion to the great principle of religious liberty should not lead us into a rigid interpretation of the constitutional guarantee that conflicts with accepted habits of our people. This is an instance where, for me, the history of past practices is determinative of the meaning of a constitutional clause. . . .

c. The McCollum Case Limited
ZORACH v. CLAUSON
343 US 306 (1952)

[In the *McCollum Case* religious instruction was given *within* the public school building. The New York City "released time" program called for the religious courses to be operated *outside* the public school building. The pupils who did not choose to attend the religious courses of their respective denominations were required to remain in their public school classrooms. Six Justices found this system sufficiently different from that presented in the *McCollum Case* to conclude that it violated no constitutional provision.

[Justices Black and Jackson dissented, maintaining that there was no essential difference between this case and the previous one. Justice Frankfurter's dissent emphasized that the state courts had not permitted proof that the New York City program involved coercion of pupils to join the sectarian classes. He also sharply differentiated a "dismissed time" from a "released time" system. Under the former *all* students are dismissed and are free to do with their "dismissed time" as they or their parents may see fit; some of them may go to their church schools, others may go home. This system would involve no coercion. The "released time" system may, however, involve coercion of the reluctant. If it is coercive, it should be declared unconstitutional.

[Again all Justices avowed belief in the principle of separation of church and state. The dissenters, however, maintained that the principle was, in this case, honored in the breach rather than in the observance.]

Mr. Justice Douglas delivered the opinion of the Court:

New York City has a program which permits its public schools to release students during the school day so that they may leave the school buildings and school grounds and go to religious centers for religious instruction or devotional exercises. A student is released on written request of his parents. Those not released stay in the classrooms. The churches make weekly reports to the schools, sending a list of children who have been released from public school but who have not reported for religious instruction.

This "released time" program involves neither religious instruction in public school classrooms nor the expenditure of public funds. All costs, including the application blanks, are paid by the religious organizations. The case is therefore unlike *McCollum v. Board of Education,* 333 U.S. 203, which involved a "released time" program from

Illinois. In that case the classrooms were turned over to religious instructors. We accordingly held that the program violated the First Amendment which (by reason of the Fourteenth Amendment) prohibits the states from establishing religion or prohibiting its free exercise.

Appellants, who are taxpayers and residents of New York City and whose children attend its public schools, challenge the present law, contending it is in essence not different from the one involved in the *McCollum Case*. Their argument, stated elaborately in various ways, reduces itself to this: the weight and influence of the school is put behind a program for religious instruction; public school teachers police it, keeping tab on students who are released; the classroom activities come to a halt while the students who are released for religious instruction are on leave; the school is a crutch on which the churches are leaning for support in their religious training; without the cooperation of the schools this "released time" program, like the one in the *McCollum Case*, would be futile and ineffective. . . .

The briefs and arguments are replete with data bearing on the merits of this type of "released time" program. Views *pro* and *con* are expressed, based on practical experience with these programs and with their implications. We do not stop to summarize these materials nor to burden the opinion with an anlysis of them. For they involve considerations not germane to the narrow constitutional issue presented. They largely concern the wisdom of the system, its efficiency from an educational point of view, and the political considerations which have motivated its adoption or rejection in some communities. Those matters are of no concern here, since our problem reduces itself to whether New York by this system has either prohibited the "free exercise" of religion or has made a law "respecting an establishment of religion" within the meaning of the First Amendment.

It takes obtuse reasoning to inject any issue of the "free exercise" of religion into the present case. No one is forced to go to the religious classroom and no religious exercise or instruction is brought to the classrooms of the public schools. A student need not take religious instruction. He is left to his own desires as to the manner or time of his religious devotions, if any.

There is a suggestion that the system involves the use of coercion to get public school students into religious classrooms. There is no evidence in the record before us that supports that conclusion. The present record indeed tells us that the school authorities are neutral in this regard and do no more than release students whose parents so request. If in fact coercion were used, if it were established that any one or more teachers were using their office to persuade or force students to take the religious instruction, a wholly different case would be presented. Hence we put aside that claim of coercion both as respects the "free exercise" of religion and "an establishment of religion" within the meaning of the First Amendment.

Moreover, apart from that claim of coercion, we do not see how New York by this type of "released time" program has made a law respecting an establishment of religion within the meaning of the First Amendment. There is much talk of the separation of Church and State in the history of the Bill of Rights and in the decisions clustering around the First Amendment. . . . There cannot be the slightest doubt that the First Amendment reflects the philosophy that Church and State should be separated. And so far as interference with the "free exercise" of religion and an "establishment" of religion are concerned, the separation must be complete and unequivocal. The First Amendment within the scope of its coverage permits no exception; the prohibition is absolute. The First Amendment, however, does not say that in every and all respects there shall be a separation of Church and State. Rather, it studiously defines the manner, the specific ways, in which there shall be no concert or union or dependency one on the other. That is the common sense of the matter. Otherwise the state and religion would be aliens to each other—hostile, suspicious, and even unfriendly. Churches could not be required to pay even property taxes. Municipalities would not be permitted to render police or fire protection to religious groups. Policemen who helped parishioners into their places of worship would violate the Constitution. Prayers in our legislative halls; the appeals to the Almighty in the messages of the Chief Executive; the proclamations making Thanksgiving Day a holiday; "so help me God" in our courtroom oaths—these and all other references to the Almighty that run through our laws, our public rituals, our ceremonies would be flouting the First Amendment. A fastidious atheist or agnostic could even object to the supplication with which the Court opens each session: "God save the United States and this Honorable Court."

We would have to press the concept of separation of Church and State to these extremes to condemn the present law on constitutional grounds. The nullification of this law would have wide and profound effects. A Catholic student applies to his teacher for permission to leave the school during hours on a Holy Day of Obligation to attend a mass. A Jewish student asks his teacher for permission to be excused for Yom Kippur. A Protestant wants the afternoon off for a family baptismal ceremony. In each case the teacher requires parental consent in writing. In each case the teacher, in order to make sure the student is not a truant, goes further and requires a report from the priest, the rabbi, or the minister. The teacher in other words cooperates in a religious program to the extent of making it possible for her students to participate in it. Whether she does it occasionally for a few students, regularly for one, or pursuant to a systematized program designed to further the religious needs of all the students does not alter the character of the act.

We are a religious people whose institutions presuppose a Supreme Being. We guarantee the freedom to worship as one chooses. We make room for as wide a variety of beliefs and creeds as the spiritual needs of man deem necessary. We sponsor an attitude on the part of government that shows no partiality to any one group and that lets each flourish according to the zeal of its adherents and the appeal of its dogma. When the state encourages religious instruction or cooperates with religious authorities by adjusting the schedule of public events to sectarian needs, it follows the best of our traditions. For it then respects the religious nature of our people and accommodates the public service to their spiritual needs. To hold that it may not would be to find in the Constitution a requirement that the government show a callous indifference to religious groups. That would be preferring those who believe in no religion over those who do believe. Government may not finance religious groups nor undertake religious instruction nor blend secular and sectarian education nor use secular institutions to force one or some religion on any person. But we find no constitutional requirement which makes it necessary for government to be hostile to religion and to throw its weight against efforts to widen the effective scope of religious influence. The government must be neutral when it comes to competition between sects. It may not thrust any sect on any person. It may not make a religious observance compulsory. It may not coerce anyone to attend church, to observe a religious holiday, or to take religious instruction. But it can close its doors or suspend its operations as to those who want to repair to their religious sanctuary for worship or instruction. No more than that is undertaken here.

This program may be unwise and improvident from an educational or a community viewpoint. That appeal is made to us on a theory, previously advanced, that each case must be decided on the basis of "our own prepossessions." . . . Our individual preferences, however, are not the constitutional standard. The constitutional standard is the separation of Church and State. The problem, like many problems in constitutional law, is one of degree. . . .

In the *McCollum Case* the classrooms were used for religious instruction and the force of the public school was used to promote that instruction. Here, as we have said, the public schools do no more than accommodate their schedules to a program of outside religious instruction. We follow the *McCollum Case*. But we cannot expand it to cover the present released time program unless separation of Church and State means that public institutions can make no adjustments of their schedules to accommodate the religious needs of the people. We cannot read into the Bill of Rights such a philosophy of hostility to religion.

Affirmed [constitutionality sustained].

Mr. Justice Black, dissenting:

. . . I see no significant difference between the invalid Illinois system and that of New York here sustained. Except for the use of the school buildings in Illinois, there is no difference between the systems which I consider even worthy of mention. In the New York program, as in that of Illinois, the school authorities release some of the children on the condition that they attend the religious classes, get reports on whether they attend, and hold the other children in the school building until the religious hour is over. As we attempted to make categorically clear, the *McCollum* decision would have been the same if the religious classes had not been held in the school buildings. We said:

> Here *not only* are the state's tax-supported public school buildings used for the dissemination of religious doctrines. The State *also* affords sectarian groups an invaluable aid in that it helps to provide pupils for their religious classes through use of the state's compulsory public school machinery. *This* is not separation of Church and State. (Emphasis supplied.)

McCollum thus held that Illinois could not constitutionally manipulate the compelled classroom hours of its compulsory school machinery so as to channel children into sectarian classes. Yet that is exactly what the Court holds New York can do.

I am aware that our *McCollum* decision on separation of church and state has been subjected to a most searching examination throughout the country. Probably few opinions from this Court in recent years have attracted more attention or stirred wider debate. Our insistence on "a wall between Church and State which must be kept high and inpregnable" has seemed to some a correct exposition of the philosophy and a true interpretation of the language of the First Amendment to which we should strictly adhere. With equal conviction and sincerity, others have thought the *McCollum* decision fundamentally wrong and have pledged continuous warfare against it. The opinions in the court below and the briefs here reflect these diverse viewpoints. In dissenting today, I mean to do more than give routine approval to our *McCollum* decision. I mean also to reaffirm my faith in the fundamental philosophy expressed in *McCollum* and *Everson* v. *Board of Education*. . . .

Difficulty of decision in the hypothetical situations mentioned by the Court, but not now before us, should not confuse the issues in this case. Here the sole question is whether New York can use its compulsory education laws to help religious sects get attendants presumably too unenthusiastic to go unless moved to do so by the pressure of this state machinery. That this is the plan, purpose, design and consequence of the New York program cannot be denied. The state thus makes religious sects beneficiaries of its power to compel children to attend secular schools. Any use of such coercive power by the state to help or hinder some religious sects or to prefer all religious sects over nonbelievers or vice versa is just what I think the First Amendment forbids. In considering whether a state has entered this forbidden field the question is not whether it has entered too far but whether it has entered at all. New York is manipulating its compulsory education laws to help religious sects get pupils. This is not separation but combination of Church and State.

The Court's validation of the New York system rests in part on its statement that Americans are "a religious people whose institutions presuppose a Supreme Being." This was at least as true when the First Amendment was adopted; and it was just as true when eight justices of this Court invalidated the released time system in *McCollum* on the premise that a state can no more "aid all religions" than it can aid one. It was precisely because Eighteenth Century Americans were a religious people divided into many fighting sects that we were given the constitutional mandate to keep Church and State completely separate. Colonial history had already shown that, here as elsewhere, zealous sectarians entrusted with governmental power to further their causes, would sometimes torture, maim and kill those they branded "heretics," "atheists" or "agnostics." The First Amendment was therefore to insure that no one powerful sect or combination of sects could use political or governmental power to punish dissenters whom they could not convert to their faith. Now as then, it is only by wholly isolating the state from the religious sphere and compelling it to be completely neutral, that the freedom of each and every denomination and of all nonbelievers can be maintained. It is this neutrality the Court abandons today when it treats New York's coercive system as a program which *merely* "encourages religious instruction or cooperates with religious authorities." The abandonment is all the more dangerous to liberty because of the Court's legal exaltation of the orthodox and its derogation of unbelievers.

Under our system of religious freedom, people have gone to their religious sanctuaries not because they feared the law but because they loved their God. The choice of all has been as free as the choice of those who answered the call to worship moved only by the music of the old Sunday morning church bells. The spiritual mind of man has thus been free to believe, disbelieve, or doubt, without repression, great or small, by the heavy hand of government. Statutes authorizing such repression have been stricken. Before today, our judicial opinions have refrained from drawing invidious distinctions between those who believe in no religion and those who do believe. The First Amendment has lost much if the religious follower and the atheist are no longer to be judicially regarded as entitled to equal justice under law.

State help to religion injects political and party prejudices into a holy field. It too often substitutes force for prayer, hate for love, and persecution for persuasion. Government should not be allowed, under cover of the soft euphemism of "co-operation," to steal into the sacred area of religious choice.

Mr. Justice Frankfurter, dissenting:

By way of emphasizing my agreement with Mr. Justice Jackson's dissent, I add a few words.

The Court tells us that in the maintenance of its public schools, "[The State government] can close its doors or suspend its operations" so that its citizens may be free for religious devotions or instruction. If that were the issue, it would not rise to the dignity of a constitutional controversy. Of course a State may provide that the classes in its schools shall be dismissed, for any reason, or no reason, on fixed days, or for special occasions. The essence of this case is that the school system did not "close its doors" and did not "suspend its operations." There is all the difference in the world between letting the children out of school and letting some of them out of school into religious classes. If every one is free to make what use he will of time wholly unconnected from schooling required by law—those who wish sectarian instruction devoting it to that purpose, those who have ethical instruction at home, to that, those who study music, to that—then of course there is no conflict with the Fourteenth Amendment.

The pith of the case is that formalized religious instruction is substituted for other school activity which those who do not participate in the released-time program are compelled to attend. The school system is very much in operation during this kind of released time. If its doors are closed, they are closed upon those students who do not attend the religious instruction in order to keep them within the school. That is the very thing which raises the constitutional issue. It is not met by disregarding it. Failure to discuss this issue does not take it out of the case.

Again, the Court relies upon the absence from the record of evidence of coercion in the operation of the system. "If in fact coercion were used," according to the Court, "if it were established that any one or more teachers were using their office to persuade or force students to take the religious instruction, a wholly different case would be presented." Thus, "coercion" in the abstract is acknowledged to be fatal. But the Court disregards the fact that as the case comes to us, there could be no proof of coercion, for the petitioners were not allowed to make proof of it. Petitioners alleged that "The operation of the released time program has resulted and inevitably results in the exercise of pressure and coercion upon parents and children to secure attendance by the children for religious instruction." This allegation—that coercion was in fact present and is inherent in the system, no matter what disavowals might be made in the operating regulations—was denied by respondents. Thus were drawn issues of fact which cannot be determined, on any conceivable view of judicial notice, by judges out of their own knowledge or experience. Petitioners sought an opportunity to adduce evidence in support of these allegations at an appropriate trial. And though the courts below cited the concurring opinion in *McCollum* v. *Board of Education* to "emphasize the importance of detailed analysis of the facts to which the Constitutional test of Separation is to be applied," they denied that opportunity on the ground that such proof was irrelevant to the issue of constitutionality. . . .

The result in the *McCollum Case* . . . was based on principles that received unanimous acceptance by this Court, barring only a single vote. I agree with Mr. Justice Black that those principles are disregarded in reaching the result in this case. Happily they are not disavowed by the Court. From this I draw the hope that in future variations of the problem which are bound to come here, these principles may again be honored in the observance.

The deeply divisive controversy aroused by the attempts to secure public school pupils for sectarian instruction would promptly end if the advocates of such instruction were content to have the school "close its doors or suspend operations"—that is, dismiss classes in their entirety, without discrimination—instead of seeking to use the public schools as the instrument for security of attendance at denominational classes. The unwillingness of the promoters of this movement to dispense with such use of the public schools betrays a surprising want of confidence in the inherent power of the various faiths to draw children to outside sectarian classes—an attitude that hardly reflects the faith of the greatest religious spirits.

Mr. Justice Jackson, dissenting:

This released time program is founded upon a use of the State's power of coercion, which, for me, determines its unconstitutionality. Stripped to its essentials, the plan has two stages, first, that the State compels each student to yield a large part of his time for public secular education and, second, that some of it be "released" to him on condition that he devote it to sectarian religious purposes.

No one suggests that the Constitution would permit the State directly to require this "released" time to be spent "under the control of a duly constituted religious body." This program accomplishes that forbidden result by indirection. If public education were taking so much of the pupils' time as to injure the public or the students' welfare by encroaching upon their religious opportunity, simply shortening everyone's school day would facilitate voluntary and optional attendance at Church classes. But that suggestion is rejected upon the ground that if they are made free many students will not go to the Church. Hence, they must be deprived of freedom for this period, with Church attendance put to them as one of the two permissible ways of using it.

The greater effectiveness of this system over voluntary attendance after school hours is due to the truant officer who, if the youngster fails to go to the Church school, dogs him back to the public schoolroom. Here schooling is more or less suspended during the "released time" so the nonreligious attendants will not forge ahead of the churchgoing absentees. But it serves as a temporary jail for a pupil who will not go to Church. It takes more subtlety of mind than I possess to deny that this is governmental constraint in support of religion. It is as unconstitutional, in my view, when exerted by indirection as when exercised forthrightly.

As one whose children, as a matter of free choice, have been sent to privately supported Church schools, I may challenge the Court's suggestion that opposition to this plan can only be antireligious, atheistic, or agnostic. My evangelistic brethren confuse an objection to compulsion with an objection to religion. It is possible to hold a faith with enough confidence to believe that what should be rendered to God does not need to be decided and collected by Caesar.

The day that this country ceases to be free for irreligion it will cease to be free for religion—except for the sect that can win political power. The same epithetical jurisprudence used by the Court today to beat down those who oppose pressuring children into some religion can devise as good epithets tomorrow against those who object to pressuring them into a favored religion. And, after all, if we concede to the State power and wisdom to single out "duly constituted religious" bodies as exclusive alternatives for compulsory secular instruction, it would be logical to also uphold the power and wisdom to choose the true faith among those "duly constituted." We start down a rough road when we begin to mix compulsory public education with compulsory godliness. . . .

The distinction attempted between that case [McCollum] and this is trivial, almost to the point of cynicism, magnifying its nonessential details and disparaging compulsion which was the underlying reason for invalidity. A reading of the Court's opinion in that case along with its opinion in this case will show such difference of overtones and undertones as to make clear that the McCollum Case has passed like a storm in a teacup. The wall which the Court was professing to erect between Church and State has become even more warped and twisted than I expected. Today's judgment will be more interesting to students of psychology and of the judicial processes than to students of constitutional law.

d. Bible Reading in Public Schools

ABINGTON SCHOOL DISTRICT v. SCHEMPP

MURRAY v. CURLETT

83 S. Ct. — ; 31 US Law Week 4683 (1963)

[Many states permit or require teachers in the public schools to read passages from the Bible or from the Old Testament. Some also permit or require recitation of the Lord's Prayer. Most of the statutes have been adopted in the twentieth century. The Schempp Case involved a Pennsylvania act; the Murray Case involved a Maryland act. The Supreme Court, by an 8-to-1 vote, held the statutes unconstitutional as a violation of the First Amendment, made applicable to the states by the Fourteenth Amendment. The opinion for the Court was by Justice Clark. Justices Brennan and Goldberg wrote concurring opinions.

Justice Stewart wrote a dissenting opinion, in which he contended that the records in both cases were inadequate for the decisions and that both cases should have been remanded for further hearings.]

Mr. Justice Clark delivered the opinion of the Court:

Once again we are called upon to consider the scope of the provision of the First Amendment to the United States Constitution which declares that "Congress shall make no law respecting an establishment of religion or prohibiting the free exercise thereof. . . ." These companion cases present the issues in the context of state action requiring that schools begin each day with readings from the Bible. While raising the basic questions under slightly different factual situations, the cases permit of joint treatment. In light of the history of the First Amendment and of our cases interpreting and applying its requirements, we hold that the practices at issue and the laws requiring them are unconstitutional under the Establishment Clause, as applied to the states through the Fourteenth Amendment.

I.

The Facts in Each Case: No. 142. The Commonwealth of Pennsylvania by law, 24 Pa. Stat. § 15–1516, as amended, Pub. Law 1928 (Supp. 1960) Dec. 17, 1959, requires that "at least ten verses from the Holy Bible shall be read, without comment, at the opening of each public school on each school day. Any child shall be excused from such Bible reading, or attending such Bible reading, upon the written request of his parent or guardian." The Schempp family, husband and wife and two of their three children, brought suit to enjoin enforcement of the statute, contending that their rights under the Fourteenth Amendment to the Constitution of the United States are, have been, and will continue to be violated unless this statute be declared unconstitutional as violative of these provisions of the First Amendment. They sought to enjoin the appellant school district, wherein the Schempp children attend school, and its officers and the Superintendent of Public Instruction of the Commonwealth from continuing to conduct such readings and recitation of the Lord's Prayer in the public schools of the district pursuant to the statute. A three-judge statutory District Court for the Eastern District of Pennsylvania held that the statute is violative of the Establishment Clause of the First Amendment as applied to the states by the Due Process Clause of the Fourteenth Amendment and directed that appropriate injunctive relief issue. . . .

The appellees Edward Lewis Schempp, his wife Sidney, and their children, Roger and Donna, are of the Unitarian faith and are members of the Unitarian Church in Germantown, Philadelphia, Pennsylvania, where they, as well as another son, Ellory, regularly attend religious services. The latter was originally a party, but having graduated from the school system *pendente lite,* was voluntarily dismissed from the action. The other children attend the Abington Senior High School, which is a public school operated by appellant district.

On each school day at the Abington Senior High School between 8:15 and 8:30 a.m., while the pupils are attending their home rooms or advisory sections, opening exercises are conducted pursuant to the statute. The exercises are broadcast into each room in the school building through an intercommunications system and are conducted under the supervision of a teacher by students attending the school's radio and television workshop. Selected students from this course gather each morning in the school's workshop studio for the exercises, which include readings by one of the students of 10 verses of the Holy Bible, broadcast to each room in the building. This is followed by the recitation of the Lord's Prayer, likewise over the intercommunications system, but also by the students in the various classrooms, who are asked to stand and join in repeating the prayer in unison. The exercises are closed with the flag salute and such pertinent announcements as are of interest to the students. Participation in the opening exercises, as directed by the statute, is voluntary. The student reading the verses from the Bible may select the passages and read from any version he chooses, although the only copies furnished by the school are the King James version, copies of which were circulated to each teacher by the school district. During the period in which the exercises have been conducted the King James, the Douay and the Revised Standard versions of the Bible have been used, as well as the Jewish Holy Scriptures. There are no prefatory statements, no questions asked or solicited, no comments or explanations made and no interpretations given at or during the exercises. The students and parents are advised that the student may absent himself from the classroom or, should he elect to remain, not participate in the exercises.

It appears from the record that in schools not having an intercommunications system the Bible reading and the recitation of the Lord's Prayer were conducted by the home-room teacher, who chose the text of the verses and read them herself or had students read them in rotation or by volunteers. This was followed by a standing recitation of the Lord's Prayer, together with the Pledge of Allegiance to the flag by the class in unison and a closing announcement of routine school items of interest.

At the first trial Edward Schempp and the children testified as to specific religious doctrines purveyed by a literal reading of the Bible "which were contrary to the religious beliefs they held and to their familial teaching." . . . The children testified that all of the doctrines to which they referred were read to them at various times as part of the exercises. Edward Schempp testified at the second trial that he had considered having Roger and Donna excused from attendance at the exercises but decided against it for several reasons, including his belief that the children's relationships with their teachers and classmates would be adversely affected. . . .

The trial court, in striking down the practices and the statute requiring them, made specific findings of fact that the children's attendance at Abington Senior High School is compulsory and that the practice of reading 10 verses from the Bible is also compelled by law. It also found that

The reading of the verses, even without comment, possesses a devotional and religious character and constitutes in effect a religious observance. The devotional and religious nature of the morning exercises is made all the more apparent by the fact that the Bible reading is followed immediately by a recital in unison by the pupils of the Lord's Prayer. The fact that some pupils, or theoretically all pupils, might be excused from attendance at the exercises does not mitigate the obligatory nature of the ceremony for . . . Section 1516 . . . unequivocally requires the exercises to be held every school day in every school in the Commonwealth. The exercises are held in the school buildings and perforce are conducted by and under the authority of the local school authorities and during school sessions. Since the statute requires the reading of the "Holy Bible," a Christian document, the practice . . . prefers the Christian religion. The record demonstrates that it was the intention of . . . the Commonwealth . . . to introduce a religious ceremony into the public schools of the Commonwealth. . . .

No. 119. In 1905 the Board of School Commissioners of Baltimore City adopted a rule pursuant to Art. 77, § 202 of the Annotated Code of Maryland. The rule provided for the holding of opening exercises in the schools of the city consisting primarily of the "reading, without comment, of a chapter in the Holy Bible and/or the use of the Lord's Prayer." The petitioners, Mrs. Madalyn Murray and her son, William J. Murray, III, are both professed atheists. Following unsuccessful attempts to have the respondent school board rescind the rule this suit was filed for mandamus to compel its rescission and cancellation. It was alleged that William was a student in a public school of the city and Mrs. Murray, his mother, was a taxpayer therein; that it was the practice under the rule to have a reading on each school morning from the King James version of the Bible; that at petitioners' insistence the rule was amended to permit children to be excused from the exercise on request of the parent and that William had been excused pursuant thereto; that nevertheless the rule as amended was in violation of the petitioners' rights "to freedom of religion under the First and Fourteenth Amendments" and in violation of "the principle of separation between church and state, contained therein. . . ." The petition particularized the petitioners' atheistic beliefs and stated that the rule, as practiced, violated their rights

in that it threatens their religious liberty by placing a premium on belief as against non-belief and subjects their freedom of conscience to the rule of the majority; it pronounces belief in God as the source of all moral and spiritual values, equating these values with religious values, and thereby renders sinister, alien and suspect the belief and ideals of . . . Petitioners, promoting doubt and question of their morality, good citizenship and good faith.

The respondents demurred and the trial court, recognizing that the demurrer admitted all facts well pleaded, sustained it without leave to amend. The Maryland Court of Appeals affirmed, the majority of four justices holding the exercise not in violation of the First and Fourteenth Amendments, with three justices dissenting. . . .

II.

It is true that religion has been closely identified with our history and government. As we said in *Engel* v. *Vitale*, 370 U.S. 421, 434 (1962), "The history of man is inseparable from the history of religion. And . . . since the beginning of that history many people have devoutly believed that 'More things are wrought by prayer than this world dreams of.'" In *Zorach* v. *Clauson*, 343 U.S. 306, 313 (1952), we gave specific recognition to the proposition that "[w]e are a religious people whose institutions presuppose a Supreme Being." The fact that the Founding Fathers believed devotedly that there was a God and that the unalienable, rights of man were rooted in Him is clearly evidenced in their writings, from the Mayflower Compact to the Constitution itself. This background is evidenced today in our public life through the continuance in our oaths of office from the Presidency to the Alderman of the final supplication, "So help me God." Likewise each House of the Congress provides through its Chaplain an opening prayer, and the sessions of this Court are declared open by the crier in a short ceremony, the final phrase of which invokes the grace of God. Again, there are such manifestations in our military forces, where those of our citizens who are under the restrictions of military service wish to engage in voluntary worship. Indeed, only last year an official survey of the country indicated that 64% of our people have church membership, Bureau of Census, U.S. Department of Commerce, Statistical Abstract of the United States, 48 (83d ed. 1962), while less than 3% profess no religion whatever. *Id.*, at p. 46. It can be truly said, therefore, that today, as in the beginning, our national life reflects a religious people who, in the words of Madison, are "earnestly praying, as . . . in duty bound, that the Supreme Lawgiver of the Universe . . . guide them into every measure which may be worthy of his . . . blessing. . . .

III.

Almost a hundred years ago in *Minor* v. *Board of Education of Cincinnati,* Judge Alphonzo Taft, father of the revered Chief Justice, in an unpublished opinion stated the ideal of our people as to religious freedom as one of absolute equality before the law of all religious opinions and sects. . . .

The government is neutral, and, while protecting all, it prefers none, and it disparages none.

Before examining this "neutral" position in which the Establishment and Free Exercise Clauses of the First Amendment place our government it is well that we discuss the reach of the Amendment under the cases of this Court.

First, this Court has decisively settled that the First Amendment's mandate that "Congress shall make no law respecting an establishment of religion, or prohibiting the free exercise thereof" has been made wholly applicable to the states by the Fourteenth Amendment. Twenty-three years ago in *Cantwell* v. *Connecticut*, 310 U.S. 296, 303 (1940), this Court, through Mr. Justice Roberts, said:

The fundamental concept of liberty embodied in that [Fourteenth] Amendment embraces the liberties guaranteed by the First Amendment. The First Amendment declares that Congress shall make no law respecting an establishment of religion or prohibiting the free exercise thereof. The Fourteenth Amendment has rendered the legislatures of the states as incompetent as Congress to enact such laws. . . .

In a series of cases since *Cantwell* the Court has repeatedly reaffirmed that doctrine, and we do so now. . . .

Second, this Court has rejected unequivocally the contention that the establishment clause forbids only governmental preference of one religion over another. Almost 20 years ago in *Everson*, the Court said that "[n]either a state nor the Federal government can set up a church. Neither can pass laws which aid one religion, aid all religions, or prefer one religion over another." . . . The same conclusion has been firmly maintained ever since that time . . . and we reaffirm it now.

While none of the parties to either of these cases has questioned these basic conclusions of the Court, both of which have been long established, recognized and consistently reaffirmed, others continue to question their history, logic and efficacy. Such contentions, in the light of the consistent interpretation in cases of this Court, seem entirely untenable and of value only as academic exercises.

IV.

The interrelationship of the Establishment and the Free Exercise Clauses was first touched upon by Mr. Justice Roberts for the Court in *Cantwell* v. *Connecticut*, where it was said that their "inhibition of legislation" had

a double aspect. On the one hand, it forestalls compulsion by law of the acceptance of any creed or the practice of any form of worship. Freedom of conscience and freedom to adhere to such religious organization or form of worship as the individual may choose cannot be restricted by law. On the other hand, it safeguards the free exercise of the chosen form of religion. Thus the Amendment embraces two concepts—freedom to believe and freedom to act. The first is absolute but, in the nature of things, the second cannot be.

A half dozen years later in *Everson* v. *Board of Education*, this Court, through Mr. Justice Black, stated that the "scope of the First Amendment . . . was designed forever to suppress" the establishment of religion or the prohibition of the free exercise thereof. In short, the Court held that the Amendment

requires the state to be a neutral in its relations with groups of religious believers and nonbelievers; it does not require the state to be their adversary. State power is no more to be used so as to handicap religions than it is to favor them. . . .

Finally, in *Engel* v. *Vitale*, only last year, these principles were so universally recognized that the Court without the citation of a single case and over the sole dissent of Mr. Justice Stewart reaffirmed them. The Court found the 22-word prayer used in "New York's program of daily classroom invocation of God's blessings as prescribed in the Regents' prayer . . . [to be] a religious activity." It held that "it is no part of the business of government to compose official prayers for any group of the American people to recite as a part of a religious program carried on by the government." In discussing the reach of the Establishment and Free Exercise Clauses of the First Amendment the Court said:

Although these two clauses may in certain instances overlap, they forbid two quite different kinds of governmental encroachment upon religious freedom. The Establishment Clause, unlike the Free Exercise Clause, does not depend upon any showing of direct governmental compulsion and is violated by the enactment of laws which establish an official religion whether those laws operate directly to coerce non-observing individuals or not. This is not to say, of course, that laws officially prescribing a particular form of religious worship do not involve coercion of such individuals. When the power, prestige and financial support of government is placed behind a particular religious belief, the indirect coercive pressure upon religious minorities to conform to the prevailing officially approved religion is plain.

And in further elaboration the Court found that the "first and most immediate purpose [of the Establishment Clause] rested on a belief that a union of government and religion tends to destroy government and to degrade religion." When government, the Court said, allies itself with one particular form of religion, the inevitable result is that it incurs "the hatred, disrespect, and even contempt of those who held contrary beliefs."

V.

The wholesome "neutrality" of which this Court's cases speak thus stems from a recognition of the teachings of history that powerful sects or groups might bring about a fusion of governmental and religious functions or a concert or dependency of one upon the other to the end that official support of the State or Federal Government would be placed behind the tenets of one or of all orthodoxies. This the Establishment Clause prohibits. And a further reason for neutrality is found in the Free Exercise Clause, which recognizes the value of religious training, teaching and observance and, more particularly, the right of every person to freely choose his own course with reference thereto, free of any compulsion from the state. This the Free Exercise Clause guarantees. Thus, as we have seen, the two clauses may overlap. As we have indicated, the Establishment Clause has been directly considered by this Court eight times in the past score of years and, with only one Justice dissenting on the point, it has consistently held that the clause withdrew all legislative power respecting religious belief or the expression thereof. The test may be stated as follows: what are the purpose and the primary effect of the enactment? If either is the advancement or inhibition of religion then the enactment exceeds the scope of legislative power as circumscribed by the Constitution. That is to say that to withstand the strictures of the Establishment Clause there must be a secular legislative purpose and a primary effect that neither advances nor inhibits religion. . . . The Free Exercise Clause, likewise considered many times here, withdraws from legislative power, state and federal, the exertion of any restraint on the free exercise of religion. Its purpose is to secure religious liberty in the individual by prohibiting any invasions thereof by civil authority. Hence it is necessary in a free exercise case for one to show the coercive effect of the enactment as it operates against him in the practice of his religion. The distinction between the two clauses is apparent—a violation of the Free Exercise Clause is predicated on coercion while the Establishment Clause violation need not be so attended.

Applying the Establishment Clause principles to the cases at bar we find that the States are requiring the selection and reading at the opening of the school day of verses from the Holy Bible and the recitation of the Lord's Prayer by the students in unison. These exercises are prescribed as part of the curricular activities of students who are required by law to attend school. They are held in the school buildings under the supervision and with the participation of teachers employed in those schools. None of these factors, other than compulsory school attendance, was present in the program upheld in *Zorach* v. *Clauson*. The trial court in No. 142 has found that such an opening exercise is a religious ceremony and was intended by the State to be so. We agree with the trial court's finding as to the religious character of the exercises. Given that finding the exercises and the law requiring them are in violation of the Establishment Clause.

There is no such specific finding as to the religious character of the exercises in No. 119, and the State contends (as does the State in No. 142) that the program is an effort to extend its benefits to all public school children without regard to their religious belief. Included within its secular purposes, it says, are the promotion of moral values, the contradiction to the materialistic trends of our times, the perpetuation of our institutions and the teaching of literature. The case came up on demurrer, of course, to a petition which alleged that the uniform practice under the rule had been to read from the King James version of the Bible and that the exercise was sectarian. The short answer, therefore, is that the religious character of the exercise was admitted by the State. But even if its purpose is not strictly religious, it is sought to be accomplished through readings, without comment, from the Bible. Surely the place of the Bible as an instrument of religion cannot be gainsaid, and the State's recognition of the pervading religious character of the ceremony is evident from the rule's specific permission of the alternative use of the Catholic Douay version as well as the recent amendment permitting non-attendance at the exercises. None of these factors is consistent with the contention that the Bible is here used either as an instrument for nonreligious moral inspiration or as a reference for the teaching of secular subjects.

The conclusion follows that in both cases the laws require religious exercises and such exercises are being conducted in direct violation of the rights of the appellees and petitioners. Nor are these required exercises mitigated by the fact that individual students may absent themselves upon parental request, for that fact furnishes no defense to a claim of unconstitutionality under the Establishment Clause. . . . Further, it is no defense to urge that the religious practices here may be relatively minor encroachments on the First Amendment. The breach of neutrality that is today a trickling stream may all too soon become a raging torrent and, in the words of Madison, "it is proper to take alarm at the first experiment on our liberties." . . .

It is insisted that unless these religious exercises are permitted a "religion of secularism" is established in the schools. . . . We do not agree, however, that this decision in any sense has that effect. In addition, it might well be said that one's education is not complete without a study of comparative religion or the history of religion and its relationship to the advancement of civilization. It certainly may be said that the Bible is worthy of study for its literary and historic qualities. Nothing we have said here indicates that such study of the Bible or of religion, when presented objectively as part of a secular program of education may not be effected consistent with the First Amendment. But the exercises here do not fall into those categories. They are religious exercises, required by the States in violation of the command of the First Amendment that the Government maintain strict neutrality, neither aiding nor opposing religion.

Finally, we cannot accept that the concept of neutrality, which does not permit a State to require a religious exercise even with the consent of the majority of those affected, collides with the majority's right to free exercise of religion. While the Free Exercise Clause clearly prohibits the use of state action to deny the right of free exercise to *anyone*, it has never meant that a majority could use the machinery of the State to practice its beliefs. . . .

The place of religion in our society is an exalted one, achieved through a long tradition of reliance on the home, the church and the inviolable citadel of the individual heart and mind. We have come to recognize through bitter experience that it is not within the power of government to invade that citadel, whether its purpose or effect be to aid or oppose, to advance or retard. In the relationship between man and religion, the State is firmly committed to a position of neutrality. Though the application of that rule requires interpretation of a delicate sort, the rule itself is clearly and concisely stated in the words of the First Amendment. Applying that rule to the facts of these cases, we affirm the judgment in No. 142. In No. 119, the judgment is reversed and the cause remanded to the Maryland Court of Appeals for further proceedings consistent with this opinion.

It is so ordered.

e. Bible Distribution in Public Schools

TUDOR v. BOARD OF EDUCATION OF RUTHERFORD

14 NJ 31 (1953)

[A Protestant organization, the Gideons International, attempts "to win men and women for the Lord Jesus Christ" by the distribution of the Bible in hotels, hospitals, and, more recently, public schools. For public schools the "Gideons Bible" consists of the New Testament, the Book of Psalms, and the Book of Proverbs. Pupils are given an opportunity to get free copies to take home. Objections to distribution of the "Gideons Bible" to public school pupils have been voiced by both Roman Catholics and Jews. In the *Rutherford Case* the Supreme Court of New Jersey unanimously held that the local board of education violated the Federal and State Constitutions when it gave permission for the distribution of the "Gideons Bible," a sectarian book, to public school pupils. The opinion of Chief Justice Vanderbilt is notable as being the first judicial opinion by a high court on the issue and also for using expert testimony on the harm done to children by the action of the Gideons in the public schools.]

The opinion of the Court was delivered by Chief Justice Vanderbilt:

I

The Gideons International is a nonprofit corporation organized under the laws of the State of Illinois, whose object is "to win men and women for the Lord Jesus Christ, through . . . (c) placing the Bible—God's Holy Words—or portions thereof in hotels, hospitals, schools, institutions, and also through the distribution of same for personal use." In recent years it began a campaign to make available to pupils in the public schools of this country the so-called "Gideon Bible," which was characterized by the International in its pleadings as "a book containing all of the New Testament, all of the Book of Psalms from the Old Testament, all of the Book of Proverbs from the Old Testament; all without note or comment, conformable to the edition of 1611, commonly known as the Authorized, or King James version of the Holy Bible." In furtherance of this campaign it applied by letter to the Board of Education of the Borough of Rutherford for permission to distribute its Bible to the public schools of that municipality: . . .

Gentlemen:

The Gideons of Passaic and Bergen County, consisting of local business men, hereby offer to furnish, without charge, a volume containing the book of Psalms, Proverbs and the New Testament to each of the children in the schools of Rutherford from the fifth grade up through the eighth grade, and High School.

This offer is part of a national campaign conducted by the Gideons International to furnish the Word of God free to the young people of our country from the fifth grade through the high school. If God's word is heard and heeded, if it is read and believed, we believe that this is the answer to the problem of juvenile delinquency.

If your board approves this distribution, we will be glad to have our committee work out the details with the principals of the schools.

Yours very truly,
PASSAIC COUNTY CAMP OF GIDEONS . . .

The proposal was considered at a meeting of the Board of Education on November 5, 1951, at which time there was voiced some opposition to the proposal by a Catholic priest and a Jewish rabbi on the grounds that the Gideons' New Testament was sectarian and forbidden to Catholic and Jewish children under the laws of their respective religions. The proposal, however, was passed by the board with one dissenting vote, the resolution adopted providing that "the Gideons International be allowed to furnish copies of the New Testament, Psalms and Proverbs to those pupils who request them." Under date of November 21, 1951, the following request form for signature of the parents was prepared by the Board of Education and distributed to the pupils of the public schools of Rutherford:

Rutherford Public Schools,
Rutherford, N.J.
November 21, 1951

To all Parents:

At the regular meeting of the Board of Education on November 5, 1951, The Gideon Bible Society presented a request that the New Testament, Psalms and Proverbs be made available, without cost, to all children who wish a copy. The Board approved this request provided the distribution be voluntary. *If you wish a copy of this Bible, will you please sign the slip below and return it with your child to the school he attends by Friday, December 21.*

_____

School

_____   _____
                                        Date

Please request The Gideon Bible Society to provide my child _____ _____, with a copy of the New Testament, Psalms and Proverbs. This request involves no obligation on my part or on the part of the Board of Education.

Signed_____
Parent or Guardian

On January 14, 1952, the Board of Education was advised by its counsel that the proposed distribution was in his opinion legal. At a principal's meeting on February 6, 1952, the following instructions were issued:

(a) Only names of pupils whose parents had previously signed for the Bibles should be used in any announcement.

(b) Pupils whose parents had signed for Bibles are to report to the home room at the close of the session and no other pupils are to be in the room when the Bibles are distributed.

(c) Any announcement of names for the purpose of reporting after school should not include a reference as to the purpose of reporting.

Prior to the distribution of the books the present action was commenced demanding judgment as to the validity of the distribution under the Federal and New Jersey Constitutions and seeking an injunction against it. . . .

The plaintiff Bernard Tudor is an adherent of the Jewish religion, while plaintiff Ralph Lecoque is a member of the Catholic faith, each being a New Jersey citizen and taxpayer of Rutherford and a parent of a pupil in a Rutherford public school. Each contends that the Gideon Bible is "a sectarian work of peculiar religious value and significance to members of the Protestant faith," Mr. Tudor claiming that "its distribution to children of the Jewish faith violates the teachings, tenets and principles of Judaism," while Mr. Lecoque states that "its distribution to children of Catholic faith violates the teachings, tenets and principles of Catholicism." After this action was commenced, the child of plaintiff Ralph Lecoque transferred from the public school to a Catholic parochial school and to the extent that the complaint was based upon his status as a parent, the issue became moot. The State of New Jersey was originally named as a party defendant but the action as to it has been dismissed. The Synagogue Council of America and the National Community Relations Advisory Council have submitted a brief amici curiae.

II

The American doctrine of the separation of Church and State cannot be understood apart from its history for it is the epitome of centuries of struggle and conflict. In 311 A.D. Christians were still being persecuted; but shortly thereafter the Fourth Century witnessed the toleration of Christianity in the Roman World. In 313 A.D. Constantine, the ruler of the West, and Licinius, the emperor of the East, met in Italy and proclaimed the Edict of Milan, which made the toleration of the Christian religion "a part of a universal toleration of all religions, and it establishes absolute freedom of worship," Innes, *Church and State*, p. 23. In 410 A.D. Rome was sacked by Alaric. Italy, as well as Spain and Africa, fell to the Teutonic barbarians, but these conquests did not spell defeat for Christianity. The attitude of the invaders is illustrated by the words of Theodoric, speaking shortly after the fall of Rome:

That to pretend to a dominion over the conscience is to usurp the prerogative of God; that by the nature of things the power of sovereigns is confined to external government; that they have no right of punishment, but over those who disturb the public peace, of which they are the guardians; and that the most dangerous heresy is that of a sovereign who separates himself from a part of his subjects, because they believe not according to his belief. Innes, *Church and State*, p. 51.

After the collapse of the Roman Empire the Church remained as the one stable, permanent element in society. Gradually it came to claim not merely equality with the State, but actual superiority. Thomas Aquinas summed up the Church's attitude:

The highest aim of mankind is eternal happiness. To this chief aim of mankind all earthly aims must be subordinated. This chief aim cannot be realized through human direction alone but must obtain divine assistance which is only to be obtained through the Church. Therefore the State, through which earthly aims are obtained, must be subordinated to the Church. Church and State are as two swords which God has given to Christendom for protection; both of these, however, are given by him to the Pope and the temporal sword by him handed to the rulers of the State. Bates, *Religious Liberty: An Inquiry* (1945), p. 140.

The Church's claim of supremacy did not go unchallenged. Charlemagne, who had been crowned by the Pope, deliberately crowned his own son as successor without consulting the Pope. The struggle for supremacy was on between Church and State, and the history of the Middle Ages in Europe is largely a history of this continuing conflict. The struggles between Pope Gregory VII and Emperor Henry IV in the Eleventh Century, and between the English kings Henry II and John and Celestine III and Innocent III a century later were but phases of the conflict. The Church reached the height of its supremacy over the State in the Thirteenth Century, under Innocent III, who informed the Patriarch of Constantinople that "the Lord left to Peter (the Pope) the government not of the Church only but of the whole world," and advised Philip Augustus of France that "single rulers have single provinces and single kings have single kingdoms, but Peter, as in the plentitude, so in the extent of his power, is preëminent over all since he is the vicar of Him Whose is the earth and fullness thereof, the whole world and all that dwell therein." Bates, *Religious Liberty: An Inquiry*, pp. 140–141. During his rule Innocent was not only a spiritual leader but he was also the supreme temporal chief of the Italian State, the Spanish Peninsula, the Scandinavian States, Hungary, Bohemia, Poland, Servia, Bosnia, Bulgaria, and the Christian state of Syria. 17 *Encyclopedia Britannica*, (14th ed.) "Papacy," p. 203.

The fourteenth century witnessed the growth of new ideas. In 1324 Marsilius of Padua in his *Defensor Pacis* denied the right of the Church to interfere in any matters which were not spiritual. He expounded the very ideas that centuries later were credited to Locke, Montesquieu, Rousseau and Jefferson. Marsilius was far ahead of his age when he claimed that "no man may be punished for his religion." Acton, "History of Freedom in Christianity," in *Essays on Freedom and Power*, p. 65.

But the doctrine of religious liberty and the separation of Church and State were not established in Europe even with the advent of the Reformation. The Reformation brought forth the more prevalent Erastian doctrine of state supremacy and the use of religion to help carry out state policy. The peace of Augsburg in 1555 was a compromise between Lutherans and Catholics, based on the theory that the religion of a province was to be determined by the religion of its ruler (*cuius regio, eius religio*). To the same effect was the peace of Westphalia in 1648 ending a thirty year religious war which swept Central Europe. . . . In England under Queen Elizabeth the Thirty-nine Articles of the Church of England were adopted and the supremacy of the Crown over the Church was clearly established. Bloody struggles between Anglicans, Catholics and Dissenters continued. By the Seventeenth Century Catholics were regarded with disfavor and in 1647 the Constitution established by Cromwell granted religious freedom to all except Catholics. In the Glorious Revolution of 1689 the Act of Toleration under William and Mary established religious toleration in England, but again Catholics were excepted.

By 1787 in Europe no nation had established complete freedom of worship or the mutual independence of religion and civil government. There had been steps in that direction and there were those who strongly advocated the separation of Church and State but the Erastian doctrine still prevailed. In almost every country there was a state-supported or at least a state-favored religion while the other faiths were treated with varying degrees of toleration. In Spain the Inquisition was still in existence in 1787 while at the other extreme Holland represented the utmost in religious toleration and freedom for all faiths. In 1784 James Madison summed up the centuries of bloody religious battles in Europe: "Torrents of blood have been spilt in the world in vain attempts of the secular arm to extinguish religious discord, by proscribing all differences in religious opinions." Blau, *Cornerstones of Religious Freedom in America* (1949), p. 85. While America has been free from religious wars, our history has had its dark pages of religious persecution.

III

Religion was a strong motivating force in the American colonies. People of all faiths flocked to the New World, many with the hope that here for the first time they could enjoy religious freedom. Unfortunately to America these earlier settlers also brought the Old World idea of a state established and state dominated religion. Many of the original charters granted by the Crown required the settlers to establish a religion that was to be supported by all, believers and nonbelievers alike. Thus in early Virginia all ministers were required to conform to the canons of the Church of England. Quakers were banished and Catholics were disqualified from public office, while priests were not permitted in the colony. In New York Peter Stuyvesant established the Dutch Reformed Church, which all settlers were required to support. Baptists who attempted to hold services in their homes were subject to fines, whipping and banishment. Quakers were unwelcome and subject to persecution. . . . In New England generally the Calvinist Congregational Church was the established religion.

Religious freedom in the colonies was far from an established fact. In the Massachusetts Bay Colony Anne Hutchinson in 1638 was tried and convicted as a blasphemer and seducer of the faithful and as a teacher of erroneous doctrines, because she held meetings in her home where she advocated the direct intuition of God's grace and love instead of obedience to the laws of the Church and the State. Roger Williams was banished because "he broached and divulged divers new and dangerous opinions, against the authority of the magistrates." Stokes, *Church and State in the United States* (1950), Vol. I, p. 195. Catholics were persecuted and in 1647 the General Court ordered that:

No Jesuit or spiritual or ecclesiastical person ordained by the pope or see of Rome shall henceforth come into Massachusetts. Any person not freeing himself of suspicion shall be jailed, then banished. If taken a second time he shall be put to death. Pfeffer, *Church, State and Freedom* (1953), p. 68.

Despite these instances of intolerance and persecution there were successful examples of religious freedom. In 1649, largely due to the efforts of Cecil Calvert, the second Lord Baltimore, Maryland granted toleration to all Trinitarian Christians. In Rhode Island through the efforts of John Clarke, a follower of Roger Williams, Charles II granted a charter in 1663 which provided for complete religious freedom. In 1683 Pennsylvania received from William Penn its "Frame of Government" which stated that all who believed in "One Almighty God" should be protected and all who believed in "Jesus Christ the Savior of the World" could hold civil office.

The history of religious freedom in the province of New Jersey was not fundamentally different from that in the other colonies, although Stokes states that we "had a better colonial record in the matter of toleration than most of the colonies." *Church and State in the United States, supra,* Vol. 1, p. 435. The grantees of the Concessions of 1665, Lord Berkeley and Sir George Carteret, offered liberty of worship as an inducement to settlers. This was continued under the Quakers by a Law of 1681 in West Jersey and in East Jersey by a Law of 1683. Nevertheless, despite what appeared to be the establishment of religious freedom in the Province of New Jersey, . . . there was strong anti-Catholic feeling in the colony, and holders of civil office were required to take an oath against the Pope. . . . By the king's instructions to Lord Cornbury . . . in 1702 he was to permit a liberty of conscience to all persons except Papists. Our Constitution of 1776 provides:

XVIII. Free Exercise of Religion. That no person shall ever within this colony be deprived of the inestimable privilege of worshipping Almighty God in a manner agreeable to the dictates of his own conscience; nor under any pretense whatsoever, compelled to attend any place of worship, contrary to his own faith and judgment; nor shall any person within this colony, ever be obliged to pay tithes, taxes or any other rates, for the purpose of building or repairing any church or churches, place or places of worship, or for the maintenance of any minister or ministry, contrary to what he believes to be right, or has deliberately or voluntarily engaged himself to perform.

But the very next article of this same Constitution, after providing that there shall be "no establishment of any one religious sect in this province in preference to another," goes on to guarantee civil rights and the right to hold civil office to all who are of the "protestant sect." The exclusion of Catholics from this guarantee of civil rights and from holding civil office was not eliminated until the Constitution of 1844.

Generally speaking it can then be said that religious toleration varied from one province to another with very few approaching a system of full religious freedom. Pfeffer reviews the religious atmosphere in the colonies:

Summarizing the colonial period, we may note that the proprietary regimes permitted a considerable degree of toleration, at least in comparison with the other colonies. This difference may be explained partly by the idealism of the proprietors and partly by the economic necessity of attracting large numbers of settlers in order to preserve and make profitable the proprietor's substantial investment.

Even in the proprietary colonies, however, the death of the idealistic founder, Calvert, Williams, or Penn, resulted in considerable backsliding, and the imposition of restrictions on civil and religious rights, particularly of non-Protestants. The limited tolerance which did exist did not include Catholics, Jews, Unitarians, or Deists. The variety and degree of discrimination against them varied. Primarily, the discrimination was political—the non-Protestants could not vote or hold office. But the restrictions were not always limited to political disabilities. Public performance of Catholic worship was prohibited almost everywhere, and as late as 1756 the colony which had been founded by the Catholic Calverts enacted a law subjecting Catholics to double taxation.

Perhaps the incident that most ironically illustrates the turnabout after the death of the idealistic founder is the action of a Rhode Island court which in 1762 denied the petition of two Jews for naturalization on the ground that to grant the petition would be "inconsistent with the first principles on which the colony was founded." *Church, State and Freedom*, p. 79.

It was left to Virginia to lead the struggle for religious freedom and the separation of church and state. In 1784 there was proposed in its House of Delegates a "bill establishing provision for teachers of the Christian religions." Action thereon was postponed until the next session in order that the bill could be publicized and distributed to the people who could then make known their views. The issue was fought on a very high plane of principle with Thomas Jefferson, James Madison and George Mason aligned with the opposition. It was then that James Madison wrote his famous *A Memorial and Remonstrance* in which he presented his views that religion was not a matter within the scope of civil government. For complete historical background and full text reference is made to Mr. Justice Rutledge's dissenting opinion in *Everson* v. *Board of Education*, 330 U.S. 1. At the next session the proposed bill was defeated and in its place an Act "for establishing religious freedom" drafted by Thomas Jefferson was passed, the preamble of which stated: "that to suffer the civil magistrate to intrude his powers into the field of opinion, and to restrain the profession or propagation of principles on supposition of their ill tendency, is a dangerous fallacy which at once destroys all religious liberty." The bill further provided "that it is time enough for the rightful purposes of civil government for its officers to interfere when principles break out into overt acts against peace and good order." In his opinion for the court in *Reynolds* v. *United States*, 98 U.S. 145, Mr. Chief Justice Waite states that "in these two sentences is found the true distinction between what properly belongs to the Church and what to the State."

It was a little over a year later that the Convention met in Philadelphia to draft the Constitution of the United States. The Convention failed to include in the proposed Constitution any Bill of Rights or any provision concerning freedom of religion. Although adopting the Constitution, several states did so only on the understanding that a Bill of Rights would be added including a provision for a declaration of religious liberty. At the very first session of Congress the first ten amendments, or Bill of Rights, were proposed and largely through the efforts of James Madison were adopted, the First Amendment providing that "Congress shall make no law respecting an establishment of religion, or prohibiting the free exercise thereof." It took us over fourteen centuries and an incalculable amount of persecution to gain the religious tolerance and freedom expounded in 313 A.D. by the rulers of the Roman world.

The First Amendment, of course, applied only to the federal government, but it has been held that upon the adoption of the Fourteenth Amendment the prohibitions of the First Amendment were applicable to state action abridging religious freedom, *Cantwell* v. *Connecticut*, 310 U.S. 296.

IV

The charge here is sectarianism. The defendant Board of Education is accused of showing a preference by permitting the distribution of the King James version of the New Testament, which is unacceptable to those of the Jewish faith and, in fact, in conflict with their tenets. This violates the mandate of the First Amendment, as incorporated into the Fourteenth Amendment, prohibiting the making of any law "respecting an establishment of religion" and the requirement of Article I, paragraph 4 of the New Jersey Constitution that "there shall be no establishment of one religious sect in preference to another." By its very terms the New Jersey constitutional provision prohibits any such religious preference, while the First Amendment to the Federal Constitution has been judicially interpreted as so providing. As stated by Mr. Justice Black in his opinion for the majority of the Court in *Everson* v. *Board of Education:*

The "establishment of religion" clause of the First Amendment means at least this: Neither a state nor the Federal Government can set up a church. Neither can pass laws which aid one religion, aid all religions, or prefer one religion over another. . . .

That amendment [First] requires the state to be a neutral in its relations with groups of religious believers and non-believers.

In *Zorach* v. *Clausen*, 343 U.S. 306, Mr. Justice Douglas in his opinion for the majority of the court stated: "The government must be neutral when it comes to competition between sects." . . .

We are well aware of the ever continuing debates that have been taking place in this country for many years as to the meaning which should be given to the First Amendment. There are those who contend that our forefathers never intended to erect a "wall of separation" between Church and State. On the other hand, there are those who insist upon this absolute separation between Church and State. The plaudits and the criticisms of the various majority, concurring, and dissenting opinions rendered by the United States Supreme Court in *Everson* v. *Board of Education, McCollum* v. *Board of Education,* and *Zorach* v. *Clausen,* still continue.

But regardless of what our views on this fundamental question may be, our decision in this case must be based upon the undoubted doctrine of both the Federal Constitution and our New Jersey Constitution, that the state or any instrumentality thereof cannot under any circumstances show a preference for one religion over another. Such favoritism cannot be tolerated and must be disapproved as a clear violation of the Bill of Rights of our Constitutions.

This brings us to the heart of our problem here—namely, whether the resolution of the Board of Education displays that favoritism that is repugnant to our constitution. By permitting the distribution of the Gideon Bible, has the Board of Education established one religious sect in preference to another? Although as to the Catholic plaintiff this action has become moot due to the withdrawal of his child from the public schools of Rutherford, some testimony was presented at the trial as to his claim of sectarianism so we will at times refer to such testimony in our opinion. Our decision, however, is based upon the claim of the Jewish plaintiff that the resolution of the Rutherford Board of Education constitutes a preference of one religion over the Hebrew faith.

A review of the testimony at the trial convinces us that the King James version or Gideon Bible is unacceptable to those of the Jewish faith. In this regard Rabbi Joachim Prinz testified:

The New Testament is in profound conflict with the basic principles of Judaism. It is not accepted by the Jewish people as a sacred book. The Bible of the Jewish people is the Old Testament. The New Testament is not recognized as part of the Bible. The teachings of the New Testament are in complete and profound conflict with what Judaism teaches. It presupposes the concept of Jesus of Nazareth as a divinity, a concept which we do not accept.

They are in complete and utter conflict with what we teach, for we teach the oneness of God, which to our—and in accordance with our belief, excludes the existence of a Son of God. We accept Jesus of Nazareth as one of the figures of Jewish history, a Jew born, a Jew, died as a Jew, but we do not accept Jesus of Nazareth as the Christ. . . .

No, it is certainly not a nonsectarian book. It is a book that is—expresses the view of one denomination among the many religious denominations of the world.

Dr. Bernard J. Bamberger, rabbi of the West End Synagogue in New York City and former president of the Synagogue Council of America, stated:

Well, the New Testament, of course, is itself a complex document which contains a great many different writings, and so forth. Some of the passages and some of those writings are in themselves not necessarily in conflict with Judaism, but a very great many of them are in conflict with Judaism, first, because they teach certain doctrines which are contradictory to doctrines taught by Judaism, and also because in certain passages the New Testament writers directly attack certain Jewish beliefs which are very sacred to Jews.

He concluded that the King James Version was "completely not a non-sectarian book." Rabbi Irving Schnipper, in answer to a question whether the teachings of the New Testament are in conflict with his teaching of the children of the plaintiff Bernard Tudor, testified: "Definitely, the New Testament itself is in direct opposition to the teachings of Judaism." Nor is there any doubt that the King James version of the Bible is as unacceptable to Catholics as the Douay version is to Protestants. According to the testimony in this case the canon law of the Catholic Church provides that "Editions of the original text of the sacred scriptures published by non-Catholics are forbidden *ipso jure.*"

The defendant refers us to various statements by legal scholars and others to show that the Bible is not sectarian, but rather is the universal book of the Christian world, but in many of these statements the question of the New Testament was not discussed. In *Doremus* v. *Board of Education of the Borough of Hawthorne,* 5 N.J. 435, relied on by the defendant, the issue was whether R.S. 18:14–77 and 78, providing for compulsory reading in the public schools of five verses of the Old Testament and permissive reading of the Lord's Prayer violated the Federal Constitution. In upholding the constitutionality of the statutes we specifically stated . . . : "We consider that the Old Testament and the Lord's Prayer, pronounced without comment, are not sectarian, and that the short exercise provided by the statute does not constitute sectarian instruction or sectarian worship. . . ." We adhere to the *Doremus Case,* but its holding does not apply here, where clearly the issue of sectarianism is present. Here the issue is the distribution of the New Testament. The uncontradicted evidence presented by the plaintiff reveals that as far as the Jewish faith is concerned, the Gideon Bible is a sectarian book, the teachings of which are in conflict with the doctrines of his religion as well as that of his child, who is a pupil in the Rutherford public school. The full force of the violation of both the state and federal constitutions is revealed when we perceive what might happen if a single school board were besieged by three separate applications for the distribution of Bibles—one from Protestants as here, another from Catholics for the distribution of the Douay Bible and a third from Jews for the same privilege for their Bible.

We find from the evidence presented in this case that the Gideon Bible is a sectarian book, and that the resolution of the defendant Board of Education to permit its distribution through the public school system of the Borough of Rutherford was in violation of the First Amendment of the United States Constitution, as incorporated into the Fourteenth Amendment, and of Article I, paragraph 4, of the New Jersey Constitution. It therefore must be set aside.

V

The defendant contends that the distribution of the Gideon Bible in no way injects any issue of the "free exercise" of religion, that "no one is forced to take a New Testament and no religious exercise or instrument is brought to the classrooms of the public schools." In other words, it asserts the arguments of *Zorach* v. *Clausen,* that the "accommodation" of religion is permissible. This argument, however, ignores the realities of life. . . . Prof. Isidore Chein, Supervisor of Psychology and Acting Director of the Research Center for Mental Health at New York University, testified on behalf of the plaintiff:

. . . I would expect that a slip of this kind, distributed under the authority of the school, would create a subtle pressure on the child which would leave him with a sense that he is not quite as free as the statement on that slip says; in other words, that he will be something of an outcast and a pariah if he does not go along with this procedure.

. . . I think that they would be in a situation where they have to play along with this or else feel themselves to be putting themselves in a public position where they are different, where they are not the same as other people, and the whole pressure would exist on them to conform.

Dr. Dan Dodson, professor in the School of Education of New York University and director of curriculum and research in the Center for Human Relations Studies, when questioned as to the divisive effect of the distribution of the Gideon Bible stated:

I would say that any instance of this kind in which the—a document that has the importance that this has to certain religious groups, including my own, would be distributed or used as a means of propaganda or indoctrination by official channels, such as the school system, would create tensions among the religious groups; there would be a controversial problem.

I would say that it would raise questions among the children as to who is and who isn't, in terms of receiving the Bible. It would also create problems as to why some accepted it and others didn't. That would be divisive.

See also *People ex rel. Ring* v. *Board of Education,* 245 Ill. 334, where the court maintained that the fact that pupils could request to be excused from religious exercise did not make the requirement of sectarian Bible reading constitutional, and *Miller* v. *Cooper,* 52 N.M. 355, where the plaintiffs brought an action seeking, among other things, an injunction against the dissemination of allegedly sectarian literature among the public school pupils in violation of the provisions of the Federal and State Constitutions. The court there granted this relief, saying:

The charge that the defendants were using the school as a medium for the dissemination of religious pamphlets published by the Presbyterian Church presents a different situation. It is true that the teachers did not hand them to the pupils or instruct that they be taken or read. The pamphlets were, however, kept in plain sight in a school room and were available to pupils and the supply was evidently replenished from time to time. We condemned such practice . . . and condemn it here and hold that the trial court was in error when it failed to enjoin such acts. . . .

We cannot accept the argument that here, as in the *Zorach Case,* the State is merely "accommodating" religion. It matters little whether the teachers themselves will distribute the Bibles or whether that will be done by members of the Gideons International. The same vice exists, that of preference of one religion over another. This is all the more obvious when we realize the motive of the Gideons. Its purpose is "to win men and women for the Lord Jesus Christ, through . . . (c) placing the Bible—God's Holy Word . . . or portions thereof in hotels, hospitals, schools, institutions, and also through distribution of some for personal use." The society is engaged in missionary work, accomplished in part by placing the King James version of the Bible in the hands of public school children throughout the United States. To achieve this end it employs the public school system as the medium of distribution. It is at the school that the pupil receives the request slip to take to his parents for signature. It is at the school that the pupil actually receives his Gideon Bible. In other words, the public school machinery is used to bring about the distribution of these Bibles to the children of Rutherford. In the eyes of the pupils and their parents the Board of Education has placed its stamp of approval upon this distribution and, in fact, upon the Gideon Bible itself. Dr. Dodson further testified:

I would say it would leave a lefthanded implication that the school thought this was preferential in terms of what is the divine word, and that the backing of the State would inevitably be interpreted as being behind it.

Dr. William Heard Kilpatrick stated:

The Protestants would feel that the school is getting behind this thing; the Catholics would feel that the school is getting behind a Protestant affair; the Jews would feel that the school is getting behind the Protestant religion as opposed to their religion; and the people who don't accept any religion would feel that the school is actually trying to teach the religion through this means.

This is more than mere "accommodation" of religion permitted in the *Zorach Case.* The school's part in this distribution is an active one and cannot be sustained on the basis of a mere assistance to religion.

We are here concerned with a vital question involving the very foundation of our civilization. Centuries ago our forefathers fought and died for the principles now contained in the Bill of Rights of the Federal and New Jersey Constitutions. It is our solemn duty to preserve these rights and to prohibit any encroachment upon them. To permit the distribution of the King James version of the Bible in the public schools of this state would be to cast aside all the progress made in the United States and throughout New Jersey in the field of religious toleration and freedom. We would be renewing the ancient struggles among the various religious faiths to the detriment of all. This we must decline to do.

The . . . resolution of the Board of Education of the Borough of Rutherford under review is stricken [and order of injunction issued].

f. The Regents' Prayer in Public Schools

ENGEL v. VITALE

370 US 421 (1962)

[The Court, in a 6-to-1 decision, held that the "non-denominational" prayer used in some of the public schools in New York State, on the recommendation of the Board of Regents, was unconstitutional as a violation of the Establishment Clause of the First Amendment, as read into the Fourteenth Amendment. The Court held that the recital of the prayer was a religious activity. The fact that nonobserving pupils might be excused did not save the constitutionality of the practice, since the practice was found to constitute an "establishment" in the constitutional sense. Justice Douglas wrote a concurring opinion. Justice Stewart dissented and contended that the decision denied the pupils who wished to recite the prayer "the opportunity of sharing in the spiritual heritage of our Nation."]

Mr. Justice Black delivered the opinion of the Court:

The respondent Board of Education of Union Free School District No. 9, New Hyde Park, New York, acting in its official capacity under state law, directed the School District's principal to cause the following prayer to be said aloud by each class in the presence of a teacher at the beginning of each school day:

> Almighty God, we acknowledge our dependence upon
> Thee, and we beg Thy blessings upon us, our parents,
> our teachers and our country.

This daily procedure was adopted on the recommendation of the State Board of Regents, a governmental agency created by the State Constitution to which the New York Legislature has granted broad supervisory, executive, and legislative powers over the State's public school system. These state officials composed the prayer which they recommended and published as a part of their "Statement on Moral and Spiritual Training in the Schools," saying: "We believe that this Statement will be subscribed to by all men and women of good will, and we call upon all of them to aid in giving life to our program."

Shortly after the practice of reciting the Regents' prayer was adopted by the School District, the parents of ten pupils brought this action in a New York State Court insisting that use of this official prayer in the public schools was contrary to the beliefs, religions, or religious practices of both themselves and their children. Among other things, these parents challenged the constitutionality of both the state law authorizing the School District to direct the use of prayer in public schools and the School District's regulation ordering the recitation of this particular prayer on the ground that these actions of official governmental agencies violate that part of the First Amendment of the Federal Constitution which commands that "Congress shall make no law respecting an establishment of religion"—a command which was "made applicable to the State of New York by the Fourteenth Amendment of the said Constitution." The New York Court of Appeals, over the dissents of Judges Dye and Fuld, sustained an order of the lower state courts which had upheld the power of New York to use the Regents' prayer as a part of the daily procedures of its public schools so long as the schools did not compel any pupil to join in the prayer over his or his parents' objection.* We granted certiorari to review this important decision involving rights protected by the First and Fourteenth Amendments.

* 10 N.Y. 2d 174, 176 N.E. 2d 579. The trial court's opinion, which is reported at 18 Misc. 2d 659, 191 N.Y.S. 2d 453, had made it clear that the Board of Education must set up some sort of procedures to protect those who objected to reciting the prayer: "This is not to say that the rights accorded petitioners and their children under the 'free exercise' clause do not mandate safeguards against such embarrassments and pressures. It is enough on this score, however, that regulations, such as were adopted by New York City's Board of Education in connection with its released time program, be adopted, making clear that neither teachers nor any other school authority may comment on participation or nonparticipation in the exercise nor suggest or require that any posture or language be used or dress be worn or be not used or not worn. Nonparticipation may take the form either of remaining silent during the exercise, or if the parent or child so desires, of being excused entirely from the exercise. Such regulations must also make provision for those nonparticipants who are to be excused from the prayer exercise. The exact provision to be made is a matter for decision by the board, rather than the court, within the framework of constitutional requirements. Within that framework would fall a provision that prayer participants proceed to a common assembly while nonparticipants attend other rooms, or that nonparticipants be permitted to arrive at school a few minutes late or to attend separate opening exercises, or any other method which treats with equality both participants and nonparticipants." . . .

We think that by using its public school system to encourage recitation of the Regents' prayer, the State of New York has adopted a practice wholly inconsistent with the Establishment Clause. There can, of course, be no doubt that New York's program of daily classroom invocation of God's blessings as perscribed in the Regents' prayer is a religious activity. It is a solemn avowal of divine faith and supplication for the blessings of the Almighty. The nature of such a prayer has always been religious, none of the respondents has denied this and the trial court expressly so found:

The religious nature of prayer was recognized by Jefferson and has been concurred in by theological writers, the United States Supreme Court and State courts and administrative officials, including New York's Commissioner of Education. A committee of the New York Legislature has agreed.

The Board of Regents as *amicus curiae*, the respondents and intervenors all concede the religious nature of prayer, but seek to distinguish this prayer because it is based on our spiritual heritage. . . .

The petitioners contend among other things that the state laws requiring or permitting use of the Regents' prayer must be struck down as a violation of the Establishment Clause because that prayer was composed by governmental officials as a part of a governmental program to further religious beliefs. For this reason, petitioners argue, the State's use of the Regents' prayer in its public school system breaches the constitutional wall of separation between Church and State. We agree with that contention since we think that the constitutional prohibition against laws respecting an establishment of religion must at least mean that in this country it is no part of the business of government to compose official prayers for any group of the American people to recite as a part of a religious program carried on by government.

It is a matter of history that this very practice of establishing governmentally composed prayers for religious services was one of the reasons which caused many of our early colonists to leave England and seek religious freedom in America. The Book of Common Prayer, which was created under governmental direction and which was approved by Acts of Parliament in 1548 and 1549, set out in minute detail the accepted form and content of prayer and other religious ceremonies to be used in the established, tax-supported Church of England. The controversies over the Book and what should be its content repeatedly threatened to disrupt the peace of that country as the accepted forms of prayer in the established church changed with the views of the particular ruler that happened to be in control at the time. Powerful groups representing some of the varying religious views of the people struggled among themselves to impress their particular views upon the Government and obtain amendments of the Book more suitable to their respective notions of how religious services should be conducted in order that the official religious establishment would advance their particular religious beliefs. Other groups, lacking the necessary political power to influence the Government on the matter, decided to leave England and its established church and seek freedom in America from England's governmentally ordained and supported religion.

It is an unfortunate fact of history that when some of the very groups which had most strenuously opposed the established Church of England found themselves sufficiently in control of colonial governments in this country to write their own prayers into law, they passed laws making their own religion the official religion of their respective colonies. Indeed, as late as the time of the Revolutionary War, there were established churches in at least eight of the thirteen former colonies and established religions in at least four of the other five. But the successful Revolution against English political domination was shortly followed by intense opposition to the practice of establishing religion by law. This opposition crystallized rapidly into an effective political force in Virginia where the minority religious groups such as Presbyterians, Lutherans, Quakers and Baptists had gained such strength that the adherents to the established Episcopal Church were actually a minority themselves. In 1785–1786, those opposed to the established Church, led by James Madison and Thomas Jefferson, who, though themselves not members of any of these dissenting religious groups, opposed all religious establishments by law on grounds of principle, obtained the enactment of the famous "Virginia Bill for Religious Liberty" by which all religious groups were placed on an equal footing so far as the State was concerned. Similar though less far-reaching legislation was being considered and passed in other States.

By the time of the adoption of the Constitution, our history shows that there was a widespread awareness among many Americans of the dangers of a union of Church and State. These people knew, some of them from bitter personal experience, that one of the greatest dangers to the freedom of the individual to worship in his own way lay in the Government's placing its official stamp of approval upon one particular kind of prayer or one particular form of religious services. They knew the anguish, hardship and bitter strife that could come when zealous religious groups struggled with one another to obtain the Government's stamp of approval from each King, Queen, or Protector that came to temporary power. The Constitution was intended to avert a part of this danger by leaving the government of this country in the hands of the people rather than in the hands of any monarch. But this safeguard was not enough. Our Founders were no more willing to let the content of their prayers and their privilege of praying whenever they pleased be influenced by the ballot box than they were to let these vital matters of personal conscience depend upon the succession of monarchs. The First Amendment was added to the Constitution to stand as a guarantee that neither the power nor the prestige of the Federal Government would be used to control, support or influence the kinds of prayer the American people can say—that the people's religions must not be subjected to the pressures of government for change each time a new political administration is elected to office. Under that Amendment's prohibition against governmental establishment of religion, as reinforced by the provisions of the Fourteenth Amendment, government in this country, be it state or federal, is without power to prescribe by law any particular form of prayer which is to be used as an official prayer in carrying on any program of governmentally sponsored religious activity.

There can be no doubt that New York's state prayer program officially establishes the religious beliefs embodied in the Regents' prayer. The respondents' argument to the contrary, which is largely based upon the contention that the Regents' prayer is "non-denominational" and the fact that the program, as modified and approved by state courts, does not require all pupils to recite the prayer but permits those who wish to do so to remain silent or be excused from the room, ignores the essential nature of the program's constitutional defects. Neither the fact that the prayer may be denominationally neutral, nor the fact that its observance on the part of the students is voluntary can serve to free it from the limitations of the Establishment Clause, as it might from the Free Exercise Clause, of the First Amendment, both of which are operative against the States by virtue of the Fourteenth Amendment. Although these two clauses may in certain instances overlap, they forbid two quite different kinds of governmental encroachment upon religious freedom. The Establishment Clause, unlike the Free Exercise Clause, does not depend upon any showing of direct governmental compulsion and is violated by the enactment of laws which establish an official religion whether those laws operate directly to coerce nonobserving individuals or not. This is not to say, of course, that laws officially prescribing a particular form of religious worship do not involve coercion of such individuals. When the power, prestige and financial support of government is placed behind a particular religious belief, the indirect coercive pressure upon religious minorities to conform to the prevailing officially approved religion is plain. But the purposes underlying the Establishment Clause go much further than that. Its first and most immediate purpose rested on the belief that a union of government and religion tends to destroy government and to degrade religion. The history of governmentally established religion, both in England and in this country, showed that whenever government had allied itself with one particular form of religion, the inevitable result had been that it had incurred the hatred, disrespect and even contempt of those who held contrary beliefs. That same history showed that many people had lost their respect for any religion that had relied upon the support of government to spread its faith. The Establishment Clause thus stands as an expression of principle on the part of the Founders of our Constitution that religion is too personal, too sacred, too holy, to permit its "unhallowed perversion" by a civil magistrate. Another purpose of the Establishment Clause rested upon an awareness of the historical fact that governmentally established religions and religious persecutions go hand in hand. The Founders knew that only a few years after the Book of Common Prayer became the only accepted form of religious services in the established Church of England, an Act of Uniformity was passed to compel all Englishmen to attend those services and to make it a criminal offense to conduct or attend religious gatherings of any other kind—a law which was consistently flouted by dissenting religious groups in England and which contributed to widespread persecutions of people like John Bunyan who persisted in holding "unlawful [religious] meetings . . . to the great disturbance and distraction of the good subjects of this kingdom. . . ." And they knew that similar persecutions had received the sanction of law in several of the colonies in this country soon after the establishment of official religions in those colonies. It was in large part to get completely away from this sort of systematic religious persecution that the Founders brought into being our Nation, our Constitution, and our Bill of Rights with its prohibition against any governmental establishment of religion. The New York laws officially prescribing the Regents' prayer are inconsistent with both the purposes of the Establishment Clause and with the Establishment Clause itself.

It has been argued that to apply the Constitution in such a way as to prohibit state laws respecting an establishment of religious services in public schools is to indicate a hostility toward religion or toward prayer. Nothing, of course, could be more wrong. The history of man is inseparable from the history of religion. And perhaps it is not too much to say that since the beginning of that history many people have devoutly believed that "More things are wrought by prayer than this world dreams of." It was doubtless largely due to men who believed this that there grew up a sentiment that caused men to leave the cross-currents of officially established state religions and religious persecution in Europe and come to this country filled with the hope that they could find a place in which they could pray when they pleased to the God of their faith in the language they chose. And there were men of this same faith in the power of prayer who led the fight for adoption of our Constitution and also for our Bill of Rights with the very guarantees of religious freedom that forbid the sort of governmental activity which New York has attempted here. These men knew that the First Amendment, which tried to put an end to governmental control of religion and of prayer, was not written to destroy either. They knew rather that it was written to quiet well-justified fears which nearly all of them felt arising out of an awareness that governments of the past had shackled men's tongues to make them speak only the religious thoughts that government wanted them to speak and to pray only to the God that government wanted them to pray to. It is neither sacrilegious nor antireligious to say that each separate government in this country should stay out of the business of writing or sanctioning official prayers and leave that purely religious function to the people themselves and to those the people chose to look to for religious guidance.*

It is true that New York's establishment of its Regents' prayer as an officially approved religious doctrine of that State does not amount to a total establishment of one particular religious sect to the exclusion of all others—that, indeed, the governmental endorsement of that prayer seems relatively insignificant when compared to the governmental encroachments upon religion which were commonplace 200 years ago. To those who may subscribe to the view that because the Regents' official prayer is so brief and general there can be no danger to religious freedom in its governmental establishment, however, it may be appropriate to say in the words of James Madison, the author of the First Amendment:

[I]t is proper to take alarm at the first experiment on our liberties. . . . Who does not see that the same authority which can establish Christianity, in exclusion of all other Religions, may establish with the same ease any particular sect of Christians, in exclusion of all other Sects? That the same authority which can force a citizen to contribute three pence only of his property for the support of any one establishment, may force him to conform to any other establishment in all cases whatsoever?

* There is of course nothing in the decision reached here that is inconsistent with the fact that school children and others are officially encouraged to express love for our country by reciting historical documents such as the Declaration of Independence which contain references to the Deity or by singing officially espoused anthems which include the composer's professions of faith in a Supreme Being, or with the fact that there are many manifestations in our public life of belief in God. Such patriotic or ceremonial occasions bear no true resemblance to the unquestioned religious exercise that the State of New York has sponsored in this instance.

The judgment of the Court of Appeals of New York is reversed and the cause remanded for further proceedings not inconsistent with this opinion.

Mr. Justice Douglas, concurring:

It is customary in deciding a constitutional question to treat it in its narrowest form. Yet at times the setting of the question gives it a form and content which no abstract treatment could do. The point for decision is whether the Government can constitutionally finance a religious exercise. Our system at the federal and state levels is presently honeycombed with such financing.* Nevertheless, I think it is an unconstitutional undertaking whatever form it takes.

First, a word as to what this case does not involve.

Plainly, our Bill of Rights would not permit a State or the Federal Government to adopt an official prayer and penalize anyone who would not utter it. This, however, is not that case, for there is no element of compulsion or coercion in New York's regulation requiring that public schools be opened each day with the following prayer:

> Almighty God, we acknowledge our dependence upon
> Thee, and we beg Thy blessings upon us, our parents,
> our teachers and our Country.

* "There are many 'aids' to religion in this country at all levels of government. To mention but a few at the federal level, one might begin by observing that the very First Congress which wrote the First Amendment provided for chaplains in both Houses and in the armed services. There is compulsory chapel at the service academies, and religious services are held in federal hospitals and prisons. The President issues religious proclamations. The Bible is used for the administration of oaths. N.Y.A. and W.P.A. funds were available to parochial schools during the depression. Veterans receiving money under the 'G.I.' Bill of 1944 could attend denominational schools, to which payments were made directly by the government. During World War II, federal money was contributed to denominational schools for the training of nurses. The benefits of the National School Lunch Act are available to students in private as well as public schools. The Hospital Survey and Construction Act of 1946 specifically made money available to non-public hospitals. The slogan 'In God We Trust' is used by the Treasury Department, and Congress recently added God to the pledge of allegiance. There is Bible-reading in the schools of the District of Columbia, and religious instruction is given in the District's National Training School for Boys. Religious organizations are exempt from the federal income tax and are granted postal privileges. Up to defined limits— 15 per cent of the adjusted gross income of individuals and 5 per cent of the net income of corporations—contributions to religious organizations are deductible for federal income tax purposes. There are limits to the deductibility of gifts and bequests to religious institutions made under the federal gift and estate tax laws. This list of federal 'aids' could easily be expanded, and of course there is a long list in each state." Fellman, *The Limits of Freedom* (1959), pp. 40–41.

The prayer is said upon the commencement of the school day, immediately following the pledge of allegiance to the flag. The prayer is said aloud in the presence of a teacher, who either leads the recitation or selects a student to do so. No student, however, is compelled to take part. The respondents have adopted a regulation which provides that "neither teachers nor any school authority shall comment on participation or non-participation . . . nor suggest or request that any posture or language be used or dress be worn or be not used or not worn." Provision is also made for excusing children, upon written request of a parent or guardian, from the saying of the prayer or from the room in which the prayer is said. A letter implementing and explaining this regulation has been sent to each taxpayer and parent in the school district. As I read this regulation, a child is free to stand or not stand, to recite or not recite, without fear of reprisal or even comment by the teacher or any other school official.

In short, the only one who need utter the prayer is the teacher; and no teacher is complaining of it. Students can stand mute or even leave the classroom, if they desire.*

McCollum v. *Board of Education*, 333 U.S. 203, does not decide this case. It involved the use of public school facilities for religious education of students. Students either had to attend religious instruction or "go to some other place in the school building for pursuit of their secular studies. . . . Reports of their presence or absence were to be made to their secular teachers." . . . The influence of the teaching staff was therefore brought to bear on the student body, to support the instilling religious principles. In the present case, school facilities are used to say the prayer and the teaching staff is employed to lead the pupils in it. There is, however, no effort at indoctrination and no attempt at exposition. Prayers of course may be so long and of such a character as to amount to an attempt at the religious instruction that was denied the public schools by the *McCollum* case. But New York's prayer is of a character that does not involve any element of proselytizing as in the *McCollum* case.

The question presented by this case is therefore an extremely narrow one. It is whether New York oversteps the bounds when it finances a religious exercise.

What New York does on the opening of its public schools is what we do when we open court. Our Marshal has from the beginning announced the convening of the Court and then added "God save the United States and this honorable court." That utterance is a supplication, a prayer in which we, the judges, are free to join, but which we need not recite any more than the students need recite the New York prayer.

What New York does on the opening of its public schools is what each

---

* West Point Cadets are required to attend chapel each Sunday. Reg., c. 21, § 2101. The same requirement obtains at the Naval Academy (Reg., c. 9, § 0901, (1) (a)), and at the Air Force Academy except First Classmen. Catalogue, 1962–1963, p. 110. . . .

House of Congress does at the opening of each day's business. Reverend Frederick B. Harris is Chaplain of the Senate; Reverend Bernard Braskamp is Chaplain of the House. Guest chaplains of various denominations also officiate. *

In New York the teacher who leads in prayer is on the public payroll; and the time she takes seems minuscule as compared with the salaries appropriated by state legislatures and Congress for chaplains to conduct prayers in

---

* It would, I assume, make no difference in the present case if a different prayer were said every day or if the ministers of the community rotated, each giving his own prayer. For some of the petitioners in the present case profess no religion.

The Pledge of Allegiance, like the prayer, recognizes the existence of a Supreme Being. Since 1954 it has contained the words "one nation *under God,* indivisible, with liberty and justice for all." 36 U.S.C. 172. The House Report, recommending the addition of the words "under God" stated that those words in no way run contrary to the First Amendment but recognize "only the guidance of God in our national affairs." . . . Senator Ferguson, who sponsored the measure in the Senate, pointed out that the words "In God We Trust" are over the entrance to the Senate Chamber. 100 Cong. Rec. 6348. He added:

"I have felt that the Pledge of Allegiance to the Flag which stands for the United States of America should recognize the Creator who we really believe is in control of the destinies of this great Republic.

"It is true that under the Constitution no power is lodged anywhere to establish a religion. This is not an attempt to establish a religion; it has nothing to do with anything of that kind. It relates to belief in God, in whom we sincerely repose our trust. We know that America cannot be defended by guns, planes, and ships alone. Appropriations and expenditures for defense will be of value only if the God under whom we live believes that we are in the right. We should at all times recognize God's province over the lives of our people and over this great Nation." . . .

The Act of March 3, 1865, 13 Stat. 517, authorized the phrase "In God We Trust" to be placed on coins. And see 17 Stat. 427. The first mandatory requirement for the use of that motto on coins was made by the Act of May 18, 1908, 35 Stat. 164. . . . The use of the motto on all currency and coins was directed by the Act of July 11, 1955, 69 Stat. 290. . . . Moreover, by the Joint Resolution of July 30, 1956, our national motto was declared to be "In God We Trust." 70 Stat. 732. In reporting the Joint Resolution, the Senate Judiciary Committee stated:

"Further official recognition of this motto was given by the adoption of the Star-Spangled Banner as our national anthem. One stanza of our national anthem is as follows:

> 'O, thus be it ever when freemen shall stand
> Between their lov'd home and the war's desolation:
> Blest with vict'ry and peace may the heav'n rescued land
> Praise the power that hath made and preserved us a nation!
> Then conquer we must when our cause it is just,
> And this be our motto—"In God is our trust."
> And the Star-Spangled Banner in triumph shall wave
> O'er the land of the free and the home of the brave.'

"In view of these words in our national anthem, it is clear that 'In God we trust' has a strong claim as our national motto." . . .

the legislative halls. Only a bare fraction of the teacher's time is given to reciting this short 22-word prayer, about the same amount of time that our Marshal spends announcing the opening of our sessions and offering a prayer for this Court. Yet for me the principle is the same, no matter how briefly the prayer is said, for in each of the instances given the person praying is a public official on the public payroll, performing a religious exercise in a governmental institution.° It is said that the element of coercion is inherent in the giving of this prayer. If that is true here, it is also true of the prayer with which this Court is convened, and with those that open the Congress. Few adults, let alone children, would leave our courtroom or the Senate or the House while those prayers are being given. Every such audience is in a sense a "captive" audience.

At the same time I cannot say that to authorize this prayer is to establish a religion in the strictly historic meaning of those words.† A religion is not established in the usual sense merely by letting those who chose to do so say the prayer that the public school teacher leads. Yet once government finances a religious exercise it inserts a divisive influence into our communities.‡ The New York court said that the prayer given does not conform to all of the tenets of the Jewish, Unitarian, and Ethical Culture groups. One of petitioners is an agnostic.

"We are a religious people whose institutions presuppose a Supreme Being." *Zorach* v. *Clauson*, 343 U.S. 306. Under our Bill of Rights free play is given for making religion an active force in our lives. But "if a religious leaven is to be worked into the affairs of our people, it is to be done by individuals and groups, not by the Government." *McGowan* v. *Maryland*, 366 U.S. 420, 563 (dissenting opinion). By reason of the First Amendment government is commanded "to have no interest in theology or ritual" (*id.*, at 564), for on those matters "government must be neutral." *Ibid.* The First Amendment leaves the Government in a position not of hostility to religion

---

° The fact that taxpayers do not have standing in the federal courts to raise the issue (*Frothingham* v. *Mellon*, 262 U.S. 447) is of course no justification for drawing a line between what is done in New York on one hand and on the other what we do and what Congress does in this matter of prayer.

† The Court analogizes the present case to those involving the traditional Established Church. We once had an Established Church, the Anglican. All baptisms and marriages had to take place there. That church was supported by taxation. In these and other ways the Anglican Church was favored over the others. The First Amendment put an end to placing any one church in a preferred position. It ended support of any church or all churches by taxation. It went further and prevented secular sanction to any religious ceremony, dogma, or rite. Thus, it prevents civil penalties from being applied against recalcitrants or nonconformists.

‡ Some communities, including Washington, D.C., have a Christmas tree purchased with the taxpayers' money. The tree is sometimes decorated with the words "Peace on earth, goodwill to men." At other times the authorities draw from a different version of the Bible which says "Peace on earth to men of goodwill." Christmas, I suppose, is still a religious celebration, not merely a day put on the calendar for the benefit of merchants.

but of neutrality. The philosophy is that the atheist or agnostic—the nonbeliever—is entitled to go his own way. The philosophy is that if government
interferes in matters spiritual, it will be a divisive force. The First Amendment teaches that a government neutral in the field of religion better serves
all religious interests.

My problem today would be uncomplicated but for *Everson* v. *Board of
Education,* 330 U.S. 1, which allowed taxpayers' money to be used to pay
"the bus fares of parochial school pupils as a part of a general program under
which" the fares of pupils attending public and other schools were also paid.
The *Everson* case seems in retrospect to be out of line with the First Amendment. Its result is appealing, as it allows aid to be given to needy children.
Yet by the same token, public funds could be used to satisfy other needs of
children in parochial schools—lunches, books, and tuition being obvious
examples. Mr. Justice Rutledge stated in dissent what I think is durable
First Amendment philosophy:

> The reasons underlying the Amendment's policy have not vanished
> with time or diminished in force. Now as when it was adopted the
> price of religious freedom is double. It is that the church and religion
> shall live both within and upon that freedom. There cannot be free-
> dom of religion, safeguarded by the state, and intervention by the
> church or its agencies in the state's domain or dependency on its
> largesse. Madison's Remonstance, Par. 6, 8. The great condition of
> religious liberty is that it be maintained free from sustenance, as also
> from other interferences, by the state. For when it comes to rest upon
> that secular foundation it vanishes with the resting. *Id.,* Par. 7, 8.
> Public money devoted to payment of religious costs, educational or
> other, brings the quest for more. It brings too the struggle of sect
> against sect for the larger share or for any. Here one by numbers alone
> will benefit most, there another. That is precisely the history of so-
> cieties which have had an established religion and dissident groups.
> *Id.* Par. 8, 11. It is the very thing Jefferson and Madison experienced
> and sought to guard against, whether in its blunt or in its more
> screened forms. *Ibid.* The end of such strife cannot be other than to
> destroy the cherished liberty. The dominating group will achieve the
> dominant benefit; or all will embroil the state in their dissensions.
> *Id.* Par. 11. . . .

What New York does with this prayer is a break with that tradition. I
therefore join the Court in reversing the judgment below.

Mr. Justice Stewart, dissenting:

A local school board in New York has provided that those pupils who
wish to do so may join in a brief prayer at the beginning of each school
day, acknowledging their dependence upon God and asking His blessing

upon them and upon their parents, their teachers, and their country. The Court today decides that in permitting this brief non-denominational prayer the school board has violated the Constitution of the United States. I think this decision is wrong.

The Court does not hold, nor could it, that New York has interfered with the free exercise of anybody's religion. For the state courts have made clear that those who object to reciting the prayer must be entirely free of any compulsion to do so, including any "embarrassments and pressures." . . . But the Court says that in permitting school children to say this simple prayer, the New York authorities have established "an official religion."

With all respect, I think the Court has misapplied a great constitutional principle. I cannot see how an "official religion" is established by letting those who want to say a prayer say it. On the contrary, I think that to deny the wish of these school children to join in reciting this prayer is to deny them the opportunity of sharing in the spiritual heritage of our Nation.

The Court's historical review of the quarrels over the Book of Common Prayer in England throws no light for me on the issue before us in this case. England had then and has now an established church. Equally unenlightening, I think, is the history of the early establishment and later rejection of an official church in our own States. For we deal here not with the establishment of a state church, which would, of course, be constitutionally impermissible, but with whether school children who want to begin their day by joining in prayer must be prohibited from doing so. Moreover, I think that the Court's task, in this as in all areas of constitutional adjudication, is not responsibly aided by the uncritical invocation of metaphors like the "wall of separation," a phrase nowhere to be found in the Constitution. What is relevant to the issue here is not the history of an established church in sixteenth century England or in eighteenth century America, but the history of the religious traditions of our people, reflected in countless practices of the institutions and officials of our government.

At the opening of each day's Session of this Court we stand, while one of our officials invokes the protection of God. Since the days of John Marshall our Crier has said, "God save the United States and this Honorable Court." Both the Senate and the House of Representatives open their daily Sessions with prayer. Each of our Presidents, from George Washington to John F. Kennedy, has upon assuming his Office asked the protection and help of God.

The Court today says that the state and federal governments are without constitutional power to prescribe any particular form of words to be recited by any group of the American people on any subject touching religion. The third stanza of "The Star-Spangled Banner," made our National Anthem by Act of Congress in 1931, contains these verses:

> Blest with victory and peace, may the heav'n rescued land
>   Praise the Pow'r that hath made and preserved us a nation!
> Then conquer we must, when our cause it is just,
>   And this be our motto "In God is our Trust."

In 1954 Congress added a phrase to the Pledge of Allegiance to the Flag so that it now contains the words "one Nation *under God,* indivisible, with liberty and justice for all." In 1952 Congress enacted legislation calling upon the President each year to proclaim a National Day of Prayer. Since 1865 the words "IN GOD WE TRUST" have been impressed on our coins.

Countless similar examples could be listed, but there is no need to belabor the obvious.* It was all summed up by this Court just ten years ago in a single sentence: "We are a religious people whose institutions presuppose a Supreme Being." *Zorach* v. *Clauson,* 343 U.S. 306.

I do not believe that this Court, or the Congress, or the President has by the actions and practices I have mentioned established an "official religion" in violation of the Constitution. And I do not believe the State of New York has done so in this case. What each has done has been to recognize and to follow the deeply entrenched and highly cherished spiritual traditions of our Nation—traditions which come down to us from those who almost two hundred years ago avowed their "firm reliance on the Protection of Divine Providence" when they proclaimed the freedom and independence of this brave new world.

I dissent.

g. Religious Test Oaths
TORCASO *v.* WATKINS
367 US 488 (1961)

[The Maryland Constitution, as construed by the highest state court, required a declaration of belief in God as a qualification for public office. The Supreme Court unanimously held that this requirement invaded freedom of religion and was therefore in violation of the First and Fourteenth Amendments. Justices Frankfurter and Harlan concurred in the result without an opinion.]

Mr. Justice Black delivered the opinion of the Court:

Article 37 of the Declaration of Rights of the Maryland Constitution provides:

[N]o religious test ought ever to be required as a qualification for any office of profit or trust in this State, other than a declaration of belief in the existence of God. . . .

* I am at a loss to understand the Court's unsupported *ipse dixit* that these official expressions of religious faith in and reliance upon a Supreme Being "bear no true resemblance to the unquestioned religious exercise that the State of New York has sponsored in this instance." . . . I can hardly think that the Court means to say that the First Amendment imposes a lesser restriction upon the Federal Government than does the Fourteenth Amendment upon the States. Or is the Court suggesting that the Constitution permits judges and Congressmen and Presidents to join in prayer, but prohibits school children from doing so?

The appellant Torcaso was appointed to the office of Notary Public by the Governor of Maryland but was refused a commission to serve because he would not declare his belief in God. He then brought this action in a Maryland Circuit Court to compel issuance of his commission, charging that the State's requirement that he declare this belief violated "the First and Fourteenth Amendments to the Constitution of the United States. . . ." The Circuit Court rejected these federal constitutional contentions, and the highest court of the State, the Court of Appeals, affirmed, holding that the state constitutional provision is self-executing and requires declaration of belief in God as a qualification for office without need for implementing legislation. . . .

There is, and can be, no dispute about the purpose or effect of the Maryland Declaration of Rights requirement before us—it sets up a religious test which was designed to and, if valid, does bar every person who refuses to declare a belief in God from holding a public "office of profit or trust" in Maryland. The power and authority of the State of Maryland thus is put on the side of one particular sort of believers—those who are willing to say they believe in "the existence of God." It is true that there is much historical precedent for such laws. Indeed, it was largely to escape religious test oaths and declarations that a great many of the early colonists left Europe and came here hoping to worship in their own way. It soon developed, however, that many of those who had fled to escape religious test oaths turned out to be perfectly willing, when they had the power to do so, to force dissenters from their faith to take test oaths in conformity with that faith. This brought on a host of laws in the new Colonies imposing burdens and disabilities of various kinds upon varied beliefs depending largely upon what group happened to be politically strong enough to legislate in favor of its own beliefs. The effect of all this was the formal or practical "establishment" of particular religious faiths in most of the Colonies, with consequent burdens imposed on the free exercise of the faiths of nonfavored believers.

There were, however, wise and far-seeing men in the Colonies—too many to mention—who spoke out against test oaths and all the philosophy of intolerance behind them. One of these, it so happens, was George Calvert (the first Lord Baltimore), who took a most important part in the original establishment of the Colony of Maryland. He was a Catholic and had, for this reason, felt compelled by his conscience to refuse to take the Oath of Supremacy in England at the cost of resigning from high governmental office. He again refused to take that oath when it was demanded by the Council of the Colony of Virginia, and as a result he was denied settlement in that Colony. A recent historian of the early period of Maryland's life has said that it was Calvert's hope and purpose to establish in Maryland a colonial government free from the religious persecutions he had known—one "securely beyond the reach of oaths. . . ."

When our Constitution was adopted, the desire to put the people "securely beyond the reach" of religious test oaths brought about the inclusion in Article VI of that document of a provision that "no religious Test shall ever be required as a Qualification to any Office or public Trust under the United States." Article VI supports the accuracy of our observations in *Girouard* v. *United States,* 328 U.S. 61, that "[t]he test oath is abhorrent to our tradition." Not satisfied, however, with Article VI and other guarantees in the original Constitution, the First Congress proposed and the states very shortly thereafter adopted our Bill of Rights, including the First Amendment. That Amendment broke new constitutional ground in the protection it sought to afford to freedom of religion, speech, press, petition and assembly. Since prior cases in this Court have thoroughly explored and documented the history behind the First Amendment, the reasons for it, and the scope of the religious freedom it protects, we need not cover that ground again. What was said in our prior cases we think controls our decision here.

In *Cantwell* v. *Connecticut,* 310 U.S. 296, we said:

The First Amendment declares that Congress shall make no law respecting an establishment of religion or prohibiting the free exercise thereof. The Fourteenth Amendment has rendered the legislatures of the states as incompetent as Congress to enact such laws. . . . Thus the Amendment embraces two concepts,—freedom to believe and freedom to act. The first is absolute but, in the nature of things, the second cannot be.

Later we decided *Everson* v. *Board of Education,* 330 U.S. 1, and said this at pages 15 and 16:

The "establishment of religion" clause of the First Amendment means at least this: Neither a state nor the Federal Government can set up a church. Neither can pass laws which aid one religion, aid all religions, or prefer one religion over another. Neither can force nor influence a person to go to or to remain away from church against his will or force him to profess a belief or disbelief in any religion. No person can be punished for entertaining or professing religious beliefs or disbeliefs, for church attendance or non-attendance. No tax in any amount, large or small, can be levied to support any religious activities or institutions, whatever they may be called, or whatever form they may adopt to teach or practice religion. Neither a state nor the Federal Government can, openly or secretly, participate in the affairs of any religious organizations or groups and *vice versa.* In the words of Jefferson, the clause against establishment of religion by law was intended to erect "a wall of separation between church and State."

While there were strong dissents in the *Everson* case, they did not challenge the Court's interpretation of the First Amendment's coverage as being too broad, but thought the Court was applying that interpretation too narrowly to the facts of that case. Not long afterward, in *Illinois ex rel. McCollum* v. *Board of Education,* 333 U.S. 203, we were urged to repudiate as dicta the above-quoted *Everson* interpretation of the scope of the First Amendment's coverage. We declined to do this, but instead strongly reaffirmed what had been said in *Everson,* calling attention to the fact that both the majority and the minority in *Everson* had agreed on the principles declared in this part of the *Everson* opinion. And a concurring opinion in *McCollum,* written by Mr. Justice Frankfurter and joined by the other *Everson* dissenters, said this:

We are all agreed that the First and Fourteenth Amendments have a secular reach far more penetrating in the conduct of Government than merely to forbid an "established church." . . . We renew our conviction that "we have staked the very existence of our country on the faith that complete separation between the state and religion is best for the state and best for religion."

The Maryland Court of Appeals thought, and it is argued here, that this Court's later holding and opinion in *Zorach* v. *Clauson,* 343 U.S. 306, had in part repudiated the statement in the *Everson* opinion quoted above and previously reaffirmed in *McCollum.* But the Court's opinion in *Zorach* specifically stated: "We follow the *McCollum* case." . . . Nothing decided or written in *Zorach* lends support to the idea that the Court there intended to open up the way for government, state or federal, to restore the historically and constitutionally discredited policy of probing religious beliefs by test oaths or limiting public offices to persons who have, or perhaps more properly, profess to have a belief in some particular kind of religious concept.

We repeat and again reaffirm that neither a State nor the Federal Government can constitutionally force a person "to profess a belief or disbelief in any religion." Neither can constitutionally pass laws nor impose requirements which aid all religions as against non-believers, and neither can aid those religions based on a belief in the existence of God as against those religions founded on different beliefs.

In upholding the State's religious test for public office the highest court of Maryland said:

The petitioner is not compelled to believe or disbelieve, under threat of punishment or other compulsion. True, unless he makes the declaration of belief he cannot hold public office in Maryland, but he is not compelled to hold office.

The fact, however, that a person is not compelled to hold public office cannot possibly be an excuse for barring him from office by state-imposed criteria forbidden by the Constitution. This was settled by our holding in *Wieman* v. *Updegraff*, 344 U.S. 183. We there pointed out that whether or not "an abstract right to public employment exists," Congress could not pass a law providing " '. . . that no federal employee shall attend Mass or take any active part in missionary work.' "

This Maryland religious test for public office unconstitutionally invades the appellant's freedom of belief and religion and therefore cannot be enforced against him.

The judgment of the Supreme Court of Maryland is accordingly reversed and the cause is remanded for further proceedings not inconsistent with this opinion.

h. Sunday Closing Laws

McGOWAN v. MARYLAND

366 US 420 (1961)

[Employees of a large discount department store located on a highway were convicted in Maryland state courts of making sales on Sunday in violation of the state's Sunday closing laws. The Supreme Court affirmed the conviction. It upheld the constitutionality of the laws against the charges that they were unconstitutionally vague and that they violated the Equal Protection Clause of the Fourteenth Amendment. The Court held that the laws did not violate the Establishment Clause of the First Amendment, for the purpose and effect of the statutes were not to aid religion or Christianity but to set aside Sunday as a secular day of rest and recreation.

[Justice Frankfurter wrote a concurring opinion, joined by Justice Harlan.

[Justice Douglas was the only dissenter. For his opinion see *Braunfeld* v. *Brown, post.*

[This case is to be read along with the next three cases that follow. All four cases were decided together.]

Mr. Chief Justice Warren delivered the opinion of the Court:

The issues in this case concern the constitutional validity of Maryland criminal statutes, commonly known as Sunday Closing Laws, or Sunday Blue Laws. These statutes, with exceptions to be noted hereafter, generally proscribe all labor, business and other commercial activities on Sunday. The questions presented are whether the classifications within the statutes bring about a denial of equal protection of the law, whether the laws are so vague as to fail to give reasonable notice of the forbidden conduct and therefore violate due process, and whether the statutes are laws respecting an establishment of religion or prohibiting the free exercise thereof.

Appellants are seven employees of a large discount department store located on a highway in Anne Arundel County, Maryland. They were indicted for the Sunday sale of a three-ring loose-leaf binder, a can of floor wax, a stapler and staples, and a toy submarine in violation of Md. Ann. Code, Art. 27, § 521. Generally, this section prohibited, throughout the State, the Sunday sale of all merchandise except the retail sale of tobacco products, confectioneries, milk, bread, fruits, gasoline, oils, greases, drugs and medicines, and newspapers and periodicals. Recently amended, this section also now excepts from the general prohibition the retail sale in Anne Arundel County of all foodstuffs, automobile and boating accessories, flowers, toilet goods, hospital supplies and souvenirs. It now further provides that any retail establishment in Anne Arundel County which does not employ more than one person other than the owner may operate on Sunday.

Although appellants were indicted only under § 521, in order properly to consider several of the broad constitutional contentions, we must examine the whole body of Maryland Sunday laws. Several sections of the Maryland statutes are particularly relevant to evaluation of the issues presented. Section 492 of Md. Ann. Code, Art. 27, forbids all persons from doing any work or bodily labor on Sunday and forbids permitting children or servants to work on that day or to engage in fishing, hunting and unlawful pastimes or recreations. The section excepts all works of necessity and charity. Section 522 of Md. Ann. Code, Art. 27, disallows the opening or use of any dancing saloon, opera house, bowling alley or barber shop on Sunday. However, in addition to the exceptions noted above, Md. Ann. Code, Art. 27, § 509 exempts, for Anne Arundel County, the Sunday operation of any bathing beach, bathhouse, dancing saloon and amusement park, and activities incident thereto and retail sales of merchandise customarily sold at, or incidental to, the operation of the aforesaid occupations and businesses. Section 90 of Md. Ann. Code, Art. 2B, makes generally unlawful the sale of alcoholic beverages on Sunday. However, this section, and immediately succeeding ones, provide various immunities for the Sunday sale of different kinds of alcoholic beverages, at different hours during the day, by vendors holding different types of licenses, in different political divisions of the State—particularly in Anne Arundel County. . . .

The remaining statutory sections concern a myriad of exceptions for various counties, districts of counties, cities and towns throughout the State. Among the activities allowed in certain areas on Sunday are such sports as football, baseball, golf, tennis, bowling, croquet, basketball, lacrosse, soccer, hockey, swimming, softball, boating, fishing, skating, horseback riding, stock car racing and pool or billiards. Other immunized activities permitted in some regions of the State include group singing or playing of musical instruments; the exhibition of motion pictures; dancng; the operation of recreation centers, picnic grounds, swimming pools, skating rinks and miniature golf courses. The taking of oysters and the hunting or killing of game is generally forbidden, but shooting conducted by organized rod and gun clubs is permitted in one county. In some of the subdivisions within the State, the exempted Sunday activities are sanctioned throughout the day; in others, they may not commence until early afternoon or evening; in many, the activities may only be conducted during the afternoon and late in the evening. Certain localities do not permit the allowed Sunday activity to be carried on within one hundred yards of any church where religious services are being held. Local ordinances and regulations concerning certain limited activities supplement the State's statutory scheme. In Anne Arundel County, for example, slot machines, pinball machines and bingo may be played on Sunday.

Among other things, appellants contended at the trial that the Maryland statutes under which they were charged were contrary to the Fourteenth Amendment for the reasons stated at the outset of this opinion. Appellants were convicted and each was fined five dollars and costs. The Maryland Court of Appeals affirmed, . . .

I.

Appellants argue that the Maryland statutes violate the "Equal Protection" Clause of the Fourteenth Amendment on several counts. First, they contend that the classifications contained in the statutes concerning which commodities may or may not be sold on Sunday are without rational and substantial relation to the object of the legislation. Specifically, appellants allege that the statutory exemptions for the Sunday sale of the merchandise mentioned above render arbitrary the statute under which they were convicted. Appellants further allege that § 521 is capricious because of the exemptions for the operation of the various amusements that have been listed and because slot machines, pinball machines, and bingo are legalized and are freely played on Sunday.

The standards under which this proposition is to be evaluated have been set forth many times by this Court. Although no precise formula has been developed, the Court has held that the Fourteenth Amendment permits the States a wide scope of discretion in enacting laws which affect some groups of citizens differently than others. The constitutional safeguard is offended only if the classification rests on grounds wholly irrelevant to the achievement of the State's objective.

State legislatures are presumed to have acted within their constitutional power despite the fact that, in practice, their laws result in some inequality. A statutory discrimination will not be set aside if any state of facts reasonably may be conceived to justify it. . . .

It would seem that a legislature could reasonably find that the Sunday sale of the exempted commodities was necessary either for the health of the populace or for the enhancement of the recreational atmosphere of the day—that a family which takes a Sunday ride into the country will need gasoline for the automobile and may find pleasant a soft drink or fresh fruit; that those who go to the beach may wish ice cream or some other item normally sold there; that some people will prefer alcoholic beverages or games of chance to add to their relaxation; that newspapers and drug products should always be available to the public.

The record is barren of any indication that this apparently reasonable basis does not exist, that the statutory distinctions are invidious, that local tradition and custom might not rationally call for this legislative treatment. . . . Likewise, the fact that these exemptions exist and deny some vendors and operators the day of rest and recreation contemplated by the legislature does not render the statutes violative of equal protection since there would appear to be many valid reasons for these exemptions, as stated above, and no evidence to dispel them.

Secondly, appellants contend that the statutory arrangement which permits only certain Anne Arundel County retailers to sell merchandise essential to, or customarily sold at, or incidental to, the operation of bathing beaches, amusement parks et cetera is contrary to the "Equal Protection" Clause because it discriminates unreasonably against retailers in other Maryland counties. But we have held that the Equal Protection Clause relates to equality between persons as such, rather than between areas and that territorial uniformity is not a constitutional prerequisite. With particular reference to the State of Maryland, we have noted that the prescription of different substantive offenses in different counties is generally a matter for legislative discretion. We find no invidious discrimination here. . . .

Thirdly, appellants contend that this same statutory provision, Art. 27, § 509, violates the "Equal Protection" Clause because it permits only certain merchants within Anne Arundel County (operators of bathing beaches and amusement parks et cetera) to sell merchandise customarily sold at these places while forbidding its sale by other vendors of this merchandise, such as appellant's employer. Here again, it would seem that a legislature could reasonably find that these commodities, necessary for the health and recreation of its citizens, should only be sold on Sunday by those vendors at the locations where the commodities are most likely to be immediately put to use. Such a determination would seem to serve the consuming public and at the same time secure Sunday rest for those employees, like appellants, of all other retail establishments. In addition, the enforcement problems which would accrue if large retail establishments, like appellants' employer, were permitted to remain open on Sunday but were restricted to the sale of the merchandise in question would be far greater than the problems accuring if only beach and amusement park vendors were exempted. Here again, there has been no indication of the unreasonableness of this differentiation. On the record before us, we cannot say that these statutes do not provide equal protection of the laws.

II.

Another question presented by appellants is whether Art. 27, § 509, which exempts the Sunday retail sale of "merchandise essential to, or customarily sold at, or incidental to, the operation of" bathing beaches, amusement parks et cetera in Anne Arundel County, is unconstitutionally vague. We believe that business people of ordinary intelligence in the position of appellants' employer would be able to know what exceptions are encompassed by the statute either as a matter of ordinary commercial knowledge or by simply making a reasonable investigation at a nearby bathing beach or amusement park within the county. . . . Under these circumstances, there is no necessity to guess at the statute's meaning in order to determine what conduct it makes criminal. . . .

III.

The final questions for decision are whether the Maryland Sunday Closing Laws conflict with the Federal Constitution's provisions for religious liberty. First, appellants contend here that the statutes applicable to Anne Arundel County violate the constitutional guarantee of freedom of religion in that the statutes' effect is to prohibit the free exercise of religion in contravention of the First Amendment, made applicable to the States by the Fourteenth Amendment. But appellants allege only economic injury to themselves; they do not allege any infringement of their own religious freedoms due to Sunday closing. In fact, the record is silent as to what appellants' religious beliefs are. Since the general rule is that "a litigant may only assert his own constitutional rights or immunities," . . . we hold that appellants have no standing to raise this contention. . . . Furthermore, since appellants do not specifically allege that the statutes infringe upon the religious beliefs of the department store's present or prospective patrons, we have no occasion here to consider the standing question of *Pierce* v. *Society of Sisters*, 268 U.S. 510, 535–536. Those persons whose religious rights are allegedly impaired by the statutes are not without effective ways to assert these rights. Cf. *N.A.A.C.P.* v. *Alabama,* 357 U.S. 449; *Barrows* v. *Jackson,* 346 U.S. 249. Appellants present no weighty countervailing policies here to cause an exception to our general principles. . . .

Secondly, appellants contend that the statutes violate the guarantee of separation of church and state in that the statutes are laws respecting an establishment of religion contrary to the First Amendment, made applicable to the states by the Fourteenth Amendment. If the purpose of the "establishment" clause was only to insure protection for the "free exercise" of religion, then what we have said above concerning appellant's standing to raise the "free exercise" contention would appear to be true here. However, the writings of Madison, who was the First Amendment's architect, demonstrate that the establishment of a religion was equally feared because of its tendencies to political tyranny and subversion of civil authority. Thus, in *Everson* v. *Board of Education,* the Court permitted a district taxpayer to challenge, on "establishment" grounds, a state statute which authorized district boards of education to reimburse parents for fares paid for the transportation of their children to both public and Catholic schools. Appellants here concededly have suffered direct economic injury, allegedly due to the imposition on them of the tenets of the Christian religion. We find, in these circumstances, these appellants have standing to complain that the statutes are laws respecting an establishment of religion.

The essence of appellant's "establishment" argument is that Sunday is the Sabbath day of the predominant Christian sects; that the purpose of the enforced stoppage of labor on that day is to facilitate and encourage church attendance; that the purpose of setting Sunday as a day of universal rest is to induce people with no religion or people with marginal religious beliefs to join the predominant Christian sects; that the purpose of the atmosphere of tranquility created by Sunday closing is to aid the conduct of church services and religious observance of the sacred day. In substantiating their "establishment" argument, appellants rely on the wording of the present Maryland statutes, on earlier versions of the current Sunday laws and on prior judicial characterizations of these laws by the Maryland Court of Appeals. Although only the constitutionality of § 521, the section under which appellants have been convicted, is immediately before us in this litigation, inquiry into the history of Sunday Closing Laws in our country, in addition to an examination of the Maryland Sunday closing statutes in their entirety and of their history, is relevant to the decision of whether the Maryland Sunday law in question is one respecting an establishment of religion. There is no dispute that the original laws which dealt with Sunday labor were motivated by religious forces. But what we must decide is whether present

Sunday legislation, having undergone extensive changes from the earliest forms, still retains its religious character.

Sunday Closing Laws go far back into American history having been brought to the colonies with a background of English legislation dating to the thirteenth century. In 1237, Henry III forbade the frequenting of markets on Sunday; the Sunday showing of wools at the staple was banned by Edward III in 1354; in 1409, Henry IV prohibited the playing of unlawful games on Sunday; Henry VI proscribed Sunday fairs in churchyards in 1444 and, four years later, made unlawful all fairs and markets and all showings of any goods or merchandise; Edward VI disallowed Sunday bodily labor by several injunctions in the mid-sixteenth century; various Sunday sports and amusements were restricted in 1625 by Charles I. . . . The law of the colonies to the time of the Revolution and the basis of the Sunday laws in the States was 29 Charles II, c. 7 (1677). It provided, in part:

> For the better observation and keeping holy the Lord's day, commonly called Sunday: be it enacted . . . that all the laws enacted and in force concerning the observation of the Lord's day, *and repairing to the church thereon,* be carefully put in execution; and that all and every person and persons whatsoever shall upon every Lord's day apply themselves to the observation of the same, by exercising themselves thereon in the duties of piety and true religion, publicly and privately; and that no tradesman, artificer, workman, laborer, or other person whatsoever, *shall do or exercise any worldly labor or business or work* of their ordinary callings upon the Lord's day, or any part thereof (works of necessity and charity only excepted); . . . and that no person or persons whatsoever shall publicly cry, show forth, or expose for sale any wares, merchandise, fruit, herbs, goods, or chattels, whatsoever, upon the Lord's day, or any part thereof. . . . (Emphasis added.)

Observation of the above language, and of that of the prior mandates, reveals clearly that the English Sunday legislation was in aid of the established church.

The American colonial Sunday restrictions arose soon after settlement. Starting in 1650, the Plymouth Colony proscribed servile work, unnecessary travelling, sports, and the sale of alcoholic beverages on the Lord's day and enacted laws concerning church attendance. The Massachusetts Bay Colony and the Connecticut and New Haven Colonies enacted similar prohibitions, some even earlier in the seventeenth century. The religious orientation of the colonial statutes was equally apparent. For example, a 1629 Massachusetts Bay instruction began, "And to the end the Sabbath may be celebrated in a religious manner. . . ." A 1653 enactment spoke of Sunday activities "which things

tend much to the dishonor of God, the reproach of religion, and the profanation of his holy Sabbath, the sanctification whereof is sometimes put for all duties immediately respecting the service of God. . . ."
. . . These laws persevered after the Revolution and, at about the time of the First Amendment's adoption, each of the colonies had laws of some sort restricting Sunday labor. . . .

But, despite the strongly religious origin of these laws, beginning before the eighteenth century, nonreligious arguments for Sunday closing began to be heard more distinctly and the statutes began to lose some of their totally religious flavor. In the middle 1700's, Blackstone wrote, "[T]he keeping one day in the seven holy, as a time of relaxation and refreshment as well as for public worship, is of admirable service to a state considered merely as a civil institution. It humanizes, by the help of conversation and society, the manners of the lower classes; which would otherwise degenerate into a sordid ferocity and savage selfishness of spirit; it enables the industrious workman to pursue his occupation in the ensuing week with health and cheerfulness." . . . A 1788 English statute dealing with chimney sweeps, 28 Geo. III, c. 48, in addition to providing for their Sunday religious affairs, also regulated their hours of work. The preamble to a 1679 Rhode Island enactment stated that the reason for the ban on Sunday employment was that "persons being evill minded, have presumed to employ in servile labor, more than necessity requireth, their servants. . . ." . . . The New York law of 1788 omitted the term "Lord's day" and substituted "the first day of the week commonly called Sunday." . . . Similar changes marked the Maryland statutes, discussed below. With the advent of the First Amendment, the colonial provisions requiring church attendance were soon repealed. . . .

More recently, further secular justifications have been advanced for making Sunday a day of rest, a day when people may recover from the labors of the week just passed and may physically and mentally prepare for the week's work to come. In England, during the First World War, a committee investigating the health conditions of munitions workers reported that "if the maximum output is to be secured and maintained for any length of time, a weekly period of rest must be allowed. . . . On economic and social grounds alike this weekly period of rest is best provided on Sunday."

The proponents of Sunday closing legislation are no longer exclusively representatives of religious interests. Recent New Jersey Sunday legislation was supported by labor groups and trade associations . . . ; modern English Sunday legislation was promoted by the National Federation of Grocers and supported by the National Chamber of Trade, the Drapers' Chamber of Trade, and the National Union of Shop Assistants. . . .

Throughout the years, state legislatures have modified, deleted from and added to their Sunday statutes. As evidenced by the New Jersey laws mentioned above, current changes are commonplace. Almost every State in our country presently has some type of Sunday regulation and over forty possess a relatively comprehensive system. . . . Some of our States now enforce their Sunday legislation through Departments of Labor, e.g., S.C. Code Ann. (1952), § 64–5. Thus have Sunday laws evolved from the wholly religious sanctions that originally were enacted.

Moreover, litigation over Sunday closing laws is not novel. Scores of cases may be found in the state appellate courts relating to sundry phases of Sunday enactments. Religious objections have been raised there on numerous occasions but sustained only once, in *Ex parte Newman*, 9 Cal. 502 (1858); and that decision was overruled three years later, in *Ex parte Andrews*, 18 Cal. 678. A substantial number of cases in varying postures bearing on state Sunday legislation have reached this Court. Although none raising the issues now presented have gained plenary hearing, language used in some of these cases further evidences the evolution of Sunday laws as temporal statutes. Mr. Justice Field wrote in *Soon Hing* v. *Crowley* [113 U.S. 703]:

Laws setting aside Sunday as a day of rest are upheld, not from any right of the government to legislate for the promotion of religious observances, but from its right to protect all persons from the physical and moral debasement which comes from uninterrupted labor. Such laws have always been deemed beneficient and merciful laws, especially to the poor and dependent, to the laborers in our factories and workshops and in the heated rooms of our cities; and their validity has been sustained by the highest courts of the States.

While a member of the California Supreme Court, Mr. Justice Field dissented in *Ex parte Newman, supra,* saying:

Its requirement is a cessation from labor. In its enactment, the Legislature has given the sanction of law to a rule of conduct, which the entire civilized world recognizes as essential to the physical and moral well-being of society. Upon no subject is there such a concurrence of opinion, among philosophers, moralists and statesmen of all nations, as on the necessity of periodical cessations from labor. One day in seven is the rule, founded in experience, and sustained by science. . . . The prohibition of secular business on Sunday is advocated on the ground that by it the general welfare is advanced, labor protected, and the moral and physical well-being of society promoted.

This was quoted with approval by Mr. Justice Harlan in *Hennington* v. *Georgia* (163 US 299), who also stated:

It is none the less a civil regulation because the day on which the running of freight trains is prohibited is kept by many under a sense of religious duty. The legislature having, as will not be disputed, power to enact laws to promote the order and to secure the comfort, happiness and health of the people, it was within its discretion to fix the day when all labor, within the limits of the State, works of necessity and charity excepted, should cease. . . .

Before turning to the Maryland legislation now here under attack, an investigation of what historical position Sunday Closing Laws have occupied with reference to the First Amendment should be undertaken. . . .

This Court has considered the happenings surrounding the Virginia General Assembly's enactment of "A Bill for Establishing Religious Freedom," . . . written by Thomas Jefferson and sponsored by James Madison, as best reflecting the long and intensive struggle for religious freedom in America, as particularly relevant in the search for the First Amendment's meaning. . . . In 1776, nine years before the bill's passage, Madison co-authored Virginia's Declaration of Rights which provided, *inter alia,* that "all men are equally entitled to the free exercise of religion, according to the dictates of conscience. . . ." . . . Virginia had had Sunday legislation since early in the seventeenth century; in 1776, the laws penalizing "maintaining any opinions in matters of religion, *forbearing to repair to church,* or the exercising any mode of worship whatsoever . . . (emphasis added), were repealed, and all dissenters were freed from the taxes levied for the support of the established church. The Sunday labor prohibitions remained; apparently, they were not believed to be inconsistent with the newly enacted Declaration of Rights. Madison had sought also to have the Declaration expressly condemn the existing Virginia establishment. This hope was finally realized when "A Bill for Establishing Religious Freedom" was passed in 1785. In this same year, Madison presented to Virginia legislators "A Bill for Punishing . . . Sabbath Breakers" which provided, in part:

If any person on Sunday shall himself be found labouring at his own or any other trade or calling, or shall employ his apprentices, servants or slaves in labour, or other business, except it be in the ordinary household offices of daily necessity, or other work of necessity or charity, he shall forfeit the sum of ten shillings for every such offence, deeming every apprentice, servant, or slave so employed, and every day he shall be so employed as constituting a distinct offence.

This became law the following year and remained during the time that Madison fought for the First Amendment in the Congress. It was the law of Virginia, and similar laws were in force in other States, when Madison stated at the Virginia ratification convention:

Happily for the states, they enjoy the utmost freedom of religion. . . . Fortunately for this commonwealth, a majority of the people are decidedly against any exclusive establishment. I believe it to be so in other states. . . . I can appeal to my uniform conduct on this subject, that I have warmly supported religious freedom.

In 1799, Virginia pronounced "A Bill for Establishing Religious Freedom" as "a true exposition of the principles of the bill of rights and constitution," and repealed all subsequently enacted legislation deemed inconsistent with it. . . . Virginia's statute banning Sunday labor stood.

In *Reynolds* v. *United States,* 98 U.S. 145, the Court relied heavily on the history of the Virginia bill. That case concerned a Mormon's attack on a statute making bigamy a crime. The Court said:

In connection with the case we are now considering, it is a significant fact that on the 8th of December, 1788, after the passage of the act establishing religious freedom, and after the convention of Virginia had recommended as an amendment to the Constitution of the United States the declaration in a bill of rights that "all men have an equal, natural, and unalienable right to the free exercise of religion, according to the dictates of conscience," the legislature of that State substantially enacted the statute of James I., death penalty included, because, as recited in the preamble, "it hath been doubted whether bigamy or poligamy be punishable by the laws of this Commonwealth." . . . From that day to this we think may safely be said there never has been a time in any State of the Union when polygamy has not been an offence against society, cognizable by the civil courts and punishable with more or less severity. In the face of all of this evidence, it is impossible to believe that the constitutional guaranty of religious freedom was intended to prohibit legislation in respect to this most important feature of social life.

In the case at bar, we find the place of Sunday Closing Laws in the First Amendment's history both enlightening and persuasive.

But in order to dispose of the case before us, we must consider the standards by which the Maryland statutes are to be measured. Here, a brief review of the First Amendment's background proves helpful. The First Amendment states that "Congress shall make no law respecting an establishment of religion. . . ." U.S. Const., Amend. I. The Amendment was proposed by James Madison on June 8, 1789, in the House of Representatives. It then read, in part:

The civil rights of none shall be abridged on account of religious belief or worship, *nor shall any national religion be established,* nor shall the full and equal rights of conscience be in any manner, or on any pretext, infringed. (Emphasis added.) I Annals of Congress 434.

We are told that Madison added the word "national" to meet the scruples of States which then had an established church. . . . After being referred to committee, it was considered by the House, on August 15, 1789, acting as a Committee of the Whole. Some assistance in determining the scope of the Amendment's proscription of establishment may be found in that debate.

Mr. Boudinot proposed the insertion of the language, "no religion shall be established by law." . . . Mr. Gerry "said it would read better if it was, that no religious doctrine shall be established by law." . . . Mr. Madison "said, he apprehended the meaning of the words to be, that Congress should not establish a religion, and enforce the legal observation of it by law, nor compel men to worship God in any manner contrary to their conscience. . . . He believed that the people feared one sect might obtain a pre-eminence, or two combine together, and establish a religion to which they would compel others to conform." . . .

The Amendment, as it passed the House of Representatives nine days later, read, in part:

Congress shall make no law establishing religion. . . .

It passed the Senate on September 9, 1879, reading, in part:

Congress shall make no law establishing articles of faith, or a mode of worship. . . .

An early commentator opined that the "real object of the amendment was . . . to prevent any national ecclesiastical establishment, which should give to an hierarchy the exclusive patronage of the national government." 3 Story, *Commentaries on the Constitution of the United States,* 728. But, the First Amendment, in its final form, did not simply bar a congressional enactment *establishing a church;* it forbade all laws *respecting an establishment of religion.* Thus, this Court has given the Amendment a "broad interpretation" . . . "in the light of its history and the evils it was designed forever to suppress. . . ." . . . It has found that the First and Fourteenth Amendments afford protection against religious establishment far more extensive than merely to forbid a national or state church. Thus, in *McCollum* v. *Board of Education,* 333 U.S. 203, the Court held that the action of a board of education, permitting religious instruction during school hours in public school buildings and requiring those children who chose not to attend to remain in their classrooms, to be contrary to the "Establishment" Clause.

However, it is equally true that the "Establishment" Clause does not ban federal or state regulation of conduct whose reason or effect merely happens to coincide or harmonize with the tenets of some or all religions. In many instances, the Congress or state legislatures conclude that the general welfare of society, wholly apart from any religious considerations, demands such regulation. Thus, for temporal purposes, murder is illegal. And the fact that this agrees with the dictates of the Judaeo-Christian religions while it may disagree with others does not invalidate the regulation. So too with the questions of adultery and polygamy. . . . The same could be said of theft, fraud, etc., because those offenses were also proscribed in the Decalogue.

Thus, these broad principles have been set forth by this Court. Those cases dealing with the specific problems arising under the "Establishment" Clause which have reached this Court are few in number. The most extensive discussion of the "Establishment" Clause's latitude is to be found in *Everson* v. *Board of Education* . . .

In light of the evolution of our Sunday Closing Laws through the centuries, and of their more or less recent emphasis upon secular considerations, it is not difficult to discern that as presently written and administered, most of them, at least, are of a secular rather than of a religious character, and that presently they bear no relationship to establishment of religion as those words are used in the Constitution of the United States.

Throughout this century and longer, both the federal and state governments have oriented their activities very largely toward improvement of the health, safety, recreation and general well-being of our citizens. Numerous laws affecting public health, safety factors in industry, laws affecting hours and conditions of labor of women and children, weekend diversion at parks and beaches, and cultural activities of various kinds, now point the way toward the good life for all. Sunday Closing Laws, like those before us, have become part and parcel of this great governmental concern wholly apart from their original purposes or connotations. The present purpose and effect of most of them is to provide a uniform day of rest for all citizens; the fact that this day is Sunday, a day of particular significance for the dominant Christian sects, does not bar the State from achieving its secular goals. To say that the States cannot prescribe Sunday as a day of rest for these purposes solely because centuries ago such laws had their genesis in religion would give a constitutional interpretation of hostility to the public welfare rather than one of mere separation of church and State.

We now reach the Maryland statutes under review. The title of the major series of sections of the Maryland Code dealing with Sunday closing—Art. 27, §§ 492–534C—is "Sabbath Breaking"; § 492 proscribes work or bodily labor on the "Lord's day," and forbids persons to "profane the Lord's day" by gaming, fishing et cetera; § 522 refers to Sunday as the "Sabbath day." As has been mentioned above, many of the exempted Sunday activities in the various localities of the State may only be conducted during the afternoon and late evening; most Christian church services, of course, are held on Sunday morning and early Sunday evening. Finally, as previously noted, certain localities do not permit the allowed Sunday activities to be carried on within one hundred yards of any church where religious services are being held. This is the totality of the evidence of religious purpose which may be gleaned from the face of the present statute and from its operative effect.

The predecessors of the existing Maryland Sunday laws are undeniably religious in origin. The first Maryland statute dealing with Sunday activities, enacted in 1649, was entitled "An Act concerning Religion." . . . It made it criminal to "profane the Sabbath or Lord's day called Sunday by frequent swearing, drunkenness or by an uncivill or disorderly recreation, or by working on that day when absolute necessity doth not require it." A 1692 statute entitled "An Act for the Service of Almighty God and the Establishment of the Protestant Religion within this Province," . . . after first stating the importance of keeping the Lord's Day holy and sanctified and expressing concern with the breach of its observance throughout the State, then enacted a Sunday labor prohibition which was the obvious precursor of the present § 492. There was a re-enactment in 1696 entitled "An Act for Sanctifying & keeping holy the Lord's Day Commonly called Sunday." . . . By 1723, the Sabbath-breaking section of the statute assumed the present form of § 492, omitting the specific prohibition against Sunday swearing and the patently religiously motivated title. . . .

There are judicial statements in early Maryland decisions which tend to support appellants' position. In an 1834 case involving a contract calling for delivery on Sunday, the Maryland Court of Appeals remarked that "Ours is a christian community, and a day set apart as the day of rest, is the day consecrated by the resurrection of our Saviour, and embraces the twenty-four hours next ensuing the midnight of Saturday." *Kilgour v. Miles*, 6 Gill and Johnson 268. This language was cited with approval in *Judefind v. State*, 78 Md. 510 (1894). It was also stated there:

It is undoubtedly true that rest from secular employment on Sunday does have a tendency to foster and encourage the Christian religion—of all sects and denominations that observe that day—as rest from work and ordinary occupation enables many to engage in public worship who probably would not otherwise do so. But it would scarcely be asked of a Court, in what professes to be a Christian land, to declare a law unconstitutional because it requires rest from bodily labor on Sunday, (except works of necessity and charity,) and *thereby* promotes the cause of Christianity. If the

Christian religion is, incidentally or otherwise, benefited or fostered by having this day of rest, as it undoubtedly is, there is all the more reason for the enforcement of laws that help to preserve it. Whilst Courts have generally sustained Sunday laws as "civil regulations," their decisions will have no less weight if they are shown to be in accordance with divine law as well as human.

But it should be noted that, throughout the *Judefind* decision, the Maryland court specifically rejected the contention that the laws interfered with religious liberty and stated that the laws' purpose was to provide the "advantages of having a weekly day of rest, 'from a mere physical and political standpoint.' "

Considering the language and operative effect of the current statutes, we no longer find the blanket prohibition against Sunday work or bodily labor. To the contrary, we find that § 521 of Art. 27, the section which appellants violated, permits the Sunday sale of tobaccos and sweets and a long list of sundry articles which we have enumerated above; we find that § 509 of Art. 25 permits the Sunday operation of bathing beaches, amusement parks and similar facilities; we find that Art. 2B, § 28, permits the Sunday sale of alcoholic beverages, products strictly forbidden by predecessor statutes; we are told that Anne Arundel County allows Sunday bingo and the Sunday playing of pinball machines and slot machines, activities generally condemned by prior Maryland Sunday legislation. Certainly, these are not works of charity or necessity. Section 521's current stipulation that shops with only one employee may remain open on Sunday does not coincide with a religious purpose. These provisions, along with those which permit various sports and entertainments on Sunday, seem clearly to be fashioned for the purpose of providing a Sunday atmosphere of recreation, cheerfulness, repose and enjoyment. Coupled with the general proscription against other types of work, we believe that the air of the day is one of relaxation rather than one of religion.

The existing Maryland Sunday laws are not simply verbatim re-enactments of their religiously oriented antecedents. Only § 492 retains the appellation of "Lord's day" and even that section no longer makes recitation of religious purpose. It does talk in terms of "profan[ing] the Lord's day," but other sections permit the activities previously thought to be profane. Prior denunciation of Sunday drunkenness is now gone. Contemporary concern with these statutes is evidenced by the dozen changes made in 1959 and by the recent enactment of a majority of the exceptions.

Finally, the relevant pronouncements of the Maryland Court of Appeals dispel any argument that the statutes' announced purpose is religious. In *Hiller* v. *Maryland*, 124 Md. 385 (1914), the court had before it a Baltimore ordinance prohibiting Sunday baseball. The court said:

What the eminent chief judge said with respect to police enactments which deal with the protection of the public health, morals and safety apply with equal force to those which are concerned with the peace, order and quiet of the community on Sunday, for these social conditions are well recognized heads of the police power. Can the Court say that this ordinance has no real and substantial relation to the peace and order and quiet of Sunday, as a day of rest, in the City of Baltimore?

And, the Maryland court declared in its decision in the instant case: "The legislative plan is plain. It is to compel a day of rest from work, permitting only activities which are necessary or recreational." . . . After engaging in the close scrutiny demanded of us when First Amendment liberties are at issue, we accept the State Supreme Court's determination that the statutes' present purpose and effect is not to aid religion but to set aside a day of rest and recreation.

But, this does not answer all of appellants' contentions. We are told that the State has other means at its disposal to accomplish its secular purpose, other courses that would not even remotely or incidentally give state aid to religion. On this basis, we are asked to hold these statutes invalid on the ground that the State's power to regulate conduct in the public interest may only be executed in a way that does not unduly or unnecessarily infringe upon the religious provisions of the First Amendment. . . . However relevant this argument may be, we believe that the factual basis on which it rests is not supportable. It is true that if the State's interest were simply to provide for its citizens a periodic respite from work, a regulation demanding that everyone rest one day in seven, leaving the choice of the day to the individual, would suffice.

However, the State's purpose is not merely to provide a one-day-in-seven work's stoppage. In addition to this, the State seeks to set one day apart from all others as a day of rest, repose, recreation and tranquility—a day which all members of the family and community have the opportunity to spend and enjoy together, a day in which there exists relative quiet and disassociation from the everyday intensity of commercial activities, a day in which people may visit friends and relatives who are not available during working days.*

Obviously, a state is empowered to determine that a rest-one-day-in-

* This purpose has been articulated in various ways at different times. The parliamentary debates on the British Shops (Sunday Trading Restriction) Bill in 1936 are particularly instructive. The sponsor of the Bill stated:

"I realise also that the State to-day is interfering more and more with family life and more and more controlling the family liberty, and were this a Bill to restrict

seven statute would not accomplish this purpose; that it would not provide a general cessation of activity, a special atmosphere of tranquility, a day which all members of the family or friends and relatives might spend together. Furthermore, it seems plain that the problems involved in enforcing such a provision would be exceedingly more difficult than those in enforcing a common-day-of-rest provision.

Moreover, it is common knowledge that the first day of the week has come to have special significance as a rest day in this country. People of all religions and people with no religion regard Sunday as a time for family activity, for visiting friends and relatives, for late-sleeping, for passive and active entertainments, for dining out and the like. "Vast masses of our people, in fact, literally millions, go out into the countryside on fine Sunday afternoons in the Summer. . . ." 308 Parliamentary Debates, Commons 2159. Sunday is a day apart from all others.* The

---

liberty, and above all to restrict the liberty of the family, I would not be responsible for introducing it. But I hope to show to the House that it is a Bill which is necessary to secure the family life and liberty of hundreds of thousands of our people. . . . They have the right to a holiday on Sunday, to be able to rest from work on that day and to go out into the parks or into the country on a summer day. That is the liberty for which they are asking, and that is the liberty which this Bill would give to them." 308 Parliamentary Debates, Commons 2157-2158.

Another member stated:

"As a family man let me say that my family life would be unduly disturbed if any member had his Sunday on a Tuesday. The value of a Sunday is that everybody in the family is at home on the same day. What is the use of talking about a six-day working week in which six members of a family would each have his day of rest on a different day of the week?" *Id.*, at 2198.

Reports of the International Labour Conferences are also revealing:

"Social custom requires that the same rest-day should as far as possible be accorded to the members of the same working family and to the working class community as a whole. It is a fact that originally religious motives determined the rest-day and that the tradition thus established has subsequently been maintained by law. It appears to be a universal rule that workers in the same area or in the same country have the same rest-day, and that the rest-day coincides with the day established by tradition or custom; and the International Labour Office proposes that this rule should be maintained." Rep. VII, International Labour Conference, 3d Sess. 1921, 127–128.

"A study of national standards shows that the most usual practice is to grant the weekly rest collectively on specified days of the week. This tendency to ensure that the weekly rest is taken at the same time by all workers on the day established by tradition or custom has an obvious social purpose, namely to enable the workers to take part in the life of the community and in the special forms of recreation which are available on certain days." Rep. VII (1), International Labour Conference, 39th Sess. 1956, 24.

* The Constitution itself provides for a Sunday exception in the calculation of the ten days for presidential veto. U.S. Const., Art. I, § 7.

cause is irrelevant; the fact exists. It would seem unrealistic for enforcement purposes and perhaps detrimental to the general welfare to require a state to choose a common-day-of-rest other than that which most persons would select of their own accord. For these reasons, we hold that the Maryland statutes are not laws respecting an establishment of religion.

The distinctions between the statutes in the case before us and the state action in *McCollum* v. *Board of Education*, the only case in this Court finding a violation of the "Establishment" Clause, lend further substantiation to our conclusion. In *McCollum*, state action permitted religious instruction in public school buildings during school hours and required students not attending the religious instructions to remain in their classrooms during that time. The Court found that this system had the effect of coercing the children to attend religious classes; no such coercion to attend church services is present in the situation at bar. In *McCollum*, the only alternative available to the nonattending students was to remain in their classrooms; the alternatives open to nonlaboring persons in the instant case are far more diverse. In *McCollum*, there was direct cooperation between state officials and religious ministers; no such direct participation exists under the Maryland laws. In *McCollum*, tax supported buildings were used to aid religion; in the case, no tax monies are being used in aid of religion.

Finally, we should make clear that this case deals only with the constitutionality of § 521 of the Maryland statute before us. We do not hold that Sunday legislation may not be a violation of the "Establishment" Clause if it can be demonstrated that its purpose—evidenced either on the face of the legislation, in conjunction with its legislative history, or in its operative effect—is to use the State's coercive power to aid religion.

Accordingly, the decision is affirmed.

GALLAGHER *v.* CROWN KOSHER SUPER MARKET

366 US 617 (1961)

[The Massachusetts Sunday closing laws were attacked as unconstitutional insofar as they applied to a corporation operating a kosher meat market, whose stockholders, officers, and directors were members of the Orthodox Jewish faith, which compelled them to keep the shop closed on Saturday.

[In an opinion by Chief Justice Warren, joined by Justices Black, Clark, and Whittaker, it was held that the laws, as applied to Orthodox Jews, did not prohibit the free exercise of religion. Justice Frankfurter wrote a concurring opinion, joined by Justice Harlan.

[Justices Douglas, Brennan, and Stewart dissented, on the ground that the laws, as applied to the plaintiffs, prohibited the free exercise of religion by not permitting them to open their shop on Sunday if they kept it closed on Saturday for religious reasons.]

Mr. Chief Justice Warren announced the judgment of the Court and an opinion in which Mr. Justice Black, Mr. Justice Clark, and Mr. Justice Whittaker concur:

The principal issues presented in this case are whether the Massachusetts Sunday Closing Laws violate equal protection, are statutes respecting the establishment of religion or prohibit the free exercise thereof.

Appellees are Crown Kosher Super Market, a corporation whose four stockholders, officers and directors are members of the Orthodox Jewish faith, which operates in Springfield, Massachusetts, and sells kosher meat and other food products that are almost exclusively kosher and which has many Orthodox Jewish customers; three of Crown's customers of the Orthodox Jewish faith, whose religion forbids them to shop on the Sabbath and requires them to eat kosher food, as representatives of that class of patrons; and the chief Orthodox rabbi of Springfield, as representative of a class of Orthodox rabbis whose duties include the inspecting of kosher food markets to insure compliance with Orthodox Jewish dietary laws.

Crown had previously been open for business on Sunday, on which day it had conducted about one-third of its weekly business. No other supermarket in the Springfield area had kept open on Sunday. Since the Orthodox Jewish religion requires its members to refrain from any commercial activity on the Sabbath—from sundown on Friday until sundown on Saturday, Crown was not open during those hours. Although there is a statutory provision which permits Sabbatarians to keep their shops open until 10 A.M. on Sunday for the sale of kosher meat, Crown did not do so because it was economically impractical; for the same reasons, Crown did not open after sundown on Saturday.

Those provisions of the law immediately under attack are in a section entitled "Observance of the Lord's Day." They forbid, under penalty of a fine of up to fifty dollars, the keeping open of shops and the doing of any labor, business or work on Sunday. Works of necessity and charity are excepted as is the operation of certain public utilities. There are also exemptions for the retail sale of drugs, the retail sale of tobacco by certain vendors, the retail sale and making of bread at given hours by certain dealers, and the retail sale of frozen desserts, confectioneries and fruits by various listed sellers. The statutes under attack further permit the Sunday sale of live bait for noncommercial fishing; the sale of meals to be consumed off the premises; the operation and letting of motor vehicles and the sale of items and emergency services necessary thereto;

the letting of horses, carriages, boats and bicycles; unpaid work on pleasure boats and about private gardens and grounds if it does not cause unreasonable noise; the running of trains and boats; the printing, sale and delivery of newspapers; the operation of bootblacks before 11 A.M., unless locally prohibited; the wholesale and retail sale of milk, ice and fuel; the wholesale handling and delivery of fish and perishable foodstuffs; the sale at wholesale of dressed poultry; the making of butter and cheese; general interstate truck transportation before 8 A.M. and after 8 P.M. and at all times in cases of emergency; intrastate truck transportation of petroleum products before 6 A.M. and after 10 P.M.; the transportation of livestock and farm items for participation in fairs and sporting events; the sale of fruits and vegetables on the grower's premises; the keeping open of public bathhouses; the digging of clams; the icing and dressing of fish; the sale of works of art at exhibitions; the conducting of private trade expositions between 1 P.M. and 10 P.M.

These statutes do not prohibit Sunday business and labor by Sabbatarian observers so long as it disturbs no other person. However, this has been construed to forbid the keeping open of shops for the sale of merchandise. *Commonwealth* v. *Has,* 122 Mass. 40. Permission is granted by local option for the Sunday operation after 1 P.M. of amusement parks and beach resorts, including participation in bowling and games of amusement for which prizes are awarded. Special licenses for emergency Sunday work may be obtained from local officials.

Other provisions of the Massachusetts Sunday legislation make generally unlawful Sunday attendance or participation in any public entertainments except for those which are duly licensed locally, conducted after 1 P.M., and are in keeping with the character of the day and not inconsistent with its due observance.

Although there is a general bar of games and sports on Sunday, professional sports may be played between 1:30 P.M. and 6:30 P.M. and indoor hockey and basketball any time after 1:30 P.M.; amateur sports may be played between 2 P.M. and 6 P.M.; this is all subject to local option and no game may be conducted within one thousand feet of any regular place of worship except in a public playground or park. There are specific bans on auto racing, horseracing, boxing and hunting with firearms. And there are a number of additional exemptions from the general proscription. Golf, tennis, dancing at weddings, concerts of sacred music and the celebration of religious customs or rituals are all allowed on Sunday as are the operation of miniature golf courses and golf driving ranges after 1 P.M. Motion pictures may be exhibited after this hour if a local license is obtained. Parades with music for certain commemorative purposes may be held on Sunday by veterans', civic, fraternal, policemen's and firemen's organizations providing that they are suspended while passing within two hundred feet of public worship services.

Persons who keep places of public entertainment or refreshment lose their licenses if they entertain, on Sunday, people other than travelers, strangers or lodgers. With limited exceptions, discharging firearms for sport except on one's own land, fishing for commercial purposes, and fishing with nets or spears are prohibited on Sunday. The use of gaming devices is not allowed. Outdoor exercise without the element of contest is generally permitted as is the taking of mammals by means of traps. Heavier penalties are imposed for the willful cutting and destruction of timber, shrubs, fruits or vegetables on Sunday than on other days of the week.

Still other statutory sections make it a crime for most employers to require their employees to engage in ordinary occupation on Sunday unless the employee is allowed twenty-four consecutive hours off during the following six days. The sale of alcoholic beverages by certain licensees is permitted on Sunday after 1 P.M., by local option. However, patrons consuming the beverages on the premises must be seated at tables.

Appellees sought permanently to enjoin the enforcement of the statute against them, alleging that appellant, Springfield's chief of police, had previously arrested and prosecuted Crown's manager for keeping open on Sunday; that, unless restrained, appellant would continue to enforce the statute against Crown; that the statute was unconstitutional for the reasons stated above. The three-judge Federal District Court, one judge dissenting, agreed with appellees. . . . On appeal brought under 28 U.S.C. § 1253, we noted probable jurisdiction. . . .

I.

The equal protection arguments advanced by appellees are much the same as those made by appellants in *McGowan* v. *Maryland*. They contend that the exceptions to the statute are so numerous and arbitrary as to be found to have no rational basis; that the law permits the sale of certain food items sold by Crown but limits this permission to selected types of stores; that the employees in the exempted activities are just as much in need of a day of rest as are Crown's employees. The three-judge District Court described the present statutory system as an "unbelievable hodgepodge" and sustained appellees' allegations.

The answers to these arguments are likewise similar to those given in *McGowan* when the contentions are examined under the standards set forth in that opinion. Many of the exceptions in the Massachusetts Sunday Laws are reasonably explainable on their face. Such items as tobaccos, confectioneries, fruits and frozen desserts could have been found by the legislature to be useful in adding to Sunday's enjoyment; such items as newspapers, milk and bread could have been found to be required to be sold fresh daily. It is conceivable that the legislature believed that the sale of fish and perishable foodstuffs at wholesale would not detract from the atmosphere of the day, while the retail sale of these items would inject the distinctly commercial element that exists during the other six days of the week. It is fair to believe that the allowance of professional and amateur sports on Sunday would add to the day's special character rather than detract from it. And the legislature could find that the circumstances attendant to the conduct of professional sports are sufficiently different from those of amateur sports to justify different treatment as to the hours during which they may be played. Furthermore, the legislature could determine that, although many retailers, including Crown, sell frozen desserts, to permit only a limited number of innholders, druggists and common victuallers to sell them on Sunday would serve the public purpose of providing these items on Sunday and, at the same time, limit the commercial activities ordinarily attendant to their sale. And, if such determination requires this limited number of stores to be open to serve the public interest, the employees of most of the stores are still protected by the statutory provision giving the employees another day of rest. To permit all stores which sell the exempted products to remain open on Sunday but to limit them to the sale of the exempted items might well be believed to impose near insuperable enforcement problems.

The fact is that the irrationality of these and the many other apparently reasonable distinctions has not been shown. The presumption of validity upon which the other classifications stand has not been dispelled. "A classification having some reasonable basis does not offend against [the equal protection] clause merely because it is not made with mathematical nicety or because in practice it results in some inequality." *Lindsley* v. *Natural Carbonic Gas Co.*, 220 U.S. 61. Thus, we hold that the Massachusetts Sunday Laws do not violate equal protection of the laws.

II.

Appellees make several contentions that the statutes violate the constitutional guarantees of religious freedom. *First,* they allege that the statute is a law respecting an establishment of religion in that both its original and current purpose is to enforce the observance of Sunday as the Sabbath.

We agree with the court below that, like the Sunday laws of other States, the Massachusetts statutes have an unmistakable religious origin. The first enactment of the Plymouth Colony in 1650 stated simply that "whosoever shall prophane the Lords day by doeing any servill worke or any such like abusses" shall either be fined or whipped. . . . Eight years later, a ban on Sunday traveling was enacted with the following preamble:

Wheras complaint is made of great abuses in sundry places of this Govrment of prophaning the Lords day by travellers both horse and foot by bearing of burdens carrying of packes &c. upon the Lords day to the great offence of the Godly welafected among us.

And, in 1671, the religious purpose was made clear beyond doubt:

9. This Court taking notice of great abuse, and many misdemeanours, committed by divers persons in these many wayes, Profaneing the Sabbath or Lord's-day, to the great dishonour of God, Reproach of Religion, and Grief of the Spirits of God's People

Do therefore Order, That whosoever shall Prophane the Lord's-day, by doing unnecessary servile Work, by unnecessary travailing, or by sports and recreations, he or they that so transgress, shall forfeit for every such default forty shillings, or be publickly whipt: But if it clearly appear that the sin was proudly, Presumptuously and with a high hand committed, against the known Command and Authority of the blessed God, such a person therein Despising and Reproaching the Lord, shall be put to death or grievously punished at the Judgement of the Court.

10. And whosoever shall frequently neglect the public Worship of God on the Lords day, that is approved by this Government, shall forfeit for every such default convicted of, ten shillings, especially where it appears to arise from negligance, Idleness or Prophaness of Spirit.

The Sunday regulations of the Massachusetts Colony were no different. The 1653 version spoke of the abuses of the Dishonor of God and the Reproach of Religion which were Grieving the Souls of God's Servants. Among other things, the statute forbade Drinking and Sporting on Sunday. . . . In 1665, Neglect of God's Public Worship was made a crime. Every person was required to apply himself to Duties of Religion and Piety on Sunday according to the 1692 statute which continued the ban on Sunday sports. . . . The preamble to the new statute in 1761 retained the Religion and Piety language and added that Profanation of the Lord's Day is highly offensive to Almighty God. This statute retained and strengthened the former prohibitions.

A change came about in 1782. The preamble added the following:

Whereas the Observance of the Lord's Day is highly promotive of the Welfare of a Community, by affording necessary Seasons for Relaxation from Labor and the Cares of Business; for moral Reflections and Conversation on the Duties of Life, and the frequent Errors of human Conduct; . . . Acts and Laws of the Commonwealth of Massachusetts 63.

Thus, the statute's announced purpose was no longer solely religious. But this statute proscribed the Sunday attendance at any Concert of Music and Dancing in addition to the previously mentioned activities. This law was re-enacted in 1792. . . .

However, when we examine the statutes now before the Court, we find that, for the most part, they have been divorced from the religious orientation of their predecessors. The preambles' statements, in certain terms, of religious purpose exist no longer. Sports of almost all kinds are now generally allowed on Sunday. The absolute prohibition against alcoholic beverages has disappeared. Concerts and dancing are permitted. Church attendance is no longer required.

Admittedly, the statutes still contain references to the Lord's Day and some provisions speak of weekdays as being secular days. Although § 2 of c. 136 excepts concerts of *sacred* music, the next clause of the section permits free open-air concerts. It would seem that the objectionable language is merely a relic. The fact that certain Sunday activities are permitted only if they are "in keeping with the character of the day and not inconsistent with its due observance," does not necessarily mean that the day is intended to be religious; the "character" of the day would appear more likely to be intended to be one of repose and recreation. We are told that those provisions forbidding certain activities to be conducted within a set distance from a place of public worship are especially devoted to maintaining Sunday as the Sabbath. But because the State wishes to protect those who do worship on Sunday does not mean that the State means to impose religious worship on all. . . . Although many of the more recently allowed Sunday activities may not commence prior to 1 P.M., others may be undertaken at any time during the day. And the contention that evening church services are being protected cannot be maintained since most of those activities that begin after 1 P.M. may continue throughout the day.

Furthermore, the long list of exemptions that have been recently granted evidences that the present scheme is one to provide an atmosphere of recreation rather than religion. The court below pointed out that, since 1858, the statutes have been amended more than seventy times. It would not seem that the Sunday sales of tobacco, soda water, fruit, et cetera, are in aid of religion. It would seem that the operation of amusement parks and beach resorts is in aid of recreation.

An examination of recent Massachusetts legislative history bolsters the State's position that these statutes are not religious. In 1960, a report of the Legislative Research Council stated:

In general, Sunday laws protect the public by guaranteeing one day in seven to provide a period of rest and quiet. Health, peace and good order of society are thereby promoted. Such provision is essentially civil in character and the statutes are not regarded as religious ordinances. Report of the Legislative Research Council relative to Legal Holidays and their observance, Mass. Leg. Docs., Sen. Doc. No. 525 (1960), 24.*

The earliest pronouncements of the Supreme Judicial Court of Massachusetts are further indication of the religious origin of the Sunday Laws. In *Pearce* v. *Atwood,* 13 Mass. 324 (1816), it was stated that the statute's sole object was "ensuring reverence and respect for one day of the week, in order that religious exercises should be performed without interruption from common and secular employments." In *Bennett* v. *Brooks,* 91 Mass. 118 (1864), the day was characterized as one "set apart for religious services and observances."

In 1877, a case arose in which a charge of violation of religious freedom was made. The Supreme Judicial Court relied on the Pennsylvania case of *Specht* v. *Commonwealth,* 8 Pa. 312, and stated clearly:

It is essentially a civil regulation, providing for a fixed period of rest in the business, the ordinary avocations and the amusements of the community. If there is to be such a cessation from labor and amusement, some one day must be selected for the purpose; and even if the day thus selected is chosen because a great majority of the people celebrate it as a day of peculiar sanctity, the legislative authority to provide for its observance is derived from its general authority to regulate the business of the community and to provide for its moral and physical welfare. The act imposes upon no one any religious ceremony or attendance upon any form of worship, and any one, who deems another day more suitable for rest or worship, may devote that day to the religious observance which he deems appropriate. That one who conscientiously observes the seventh day of the week may also be compelled to abstain from business of the kind expressly forbidden on the first day, is not occasioned by any subordination of his religion, but because as a member of the community he must submit to the rules which are made by lawful authority to regulate and govern the business of that community. *Commonwealth* v. *Has,* 122 Mass. 40 (1877).

The court below characterized this decision as an *ad hoc* improvisation by the Massachusetts court. Of course, the court below was correct in deciding that it was not bound by the Massachusetts characterization of the statutes. . . . But ten years later, in *Commonwealth* v. *Starr,* 144 Mass. 359 (1887), another religious charge against the statute was made; it was rejected on the authority of *Has.*

* A 1953 report concluded:
"The wave of materialism which is sweeping the country makes it most important that one day be set aside for worship, rest and to give all persons an opportunity to strengthen the bulwark of our American civilization—the home." Report of the Unpaid Special Commission to Investigate and Study the Provisions of the Laws Relating to the Observance of the Lord's Day, Mass. Leg. Docs., H. Doc. No. 2413 (1954) 9.

As the court below pointed out, there have been several cases, be-tween 1877 and 1923, which gave a religious characterization to the statute. But in none of these cases was there a contention regarding religious freedom, and none of the cases stated the statute's purpose to be exclusively religious. Finally, in the only recent case passing on the Massachusetts Sunday Closing Laws, *Commonwealth* v. *Chernock*, 336 Mass. 384 (1957), the court summarily dismissed the complainant's religious contention, relying on *Has.*

The relevant factors having been most carefully considered, we do not find that the present statutes' purpose or effect is religious. Although the three-judge court found that Massachusetts had no legitimate secular interest in maintaining Sunday closing, we have held differently in *McGowan* v. *Maryland, supra*. And, for the reasons stated in that case, we reject appellees' request to hold these statutes invalid on the ground that the State may accomplish its secular purpose by alternative means that would not even remotely or incidentally aid religion.

Secondly, appellees contend that the application to them of the Sun-day Closing Laws prohibits the free exercise of their religion. Crown alleges that if it is required by law to abstain from business on Sunday, then, because its owners' religion demands closing from sundown Fri-day to sundown Saturday, Crown will be open only four and one-half days a week, thereby suffering extreme economic disadvantage. Crown's Orthodox Jewish customers allege that because their religious beliefs forbid their shopping on the Jewish Sabbath, the statute's effect is to deprive them, from Friday afternoon until Monday of each week, of the opportunity to purchase the kosher food sanctioned by their faith. The Orthodox rabbis allege that the statutes' effect greatly complicates their task of supervising the condition of kosher meat because the meat delivered on Friday would have to be kept until Monday. Furthermore, appellees contend that, because of all this, the statute discriminates against their religion.

These allegations are similar, although not as grave, as those made by appellants in *Braunfeld* v. *Brown*. Since the decision in that case rejects the contentions presented by these appellees on the merits, we need not decide whether appellees have standing to raise these ques-tions.

Accordingly, the decision below is reversed.

TWO GUYS FROM HARRISON-ALLENTOWN *v.* McGINLEY

366 US 582 (1961)

[This case, involving the Pennsylvania Sunday closing laws, is to be read together with *McGowan* v. *Maryland, supra*. The decision in this case, too, was 8 to 1, with only Justice Douglas dissenting. Justice Frankfurter wrote a concurring opinion, joined by Justice Harlan.]

Mr. Chief Justice Warren delivered the opinion of the Court:

The primary questions presented in this case are whether a Pennsylvania statute enacted in 1959 which makes unlawful the Sunday retail sale of certain commodities, imposing a fine of up to one hundred dollars for the first offense, is violative of the constitutional guarantees of equal protection of the laws and religious freedom.

This case is essentially the same as *McGowan* v. *Maryland,* decided today. The major differences between the Pennsylvania and Maryland Sunday Closing Laws concern the specific provisions for exemptions from the general proscription of Sunday sales and activities. . . .

Appellant contends that the Pennsylvania Sunday Closing Law is one respecting an establishment of religion because it commemorates the Resurrection, obliges everyone to honor this basic doctrine of the major Christian denominations by abstaining from work and encourages Christian religious worship. Appellant also alleges that the statute discriminates against certain religions. For the same reasons stated in *McGowan* v. *Maryland,* . . . we hold that appellant has standing to raise only the first contention. . . .

The court below found that the connection between religion and the original Pennsylvania Sunday closing statutes was obvious and indisputable. This is clearly demonstrated by the first Pennsylvania Sunday Law, enacted in 1682. There were re-enactments several years later, and again in 1700, which once more stated the purposes of preventing "Looseness, Irreligion, and Atheism," and of better permitting on Sunday the reading of the scriptures at home or the frequenting of meetings of religious worship. . . . In 1705, some changes appeared. The preamble of the statute remained religious and the stated purposes of bible reading and religious worship continued. However, some of the exceptions still present in the 1939 statute first appeared, but a specific ban on the drinking of alcoholic beverages in public houses was enacted. The most apparent forerunner of the 1939 statute was passed in 1779. The preamble stated only that the purpose was "for the due observation of the Lord's day." . . . No mention was made of bible reading or religious worship and the specific Sunday prohibition concerning alcoholic beverages was omitted. By 1786, the preamble completely disappeared. . . .

The present statutory sections still contain some traces of the early religious influence. The 1939 statute refers to Sunday as "the Lord's day"; but it is included in the general section entitled, "Offenses Against

Public Policy, Economy and Health.". . . § 4651 uses the term "Sabbath Day" and refers to the other days of the week as "secular days." But almost every other statutory section simply uses the word, "Sunday," and contains no language with religious connotation. It would seem that those traces that have remained are simply the result of legislative oversight in failing to remove them. Section 4651 was re-enacted in 1959 and happened to retain the religious language; many other statutory sections, passed both before and after this date, omit it. Certain political subdivisions are authorized to restrain "desecrations of the Sabbath day," and there is a jurisdictional section authorizing the punishment of persons who "profane the Lord's day." But many of the activities historically considered to be profane—e.g., the consumption of alcoholic beverages—are now no longer totally prohibited. There is a general immunity for religious motion pictures and some of the recently exempted activities are permitted only during Sunday afternoons.

On the other hand, we find that the 1939 statute was recently amended to permit all healthful and recreational exercises and activities on Sunday. This is not consistent with aiding church attendance; in fact, it might be deemed inconsistent. And the statutory section, § 4699.10, the constitutionality of which is immediately before us, was promoted principally by the representatives of labor and business interests. Those Pennsylvania legislators who favored the bill specifically disavowed any religious purpose for its enactment but stated instead that economics required its passage.

As early as 1848, the Pennsylvania Supreme Court vociferously disclaimed that the purpose of Sunday closing was religious:

All agree that to the well-being of society, periods of rest are absolutely necessary. To be productive of the required advantage, these periods must recur at stated intervals, so that the mass of which the community is composed, may enjoy a respite from labour at the same time. They may be established by common consent, or, as is conceded, the legislative power of the state may, without impropriety, interfere to fix the time of their stated return and enforce obedience to the direction. When this happens, some one day must be selected, and it has been said the round of the week presents none which, being preferred, might not be regarded as favouring some one of the numerous religious sects into which mankind are divided. In a Christian community, where a very large majority of the people celebrate the first day of the week as their chosen period of rest from labour, it is not surprising that that day should have received the legislative sanction: and as it is also devoted to religious observances, we are prepared to estimate the reason why the statute should speak of it as the Lord's day, and denominate the infraction of its legalized rest, a profanation. *Yet this does not change the character of the enactment. It is still, essentially, but a civil regulation made for the government of man as a member of society,* and obedience to it may properly be enforced by penal sanctions. *Specht* v. *Commonwealth,* 8 Pa. 312. (Emphasis added.)

Concededly, there were a number of cases decided after *Specht* which used language strongly supporting appellant's position. But, these cases, the last of which was decided more than thirty years ago, did not squarely decide a constitutional contention. More persuasively, in the only recent appellate case dealing with the constitutionality of the 1939 statute, the Pennsylvania Superior Court affirmed an opinion which specifically relied on the language and reasoning of *Specht.* . . .

Having carefully examined the entirety of the present legislation, the relevant judicial characterizations and, particularly, the legislative history leading to the passage of the 1959 Act immediately before us, we hold that neither the statute's purpose nor its effect is religious. See *McGowan* v. *Maryland.* . . . Moreover, for the same reasons stated in *McGowan* v. *Maryland,* . . . we reject appellant's contention that the State has other means at its disposal to accomplish its secular purpose that would not even remotely or incidentally give state aid to religion.

Accordingly, the decision is affirmed.

BRAUNFELD *v.* BROWN

366 US 599 (1961)

[Like the immediately preceding case, this case also involved the Sunday closing laws of Pennsylvania, but also was a companion case to *Gallagher* v. *Crown Kosher Super Market* in that it involved an attack on the statutes by merchants who adhered to the Orthodox Jewish faith and who contended that the compulsory Sunday closing violated their right to the free exercise of religion. The Court upheld the constitutionality of the laws. Justice Frankfurter wrote a concurring opinion, joined by Justice Harlan. Justices Douglas, Brennan, and Stewart dissented.]

Mr. Chief Justice Warren announced the judgment of the Court and an opinion in which Mr. Justice Black, Mr. Justice Clark, and Mr. Justice Whittaker concur:

This case concerns the constitutional validity of the application to appellants of the Pennsylvania criminal statute, enacted in 1959, which proscribes the Sunday retail sale of certain enumerated commodities. Among the questions presented are whether the statute is a law respecting an establishment of religion and whether the statute violates equal protection. Since both of these questions, in reference to this very statute, have already been answered in the negative, *Two Guys from Harrison-Allentown, Inc.,* v. *McGinley,* and since appellants present nothing new regarding them, they need not be considered here. Thus, the only question for consideration is whether the statute interferes with the free exercise of appellants' religion.

Appellants are merchants in Philadelphia who engage in the retail sale of clothing and home furnishings within the proscription of the statute in issue. Each of the appellants is a member of the Orthodox Jewish faith, which requires the closing of their places of business and a total abstention from all manner of work from nightfall each Friday until nightfall each Saturday. They instituted a suit in the court below seeking a permanent injunction against the enforcement of the 1959 statute. Their complaint, as amended, alleged that appellants had previously kept their places of business open on Sunday; that each of appellants had done a substantial amount of business on Sunday, compensating somewhat for their closing on Saturday; that Sunday closing will result in impairing the ability of all appellants to earn a livelihood and will render appellant Braunfeld unable to continue in his business, thereby losing his capital investment; that the statute is unconstitutional for the reasons stated above.

A three-judge court was properly convened and it dismissed the complaint on the authority of the *Two Guys from Harrison* case. . . . On appeal brought under 28 U.S.C. § 1253, we noted probable jurisdiction.

Appellants contend that the enforcement against them of the Pennsylvania statute will prohibit the free exercise of their religion because, due to the statute's compulsion to close on Sunday, appellants will suffer substantial economic loss, to the benefit of their non-Sabbatarian competitors, if appellants also continue their Sabbath observance by closing their businesses on Saturday; that this result will either compel appellants to give up their Sabbath observance, a basic tenet of the Orthodox Jewish faith, or will put appellants at a serious economic disadvantage if they continue to adhere to their Sabbath. Appellants also assert that the statute will operate so as to hinder the Orthodox Jewish faith in gaining new adherents. And the corollary to these arguments is that if the free exercise of appellants' religion is impeded, that religion is being subjected to discriminatory treatment by the State.

In *McGowan* v. *Maryland,* we noted the significance that this Court has attributed to the development of religious freedom in Virginia in determining the scope of the First Amendment's protection. We observed that when Virginia passed its Declaration of Rights in 1776, providing that "all men are equally entitled to the free exercise of religion," Virginia repealed its laws which in any way penalized "maintaining any opinions in matters of religion, forebearing to repair to church, or the exercising any mode of worship whatsoever." But, Virginia retained its laws prohibiting Sunday labor.

We also took cognizance, in *McGowan,* of the evolution of Sunday Closing Laws from wholly religious sanctions to legislation concerned with the establishment of a day of community tranquillity, respite and recreation, a day when the atmosphere is one of calm and relaxation rather than one of commercialism, as it is during the other six days of the week. We reviewed the still growing state preoccupation with improving the health, safety, morals and general well-being of our citizens.

Concededly, appellants and all other persons who wish to work on Sunday will be burdened economically by the State's day of rest mandate; and appellants point out that their religion requires them to refrain from work on Saturday as well. Our inquiry then is whether, in these circumstances, the First and Fourteenth Amendments forbid application of the Sunday Closing Law to appellants.

Certain aspects of religious exercise cannot, in any way, be restricted or burdened by either federal or state legislation. Compulsion by law of the acceptance of any creed or the practice of any form of worship is strictly forbidden. The freedom to hold religious beliefs and opinions is absolute. *Cantwell* v. *Connecticut,* 310 U.S. 296; *Reynolds* v. *United States,* 98 U.S. 145. Thus, in *West Virginia State Board of Education* v. *Barnette,* 319 U.S. 624, this Court held that state action compelling school children to salute the flag, on pain of expulsion from public school, was contrary to the First and Fourteenth Amendments when applied to those students whose religious beliefs forbade saluting a flag. But, this is not the case at bar; the statute before us does not make criminal the holding of any religious belief or opinion, nor does it force anyone to embrace any religious belief or to say or believe anything in conflict with his religious tenets.

However, the freedom to act, even when the action is in accord with one's religious convictions, is not totally free from legislative restrictions. . . . As pointed out in *Reynolds* v. *United States, supra,* at p. 164, legislative power over mere opinion is forbidden but it may reach people's actions when they are found to be in violation of important social duties or subversive of good order, even when the actions are demanded by one's religion. This was articulated by Thomas Jefferson when he said:

Believing with you that religion is a matter which lies solely between man and his God, that he owes account to none other for his faith or his worship, that *the legislative powers of the government reach actions only, and not opinions,* I contemplate with sovereign reverence that act of the whole American people which declared that their legislature should "make no law respecting an establishment of religion, or prohibiting the free exercise thereof," thus building a wall of separation between church and State. Adhering to this expression of the supreme will of the nation in behalf of the rights of conscience, I shall see with sincere satisfaction the progress of those sentiments, which tend to restore to man all his natural rights, convinced *he has no natural right in opposition to his social duties."* (Emphasis added.) 8 *Works of Thomas Jefferson* 113.*

And, in the *Barnette* case, the Court was careful to point out that "the freedom asserted by these appellees does not bring them into collision with rights asserted by any other individual. It is such conflicts which most frequently require intervention of the State to determine where the rights of one end and those of another begin. . . . It is . . . to be noted that the compulsory flag salute and pledge requires *affirmation of a belief* and an *attitude of mind."* (Emphasis added.)

Thus, in *Reynolds* v. *United States,* this Court upheld the polygamy conviction of a member of the Mormon faith despite the fact that an accepted doctrine of his church then imposed upon its male members the *duty* to practice polygamy. And, in *Prince* v. *Massachusetts,* 321 U.S. 158, this Court upheld a statute making it a crime for a girl under eighteen years of age to sell any newspapers, periodicals or merchandise in public places despite the fact that a child of the Jehovah's Witnesses faith believed that it was her religious *duty* to perform this work.

It is to be noted that, in the two cases just mentioned, the religious practices themselves conflicted with the public interest. In such cases, to make accommodation between the religious action and an exercise of state authority is a particularly delicate task, . . . because resolution in favor of the State results in the choice of the individual of either abandoning his religious principle or facing criminal prosecution.

But, again, this is not the case before us because the statute at bar does not make unlawful any religious practices of appellants; the Sunday law simply regulates a secular activity and, as applied to appellants, operates so as to make the practice of their religious beliefs more expensive. Furthermore, the law's effect does not inconvenience all members of the Orthodox Jewish faith but only those who believe it necessary to work on Sunday. And even these are not faced with as serious a

---

* Oliver Ellsworth, a member of the Constitutional Convention and later Chief Justice, wrote:

"But while I assert the rights of religious liberty, I would not deny that the civil power has a right, in some cases, to interfere in matters of religion. It has a right to prohibit and punish gross immoralities and impieties; because the open *practice* of these is of evil example and detriment." (Emphasis added.) Written in the Connecticut Courant, Dec. 17, 1787, as quoted in 1 Stokes, *Church and State in the United States,* 535.

choice as forsaking their religious practices or subjecting themselves to criminal prosecution. Fully recognizing that the alternatives open to appellants and others similarly situated—retaining their present occupations and incurring economic disadvantage or engaging in some other commercial activity which does not call for either Saturday or Sunday labor—may well result in some financial sacrifice in order to observe their religious beliefs, still the option is wholly different than when the legislation attempts to make a religious practice itself unlawful.

To strike down, without the most critical scrutiny, legislation which imposes only an indirect burden on the exercise of religion, i.e., legislation which does not make unlawful the religious practice itself, would radically restrict the operating latitude of the legislature. Statutes which tax income and limit the amount which may be deducted for religious contributions impose an indirect economic burden on the observance of the religion of the citizen whose religion requires him to donate a greater amount to his church; statutes which require the courts to be closed on Saturday and Sunday impose a similar indirect burden on the observance of the religion of the trial lawyer whose religion requires him to rest on a weekday. The list of legislation of this nature is nearly limitless.

Needless to say, when entering the area of religious freedom, we must be fully cognizant of the particular protection that the Constitution has accorded it. Abhorrence of religious persecution and intolerance is a basic part of our heritage. But we are a cosmopolitan nation made up of people of almost every conceivable religious preference. These denominations number almost three hundred. . . . Consequently, it cannot be expected, much less required, that legislators enact no law regulating conduct that may in some way result in an economic disadvantage to some religious sects and not to others because of the special practices of the various religions. We do not believe that such an effect is an absolute test for determining whether the legislation violates the freedom of religion protected by the First Amendment.

Of course, to hold unassailable all legislation regulating conduct which imposes solely an indirect burden on the observance of religion would be a gross oversimplification. If the purpose or effect of a law is to impede the observance of one or all religions or is to discriminate invidiously between religions, that law is constitutionally invalid even though the burden may be characterized as being only indirect. But if the State regulates conduct by enacting a general law within its power, the purpose and effect of which is to advance the State's secular goals, the statute is valid despite its indirect burden on religious observance unless the State may accomplish its purpose by means which do not impose such a burden. . . .

As we pointed out in *McGowan* v. *Maryland,* we cannot find a State without power to provide a weekly respite from all labor and, at the same time, to set one day of the week apart from the others as a day of rest, repose, recreation and tranquillity—a day when the hectic tempo of everyday existence ceases and a more pleasant atmosphere is created, a day which all members of the family and community have the opportunity to spend and enjoy together, a day in which people may visit friends and relatives who are not available during working days, a day when the weekly laborer may best regenerate himself. This is particularly true in this day and age of increasing state concern with public welfare legislation.

Also, in *McGowan,* we examined several suggested alternative means by which it was argued that the State might accomplish its secular goals without even remotely or incidentally affecting religious freedom. We found there that a State might well find that those alternatives would not accomplish bringing about a general day of rest. We need not examine them again here.

However, appellants advance yet another means at the State's disposal which they would find unobjectionable. They contend that the State should cut an exception from the Sunday labor proscription for those people who, because of religious conviction, observe a day of rest other than Sunday. By such regulation, appellants contend, the economic disadvantages imposed by the present system would be removed and the State's interest in having all people rest one day would be satisfied.

A number of States provide such an exemption, and this may well be the wiser solution to the problem. But our concern is not with the wisdom of legislation but with its constitutional limitation. Thus, reason and experience teach that to permit the exemption might well undermine the State's goal of providing a day that, as best possible, eliminates the atmosphere of commercial noise and activity. Although not dispositive of the issue, enforcement problems would be more difficult since there would be two or more days to police rather than one and it would be more difficult to observe whether violations were occurring.

Additional problems might also be presented by a regulation of this sort. To allow only people who rest on a day other than Sunday to keep their businesses open on that day might well provide these people with an economic advantage over their competitors who must remain closed on that day; * this might cause the Sunday-observers to complain that

---

* "If he [the Orthodox Jewish storekeeper] opens on Saturday, he is subjected to very fierce competition indeed from Christian shopkeepers, whereas on Sunday, supposing he closes on Saturday, he has an absolutely free run and no competition

their religions are being discriminated against. With this competitive advantage existing, there could well be the temptation for some, in order to keep their businesses open on Sunday, to assert that they have religious convictions which compel them to close their businesses on what had formerly been their least profitable day. This might make necessary a state-conducted inquiry into the sincerity of the individual's religious beliefs, a practice which a State might believe would itself run afoul of the spirit of constitutionally protected religious guarantees. Finally, in order to keep the disruption of the day at a minimum, exempted employers would probably have to hire employees who themselves qualified for the exemption because of their own religious beliefs, a practice which a State might feel to be opposed to its general policy prohibiting religious discrimination in hiring. For all of these reasons, we cannot say that the Pennsylvania statute before us is invalid, either on its face or as applied.

Accordingly, the decision is affirmed.

Mr. Justice Douglas, dissenting:

The question is not whether one day out of seven can be imposed by a State as a day of rest. The question is not whether Sunday can by force of custom and habit be retained as a day of rest. The question is whether a State can impose criminal sanctions on those who, unlike the Christian majority that makes up our society, worship on a different day or do not share the religious scruples of the majority.

If the "free exercise" of religion were subject to reasonable regulations, as it is under some constitutions, or if all laws "respecting the establishment of religion" were not proscribed, I could understand how rational men, representing a predominantly Christian civilization, might think these Sunday laws did not unreasonably interfere with any one's free exercise of religion and took no step toward a burdensome establishment of any religion.

But that is not the premise from which we start, as there is agreement that the fact that a State, and not the Federal Government, has promulgated these Sunday laws does not change the scope of the power asserted. For the classic view is that the First Amendment should be applied to the States with the same firmness as it is enforced against the Federal Government. . . . The most explicit statement perhaps was in *Board of Education* v. *Barnette* . . . [:]

In weighing arguments of the parties it is important to distinguish between the due process clause of the Fourteenth Amendment as

from Christian shopkeepers at all." 311 Parliamentary Debates, Commons, 492.

"It is true that the orthodox Jew will only be allowed to trade until two o'clock on Sunday, but during that time he will have a monopoly. That is a tremendous advantage. In many districts he will be the only trader with a shop open in that district." 101 Parliamentary Debates, Lords, 430.

an instrument for transmitting the principles of the First Amendment and those cases in which it is applied for its own sake. The test of legislation which collides with the Fourteenth Amendment, because it also collides with the principles of the First, is much more definite than the test when only the Fourteenth is involved. Much of the vagueness of the due process clause disappears when the specific prohibitions of the First become its standard. The right of a State to regulate, for example, a public utility may well include, so far as the due process test is concerned, power to impose all of the restrictions which a legislature may have a "rational basis" for adopting. But freedoms of speech and of press, of assembly, and of worship may not be infringed on such slender grounds. They are susceptible of restriction only to prevent grave and immediate danger to interests which the State may lawfully protect. It is important to note that while it is the Fourteenth Amendment which bears directly upon the State it is the more specific limiting principles of the First Amendment that finally govern this case.

With that as my starting point I do not see how a State can make protesting citizens refrain from doing innocent acts on Sunday because the doing of those acts offends sentiments of their Christian neighbors.

The institutions of our society are founded on the belief that there is an authority higher than the authority of the State; that there is a moral law which the state is powerless to alter; that the individual possesses rights, conferred by the Creator, which government must respect. The Declaration of Independence stated the now familiar theme:

> We hold these truths to be self evident, that all men are created equal, that they are endowed by their Creator with certain inalienable rights, that among these are life, liberty, and the pursuit of happiness.

And the body of the Constitution as well as the Bill of Rights enshrined those principles.

The Puritan influence helped shape our constitutional law and our common law as Dean Pound has said: The Puritan "put individual conscience and individual judgment in the first place." *The Spirit of the Common Law* (1921), p. 42. For these reasons we stated in *Zorach* v. *Clauson*, 343 U.S. 306, "We are a religious people whose institutions presuppose a Supreme Being."

But those who fashioned the Constitution decided that if and when God is to be served, His service will not be motivated by coercive measures of government. "Congress shall make no law respecting an establishment of religion, or prohibiting the free exercise thereof"—such is the command of the First Amendment made applicable to the state by reason of the Due Process Clause of the Fourteenth. This means, as I understand it, that if a religious leaven is to be worked into the affairs of our people, it is to be done by individuals and groups, not by the government. This necessarily means, *first,* that the dogma, creed, scruples, or practices of no religious group or sect are to be preferred over those of any others; *second,* that

no one shall be interfered with by government for practicing the religion of
his choice; *third*, that the state may not require anyone to practice a religion
or even any religion; and *fourth*, that the state cannot compel one so to
conduct himself as not to offend the religious scruples of another. The idea,
as I understand it, was to limit the power of government to act in religious
matters . . . not to limit the freedom of religious men to act religiously
nor to restrict the freedom of atheists or agnostics.

The First Amendment commands government to have no interest in theology or ritual; it admonishes government to be interested in allowing religious freedom to flourish—whether the result is to produce Catholics,
Jews, or Protestants, or to turn the people toward the path of Buddha, or
to end in a predominantly Moslem nation, or to produce in the long run
atheists or agnostics. On matters of this kind government must be neutral.
This freedom plainly includes freedom *from* religion with the right to believe, speak, write, publish and advocate antireligious programs. . . . Certainly the "free exercise" clause does not require that everyone embrace the
theology of some church or of some faith, or observe the religious practices
of any majority or minority sect. The First Amendment by its "establishment" clause prevents, of course, the selection of government of an "official"
church. Yet the ban plainly extends farther than that. We said in *Everson*
v. *Board of Education,* that it would be an "establishment" of a religion if
the government financed one church or several churches. For what better
way to "establish" an institution than to find the fund that will support it?
The "establishment" clause protects citizens also against any law which
selects any religious custom, practice, or ritual, puts the force of government behind it, and fines, imprisons, or otherwise penalizes a person for not
observing it. The Government plainly could not join forces with one religious
group and decree a universal and symbolic circumcision. Nor could it require all children to be baptized or give tax exemptions only to those whose
children were baptized.

Could it require a fast from sunrise to sunset throughout the Moslem
month of Ramadan? I should think not. Yet why then can it make criminal
the doing of other acts, as innocent as eating, during the day that Christians
revere?

Sunday is a word heavily overlaid with connotations and traditions deriving from the Christian roots of our civilization that color all judgments concerning it. This is what the philosophers call "word magic."

> For most judges, for most lawyers, for most human beings, we are
> as unconscious of our value patterns as we are of the oxygen that we
> breathe. Cohen, *Legal Conscience* (1960), p. 169.

The issue of these cases would therefore be in better focus if we imagined
that a state legislature, controlled by Orthodox Jews and Seventh Day Ad-
ventists, passed a law making it a crime to keep a shop open on Saturdays.
Would a Baptist, Catholic, Methodist, or Presbyterian be compelled to obey
that law or go to jail or pay a fine? Or suppose Moslems grew in political

strength here and got a law through a state legislature making it a crime to keep a shop open on Fridays? Would the rest of us have to submit under the fear of criminal sanctions?

Dr. John Cogley recently summed up the dominance of the three-religion influence in our affairs:

> For the foreseeable future, it seems, the United States is going to be a three-religion nation. At the present time all three are characteristically "American," some think flavorlessly so. For religion in America is almost uniformly "respectable," bourgeois, and prosperous. In the Protestant world the "church" mentality has triumphed over the more venturesome spirit of the "sect." In the Catholic world, the mystical is muted in favor of booming organization and efficiently administered good works. And in the Jewish world the prophet is too frequently without honor, while the synagogue emphasis is focused on suburban togetherness. There are exceptions to these rules, of course; each of the religious communities continues to cast up its prophets, it rebels and radicals. But a Jeremiah, one fears, would be positively embarrassing to the present position of the Jews; a Francis of Assisi upsetting the complacency of American Catholics would be rudely dismissed as a fantatic; and a Kierkegaard, speaking with an American accent, would be considerably less welcome than Norman Vincent Peale in most Protestant pulpits.

This religious influence has extended far, far back of the First and Fourteenth Amendments. Every Sunday School student knowns the Fourth Commandment:

> Remember the sabbath day, to keep it holy.
> Six days shalt thou labour, and do all thy work:
> But the seventh day is the sabbath of the LORD thy God: in it thou shalt not do any work, thou, nor thy son, nor thy daughter, thy manservant, nor thy maidservant, nor thy cattle, nor thy stranger that is within thy gates:
> For in six days the LORD made heaven and earth, the sea, and all that in them is, and rested the seventh day: wherefore the LORD blessed the sabbath day, and hallowed it. Exodus 20:8–11.

This religious mandate for observance of the Seventh Day became, under Emperor Constantine, a mandate for observance of the First Day "in conformity with the practice of the Christian Church." . . . This religious mandate has had a checkered history, but in general its command, enforced now by the ecclesiastical authorities, now by the civil authorities, and now by both, has held good down through the centuries. The general pattern of these laws in the United States was set in the eighteenth century and derives, most directly, from a seventeenth century English statute. . . . Judicial comment on the Sunday laws has always been a mixed bag. Some judges have asserted that the statutes have a "purely" civil aim, *i.e.*, limitation of work time and provision for a common and universal leisure. But other judges have recognized the religious significance of Sunday and that the laws existed to enforce the maintenance of that significance. In general, both threads of argument have continued to interweave in the case law on the subject. Prior to the time when the First Amendment was held applicable to the States by reason of the Due Process Clause of the Fourteenth, the Court at least by *obiter dictum* approved State Sunday laws on three occasions: *Soon Hing* v. *Crowley*, 113 U.S. 703, in 1885; *Hennington* v. *Georgia*, 163 U.S. 299, in 1896; *Petit* v. *Minnesota*, 177 U.S. 164, in 1900. And in *Friedman* v. *New York*, 341 U.S. 907, the Court, by a divided vote, dismissed "for want of a substantial federal question" an appeal from a New York decision upholding the validity of a Sunday law against an attack based on the First Amendment.

The *Soon Hing, Hennington,* and *Petit* cases all rested on the police power of the State—the right to safeguard the health of the people by requiring the cessation of normal activities one day of seven. The Court in the *Soon Hing* case rejected the idea that Sunday laws rested on the power of government "to legislate for the promotion of religious observances." The New York Court of Appeals in the *Friedman* case followed the reasoning of the earlier cases.

The Massachusetts Sunday law involved in one of these appeals was once characterized by the Massachusetts court as merely a civil regulation providing for a "fixed period of rest." *Commonwealth* v. *Has,* 122 Mass. 40. That decision was, according to the District Court in the *Gallagher* case, "an *ad hoc* improvisation" made "because of the realization that the Sunday law would be more vulnerable to constitutional attack under the State Constitution if the religious motivation of the statute were more explicitly avowed." Certainly prior to the *Has* case, the Massachusetts courts had indicated that the aim of the Sunday law was religious. . . . After the *Has* case the Massachusetts court construed the Sunday law as a religious measure. In *Davis* v. *Somerville,* 128 Mass. 594, it was said:

> Our Puritan ancestors intended that the day should be not merely a day of rest from labor, but also a day devoted to public and private worship and to religious meditation and repose, undisturbed by secular cares or amusements. They saw fit to enforce the observance of the day by penal legislation, and the statute regulations which they devised for that purpose have continued in force, without any substantial modification, to the present time. . . .

In *Commonwealth* v. *White,* 190 Mass. 578, 581, 177 N.E. 636, 637, the court refused to liberalize its construction of an exception in its Sunday law for works of "necessity." That word, it said, "was originally inserted to secure the observance of the Lord's day in accordance with the views of our ancestors, and it ever since has stood and still stands for the same purpose." In *Commonwealth* v. *McCarthy,* 244 Mass. 484, the court reiterated that the aim of the law was "to secure respect and reverence for the Lord's day."

The Pennsylvania Sunday laws before us . . . have received the same construction. "Rest and quiet, on the Sabbath day, with the right and privilege of public and private worship, undisturbed by any mere worldly employment, are exactly what the statute was passed to protect." *Sparhawk* v. *Union Passenger R. Co.*, 54 Pa. 401, . . . A recent pronouncement by the Pennsylvania Supreme Court is found in *Commonwealth* v. *American Baseball Club*, 290 Pa. 136: "Christianity is part of the common law of Pennsylvania . . . and its people are christian people. Sunday is the holy day among christians."

The Maryland court is sustaining the challenged law . . . relied on *Judefind* v. *State*, 78 Md. 510, and *Levering* v. *Park Commissioner*, 134 Md. 48. In the former the court said:

> It is undoubtedly true that rest from secular employment on Sunday does have a tendency to foster and encourage the Christian religion— of all sects and denominations that observe that day—as rest from work and ordinary occupation enables many to engage in public worship who probably would not otherwise do so. But it would scarcely be asked of a Court, in what professes to be a Christian land, to declare a law unconstitutional because it requires rest from bodily labor on Sunday, (except works of necessity and charity,) and *thereby* promotes the cause of Christianity. If the Christian religion is, incidentally or otherwise, benefited or fostered by having this day of rest, as it undoubtedly is, there is all the more reason for the enforcement of laws that help to preserve it. . . .

We have then in each of the four cases Sunday laws that find their source in Exodus, that were brought here by the Puritans, and that are today maintained, construed, and justified because they respect the views of our dominant religious groups and provide a needed day of rest.

The history was accurately summarized a century ago by Chief Justice Terry of the Supreme Court of California in *Ex parte Newman*, 9 Cal. 502.

> The truth is, however much it may be disguised, that this one day of rest is a purely religious idea. Derived from the Sabbatical institutions of the ancient Hebrew, it has been adopted into all the creeds of succeeding religious sects throughout the civilized world; and whether it be the Friday of the Mohammedan, the Saturday of the Israelite, or the Sunday of the Christian, it is alike fixed in the affections of its followers, beyond the power of eradication, and in most of the States of our Confederacy, the aid of the law to enforce its observance has been given under the pretence of a civil, municipal, or police regulation.

That case involved the validity of a Sunday law under a provision of the California Constitution guaranteeing the "free exercise" of religion. . . . Justice Burnett stated why he concluded that the Sunday law, there sought to be enforced against a man selling clothing on Sunday, infringed California's constitution:

> Had the act made Monday, instead of Sunday, a day of compulsory rest, the constitutional question would have been the same. The fact that the Christian *voluntarily* keeps holy the first day of the week, does not authorize the Legislature to make that observance *compulsory*. The Legislature can not compel the citizen to do that which the Constitution leaves him free to do or omit, at his election. The act violates as much the religious freedom of the Christian as of the Jew. Because the conscientious views of the Christian compel him to keep Sunday as a Sabbath, he has the right to object, when the Legislature invades his freedom of religious worship, and assumes the power to compel him to do that which he has the right to omit if he pleases. The principle is the same, whether the act of the Legislature *compels* us to do that which we wish to do, or not to do. . . .
>
> Under the Constitution of this State, the Legislature can not pass any act, the legitimate effect of which is *forcibly* to establish any merely religious truth, or enforce any merely religious observances. The Legislature has no power over such a subject. When, therefore, the citizen is sought to be compelled by the Legislature to do any affirmative religious act, or to refrain from doing anything, because it violates simply a religious principle or observance, the act is unconstitutional.

The Court picks and chooses language from various decisions to bolster its conclusion that these Sunday Laws in the modern setting are "civil regulations." No matter how much is written, no matter what is said, the parentage of these laws is the Fourth Commandment; and they serve and satisfy the religious predispositions of our Christian communities. After all, the labels a State places on its laws are not binding on us when we are confronted with a constitutional decision. We reach our own conclusion as to the character, effect, and practical operation of the regulation in determining its constitutionality. . . .

It seems to me plain that by these laws the States compel one, under sanction of law, to refrain from work or recreation on Sunday because of the majority's religious views about that day. The State by law makes Sunday a symbol of respect or adherence. Refraining from work or recreation in deference to the majority's religious feelings about Sunday is within every person's choice. By what authority can government compel it?

Cases are put where acts that are immoral by our standards but not by the standards of other religious groups are made criminal. That category of cases, until today, has been a very restricted one confined to polygamy (*Reynolds* v. *United States*, 98 U.S. 145) and other extreme situations. The latest example is *Prince* v. *Massachusetts*, 321 U.S. 158, which upheld a statute making it criminal for a child under twelve to sell papers, periodicals, or merchandise on a street or in any public place. It was sustained in spite of the finding that the child thought it was her religious duty to perform the act. But that was a narrow holding which turned on the effect which street solicitation might have on the child-solicitor. . . . None of the acts involved here implicates minors. None of the actions made constitutionally criminal today involves the doing of any act that any society has deemed to be immoral.

The conduct held constitutionally criminal today embraces the selling of pure, not impure, food; wholesome, not noxious, articles. Adults, not minors, are involved. The innocent acts, now constitutionally classified as criminal, emphasize the drastic break we make with tradition.

These laws are sustained because, it is said, the First Amendment is concerned with religious convictions or opinion, not with conduct. But it is a strange Bill of Rights that makes it possible for the dominant religious group to bring the minority to heel because the minority, in the doing of acts which intrinsically are wholesome and not antisocial, does not defer to the majority's religious beliefs. Some have religious scruples against eating pork. Those scruples, no matter how bizarre they might seem to some, are within the ambit of the First Amendment. . . . Is it possible that a majority of a state legislature having those religious scruples could make it criminal for the nonbeliever to sell pork? Some have religious scruples against slaughtering cattle. Could a state legislature, dominated by that group, make it criminal to run an abattoir?

The Court balances the need of the people for rest, recreation, late-sleeping, family visiting and the like against the command of the First Amendment that no one need bow to the religious beliefs of another. There is in this realm no room for balancing. I see no place for it in the constitutional scheme. A legislature of Christians can no more make minorities conform to their weekly regime than a legislature of Moslems, or a legislature of Hindus. The religious regime of every group must be respected—unless it crosses the line of criminal conduct. But no one can be forced to come to a halt before it, or refrain from doing things that would offend it. That is my reading of the Establishment Clause and the Free Exercise Clause. Any other reading imports, I fear, an element common in other societies but foreign to us. Thus Nigeria in Article 23 of her Constitution, after guaranteeing religious freedom, adds, "Nothing in this section shall invalidate any law that is reasonably justified in a democratic society in the interest of defence, public safety, public order, public morality, or public health." And see Article 25 of the Indian Constitution. That may be a desirable provision. But when the Court adds it to our First Amendment, as it does today, we make a sharp break with the American ideal of religious liberty as enshrined in the First Amendment.

The State can of course require one day of rest a week: one day when every shop or factory is closed. Quite a few States make that requirement. Then the "day of rest" becomes purely and simply a health measure. But the Sunday laws operate differently. They force minorities to obey the majority's religious feelings of what is due and proper for a Christian community; they provide a coercive spur to the "weaker brethren," to those who are indifferent to the claims of a Sabbath through apathy or scruple. Can there be any doubt that Christians, now aligned vigorously in favor of these laws, would be as strongly opposed, if they were prosecuted under a Moslem law that forbade them from engaging in secular activities on days that violated Moslem scruples?

There is an "establishment" of religion in the constitutional sense if any practice of any religious group has the sanction of law behind it. There is an interference with the "free exercise" of religion if what in conscience one can do or omit doing is required because of the religious scruples of the community. Hence I would declare each of those laws unconstitutional as applied to the complaining parties, whether or not they are members of a sect which observes as their Sabbath a day other than Sunday.

When these laws are applied to Orthodox Jews . . . or to Sabbatarians their vice is accentuated. If the Sunday laws are constitutional, Kosher markets are on a five-day week. Thus those laws put an economic penalty on those who observe Saturday rather than Sunday as the Sabbath. For the economic pressures on these minorities, created by the fact that our communities are predominantly Sunday-minded, there is no recourse. When, however, the State uses its coercive powers—here the criminal law—to compel minorities to observe a second Sabbath, not their own, the State undertakes to aid and "prefer one religion over another"—contrary to the command of the Constitution. . . .

In large measure the history of the religious clause of the First Amendment was a struggle to be free of economic sanctions for adherence to one's religion. . . . A small tax was imposed in Virginia for religious education. Jefferson and Madison led the fight against the tax, Madison writing his famous Memorial and Remonstrance against that law. As a result, the tax measure was defeated and instead Virginia's famous "Bill for Religious Liberty," written by Jefferson, was enacted. That Act provided:

> That no man shall be compelled to frequent or support any religious worship, place, or ministry whatsoever, nor shall be enforced, restrained, molested, or burthened in his body or goods, nor shall otherwise suffer on account of his religious opinions or belief. . . .

The reverse side of an "establishment" is a burden on the "free exercise" of religion. Receipt of funds from the state benefits the established church directly; laying an extra tax on nonmembers benefits the established church indirectly. Certainly the present Sunday laws place Orthodox Jews and Sabbatarians under extra burdens because of their religious opinions or beliefs. Requiring them to abstain from their trade or business on Sunday reduces their work-week to five days, unless they violate their religious scruples. This places them at a competitive disadvantage and penalizes them for adhering to their religious beliefs.

"The sanction imposed by the state for observing a day other than Sunday as holy time is certainly more serious economically than the imposition of a license tax for preaching," which we struck down in *Murdock* v. *Pennsylvania*, 319 U.S. 105, and in *Follett* v. *McCormick*, 321 U.S. 573. The special protection which Sunday laws give the dominant religious groups and the penalty they place on minorities whose holy day is Saturday constitute in my view state interference with the "free exercise" of religion.

I dissent from applying criminal sanctions against any of these complainants since to do so implicates the States in religious matters contrary to the constitutional mandate. Allan C. Parker, Jr., Pastor of the South Park Presbyterian Church, Seattle, Washington, has stated my views:

> We forget that, though Sunday-worshipping Christians are in the majority in this country among religious people, we do not have the right to force our practice upon the minority. Only a Church which deems itself without error and intolerant of error can justify its intolerance of the minority.
>
> A Jewish friend of mine runs a small business establishment. Because my friend is a Jew he closes his store voluntarily so that he will be able to worship his God in his fashion. Fine! But, as a Jew living under Christian inspired Sunday closing laws, he is required to close his store on Sunday so that I will be able to worship my God in my fashion.
>
> Around the corner from my church there is a small Seventh Day Baptist church. I disagree with the Seventh Day Baptists on many points of doctrine. Among the tenets of their faith with which I disagree is the "seventh day worship." But they are good neighbors and fellow Christians, and while we disagree we respect one another. The good people of my congregation set aside their jobs on the first of the week and gather in God's house for worship. Of course, it is easy for them to set aside their jobs since Sunday closing laws—inspired by the Church—keep them from their work. At the Seventh Day Baptist church the people set aside their jobs on Saturday to worship God. This takes real sacrifice because Saturday is a good day for business. But that is not all—they are required by law to set aside their jobs on Sunday while more orthodox Christians worship. . . .
>
> I do not believe that because I have set aside Sunday as a holy day I have the right to force all man to set aside that day also. Why should my faith be favored by the State over any other man's faith?

With all deference none of the opinions filed today in support of the Sunday laws have answered that question.

3. Constitutional Status of Private Schools

a. Liberty of the Teacher

MEYER v. NEBRASKA

262 US 390 (1923)

[During and immediately after World War I some state legislatures and local school boards sought to prohibit the teaching of the German language. In some instances the prohibition had a special impact on the Lutheran parochial schools, which used German extensively in their teaching program. The supreme courts of Iowa, Ohio, and Nebraska upheld such prohibiting acts as constitutional on the broad ground that the legislature alone could decide what the common welfare demanded. These laws and decisions were challenged before the Supreme Court of the United States in the *Meyer Case.* The Court reversed all the state decisions by declaring the Nebraska statute unconstitutional as violative of the teacher's right to teach and of the parents' right to engage him. "Mere knowledge of the German language," said the Court, "cannot reasonably be regarded as harmful." The teacher of German engages, therefore, in a legal profession—a calling which cannot be outlawed by mere legislative fiat. The act also interfered wrongfully "with the opportunities of pupils to acquire knowledge, and with the power of parents to control the education of their own."

[A state may make reasonable regulations for all schools and may require that instruction be in English. But it may not prohibit the teaching of subjects in addition to those in the curriculum required by the state, when the teaching of such subjects will not be injurious to the health or morals of the child.

[Justices Holmes and Sutherland dissented. Holmes contended that reasonable minds might differ as to the wisdom of the Nebraska law, and therefore he was "unable to say that the Constitution of the United States prevents the experiment being tried." His dissent appears in *Bartels* v. *Iowa*, 262 US 404 (1923), a companion case to the *Meyer Case*.]

Mr. Justice McReynolds delivered the opinion of the Court:

Plaintiff in error was tried and convicted in the district court for Hamilton county, Nebraska, under an information which charged that on May 25, 1920, while an instructor in Zion Parochial School, he unlawfully taught the subject of reading in the German language to Raymond Parpart, a child of ten years, who had not attained and successfully passed the eighth grade. The information is based upon "An Act Relating to the Teaching of Foreign Languages in the State of Nebraska," approved April 9, 1919, which follows:

Section 1. No person, individually or as a teacher, shall, in any private, denominational, parochial or public school, teach any subject to any person in any language other than the English language.

Sec. 2. Languages, other than the English language, may be taught as languages only after a pupil shall have attained and successfully passed the eighth grade as evidenced by a certificate of graduation issued by the county superintendent of the county in which the child resides.

Sec. 3. Any person who violates any of the provisions of this act shall be deemed guilty of a misdemeanor and upon conviction, shall be subject to a fine of not less than twenty-five ($25) dollars, nor more than one hundred ($100) dollars or be confined in the county jail for any period not exceeding thirty days for each offense.

Sec. 4. Whereas, an emergency exists, this act shall be in force from and after its passage and approval.

The supreme court of the state affirmed the judgment of conviction. It declared the offense charged and established was "the direct and intentional teaching of the German language as a distinct subject to a child who had not passed the eighth grade," in the parochial school maintained by Zion Evangelical Lutheran Congregation, a collection of Biblical stories being used therefor. And it held that the statute forbidding this did not conflict with the 14th Amendment, but was a valid exercise of the police power. . . .

The problem for our determination is whether the statute, as construed and applied, unreasonably infringes the liberty guaranteed to the plaintiff in error by the 14th Amendment. "No state . . . shall deprive any person of life, liberty, or property without due process of law."

While this court has not attempted to define with exactness the liberty thus guaranteed, the term has received much consideration, and some of the included things have been definitely stated. Without doubt, it denotes not merely freedom from bodily restraint, but also the right of the individual to contract, to engage in any of the common occupations of life, to acquire useful knowledge, to marry, establish a home and bring up children, to worship God according to the dictates of his own conscience, and, generally, to enjoy those privileges long recognized at common law as essential to the orderly pursuit of happiness by free men. . . . The established doctrine is that this liberty may not be interfered with, under the guise of protecting the public interest, by legislative action which is arbitrary or without reasonable relation to some purpose within the competency of the state to effect. Determination by the legislature of what constitutes proper exercise of police power is not final or conclusive, but is subject to supervision by the courts. . . .

The American people have always regarded education and acquisition of knowledge as matters of supreme importance, which should be diligently promoted. The Ordinance of 1787 declares: "Religion, morality and knowledge being necessary to good government and the happiness of mankind, schools and the means of education shall forever be encouraged." Corresponding to the right of control, it is the natural duty of the parent to give his children education suitable to their station in life; and nearly all the states, including Nebraska, enforce this obligation by compulsory laws.

Practically, education of the young is only possible in schools conducted by especially qualified persons who devote themselves thereto. The calling always has been regarded as useful and honorable,—essential, indeed, to the public welfare. Mere knowledge of the German language cannot reasonably be regarded as harmful. Heretofore it has been commonly looked upon as helpful and desirable. Plaintiff in error taught this language in school as part of his occupation. His right thus to teach and the right of parents to engage him so to instruct their children, we think, are within the liberty of the Amendment.

The challenged statute forbids the teaching in school of any subject except in English; also the teaching of any other language until the pupil has attained and successfully passed the eighth grade, which is not usually accomplished before the age of twelve. The supreme court of the state has held that "the so-called ancient or dead languages" are not "within the spirit or the purpose of the act." . . . Latin, Greek, Hebrew are not proscribed; but German, French, Spanish, Italian, and every other alien speech are within the ban. Evidently the legislature has attempted materially to interfere with the calling of modern language teachers, with the opportunities of pupils to acquire knowledge, and with the power of parents to control the education of their own.

It is said the purpose of the legislation was to promote civic development by inhibiting training and education of the immature in foreign tongues and ideals before they could learn English and acquire American ideals; and "that the English language should be and become the mother tongue of all children reared in this state." It is also affirmed that the foreign-born population is very large, that certain communities commonly use foreign words, follow foreign leaders, move in a foreign atmosphere, and that the children are thereby hindered from becoming citizens of the most useful type, and the public safety is imperiled.

That the state may do much, go very far, indeed, in order to improve the quality of its citizens, physically, mentally, and morally, is clear; but the individual has certain fundamental rights which must be respected. The protection of the Constitution extends to all,—to those who speak other languages as well as to those born with English on the tongue. Perhaps it would be highly advantageous if all had ready understanding of our ordinary speech, but this cannot be coerced by methods which conflict with the Constitution,—a desirable end cannot be promoted by prohibited means.

For the welfare of his Ideal Commonwealth, Plato suggested a law which should provide

that the wives of our guardians are to be common, and their children are to be common, and no parent is to know his own child nor any child his parent. . . . The proper officers will take the offspring of the good parents to the pen or fold, and there they will deposit them with certain nurses who dwell in a separate quarter; but the offspring of the inferior, or of the better when they chance to be deformed, will be put away in some mysterious, unknown place, as they should be.

In order to submerge the individual and develop ideal citizens, Sparta assembled the males at seven into barracks and intrusted their subsequent education and training to official guardians. Although such measures have been deliberately approved by men of great genius, their ideas touching the relation between individual and state were wholly different from those upon which our institutions rest; and it hardly will be affirmed that any legislature could impose such restrictions upon the people of a state without doing violence to both letter and spirit of the Constitution.

The desire of the legislature to foster a homogeneous people with American ideals, prepared readily to understand current discussions of civic matters, is easy to appreciate. Unfortunate experiences during the late war, and aversion toward every characteristic of truculent adversaries, were certainly enough to quicken that aspiration. But the means adopted, we think, exceed the limitations upon the power of the state, and conflict with rights assured to plaintiff in error. The interference is plain enough, and no adequate reason therefor in time of peace and domestic tranquillity has been shown.

The power of the state to compel attendance at some school and to make reasonable regulations for all schools, including a requirement that they shall give instructions in English, is not questioned. Nor has challenge been made of the state's power to prescribe a curriculum for institutions which it supports. Those matters are not within the present controversy. . . . No emergency has arisen which renders knowledge by a child of some language other than English so clearly harmful as to justify its inhibition, with the consequent infringement of rights long freely enjoyed. We are constrained to conclude that the statute as applied is arbitrary, and without reasonable relation to any end within the competency of the state.

As the statute undertakes to interfere only with teaching which involves a modern language, leaving complete freedom as to other matters, there seems no adequate foundation for the suggestion that the purpose was to protect the child's health by limiting his mental activities. It is well known that proficiency in a foreign language seldom comes to one not instructed at an early age, and experience shows that this is not injurious to the health, morals, or understanding of the ordinary child. . . .

Reversed.

b. Liberty of the Parents

PIERCE *v.* SOCIETY OF THE SISTERS OF THE HOLY NAMES

268 US 510 (1925)

[Oregon by statute attempted to prohibit parochial and private schools for children between eight and sixteen by requiring their attendance at public schools only. The Supreme Court unanimously held the statute unconstitutional; children, said the Court, are not mere creatures of the state. A state may not attempt to standardize its children by forcing them to accept public school instruction only.

[Occasionally the courts face the problem of adjusting conflicting claims of the state and the parents. Members of the Old Order Amish Church have claimed that their children, when they reach the age of fourteen years, should be exempt from compulsory school attendance laws, which, in Pennsylvania, require attendance up to the age of seventeen years. The court held that the school law was paramount to the claim of religious conscience. *Commonwealth* v. *Beiler*, 168 Pa. Super. 462, 79 A. 2d 134 (1951).]

Mr. Justice McReynolds delivered the opinion of the Court:

The challenged act, effective September 1, 1926, requires every parent, guardian, or other person having control or charge or custody of a child between eight and sixteen years to send him "to a public school for the period of time a public school shall be held during the current year" in the district where the child resides; and failure so to do is declared a misdemeanor. There are exemptions—not specially important here—for children who are not normal, or who have completed the eighth grade, or whose parents or private teachers reside at considerable distances from any public school, or who hold special permits from the county superintendent. The manifest purpose is to compel general attendance at public schools by normal children, between eight and sixteen, who have not completed the eighth grade. And without doubt enforcement of the statute would seriously impair, perhaps destroy, the profitable features of appellees' business, and greatly diminish the value of their property.

Appellee the Society of Sisters is an Oregon corporation, organized in 1880, with power to care for orphans, educate and instruct the youth, establish and maintain academies or schools, and acquire necessary real and personal property. It has long devoted its property and effort to the secular and religious education and care of children, and has acquired the valuable good will of many parents and guardians. It conducts interdependent primary and high schools and junior colleges, and maintains orphanages for the custody and control of children between eight and sixteen. In its primary schools many children between those ages are taught the subjects usually pursued in Oregon public schools during the first eight years. Systematic religious instruction and moral training according to the tenets of the Roman Catholic Church are also regularly provided. All courses of study, both temporal and religious, contemplate continuity of training under appellee's charge; the primary schools are essential to the system and the most profitable. It owns valuable buildings, especially constructed and equipped for school purposes. The business is remunerative,—the annual income from primary schools exceeds $30,000,—and the successful conduct of this requires long-time contracts with teachers and parents. The Compulsory Education Act of 1922 has already caused the withdrawal from its schools of children who would otherwise continue, and their income has steadily declined. The appellants, public officers, have proclaimed their purpose strictly to enforce the statute.

After setting out the above facts, the Society's bill alleges that the enactment conflicts with the right of parents to choose schools where their children will receive appropriate mental and religious training, the right of the child to influence the parents' choice of a school, the right of schools and teachers therein to engage in a useful business or profession, and is accordingly repugnant to the Constitution and void. And, further, that unless enforcement of the measure is enjoined, the corporation's business and property will suffer irreparable injury.

Appellee Hill Military Academy is a private corporation organized in 1908 under the laws of Orègon, engaged in owning, operating, and conducting for profit an elementary, college preparatory, and military training school for boys between the ages of five and twenty-one years. The average attendance is one hundred, and the annual fees received for each student amount to some $800. The elementary department is divided into eight grades, as in the public schools; the college preparatory department has four grades, similar to those of the public high schools; the courses of study conform to the requirements of the state board of education. Military instruction and training are also given, under the supervision of an Army officer. It owns considerable real and personal property, some useful only for school purposes. The business and incident good will are very valuable. In order to conduct its affairs long-time contracts must be made for supplies, equipment, teachers, and pupils. Appellants, law officers of the state and county, have publicly announced that the Act of November 7, 1922, is valid, and have declared their intention to enforce it. By reason of the statute and threat of enforcement, appellee's business is being destroyed and its property depreciated; parents and guardians are refusing to make contracts for the future instruction of their sons, and some are being withdrawn. . . .

No question is raised concerning the power of the state reasonably to regulate all schools, to inspect, supervise, and examine them, their teachers and pupils; to require that all children of proper age attend some school, that teachers shall be of good moral character and patriotic disposition, that certain studies plainly essential to good citizenship must be taught, and that nothing be taught which is manifestly inimical to the public welfare.

The inevitable practical result of enforcing the act under consideration would be destruction of appellees' primary schools, and perhaps all other private primary schools for normal children within the state of Oregon. Appellees are engaged in a kind of undertaking not inherently harmful, but long regarded as useful and meritorious. Certainly there is nothing in the present records to indicate that they have failed to discharge their obligations to patrons, students, or the state. And there are no peculiar circumstances or present emergencies which demand extraordinary measures relative to primary education.

. . . The fundamental theory of liberty upon which all governments in this Union repose excludes any general power of the state to standardize its children by forcing them to accept instruction from public teachers only. The child is not the mere creature of the state; those who nurture him and direct his destiny have the right, coupled with the high duty, to recognize and prepare him for additional obligations.

Appellees are corporations, and therefore, it is said, they cannot claim for themselves the liberty which the 14th Amendment guarantees. Accepted in the proper sense, this is true. . . . But they have business and property for which they claim protection. These are threatened with destruction through the unwarranted compulsion which appellants are exercising over present and prospective patrons of their schools. And this court has gone very far to protect against loss threatened by such action. . . .

[Decrees enjoining enforcement of the statute affirmed.]

4. Freedom to Engage in Missionary Work

TUCKER v. TEXAS

326 US 517 (1945)

[In many parts of the world there is freedom of religious worship but no freedom to make converts, to evangelize, or to follow the calling of a religious missionary. This freedom has been tested in many cases brought before the Supreme Court by Jehovah's Witnesses, who claimed local or state interference with their efforts to distribute their religious literature on the streets of municipalities, or from door to door, or their playing of phonograph records on streets to willing auditors. The Court has been reluctant to sustain police restrictions against such activities, whether imposed by a municipality (e.g., Lovell v. Griffin, 303 US 444, 1938), or a company-owned town (Marsh v. Alabama, 326 US 501, 1946), or, as in the present case, by a defense housing development.

[Restrictions in the interests of public peace and order are considered below, under "Freedom of Speech and Press."

[In the present case Chief Justice Stone and Justices Reed and Burton dissented, on the ground that there was no showing that the property, owned by the United States, had been dedicated to general use by the public.]

Mr. Justice Black delivered the opinion of the Court:

The appellant was charged in the Justice Court of Medina County, Texas, with violating . . . the Texas Penal Code which makes it an offense for any "peddler or hawker of goods or merchandise" wilfully to refuse to leave premises after having been notified to do so by the owner or possessor thereof. The appellant urged in his defense that he was not a peddler or hawker of merchandise, but a minister of the gospel engaged in the distribution of religious literature to willing recipients. He contended that to construe the Texas statute as applicable to his activities would, to that extent, bring it into conflict with the Constitutional guarantees of freedom of press and religion. Const. Amend. 1. His contention was rejected and he was convicted. . . .

The facts shown by the record need be but briefly stated. Appellant is an ordained minister of the group known as Jehovah's Witnesses. In accordance with the practices of this group he calls on people from door to door, presents his religious views to those willing to listen, and distributes religious literature to those willing to receive it. In the course of his work, he went to the Hondo Navigation Village located in Medina County, Texas. The village is owned by the United States under a Congressional program which was designed to provide housing for persons engaged in National Defense activities. According to all indications the village was freely accessible and open to the public and had the characteristics of a typical American town. The Federal Public Housing Authority had placed the buildings in charge of a manager whose duty it was to rent the houses, collect the rents, and generally to supervise operations, subject to over-all control by the Authority. He ordered appellant to discontinue all religious activities in the village. Appellant refused. Later the manager ordered appellant to leave the village. Insisting that the manager had no right to suppress religious activities, appellant declined to leave, and his arrest followed. At the trial the manager testified that the controlling Federal agency had given him full authority to regulate the conduct of those living in the village, and that he did not allow preaching by ministers of any denomination without a permit issued by him in his discretion. He thought this broad authority was entrusted to him, at least in part, by a regulation, which the Authority's Washington office had allegedly promulgated. He testified that this regulation provided that no peddlers or hawkers could come into or remain in the village without getting permission from the manager. . . .

The foregoing statement of facts shows their close similarity to the facts which led us this day to decide in *Marsh* v. *Alabama*, 326 US

501, that managers of a company-owned town could not bar all distribution of religious literature within the town, or condition distribution upon a permit issued at the discretion of its management.

The only difference between this case and *Marsh* v. *Alabama* is that here instead of a private corporation, the Federal Government owns and operates the village. This difference does not affect the result. Certainly neither Congress nor Federal agencies acting pursuant to Congressional authorization may abridge the freedom of press and religion safeguarded by the First Amendment. True, under certain circumstances it might be proper for security reasons to isolate the inhabitants of a settlement, such as Hondo Village, which houses workers engaged in producing war materials. But no such necessity and no such intention on the part of Congress or the Public Housing Authority are shown here.

It follows from what we have said that to the extent that the Texas statute was held to authorize appellant's punishment for refusing to refrain from religious activities in Hondo Village it is an invalid abridgement of the freedom of press and religion. . . .

5. *Ecclesiastical Self-Government—* *The Liberty of Churches*

WATSON *v.* JONES
13 Wall (US) 679 (1872)

[It is estimated that the number of churches in the United States is over 325,000, with a total membership of more than 80,000,000 persons, belonging to at least 230 denominations. Many of these churches and denominations had their origin in schisms. Factional disputes have often involved the question of the ultimate disposition or control of the church funds or property. American courts could have used property law issues in such a way as to make the courts arbiters of religious doctrines and practices. They have scrupulously avoided doing this. Rather they have held that when a church belongs to a denomination which is governed by a hierarchy, the members must abide by the decision of their own ecclesiastical authorities. This was the decision of the Supreme Court in *Watson* v. *Jones,* in which the factional dispute grew out of difference over slavery.

[This case was followed by the Court in 1952 when a similar issue was presented to it involving a split in the Russian Orthodox Church in North America. After the Bolshevik Revolution in 1917 a separatist movement developed within the Russian Orthodox Church in the United States. The schismatics declared themselves independent of the mother church and the Patriarch in Moscow, and they sought to win control of the church property and ecclesiastical positions. The New York Legislature passed statutes in 1945 and 1948 to aid the schismatics in their efforts to gain autonomy and thus free the church of atheistic and subversive influences. With this legislative aid separatists tried to eject from the Cathedral in New York those who occupied it by authority of the church authorities in Moscow. The Supreme Court, by an 8-to-1 vote, held that the New York legislation was unconstitutional as a violation of the guaranty of freedom of religion.

[Separatists, schismatics, dissenters may leave a church and organize their own congregation. They have a constitutional right to do this. But if the church was subject to an ecclesiastical authority—e.g., the Patriarch in Moscow—then the church property cannot be taken over by the separatists; it remains with those who are loyal to the church. *Kedroff* v. *Saint Nicholas Cathedral,* 344 US 94 (1952).

[This decision is in the interests of religious freedom. It reaffirms the decision of the *Watson Case:* the state is not to be an arbiter of religious beliefs and practices. If clergymen are guilty of subversive activities, they may be punished in the same way as the law may punish others; but neither the legislature nor the courts may take church property and positions away from one faction and turn them over to another faction on the ground that the action would free the church from subversive influences.]

Mr. Justice Miller delivered the opinion of the Court:

. . . This is a case of a division or schism in a church. It is a question as to which of two bodies shall be recognized as the Third or Walnut Street Presbyterian Church [Louisville, Ky.] . . . The issue here is no longer a mere question of eldership, but it is a separation of the original church members and officers into two distinct bodies, with distinct members and officers, each claiming to be the true Walnut Street Presbyterian Church, and denying the right of the other to any such claim. . . .

From the commencement of the late war of insurrection to its close, the General Assembly of the Presbyterian Church at its annual meetings expressed, in declaratory statements or resolutions, its sense of the obligation of all good citizens to support the Federal Government in that struggle; and when, by the Proclamation of President Lincoln, emancipation of the slaves of the States in insurrection was announced, that body also expressed views favorable to emancipation, and adverse to the institution of slavery. At its meeting in Pittsburg, in May, 1865, instructions were given to the Presbyteries, the Board of Missions, and to the sessions of the Churches, that when any persons from the Southern States should make application for employment as missionaries, or for admission as members or ministers of churches, inquiry should be made as to their sentiments in regard to loyalty to the government, and on the subject of slavery; and if it was found that they had been guilty of voluntarily aiding the war of the rebellion, or held the doctrine announced by the large body of the churches in the insurrectionary States, which had organized a new General Assembly, that "the system of Negro slavery in the South is a divine institution, and that it is the peculiar mission of the Southern Church to conserve that institution" they should be required to repent and forsake these sins before they could be received.

In the month of September, thereafter, the Presbytery of Louisville, under whose immediate jurisdiction was the Walnut Street Church, adopted and published in pamphlet form, what is called "a declaration and testimony against the erroneous and heretical doctrines and practices which have obtained and been propagated in the Presbyterian Church of the United States during the last five years." This declaration denounced, in the severest terms, the action of the General Assembly in the matters we have just mentioned, declared their intention to refuse to be governed by that action, and invited the co-operation of all the members of the Presbyterian Church who shared these sentiments of the declaration, in a concerted resistance to what they called the usurpation of authority by the Assembly. . . .

The General Assembly of 1866 denounced the declaration and testimony, and declared that every Presbytery which refused to obey its order should be *ipso facto* dissolved and called to answer before the next General Assembly, giving the Louisville Presbytery an opportunity for repentance and conformity. The Louisville Presbytery divided, and the adherents of the declaration and testimony sought and obtained admission in 1868, into "The Presbyterian Church of the Confederate States." . . .

In January, 1866, the congregation of the Walnut Street Church become divided in the manner stated above, each claiming to constitute the Church. . . .

On the 19th June, 1866, the Synod of Kentucky became divided, the opposing parties in each claiming to constitute respectively the true Presbytery and the true Synod; each meanwhile recognizing and claiming to adhere to the same General Assembly. Of these contesting bodies, the appellants adhered to one; the appellees to another.

On the 1st of June, 1867, the Presbytery and Synod recognized by the appellants, were declared by the General Assembly to be "in no sense the true and lawful Synod and Presbytery in connection with and under the care and authority of the General Assembly of the Presbyterian

Church in the United States of America"; and were permanently excluded from connection with or representation in the Assembly; by the same resolution the Synod and Presbytery adhered to by appellees were declared to be the true and lawful Presbytery of Louisville, and Synod of Kentucky.

The Synod of Kentucky thus excluded by a resolution adopted the 28th June, 1867, declared "That, in its future action, it will be governed by this recognized sundering of all its relation to the aforesaid revolutionary body (the General Assembly) by the acts of that body itself." The Presbytery took substantially the same action. . . .

The division and separation finally extended to the Presbytery of Louisville and the Synod of Kentucky. It is now complete and apparently irreconcilable, and we are called upon to declare the beneficial uses of the church property in this condition of total separation between the members of what was once a united and harmonious congregation of the Presbyterian Church.

The questions which have come before the civil courts concerning the rights to property held by ecclesiastical bodies, may, so far as we have been able to examine them, be profitably classified under three general heads, which of course do not include cases governed by considerations applicable to a church established and supported by law as the religion of the State.

1. The first of these is when the property which is the subject of controversy has been, by the deed or will of the donor, or other instrument by which the property is held, by the express terms of the instrument devoted to the teaching, support or spread of some specific form of religious doctrine or belief.

2. The second is when the property is held by a religious congregation which, by the nature of its organization, is strictly independent of other ecclesiastical associations, and so far as church government is concerned, owes no fealty or obligation to any higher authority.

3. The third is where the religious congregation or ecclesiastical body holding the property is but a subordinate member of some general church organization in which there are superior ecclesiastical tribunals with a general and ultimate power of control more or less complete in some supreme judicatory over the whole membership of that general organization.

In regard to the first of these classes it seems hardly to admit of a rational doubt that an individual or an association of individuals may dedicate property by way of trust to the purpose of sustaining, supporting and propagating definite religious doctrines or principles, providing that in doing so they violate no law of morality, and give to the instrument by which their purpose is evidenced, the formalities which the laws require. And it would seem also to be the obvious duty of the court, in a case properly made, to see that the property so dedicated is not diverted from the trust which is thus attached to its use. So long as there are persons qualified within the meaning of the original dedication, and who are also willing to teach the doctrines or principles prescribed in the act of dedication, and so long as there is any one so interested in the execution of the trust as to have a standing in court, it must be that they can prevent the diversion of the property or fund to other and different uses. This is the general doctrine of courts of equity as to charities, and it seems equally applicable to ecclesiastical matters.

In such case, if the trust is confided to a religious congregation of the independent or congregational form of church government, it is not in the power of the majority of that congregation, however preponderant, by reason of a change of views on religious subjects, to carry the property so confided to them to the support of new and conflicting doctrine. A pious man building and dedicating a house of worship to the sole and exclusive use of those who believe in the doctrine of the Holy Trinity, and placing it under the control of a congregation which at the time holds the same belief, has a right to expect that the law will prevent that property from being used as a means of support and dissemination of the Unitarian doctrine, and as a place of Unitarian worship. Nor is the principle varied when the organization to which the trust is confided is of the second or associated form of church government. The protection which the law throws around the trust is the same. And though the task may be a delicate one and a difficult one, it will be the duty of the court in such cases, when the doctrine to be taught or the form of worship to be used is definitely and clearly laid down, to inquire whether the party accused of violating the trust is holding or teaching a different doctrine, or using a form of worship which is so far variant as to defeat the declared objects of the trust. . . .

The second class of cases which we have described has reference to the case of a church of a strictly congregational or independent organization, governed solely within itself, either by a majority of its members or by such other local organism as it may have instituted for the purpose of ecclesiastical government; and to property held by such a church, either by way of purchase or donation, with no other specific trust attached to it in the hands of the church than that it is for the use of that congregation as a religious society.

In such cases, where there is a schism which leads to a separation into distinct and conflicting bodies, the rights of such bodies to the use of the property must be determined by the ordinary principles which govern voluntary associations. If the principle of government in such cases is that the majority rules, then the numerical majority of members must control the right to the use of the property. If there be within the congregation officers in whom are vested the powers of such control, then those who adhere to the acknowledged organism by which the body is governed are entitled to the use of the property. The minority in choosing to separate themselves into a distinct body, and refusing to recognize the authority of the governing body, can claim no rights in the property from the fact that they had once been members of the Church or congregation. This ruling admits of no inquiry into the existing religious opinions of those who comprise the legal or regular organization; for, if such was permitted, a very small minority, without any officers of the church among them, might be found to be the only faithful supporters of the religious dogmas of the founders of the Church. There being no such trust imposed upon the property when purchased or given, the court will not imply one for the purpose of expelling from its use those who by regular succession and order constitute the Church, because they may have changed in some respect their views of religious truth. . . .

But the third of these classes of cases is the one which is oftenest found in the courts, and which, with reference to the number and difficulty of the questions involved, and to other considerations, is every way the most important.

It is the case of property acquired in any of the usual modes for the general use of a religious congregation which is itself part of a large and general organization of some religious denomination, with which it is more or less intimately connected by religious views and ecclesiastical government.

The case before us is one of this class, growing out of a schism which has divided the congregation and its officers, and the presbytery and synod, and which appeals to the courts to determine the right to the use of the property so acquired. Here is no case of property devoted forever by the instrument which conveyed it, or by any specific declaration of its owner, to the support of any special religious dogmas, or any peculiar form of worship, but of property purchased for the use of a religious congregation, and so long as any existing religious congregation can be ascertained to be that congregation, or its regular and legitimate successor, it is entitled to the use of the property. In the case of an independent congregation we have pointed out how this identity, or succession, is to be ascertained, but in cases of this character we are bound to look at the fact that the local congregation is itself but a member of a much larger and more important religious organization, and is under its government and control, and is bound by its orders and judgments. There are in the Presbyterian system of ecclesiastical government, in regular succession, the Presbytery over the session or local church, the Synod over the Presbytery, and the General Assembly over all. These are called, in the language of the church organs, "judicatories," and they entertain appeals from the decisions of those below, and prescribe corrective measures in other cases.

In this class of cases we think the rule of action which should govern the civil courts, founded in a broad and sound view of the relations of church and state under our system of laws, and supported by a preponderating weight of judicial authority is, that, whenever the questions of discipline or of faith, or ecclesiastical rule, custom or law have been decided by the highest of these church judicatories to which the matter has been carried, the legal tribunals must accept such decisions as final, and as binding on them, in their application to the case before them. . . .

In this country the full and free right to entertain any religious belief, to practice any religious principle, and to teach any religious doctrine which does not violate the laws of morality and property, and which does not infringe personal rights, is conceded to all. The law knows no heresy, and is committed to the support of no dogma, the establishment of no sect. The right to organize voluntary religious associations to assist in the expression and dissemination of any religious doctrine, and to create tribunals for the decision of controverted questions of faith within the association, and for the ecclesiastical government of all the individual members, congregations and officers within the general association, is unquestioned. All who unite themselves to such a body do so with an implied consent to this government, and are bound to submit to it. But it would be a vain consent and would lead to the total subversion of such religious bodies, if any one aggrieved by one of their decisions could appeal to the secular courts and have them reversed. It is of the essence of these religious unions, and of their right to establish tribunals for the decision of questions arising among themselves, that those decisions should be binding in all cases of ecclesiastical cognizance, subject only to such appeals as the organism itself provides for. . . .

But it is a very different thing where a subject matter of dispute, strictly and purely ecclesiastical in its character—a matter over which the civil courts exercise no jurisdiction—a matter which concerns theological controversy, church discipline, ecclesiastical government, or the conformity of the members of the church to the standard of morals required of them—becomes the subject of its action. It may be said here, also, that no jurisdiction has been conferred on the tribunal to try the particular case before it, or that, in its judgment, it exceeds the powers conferred upon it, or that the laws of the church do not authorize the particular form of proceeding adopted; and, in a sense often used in the courts, all of those may be said to be questions of jurisdiction. But it is easy to see that if the civil courts are to inquire into all these matters, the whole subject of the doctrinal theology, the usages and customs, the written laws, and fundamental organization of every religious denomination may, and must, be examined into with minuteness and care, for they would become, in almost every case, the *criteria* by which the validity of the ecclesiastical decree would be determined in the civil court. This principle would deprive these bodies of the right of construing their own church laws, would open the way to all the evils which we have depicted . . . and would in effect transfer to the civil courts where property rights were concerned the decision of all ecclesiastical questions. . . .

But we need pursue this subject no further. Whatever may have been the case before the Kentucky court, the appellants in the case presented to us have separated themselves wholly from the church organization to which they belonged when this controversy commenced. They now deny its authority, denounce its action and refuse to abide by its judgments. They have first erected themselves into a new organization, and have since joined themselves to another totally different, if not hostile, to the one to which they belonged when the difficulty first began. Under any of the decisions which we have examined, the appellants, in their present position, have no right to the property, or to the use of it, which is the subject of this suit. . . .

Freedom of Assembly, Petition,

and Association

DE JONGE v. OREGON

299 US 353 (1937)

[The First Amendment provides that Congress shall make no law "abridging . . . the right of the people peaceably to assemble, and to petition the Government for a redress of grievances." Not until 1876 was the Supreme Court called upon to construe this provision. In *United States* v. *Cruikshank*, 92 US 542 (1876) the Court gave this provision a restricted meaning, holding that the First Amendment guarantees to citizens the freedom to assemble in order that they may petition Congress for a redress of grievances. Apparently, only a peaceful assembly called for this purpose was constitutionally protected. Freedom of assembly was thus dependent upon the right of petition, which had its origin in Magna Carta, reaffirmed in the Bill of Rights of 1689.

[In the *De Jonge Case*, however, freedom of assembly was liberated from dependence upon the right of petition and was held to be as fundamental as are freedom of speech and freedom of the press. In this case the meeting was called under the auspices of the Communist Party, but the Court held that it is a matter of constitutional indifference under whose auspices a meeting is called, or who the speakers are; the only question is whether "their utterances transcend the bounds of the freedom of speech which the Constitution protects."

[In this significant unanimous decision the Court also held that freedom of speech and of the press and the right of peaceable assembly are safeguarded against infringement by state action: these freedoms are assimilated into the Due Process Clause of the Fourteenth Amendment.]

Mr. Chief Justice Hughes delivered the opinion of the Court:

Appellant, Dirk De Jonge, was indicted in Multnomah County, Oregon, for violation of the Criminal Syndicalism Law of that State. The act . . . defines "criminal syndicalism" as "the doctrine which advocates crime, physical violence, sabotage, or any unlawful acts or methods as a means of accomplishing or effecting industrial or political change or revolution." With this preliminary definition the Act proceeds to describe a number of offenses, embracing the teaching of criminal syndicalism, the printing or distribution of books, pamphlets, etc., advocating that doctrine, the organization of a society or assemblage which advocates it, and presiding at or assisting in conducting a meeting of such an organization, society or group. The prohibited acts are made felonies, punishable by imprisonment for not less than one year nor more than ten years, or by a fine of not more than $1,000, or by both.

We are concerned with but one of the described offenses and with the validity of the statute in this particular application. The charge is that appellant assisted in the conduct of a meeting which was called under the auspices of the Communist Party, an organization advocating criminal syndicalism. The defense was that the meeting was public and orderly and was held for a lawful purpose; that, while it was held under the auspices of the Communist Party, neither criminal syndicalism nor any unlawful conduct was taught or advocated at the meeting either by appellant or by others. Appellant moved for a direction of acquittal, contending that the statute as applied to him, for merely assisting at a meeting called by the Communist Party at which nothing unlawful was done or advocated, violated the due process clause of the Fourteenth Amendment of the Constitution of the United States.

This contention was overruled. Appellant was found guilty as charged and was sentenced to imprisonment for seven years. The judgment was affirmed by the Supreme Court of the State. . . . The case comes here on appeal.

The record does not present the evidence adduced at the trial. The parties have substituted a stipulation of facts. . . .

The stipulation, after setting forth the charging part of the indictment, recites in substance the following: That on July 27, 1934, there was held in Portland a meeting which had been advertised by handbills issued by the Portland section of the Communist Party; that the number of persons in attendance was variously estimated at from 150 to 300;

that some of those present, who were members of the Communist Party, estimated that not to exceed 10 to 15 per cent of those in attendance were such members; that the meeting was open to the public without charge and no questions were asked of those entering, with respect to their relation to the Communist Party; that the notice of the meeting advertised it as a protest against illegal raids on workers' halls and homes and against the shooting of striking longshoremen by Portland police; that the chairman stated that it was a meeting held by the Communist Party; that the first speaker dwelt on the activities of the Young Communist League; that the defendant De Jonge, the second speaker, was a member of the Communist Party and went to the meeting to speak in its name; that in his talk he protested against conditions in the county jail, the action of city police in relation to the maritime strike then in progress in Portland and numerous other matters; that he discussed the reason for the raids on the Communist headquarters and workers' halls and offices; that he told the workers that these attacks were due to efforts on the part of the steamship companies and stevedoring companies to break the maritime longshoremen's and seamen's strike; that they hoped to break the strike by pitting the longshoremen and seamen against the Communist movement; that there was also testimony to the effect that defendant asked those present to do more work in obtaining members for the Communist Party and requested all to be at the meeting of the party to be held in Portland on the following evening and to bring their friends to show their defiance to local police authority and to assist them in their revolutionary tactics; that there was also testimony that defendant urged the purchase of certain communist literature which was sold at the meeting; that while the meeting was still in progress it was raided by the police; that the meeting was conducted in an orderly manner; that defendant and several others who were actively conducting the meeting were arrested by the police; and that on searching the hall the police found a quantity of communist literature.

The stipulation then set forth various extracts from the literature of the Communist Party to show its advocacy of criminal syndicalism. The stipulation does not disclose any activity by the defendant as a basis for his prosecution other than his participation in the meeting in question. Nor does the stipulation show that the communist literature distributed at the meeting contained any advocacy of criminal syndicalism or of any unlawful conduct. It was admitted by the Attorney General of the State in his argument at the bar of this Court that the literature distributed in the meeting was not of that sort and that the extracts contained in the stipulation were taken from communist literature found elsewhere. Its introduction in evidence was for the purpose of showing that the Communist Party as such did advocate the doctrine of criminal syndicalism, a fact which is not disputed on this appeal.

The indictment charged as follows:

The said Dirk De Jonge, Don Cluster, Edward R. Denny and Earl Stewart on the 27th day of July, A.D. 1934, in the county of Multnomah and state of Oregon, then and there being, did then and there unlawfully and feloniously preside at, conduct and assist in conducting an assemblage of persons, organization, society and group, to wit: The Communist Party, a more particular description of which said assemblage of persons, organization, society and group is to this grand jury unknown, which said assemblage of persons, organization, society and group did then and there unlawfully and feloniously teach and advocate the doctrine of criminal syndicalism and sabotage, contrary to the statutes in such cases made and provided, and against the peace and dignity of the state of Oregon.

On the theory that this was a charge that criminal syndicalism and sabotage were advocated at the meeting in question, defendant moved for acquittal, insisting that the evidence was insufficient to warrant his conviction. The trial court denied his motion, and error in this respect was assigned on appeal. The Supreme Court of the State put aside that contention by ruling that the indictment did not charge that criminal syndicalism or sabotage was advocated at the meeting described in the evidence, either by defendant or by anyone else. The words of the indictment that "said assemblage of persons, organization, society, and group did then and there unlawfully and feloniously teach and advocate the doctrine of criminal syndicalism and sabotage," referred not to the meeting in question, or to anything then and there said or done by defendant or others, but to the advocacy of criminal syndicalism and sabotage by the Communist Party in Multnomah County. The ruling of the State court upon this point was precise. . . .

In this view, lack of sufficient evidence as to illegal advocacy or action at the meeting became immaterial. Having limited the charge to defendant's participation in a meeting called by the Communist Party, the state court sustained the conviction upon that basis regardless of what was said or done at the meeting.

We must take the indictment as thus construed. Conviction upon a. charge not made would be sheer denial of due process. It thus appears that, while defendant was a member of the Communist Party, he was not indicted for participating in its organization, or for joining it, or for soliciting members or for distributing its literature. He was not charged with teaching or advocating criminal syndicalism or sabotage or any unlawful acts, either at the meeting or elsewhere. He was accordingly deprived of the benefit of evidence as to the orderly and unlawful conduct of the meeting and that it was not called or used for the advocacy of criminal syndicalism or sabotage or any unlawful action. His sole offense as charged, and for which he was convicted and sentenced to imprisonment for seven years, was that he had assisted in the conduct of a public meeting, albeit otherwise lawful, which was held under the auspices of the Communist Party.

The broad reach of the statute as thus applied is plain. While defendant was a member of the Communist Party, that membership was not necessary to conviction on such a charge. A like fate might have attended any speaker, although not a member, who "assisted in the conduct" of the meeting. However innocuous the object of the meeting, however lawful the subjects and tenor of the addresses, however reasonable and timely the discussion, all those assisting in the conduct of the meeting would be subject to imprisonment as felons if the meeting were held by the Communist Party. . . . Thus, if the Communist Party had called a public meeting in Portland to discuss the tariff, or the foreign policy of the Government, or taxation, or relief, or candidacies for the offices of President, members of Congress, Governor, or state legislators, every speaker who assisted in the conduct of the meeting would be equally guilty with the defendant in this case, upon the charge as here defined and sustained. The list of illustrations might be indefinitely extended to every variety of meetings under the auspices of the Communist Party although held for the discussion of political issues or to adopt protests and pass resolutions of an entirely innocent and proper character.

While the States are entitled to protect themselves from the abuse of the privileges of our institutions through an attempted substitution of force and violence in the place of peaceful political action in order to effect revolutionary changes in government, none of our decisions go to the length of sustaining such a curtailment of the right of free speech and assembly as the Oregon statute demands in its present application. . . . The right of peaceable assembly is a right cognate to those of free speech and free press and is equally fundamental. As this Court said in *United States* v. *Cruikshank,* 92 U.S. 542: "The very idea of a government, republican in form, implies a right on the part of its citizens to meet peaceably for consultation in respect to public affairs and to petition for a redress of grievances." The First Amendment of the Federal Constitution expressly guarantees that right against abridgment by Congress. But explicit mention there does not argue exclusion elsewhere. For the right is one that cannot be denied without violating those fundamental principles of liberty and justice which lie at the base of all civil and political institutions—principles which the Fourteenth Amendment embodies in the general terms of its due process clause. . . .

These rights may be abused by using speech or press or assembly in order to incite to violence and crime. The people through their legislatures may protect themselves against that abuse. But the legislative intervention can find constitutional justification only by dealing with the abuse. The rights themselves must not be curtailed. The greater the importance of safeguarding the community from incitements to the overthrow of our institutions by force and violence, the more imperative is the need to preserve inviolate the constitutional rights of free speech, free press and free assembly in order to maintain the opportunity for free political discussion, to the end that government may be responsive to the will of the people and that changes, if desired, may be obtained by peaceful means. Therein lies the security of the Republic, the very foundation of constitutional government.

It follows from these considerations that, consistently with the Federal Constitution, peaceable assembly for lawful discussion cannot be made a crime. The holding of meetings for peaceable political action cannot be proscribed. Those who assist in the conduct of such meetings cannot be branded as criminals on that score. The question, if the rights of free speech and peaceable assembly are to be preserved, is not as to the auspices under which the meeting is held but as to its purpose; not as to the relations of the speakers, but whether their utterances transcend the bounds of the freedom of speech which the Constitution protects. If the persons assembling have committed crimes elsewhere, if they have formed or are engaged in a conspiracy against the public peace and order, they may be prosecuted for their conspiracy or other violation of valid laws. But it is a different matter when the State, instead of prosecuting them for such offenses, seizes upon mere participation in a peaceable assembly and a lawful public discussion as the basis for a criminal charge.

We are not called upon to review the findings of the state court as to the objectives of the Communist Party. Notwithstanding those objectives, the defendant still enjoyed his personal right of free speech and to take part in a peaceable assembly having a lawful purpose, although called by that party. The defendant was none the less entitled to discuss the public issues of the day and thus in a lawful manner, without incitement to violence or crime, to seek redress of alleged grievances. That was of the essence of his guaranteed personal liberty.

We hold that the Oregon statute as applied to the particular charge as defined by the state court is repugnant to the due process clause of the Fourteenth Amendment. The judgment of conviction is reversed. . . .

HAGUE *v.* COMMITTEE FOR INDUSTRIAL ORGANIZATION
307 US 496 (1939)

[An ordinance of Jersey City, New Jersey, prohibited public assembly on the streets or in the public buildings or parks of the city without a permit from the director of public safety, and this public official was authorized to refuse to issue a permit "for the purpose of preventing riots, disturbances or disorderly assemblage." Alleging that the individuals requesting permits were Communists, the police denied numerous persons the right to hold public assemblies called for the purpose of organizing workers into unions, the right to distribute pamphlets, and the right to rent a hall for a public meeting. The police stopped persons as they entered the city, seized literature in their possession, and arrested or "deported" them. The persons against whom these actions were taken denied that they were Communists and contended that their sole purpose was to explain to workers their rights under the National Labor Relations Act and why they should join the C.I.O.

[The Court in a 5-to-2 decision (Justices McReynolds and Butler dissented) held the ordinance unconstitutional. There were opinions by Justices Roberts and Stone and Chief Justice Hughes. All the five Justices seem to have agreed on the fundamental issue of the controversy, namely, that the ordinance could be used as an "instrument of arbitrary suppression of free expression of views on national affairs for the prohibition of all speaking will undoubtedly 'prevent' such eventualities," that is, "riots, disturbances or disorderly assemblage."

[Justices Roberts and Black were of the opinion that the ordinance violated the right of citizens of the United States to assemble to discuss their rights and privileges under the National Labor Relations Act. This privilege belongs to citizens of the United States and is protected against infringement by the state under the Fourteenth Amendment.

[Justices Stone and Reed would put the decision on the broader principle that "freedom of speech and of assembly for any lawful purpose are rights of personal liberty secured to all persons, without regard to citizenship, by the due process clause of the Fourteenth Amendment." These freedoms are not privileges or immunities peculiar to national citizenship; they are protected against infringement by the state whether their exercise is attempted by citizens or aliens. Nor was it material to Stone and Reed that the purpose of the meetings was to discuss the National Labor Relations Act; it was enough that the meetings were called for any "lawful purpose."

[On the scope of the Privileges and Immunities Clause of the Fourteenth Amendment, see Milton R. Konvitz, *The Constitution and Civil Rights* (New York: Columbia University Press, 1947), ch. ii.]

Mr. Justice Roberts . . . :

The question now presented is whether freedom to disseminate information concerning the provisions of the National Labor Relations Act, to assemble peaceably for discussion of the Act, and of the opportunities and advantages offered by it, is a privilege or immunity of a citizen of the United States secured against State abridgment by sec. 1 of the Fourteenth Amendment; and whether Rev. Stat. § 1979 and § 24 (14) of the Judicial Code, 28 U.S.C.A. § 41 (14) afford redress in a federal court for such abridgment. This is the narrow question presented by the record, and we confine our decision to it, without consideration of broader issues which the parties urge. . . . The bill alleges, and the findings sustain the allegation, that the respondents [labor organizers] had no other purpose than to inform citizens of Jersey City by speech, and by the written word, respecting matters growing out of national legislation, the constitutionality of which this court has sustained.

Although it has been held that the Fourteenth Amendment created no rights in citizens of the United States, but merely secured existing rights against state abridgment, it is clear that the right peaceably to assemble and to discuss these topics, and to communicate respecting them, whether orally or in writing, is a privilege inherent in citizenship of the United States which the Amendment protects.

In the *Slaughter-House Cases* it was said, 16 Wall. 79, 21 L. ed. 409: "The right to peaceably assemble and petition for redress of grievances, the privilege of the writ of habeas corpus, are rights of the citizen guaranteed by the Federal Constitution."

In *United States* v. *Cruikshank*, 92 U.S. 542, the court said:

The right of the people peaceably to assemble for the purpose of petitioning Congress for a redress of grievances, or for any thing else connected with the powers or the duties of the national government, is an attribute of national citizenship, and, as such, under the protection of, and guaranteed by, the United States. The very idea of a government, republican in form, implies a right on the part of its citizens to meet peaceably for consultation in respect to public affairs and to petition for a redress of grievances. . . .

No expression of a contrary view has ever been voiced by this court.

The National Labor Relations Act declares the policy of the United States to be to remove obstructions to commerce by encouraging collective bargaining, protecting full freedom of association and self-organization of workers, and, through their representatives, negotiating as to conditions of employment.

Citizenship of the United States would be little better than a name if it did not carry with it the right to discuss national legislation and the benefits, advantages, and opportunities to accrue to citizens therefrom. All of the respondents' proscribed activities had this single end and aim. The District Court had jurisdiction under sec. 24 (14).

Natural persons, and they alone, are entitled to the privileges and immunities which sec. 1 of the Fourteenth Amendment secures for "citizens of the United States." Only the individual respondents may, therefore, maintain this suit.

What has been said demonstrates that, in the light of the facts found, privileges and immunities of the individual respondents as citizens of the United States, were infringed by the petitioners [Mayor Frank Hague and other officials of Jersey City], by virtue of their official positions, under color of ordinances of Jersey City, unless, as petitioners contend, the city's ownership of streets and parks is as absolute as one's ownership of his home, with consequent power altogether to exclude citizens from the use thereof, or unless, though the city holds the streets in trust for public use, the absolute denial of their use to the respondents is a valid exercise of the police power.

The findings of fact negative the latter assumption. In support of the former the petitioners rely upon *Davis* v. *Massachusetts,* 167 U.S. 43. There it appeared that, pursuant to enabling legislation, the city of Boston adopted an ordinance prohibiting anyone from speaking, discharging fire arms, selling goods, or maintaining any booth for public amusement on any of the public grounds of the city except under a permit from the Mayor. Davis spoke on Boston Common without a permit and without applying to the Mayor for one. He was charged with a violation of the ordinance and moved to quash the complaint, inter alia, on the ground that the ordinance abridged his privileges and immunities as a citizen of the United States and denied him due process of law because it was arbitrary and unreasonable. His contentions were overruled and he was convicted. The judgment was affirmed by the Supreme Court of Massachusetts and by this court.

The decision seems to be grounded on the holding of the State court that the Common "was absolutely under the control of the legislature," and that it was thus "conclusively determined there was no right in the plaintiff in error to use the common except in such mode and subject to such regulations as the legislature in its wisdom may have deemed proper to prescribe." The Court added that the Fourteenth Amendment did not destroy the power of the states to enact police regulations as to a subject within their control or enable citizens to use public property in defiance of the constitution and laws of the State.

The ordinance there in question apparently had a different purpose from that of the one here challenged, for it was not directed solely at the exercise of the right of speech and assembly, but was addressed as well to other activities, not in the nature of civil rights, which doubtless might be regulated or prohibited as respects their enjoyment in parks. In the instant case the ordinance deals only with the exercise of the right of assembly for the purpose of communicating views entertained by speakers, and is not a general measure to promote the public convenience in the use of the streets or parks.

We have no occasion to determine whether, on the facts disclosed, the *Davis Case* was rightly decided, but we cannot agree that it rules the instant case. Wherever the title of streets and parks may rest, they have immemorially been held in trust for the use of the public and, time out of mind, have been used for purposes of assembly, communicating thoughts between citizens, and discussing public questions. Such use of the streets and public places has, from ancient times, been a part of the privileges, immunities, rights, and liberties of citizens. The privilege of a citizen of the United States to use the streets and parks for communication of views on national questions may be regulated in the interest of all; it is not absolute, but relative, and must be exercised in subordination to the general comfort and convenience, and in consonance with peace and good order; but it must not, in the guise of regulation, be abridged or denied.

We think the court below was right in holding the ordinance void on its face. It does not make comfort or convenience in the use of streets or parks the standard of official action. It enables the Director of Safety to refuse a permit on his mere opinion that such refusal will prevent "riots, disturbances or disorderly assemblage." It can thus, as the record discloses, be made the instrument of arbitrary suppression of free expression of views on national affairs for the prohibition of all speaking will undoubtedly "prevent" such eventualities. But uncontrolled official suppression of the privilege cannot be made a substitute for the duty to maintain order in connection with the exercise of the right. . . .

STAUB v. BAXLEY

355 US 313 (1958)

[Essential to the freedom of association is the right to solicit members for an organization. An ordinance of the city of Baxley, Georgia, made it a criminal offense to solicit members for any organization that requires the payment of dues, without first applying for and procuring a permit from the mayor and city council, who had the right to refuse a permit if they did not approve of the applicant or his organization or the organization's effect on the general welfare of the city. In a 7-to-2 decision the Court, in an opinion by Justice Whittaker, held that the ordinance violated the Fourteenth Amendment, which protects freedom of speech against invasion by a state (including a municipality acting under state authority). Cf. *Thomas v. Collins*, 323 US 516 (1945).

[Justice Frankfurther dissented (joined by Justice Clark) for the reason that, because of the procedure followed in the case, the decision of the Supreme Court of Georgia rested on an adequate non-federal ground, which should not be reviewed by the United States Supreme Court.]

Mr. Justice Whittaker delivered the opinion of the Court:

Appellant, Rose Staub, was convicted in the Mayor's Court of the City of Baxley, Georgia, of violation of a city ordinance and was sentenced to imprisonment for 30 days or to pay a fine of $300. The Superior Court of the county affirmed the judgment of conviction; the Court of Appeals of the State affirmed the judgment of the Superior Court, . . . and the Supreme Court of the State denied an application for certiorari. The case comes here on appeal. . . .

Appellant was a salaried employee of The International Ladies' Garment Workers Union which was attempting to organize the employees of a manufacturing company located in the nearby town of Hazelhurst. A number of those employees lived in Baxley. On February 19, 1954, appellant and one Mamie Merritt, also a salaried employee of the union, went to Baxley and, without applying for permits required under the ordinance, talked with several of the employees at their homes about joining the union. While in a restaurant in Baxley on that day they were sought out and questioned by the Chief of Police concerning their activities in Baxley, and appellant told him that they were "going around talking to some of the women to organize the factory workers . . . and hold[ing] meetings with them for that purpose." Later that day a meeting was held at the home of one of the employees, attended by three other employees, at which, in the words of the hostess, appellant "just told us they wanted us to join the union, and said it would be a good thing for us to do . . . and went on to tell us how this union would help us." Appellant told those present that the membership dues would be 64 cents per week but would not be payable until the employees were organized. No money was asked or received from the persons at the meeting, but they were invited "to get other girls . . . there to join the union" and blank membership cards were offered for that use. Appellant further explained that the immediate objective was to "have enough cards signed to petition for an election . . . with the Labor Board."

On the same day a summons was issued and served by the Chief of Police commanding appellant to appear before the Mayor's Court three days later to answer "to the offense of soliciting members for an organization without a Permit & License." . . .

The First Amendment of the Constitution provides: "Congress shall make no law . . . abridging the freedom of speech. . . ." This freedom is among the fundamental personal rights and liberties which are protected by the Fourteenth Amendment from invasion by state action; and municipal ordinances adopted under state authority constitute state action. . . .

This ordinance in its broad sweep makes it an offense to "solicit" citizens of the City of Baxley to become members of any "organization, union or society" which requires "fees [or] dues" from its members without first applying for and receiving from the Mayor and Council of the City a "permit" . . . which they may grant or refuse to grant . . . after considering "the character of the applicant, the nature of the . . . organization for which members are desired to be solicited, and its effects upon the general welfare of [the] citizens of the City of Baxley." . . .

Appellant's first contention in this Court is that the ordinance is invalid on its face because it makes enjoyment of the constitutionally guaranteed freedom of speech contingent upon the will of the Mayor and Council of the City and thereby constitutes a prior restraint upon, and abridges, that freedom. Believing that appellant is right in that contention and that the judgment must be reversed for that reason, we confine our considerations to that particular question and do not reach other questions presented.

It will be noted that appellant was not accused of any act against the peace, good order or dignity of the community, nor for any particular thing she said in soliciting employees of the manufacturing company to join the union. She was simply charged and convicted for "soliciting members for an organization without a Permit." This solicitation, as shown by the evidence, consisted solely of speaking to those employees in their private homes about joining the union.

It will also be noted that the permit is not to be issued as a matter of course, but only upon the affirmative action of the Mayor and Council of the City. They are expressly authorized to refuse to grant the permit if they do not approve of the applicant or of the union or of the union's "effects upon the general welfare of the citizens of the City of Baxley." These criteria are without semblance of definitive standards or other controlling guides governing the action of the Mayor and Council in granting or withholding a permit. . . . It is thus plain that they act in this respect in their uncontrolled discretion.

It is settled by a long line of recent decisions of this Court that an ordinance which, like this one, makes the peaceful enjoyment of freedoms which the Constitution guarantees contingent upon the uncontrolled will of an official—as by requiring a permit or license which may be granted or withheld in the discretion of such official—is an unconstitutional censorship or prior restraint upon the enjoyment of those freedoms. . . .

It is undeniable that the ordinance authorized the Mayor and Council of the City of Baxley to grant "or refuse to grant" the required permit in their uncontrolled discretion. It thus makes enjoyment of speech contingent upon the will of the Mayor and Council of the City, although that fundamental right is made free from congressional abridgment by the First Amendment and is protected by the Fourteenth from invasion by state action. For these reasons, the ordinance, on its face, imposes an unconstitutional prior restraint upon the enjoyment of First Amendment freedoms and lays "a forbidden burden upon the exercise of liberty protected by the Constitution." . . . Therefore, the judgment of conviction must fall.

Reversed.

NATIONAL ASSN. FOR ADVANCEMENT OF
COLORED PEOPLE *v.* ALABAMA
357 US 449 (1958)

[In the aftermath of the Court's decision in *Brown* v. *Topeka,* 347 US 483 (1954), prohibiting segregation in the schools, southern states attacked and tried to outlaw the NAACP. The attorney general of Alabama sought an injunction to oust the association from the state. In the course of proceedings in the state courts, the NAACP was ordered to produce records and papers, including names and addresses of all of the association's members and agents in the state. The association produced all records except the membership lists. As to these lists, the NAACP contended that the state could not constitutionally compel disclosure.

[In a unanimous decision the Court upheld the claim of the association. In his opinion for the Court, Justice Harlan said that the NAACP had the right to protect its membership lists on behalf of the right of the members to pursue their lawful private interests and to associate freely with others in the pursuit of their private interests. This right of the members, asserted for them by the association, is protected by the Fourteenth Amendment against state action. The Due Process Clause of the Fourteenth Amendment protects the freedom to engage in association for the advancement of beliefs and ideas pertaining to political, economic, religious, or cultural matters.]

Mr. Justice Harlan delivered the opinion of the Court:

We review from the standpoint of its validity under the Federal Constitution a judgment of civil contempt entered against petitioner, the National Association for the Advancement of Colored People, in the courts of Alabama. The question presented is whether Alabama, consistently with the Due Process Clause of the Fourteenth Amendment, can compel petitioner to reveal to the State's Attorney General the names and addresses of all its Alabama members and agents, without regard to their positions or functions in the Association. The judgment of contempt was based upon petitioner's refusal to comply fully with a court order requiring in part the production of membership lists. Petitioner's claim is that the order, in the circumstances shown by this record, violated rights assured to petitioner and its members under the Constitution.

Alabama has a statute similar to those of many other States which requires foreign corporations, except as exempted, to qualify before doing business by filing the corporate charter with the Secretary of State and designating a place of business and an agent to receive service of process. The statute imposes a fine on a corporation transacting intrastate business before qualifying and provides for criminal prosecution of officers of such a corporation. . . . The National Association for the Advancement of Colored People is a nonprofit membership corporation organized under the laws of New York. Its purposes, fostered on a nationwide basis, are those indicated by its name, and it operates through chartered affiliates which are independent unincorporated associations, with membership therein equivalent to membership in petitioner. The first Alabama affiliates were chartered in 1918. Since that time the aims of the Association have been advanced through activities of its affiliates, and in 1951 the Association itself opened a regional office in Alabama, at which it employed two supervisory persons and one clerical worker. The Association has never complied with the qualification statute, from which it considered itself exempt.

In 1956 the Attorney General of Alabama brought an equity suit in the State Circuit Court, Montgomery County, to enjoin the Association from conducting further activities within, and to oust it from, the State. Among other things the bill in equity alleged that the Association had opened a regional office and had organized various affiliates in Alabama; had recruited members and solicited contributions within the State; had given financial support and furnished legal assistance to Negro students seeking admission to the state university; and had supported a Negro boycott of the bus lines in Montgomery to compel the seating of passengers without regard to race. The bill recited that the Association, by continuing to do business in Alabama without complying with the qualification statute, was ". . . causing irreparable injury to the property and civil rights of the residents and citizens of the State of Alabama for which criminal prosecution and civil actions at law afford no adequate relief. . . ." On the day the complaint was filed, the Circuit Court issued *ex parte* an order restraining the Association, *pendente lite*, from engaging in further activities within the State and forbidding it to take any steps to qualify itself to do business therein.

Petitioner demurred to the allegations of the bill and moved to dissolve the restraining order. It contended that its activities did not subject it to the qualification requirements of the statute and that in any event what the State sought to accomplish by its suit would violate rights to freedom of speech and assembly guaranteed under the Fourteenth Amendment to the Constitution of the United States. Before the date set for a hearing on this motion, the State moved for the production of a large number of the Association's records and papers, including bank statements, leases, deeds, and records containing the names and addresses of all Alabama "members" and "agents" of the Association. It alleged that all such documents were necessary for adequate preparation for the hearing, in view of petitioner's denial of the conduct of intrastate business within the meaning of the qualification statute. Over petitioner's objections, the court ordered the production of a substantial part of the requested records, including the membership lists, and postponed the hearing on the restraining order to a date later than the time ordered for production.

Thereafter petitioner filed its answer to the bill in equity. It admitted its Alabama activities substantially as alleged in the complaint and that it had not qualified to do business in the State. Although still disclaiming the state's application to it, petitioner offered to qualify if the bar from qualification made part of the restraining order were lifted, and it submitted with the answer an executed set of the forms required by the statute. However petitioner did not comply with the production order, and for this failure was adjudged in civil contempt and fined $10,000. The contempt judgment provided that the fine would be subject to reduction or remission if compliance were forthcoming within five days but otherwise would be increased to $100,000.

At the end of the five-day period petitioner produced substantially all the data called for by the production order except its membership lists, as to which it contended that Alabama could not constitutionally compel disclosure, and moved to modify or vacate the contempt judgment, or stay its execution pending appellate review. This motion was denied. While a similar stay application, which was later denied, was pending before the Supreme Court of Alabama, the Circuit Court made a further order adjudging petitioner in continuing contempt and increasing the fine already imposed to $100,000. Under Alabama law, . . . the effect of the contempt adjudication was to foreclose petitioner from obtaining a hearing on the merits of the underlying ouster action, or from taking any steps to dissolve the temporary restraining order which had been issued *ex parte,* until it purged itself of contempt. . . .

The State Supreme Court thereafter twice dismissed petitions for certiorari to review this final contempt judgment, the first time, . . . for insufficiency of the petition's allegations and the second time on procedural grounds. . . . We granted certiorari because of the importance of the constitutional questions presented. . . .

The Association both urges that it is constitutionally entitled to resist official inquiry into its membership lists, and that it may assert, on behalf of its members, a right personal to them to be protected from compelled disclosure by the State of their affiliation with the Association as revealed by the membership lists. We think that petitioner argues more appropriately the rights of its members, and that its nexus with them is sufficient to permit that it act as their representative before this Court. In so concluding, we reject respondent's argument that the Association lacks standing to assert here constitutional rights pertaining to the members, who are not of course parties to the litigation.

To limit the breadth of issues which must be dealt with in particular litigation, this Court has generally insisted that parties rely only on constitutional rights which are personal to themselves. . . . This rule is related to the broader doctrine that constitutional adjudication should where possible be avoided. . . . The principle is not disrespected where constitutional rights of persons who are not immediately before the Court could not be effectively vindicated except through an appropriate representative before the Court. . . .

If petitioner's rank-and-file members are constitutionally entitled to withhold their connection with the Association despite the production order, it is manifest that this right is properly assertable by the Association. To require that it be claimed by the members themselves would result in nullification of the right at the very moment of its assertion. Petitioner is the appropriate party to assert these rights, because it and its members are in every practical sense identical. The Association, which provides in its constitution that "[a]ny person who is in accordance with [its] principles and policies . . ." may become a member, is but the medium through which its individual members seek to make more effective the expression of their own views. The reasonable likelihood that the Association itself through diminished financial support and membership may be adversely affected if production is compelled is a further factor pointing towards our holding that petitioner has standing to complain of the production order on behalf of its members. . . .

We thus reach petitioner's claim that the production order in the state litigation trespasses upon fundamental freedoms protected by the Due Process Clause of the Fourteenth Amendment. Petitioner argues that in view of the facts and circumstances shown in the record, the effect of compelled disclosure of the membership lists will be to abridge the rights of its rank-and-file members to engage in lawful association in support of their common beliefs. It contends that governmental action which, although not directly suppressing association, nevertheless carries this consequence, can be justified only upon some overriding valid interest of the State.

Effective advocacy of both public and private points of view, particularly controversial ones, is undeniably enhanced by group association, as this Court had more than once recognized by remarking upon the close nexus between the freedoms of speech and assembly. . . . It is beyond debate that freedom to engage in association for the advancement of beliefs and ideas is an inseparable aspect of the "liberty" assured by the Due Process Clause of the Fourteenth Amendment, which embraces freedom of speech. . . . Of course, it is immaterial whether the beliefs sought to be advanced by association pertain to political, economic, religious or cultural matters, and state action which may have the effect of curtailing the freedom to associate is subject to the closest scrutiny.

The fact that Alabama, so far as is relevant to the validity of the contempt judgment presently under review, has taken no direct action, . . . to restrict the right of petitioner's members to associate freely, does not end inquiry into the effect of the production order. See *American Communications Assn.* v. *Douds,* 339 US 382. In the domain of these indispensable liberties, whether of speech, press, or association, the decisions of this Court recognize that abridgement of such rights, even though unintended, may inevitably follow from varied forms of governmental action. Thus in *Douds,* the Court stressed that the legislation there challenged, which on its face sought to regulate labor unions and to secure stability in interstate commerce, would have the practical effect "of discouraging" the exercise of constitutionally protected political rights, . . . and it upheld the statute only after concluding that the reasons advanced for its enactment were constitutionally sufficient to justify its possible deterrent effect upon such freedoms. Similar recognition of possible unconstitutional intimidation of the free exercise of the right to advocate underlay this Court's narrow construction of the authority of a congressional committee investigating lobbying and of an Act regulating lobbying, although in neither case was there an effort to suppress speech. *United States* v. *Rumely*, 345 US 41; *United States* v. *Harriss*, 347 US 612. The governmental action challenged may appear to be totally unrelated to protected liberties. Statutes imposing taxes upon rather than prohibiting particular activity have been struck down when perceived to have the consequence of unduly curtailing the liberty of freedom of press assured under the Fourteenth Amendment. *Grosjean* v. *American Press Co.*, 297 US 233; *Murdock* v. *Pennsylvania*, 319 US 105.

It is hardly a novel perception that compelled disclosure of affiliation with groups engaged in advocacy may constitute as effective a restraint on freedom of association as the forms of governmental action in the cases above were thought likely to produce upon the particular constitutional rights there involved. This Court has recognized the vital relationship between freedom to associate and privacy in one's associations. When referring to the varied forms of governmental action which might interfere with freedom of assembly, it is said in *American Communications Assn.* v. *Douds*, . . . : "A requirement that adherents of particular religious faiths or political parties wear identifying arm-bands, for example, is obviously of this nature." Compelled disclosure of membership in an organization engaged in advocacy of particular beliefs is of the same order. Inviolability of privacy in group association may in many circumstances be indispensable to preservation of freedom of association, particularly where a group espouses dissident beliefs. . . .

We think that the production order, in the respects here drawn in question, must be regarded as entailing the likelihood of a substantial restraint upon the exercise by petitioner's members of their right to freedom of association. Petitioner has made an uncontroverted showing that on past occasions revelation of the identity of its rank-and-file members has exposed these members to economic reprisals, loss of employment, threat of physical coercion, and other manifestations of public hostility. Under these circumstances, we think it apparent that compelled disclosure of petitioner's Alabama membership is likely to affect adversely the ability of petitioner and its members to pursue their collective effort to foster beliefs which they admittedly have the right to advocate, in that it may induce members to withdraw from the Association and dissuade others from joining because of fear of exposure of their beliefs shown through their associations and of the consequences of this exposure.

It is not sufficient to answer, as the State does here, that whatever repressive effect compulsory disclosure of names of petitioner's members may have upon participation by Alabama citizens in petitioner's activities follows not from *state* action but from *private* community pressures. The crucial factor is the interplay of governmental and private action, for it is only after the initial exertion of state power represented by the production order that private action takes hold.

We turn to the final question whether Alabama has demonstrated an interest in obtaining the disclosures it seeks from petitioner which is sufficient to justify the deterrent effect which we have concluded these disclosures may well have on the free exercise by petitioner's members of their constitutionally protected right of association. . . . Such a ". . . subordinating interest of the State must be compelling," *Sweezy* v. *New Hampshire*, 354 US 234 (concurring opinion). It is not of moment that the State has here acted solely through its judicial branch, for whether legislative or judicial, it is still the application of state power which we are asked to scrutinize.

It is important to bear in mind that petitioner asserts no right to absolute immunity from state investigation, and no right to disregard Alabama's laws. As shown by its substantial compliance with the production order, petitioner does not deny Alabama's right to obtain from it such information as the State desires concerning the purposes of the Association and its activities within the State. Petitioner has not objected to divulging the identity of its members who are employed by or hold official positions with it. It has urged the rights solely of its ordinary rank-and-file members. This is therefore not analogous to a case involving the interest of a State in protecting its citizens in their dealings with paid solicitors or agents of foreign corporations by requiring identification. . . .

Whether there was "justification" in this instance turns solely on the substantiality of Alabama's interest in obtaining the membership lists. During the course of a hearing before the Alabama Circuit Court on a motion of petitioner to set aside the production order, the State Attorney General presented at length, under examination by petitioner, the State's reason for requesting the membership lists. The exclusive purpose was to determine whether petitioner was conducting intrastate business in violation of the Alabama foreign corporation registration statute, and the membership lists were expected to help resolve this question. The issues in the litigation commenced by Alabama by its bill in equity were whether the character of petitioner and its activities in Alabama had been such as to make petitioner subject to the registration statute, and whether the extent of petitioner's activities without qualifying suggested its permanent ouster from the State. Without intimating the slightest view upon the merits of these issues, we are unable to perceive that the disclosure of the names of petitioner's rank-and-file members has a substantial bearing on either of them. As matters stand in the state court, petitioner (1) has admitted its presence and conduct of activities in Alabama since 1918; (2) has offered to comply in all respects with the state qualification statute, although preserving its contention that the statute does not apply to it; and (3) has apparently complied satisfactorily with the production order, except for the membership lists, by furnishing the Attorney General with varied business records, its charter and statement of purposes, the names of all of its directors and officers, and with the total number of its Alabama members and the amount of their dues. These last items would not on this record appear subject to constitutional challenge and have been furnished, but whatever interest the State may have in obtaining names of ordinary members has not been shown to be sufficient to overcome petitioner's constitutional objections to the production order. . . .

We hold that the immunity from state scrutiny of membership lists which the Association claims on behalf of its members is here so related to the right of the members to pursue their lawful private interest privately and to associate freely with others in so doing as to come within the protection of the Fourteenth Amendment. And we conclude that Alabama has fallen short of showing a controlling justification for the deterrent effect on the free enjoyment of the right to associate which disclosure of membership lists is likely to have. Accordingly, the judgment of civil contempt and the $100,000 fine which resulted from petitioner's refusal to comply with the production order in this respect must fall. . . .

Reversed.

BATES v. LITTLE ROCK

361 US 516 (1960)

[Defendants were convicted in an Arkansas state court for violating occupation license tax ordinances of two cities, by which they were required to submit the names of all members of the National Association for the Advancement of Colored People. The Supreme Court unanimously reversed. The requirement was a restraint on freedom of association. Justice Black wrote a concurring opinion, joined by Justice Douglas.]

Mr. Justice Stewart delivered the opinion of the Court:

Each of the petitioners has been convicted of violating an identical ordinance of an Arkansas municipality by refusing a demand to furnish city officials with a list of the names of the members of a local branch of the National Association for the Advancement of Colored People. The question for decision is whether these convictions can stand under the Due Process Clause of the Fourteenth Amendment to the United States Constitution.

Municipalities in Arkansas are authorized by the State to levy a license tax on any person, firm, individual, or corporation engaging in any "trade, business, profession, vocation, or calling" within their corporate limits. Pursuant to this authority, the City of Little Rock and the City of North Little Rock have for some years imposed annual license taxes on a broad variety of businesses, occupations, and professions. Charitable organizations which engage in the activities affected are relieved from paying the taxes.

In 1957 the two cities added identical amendments to their occupation license tax ordinances. These amendments require that any organization operating within the municipality in question must supply to the City Clerk, upon request and within a specified time, (1) the official name of the organization; (2) its headquarters or regular meeting place; (3) the names of the officers, agents, servants, employees, or representatives, and their salaries; (4) the purpose of the organization; (5) a statement as to dues, assessments, and contributions paid, by whom and when paid, together with a statement reflecting the disposition of the funds and the total net income; (6) an affidavit stating whether the organization is subordinate to a parent organization, and if so, the latter's name. The ordinances expressly provide that all information furnished shall be public and subject to the inspection of any interested party at all reasonable business hours.

Petitioner Bates was the custodian of the records of the local branch of the National Association for the Advancement of Colored People in Little Rock, and petitioner Williams was the custodian of the records of the North Little Rock branch. These local organizations supplied the two municipalities with all the information required by the ordinances, except that demanded under § 2E of each ordinance which would have required disclosure of the names of the organizations' members and contributors. Instead of furnishing the detailed breakdown required by this section of the North Little Rock ordinance, the petitioner Williams wrote to the City Clerk as follows:

E. The financial statement is as follows:

January 1, 1957 to December 4, 1957.

Total receipts from membership and contributors $252.00.

Total expenditures $183.60
   (to National Office)

Secretarial help 5.00

Stationery, stamps, etc. 3.00

Total $191.60

On Hand 60.40

F. I am attaching my affidavit as president indicating that we are a Branch of the National Association for the Advancement of Colored People, a New York Corporation.

We cannot give you any information with respect to the names and addresses of our members and contributors or any information which may lead to the ascertainment of such information. We base this refusal on the anti-NAACP climate in this state. It is our good faith and belief that the public disclosure of the names of our members and contributors might lead to their harassment, economic reprisals, and even bodily harm. Moreover, even aside from that possibility, we have been advised by our counsel, and we do so believe that the city has no right under the Constitution and laws of the United States, and under the Constitution and laws of the State of Arkansas to demand the names and addresses of our members and contributors. We assert on behalf of the organization and its members the right to contribute to the NAACP and to seek under its aegis to accomplish the aims and purposes herein described free from any restraints or interference from city or state officials. In addition we assert the right of our members and contributors to participate in the activities of the NAACP, anonymously, a right which has been recognized as the basic right of every American citizen since the founding of this country. . . .

A substantially identical written statement was submitted on behalf of the Little Rock branch of the Association to the Clerk of that city.

After refusing upon further demand to submit the names of the members of their organizations, each petitioner was tried, convicted, and fined for a violation of the ordinance of her respective municipality. At the Bates trial evidence was offered to show that many former members of the local organization had declined to renew their membership because of the existence of the ordinance in question. Similar evidence was received in the Williams trial, as well as evidence that those who had been publicly identified in the community as members of the National Association for the Advancement of Colored People had been subjected to harassment and threats of bodily harm.

On appeal the cases were consolidated in the Supreme Court of Arkansas, and, with two justices dissenting, the convictions were upheld. The court concluded that compulsory disclosure of the membership lists under the circumstances was "not an unconstitutional invasion of the freedoms guaranteed . . ." but "a mere incident to a permissible legal result." Because of the significant constitutional question involved, we granted certiorari.

Like freedom of speech and a free press, the right of peaceable assembly was considered by the Framers of our Constitution to lie at the foundation of a government based upon the consent of an informed citizenry—a government dedicated to the establishment of justice and the preservation of liberty. U.S. Const., Amend. I. And it is now beyond dispute that freedom of association for the purpose of advancing ideas and airing grievances is protected by the Due Process Clause of the Fourteenth Amendment from invasion by the States. *De Jonge* v. *Oregon*, 299 U.S. 353; *N.A.A.C.P.* v. *Alabama*, 357 U.S. 449.

Freedoms such as these are protected not only against heavy-handed frontal attack, but also from being stifled by more subtle governmental interference. . . . "It is hardly a novel perception that compelled disclosure of affiliation with groups engaged in advocacy may constitute [an] effective . . . restraint on freedom of association. . . . This Court has recognized the vital relationship between freedom to associate and privacy in one's associations. . . . Inviolability of privacy in group association may in many circumstances be indispensable to preservation of freedom of association, particularly where a group espouses dissident beliefs." *N.A.A.C.P.* v. *Alabama.*

On this record it sufficiently appears that compulsory disclosure of the membership lists of the local branches of the National Association for the Advancement of Colored People would work a significant interference with the freedom of association of their members. There was substantial uncontroverted evidence that public identification of persons in the community as members of the organizations had been followed by harassment and threats of bodily harm. There was also evidence that fear of community hostility and economic reprisals that would follow public disclosure of the membership lists had discouraged new members from joining the organizations and induced former members to withdraw. This repressive effect, while in part the result of private attitudes and pressures, was brought to bear only after the exercise of governmental power had threatened to force disclosure of the members' names. . . . Thus, the threat of substantial government encroachment upon important and traditional aspects of individual freedom is neither speculative nor remote.

Decision in this case must finally turn, therefore, on whether the cities as instrumentalities of the State have demonstrated so cogent an interest in obtaining and making public the membership lists of these organizations as to justify the substantial abridgment of associational freedom which such disclosures will effect. Where there is a significant encroachment upon personal liberty, the State may prevail only upon showing a subordinating interest which is compelling. . . .

It cannot be questioned that the governmental purpose upon which the municipalities rely is a fundamental one. No power is more basic to the ultimate purpose and function of government than is the power to tax. . . . Nor can it be doubted that the proper and efficient exercise of this essential governmental power may sometimes entail the possibility of encroachment upon individual freedom. . . .

It was as an adjunct of their power to impose occupation license taxes that the cities enacted the legislation here in question. But governmental action does not automatically become reasonably related to the achievement of a legitimate and substantial governmental purpose by mere assertion in the preamble of an ordinance. When it is shown that state action threatens significantly to impinge upon constitutionally protected freedom it becomes the duty of this Court to determine whether the action bears a reasonable relationship to the achievement of the governmental purpose asserted as its justification.

In this record we can find no relevant correlation between the power of the municipalities to impose occupation license taxes and the compulsory disclosure and publication of the membership lists of the local branches of the National Association for the Advancement of Colored People. The occupation license tax ordinances of the municipalities are squarely aimed at reaching all the commercial, professional, and business occupations within the communities. The taxes are not, and as a matter of state law cannot be, based on earnings or income, but upon the nature of the occupation or enterprise conducted.

Inquiry of organizations within the communities as to the purpose and nature of their activities would thus appear to be entirely relevant to enforcement of the ordinances. Such an inquiry was addressed to these organizations and was answered as follows:

We are an affiliate of a national organization seeking to secure for American Negroes their rights as guaranteed by the Constitution of the United States. Our purposes may best be described by quoting from the Articles of Incorporation of our National Organization where these purposes are set forth as:

". . . voluntarily to promote equality of rights and eradicate caste or race prejudice among the citizens of the United States; to advance the interest of colored citizens; to secure for them impartial suffrage; and to increase their opportunities for securing justice in the courts, education for their children, employment according to their ability, and complete equality before the law. To ascertain and publish all facts bearing upon these subjects and to take any lawful action thereon; together with any kind and all things which may lawfully be done by a membership corporation organized under the laws of the State of New York for the further advancement of these objects."

The Articles of Incorporation hereinabove referred to are on file in the office of the Secretary of State of the State of Arkansas. In accord with these purposes and aims, [this] . . . Branch, NAACP was chartered and organized, and we are seeking to effectuate these principles within [this municipality].

The municipalities have not suggested that an activity so described, even if conducted for profit, would fall within any of the occupation classifications for which a license is required or a tax payable. On oral argument counsel for the City of Little Rock was unable to relate any activity of these organizations to which a license tax might attach. And there is nothing in the record to indicate that a tax claim has ever been asserted against either organization. If the organizations were to claim the exemption which the ordinance grants to charitable endeavors, information as to the specific sources and expenditures of their funds might well be a subject of relevant inquiry. But there is nothing to show that any exemption has ever been sought, claimed, or granted—and positive evidence in the record to the contrary.

In sum, there is a complete failure in this record to show (1) that the organizations were engaged in any occupation for which a license would be required, even if the occupation were conducted for a profit; (2) that the cities have ever asserted a claim against the organizations for payment of an occupation license tax; (3) that the organizations have ever asserted exemption from a tax imposed by the municipalities, either because of their alleged nonprofit character or for any other reason.

We conclude that the municipalities have failed to demonstrate a controlling justification for the deterrence of free association which compulsory disclosure of the membership lists would cause. The petitioners cannot be punished for refusing to produce information which the municipalities could not constitutionally require. The judgment cannot stand.

Reversed.

SHELTON v. TUCKER

364 US 479 (1960)

[An Arkansas statute compelled every teacher, as a condition of employment in a state-supported school or college, to file annually an affidavit listing every organization to which he had belonged or regularly contributed within the preceding five years. By 5 to 4, the Supreme Court held the act unconstitutional. Justices Frankfurter and Harlan wrote dissenting opinions, in which they were joined by Justices Clark and Whittaker.]

Mr. Justice Stewart delivered the opinion of the Court:

An Arkansas statute compels every teacher, as a condition of employment in a State supported school or college, to file annually an affidavit listing without limitation every organization to which he has belonged or regularly contributed within the preceding five years. At issue in these two cases is the validity of that statute under the Fourteenth Amendment to the Constitution. No. 14 is an appeal from the judgment of a three-judge Federal District Court upholding the statute's validity. No. 83 is here on writ of certiorari to the Supreme Court of Arkansas, which also held the statute constitutionally valid.

The statute in question is Act 10 of the Second Extraordinary Session of the Arkansas General Assembly of 1958. The provisions of the Act are summarized in the opinion of the District Court as follows:

Act 10 provides in substance that no person shall be employed or elected to employment as a superintendent, principal or teacher in any public school in Arkansas, or as an instructor, professor or teacher in any public institution of higher learning in that State until such person shall have submitted to the appropriate hiring authority an affidavit listing all organizations to which he at the time belongs and to which he has belonged during the past five years, and also listing all organizations to which he at the time is paying regular dues or is making regular contributions, or to which within the past five years he has paid such dues or made such contributions. The Act further provides, among other things, that any contract entered into with any person who has not filed the prescribed affidavit shall be void; that no public moneys shall be paid to such person as compensation for his services; and that any such funds so paid may be recovered back either from the person receiving such funds or from the board of trustees or other governing body making the payment. The filing of a false affidavit is denounced as perjury, punishable by a fine of not less than five hundred nor more than one thousand dollars, and, in addition, the person filing the false affidavit is to lose his teaching license.

These provisions must be considered against the existing system of teacher employment required by Arkansas law. Teachers there are hired on a year-to-year basis. They are not covered by a civil service system, and they have no job security beyond the end of each school year. The closest approach to tenure is a statutory provision for the automatic renewal of a teacher's contract if he is not notified within ten days after the end of a school year that the contract has not been renewed. . . .

The plaintiffs in the Federal District Court (appellants here) were

B. T. Shelton, a teacher employed in the Little Rock Public School
System, suing for himself and others similarly situated, together with
the Arkansas Teachers Association and its Executive Secretary, suing
for the benefit of members of the Association. Shelton had been employed in the Little Rock Special School District for twenty-five years.
In the spring of 1959 he was notified that, before he could be employed
for the 1959–1960 school year, he must file the affidavit required by Act
10, listing all his organizational connections over the previous five years.
He declined to file the affidavit, and his contract for the ensuing school
year was not renewed. At the trial the evidence showed that he was not
a member of the Communist Party or of any organization advocating
the overthrow of the Government by force, and that he was a member
of the National Association for the Advancement of Colored People.
The court upheld Act 10, finding the information it required was "relevant," and relying on several decisions of this Court, . . .

The plaintiffs in the State court proceedings (petitioners here) were
Max Carr, an associate professor at the University of Arkansas, and
Ernest T. Gephardt, a teacher at Central High School in Little Rock,
each suing for himself and others similarly situated. Each refused to
execute and file the affidavit required by Act 10. Carr executed an affirmation in which he listed his membership in professional organizations,
denied ever having been a member of any subversive organization, and
offered to answer any questions which the University authorities might
constitutionally ask touching upon his qualifications as a teacher. Gephardt filed an affidavit stating that he had never belonged to a subversive organization, disclosing his membership in the Arkansas Education
Assocation and the American Legion, and also offering to answer any
questions which the school authorities might constitutionally ask touching upon his qualifications as a teacher. Both were advised that their
failure to comply with the requirements of Act 10 would make impossible their re-employment as teachers for the following school year. The
Supreme Court of Arkansas upheld the constitutionality of Act 10, on
its face and as applied to the petitioners.

I.

It is urged here, as it was unsuccessfully urged throughout the proceedings in both the Federal and State courts, that Act 10 deprives
teachers in Arkansas of their rights to personal, associational, and academic liberty, protected by the Due Process Clause of the Fourteenth
Amendment from invasion by state action. In considering this contention, we deal with two basic postulates.

First. There can be no doubt of the right of a state to investigate the
competence and fitness of those whom it hires to teach in its schools, as
this Court before now has had occasion to recognize. "A teacher works

in a sensitive area in a schoolroom. There he shapes the attitude of young minds towards the society in which they live. In this, the state has a vital concern." *Adler* v. *Board of Education,* 342 U.S. 485. There is "no requirement in the Federal Constitution that a teacher's classroom conduct be the sole basis for determining his fitness. Fitness for teaching depends on a broad range of factors." *Beilan* v. *Board of Education,* 357 U.S. 399.

This controversy is thus not of a pattern with such cases as *N.A.A.C.P.* v. *Alabama,* 357 U.S. 449, and *Bates* v. *Little Rock,* 361 U.S. 516. In those cases the Court held that there was no substantially relevant correlation between the governmental interest asserted and the state's effort to compel disclosure of the membership lists involved. Here, by contrast, there can be no question of the relevance of a state's inquiry into the fitness and competence of its teachers.

⮩ *Second.* It is not disputed that to compel a teacher to disclose his every associational tie is to impair that teacher's right of free association, a right closely allied to freedom of speech and a right which, like free speech, lies at the foundation of a free society. *De Jonge* v. *Oregon,* 299 U.S. 353; *Bates* v. *Little Rock, supra.* Such interference with personal freedom is conspicuously accented when the teacher serves at the absolute will of those to whom the disclosure must be made—those who any year can terminate the teacher's employment without bringing charges, without notice, without a hearing, without affording an opportunity to explain.

The statute does not provide that the information it requires be kept confidential. Each school board is left free to deal with the information as it wishes. The record contains evidence to indicate that fear of public disclosure is neither theoretical nor groundless. Even if there were no disclosure to the general public, the pressure upon a teacher to avoid any ties which might displease those who control his professional destiny would be constant and heavy. Public exposure, bringing with it the possibility of public pressures upon school boards to discharge teachers who belong to unpopular or minority organizations; would simply operate to widen and aggravate the impairment of constitutional liberty.

The vigilant protection of constitutional freedoms is nowhere more vital than in the community of American schools. "By limiting the power of the States to interfere with freedom of speech and freedom of inquiry and freedom of association, the Fourteenth Amendment protects all persons, no matter what their calling. But, in view of the nature of the teacher's relation to the effective exercise of the rights which are safeguarded by the Bill of Rights and by the Fourteenth Amendment, inhibition of freedom of thought, and of action upon thought, in the case of teachers brings the safeguards of those amendments vividly into operation. Such unwarranted inhibition upon the free spirit of teachers . . . has an unmistakable tendency to chill that free play of the spirit which all teachers ought especially to cultivate and practice; it makes for caution and timidity in their associations by potential teachers." *Wieman* v. *Updegraff,* 344 U.S. 183 (concurring opinion). "Scholarship cannot flourish in an atmosphere of suspicion and distrust. Teachers and students must always remain free to inquire, to study and to evaluate. . . ." *Sweezy* v. *New Hampshire,* 354 U.S. 234.

II.

The question to be decided here is not whether the State of Arkansas can ask certain of its teachers about all their organizational relationships. It is not whether the State can ask all of its teachers about certain of their associational ties. It is not whether teachers can be asked how many organizations they belong to, or how much time they spend in organizational activity. The question is whether the State can ask every one of its teachers to disclose every single organization with which he has been associated over a five-year period. The scope of the inquiry by Act 10 is completely unlimited. The statute requires a teacher to reveal the church to which he belongs, or to which he has given financial support. It requires him to disclose his political party, and every political organization to which he may have contributed over a five-year period. It requires him to list, without number, every conceivable kind of associational tie—social, professional, political, avocational, or religious. Many such relationships could have no possible bearing upon the teacher's occupational competence or fitness.

In a series of decisions this Court has held that, even though the governmental purpose be legitimate and substantial, that purpose cannot be pursued by means that broadly stifle fundamental personal liberties when the end can be more narrowly achieved. The breadth of legislative abridgment must be viewed in the light of less drastic means for achieving the same basic purpose. . . .

The unlimited and indiscriminate sweep of the statute now before us brings it within the ban of our prior cases. The statute's comprehensive interference with associational freedom goes far beyond what might be justified in the exercise of the State's legitimate inquiry into the fitness and competency of its teachers. The judgments in both cases must be reversed.

Mr. Justice Harlan, whom Mr. Justice Frankfurter, Mr. Justice Clark and Mr. Justice Whittaker join, dissenting:

Of course this decision has a natural tendency to enlist support, involving as it does an unusual statute that touches constitutional rights whose protection in the context of the racial situation in various parts of the country demands the unremitting vigilance of the courts. Yet that very circumstance also serves to remind of the restraints that attend constitutional adjudication. It must be emphasized that neither of these cases actually presents an issue of racial discrimination. The statute on its face applies to *all* Arkansas teachers irrespective of race, and there is no showing that it has been discriminatorily administered.

The issue is whether, consistently with the Fourteenth Amendment, a State may require teachers in its public schools or colleges to disclose, as a condition precedent to their initial or continued employment, all organizations to which they have belonged, paid dues, or contributed within the past five years. Since I believe that such a requirement cannot be said to transgress the constitutional limits of a State's conceded authority to determine the qualifications of those serving it as teachers, I am bound to consider that Arkansas had the right to pass the statute in question, and therefore conceive it my duty to dissent.

The legal framework in which the issue must be judged is clear. The rights of free speech and association embodied in the "liberty" assured against state action by the Fourteenth Amendment . . . is not absolute. . . . Where official action is claimed to invade these rights, the controlling inquiry is whether such action is justifiable on the basis of a superior governmental interest to which such individual rights must yield. When the action complained of pertains to the realm of investigation, our inquiry has a double aspect: first, whether the investigation relates to a legitimate governmental purpose; second, whether, judged in the light of that purpose, the questioned action has substantial relevance thereto. . . .

In the two cases at hand, I think both factors are satisfied. It is surely indisputable that a State has the right to choose its teachers on the basis of fitness. And I think it equally clear, as the Court appears to recognize, that information about a teacher's associations may be useful to school authorities in determining the moral, professional, and social qualifications of the teacher, as well as in determining the type of service for which he will be best suited in the educational system. . . . Furthermore, I take the Court to acknowledge that, agreeably to our previous decisions, the State may enquire into associations to the extent that the resulting information may be in aid of that legitimate purpose. These cases therefore do not present a situation such as we had in *N.A.A.C.P.* v. *Alabama,* 357 U.S. 449, and *Bates* v. *Little Rock,* 361 U.S. 516, where the required disclosure bears no substantial relevance to a legitimate state interest.

Despite these considerations this statute is stricken down because, in the Court's view, it is too broad, because it asks more than may be necessary to effectuate the State's legitimate interest. Such a statute, it is said, cannot justify the inhibition on freedom of association which so blanket an inquiry may entail. Cf. *N.A.A.C.P.* v. *Alabama, supra; Bates* v. *Little Rock, supra.*

I am unable to subscribe to this view because I believe it impossible to determine *a priori* the place where the line should be drawn between what would be permissible inquiry and over-broad inquiry in a situation like this. Certainly the Court does not point that place out. There can be little doubt that much of the associational information called for by the statute will be of little or no use whatever to the school authorities, but I do not understand how those authorities can be expected to fix in advance the terms of their enquiry so that it will yield only relevent information.

I do not mean to say that alternatives such as an enquiry limited to the names of organizations of whose character the State is presently aware, or to a class of organizations defined by their purposes, would not be more consonant with a decent respect for the privacy of the teacher, nor that such alternatives would be utterly unworkable. I do see, however, that these alternatives suffer from deficiencies so obvious where a State is bent upon discovering everything which would be relevant to its proper purposes, that I cannot say that it must, as a matter of constitutional compulsion, adopt some such means instead of those which have been chosen here.

Finally, I need hardly say that if it truns out that this statute is abused, either by an unwarranted publicizing of the required associational disclosures or otherwise, we would have a different kind of case than those presently before us. . . . All that is now here is the validity of the statute on its face, and I am unable to agree that in this posture of things the enactment can be said to be unconstitutional.

I would affirm in both cases.

INTERNATIONAL ASSN. OF MACHINISTS *v.* STREET
367 US 740 (1961)

[Labor unions which had negotiated union-shop agreements, pursuant to the Railway Labor Act, expended union funds in support of political causes to which plaintiffs were opposed, and the funds were so spent over their objection. They brought suit in a Georgia court to enjoin enforcement of the union-shop agreement on constitutional grounds. The state court granted the injunction, holding the Railway Labor Act provision for the union-shop agreement unconstitutional insofar as it permitted such use of union funds exacted from employees. On appeal, the Supreme Court reversed. This decision essentially was on a vote of 7 to 2, with Justice Frankfurter writing a dissenting opinion, in which he was joined by Justice Harlan.

[Speaking for four members of the Court, Justice Brennan said that it was not necessary to pass on the constitutionality of the Railway Labor Act union-shop provision, since the act could reasonably be construed as denying to the union the right to use a member's money for political causes to which he was opposed. Justices Douglas and Whittaker concurred with the four on the main issue. Justice Black would have gone further and have held the union-shop provision, as interpreted, a violation of the freedom of speech guarantee of the First Amendment.

[The case is important as one that involves the right of dissent within an organization to which a citizen may belong by reason of the statutory status the organization enjoys.

[Cf. a companion case, *Lathrop* v. *Donohue*, 367 US 820 (1961), involving the integrated bar of Wisconsin.]

Mr. Justice Brennan delivered the opinion of the Court:

A group of labor organizations, appellants here, and the carriers comprising the Southern Railway System, entered into a union-shop agreement pursuant to the authority of § 2, Eleventh of the Railway Labor Act. The agreement requires each of the appellees, employees of the carriers, as a condition of continued employment, to pay the appellant union representing his particular class or craft the periodic dues, initiation fees and assessments uniformly required as a condition of acquiring or retaining union membership. The appellees, in behalf of themselves and of employees similarly situated, brought this action in the Superior Court of Bibb County, Georgia, alleging that the money each was thus compelled to pay to hold his job was in substantial part used to finance the campaigns of candidates for federal and state offices whom he opposed, and to promote the propagation of political and economic doctrines, concepts and ideologies with which he disagreed. The Superior Court found that the allegations were fully proved and entered a judgment and decree enjoining the enforcement of the union-shop agreement on the ground that § 2, Eleventh violates the Federal Constitution to the extent that it permits such use by the appellants of the funds exacted from employees. The Supreme Court of Georgia affirmed, ... On appeal to this Court under 28 U.S.C. § 157 (1) we noted probable jurisdiction, 361 U.S. 807.

I. *The Hanson Decision.*

We held in *Railyway Employees' Dept.* v. *Hanson*, 351 U.S. 225, that enactment of the provision of § 2, Eleventh authorizing union-shop agreements between interstate railroads and unions of their employees was a valid exercise by Congress of its powers under the Commerce Clause and did not violate the First Amendment or the Due Process Clause of the Fifth Amendment. It is argued that our disposition of the First Amendment claims in *Hanson* disposes of appellees' constitutional claims in this case adversely to their contentions. We disagree. As appears from its history, that case decided only that § 2, Eleventh, in authorizing collective agreements conditioning employees' continued employment on payment of union dues, initiation fees and assessments, did not on its face impinge upon protected rights of association. The Nebraska Supreme Court in *Hanson,* upholding the employees' contention that the union shop could not constitutionally be enforced against them, stated that the union shop "improperly burdens their right to work and infringes upon their freedoms. This is particularly true as to the latter because it is apparent that some of these labor organizations advocate political ideas, support political candidates, and advance national economic concepts which may or may not be of an employee's choice." . . . That statement was made in the context of the argument that compelling an individual to become a member of an organization with political aspects is an infringement of the constitutional freedom of association, whatever may be the constitutionality of compulsory financial support of group activities outside the political process. The Nebraska court's reference to the support of political ideas, candidates, and economic concepts "which may or may not be of an employee's choice" indicates that it was considering at most the question of compelled membership in an organization with political facets. In their brief in this Court the appellees in *Hanson* argued that First Amendment rights would be infringed by the enforcement of an agreement which would enable compulsorily collected funds to be used for political purposes. But there was nothing concrete in the record to show the extent to which the unions were actually spending money for political purposes and what these purposes were, nothing to show the extent to which union funds collected from members were being used to meet the costs of political activity and the mechanism by which this was done, and nothing to show that the employees there involved opposed the use of their money for any particular political objective. In contrast, the present record contains detailed information on all these points, and specific findings were made in the courts below as to all of them. . . . Thus all that was held in *Hanson* was that § 2, Eleventh was constitutional in its bare authorization of union-shop contracts requiring workers to give "financial support" to unions legally authorized to act as their collective bargaining agents. We sustained this requirement—and only this requirement—embodied in the statutory authorization of agreements under which "all employees shall become members of the labor organization representing their craft or class." We clearly passed neither upon forced association in any other aspect nor upon the issue of the use of exacted money for political causes which were opposed by the employees.

The record in this case is adequate squarely to present constitutional questions reserved in *Hanson.* These are questions of the utmost gravity.

However, the restraints against unnecessary constitutional decision counsel against their determination unless we must conclude that Congress, in authorizing a union shop under § 2, Eleventh, also meant that the labor organization receiving an employee's money should be free, despite that employee's objection, to spend his money for political causes which he opposes. Federal statutes are to be so construed as to avoid serious doubt of their constitutionality. "When the validity of an act of the Congress is drawn in question, and even if a serious doubt of constitutionality is raised, it is a cardinal principle that this Court will first ascertain whether a construction of the statute is fairly possible by which the question may be avoided." . . . Each named appellee in this action has made known to the union representing his craft or class his dissent from the use of his money for political causes which he opposes. We have therefore examined the legislative history of § 2, Eleventh in the context of the development of unionism in the railroad industry under the regulatory scheme created by the Railway Labor Act to determine whether a construction is "fairly possible" which denies the authority to a union, over the employee's objection, to spend his money for political causes which he opposes. We conclude that such a construction is not only "fairly possible" but entirely reasonable, and we therefore find it unnecessary to decide the correctness of the constitutional determinations made by the Georgia courts.

II. *The Rail Unions and Union Security.*

The history of union security in the railway industry is marked *first*, by a strong and long-standing tradition of voluntary unionism on the part of the standard rail unions; *second*, by the declaration in 1934 of a congressional policy of complete freedom of choice of employees to join or not to join a union; *third*, by the modification of the firm legislative policy against compulsion, but only as a specific response to the recognition of the expenses to the recognition of the expenses and burdens incurred by the unions in the administration of the complex scheme of the Railway Labor Act.

When the question of union security in the rail industry was first given detailed consideration by Congress in 1934 only one of the standard unions had security provisions in any of its contracts. The Brotherhood of Railroad Trainmen maintained a number of so-called "percentage" contracts, requiring that in certain classes of employees represented by the Brotherhood, a specified percentage of employees had to belong to the union. These contracts applied only to yard conductors, yard brakemen and switchmen, and covered no more than 10,000 workers, about 1% of all rail employees. . . .

During congressional consideration of the 1934 legislation, the rail unions attempted to persuade Congress not to preclude them from negotiating security arrangements. By amendments to the original proposal, they sought to assure that the provision which became § 2, Fifth should prevent the carriers from conditioning employment on membership in a company union but should exempt the standard unions from its prohibitions. The Trainmen, the only union which stood to lose existing contracts if the section was not limited to company unions, especially urged such a limitation. . . .

The unions succeeded in having the House incorporate such a limitation in the bill it passed. . . . But the Senate did not acquiesce. Eastman, a firm believer in complete freedom of employees in their choice of representatives, strongly opposed the limitation. He characterized it as "vicious, because it strikes at the principle of freedom of choice which the bill is designed to protect. The prohibited practices acquire no virtue by being confined to so-called 'standard unions.' . . . Within recent years, the practice of tying up men's jobs with labor-union membership has crept into the railroad industry which theretofore was singularly clean in this respect. The practice has been largely in connection with company unions but not entirely. If genuine freedom of choice is to be the basis of labor relations under the Railway Labor Act, as it should be, then the yellow-dog contract, and its corollary, the closed shop, and the so-called 'percentage contract' have no place in the picture." . . . Eastman's views prevailed in the Senate, and the House concurred in a final version of § 2, Fifth, providing that "[n]o carrier . . . shall require any person seeking employment to sign any contract or agreement promising to join or not to join a labor organization." . . .

During World War II, the nonoperating unions made an unsuccessful attempt to obtain union security, incidental to an effort to secure a wage increase. Following the failure of negotiations and mediation, a Presidential Emergency Board was appointed. Two principal reasons were advanced by the unions. They urged that in view of their pledge not to strike for the duration and their responsibilities to assure uninterrupted operation of the railroads, they were justified in seeking to maintain their positions by union security arrangements. They also maintained that since they secured benefits through collective bargaining for all employees they represented, it was fair that the costs of their operations be shared by all workers. The Board recommended withdrawal of the request, concluding that the union shop was plainly forbidden by the Railway Labor Act and that in any event the unions had failed to show its necessity or utility. . . . The Report said: "[T]he Board is convinced that the essential elements of the union shop as defined in the employees' request are prohibited by section 2 of the Railway Labor Act.

The intent of Congress in this respect is made evident, with unusual clarity." . . . On the merits of the issue, the Board expressly rejected the claim that union security was necessary to protect the bargaining position of the unions: "[T]he unions are not suffering from a falling off in members. On the contrary, . . . membership has been growing and at the present time appears to be the largest in railroad history, with less than 10 percent nonmembership among the employees here represented." . . . "[T]he evidence presented with respect to danger from predatory rivals seemed to the Board lacking in sufficiency, especially so in the light of the evidence concerning membership growth." . . . "[N]o evidence was presented indicating that the unions stand in jeopardy by reason of carrier opposition. A few railroads were mentioned on which some of the unions do not represent a majority of their craft or class, and do not have bargaining relationships with the carrier. But the exhibits show that these unions are the chosen representatives of the employees on the overwhelming majority of the railroads, and that recognition of the unions is general. The Board does not find therefore that a sufficient case has been made for the necessity of additional protection of union status on the railroads." . . . The unions acceded to the Board's recommendation.

The question of union security was reopened in 1950. Congress then evaluated the proposal for authorizing the union shop primarily in terms of its relationship to the financing of the unions' participation in the machinery created by the Railway Labor Act to achieve its goals. The framework for fostering voluntary adjustments between the carriers and their employees in the interest of the efficient discharge by the carriers of their important functions with minimum disruption from labor strife has no statutory parallel in other industry. That machinery, the product of a long legislative evolution, is more complex than that of any other industry. The labor relations of interstate carriers have been a subject of congressional enactments since 1888. For a time, after World War I, Congress experimented with a form of compulsory arbitration. The experiment was unsuccessful. Congress has since that time consistently adhered to a regulatory policy which places the responsibility squarely upon the carriers and the unions mutually to work out settlements of all aspects of the labor relationship. That policy was embodied in the Railway Labor Act of 1926, 44 Stat. 577, which remains the basic regulatory enactment. As the Senate Report on the bill which became that law stated: "The question was . . . presented whether the substitute [for the Act of 1920] should consist of a compulsory system with adequate means provided for its enforcement, or whether it was in the public interest to create the machinery for amicable adjustment of labor disputes agreed upon by the parties to the success of which both parties were committed. . . . The committee is of opinion that it is in the public interest to permit a fair trial of the method of amicable adjustment agreed upon by the parties, rather than to attempt under existing conditions to use the entire power of the Government to deal with these labor disputes." . . . The reference to the plan "agreed upon by the parties" was to "the fact that the Railway Labor Act of 1926 came on the statute books through agreement between the railroads and the railroad unions on the need of such legislation. It is accurate to say that the railroads and the railroad unions between them wrote the Railway Labor Act of 1926 and Congress formally enacted their agreement." . . .

"All through the [1926] act is the theory that the agreement is the vital thing in life." . . . The Act created affirmative legal duties on the part of the carriers and their employees "to exert every reasonable effort to make and maintain agreements concerning rates of pay, rules, and working conditions, and to settle all disputes, whether arising out of the application of such agreements or otherwise. . . ." § 2, First. . . . The Act also established a comprehensive administrative apparatus for the adjustment of disputes, in conferences between the parties, § 2, Second, Third and Fourth (now Sixth), and if not so settled, in submissions to boards of adjustment, § 3, or the National Mediation Board, §4. And the legislation expanded the already existing voluntary arbitration machinery, §§ 7, 8, 9.

A primary purpose of the major revisions made in 1934 was to strengthen the position of the labor organization *vis-à-vis* the carriers, to the end of furthering the success of the basic congressional policy of self-adjustment of the industry's labor problems between carrier organizations and effective labor organizations. The unions claimed that the carriers interfered with the employees' freedom of choice of representatives by creating company unions, and otherwise attempting to undermine the employees' participation in the process of collective bargaining. Congress amended § 2, Third to reinforce the prohibitions against interference with the choice of representatives, and to permit the employees to select nonemployee representatives. A new § 2, Fourth was added guaranteeing employees the right to organize and bargain collectively, and Congress made it the enforceable duty of the carriers "to treat with" the representatives of the employees, § 2, Ninth. . . . It was made explicit that the representative selected by a majority of any class or craft of employees should be the exclusive bargaining representative of all the employees of that craft or class. "The minority members of a craft are thus deprived by the statute of the right, which they would otherwise possess, to choose a representative of their own, and its members cannot bargain individually on behalf of themselves as to matters which are properly the subject of collective bargaining." . . . "Congress has seen fit to clothe the bargaining representative with powers comparable to those possessed by a legislative body both to create and restrict the rights of those whom it represents. . . ." In addition to thus strengthening the unions' status in relation to both the carriers and the employees, the 1934 Act created the National Railroad Adjustment Board and provided that the 18 employee representatives were to be chosen by the labor organizations national in scope. § 3. This Board was given jurisdiction to settle what are termed minor disputes in the railroad industry, primarily grievances arising from the application of collective bargaining agreements to particular situations. . . .

In sum, in prescribing collective bargaining as the method of settling railway disputes, in conferring upon the unions the status of exclusive representatives in the negotiation and administration of collective agreements, and in giving them representation on the statutory board to adjudicate grievances, Congress has given the unions a clearly defined and delineated role to play in effectuating the basic congressional policy of stabilizing labor relations in the industry. "It is fair to say that every stage in the evolution of this railroad labor code was progressively infused with the purpose of securing self-adjustment between the effectively organized railroads and the equally effective railroad unions and, to that end, of establishing facilities of such self-adjustment by the railroad community of its own industrial controversies. . . . The assumption as well as the aim of that Act [of 1934] is a process of permanent conference and negotiation between the carriers on the one hand and the employees through their unions on the other." . . .

Performance of these functions entails the expenditure of considerable funds. Moreover, this Court has held that under the statutory scheme, a union's status as exclusive bargaining representative carries with it the duty fairly and equitably to represent all employees of the craft or class, union and nonunion. . . . The principal argument made by the unions in 1950 was based on their role in this regulatory framework. They maintained that because of the expense of performing their duties in the congressional scheme, fairness justified the spreading of the costs to all employees who benefited. They thus advanced as their purpose the elimination of the "free riders"—those employees who obtained the benefits of the unions' participation in the machinery of the Act without financially supporting the unions.

George M. Harrison, spokesman for the Railway Labor Executives' Association, stated the unions' case in this fashion:

Activities of labor organizations resulting in the procurement of employee benefits are costly, and the only source of funds with which to carry on these activities is the dues received from members of the organization. We believe that it is essentially unfair for nonmembers to participate in the benefits of these activities without contributing anything to the cost. This is especially true when the collective bargaining representative is one from whose existence and activities he derives most important benefits and one which is obligated by law to extend these advantages to him.

Furthermore, collective bargaining to the railroad industry is more costly from a monetary standpoint than that carried on in any other industry. The administrative machinery is more complete and more complex. The mediation, arbitration, and Presidential Emergency Board provisions of the act, while greatly in the public interest, are very costly to the unions. The handling of agreement disputes through the National Railroad Adjustment Board also requires expense which is not known to unions in outside industry. . . .

This argument was decisive with Congress. The House Committee Report traced the history of previous legislation in the industry and pointed out the duty of the union acting as exclusive bargaining representative to represent equally all members of the class. "Under the act, the collective bargaining representative is required to represent the entire membership of the craft or class, including non-union members, fairly, equitably, and in good faith. Benefits resulting from collective bargaining may not be withheld from employees because they are not members of the union." . . . Observing that about 75% or 80% of all railroad employees were believed to belong to a union, the report continued: "Nonunion members, nevertheless, share in the benefits derived from collective agreements negotiated by the railway labor unions but bear no share of the cost of obtaining such benefits." These considerations overbore the arguments in favor of the earlier policy of complete individual freedom of choice. As we said in *Railway Employees' Dept. v. Hanson*, "[t]o require, rather than to induce, the beneficiaries of trade unionism to contribute to its costs may not be the wisest course. But Congress might well believe that it would help to insure the right to work in and along the arteries of interstate commerce. No more has been attempted here. . . . The financial support required relates . . . to the work of the union in the realm of collective bargaining." The conclusion to which this history clearly points is that § 2, Eleventh contemplated compulsory unionism to force employees to share the costs of negotiating and administering collective agreements, and the costs of the adjustment and settlement of disputes. One looks in vain for any suggestion that Congress also meant in § 2, Eleventh to provide the unions with a means for forcing employees, over their objection, to support political causes which they oppose.

III. *The Safeguarding of Rights of Dissent.*

To the contrary, Congress incorporated safeguards in the statute to protect dissenters' interests. Congress became concerned during the hearings and debates that the union shop might be used to abridge freedom of speech and beliefs. The original proposal for authorization of the union shop was qualified in only one respect. It provided "That no such agreement shall require such condition of employment with respect to employees to whom membership is not available upon the same terms and conditions as are generally applicable to any other member. . . ." This was primarily designed to prevent discharge of employees for nonmembership where the union did not admit the employee to membership on racial grounds. . . . But it was strenuously protested that the proposal provided no protection for an employee who disagreed with union policies or leadership. It was argued, for example, that "the right of free speech is at stake. . . . A man could feel that he was no longer able freely to express himself because he could be dismissed on account of criticism of the union. . . ." Objections of this kind led the rail unions to propose an addition to the proviso to § 2, Eleventh to prevent loss of job for nonunion membership "with respect to employees to whom membership was denied or terminated for any reason other than the failure of the employee to tender the periodic dues, fees, and assessments uniformly required as a condition of acquiring or retaining membership." . . . Mr. Harrison presented this text and stated, "It is submitted that this bill with the amendment as suggested in this statement remedies the alleged abuses of compulsory union membership as claimed by the opposing witnesses, yet makes possible the elimination of the 'free rider' and the sharing of the burden of maintenance of all the beneficiaries of union activity." . . . Mr. Harrison also sought to reassure Committee members as to the possible implications of other language of the proposed bill; he explained that "fees" meant, "initiation fees," and "assessments" was intended primarily to cover the situation of a union which had only nominal dues, so that its members paid "an assessment to finance the activities of the general negotiating committee . . . it will vary month by month, based on the expenses and work of that committee." Or, he explained, an assessment might cover convention expenses. "So we had to use the word 'assessment' in addition to dues and fees because some of the unions collect a nominal amount of dues and an assessment month after month to finance part of the activities, although in total it perhaps is no different than the dues paid in the first instance which comprehended all of those expenses." In reporting the bill, the Senate Committee expressly noted the protective proviso, . . . and affixed additional limitations. The words "not including fines and penalties" were added, to make it clear that termination of union membership for their nonpayment would not be grounds for discharge. It was also made explicit that "fees" meant "initiation fees." . . .

A congressional concern over possible impingements on the interests of individual dissenters from union policies is therefore discernible. It is true that opponents of the union shop urged that Congress should not allow it without explicitly regulating the amount of dues which might be exacted or prescribing the uses for which the dues might be expended. We may assume that Congress was also fully conversant with the long history of intensive involvement of the railroad unions in political activities. But it does not follow that § 2, Eleventh places no restriction on the use of any employee's money, over his objection, to support political causes he opposes merely because Congress did not enact a comprehensive regulatory scheme governing expenditures. For it is abundantly clear that Congress did not completely abandon the policy of full freedom of choice embodied in the 1934 Act, but rather made inroads on it for the limited purpose of eliminating the problems created by the "free rider." That policy survives in § 2, Eleventh in the safeguards intended to protect freedom of dissent. Congress was aware of the conflicting interests involved in the question of the union shop and sought to achieve their accommodation. . . . We respect this congressional purpose when we construe § 2, Eleventh as not vesting the unions with unlimited power to spend exacted money. We are not called upon to delineate the precise limits of that power in this case. We have before us only the question whether the power is restricted to the extent of denying the unions the right, over the employee's objection, to use his money to support political causes which he opposes. Its use to support candidates for public office, and advance political programs, is not a use which helps defray the expenses of the negotiation or administration of collective agreements, or the expenses entailed in the adjustment of grievances and disputes. In other words, it is a use which falls clearly outside the reasons advanced by the unions and accepted by Congress why authority to make union-shop agreements was justified. On the other hand, it is equally clear that it is a use to support activities within the area of dissenters' interests which Congress enacted the proviso to protect. We give § 2, Eleventh the construction which achieves both congressional purposes when we hold, as we do, that § 2, Eleventh is to be construed to deny the unions, over an employee's objection, the power to use his exacted funds to support political causes which he opposes.

We express no view as to other union expenditures objected to by an employee and not made to meet the costs of negotiation and administration of collective agreements, or the adjustment and settlement of grievances and disputes. We do not understand, in view of the findings of the Georgia courts and the question decided by the Georgia Supreme Court, that there is before us the matter of expenditures for activities in the area between the costs which led directly to the complaint as to "free riders," and the expenditures to support union political activities. We are satisfied, however, that § 2, Eleventh is to be interpreted to deny the unions the power claimed in this case. The appellant unions, in insisting that § 2, Eleventh contemplates their use of exacted funds to support political causes objected to by the employee, would have us hold that Congress sanctioned an expansion of historical practices in the political area by the rail unions. This we decline to do. Both by tradition and, from 1934 to 1951, by force of law, the rail unions did not rely upon the compulsion of union security agreements to exact money to support the political activities in which they engage. Our construction therefore involves no curtailment of the traditional political activities of the railroad unions. It means only that those unions must not support those activities, against the expressed wishes of a dissenting employee, with his exacted money.

IV. *The Appropriate Remedy.*

Under our view of the statute, however, the decision of the court below was erroneous and cannot stand. The appellees who have participated in this action have in the course of it made known to their respective unions their objection to the use of their money for the support of political causes. In that circumstance, the respective unions were without power to use payments thereafter tendered by them for such political causes. However, the union-shop agreement itself is not unlawful. *Railway Employees' Dept.* v. *Hanson, supra.* The appellees therefore remain obliged, as a condition of continued employment, to make the payments to their respective unions called for by the agreement. Their right of action stems not from constitutional limitations on Congress' power to authorize the union shop, but from § 2, Eleventh itself. In other words, appellees' grievance stems from the spending of their funds for purposes not authorized by the Act in the face of their objection, not from the enforcement of the union-shop agreement by the mere collection of funds. If their money were used for purposes contemplated by § 2, Eleventh, the appellees would have no grievance at all. We think that an injunction restraining enforcement of the union-shop agreement is therefore plainly not a remedy appropriate to the violation of the Act's restriction on expenditures. Restraining the collection of all funds from the appellees sweeps too broadly, since their objection is only to the uses to which some of their money is put. Moreover, restraining collection of the funds as the Georgia courts have done might well interfere with the appellant unions' performance of those functions and duties which the Railway Labor Act places upon them to attain its goal of stability in the industry. Even though the lower court decree is subject to modification upon proof by the appellants of cessation of improper expenditures, in the interim the prohibition is absolute against the collection of all funds from anyone who can show that he is opposed to the expenditure of any of his money for political purposes which he disapproves. The complete shutoff of this source of income defeats the congressional plan to have all employees benefited share costs "in the realm of collective bargaining," *Hanson,* 351 U.S., at p. 235, and threatens the basic congressional policy of the Railway Labor Act for self-adjustments between effective carrier organizations and effective labor organizations.

Since the case must therefore be remanded to the court below for consideration of a proper remedy, we think that it is appropriate to suggest the limits within which remedial discretion may be exercised consistently with the Railway Labor Act and other relevant public policies. As indicated, an injunction against enforcement of the union shop itself through the collection of funds is unwarranted. We also think that a blanket injunction against all expenditures of funds for the disputed purposes, even one conditioned on cessation of improper expenditures, would not be a proper exercise of equitable discretion. Nor would it be proper to issue an interim or temporary blanket injunction of this character pending a final adjudication. The Norris-LaGuardia Act, 29 U.S.C. §§ 101–115, expresses a basic policy against the injunction of activities of labor unions. We have held that the Act does not deprive the federal courts of jurisdiction to enjoin compliance with various mandates of the Railway Labor Act. . . . However, the policy of the Act suggests that the courts should hesitate to fix upon the injunctive remedy for breaches of duty owing under the labor laws unless that remedy alone can effectively guard the plaintiff's right. In *Graham* this Court found an injunction necessary to prevent the breach of the duty of fair representation, in order that Congress might not seem to have held out to the petitioners there "an illusory right for which it was denying them a remedy." No such necessity for a blanket injunctive remedy because of the absence of reasonable alternatives appears here. Moreover, the fact that these expenditures are made for political activities is an additional reason for reluctance to impose such an injunctive remedy. Whatever may be the powers of Congress or the States to forbid unions altogether to make various types of political expenditures, as to which we express no opinion here, many of the expenditures involved in the present case are made for the purpose of disseminating information as to candidates and programs and publicizing the positions of the unions on them. As to such expenditures an injunction would work a restraint on the expression of political ideas which might be offensive to the First Amendment. For the majority also has an interest in stating its views without being silenced by the dissenters. To attain the appropriate reconciliation between majority and dissenting interests in the area of political expression, we think the courts in administering the Act should select remedies which protect both interests to the maximum extent possible without undue impingement of one on the other.

Among possible remedies which would appear appropriate to the injury complained of, two may be enforced with a minimum of administrative difficulty and with little danger of encroachment on the legitimate activities or necessary functions of the unions. Any remedies, however, would properly be granted only to employees who have made known to the union officials that they do not desire their funds to be used for political causes to which they object. The safeguards of § 2, Eleventh were added for the protection of dissenters' interest, but dissent is not to be presumed—it must affirmatively be made known to the union by the dissenting employee. The union receiving money exacted from an employee under a union-shop agreement should not in fairness be subjected to sanctions in favor of an employee who makes no complaint of the use of his money for such activities. From these considerations, it follows that the present action is not a true class action, for there is no attempt to prove the existence of a class of workers who had specifically objected to the exaction of dues for political purposes. . . . Thus we think that only those who have identified themselves as opposed to political uses of their funds are entitled to relief in this action.

One remedy would be an injunction against expenditure for political causes opposed by the complaining employee of a sum, from those moneys to be spent by the union for political purposes, which is so much of the moneys exacted from him as is the proportion of the union's total expenditures made for such political activities to the union's total budget. The union should not be in a position to make up such sum from money paid by a nondissenter, for this would shift a disproportionate share of the costs of collective bargaining to the dissenter and have the same effect of applying his money to support such political activities. A second remedy would be restitution to an individual employee of that portion of his money which the union expended, despite his notification, for the political causes to which he had advised the union he was opposed. There should be no necessity, however, for the employee to trace his money up to and including its expenditure; if the money goes into general funds and no separate accounts of receipts and expenditures of the funds of individual employees are maintained, the portion of his money the employee would be entitled to recover would be in the same proportion that the expenditures for political purposes which he had advised the union he disapproved bore to the total union budget.

The judgment is reversed and the case is remanded to the court below for proceedings not inconsistent with this opinion.

LATHROP *v.* DONOHUE

367 US 820 (1961)

[Like the *Street Case, supra,* this case involves compulsory membership in an organization and a member's rights and liberties under the First Amendment. The Supreme Court of Wisconsin ordered the integration of the Wisconsin bar, which had the effect of compelling every lawyer in the state to pay dues to the association known as "The State Bar of Wisconsin." A member of the Wisconsin bar objected to paying dues and raised constitutional issues. The state supreme court ruled against him on these issues.

[In a 7-to-2 decision, the Supreme Court affirmed. In an opinion by Justice Brennan, the Court held that a state may condition the right to practice law upon membership in an integrated bar association. Justice Harlan wrote a concurring opinion, joined by Justice Frankfurter. Justice Whittaker concurred in the result. Justices Black and Douglas each wrote a dissenting opinion, condemning compulsory bar association membership as violative of the First Amendment freedoms.]

Mr. Justice Brennan announced the judgment of the Court and an opinion in which The Chief Justice, Mr. Justice Clark and Mr. Justice Stewart join:

The Wisconsin Supreme Court integrated the Wisconsin Bar by an order which created "The State Bar of Wisconsin" on January 1, 1957, under Rules and Bylaws promulgated by the court. . . . The order originally was effective for a two-year trial period, but in 1958 was continued indefinitely. . . . Alleging that the "rules and by-laws required the plaintiff to enroll in the State Bar of Wisconsin and to pay dues to the treasurer of the State Bar of Wisconsin on the penalty of being deprived of his livelihood as a practicing lawyer, if he should fail to do so," the appellant, a Wisconsin lawyer, brought this action in the Circuit Court of Dane County for the refund of $15 annual dues for 1959 paid by him under protest to appellee, the Treasurer of the State Bar. He attached to his complaint a copy of the letter with which he had enclosed his check for the dues. He stated in the letter that he paid under protest because "I do not like to be coerced to support an organization which is authorized and directed to engage in political and propaganda activities. . . . A major portion of the activities of the State Bar as prescribed by the Supreme Court of Wisconsin are of a political and propaganda nature." His complaint alleges more specifically that the State Bar promotes "law reform" and "makes and opposes proposals for changes in . . . laws and constitutional provisions and argues to legislative bodies and their committees and to the lawyers and to the people with respect to the adoption of changes in . . . codes, laws and constitutional provisions." He alleges further that in the course of this activity "the State Bar of Wisconsin has used its employees, property and funds in active, unsolicited opposition to the adoption of legislation by the Legislature of the State of Wisconsin, which was favored by the plaintiff, all contrary to plaintiff's convictions and beliefs." His complaint concludes: "The plaintiff bases this action on his claim that the defendant has unjustly received, held, and disposed of funds of the plaintiff in the amount of $15.00, which to the knowledge of the defendant were paid to the defendant by the plaintiff unwillingly and under coercion, and that such coercion was and is entailed in the rules and by-laws of the State Bar of Wisconsin continued in effect by the aforesaid order of the Supreme Court of the State of Wisconsin . . . ; and the said order insofar as it coerces the plaintiff to support the State Bar of Wisconsin, is unconstitutional and in violation of the Fourteenth Amendment of the Constitution of the United States. . . ."

The appellee demurred to the complaint on the ground, among others, that it failed to state a cause of action. The demurrer was sustained and the complaint was dismissed. The Supreme Court of Wisconsin, on appeal, stated that the Circuit Court was without jurisdiction to determine the questions raised by the complaint. However, treating the case as if originally and properly brought in the Supreme Court, the court considered appellant's constitutional claims, not only on the allegations of the complaint, but also upon the facts, of which it took judicial notice, as to its own actions leading up to the challenged order, and as to all activities, including legislative activities, of the State Bar since its creation. The judgment of the Circuit Court dismissing the complaint was affirmed. . . . The Supreme Court held that the requirement that appellant be an enrolled dues-paying member of the State Bar did not abridge his rights of freedom of association, and also that his rights to free speech were not violated because the State Bar used his money to support legislation with which he disagreed.

An appeal was brought here by appellant under 28 U.S.C. § 1257 (2), which authorizes our review of a final judgment rendered by the highest court of a State "By appeal, where is drawn in question the validity of a [state] statute. . . ." We postponed to the hearing on the merits the question whether the order continuing the State Bar indefinitely under the Rules and Bylaws is a "statute" for the purposes of appeal under § 1257 (2).

We think that the order is "a statute" for the purposes of § 1257 (2). . . . We conclude that the appeal is cognizable under § 1257 (2). We therefore proceed to the consideration of the merits.

The core of appellant's argument is that he cannot constitutionally be compelled to join and give support to an organization which has among its functions the expression of opinion on legislative matters and which utilizes its property, funds and employees for the purposes of influencing legislation and public opinion toward legislation. But his compulsory enrollment imposes only the duty to pay dues. The Supreme Court of Wisconsin so interpreted its order and its interpretation is of course binding on us. The court said: "The rules and by-laws of the State Bar, as approved by this court, do not compel the plaintiff to associate with anyone. He is free to attend or not attend its meetings or vote in its elections as he chooses. The only compulsion to which he has been subjected by the integration of the bar is the payment of the annual dues of $15 per year." We therefore are confronted, as we were in *Railway Employees Department* v. *Hanson*, 351 U.S. 225, only with a question of compelled financial support of group activities, not with involuntary membership in any other aspect. . . .

A review of the activities of the State Bar authorized under the Rules and Bylaws is necessary to decision. The purposes of the organization are stated as follows in Rule 1, § 2: "to aid the courts in carrying on and improving the administration of justice; to foster and maintain on the part of those engaged in the practice of law high ideals of integrity, learning, competence and public service and high standards of conduct; to safeguard the proper professional interests of the members of the bar; to encourage the formation and activities of local bar associations; to provide a forum for the discussion of subjects pertaining to the practice of law, the science of jurisprudence and law reform, and the relations of the bar to the public, and to publish information relating thereto; to the end that the public responsibilities of the legal profession may be more effectively discharged." To achieve these purposes standing committees and sections are established. The Rules also assign the organization a major role in the State's procedures for the discipline of members of the bar for unethical conduct. A Committee on Grievances is provided for each of the nine districts into which the State is divided. Each committee receives and investigates complaints of alleged misconduct of lawyers within its district. Each committee also investigates and processes petitions for reinstatement of lawyers and petitions for late enrollment in the State Bar of lawyers who fail to enroll within a designated period after becoming eligible to enroll.

The State Legislature and the State Supreme Court have informed us of the public interest sought to be served by the integration of the Bar. The statute states its desirability "to the end that such association shall promote the public interest by maintaining high standards of conduct in the legal profession and by aiding in the efficient administration of justice." This theme is echoed in the several Supreme Court opinions. The first opinion after the passage of the statute noted the "widespread general recognition of the fact that the conduct of the bar is a matter of general public interest and concern." But the court's examination at that time of existing procedures governing admission and discipline of lawyers and the prevention of the unauthorized practice of the law persuaded the court that the public interest was being adequately served without integration. The same conclusion was reached when the matter was reviewed again in 1946. At that time, in addition to reviewing the desirability of integration in the context of the problems of admission and discipline, the court considered its utility in other fields. The matter of post-law school or post-admission education of lawyers was one of these. The court believed, however, that while an educational program was a proper objective, the one proposed was "nebulous in outline and probably expensive in execution." The court also observed, "There are doubtless many other useful activities for which dues might properly be used, but what they are does not occur to us and no particular one seems to press for action."

The court concluded in 1956, however, that integration might serve the public interest and should be given a two-year trial. It decided to "require the bar to act as a unit to promote high standards of practice and the economical and speedy enforcement of legal rights," because it had come to the conclusion that efforts to accomplish these ends in the public interest through voluntary association had not been effective. "[T]oo many lawyers have refrained or refused to join, . . . membership in the voluntary association has become static, and . . . a substantial minority of the lawyers in the state are not associated with the State Bar Association." When the order was extended indefinitely in 1958 the action was expressly grounded on the finding that, "Members of the legal profession by their admission to the bar become an important part of [the] process [of administering justice]. . . . An independent, active, and intelligent bar is necessary to the efficient administration of justice by the courts."

The appellant attacks the power of the State to achieve these goals through integration on the ground that because of its legislative activities, the State Bar partakes of the character of a political party. But on their face the purposes and the designated activities of the State Bar hardly justify this characterization. The inclusion among its purposes that it be a forum for a "discussion of . . . law reform" and active in safeguarding the "proper professional interests of, the members of the bar," in unspecified ways, does not support it. Only two of the 12 committees, Administration of Justice, and Legislation, are expressly directed to concern themselves in a substantial way with legislation. Authority granted the other committees directs them to deal largely with matters which appear to be wholly outside the political process and to concern the internal affairs of the profession.

We do not understand the appellant to contend that the State Bar is a sham organization deliberately designed to further a program of political action. Nor would such a contention find support in this record. Legislative activity is carried on under a statement of policy which followed the recommendations of a former president of the voluntary Wisconsin Bar Association, Alfred LaFrance. He recommended that the legislative activity of the State Bar should have two distinct aspects: (1) "the field of legislative reporting or the dissemination of information concerning legislative proposals. . . . This is a service-information function that is both useful to the general membership and to the local bar associations" and (2) "promotional or positive legislative activity." As to the latter he advised that "the rule of substantial unanimity should be observed. Unless the lawyers of Wisconsin are substantially for or against a proposal, the State Bar should neither support nor oppose the proposal." "We must remember that we are an integrated Bar, that the views of the minority must be given along with the views of the majority where unanimity does not appear. The State Bar represents all of the lawyers of this state and in that capacity we must safeguard the interests of all." The rules of policy and procedure for legislative activity follow these recommendations.

Under its charter of legislative action, the State Bar has participated in political activities in these principal categories:

(1) its executive director is registered as a lobbyist in accordance with state law. For the legislative session 1959–1960, the State Bar listed a $1,400 lobbying expense; this was a percentage of the salary of the executive director, based on an estimate of the time he spent in seeking to influence legislation, amounting to 5% of his salary for the two years. The registration statement signed by the then president of the State Bar added the explanatory note: "His activities as a lobbyist on behalf of the State Bar are incidental to his general work and occupy only a small portion of his time."

(2) The State Bar, through its Board of Governors or Executive Committee, has taken a formal position with respect to a number of

questions of legislative policy. These have included such subjects as an increase in the salaries of State Supreme Court justices; making attorneys notaries public; amending the Federal Career Compensation Act to apply to attorneys employed with the Armed Forces the same provisions for special pay and promotion available to members of other professions; improving pay scales of attorneys in state service; court reorganization; extending personal jurisdiction over nonresidents; allowing the recording of unwitnessed conveyances; use of deceased partners' names in firm names; revision of the law governing federal tax liens; law clerks for State Supreme Court justices; curtesy and dower; securities transfers by fiduciaries; jurisdiction of county courts over the administration of *inter vivos* trusts; special appropriations for research for the State Legislative Council.

(3) The standing committees, particularly the Committees on Legislation and Administration of Justice, and the sections have devoted considerable time to the study of legislation, the formulation of recommendations, and the support of various proposals. For example, the president reported in 1960 that the Committee on Legislation "has been extremely busy, and through its efforts in cooperation with other interested agencies has been instrumental in securing the passage of the Court Reorganization bill, the bill of the Judicial Council expanding personal jurisdiction, and at this recently resumed session a bill providing clerks for our Supreme Court, and other bills of importance to the administration of justice." A new subcommittee, on federal legislation, was set up by this committee following a study which found need for such a group "to deal with federal legislation affecting the practice of law, or lawyers as a class, or the jurisdiction, procedure and practice of the Federal courts and other Federal tribunals, or creation of new Federal courts or judgeships affecting this state, and comparable subjects. . . ." Furthermore, legislative recommendations and activities have not been confined to those standing committees with the express function in the by-laws of considering legislative proposals. Many of the positions on legislation taken on behalf of the State Bar by the Board of Governors or the Executive Committee have also followed studies and recommendations by the sections.

(4) A number of special committees have been constituted, either *ad hoc* to consider particular legislative proposals, or to perform continuing functions which may involve the consideration of legislation. Thus special committees have considered such subjects as extension of personal jurisdiction over nonresidents, law clerks for State Supreme Court justices, and revision of the federal tax lien laws. The Special Committee on World Peace through Law, which

has encouraged the formation of similar committees on the local level, has sponsored debates on subjects such as the repeal of the Connally reservation, believing that "the general knowledge of laymen as well as of lawyers concerning the possibility of world peace through law is limited and requires a constant program of education and discussion."

(5) The Wisconsin Bar Bulletin, sent to each member, prints articles suggesting changes in state and federal law. And other publications of the State Bar deal with the progress of legislation.

But it seems plain that legislative activity is not the major activity of the State Bar. The activities without apparent political coloration are many. The Supreme Court provided in an appendix to the opinion below, "an analysis of [State Bar] . . . activities and the public purpose served thereby." The court found that "The most extensive activities of the State Bar are those directed toward postgraduate education of lawyers," and that "Postgraduate education of lawyers is in the public interest because it promotes the competency of lawyers to handle the legal matters entrusted to them by those of the general public who employ them." It found that the State Bar's participation in the handling of grievances improved the efficiency and effectiveness of this work. It found that the public interest was furthered by the Committee on Unauthorized Practice of Law which was carrying on "a constant program since numerous trades and occupations keep expanding their services and frequently start offering services which constitutue the practice of the law." The court also concluded that the Legal Aid Committee had "done effective and noteworthy work to encourage the local bar associations of the state to set up legal-aid systems in their local communities. . . . Such committee has also outlined recommended procedures for establishing and carrying through such systems of providing legal aid." In the field of public relations the court found that the "chief activity" of the State Bar was the "preparation, publication and distribution to the general public of pamphlets dealing with various transactions and happenings with which laymen are frequently confronted, which embody legal problems." Moreover, a number of studies have been made of programs, not involving political action, to further the economic well-being of the profession.

This examination of the purposes and functions of the State Bar shows its multifaceted character, in fact as well as in conception. In our view the case presents a claim of impingement upon freedom of association no different from that which we decided in *Railway Employees Dept.* v. *Hanson,* 351 U.S. 225. We there held that § 2, Eleventh of the Railway Labor Act, 45 U.S.C. § 152, Eleventh, did not on its face abridge protected rights of association in authorizing union-shop agreements between interstate railroads and unions of their employees conditioning the employees' continued employment on payment of union dues, initiation fees and assessments. There too the record indicated that the organizations engaged in some activities similar to the legislative activities of which the appellant complains. . . . In rejecting Hanson's claim of abridgment of his rights of freedom of association, we said, "On the present record, there is no more an infringement or impairment of First Amendment rights than there would be in the case of a lawyer who by state law is required to be a member of an integrated bar." Both in purport and in practice the bulk of State Bar activities serve the function, or at least so Wisconsin might reasonably believe, of elevating the educational and ethical standards of the Bar to the end of improving the quality of the legal service available to the people of the State, without any reference to the political process. It cannot be denied that this is a legitimate end of state policy. We think that the Supreme Court of Wisconsin, in order to further the State's legitimate interests in raising the quality of professional services, may constitutionally require that the costs of improving the profession in this fashion should be shared by the subjects and beneficiaries of the regulatory program, the lawyers, even though the organization created to attain the objective also engages in some legislative activity. Given the character of the integrated bar shown on this record, in the light of the limitation of the membership requirement to the compulsory payment of reasonable annual dues, we are unable to find any impingement upon protected rights of association.

However appellant would have us go farther and decide whether his constitutional rights of free speech are infringed if his dues money is used to support the political activities of the State Bar. The State Supreme Court treated the case as raising the question whether First Amendment rights were violated "because part of his dues money is used to support causes to which he is opposed." The Court in rejecting appellant's argument reasoned that "[t]he right to practice law is not a right but is a privilege subject to regulation. . . . The only limitation upon the state's power to regulate the privilege of the practice of law is that the regulations adopted do not impose an unconstitutional burden or deny due process." The Court found no such burden because ". . . the public welfare will be promoted by securing and publicizing the composite judgment of the members of the bar of the state on measures directly affecting the administration of justice and the practice of law. The general public and the legislature are entitled to know how the profession as a whole stands on such type of proposed legislation. . . . The only challenged interference with his liberty is the exaction of annual dues to the State Bar, in the nature of the imposition of an annual license fee, not unreasonable or unduly burdensome in amount, part of which is used to advocate causes to which he is opposed. However, this court, in which is vested the power of the state to regulate the practice of law, has determined that it promotes the public interest to have public expression of the views of a majority of the lawyers of the state, with respect to legislation affecting the administration of justice and the practice of law, the same to be voiced through their own democratically chosen representatives comprising the board of governors of the State Bar. The public interest so promoted far outweighs the slight inconvenience to the plaintiff resulting from his required payment of the annual dues."

We are persuaded that on this record we have no sound basis for deciding appellant's constitutional claim insofar as it rests on the assertion that his rights of free speech are violated by the use of his money for causes which he opposes. Even if the demurrer is taken as admitting all the factual allegations of the complaint, even if these allegations are construed most expansively, and even if, like the Wisconsin Supreme Court, we take judicial notice of the political activities of the State Bar, still we think that the issue of impingement upon rights of free speech through the use of exacted dues is no more concretely presented for adjudication than it was in *Hanson*. . . . Nowhere are we clearly apprised as to the views of the appellant on any particular legislative issues on which the State Bar has taken a position, or as to the way in which and the degree to which funds compulsorily exacted from its members are used to support the organization's political activities. There is an allegation in the complaint that the State Bar had "used its employees, property and funds in active unsolicited opposition to the adoption of legislation by the Legislature of the State of Wisconsin which was favored by the plaintiff, all contrary to the plaintiff's convictions and beliefs," but there is no indication of the nature of this legislation, nor of appellant's views on particular proposals, nor of whether any of his dues were used to support the State Bar's positions. There is an allegation that the State Bar's revenues amount to about $90,000 a year, of which $80,000 is derived from dues, but there is no indication in the record as to how political expenditures are financed and how much has been expended for political causes to which appellant objects. The facts of which the Supreme Court took judicial notice do not enlighten us on these gaps in the record. The minutes of the Board of Governors and Executive Committee of the State Bar show that the organization has taken one position or another on a wide variety of issues, but those minutes give no indication of appellant's views as to any of such issues or of what portions of the expenditure of funds to propagate the State Bar's views may be properly apportioned to his dues payments. Nor do the other publications of the State Bar. The Supreme Court assumed, as apparently the trial court did in passing on the demurrer, that the appellant was personally opposed to some of the legislation supported by the State Bar. But its opinion still gave no description of any specific measures he opposed, or the extent to which the State Bar actually utilized dues funds for specific purposes to which he had objected. Appellant's phrasing of the question presented on appeal in this Court is not responsive to any of these inquiries as to facts which may be relevant to the determination of constitutional questions surrounding the political expenditures. It merely asks whether a requirement of financial support of an association which "among other things uses its property, funds and employees for the purpose of influencing a broad range of legislation and public opinion" can be constitutionally imposed on him. This statement of the question, just as does his complaint, appears more a claim of the right to be free from compelled financial support of the organization because of its political activities, than a challenge by appellant to the use of his dues money for particular political causes of which he disapproves. Moreover, although the court below purported to decide as against all Fourteenth Amendment claims that the appellant could be compelled to pay his annual dues, even though "part of [it] . . . is used to advocate causes to which he is opposed," on oral argument here appellant disclaimed any necessity to show that he had opposed the position of the State Bar on any particular issue and asserted that it was sufficient that he opposed the use of his money for any political purposes at all. In view of the state of the record and this disclaimer, we think that we would not be justified in passing on the constitutional question considered below. "[T]he questions involving the power of . . . [the State] come here not so shaped by the record and by the proceedings below as to bring those powers before this Court as leanly and as sharply as judicial judgment upon an exercise of . . . [state] power requires." *United States* v. *C.I.O.*, 335 U.S. 106, 126 (concurring opinion). . . .

We, therefore, intimate no view as to the correctness of the conclusion of the Wisconsin Supreme Court that the appellant may constitutionally be compelled to contribute his financial support to political activities which he opposes. That issue is reserved, just as it was in *Hanson*, see *Street*, pp. 5–8. Upon this understanding we four vote to affirm. Since three of our colleagues are of the view that the claim which we do not decide is properly here and has no merit, and on that ground affirm, the judgment of the Wisconsin Supreme Court is affirmed.

Mr. Justice Douglas, dissenting:

The question in the present case concerns the power of a State to compel lawyers to belong to a statewide bar association, the organization commonly referred to in this country as the "integrated bar." There can be no doubt that lawyers, like doctors and dentists, can be required to pass examinations that test their character and their fitness to practice the profession. No question of that nature is presented. There is also no doubt that a State for cause shown can deprive a lawyer of his license. No question of that kind is involved in the present case. The sole question is the extent of the power of a State over a lawyer who rebels at becoming a member of the integrated bar and paying dues to support activities that are offensive to him. Thus the First Amendment, made applicable to the States by the Fourteenth, is brought into play. And for the reasons stated by Mr. Justice Black, I think all issues in the case are ripe for decision.

If the State can compel all lawyers to join a guild, I see no reason why it cannot make the same requirement of doctors, dentists, and nurses. They too have responsibilities to the public; and they also have interests beyond making a living. The groups whose activities are or may be deemed affected with a public interest are indeed numerous. Teachers are an obvious example. Insurance agents, brokers, and pharmacists have long been under licensing requirements or supervisory regimes. As the interdependency of each person on the other increases with the complexities of modern society, the circle of people performing vital services increases. Precedents once established often gain momentum by the force of their existence. Doctrine has a habit of following the path of inexorable logic.

We established no such precedent in *Railway Employes' Dept.* v. *Hanson,* 351 U.S. 225. We dealt there only with a problem in collective bargaining, *viz.,* is it beyond legislative competence to require all who benefit from the process of collective bargaining and enjoy its fruits to contribute to its costs? We held that the evil of those who are "free riders" may be so disruptive of labor relations and therefore so fraught with danger to the movement of commerce that Congress has the power to permit a union-shop agreement that exacts from each beneficiary his share of the cost of getting increased wages and improved working conditions. The power of a State to manage its internal affairs by requiring a union-shop agreement would seem to be as great.

In the *Hanson* case we said, to be sure, that if a lawyer could be required to join an integrated bar, an employee could be compelled to join a union shop. But on reflection the analogy fails.

Of course any group purports to serve a group cause. A medical association that fights socialized medicine protects the fees of the profession. Yet not even an immediate cause of that character is served by the integrated bar. Its contribution is in policing the members of the legal profession and in promoting what the majority of the Bar thinks is desirable legislation.

The Supreme Court of Wisconsin said that the integrated bar, unlike a voluntary bar association, was confined in its legislative activities. Though the Wisconsin Bar was active in the legislative field, it was restricted to administration of justice, court reform, and legal practice. The court however added:

The plaintiff complains that certain proposed legislation, upon which the State Bar has taken a stand, embody changes in substantive law, and points to the recently enacted Family Code. Among other things, such measure made many changes in divorce procedure, and, therefore, legal practice. We do not deem that the State Bar should be compelled to refrain from taking a stand on a measure which does substantially deal with legal practice and the administration of justice merely because it also makes some changes in substantive law.

It is difficult for me to see how the State can compel even that degree of subservience of the individual to the group.

It is true that one of the purposes of the State Bar Association is "to safeguard the proper professional interests of the members of the bar." State Bar of Wisconsin, Rule 1, § 2. In this connection, the association has been active in exploiting the monopoly position given by the licensed character of the profession. Thus, the Bar has compiled and published a schedule of recommended minimum fees. . . . Along the same line, the Committee on Unauthorized Practice of the State Bar, along with a Committee on Interprofessional and Business Relations, have been set up to police activities by nonprofessionals within "the proper scope of the practice of law." . . .

Yet this is a far cry from the history which stood behind the decision of Congress to foster the well-established institution of collection bargaining as one of the means of preserving industrial peace. That history is partially crystallized in the language of the Wagner and Taft-Hartley Acts: "Experience has proved that protection by law of the right of employees to organize and bargain collectively safeguards commerce . . . by encouraging practices fundamental to the friendly adjustment of industrial disputes arising out of differences as to wages, hours, or other working conditions, and by restoring equality of bargaining power between employers and employees." National Labor Relations Act, as amended by the Taft-Hartley Act, 61 Stat. 136, 29 U.S.C. § 151. It was with this history in mind that we spoke when we said that "One would have to be blind to history to assert that trade unionism did not enhance and strengthen the right to work." *Railway Employes' Dept.* v. *Hanson, supra.*

Nor can the present association be defended on grounds that it renders only public services.

If we had here a law which required lawyers to contribute to a fund out of which clients would be paid in case attorneys turned out to be embezzlers, the present objection might not be relevant. In that case one risk of the profession would be distributed among all members of the group. The fact that a dissident member did not feel he had within him the seeds of an embezzler might not bar a levy on the whole profession for one sad but notorious risk of the profession. We would also have a different case if lawyers were assessed to raise money to finance the defense of indigents. Cf. *In re Florida Bar*, 62 So. 2d. 20. That would be an imposition of a duty on the calling which partook of service to the public. Here the objection strikes deeper. An attorney objects to a forced association with a group that demands his money for the promotion of causes with which he disagrees, from which he obtains no gain, and which is not a part and parcel of service owing litigants or courts.

The right of association is an important incident of First Amendment rights. The right to belong—or not to belong—is deep in the American tradition. Joining is one method of expression. This freedom of association is not an absolute. For as I have noted in my opinion in *International Assn. of Machinists* v. *Street, ante,* decided this day, the necessities of life put us into relations with others that may be undesirable or even abhorrent, if individual standards were to obtain. Yet if this right is to be curtailed by law, if the individual is to be compelled to associate with others in a common cause, then I think exceptional circumstances should be shown. I would treat laws of this character like any that touch on First Amendment rights. Congestion of traffic, street fights, riots and such may justify curtailment of opportunities or occasions to speak freely. Cf. *Chaplinsky* v. *New Hampshire,* 315 U.S. 568. But when those laws are sustained, we require them to be "narrowly drawn" (*Cantwell* v. *Connecticut,* 310 U.S. 296) so as to be confined to the precise evil within the competence of the legislature. . . . There is here no evil shown. It has the mark of "a lawyer class or caste"—the system of "a self-governing and self-disciplining bar" such as England has. The pattern of this legislation is regimentation. The inroads of an integrated bar on the liberty and freedom of lawyers to espouse such causes as they choose was emphasized by William D. Guthrie of the New York Bar:

> The idea seems to be, contrary to all human experience, that if power be vested in this at present unknown and untried as well as indifferent outside body, holding themselves aloof from their profession, they will somehow become inspired with a high professional sentiment or sense of duty and cooperation and will unselfishly exercise their majority power for the good of their profession and the public, that they can be trusted to choose as their officers and leaders lawyers of the type who are now leaders, that the responsibility of power will necessarily sober and elevate their minds, and finally that democracy calls for the rule of the majority.
>
> Thus, the traditions and ethics of our great profession would be left to the mercy of mere numbers officially authorized to speak for us! This would be adopting all the vices of democracy without the reasonable hope in common sense of securing any of its virtues. It would be forcing the democratic dogma of mass or majority rule to a dangerous and pernicious extreme.
>
> Although in political democracy the rule of the majority is necessary, the American system of democracy is based upon the recognition of the imperative necessity of limitations upon the will of the majority. In the proposed compulsory or involuntary incorporation of the bar, there would be no limitation whatever, and the best sentiments and traditions of the profession, of the public-spirited and high-minded

lawyers who are now active in the voluntary bar associations of the state, could be wholly and wantonly disregarded and overruled.

This regimentation appears in humble form today. Yet we know that the Bar and Bench do not move to a single "nonpartisan" objective. The obvious fact that they are not so motivated is plain from *Cohen* v. *Hurley*, 366 U.S. 117, which we decided only the other day. Once we approve this measure we sanction a device where men and women in almost any profession or calling can be at least partially regimented behind causes which they oppose. I look on the *Hanson* case as a narrow exception to be closely confined. Unless we so treat it, we practically give *carte blanche* to any legislature to put at least professional people into goose-stepping brigades. Those brigades are not compatible with the First Amendment. While the legislature has few limits where strictly social legislation is concerned (*Giboney* v. *Empire Storage Co.*, 336 U.S. 490; *Tot* v. *United States*, 319 U.S. 463) the First Amendment applies strictures designed to keep our society from becoming moulded into patterns of conformity which satisfy the majority.

NATIONAL ASSN. FOR ADVANCEMENT OF
COLORED PEOPLE *v.* BUTTON
371 US 415 (1963)

[In the case as it finally reached the United States Supreme Court, what was involved was the constitutionality of a statute of Virginia, adopted in 1956, which made it a crime for the NAACP to advise a person that his legal rights have been infringed and to refer him to a particular attorney or group of attorneys for assistance, or knowingly to render legal assistance to the person thus referred. In a 6-to-3 decision, the Court held the statute unconstitutional as a restriction on the NAACP's freedom of expression and of association.

[Justice Douglas wrote a concurring opinion. Justice White, in a separate opinion, agreed that the statute was unconstitutional but expressed the view that a narrowly drawn statute would be constitutional. Justice Harlan—joined by Justices Clark and Stewart—dissented on the ground that the statute constitutionally regulated the litigating activities of the NAACP.]

Mr. Justice Brennan delivered the opinion of the Court:

This case originated in companion suits by the National Association for the Advancement of Colored People, Inc. (N.A.A.C.P.) and the N.A.A.C.P. Legal Defense and Educational Fund, Inc. (Defense Fund), brought in 1957 in the United States District Court for the Eastern District of Virginia. The suits sought to restrain the enforcement of Chapters 31, 32, 33, 35 and 36 of the Virginia Acts of Assembly, 1956 Extra Session, on the ground that the statutes, as applied to the activities of the plaintiffs, violated the Fourteenth Amendment. A three-judge court convened pursuant to 28 USC § 2281, after hearing evidence and making factfindings, struck down Chapters 31, 32 and 35 but abstained from passing upon the validity of Chapters 33 and 36 pending an authoritative interpretation of these statutes by the Virginia courts. The complainants thereupon petitioned in the Circuit Court of the City of Richmond to declare Chapters 33 and 36 inapplicable to their activities, or, if applicable, unconstitutional. The record in the Circuit Court was that made before the three-judge court supplemented by additional evidence. The Circuit Court held the chapters to be both applicable and constitutional. The holding was sustained by the Virginia Supreme Court of Appeals as to Chapter 33, but reversed as to Chapter 36, which was held unconstitutional under both state and federal law. Thereupon the Defense Fund returned to the Federal District Court, where its case is presently pending, while the N.A.A.C.P. filed the instant petition. We granted certiorari. We heard argument in the 1961 Term and ordered reargument this Term. Since no cross-petition was filed to review the Supreme Court of Appeals' disposition of Chapter 36, the only issue before us is the constitutionality of Chapter 33 as applied to the activities of the N.A.A.C.P.

There is no substantial dispute as to the facts; the dispute centers about the constitutionality under the Fourteenth Amendment of Chapter 33, as construed and applied by the Virginia Supreme Court of Appeals to include N.A.A.C.P.'s activities within the statute's ban against "the improper solicitation of any legal business."

The N.A.A.C.P. was formed in 1909 and incorporated under New York law as a nonprofit membership corporation in 1911. It maintains its headquarters in New York and presently has some 1,000 active unincorporated branches throughout the Nation. The corporation is licensed to do business in Virginia, and has 89 branches there. The Virginia branches are organized into the Virginia State Conference of N.A.A.C.P. Branches (the Conference), an unincorporated association, which in 1957 had some 13,500 members. The activities of the Conference are financed jointly by the national organization and the local branches from contributions and membership dues. N.A.A.C.P. policy, binding upon local branches and conferences, is set by the annual national convention.

The basic aims and purposes of N.A.A.C.P. are to secure the elimination of all racial barriers which deprive Negro citizens of the privileges and burdens of equal citizenship rights in the United States. To this end the Association engages in extensive educational and lobbying activities. It also devotes much of its funds and energies to an extensive program of assisting certain kinds of litigation on behalf of its declared purposes.

For more than 10 years, the Virginia Conference has concentrated upon financing litigation aimed at ending racial segregation in the public schools of the Commonwealth.

The Conference ordinarily will finance only cases in which the assisted litigant retains an N.A.A.C.P. staff lawyer to represent him. The Conference maintains a legal staff of 15 attorneys, all of whom are Negroes and members of the N.A.A.C.P. The staff is elected at the Conference's annual convention. Each legal staff member must agree to abide by the policies of the N.A.A.C.P., which, insofar as they pertain to professional services, limit the kinds of litigation which the N.A.A.C.P. will assist. Thus the N.A.A.C.P. will not underwrite ordinary damages actions, criminal actions in which the defendant raises no question of possible racial discrimination, or suits in which the plaintiff seeks separate but equal rather than fully desegregated public school facilities. The staff decides whether a litigant, who may or may not be an N.A.A.C.P. member, is entitled to N.A.A.C.P. assistance. The Conference defrays all expenses of litigation in an assisted case, and usually, although not always, pays each lawyer on the case a per diem fee not to exceed $60, plus out-of-pocket expenses. The assisted litigant receives no money from the Conference or the staff lawyers. The staff member may not accept, from the litigant or any other source, any other compensation for his services in an N.A.A.C.P.-assisted case. None of the staff receives a salary or retainer from the N.A.A.C.P.; the per diem fee is paid only for professional services in a particular case. This per diem payment is smaller than the compensation ordinarily received for equivalent private professional work. The actual conduct of assisted litigation is under the control of the attorney, although the N.A.A.C.P. continues to be concerned that the outcome of the lawsuit should be consistent with N.A.A.C.P.'s policies already described. A client is free at any time to withdraw from an action.

The members of the legal staff of the Virginia Conference and other N.A.A.C.P. or Defense Fund lawyers called in by the staff to assist are drawn into litigation in various ways. One is for an aggrieved Negro to apply directly to the Conference or the legal staff for assistance. His application is referred to the Chairman of the legal staff. The Chairman, with the concurrence of the President of the Conference, is authorized to agree to give legal assistance in an appropriate case. In litigation involving public school segregation, the procedure tends to be different. Typically, a local N.A.A.C.P. branch will invite a member of the legal staff to explain to a meeting of parents and children the legal steps necessary to achieve desegregation. The staff member will bring printed forms to the meeting authorizing him, and other N.A.A.C.P. or Defense Fund attorneys of his designation, to represent the signers in legal proceedings to achieve desegregation. On occasion, blank forms have been signed by litigants, upon the understanding that a member or members of the legal staff, with or without assistance from other N.A.A.C.P. lawyers, or from the Defense Fund, would handle the case. It is usual, after obtaining authorizations, for the staff lawyer to bring into the case the other staff members in the area where suit is to be brought, and sometimes to bring in lawyers from the national organization or the Defense Fund. In effect, then, the prospective litigant retains not so much a particular attorney as the "firm" of N.A.A.C.P. and Defense Fund lawyers, which has a corporate reputation for expertness in presenting and arguing the difficult questions of law that frequently arise in civil rights litigation.

These meetings are sometimes prompted by letters and bulletins from the Conference urging active steps to fight segregation. The Conference has on occasion distributed to the local branches petitions for desegregation to be signed by parents and filed with local school boards, and advised branch officials to obtain, as petitioners, persons willing to "go all the way" in any possible litigation that may ensue. While the Conference in these ways encourages the bringing of lawsuits, the plaintiffs in particular actions, so far as appears, make their own decisions to become such.

Statutory regulation of unethical and nonprofessional conduct by attorneys has been in force in Virginia since 1849. These provisions outlaw, inter alia, solicitation of legal business in the form of "running" or "capping." Prior to 1956, however, no attempt was made to proscribe under such regulations the activities of the N.A.A.C.P., which had been carried on openly for many years in substantially the manner described. In 1956, however, the legislature amended, by the addition of Chapter 33, the provisions of the Virginia Code forbidding solicitation of legal business by a "runner" or "capper" to include, in the definition of "runner" or "capper," an agent for an individual or organization which retains a lawyer in connection with an action to which it is not a party and in which it has no pecuniary right or liability. The Virginia Supreme Court of Appeals held that the chapter's purpose "was to strengthen the existing statutes to further control the evils of solicitation of legal business. . . ." The court held that the activities of N.A.A.C.P., the Virginia Conference, the Defense Fund, and the lawyers furnished by them, fell within, and could constitutionally be proscribed by, the chapter's expanded definition of improper solicitation of legal business, and also violated Canons 35 and 47 of the American Bar Association's Canons of Professional Ethics, which the court had adopted in 1938. Specifically the court held that, under the expanded definition, such activities on the part of N.A.A.C.P., the Virginia Conference, and the Defense Fund constituted "fomenting and soliciting legal business in which they are not parties and have no pecuniary right or liability, and which they channel to the enrichment of certain lawyers employed by them, at no cost to the litigants and over which the litigants have no control." Finally, the court restated the decree of the Richmond Circuit Court. . . .

II.

Petitioner challenges the decision of the Supreme Court of Appeals on many grounds. But we reach only one: that Chapter 33 as construed and applied abridges the freedoms of the First Amendment, protected against state action by the Fourteenth. More specifically, petitioner claims that the chapter infringes the right of the N.A.A.C.P. and its members and lawyers to associate for the purpose of assisting persons who seek legal redress for infringements of their constitutionally guaranteed and other rights. We think petitioner may assert this right on its own behalf, because, though a corporation, it is directly engaged in those activities, claimed to be constitutionally protected, which the statute would curtail. Cf. *Grosjean* v. *American Press Co.*, 297 US 233. We also think petitioner has standing to assert the corresponding rights of its members. See *National Asso. for Advancement of Colored People* v. *Alabama*, 357 US 449; *Bates* v. *Little Rock*, 361 US 516; *Louisiana ex rel. Gremillion* v. *National Asso. for Advancement of Colored People*, 366 US 293.

We reverse the judgment of the Virginia Supreme Court of Appeals. We hold that the activities of the N.A.A.C.P., its affiliates and legal staff shown on this record are modes of expression and association protected by the First and Fourteenth Amendments which Virginia may not prohibit, under its power to regulate the legal profession, as improper solicitation of legal business violative of Chapter 33 and the Canons of Professional Ethics.

A.

We meet at the outset the contention that "solicitation" is wholly outside the area of freedoms protected by the First Amendment. To this contention there are two answers. The first is that a state cannot foreclose the exercise of constitutional rights by mere labels. The second is that abstract discussion is not the only species of communication which the Constitution protects; the First Amendment also protects vigorous advocacy, certainly of lawful ends, against governmental intrusion. . . . In the context of N.A.A.C.P. objectives, litigation is not a technique of resolving private differences; it is a means for achieving the lawful objectives of equality of treatment by all governmental, federal, state and local, for the members of the Negro community in this country. It is thus a form of political expression. Groups which find themselves unable to achieve their objectives through the ballot frequently turn to the courts. Just as it was true of the opponents of New Deal legislation during the 1930's, for example, no less is it true of the Negro minority today. And under the conditions of modern government, litigation may well be the sole practicable avenue open to a minority to petition for redress of grievances.

We need not, in order to find constitutional protection for the kind of cooperative, organizational activity disclosed by this record, whereby Negroes seek through lawful means to achieve legitimate political ends, subsume such activity under a narrow, literal conception of freedom of speech, petition or assembly. For there is no longer any doubt that the First and Fourteenth Amendments protect certain forms of orderly group activity. Thus we have affirmed the right "to engage in association for the advancement of beliefs and ideas." *National Asso. for Advancement of Colored People* v. *Alabama, supra.* We have deemed privileged, under certain circumstances, the efforts of a union official to organize workers. *Thomas* v. *Collins,* 323 US 516. We have said that the Sherman Act does not apply to certain concerted activities of railroads "at least insofar as those activities comprised mere solicitation of governmental action with respect to the passage and enforcement of laws" because "such a construction of the Sherman Act would raise important constitutional questions," specifically, First Amendment questions. *Eastern R. Presidents Conference* v. *Noerr Motor Freight, Inc.,* 365 US 127. And we have refused to countenance compelled disclosure of a person's political associations in language closely applicable to the instant case:

Our form of government is built on the premise that every citizen shall have the right to engage in political expression and association. This right was enshrined in the First Amendment of the Bill of Rights. Exercise of these basic freedoms in America has traditionally been through the media of political associations. Any interference with the freedom of a party is simultaneously an interference with the freedom of its adherents. All political ideas cannot and should not be channeled into the programs of our two major parties. History has amply proved the virtue of political activity by minority, dissident groups. . . . *Sweezy* v. *New Hampshire,* 354 US 234 (plurality opinion). Cf. *De Jonge* v. *Oregon,* 299 US 353.

The N.A.A.C.P. is not a conventional political party; but the litigation it assists, while serving to vindicate the legal rights of members of the American Negro community, at the same time and perhaps more importantly, makes possible the distinctive contribution of a minority group to the ideas and beliefs of our society. For such a group, association for litigation may be the most effective form of political association.

B.

Our concern is with the impact of enforcement of Chapter 33 upon First Amendment freedoms. We start, of course, from the decree of the Supreme Court of Appeals. Although the action before it was one basically for declaratory relief, that court not only expounded the purpose and reach of the chapter but held concretely that certain of petitioner's activities had, and certain others had not, violated the chapter. These activities had been explored in detail at the trial and were spread out plainly on the record. We have no doubt that the opinion of the Supreme Court of Appeals in the instant case was intended as a full and authoritative construction of Chapter 33 as applied in a detailed factual context. That construction binds us. For us, the words of Virginia's highest court are the words of the statute. . . . We are not left to speculate at large upon the possible implications of bare statutory language.

But it does not follow that this Court now has only a clear-cut task to decide whether the activities of the petitioner deemed unlawful by the Supreme Court of Appeals are constitutionally privileged. If the line drawn by the decree between the permitted and prohibited activities of the N.A.A.C.P., its members and lawyers is an ambiguous one, we will not presume that the statute curtails constitutionally protected activity as little as possible. For standards of permissible statutory vagueness are strict in the area of free expression. . . . Furthermore, the instant decree may be invalid if it prohibits privileged exercises of First Amendment rights whether or not the record discloses that the petitioner has engaged in privileged conduct. For in appraising a statute's inhibitory effect upon such rights, this Court has not hesitated to take into account possible applications of the statute in other factual contexts besides that at bar. . . . It makes no difference that the instant case was not a criminal prosecution and not based on a refusal to comply with a licensing requirement. The objectionable quality of vagueness and overbreadth does not depend upon absence of fair notice to a criminally accused or upon unchanneled delegation of legislative powers, but upon the danger of tolerating, in the area of First Amendment freedoms, the existence of a penal statute susceptible of sweeping and improper application. . . . These freedoms are delicate and vulnerable, as well as supremely precious in our society. The threat of sanctions may deter their exercise almost as potently as the actual application of sanctions. . . . Because First Amendment freedoms need breathing space to survive, government may regulate in the area only with narrow specificity. . . .

We read the decree of the Virginia Supreme Court of Appeals in the instant case as proscribing any arrangement by which prospective litigants are advised to seek the assistance of particular attorneys. No narrower reading is plausible. We cannot accept the reading suggested on behalf of the Attorney General of Virginia on the second oral argument that the Supreme Court of Appeals construed Chapter 33 as proscribing control only of the actual litigation by the N.A.A.C.P. after it is instituted. In the first place, upon a record devoid of any evidence of interference by the N.A.A.C.P. in the actual conduct of litigation, or neglect or harrassment of clients, the court nevertheless held that petitioner, its members, agents and staff attorneys had practiced criminal solicitation. Thus, simple referral to or recommendation of a lawyer may be solicitation within the meaning of Chapter 33. In the second place, the decree does not seem to rest on the fact that the attorneys were organized as a staff and paid by petitioner. The decree expressly forbids solicitation on behalf of "any particular attorneys" in addition to attorneys retained or compensated by the N.A.A.C.P. In the third place, although Chapter 33 purports to prohibit only solicitation by attorneys or their "agents," it defines agent broadly as anyone who "represents" another in his dealings with a third person. Since the statute appears to depart from the common-law concept of the agency relationship and since the Virginia court did not clarify the statutory definition, we cannot say that it will not be applied with the broad sweep which the statutory language imports.

We conclude that under Chapter 33, as authoritatively construed by the Supreme Court of Appeals, a person who advises another that his legal rights have been infringed and refers him to a particular attorney or group of attorneys (for example, to the Virginia Conference's legal staff) for assistance has committed a crime, as has the attorney who knowingly renders assistance under such circumstances. There thus inheres in the statute the gravest danger of smothering all discussion looking to the eventual institution of litigation on behalf of the rights of members of an unpopular minority. Lawyers on the legal staff or even mere N.A.A.C.P. members or sympathizers would understandably hesitate, at an N.A.A.C.P. meeting or on any other occasion, to do what the decree purports to allow, namely, acquaint "persons with what they believe to be their legal rights and . . . [advise] them to assert their rights by commencing or further prosecuting a suit. . . ." For if the lawyers, members or sympathizers also appeared in or had any connection with any litigation supported with N.A.A.C.P. funds contributed under the provision of the decree by which the N.A.A.C.P. is not prohibited "from contributing money to persons to assist them in commencing or further prosecuting such suits," they plainly would risk (if lawyers) disbarment proceedings and, lawyers and nonlawyers alike, criminal prosecution for the offense of "solicitation," to which the Virginia court gave so broad and uncertain a meaning. It makes no difference whether such prosecutions or proceedings would actually be commenced. It is enough that a vague and broad statute lends itself to selective enforcement against unpopular causes. We cannot close our eyes to the fact that the militant Negro civil rights movement has engendered the intense resentment and opposition of the politically dominant white community of Virginia, litigation assisted by the N.A.A.C.P. has been bitterly fought. In such circumstances, a statute broadly curtailing group activity leading to litigation may easily become a weapon of oppression, however evenhanded its terms appear. Its mere existence could well freeze out of existence all such activity on behalf of the civil rights of Negro citizens.

It is apparent, therefore, that Chapter 33 as construed limits First Amendment freedoms. As this Court said in *Thomas* v. *Collins*, 323 US 516, " 'Free trade in ideas' means free trade in the opportunity to persuade to action, not merely to describe facts." Thomas was convicted for delivering a speech in connection with an impending union election under National Labor Relations Board auspices, without having first registered as a "labor organizer." He urged workers to exercise their rights under the National Labor Relations Act and join the union he represented. This Court held that the registration requirement as applied to his activities was constitutionally invalid. In the instant case, members of the N.A.A.C.P. urged Negroes aggrieved by the allegedly unconstitutional segregation of public schools in Virginia to exercise their legal rights and to retain members of the Association's legal staff. Like Thomas, the Association and its members were advocating lawful means of vindicating legal rights.

We hold that Chapter 33 as construed violates the Fourteenth Amendment by unduly inhibiting protected freedoms of expression and association. In so holding, we reject two further contentions of respondents. The first is that the Virginia Supreme Court of Appeals has guaranteed free expression by expressly confirming petitioner's right to continue its advocacy of civil-rights litigation. But in light of the whole decree of the court, the guarantee is of purely speculative value. As construed by the Court, Chapter 33, at least potentially, prohibits every cooperative activity that would make advocacy of litigation meaningful. If there is an internal tension between proscription and protection in the statute, we cannot assume that, in its subsequent enforcement, ambiguities will be resolved in favor of adequate protection of First Amendment rights. Broad prophylactic rules in the area of free expression are suspect. . . . Precision of regulation must be the touchstone in an area so closely touching our most precious freedoms.

C.

The second contention is that Virginia has a subordinating interest in the regulation of the legal profession, embodied in Chapter 33, which justifies limiting petitioner's First Amendment rights. Specifically, Virginia contends that the N.A.A.C.P.'s activities in furtherance of litigation, being "improper solicitation" under the state statute, fall within the traditional purview of state regulation of professional conduct. However, the State's attempt to equate the activities of the N.A.A.C.P. and its lawyers with common-law barratry, maintenance and champerty, and to outlaw them accordingly, cannot obscure the serious encroachment worked by Chapter 33 upon protected freedoms of expression. The decisions of this Court have consistently held that only a compelling state interest in the regulation of a subject within the State's constitutional power to regulate can justify limiting First Amendment freedoms. Thus it is no answer to the constitutional claims asserted by petitioners to say, as the Virginia Supreme Court of Appeals has said, that the purpose of these regulations was merely to insure high professional standards and not to curtail free expression. For a State may not, under the guise of prohibiting professional misconduct, ignore constitutional rights. . . .

However valid may be Virginia's interest in regulating the traditionally illegal practices of barratry, maintenance and champerty, that interest does not justify the prohibition of the N.A.A.C.P. activities disclosed by this record. Malicious intent was of the essence of the common-law offenses of fomenting or stirring up litigation. And whatever may be or may have been true of suits against government in other countries, the exercise in our own, as in this case, of First Amendment rights to enforce constitutional rights through litigation, as a matter of law, cannot be deemed malicious. Even more modern, subtler regulations of unprofessional conduct or interference with professional relations, not involving malice, would not touch the activities at bar; regulations which reflect hostility to stirring up litigation have been aimed chiefly at those who urge recourse to the courts for private gain, serving no public interest. Hostility still exists to stirring up private litigation where it promotes the use of legal machinery to oppress: as, for example, to sow discord in a family; to expose infirmities in land titles, as by hunting up claims of adverse possession; to harass large companies through a multiplicity of small claims; or to oppress debtors as by seeking out unsatisfied judgments. For a member of the bar to participate, directly or through intermediaries, in such misuses of the legal process is conduct traditionally condemned as injurious to the public. And beyond this, for a lawyer to attempt to reap gain by urging another to engage in private litigation has also been condemned: that seems to be the import of Canon 28, which the Virginia Supreme Court of Appeals has adopted as one of its Rules.

Objection to the intervention of a lay intermediary, who may control litigation or otherwise interfere with the rendering of legal services in a confidential relationship, also derives from the element of pecuniary gain. Fearful of dangers thought to arise from that element, the courts of several States have sustained regulations aimed at these activities. We intimate no view one way or the other as to the merits of those decisions with respect to the particular arrangements against which they are directed. It is enough that the superficial resemblance in form between those arrangements and that at bar cannot obscure the vital fact that here the entire arrangement employs constitutionally privileged means of expression to secure constitutionally guaranteed civil rights. There has been no showing of a serious danger here of professionally reprehensible conflicts of interest which rules against solicitation frequently seek to prevent. This is so partly because no monetary stakes are involved, and so there is no danger that the attorney will desert or subvert the paramount interests of his client to enrich himself or an outside sponsor. And the aims and interests of N.A.A.C.P. have not been shown to conflict with those of its members and non-member Negro litigants; . . .

Resort to the courts to seek vindication of constitutional rights is a different matter from the oppressive, malicious, or avaricious use of the legal process for purely private gain. Lawsuits attacking racial discrimination, at least in Virginia, are neither very profitable nor very popular. They are not an object of general competition among Virginia lawyers; the problem is rather one of an apparent dearth of lawyers who are willing to undertake such litigation. There has been neither claim nor proof that any assisted Negro litigants have desired, but have been prevented from retaining, the services of other counsel. We realize that an N.A.A.C.P. lawyer must derive personal satisfaction from participation in litigation on behalf of Negro rights, else he would hardly be inclined to participate at the risk of financial sacrifice. But this would not seem to be the kind of interest or motive which induces criminal conduct.

We conclude that although the petitioner has amply shown that its activities fall within the First Amendment's protections, the State has failed to advance any substantial regulatory interest, in the form of substantive evils flowing from petitioner's activities, which can justify the broad prohibitions which it has imposed. Nothing that this record shows as to the nature and purpose of N.A.A.C.P. actvities permits an inference of any injurious intervention in or control of litigation which would constitutionally authorize the application of Chapter 33 to those activities. A fortiori, nothing in this record justifies the breadth and vagueness of the Virginia Supreme Court of Appeals' decree.

A final observation is in order. Because our disposition is rested on the First Amendment as absorbed in the Fourteenth, we do not reach the considerations of race or racial discrimination which are the predicate of petitioner's challenge to the statute under the Equal Protection Clause. That the petitioner happens to be engaged in activities of expression and association on behalf of the rights of Negro children to equal opportunity is constitutionally irrelevant to the ground of our decision. The course of our decisions in the First Amendment area makes plain that its protections would apply as fully to those who would arouse our society against the objectives of the petitioner. . . . For the Constitution protects expression and association without regard to the race, creed, or political or religious affiliation of the members of the group which invokes its shield, or to the truth, popularity, or social utility of the ideas and beliefs which are offered.

Reversed.

★ III ★

Freedom of Speech and Press:

Some Basic Principles

1. *The Freedom* Not *to Speak*

WEST VIRGINIA STATE BOARD OF EDUCATION *v.* BARNETTE

319 US 624 (1943)

[In 1940 there came before the Supreme Court *Minersville School District* v. *Gobitis*, 310 US 586, in which the Court upheld the requirement of participation by pupils in public schools in the ceremony of saluting the national flag. The Court held that a pupil belonging to Jehovah's Witnesses could not constitutionally claim exemption from this requirement on the ground that the flag salute would violate her religious beliefs and scruples. Justice Stone was the only dissenter.

[This decision was widely attacked. Three years later, in the *Barnette Case*, the Court dramatically reversed itself and expressly overruled the *Gobitis* decision. Justices Roberts, Reed, and Frankfurter dissented. In the *Barnette Case* the majority decision was put on the broad ground that the compulsory flag salute was an invasion of the sphere of intellect and spirit—a sphere protected from official control by the First and Fourteenth Amendments. National unity may be fostered by persuasion and example, but there may be no coerced uniformity. The Constitution guarantees the freedom to differ even "as to things that touch the heart of the existing order." Citizens may not be forced "to confess by word or act" their faith in any "orthodox" politics, nationalism, religion, or other matters of opinion.

[Justice Frankfurter, dissenting, said that the remedy for the unwise legislation involved in this case was to be found in the legislature and not in the courts. Much legislation affecting freedom of thought and speech, he said, "should offend a free-spirited society" and is yet constitutional. "Reliance for the most precious interests of civilization, therefore, must be found outside of their vindication in courts of law. Only a persistent positive translation of the faith of a free society into the convictions and habits of a community is the ultimate reliance against unabated temptations to fetter the human spirit."]

Mr. Justice Jackson delivered the opinion of the Court:

Following the decision by this Court on June 3, 1940, in *Minersville School Dist.* v. *Gobitis,* 310 US 586, the West Virginia legislature amended its statutes to require all schools therein to conduct courses of instruction in history, civics, and in the Constitutions of the United States and of the State "for the purpose of teaching, fostering and perpetuating the ideals, principles and spirit of Americanism, and increasing the knowledge of the organization and machinery of the government." Appellant Board of Education was directed, with advice of the State Superintendent of Schools, to "prescribe the courses of study covering these subjects" for public schools. The Act made it the duty of private, parochial and denominational schools to prescribe courses of study "similar to those required for the public schools."

The Board of Education on January 9, 1942, adopted a resolution containing recitals taken largely from the Court's *Gobitis* opinion and ordering that the salute to the flag become "a regular part of the program of activities in the public schools," that all teachers and pupils "shall be required to participate in the salute honoring the Nation represented by the Flag; provided, however, that refusal to salute the Flag be regarded as an Act of insubordination, and shall be dealt with accordingly."

The resolution originally required the "commonly accepted salute to the Flag" which it defined. Objections to the salute as "being too much like Hitler's" were raised by the Parent and Teachers Association, the Boy and Girl Scouts, the Red Cross, and the Federation of Women's Clubs. Some modification appears to have been made in deference to these objections, but no concession was made to Jehovah's Witnesses. What is now required is the "stiff-arm" salute, the saluter to keep the right hand raised with palm turned up while the following is repeated: "I pledge allegiance to the Flag of the United States of America and to the Republic for which it stands; one Nation, indivisible, with liberty and justice for all."

Failure to conform is "insubordination" dealt with by expulsion. Readmission is denied by statute until compliance. Meanwhile the expelled child is "unlawfully absent" and may be proceeded against as a delinquent. His parents or guardians are liable to prosecution, and if convicted are subject to fine not exceeding $50 and jail term not exceeding thirty days.

Appellees, citizens of the United States and of West Virginia, brought suit in the United States District Court for themselves and others similarly situated asking its injunction to restrain enforcement of these laws and regulations against Jehovah's Witnesses. The Witnesses are an unincorporated body teaching that the obligation imposed by law of God is superior to that of laws enacted by temporal government. Their religious beliefs include a literal version of Exodus, Chapter 20, verses 4 and 5, which says: "Thou shalt not make unto thee any graven image, or any likeness of anything that is in heaven above, or that is in the earth beneath, or that is in the water under the earth; thou shalt not bow down thyself to them, nor serve them." They consider that the flag is an "image" within this command. For this reason they refuse to salute it.

Children of this faith have been expelled from school and are threatened with exclusion for no other cause. Officials threaten to send them to reformatories maintained for criminally inclined juveniles. Parents of such children have been prosecuted and are threatened with prosecutions for causing delinquency. . . .

This case calls upon us to reconsider a precedent decision, as the Court throughout its history often has been required to do. Before turning to the *Gobitis Case,* however, it is desirable to notice certain characteristics by which this controversy is distinguished.

The freedom asserted by these appellees does not bring them into collision with rights asserted by any other individuals. It is such conflicts which most frequently require intervention of the State to determine where the rights of one end and those of another begin. But the refusal of these persons to participate in the ceremony does not interfere with or deny rights of others to do so. Nor is there any question in this case that their behavior is peaceable and orderly. The sole conflict is between authority and rights of the individual. The State asserts power to condition access to public education on making a prescribed sign and profession and at the same time to coerce attendance by punishing both parent and child. The latter stand on a right of self-determination in matters that touch individual opinion and personal attitude.

As the present Chief Justice [Stone] said in dissent in the *Gobitis Case,* the State may "require teaching . . . in our history and in the structure and organization of our government, including the guaranties of civil liberty, which tend to inspire patriotism and love of country."

Here, however, we are dealing with a compulsion of students to declare a belief. They are not merely made acquainted with the flag salute so that they may be informed as to what it is or even what it means. The issue here is whether this slow and easily neglected route to aroused loyalties constitutionally may be short-cut by substituting a compulsory salute and slogan. This issue is not prejudiced by the Court's previous holding that where a State, without compelling attendance, extends college facilities to pupils who voluntarily enroll, it may prescribe military training as part of the course without offense to the Constitution. It was held that those who take advantage of its opportunities may not on ground of conscience refuse compliance with such conditions. *Hamilton* v. *University of California,* 293 US 245. In the present case attendance is not optional. That case is also to be distinguished from the present one because, independently of college privileges or requirements, the State has power to raise militia and impose the duties of service therein upon its citizens.

There is no doubt that, in connection with the pledges, the flag salute is a form of utterance. Symbolism is a primitive but effective way of communicating ideas. The use of an emblem or flag to symbolize some system, idea, institution, or personality, is a short cut from mind to mind. Causes and nations, political parties, lodges and ecclesiastical groups seek to knit the loyalty of their followings to a flag or banner, a color or design. The State announces rank, function, and authority through crowns and maces, uniforms and black robes; the church speaks through the Cross, the Crucifix, the altar and shrine, and clerical raiment. Symbols of State often convey political ideas just as religious symbols come to convey theological ones. Associated with many of these symbols are appropriate gestures of acceptance or respect: a salute, a bowed or bared head, a bended knee. A person gets from a symbol the meaning he puts into it, and what is one man's comfort and inspiration is another's jest and scorn.

Over a decade ago Chief Justice Hughes led this Court in holding that the display of a red flag as a symbol of opposition by peaceful and legal means to organized government was protected by the free speech guaranties of the Constitution. *Stromberg* v. *California,* 283 US 359. Here it is the State that employs a flag as a symbol of adherence to government as presently organized. It requires the individual to communicate by word and sign his acceptance of the political ideas it thus bespeaks. Objection to this form of communication when coerced is an old one, well known to the framers of the Bill of Rights.

It is also to be noted that the compulsory flag salute and pledge requires affirmation of a belief and an attitude of mind. It is not clear whether the regulation contemplates that pupils forego any contrary convictions of their own and become unwilling converts to the prescribed ceremony or whether it will be acceptable if they simulate assent by words without belief and by a gesture barren of meaning. It is now a commonplace that censorship or suppression of expression of opinion is tolerated by our Constitution only when the expression presents a clear and present danger of action of a kind the State is empowered to prevent and punish. It would seem that involuntary affirmation could be commanded only on even more immediate and urgent grounds than silence. But here the power of compulsion is invoked without any allegation that remaining passive during a flag salute ritual creates a clear and present danger that would justify an effort even to muffle expression. To sustain the compulsory flag salute we are required to say that a Bill of Rights which guards the individual's right to speak his own mind, left it open to public authorities to compel him to utter what is not in his mind.

Whether the First Amendment to the Constitution will permit officials to order observance of ritual of this nature does not depend upon whether as a voluntary exercise we would think it to be good, bad or merely innocuous. Any credo of nationalism is likely to include what some disapprove or to omit what others think essential, and to give off different overtones as it takes on different accents or interpretations. If official power exists to coerce acceptance of any patriotic creed, what it shall contain cannot be decided by courts, but must be largely discretionary with the ordaining authority, whose power to prescribe would no doubt include power to amend. Hence validity of the asserted power to force an American citizen publicly to profess any statement of belief or to engage in any ceremony of assent to one, presents questions of power that must be considered independently of any idea we may have as to the utility of the ceremony in question.

Nor does the issue as we see it turn on one's possession of particular religious views or the sincerity with which they are held. While religion supplies appellees' motive for enduring the discomforts of making the issue in this case, many citizens who do not share these religious views hold such a compulsory rite to infringe constitutional liberty of the individual. It is not necessary to inquire whether non-conformist beliefs will exempt from the duty to salute unless we first find power to make the salute a legal duty.

The *Gobitis* decision, however, *assumed,* as did the argument in that case and in this, that power exists in the State to impose the flag salute discipline upon school children in general. The Court only examined and rejected a claim based on religious beliefs of immunity from an unquestioned general rule. The question which underlies the flag salute controversy is whether such a ceremony so touching matters of opinion and political attitude may be imposed upon the individual by official authority under powers committed to any political organization under our Constitution. We examine rather than assume existence of this power and, against this broader definition of issues in this case, re-examine specific grounds assigned for the *Gobitis* decision.

1. It was said that the flag-salute controversy confronted the Court with "the problem which Lincoln cast in memorable dilemma: 'Must a government of necessity be too *strong* for the liberties of its people, or too *weak* to maintain its own existence?'" and that the answer must be in favor of strength. *Minersville School Dist.* v. *Gobitis*.

We think these issues may be examined free of pressure or restraint growing out of such considerations.

It may be doubted whether Mr. Lincoln would have thought that the strength of government to maintain itself would be impressively vindicated by our confirming power of the state to expel a handful of children from school. Such oversimplification, so handy in political debate, often lacks the precision necessary to postulates of judicial reasoning. If validly applied to this problem, the utterance cited would resolve every issue of power in favor of those in authority and would require us to override every liberty thought to weaken or delay execution of their policies.

Government of limited power need not be anemic government. Assurance that rights are secure tends to diminish fear and jealousy of strong government, and by making us feel safe to live under it makes for its better support. Without promise of a limiting Bill of Rights it is doubtful if our Constitution could have mustered enough strength to enable its ratification. To enforce those rights today is not to choose weak government over strong government. It is only to adhere as a means of strength to individual freedom of mind in preference to officially disciplined uniformity for which history indicates a disappointing and disastrous end.

The subject now before us exemplifies this principle. Free public education, if faithful to the ideal of secular instruction and political neutrality, will not be partisan or enemy of any class, creed, party, or faction. If it is to impose any ideological discipline, however, each party or denomination must seek to control, or failing that, to weaken the influence of the educational system. Observance of the limitations of the Constitution will not weaken government in the field appropriate for its exercise.

2. It was also considered in the *Gobitis Case* that functions of educational officers in states, counties and school districts were such that to interfere with their authority "would in effect make us the school board for the country."

The Fourteenth Amendment, as now applied to the States, protects the citizen against the State itself and all of its creatures—Boards of Education not excepted. These have, of course, important, delicate, and highly discretionary functions, but none that they may not perform within the limits of the Bill of Rights. That they are educating the young for citizenship is reason for scrupulous protection of Constitutional freedoms of the individual, if we are not to strangle the free mind at its source and teach youth to discount important principles of our government as mere platitudes.

Such Boards are numerous and their territorial jurisdiction often small. But small and local authority may feel less sense of responsibility to the Constitution, and agencies of publicity may be less vigilant in calling it to account. The action of Congress in making flag observance voluntary and respecting the conscience of the objector in a matter so vital as raising the Army contrasts sharply with these local regulations in matters relatively trivial to the welfare of the nation. There are village tyrants as well as village Hampdens, but none who acts under color of law is beyond reach of the Constitution.

3. The *Gobitis* opinion reasoned that this is a field "where courts possess no marked and certainly no controlling competence," that it is committed to the legislatures as well as the courts to guard cherished liberties and that it is constitutionally appropriate to "fight out the wise use of legislative authority in the forum of public opinion and before legislative assemblies rather than to transfer such a contest to the judicial arena," since all the "effective means of inducing political changes are left free."

The very purpose of a Bill of Rights was to withdraw certain subjects from the vicissitudes of political controversy, to place them beyond the reach of majorities and officials and to establish them as legal principles to be applied by the courts. One's right to life, liberty, and property, to free speech, a free press, freedom of worship and assembly, and other fundamental rights may not be submitted to vote; they depend on the outcome of no elections.

In weighing arguments of the parties it is important to distinguish between the due process clause of the Fourteenth Amendment as an instrument for transmitting the principles of the First Amendment and those cases in which it is applied for its own sake. The test of legislation which collides with the Fourteenth Amendment, because it also collides with the principles of the First, is much more definite than the test when only the Fourteenth is involved. Much of the vagueness of the due process clause disappears when the specific prohibitions of the First become its standard. The right of a State to regulate, for example, a public utility may well include, so far as the due process test is concerned, power to impose all of the restrictions which a legislature may have a "rational basis" for adopting. But freedoms of speech and of press, of assembly, and of worship may not be infringed on such slender grounds. They are susceptible of restriction only to prevent grave and immediate danger to interests which the state may lawfully protect. It is important to note that while it is the Fourteenth Amendment which bears directly upon the State it is the more specific limiting principles of the First Amendment that finally govern this case.

Nor does our duty to apply the Bill of Rights to assertions of official authority depend upon our possession of marked competence in the field where the invasion of rights occurs. True, the task of translating the majestic generalities of the Bill of Rights, conceived as part of the pattern of liberal government in the eighteenth century, into concrete restraints on officials dealing with the problems of the twentieth century, is one to disturb self-confidence. These principles grew in soil which also produced a philosophy that the individual was the center of society, that his liberty was attainable through mere absence of governmental restraints, and that government should be entrusted with few controls and only the mildest supervision over men's affairs. We must transplant these rights to a soil in which the laissez-faire concept or principle of non-interference has withered at least as to economic affairs, and social advancements are increasingly sought through closer integration of society and through expanded and strengthened governmental controls. These changed conditions often deprive precedents of reliability and cast us more than we would choose upon our judgment. But we act in these matters not by authority of our competence but by force of our commissions. We cannot, because of modest estimates of our competence in such specialties as public education, withhold the judgment that history authenticates as the function of this Court when liberty is infringed.

4. Lastly, and this is the very heart of the *Gobitis* opinion, it reasons that "national unity is the basis of national security," that the authorities have "the right to select appropriate means for its attainment," and hence reaches the conclusion that such compulsory measures toward "national unity" are constitutional. Upon the verity of this assumption depends our answer in this case.

National unity as an end which officials may foster by persuasion and example is not in question. The problem is whether under our Constitution compulsion as here employed is a permissible means for its achievement.

Struggles to coerce uniformity of sentiment in support of some end thought essential to their time and country have been waged by many good as well as by evil men. Nationalism is a relatively recent phenomenon but at other times and places the ends have been racial or territorial security, support of a dynasty or regime, and particular plans for saving souls. As first and moderate methods to attain unity have failed, those bent on its accomplishment must resort to an ever increasing severity. As governmental pressure toward unity becomes greater, so strife becomes more bitter as to whose unity it shall be. Probably no deeper division of our people could proceed from any provocation than from finding it necessary to choose what doctrine and whose program public educational officials shall compel youth to unite in embracing. Ultimate futility of such attempts to compel coherence is the lesson of every such effort from the Roman drive to stamp out Christianity as a disturber of its pagan unity, the Inquisition, as a means to religious and dynastic unity, the Siberian exiles as a means to Russian unity, down to the fast failing efforts of our present totalitarian enemies. Those who begin coercive elimination of dissent soon find themselves exterminating dissenters. Compulsory unification of opinion achieves only the unanimity of the graveyard.

It seems trite but necessary to say that the First Amendment to our Constitution was designed to avoid these ends by avoiding these beginnings. There is no mysticism in the American concept of the State or of the nature or origin of its authority. We set up government by consent of the governed, and the Bill of Rights denies those in power any legal opportunity to coerce that consent. Authority here is to be controlled by public opinion, not public opinion by authority.

The case is made difficult not because the principles of its decision are obscure but because the flag involved is our own. Nevertheless, we apply the limitations of the Constitution with no fear that freedom to be intellectually and spiritually diverse or even contrary will disintegrate the social organization. To believe that patriotism will not flourish if patriotic ceremonies are voluntary and spontaneous instead of a compulsory routine is to make an unflattering estimate of the appeal of our institutions to free minds. We can have intellectual individualism and the rich cultural diversities that we owe to exceptional minds only at the price of occasional eccentricity and abnormal attitudes. When they are so harmless to others or to the State as those we deal with here, the price is not too great. But freedom to differ is not limited to things that do not matter much. That would be a mere shadow of freedom. The test of its substance is the right to differ as to things that touch the heart of the existing order.

If there is any fixed star in our constitutional constellation, it is that no official, high or petty, can prescribe what shall be orthodox in politics, nationalism, religion, or other matters of opinion or force citizens to confess by word or act their faith therein. If there are any circumstances which permit an exception, they do not now occur to us.

We think the action of the local authorities in compelling the flag salute and pledge transcends constitutional limitations on their power and invades the sphere of intellect and spirit which it is the purpose of the First Amendment to our Constitution to reserve from all official control.

The decision of this Court in *Minersville School Dist.* v. *Gobitis* and the holdings of those few *per curiam* decisions which preceded and foreshadowed it are overruled, and the judgment enjoining enforcement of the West Virginia Regulation is affirmed.

2. *The Freedom* Not *to Listen*

PUBLIC UTILITIES COMMISSION *v.* POLLAK

343 US 451 (1952)

[In this "captive audience" case it appears that the Public Utilities Commission of the District of Columbia issued an order permitting the Capital Transit Company to broadcast on its buses and street cars radio programs consisting of 90 percent music and 10 percent announcements and commercial advertising.

[The Supreme Court held that these facts did not show a violation of any constitutional guaranty. Justice Black concurred, agreeing that the musical programs did not violate the First Amendment but making it clear that the broadcasting of news, speeches, commentators' views, or propaganda of any kind would, in his opinion, violate the Constitution. Justice Douglas dissented. He agreed with the views of Judge Edgerton of the United States Court of Appeals, who said that forcing a "captive audience" to listen is a violation of the "freedom of attention," which is destroyed by forced listening. "If Transit obliged its passengers to read what it liked," said Judge Edgerton, "or get off the car, invasion of their freedom would be obvious." Freedom of speech is guaranteed to every citizen so that he may reach the minds of willing, not coerced, listeners.

[Justice Frankfurter did not participate on the ground that, "as a victim of the practice," his feelings were "so strongly engaged" that he feared that his unconscious feelings may "operate in the ultimate judgment" or create the impression that they have so operated.]

Mr. Justice Burton delivered the opinion of the Court:

The principal question here is whether, in the District of Columbia, the Constitution of the United States precludes a street railway company from receiving and amplifying radio programs through loud speakers in its passenger vehicles under the circumstances of this case. The service and equipment of the company are subject to regulation by the Public Utilities Commission of the District of Columbia. The Commission, after an investigation and public hearings disclosing substantial grounds for doing so, has concluded that the radio service is not inconsistent with public convenience, comfort and safety and "tends to improve the conditions under which the public ride." The Commission, accordingly, has permitted the radio service to continue despite vigorous protests from some passengers that to do so violates their constitutional rights. For the reasons hereafter stated, we hold that neither the operation of the service nor the action of the Commission permitting its operation is precluded by the Constitution.

The Capital Transit Company, here called Capital Transit, is a privately owned public utility corporation, owning an extensive street railway and bus system which it operates in the District of Columbia under a franchise from Congress. Washington Transit Radio, Inc., here called Radio, also is a privately owned corporation doing business in the District of Columbia.

In March, 1948, Capital Transit experimented with "music as you ride" radio programs received and amplified through loud speakers in a streetcar and in a bus. Those vehicles were operated on various lines at various hours. A poll of passengers who heard the programs showed that 92% favored their continuance. Experience in other cities was studied. Capital Transit granted Radio the exclusive right to install, maintain, repair and use radio reception equipment in Capital Transit's streetcars, busses, terminal facilities, waiting rooms and division headquarters. Radio, in return, agreed to contract with a broadcasting station for programs to be received during a minimum of eight hours every day, except Sundays. To that end Radio secured the services of Station WWDC-FM. Its programs were to meet the specifications stated in Capital Transit's contract. Radio agreed to pay Capital Transit, after a 90-day trial, $6 per month per radio installation, plus additional compensation dependent upon the station's receipts from sources such as commercial advertising on the programs. In February, 1949, when more than 20 installations had been made, the service went into regular operation. At the time of the Commission's hearings, October 27–November 1, 1949, there were 212. On that basis the minimum annual payment to Capital Transit came to $15,264. The potential minimum would be $108,000 based upon 1,500 installations. The contract covered five years, with an automatic five-year renewal in the absence of notice to the contrary from either party.

This proceeding began in July, 1949, when the Commission, on its own motion, ordered an investigation. . . .

The Commission concluded "that the installation and use of radios in streetcars and busses of the Capital Transit Company is not inconsistent with public convenience, comfort, and safety" and dismissed its investigation. . . .

In this proceeding the courts are expressly restricted to the facts found by the Commission, insofar as those findings do not appear to be unreasonable, arbitrary or capricious.

After reciting that it had given careful consideration to the testimony bearing on public convenience, comfort and safety, the Commission said that—

From the testimony of record, the conclusion is inescapable that radio reception in streetcars and busses is not an obstacle to safety of operation.

Further, it is evident that public comfort and convenience is not impaired and that, in fact, through the creation of better will among passengers, it tends to improve the conditions under which the public ride. . . .

In view of the findings and conclusions of the Commission, there can be little doubt that, apart from the constitutional questions here raised, there is no basis for setting aside the Commission's decision. It is within the statutory authority of the Commission to prohibit or to permit and regulate the receipt and amplification of radio programs under such conditions that the total utility service shall not be unsafe, uncomfortable or inconvenient. . . .

Applicability of the First and Fifth Amendments.—It was held by the court below that the action of Capital Transit in installing and operating the radio receivers, coupled with the action of the Public Utilities Commission in dismissing its own investigation of the practice, sufficiently involved the Federal Government in responsibility for the radio programs to make the First and Fifth Amendments to the Constitution of the United States applicable to this radio service. These Amendments concededly apply to and restrict only the Federal Government and not private persons. . . .

We find in the reasoning of the court below a sufficiently close relation between the Federal Government and the radio service to make it necessary for us to consider those Amendments. In finding this relation we do not rely on the mere fact that Capital Transit operates a public utility on the streets of the District of Columbia under authority of Congress. Nor do we rely upon the fact that, by reason of such federal authorization, Capital Transit now enjoys a substantial monopoly of street railway and bus transportation in the District of Columbia. We do, however, recognize that Capital Transit operates its service under the regulatory supervision of the Public Utilities Commission of the District of Columbia which is an agency authorized by Congress. We rely particularly upon the fact that that agency, pursuant to protests against the radio program, ordered an investigation of it and, after formal public hearings, ordered its investigation dismissed on the ground that the public safety, comfort and convenience were not impaired thereby. . . .

No violation of the First Amendment.—Pollak and Martin contend that the radio programs interfere with their freedom of conversation and that of other passengers by making it necessary for them to compete against the programs in order to be heard. The Commission, however, did not find, and the testimony does not compel a finding, that the programs interfered substantially with the conversation of passengers or with rights of communication constitutionally protected in public places. It is suggested also that the First Amendment guarantees a freedom to listen only to such points of view as the listener wishes to hear. There is no substantial claim that the programs have been used for objectionable propaganda. There is no issue of that kind before us. The inclusion in the program of a few announcements explanatory and commendatory of Capital Transit's own services does not sustain such an objection.

No violation of the Fifth Amendment.—The court below has emphasized the claim that the radio programs are an invasion of constitutional rights of privacy of the passengers. This claim is that no matter how much Capital Transit may wish to use radio in its vehicles as part of its service to its passengers and as a source of income, no matter how much the great majority of its passengers may desire radio in those vehicles, and however positively the Commission, on substantial evidence, may conclude that such use of radio does not interfere with the convenience, comfort and safety of the service but tends to improve it, yet if one passenger objects to the programs as an invasion of his constitutional right of privacy, the use of radio on the vehicles must be discontinued. This position wrongly assumes that the Fifth Amendment secures to each passenger on a public vehicle regulated by the Federal Government a right of privacy substantially equal to the privacy to which he is entitled in his own home. However complete his right of privacy may be at home, it is substantially limited by the rights of others when its possessor travels on a public thoroughfare or rides in a public conveyance. Streetcars and busses are subject to the immediate control of their owner and operator and, by virtue of their dedication to public service, they are for the common use of all of their passengers. The Federal Government in its regulation of them is not only entitled, but is required, to take into consideration the interests of all concerned.

In a public vehicle there are mutual limitations upon the conduct of everyone, including the vehicle owner. These conflicting demands limit policies on such matters as operating schedules and the location of car or bus stops, as well as policies relating to the desirability or nature of radio programs in the vehicles. Legislation prohibiting the making of artificially amplified raucous sounds in public places has been upheld. *Kovacs* v. *Cooper*, 336 U.S. 77. . . . Conversely, where a regulatory body has jurisdiction, it will be sustained in its protection of activities in public places when those activities do not interfere with the general public convenience, comfort and safety. The supervision of such practices by a Public Utilities Commission in the manner prescribed in the District of Columbia meets the requirements both of substantive and procedural due process when it is not arbitrarily and capriciously exercised.

The contention of Pollak and Martin would permit an objector, with a status no different from that of other passengers, to override not only the preference of the majority of the passengers but also the considered judgment of the federally authorized Public Utilities Commission, after notice, investigation and public hearings, and upon a record reasonably justifying its conclusion that the policy of the owner and operator did not interfere with public convenience, comfort and safety but tended, in general, to improve the utility service.

We do not agree with that contention. The protection afforded to the liberty of the individual by the Fifth Amendment against the action of the Federal Government does not go that far. The liberty of each individual in a public vehicle or public place is subject to reasonable limitations in relation to the rights of others.

This Court expresses no opinion as to the desirability of radio programs in public vehicles. In this case that is a matter for decision between Capital Transit, the public and the Public Utilities Commission. The situation is not unlike that which arises when a utility makes a change in its running schedules or in the locations of its shops in the interest of the majority of the passengers but against the vigorous protests of the few who are inconvenienced by the change.

While the court below expressly refrained from stating its view of the constitutionality of the receipt and amplification in public vehicles of musical programs containing no commercial advertising and other announcements, it is clear that if programs containing commercial advertising and other announcements are permissible, then programs limited to the type of music here contracted for would not be less so. . . .

Reversed.

Separate opinion of Mr. Justice Black:

I concur in the Court's holding that this record shows no violation of the Due Process Clause of the Fifth Amendment. I also agree that Capital Transit's musical programs have not violated the First Amendment. I am of the opinion, however, that subjecting Capital Transit's passengers to the broadcasting of news, public speeches, views, or propaganda of any kind and by any means would violate the First Amendment. To the extent, if any, that the Court holds the contrary, I dissent.

Mr. Justice Douglas, dissenting:

This is a case of first impression. There are no precedents to construe; no principles previously expounded to apply. We write on a clean slate.

The case comes down to the meaning of "liberty" as used in the Fifth Amendment. Liberty in the constitutional sense must mean more than freedom from unlawful governmental restraint; it must include privacy as well, if it is to be a repository of freedom. The right to be let alone is indeed the beginning of all freedom. Part of our claim to privacy is in the prohibition of the Fourth Amendment against unreasonable searches and seizures. It gives the guarantee that a man's home is his castle beyond invasion either by inquisitive or by officious people. A man loses that privacy of course when he goes upon the streets or enters public places. But even in his activities outside the home he has immunities from controls bearing on privacy. He may not be compelled against his will to attend a religious service; he may not be forced to make an affirmation or observe a ritual that violates his scruples; he may not be made to accept one religious, political, or philosophical creed as against another. Freedom of religion and freedom of speech guaranteed by the First Amendment give more than the privilege to worship, to write, to speak as one chooses; they give freedom not to do nor to act as the government chooses. The First Amendment in its respect for the conscience of the individual honors the sanctity of thought and belief. To think as one chooses, to believe what one wishes are important aspects of the constitutional right to be let alone.

If we remembered this lesson taught by the First Amendment, I do not believe we would construe "liberty" within the meaning of the Fifth Amendment as narrowly as the Court does. The present case involves a form of coercion to make people listen. The listeners are of course in a public place; they are on streetcars traveling to and from home. In one sense it can be said that those who ride the streetcars do so voluntarily. Yet in a practical sense they are forced to ride, since this mode of transportation is today essential for many thousands. Compulsion which comes from circumstances can be as real as compulsion which comes from a command.

The streetcar audience is a captive audience. It is there as a matter of necessity, not of choice. One who is in a public vehicle may not of course complain of the noise of the crowd and the babble of tongues. One who enters any public place sacrifices some of his privacy. My protest is against the invasion of his privacy over and beyond the risks of travel.

The government may use the radio (or television) on public vehicles for many purposes. Today it may use it for a cultural end. Tomorrow it may use it for political purposes. So far as the right of privacy is concerned the purpose makes no difference. The music selected by one bureaucrat may be as offensive to some as it is soothing to others. The news commentator chosen to report on the events of the day may give overtones to the news that please the bureau head but which rile the streetcar captive audience. The political philosophy which one radio speaker exudes may be thought by the official who makes up the streetcar programs to be best for the welfare of the people. But the man who listens to it on his way to work in the morning and on his way home at night may think it marks the destruction of the Republic.

One who tunes in on an offensive program at home can turn it off or tune in another station, as he wishes. One who hears disquieting or unpleasant programs in public places, such as restaurants, can get up and leave. But the man on the streetcar has no choice but to sit and listen, or perhaps to sit and to try *not* to listen.

When we force people to listen to another's ideas, we give the propagandist a powerful weapon. Today it is a business enterprise working out a radio program under the auspices of government. Tomorrow it may be a dominant political or religious group. Today the purpose is benign; there is no invidious cast to the programs. But the vice is inherent in the system. Once privacy is invaded, privacy is gone. Once a man is forced to submit to one type of radio program, he can be forced to submit to another. It may be but a short step from a cultural program to a political program.

If liberty is to flourish, government should never be allowed to force people to listen to any radio program. The right of privacy should include the right to pick and choose from competing entertainments, competing propaganda, competing political philosophies. If people are let alone in those choices, the right of privacy will pay dividends in character and integrity. The strength of our system is in the dignity, the resourcefulness, and the independence of our people. Our confidence is in their ability as individuals to make the wisest choice. That system cannot flourish if regimentation takes hold. The right of privacy, today violated, is a powerful deterrent to any one who would control men's minds.

3. The Police Power and Freedom of Speech and Press

a. Protecting the Privacy of Home

BREARD v. CITY OF ALEXANDRIA

341 US 622 (1951)

[In an earlier case, *Martin* v. *Struthers*, 319 US 141 (1943), the Court held that a municipality lacks the power constitutionally to prohibit a person from going from door to door ringing the doorbell for the purpose of distributing to the householder a handbill announcing a religious meeting. In effect the decision said that while it is admittedly an inconvenience to be summoned to one's door to receive a handbill or pamphlet, this is a small price to pay for the sustenance of a free press and freedom of speech. The occupant could, however, post a notice on his door that he did not wish to be disturbed by uninvited peddlers or distributors.

[A majority of the Court distinguished the *Martin Case* from the *Breard Case* because the latter involved the ringing of doorbells by persons who solicited subscriptions for nationally-known magazines. Door-to-door solicitation for this commercial purpose could be prohibited by municipal ordinance.

[Justices Black and Douglas dissented on the ground that the ordinance infringed the constitutional guaranty of liberty of the press. Chief Justice Vinson also dissented on the ground that the ordinance discriminated against interstate commerce in favor of local vendors.]

Mr. Justice Reed delivered the opinion of the Court:

The appellant here, Jack H. Breard, a regional representative of Keystone Readers Service, Inc., a Pennsylvania corporation, was arrested while going from door to door in the City of Alexandria, Louisiana, soliciting subscriptions for nationally known magazines. The arrest was solely on the ground that he had violated an ordinance because he had not obtained the prior consent of the owners of the residences solicited. Breard, a resident of Texas, was in charge of a crew of solicitors who go from house to house in the various cities and towns in the area under Breard's management and solicit subscriptions for nationally known magazines and periodicals including among others the *Saturday Evening Post, Ladies Home Journal, Country Gentleman, Holiday, Newsweek, American Home, Cosmopolitan, Esquire, Pic, Parents, Today's Woman* and *True*. These solicitors spend only a few days in each city depending upon its size. Keystone sends a card from its home office to the new subscribers acknowledging receipt of the subscription and thereafter the periodical is forwarded to the subscriber by the publisher in interstate commerce through the mails.

The ordinance under which the arrest was made, so far as is here pertinent, reads as follows:

Section 1. Be it ordained by the council of the city of Alexandria, Louisiana, in legal session convened that the practice of going in and upon private residences in the City of Alexandria, Louisiana by solicitors, peddlers, hawkers, itinerant merchants or transient vendors of merchandise not having been requested or invited so to do by the owner or owners, occupant or occupants of said private residences for the purpose of soliciting orders for the sale of goods, wares and merchandise and/or disposing of and/or peddling or hawking the same is declared to be a nuisance and punishable as such nuisance as a misdemeanor.

It, or one of similar import, has been on the statute books of Alexandria for many years. It is stipulated that:

Such ordinance was enacted by the City Council, among other reasons, because some householders complained to those in authority that in some instances, for one reason or another, solicitors were undesirable or discourteous, and some householders complained that, whether a solicitor was courteous or not, they did not desire any uninvited intrusion into the privacy of their home. . . .

At appellant's trial for violation of the ordinance there was a motion to quash on the ground that the ordinance violates the Due Process Clause of the Fourteenth Amendment to the Federal Constitution; that it violates the Federal Commerce Clause, art. 1, § 8, cl. 3; and that it violates the guarantees of the First Amendment of freedom of speech and of the press, made applicable to the states by the Fourteenth Amendment to the Constitution of the United States. Appellant's motion to quash was overruled by the trial court and he was found guilty and sentenced to pay a $25 fine or serve 30 days in jail. The Supreme Court of Louisiana affirmed appellant's conviction and expressly rejected the federal constitutional objections. . . .

All declare for liberty and proceed to disagree among themselves as to its true meaning. There is equal unanimity that opportunists, for private gain, cannot be permitted to arm themselves with an acceptable principle, such as that of a right to work, a privilege to engage in interstate commerce, or a free press, and proceed to use it as an iron standard to smooth their path by crushing the living rights of others to privacy and repose. This case calls for an adjustment of constitutional rights in the light of the particular living conditions of the time and place. Everyone cannot have his own way and each must yield something to the reasonable satisfaction of the needs of all.

It is true that the knocker on the front door is treated as an invitation or license to attempt an entry, justifying ingress to the home by solicitors, hawkers and peddlers for all kinds of salable articles. When such visitors are barred from premises by notice or order, however, subsequent trespasses have been punished. Door-to-door canvassing has flourished increasingly in recent years with the ready market furnished by the rapid concentration of housing. The infrequent and still welcome solicitor to the rural home became to some a recurring nuisance in towns when the visits were multiplied. Unwanted knocks on the door by day or night are a nuisance or worse to peace and quiet. The local retail merchant, too, has not been unmindful of the effective competition furnished by house-to-house selling in many lines. As a matter of business fairness, it may be thought not really sporting to corner the quarry in his home and through his open door put pressure on the prospect to purchase. As the exigencies of trade are not ordinarily expected to have a higher rating constitutionally than the tranquillity of the fireside, responsible municipal officers have sought a way to curb the annoyances while preserving complete freedom for desirable visitors to the homes. The idea of barring classified salesmen from homes by means of notices posted by individual householders was rejected early as less practical than an ordinance regulating solicitors. . . .

First Amendment.— . . . We come to a point not heretofore urged. . . . This is that such an ordinance is an abridgment of freedom of speech and the press. Only the press or oral advocates of ideas could urge this point. It was not open to the solicitors for gadgets or brushes. The point is not that the press is free of the ordinary restraints and regulations of the modern state, such as taxation or labor regulation, . . . but, as stated in appellant's brief, "because the ordinance places an arbitrary, unreasonable and undue burden upon a well established and essential method of distribution and circulation of lawful magazines and periodicals and, in effect, is tantamount to a prohibition of the utilization of such method." Regulation necessarily has elements of prohibition. Thus the argument is not that the money-making activities of the solicitor entitles him to go "in or upon private residences" at will, but that the distribution of periodicals through door-to-door canvassing is entitled to First Amendment protection. This kind of distribution is said to be protected because the mere fact that money is made out of the distribution does not bar the publications from First Amendment protection. We agree that the fact that periodicals are sold does not put them beyond the protection of the First Amendment. The selling, however, brings into the transaction a commercial feature.

The First and Fourteenth Amendments have never been treated as absolute. Freedom of speech or press does not mean that one can talk or distribute where, when and how one chooses. Rights other than those of the advocates are involved. By adjustment of rights, we can have both full liberty of expression and an orderly life.

The case that comes nearest to supporting appellant's contention is *Martin* v. *Struthers*, 319 U.S. 141. . . . There a municipal ordinance forbidding anyone summoning the occupants of a residence to the door to receive advertisements was held invalid as applied to the free distribution of dodgers "advertising a religious meeting." Attention was directed in note 1 of that case to the fact that the ordinance was not aimed "solely at commercial advertising." It was said: "The ordinance does not control anything but the distribution of literature, and in that respect it substitutes the judgment of the community for the judgment of the individual householder."

The decision to release the distributor was because: "Freedom to distribute information to every citizen wherever he desires to receive it is so clearly vital to the preservation of a free society that, putting aside reasonable police and health regulations of time and manner of distribution, it must be fully preserved."

There was dissent even to this carefully phrased application of the principles of the First Amendment. As no element of the commercial entered into this free solicitation and the opinion was narrowly limited to the precise fact of the free distribution of an invitation to religious services, we feel that it is not necessarily inconsistent with the conclusion reached in this case. . . .

This makes the constitutionality of Alexandria's ordinance turn upon a balancing of the conveniences between some householders' desire for privacy and the publisher's right to distribute publications in the precise way that those soliciting for him think brings the best results. The issue brings into collision the rights of the hospitable housewife, peering on Monday morning around her chained door with those of Mr. Breard's courteous, well-trained but possibly persistent solicitor, offering a bargain on culture and information through a joint subscription to *Satevepost, Pic* and *Today's Woman.* Behind the housewife are many housewives and homeowners in the towns where . . . ordinances offer their aid. Behind Mr. Breard are "Keystone" with an annual business of $5,000,000 in subscriptions and the periodicals with their use of house-to-house canvassing to secure subscribers for their valuable publications, together with other housewives who desire solicitors to offer them the opportunity and remind and help them, at their doors, to subscribe for publications.

Subscriptions may be made by anyone interested in receiving the magazines without the annoyances of house-to-house canvassing. We think those communities that have found these methods of sale obnoxious may control them by ordinance. It would be, it seems to us, a misuse of the great guarantees of free speech and free press to use that guarantee to force a community to admit the solicitors of publications to the home premises of its residents. We see no abridgement of the principles of the First Amendment in this ordinance.

Affirmed.

Mr. Justice Black, with whom Mr. Justice Douglas joins, dissenting:

On May 3, 1943, this Court held that cities and states could not enforce laws which impose flat taxes on the privilege of door-to-door sales of religious literature, *Jones* v. *Opelika*, 319 U.S. 103; *Murdock* v. *Pennsylvania*, 319 U.S. 105; or which make it unlawful for persons to go from home to home knocking on doors and ringing doorbells to invite occupants to religious, political or other kinds of public meetings. *Martin* v. *Struthers*, 319 U.S. 141. Over strong dissents, these laws were held to invade liberty of speech, press and religion in violation of the First and Fourteenth Amendments. Today a new majority adopts the position of the former dissenters and sustains a city ordinance forbidding door-to-door solicitation of subscriptions to the *Saturday Evening Post, Newsweek* and other magazines. Since this decision cannot be reconciled with the *Jones, Murdock* and *Martin* v. *Struthers* cases, it seems to me that good judicial practice calls for their forthright overruling. But whether this is done or not, it should be plain that my disagreement with the majority of the Court as now constituted stems basically from a different concept of the reach of the constitutional liberty of the press rather than from any difference of opinion as to what former cases have held.

Today's decision marks a revitalization of the judicial views which prevailed before this Court embraced the philosophy that the First Amendment gives a preferred status to the liberties it protects. I adhere to that preferred position philosophy. It is my belief that the freedom of the people of this Nation cannot survive even a little governmental hobbling of religious or political ideas, whether they be communicated orally or through the press.

The constitutional sanctuary for the press must necessarily include liberty to publish and circulate. In view of our economic system, it must also include freedom to solicit paying subscribers. Of course homeowners can if they wish forbid newsboys, reporters or magazine solicitors to ring their doorbells. But when the homeowner himself has not done this, I believe that the First Amendment, interpreted with due regard for the freedoms it guarantees, bars laws like the present ordinance which punish persons who peacefully go from door to door as agents of the press.

b. Protecting the Repose and Quiet of Streets and Neighborhoods

KOVACS v. COOPER

336 US 77 (1949)

[In 1897 the Supreme Court held that a city may absolutely or conditionally prohibit public speaking in a public street or park. *Davis* v. *Massachusetts,* 167 US 43 (1897). In the *Hague Case,* above, the Court, except for Justice Butler, held that the *Davis Case* did not govern the Jersey City case. Justice Roberts in the *Hague Case* said that the streets and parks have from ancient times been used for the communication of thoughts and views and the discussion of public issues. While this use may be regulated, it may not be abridged or denied.

[In 1948 the Court had before it an ordinance which prohibited the use of loud-speaker devices in public places without police permission. The police had denied a permit for the use of a sound truck to deliver a religious lecture in a public park. The Court held the ordinance unconstitutional. Justices Frankfurter, Reed, Burton, and Jackson dissented. *Saia* v. *New York,* 334 US 558 (1948). In the following year the Court considered *Kovacs* v. *Cooper.* This time eight Justices agreed that sound amplification in public places is subject to reasonable regulation, but Justices Frankfurter and Jackson went further and said that the use of sound trucks on public streets may be prohibited altogether. Justices Murphy, Black, Douglas, and Rutledge dissented—Murphy absolutely, the others on a construction of the facts in the case.]

Mr. Justice Reed announced the judgment of the Court . . . :

This appeal involves the validity of a provision of Ordinance No. 430 of the City of Trenton, New Jersey. It reads as follows:

4. That it shall be unlawful for any person, firm or corporation, either as principal, agent or employee, to play, use or operate for advertising purposes, or for any other purpose whatsoever, on or upon the public streets, alleys or thoroughfares in the City of Trenton, any device known as a sound truck, loud speaker or sound amplifier, or radio or phonograph with a loud speaker or sound amplifier, or any other instrument known as a calliope or any instrument of any kind or character which emits therefrom loud and raucous noises and is attached to and upon any vehicle operated or standing upon said streets or public places aforementioned.

The appellant was found guilty of violating this ordinance by the appellee, a police judge of the City of Trenton. . . .

We took jurisdiction to consider the challenge made to the constitutionality of the section on its face and as applied on the ground that § 1 of the Fourteenth Amendment of the United States Constitution was violated because the section and the conviction are in contravention of rights of freedom of speech, freedom of assemblage and freedom to communicate information and opinions to others. The ordinance is also challenged as violative of the Due Process Clause of the Fourteenth Amendment on the ground that it is so obscure, vague, and indefinite as to be impossible of reasonably accurate interpretation. . . .

At the trial in the Trenton police court, a city patrolman testified that while on his post he heard a sound truck broadcasting music. Upon going in the direction of said sound, he located the truck on a public street near the municipal building. As he approached the truck, the music stopped and he heard a man's voice broadcasting from the truck. The appellant admitted that he operated the mechanism for the music and spoke into the amplifier. The record from the police court does not show the purpose of the broadcasting but the opinion in the Supreme Court suggests that the appellant was using the sound apparatus to comment on a labor dispute then in progress in Trenton.

The contention that the section is so vague, obscure and indefinite as to be unenforceable merits only a passing reference. This objection centers around the use of the words "loud and raucous." While these are abstract words, they have through daily use acquired a content that conveys to any interested person a sufficiently accurate concept of what is forbidden. . . .

We think the words of § 4 of this Trenton ordinance comply with the requirements of definiteness and clarity, set out above.

The scope of the protection afforded by the Fourteenth Amendment, for the right of a citizen to play music and express his views on matters which he considers to be of interest to himself and others on a public street through sound amplification devices mounted on vehicles, must be considered. Freedom of speech, freedom of assembly and freedom to communicate information and opinion to others are all comprehended on this appeal in the claimed right of free speech. They will be so treated in this opinion.

The use of sound trucks and other peripatetic or stationary broadcasting devices for advertising, for religious exercises and for discussion of issues or controversies has brought forth numerous municipal ordinances. The avowed and obvious purpose of these ordinances is to prohibit or minimize such sounds on or near the streets since some citizens find the noise objectionable and to some degree an interference with the business or social activities in which they are engaged or the quiet that they would like to enjoy. A satisfactory adjustment of the conflicting interests is difficult as those who desire to broadcast can hardly acquiesce in a requirement to modulate their sounds to a pitch that would not rise above other street noises nor would they deem a restriction to sparsely used localities or to hours after work and before sleep—say 6 to 9 P.M.—sufficient for the exercise of their claimed privilege. Municipalities are seeking actively a solution. . . . Unrestrained use throughout a municipality of all sound amplifying devices would be intolerable. Absolute prohibition within municipal limits of all sound amplification, even though reasonably regulated in place, time and volume, is undesirable and probably unconstitutional as an unreasonable interference with normal activities. . . .

This ordinance . . . is an exercise of the authority granted to the city by New Jersey "to prevent disturbing noises," . . . nuisances well within the municipality's power to control. The police power of a state extends beyond health, morals and safety, and comprehends the duty, within constitutional limitations, to protect the well-being and tranquility of a community. A state or city may prohibit acts or things reasonably thought to bring evil or harm to its people. . . .

We accept the determination of New Jersey that § 4 applies only to vehicles with sound amplifiers emitting loud and raucous noises. Courts are inclined to adopt that reasonable interpretation of a statute which removes it farthest from possible constitutional infirmity. . . . We need not determine whether this ordinance so construed is regulatory or prohibitory. All regulatory enactments are prohibitory so far as their restrictions are concerned, and the prohibition of this ordinance as to a use of streets is merely regulatory. Sound trucks may be utilized in places such as parks or other open spaces off the streets. The constitutionality of the challenged ordinance as violative of appellant's right of free speech does not depend upon so narrow an issue as to whether its provisions are cast in the words of prohibition or regulation. The question is whether or not there is a real abridgment of the rights of free speech.

Of course, even the fundamental rights of the Bill of Rights are not absolute. . . .

Hecklers may be expelled from assemblies and religious worship may not be disturbed by those anxious to preach a doctrine of atheism. The right to speak one's mind would often be an empty privilege in a place and at a time beyond the protecting hand of the guardians of public order. . . .

City streets are recognized as a normal place for the exchange of ideas by speech or paper. But this does not mean the freedom is beyond all control. We think it is a permissible exercise of legislative discretion to bar sound trucks with broadcasts of public interest, amplified to a loud and raucous volume, from the public ways of municipalities. On the business streets of cities like Trenton, with its more than 125,000 people, such distractions would be dangerous to traffic at all hours useful for the dissemination of information, and in the residential thoroughfares the quiet and tranquility so desirable for city dwellers would likewise be at the mercy of advocates of particular religious, social or political persuasions. We cannot believe that rights of free speech compel a municipality to allow such mechanical voice amplification on any of its streets.

The right of free speech is guaranteed every citizen that he may reach the minds of willing listeners and to do so there must be opportunity to win their attention. This is the phase of freedom of speech that is involved here. We do not think the Trenton ordinance abridges that freedom. It is an extravagant extension of due process to say that because of it a city cannot forbid talking on the streets through a loud speaker in a loud and raucous tone. Surely such an ordinance does not violate our people's "concept of ordered liberty" so as to require federal intervention to protect a citizen from the action of his own local government. . . . Opportunity to gain the public's ears by objectionably amplified sound on the streets is no more assured by the right of free speech than is the unlimited opportunity to address gatherings on the streets. The preferred position of freedom of speech in a society that cherishes liberty for all does not require legislators to be insensible to claims by citizens to comfort and convenience. To enforce freedom of speech in disregard of the rights of others would be harsh and arbitrary in itself. That more people may be more easily and cheaply reached by sound trucks, perhaps borrowed without cost from some zealous supporter, is not enough to call forth constitutional protection for what those charged with public welfare reasonably think is a nuisance when easy means of publicity are open. Section 4 of the ordinance bars sound trucks from broadcasting in a loud and raucous manner on the streets. There is no restriction upon the communication of ideas or discussion of issues by the human voice, by newspapers, by pamphlets, by dodgers. We think that the need for reasonable protection in the homes or business houses from the distracting noises of vehicles equipped with such sound amplifying devices justifies the ordinance.

Affirmed.

Mr. Justice Black, with whom Mr. Justice Douglas, and Mr. Justice Rutledge, concur, dissenting:

. . . The appellant was charged and convicted by interpreting the ordinance as an absolute prohibition against the use of sound amplifying devices. . . .

Nevertheless, in this Court the requisite majority for affirmance of appellant's conviction is composed in part of Justices who give the New Jersey ordinance a construction different from that given it by the state courts. That is not all. Affirmance here means that the appellant will be punished for an offense with which he was not charged, to prove which no evidence was offered, and of which he was not convicted. . . .

The New Jersey ordinance is on its face, and as construed and applied in this case by that state's courts, an absolute and unqualified prohibition of amplifying devices on any of Trenton's streets at any time, at any place, for any purpose, and without regard to how noisy they may be. . . .

There are many people who have ideas that they wish to disseminate but who do not have enough money to own or control publishing plants, newspapers, radios, moving picture studios, or chains of show places. Yet everybody knows the vast reaches of these powerful channels of communication which from the very nature of our economic system must be under the control and guidance of comparatively few people. On the other hand, public speaking is done by many men of divergent minds with no centralized control over the ideas they entertain so as to limit the causes they espouse. It is no reflection on the value of preserving freedom for dissemination of the ideas of publishers of newspapers, magazines, and other literature, to believe that transmission of ideas through public speaking is also essential to the sound thinking of a fully informed citizenry.

It is of particular importance in a government where people elect their officials that the fullest opportunity be afforded candidates to express and voters to hear their views. It is of equal importance that criticism of governmental action not be limited to criticisms by press, radio, and moving pictures. In no other way except public speaking can the desirable objective of widespread public discussion be assured. For the press, the radio, and the moving picture owners have their favorites, and it assumes the impossible to suppose that these agencies will at all times be equally fair as between the candidates and officials they favor and those whom they vigorously oppose. And it is an obvious fact that public speaking today without the sound amplifiers is a wholly inadequate way to reach the people on a large scale. Consequently, to tip the scales against transmission of ideas through public speaking, as the Court does today, is to deprive the people of a large part of the basic advantages of the receipt of ideas that the First Amendment was designed to protect.

There is no more reason that I can see for wholly prohibiting one useful instrument of communication than another. If Trenton can completely bar the streets to the advantageous use of loud speakers, all cities can do the same. In that event preference in the dissemination of ideas is given those who can obtain the support of newspapers, etc., or those who have money enough to buy advertising from newspapers, radios, or moving pictures. This Court should no more permit this invidious prohibition against the dissemination of ideas by speaking than it would permit a complete blackout of the press, the radio, or moving pictures. It is wise for all who cherish freedom of expression to reflect upon the plain fact that a holding that the audiences of public speakers can be constitutionally prohibited is not unrelated to a like prohibition in other fields. And the right to freedom of expression should be protected from absolute censorship for persons without, as for persons with, wealth and power. At least, such is the theory of our society.

I am aware that the "blare" of this new method of carrying ideas is susceptible of abuse and may under certain circumstances constitute an intolerable nuisance. But ordinances can be drawn which adequately protect a community from unreasonable use of public speaking devices without absolutely denying to the community's citizens all information that may be disseminated or received through this new avenue for trade in ideas. I would agree without reservation to the sentiment that "unrestrained use throughout a municipality of all sound amplifying devices would be intolerable." And of course cities may restrict or absolutely ban the use of amplifiers on busy streets in the business area. A city ordinance that reasonably restricts the volume of sound, or the hours during which an amplifier may be used, does not, in my mind, infringe the constitutionally protected area of free speech. It is because this ordinance does none of these things, but is instead an absolute prohibition of all uses of an amplifier on any of the streets of Trenton at any time that I must dissent.

I would reverse the judgment.

c. Speech That Is a Violation of Public Peace and Order

FEINER v. NEW YORK

340 US 315 (1951)

[A university student, using a loud speaker, addressed a crowd, which included some Negroes, from a box on the sidewalk in Syracuse, New York. He called then-President Truman "a bum" and said that Negroes "should rise up in arms and fight for their rights." Policemen asked him to stop speaking; as he ignored their requests, they arrested him. He was convicted for disorderly conduct. By a 6-to-3 decision the Supreme Court upheld the conviction on the ground that the speaker had created a clear danger of disorder on the public streets of the city. The dissenting Justices (Black, Douglas, and Minton) maintained that the speaker was punished for his unpopular views, expressed to an unsympathetic audience; that he was arrested before there was a present danger of a riot; that the police should have protected him in the exercise of his constitutional rights against anyone in the crowd who may have threatened him with violence rather than have thrown their weight against him. The majority, however, were impressed with the fact that the state trial and appeals courts found that the speaker had created danger to public order.

[Justice Frankfurter's concurring opinion is a scholarly, helpful analysis and classification of the different types of free speech cases considered by the Court. It appears as part of another case decided the same day, *Niemotko* v. *Maryland,* which appears later in this volume.]

Mr. Chief Justice Vinson delivered the opinion of the Court:

Petitioner was convicted of the offense of disorderly conduct, a misdemeanor under the New York penal laws, in the Court of Special Sessions of the City of Syracuse and was sentenced to thirty days in the county penitentiary. . . .

On the evening of March 8, 1949, petitioner Irving Feiner was addressing an open-air meeting at the corner of South McBride and Harrison Streets in the City of Syracuse. At approximately 6:30 P.M., the police received a telephone complaint concerning the meeting, and two officers were detailed to investigate. One of these officers went to the scene immediately, the other arriving some twelve minutes later. They found a crowd of about seventy-five or eighty people, both Negro and white, filling the sidewalk and spreading out into the street. Petitioner, standing on a large wooden box on the sidewalk, was addressing the crowd through a loud-speaker system attached to an automobile. Although the purpose of his speech was to urge his listeners to attend a meeting to be held that night in the Syracuse Hotel, in its course he was making derogatory remarks concerning President Truman, the American Legion, the Mayor of Syracuse, and other local political officials.

The police officers made no effort to interfere with petitioner's speech, but were first concerned with the effect of the crowd on both pedestrian and vehicular traffic. They observed the situation from the opposite side of the street, noting that some pedestrians were forced to walk in the street to avoid the crowd. Since traffic was passing at the time, the officers attempted to get the people listening to petitioner back on the sidewalk. The crowd was restless and there was some pushing, shoving and milling around. One of the officers telephoned the police station from a nearby store, and then both policemen crossed the street and mingled with the crowd without any intention of arresting the speaker.

At this time, petitioner was speaking in a "loud, high-pitched voice." He gave the impression that he was endeavoring to arouse the Negro people against the whites, urging that they rise up in arms and fight for equal rights. The statements before such a mixed audience "stirred up a little excitement." Some of the onlookers made remarks to the police about their inability to handle the crowd and at least one threatened violence if the police did not act. There were others who appeared to be favoring petitioner's arguments. Because of the feeling that existed in the crowd both for and against the speaker, the officers finally "stepped in to prevent it from resulting in a fight." One of the officers approached the petitioner, not for the purpose of arresting him, but to get him to break up the crowd. He asked petitioner to get down off the box, but the latter refused to accede to his request and continued talking. The officer waited for a minute and then demanded that he cease talking. Although the officer had thus twice requested petitioner to stop over the course of several minutes, petitioner not only ignored him but continued talking. During all this time, the crowd was pressing closer around petitioner and the officer. Finally, the officer told petitioner he was under arrest and ordered him to get down from the box, reaching up to grab him. Petitioner stepped down, announcing over the microphone that "the law has arrived, and I suppose they will take over now." In all, the officer had asked petitioner to get down off the box three times over a space of four or five minutes. Petitioner had been speaking for over a half hour.

On these facts, petitioner was specifically charged with violation . . . of the Penal Law of New York. . . .

We are not faced here with blind condonation by a state court of arbitrary police action. Petitioner was accorded a full, fair trial. The trial judge heard testimony supporting and contradicting the judgment of the police officers that a clear danger of disorder was threatened. After weighing this contradictory evidence, the trial judge reached the conclusion that the police officers were justified in taking action to prevent a breach of the peace. The exercise of the police officers' proper discretionary power to prevent a breach of the peace was thus approved by the trial court and later by two courts on review. The courts below recognized petitioner's right to hold a street meeting at this locality, to make use of loud-speaking equipment in giving his speech, and to make derogatory remarks concerning public officials and the American Legion. They found that the officers in making the arrest were motivated solely by a proper concern for the preservation of order and protection of the general welfare, and that there was no evidence which could lend color to a claim that the acts of the police were a cover for suppression of petitioner's views and opinions. Petitioner was thus neither arrested nor convicted for the making or the content of his speech. Rather, it was the reaction which it actually engendered.

. . . The findings of the New York courts as to the condition of the crowd and the refusal of petitioner to obey the police requests, supported as they are by the record of this case, are persuasive that the conviction of petitioner for violation of public peace, order and authority does not exceed the bounds of proper state police action. This Court respects, as it must, the interest of the community in maintaining peace and order on its streets. . . . We cannot say that the preservation of that interest here encroaches on the constitutional rights of this petitioner.

We are well aware that the ordinary murmurings and objections of a hostile audience cannot be allowed to silence a speaker, and are also mindful of the possible danger of giving overzealous police officials complete discretion to break up otherwise lawful public meetings. "A State may not unduly suppress free communication of views, religious or other, under the guise of conserving desirable conditions." *Cantwell* v. *Connecticut.* . . . But we are not faced here with such a situation. It is one thing to say that the police cannot be used as an instrument for the suppression of unpopular views, and another to say that, when as here the speaker passes the bounds of argument or persuasion and undertakes incitement to riot, they are powerless to prevent a breach of the peace. Nor in this case can we condemn the considered judgment of three New York courts approving the means which the police, faced with a crisis, used in the exercise of their power and duty to preserve peace and order. The findings of the state courts as to the existing situation and the imminence of greater disorder coupled with petitioner's deliberate defiance of the police officers convince us that we should not reverse this conviction in the name of free speech.

Affirmed. . . .

Mr. Justice Black, dissenting:

The record before us convinces me that petitioner, a young college student, has been sentenced to the penitentiary for the unpopular views he expressed on matters of public interest while lawfully making a street-corner speech in Syracuse, New York. Today's decision, however, indicates that we must blind ourselves to this fact because the trial judge fully accepted the testimony of the prosecution witnesses on all important points. Many times in the past this Court has said that despite findings below, we will examine the evidence for ourselves to ascertain whether federally protected rights have been denied; otherwise review here would fail of its purpose in safeguarding constitutional guarantees. Even a partial abandonment of this rule marks a dark day for civil liberties in our Nation.

But still more has been lost today. Even accepting every "finding of fact" below, I think this conviction makes a mockery of the free speech guarantees of the First and Fourteenth Amendments. The end result of the affirmance here is to approve a simple and readily available technique by which cities and states can with impunity subject all speeches, political or otherwise, on streets or elsewhere, to the supervision and censorship of the local police. I will have no part or parcel in this holding which I view as a long step toward totalitarian authority.

Considering only the evidence which the state courts appear to have accepted, the pertinent 'facts" are: Syracuse city authorities granted a permit for O. John Rogge, a former assistant attorney general, to speak in a public school building on March 8, 1948, on the subject of racial discrimination and civil liberties. On March 8th, however, the authorities cancelled the permit. The Young Progressives under whose auspices the meeting was scheduled then arranged for Mr. Rogge to speak at the Hotel Syracuse. The gathering on the street where petitioner spoke was held to protest the cancellation and to publicize the meeting at the hotel. In this connection, petitioner used derogatory but not profane language with reference to the city authorities, President Truman and the American Legion. After hearing some of these remarks, a policeman, who had been sent to the meeting by his superiors, reported to Police Headquarters by telephone. To whom he reported or what was said does not appear in the record, but after returning from the call, he and another policeman started through the crowd toward petitioner. Both officers swore they did not intend to make an arrest when they started, and the trial court accepted their statements. They also said, and the court believed, that they heard and saw "angry mutterings," "pushing," "shoving and milling around" and "restlessness." Petitioner spoke in a "loud, high pitched voice." He said that "colored people don't have equal rights and they should rise up in arms and fight for them." One man who heard this told the officers that if they did not take that "S . . . O . . . B . . ." off the box, he would. The officers then approached petitioner for the first time. One of them first "asked" petitioner to get off the box, but petitioner continued urging his audience to attend Rogge's speech. The officer next "told" petitioner to get down, but he did not. The officer finally "demanded" that petitioner get down, telling him he was under arrest. Petitioner then told the crowd that "the law had arrived and would take over" and asked why he was arrested. The officer first replied that the charge was "unlawful assembly" but later changed the ground to "disorderly conduct."

The Court's opinion apparently rests on this reasoning: The policeman, under the circumstances detailed, could reasonably conclude that serious fighting or even riot was imminent; therefore he could stop petitioner's speech to prevent a breach of peace; accordingly, it was "disoderly conduct" for petitioner to continue speaking in disobedience of the officer's request. As to the existence of a dangerous situation on the street corner, it seems far-fetched to suggest that the "facts" show any imminent threat of riot or uncontrollable disorder. It is neither unusual nor unexpected that some people at public street meetings mutter, mill about, push, shove, or disagree, even violently, with the speaker. Indeed, it is rare where controversial topics are discussed that an outdoor crowd does not do some or all of these things. Nor does one isolated threat to assault the speaker forebode disorder. Especially should the danger be discounted where, as here, the person threatening was a man whose wife and two small children accompanied him and who, so far as the record shows, was never close enough to petitioner to carry out the threat.

Moreover, assuming that the "facts" did indicate a critical situation, I reject the implication of the Court's opinion that the police had no obligation to protect petitioner's constitutional right to talk. The police of course have power to prevent breaches of the peace. But if, in the name of preserving order, they ever can interfere with a lawful public speaker, they first must make all reasonable efforts to protect him. Here the policeman did not even pretend to try to protect petitioner. According to the officers' testimony, the crowd was restless but there is no showing of any attempt to quiet it; pedestrians were forced to walk into the street, but there was no effort to clear a path on the sidewalk; one person threatened to assault petitioner but the officers did nothing to discourage this when even a word might have sufficed. Their duty was to protect petitioner's right to talk, even to the extent of arresting the man who threatened to interfere. Instead, they shirked that duty and acted only to suppress the right to speak.

Finally, I cannot agree with the Court's statement that petitioner's disregard of the policeman's unexplained request amounted to such "deliberate defiance" as would justify an arrest or conviction for disorderly conduct. On the contrary, I think that the policeman's action was a "deliberate defiance" of ordinary official duty as well as of the constitutional right of free speech. For at least where time allows, courtesy and explanation of commands are basic elements of good official conduct in a democratic society. Here petitioner was "asked" then "told" then "commanded" to stop speaking, but a man making a lawful address is certainly not required to be silent merely because an officer directs it. Petitioner was entitled to know why he should cease doing a lawful act. Not once was he told. I understand that people in authoritarian countries must obey arbitrary orders. I had hoped that there was no such duty in the United States.

In my judgment, today's holding means that as a practical matter, minority speakers can be silenced in any city. Hereafter, despite the First and Fourteenth Amendments, the policeman's club can take heavy toll of a current administration's public critics. Criticism of public officials will be too dangerous for all but the most courageous. . . .

In this case I would reverse the conviction, thereby adhering to the great principles of the First and Fourteenth Amendments as announced for this Court in 1940 by Mr. Justice Roberts:

> In the realm of religious faith and in that of political belief, sharp differences arise. In both fields, the tenets of one man may seem the rankest error to his neighbor. To persuade others to his own point of view, the pleader, as we know, at times resorts to exaggeration, to vilification of men who have been, or are, prominent in church or state, and even to false statement. But the people of this nation have ordained in the light of history, that, in spite of the probability of excesses and abuses, these liberties are, in the long view, essential to enlightened opinion and right conduct on the part of the citizens of a democracy. *Cantwell* v. *Connecticut*, 310 US 296. . . .

Mr. Justice Douglas, with whom Mr. Justice Minton concurs, dissenting:

Feiner, a university student, made a speech on a street corner in Syracuse, New York, on March 8, 1949. The purpose of the speech was to publicize a meeting of the Young Progressives of America to be held that evening. A permit authorizing the meeting to be held in a public school auditorium had been revoked and the meeting shifted to a local hotel.

Feiner delivered his speech in a small shopping area in a predominantly colored residential section of Syracuse. He stood on a large box and spoke over loudspeakers mounted on a car. His audience was composed of about 75 people, colored and white. A few minutes after he started two police officers arrived.

The speech was mainly devoted to publicizing the evening's meeting and protesting the revocation of the permit. It also touched on various public issues. The following are the only excerpts revealed by the record:

> Mayor Costello [of Syracuse] is a champagne-sipping bum; he does not speak for the Negro people.
>
> The 15th Ward is run by corrupt politicians, and there are horse rooms operating there.
>
> President Truman is a bum.
>
> Mayor O'Dwyer is a bum.
>
> The American Legion is a Nazi Gestapo.
>
> The Negroes don't have equal rights; they should rise up in arms and fight for their rights.

There was some pushing and shoving in the crowd and some angry muttering. That is the testimony of the police. But there were no fights and no "disorder" even by the standards of the police. There was not even any heckling of the speaker.

But after Feiner had been speaking about 20 minutes a man said to the police officers, "If you don't get that son of a bitch off, I will go over and get him off there myself." It was then that the police ordered Feiner to stop speaking; when he refused, they arrested him.

Public assemblies and public speech occupy an important role in American life. One high function of the police is to protect these lawful gatherings so that the speakers may exercise their constitutional rights. When unpopular causes are sponsored from the public platform there will commonly be mutterings and unrest and heckling from the crowd. When a speaker mounts a platform it is not unusual to find him resorting to exaggeration, to vilification of ideas and men, to the making of false charges. But those extravagances . . . do not justify penalizing the speaker by depriving him of the platform or by punishing him for his conduct.

A speaker may not, of course, incite a riot any more than he may incite a breach of the peace by the use of "fighting words." . . . But this record shows no such extremes. It shows an unsympathetic audience and the threat of one man to haul the speaker from the stage. It is against that kind of threat that speakers need police protection. If they do not receive it and instead the police throw their weight on the side of those who would break up the meetings, the police become the new censors of speech. Police censorship has all the vices of the censorship from city halls which we have repeatedly struck down. . . .

TERMINIELLO v. CHICAGO
337 US 1 (1949)

[In the *Feiner Case*, it will be recalled, the Court found that the speaker had created a clear danger of public disorder; in the face of such danger, he should not have persisted in continuing his outdoor speech. In the *Terminiello Case* the speech was delivered in a hall hired for the occasion. This, it seems, is an important difference; for people who hear parts of a speech through an amplifying device as they walk on the street are members of a "captive audience," while people who attend a speech in a hall do so voluntarily. Another important difference is that Terminiello was convicted, not for creating a clear danger of public disorder, but for causing a breach of peace by delivering a speech which "stirs the public to anger, invites dispute, [or] brings about a condition of unrest." Terminiello, said the Court, could not, under these circumstances, be punished: "A function of free speech . . . is to invite dispute," induce a condition of unrest, create "dissatisfaction with conditions as they are," or even stir people to anger.

[The decision was 5 to 4, with Chief Justice Vinson and Justices Frankfurter, Jackson, and Burton dissenting. Three of these Justices dissented on what amounts to a procedural point, while Jackson dissented on this ground and also because he read the facts as showing that Terminiello had in fact incited the friendly audience in the hall and had provoked the hostile mob outside the hall, and that violence between the two crowds was threatened.]

Mr. Justice Douglas delivered the opinion of the Court:

Petitioner after jury trial was found guilty of disorderly conduct in violation of a city ordinance of Chicago and fined. The case grew out of an address he delivered in an auditorium in Chicago under the auspices of the Christian Veterans of America. The meeting commanded considerable public attention. The auditorium was filled to capacity with over eight hundred persons present. Others were turned away. Outside of the auditorium a crowd of about one thousand persons gathered to protest against the meeting. A cordon of policemen was assigned to the meeting to maintain order; but they were not able to prevent several disturbances. The crowd outside was angry and turbulent.

Petitioner in his speech condemned the conduct of the crowd outside and vigorously, if not viciously, criticized various political and racial groups whose activities he denounced as inimical to the nation's welfare.

The trial court charged that "breach of the peace" consists of any "misbehavior which violates the public peace and decorum"; and that the "misbehavior may constitute a breach of the peace if it stirs the public to anger, invites dispute, brings about a condition of unrest, or creates a disturbance, or if it molests the inhabitants in the enjoyment of peace and quiet by arousing alarm." Petitioner did not take exception to that instruction. But he maintained at all times that the ordinance as applied to his conduct violated his right of free speech under the Federal Constitution. . . .

The argument here has been focused on the issue of whether the content of petitioner's speech was composed of derisive, fighting words, which carried it outside the scope of the constitutional guarantees. See *Chaplinsky v. New Hampshire*, 315 U.S. 568. . . . We do not reach that question, for there is a preliminary question that is dispositive of the case.

As we have noted, the statutory words "breach of the peace" were defined in instructions to the jury to include speech which "stirs the public to anger, invites dispute, brings about a condition of unrest, or creates a disturbance. . . ." That construction of the ordinance is a ruling on a question of state law that is as binding on us as though the precise words had been written into the ordinance. . . .

The vitality of civil and political institutions in our society depends on free discussion. As Chief Justice Hughes wrote in *De Jonge v. Oregon*, 299 U.S. 353, . . . it is only through free debate and free exchange of ideas that government remains responsive to the will of the people and peaceful change is effected. The right to speak freely and to promote diversity of ideas and programs is therefore one of the chief distinctions that sets us apart from totalitarian regimes.

Accordingly a function of free speech under our system of government is to invite dispute. It may indeed best serve its high purpose when it induces a condition of unrest, creates dissatisfaction with conditions as they are, or even stirs people to anger. Speech is often provocative and challenging. It may strike at prejudices and preconceptions and have profound unsettling effects as it presses for acceptance of an idea. That is why freedom of speech, though not absolute, . . . is nevertheless protected against censorship or punishment, unless

shown likely to produce a clear and present danger of a serious substantive evil that arises far above public inconvenience, annoyance, or
unrest. . . . There is no room under our Constitution for a more restrictive view. For the alternative would lead to standardization of
ideas either by legislatures, courts, or dominant political or community
groups.

The ordinance as construed by the trial court seriously invaded this
province. It permitted conviction of petitioner if his speech stirred
people to anger, invited public dispute, or brought about a condition
of unrest. A conviction resting on any of those grounds may not
stand. . . .

But it is said that throughout the appellate proceedings the Illinois
courts assumed that the only conduct punishable and punished under
the ordinance was conduct constituting "fighting words." . . . Petitioner was not convicted under a statute so narrowly construed. For
all anyone knows he was convicted under the parts of the ordinance (as
construed) which, for example, make it an offense merely to invite
dispute or to bring about a condition of unrest. We cannot avoid that
issue by saying that all Illinois did was to measure petitioner's conduct, not the ordinance, against the Constitution. Petitioner raised both
points—that his speech was protected by the Constitution; that the
inclusion of his speech within the ordinance was a violation of the Constitution. . . .

—Reversed.

Mr. Justice Jackson, dissenting:

The Court reverses this conviction by reiterating generalized approbations
of freedom of speech with which, in the abstract, no one will disagree. Doubts
as to their applicability are lulled by avoidance of more than passing reference to the circumstances of Terminiello's speech and judging it as if he had
spoken to persons as dispassionate as empty benches, or like a modern
Demosthenes practicing his Philippics on a lonely seashore.

But the local court that tried Terminiello was not indulging in theory.
It was dealing with a riot and with a speech that provoked a hostile mob
and incited a friendly one, and threatened violence between the two. When
the trial judge instructed the jury that it might find Terminiello guilty of
inducing a breach of the peace if his behavior stirred the public to anger,
invited dispute, brought about unrest, created a disturbance or molested
peace and quiet by arousing alarm, he was not speaking of these as harmless or abstract conditions. He was addressing his words to the concrete
behavior and specific consequences disclosed by the evidence. He was saying to the jury, in effect, that if this particular speech added fuel to the
situation already so inflamed as to threaten to get beyond police control, it
could be punished as inducing a breach of peace. When the light of the

evidence not recited by the Court is thrown upon the Court's opinion, it discloses that underneath a little issue of Terminiello and his hundred-dollar fine lurk some of the most far-reaching constitutional questions that can confront a people who value both liberty and order. This Court seems to regard these as enemies of each other and to be of the view that we must forego order to achieve liberty. So it fixes its eyes on a conception of freedom of speech so rigid as to tolerate no concession to society's need for public order.

An old proverb warns us to take heed lest we "walk into a well from looking at the stars." To show why I think the Court is in some danger of doing just that, I must bring these deliberations down to earth by a long recital of facts.

Terminiello, advertised as a Catholic Priest, but revealed at the trial to be under suspension by his Bishop, was brought to Chicago from Birmingham, Alabama, to address a gathering that assembled in response to a call signed by Gerald L. K. Smith, which, among other things, said:

> . . . The same people who hate Father Coughlin hate Father Terminiello. They have persecuted him, hounded him, threatened him, but he has remained unaffected by their anti-Christian campaign against him. You will hear all sorts of reports concerning Father Terminiello. But remember that he is a Priest in good standing and a fearless lover of Christ and America.

The jury may have considered that this call attempted to capitalize the hatreds this man had stirred and foreshadowed, if it did not intend to invite the kind of demonstration that followed.

Terminiello's own testimony shows the conditions under which he spoke. So far as material it follows:

> . . . We got there [the meeting place] approximately fifteen or twenty minutes past eight. The car stopped at the front entrance. There was a crowd of three or four hundred congregated there shouting and cursing and picketing. . . .
>
> When we got there the pickets were not marching; they were body to body and covered the sidewalk completely, some on the steps so that we had to form a flying wedge to get through. Police escorted us to the building, and I noticed four or five others there.
>
> They called us "God damned Fascists, Nazis, ought to hang the so and sos." When I entered the building I heard the howls of the people outside. . . . There were four or five plain clothes officers standing at the entrance to the stage and three or four at the entrance to the back door.
>
> The officers threatened that if they broke the door again they would arrest them and every time they opened the door a little to look out something was thrown at the officers, including ice-picks and rocks.
>
> A number of times the door was broken, was partly broken through. There were doors open this way and they partly opened and the officers looked out two or three times and each time ice-picks, stones and

bottles were thrown at the police at the door. I took my place on the stage, before this I was about ten or fifteen minutes in the body of the hall.

I saw a number of windows broken by stones or missiles. I saw the back door being forced open, pushed open.

The front door was broken partly open after the doors were closed. There were about seven people seated on the stage. Smith opened the meeting with prayer, the Pledge of Allegiance to the Flag and singing of America. There were other speakers who spoke before me and before I spoke I heard things happening in the hall and coming from the outside.

I saw rocks being thrown through windows and that continued throughout at least the first half of the meeting, probably longer, and again attempts were made to force the front door, rather the front door was forced partly. The howling continued on the outside, cursing could be heard audibly in the hall at times. Police were rushing in and out of the front door protecting the front door, and there was a general commotion, all kinds of noises and violence—all from the outside.

Between the time the first speaker spoke and I spoke, stones and bricks were thrown in all the time. I started to speak about 35 or 40 minutes after the meeting started, a little later than nine o'clock. . . .

The Court below, in addition to this recital, heard other evidence, that the crowd reached an estimated number of 1,500. Picket lines obstructed and interfered with access to the building. The crowd constituted "a surging, howling mob hurling epithets at those who would enter and tried to tear their clothes off." One young woman's coat was torn off and she had to be assisted into the meeting by policemen. Those inside the hall could hear the loud noises and hear those on the outside yell, "Fascists, Hitlers!" and curse words like "damn Fascists." Bricks were thrown through the windowpanes before and during the speaking. About 28 windows were broken. The street was black with people on both sides for at least a block either way; bottles, stink bombs and brickbats were thrown. Police were unable to control the mob, which kept breaking the windows at the meeting hall, drowning out the speaker's voice at times and breaking in through the back door of the auditorium. About 17 of the group outside were arrested by the police.

Knowing of this environment, Terminiello made a long speech, from the stenographic record of which I omit relatively innocuous passages and add emphasis to what seems especially provocative:

Father Terminiello: Now, I am going to whisper my greetings to you, Fellow Christians. I will interpret it. I said, "Fellow *Christians*," and I suppose there are *some of the scum got in by mistake*, so I want to tell a story about *the scum:*

. . . And nothing I could say tonight could begin to express the contempt I have for the *slimy scum* that got in by mistake.

. . . The subject I want to talk to you tonight about is the attempt *that is going on right outside this hall tonight,* the attempt that is going on to *destroy America by revolution.* . . .

I know I was told one time that my winter quarters were ready for me in Siberia. I was told that. Now, I am talking about the fifty-seven varieties that we have in America and we have fifty-seven varieties of pinks and reds and pastel shades in this country; and all of it can be traced back to the twelve years we spent under the New Deal, because that was the build-up for what is going on in the world today. . . .

Now, we are going to get the threats of the people of Argentine, the people of Spain. We have now declared, according to our officials, to have declared Franco to have taken the place of Hitler. *Franco was the savior of what was left of Europe.*

Now, let me say, I am going to talk about—I almost said, about the Jews. Of course, I would not want to say that. However, I am going to talk about some Jews, I hope that—I am a Christian minister. We must take a Christian attitude. I don't want you to go from this hall with hatred in your heart for any person, for no person. . . .

Now, this danger which we face—let us call them Zionist Jews if you will, let's call them atheistic, communistic Jewish or Zionist Jews, then let us not fear to condemn them. You remember the Apostles when they went into the upper room after the death of the Master, they went in there, after locking the doors; they closed the windows. (At this time there was a very loud noise as if something was being thrown into the building.)

Don't be disturbed. That happened by the way, while Mr. Gerald Smith was saying "Our Father who art in heaven;" (just then a rock went through the window.) *Do you wonder they were persecuted in other countries in the world?* . . .

That is why I say to you, men, don't you do it. Walk out of here dignified. The police will protect you. Put the women on the inside, where there will be no hurt to them. Just walk; don't stop and argue. . . . They want to picket our meetings. They don't want us to picket their meetings. It is the same kind of tolerance, if we said there was a bedbug in bed, "We don't care for you," or if we looked under the bed and found a snake and said, "I am going to be tolerant and leave the snake there." We will not be tolerant of that mob out there. We are not going to be tolerant any longer.

We are strong enough. We are not going to be tolerant of their smears any longer. We are going to *stand up and dare them to smear us.*

So, my friends, since we spent much time tonight trying to quiet the howling mob, I am going to bring my thoughts to a conclusion, and the conclusion is this. We must all be like the Apostles before the coming of the Holy Ghost. We must not lock ourselves in an upper room for fear of the Jews. I speak of the Communistic Zionistic Jew, and those are not American Jews. We don't want them here; we want them to go back where they came from. . . .

Such was the speech. Evidence showed that it stirred the audience not only to cheer and applaud but to expressions of immediate anger, unrest and alarm. One called the speaker a "God damned liar" and was taken out by the police. Another said that "Jews, niggers and Catholics would have to be gotten rid of." One response was, "yes, the Jews are all killers, murderers. If we don't kill them first, they will kill us." The anti-Jewish stories elicited exclamations of "Oh!" and "Isn't that terrible!" and shouts of "Yes, send the Jews back to Russia," "Kill the Jews," "Dirty kikes," and much more of ugly tenor. This is the specific and concrete kind of anger, unrest and alarm, coupled with that of the mob outside, that the trial court charged the jury might find to be a breach of peace induced by Terminiello. It is difficult to believe that this Court is speaking of the same occasion, but it is the only one involved in this litigation.

Terminiello, of course, disclaims being a fascist. Doubtless many of the indoor audience were not consciously such. His speech, however, followed, with fidelity that is more than coincidental, the pattern of European fascist leaders.

The street mob, on the other hand, included some who deny being communists, but Terminiello testified and offered to prove that the demonstration was communist-organized and communist-led. He offered literature of left-wing organizations calling members to meet and "mobilize" for instruction as pickets and exhorting followers: "All out to fight Fascist Smith."

As this case declares a nation-wide rule that disables local and state authorities from punishing conduct which produces conflicts of this kind, it is unrealistic not to take account of the nature, methods and objectives of the forces involved. This was not an isolated, spontaneous and unintended collision of political, racial or ideological adversaries. It was a local manifestation of a world-wide and standing conflict between two organized groups of revolutionary fanatics, each of which has imported to this country the strong-arm technique developed in the struggle by which their kind has devastated Europe. Increasingly, American cities have to cope with it. One faction organizes a mass meeting, the other organizes pickets to harass it; each organizes squads to counteract the other's pickets; parade is met with counterparade. Each of these mass demonstrations has the potentiality, and more than a few the purpose, of disorder and violence. This technique appeals not to reason but to fears and mob spirit; each is a show of force designed to bully adversaries and to overawe the indifferent. We need not resort to speculation as to the purposes for which these tactics are calculated nor as to their consequences. Recent European history demonstrates both.

Hitler summed up the strategy of the mass demonstration as used by both fascism and communism: "We should not work in secret conventicles but in mighty mass demonstrations, and it is not by dagger and poison or pistol that the road can be cleared for the movement but *by the conquest of the streets*. We must teach the Marxists that the future *master of the streets* is National Socialism, just as it will some day be the master of the state." . . .

The present obstacle to mastery of the streets by either radical or reactionary mob movements is not the opposing minority. It is the authority of local governments which represent the free choice of democratic and law-abiding elements, of all shades of opinion but who, whatever their differences, submit them to free elections which register the results of their free discussion. The fascist and communist groups, on the contrary, resort to these terror tactics to confuse, bully and discredit those freely chosen governments. Violent and noisy shows of strength discourage participation of moderates in discussions so fraught with violence and real discussion dries up and disappears. And people lose faith in the democratic process when they see public authority flouted and impotent and begin to think the time has come when they must choose sides in a false and terrible dilemma such as was posed as being at hand by the call for the Terminiello meeting: "Christian Nationalism or World Communism—Which?"

This drive by totalitarian groups to undermine the prestige and effectiveness of local democratic governments is advanced whenever either of them can win from this Court a ruling which paralyzes the power of these officials. This is such a case. The group of which Terminiello is a part claims that his behavior, because it involved a speech, is above the reach of local authorities. If the mild action those authorities have taken is forbidden, it is plain that hereafter there is nothing effective left that they can do. If they can do nothing as to him, they are equally powerless as to rival totalitarian groups. Terminiello's victory today certainly fulfills the most extravagant hopes of both right and left totalitarian groups, who want nothing so much as to paralyze and discredit the only democratic authority that can curb them in their battle for the streets.

I am unable to see that the local authorities have transgressed the Federal Constitution. Illinois imposed no prior censorship or suppression upon Terminiello. On the contrary, its sufferance and protection was all that enabled him to speak. It does not appear that the motive in punishing him is to silence the ideology he expressed as offensive to the State's policy or as untrue, or has any purpose of controlling his thought or its peaceful communication to others. There is no claim that the proceedings against Terminiello are designed to discriminate against him or the faction he represents or the ideas that he bespeaks. There is no indication that the charge against him is a mere pretext to give the semblance of legality to a covert effort to silence him or to prevent his followers or the public from hearing any truth that is in him.

A trial court and jury has found only that in the context of violence and disorder in which it was made, this speech was a provocation to immediate breach of the peace and therefore cannot claim constitutional immunity from punishment. Under the Constitution as it has been understood and applied, at least until most recently, the State was within its powers in taking this action.

Rioting is a substantive evil, which I take it no one will deny that the State and the City have the right and the duty to prevent and punish. Where an offense is induced by speech, the Court has laid down and often reiterated a test of the power of the authorities to deal with the speaking as also an offense. "The question in every case is whether the words *used are used in such circumstances* and are of *such a nature* as to create a *clear and present danger* that they will bring about the substantive evils that Congress [or the State or City] has a right to prevent." (Emphasis supplied.) Mr. Justice Holmes in *Schenck* v. *United States,* 249 U.S. 47. No one ventures to contend that the State on the basis of this test, for whatever it may be worth, was not justified in punishing Terminiello. In this case the evidence proves beyond dispute that danger of rioting and violence in response to the speech was clear, present and immediate. If this Court has not silently abandoned this long standing test and substituted for the purposes of this case an unexpressed but more stringent test, the action of the State would have to be sustained.

Only recently this Court held that a state could punish as a breach of the peace use of epithets such as "damned racketeer" and "damned fascists," addressed to only one person, an official, because likely to provoke the average person to retaliation. But these are mild in comparison to the epithets "slimy scum," "snakes," "bedbugs," and the like, which Terminiello hurled at an already inflamed mob of his adversaries. Mr. Justice Murphy, writing for a unanimous Court in *Chaplinsky* v. *New Hampshire,* 315 U.S. 568, said:

> There are certain well-defined and narrowly limited classes of speech, the prevention and punishment of which have never been thought to raise any Constitutional problem. These include the lewd and obscene, the profane, the libelous and the insulting or 'fighting' words—those which by their very utterance inflict injury or tend to incite an immediate breach of the peace. It has been well observed that such utterances are no essential part of any exposition of ideas, and are of such slight social value as a step to truth that any benefit that may be derived from them is clearly outweighed by the social interest in order and morality. "Resort to epithets or personal abuse is not in any proper sense communication of information or opinion safeguarded by the Constitution, and its punishment as a criminal act would raise no question under that instrument." *Cantwell* v. *Connecticut,* 310 U.S. 296.

. . . How this present decision, denying state power to punish civilly one who precipitated a public riot involving hundreds of fanatic fighters in a most violent melee, can be squared with those unanimous statements of law, is incomprehensible to me. . . .

However, these wholesome principles are abandoned today and in their place is substituted a dogma of absolute freedom for irresponsible and provocative utterance which almost completely sterilizes the power of local authorities to keep the peace as against this kind of tactics. . . .

This case demonstrates also that this Court's service to free speech is essentially negative and can consist only of reviewing actions by local magistrates. But if free speech is to be a practical reality, affirmative and immediate protection is required; and it can come only from nonjudicial sources. It depends on local police, maintained by law-abiding taxpayers, and who, regardless of their own feelings, risk themselves to maintain supremacy of law. Terminiello's theoretical right to speak free from interference would have no reality if Chicago should withdraw its officers to some other section of the city, or if the men assigned to the task should look the other way when the crowd threatens Terminiello. Can society be expected to keep these men at Terminiello's service if it has nothing to say of his behavior which may force them into dangerous action?

No one will disagree that the fundamental, permanent and overriding policy of police and courts should be to permit and encourage utmost freedom of utterance. It is the legal right of any American citizen to advocate peaceful adoption of fascism or communism, socialism or capitalism. He may go far in expressing sentiments whether pro-semitic or anti-semitic, pro-Negro or anti-Negro, pro-Catholic or anti-Catholic. He is legally free to argue for some anti-American system of government to supersede by constitutional methods the one we have. It is our philosophy that the course of government should be controlled by a consensus of the governed. This process of reaching intelligent popular decisions requires free discussion. Hence we should tolerate no law or custom of censorship or suppression.

But we must bear in mind also that no serious outbreak of mob violence, race rioting, lynching or public disorder is likely to get going without help of some speech-making to some mass of people. A street may be filled with men and women and the crowd still not be a mob. Unity of purpose, passion and hatred, which merges the many minds of a crowd into the mindlessness of a mob, almost invariably is supplied by speeches. It is naive, or worse, to teach that oratory with this object or effect is a service to liberty. No mob has ever protected any liberty, even its own, but if not put down it always winds up in an orgy of lawlessness which respects no liberties.

In considering abuse of freedom by provocative utterances it is necessary to observe that the law is more tolerant of discussion than are most individuals or communities. Law is so indifferent to subjects of talk that I think of none that it should close to discussion. Religious, social and political topics that in other times or countries have not been open to lawful debate may be freely discussed here.

Because a subject is legally arguable, however, does not mean that public sentiment will be patient of its advocacy at all times and in all manners. So it happens that, while peaceful advocacy of communism or fascism is tolerated by the law, both of these doctrines arouse passionate reactions. A great number of people do not agree that introduction to America of communism or fascism is even debatable. Hence many speeches, such as that of Terminiello, may be legally permissible but may nevertheless in some surroundings, be a menace to peace and order. When conditions show the speaker that this is the case, as it did here, there certainly comes a point beyond which he cannot indulge in provocations to violence without being answerable to society. . . .

The ways in which mob violence may be worked up are subtle and various. Rarely will a speaker directly urge a crowd to lay hands on a victim or class of victims. An effective and safer way is to incite mob action while pretending to deplore it, after the classic example of Antony, and this was not lost on

Terminiello. And whether one may be the cause of mob violence by his own personification or advocacy of ideas which a crowd already fears and hates, is not solved merely by going through a transcript of the speech to pick out "fighting words." The most insulting words can be neutralized if the speaker will smile when he says them, but a belligerent personality and an aggressive manner may kindle a fight without use of words that in cold type shock us. True judgment will be aided by observation of the individual defendant, as was possible for this jury and trial court but impossible for us. . . .

Invocation of constitutional liberties as part of the strategy for overthrowing them presents a dilemma to a free people which may not be soluble by constitutional logic alone.

But I would not be understood as suggesting that the United States can or should meet this dilemma by suppression of free, open and public speaking on the part of any group or ideology. Suppression has never been a successful permanent policy; any surface serenity that it creates is a false security, while conspirational forces go underground. My confidence in American institutions and in the sound sense of the American people is such that if with a stroke of the pen I could silence every fascist and communist speaker, I would not do it. . . .

This Court has gone far toward accepting the doctrine that civil liberty means the removal of all restraints from these crowds and that all local attempts to maintain order are impairments of the liberty of the citizen. The choice is not between order and liberty. It is between liberty with order and anarchy without either. There is danger that, if the Court does not temper its doctrinaire logic with a little practical wisdom it will convert the constitutional Bill of Rights into a suicide pact.

I would affirm the conviction.

d. Group Libel

BEAUHARNAIS v. ILLINOIS

343 US 250 (1952)

[The guaranty of freedom of the press does not protect a person when he makes statements about another person that are libelous. A libel may be the basis of a civil suit for damages or of a criminal prosecution. While the truth may be a complete defense in a civil libel case, in a criminal libel case some states provide that truth is a defense only when the statement is published with good motives for justifiable ends. Illinois extended this law of criminal libel to punish publications which libel a group by identifying its members by their race, creed, or religion. Beauharnais, a white-supremacy agitator, was convicted under this law. The Supreme Court upheld the group libel statute as constitutional.

[The decision was 5 to 4, with Justices Reed, Jackson, Black, and

Douglas dissenting. Students of free speech are as divided about the constitutionality and wisdom of group libel laws as are members of the Court. For some years a group libel law was under consideration by Congress—to punish use of the mails by publications that libel certain groups—but counsel on the bill was divided and Congress has not enacted the bill. Should groups that agitate race or religious hatred aggravate the dangers to public peace, the debate over group libel statutes will again become a subject of immediate public interest.]

Mr. Justice Frankfurter delivered the opinion of the Court:

The petitioner was convicted upon information in the Municipal Court of Chicago of violating the Illinois Penal Code. He was fined $200. The section provides:

It shall be unlawful for any person, firm or corporation to manufacture, sell, or offer for sale, advertise or publish, present or exhibit in any public place in this state any lithograph, moving picture, play, drama or sketch, which publication or exhibition portrays depravity, criminality, unchastity, or lack of virtue of a class of citizens, of any race, color, creed or religion which said publication or exhibition exposes the citizens of any race, color, creed or religion to contempt, derision, or obloquy or which is productive of breach of the peace or riots. . . .

Beauharnais challenged the statute as violating the liberty of speech and of the press guaranteed as against the States by the Due Process Clause of the Fourteenth Amendment, and as too vague, under the restrictions implicit in the same Clause, to support conviction for crime. The Illinois courts rejected these contentions and sustained defendant's conviction. . . . We granted certiorari in view of the serious questions raised concerning the limitations imposed by the Fourteenth Amendment on the power of a State to punish utterances promoting friction among racial and religious groups. . . .

The information, cast generally in the terms of the statute, charged that Beauharnais "did unlawfully . . . exhibit in public places lithographs, which publications portray depravity, criminality, unchastity or lack of virtue of citizens of Negro race and color and which exposes [*sic*] citizens of Illinois of the Negro race and color to contempt, derision, or obloquy. . . ." The lithograph complained of was a leaflet setting forth a petition calling on the Mayor and City Council of Chicago "to halt the further encroachment, harassment and invasion of white people, their property, neighborhoods and persons, by the Negro. . . ." Below was a call for "One million self respecting white people in Chicago to unite . . ." with the statement added that "If persuasion and the need to prevent the white race from becoming mongrelized by the negro will not unite us, then the aggression . . . rapes, robberies, knives, guns and marijuana of the negro, surely will." This, with more language, similar if not so violent, concluded with an attached application for membership in the White Circle League of America, Inc.

The testimony at the trial was substantially undisputed. From it the jury could find that Beauharnais was president of the White Circle League; that, at a meeting on January 6, 1950, he passed out bundles of the lithographs in question, together with other literature, to volunteers for distribution on downtown Chicago street corners the following day; that he carefully organized that distribution, giving detailed instructions for it; and that the leaflets were in fact distributed . . . in accordance with his plan and instructions. The court, together with other charges on burden of proof and the like, told the jury "if you find . . . that the defendant, Joseph Beauharnais, did . . . manufacture, sell, or offer for sale, advertise or publish, present or exhibit in any public place the lithograph . . . then you are to find the defendant guilty. . . ." He refused to charge the jury, as requested by the defendant, that in order to convict they must find "that the article complained of was likely to produce a clear and present danger of a serious substantive evil that rises far above public inconvenience, annoyance or unrest." Upon this evidence and these instructions, the jury brought in the conviction here for review.

The statute before us is not a catchall enactment left at large by the State court which applied it. . . . It is a law specifically directed at a defined evil, its language drawing from history and practice in Illinois and in more than a score of other jurisdictions a meaning confirmed by the Supreme Court of that State in upholding this conviction. We do not, therefore, parse the statute as grammarians or treat it as an abstract exercise in lexicography. . . .

The Illinois Supreme Court tells us that § 224a "is a form of criminal libel law." . . . The defendant, the trial court and the Supreme Court consistently treated it as such. The defendant offered evidence tending to prove the truth of parts of the utterance, and the courts below considered and disposed of this offer in terms of ordinary criminal libel precedents. Section 224a does not deal with the defense of truth, but by the Illinois Constitution, . . . "in all trials for libel, both civil and criminal, the truth, when published with good motives and for justifiable ends, shall be a sufficient defense." . . . Similarly, the action of the trial court in deciding as a matter of law the libelous character of the utterance, leaving to the jury only the question of publication, follows the settled rule in prosecutions for libel in Illinois and other States. Moreover, the Supreme Court's characterization of the words prohibited by the statute as those "liable to cause violence and disorder" paraphrases the traditional justification for punishing libels criminally, namely their "tendency to cause breach of the peace."

Libel of an individual was a common-law crime, and thus criminal in the colonies. Indeed, at common law, truth or good motives was no defense. In the first decades after the adoption of the Constitution, this was changed by judicial decision, statute or constitution in most States, but nowhere was there any suggestion that the crime of libel be abolished. Today, every American jurisdiction—the forty-eight States, the District of Columbia, Alaska, Hawaii and Puerto Rico—punish libels directed at individuals.

There are certain well-defined and narrowly limited classes of speech, the prevention and punishment of which has never been thought to raise any Constitutional problem. These include the lewd and obscene, the profane, the libelous, and the insulting or 'fighting' words—those which by their very utterance inflict injury or tend to incite an immediate breach of the peace. It has been well observed that such utterances are no essential part of any exposition of ideas, and are of such slight social value as a step to truth that any benefit that may be derived from them is clearly outweighed by the social interest in order and morality. 'Resort to epithets or personal abuse is not in any proper sense communication of information or opinion safeguarded by the Constitution, and its punishment as a criminal act would raise no question under that instrument.' *Cantwell* v. *Connecticut*, 310 U.S. 296. . . .

Such were the views of a unanimous Court in *Chaplinsky* v. *New Hampshire*, 315 U.S. 571.

No one will gainsay that it is libelous falsely to charge another with being a rapist, robber, carrier of knives and guns, user of marijuana. The precise question before us, then, is whether the protection of "liberty" in the Due Process Clause of the Fourteenth Amendment prevents a State from punishing such libels—as criminal libel has been defined, limited and constitutionally recognized time out of mind—directed at designated collectivities and flagrantly disseminated. There is even authority, however dubious, that such utterances were also crimes at common law. It is certainly clear that some American jurisdictions have sanctioned their punishment under ordinary criminal libel statutes. We cannot say, however, that the question is concluded by history and practice. But if an utterance directed at an individual may be the object of criminal sanctions, we cannot deny to a State power to punish the same utterance directed at a defined group, unless we can say that this is a wilful and purposeless restriction unrelated to the peace and well-being of the State.

Illinois did not have to look beyond her own borders or await the tragic experience of the last three decades to conclude that wilful purveyors of falsehood concerning racial and religious groups promote strife and tend powerfully to obstruct the manifold adjustments required of free, ordered life in a metropolitan, polyglot community. From the murder of the abolitionist Lovejoy in 1837 to the Cicero riots of 1951, Illinois has been the scene of exacerbated tension between races, often flaring into violence and destruction. In many of these outbreaks, utterances of the character here in question, so the Illinois legislature could conclude, played a significant part. The law was passed on June 29, 1917, at a time when the State was struggling to assimilate vast numbers of new inhabitants, as yet concentrated in discrete racial or national or religious groups—foreign-born brought to it by the crest of the great wave of immigration, and Negroes attracted by jobs in war plants and the allurements of northern claims. Nine years earlier, in the very city where the legislature sat, what is said to be the first northern race riot had cost the lives of six people, left hundreds of Negroes homeless and shocked citizens into action far beyond the borders of the State. Less than a month before the bill was enacted, East St. Louis had seen a day's rioting, prelude to an outbreak, only four days after the bill became law, so bloody that it led to Congressional investigation. A series of bombings had begun which was to culminate two years later in the awful race riot which held Chicago in its grip for seven days in the summer of 1919. Nor has tension and violence between the groups defined in the statute been limited in Illinois to clashes between whites and Negroes.

In the face of this history and its frequent obligato of extreme racial and religious propaganda, we would deny experience to say that the Illinois legislature was without reason in seeking ways to curb false or malicious defamation of racial and religious groups, made in public places and by means calculated to have a powerful emotional impact on those to whom it was presented. "There are limits to the exercise of these liberties [of speech and of the press]. The danger in these times from the coercive activities of those who in the delusion of racial or religious conceit would incite violence and breaches of the peace in order to deprive others of their equal right to the exercise of their liberties, is emphasized by events familiar to all. These and other transgressions of those limits the states appropriately may punish." This was the conclusion, again of a unanimous Court, in 1940. *Cantwell v. Connecticut.* . . .

It may be argued, and weightily, that this legislation will not help matters; that tension and on occasion violence between racial and religious groups must be traced to causes more deeply embedded in our society than the rantings of modern Know-nothings. Only those lacking responsible humility will have a confident solution for problems as intractable as the frictions attributable to differences of race, color or religion. This being so, it would be out of bounds for the judiciary to deny the legislature a choice of policy, provided it is not unrelated to the problem and not forbidden by some explicit limitation on the State's power. That the legislative remedy might not in practice mitigate the evil, or might itself raise new problems, would only manifest once more the paradox of reform. It is the price to be paid for the trial-and-error inherent in legislative efforts to deal with obstinate social issues. "The science of government is the most abstruse of all sciences; if, indeed, that can be called a science which has but few fixed principles, and practically consists in little more than the exercise of a sound discretion, applied to the exigencies of the state as they arise. It is the science of experiment." *Anderson* v. *Dunn*, 6 Wheat. 204. Certainly the Due Process Clause does not require the legislature to be in the vanguard of science—especially sciences as young as human ecology and cultural anthropology. . . .

Long ago this Court recognized that the economic rights of an individual may depend for the effectiveness of their enforcement on rights in the group, even though not formally corporate, to which he belongs. . . . Such group-protection on behalf of the individual may, for all we know, be a need not confined to the part that a trade union plays in effectuating rights abstractly recognized as belonging to its members. It is not within our competence to confirm or deny claims of social scientists as to the dependence of the individual on the position of his racial or religious group in the community. It would, however, be arrant dogmatism, quite outside the scope of our authority in passing on the powers of a State, for us to deny that the Illinois Legislature may warrantably believe that a man's job and his educational opportunities and the dignity accorded him may depend as much on the reputation of the racial and religious group to which he willy-nilly belongs, as it does on his own merits. This being so, we are precluded from saying that speech concededly punishable when immediately directed at individuals cannot be outlawed if directed at groups with whose position and esteem in society the affiliated individual may be inextricably involved.

We are warned that the choice open to the Illinois legislature here may be abused, that the law may be discriminatorily enforced; prohibiting libel of a creed or of a racial group, we are told, is but a step from prohibiting libel of a political party.

Every power may be abused, but the possibility of abuse is a poor reason for denying Illinois the power to adopt measures against criminal libels sanctioned by centuries of Anglo-American law. "While this Court sits" it retains and exercises authority to nullify action which encroaches on freedom of utterance under the guise of punishing libel. Of course discussion cannot be denied and the right, as well as the duty, of criticism must not be stifled.

The scope of the statute before us, as construed by the Illinois court, disposes of the contention that the conduct prohibited by the law is so ill-defined that judges and juries in applying the statute and men in acting cannot draw from it adequate standards to guide them. . . .

It is suggested that while it was clearly within the constitutional power of Illinois to punish this utterance if the proceeding were properly safeguarded, in this particular case Illinois denied the defendant rights which the Due Process Clause commands. Specifically, it is argued that the defendant was not permitted to raise at the trial defenses constitutionally guaranteed in a criminal libel prosecution: (1) the defense of truth; (2) justification of the utterance as "fair comment"; and (3) its privilege as a means for redressing grievances.

Neither by proffer of evidence, requests for instructions, motion before or after verdict did the defendant seek to justify his utterance as "fair comment" or as privileged. Nor has the defendant urged as a ground for reversing his conviction in this Court that his opportunity to make those defenses was denied below. And so, whether a prosecution for libel of a racial or religious group is unconstitutionally invalid where the State did deny the defendant such opportunities is not before us. Certainly the State may cast the burden of justifying what is patent defamation upon the defamer. The benefits of hypothetical defenses, never raised below or pressed upon us, are not to be invoked in the abstract.

As to the defense of truth, Illinois in common with many States requires a showing not only that the utterance state the facts, but also that the publication be made "with good motives and for justifiable ends." Ill. Const. Art. II, § 4. Both elements are necessary if the defense is to prevail. What has been called "the common sense of American criminal law," as formulated, with regard to necessary safeguards in criminal libel prosecutions, in the New York constitution of 1821, Art. VII, § 8, has been adopted in terms by Illinois. The teaching of a century and a half of criminal libel prosecutions in this country would go by the board if we were to hold that Illinois was not within her rights in making this combined requirement. Assuming that defendant's offer of proof directed to a part of the defense was adequate, it did not satisfy the entire requirement which Illinois could exact.

Libellous utterances, not being within the area of constitutionally protected speech, it is unnecessary, either for us or for the State courts, to consider the issues behind the phrase "clear and present danger." Certainly no one would contend that obscene speech, for example, may be punished only upon a showing of such circumstances. Libel, as we have seen, is in the same class.

We find no warrant in the Constitution for denying to Illinois the power to pass the law here under attack. But it bears repeating—although it should not—that our finding that the law is not constitutionally objectionable carries no implication of approval of the wisdom of the legislation or of its efficacy. These questions may raise doubts in our minds as well as in others. It is not for us, however, to make the legislative judgment. We are not at liberty to erect those doubts into fundamental law.

Affirmed.

Mr. Justice Black, with whom Mr. Justice Douglas concurs, dissenting:

This case is here because Illinois inflicted criminal punishment on Beauharnais for causing the distribution of leaflets in the city of Chicago. The conviction rests on the leaflet's contents, not on the time, manner or place of distribution. Beauharnais is head of an organization that opposes amalgamation and favors segregation of white and colored people. After discussion, an assembly of his group decided to petition the mayor and council of Chicago to pass laws for segregation. Volunteer members of the group agreed to stand on street corners, solicit signers to petitions addressed to the city authorities, and distribute leaflets giving information about the group, its beliefs and its plans. In carrying out this program a solicitor handed out a leaflet which was the basis of this prosecution. . . .

That Beauharnais and his group were making a genuine effort to petition their elected representatives is not disputed. Even as far back as 1689, the Bill of Rights exacted of William & Mary said: "It is the right of the subjects to petition the King; and all commitments and prosecutions for such petitioning are illegal." And 178 years ago the Declaration of Rights of the Colonial Congress proclaimed to the monarch of that day that his American subjects had "a right peaceably to assemble, consider of their grievances, and petition the King; and that all prosecutions, prohibitory proclamations, and commitments for the same, are illegal." After independence was won, Americans stated as the first unequivocal command of their Bill of Rights: "Congress shall make no law . . . abridging the freedom of speech, or of the press; or the right of the people peaceably to assemble, and to petition the Government for a redress of grievances." Without distortion, this First Amendment could not possibly be read so as to hold that Congress has power to punish Beauharnais and others for petitioning Congress as they have here sought to petition the Chicago authorities. . . . And we have held in a number of prior cases that the Fourteenth Amendment makes the specific prohibitions of the First Amendment equally applicable to the states.

In view of these prior holdings, how does the Court justify its holding today that states can punish people for exercising the vital freedoms intended to be safeguarded from suppression by the First Amendment? The prior holdings are not referred to; the Court simply acts on the bland assumption that the First Amendment is wholly irrelevant. It is not even accorded the respect of a passing mention. This follows logically, I suppose, from recent constitutional doctrine which appears to measure state laws solely by this Court's notions of civilized "canons of decency," reasonableness, etc. . . . Under this "reasonableness" test, state laws abridging First Amendment freedoms are sustained if found to have a "rational basis." . . . Today's case degrades First Amendment freedoms to the "rational basis" level. It is now a certainty that the new "due process" coverall offers far less protection to liberty than would adherence to our former cases compelling states to abide by the unequivocal First Amendment command that its defined freedoms shall not be abridged.

The Court's holding here and the constitutional doctrine behind it leave the right of assembly, petition, speech and press almost completely at the mercy of state legislative, executive, and judicial agencies. I say "almost" because state curtailment of these freedoms may still be invalidated if a majority of this Court conclude that a particular infringement is "without reason," or is "a wilful and purposeless restriction unrelated to the peace and well being of the State." But lest this encouragement should give too much hope as to how and when this Court might protect these basic freedoms from state invasion, we are cautioned that state legislatures must be left free to "experiment" and to make "legislative" judgments. We are told that mistakes may be made during the legislative process of curbing public opinion. In such event the Court fortunately does not leave those mistakenly curbed, or any of us for that matter, unadvised. Consolation can be sought and must be found in the philosophical reflection that state legislative error in stifling speech and press "is the price to be paid for the trial-and-error inherent in legislative efforts to deal with obstinate social issues." My own belief is that no legislature is charged with the duty or vested with the power to decide what public issues Americans can discuss. In a free country that is the individual's choice, not the state's. State experimentation in curbing freedom of expression is startling and frightening doctrine in a country dedicated to self-government by its people. I reject the holding that either state or nation can punish people for having their say in matters of public concern. . . .

Unless I misread history the majority is giving libel a more expansive scope and more respectable status than it was ever accorded even in the Star Chamber. For here it is held to be punishable to give publicity to any picture, moving picture, play, drama or sketch, or any printed matter which a judge may find unduly offensive to any race, color, creed or religion. In other words, in arguing for or against the enactment of laws that may differently affect huge groups, it is now very dangerous indeed to say something critical of one of the groups. And any "person, firm or corporation" can be tried for this crime. "Person, firm or corporation" certainly includes a book publisher, newspaper, radio or television station, candidate or even a preacher.

It is easy enough to say that none of this latter group have been proceeded against under the Illinois Act. And they have not—yet. But emotions bubble and tempers flare in racial and religious controversies, the kind here involved. It would not be easy for any court, in good conscience, to narrow this Act so as to exclude from it any of those I have mentioned. Furthermore, persons tried under the Act could not even get a jury trial except as to the bare fact of publication. Here, the court simply charged the jury that Beauharnais was guilty if he had caused distribution of the leaflet. Such trial by judge rather than by jury was outlawed in England in 1792 by Fox's Libel Law.

This Act sets up a system of state censorship which is at war with the kind of free government envisioned by those who forced adoption of our Bill of Rights. The motives behind the state law may have been to do good. But the same can be said about most laws making opinions punishable as crimes. History indicates that urges to do good have led to the burning of books and even to the burning of "witches."

No rationalization on a purely legal level can conceal the fact that state laws like this one present a constant overhanging threat to freedom of speech, press and religion. Today Beauharnais is punished for publicity expressing strong views in favor of segregation. Ironically enough, Beauharnais, convicted of crime in Chicago, would probably be given a hero's reception in many other localities, if not in some parts of Chicago itself. Moreover, the same kind of state law that makes Beauharnais a criminal for advocating segregation in Illinois can be utilized to send people to jail in other states for advocating equality and nonsegregation. What Beauharnais said in his leaflet is mild compared with usual arguments on both sides of racial controversies.

We are told that freedom of petition and discussion are in no danger "while this Court sits." This case raises considerable doubt. Since those who peacefully petition for changes in the law are not to be protected "while this Court sits," who is? I do not agree that the Constitution leaves freedom of petition, assembly, speech, press or worship at the mercy of a case-by-case, day-by-day majority of this Court. I had supposed that our people could rely for their freedom on the Constitution's commands, rather than on the grace of this Court on an individual case basis. To say that a legislative body can, with this Court's approval, make it a crime to petition for and publicly discuss proposed legislation seems as farfetched to me as it would be to say that a valid law could be enacted to punish a candidate for President for telling the people his views. I think the First Amendment, with the Fourteenth, "absolutely" forbids such laws without any "ifs" or "buts" or "whereases." Whatever the danger, if any, in such public discussions, it is a danger the Founders deemed outweighed by the danger incident to the stifling of thought and speech. The Court does not act on this view of the Founders. It calculates what it deems to be the danger of public discussion, holds the scales are tipped on the side of state suppression, and upholds state censorship. This method of decision offers little protection to First Amendment liberties "while this Court sits."

If there be minority groups who hail this holding as their victory, they might consider the possible relevancy of this ancient remark: "Another such victory and I am undone."

Mr. Justice Douglas, dissenting:

Hitler and his Nazis showed how evil a conspiracy could be which was aimed at destroying a race by exposing it to contempt, derision, and obloquy. I would be willing to concede that such conduct directed at a race or group in this country could be made an indictable offense. For such a project would be more than the exercise of free speech. Like picketing, it would be free speech plus.

I would also be willing to concede that even without the element of conspiracy there might be times and occasions when the legislative or executive branch might call a halt to inflammatory talk, such as the shouting of "fire" in a school or a theatre.

My view is that if in any case other public interests are to override the plain command of the First Amendment, the peril of speech must be clear and present, leaving no room for argument, raising no doubts as to the necessity of curbing speech in order to prevent disaster.

The First Amendment is couched in absolute terms—freedom of speech shall not be abridged. Speech has therefore a preferred position as contrasted to some other civil rights. For example, privacy, equally sacred to some, is protected by the Fourth Amendment only against unreasonable searches and seizures. There is room for regulation of the ways and means of invading privacy. No such leeway is granted the invasion of the right of free speech guaranteed by the First Amendment. Until recent years that had been the course and direction of constitutional law. Yet recently the Court in this and in other cases has engrafted the right of regulation onto the First Amendment by placing in the hands of the legislative branch the right to regulate "within reasonable limits" the right of free speech. This to me is an ominous and alarming trend. The free trade in ideas which the Framers of the Constitution visualized disappears. In its place there is substituted a new orthodoxy—an orthodoxy that changes with the whims of the age or the day, an orthodoxy which the majority by solemn judgment proclaims to be essential to the safety, welfare, security, morality, or health of society. Free speech in the constitutional sense disappears. Limits are drawn—limits dictated by expediency, political opinion, prejudices or some other desideratum of legislative action.

An historic aspect of the issue of judicial supremacy was the extent to which legislative judgment would be supreme in the field of social legislation. The vague contours of the Due Process Clause were used to strike down laws deemed by the Court to be unwise and improvident. That trend has been reversed. In matters relating to business, finance, industrial and labor conditions, health and the public welfare, great leeway is now granted the legislature, for there is no guarantee in the Constitution that the *status quo* will be preserved against regulation by government. Freedom of speech, however, rests on a different constitutional basis. The First Amendment says that freedom of speech, freedom of press, and the free exercise of religion shall not be abridged. That is a negation of power on the part of each and every department of government. Free speech, free press, free exercise of religion are placed separate and apart; they are above and beyond the police power; they are not subject to regulation in the manner of factories, slums, apartment houses, production of oil, and the like.

The Court in this and in other cases places speech under an expanding legislative control. Today a white man stands convicted for protesting in unseemly language against our decisions invalidating restrictive covenants. Tomorrow a Negro will be hailed before a court for denouncing lynch law in heated terms. Farm laborers in the west who compete with field hands drifting up from Mexico; whites who feel the pressure of orientals; a minority which finds employment going to members of the dominant religious group —all of these are caught in the mesh of today's decision. Debate and argument even in the courtroom are not always calm and dispassionate. Emotions sway speakers and audiences alike. Intemperate speech is a distinctive characteristic of man. Hot heads blow off and release destructive energy in the process. They shout and rave, exaggerating weaknesses, magnifying error, viewing with alarm. So it has been from the beginning; and so it will be throughout time. The Framers of the Constitution knew human nature as well as we do. They too had lived in dangerous days; they too knew the suffocating influence of orthodoxy and standardized thought. They weighed the compulsions for restrained speech and thought against the abuses of liberty. They chose liberty. That should be our choice today no matter how distasteful to us the pamphlet of Beauharnais may be. It is true that this is only one decision which may later be distinguished or confined to narrow limits. But it represents a philosophy at war with the First Amendment—a constitutional interpretation which puts free speech under the legislative thumb. It reflects an influence moving ever deeper into our society. It is notice to the legislatures that they have the power to control unpopular blocs. It is a warning to every minority that when the Constitution guarantees free speech it does not mean what it says.

Mr. Justice Jackson, dissenting:

. . . Punishment of printed words, based on their *tendency* either to cause breach of the peace or injury to persons or groups, in my opinion, is justifiable only if the prosecution survives the "clear and present danger" test. It is the most just and workable standard yet evolved for determining criminality of words whose injurious or inciting tendencies are not demonstrated by the event but are ascribed to them on the basis of probabilities.

Its application is important in this case because it takes account of the particular form, time, place, and manner of communication in question. "The moving picture screen, the radio, the newspaper, the handbill, the sound truck and the street corner orator have differing natures, values, abuses and dangers. Each, in my view, is a law unto itself. . . ." *Kovacs v. Cooper*, 336 U.S. 77. . . . It would consider whether a leaflet is so emotionally exciting to immediate action as the spoken word, especially the incendiary street or public speech. . . . It will inquire whether this publication was obviously so foul and extreme as to defeat its own ends, whether its appeals for money

—which has a cooling effect on many persons—would not negative its inflammatory effect, whether it would not impress the passer-by as the work of an irresponsible who needed mental examination.

One of the merits of the clear and present danger test is that the triers of fact would take into account the realities of race relations and any smouldering fires to be fanned into holocausts. Such consideration might well warrant a conviction here when it would not in another and different environment.

Group libel statutes represent a commendable desire to reduce sinister abuses of our freedoms of expression—abuses which I have had occasion to learn can tear apart a society, brutalize its dominant elements, and persecute, even to extermination, its minorities. While laws or prosecutions might not alleviate racial or sectarian hatreds and may even invest scoundrels with a specious martyrdom, I should be loath to foreclose the States from a considerable latitude of experimentation in this field. Such efforts, if properly applied, do not justify frenetic forebodings of crushed liberty. But these acts present most difficult policy and technical problems, as thoughtful writers who have canvassed the problem more comprehensively than is appropriate in a judicial opinion have well pointed out.

No group interest in any particular prosecution should forget that the shoe may be on the other foot in some prosecution tomorrow. In these, as in other matters, our guiding spirit should be that each freedom is balanced with a responsibility, and every power of the State must be checked with safeguards. Such is the spirit of our American law of criminal libel, which concedes the power to the State, but only as a power restrained by recognition of individual rights. I cannot escape the conclusion that as the Act has been applied in this case it lost sight of the rights.

4. Previous Restraints or Censorship

NEAR v. MINNESOTA

283 US 697 (1931)

[Historically, censorship of publications was associated with licensing: a book or pamphlet could not be published unless it was first submitted to a censor or licensing official and his approval was procured. Publication without such a license from the censor was a criminal offense. It was against such censorship or previous restraint on publication that John Milton protested in his *Areopagitica* in 1644. In the minds of Englishmen licensing by censors was associated with ecclesiastical supervision, the Inquisition, the Star Chamber, and monopolies. In 1695 the licensing system in England ended forever. Liberty of the press, wrote Blackstone in 1769, "consists in laying no previous restraints upon publication, and not in freedom from censure for criminal matters when published."

[This is still an essential aspect of liberty of the press under the

Constitution: freedom from preliminary restraint, Justice Holmes has said, "extends as well to the false as to the true; the subsequent punishment may extend as well to the true as to the false." *Patterson* v. *Colorado,* 205 US 454 (1907).

[Licensing requirements are frowned upon by the courts more than any other restrictive device. Even in the case of moving pictures, as we shall see, the Supreme Court has reached the point where it thinks that censorship is inconsistent with the demands of the Constitution. Licensing in radio broadcasting remains an exception to the rule. *Communications Commission* v. *N.B.C.,* 319 US 239 (1943). Injunctions against picketing in labor disputes are a form of previous restraint by judicial act and fall into a separate category. This matter is considered at a later point.

[In *Near* v. *Minnesota,* which condemns censorship as unconstitutional, the decision was 5 to 4, with Justices Butler, Van Devanter, McReynolds, and Sutherland dissenting. It is doubtful whether any Justice would dissent from the opinion of Chief Justice Hughes today.]

Mr. Chief Justice Hughes delivered the opinion of the Court:

Chapter 285 of the Session Laws of Minnesota for the year 1925 provides for the abatement, as a public nuisance, of a "malicious, scandalous and defamatory newspaper, magazine or other periodical." Section one of the act is as follows:

Section 1: Any person who, as an individual, or as a member or employee of a firm, or association or organization, or as an officer, director, member or employee of a corporation, shall be engaged in the business of regularly or customarily producing, publishing or circulating, having in possession, selling or giving away,

(a) an obscene, lewd and lascivious newspaper, magazine, or other periodical, or

(b) a malicious, scandalous and defamatory newspaper, magazine or other periodical,

is guilty of a nuisance, and all persons guilty of such nuisance may be enjoined, as hereinafter provided.

Participation in such business shall constitute a commission of such nuisance and render the participant liable and subject to the proceedings, orders and judgments provided for in this act. Ownership, in whole or in part, directly or indirectly, of any such periodical, or of any stock or interest in any corporation or organization which owns the same in whole or in part, or which publishes the same, shall constitute such participation.

In actions brought under (b) above, there shall be available the defense that the truth was published with good motives and for justifiable ends and in such actions the plaintiff shall not have the right to report [*sic*] to issues or editions of periodicals taking place more than three months before the commencement of the action.

Section two provides that whenever any such nuisance is committed or exists, the county attorney of any county where any such periodical is published or circulated, or, in case of his failure or refusal to proceed upon written request in good faith of a reputable citizen, the attorney general, or upon like failure or refusal of the latter, any citizen of the county, may maintain an action in the district court of the county in the name of the state to enjoin perpetually the persons committing or maintaining any such nuisance from further committing or maintaining it. Upon such evidence as the court shall deem sufficient, a temporary injunction may be granted. The defendants have the right to plead by demurrer or answer, and the plaintiff may demur or reply as in other cases.

The action, by section three, is to be "governed by the practice and procedure applicable to civil actions for injunctions," and after trial the court may enter judgment permanently enjoining the defendants found guilty of violating the act from continuing the violation and, "in and by such judgment, such nuisance may be wholly abated." The court is empowered, as in other cases of contempt, to punish disobedience to a temporary or permanent injunction by fine of not more than $1,000 or by imprisonment in the county jail for not more than twelve months.

Under this statute, . . . the county attorney of Hennepin county brought this action to enjoin the publication of what was described as a "malicious, scandalous and defamatory newspaper, magazine and periodical," known as *The Saturday Press,* published by the defendants in the city of Minneapolis. The complaint alleged that the defendants, on September 24, 1927, and on eight subsequent dates in October and November, 1927, published and circulated editions of that periodical which were "largely devoted to malicious, scandalous and defamatory articles" concerning Charles G. Davis, Frank W. Brunskill, the *Minneapolis Tribune,* the *Minneapolis Journal,* Melvin C. Passolt, George E. Leach, the Jewish Race, the members of the grand jury of Hennepin county impaneled in November, 1927, and then holding office, and other persons, as more fully appeared in exhibits annexed to the complaint, consisting of copies of the articles described and constituting 327 pages of the record. While the complaint did not so allege, it appears from the briefs of both parties that Charles G. Davis was a special law enforcement officer employed by a civic organization, that George E. Leach was mayor of Minneapolis, that Frank W. Brunskill was its chief of police, and that Floyd B. Olson (the relator in this action) was county attorney.

Without attempting to summarize the contents of the voluminous exhibits attached to the complaint, we deem it sufficient to say that the articles charged in substance that a Jewish gangster was in control of gambling, bootlegging and racketeering in Minneapolis, and that law enforcing officers and agencies were not energetically performing their duties. Most of the charges were directed against the chief of police; he was charged with gross neglect of duty, illicit relations with gangsters, and with participation in graft. The county attorney was charged with knowing the existing conditions and with failure to take adequate measures to remedy them. The mayor was accused of inefficiency and dereliction. One member of the grand jury was stated to be in sympathy with the gangsters. A special grand jury and a special prosecutor were demanded to deal with the situation in general, and, in particular, to investigate an attempt to assassinate one Guilford, one of the original defendants, who, it appears from the articles, was shot by gangsters after the first issue of the periodical had been published. There is no question but that the articles made serious accusations against the public officers named and others in connection with the prevalence of crimes and the failure to expose and punish them. . . .

This statute, for the suppression as a public nuisance of a newspaper or periodical, is unusual, if not unique, and raises questions of grave importance transcending the local interests involved in the particular action. It is no longer open to doubt that the liberty of the press and of speech is within the liberty safeguarded by the due process clause of the 14th Amendment from invasion by state action. It was found impossible to conclude that this essential personal liberty of the citizen was left unprotected by the general guaranty of fundamental rights of person and property. . . . Liberty of speech and of the press is . . . not an absolute right, and the state may punish its abuse. . . . Liberty, in each of its phases, has its history and connotation and, in the present instance, the inquiry is as to the historic conception of the liberty of the press and whether the statute under review violates the essential attributes of that liberty. . . .

The statute is not aimed at the redress of individual or private wrongs. Remedies for libel remain available and unaffected. The statute, said the state court, "is not directed at threatened libel but at an existing business which, generally speaking, involves more than libel." It is aimed at the distribution of scandalous matter as "detrimental to public morals and to the general welfare," tending "to disturb the peace of the community" and "to provoke assaults and the commission of crime." In order to obtain an injunction to suppress the future publication of the newspaper or periodical, it is not necessary to prove the

falsity of the charges that have been made in the publication condemned. In the present action there was no allegation that the matter
published was not true. It is alleged, and the statute requires the allegation, that the publication was "malicious." But, as in prosecutions
for libel, there is no requirement of proof by the state of malice in
fact as distinguished from malice inferred from the mere publication
of the defamatory matter. The judgment in this case proceeded upon
the mere proof of publication. The statute permits the defense, not of
the truth alone, but only that the truth was published with good motives and for justifiable ends. It is apparent that under the statute the
publication is to be regarded as defamatory if it injures reputation,
and that it is scandalous if it circulates charges of reprehensible conduct, whether criminal or otherwise, and the publication is thus
deemed to invite public reprobation and to constitute a public scandal.
The court sharply defined the purpose of the statute, bringing out the
precise point, in these words: "There is no constitutional right to
publish a fact merely because it is true. It is a matter of common knowledge that prosecutions under the criminal libel statutes do not result
in efficient repression or suppression of the evils of scandal. Men who
are the victims of such assaults seldom resort to the courts. This is
especially true if their sins are exposed and the only question relates
to whether it was done with good motives and for justifiable ends. This
law is not for the protection of the person attacked nor to punish the
wrongdoer. It is for the protection of the public welfare." . . .

If we cut through mere details of procedure, the operation and
effect of the statute in substance is that public authorities may bring
the owner or publisher of a newspaper or periodical before a judge
upon a charge of conducting a business of publishing scandalous and
defamatory matter—in particular that the matter consists of charges
against public officers of official dereliction—and unless the owner or
publisher is able and disposed to bring competent evidence to satisfy
the judge that the charges are true and are published with good motives and for justifiable ends, his newspaper or periodical is suppressed
and further publication is made punishable as a contempt. This is of
the essence of censorship.

The question is whether a statute authorizing such proceedings in
restraint of publication is consistent with the conception of the liberty
of the press as historically conceived and guaranteed. In determining
the extent of the constitutional protection, it has been generally, if
not universally, considered that it is the chief purpose of the guaranty
to prevent previous restraints upon publication. The struggle in England, directed against the legislative power of the licenser, resulted
in renunciation of the censorship of the press. The liberty deemed to

be established was thus described by Blackstone: "The liberty of the press is indeed essential to the nature of a free state; but this consists in laying no *previous* restraints upon publications, and not in freedom from censure for criminal matter when published. Every freeman has an undoubted right to lay what sentiments he pleases before the public; to forbid this, is to destroy the freedom of the press; but if he publishes what is improper, mischievous or illegal, he must take the consequence of his own temerity." . . . The distinction was early pointed out between the extent of the freedom with respect to censorship under our constitutional system and that enjoyed in England. Here, as Madison said, "The great and essential rights of the people are secured against legislative as well as against executive ambition. They are secured, not by laws paramount to prerogative, but by constitutions paramount to laws. This security of the freedom of the press requires that it should be exempt not only from previous restraint by the executive, as in Great Britain, but from legislative restraint also." . . . This court said, in *Patterson* v. *Colorado*, 205 U.S. 454: "In the first place, the main purpose of such constitutional provisions is 'to prevent all such *previous restraints* upon publications as had been practised by other governments,' and they do not prevent the subsequent punishment of such as may be deemed contrary to the public welfare. . . . The preliminary freedom extends as well to the false as to the true; the subsequent punishment may extend as well to the true as to the false. This was the law of criminal libel apart from statute in most cases, if not in all. . . ."

The criticism upon Blackstone's statement has not been because immunity from previous restraint upon publication has not been regarded as deserving of special emphasis, but chiefly because that immunity cannot be deemed to exhaust the conception of the liberty guaranteed by state and Federal constitutions. The point of criticism has been "that the mere exemption from previous restraints cannot be all that is secured by the constitutional provisions"; and that "the liberty of the press might be rendered a mockery and a delusion, and the phrase itself a by-word, if, while every man was at liberty to publish what he pleased, the public authorities might nevertheless punish him for harmless publications." 2 Cooley, *Constitutional Limitations*, 8th ed., p. 885. But it is recognized that punishment for the abuse of the liberty accorded to the ·press is essential to the protection of the public, and that the common law rules that subject the libeler to responsibility for the public offense, as well as for the private injury, are not abolished by the protection extended in our constitutions. . . . The law of criminal libel rests upon that secure foundation. There is also the conceded authority of courts to punish for contempt when publications directly tend to prevent the proper discharge of judicial functions. . . . In the present case, we have no occasion to inquire as to the permissible scope of subsequent punishment. For whatever wrong the appellant has committed or may commit, by his publications, the state appropriately affords both public and private redress by its libel laws. As has been noted, the statute in question does not deal with punishments; it provides for no punishment, except in case of contempt for violation of the court's order, but for suppression and injunction, that is, for restraint upon publication.

The objection has also been made that the principle as to immunity from previous restraint is stated too broadly, if every such restraint is deemed to be prohibited. That is undoubtedly true; the protection even as to previous restraint is not absolutely unlimited. But the limitation has been recognized only in exceptional cases. "When a nation is at war many things that might be said in time of peace are such a hindrance to its effort that their utterance will not be endured so long as men fight and that no court could regard them as protected by any constitutional right." *Schenck* v. *United States,* 249 U.S. 47. No one would question but that a government might prevent actual obstruction to its recruiting service or the publication of the sailing dates of transports or the number and location of troops. On similar grounds, the primary requirements of decency may be enforced against obscene publications. The security of the community life may be protected against incitements to acts of violence and the overthrow by force of orderly government. The constitutional guaranty of free speech does not "protect a man from an injunction against uttering words that may have all the effect of force. . . ." *Schenck* v. *United States.* These limitations are not applicable here. Nor are we now concerned with questions as to the extent of authority to prevent publications in order to protect private rights according to the principles governing the exercise of the jurisdiction of courts of equity.

The exceptional nature of its limitations places in a strong light the general conception that liberty of the press, historically considered and taken up by the Federal Constitution, has meant, principally, although not exclusively, immunity from previous restraints or censorship. The conception of the liberty of the press in this country had broadened with the exigencies of the colonial period and with the efforts to secure freedom from oppressive administration. That liberty was especially cherished for the immunity it afforded from previous restraint of the publication of censure of public officers and charges of official misconduct. . . .

The fact that for approximately one hundred and fifty years there has been almost an entire absence of attempts to impose previous restraints upon publications relating to the malfeasance of public officers is significant of the deep-seated conviction that such restraints would violate constitutional right. Public officers, whose character and conduct remain open to debate and free discussion in the press, find their remedies for false accusations in actions under libel laws providing for redress and punishment, and not in proceedings to restrain the publication of newspapers and periodicals. The general principle that the constitutional guaranty of the liberty of the press gives immunity from previous restraints has been approved in many decisions under the provision of state constitutions.

The importance of this immunity has not lessened. While reckless assaults upon public men, and efforts to bring obloquy upon those who are endeavoring faithfully to discharge official duties, exert a baleful influence and deserve the severest condemnation in public opinion, it cannot be said that this abuse is greater, and it is believed to be less, than that which characterized the period in which our institutions took shape. Meanwhile, the administration of government has become more complex, the opportunities for malfeasance and corruption have multiplied, crime has grown to most serious proportions, and the danger of its protection by unfaithful officials and of the impairment of the fundamental security of life and property by criminal alliances and official neglect, emphasizes the primary need of a vigilant and courageous press, especially in great cities. The fact that the liberty of the press may be abused by miscreant purveyors of scandal does not make any the less necessary the immunity of the press from previous restraint in dealing with official misconduct. Subsequent punishment for such abuses as may exist is the appropriate remedy, consistent with constitutional privilege. . . .

Judgment reversed.

LOVELL v. GRIFFIN

303 US 444 (1938)

[This case illustrates the scope of the decision in the previous case of *Near* v. *Minnesota.* An ordinance that required official permission to distribute publications was condemned as unconstitutional by a unanimous Court. An ordinance might meet the constitutional test only if it left no discretion to the licensing official but merely attempted to impose reasonable and well-defined restrictions as to time and place in order to maintain public order and prevent disorderly conduct. *Lovell* v. *Griffin* should be compared with *Tucker* v. *Texas* and *Breard* v. *City of Alexandria,* above.

[This case is important also because it expressly assimilates distribution of literature to publication for constitutional protection.]

Mr. Chief Justice Hughes delivered the opinion of the Court:

Appellant, Alma Lovell, was convicted in the recorder's court of the City of Griffin, Ga., of the violation of a city ordinance and was sentenced to imprisonment for fifty days in default of the payment of a fine of $50. . . .

The ordinance in question is as follows:

1. That the practice of distributing, either by hand or otherwise, circulars, handbooks, advertising, or literature of any kind, whether said articles are being delivered free, or whether same are being sold, within the limits of the City of Griffin, without first obtaining written permission from the City Manager of the City of Griffin, such practice shall be deemed a nuisance, and punishable as an offense against the City of Griffin.

2. The Chief of Police of the City of Griffin and the police force of the City of Griffin are hereby required and directed to suppress the same and to abate any nuisance as is described in the first section of this ordinance.

The violation, which is not denied, consisted of the distribution without the required permission of a pamphlet and magazine in the nature of religious tracts, setting forth the gospel of the "Kingdom of Jehovah." Appellant did not apply for a permit, as she regarded herself as sent "by Jehovah to do His work" and that such an application would have been "an act of disobedience to His commandment."

Upon the trial, with permission of the court, appellant demurred to the charge and moved to dismiss it upon a number of grounds, among which was the contention that the ordinance violated the Fourteenth Amendment of the Constitution of the United States in abridging "the freedom of the press" and prohibiting "the free exercise of petitioner's religion." . . .

The ordinance in its broad sweep prohibits the distribution of "circulars, handbooks, advertising, or literature of any kind." It manifestly applies to pamphlets, magazines, and periodicals. The evidence against appellant was that she distributed a certain pamphlet and a magazine called the *Golden Age*. Whether in actual administration the ordinance is applied, as apparently it could be, to newspapers does not appear. The city manager testified that "every one applies to me for a license to dilstribute literature in this City. None of these people (including defendant) secured a permit from me to distribute literature in the City of Griffin." The ordinance is not limited to "literature" that is obscene or offensive to public morals or that advocates unlawful conduct. There is no suggestion that the pamphlet and magazine distributed in the instant case were of that character. The ordinance embraces "literature" in the widest sense.

The ordinance is comprehensive with respect to the method of distribution. It covers every sort of circulation "either by hand or otherwise." There is thus no restriction in its application with respect to time or place. It is not limited to ways which might be regarded as inconsistent with the maintenance of public order, or as involving disorderly conduct, the molestation of the inhabitants, or the misuse or littering of the streets. The ordinance prohibits the distribution of literature of any kind at any time, at any place, and in any manner without a permit from the city manager.

We think that the ordinance is invalid on its face. Whatever the motive which induced its adoption, its character is such that it strikes at the very foundation of the freedom of the press by subjecting it to license and censorship. The struggle for the freedom of the press was primarily directed against the power of the licensor. It was against that power that John Milton directed his assault by his [*Areopagitica*] "Appeal for the Liberty of Unlicensed Printing." And the liberty of the press became initially a right to publish "*without* a license what formerly could be published only *with* one." While this freedom from previous restraint upon publication cannot be regarded as exhausting the guaranty of liberty, the prevention of that restraint was a leading purpose in the adoption of the constitutional provision. . . . Legislation of the type of the ordinance in question would restore the system of license and censorship in its baldest form.

The liberty of the press is not confined to newspapers and periodicals. It necessarily embraces pamphlets and leaflets. These indeed have been historic weapons in the defense of liberty, as the pamphlets of Thomas Paine and others in our own history abundantly attest. The press in its historic connotation comprehends every sort of publication which affords a vehicle of information and opinion. . . .

The ordinance cannot be saved because it relates to distribution and not to publication. "Liberty of circulating is as essential to that freedom as liberty of publishing; indeed, without the circulation, the publication would be of little value." *Ex parte Jackson,* 96 U.S. 727. . . .

Reversed.

NIEMOTKO *v.* MARYLAND

340 US 268 (1951)

[The city of Havre de Grace, Maryland, followed the practice of requiring a license for use of a public park for meetings. There was no narrowly drawn ordinance, with reasonable and definite standards to guide the officials. The Court unanimously condemned the official practice as unconstitutional.

[The concurring opinion of Justice Frankfurter covers this case and also *Feiner* v. *New York,* given above, and *Kunz* v. *New York,* which follows. See the editorial note introducing the *Feiner Case.*]

Mr. Chief Justice Vinson delivered the opinion of the Court:

Appellants are two members of the religious group known as Jehovah's Witnesses. At the invitation of local coreligionists, they scheduled Bible talks in the public park of the city of Havre de Grace, Maryland. Although there is no ordinance prohibiting or regulating the use of this park, it has been the custom for organizations and individuals desiring to use it for meetings and celebrations of various kinds to obtain a permit from the Park Commissioner. In conformity with this practice, the group requested permission of the Park Commissioner for use of the park on four consecutive Sundays in June and July, 1949. This permission was refused.

Having been informed that an Elks' Flag Day ceremony was scheduled for the first Sunday, the applicants did not pursue their request for the use of the park for that particular day, but, instead, filed a written request with the City Council for the following three Sundays. This request was filed at the suggestion of the Mayor, it appearing that under the custom of the municipality there is a right of appeal to the City Council from the action of the Park Commissioner. The Council held a hearing at which the request was considered. At this hearing the applicants and their attorney appeared. The request was denied.

Because they were awaiting the decision of the Council on their application, the applicants took no further steps on the second Sunday, but, after the denial of the request, they proceeded to hold their meeting on the third Sunday. No sooner had appellant Niemotko opened the meeting and commenced delivering his discourse, than the police, who had been ordered to the park by the Mayor, arrested him. At the meeting held in the park on the fourth and following Sunday, appellant Kelley was arrested before he began his lecture.

Appellants were subsequently brought to trial before a jury on a charge of disorderly conduct under the Maryland disorderly conduct statute. . . . They were convicted and each fined $25 and costs. . . .

A brief recital of the facts as they were adduced at this trial will suffice to show why these convictions cannot stand. At the time of the arrest of each of these appellants, there was no evidence of disorder, threats of violence or riot. There was no indication that the appellants conducted themselves in a manner which could be considered as detrimental to the public peace or order. On the contrary, there was positive testimony by the police that each of the appellants had conducted himself in a manner beyond reproach. It is quite apparent that any disorderly conduct which the jury found must have been based on the fact that appellants were using the park without a permit, although as we have indicated above, there is no statute or ordinance prohibiting or regulating the use of the park without a permit.

This Court has many times examined the licensing systems by which local bodies regulate the use of their parks and public places. . . . In those cases this Court condemned statutes and ordinances which required that permits be obtained from local officials as a prerequisite to the use of public places, on the grounds that a license requirement constituted a prior restraint on freedom of speech, press and religion, and, in the absence of narrowly drawn, reasonable and definite standards for the officials to follow, must be invalid. . . . In the instant case we are met with no ordinance or statute regulating or prohibiting the use of the park; all that is here is an amorphous "practice," whereby all authority to grant permits for the use of the parks is in the Park Commission and the City Council. No standards appear anywhere; no narrowly drawn limitations; no circumscribing of this absolute power; no substantial interest of the community to be served. It is clear that all that has been said about the invalidity of such limitless discretion must be equally applicable here.

This case points up with utmost clarity the wisdom of this doctrine. For the very possibility of abuse, which those earlier decisions feared, has occurred here. Indeed, rarely has any case been before this Court which shows so clearly an unwarranted discrimination in a refusal to issue such a license. It is true that the City Council held a hearing at which it considered the application. But we have searched the record in vain to discover any valid basis for the refusal. In fact, the Mayor testified that the permit would probably have been granted if, at the hearing, the applicants had not started to "berate" the Park Commissioner for his refusal to issue the permit. The only question asked of the Witnesses at the hearing pertained to their alleged refusal to salute the flag, their views on the Bible, and other issues irrelevant to unencumbered use of the public parks. The conclusion is inescapable that the use of the park was denied because of the City Council's dislike for or disagreement with the Witnesses or their views. The right to equal protection of the laws, in the exercise of those freedoms of speech and religion protected by the First and Fourteenth Amendments, has a firmer foundation than the whims or personal opinions of a local governing body.

In this Court, it is argued that state and city officials should have the power to exclude religious groups, as such, from the use of the public parks. But that is not this case. For whatever force this contention could possibly have is lost in the light of the testimony of the Mayor at the trial that within his memory permits had always been issued for religious organizations and Sunday-school picnics. We might also point out that the attempt to designate the park as a sanctuary for peace and quiet not only does not defeat these appellants, whose own conduct created no disturbance, but this position is also more than slightly inconsistent, since, on the first Sunday here involved, the park was the situs for the Flag Day ceremony of the Order of Elks.

It thus becomes apparent that the lack of standards in the license-issuing "practice" renders that "practice" a prior restraint in contravention of the Fourteenth Amendment, and that the completely arbitrary and discriminatory refusal to grant the permits was a denial of equal protection. Inasmuch as the basis of the convictions was the lack of the permits, and that lack was, in turn, due to the unconstitutional defects discussed, the convictions must fall.

Reversed. . . .

Mr. Justice Frankfurter concurring in the result:

The issues in these cases concern living law in some of its most delicate aspects. To smother differences of emphasis and nuance will not help its wise development. When the way a result is reached may be important to results hereafter to be reached, law is best respected by individual expression of opinion.

These cases present three variations upon a theme of great importance. Legislatures, local authorities, and the courts have for years grappled with claims of the right to disseminate ideas in public places as against claims of an effective power in government to keep the peace and to protect other interests of a civilized community. These cases are of special interest because they show the attempts of three communities to meet the problem in three different ways. It will, I believe, further analysis to use the three situations as cross-lights on one another.

I.

1. Nos. 17 and 18.—Havre de Grace, Maryland, sought to solve this tangled problem by permitting its park commissioner and city council to act as censors. The city allowed use of its park for public meetings, including those of religious groups, but by custom a permit was required. In this case, the city council questioned the representatives of Jehovah's Witnesses, who had requested a license, about their views on saluting the flag, the Catholic Church, service in the armed forces, and other matters in no way related to public order or public convenience in use of the park. The Mayor testified that he supposed the permit was denied "because of matters that were

brought out at [the] meeting." When Niemotko and Kelley, Jehovah's Witnesses, attempted to speak, they were arrested for disturbing the peace. There was no disturbance of the peace and it is clear that they were arrested only for want of a permit.

2. No. 50.—New York City set up a licensing system to control the use of its streets and parks for public religious services. The New York Court of Appeals construed the city's ordinance so as to sanction the right of the Police Commissioner to revoke or refuse a license for street-preaching if he found the person was likely to "ridicule" or "denounce" religion. In 1946, after hearings before a Fourth Deputy Police Commissioner, Kunz's license was revoked because he had "ridiculed" and "denounced" religion while speaking in one of New York's crowded centers, and it was thought likely that he would continue to do so. In 1947 and 1948 he was refused a license on the sole ground of the determination made in 1946. In September of 1948 he was arrested for speaking at Columbus Circle without a license.

3. No. 93.—Syracuse, New York, did not set up a licensing system but relied on a statute which is in substance an enactment of the commonlaw offense of breach of the peace. Feiner, the defendant, made a speech near the intersection of South McBride and Harrison Streets in Syracuse. He spoke from a box located on the parking between the sidewalk and the street, and made use of sound amplifiers attached to an automobile. A crowd of 75 to 80 persons gathered around him, and several pedestrians had to go into the highway in order to pass by. Two policemen observed the meeting. In the course of his speech, Feiner referred to the Mayor of Syracuse as a "champagne-sipping bum," to the President as a "bum," and to the American Legion as "Nazi Gestapo agents." Feiner also indicated in an excited manner that Negroes did not have equal rights and should rise up in arms. His audience included a number of Negroes.

One man indicated that if the police did not get the speaker off the stand, he would do it himself. The crowd, which consisted of both those who opposed and those who supported the speaker, was restless. There was not yet a disturbance but, in the words of the arresting officer whose story was accepted by the trial judge, he "stepped in to prevent it from resulting in a fight. After all there was angry muttering and pushing." Having ignored two requests to stop speaking, Feiner was arrested.

II.

Adjustment of the inevitable conflict between free speech and other interests is a problem as persistent as it is perplexing. It is important to bear in mind that this Court can only hope to set limits and point the way. It falls to the lot of legislative bodies and administrative officials to find practical solutions within the frame of our decisions. There are now so many of these decisions, arrived at by the *ad hoc* process of adjudication, that it is desirable to make a cruise of the timber.

In treating the precise problem presented by the three situations before us —how to reconcile the interest in allowing free expression of ideas in public places with the protection of the public peace and of the primary uses of streets and parks—we should first set to one side decisions which are apt to mislead rather than assist. Contempt cases and convictions under State and Federal statutes aimed at placing a general limitation upon what may be said or written, bring additional factors into the equation. Cases like *Near* v. *Minnesota*, 283 US 697, . . . and *Grosjean* v. *American Press Co.*, 297 US 233, . . . are rooted in historic experience regarding prior restraints on publication. They give recognition to the role of the press in a democracy, a consideration not immediately pertinent. The picketing cases are logically relevant since they usually involve, in part, dissmination of information in public places. But here also enter economic and social interests outside the situations before us. . . .

The cases more exclusively concerned with restrictions upon expression in its divers forms in public places have answered problems varying greatly in content and difficulty.

1. The easiest cases have been those in which the only interest opposing free communication was that of keeping the streets of the community clean. This could scarcely justify prohibiting the dissemination of information by handbills or censoring their contents. In *Lovell* v. *Griffin*, 303 US 444, . . . an ordinance requiring a permit to distribute pamphlets was held invalid where the licensing standard was "not limited to ways which might be regarded as inconsistent with the maintenance of public order or as involving disorderly conduct, the molestation of the inhabitants, or the misuse or littering of the streets." . . . In *Hague* v. *C.I.O.*, 307 US 496, . . . a portion of the ordinance declared invalid prohibited the distribution of pamphlets. In *Schneider* v. *Irvington*, 308 US 147, . . . three of the four ordinances declared invalid by the Court prohibited the distribution of pamphlets. In *Jamison* v. *Texas*, 318 US 413, . . . the Court again declared invalid a municipal ordinance prohibiting the distribution of all handbills.

2. In a group of related cases, regulation of solicitation has been the issue. Here the opposing interest is more substantial—protection of the public from fraud and from criminals who use solicitation as a device to enter homes. The fourth ordinance considered in *Schneider* v. *Irvington* allowed the chief of police to refuse a permit if he found, in his discretion, that the canvasser was not of good character or was canvassing for a project not free from fraud. The ordinance was found invalid because the officer who could, in his discretion, make the determinations concerning "good character" and "project not free from fraud" in effect held the power of censorship. In *Cantwell* v. *Connecticut*, 310 US 296, . . . conviction was, in part, under a State statute requiring a permit for religious solicitation. The statute was declared invalid because the licensing official could determine what causes were religious, allowing a "censorship of religion." . . . Again, in *Largent* v. *Texas*, 318 US 418, . . . an ordinance requiring a permit from the mayor, who was to issue the permit only if he deemed it "proper or advisable," was declared invalid as creating an administrative censorship. The Court has also denied the right of those in control of a company town or Government housing project to prohibit solicitation by Jehovah's Witnesses. . . . In *Thomas* v. *Collins*, 323 US 516, . . . the solicitation was in the

interest of labor rather than religion. There a State statute requiring registration of labor organizers was found unconstitutional when invoked to enjoin a speech in a public hall. The interest of the State in protecting its citizens through the regulation of vocations was deemed insufficient to support the statute.

3. Whether the sale of religious literature by Jehovah's Witnesses can be subjected to nondiscriminatory taxes on solicitation has introduced another opposing interest—the right of the community to raise funds for the support of the government. In *Jones* v. *Opelika,* 319 US 103, . . . and in *Murdock* v. *Pennsylvania,* 319 US 105, . . . the Court held that imposition of the tax upon itinerants was improper. In *Follett* v. *McCormick,* 321 US 573, . . . the Court went further to hold unconstitutional the imposition of a flat tax on book agents upon a resident who made his living selling religious books.

4. *Martin* v. *Struthers,* 319 US 141, . . . represents another situation. An ordinance of the City of Struthers, Ohio, forbade knocking on the door or ringing the doorbell of a residence in order to deliver a handbill. Prevention of crime and assuring privacy in an industrial community where many worked on night shifts, and had to obtain their sleep during the day, were held insufficient to justify the ordinance in the case of handbills distributed on behalf of Jehovah's Witnesses.

5. In contrast to these decisions, the Court held in *Prince* v. *Massachusetts,* 321 US 158, . . . that the application to Jehovah's Witnesses of a State statute providing that no boy under 12 or girl under 18 should sell periodicals on the street was constitutional. Claims of immunity from regulation of religious activities were subordinated to the interest of the State in protecting its children.

6. Control of speeches made in streets and parks draws on still different considerations—protection of the public peace and of the primary uses of travel and recreation for which streets and parks exist.

(a) The pioneer case concerning speaking in parks and streets is *Davis* v. *Massachusetts,* 167 US 43, . . . in which this Court adopted the reasoning of the opinion below written by Mr. Justice Holmes, while on the Massachusetts Supreme Judicial Court. . . . The Boston ordinance which was upheld required a permit from the mayor for any person to "make any public address, discharge any cannon or firearm, expose for sale any goods, . . ." on public grounds. This Court respected the finding that the ordinance was not directed against free speech but was intended as "a proper regulation of the use of public grounds." . . .

An attempt to derive from dicta in the *Davis Case* the right of a city to exercise any power over its parks, however arbitrary or discriminatory, was rejected in *Hague* v. *C.I.O.* . . . The ordinance presented in the *Hague Case* required a permit for meetings on public ground, the permit to be refused by the licensing official only "for the purpose of preventing riots, disturbances or disorderly assemblage." The facts of the case, however, left no doubt that the licensing power had been made an "instrument of arbitrary suppression of free expression of views on national affairs." . . . The holding of the *Hague Case* was not that a city could not subject the use of its streets and parks to reasonable regulation. The holding was that the licensing officials could not be given power arbitrarily to suppress free expression, no matter under what cover of law they purported to act.

Cox v. *New Hampshire*, 312 US 569, . . . made it clear that the United States Constitution does not deny localities the power to devise a licensing system if the exercise of discretion by the licensing officials is appropriately confined. A statute requiring a permit and license fee for parades had been narrowly construed by the State courts. The license could be refused only for "considerations of time, place and manner so as to conserve the public convenience," and the license fee was "to meet the expense incident to the maintenance of public order in the matter licensed." . . . The licensing system was sustained even though the tax, ranging from a nominal amount to $300, was determined by the licensing officials on the facts of each case.

(b) Two cases have involved the additional considerations incident to the use of sound trucks. In *Saia* v. *New York*, 334 US 558, . . . the ordinance required a license from the chief of police for use of sound amplification devices in public places. The ordinance was construed not to prescribe standards to be applied in passing upon a license application. In the particular case, a license to use a sound truck in a small city park had been denied because of complaints about the noise which resulted when sound amplifiers had previously been used in the park. There was no indication that the license had been refused because of the content of the speeches. Nevertheless, the Court held the ordinance unconstitutional. In *Kovacs* v. *Cooper*, 336 US 77, . . . part of the Court construed the ordinance as allowing conviction for operation of any sound truck, emitting "loud and raucous" noises, and part construed the ordinance to ban all sound trucks. The limits of the decision of the Court upholding the ordinance are therefore not clear, but the result in any event does not leave the *Saia* decision intact.

(c) On a few occasions the Court has had to pass on a limitation upon speech by a sanction imposed after the event rather than by a licensing statute. In *Cantwell* v. *Connecticut*, 310 US 296, . . . one of the convictions was for common-law breach of the peace. The problem was resolved in favor of the defendant . . . in view of the inquiry whether, on the facts of the case, there was "such clear and present menace to public peace and order as to render him liable to conviction of the common law offense in question." . . .

In *Chaplinsky* v. *New Hampshire*, 315 US 568, . . . a State statute had enacted the common-law doctrine of "fighting words": "No person shall address any offensive, derisive or annoying word to any other person who is lawfully in any street or other public place, nor call him by any offensive or derisive name. . . ." The State courts had previously held the statute applicable only to the use in a public place of words directly tending to cause a breach of the peace by the persons to whom the remark was addressed. The conviction of a street speaker who called a policeman a "damned racketeer" and "damned Fascist" was upheld.

7. One other case should be noted, although it involved a conviction for

breach of peace in a private building rather than in a public place. In *Terminiello* v. *Chicago,* 337 US 1, . . . the holding of the Court was on an abstract proposition of law, unrelated to the facts in the case. A conviction was overturned because the judge had instructed the jury that "breach of the peace" included speech which "stirs the public to anger, invites disputes, brings about a condition of unrest, or creates a disturbance. . . ." The holding apparently was that breach of the peace may not be defined in such broad terms, certainly as to speech in a private hall.

The results in these multifarious cases have been expressed in language looking in two directions. While the Court has emphasized the importance of "free speech," it has recognized that "free speech" is not in itself a touchstone. The Constitution is not unmindful of other important interests, such as public order, if interference with free expression of ideas is not found to be the overbalancing consideration. More important than the phrasing of the opinions are the questions on which the decisions appear to have turned.

(1) What is the interest deemed to require the regulation of speech? The State cannot of course forbid public proselyting or religious argument merely because public officials disapprove the speaker's views. It must act in patent good faith to maintain the public peace, to assure the availability of the streets for their primary purposes of passenger and vehicular traffic, or for equally indispensable ends of modern community life.

(2) What is the method used to achieve such ends as a consequence of which public speech is constrained or barred? A licensing standard which gives an official authority to censor the content of a speech differs *toto coelo* from one limited by its terms, or by nondiscriminatory practice, to considerations of public safety and the like. Again, a sanction applied after the event assures consideration of the particular circumstances of a situation. The net of control must not be cast too broadly.

(3) What mode of speech is regulated? A sound truck may be found to affect the public peace as normal speech does not. A man who is calling names or using the kind of language which would reasonably stir another to violence does not have the same claim to protection as one whose speech is an appeal to reason.

(4) Where does the speaking which is regulated take place? Not only the general classifications—streets, parks, private buildings—are relevant. The location and size of a park; its customary use for the recreational, esthetic and contemplative needs of a community; the facilities, other than a park or street corner, readily available in a community for airing views, are all pertinent considerations in assessing the limitations the Fourteenth Amendment puts on State power in a particular situation.

III.

Due regard for the interests that were adjusted in the decisions just canvassed affords guidance for deciding the cases before us.

1. In the *Niemotko Case,* neither danger to the public peace, nor consideration of time and convenience to the public, appears to have entered into denial of the permit. Rumors that there would be violence by those

opposed to the meeting appeared only after the Council made its decision, and in fact never materialized. The city allowed other religious groups to use the park. To allow expression of religious views by some and deny the same privilege to others merely because they or their views are unpopular, even deeply so, is a denial of equal protection of the law forbidden by the Fourteenth Amendment.

2. The *Kunz Case* presents a very different situation. We must be mindful of the enormous difficulties confronting those charged with the task of enabling the polyglot millions in the City of New York to live in peace and tolerance. Street-preaching in Columbus Circle is done in a milieu quite different from preaching on a New England village green. Again, religious polemic does not touch the merely ratiocinative nature of man, and the ugly facts disclosed by the record of this case show that Kunz was not reluctant to offend the deepest religious feelings of frequenters of Columbus Circle. Especially in such situations, this Court should not substitute its abstract views for the informed judgment of local authorities confirmed by local courts.

I cannot make too explicit my conviction that the City of New York is not restrained by anything in the Constitution of the United States from protecting completely the community's interests in relation to its streets. But if a municipality conditions holding street meetings on the granting of a permit by the police, the basis which guides licensing officials in granting or denying a permit must not give them a free hand, or a hand effectively free when the actualities of police administration are taken into account. It is not for this Court to formulate with particularity the terms of a permit system which would satisfy the Fourteenth Amendment. No doubt, finding a want of such standards presupposes some conception of what is necessity to meet the constitutional requirement we draw from the Fourteenth Amendment. But many a decision of this Court rests on some inarticulate major premise and is none the worse for it. A standard may be found inadequate without the necessity of explicit delineation of the standards that would be adequate, just as doggerel may be felt not to be poetry without the need of writing an essay on what poetry is.

Administrative control over the right to speak must be based on appropriate standards, whether the speaking be done indoors or out-of-doors. The vice to be guarded against is arbitrary action by officials. The fact that in a particular instance an action appears not arbitrary does not save the validity of the authority under which the action was taken.

In the present case, Kunz was not arrested for what he said on the night of arrest, nor because at that time he was disturbing the peace or interfering with traffic. He was arrested because he spoke without a license, and the license was refused because the police commissioner thought it likely on the basis of past performance that Kunz would outrage the religious sensibilities of others. If such had been the supportable finding on the basis of fair standards in safeguarding peace in one of the most populous centers of New York City, this Court would not be justified in upsetting it. It would not be censorship in advance. But here the standards are defined neither by language nor by settled construction to preclude discriminatory or arbitrary action by officials. The ordinance, as judicially construed, provides that anyone who, in the judgment of the licensing officials, would "ridicule" or "denounce" religion creates such a danger of public disturbance that he cannot speak in any park or street in the City of New York. Such a standard, considering the informal procedure under which it is applied, too readily permits censorship of religion by the licensing authorities. . . . The situation here disclosed is not, to reiterate, beyond control on the basis of regulation appropriately directed to the evil.

3. Feiner was convicted under New York Penal Law § 722. . . .

Here, Feiner forced pedestrians to walk in the street by collecting a crowd on the public sidewalk, he attracted additional attention by using sound amplifiers, he indulged in name-calling, he told part of his audience that it should rise up in arms. In the crowd of 75 to 80 persons, there was angry muttering and pushing. Under these circumstances, and in order to prevent a disturbance of the peace, an officer asked Feiner to stop speaking. When he had twice ignored the request, Feiner was arrested. The trial judge concluded that "the officers were fully justified in feeling that a situation was developing which could very, very easily result in a serious disorder." His view was sustained by an intermediate appellate court and by a unanimous decision of the New York Court of Appeals. . . . The estimate of a particular local situation thus comes here with the momentum of the weightiest judicial authority of New York.

This Court has often emphasized that in the exercise of our authority over state court decisions the Due Process Clause must not be construed in an abstract and doctrinaire way by disregarding local conditions. In considering the degree of respect to be given findings by the highest court of a State in cases involving the Due Process Clause, the course of decisions by that court should be taken into account. Particularly within the area of due process colloquially called "civil liberties," it is important whether such a course of decisions reflects a cavalier attitude toward civil liberties or real regard for them. Only unfamiliarity with its decisions and the outlook of its judges could generate a notion that the Court of Appeals of New York is inhospitable to claims of civil liberties or is wanting in respect for this Court's decisions in support of them. It is pertinent, therefore, to note that all members of the New York Court accepted the finding that Feiner was stopped not because the listeners or police officers disagreed with his views but because these officers were honestly concerned with preventing a breach of the peace. This unanimity is all the more persuasive since three members of the Court had dissented, only three months earlier, in favor of Kunz, a man whose vituperative utterances must have been highly offensive to them.

. . . Where conduct is within the allowable limits of free speech, the police are peace officers for the speaker as well as for his hearers. But the power effectively to preserve order cannot be displaced by giving a speaker complete immunity. Here, there were two police officers present for 20 minutes. They interfered only when they apprehended imminence of violence. It is not a constitutional principle that, in acting to preserve order, the police must proceed against the crowd, whatever its size and temper, and not against the speaker.

It is true that breach-of-peace statutes, like most tools of government, may be misused. Enforcement of these statutes calls for public tolerance and intelligent police administration. These, in the long run, must give substance to whatever this Court may say about free speech. But the possibility of misuse is not alone a sufficient reason to deny New York the power here asserted or so limit it by constitutional construction as to deny its practical exercise.

KUNZ v. NEW YORK

340 US 290 (1951)

[An ordinance of the City of New York required a permit for public meetings on streets. It failed to define the circumstances under which officials might refuse to issue permits. The officials construed the ordinance as authorizing them to refuse a permit, in their discretion, if the applicant *in the past* had ridiculed or denounced some religious belief. Kunz had engaged in attacks on Catholics and Jews; when he applied for a permit to speak, he was denied one for this reason; he spoke at Columbus Circle without a permit and was arrested. The Court held that the ordinance was unconstitutional as a previous restraint on rights guaranteed by the First Amendment. Only Justice Jackson dissented. For Justice Frankfurter's concurring opinion, see the preceding case.]

Mr. Chief Justice Vinson delivered the opinion of the Court:

New York City has adopted an ordinance which makes it unlawful to hold public worship meetings on the streets without first obtaining a permit from the city police commissioner. Appellant, Carl Jacob Kunz, was convicted and fined $10 for violating this ordinance by holding a religious meeting without a permit. . . .

Appellant is an ordained Baptist minister who speaks under the auspices of the "Outdoor Gospel Work," of which he is the director. He has been preaching for about six years, and states that it is his conviction and duty to "go out on the highways and byways and preach the word of God." In 1946, he applied for and received a permit under the ordinance in question, there being no question that appellant comes within the classes of persons entitled to receive permits under the ordinance. This permit, like all others, was good only for the calendar year in which issued. In November, 1946, his permit was revoked after a hearing by the police commissioner. The revocation was based on evidence that he had ridiculed and denounced other religious beliefs in his meetings.

Although the penalties of the ordinance apply to anyone who "ridicules and denounces other religious beliefs," the ordinance does not specify this as a ground for permit revocation. Indeed, there is no mention in the ordinance of any power of revocation. However, appellant did not seek judicial or administrative review of the revocation proceedings, and any question as to the propriety of the revocation is not before us in this case. In any event, the revocation affected appellant's rights to speak in 1946 only. Appellant applied for another permit in 1947, and again in 1948, but was notified each time that his application was "disapproved," with no reason for the disapproval being given. On September 11, 1948, appellant was arrested for speaking at Columbus Circle in New York City without a permit. It is from the conviction which resulted that this appeal has been taken.

Appellant's conviction was thus based upon his failure to possess a permit for 1948. We are here concerned only with the propriety of the action of the police commissioner in refusing to issue that permit. Disapproval of the 1948 permit application by the police commissioner was justified by the New York courts on the ground that a permit had previously been revoked "for good reasons." It is noteworthy that there is no mention in the ordinance of reasons for which such a permit application can be refused. This interpretation allows the police commissioner, an administrative official, to exercise discretion in denying subsequent permit applications on the basis of his interpretation, at that time, of what is deemed to be conduct condemned by the ordinance. We have here, then, an ordinance which gives an administrative official discretionary power to control in advance the right of citizens to speak on religious matters on the streets of New York. As such, the ordinance is clearly invalid as a prior restraint on the exercise of First Amendment rights.

In considering the right of a municipality to control the use of public streets for the expression of religious views, we start with the words of Mr. Justice Roberts that "Wherever the title of streets and parks may rest, they have immemorially been held in trust for the use of the public and, time out of mind, have been used for purposes of assembly, communicating thoughts between citizens, and discussing public questions." *Hague* v. *C.I.O.*, 307 US 496. . . .

The court below has mistakenly derived support for its conclusion from the evidence produced at the trial that appellant's religious meetings had, in the past, caused some disorder. There are appropriate public remedies to protect the peace and order of the community if appellant's speeches should result in disorder or violence. "In the present case, we have no occasion to inquire as to the permissible scope of subsequent punishment." *Near* v. *Minnesota*, 283 US 697. We do not express any opinion on the propriety of punitive remedies which the New York authorities may utilize. We are here concerned with suppression—not punishment. It is sufficient to say that New York cannot vest restraining control over the right to speak on religious subjects in an administrative official where there are no appropriate standards to guide his action.

Reversed. . . .

Mr. Justice Jackson, dissenting:

Essential freedoms are today threatened from without and within. It may become difficult to preserve here what a large part of the world has lost—the right to speak, even temperately, on matters vital to spirit and body. In such a setting, to blanket hateful and hate-stirring attacks on races and faiths under the protections for freedom of speech may be a noble innovation. On the other hand, it may be a quixotic tilt at windmills which belittles great principles of liberty. Only time can tell. But I incline to the latter view and cannot assent to the decision. . . .

This Court today initiates the doctrine that language such as this, in the environment of the street meeting, is immune from prior municipal control. We would have a very different question if New York had presumed to say that Kunz could not speak his piece in his own pulpit or hall. But it has undertaken to restrain him only if he chooses to speak at street meetings. There is a world of difference. The street preacher takes advantage of people's presence on the streets to impose his message upon what, in a sense, is a captive audience. A meeting on private property is made up of an audience that has volunteered to listen. The question, therefore, is not whether New York could, if it tried, silence Kunz, but whether it must place its streets at his service to hurl insults at the passerby.

What Mr. Justice Holmes said for a unanimous Court in *Schenck* v. *United States*, 249 US 47, . . . has become an axiom: "The most stringent protection of free speech would not protect a man in falsely shouting fire in a theatre and causing a panic." This concept was applied in one of its few unanimous decisions in recent years, when, through Mr. Justice Murphy, the Court said: "There are certain well-defined and narrowly limited classes of speech, *the prevention and punishment* of which *have never been thought to raise any Constitutional problem*. These include the lewd and obscene, the profane, the libelous, and *the insulting or 'fighting' words*—those which by their very utterance inflict injury or *tend to incite* an immediate breach of the peace. . . ." (Emphasis supplied.) *Chaplinsky* v. *New Hampshire*, 315 US 568. . . .

There held to be "insulting or 'fighting' words" were calling one a "God damned racketeer" and a "damned Fascist." Equally inciting and more clearly "fighting words," when thrown at Catholics and Jews who are rightfully on the streets of New York, are statements that "The Pope is the anti-Christ" and the Jews are "Christ-killers." These terse epithets come down to our generation weighted with hatreds accumulated through centuries of bloodshed. They are recognized words of art in the profession of defamation. They are not the kind of insult that men bandy and laugh off when the spirits are high and the flagons are low. They are not in that class of epithets whose literal sting will be drawn if the speaker smiles when he uses them. They are always, and in every context, insults which do not spring from reason and can be answered by none. Their historical associations with violence are well understood, both by those who hurl and those who are struck by these missiles. Jews, many of whose families perished in extermination furnaces of Dachau and Auschwitz, are more than tolerant if they pass off lightly the suggestion that unbelievers in Christ should all have been burned. Of course, people might pass this speaker by as a mental case, and so they might file out of a theatre in good order at the cry of "fire." But in both cases there is genuine likelihood that someone will get hurt. . . .

A hostile reception of his subject certainly does not alone destroy one's right to speak. A temperate and reasoned criticism of Roman Catholicism or Judaism might, and probably would, cause some resentment and protest. But in a free society all sects and factions, as the price of their own freedom to preach their views, must suffer that freedom in others. Tolerance of unwelcome, unorthodox ideas or information is a constitutionally protected policy not to be defeated by persons who would break up meetings they do not relish.

But emergencies may arise on streets which would become catastrophes if there was not immediate police action. The crowd which should be tolerant may be prejudiced and angry or malicious. If the situation threatens to get out of hand for the force present, I think the police may require the speaker, even if within his rights, to yield his right temporarily to the greater interest of peace. Of course, the threat must be judged in good faith to be real, immediate and serious. But silencing a speaker by authorities as a measure of mob control, is like dynamiting a house to stop the spread of a conflagration. It may be justified by the overwhelming community interest that flames not be fed as compared with the little interest to be served by continuing to feed them. But this kind of disorder does not abridge the right to speak except for the emergency and, since the speaker was within his constitutional right to speak, it could not be grounds for revoking or refusing him a permit or convicting him of any offense because of his utterance. If he resisted an officer's reasonable demand to cease, he might incur penalties.

And so the matter eventually comes down to the question whether the "words used are used in such circumstances and are of such a nature" that we can say a reasonable man would anticipate the evil result. In this case the Court does not justify, excuse, or deny the inciting and provocative character of the language, and it does not, and, on this record could not, deny that when Kunz speaks he poses a "clear and present" danger to peace and order. Why, then, does New York have to put up with it?

It is well to be vigilant to protect the right of Kunz to speak, but is he to be sole judge as to how far he will carry verbal attacks in the public streets? Is official action the only source of interference with religious freedom? Does the Jew, for example, have the benefit of these freedoms when, lawfully going about, he and his children are pointed out as "Christ-killers" to gatherings on public property by a religious sectarian sponsored by a police bodyguard?

We should weigh the value of insulting speech against its potentiality for harm. Is the Court, when declaring Kunz has the *right* he asserts, serving the great end for which the First Amendment stands?

The purpose of constitutional protection of speech is to foster peaceful interchange of all manner of thoughts, information and ideas. Its policy is rooted in faith in the force of reason. This Court wisely has said, "Resort to epithets or personal abuse is not in any proper sense communication of information or opinion safeguarded by the Constitution." . . .

The question remains whether the Constitution prohibits a city from control of its streets by a permit system which takes into account damages to public peace and order. I am persuaded that it does not do so, provided, of course, that the city does not so discriminate as to deny equal protection of the law or undertake a censorship of utterances that are not so defamatory, insulting, inciting, or provocative as to be reasonably likely to cause disorder and violence.

The Court does not hold that New York has abused the permit system by discrimination or actual censorship, nor does it deny the abuses on Kunz's part. But neither, says the Court, matters, holding that any prior restraint is bad, regardless of how fairly administered or what abuses it seeks to prevent.

It strikes rather blindly at permit systems which indirectly may affect First Amendment freedoms. Cities throughout the country have adopted permit requirements to control private activities on public streets and for other purposes. The universality of this type of regulation demonstrates a need and indicates widespread opinion in the profession that it is not necessarily incompatible with our constitutional freedoms. Is everybody out of step but this Court?

Until recently this custom of municipalities was regarded by this Court as consistent with the Constitution. . . .

In the *Chaplinsky Case, prevention* as well as *punishment* of "limited classes of speech . . . have never been thought to raise *any* constitutional problem." (Empahsis supplied.) Mr. Justice Holmes pointed out in the *Schenck Case* that the Constitution would not protect one from an injunction against uttering words that lead to riot. . . .

Of course, as to the press, there are the best of reasons against any licensing or prior restraint. Decisions such as *Near* v. *Minnesota*, 283 US 697, . . . hold any licensing or prior restraint of the press unconstitutional, and I heartily agree. But precedents from that field cannot reasonably be transposed to the street-meeting field. The impact of publishing on public order has no similarity with that of a street meeting. Publishing does not make private use of public property. It reaches only those who choose to read, and, in that way, is analogous to a meeting held in a hall where those who come do so by choice. Written words are less apt to incite or provoke to mass action than spoken words, speech being the primitive and direct communication with the emotions. Few are the riots caused by publication alone, few are the mobs that have not had their immediate origin in harangue. The vulnerability of various forms of communication to community control must be proportioned to their impact upon other community interests. . . .

It seems hypercritical to strike down local laws on their faces for want of standards when we have no standards. And I do not find it required by existing authority. I think that where speech is outside of constitutional immunity the local community or the State is left a large measure of discretion as to the means for dealing with it. . . .

Turning then to the permit system as applied by the Court of Appeals, whose construction binds us, we find that issuance the first time is required. Denial is warranted only in such unusual cases as where an applicant has had a permit which has been revoked for cause and he asserts the right to continue the conduct which was cause for revocation. If anything less than a reasonable certainty of disorder was shown, denial of a permit would be improper. The procedure by which that decision is reached commends itself to the orderly mind—complaints are filed, witnesses are heard, opportunity to cross-examine is given, and decision is reached by what we must assume to be an impartial and reasonable administrative officer, and, if he denies the permit, the applicant' may carry his cause to the courts. He may thus have a civil test of his rights without the personal humiliation of being arrested as presenting a menace to public order. It seems to me that this procedure better protects freedom of speech than to let everyone speak without leave, but subject to surveillance and to being ordered to stop in the discretion of the police.

It is obvious that a permit is a source of security and protection for the civil liberties of the great number who are entitled to receive them. It informs the police of the time and place one intends to speak, which allows necessary steps to insure him a place to speak where overzealous police officers will not order everyone who stops to listen to move on, and to have officers present to insure an orderly meeting. Moreover, disorder is less likely, for the speaker knows that if he provokes disorder his permit may be revoked, and the objector may be told that he has a remedy by filing a complaint and does not need to take the law in his own hands. Kunz was not arrested in 1946, when his speeches caused serious objections, nor was he set upon by the crowd. Instead, they did the orderly thing and made complaints which resulted in the revocation of his permit. This is the method that the Court frustrates today.

Of course, emergencies may arise either with or without the permit system. A speaker with a permit may go beyond bounds and incite violence, or a mob may undertake to break up an authorized and properly conducted meeting. In either case, the policeman on the spot must make the judgment as to what measures will most likely avoid violent disorders. But these emergencies seem less likely to occur with the permit system than if every man and his adversary take the law in their own hands.

The law of New York does not segregate according to their diverse nationalities, races, religions, or political associations, the vast hordes of people living in its narrow confines. Every individual in frightening aggregation is legally free to live, to labor, to travel, when and where he chooses. In streets and public places, all races and nationalities and all sorts and conditions of men walk, linger and mingle. Is it not reasonable that the City protect the dignity of these persons against fanatics who take possession of its streets to hurl into its crowds defamatory epithets that hurt like rocks?

If any two subjects are intrinsically incendiary and divisive, they are race and religion. Racial fears and hatreds have been at the root of the most terrible riots that have disgraced American civilization. They are ugly possibilities that overhang every great American city. The "consecrated hatreds of sect" account for more than a few of the world's bloody disorders. These are the explosives which the Court says Kunz may play with in the public streets, and the community must not only tolerate but aid him. I find no such doctrine in the Constitution.

In this case there is no evidence of a purpose to suppress speech, except to keep it in bounds that will not upset good order. If there are abuses of censorship or discrimination in administering the ordinance, as well there may be, they are not proved in this case. This Court should be particularly sure of its ground before it strikes down, in a time like this, the going, practical system by which New York has sought to control its street-meeting problem.

Addressing himself to the subject, *Authority and the Individual,* one of the keenest philosophers of our time [Bertrand Russell] observes: "The problem, like all those with which we are concerned, is one of balance; too little liberty brings stagnation, and too much brings chaos." Perhaps it is the fever of our times that inclines the Court today to favor chaos. My hope is that few will take advantage of the license granted by today's decision. But life teaches one to distinguish between hope and faith.

ROCKWELL v. MORRIS

211 NYS 2d 25 (1961)

[George Lincoln Rockwell, leader of the American Nazi Party, applied to Newbold Morris, commissioner of parks of the City of New York, for a permit to speak at Union Square on July 4, 1960. His application was denied. Rockwell sought relief in the state supreme court but was denied a remedy, the judge saying that it was not within the Constitution "to loose self-confessed advocates of violence upon a community at a time and place where it is inevitable that public disorder and riot will occur." The appellate division of the state supreme court reversed by a 4-to-1 vote. The opinion of the court is printed

below. The New York Court of Appeals affirmed, 219 NYS 2d 268, and
the United States Supreme Court denied certiorari, 368 US 913 (1961).]

Breitel, J. P.:

Rockwell, a self-styled American Nazi and, reputedly, a rabid racist,
applied to the Commissioner of Parks on May 17, 1960, for a permit to
use Union Square Park to make a public political speech the following
July 4th. The Park is located in New York City in a traffic and pedestrian-
congested area which is also a transfer point for a number of rapid
transit lines. Respondent Commissioner denied the application June
22, 1960, without offering Rockwell an alternative time or place. This
proceeding under Article 78 of the Civil Practice Act was instituted
August 11, 1960 to review the Commissioner's determination.

Special Term dismissed the petitioner. The nub of its reasoning was
that Rockwell had by speech and pamphlet accused more than two and
a half million residents of New York City of being traitors, identified
by their ethnic and religious classification; that he was a "self-confessed
advocate of violence" and Hitlerian methods; and that if he spoke it was
"inevitable that public disorder and riot will result."

Rockwell has appealed urging that the Commissioner did not comply
with the very regulation under which he purported to act, and that, if
he had such power under the regulation, it is void for unconstitutionality. Respondent Commissioner contends that under the regulation
he has the power, constitutionally, to refuse a permit to one whose
activities would create serious disorder—a clear and present danger.
Respondent also urges that the date requested, July 4th, 1960, having
passed, the matter has been rendered moot, and the petition should be
dismissed.

The order of Special Term must be reversed and the petition granted
in part. The Commissioner did not comply with his own regulation. In
any event, such a power, as arrogated by the Commissioner, would be
unconstitutional. Because the regulation requires provision of an alternative time and place, and the issue is of such vital constitutional significance, the proceeding has not been mooted.

First: The record does not support the grounds subsequently assigned
by the Commissioner for his action.

At or about the time Rockwell made his application for a permit
the metropolitan newspapers were filled with material about him, all
to his evident satisfaction and purpose. His activities in his favorite
haunt, Washington, D.C., near his home in Virginia, were publicized,
including his arrest for creating public disorder by highly offensive,
rabid, racist speeches. As a result, several organized groups in this City

were aroused, the Mayor made public pronouncements, and the Commissioner in due course denied Rockwell's application, without at that time assigning any reasons. In fact, all the Commissioner had before him, and that is still the only original administrative record, is a stark application, which, except for the designation "American Nazi Party," and a reference to "Storm Leader," suggests none of the things for which Rockwell stands or may be responsible.

Later, in the judicial proceeding the Corporation Counsel endeavored to supplement the bare administrative record by annexing newspaper cuttings and leaflets distributed, purportedly, by Rockwell and his group. These reveal or represent the characteristic emission of certain extremist, often paranoid, groups, not large in number, but often responsible for disorder in sensitive places in the nation. Characteristically too, equivocal language is used suggesting dire acts of violence and destruction but not quite related to any immediacy in time. Group hate and fear are stimulated and expressly intended to be stimulated in those ripe for it. Whether the authors intend to attain their ends by unlawful means is not made clear, and undoubtedly purposely so. In this case the evidentiary relevance for these additions is never quite established. Not only were they not before the Commissioner, but no proper authenticating foundation was laid. . . .

Consequently, there is no competent record upon which the Commissioner, Special Term, or this Court, could reach the conclusion, even if otherwise legally permissible, that Rockwell's proposed speech on July 4th, 1960 was likely to create the disorders, upon the basis of which his application was denied.

Second: The Commissioner did not follow the regulation of his own department.

The Commissioner acted under section 21-a of the Rules of the Department of Parks. It provides express standards. These bar all private or commercial uses. In addition, the rule bars various uses affecting adversely the physical facilities in the park, or the priorities of convenience. No standards are provided or suggested related to speech content. The rule mandates that, whenever a permit is denied for any but commercial or private uses, alternative suitable location and date must be offered to the applicant. This last the Commissioner did not do.

The regulation is one carefully and consciously drawn in the light of recent judicial constitutional pronouncements (*People* v. *Nahman*, 298 N.Y. 95; *Saia* v. *New York*, 334 U.S. 558; *Cox* v. *New Hampshire*, 312 U.S. 569). Thus, the regulation depends for validity upon the fact that it does not authorize censorship of speech content, condemned in the *Saia* case. There, in striking down a municipal ordinance adopted in this State, Mr. Justice Douglas said on behalf of the court:

"The present ordinance has the same defects (as in *Cantwell* v. *Connecticut, infra,* 310 U.S. 296; and *Hague* v. *C.I.O., infra,* 307 U.S. 496). The right to be heard is placed in the uncontrolled discretion of the Chief of Police. He stands athwart the channels of communication as an obstruction which can be removed only after criminal trial and conviction and lengthy appeal. A more effective previous restraint is difficult to imagine."

Notably, in the *Nahman* case, a prosecution for displaying placards without a permit and involving section 21 (not section 21-a) of the Park Department regulations, the then Commission represented to the court as follows:

"Meetings and other public events are never prohibited through the permit procedure but are merely scheduled and located as to area and time in an orderly way by making necessary adjustments in the place and time stated in the application for a permit where such adjustment is necessary in the interest of the comfort, convenience and protection of the general public in the use of the parks. The application procedure is used so as to limit the use of available areas to one group at a time and provide for proper police and other supervision where necessary so that meetings and other events will be orderly and without danger to the safety of others using the parks."

Thereafter, section 21-a was adopted. From its terms it appears to be a codification of the practice under section 21 then described by the Commission. It follows the strictures of the court that in the regulations

". . . No power to suppress the publication of facts or opinions is thereby conferred and the sole standard of official action thereby countenanced is the promotion of beauty and utility of the public parks of the city—an objective which undoubtedly goes far to secure the safety, comfort and convenience of a population of more than eight million people."

Moreover, whatever doubt may have remained as to the right to speak in public parks without prior restraint was eventually made clear in *Niemotko v. Maryland* (340 U.S. 268), thus justifying the narrow and cautious handling of the permit procedure by the Park Department in the *Nahman* case, *supra,* and in the later draftmanship of section 21-a. There it was held that a park commissioner could not withhold a permit to Jehovah's Witnesses to speak, by reason of a municipal custom in which there were no limited standards confined to proper physical use of a park, and that, therefore, the permit was refused because of dislike for Jehovah's Witnesses. A conviction for speaking without a permit was vacated. There is little to distinguish that case from this except that some may resent "American Nazis" more than Jehovah's Witnesses.

Consequently, there is no doubt that the Commissioner arrogated a power he did not have under the very regulation of his own department. On this view the regulation is valid under well-recognized constitutional principles, but the Commissioner's action is vulnerable.

Third: Regulations aside, there is no power in government under our Constitution to exercise prior restraint of the expression of views, unless it is demonstrable on a record that such expression will immediately and irreparably create injury to the public weal—not that such expression, without itself being unlawful, will incite criminal acts in others.

The cases in support of this teaching are many. It is enough to refer to those in which the facts come quite close to these at hand (if a proper record could have and had been made).

In *Near* v. *Minnesota* (283 U.S. 697) there was involved a statute authorizing injunction to restrain publication of malicious, scandalous, and defamatory matter. The state courts enjoined defendant from publishing a periodical which, in undisguised language, charged an ethnic group with gangster control of Minneapolis. Capitalization of words, epithets, references to violence and death were interspersed not only to be offensive but to be stimulative of group hate and fear. It was quite equal, in impact, to much of the literature attributed to Rockwell. The statute was struck down as an unconstitutional prior restraint on expression of views.

Much closer in time and much closer to home is *Kunz* v. *New York* (340 U.S. 290). In that case, Kunz, a self-styled religious preacher, used Columbus Circle in congested mid-Manhattan in New York City, to denounce in vicious and unbridled terms, Jews and Catholics. He too spoke of the incinerators of Hitler Germany, and regretted that the job was not complete. He had no permit as required by local ordinance, and was convicted for that violation. He was not prosecuted for any violation of law based on speech content. The Supreme Court struck the ordinance down as invalid previous restraint. . . .

It makes no difference that the *Kunz* case involved religious freedom. Indeed, it has been said neatly that there is an absolute right to religious belief, but that the right to religious speech or activity may be qualified, albeit only to a very limited degree (*Cantwell* v. *Connecticut*, 310 U.S. 296). Thus, for this purpose, the right of expression in religion or politics is about the same. Either right is equally qualified, just the same as the right to religious or political *belief* is equally absolute. But even the qualified right to speak on religion or politics is not subject to prior restraint with but the narrowest of exceptions.

The narrowest of exceptions relate to immediate and irreparable injury to the public weal (e.g., *Schenck* v. *United States*, 249 U.S. 47, involving anticonscription activity in time of war; but compare *De Jonge* v. *Oregon*, 299 U.S. 353, in which it was held that participation in a "lawful" meeting of a subversive organization could not be made the subject of criminal prosecution). But this does not justify the perversion that if the actor's speech, otherwise innocent, incites others to unlawful action he may be suppressed (*Terminiello* v. *Chicago*, 337 U.S. 1).

In the *Terminiello* case, a racist, rabid, suspended clergyman spoke in a private hall. His speech would satisfy the generic definition in which the Kunz and Rockwell emissions fall. A crowd outside threw missiles, fights started, and doors were broken. The situation inside the hall was only a little better. It was no trivial affair. Terminiello's conviction, *post factum*, was vacated because the charge to the Jury was broad enough to encompass a finding of guilt, even if the defendant has said nothing unlawful. Said the court (per Douglas, J.):

> "It [the charge] permitted conviction of petitioner if his speech stirred people to anger, invited public dispute, or brought about a condition of unrest."

Even the dissenters (Vinson, Ch. J., and Frankfurter, Burton, and Jackson, JJ.) in the *Terminiello* case did not seem to dispute that the measure of the speaker is not the conduct of his audience.

In the *Kunz* case, *supra*, Mr. Justice Jackson, in an eloquent dissenting opinion, made the most of the position now taken by respondent in favor of previous restraint. It did not prevail then, and has not since. This is not because the speeches of Kunz were any more tolerable than those of Rockwell. The problem is much deeper and more difficult.

Fourth: While there may not be a prior restraint on the expression of views, but for the narrowest of exceptions, there may be complete responsibility for the content of such expression.

Again, the cases are many. It is on such cases that respondent largely and mistakenly relies. They involve subsequent punishment for what was said, which expression unlawfully injured others or the public weal (*Beauharnais* v. *Illinois*, 343 U.S. 250; *Chaplinsky* v. *New Hampshire*, 315 U.S. 568; *Whitney* v. *California*, 274 U.S. 357; *Gitlow* v. *New York*, 268 U.S. 652; *People* v. *McWilliams* (Mag. Ct.), 22 N.Y.S. 2d 571, revd. on other gds. 31 N.Y.S. 2d 37; *People* v. *Doss*, 384 Ill. 400).

Once again, there is precedent closer in time and closer to home. In *Feiner* v. *New York* (340 U.S. 315), the speaker was convicted of disorderly conduct when he refused to stop his provocative speaking as riot impended, although requested by police officers. (Perhaps it is of controlling significance that Feiner was inciting a "mob" to disorderly action in favor of his teaching; a "mob" was not reacting unlawfully to his speech, although adverse action was threatened by one or more individuals.) The conviction was sustained in the state courts, and in the Supreme Court. In the last court it was said (per Vinson, Ch. J.):

"We are well aware that the ordinary murmurings and objections of a hostile audience cannot be allowed to silence a speaker, and are also mindful of the possible danger of giving overzealous police officials complete discretion to break up otherwise lawful public meetings.

". . . But we are not faced here with such a situation. It is one thing to say that the police cannot be used as an instrument for the suppression of unpopular views, and another to say that, when as here the speaker passes the bounds of argument or persuasion and undertakes incitement to riot, they are powerless to prevent a breach of the peace."

Now, there is no question that government, in each of its branches —executive, legislative, and judicial—faces here one of its gravest domestic problems. Although marked advances in thinking and solution have occurred, total resolution has not yet been achieved. To some, the cases may seem to have zigzagged since the days of *Davis* v. *Massachusetts*, 167 U.S. 43, in which, incidentally, it was the opinion of Mr. Justice Holmes, written with a much finer pen, in the Supreme Judicial Court of Massachusetts that was upheld when it seemed, and it was said, that the municipality had absolute control of its streets and parks, even to the arbitrary exclusion of a speaker from Boston Common. Actually, a consistently forward-moving pattern emerges, and that pattern serves thus far to balance protection for the speaker and for the public.

A community need not wait to be subverted by street riots and stormtroopers; but, also, it cannot, by its policemen, or commissioners, suppress a speaker, in prior restraint, on the basis of news reports, hysteria, or inference that what he did yesterday, he will do today. Thus, too, if the speaker incites others to immediate unlawful action he may be punished—in a proper case, stopped when disorder actually impends; but this is not to be confused with unlawful action from others who seek unlawfully to suppress or punish the speaker.

So, the unpopularity of views, their shocking quality, their obnoxiousness, and even their alarming impact is not enough. Otherwise, the preacher of any strange doctrine could be stopped; the anti-racist himself could be suppressed, if he undertakes to speak in "restricted" areas; and one who asks that public schools be open indiscriminately to all ethnic groups could be lawfully suppressed, if only he choose to speak where persuasion is needed most.

It is worth noting that Mr. Justice Frankfurter, in his concurring opinion in *Niemotko* v. *Maryland, supra* (340 U.S. 268, 273, *et seq.*), which also covers his views in the *Kunz* and *Feiner* cases, *supra*, stated a suggestive proposition with which one may agree. It is to the effect that municipalities or states can legislate effectively to prevent the mad, the criminal, or the subversive from taking over the streets, and this can be done in accordance with the requirements of the Fourteenth Amendment, but that it is not for the courts to tell them how.

Quite interesting in that connection is *Poulos* v. *New Hampshire* (345 U.S. 395), involving a park permit procedure, the same as that involved and sustained in the *Cox* case, *supra*. Substantially, the analyses here and in that case are in accord. Much more important is that the case has maximum significance for those who would legislate in this area. For, in the *Poulos* case, a conviction for speaking without a permit was sustained although the permit was arbitrarily refused, because, it was held, defendant should have exhausted his judicial remedies to review the administrator's action. Of course, and emphatically, the case may not be misread to permit advance censorship of speech content, even in these circumstances.

Notably, when section 21-a itself was drawn, it was done with recent teachings in mind. But now, once again, against a speaker despised, hated or feared, the lawless short-circuit is seized upon. The evil to be ended provokes evil means to that end. This is not good law or good morals. No doubt, too, suppression is easier than punishment. No doubt suppressing a minority is easier than keeping a misbehaving majority in line. But that is exactly the purpose of law, and of government under law. Indeed, the moral imperative is for all to obey the law, the audience as well as the speaker, and especially those who do not wish to be even a part of the audience.

Only if Rockwell speaks criminally (or, perhaps, if it is established on a proper record, in that very rare case, that he will speak criminally, not because he once did, but that he will this time, and irreparable harm will ensue) can his right to speak be cut off. If he does not speak criminally, then, of course, his right to speak may not be cut off, no matter how offensive his speech may be to others. Instead, his right, and that of those who wish to listen to him, must be protected, no matter how unpleasant the assignment.

Fifth: Because of the important public issue involved and the future significance of the constitutional questions raised, and also because the Commissioner failed to provide petitioner with an alternative time and place for his speech, the proceeding is not mooted.

On public significance justifying retention of jurisdisction see: *Matter of Rosenbluth* v. *Finkelstein* (300 N.Y. 402, 404) and *Matter of Adirondack L. Club* v. *Black Riv. R. Dist.* (301 N.Y. 219, 222). In any event, the matter is not moot because the park regulation petitioner would be entitled to an alternative time and place, if the Commissioner should find that Union Square Park was unsuitable as to either or both (section 21-a, *supra*). In other words, the date requested in the application is not determinative of the matter.

In summary, the key to understanding is really very simple: The right of free expression is not to be entrusted to administrative previous restraint for contemplated violation of law, but such expression is not immune from punishment after the fact for what has been said, by judicial process. This is not unreasonable. History elsewhere has shown the executive sometimes to establish tyranny and dictatorship by the powers of suppression.

Surely, there is risk in denying prior restraint. It is a price paid for liberty while order is to be preserved by the sanction of punshment after the fact. It is the price paid for not having the policeman or the Commissioner as censor, while leaving the courts, disciplined by appellate review and the rules of evidence, to provide punishment under criminal standards for the unlawful act already committed.

But the risk is not so great as to be intolerable in a civilized, law-abiding community. Indeed, recent events, when especially provocative personalities attended an international meeting in this city, prove otherwise. Then these personalities did not represent mere mad ravings but effective, and not too remote, threats of widespread death and destruction. Nevertheless, the people, at least the residents, in this community, to many of whom these personalities were directly offensive and repugnant, did not resort to riot. They knew what was expected of them. It had also been made quite clear to them that the law was to be enforced without discrimination. The reward was not only the order which obtained, but the national respect that ensued for the people and their police force.

Of course, recent events, elsewhere, have shown that riotous conditions can be produced or will occur, merely by law enforcement agencies declaring their inability to prevent riot, and asking, even in courts of law, for the right to be denied so that riot will not occur. . . .

It is not law or order that is fashioned to avoid riot at the expense of comprising [sic] constitutional guarantees. Instead, it is something which can end only in anarchy and then tyranny.

5. Taxes on Knowledge

GROSJEAN v. AMERICAN PRESS CO.

297 US 233 (1936)

[In 1712 Parliament imposed a tax on printed papers, pamphlets, and advertisements and required a stamp to be placed on every newspaper. Such taxes came to be known as "taxes on knowledge." The tax on pamphlets continued until 1833, on advertisements until 1852, and the stamp duty on newspapers until 1855. The effect of these duties was to restrict circulation of printed matter among the relatively poor.

[Pointing out that the American Revolution began in effect when England started to send stamps for newspaper duties to the American Colonies, the Court in the present case unanimously condemned as unconstitutional any device that falls within the category of "taxes on knowledge." The decision has been followed in later cases; e.g., *Follett* v. *McCormick*, 321 US 573 (1944), in which the Court extended the prohibition to a tax on the exercise of religion.]

Mr. Justice Sutherland delivered the opinion of the Court:

This suit was brought by appellees, nine publishers of newspapers in the State of Louisiana, to enjoin the enforcement against them of the provisions of § 1 of the act of the legislature of Louisiana known as Act No. 23, passed and approved July 12, 1934, as follows:

That every person, firm, association or corporation, domestic or foreign, engaged in the business of selling, or making any charge for, advertising or for advertisements, whether printed or published, or to be printed or published, in any newspaper, magazine, periodical or publication whatever having a circulation of more than 20,000 copies per week, or displayed and exhibited, or to be displayed and exhibited by means of moving pictures, in the State of Louisiana, shall, in addition to all other taxes and licenses levied and assessed in this State, pay a license tax for the privilege of engaging in such business in this State of two per cent. (2%) of the gross receipts of such business.

The nine publishers who brought the suit publish thirteen newspapers; and these thirteen publications are the only ones within the State of Louisiana having each a circulation of more than 20,000 copies per week, although the lower court finds there are four other daily newspapers each having a circulation of "slightly less than 20,000 copies per week" which are in competition with those published by appellees both as to circulation and as to advertising. In addition, there are 120 weekly newspapers published in the state, also in competition, to a greater or less degree, with the newspapers of appellees. The revenue derived from appellees' newspapers comes almost entirely from regular subscribers or purchasers thereof and from payments received for the insertion of advertisements therein.

The act requires everyone subject to the tax to file a sworn report every three months showing the amount and the gross receipts from the business described in § 1. The resulting tax must be paid when the report is filed. Failure to file the report or pay the tax as thus provided constitutes a misdemeanor and subjects the offender to a fine not exceeding $500, or imprisonment not exceeding six months, or both, for each violation. Any corporation violating the act subjects itself to the payment of $500 to be recovered by suit. . . .

The validity of the act is assailed as violating the federal Constitution in two particulars—(1) that it abridges the freedom of the press in contravention of the due process clause contained in § 1 of the Fourteenth Amendment; (2) that it denies appellees the equal protection of the laws in contravention of the same Amendment.

1. The first point presents a question of the utmost gravity and importance; for, if well made, it goes to the heart of the natural right of the members of an organized society, united for their common good, to impart and acquire information about their common interests. The First Amendment to the federal Constitution provides that "Congress shall make no law . . . abridging the freedom of speech, or of the press. . . ." While this provision is not a restraint upon the powers of the states, the states are precluded from abridging the freedom of speech or of the press by force of the due process clause of the Fourteenth Amendment. . . .

That freedom of speech and of the press are rights of the same fundamental character, safeguarded by the due process of law clause of the Fourteenth Amendment against abridgment by state legislation, has . . . been settled by a series of decisions of this court. . . . The word "liberty" contained in that amendment embraces not only the right of a person to be free from physical restraint, but the right to be free in the enjoyment of all his faculties as well. . . .

For more than a century prior to the adoption of the amendment—and, indeed, for many years thereafter—history discloses a persistent effort on the part of the British government to prevent or abridge the free expression of any opinion which seemed to criticize or exhibit in an unfavorable light, however truly, the agencies and operations of the government. The struggle between the proponents of measures to that end and those who asserted the right of free expression was continuous and unceasing. As early as 1644, John Milton, in [*Areopagitica,*] an "Appeal for the Liberty of Unlicensed Printing," assailed an act of Parliament which had just been passed providing for censorship of the press previous to publication. He vigorously defended the right of every man to make public his honest views "without previous censure"; and declared the impossibility of finding any man base enough to accept the office of censor and at the same time good enough to be allowed to perform its duties. . . . The act expired by its own terms in 1695. It was never renewed; and the liberty of the press thus became . . . merely "a right or liberty to publish *without* a license what formerly could be published only *with* one." But mere exemption from previous censorship was soon recognized as too narrow a view of the liberty of the press.

In 1712, in response to a message from Queen Anne . . . , Parliament imposed a tax upon all newspapers and upon advertisements. . . . That the main purpose of these taxes was to suppress the publication of comments and criticisms objectionable to the Crown does not admit of doubt. . . . There followed more than a century of resistance to, and evasion of, the taxes, and of agitation for their repeal. . . . [It has been said that] these taxes constituted one of the factors that aroused the American colonists to protest against taxation for the purposes of the home government; and that the revolution really began when, in 1765, that government sent stamps for newspaper duties to the American colonies.

These duties were quite commonly characterized as "taxes on knowledge," a phrase used for the purpose of describing the effect of the exactions and at the same time condemning them. That the taxes had, and were intended to have, the effect of curtailing the circulation of newspapers, and particularly the cheaper ones whose readers were generally found among the masses of the people, went almost without question, even on the part of those who defended the act. May (*Constitutional History of England*, 7th ed., vol. 2, p. 245), after discussing the control by "previous censure," says: ". . . a new restraint was devised in the form of a stamp duty on newspapers and advertisements, —avowedly for the purpose of repressing libels. This policy, being found effectual in limiting the circulation of cheap papers was improved upon in the two following reigns, and continued in high esteem until our own time." Collett ([*History of the Taxes on Knowledge,*] vol. 1, p. 14) says: "Any man who carried on printing or publishing for a livelihood was actually at the mercy of the Commissioners of Stamps, when they chose to exert their powers."

Citations of similar import might be multiplied many times; but the foregoing is enough to demonstrate beyond peradventure that in the adoption of the English newspaper stamp tax and the tax on advertisements, revenue was of subordinate concern; and that the dominant and controlling aim was to prevent, or curtail the opportunity for, the acquisition of knowledge by the people in respect of their governmental affairs. It is idle to suppose that so many of the best men of England would for a century of time have waged, as they did, stubborn and often precarious warfare against these taxes if a mere matter of taxation had been involved. The aim of the struggle was not to relieve taxpayers from a burden, but to establish and preserve the right of the English people to full information in respect of the doings or misdoings of their government. Upon the correctness of this conclusion the very characterization of the exactions as "taxes on knowledge" sheds a flood of corroborative light. In the ultimate, an informed and enlightened public opinion was the thing at stake; for, as Erskine, in his great speech in defense of Paine, has said: "The liberty of opinion keeps governments themselves in due subjection to their duties." . . .

In 1785, only four years before Congress had proposed the First Amendment, the Massachusetts legislature, following the English example, imposed a stamp tax on all newspapers and magazines. The following year an advertisement tax was imposed. Both taxes met with such violent opposition that the former was repealed in 1786, and the latter in 1788. Duniway, *Freedom of the Press in Massachusetts*, pp. 136, 137.

The framers of the First Amendment were familiar with the English struggle, which then had continued for nearly eighty years and was destined to go on for another sixty-five years, at the end of which time it culminated in a lasting abandonment of the obnoxious taxes. The framers were likewise familiar with the then recent Massachusetts episode; and while that occurrence did much to bring about the adoption of the amendment . . . , the predominant influence must have come from the English experience. It is impossible to concede that by the words "freedom of the press" the framers of the amendment intended to adopt merely the narrow view then reflected by the law of England that such freedom consisted only in immunity from previous censorship; for this abuse had then permanently disappeared from English practice. It is equally impossible to believe that it was not intended to bring within the reach of these words such modes of restraint as were embodied in the two forms of taxation already described. Such belief must be rejected in the face of the then well known purpose of the exactions and the general adverse sentiment of the colonies in respect to them. . . .

In the light of all that has now been said, it is evident that the restricted rules of the English law in respect of the freedom of the press in force when the Constitution was adopted were never accepted by the American colonists, and that by the First Amendment it was meant to preclude the national government, and by the Fourteenth Amendment to preclude the states, from adopting any form of previous restraint upon printed publications, or their circulation, including that which had theretofore been effected by these two well-known and odious methods. . . .

It is not intended by anything we have said to suggest that the owners of newspapers are immune from any of the ordinary forms of taxation for support of the government. But this is not an ordinary form of tax, but one single in kind, with a long history of hostile misuse against the freedom of the press.

The predominant purpose of the grant of immunity here invoked was to preserve an untrammeled press as a vital source of public information. The newspapers, magazines and other journals of the country, it is safe to say, have shed and continue to shed, more light on the public and business affairs of the nation than any other instrumentality of publicity; and since informed public opinion is the most potent of all restraints upon misgovernment, the suppression or abridgment of the publicity afforded by a free press cannot be regarded otherwise than with grave concern. The tax here involved is bad not because it takes money from the pockets of the appellees. If that were all, a wholly different question would be presented. It is bad because, in the light of its history and of its present setting, it is seen to be a deliberate and calculated device in the guise of a tax to limit the circulation of information to which the public is entitled in virtue of the constitutional guaranties. A free press stands as one of the great interpreters between the government and the people. To allow it to be fettered is to fetter ourselves.

In view of the persistent search for new subjects of taxation, it is not without significance that, with the single exception of the Louisiana statute, so far as we can discover, no state during the one hundred fifty years of our national existence has undertaken to impose a tax like that now in question.

The form in which the tax is imposed is in itself suspicious. It is not measured or limited by the volume of advertisements. It is measured alone by the extent of the circulation of the publication in which the advertisements are carried, with the plain purpose of penalizing the publishers and curtailing the circulation of a selected group of newspapers.

2. Having reached the conclusion that the act imposing the tax in question is unconstitutional under the due process of law clause because it abridges the freedom of the press, we deem it unnecessary to consider the further ground assigned that it also constitutes a denial of the equal protection of the laws.

Decree affirmed.

6. Freedom of Anonymous Publication

TALLEY v. CALIFORNIA

362 US 60 (1960)

[A Los Angeles municipal ordinance made it a crime to distribute handbills that did not contain the names and addresses of the persons who prepared, distributed, or sponsored the handbills. By a 6-to-3 decision, the Supreme Court held this requirement unconstitutional. Justice Harlan wrote a concurring opinion. Justice Clark wrote a dissenting opinion, joined by Justices Frankfurter and Whittaker.]

Mr. Justice Black delivered the opinion of the Court:

The question presented here is whether the provisions of a Los Angeles City ordinance restricting the distribution of handbills "abridge the freedom of speech and of the press secured against state invasion by the Fourteenth Amendment of the Constitution." The ordinance, § 28.06 of the Municipal Code of the City of Los Angeles, provides:

No person shall distribute any hand-bill in any place under any circumstances, which does not have printed on the cover, or the face thereof, the name and address of the following:

(a) The person who printed, wrote, compiled or manufactured the same.

(b) The person who caused the same to be distributed; provided, however, that in the case of a fictitious person or club, in addition to such fictitious name, the true names and addresses of the owners, managers or agents of the person sponsoring said hand-bill shall also appear thereon.

The petitioner was arrested and tried in a Los Angeles Municipal Court for violating this ordinance. It was stipulated that the petitioner had distributed handbills in Los Angeles, and two of them were presented in evidence. Each had printed on it the following:

> National Consumers Mobilization,
> Box 6533,
> Los Angeles 55, Calif.
> PLeasant 9-1576.

The handbills urged readers to help the organization carry on a boycott against certain merchants and businessmen, whose names were given, on the ground that, as one set of handbills said, they carried products of "manufacturers who will not offer equal employment opportunities to Negroes, Mexicans, and Orientals." There also appeared a blank, which, if signed, would request enrollment of the signer as a "member of National Consumers Mobilization," and which was preceded by a statement that "I believe that every man should have an equal opportunity for employment no matter what his race, religion, or place of birth."

The Municipal Court held that the information printed on the handbills did not meet the requirements of the ordinance, found the petitioner guilty as charged, and fined him $10. The Appellate Department of the Superior Court of the County of Los Angeles affirmed the conviction, rejecting petitioner's contention, timely made in both state courts, that the ordinance invaded his freedom of speech and press in violation of the Fourteenth and First Amendments to the Federal Constitution. Since this was the highest state court available to petitioner, we granted certiorari to it to consider this constitutional contention.

In *Lovell* v. *Griffin*, 303 U.S. 444, we held void on its face an ordinance that comprehensively forbade any distribution of literature at any time or place in Griffin, Georgia, without a license. Pamphlets and leaflets, it was pointed out, "have been historic weapons in the defense of liberty" and enforcement of the Griffin ordinance "would restore the system of license and censorship in its baldest form." A year later we had before us four ordinances each forbidding distribution of leaflets— one in Irvington, New Jersey, one in Los Angeles, California, one in Milwaukee, Wisconsin, and one in Worcester, Massachusetts. *Schneider v. Irvington*, 308 U.S. 147. Efforts were made to distinguish these four ordinances from the one held void in the *Griffin* case. The chief grounds urged for distinction were that the four ordinances had been passed to prevent either frauds, disorder, or littering, according to the records in these cases, and another ground urged was that two of the ordinances applied only to certain city areas. This Court refused to uphold the four ordinances on those grounds pointing out that there were other ways to accomplish these legitimate aims without abridging freedom of speech and press. Frauds, street littering and disorderly conduct could be denounced and punished as offenses, the Court said. Several years later we followed the *Griffin* and *Schneider* cases in striking down a Dallas, Texas, ordinance which was applied to prohibit the dissemination of information by the distribution of handbills. We said that although a city could punish any person for conduct on the streets if he violates a valid law, "one who is rightfully on a street . . . carries with him there as elsewhere the constitutional right to express his views in an orderly fashion . . . by handbills and literature as well as by the spoken words." *Jamison* v. *Texas*, 318 U.S. 413.

The broad ordinance now before us, barring distribution of "any hand-bill in any place under any circumstances," falls precisely under the ban of our prior cases unless this ordinance is saved by the qualification that handbills can be distributed if they have printed on them the names and addresses of the persons who prepared, distributed or sponsored them. For, as in *Griffin*, the ordinance here is not limited to handbills whose content is "obscene or offensive to public morals or that advocates unlawful conduct." Counsel has urged that this ordinance is aimed at providing a way to identify those responsible for fraud, false advertising and libel. Yet the ordinance is in no manner so limited, nor have we been referred to any legislative history indicating such a purpose. Therefore we do not pass on the validity of an ordinance limited to prevent these or any other supposed evils. This ordinance simply bars all handbills under all circumstances anywhere that do not have the printed names and addresses on them in the place the ordinance requires.

There can be no doubt that such an identification requirement would tend to restrict freedom to distribute information and thereby freedom of expression. "Liberty of circulating is as essential to that freedom as liberty of publishing; indeed, without the circulation, the publication would be of little value." *Lovell* v. *Griffin,* 303 U.S.

Anonymous pamphlets, leaflets, brochures and even books have played an important role in the progress of mankind. Persecuted groups and sects from time to time throughout history have been able to criticize oppressive practices and laws either anonymously or not at all. The obnoxious press licensing law of England, which was also enforced on the Colonies, was due in part to the knowledge that exposure of the names of printers, writers and distributors would lessen the circulation of literature critical of the government. The old seditious libel cases in England show the length to which government had to go to find out who was responsible for books that were obnoxious to the rulers. John Lilburne was whipped, pilloried and fined for refusing to answer questions designed to get evidence to convict him or someone else for the secret distribution of books in England. Two Puritan Ministers, John Penry and John Udall, were sentenced to death on charges that they were responsible for writing, printing or publishing books. Before the Revolutionary War colonial patriots frequently had to conceal their authorship or distribution of literature that easily could have brought down on them prosecutions by English controlled courts. Along about that time the Letters of Junius were written and the identity of their author is unknown to this day. Even the Federalist Papers, written in favor of the adoption of our Constitution, were published under fictitious names. It is plain that anonymity has sometimes been assumed for the most constructive purposes.

We have recently had occasion to hold in two cases that there are times and circumstances when States may not compel members of groups engaged in the dissemination of ideas to be publicly identified. *Bates* v. *Little Rock,* 361 U.S. 516; *N.A.A.C.P.* v. *Alabama,* 357 U.S. 449. The reason for those holdings was that identification and fear of reprisal might deter perfectly peaceful discussions of public matters of importance. This broad Los Angeles ordinance is subject to the same infirmity. We hold that it, like the Griffin, Georgia, ordinance, is void on its face.

The judgment of the Appellate Department of the Superior Court of the State of California is reversed and the cause is remanded to it for further proceedings not inconsistent with this opinion.

Mr. Justice Clark, whom Mr. Justice Frankfurter and Mr. Justice Whittaker join, dissenting:

To me, Los Angeles' ordinance cannot be read as being void on its face. Certainly a fair reading of it does not permit a conclusion that it prohibits the distribution of handbills "of any kind at any time, at any place, and in any manner," . . . as the Court seems to conclude. . . . As I read it, the ordinance here merely prohibits the distribution of a handbill which does not carry the identification of the name of the person who "printed, wrote, compiled . . . manufactured [or] . . . caused" the distribution of it. There could well be a compelling reason for such a requirement. The Court implies as much when it observes that Los Angeles has not "referred to any legislative history indicating" that the ordinance was adopted for the purpose of preventing "fraud, false advertising and libel." But even as to its legislative background there is pertinent material which the Court overlooks. At oral argument, the City's chief law enforcement officer stated that the ordinance was originally suggested in 1931 by the Los Angeles Chamber of Commerce in a complaint to the City Council urging it to "do something about these handbills and advertising matters which were false and misleading." Upon inquiry by the Council, he said, the matter was referred to his office, and the Council was advised that such an ordinance as the present one would be valid. He further stated that this ordinance, relating to the original inquiry of the Chamber of Commerce, was thereafter drafted and submitted to the Council. It was adopted in 1932. In the face of this and the presumption of validity that the ordinance enjoys, the Court nevertheless strikes it down, stating that it "falls precisely under the ban of our prior cases." This cannot follow, for in each of the three cases cited, the ordinances either "forbade any distribution of literature . . . without a license," *Lovell* v. *Griffin, supra,* or forbade, without exception, any distribution of handbills on the streets, *Jamison* v. *Texas,* 318 U.S. 413 (1943); or, as in *Schneider* v. *State,* 308 U.S. 147 (1939), which covered different ordinances in four cities, they were either outright bans or prior restraints upon the distribution of handbills. I, therefore, cannot see how the Court can conclude that the Los Angeles ordinance here "falls precisely" under any of these cases. On the contrary to my mind they neither control this case nor are apposite to it. In fact, in *Schneider,* depended upon by the Court, it was held, through Mr. Justice Roberts, that, "In every case . . . where legislative abridgment of the rights is asserted, the courts should be astute to examine the effect of the challenged legislation . . . weigh the circumstances and . . . appraise the substantiality of the reasons advanced. . . ." The Court here, however, makes no appraisal of the *circumstances,* or *the substantiality* of the claims of the litigants, but strikes down the ordinance as being "void on its face." I cannot be a party to using such a device as an escape from the requirements of our cases, . . .

Therefore, before passing upon the validity of the ordinance, I would weigh the interests of the public in its enforcement against the claimed right of Talley. The record is barren of any claim, much less proof, that he will suffer any injury whatever by identifying the handbill with his name. Unlike *N.A.A.C.P.* v *Alabama,* 357 U.S. 449 (1958), which is relied upon, there is neither allegation nor proof that Talley or any group sponsoring him would suffer "economic reprisal, loss of employment, threat of physical coercion [or] other manifestations of public hostility." Talley makes no showing whatever to support his contention that a restraint upon his freedom of speech will result from the enforcement of the ordinance. The existence of such a restraint is necessary before we can strike the ordinance down.

But even if the State had this burden, which it does not, the substantiality of Los Angeles' interest in the enforcement of the ordinance sustains its validity. Its chief law enforcement officer says that the enforcement of the ordinance prevents "fraud, deceit, false advertising, negligent use of words, obscenity and libel," and, as we have said, that such was its purpose. In the absence of any showing to the contrary by Talley, this appears to me entirely sufficient.

I stand second to none in supporting Talley's right of free speech—but not his freedom of anonymity. The Constitution says nothing about freedom of anonymous speech. In fact, this Court has approved laws requiring no more than Los Angeles' ordinance. I submit that they control this case and require our approval of Los Angeles' ordinance under the attack made here. First, *Lewis Publishing Co.* v. *Morgan*, 229 U.S. 288 (1913), upheld an Act of Congress requiring any newspaper using the second-class mails to publish the names of its editor, publisher, owner, and stockholders. . . . Second, in the Federal Regulation of Lobbying Act, 2 U.S.C. § 267, Congress requires those engaged in lobbying to divulge their identities and give "a modicum of information" to Congress. *United States* v. *Harriss*, 347 U.S. 612 (1954). Third, the several States have corrupt practices Acts outlawing, *inter alia*, the distribution of anonymous publications with reference to political candidates.* While these statutes are leveled at political campaign and election practices, the underlying ground sustaining their validity applies with equal force here.

No civil right has a greater claim to constitutional protection or calls for more rigorous safeguarding than voting rights. In this area the danger of coercion and reprisals—economic and otherwise—is a matter of common knowledge. Yet these statutes, disallowing anonymity in promoting one's views in election campaigns, have expressed the overwhelming public policy of the Nation. Nevertheless the Court is silent about this impressive authority relevant to the disposition of this case.

All three of the types of statutes mentioned are designed to prevent the same abuses—libel, slander, false accusations, etc. The fact that some of these statutes are aimed at elections, lobbying, and the mails makes their restraint no more palatable, nor the abuses they prevent less deleterious to the public interest, than the present ordinance.

All that Los Angeles requires is that one who exercises his right of free speech through writing or distributing handbills identify himself just as does one who speaks from the platform. The ordinance makes for the responsibility in writing that is present in public utterance. When and if the application of such an ordinance in a given case encroaches on First Amendment freedoms, then will be soon enough to strike that application down. But no such restraint has been shown here. After all, the public has some rights against which the enforcement of freedom of speech would be "harsh and

* Thirty-six States have statutes prohibiting the anonymous distribution of materials relating to elections. . . .

arbitrary in itself." *Kovacs* v. *Cooper,* 336 U.S. 77, 88 (1949). We have upheld complete proscription of uninvited door-to-door canvassing as an invasion of privacy. *Breard* v. *Alexandria,* 341 U.S. 622 (1951). Is this less restrictive than complete freedom of distribution—regardless of content— of a signed handbill? And commercial handbills may be declared *verboten, Valentine* v. *Chrestensen,* 316 U.S. 52 (1942), regardless of content or identification. Is Talley's anonymous handbill, designed to destroy the business of a commercial establishment, passed out at its very front door, and attacking its then lawful commercial practices, more comportable with First Amendment freedoms? I think not. Before we may expect international responsibility among nations, might not it be well to require individual responsibility at home? Los Angeles' ordinance does no more.

Contrary to Petitioner's contention, the ordinance as applied does not arbitrarily deprive him of equal protection of the law. He complains that handbills are singled out, while other printed media—books, magazines, and newspapers—remain unrestrained. However, "[t]he problem of legislative classification is a perennial one, admitting of no doctrinaire definition. Evils in the same field may be of different dimensions and proportions, requiring different remedies. . . . Or the reform may take one step at a time, addressing itself to the phase of the problem which seems most acute to the legislative mind. . . . The prohibition of the Equal Protection Clause goes no further than the invidious discrimination. [I] cannot say that that point has been reached here." *Williamson* v. *Lee Optical Co.,* 348 U.S. 483 (1955).

I dissent.

7. *Group Exercise of Free Speech, Free Assembly, and Freedom to Petition for Redress of Grievances*

EDWARDS *v.* SOUTH CAROLINA

372 US 229 (1963)

[Occasionally, as part of the movement to end racial segregation, groups of Negro students march peacefully to a state house or a city hall to publicize their discontent and their dissatisfaction with discriminatory practices. When 187 Negro high school and college students participated in such a march in Columbia, South Carolina, they were arrested and convicted of the common law crime of breach of the peace. With only Justice Clark dissenting, the Supreme Court reversed the convictions on the ground that the demonstrators' rights of free speech, free assembly, and freedom to petition for redress of grievances had been infringed.]

Mr. Justice Stewart delivered the opinion of the Court:

The petitioners, 187 in number, were convicted in a magistrate's court in Columbia, South Carolina, of the commonlaw crime of breach of the peace. Their convictions were ultimately affirmed by the South Carolina Supreme Court. We granted certiorari to consider the claim that these convictions cannot be squared with the Fourteenth Amendment of the United States Constitution.

There was no substantial conflict in the trial evidence. Late in the morning of March 2, 1961, the petitioners, high school and college students of the Negro race, met at the Zion Baptist Church in Columbia. From there, at about noon, they walked in separate groups of about 15 to the South Carolina State House grounds, an area of two city blocks open to the general public. Their purpose was "to submit a protest to the citizens of South Carolina, along with the Legislative Bodies of South Carolina, our feelings and our dissatisfaction with the present condition of discriminatory actions against Negroes, in general, and to let them know that we were dissatisfied and that we would like for the laws which prohibited Negro privileges in this State to be removed."

Already on the State House grounds when the petitioners arrived were 30 or more law enforcement officers, who had advance knowledge that the petitioners were coming. Each group of petitioners entered the grounds through a driveway and parking area known in the record as the "horseshoe." As they entered, they were told by the law enforcement officials that "they had a right, as a citizen, to go through the State House grounds, as any other citizen has, as long as they were peaceful." During the next half hour or 45 minutes, the petitioners, in the same small groups, walked single file or two abreast in an orderly way through the grounds, each group carrying placards bearing such messages as "I am proud to be a Negro," and "Down with segregation."

During this time a crowd of some 200 to 300 onlookers had collected in the horseshoe area and on the adjacent sidewalks. There was no evidence to suggest that these onlookers were anything but curious, and no evidence at all of any threatening remarks, hostile gestures, or offensive language on the part of any member of the crowd. The City Manager testified that he recognized some of the onlookers, whom he did not identify, as "possible trouble makers," but his subsequent testimony made clear that nobody among the crowd actually caused or threatened any trouble. There was no obstruction of pedestrian or vehicular traffic within the State House grounds. No vehicle was prevented from entering or leaving the horseshoe area. Although vehicular traffic at a nearby street intersection was slowed down somewhat, an officer was dispatched to keep traffic moving. There were a number of bystanders on the public sidewalks adjacent to the State House grounds, but they all moved on when asked to do so, and there was no impediment of pedestrian traffic. Police protection at the scene was at all times sufficient to meet any foreseeable possibility of disorder.

In the situation and under the circumstances thus described, the police authorities advised the petitioners that they would be arrested if they did not disperse within 15 minutes. Instead of dispersing, the petitioners engaged in what the City Manager described as "boisterous," "loud," and "flamboyant" conduct, which, as his later testimony made clear, consisted of listening to a "religious harangue" by one of their leaders, and loudly singing "The Star Spangled Banner" and other patriotic and religious songs, while stamping their feet and clapping their hands. After 15 minutes had passed, the police arrested the petitioners and marched them off to jail.

Upon this evidence the state trial court convicted the petitioners of breach of the peace, and imposed sentences ranging from a $10 fine or five days in jail, to a $100 fine or 30 days in jail. In affirming the judgments, the Supreme Court of South Carolina said that under the law of that State the offense of breach of the peace "is not susceptible of exact definition," but that the "general definition of the offense" is as follows:

In general terms, a breach of the peace is a violation of public order, a disturbance of the public tranquility, by any act or conduct inciting to violence . . . , it includes any violation of any law enacted to preserve peace and good order. It may consist of an act of violence or an act likely to produce violence. It is not necessary that the peace be actually broken to lay the foundation for a prosecution for this offense. If what is done is unjustifiable and unlawful, tending with sufficient directness to break the peace, no more is required. Nor is actual personal violence an essential element in the offense. . . .

By "peace," as used in the law in this connection, is meant the tranquility enjoyed by citizens of a municipality or community where good order reigns among its members, which is the natural right of all persons in political society.

The petitioners contend that there was a complete absence of any evidence of the commission of this offense, and that they were thus denied one of the most basic elements of due process of law. *Thompson* v. *Louisville*, 362 U.S. 199; see *Garner* v. *Louisiana*, 368 U.S. 157; *Taylor* v. *Louisiana*, 370 U.S. 154. Whatever the merits of this contention, we need not pass upon it in the present case. The state courts have held that the petitioners' conduct constituted breach of the peace under state law, and we may accept their decision as binding upon us to that extent. But it nevertheless remains our duty in a case such as this to make an independent examination of the whole record. . . . And it is clear to us that in arresting, convicting, and punishing the petitioners under the circumstances disclosed by this record, South Carolina infringed the petitioners' constitutionally protected rights of free speech, free assembly, and freedom to petition for redress of their grievances.

It has long been established that these First Amendment freedoms are protected by the Fourteenth Amendment from invasion by the States. . . . The circumstances in this case reflect an exercise of these basic constitutional rights in their most pristine and classic form. The petitioners felt aggrieved by laws of South Carolina which allegedly "prohibited Negro privileges in this State." They peaceably assembled at the site of the State Government and there peaceably expressed their grievances "to the citizens of South Carolina, along with the Legislative Bodies of South Carolina." Not until they were told by police officials that they must disperse on pain of arrest did they do more. Even then, they but sang patriotic and religious songs after one of their leaders had delivered a "religious harangue." There was no violence or threat of violence on their part, or on the part of any member of the crowd watching them. Police protection was "ample."

This, therefore, was a far cry from the situation in *Feiner* v. *New York*, 340 U.S. 315, where two policemen were faced with a crowd which was "pushing, shoving, and milling around," where at least one member of the crowd "threatened violence if the police did not act," where "the crowd was pressing closer around petitioner and the officer," and where "the speaker passes the bounds of argument or persuasion and undertakes incitement to riot." And the record is barren of any evidence of "fighting words." See *Chaplinsky* v. *New Hampshire*, 315 U.S. 568.

We do not review in this case criminal convictions resulting from the even-handed application of a precise and narrowly drawn regulatory statute evincing a legislative judgment that certain specific conduct be limited or proscribed. If, for example, the petitioners had been convicted upon evidence that they had violated a law regulating traffic, or had disobeyed a law reasonably limiting the periods during which the State House grounds were open to the public, this would be a different case. . . . These petitioners were convicted of an offense so generalized as to be, in the words of the South Carolina Supreme Court, "not susceptible of exact definition." And they were convicted upon evidence which showed no more than that the opinions which they were peaceably expressing were sufficiently opposed to the views of the majority of the community to attract a crowd and necessitate police protection.

The Fourteenth Amendment does not permit a State to make criminal the peaceful expression of unpopular views. "[A] function of free speech under our system of government is to invite dispute. It may indeed best serve its high purpose when it induces a condition of unrest, creates dissatisfaction with conditions as they are, or even stirs people to anger. Speech is often provocative and challenging. It may strike at prejudices and preconceptions and have profound unsettling effects as it presses for acceptance of an idea. That is why freedom of speech, . . . is . . . protected against censorship or punishment, unless shown likely to produce a clear and present danger of a serious substantive evil that rises far above public inconvenience, annoyance, or unrest. . . . There is no room under our Constitution for a more restrictive view. For the alternative would lead to standardization of ideas either by legislatures, courts, or dominant political or community groups." . . . As in the *Terminiello* case, the courts of South Carolina have defined a criminal offense so as to permit conviction of the petitioners if their speech "stirred people to anger, invited public dispute, or brought about a condition of unrest. A conviction resting on any of those grounds may not stand."

As Chief Justice Hughes wrote in *Stromberg* v. *California,* "The maintenance of the opportunity for free political discussion to the end that government may be responsive to the will of the people and that changes may be obtained by lawful means, an opportunity essential to the security of the Republic, is a fundamental principle of our constitutional system. A statute which upon its face, and as authoritatively construed, is so vague and indefinite as to permit the punishment of the fair use of this opportunity is repugnant to the guaranty of liberty contained in the Fourteenth Amendment. . . ." 283 U.S. 359.

For these reasons we conclude that these criminal convictions cannot stand.

Reversed.

8. *Limits on Picketing*

HUGHES *v.* SUPERIOR COURT OF CALIFORNIA
339 US 460 (1950)

[In 1940 the Court said that peaceful picketing is "dissemination of information concerning a labor dispute" and is, therefore, protected as free speech by the Constitution; it may be abridged only when it creates a clear and present danger of substantive evils. *Thornhill* v. *Alabama,* 310 US 88 (1940). Soon thereafter, however, the Court began to impose restrictions on this doctrine; in 1950 the Court said that picketing "cannot dogmatically be equated with the constitutionally protected freedom of speech." *Teamsters Union* v. *Hanke,* 339 US 470 (1950). If a state has a valid law "designed to protect important interests of society," a court may enjoin picketing which attempts to induce breach of this law. *Giboney* v. *Empire Storage Co.,* 336 US 490 (1949). This principle finds application and extension in the present case, in which the injunction on picketing was upheld by a unanimous Supreme Court (Justice Douglas not participating).

[Insofar as picketing contains "an ingredient of communication," it cannot be prohibited in all instances without regard to circumstances. Such a sweeping, absolute prohibition would be declared unconstitutional. Thus, constitutionally, picketing finds itself in a twilight zone; it is subject to some protection, but it is also subject to considerable restriction that falls far short of the clear and present danger test.]

Mr. Justice Frankfurter delivered the opinion of the Court:

Does the Fourteenth Amendment of the Constitution bar a State from use of the injunction to prohibit picketing of a place of business solely in order to secure compliance with a demand that its employees be in proportion to the racial origin of its then customers? Such is the broad question of this case.

The petitioners, acting on behalf of a group calling themselves Progressive Citizens of America, demanded of Lucky Stores, Inc., that it hire Negroes at its grocery store near the Canal Housing Project in Richmond, California, as white clerks quit or were transferred, until the proportion of Negro clerks to white clerks approximated the proportion of Negro to white customers. At the time in controversy about 50% of the customers of the Canal store were Negroes. Upon refusal of this demand and in order to compel compliance, the Canal store was systematically patrolled by pickets carrying placards stating that Lucky refused to hire Negro clerks in proportion to Negro customers.

Suit was begun by Lucky to enjoin the picketing on appropriate allegations for equitable relief. The Superior Court of Contra Costa County issued a preliminary injunction restraining petitioners and others from picketing any of Lucky's stores to compel "the selective hiring of Negro clerks, such hiring to be based on the proportion of white and Negro customers who patronize plaintiff's stores." In the face of this injunction, petitioners continued to picket the Canal store, carrying placards reading: "Lucky Won't Hire Negro Clerks in Proportion to Negro Trade—Don't Patronize." In conformity with State procedure, petitioners were found guilty of contempt for "wilfully disregarding" the injunction and were sentenced to imprisonment for two days and fined $20 each. They defended their conduct by challenging the injunction as a deprivation of the liberty assured them by

the Due Process Clause of the Fourteenth Amendment. The intermediate appellate court annulled the judgment of contempt, . . . but it
was reinstated on review by the Supreme Court of California. That
court held that the conceded purpose of the picketing in this case—to
compel the hiring of Negroes in proportion to Negro customers—was
unlawful even though pursued in a peaceful manner. Having violated
a valid injunction petitioners were properly punishable for contempt.
"The controlling points," according to the decision of the Supreme
Court of California, "are that the injunction is limited to prohibiting
picketing for a specific unlawful purpose and that the evidence justified
the trial court in finding that such narrow prohibition was deliberately
violated." . . .

First. Discrimination against Negroes in employment has brought
a variety of legal issues before this Court in recent years. . . . Such
discrimination raises sociological problems which in some aspects and
within limits have received legal solutions. California has been sensitive to these problems and decisions of its Supreme Court have been
hostile to discrimination on the basis of color. . . . This background
of California's legal policy is relevant to the conviction of its court
that it would encourage discriminatory hiring to give constitutional
protection to petitioners' efforts to subject the opportunity of getting
a job to a quota system. . . .

These considerations are most pertinent in regard to a population
made up of so many diverse groups as ours. To deny to California the
right to ban picketing in the circumstances of this case would mean
that there could be no prohibition of the pressure of picketing to secure
proportional employment on ancestral grounds of Hungarians in Cleve-
land, of Poles in Buffalo, of Germans in Milwaukee, of Portuguese in
New Bedford, of Mexicans in San Antonio, of the numerous minority
groups in New York, and so on through the whole gamut of racial and
religious concentrations in various cities. States may well believe that
such constitutional sheltering would inevitably encourage use of picketing to compel employment on the basis of racial discrimination.
In disallowing such picketing States may act under the belief that
otherwise community tensions and conflicts would be exacerbated. The
differences in cultural traditions instead of adding flavor and variety
to our common citizenry might well be hardened into hostilities by
leave of law. The Constitution does not demand that the element of
communication in picketing prevail over the mischief furthered by its
use in these situations.

Second. "[T]he domain of liberty, withdrawn by the Fourteenth
Amendment from encroachment by the states" . . . no doubt includes
liberty of thought and appropriate means for expressing it. But while

picketing is a mode of communication it is inseparably something more and different. Industrial picketing "is more than free speech, since it involves patrol of a particular locality and since the very presence of a picket line may induce action of one kind or another, quite irrespective of the nature of the ideas which are being disseminated."
. . . Publication in a newspaper, or by distribution of circulars, may convey the same information or make the same charge as do those patrolling a picket line. But the very purpose of a picket line is to exert influences, and it produces consequences, different from other modes of communication. The loyalties and responses evoked and exacted by picket lines are unlike those flowing from appeals by printed word. . . .

Third. A State may constitutionally permit picketing despite the ingredients in it that differentiate it from speech in its ordinary context.
. . . And we have found that because of its element of communication picketing under some circumstances finds sanction in the Fourteenth Amendment. . . . However general or loose the language of opinions, the specific situations have controlled decision. It has been amply recognized that picketing, not being the equivalent of speech as a matter of fact, is not its inevitable legal equivalent. Picketing is not beyond the control of a State if the manner in which picketing is conducted or the purpose which it seeks to effectuate gives ground for its disallowance. . . . "A state is not required to tolerate in all places and all circumstances even peaceful picketing by an individual." . . .

The constitutional boundary line between the competing interests of society involved in the use of picketing cannot be established by general phrases. Picketing when not in numbers that of themselves carry a threat of violence may be a lawful means to a lawful end. . . . We cannot construe the Due Process Clause as precluding California from securing respect for its policy against involuntary employment on racial lines by prohibiting systematic picketing that would subvert such policy. . . .

The policy of a State may rely for the common good on the free play of conflicting interests and leave conduct unregulated. Contrariwise, a State may deem it wiser policy to regulate. Regulation may take the form of legislation, e.g., restraint of trade statutes, or be left to the *ad hoc* judicial process, e.g., common law mode of dealing with restraints of trade. Either method may outlaw an end not in the public interest or merely address itself to the obvious means toward such end. The form the regulation should take and its scope are surely matters of policy and, as such, within a State's choice.

If because of the compulsive features inherent in picketing, beyond the aspect of mere communication as an appeal to reason, a State chooses to enjoin picketing to secure submission to a demand for employment proportional to the racial origin of the then customers of a business, it need not forbid the employer to adopt such a quota system of his own free will. A State is not required to exercise its intervention on the basis of abstract reasoning. The Constitution commands neither logical symmetry nor exhaustion of a principle. "The problems of government are practical ones and may justify, if they do not require, rough accommodations—illogical, it may be, and unscientific." . . . A State may "direct its law against what it deems the evil as it actually exists without covering the whole field of possible abuses, and it may do so none the less that the forbidden act does not differ in kind from those that are allowed." . . . Lawmaking is essentially empirical and tentative, and in adjudication as in legislation the Constitution does not forbid "cautious advance, step by step, and the distrust of generalities." . . .

The injunction here was drawn to meet what California deemed the evil of picketing to bring about proportional hiring. We do not go beyond the circumstances of the case. Generalizations are treacherous in the application of large constitutional concepts.

Affirmed.

⋆ IV ⋆

Freedom of Speech and Press:

The Clear and Present

Danger Doctrine

The Clear and Present Danger Doctrine and the Communist Conspiracy

DENNIS *v.* UNITED STATES

341 US 494 (1951)

[Some classes of speech and publications are beyond constitutional protection: "the lewd and obscene, the profane, the libelous, and the insulting or 'fighting' words—those which by their very utterance inflict injury or tend to incite an immediate breach of the peace." They are "no essential part of any exposition of ideas, and are of such slight social value as a step to truth that any benefit that may be derived from them is clearly outweighed by the social interest in order and morality." Justice Murphy in *Chaplinsky* v. *New Hampshire*, 315 US 568 (1942). Cases heretofore considered which exemplify the force of this statement are *Feiner* v. *New York* and *Beauharnais* v. *Illinois*. Cases involving lewd or obscene language, e.g., the *"Ulysses" Case*, are discussed later.

[Other classes of speech and publications are protected by the Constitution unless "the expression presents a clear and present danger of action of a kind the State is empowered to prevent and punish." Justice Jackson in *Board of Education* v. *Barnette,* above. While the rights of free speech and press are fundamental, "their exercise is subject to restriction, if the particular restriction proposed is required in order to protect the state from destruction or from serious injury, political, economic or moral." The necessity for restriction does not exist "unless speech would produce, or is intended to produce, a clear and imminent danger of some substantive evil which the State constitutionally may seek to prevent." Justice Brandeis in *Whitney* v. *California,* 274 US 357 (1927). To justify suppression of free speech, Brandeis added, there must be "reasonable ground to fear that serious evil will result if free speech is practiced . . . ; that the danger apprehended is imminent . . . ; that the evil to be prevented is a serious one." He distinguished advocacy from incitement, preparation from attempt, assembly from conspiracy. To some authorities these are still the essential elements of the clear and present danger doctrine.

[The doctrine was first stated in the Supreme Court by Justice Holmes in *Schenck* v. *United States,* 249 US 47 (1919). His opinion was that of a unanimous Court. In some later cases, however, the Court failed effectively to use the clear and present danger test, and accordingly Holmes and Brandeis dissented, as in *Abrams* v. *United States,* 250 US 616 (1919). In *Gitlow* v. *New York,* 268 US 652 (1925), a majority of the Court declined to follow the test. Holmes and Brandeis dissented. While the *Gitlow Case* has not been expressly overruled, later cases have used the clear and present danger test as formulated by Holmes and Brandeis—e.g., *Herndon* v. *Lowry,* 301 US 242 (1937). It is still the standard by which the Court judges the constitutionality of restrictions on free speech.

[But the force and reach of the clear and present danger doctrine are matters concerning which members of the Court have differing views. Courts differ as to how it can be determined when a danger is "clear," or when it is "present," or when the evil sought to be prevented by a restriction on free speech is "substantial." Justice Frankfurter even doubts if Holmes meant the clear and present danger doctrine to be "a technical legal doctrine" or to "convey a formula for adjudicating cases." *Pennekamp* v. *Florida,* 328 US 331 (1946).

[The *Dennis Case,* involving the conviction of eleven Communist Party leaders, reflects the diversity of views and the strains and stresses to which the Holmes-Brandeis doctrine has been subjected. In a 6-to-2 decision (Justice Clark not participating and Justices Black and Douglas dissenting) the Court upheld the conviction for conspiracy under the Smith Act of 1940. Seven of the Justices agreed that the standard to be used is that of the clear and present danger; only Justice Jackson maintained that in a conspiracy case such as this one the conspirators could be convicted even if there was no clear and present danger of overthrow of the Government. The dissenting Justices, on the other hand, ignored the conspiracy element and put all their weight on the clear and present danger test.

[It should be borne in mind that the Court had before it a conviction for *criminal conspiracy;* for the law has always considered conspiracy a much graver threat to the state than the acts of a solitary criminal. Following the *Dennis Case,* other Communists have been convicted—state and local as well as national leaders of the party.]

Mr. Chief Justice Vinson:

Petitioners were indicted in July, 1948, for violation of the conspiracy provisions of the Smith Act, 54 Stat. 671, 18 U.S.C. (1946 ed.) § 11, during the period of April, 1945, to July, 1948. . . . A verdict of guilty as to all the petitioners was returned by the jury on October 14, 1949. The Court of Appeals affirmed the convictions. . . . We granted certiorari, . . . limited to the following two questions: (1) Whether either § 2 or § 3 of the Smith Act, inherently or as construed and applied in the instant case, violates the First Amendment and other provisions of the Bill of Rights; (2) whether either § 2 or § 3 of the Act, inherently or as construed and applied in the instant case, violates the First and Fifth Amendments because of indefiniteness.

Sections 2 and 3 of the Smith Act provide as follows:

Sec. 2.

(a) It shall be unlawful for any person—

(1) to knowingly or willfully advocate, abet, advise, or teach the duty, necessity, desirability, or propriety of overthrowing or destroying any government in the United States by force or violence, or by the assassination of any officer of any such government;

(2) with the intent to cause the overthrow or destruction of any government in the United States, to print, publish, edit, issue, circulate, sell, distribute, or publicly display any written or printed matter advocating, advising, or teaching the duty, necessity, desirability, or propriety of overthrowing or destroying any government in the United States by force or violence;

(3) to organize or help to organize any society, group, or assembly of persons who teach, advocate, or encourage the overthrow or destruction of any government in the United States by force or violence; or to be or become a member of, or affiliate with, any such society, group, or assembly of persons, knowing the purposes thereof.

(b) For the purposes of this section, the term "government in the United States" means the Government of the United States, the government of any State, Territory, or possession of the United States, the government of the

District of Columbia, or the government of any political sub-division of any of them.

Sec. 3. It shall be unlawful for any person to attempt to commit, or to conspire to commit, any of the acts prohibited by the provisions of . . . this title.

The indictment charged the petitioners with wilfully and knowingly conspiring (1) to organize as the Communist Party of the United States of America a society, group and assembly of persons who teach and advocate the overthrow and destruction of the Government of the United States by force and violence, and (2) knowingly and wilfully to advocate and teach the duty and necessity of overthrowing and destroying the Government of the United States by force and violence. The indictment further alleged that § 2 of the Smith Act proscribes these acts and that any conspiracy to take such action is a violation of § 3 of the Act.

The trial of the case extended over nine months, six of which were devoted to the taking of evidence, resulting in a record of 16,000 pages. Our limited grant of the writ of certiorari has removed from our consideration any question as to the sufficiency of the evidence to support the jury's determination that petitioners are guilty of the offense charged. Whether on this record petitioners did in fact advocate the overthrow of the Government by force and violence is not before us, and we must base any discussion of this point upon the conclusions stated in the opinion of the Court of Appeals, which treated the issue in great detail. That court held that the record in this case amply supports the necessary finding of the jury that petitioners, the leaders of the Communist Party in this country, were unwilling to work within our framework of democracy, but intended to initiate a violent revolution whenever the propitious occasion appeared. Petitioners dispute the meaning to be drawn from the evidence, contending that the Marxist-Leninist doctrine they advocated taught that force and violence to achieve a Communist form of government in an existing democratic state would be necessary only because the ruling classes of that state would never permit the transformation to be accomplished peacefully, but would use force and violence to defeat any peaceful political and economic gain the Communists could achieve. But the Court of Appeals held that the record supports the following broad conclusions: By virtue of their control over the political apparatus of the Communist Political Association, petitioners were able to transform that organization into the Communist Party; that the policies of the Association were changed from peaceful cooperation with the United States and its economic and political structure to a policy which had existed before the United States and the Soviet Union were fighting a common enemy, namely, a policy which worked for the overthrow of the Government by force and violence; that the Communist Party is a highly disciplined organization, adept at infiltration into strategic positions, use of aliases, and double-meaning language; that the Party is rigidly controlled; that Communists, unlike other political parties, tolerate no dissension from the policy laid down by the guiding forces, but that the approved program is slavishly followed by the members of the Party; that the literature of the Party and the statements and activities of its leaders . . . advocate, and the general goal of the Party was, during the period in question, to achieve a successful overthrow of the existing order by force and violence.

. . . The structure and purpose of the statute demand the inclusion of intent as an element of the crime. Congress was concerned with those who advocate and organize for the overthrow of the Government. Certainly those who recruit and combine for the purpose of advocating overthrow intend to bring about that overthrow. We hold that the statute requires as an essential element of the crime proof of the intent of those who are charged with its violation to overthrow the Government by force and violence. . . .

Nor does the fact that there must be an investigation of a state of mind under this interpretation afford any basis for rejection of that meaning. A survey of Title 18 of the U.S. Code indicates that the vast majority of the crimes designated by that Title require, by express language, proof of the existence of a certain mental state in words such as "knowingly," "maliciously," "wilfully," "with the purpose of," "with intent to," or combinations or permutations of these and synonymous terms. The existence of a *mens rea* is the rule of, rather than the exception to, the principles of Anglo-American criminal jurisprudence. . . .

The obvious purpose of the statute is to protect existing Government, not from change by peaceable, lawful and constitutional means, but from change by violence, revolution and terrorism. That it is within the *power* of the Congress to protect the Government of the United States from armed rebellion is a proposition which requires little discussion. Whatever theoretical merit there may be to the argument that there is a "right" to rebellion against dictatorial governments is without force where the existing structure of the government provides for peaceful and orderly change. We reject any principle of governmental helplessness in the face of preparation for revolution, which principle, carried to its logical conclusion, must lead to anarchy. No one could conceive that it is not within the power of Congress to prohibit acts intended to overthrow the Government by force and violence. The question with which we are concerned here is not whether Congress has such *power*, but whether the *means* which it has employed conflict with the First and Fifth Amendments to the Constitution.

One of the bases for the contention that the means which Congress has employed are invalid takes the form of an attack on the face of the statute on the grounds that by its terms it prohibits academic discussion of the merits of Marxism-Leninism, that it stifles ideas and is contrary to all concepts of a free speech and a free press. . . .

The very language of the Smith Act negates the interpretation which petitioners would have us impose on that Act. It is directed at advocacy, not discussion. Thus, the trial judge properly charged the jury that they could not convict if they found that petitioners did "no more than pursue peaceful studies and discussions or teaching and advocacy in the realm of ideas." He further charged that it was not unlawful "to conduct in an American college and university a course explaining the philosophical theories set forth in the books which have been placed in evidence." Such a charge is in strict accord with the statutory language, and illustrates the meaning to be placed on those words. Congress did not intend to eradicate the free discussion of political theories, to destroy the traditional rights of Americans to discuss and evaluate ideas without fear of governmental sanction. Rather Congress was concerned with the very kind of activity in which the evidence showed these petitioners engaged.

. . . The basis of the First Amendment is the hypothesis that speech can rebut speech, propaganda will answer propaganda, free debate of ideas will result in the wisest governmental policies. It is for this reason that this Court has recognized the inherent value of free discourse. An analysis of the leading cases in this Court which have involved direct limitations on speech, however, will demonstrate that both the majority of the Court and the dissenters in particular cases have recognized that this is not an unlimited, unqualified right, but that the societal value of speech must, on occasion, be subordinated to other values and considerations. . . .

The rule we deduce from these cases is that where an offense is specified by a statute in nonspeech or nonpress terms, a conviction relying upon speech or press as evidence of violation may be sustained only when the speech or publication created a "clear and present danger" of attempting or accomplishing the prohibited crime, e.g., interference with enlistment. . . .

. . . Neither Justice Holmes nor Justice Brandeis ever envisioned that a shorthand phrase should be crystallized into a rigid rule to be applied inflexibly without regard to the circumstances of each case. Speech is not an absolute, above and beyond control by the legislature when its judgment, subject to review here, is that certain kinds of speech are so undesirable as to warrant criminal sanction. Nothing is more certain in modern society than the principle that there are no absolutes, that a name, a phrase, a standard has meaning only when associated with the considerations which gave birth to the nomenclature. . . . To those who would paralyze our Government in the face of impending threat by encasing it in a semantic straitjacket we must reply that all concepts are relative.

. . . In this case we are squarely presented with the application of the "clear and present danger" test, and must decide what that phrase imports. We first note that many of the cases in which this Court has reversed convictions by use of this or similar tests have been based on the fact that the interest which the State was attempting to protect was itself too insubstantial to warrant restriction of speech. . . . Overthrow of the Government by force and violence is certainly a substantial enough interest for the Government to limit speech. Indeed, this is the ultimate value of any society, for if a society cannot protect its very structure from armed internal attack, it must follow that no subordinate value can be protected. If, then, this interest may be protected, the literal problem which is presented is what has been meant by the use of the phrase "clear and present danger" of the utterances bringing about the evil within the power of Congress to punish.

. . . Obviously, the words cannot mean that before the Government may act, it must wait until the *putsch* is about to be executed, the plans have been laid and the signal is awaited. If Government is aware that a group aiming at its overthrow is attempting to indoctrinate its members and to commit them to a course whereby they will strike when the leaders feel the circumstances permit, action by the Government is required. The argument that there is no need for Government to concern itself, for Government is strong, it possesses ample powers to put down a rebellion, it may defeat the revolution with ease needs no answer. For that is not the question. Certainly an attempt to overthrow the Government by force, even though doomed from the outset because of inadequate numbers or power of the revolutionists, is a sufficient evil for Congress to prevent. The damage which such attempts create both physically and politically to a nation makes it impossible to measure the validity in terms of the probability of success, or the immediacy of a successful attempt. In the instant case the trial judge charged the jury that they could not convict unless they found that petitioners intended to overthrow the Government "as speedily as circumstances would permit." This does not mean, and could not properly mean, that they would not strike until there was certainty of success. What was meant was that the revolutionists would strike when they thought the time was ripe. We must therefore reject the contention that success or probability of success is the criterion.

. . . Chief Judge Learned Hand, writing for the majority below, interpreted the phrase as follows: "In each case [courts] must ask whether the gravity of the 'evil,' discounted by its improbability, justifies such invasion of free speech as is necessary to avoid the danger." . . . We adopt this statement of the rule. As articulated by Chief Judge Hand, it is as succinct and inclusive as any other we might devise at this time. It takes into consideration those factors which we deem relevant, and relates their significances. More we cannot expect from words.

. . . Likewise, we are in accord with the court below, which affirmed the trial court's finding that the requisite danger existed. The mere fact that from the period 1945 to 1948 petitioners' activities did not result in an attempt to overthrow the Government by force and violence is of course no answer to the fact that there was a group that was ready to make the attempt. The formation by petitioners of such a highly organized conspiracy, with rigidly disciplined members subject to call when the leaders, these petitioners, felt that the time had come for action, coupled with the inflammable nature of world conditions, similar uprisings in other countries, and the touch-and-go nature of our relations with countries with whom petitioners were in the very least ideologically attuned, convince us that their convictions were justified on this score. And this analysis disposes of the contention that a conspiracy to advocate, as distinguished from the advocacy itself, cannot be constitutionally restrained, because it comprises only the preparation. It is the existence of the conspiracy which creates the danger. . . . If the ingredients of the reaction are present, we cannot bind the Government to wait until the catalyst is added.

. . . Although we have concluded that the finding that there was a sufficient danger to warrant the application of the statute was justified on the merits, there remains the problem of whether the trial judge's treatment of the issue was correct. He charged the jury, in relevant part, as follows: . . .

If you are satisfied that the evidence establishes beyond a reasonable doubt that the defendants, or any of them, are guilty of a violation of the statute as I have interpreted it to you, I find as a matter of law that there is sufficient danger of a substantive evil that the Congress has a right to prevent to justify the application of the statute under the First Amendment of the Constitution.

This is matter of law about which you have no concern. It is a finding on a matter of law which I deem essential to support my ruling that the case should be submitted to you to pass upon the guilt or innocence of the defendants. . . .

It is thus clear that he reserved the question of the existence of the danger for his own determination, and the question becomes whether the issue is of such a nature that it should have been submitted to the jury.

. . . The argument that the action of the trial court is erroneous, in declaring as a matter of law that such violation shows sufficient danger to justify the punishment despite the First Amendment, rests on the theory that a jury must decide a question of the application of the First Amendment. We do not agree. . . .

The question in this case is whether the statute which the legislature has enacted may be constitutionally applied. In other words, the Court must examine judicially the application of the statute to the particular situation, to ascertain if the Constitution prohibits the conviction. We hold that the statute may be applied where there is a "clear and present danger" of the substantive evil which the legislature had the right to prevent. Bearing, as it does, the marks of a "question of law," the issue is properly one for the judge to decide.

There remains to be discussed the question of vagueness—whether the statute as we have interpreted it is too vague, not sufficiently advising those who would speak of the limitations upon their activity. It is urged that such vagueness contravenes the First and Fifth Amendments. . . .

We agree that the standard as defined is not a neat, mathematical formulary. Like all verbalizations it is subject to criticism on the score of indefiniteness. But petitioners themselves contend that the verbalization, "clear and present danger," is the proper standard. We see no difference from the standpoint of vagueness, whether the standard of "clear and present danger" is one contained in *haec verba* within the statute, or whether it is the judicial measure of constitutional applicability. We have shown the indeterminate standard the phrase necessarily connotes. We do not think we have rendered that standard any more indefinite by our attempt to sum up the factors which are included within its scope. We think it well serves to indicate to those who would advocate constitutionally prohibited conduct that there is a line beyond which they may not go—a line, which they, in full knowledge of what they intend and the circumstances in which their activity takes place, will well appreciate and understand. . . .

We hold that §§ 2(a) (1), 2(a) (3) and 3 of the Smith Act, do not inherently, or as construed or applied in the instant case, violate the

First Amendment and other provisions of the Bill of Rights, or the First and Fifth Amendments because of indefiniteness. Petitioners intended to overthrow the Government of the United States as speedily as the circumstances would permit. Their conspiracy to organize the Communist Party and to teach and advocate the overthrow of the Government of the United States by force and violence created a "clear and present danger" of an attempt to overthrow the Government by force and violence. They were properly and constitutionally convicted for violation of the Smith Act. The judgments of conviction are affirmed.

Mr. Justice Frankfurter, concurring in affirmance of the judgment:

. . . Few questions of comparable import have come before this Court in recent years. The appellants maintain that they have a right to advocate a political theory, so long, at least, as their advocacy does not create an immediate danger of obvious magnitude to the very existence of our present scheme of society. On the other hand, the Government asserts the right to safeguard the security of the Nation by such a measure as the Smith Act. Our judgment is thus solicited on a conflict of interests of the utmost concern to the well-being of the country. This conflict of interests cannot be resolved by a dogmatic preference for one or the other, nor by a sonorous formula which is in fact only a euphemistic disguise for an unresolved conflict. If adjudication is to be a rational process we cannot escape a candid examination of the conflicting claims with full recognition that both are supported by weighty title-deeds.

I.

. . . Our whole history proves even more decisively than the course of decisions in this Court that the United States has the powers inseparable from a sovereign nation. "America has chosen to be, in many respects, and to many purposes, a nation; and for all these purposes, her government is complete; to all these objects, it is competent." Chief Justice Marshall in *Cohens* v. *Virginia,* 6 Wheat. 264. The right of a government to maintain its existence—self-preservation—is the most pervasive aspect of sovereignty. "Security against foreign danger," wrote Madison, "is one of the primitive objects of civil society." *The Federalist,* No. 41. The constitutional power to act upon this basic principle has been recognized by this Court at different periods and under diverse circumstances. . . . The most tragic experience in our history is a poignant reminder that the Nation's continued existence may be threatened from within. To protect itself from such threats, the Federal Government "is invested with all those inherent and implied powers which, at the time of adopting the Constitution, were generally considered to belong to every government as such, and as being essential to the exercise of its functions." Mr. Justice Bradley, concurring in *Legal Tender Cases,* 12 Wall. 457. . . .

But even the all-embracing power and duty of self-preservation is not absolute. Like the war power, which is indeed an aspect of the power of self-preservation, it is subject to applicable constitutional limitations. . . . Our Constitution has no provision lifting restrictions upon governmental authority during periods of emergency, although the scope of a restriction may depend on the circumstances in which it is invoked.

The First Amendment is such a restriction. It exacts obedience even during periods of war; it is applicable when war clouds are not figments of the imagination no less than when they are. The First Amendment categorically demands that "Congress shall make no law respecting an establishment of religion, or prohibiting the free exercise thereof; or abridging the freedom of speech, or of the press; or the right of the people peaceably to assemble, and to petition the Government for a redress of grievances." The right of a man to think what he pleases, to write what he thinks, and to have his thoughts made available for others to hear or read has an engaging ring of universality. The Smith Act and this conviction under it no doubt restrict the exercise of free speech and assembly. Does that, without more, dispose of the matter?

Just as there are those who regard as invulnerable every measure for which the claim of national survival is invoked, there are those who find in the Constitution a wholly unfettered right of expression. Such literalness treats the words of the Constitution as though they were found on a piece of outworn parchment instead of being words that have called into being a nation with a past to be preserved for the future. The soil in which the Bill of Rights grew was not a soil of arid pedantry. The historic antecedents of the First Amendment preclude the notion that its purpose was to give unqualified immunity to every expression that touched on matters within the range of political interest. . . .

The language of the First Amendment is to be read not as barren words found in a dictionary but as symbols of historic experience illumined by the presuppositions of those who employed them. Not what words did Madison and Hamilton use, but what was it in their minds which they conveyed? Free speech is subject to prohibition of those abuses of expression which a civilized society may forbid. As in the case of every other provision of the Constitution that is not crystallized by the nature of its technical concepts, the fact that the First Amendment is not self-defining and self-enforcing neither impairs its usefulness nor compels its paralysis as a living instrument.

"The law is perfectly well settled," this Court said over fifty years ago, "that the first 10 amendments to the constitution, commonly known as the 'Bill of Rights,' were not intended to lay down any novel principles of government, but simply to embody certain guaranties and immunities which we had inherited from our English ancestors, and which had, from time immemorial, been subject to certain well-recognized exceptions, arising from the necessities of the case. In incorporating these principles into the fundamental law, there was no intention of disregarding the exceptions, which continued to be recognized as if they had been formally expressed." *Robertson* v. *Baldwin*, 165 U.S. 275. That this represents the authentic view of the Bill of Rights and the spirit in which it must be construed has been recognized again and again in cases that have come here within the last fifty years. . . . Absolute rules would inevitably lead to absolute exceptions, and such exceptions would eventually corrode the rules. The demands of free speech in a democratic society as well as the interest in national security are better served by candid and informed weighing of the competing interests, within the confines of the judicial process, than by announcing dogmas too inflexible for the non-Euclidian problems to be solved.

But how are competing interests to be assessed? Since they are not subject to quantitative ascertainment, the issue necessarily resolves itself into asking, who is to make the adjustment?—who is to balance the relevant factors and ascertain which interest is in the circumstances to prevail? Full responsibility for the choice cannot be given to the courts. Courts are not representative bodies. They are not designed to be a good reflex of a democratic society. Their judgment is best informed, and therefore most dependable, within narrow limits. Their essential quality is detachment, founded on independence. History teaches that the independence of the judiciary is jeopardized when courts become embroiled in the passions of the day and assume primary responsibility in choosing between competing political, economic and social pressures.

Primary responsibility for adjusting the interests which compete in the situation before us of necessity belongs to the Congress. The nature of the power to be exercised by this Court has been delineated in decisions not charged with the emotional appeal of situations such as that now before us. We are to set aside the judgment of those whose duty it is to legislate only if there is no reasonable basis for it. . . . We must scrupulously observe the narrow limits of judicial authority even though self-restraint is alone set over us. Above all we must remember that this Court's power of judicial review is not "an exercise of the powers of a super-Legislature." Mr. Justice Brandeis and Mr. Justice Holmes, dissenting in *Jay Burns Baking Co.* v. *Bryan*, 264 U.S. 504. . . .

In reviewing statutes which restrict freedoms protected by the First Amendment, we have emphasized the close relation which those freedoms bear to maintenance of a free society. . . . Some members of the Court—and at times a majority—have done more. They have suggested that our function in reviewing statutes restricting freedom of expression differs sharply from our normal duty in sitting in judgment on legislation. It has been said that such statutes "must be justified by clear public interest, threatened not doubtedly or remotely, but by clear and present danger. The rational connection between the remedy provided and the evil to be curbed, which in other contexts might support legislation against attack on due process grounds, will not suffice." *Thomas* v. *Collins*, 323 U.S. 516. It has been suggested, with the casualness of a footnote, that such legislation is not presumptively valid, see *United States* v. *Carolene Products Co.*, 304 U.S. 144, and it has been weightily reiterated that freedom of speech has a "preferred position" among constitutional safeguards. *Kovacs* v. *Cooper*, 336 U.S. 77.

The precise meaning intended to be conveyed by these phrases need not now be pursued. It is enough to note that they have recurred in the Court's opinions, and their cumulative force has, not without justification, engendered belief that there is a constitutional principle, expressed by those attractive but imprecise words, prohibiting restriction upon utterance unless it creates a situation of "imminent" peril against which legislation may guard. It is on this body of the Court's pronouncements that the defendants' argument here is based. . . .

II.

We have recognized and resolved conflicts between speech and competing interests in six different types of cases.

1. The cases involving a conflict between the interest in allowing free expression of ideas in public places and the interest in protection of the public peace and the primary uses of streets and parks, were too recently considered to be rehearsed here. *Niemotko* v. *State of Maryland,* 340 U.S. 268. It suffices to recall that the result in each case was found to turn on the character of the interest with which the speech clashed, the method used to impose the restriction, and the nature and circumstances of the utterance prohibited. While the decisions recognized the importance of free speech and carefully scrutinized the justification for its regulation, they rejected the notion that vindication of the deep public interest in freedom of expression requires subordination of all conflicting values.

2. A critique of the cases testing restrictions on picketing is made more difficult by the inadequate recognition by the Court from the outset that the loyalties and responses evoked and exacted by picket lines differentiate this form of expression from other modes of communication. See *Thornhill* v. *Alabama,* 310 U.S. 88. But the crux of the decision in the *Thornhill Case* was that a State could not constitutionally punish peaceful picketing when neither the aim of the picketing nor the manner in which it was carried out conflicted with a substantial interest. In subsequent decisions we sustained restrictions designed to prevent recurrence of violence, *Milk Wagon Drivers Union* v. *Meadowmoor Dairies,* 312 U.S. 287, or reasonably to limit the area of industrial strife, *Carpenters & Joiners Union* v. *Ritter's Cafe,* 315 U.S. 722; cf. *Bakery & Pastry Drivers Local* v. *Wohl,* 315 U.S. 769. We held that a State's policy against restraints of trade justified it in prohibiting picketing which violated that policy, *Giboney* v. *Empire Storage Co.,* 336 U.S. 490; we sustained restrictions designed to encourage self-employed persons, *International Brotherhood of Teamsters Union* v. *Hanke,* 339 U.S. 470; and to prevent racial discrimination, *Hughes* v. *Superior Court,* 339 U.S. 460. The Fourteenth Amendment bars a State from prohibiting picketing when there is no fair justification for the breadth of the restriction imposed. *American Federation of Labor* v. *Swing,* 312 U.S. 321; *Cafeteria Employees Union* v. *Angelos,* 320 U.S. 293. . . . But it does not prevent a State from denying the means of communication that picketing affords in a fair balance between the interests of trade unionism and other interests of the community.

3. In three cases we have considered the scope and application of the power of the Government to exclude, deport, or denaturalize aliens because of their advocacy or their beliefs. In *Turner* v. *Williams,* 194 U.S. 279, we held that the First Amendment did not disable Congress from directing

the exclusion of an alien found in an administrative proceeding to be an anarchist. "[A]s long as human governments endure," we said, "they cannot be denied the power of self-preservation, as that question is presented here." . . .

4. History regards "freedom of the press" as indispensable for a free society and for its government. We have, therefore, invalidated discriminatory taxation against the press and prior restraints on publication of defamatory matter. *Grosjean* v. *American Press Co.*, 297 U.S. 233; *Near* v. *Minnesota*, 283 U.S. 697.

We have also given clear indication of the importance we attach to dissemination of ideas in reviewing the attempts of States to reconcile freedom of the press with protection of the integrity of the judicial process. In *Pennekamp* v. *Florida*, 328 U.S. 331, the Court agreed that the Fourteenth Amendment barred a State from adjudging in contempt of court the publisher of critical and inaccurate comment about portions of a litigation that for all practical purposes were no longer pending. We likewise agreed, in a minor phase of our decision in *Bridges* v. *California*, 314 U.S. 252, that even when statements in the press relate to matters still pending before a court, convictions for their publication cannot be sustained if their utterance is too trivial to be deemed a substantial threat to the impartial administration of justice.

The Court has, however, sharply divided on what constitutes a sufficient interference with the course of justice. In the first decision, *Patterson* v. *Colorado*, 205 U.S. 454, the Court affirmed a judgment for contempt imposed by a State supreme court for publication of articles reflecting on the conduct of the court in cases still before it on motions for rehearing. In the *Bridges Case*, however, a majority held that a State court could not protect itself from the implied threat of a powerful newspaper that failure of an elected judge to impose a severe sentence would be a "serious mistake." The same case also placed beyond a State's power to punish the publication of a telegram from the president of an important union who threatened a damaging strike in the event of an adverse decision. The majority in *Craig* v. *Harney*, 331 U.S. 367, held that the Fourteenth Amendment protected "strong," "intemperate," "unfair" criticism of the way an elected lay judge was conducting a pending civil case. None of the cases establishes that the public interest in a free press must in all instances prevail over the public interest in dispassionate adjudication. But the *Bridges* and *Craig* decisions, if they survive, tend to require a showing that interference be so imminent and so demonstrable that the power theoretically possessed by the State is largely paralyzed.

5. Our decision in *American Communications Ass'n* v. *Douds*, 339 U.S. 382, recognized that the exercise of political rights protected by the First Amendment was necessarily discouraged by the requirement of the Taft-Hartley Act that officers of unions employing the services of the National Labor Relations Board sign affidavits that they are not Communists. But we held that the statute was not for this reason presumptively invalid. The problem, we said, was "one of weighing the probable effects of the statute

upon the free exercise of the right of speech and assembly against the congressional determination that political strikes are evils of conduct which cause substantial harm to interstate commerce and that Communists and others identified by § 9 (h) pose continuing threats to that public interest when in positions of union leadership." . . . On balance, we decided that the legislative judgment was a permissible one.

6. Statutes prohibiting speech because of its tendency to lead to crime present a conflict of interests which bears directly on the problem now before us. The first case in which we considered this conflict was *Fox* v. *Washington,* 236 U.S. 273. The statute there challenged had been interpreted to prohibit publication of matter "encouraging an actual breach of law." We held that the Fourteenth Amendment did not prohibit application of the statute to an article which we concluded incited a breach of laws against indecent exposure. We said that the statute "lays hold of encouragements that, apart from statute, if directed to a particular person's conduct, generally would make him who uttered them guilty of a misdemeanor if not an accomplice or a principal in the crime encouraged, and deals with the publication of them to a wider and less selected audience." To be sure, the *Fox Case* preceded the explicit absorption of the substance of the First Amendment in the Fourteenth. But subsequent decisions extended the *Fox* principle to free-speech situations. They are so important to the problem before us that we must consider them in detail.

(a) The first important application of the principle was made in six cases arising under the Espionage Act of 1917. That Act prohibits conspiracies and attempts to "obstruct the recruiting or enlistment service." In each of the first three cases Mr. Justice Holmes wrote for a unanimous Court, affirming the convictions. The evidence in *Schenck* v. *United States,* 249 U.S. 47, showed that the defendant had conspired to circulate among men called for the draft 15,000 copies of a circular which asserted a "right" to oppose the draft. The defendant in *Frohwerk* v. *United States,* 249 U.S. 204, was shown to have conspired to publish in a newspaper twelve articls describing the sufferings of American troops and the futility of our war aims. The record was inadequate, and we said that it was therefore "impossible to say that it might not have been found that the circulation of the paper was in quarters where a little breath would be enough to kindle a flame and that the fact was known and relied upon by those who sent the paper out." In *Debs* v. *United States,* 249 U.S. 211, the indictment charged that the defendant had delivered a public speech expounding socialism and praising Socialists who had been convicted of abetting violation of the draft laws.

The ground of decision in each case was the same. The First Amendment "cannot have been, and obviously was not, intended to give immunity for every possible use of language. . . ." *Frohwerk* v. *United States.* . . . "The question in every case is whether the words used in such circumstances and are of such a nature as to create a clear and present danger that they will bring about the substantive evils that Congress has a right to prevent. It is a question of proximity and degree." *Schenck* v. *United States.* . . . When "the words used had as their natural tendency and reasonably probable effect to obstruct the recruiting service," and "the defendant had the specific intent to do so in his mind," conviction in wartime is not prohibited by the Constitution. *Debs* v. *United States.*

In the three succeeding cases Holmes and Brandeis, JJ., dissented from judgments of the Court affirming convictions. The indictment in *Abrams* v. *United States,* 250 U.S. 616, was laid under an amendment to the Espionage Act which prohibited conspiracies to advocate curtailment of production of material necessary to prosecution of the war, with the intent thereby to hinder the United States in the prosecution of the war. It appeared that the defendants were anarchists who had printed circulars and distributed them in New York City. The leaflets repeated standard Marxist slogans, condemned American intervention in Russia, and called for a general strike in protest. In *Schaefer* v. *United States,* 251 U.S. 466, the editors of a German language newspaper in Philadelphia were charged with obstructing the recruiting service and with wilfully publishing false reports with the intent to promote the success of the enemies of the United States. The evidence showed publication of articles which accused American troops of weakness and mendacity and in one instance misquoted or mistranslated two words of a Senator's speech. The indictment in *Pierce* v. *United States,* 252 U.S. 239, charged that the defendants had attempted to cause insubordination in the armed forces and had conveyed false reports with intent to interfere with military operations. Conviction was based on circulation of a pamphlet which belittled Allied war aims and criticized conscription in strong terms.

In each case both the majority and the dissenting opinions relied on *Schenck* v. *United States.* The Court divided on its view of the evidence. The majority held that the jury could infer the required intent and the probable effect of the articles from their content. Holmes and Brandeis, JJ., thought that only "expressions of opinion and exhortations," were involved, that they were "puny anonymities," "impotent to produce the evil against which the statute aimed," and that from them the specific intent required by the statute could not reasonably be inferred. The Court agreed that an incitement to disobey the draft statute could constitutionally be punished. It disagreed over the proof required to show such an incitement.

(b) In the eyes of a majority of the Court, *Gitlow* v. *New York,* 268 U.S. 652, presented a very different problem. There the defendant had been convicted under a New York statute nearly identical to the Smith Act now before us. The evidence showed that the defendant was an official of the Left Wing Section of the Socialist Party, and that he was responsible for publication of a Left Wing Manifesto. This document repudiated "moderate Socialism," and urged the necessity of a militant "revolutionary Socialism," based on class struggle and revolutionary mass action. No evidence of the effect of the Manifesto was introduced; but the jury was instructed that they could not convict unless they found that the document advocated employing unlawful acts for the purpose of overthrowing organized government.

The conviction was affirmed. The question, the Court held, was entirely different from that involved in *Schenck* v. *United States,* where the statute prohibited acts without reference to language. Here, where "the legislative body has determined generally, in the constitutional exercise of its discretion, that utterances of a certain kind involve such danger of substantive evil that they may be punished, the question whether any specific utterance coming within the prohibited class is likely, in and of itself, to bring about the substantive evil, is not open to consideration." It is sufficient that the defendant's conduct falls within the statute, and that the statute is a reasonable exercise of legislative judgment.

This principle was also applied in *Whitney* v. *California*, 274 U.S. 357, to sustain a conviction under a State criminal syndicalism statute. That statute made it a felony to assist in organizing a group assembled to advocate the commission of crime, sabotage, or unlawful acts of violence as a means of effecting political or industrial change. The defendant was found to have assisted in organizing the Communist Labor Party of California, an organization found to have the specified character. It was held that the legislature was not unreasonable in believing organization of such a party "involves such danger to the public peace and the security of the State, that these acts should be penalized in the exercise of its police power."

In neither of these cases did Mr. Justice Holmes and Mr. Justice Brandeis accept the reasoning of the Court. " 'The question,' " they said, quoting from *Schenck* v. *United States*, " 'in every case is whether the words used are used in such circumstances and are of such a nature as to create a clear and present danger that they will bring about the substantive evils that [the State] has a right to prevent.' " Since the manifesto circulated by Gitlow "had no chance of starting a present conflagration," they dissented from the affirmance of his conviction. In *Whitney* v. *California*, they concurred in the result reached by the Court, but only because the record contained some evidence that organization of the Communist Labor Party might further a conspiracy to commit immediate serious crimes, and the credibility of the evidence was not put in issue by the defendant.

(c) Subsequent decisions have added little to the principles established in these two groups of cases. In the only case arising under the Espionage Act decided by this Court during the last war, the substantiality of the evidence was the crucial issue. The defendant in *Hartzel* v. *United States*, 322 U.S. 680, was an educated man and a citizen, not actively affiliated with any political group. In 1942 he wrote three articles condemning our wartime allies and urging that the war be converted into a racial conflict. He mailed the tracts to 600 people, including high-ranking military officers. According to his testimony his intention was to "create sentiment against war amongst the white races." The majority of this Court held that a jury could not reasonably infer from these facts that the defendant had acted with a specific intent to cause insubordination or disloyalty in the armed forces.

Of greater importance is the fact that the issue of law which divided the Court in the *Gitlow* and *Whitney Cases* has not again been clearly raised, although in four additional instances we have reviewed convictions under comparable statutes. *Fiske* v. *Kansas*, 274 U.S. 380, involved a criminal syndicalism statute similar to that before us in *Whitney* v. *California*. We reversed a conviction based on evidence that the defendant exhibited an innocuous preamble to the constitution of the Industrial Workers of the World in soliciting members for that organization. In *Herndon* v. *Lowry*, 301 U.S. 242, the defendant had solicited members for the Communist Party, but there was no proof that he had urged or even approved those of the Party's aims which were unlawful. We reversed a conviction obtained under a statute prohibiting an attempt to incite to insurrection by violence, on the ground that the Fourteenth Amendment prohibited conviction where on the evidence a jury could not reasonably infer that the defendant had violated the statute the State sought to apply.

The other two decisions go no further than to hold that the statute as construed by the State courts exceeded the bounds of a legislative judgment founded in reason. The statute presented in *De Jonge* v. *Oregon*, 299 U.S. 353, had been construed to apply to anyone who merely assisted in the conduct of a meeting held under the auspices of the Communist Party. In *Taylor* v. *Mississippi*, 319 U.S. 583, the statute prohibited dissemination of printed matter "designed and calculated to encourage violence, sabotage, or disloyalty to the government of the United States, or the state of Mississippi." We reversed a conviction for what we concluded was mere criticism and prophecy, without indicating whether we thought the statute could in any circumstances validly be applied. What the defendants communicated, we said, "is not claimed or shown to have been done with an evil or sinister purpose, to have advocated or incited subversive action against the nation or state, or to have threatened any clear and present danger to our institutions or our government."

I must leave to others the ungrateful task of trying to reconcile all these decisions. In some instances we have too readily permitted juries to infer deception from error, or intention from argumentative or critical statements. . . . In other instances we weighted the interest in free speech so heavily that we permitted essential conflicting values to be destroyed. . . . Viewed as a whole, however, the decisions express an attitude toward the judicial function and a standard of values which for me are decisive of the case before us.

First.—Free-speech cases are not an exception to the principle that we are not legislators, that direct policy-making is not our province. How best to reconcile competing interests is the business of legislatures, and the balance they strike is a judgment not to be displaced by ours, but to be respected unless outside the pale of fair judgment.

On occasion we have strained to interpret legislation in order to limit its effect on interests protected by the First Amendment. . . . In some instances we have denied to States the deference to which I think they are entitled. . . . Once in this recent course of decisions the Court refused to permit a jury to draw inferences which seemed to me to be obviously reasonable. . . .

But in no case has a majority of this Court held that a legislative judgment, even as to freedom of utterance, may be overturned merely because the Court would have made a different choice between the competing interests had the initial legislative judgment been for it to make. In the cases in which the opinions go farthest towards indicating a total rejection of respect for legislative determinations, the interests between which choice was actually made were such that decision might well have been expressed in the familiar terms of want of reason in the legislative judgment. . . .

In other cases, moreover, we have given clear indication that even when free speech is involved we attach great significance to the determination of the legislature. . . .

In *Gitlow* v. *New York*, we put our respect for the legislative judgment in terms which, if they were accepted here, would make decision easy. For that case held that when the legislature has determined that advocacy of forceful overthrow should be forbidden, a conviction may be sustained without a finding that in the particular case the advocacy had a close relation to a serious attempt at overthrow. We held that it was enough that the statute be a reasonable exercise of the legislative judgment, and that the defendant's conduct fall within the statute.

One of the judges below rested his affirmance on the *Gitlow* decision, and the defendants do not attempt to distinguish the case. They place their argument squarely on the ground that the case has been overruled by subsequent decisions. It has not been explicitly overruled. But it would be disingenuous to deny that the dissent in *Gitlow* has been treated with the respect usually accorded to a decision.

The result of the *Gitlow* decision was to send a left-wing Socialist to jail for publishing a Manifesto expressing Marxist exhortations. It requires excessive tolerance of the legislative judgment to suppose that the *Gitlow* publication in the circumstances could justify serious concern.

In contrast, there is ample justification for a legislative judgment that the conspiracy now before us is a substantial threat to national order and security. If the Smith Act is justified at all, it is justified precisely because it may serve to prohibit the type of conspiracy for which these defendants were convicted. The court below properly held that as a matter of separability the Smith Act may be limited to those situations to which it can constitutionally be applied. . . . Our decision today certainly does not mean that the Smith Act can constitutionally be applied to facts like those in *Gitlow* v. *New York*. While reliance may properly be placed on the attitude of judicial self-restraint which the *Gitlow* decision reflects, it is not necessary to depend on the facts or the full extent of the theory of the case in order to find that the judgment of Congress, as applied to the facts of the case now before us, is not in conflict with the First Amendment.

Second.—A survey of the relevant decisions indicates that the results which we have reached are on the whole those that would ensue from careful weighing of conflicting interests. The complex issues presented by regulation of speech in public places, by picketing, and by legislation prohibiting advocacy of crime have been resolved by scrutiny of many factors besides the imminence and gravity of the evil threatened. The matter has been well summarized by a reflective student of the Court's work. "The truth is that the clear-and-present-danger test is an over-simplified judgment unless it takes account also of a number of other factors: the relative seriousness of the danger in comparison with the value of the occasion for speech or political activity; the availability of more moderate controls than those which the state has imposed; and perhaps the specific intent with which the speech or activity is launched. No matter how rapidly we utter the phrase 'clear and present danger,' or how closely we hyphenate the words, they are not a substitute for the weighing of values. They tend to convey a delusion of certitude when what is most certain is the complexity of the strands in the web of freedoms which the judge must disentangle." Freund, *On Understanding the Supreme Court,* 27–28.

It is a familiar experience in the law that new situations do not fit neatly into legal conceptions that arose under different circumstances to satisfy different needs. So it was when the injunction was tortured into an instrument of expression against labor in industrial conflicts. So it is with the attempt to use the direction of thought lying behind the criterion of "clear and present danger" wholly out of the context in which it originated, and to make of it an absolute dogma and definitive measuring rod for the power of Congress to deal with assaults against security through devices other than overt physical attempts.

Bearing in mind that Mr. Justice Holmes regarded questions under the First Amendment as questions of "proximity and degree," *Schenck* v. *United States,* it would be a distortion, indeed a mockery, of his reasoning to compare the "puny anonymities," to which he was addressing himself in the *Abrams Case* in 1919 or the publication that was "futile and too remote from possible consequences" in the *Gitlow Case* in 1925 with the setting of events in this case in 1950.

"It does an ill-service to the author of the most quoted judicial phrases regarding freedom of speech, to make him the victim of a tendency which he fought all his life, whereby phrases are made to do service for critical analysis by being turned into dogma. 'It is one of the misfortunes of the law that ideas become encysted in phrases and thereafter for a long time cease to provoke further analysis.' Holmes, J., dissenting, in *Hyde* v. *United States,* 225 U.S. 347." The phrase "clear and present danger," in its origin, "served to indicate the importance of freedom of speech to a free society but also to emphasize that its exercise must be compatible with the preservation of other freedoms essential to a democracy and guaranteed by our Constitution." *Pennekamp* v. *Florida* (concurring). It were far better that the phrase be abandoned than that it be sounded once more to hide from the believers in an absolute right of free speech the plain fact that the interest in speech, profoundly important as it is, is no more conclusive in judicial review than other attributes of democracy or than a determination of the people's representatives that a measure is necessary to assure the safety of government itself.

Third.—Not every type of speech occupies the same position on the scale of values. There is no substantial public interest in permitting certain kinds of utterances: "the lewd and obscene, the profane, the libelous, and the insulting or 'fighting' words—those which by their very utterance inflict injury or tend to incite an immediate breach of the peace." *Chaplinsky* v.

New Hampshire, 315 U.S. 568. We have frequently indicated that the interest in protecting speech depends on the circumstances of the occasion. . . . It is pertinent to the decision before us to consider where on the scale of values we have in the past placed the type of speech now claiming constitutional immunity.

The defendants have been convicted of conspiring to organize a party of persons who advocate the overthrow of the Government by force and violence. The jury has found that the object of the conspiracy is advocacy as "a rule or principle of action," "by language reasonably and ordinarily calculated to incite persons to such action," and with the intent to cause the overthrow "as speedily as circumstances would permit."

On any scale of values which we have hitherto recognized, speech of this sort ranks low.

Throughout our decisions there has recurred a distinction between the statement of an idea which may prompt its hearers to take unlawful action, and advocacy that such action be taken. The distinction has its root in the conception of the common law that a person who procures another to do an act is responsible for that act as though he had done it himself. This principle was extended in *Fox* v. *Washington, supra,* to words directed to the public generally which would constitute an incitement were they directed to an individual. It was adopted in *Schenck* v. *United States, supra,* into a rule of evidence designed to restrict application of the Espionage Act. It was relied on by the Court in *Gitlow* v. *New York, supra.* The distinction has been repeated in many of the decisions in which we have upheld the claims of speech. We frequently have distinguished protected forms of expression from statements which "incite to violence and crime and threaten the overthrow of organized government by unlawful means." . . .

It is true that there is no divining rod by which we may locate "advocacy." Exposition of ideas readily merges into advocacy. The same Justice who gave currency to application of the incitement doctrine in this field dissented four times from what he thought was its misapplication. As he said in the *Gitlow* dissent, "Every idea is an incitement." Even though advocacy of overthrow deserves little protection, we should hesitate to prohibit it if we thereby inhibit the interchange of rational ideas so essential to representative government and free society.

But there is underlying validity in the distinction between advocacy and the interchange of ideas, and we do not discard a useful tool because it may be misused. That such a distinction could be used unreasonably by those in power against hostile or unorthodox views does not negate the fact that it may be used reasonably against an organization wielding the power of the centrally controlled international Communist movement. The object of the conspiracy before us is clear enough that the chance of error in saying that the defendants conspired to advocate rather than to express ideas is slight. Mr. Justice Douglas quite properly points out that the conspiracy before us is not a conspiracy to overthrow the Government. But it would be equally wrong to treat it as a seminar in political theory.

III.

These general considerations underlie decision of the case before us.

On the one hand is the interest in security. The Communist Party was not designed by these defendants as an ordinary political party. For the circumstances of its organization, its aims and methods, and the relation of the defendants to its organization and aims we are concluded by the jury's verdict. The jury found that the Party rejects the basic premise of our political system—that change is to be brought about by nonviolent constitutional process. The jury found that the Party advocates the theory that there is a duty and necessity to overthrow the Government by force and violence. It found that the Party entertains and promotes this view, not as a prophetic insight or as a bit of unworldly speculation, but as a program for winning adherents and as a policy to be translated into action.

In finding that the defendants violated the statute, we may not treat as established fact that the Communist Party in this country is of significant size, well-organized, well-disciplined, conditioned to embark on unlawful activity when given the command. But in determining whether application of the statute to the defendants is within the constitutional powers of Congress, we are not limited to the facts found by the jury. We must view such a question in the light of whatever is relevant to a legislative judgment. We may take judicial notice that the Communist doctrines which these defendants have conspired to advocate are in the ascendency in powerful nations who cannot be acquitted of unfriendliness to the institutions of this country. We may take account of evidence brought forward at this trial and elsewhere, much of which has long been common knowledge. In sum, it would amply justify a legislature in concluding that recruitment of additional members for the Party would create a substantial danger to national security.

In 1947, it has been reliably reported, at least 60,000 members were enrolled in the Party. Evidence was introduced in this case that the membership was organized in small units, linked by an intricate chain of command, and protected by elaborate precautions designed to prevent disclosure of individual identity. There are no reliable data tracing acts of sabotage or espionage directly to these defendants. But a Canadian Royal Commission appointed in 1946 to investigate espionage reported that it was "overwhelmingly established" that "the Communist movement was the principal base within which the espionage network was recruited." The most notorious spy in recent history [Klaus Fuchs] was led into the service of the Soviet Union through Communist indoctrination. Evidence supports the conclusion that members of the Party seek and occupy positions of importance in political and labor organizations. Congress was not barred by the Constitution from believing that indifference to such experience would be an exercise not of freedom but of irresponsibility.

On the other hand is the interest in free speech. The right to exert all governmental powers in aid of maintaining our institutions and resisting their physical overthrow does not include intolerance of opinions and speech that cannot do harm although opposed and perhaps alien to dominant, traditional opinion. The treatment of its minorities, especially their legal position, is among the most searching tests of the level of civilization attained by a society. It is better for those who have almost unlimited power of government in their hands to err on the side of freedom. We have enjoyed so much freedom for so long that we are perhaps in danger of forgetting how much blood it cost to establish the Bill of Rights.

Of course no government can recognize a "right" of revolution, or a "right" to incite revolution if the incitement has no other purpose or effect. But speech is seldom restricted to a single purpose, and its effects may be manifold. A public interest is not wanting in granting freedom to speak their minds even to those who advocate the overthrow of the Government by force. For, as the evidence in this case abundantly illustrates, coupled with such advocacy is criticism of defects in our society. Criticism is the spur to reform; and Burke's admonition that a healthy society must reform in order to conserve has not lost its force. Astute observers have remarked that one of the characteristics of the American Republic is indifference to fundamental criticism. Bryce, *The American Commonwealth*, c.84. It is a commonplace that there may be a grain of truth in the most uncouth doctrine however false and repellent the balance may be. Suppressing advocates of overthrow inevitably will also silence critics who do not advocate overthrow but fear that their criticism may be so construed. No matter how clear we may be that the defendants now before us are preparing to overthrow our Government at the propitious moment, it is self-delusion to think that we can punish them for their advocacy without adding to the risks run by loyal citizens who honestly believe in some of the reforms these defendants advance. It is a sobering fact that in sustaining the conviction before us we can hardly escape restriction on the interchange of ideas.

We must not overlook the value of that interchange. Freedom of expression is the well-spring of our civilization—the civilization we seek to maintain and further by recognizing the right of Congress to put some limitation upon expression. Such are the paradoxes of life. For social development of trial and error, the fullest possible opportunity for the free play of the human mind is an indispensable prerequisite. The history of civilization is in considerable measure the displacement of error which once held sway as official truth by beliefs which in turn have yielded to other truths. Therefore the liberty of man to search for truth ought not to be fettered, no matter what orthodoxies he may challenge. Liberty of thought soon shrivels without freedom of expression. Nor can truth be pursued in an atmosphere hostile to the endeavor or under dangers which are hazarded only by heroes.

"The interest, which [the First Amendment] guards, and which gives it its importance, presupposes that there are no orthodoxies—religious, political, economic, or scientific—which are immune from debate and dispute. Back of that is the assumption—itself an orthodoxy, and the one permissible exception—that truth will be most likely to emerge, if no limitations are imposed upon utterances that can with any plausibility be regarded as efforts to present grounds for accepting or rejecting propositions whose truth the utterer asserts, or denies." *International Brotherhood of Electrical Workers v. National Labor Relations Board,* 181 F. 2d 34. In the last analysis it is on the validity of this faith that our national security is staked.

It is not for us to decide how we would adjust the clash of interests which this case presents were the primary responsibility for reconciling it ours. Congress has determined that the danger created by advocacy of overthrow justifies the ensuing restriction on freedom of speech. The determination was made after due deliberation, and the seriousness of the congressional purpose is attested by the volume of legislation passed to effectuate the same ends.

Can we then say that the judgment Congress exercised was denied it by the Constitution? Can we establish a constitutional doctrine which forbids the elected representatives of the people to make this choice? Can we hold that the First Amendment deprives Congress of what it deemed necessary for the Government's protection?

To make validity of legislation depend on judicial reading of events still in the womb of time—a forecast, that is, of the outcome of forces at best appreciated only with knowledge of the topmost secrets of nations—is to charge the judiciary with duties beyond its equipment. We do not expect courts to pronounce historic verdicts on bygone events. Even historians have conflicting views to this day on the origin and conduct of the French Revolution. It is as absurd to be confident that we can measure the present clash of forces and their outcome as to ask us to read history still enveloped in clouds of controversy.

In the light of their experience, the Framers of the Constitution chose to keep the judiciary dissociated from direct participation in the legislative process. In asserting the power to pass on the constitutionality of legislation, Marshall and his Court expressed the purposes of the Founders. . . . But the extent to which the exercise of this power would interpenetrate matters of policy could hardly have been foreseen by the most prescient. The distinction which the Founders drew between the Court's duty to pass on the power of Congress and its complementary duty not to enter directly the domain of policy is fundamental. But in its actual operation it is rather subtle, certainly to the common understanding. Our duty to abstain from confounding policy with constitutionality demands perceptive humility as well as self-restraint in not declaring unconstitutional what in a judge's private judgment is unwise and even dangerous.

Even when moving strictly within the limits of constitutional adjudication, judges are concerned with issues that may be said to involve vital finalities. The too easy transition from disapproval of what is undesirable to condemnation as unconstitutional, has led some of the wisest judges to question the wisdom of our scheme in lodging such authority in courts. But it is relevant to remind that in sustaining the power of Congress in a case like this nothing irrevocable is done. The democratic process at all events is not impaired or restricted. Power and responsibility remain with the people and immediately with their representation. All the Court says is that Congress was not forbidden by the Constitution to pass this enactment and a prosecution under it may be brought against a conspiracy such as the one before us.

IV.

The wisdom of the assumptions underlying the legislation and prosecution is another matter. In finding that Congress has acted within its power, a judge does not remotely imply that he favors the implications that lie beneath the legal issues. Considerations there enter which go beyond the criteria that are binding upon judges within the narrow confines of their legitimate authority. The legislation we are here considering is but a truncated aspect of a deeper issue. For me it has been most illuminatingly expressed by one in whom responsibility and experience have fructified native insight, the Director-General of the British Broadcasting Corporation:

> We have to face up to the fact that there are powerful forces in the world today misusing the privileges of liberty in order to destroy her. The question must be asked, however, whether suppression of information or opinion is the true defense. We may have come a long way from Mill's famous dictum that: "If all mankind minus one were of one opinion, and only one person were of the contrary opinion, mankind would be no more justified in silencing that one person, than he, if he had the power, would be justified in silencing mankind," but Mill's reminders from history as to what has happened when suppression was most virulently exercised ought to warn us that no debate is ever permanently won by shutting one's ears or by even the most Draconian policy of silencing opponents. The *debate* must be won. And it must be won with full information. Where there are lies, they must be shown for what they are. Where there are errors, they must be refuted. It would be a major defeat if the enemies of democracy forced us to abandon our faith in the power of informed discussion and so brought us down to their own level. Mankind is so constituted, moreover, that if, where expression and discussion are concerned, the enemies of liberty are met with a denial of liberty, many men of goodwill will come to suspect there is something in the proscribed doctrine after all. Erroneous doctrines thrive on being expunged. They die if exposed. Sir William Haley, "What Standards for Broadcasting?" *Measure*, Vol. I, No. 3, Summer 1950, pp. 211–212.

In the context of this deeper struggle, another voice has indicated the limitations of what we decide today. No one is better equipped than George F. Kennan to speak on the meaning of the menace of Communism and the spirit in which we should meet it.

> If our handling of the problem of Communist influence in our midst is not carefully moderated—if we permit it, that is, to become an emotional preoccupation and to blind us to the more important positive tasks before us—we can do a damage to our national purpose beyond comparison greater than anything that threatens us today from the Communist side. The American Communist party is today, by and large, an external danger. It represents a tiny minority in our country;

it has no real contact with the feelings of the mass of our people; and its position as the agency of a hostile foreign power is clearly recognized by the overwhelming mass of our citizens.

But the subjective emotional stresses and temptations to which we are exposed in our attempt to deal with this domestic problem are not an external danger: they represent a danger within ourselves—a danger that something may occur in our own minds and souls which will make us no longer like the persons by whose efforts this republic was founded and held together, but rather like the representatives of that very power we are trying to combat: intolerant, secretive, suspicious, cruel, and terrified of internal dissension because we have lost our own belief in ourselves and in the power of our ideals. The worst thing that our Communists could do to us, and the thing we have most to fear from their activities, is that we should become like them.

That our country is beset with external dangers I readily concede. But these dangers, at their worst, are ones of physical destruction, of the disruption of our world security, of expense and inconvenience and sacrifice. These are serious, and sometimes terrible things, but they are all things that we can take and still remain Americans.

The internal danger is of a different order. America is not just territory and people. There is lots of territory elsewhere, and there are lots of people; but it does not add up to America. America is something in our minds and our habits of outlook which causes us to believe in certain things and to behave in certain ways, and by which, in its totality, we hold ourselves distinguished from others. If that once goes there will be no America to defend. And that can go too easily if we yield to the primitive human instinct to escape from our frustrations into the realms of mass emotion and hatred and to find scapegoats for our difficulties in individual fellow-citizens who are, or have at one time been, disoriented or confused. George F. Kennan, "Where do You Stand on Communism?" *New York Times Magazine*, May 27, 1951.

Civil liberties draw at best only limited strength from legal guaranties. Preoccupation by our people with the constitutionality, instead of with the wisdom of legislation or of executive action, is preoccupation with a false value. Even those who would most freely use the judicial brake on the democratic process by invalidating legislation that goes deeply against their grain, acknowledge, at least by paying lip service, that constitutionality does not exact a sense of proportion or the sanity of humor or an absence of fear. Focusing attention on constitutionality tends to make constitutionality synonymous with wisdom. When legislation touches freedom of thought and freedom of speech, such a tendency is a formidable enemy of the free spirit. Much that should be rejected as illiberal, because repressive and envenoming, may well be not unconstitutional. The ultimate reliance for the deepest needs of civilization must be found outside their vindication in courts of law; apart from all else, judges, howsoever they may conscientiously seek to discipline themselves against it, unconsciously are too apt to be moved by the deep undercurrents of public feeling. A persistent, positive translation of the liberating faith into the feelings and thoughts and actions of men and women is the real protection against attempts to strait-jacket the human mind. Such temptations will have their way, if fear and hatred are not exorcized. The mark of a truly civilized man is confidence in the strength and security derived from the inquiring mind. We may be grateful for such honest comforts as it supports, but we must be unafraid of its uncertitudes. Without open minds there can be no open society. And if society be not open the spirit of man is mutilated and becomes enslaved. . . .

Mr. Justice Jackson, concurring:

This prosecution is the latest of never-ending, because never successful, quests for some legal formula that will secure an existing order against revolutionary radicalism. It requires us to reappraise, in the light of our own times and conditions, constitutional doctrines devised under other circumstances to strike a balance between authority and liberty.

Activity here charged to be criminal is conspiracy—that defendants conspired to teach and advocate, and to organize the Communist Party to teach and advocate, overthrow and destruction of the Government by force and violence. There is no charge of actual violence or attempt at overthrow.

The principal reliance of the defense in this Court is that the conviction cannot stand under the Constitution because the conspiracy of these defendants presents no "clear and present danger" of imminent or foreseeable overthrow.

I.

The statute before us repeats a pattern, originally devised to combat the wave of anarchistic terrorism that plagued this country about the turn of the century, which lags at least two generations behind Communist Party techniques.

Anarchism taught a philosophy of extreme individualism and hostility to government and property. Its avowed aim was a more just order, to be achieved by violent destruction of all government. Anarchism's sporadic and uncoordinated acts of terror were not integrated with an effective revolutionary machine, but the Chicago Haymarket riots of 1886, attempted murder of the industrialist Frick, attacks on state officials, and assassination of President McKinley in 1901, were fruits of its preaching.

However, extreme individualism was not conducive to cohesive and disciplined organization. Anarchism fell into disfavor among incendiary radicals, many of whom shifted their allegiance to the rising Communist Party. Meanwhile, in Europe anarchism had been displaced by Bolshevism as the doctrine and strategy of social and political upheaval. Led by intellectuals hardened by revolutionary experience it was a more sophisticated, dynamic and realistic movement. Establishing a base in the Soviet Union, it founded an aggressive international Communist apparatus which has modeled and directed a revolutionary movement able only to harass our own country. But it has seized control of a dozen other countries.

Communism, the antithesis of anarchism, appears today as a closed system of thought representing Stalin's version of Lenin's version of Marxism. As an ideology, it is not one of spontaneous protest arising from American working-class experience. It is a complicated system of assumptions, based on European history and conditions, shrouded in an obscure and ambiguous vocabulary, which allures our ultrasophisticated intelligentsia more than our hard-headed working people. From time to time it champions all manner of causes and grievances and makes alliances that may add to its foothold in government or embarrass the authorities.

The Communist Party, nevertheless, does not seek its strength primarily in numbers. Its aim is a relatively small party whose strength is in selected, dedicated, indoctrinated, and rigidly disciplined members. From established policy it tolerates no deviation and no debate. It seeks members that are, or may be, secreted in strategic posts in transportation, communications, industry, government, and especially in labor unions where it can compel employers to accept and retain its members. It also seeks to infiltrate and control organizations of professional and other groups. Through these placements in positions of power it seeks a leverage over society that will make up in power of coercion what it lacks in power of persuasion.

The Communists have no scruples against sabotage, terrorism, assassination, or mob disorder; but violence is not with them, as with the anarchists, an end in itself. The Communist Party advocates force only when prudent and profitable. Their strategy of stealth precludes premature or uncoordinated outbursts of violence, except, of course, when the blame will be placed on shoulders other than their own. They resort to violence as to truth, not as a principle but as an expedient. Force or violence, as they would resort to it, may never be necessary, because infiltration and deception may be enough.

Force would be utilized by the Communist Party not to destroy government but for its capture. The Communist recognizes that an established government in control of modern technology cannot be overthrown by force until it is about ready to fall of its own weight. Concerted uprising, therefore, is to await that contingency and revolution is seen, not as a sudden episode, but as the consummation of a long process.

The United States, fortunately, has experienced Communism only in its preparatory stages and for its pattern of final action must look abroad. Russia, of course, was the pilot Communist revolution, which to the Marxist confirms the Party's assumptions and points its destiny. But Communist technique in the overturn of a free government was disclosed by the *coup d'état* in which they seized power in Czechoslovakia. There the Communist Party during its preparatory stage claimed and received protection for its freedoms of speech, press, and assembly. Pretending to be but another political party, it eventually was conceded participation in government, where it entrenched reliable members chiefly in control of police and information services. When the government faced a foreign and domestic crisis, the Communist Party had established a leverage strong enough to threaten civil war. In a period of confusion the Communist plan unfolded and the underground organization came to the surface throughout the country in the form chiefly of labor "action committees." Communist officers of the unions took over transportation and allowed only persons with party permits to travel. Communist printers took over the newspapers and radio and put out only party-approved versions of events. Possession was taken of telegraph and telephone systems and communications were cut off wherever directed by party heads. Communist unions took over the factories, and in the cities a partisan distribution of food was managed by the Communist organization. A virtually bloodless abdication by the elected government admitted the Communists to power, whereupon they instituted a reign of oppression and terror, and ruthlessly denied to all others the freedoms which had sheltered their conspiracy.

II.

The foregoing is enough to indicate that, either by accident or design, the Communist stratagem outwits the anti-anarchist pattern of statute aimed against "overthrow by force and violence" if qualified by the doctrine that only "clear and present danger" of accomplishing that result will sustain the prosecution.

The "clear and present danger" test was an innovation by Mr. Justice Holmes in the *Schenck Case,* reiterated and refined by him and Mr. Justice Brandeis in later cases, all arising before the era of World War II revealed the subtlety and efficacy of modernized revolutionary techniques used by totalitarian parties. In those cases, they were faced with convictions under so-called criminal syndicalism statutes aimed at anarchists but which, loosely construed, had been applied to punish socialism, pacifism, and left-wing ideologies, the charges often resting on far-fetched inferences which, if true, would establish only technical or trivial violations. They proposed "clear and present danger" as a test for the sufficiency of evidence in particular cases.

I would save it, unmodified, for application as a "rule of reason" in the kind of case for which it was devised. When the issue is criminality of a hot-headed speech on a street corner, or circulation of a few incendiary pamphlets, or parading by some zealots behind a red flag, or refusal of a handful of school children to salute our flag, it is not beyond the capacity of the judicial process to gather, comprehend, and weigh the necessary materials for decision whether it is a clear and present danger of substantive evil or a harmless letting off of steam. It is not a prophecy, for the danger in such cases has matured by the time of trial or it was never present. The test applies and has meaning where a conviction is sought to be based on a speech or writing which does not directly or explicitly advocate a crime but to which such tendency is sought to be attributed by construction or by implication from external circumstances. The formula in such cases favors freedoms that are vital to our society, and, even if sometimes applied too generously, the consequences cannot be grave. But its recent expansion has extended, in particular to Communists, unprecedented immunities. Unless we are to hold our Government captive in a judge-made verbal trap, we must approach the problem of a well-organized, nation-wide conspiracy, such as I have described, as realistically as our predecessors faced the trivialities that were being prosecuted until they were checked with a rule of reason.

I think reason is lacking for applying that test to this case.

If we must decide that this Act and its application are constitutional only if we are convinced that petitioner's conduct creates a "clear and present danger" of violent overthrow, we must appraise imponderables, including international and national phenomena which baffle the best informed foreign offices and our most experienced politicians. We would have to foresee and predict the effectiveness of Communist propaganda, opportunities for in-filtration, whether, and when, a time will come that they consider propitious for action, and whether and how fast our existing government will deteri-orate. And we would have to speculate as to whether an approaching Com-munist *coup* would not be anticipated by a nationalistic fascist movement. No doctrine can be sound whose application requires us to make a prophecy of that sort in the guise of a legal decision. The judicial process simply is not adequate to a trial of such far-flung issues. The answers given would re-flect our own political predilections and nothing more.

The authors of the clear and present danger test never applied it to a case like this, nor would I. If applied as it is proposed here, it means that the Communist plotting is protected during its period of incubation; its pre-liminary stages of organization and preparation are immune from the law; the Government can move only after imminent action is manifest, when it would, of course, be too late.

III.

The highest degree of constitutional protection is due to the individual acting without conspiracy. But even an individual cannot claim that the Constitution protects him in advocating or teaching overthrow of govern-ment by force or violence. I should suppose no one would doubt that Congress has power to make such attempted overthrow a crime. But the contention is that one has the constitutional right to work up a public desire and will to do what it is a crime to attempt. I think direct incitement by speech or writing can be made a crime, and I think there can be a conviction with-out also proving that the odds favored its success by 99 to 1, or some other extremely high ratio. . . .

Of course, it is not always easy to distinguish teaching or advocacy in the sense of incitement from teaching or advocacy in the sense of exposition or explanation. It is a question of fact in each case.

IV.

What really is under review here is a conviction of conspiracy, after a trial for conspiracy, on an indictment charging conspiracy, brought under a statute outlawing conspiracy. With due respect to my colleagues, they seem to me to discuss anything under the sun except the law of conspiracy. One of the dissenting opinions even appears to chide me for "invoking the law of conspiracy." As that is the case before us, it may be more amazing that its reversal can be proposed without even considering the law of conspiracy.

The Constitution does not make conspiracy a civil right. The Court has never before done so and I think it should not do so now. Conspiracies of labor unions, trade associations, and news agencies have been condemned, although accomplished, evidenced and carried out, like the conspiracy here, chiefly by letter-writing, meetings, speeches and organization. Indeed, this Court seems, particularly in cases where the conspiracy has economic ends, to be applying its doctrines with increasing severity. While I consider criminal conspiracy a dragnet device capable of perversion into an instrument of injustice in the hands of a partisan or complacent judiciary, it has an established place in our system of law, and no reason appears for applying it only to concerted action claimed to disturb interstate commerce and withholding it from those claimed to undermine our whole Government.

The basic rationale of the law of conspiracy is that a conspiracy may be an evil in itself, independently of any other evil it seeks to accomplish. . . .

So far does this doctrine reach that it is well settled that Congress may make it a crime to conspire with others to do what an individual may lawfully do on his own. This principle is illustrated in conspiracies that violate the antitrust laws as sustained and applied by this Court. Although one may raise the prices of his own products, and many, acting without concert, may do so, the moment they conspire to that end they are punishable. The same principle is applied to organized labor. Any workman may quit his work for any reason, but concerted actions to the same end are in some circumstances forbidden. . . .

The reasons underlying the doctrine that conspiracy may be a substantive evil in itself, apart from any evil it may threaten, attempt or accomplish are peculiarly appropriate to conspiratorial Communism.

> The reason for finding criminal liability in case of a combination to effect an unlawful end or to use unlawful means, where none would exist, even though the act contemplated were actually committed by an individual, is that a combination of persons to commit a wrong, either as an end or as a means to an end, is so much more dangerous, because of its increased power to do wrong, because it is more difficult to guard against and prevent the evil designs of a group of persons than of a single person, and because of the terror which fear of such a combination tends to create in the minds of people. [Miller, *Criminal Law,* 10.]

There is lamentation in the dissents about the injustice of conviction in the absence of some overt act. Of course, there has been no general uprising against the Government, but the record is replete with acts to carry out the conspiracy alleged, acts such as always are held sufficient to consummate the crime where the statute requires an overt act.

But the shorter answer is that no overt act is or need be required. The Court, in antitrust cases, early upheld the power of Congress to adopt the ancient common law that makes conspiracy itself a crime. . . . It is not to be supposed that the power of Congress to protect the Nation's existence is more limited than its power to protect interstate commerce.

Also, it is urged that since the conviction is for conspiracy to teach and advocate, and to organize the Communist Party to teach and advocate, the First Amendment is violated, because freedoms of speech and press protect teaching and advocacy regardless of what is taught or advocated. I have never thought that to be the law.

I do not suggest that Congress could punish conspiracy to advocate something, the doing of which it may not punish. Advocacy or exposition of the doctrine of communal property ownership, or any political philosophy unassociated with advocacy of its imposition by force or seizure of government by unlawful means could not be reached through conspiracy prosecution. But it is not forbidden to put down force or violence, it is not forbidden to punish its teaching or advocacy, and the end being punishable, there is no doubt of the power to punish conspiracy for the purpose.

The defense of freedom of speech or press has often been raised in conspiracy cases, because, whether committed by Communists, by businessmen, or by common criminals, it usually consists of words written or spoken, evidenced by letters, conversations, speeches or documents. Communication is the essence of every conspiracy, for only by it can common purpose and concert of action be brought about or be proved. . . .

In conspiracy cases the Court not only has dispensed with proof of clear and present danger but even of power to create a danger. . . .

Having held that a conspiracy alone is a crime and its consummation is another, it would be weird legal reasoning to hold that Congress could punish the one only if there was "clear and present danger" of the second. This would compel the Government to prove two crimes in order to convict for one.

When our constitutional provisions were written, the chief forces recognized as antagonists in the struggle between authority and liberty were the Government on the one hand and the individual citizen on the other. It was thought that if the state could be kept in its place the individual could take care of himself.

In more recent times these problems have been complicated by the intervention between the state and the citizen of permanently organized, well-financed, semi-secret and highly disciplined political organizations. Totalitarian groups here and abroad perfected the technique of creating private paramilitary organizations to coerce both the public government and its citizens. These organizations assert as against our Government all of the constitutional rights and immunities of individuals and at the same time exercise over their followers much of the authority which they deny to the Government. The Communist Party realistically is a state within a state, an authoritarian dictatorship within a republic. It demands these freedoms, not for its members, but for the organized party. It denies to its own members at the same time the freedom to dissent, to debate, to deviate from the party line, and enforces its authoritarian rule by crude purges, if nothing more violent.

The law of conspiracy has been the chief means at the Government's disposal to deal with the growing problems created by such organizations. I happen to think it is an awkward and inept remedy, but I find no constitutional authority for taking this weapon from the Government. There is no constitutional right to "gang up" on the Government.

While I think there was power in Congress to enact this statute and that, as applied in this case, it cannot be held unconstitutional, I add that I have little faith in the long-range effectiveness of this conviction to stop the rise of the Communist movement. Communism will not go to jail with these Communists. No decision by this Court can forestall revolution whenever the existing government fails to command the respect and loyalty of the people and sufficient distress and discontent is allowed to grow up among the masses. Many failures by fallen governments attest that no government can long prevent revolution by outlawry. Corruption, ineptitude, inflation, oppressive taxation, militarization, injustice, and loss of leadership capable of intellectual initiative in domestic or foreign affairs are allies on which the Communists count to bring opportunity knocking to their door. Sometimes I think they may be mistaken. But the Communists are not building just for today—the rest of us might profit by their example.

Mr. Justice Black, dissenting:

Here . . . my basic disagreement with the Court is not as to how we should explain or reconcile what was said in prior decisions but springs from a fundamental difference in constitutional approach. Consequently, it would serve no useful purpose to state my position at length.

At the outset I want to emphasize what the crime involved in this case is, and what it is not. These petitioners were not charged with an attempt to overthrow the Government. They were not charged with overt acts of any kind designed to overthrow the Government. They were not even charged with saying anything or writing anything designed to overthrow the Government. The charge was that they agreed to assemble and to talk and publish certain ideas at a later date: The indictment is that they conspired to organize the Communist Party and to use speech or newspapers and other publications in the future to teach and advocate the forcible overthrow of the Government. No matter how it is worded, this is a virulent form of prior censorship of speech and press, which I believe the First Amendment forbids. I would hold § 3 of the Smith Act authorizing this prior restraint unconstitutional on its face and as applied.

But let us assume, contrary to all constitutional ideas of fair criminal procedure, that petitioners although not indicted for the crime of actual advocacy, may be punished for it. Even on this radical assumption, the other opinions in this case show that the only way to affirm these convictions is to repudiate directly or indirectly the established "clear and present danger" rule. This the Court does in a way which greatly restricts the protections afforded by the First Amendment. The opinions for affirmance indicate that the chief reason for jettisoning the rule is the expressed fear that advocacy of Communist doctrine endangers the safety of the Republic. Undoubtedly, a governmental policy of unfettered communication of ideas does entail dangers. To the Founders of this Nation, however, the benefits derived from free expression were worth the risk. They embodied this philosophy in the First Amendment's command that Congress "shall make no law . . . abridging the freedom of speech, or of the press. . . ." I have always believed that the First Amendment is the keystone of our Government, that the freedoms it guarantees provide the best insurance against destruction of all freedom. At least as to speech in the realm of public matters, I believe that the "clear and present danger" test does not "mark the furthermost constitutional boundaries of protected expression" but does "no more than recognize a minimum compulsion of the Bill of Rights." *Bridges* v. *California*, 314 U.S. 252. . . .

So long as this Court exercises the power of judicial review of legislation, I cannot agree that the First Amendment permits us to sustain laws suppressing freedom of speech and press on the basis of Congress' or our own notions of mere "reasonableness." Such a doctrine waters down the First Amendment so that it amounts to little more than an admonition to Congress. The Amendment as so construed is not likely to protect any but those "safe" or orthodox views which rarely need its protection. I must also express my objection to the holding because, as Mr. Justice Douglas' dissent shows, it sanctions the determination of a crucial issue of fact by the judge rather than by the jury. Nor can I let this opportunity pass without expressing my objection to the severely limited grant of certiorari in this case which precluded consideration here of at least two other reasons for reversing these convictions: (1) the record shows a discriminatory selection of the jury panel which prevented trial before a representative cross-section of the community; (2) the record shows that one member of the trial jury was violently hostile to petitioners before and during the trial.

Public opinion being what it now is, few will protest the conviction of these Communist petitioners. There is hope, however, that in calmer times, when present pressures, passions and fears subside, this or some later Court will restore the First Amendment liberties to the high preferred place where they belong in a free society.

Mr. Justice Douglas, dissenting:

If this were a case where those who claimed protection under the First Amendment were teaching the techniques of sabotage, the assassination of the President, the filching of documents from public files, the planting of bombs, the art of street warfare, and the like, I would have no doubts. The freedom to speak is not absolute; the teaching of methods of terror and other seditious conduct should be beyond the pale along with obscenity and immorality. This case was argued as if those were the facts. The argument imported much seditious conduct into the record. That is easy and it has popular appeal, for the activities of Communists in plotting and scheming against the free world are common knowledge. But the fact is that no such evidence was introduced at the trial. There is a statute which makes a seditious conspiracy unlawful. Petitioners, however, were not charged with a "conspiracy to overthrow" the Government. They were charged with a conspiracy to form a party and groups and assemblies of people who teach and advocate the overthrow of our Government by force or violence and with a conspiracy to advocate and teach its overthrow by force and violence. It may well be that indoctrination in the techniques of terror to destroy the Government would be indictable under either statute. But the teaching which is condemned here is of a different character.

So far as the present record is concerned, what petitioners did was to organize people to teach and themselves teach the Marxist-Leninist doctrine contained chiefly in four books: *Foundations of Leninism* by Stalin (1924), *The Communist Manifesto* by Marx and Engels (1848), *State and Revolution* by Lenin (1917), *History of the Communist Party of the Soviet Union* (1939).

Those books are to Soviet Communism what *Mein Kampf* was to Nazism. If they are understood, the ugliness of Communism is revealed, its deceit and cunning are exposed, the nature of its activities becomes apparent, and the chances of its success less likely. That is not, of course, the reason why petitioners chose these books for their classrooms. They are fervent Communists to whom these volumes are gospel. They preached the creed with the hope that some day it would be acted upon.

The opinion of the Court does not outlaw these texts nor condemn them to the fire, as the Communists do literature offensive to their creed. But if the books themselves are not outlawed, if they can lawfully remain on library shelves, by what reasoning does their use in a classroom become a crime? It would not be a crime under the Act to introduce these books to a class, though that would be teaching what the creed of violent overthrow of the government is. The Act, as construed, requires the element of intent —that those who teach the creed believe in it. The crime then depends not on what is taught but on who the teacher is. That is to make freedom of speech turn not on *what is said,* but on the *intent* with which it is said. Once we start down that road we enter territory dangerous to the liberties of every citizen.

There was a time in England when the concept of constructive treason flourished. Men were punished not for raising a hand against the king but for thinking murderous thoughts about him. The Framers of the Constitution were alive to that abuse and took steps to see that the practice would not flourish here. Treason was defined to require overt acts—the evolution of a plot against the country into an actual project. The present case is not one of treason. But the analogy is close when the illegality is made to turn on intent, not on the nature of the act. We then start probing men's minds for motive and purpose; they become entangled in the law not for what they did but *for what they thought; they* get convicted not for what they said but for the purpose with which they said it.

Intent, of course, often makes the difference in the law. An act otherwise excusable or carrying minor penalties may grow to an abhorrent thing if the evil intent is present. We deal here, however, not with ordinary acts but with speech, to which the Constitution has given a special sanction.

The vice of treating speech as the equivalent of overt acts of a treasonable or seditious character is emphasized by a concurring opinion, which by invoking the law of conspiracy makes speech do service for deeds which are dangerous to society. The doctrine of conspiracy has served divers and oppressive purposes and in its broad reach can be made to do great evil. But never until today has anyone seriously thought that the ancient law of conspiracy could constitutionally be used to turn speech into seditious conduct. Yet that is precisely what is suggested. I repeat that we deal here with speech alone, not with speech *plus* acts of sabotage or unlawful conduct. Not a single seditious act is charged in the indictment. To make a lawful speech unlawful because two men conceive it is to raise the law of conspiracy to appalling proportions. That course is to make a radical break with the past and to violate one of the cardinal principles of our constitutional scheme.

Free speech has occupied an exalted position because of the high service it has given our society. Its protection is essential to the very existence of a democracy. The airing of ideas releases pressures which otherwise might become destructive. When ideas compete in the market for acceptance, full and free discussion exposes the false and they gain few adherents. Full and free discussion even of ideas we hate encourages the testing of our own prejudices and preconceptions. Full and free discussion keeps a society from becoming stagnant and unprepared for the stresses and strains that work to tear all civilizations apart.

Full and free discussion has indeed been the first article of our faith. We have founded our political system on it. It has been the safeguard of every religious, political, philosophical, economic, and racial group amongst us. We have counted on it to keep us from embracing what is cheap and false; we have trusted the common sense of our people to choose the doctrine true to our genius and to reject the rest. This has been the one single outstanding tenet that has made our institutions the symbol of freedom and equality. We have deemed it more costly to liberty to suppress a despised minority than to let them vent their spleen. We have above all else feared the political censor. We have wanted a land where our people can be exposed to all the diverse creeds and cultures of the world.

There comes a time when even speech loses its constitutional immunity. Speech innocuous one year may at another time fan such destructive flames that it must be halted in the interests of the safety of the Republic. That is the meaning of the clear and present danger test. When conditions are so critical that there will be no time to avoid the evil that the speech threatens, it is time to call a halt. Otherwise, free speech which is the strength of the Nation will be the cause of its destruction.

Yet free speech is the rule, not the exception. The restraint to be constitutional must be based on more than fear, on more than passionate opposition against the speech, on more than a revolted dislike for its contents. There must be some immediate injury to society that is likely if speech is allowed. The classic statement of these conditions was made by Mr. Justice Brandeis in his concurring opinion in *Whitney v. California*, 274 U.S. 357.

Fear of serious injury cannot alone justify suppression of free speech and assembly. Men feared witches and burnt women. It is the function of speech to free men from the bondage of irrational fears. To justify suppression of free speech there must be reasonable ground to fear that serious evil will result if free speech is practiced. There must be reasonable ground to believe that the danger apprehended is imminent. There must be reasonable ground to believe that the evil to be prevented is a serious one. Every denunciation of existing law tends in some measure to increase the probability that there will be violation of it. Condonation of a breach enhances the probability. Expressions of approval add to the probability. Propagation of the criminal state of mind by teaching syndicalism increases it. Advocacy of law-breaking heightens it still further. But even advocacy of violation, however reprehensible morally, is not a justification for denying free speech where the advocacy falls short of incitement and there is nothing to indicate that the advocacy would be immediately acted on. The wide difference between advocacy and incitement, between preparation and attempt, between assembling and conspiracy, must be borne in mind. In order to support a finding of clear and present danger it must be shown either that immediate serious violence was to be expected or was advocated, or that the past conduct furnished reason to believe that such advocacy was then contemplated.

Those who won our independence by revolution were not cowards. They did not fear political change. They did not exalt order at the cost of liberty. To courageous self-reliant men, with confidence in the power of free and fearless reasoning applied through the processes of popular government, no danger flowing from speech can be deemed clear and present, unless the incidence of the evil apprehended is so imminent that it may befall before there is opportunity for full discussion. *If there be time to expose through discussion the falsehood and fallacies, to avert the evil by the processes of education, the remedy to be applied is more speech, not enforced silence.* (Italics added.)

I had assumed that the question of the clear and present danger, being so critical an issue in the case, would be a matter for submission to the jury. It was squarely held in *Pierce v. United States*, 252 U.S. 239, to be a jury question. Mr. Justice Pitney, speaking for the Court, said, "Whether the statements contained in the pamphlet had a natural tendency to produce the forbidden consequences, as alleged, was a question to be determined, not upon demurrer, but by the jury at the trial." That is the only time the Court has passed on the issue. None of our other decisions is contrary. Nothing said in any of the nonjury cases has detracted from that ruling. The statement in *Pierce* v. *United States* states the law as it has been and as it should be. The Court, I think, errs when it treats the question as one of law.

Yet, whether the question is one for the Court or the jury, there should be evidence of record on the issue. This record, however, contains no evidence whatsoever showing that the acts charged *viz.*, the teaching of the Soviet theory of revolution with the hope that it will be realized, have created any clear and present danger to the Nation. The Court, however, rules to the contrary. It says, "The formation by petitioners of such a highly organized conspiracy, with rigidly disciplined members subject to call when the leaders, these petitioners, felt that the time had come for action, coupled with the inflammable nature of world conditions, similar uprisings in other countries, and the touch-and-go nature of our relations with countries with whom petitioners were in the very least ideologically attuned, convince us that their convictions were justified on this score."

That ruling is in my view not responsive to the issue in the case. We might as well say that the speech of petitioners is outlawed because Soviet Russia and her Red Army are a threat to world peace.

The nature of Communism as a force on the world scene would, of course, be relevant to the issue of clear and present danger of petitioners' advocacy within the United States. But the primary consideration is the strength and tactical position of petitioners and their converts in this country. On that there is no evidence in the record. If we are to take judicial notice of the threat of Communists within the nation, it should not be difficult to conclude that *as a political party* they are of little consequence. Communists in this country have never made a respectable or serious showing in any election. I would doubt that there is a village, let alone a city or county or state which the Communists could carry. Communism in the world scene is no bogey-man; but Communists as a political faction or party in this country plainly is. Communism has been so thoroughly exposed in this country that it has been crippled as a political force. Free speech has destroyed it as an effective political party. It is inconceivable that those who went up and down this country preaching the doctrine of revolution which petitioners espouse would have any success. In days of trouble and confusion when bread lines were long, when the unemployed walked the streets, when people were starving the advocates of a short-cut by revolution might have a chance to gain adherents. But today there are no such conditions. The country is not in despair; the people know Soviet Communism; the doctrine of Soviet revolution is exposed in all of its ugliness and the American people want none of it.

How it can be said that there is a clear and present danger that this advocacy will succeed is, therefore, a mystery. Some nations less resilient than the United States, where illiteracy is high and where democratic traditions are only budding, might have to take drastic steps and jail these men for merely speaking their creed. But in America they are miserable merchants of unwanted ideas; their wares remain unsold. The fact that their ideas are abhorrent does not make them powerful.

The political impotence of the Communists in this country does not, of course dispose of the problem. Their numbers; their positions in industry and government; the extent to which they have in fact infiltrated the police, the armed services, transportation, stevedoring, power plants, munitions works, and other critical places—these facts all bear on the likelihood that their advocacy of the Soviet theory of revolution will endanger the Republic. But the record is silent on these facts. If we are to proceed on the basis of judicial notice, it is impossible for me to say that the Communists in this country are so potent or so strategically deployed that they must be suppressed for their speech. I could not so hold unless I were willing to conclude that the activities in recent years of committees of Congress, of the Attorney General, of labor unions, of state legislatures, and of Loyalty Boards were so futile as to leave the country on the edge of grave peril. To believe that petitioners and their following are placed in such critical positions as to endanger the Nation is to believe the incredible. It is safe to say that the followers of the creed of Soviet Communism are known to the F.B.I.; that in case of war with Russia they will be picked up overnight as were all prospective saboteurs at the commencement of World War II; that the invisible army of petitioners is the best known, the most beset, and the least thriving of any fifth column in history. Only those held by fear and panic could think otherwise.

This is my view if we are to act on the basis of judicial notice. But the mere statement of the opposing views indicates how important it is that we know the facts before we act. Neither prejudice nor hate nor senseless fear should be the basis of this solemn act. Free speech—the glory of our system of government—should not be sacrificed on anything less than plain and objective proof of danger that the evil advocated is imminent. On this record no one can say that petitioners and their converts are in such a strategic position as to have even the slightest chance of achieving their aims.

The First Amendment provides that "Congress shall make no law . . . abridging the freedom of speech." The Constitution provides no exception. This does not mean, however, that the Nation need hold its hand until it is in such weakened condition that there is no time to protect itself from incitement to revolution. Seditious conduct can always be punished. But the command of the First Amendment is so clear that we should not allow Congress to call a halt to free speech except in the extreme case of peril from the speech itself. The First Amendment makes confidence in the common sense of our people and in their maturity of judgment the great postulate of our democracy. Its philosophy is that violence is rarely, if ever, stopped by denying civil liberties to those advocating resort to force. The First Amendment reflects the philosophy of Jefferson "that it is time enough for the rightful purposes of civil government for its officers to interfere when principles break out into overt acts against peace and good order." The political censor has no place in our public debates. Unless and until extreme and necessitous circumstances are shown our aim should be to keep speech unfettered and to allow the processes of law to be invoked only when the provocateurs among us move from speech to action.

Vishinsky wrote in 1948 in *The Law of the Soviet State*, "In our state, naturally there can be no place for freedom of speech, press, and so on for the foes of socialism."

Our concern should be that we accept no such standard for the United States. Our faith should be that our people will never give support to these advocates of revolution, so long as we remain loyal to the purposes for which our Nation was founded. . . .

YATES *v.* UNITED STATES

354 US 298 (1957)

[Fourteen Communist Party leaders were convicted under the conspiracy provisions of the Smith Act, just as were the eleven defendants in the *Dennis Case, supra,* decided six years before the instant case. But here the Court, finding two decisive differences between the cases, set aside the convictions.

[In his opinion for the Court, Justice Harlan found that the charge to the jury with respect to proscribed advocacy was constitutionally defective. Mere abstract doctrine of the forcible overthrow of government cannot be put under the ban of proscribed advocacy. There must be advocacy of action to that end.

[Furthermore, the Communist Party was organized in 1945. The indictment in the instant case was returned six years later, in 1951. The term "organize," as used in the Smith Act, held the Court, refers only to acts involving the creation of a new organization; the term does not connote a continuing process that goes on throughout the life of the organization. Accordingly, the indictment was barred by the three-year statute of limitations.

[On the advocacy point Chief Justice Warren and Justices Frankfurter and Burton agreed with Justice Harlan. Justices Black and Douglas would have gone further, holding that the Smith Act provisions under which the defendants were convicted were unconstitutional.

[On the point regarding the meaning of the term "organize," Chief Justice Warren and Justices Frankfurter, Black, and Douglas agreed with Justice Harlan.

[Justice Clark dissented on both points of the decision, and Justice Burton dissented only on the second point. Justices Brennan and Whittaker did not participate.]

Mr. Justice Harlan delivered the opinion of the Court:

We brought these cases here to consider certain questions arising under the Smith Act which have not heretofore been passed upon by this Court, and otherwise to review the convictions of these petitioners for conspiracy to violate that Act. Among other things, the convictions are claimed to rest upon an application of the Smith Act which is hostile to the principles upon which its constitutionality was upheld in *Dennis* v. *United States,* 341 US 494.

These 14 petitioners stand convicted, after a jury trial in the United States Dictrict Court for the Southern District of California, upon a single count indictment charging them with conspiring (1) to advocate and teach the duty and necessity of overthrowing the Government of the United States by force and violence, and (2) to organize, as the Communist Party of the United States, a society of persons who so advocate and teach, all with the intent of causing the overthrow of the Government by force and violence as speedily as circumstances would permit. . . . 18 U.S.C. §§ 371, 2385. The conspiracy is alleged to have originated in 1940 and continued down to the date of the indictment in 1951. The indictment charged that in carrying out the conspiracy the defendants and their co-conspirators would (a) become members and officers of the Communist Party, with knowledge of its unlawful purposes, and assume leadership in carrying out its policies and activities; (b) cause to be organized units of the Party in California and elsewhere; (c) write and publish, in the *Daily Worker* and other Party organs, articles on the proscribed advocacy and teaching; (d) conduct schools for the indoctrination of Party members in such advocacy and teaching, and (e) recruit new Party members, particularly from among persons employed in the key industries of the nation. Twenty-three overt acts in furtherance of the conspiracy were alleged.

Upon conviction each of the petitioners was sentenced to five years' imprisonment and a fine of $10,000. The Court of Appeals affirmed. . . . We granted certiorari for the reasons already indicated. . . .

In the view we take of this case, it is necessary for us to consider only the following of petitioners' contentions: (1) that the term "organize" as used in the Smith Act was erroneously construed by the two lower courts; (2) that the trial court's instructions to the jury erroneously excluded from the case the issue of "incitement to action"; (3) that the evidence was so insufficient as to require this Court to direct the acquittal of these petitioners; and (4) that petitioner Schneiderman's conviction was precluded by this Court's judgment in *Schneiderman* v. *United States,* 320 US 118, under the doctrine of collateral estoppel. For reasons given hereafter, we conclude that these convictions must be reversed and the case remanded to the District

Court with instructions to enter judgments of acquittal as to certain of the petitioners, and to grant a new trial as to the rest.

I. *The Term "Organize."*

One object of the conspiracy charged was to violate the third paragraph of 18 U.S.C. § 2385, which provides:

Whoever organizes or helps or attempts to organize any society, group, or assembly of persons who teach, advocate, or encourage the overthrow or destruction of any [government in the United States] by force or violence . . . [s]hall be fined not more than $10,000 or imprisoned not more than ten years, or both. . . .

Petitioners claim that "organize" means to "establish," "found," or "bring into existence," and that in this sense the Communist Party was organized by 1945 at the latest. On this basis petitioners contend that this part of the indictment, returned in 1951, was barred by the three-year statute of limitations. The Government, on the other hand, says that "organize" connotes a continuing process which goes on throughout the life of an organization, and that, in the words of the trial court's instructions to the jury, the term includes such things as "the recruiting of new members and the forming of new units, and the regrouping or expansion of existing clubs, classes and other units of any society, party, group or other organization." The two courts below accepted the Government's position. We think, however, that petitioners' position must prevail, upon principles stated by Chief Justice Marshall more than a century ago in *United States* v. *Wiltberger*, 5 Wheat. 76, as follows:

The rule that penal laws are to be construed strictly, is perhaps not much less old than construction itself. It is founded on the tenderness of the law for the rights of individuals; and on the plain principle that the power of punishment is vested in the legislative, not in the judicial department. It is the legislature, not the Court, which is to define a crime, and ordain its punishment. . . .

The statute does not define what is meant by "organize." Dictionary definitions are of little help, for, as those offered us sufficiently show, the term is susceptible of both meanings attributed to it by the parties here. The fact that the Communist Party comprises various components and activities, in relation to which some of the petitioners bore the title of "Organizer," does not advance us towards a solution of the problem. The charge here is that petitioners conspired to organize the Communist Party, and, unless "organize" embraces the continuing concept contended for by the Government, the establishing of new units within the Party and similar activities, following the Party's initial formation in 1945, have no independent significance or vitality so far as the "organizing" charge is involved. Nor are we here concerned with the quality of petitioners' activities as such, that is, whether particular activities may properly be categorized as "organizational." Rather, the issue is whether the term "organize" as used in this statute is limited by temporal concepts. Stated most simply, the problem is to choose between two possible answers to the question: when was the Communist Party "organized"? Petitioners contend that the only natural answer to the question is the formation date—in this case, 1945. The Government would have us answer the question by saying that the Party today is still not completely "organized"; that "organizing" is a continuing process that does not end until the entity is dissolved.

The legislative history of the Smith Act is no more revealing as to what Congress meant by "organize" than is the statute itself. The Government urges that "organize" should be given a broad meaning since acceptance of the term in its narrow sense would require attributing to Congress the intent that this provision of the statute should not apply to the Communist Party as it then existed. The argument is that since the Communist Party as it then existed had been born in 1919 and the Smith Act was not passed until 1940, the use of "organize" in its narrow sense would have meant that these provisions of the statute would never have reached the act of organizing the Communist Party, except for the fortuitous rebirth of the Party in 1945—an occurrence which, of course, could not have been foreseen in 1940. This, says the Government, could hardly have been the congressional purpose since the Smith Act as a whole was particularly aimed at the Communist Party, and its "organizing" provisions were especially directed at the leaders of the movement.

We find this argument unpersuasive. While the legislative history of the Smith Act does show that concern about communism was a strong factor leading to this legislation, it also reveals that the statute, which was patterned on state anti-sedition laws directed not against Communists but against anarchists and syndicalists, was aimed equally at all groups falling within its scope. More important, there is no evidence whatever to support the thesis that the *organizing* provision of the statute was written with particular reference to the Communist Party. Indeed, the congressional hearings indicate that it was the "advocating and teaching" provision of the Act, rather than the "organizing" provision, which was especially thought to reach Communist activities.

Nor do there appear to be any other reasons for ascribing to "organize" the Government's broad interpretation. While it is understandable that Congress should have wished to supplement the general provisions of the Smith Act by a special provision directed at the activities of those responsible for creating a new organization of the proscribed type, such as was the situation involved in the *Dennis* case, we find nothing which suggests that the "organizing" provision was intended to reach beyond this, that is, to embrace the activities of those concerned with carrying on the affairs of an already existing organization. Such activities were already amply covered by other provisions of the Act, such as the "membership" clause, and the basic prohibition of "advocacy" in conjunction with the conspiracy provision, and there is thus no need to stretch the "organizing" provision to fill any gaps in the statute. Moreover, it is difficult to find any considerations, comparable to those relating to persons responsible for creating a new organization, which would have led the Congress to single out for special treatment those persons occupying so-called organizational positions in an existing organization, especially when this same section of the statute proscribes membership in such an organization without drawing any distinction between those holding executive office and others. . . .

We are thus left to determine for ourselves the meaning of this provision of the Smith Act, without any revealing guides as to the intent of Congress. In these circumstances we should follow the familiar rule that criminal statutes are to be strictly construed and give to "organize" its narrow meaning, that is, that the word refers only to acts entering into the creation of a new organization, and not to acts thereafter performed in carrying on its activities, even though such acts may loosely be termed "organizational." . . . Such indeed is the normal usage of the word "organize," and until the decisions below in this case the federal trial courts in which the question had arisen uniformly gave it that meaning. . . . We too think this statute should be read "according to the natural and obvious import of the language, without resorting to subtle and forced construction for the purpose of either limiting or extending its operation." . . .

We conclude, therefore, that since the Communist Party came into being in 1945, and the indictment was not returned until 1951, the three-year statute of limitations had run on the "organizing" charge, and required the withdrawal of that part of the indictment from the jury's consideration. . . .

II. *Instructions to the Jury.*

Petitioners contend that the instructions to the jury were fatally defective in that the trial court refused to charge that, in order to convict, the jury must find that the advocacy which the defendants conspired to promote was of a kind calculated to "incite" persons to action for the forcible overthrow of the Government. It is argued that advocacy of forcible overthrow as mere *abstract doctrine* is within the free speech protection of the First Amendment; that the Smith Act, consistently with that constitutional provision, must be taken as proscribing only the sort of advocacy which incites to illegal *action;* and that the trial court's charge, by permitting conviction for mere advocacy, unrelated to its tendency to produce forcible action, resulted in an unconstitutional application of the Smith Act. The Government, which at the trial also requested the court to charge in terms of "incitement," now takes the position, however, that the true constitutional dividing line is not between inciting and abstract advocacy of forcible overthrow, but rather between advocacy as such, irrespective of its inciting qualities, and the mere discussion or exposition of violent overthrow as an abstract theory. . . .

After telling the jury that it could not convict the defendants for holding or expressing mere opinions, beliefs, or predictions relating to violent overthrow, the trial court defined the content of the proscribed advocacy or teaching in the following terms, which are crucial here:

Any advocacy or teaching which does not include the urging of force and violence as the means of overthrowing and destroying the Government of the United States is not within the issue of the indictment here and can constitute no basis for any finding against the defendants.

The kind of advocacy and teaching which is charged and upon which your verdict must be reached is not merely a desirability but a necessity that the Government of the United States be overthrown and destroyed by force and violence and not merely a propriety but a duty to overthrow and destroy the Government of the United States by force and violence.

There can be no doubt from the record that in so instructing the jury the court regarded as immaterial, and intended to withdraw from the jury's consideration, any issue as to the character of the advocacy in terms of its capacity to stir listeners to forcible action. Both the petitioners and the Government submitted proposed instructions which would have required the jury to find that the proscribed advocacy was not of a mere abstract doctrine of forcible overthrow, but of action to that end, by the use of language reasonably and ordinarily calculated to incite persons to such action. The trial court rejected these proposed instructions on the ground that any necessity for giving them which may have existed at the time the *Dennis* case was tried was removed by this Court's subsequent decision in that case. The court made it clear in colloquy with counsel that in its view the illegal advocacy was made out simply by showing that what was said dealt with forcible overthrow and that it was uttered with a specific intent to accomplish that purpose, insisting that all such advocacy was punishable "whether in language of incitement or not." The Court of Appeals affirmed on a different theory, as we shall see later on.

We are thus faced with the question whether the Smith Act prohibits advocacy and teaching of forcible overthrow as an abstract principle, divorced from any effort to instigate action to that end, so long as such advocacy or teaching is engaged in with evil intent. We hold that it does not.

The distinction between advocacy of abstract doctrine and advocacy directed at promoting unlawful action is one that has been consistently recognized in the opinions of this Court, beginning with *Fox* v. *Washington,* 236 US 273, and *Schenck* v. *United States,* 249 US 47. This distinction was heavily underscored in *Gitlow* v. *New York,* 268 US 652, in which the statute involved was nearly identical with the one now before us, and where the Court, despite the narrow view there taken of the First Amendment, said:

> The statute does not penalize the utterance or publication of abstract "doctrine" or academic discussion having no quality of incitement to any concrete action. . . . It is not the abstract "doctrine" of overthrowing organized government by unlawful means which is denounced by the statute, but the advocacy of action for the accomplishment of that purpose. . . . This [Manifesto] . . . is [in] the language of direct incitement. . . . That the jury were warranted in finding that the Manifesto advocated not merely the abstract doctrine of overthrowing organized government by force, violence, and unlawful means, but action to that end, is clear. . . . That utterances inciting to the overthrow of organized government by unlawful means, present a sufficient danger of substantive evil to bring their punishment within the range of legislative discretion, is clear. . . .

We need not, however, decide the issue before us in terms of constitutional compulsion, for our first duty is to construe this statute. In doing so we should not assume that Congress chose to disregard a constitutional danger zone so clearly marked, or that it used the words "advocate" and "teach" in their ordinary dictionary meanings when they had already been construed as terms of art carrying a special and limited connotation. . . . The *Gitlow* case and the New York Criminal Anarchy Act there involved, which furnished the prototype for the Smith Act, were both known and adverted to by Congress in the course of the legislative proceedings. . . . The legislative history of the Smith Act and related bills shows beyond all question that Congress was aware of the distinction between the advocacy or teaching of abstract doctrine and the advocacy or teaching of action, and that it did not intend to disregard it. The statute was aimed at the advocacy and teaching of concrete action for the forcible overthrow of the Government, and not of principles divorced from action.

The Government's reliance on this Court's decision in *Dennis* is misplaced. The jury instructions which were refused here were given there, and were referred to by this Court as requiring "the jury to find the facts *essential* to establish the substantive crime." . . . It is true that at one point in the late Chief Justice's opinion it is stated that the Smith Act "is directed at advocacy, not discussion," . . . but it is clear that the reference was to advocacy of action, not ideas, for in the very next sentence the opinion emphasizes that the jury was properly instructed that there could be no conviction for "advocacy in the realm of ideas." The two concurring opinions in that case likewise emphasize the distinction with which we are concerned. . . .

In failing to distinguish between advocacy of forcible overthrow as an abstract doctrine and advocacy of action to that end, the District Court appears to have been led astray by the holding in *Dennis* that advocacy of violent action to be taken at some future time was enough. It seems to have considered that, since "inciting" speech is usually thought of as calculated to induce immediate action, and since *Dennis* held advocacy of action for future overthrow sufficient, this meant that advocacy, irrespective of its tendency to generate action, is punishable, provided only that it is uttered with a specific intent to accomplish overthrow. In other words, the District Court apparently thought that *Dennis* obliterated the traditional dividing line between advocacy of abstract doctrine and advocacy of action.

This misconceives the situation confronting the Court in *Dennis* and what was held there. Although the jury's verdict, interpreted in light of the trial court's instructions, did not justify the conclusion that the defendants' advocacy was directed at, or created any danger of, immediate overthrow, it did establish that the advocacy was aimed at building up a seditious group and maintaining it in readiness for action at a propitious time. In such circumstances, said Chief Justice Vinson, the Government need not hold its hand "until the putsch is about to be executed, the plans have been laid, and the signal is awaited. If Government is aware that a group aiming at its overthrow is attempting to indoctrinate its members and commit them to a course whereby they will strike when the leaders feel the circumstances permit, action by the Government is required." . . . The essence of the *Dennis* holding was that indoctrination of a group in preparation for future violent action, as well as exhortation to immediate action, by advocacy found to be directed to "action for the accomplishment" of forcible overthrow, to violence "as a rule or principle of action," and employing "language of incitement," . . . is not constitutionally protected when the group is of sufficient size and cohesiveness, is sufficiently oriented towards action, and other circumstances are such as reasonably to justify apprehension that action will occur. This is quite a different thing from the view of the District Court here that mere doctrinal justification of forcible overthrow, if engaged in with the intent to accomplish overthrow, is punishable *per se* under the Smith Act. That sort of advocacy, even though uttered with the hope that it may ultimately lead to violent revolution, is too remote from concrete action to be regarded as the kind of indoctrination preparatory to action which was condemned in *Dennis*. As one of the concurring opinions in *Dennis* put it: "Throughout our decisions there has recurred a distinction between the statement of an idea which may prompt its hearers to take unlawful action, and advocacy that such action be taken." . . . There is nothing in *Dennis* which makes that historic distinction obsolete.

The Court of Appeals took a different view from that of the District Court. While seemingly recognizing that the proscribed advocacy must be associated in some way with action, and that the instructions given the jury here fell short in that respect, it considered that the instructions which the trial court refused were unnecessary in this instance because establishment of the conspiracy, here charged under the general conspiracy statute, required proof of an overt act, whereas in *Dennis*, where the conspiracy was charged under the Smith Act, no overt act was required. In other words, the Court of Appeals thought that the requirement of proving an overt act was an adequate substitute for the linking of the advocacy to action which would otherwise have been necessary. This, of course, is a mistaken notion, for the overt act will not necessarily evidence the character of the advocacy engaged in, nor, indeed, is an agreement to advocate forcible overthrow itself an unlawful conspiracy if it does not call for advocacy of action. The statement in *Dennis* that "it is the existence of the conspiracy that creates the danger," . . . does not support the Court of Appeals. Bearing in mind that *Dennis*, like all other Smith Act conspiracy cases thus far, including this one, involved advocacy which had already taken place, and not advocacy still to occur, it is clear that in context the phrase just quoted referred to more than the basic agreement to advocate. "The mere fact that [during the indictment period] petitioners' activities did not result in an attempt to overthrow the Government by force and violence is of course no answer to the fact that there was a group that was *ready to make the attempt*. The formation by petitioners of such a highly organized conspiracy, with rigidly disciplined members subject to call when the leaders, these petitioners, felt that the time had come *for action*, coupled with . . . world conditions, . . . disposes of the contention that a conspiracy to advocate, as distinguished from the advocacy itself, cannot be constitutionally restrained, because it comprises only the preparation. It is the existence of the conspiracy which creates the danger. . . . If the ingredients of the reaction are present, we cannot bind the Government to wait until the catalyst is added." . . . The reference of the term "conspiracy," in context, was to an agreement to *accomplish* overthrow at some future time, implicit in the jury's findings under the instructions given, rather than to an agreement to speak. *Dennis* was thus not concerned with a conspiracy to engage at some future time in seditious advocacy, but rather with a conspiracy to advocate presently the taking of forcible action in the future. It was action, not advocacy, that was to be postponed until "circumstances" would "permit." We intimate no views as to whether a conspiracy to engage in advocacy in the future, where speech would thus be separated from action by one further remove, is punishable under the Smith Act.

We think, thus, that both of the lower courts here misconceived *Dennis*.

In light of the foregoing we are unable to regard the District Court's charge upon this aspect of the case as adequate. The jury was never told that the Smith Act does not denounce advocacy in the sense of preaching abstractly the forcible overthrow of the Government. We think that the trial court's statement that the proscribed advocacy must include the "urging," "necessity," and "duty" of forcible overthrow, and not merely its "desirability" and "propriety," may not be regarded as a sufficient substitute for charging that the Smith Act reaches only advocacy of action for the overthrow of government by force and violence. The essential distinction is that those to whom the advocacy is addressed must be urged to *do* something, now or in the future, rather than merely to *believe* in something. At best the expressions used by the trial court were equivocal, since in the absence of any instructions differentiating advocacy of abstract doctrine from advocacy of action, they were as consistent with the former as they were with the latter. Nor do we regard their ambiguity as lessened by what the trial court had to say as to the right of the defendants to announce their beliefs as to the inevitability of violent revolution, or to advocate other unpopular opinions. Especially when it is unmistakable that the court did not consider the urging of action for forcible overthrow as being a necessary element of the proscribed advocacy, but rather considered the crucial question to be whether the advocacy was uttered with a specific intent to accomplish such overthrow, we would not be warranted in assuming that the jury drew from these instructions more than the court itself intended them to convey.

Nor can we accept the Government's argument that the District Court was justified in not charging more than it did because the refused instructions proposed by both sides specified that the advocacy must be of a character reasonably calculated to "incite" to forcible overthrow, a term which, it is now argued, might have conveyed to the jury an implication that the advocacy must be of immediate action. Granting that some qualification of the proposed instructions would have been permissible to dispel such an implication, and that it was not necessary even that the trial court should have employed the particular term "incite," it was nevertheless incumbent on the court to make clear in some fashion that the advocacy must be of action and not merely abstract doctrine. The instructions given not only do not employ the word "incite," but also avoid the use of such terms and phrases as "action," "call for action," "as a rule or principle of action," and so on, all of which were offered in one form or another by both the petitioners and the Government.

What we find lacking in the instructions here is illustrated by contrasting them with the instructions given to the *Dennis* jury, upon which this Court's sustaining of the convictions in that case was bottomed. There the trial court charged:

> In further construction and interpretation of the statute [the Smith Act] I charge you that it is *not the abstract doctrine* of overthrowing or destroying organized government by unlawful means which is denounced by this law, but the teaching and advocacy *of action* for the accomplishment of that purpose, *by language reasonably and ordinarily calculated to incite persons to such action.* Accordingly, you cannot find the defendants or any of them guilty of the crime charged unless you are satisfied beyond a reasonable doubt that they conspired . . . to advocate and teach the duty and necessity of overthrowing or destroying the Government of the United States by force and violence, with the intent that such teaching and advocacy *be of a rule or principle of action* and *by language reasonably and ordinarily calculated to incite persons to such action,* all with the intent to cause the overthrow . . . as speedily as circumstances would permit. (Emphasis added.) . . .

We recognize that distinctions between advocacy or teaching of abstract doctrines, with evil intent, and that which is directed to stirring people to action, are often subtle and difficult to grasp, for in a broad sense, as Mr. Justice Holmes said in his dissenting opinion in *Gitlow* . . . : "Every idea is an incitement." But the very subtlety of these distinctions required the most clear and explicit instructions with reference to them, for they concerned an issue which went to the very heart of the charges against these petitioners. The need for precise and understandable instructions on this issue is further emphasized by the equivocal character of the evidence in this record, with which we deal in Part III of this opinion. Instances of speech that could be considered to amount to "advocacy of action" are so few and far between as to be almost completely overshadowed by the hundreds of instances in the record in which overthrow, if mentioned at all, occurs in the course of doctrinal disputation so remote from action as to be almost wholly lacking in probative value. Vague references to "revolutionary" or "militant" action of an unspecified character, which are found in the evidence, might in addition be given too great weight by the jury in the absence of more precise instructions. Particularly in light of this record, we must regard the trial court's charge in this respect as furnishing wholly inadequate guidance to the jury on this central point in the case. We cannot allow a conviction to stand on such "an equivocal direction to the jury on a basic issue." . . .

III. *The Evidence.*

The determinations already made require a reversal of these convictions. Nevertheless, in the exercise of our power under 28 U.S.C. § 2106 to "direct the entry of such appropriate judgment . . . as may be just under the circumstances," we have conceived it to be our duty to scrutinize this lengthy record with care, in order to determine whether the way should be left open for a new trial of all or some of these petitioners. Such a judgment, we think, should, on the one hand, foreclose further proceedings against those of the petitioners as to whom the evidence in this record would be palpably insufficient upon a new trial, and should, on the other hand, leave the Government free to retry the other petitioners under proper legal standards, especially since it is by no means clear that certain aspects of the evidence against them could not have been clarified to the advantage of the Government had it not been under a misapprehension as to the burden cast upon it by the Smith Act. In judging the record by these criteria we do not apply to these cases the rigorous standards of review which, for example, the Court of Appeals would be required to apply in reviewing the evidence if any of these petitioners are convicted upon a retrial. . . . Rather, we have scrutinized the record to see whether there are individuals as to whom acquittal is unequivocally demanded. We do this because it is in general too hypothetical and abstract an inquiry to try to judge whether the evidence would have been inadequate had the cases been submitted under a proper charge, and had the Government realized that all its evidence must be channeled into the "advocacy" rather than the "organizing" charge. We think we may do this by drawing on our power under 28 U.S.C. § 2106, because under that statute we would no doubt be justified in refusing to order acquittal even where the evidence might be deemed palpably insufficient, particularly since petitioners have asked in the alternative for a new trial as well as for acquittal. . . .

On this basis we have concluded that the evidence against petitioners Connelly, Kusnitz, Richmond, Spector, and Steinberg is so clearly insufficient that their acquittal should be ordered, but that as to petitioners Carlson, Dobbs, Fox, Healey (Mrs. Connelly), Lambert, Lima, Schneiderman, Stack, and Yates, we would not be justified in closing the way to their retrial. We proceed to the reasons for these conclusions.

At the outset, in view of the conclusions reached in Part I of this opinion, we must put aside as against all petitioners the evidence relating to the "organizing" aspect of the alleged conspiracy, except insofar as it bears upon the "advocacy" charge. That, indeed, dilutes in a substantial way a large part of the evidence, for the record unmistakably indicates that the Government relied heavily on its "organizing" charge. Two further general observations should also be made about the evidence as to the "advocacy" charge. The first is that both the Government and the trial court evidently proceeded on the theory that advocacy of abstract doctrine was enough to offend the Smith Act, whereas, as we have held, it is only advocacy of forcible action that is proscribed. The second observation is that both the record and the Government's brief in this Court make it clear that the Government's thesis was that the Communist Party, or at least the Communist Party of California, constituted the conspiratorial group, and that membership in the conspiracy could therefore be proved by showing that the individual petitioners were actively identified with the Party's affairs and thus inferentially parties to its tenets. This might have been well enough towards making out the Government's case if advocacy of the abstract doctrine of forcible overthrow satisfied the Smith Act, for we would at least have little difficulty in saying on this record that a jury could justifiably conclude that such was one of the tenets of the Communist Party; and there was no dispute as to petitioners' active identification with Party affairs. But when it comes to Party advocacy or teaching in the sense of a call to forcible action at some future time we cannot but regard this record as strikingly deficient. At best this voluminous record shows but a half dozen or so scattered incidents which, even under the loosest standards, could be deemed to show such advocacy. Most of these were not connected with any of the petitioners, or occurred many years before the period covered by the indictment. We are unable to regard this sporadic showing as sufficient to justify viewing the Communist Party as the nexus between these petitioners and the conspiracy charged. We need scarcely say that however much one may abhor even the abstract preaching of forcible overthrow of government, or believe that forcible overthrow is the ultimate purpose to which the Communist Party is dedicated, it is upon the evidence in the record that the petitioners must be judged in this case.

We must, then, look elsewhere than to the evidence concerning the Communist Party as such for the existence of the conspiracy to advocate charged in the indictment. As to the petitioners Connelly, Kusnitz, Richmond, Spector, and Steinberg we find no adequate evidence in the record which would permit a jury to find that they were members of such a conspiracy. For all purposes relevant here, the sole evidence as to them was that they had long been members, officers or functionaries of the Communist Party of California; and that standing alone, as Congress has enacted in § 4 (f) of the Internal Security Act of 1950, makes out no case against them. So far as this record shows, none of them has engaged in or been associated with any but what appear to have been wholly lawful activities, or has ever made a single remark or been present when someone else made a remark, which would tend to prove the charges against them. Connelly and Richmond were, to be sure, the Los Angeles and Executive Editors, respectively, of the *Daily People's World,* the West Coast Party organ, but we can find nothing in the material introduced into evidence from that newspaper which advances the Government's case.

Moreover, apart from the inadequacy of the evidence to show, at best, more than the abstract advocacy and teaching of forcible overthrow by the Party, it is difficult to perceive how the requisite specific intent to accomplish such overthrow could be deemed proved by a showing of mere membership or the holding of office in the Communist Party. We therefore think that as to these petitioners the evidence was entirely too meagre to justify putting them to a new trial, and that their acquittal should be ordered.

As to the nine remaining petitioners, we consider that a different conclusion should be reached. There was testimony from the witness Foard, and other evidence, tying Fox, Healey, Lambert, Lima, Schneiderman, Stack, and Yates to Party classes conducted in the San Francisco area during the year 1946, where there occurred what might be considered to be the systematic teaching and advocacy of illegal action which is condemned by the statute. It might be found that one of the purposes of such classes was to develop in the members of the group a readiness to engage at the crucial time, perhaps during war or during attack upon the United States from without, in such activities as sabotage and street fighting, in order to divert and diffuse the resistance of the authorities and if possible to seize local vantage points. There was also testimony as to activities in the Los Angeles area, during the period covered by the indictment, which might be considered to amount to "advocacy of action," and with which petitioners Carlson and Dobbs were linked. From the testimony of the witness Scarletto, it might be found that individuals considered to be particularly trustworthy were taken into an "underground" apparatus and there instructed in tasks which would be useful when the time for violent action arrived. Scarletto was surreptitiously indoctrinated in methods, as he said, of moving "masses of people in time of crisis." It might be found, under all the circumstances, that the purpose of this teaching was to prepare the members of the underground apparatus to engage in, to facilitate, and to cooperate with violent action directed against government when the time was ripe. In short, while the record contains evidence of little more than a general program of educational activity by the Communist Party which included advocacy of violence as a theoretical matter, we are not prepared to say, at this stage of the case, that it would be impossible for a jury, resolving all conflicts in favor of the Government and giving the evidence as to these San Francisco and Los Angeles episodes its upmost sweep, to find that advocacy of action was also engaged in when the group involved was thought particularly trustworthy, dedicated, and suited for violent tasks.

Nor can we say that the evidence linking these nine petitioners to that sort of advocacy, with the requisite specific intent, is so tenuous as not to justify their retrial under proper legal standards. Fox, Healey, Lambert, Lima, Schneiderman, Stack, and Yates, as members of the State and San Francisco County Boards, were shown to have been closely associated with Ida Rothstein, the principal teacher of the San Francisco classes, who also during this same period arranged in a devious and conspiratorial manner for the holding of Board meetings at the home of the witness Honig, which were attended by these petitioners. It was also shown that from time to time instructions emanated from the Boards or their members to instructors of groups at lower levels. And while none of the written instructions produced at the trial were invidious in themselves, it might be inferred that additional instructions were given which were not reduced to writing. Similarly, there was evidence of close association between petitioners Carlson and Dobbs and associates or superiors of the witness Scarletto, which might be taken as indicating that these two petitioners had knowledge of the apparatus in which

Scarletto was active. And finally, all of these nine petitioners were shown either to have made statements themselves, or apparently approved statements made in their presence, which a jury might take as some evidence of their participation with the requisite intent in a conspiracy to advocate illegal action.

As to these nine petitioners, then, we shall not order an acquittal.

Before leaving the evidence, we consider it advisable, in order to avoid possible misapprehension upon a new trial, to deal briefly with petitioners' contention that the evidence was insufficient to prove the overt act required for conviction of conspiracy under 18 U.S.C. § 371. Only 2 of the 11 overt acts alleged in the indictment to have occurred within the period of the statute of limitations were proved. Each was a public meeting held under Party auspices at which speeches were made by one or more of the petitioners extolling leaders of the Soviet Union and criticizing various aspects of the foreign policy of the United States. At one of the meetings an appeal for funds was made. Petitioners contend that these meetings do not satisfy the requirement of the statute that there be shown an act done by one of the conspirators "to effect the object of the conspiracy." The Government concedes that nothing unlawful was shown to have been said or done at these meetings, but contends that these occurrences nonetheless sufficed as overt acts under the jury's findings.

We think the Government's position is correct. It is not necessary that an overt act be the substantive crime charged in the indictment as the object of the conspiracy. . . . Nor, indeed, need such an act, taken by itself, even be criminal in character. . . . The function of the overt act in a conspiracy prosecution is simply to manifest "that the conspiracy is at work," . . . and is neither a project still resting solely in the minds of the conspirators nor a fully completed operation no longer in existence. The substantive offense here charged as the object of the conspiracy is speech rather than the specific action that typically constitutes the gravamen of a substantive criminal offense. Were we to hold that some concrete action leading to the overthrow of the Government was required, as petitioners appear to suggest, we would have changed the nature of the offense altogether. No such drastic change in the law can be drawn from Congress' perfunctory action in 1948 bringing Smith Act cases within 18 U.S.C. § 371.

While upon a new trial the overt act must be found, in view of what we have held, to have been in furtherance of a conspiracy to "advocate," rather than to "organize," we are not prepared to say that one of the episodes relied on here could not be found to be in furtherance of such an objective, if, under proper instructions, a jury should find that the Communist Party was a vehicle through which the alleged conspiracy was promoted. While in view of our acquittal of Steinberg, the first of these episodes, in which he is alleged to have been involved, may no longer be relied on as an overt act, this would not affect the second episode, in which petitioner Schneiderman was alleged and proved to have participated.

For the foregoing reasons we think that the way must be left open for a new trial to the extent indicated.

IV. *Collateral Estoppel.*

There remains to be dealt with petitioner Schneiderman's claim based on the doctrine of collateral estoppel by judgment. Petitioner urges that in *Schneiderman* v. *United States,* 320 US 118, a denaturalization proceeding in which he was the prevailing party, this Court made determinations favorable to him which are conclusive in this proceeding under the doctrine of collateral estoppel. Specifically, petitioner contends that the *Schneiderman* decision determined, for purposes of this proceeding, (1) that the teaching of Marxism-Leninism by the Communist Party was not necessarily the advocacy of violent overthrow of government; (2) that at least one tenable conclusion to be drawn from the evidence was that the Communist Party desired to achieve its goal of socialism through peaceful means; (3) that it could not be presumed, merely because of his membership or officership in the Communist Party, that Schneiderman adopted an illegal interpretation of Marxist doctrine; and finally, (4) that absent proof of overt acts indicating that Schneiderman personally adopted a reprehensible interpretation, the Government had failed to establish its burden by the clear and unequivocal evidence necessary in a denaturalization case. In the courts below, petitioner urged unsuccessfully that these determinations were conclusive in this proceeding under the doctrine of collateral estoppel, and entitled him either to an acquittal or to special instructions to the jury. He makes the same contentions here.

We are in agreement with petitioner that the doctrine of collateral estoppel is not made inapplicable by the fact that this is a criminal case, whereas the prior proceedings were civil in character. . . . We agree further that the nonexistence of a fact may be established by a judgment no less than its existence; that, in other words, a party may be precluded under the doctrine of collateral estoppel from attempting a second time to prove a fact that he sought unsuccessfully to prove in a prior action. . . . Nor need we quarrel with petitioner's premise that the standard of proof applicable in denaturalization cases is at least no greater than that applicable in criminal proceedings. . . . We assume, without deciding, that substantially the same standards of proof are applicable in the two types of cases. . . . Nevertheless, for reasons that will appear, we think that the doctrine of collateral estoppel does not help petitioner here.

We differ with petitioner, first of all, in his estimate of what the *Schneiderman* case determined for purposes of the doctrine of collateral estoppel. That doctrine makes conclusive in subsequent proceedings only determinations of fact, and mixed fact and law, that were essential to the decision. . . . As we read the *Schneiderman* opinion, the only determination essential to the decision was that Schneiderman had not, prior to 1927, adopted an interpretation of the Communist Party's teachings featuring "agitation and exhortation calling for present violent action." . . . If it be accepted that the holding extended in the alternative to the character of advocacy engaged in by the Communist Party, then the essential finding was that the Party had not, in 1927, engaged in "agitation and exhortation calling for present violent action." The Court in *Schneiderman* certainly did not purport to determine what the doctrinal content of "Marxism-Leninism" might be at all times and in all places. Nor did it establish that the books and pamphlets introduced against Schneiderman in that proceeding could not support in any way an inference of criminality, no matter how or by whom they might thereafter be used. At most, we think, it made the determinations we have stated, limited to the time and place that were then in issue.

It is therefore apparent that the determinations made by this Court in *Schneiderman* could not operate as a complete bar to this proceeding. Wholly aside from the fact that the Court was there concerned with the state of affairs existing in 1927, whereas we are concerned here with the period 1948–1951, the issues in the present case are quite different. We are not concerned here with whether petitioner has engaged in "agitation and exhortation calling for present violent action," whether in 1927 or later. Even if it were conclusively established against the Government that neither petitioner nor the Communist Party had ever engaged in such advocacy, that circumstance would constitute no bar to a conviction under 18 U.S.C. § 371 of conspiring to advocate forcible overthrow of government in violation of the Smith Act. It is not necessary for conviction here that advocacy of "present violent action" be proved. Petitioner's demand for judgment of acquittal must therefore be rejected. . . .

Mr. Justice Black, with whom Mr. Justice Douglas joins, concurring in part and dissenting in part:

I.

I would reverse every one of these convictions and direct that all the defendants be acquitted. In my judgment the statutory provisions on which these prosecutions are based abridge freedom of speech, press and assembly in violation of the First Amendment to the United States Constitution. . . .

The kind of trials conducted here are wholly dissimilar to normal criminal trials. Ordinarily these "Smith Act" trials are prolonged affairs lasting for months. In part this is attributable to the routine introduction in evidence of massive collections of books, tracts, pamphlets, newspapers, and manifestoes discussing Communism, Socialism, Capitalism, Feudalism and governmental institutions in general, which, it is not too much to say, are turgid, diffuse, abstruse, and just plain dull. Of course, no juror can or is expected to plow his way through this jungle of verbiage. The testimony of witnesses is comparatively insignificant. Guilt or innocence may turn on what Marx or Engels or someone else wrote or advocated as much as a hundred or more years ago. Elaborate, refined distinctions are drawn between "Communism," "Marxism," "Leninism," "Trotskyism," and "Stalinism." When the propriety of obnoxious or unorthodox views about government is in reality made the crucial issue, as it must be in cases of this kind, prejudice makes conviction inevitable except in the rarest circumstances.

II.

Since the Court proceeds on the assumption that the statutory provisions involved are valid, however, I feel free to express my views about the issues it considers.

First.—I agree with Part I of the Court's opinion that deals with the statutory term, "organize," and holds that the organizing charge in the indictment was barred by the three-year statute of limitations.

Second.—I also agree with the Court insofar as it holds that the trial judge erred in instructing that persons could be punished under the Smith Act for teaching and advocating forceful overthrow as an abstract principle. But on the other hand, I cannot agree that the instruction which the Court indicates it might approve is constitutionally permissible. The Court says that persons can be punished for advocating action to overthrow the Government by force and violence, where those to whom the advocacy is addressed are urged "to *do* something, now or in the future, rather than merely to *believe* in something." Under the Court's approach, defendants could still be convicted simply for agreeing to talk as distinguished from agreeing to act. I believe that the First Amendment forbids Congress to punish people for talking about public affairs, whether or not such discussion incites to action, legal or illegal. . . . As the Virginia Assembly said in 1785, in its "Statute for Religious Liberty," written by Thomas Jefferson, "it is time enough for the rightful purposes of civil government, for its officers to interfere when principles break out into overt acts against peace and good order. . . ."

Third.—I also agree with the Court that petitioners, Connelly, Kusnitz, Richmond, Spector, and Steinberg, should be ordered acquitted since there is no evidence that they have ever engaged in anything but "wholly lawful activities." But in contrast to the Court, I think the same action should also be taken as to the remaining nine defendants. The Court's opinion summarizes the strongest evidence offered against these defendants. This summary reveals a pitiful inadequacy of proof to show beyond a reasonable doubt that the defendants were guilty of conspiring to incite persons to act to overthrow the Government. The Court says:

> In short, while the record contains evidence of little more than a general program of educational activity by the Communist Party which included advocacy of violence as a theoretical matter, we are not prepared to say, at this stage of the case, that it would be impossible for a jury, resolving all conflicts in favor of the Government and giving the evidence as to these San Francisco and Los Angeles episodes its utmost sweep, to find that advocacy of action was also engaged in when the group involved was thought particularly trustworthy, dedicated, and suited for violent tasks.

It seems unjust to compel these nine defendants, who have just been through one four-month trial, to go through the ordeal of another trial on the basis of such flimsy evidence. As the Court's summary demonstrates, the evidence introduced during the trial against these defendants was insufficient to support their conviction. Under such circumstances, it was the duty of the trial judge to direct a verdict of acquittal. If the jury had been discharged so that the Government could gather additional evidence in an attempt to convict, such a discharge would have been a sound basis for a plea of former jeopardy in a second trial. . . . I cannot agree that "justice" requires this Court to send these cases back to put these defendants in jeopardy again in violation of the spirit if not the letter of the Fifth Admendment's provision against double jeopardy.

Fourth.—The section under which this conspiracy indictment was brought, 18 U.S.C. § 371, requires proof of an overt act done "to effect the object of the conspiracy." Originally, 11 such overt acts were charged here. These 11 have now dwindled to 2, and as the Court says:

> Each was a public meeting held under Party auspices at which speeches were made by one or more of the petitioners extolling leaders of the Soviet Union and criticizing various aspects of the foreign policy of the United States. At one of the meetings an appeal for funds was made. Petitioners contend that these meetings do not satisfy the requirement of the statute that there be shown an act done by one of the conspirators "to effect the object of the conspiracy." The Government concedes that nothing unlawful was shown to have been said or done at these meetings, but contends that these occurrences nevertheless suffice as overt acts under the jury's findings.

The Court holds that attendance at these lawful and orderly meetings constitutes an "overt act" sufficient to meet the statutory requirements. I disagree.

The requirement of proof of an overt act in conspiracy cases is no mere formality, particularly in prosecutions like these which in many respects are akin to trials for treason. Article III, § 3, of the Constitution provides that "No Person shall be convicted of Treason unless on the Testimony of two witnesses to the same overt Act, or on Confession in open Court." One of the objects of this provision was to keep people from being convicted of disloyalty to government during periods of excitement when passions and prejudices ran high, merely because they expressed "unacceptable" views. . . . The same reasons that make proof of overt acts so important in treason cases apply here. The only overt act which is now charged against these defendants is that they went to a constitutionally protected public assembly where they took part in lawful discussion of public questions, and where neither they nor anyone else advocated or suggested overthrow of the United States Government. Many years ago this Court said that "The very idea of a government, republican in form, implies a right on the part of its citizens to meet peaceably for consultation in respect to public affairs and to petition for a redress of grievances. . . ." In my judgment defendants' attendance at these public meetings cannot be viewed as an overt act to effectuate the object of the conspiracy charged.

III.

In essence, petitioners were tried upon the charge that they believe in and want to foist upon this country a different and to us a despicable form of authoritarian government in which voices criticizing the existing order are summarily silenced. I fear that the present type of prosecutions are more in line with the philosophy of authoritarian government than with that expressed by our First Amendment.

Doubtlessly, dictators have to stamp out causes and beliefs which they deem subversive to their evil regimes. But governmental suppression of causes and beliefs seems to me to be the very antithesis of what our Constitution stands for. The choice expressed in the First Amendment in favor of free expression was made against a turbulent background by men such as Jefferson, Madison, and Mason—men who believed that loyalty to the provisions of this Amendment was the best way to assure a long life for this new nation and its Government. Unless there is complete freedom for expression of all ideas, whether we like them or not, concerning the way government should be run and who shall run it, I doubt if any views in the long run can be secured against the censor. The First Amendment provides the only kind of security system that can preserve a free government—one that leaves the way wide open for people to favor, discuss, advocate, or incite causes and doctrines however obnoxious and antagonistic such views may be to the rest of us.

SCALES v. UNITED STATES

367 US 203 (1961)

[In the *Dennis* and *Yates* cases, *supra*, the Supreme Court had before it the conspiracy provisions of the Smith Act. In the present case, as well as in the *Noto Case*, immediately following, the Court had before it the membership clause of the Smith Act. By a 5-to-4 decision the Court upheld a conviction under the membership clause, which the Court interpreted as requiring proof of "active," as distinguished from mere "nominal" or "passive," membership in the Communist Party. Justice Brennan wrote a dissenting opinion, in which he was joined by Chief Justice Warren and Justice Douglas. Justices Black and Douglas wrote separate dissenting opinions.]

Mr. Justice Harlan delivered the opinion of the Court:

Our writ issued in this case to review a judgment of the Court of Appeals (260 F. 2d 21) affirming petitioner's conviction under the so-called membership clause of the Smith Act. 18 U.S.C. § 2385. The Act, among other things, makes a felony the acquisition or holding of knowing membership in any organization which advocates the overthrow of the Government of the United States by force or violence. The indictment charged that from January 1946 to the date of its filing (November 18, 1954) the Communist Party of the United States was such an organization, and that petitioner throughout that period was a member thereof, with knowledge of the Party's illegal purpose and a specific intent to accomplish overthrow "as speedily as circumstances would permit."

The validity of this conviction is challenged on statutory, constitutional, and evidentiary grounds, and further on the basis of certain alleged trial and procedural errors. We decide the issues raised upon the fullest consideration, the case having had an unusually long history in this Court. For reasons given in this opinion we affirm the Court of Appeals.

I. *Statutory Challenge.*

Petitioner contends that the indictment fails to state an offense against the United States. The claim is that § 4 (f) of Internal Security Act of 1950 constitutes a *pro tanto* repeal of the membership clause of the Smith Act by excluding from the reach of that clause membership in any Communist organization. Section 4 (f) provides:

Neither the holding of office nor membership in any Communist organization by any person shall constitute per se a violation of subsection (a) or subsection (c) of this section or of any other criminal statute. The fact of the registration of any person under section 7 or section 8 of this title as an officer or member of any Communist organization shall not be received in evidence against such person in any prosecution for any alleged violation of subsection (a) or subsection (c) of this section or for any alleged violation of any other criminal statute.

To prevail in his contention petitioner must, of course, bring himself within the first sentence of this provision, since the second sentence manifestly refers only to exclusion from evidence of the fact of registration, thus assuming that a prosecution may take place.

We turn first to the provision itself, and find that, as to petitioner's construction of it, the language is at best ambiguous if not suggestive of a contrary conclusion. Section 4 (f) provides that membership or office-holding in a Communist organization shall not constitute "per se a violation of subsection (a) or subsection (c) of this section or any other criminal statute." Petitioner would most plainly be correct if the statute under which he was indicted purported to proscribe membership in Communist organizations, as such, and to punish membership *per se* in an organization engaging in proscribed advocacy. But the membership clause of the Smith Act on its face, must less as we construe it in this case, does not do this, for it neither proscribes membership in Communist organizations, as such, but only in organizations engaging in advocacy of violent overthrow, nor punishes membership in that kind of organization except as to one "knowing the purposes thereof," and, as we have interpreted the clause, with a specific intent to further those purposes. We have also held that the proscribed membership must be active, and not nominal, passive or theoretical. Thus the words of the first sentence of § 4 (f) by no means unequivocally demand the result for which petitioner argues. When we turn from those words to their context, both in the section as a whole and in the scheme of the Act of which they are a part, whatever ambiguity there may be must be resolved, in our view, against the petitioner's contention.

In the context of § 4 as a whole, the first sentence of subsection (f) does not appear to be a provision repealing in whole or in part any other provision of the Internal Security Act. Subsection (a) of § 4 makes it a crime

for any person knowingly to combine, conspire, or agree with any other person to perform any act which would substantially contribute to the establishment within the United States of a totalitarian dictatorship . . . the direction and control of which is to be vested in, or exercised by or under the domination or control of, any foreign government, foreign organization or foreign individual. . . .

Subsection (c) makes it a crime for any officer or member of a "Communist organization" to obtain classified information. We should hesitate long before holding that subsection (f) operates to repeal *pro tanto* either one of these provisions which are found in the same section of which subsection (f) is a part; and indeed the petitioner does not argue for any such quixotic result. The natural tendency of the first sentence of subsection (f) as to the criminal provisions specifically mentioned is to provide clarification of the meaning of those provisions, that is, that an offense is not made out on proof of *mere* membership in a Communist organization. As to these particularly mentioned criminal provisions immunity, such as there is, is specifically granted in the second sentence only, where it is said that the fact of registration shall not be admitted in evidence. Yet petitioner argues that when we come to the last phrase of the first sentence, the tag "or . . . any other criminal statute," the operative part of the sentence, "membership . . . shall [not] constitute per se a violation," has an altogether different purport and effect. What operated as a clarification and guide to construction to the specifically identified provisions is, petitioner argues, a partial repealer as to the statutes referred to in the omnibus clause at the end of the sentence.

It seems apparent from the foregoing that the language of § 4 (f) in its natural import and context should not be taken to immunize members of Communist organizations from the membership clause of the Smith Act, but rather as a mandate to the courts charged with the construction of subsections (a) and (c) "or . . . any other criminal statute" that neither those two named criminal provisions nor any other shall be *construed* so as to make "membership" in a Communist organization "per se a violation." Indeed, as we read the first sentence of § 4 (f), even if the membership clause of the Smith Act could be taken as punishing naked Communist Party membership, it would then be our duty under § 4 (f) to construe it in accordance with that mandate, certainly not to strike it down. Although we think that the membership clause on its face goes beyond making mere Party membership a violation, in that it requires a showing both of illegal Party purposes and of a member's knowledge of such purposes, we regard the first sentence of § 4 (f) as a clear warrant for construing the clause as requiring not only knowing membership, but active and purposive membership, purposive that is as to the organization's criminal ends. By its terms, then, subsection (f) does not effect a *pro tanto* repeal of the membership clause; at most it modifies it.

Petitioner argues that if the § 4 (f) provision does not bar this prosecution under the membership clause, then the phrase "or of any other criminal statute" becomes meaningless, for there is no other federal criminal statute that makes this sort of membership a crime. But the argument assumes the answer. The first sentence was intended to clarify, not repeal § 4 (a) of the Internal Security Act. By a parity of reasoning, its effect on "any other criminal statute" is also clarification, not repeal.

Petitioner's contentions do not stop, however, with the words of § 4 (f) itself. The supposed partial repeal of the membership clause by that provision, it is claimed, is a consequence of the latter's purpose in the whole scheme of the Internal Security Act of 1950, as illuminated by its legislative history. The argument runs as follows: The core of the Internal Security Act is its registration provisions (§§ 7 and 8), requiring disclosure of membership in the Communist Party following a valid final determination of the Subversive Activities Control Board as to the status of the Party. The registration requirement would be rendered nugatory by a plea of self-incrimination and could only be saved by a valid grant of immunity from prosecution by reason of any such disclosure. However, the immunity provided by the second sentence of § 4 (f) is insufficient, in that it forbids only the use of the "fact of . . . registration" as evidence in any future prosecution, and not also its employment as a "lead" to other evidence. . . . Therefore to effectuate the congressional purpose it becomes necessary to consider the first sentence of § 4 (f) a *pro tanto* repealer of the membership clause of the Smith Act, thereby assuring effective immunity from the criminal consequences of registration in this instance.

Although this Court will often strain to construe legislation so as to save it against constitutional attack, it must not and will not carry this to the point of perverting the purpose of a statute. Certainly the section before us cannot be construed as petitioner argues. The fact of registration may provide a significant investigatory lead not only in prosecutions under the membership clause of the Smith Act, but equally probably to prosecutions under § 4 (a) of the Internal Security Act, let alone § 4 (c). Thus, if we accepted petitioner's argument that § 4 (f) must be read as a partial repealer of the membership clause, we would be led to the extraordinary conclusion that Congress also intended to immunize under § 4 (f) what it prohibited in these other subsections which it passed at the same time. Furthermore, the thrust of petitioner's argument cannot be limited to the membership clause, for it is equally applicable to any prosecution under any of a host of criminal provisions where Communist Party membership might provide an investigatory lead as to the elements of the crime. We cannot attribute any such sweeping purpose to Congress on the basis of the attenuated inference offered by petitioner.

Presented as we are with every indication in the statute itself that Congress had no purpose to bar a prosecution such as this, we turn to the legislative history of the Internal Security Act of 1950 to see if a different conclusion is indicated. . . .

The legislative history of § 4 (f), . . . far from weakening the conclusion flowing from analysis of the terms of the statute itself, fortifies that analysis at every point. To conclude that Congress' desire to protect the registration provisions of the Internal Security Act against pleas of self-incrimination should prevail over its advertent failure to assure that result at the expense of wiping out the membership clause of the Smith Act, as applied to Communists, would require a disregard by this Court of the evident congressional purpose. Whatever may be the consequences of that failure upon the Internal Security Act we are concerned here solely with the question whether Congress by § 4 (f) intended a partial repeal of the membership clause of the Smith Act. We conclude that it did not and hold that this prosecution is not barred by § 4 (f) of the Internal Security Act of 1950.

II. *Constitutional Challenge to the Membership Clause on its Face.*

Petitioner's constitutional attack goes both to the statute on its face and as applied. At this point we deal with the first aspect of the challenge and with one part of its second aspect. The balance of the latter, which essentially concerns the sufficiency of the evidence, is discussed in the next section of this opinion.

It will bring the constitutional issues into clearer forcus to notice first the premises on which the case was submitted to the jury. The jury was instructed that in order to convict it must find that within the three-year limitations period (1) the Communist Party advocated the violent overthrow of the Government, in the sense of present "advocacy of action" to accomplish that end as soon as circumstances were propitious; and (2) petitioner was an "active" member of the Party, and not merely "a nominal, passive, inactive or purely technical" member, with knowledge of the Party's illegal advocacy and a specific intent to bring about violent overthrow "as speedily as circumstances would permit."

The constitutional attack upon the membership clause, as thus construed, is that the statute offends (1) the Fifth Amendment, in that it impermissibly imputes guilt to an individual merely on the basis of his associations and sympathies, rather than because of some concrete personal involvement in criminal conduct; and (2) the First Amendment, in that it infringes free political expression and association. Subsidiarily, it is argued that the statute cannot be interpreted as including a requirement of a specific intent to accomplish violent overthrow, or as requiring that membership in a proscribed organization must be "active" membership, in the absence of both or either of which it is said the statute becomes *a fortiori* unconstitutional. It is further contended that even if the adjective "active" may properly be implied as a qualification upon the term "member," petitioner's conviction would nonetheless be unconstitutional, because so construed the statute would be impermissibly vague under the Fifth and Sixth Amendments, and so applied would in any event infringe the Sixth Amendment, in that the indictment charged only that Scales was a "member," not an "active" member, of the Communist Party.

1. *Statutory Construction.*

Before reaching petitioner's constitutional claims, we should first ascertain whether the membership clause permissibly bears the construction put upon it below. We think it does.

The trial court's definition of the kind of organizational advocacy that is proscribed was fully in accord with what was held in *Yates* v. *United States,* 354 U.S. 298. And the statute itself requires that a defendant must have knowledge of the organization's illegal advocacy.

The only two elements of the crime, as defined below, about which there is controversy are therefore "specific intent" and "active" membership. As to the former, this Court held in *Dennis* v. *United States,* 341 U.S. 494, that even though the "advocacy" and "organizing" provisions of the Smith Act, unlike the "literature" section did not expressly contain such a specific intent element, such a requirement was fairly to be implied. We think that the reasoning of *Dennis* applies equally to the membership clause, and are left unpersuaded by the distinctions petitioner seeks to draw between this clause and the advocacy and organizing provisions of the Smith Act.

We find hardly greater difficulty in interpreting the membership clause to reach only "active" members. We decline to attribute to Congress a purpose to punish nominal membership, even though accompanied by "knowledge" and "intent," not merely because of the close constitutional questions that such a purpose would raise . . . but also for two other reasons: It is not to be lightly inferred that Congress intended to visit upon mere passive members the heavy penalties imposed by the Smith Act. Nor can we assume that it was Congress' purpose to allow the quality of the punishable membership to be measured solely by the varying standards of that relationship as subjectively viewed by different organizations. It is more reasonable to believe that Congress contemplated an objective standard fixed by the law itself, thereby assuring an even-handed application of the statute. . . .

Petitioner's particular constitutional objections to this construction are misconceived. The indictment was not defective in failing to charge that Scales was an "active" member of the Party, for that factor was not in itself a discrete element of the crime, but an inherent quality of the membership element. As such it was a matter not for the indictment, but for elucidating instructions to the jury on what the term "member" in the statute meant. Nor do we think that the objection on the score of vagueness is a tenable one. The distinction between "active" and "nominal" membership is well understood in common parlance . . . and the point at which one shades into the other is something that goes not to the sufficiency of the statute, but to the adequacy of the trial court's guidance to the jury by way of instructions in a particular case. Moreover, whatever abstract doubts might exist on the matter, this case presents no such problem. For petitioner's actions on behalf of the Communist Party most certainly amounted to active membership by whatever standards one could reasonably anticipate, and he can therefore hardly be considered to have acted unadvisedly on this score.

We find no substance in the further suggestion that petitioner could not be expected to anticipate a construction of the statute that included within its elements activity and specific intent, and hence that he was not duly warned of what the statute made criminal. It is, of course, clear that the lower courts' construction was narrower, not broader, than the one for which petitioner argues in defining the character of the forbidden conduct and that therefore, according to petitioner's own construction, his actions were forbidden by the statute. The contention must then be that petitioner had a right to rely on the statute, as *he* construed it, being held unconstitutional. Assuming, *arguendo*, that petitioner's construction was not unreasonable, no more can be said than that—in light of the courts' traditional avoidance of constructions of dubious constitutionality and in light of their role in construing the purpose of a statute—there were two ways one could reasonably anticipate this statute being construed, and that petitioner had clear warning that his actions were in violation of both constructions. There is no additional constitutional requirement that petitioner should be entitled to rely upon the statute being construed in such a way as possibly to render it unconstitutional. In sum, this argument of a "right" to a literal construction simply boils down to a claim that the view of the statute taken below did violence to the congressional purpose. Of course a litigant is always prejudiced when a court errs, but whether or not the lower courts erred in their construction is an issue which can only be met on its merits, and not by reference to a "right" to a particular interpretation.

We hold that the statute was correctly interpreted by the two lower courts, and now turn to petitioner's basic constitutional challenge.

2. *Fifth Amendment.*

In our jurisprudence guilt is personal, and when the imposition of punishment on a status or on conduct can only be justified by reference to the relationship of that status or conduct to other concededly criminal activity (here advocacy of violent overthrow), that relationship must be sufficiently substantial to satisfy the concept of personal guilt in order to withstand attack under the Due Process Clause of the Fifth Amendment. Membership, without more, in an organization engaged in illegal advocacy, it is now said, has not heretofore been recognized by this Court to be such a relationship. This claim stands, and we shall examine it, independently of that made under the First Amendment.

Any thought that due process puts beyond the reach of the criminal law all individual associational relationships, unless accompanied by the commission of specific acts of criminality, is dispelled by familiar concepts of the law of conspiracy and complicity. While both are commonplace in the landscape of the criminal law, they are not natural features. Rather they are particular legal concepts manifesting the more general principle that society, having the power to punish dangerous behavior, cannot be powerless against those who work to bring about that behavior. The fact that Congress has not resorted to either of these familiar concepts means only that the enquiry here must direct itself to an analysis of the relationship between the fact of membership and the underlying substantive illegal conduct, in order to determine whether that relationship is indeed too tenuous to permit its use as the basis of criminal liability. In this instance it is an organization which engages in criminal activity, and we can perceive no reason why one who actively and knowingly works in the ranks of that organization, intending to contribute to the success of those specifically illegal activities, should be any more immune from prosecution than he to whom the organization has assigned the task of carrying out the substantive criminal act. Nor should the fact that Congress has focussed here on "membership," the characteristic relationship between an individual and the type of conspiratorial quasi-political associations with the criminal aspect of whose activities Congress was concerned, of itself require the conclusion that the legislature has traveled outside the familiar and permissible bounds of criminal imputability. In truth, the specificity of the proscribed relationship is not necessarily a vice; it provides instruction and warning.

What must be met, then, is the argument that membership, even when accompanied by the elements of knowledge and specific intent, affords an insufficient quantum of participation in the organization's alleged criminal activity, that is, an insufficiently significant form of aid and encouragement to permit the imposition of criminal sanctions on that basis. It must indeed be recognized that a person who merely becomes a member of an illegal organization, by that "act" alone need be doing nothing more than signifying his assent to its purposes and activities on one hand, and providing, on the other, only the sort of moral encouragement which comes from the knowledge that others believe in what the organization is doing. It may indeed be argued that such assent and encouragement do fall short of the concrete, practical impetus given to a criminal enterprise which is lent for instance by a commitment on the part of a conspirator to act in furtherance of that enterprise. A member, as distinguished from a conspirator, may indicate his approval of a criminal enterprise by the very fact of his membership without thereby necessarily committing himself to further it by any act or course of conduct whatever.

In an area of the criminal law which this Court has indicated more than once demands its watchful scrutiny . . . these factors have weight and must be found to be overborne in a total constitutional assessment of the statute. We think, however, they are duly met when the statute is found to reach only "active" members having also a guilty knowledge and intent, and which therefore prevents a conviction on what otherwise might be regarded as merely an expression of sympathy with the alleged criminal enterprise, unaccompanied by any significant action in its support or any commitment to undertake such action.

Thus, given the construction of the membership clause already discussed, we think the factors called for in rendering members criminally responsible for the illegal advocacy of the organization fall within established, and therefore presumably constitutional standards of criminal imputability.

3. First Amendment.

Little remains to be said concerning the claim that the statute infringes First Amendment freedoms. It was settled in *Dennis* that the advocacy with which we are here concerned is not constitutionally protected speech, and it was further established that a combination to promote such advocacy, albeit under the aegis of what purports to be a political party, is not such association as is protected by the First Amendment. We can discern no reason why membership, when it constitutes a purposeful form of complicity in a group engaging in this same forbidden advocacy, should receive any greater degree of protection from the guarantees of that Amendment.

If it is said that the mere existence of such an enactment tends to inhibit the exercise of constitutionally protected rights, in that it engenders an unhealthy fear that one may find himself unwittingly embroiled in criminal liability, the answer surely is that the statute provides that a defendant must be proven to have knowledge of the proscribed advocacy before he may be convicted. It is, of course, true that quasi-political parties or other groups that may embrace both legal and illegal aims differ from a technical conspiracy, which is defined by its criminal purpose, so that *all* knowing association with the conspiracy is a proper subject for criminal proscription as far as First Amendment liberties are concerned. If there were a similar blanket prohibition of association with a group having both legal and illegal aims, there would indeed be a real danger that legitimate political expression or association would be impaired, but the membership clause, as here construed, does not cut deeper into the freedom of association than is necessary to deal with "the substantive evils that Congress has a right to prevent." *Schenk* v. *United States,* 249 U.S. 47. The clause does not make criminal all association with an organization which has been shown to engage in illegal advocacy. There must be clear proof that a defendant "specifically intend[s] to accomplish [the aims of the organization] by resort to violence." . . . Thus the member for whom the organization is a vehicle for the advancement of legitimate aims and policies does not fall within the ban of the statute: he lacks the requisite specific intent "to bring about the overthrow of the government as speedily as circumstances would permit." Such a person may be foolish, deluded, or perhaps merely optimistic, but he is not by this statute made a criminal.

We conclude that petitioner's constitutional challenge must be overruled.

III. *Evidentiary Challenge.*

Only in rare instances will this Court review the general sufficiency of the evidence to support a criminal conviction, for ordinarily that is a function which properly belongs to and ends with the Court of Appeals. We do so in this case and in *Noto* v. *United States,* our first review of convictions under the membership clause of the Smith Act—not only to make sure that substantive constitutional standards have not been thwarted, but also to provide guidance for the future to the lower courts in an area which borders so closely upon constitutionally protected rights.

On this phase of the case petitioner's principal contention is that the evidence was insufficient to establish that the Communist Party was engaged in present advocacy of violent overthrow of the Government in the sense required by the Smith Act, that is, in "advocacy of action" for the accomplishment of such overthrow either immediately or as soon as circumstances proved propitious, and uttered in terms reasonably calculated to "incite" to such action. . . . This contention rests largely on the proposition that the evidence on this aspect of the case does not differ materially from that which the Court in *Yates* stated was inadequate to establish that sort of Party advocacy there. . . .

First, *Yates* makes clear what type of evidence is not *in itself* sufficient to show illegal advocacy. This category includes evidence of the following: the teaching of Marxism-Leninism and the connected use of Marxist "classics" as textbooks; the official general resolutions and pronouncements of the Party at past conventions; dissemination of the Party's general literature, including the standard outlines on Marxism; the Party's history and organizational structure; the secrecy of meetings and the clandestine nature of the Party generally; statements by officials evidencing sympathy for and alliance with the U.S.S.R. It was the predominance of evidence of this type which led the Court to order the acquittal of several *Yates* defendants, with the comment that they had not themselves "made a single remark or been present when someone else made a remark which would tend to prove the charges against them." However, this kind of evidence, while insufficient in itself to sustain a conviction, is not irrelevant. Such evidence, in the context of other evidence, may be of value in showing illegal advocacy.

Second, the *Yates* opinion also indicates what kind of evidence is sufficient. There the Court pointed to two series of events which justified the denial of directed acquittals as to nine of the *Yates* defendants. The Court noted that with respect to seven of the defendants, meetings in San Francisco . . . might be considered to be "the systematic teaching and advocacy of illegal action which is condemned by the statute." In those meetings, a small group of members were not only taught that violent revolution was inevitable, but they were also taught techniques for achieving that end. For example, the *Yates* record reveals that members were directed to be prepared to convert a general strike into a revolution and deal with Negroes so as to prepare them specifically for revolution. In addition to the San Francisco meetings, the Court referred to certain activities in the Los Angeles area "which might be considered to amount to 'advocacy of action' " and with which two *Yates* defendants were linked. Here again, the participants did not stop with teaching of the inevitability of eventual revolution, but went on to explain techniques, both legal and illegal, to be employed in preparation for or in connection with the revolution. Thus, one member was "surreptitiously indoctrinated in methods . . . of moving 'masses of people in time of crisis' "; others were told to adopt such Russian prerevolutionary techniques as the development of a special communication system through a newspaper similar to *Pravda*. Viewed together, these events described in *Yates* indicate at least two patterns of evidence sufficient to show illegal advocacy: (a) the teaching of forceful overthrow, accompanied by directions as to the type of illegal action which must be taken when the time for the revolution is reached; and (b) the teaching of forceful overthrow, accompanied by a contemporary, though legal, course of conduct clearly undertaken for the specific purpose of rendering effective the later illegal activity which is advocated. . . .

Finally, *Yates* is also relevant here in indicating, at least by implication, the type and quantum of evidence necessary to attach liability for illegal advocacy to the Party. In discussing the Government's "conspiratorial-nexus theory" the Court found that the evidence there was insufficient because the incidents of illegal advocacy were infrequent, sporadic, and not fairly related to the period covered by the indictment. In addition, the Court indicated that the illegal advocacy was not sufficiently tied to officials who spoke for the Party as such.

Thus, in short, *Yates* imposes a strict standard of proof, and indicates the kind of evidence that is insufficient to show illegal advocacy under that standard, the kind of evidence that is sufficient, and what pattern of evidence is necessary to hold the Party responsible for such advocacy. With these criteria in mind, we now proceed to an examination of the evidence in this case.

We begin with what was also present in *Yates,* the general evidence as to the doctrines, organization, and tactical procedures of the Communist Party, exposited by Lautner, the Government's foundational witness both here and in *Yates.* Together with documentary evidence, Lautner's testimony, based on high-level participation in Party affairs from 1929 to 1950, furnished the necessary background in Party theory and terminology which is crucial to the proper appreciation of the tenor of Party pronouncements, for these pronouncements, taken out of this larger context might appear harmless and peaceable without in reality being so. The distinction that was drawn in *Yates* between theoretical advocacy and advocacy of violence as a rule of action is of course basic, but when the teaching is carried out in a special vocabulary, knowledge of that vocabulary is at least relevant to an understanding of the quality and tenor of the teaching.

Lautner's testimony, having covered the pre-war history of the Party, passed to the 1945 reconstitution of the organization. Prior to that time the Party, as the Communist Political Association, had adhered to the position that the change to a Communist society could be achieved through peaceful, democratic means. The reconstitution, which was finally approved at a National Convention in July of 1945, involved a return to the principles of Marxism-Leninism. As found in the so-called Communist classics, the adoption of a program of industrial concentration, the increased effort among Negroes, especially in the South, the complete repudiation of the former Party leader, Browder, and his doctrine of "revisionism," all signified, so Lautner testified, that the United States was henceforth to be regarded as no exception to the teachings of Lenin that communism could only be achieved in an industrialized nation such as this by resort to violent revolution, and that a belief in peaceful means was foolishness or treachery. Lautner testified that the industrial concentration program, as well as the emphasis on the Negro minority, was an articulation of this doctrine, in that it involved a concentration on those elements in society which the Party believed could do most damage, in time of crisis, to the existing social fabric in relation to their numbers, and that victory at the polls was not its concern. Lautner testified that it was further resolved at the 1945 National Convention that in order to implement the principles of the reconstitution, a program of thorough re-education of the whole Party membership should be undertaken, and Lautner himself was charged with the duty of carrying out this re-education as a District Organizer and State Chairman. The balance of Lautner's testimony was devoted to a detailed description of the elaborate underground "apparatus" which he and others were charged with setting up in the various portions of the country assigned to them.

Mrs. Hartle testified as to her activities in the Party, primarily in the Pacific Northwest area, from 1934 to approximately 1952. Mrs. Hartle confirmed, in many respects, Lautner's testimony as to Party teaching and doctrine throughout this period. After the 1945 reconstitution she was sent to the National Training School in New York, where thirty "officers and functionaries" from various parts of the country were "re-educated" in accordance with the decisions and resolutions of the 1945 Convention. She was taught about "dialectical materialism," and the theory of struggle between the capitalist class and the working class. They were taught "and reference was made to a quotation . . . that it is the duty of a revolutionary not to try to gloss over this class struggle or to try to compromise it, but to unravel it, to allow this class struggle and help this class struggle to unfold, the clash to proceed." The class was told that "it is the duty of a Marxist-Leninist to be a revolutionary and not a reformist." They were further instructed "that the United States . . . was objectively at the stage for Proletarian revolution," that the time for the proletariat revolution would come when the objective conditions of political or economic crisis coincided with the "subjective condition" of a Communist Party which was large enough, with enough "influence" among the working classes, "to give the necessary leadership to lead to the seizure of power."

Much of the testimony summarized so far may indeed be considered to relate to the mere theory of revolution, abstract advocacy. However, the teaching at the National Training School also descended to a lower level of generality. Mrs. Hartle was told that the "role" of the Communist Party was "preparing the workers and the people to be ready to be able to take power, to know how to take power" when a "revolutionary situation arose." At that time, "the plan and program of the Party would be to lead the working class to seize power" and "to smash the Bourgeois state machine." With respect to this latter task, the class was told:

. . . the Bourgeois state machine is not smashed after the seizure of power, but in the course of seizing power that the armies, the police, the prisons have to be dealt with and smashed up and rendered inoperative in the course of the seizure of power, that other matters, that some other matters in replacing the, a state, such as the, some of the administrative apparatus and some other matters would take a longer period of time, but the forcible elements of the capitalist state must be smashed in the course of taking power, but some other things like reorganizing the banking system, or some matters like that, could be done in a somewhat longer process.

In pressing toward the fulfillment of the "subjective conditions" necessary for such action, Mrs. Hartle was taught that "the struggles and activities of the Communist Party prepare the working class for this act of seizure of power," and the history of the Russian Communist Party and Revolution was taught in the school and the events and principles of this history were constantly related to contemporary conditions in the United States. Thus, for example, the class was told that the coalition of workers and peasants which had proved so successful in Russia should have its counterpart in America in a coalition of workers and Negroes, especially in the South.

Following her classes at the National Training School, Mrs. Hartle returned to Washington, where she helped to recruit and organize in "underground fashion" the employees of the Boeing Aircraft Plant in that State. At the same time, Mrs. Hartle was active in Party schools in her area. She testified that she had both been instructed and had herself taught:

. . . the means by which the ultimate goal might be attained was that those means would be forcible. The teaching was that any teaching, any theory of a peaceful road to socialism, or a growing over from capitalism to socialism was a betrayal of the working class and that the Communist Party leading the working class would have to arm it in the first place with the theory that the workers must know and must be prepared to know that they can only take power forcibly. . . .

The action that Communist Party members should take in preparing for the ultimate goal that I was taught and that I taught, were to build the Communist Party as the vanguard party of the working class, a theoretically equipped party, equipped with the theory of Marxism-Leninism, a highly organized party that could act as a unit, as a monolithic whole, with democratic centralism, the principle guiding it, . . . and that the Communist Party should be the connection between the vanguard and the working class millions in this preparation by working with and winning the confidence of the working class and allies of the working class, such as, the Negro people, the poor farmers, other national groups, and in this way, in the course of struggle, constant struggle taking the forms of strikes and demonstrations and picket lines and marches and various kinds of activities to train the working class and the people for revolutionary battle.

The witness Duran, who attended a Party School in Los Angeles in 1951, described what he had been taught by one Moreau, a member of the National Education Commission of the Communist Party:

He divided in his explanation the . . . Proletariat . . . as being divided into two groups. Those in industry that would lead the revolution, and those in agriculture that would follow, and speaking about the revolution, Professor Moreau stated to the class in a very emotional manner that he could see himself carrying a gun against the Capitalist S.O.B.'s and explained to the class it was all based on the science of Marx and Lenin. . . .

In discussing the Proletarian Revolution more thoroughly Professor Moreau explained throughout the school that the Proletarian Revolution would only come about if a Bolshevik rank and file, the sincere Communists, would get out and teach, and teach the people, the desirability of changing the system and the necessity of changing them, and in doing that, we had to teach the people that you cannot change the capitalist system to a Socialist system, to socialism successfully, the peaceful way; it had to be erupted from, and had to be taken away by force and violence, away from them and the entire state machinery of the Bourgeoisie smashed, the F.B.I., the courts and the Army and the Navy, whatever was on it, what—the entire instrumentality of the Bourgeoisie had to smashed and substituted by the Proletarian machinery. . . . and during the period of the revolution the transition, the violent transition, we had to make mass work to get the masses away from the Bourgeoisie so they would not joint [sic] a counterrevolution movement.

It meant after the people of the Communist Party, the vanguard, had become satisfied, that the Bourgeoisie machinery was smashed, and they were in control, then they also had to collect guns from the people and control the people themselves.

Q. Do I understand, Mr. Moreau [sic], that during this period of revolution the people, that is, the masses of the people, would be carrying guns?

A. Yes, sir.

Q. And after the revolution do I understand that the Party would go around and collect these guns and take them away from the people?

A. Yes, sir; take them away from those that helped them overthrow the capitalist system in order to assure the revolution itself. . . .

Immediately after the overthrow of the capitalist system and establishment of the dictatorship of the Proletariat, it became necessary for a Communist to establish Red Army in this country, not only to secure and maintain the dictatorship of the Proletariat, but control the people as well, and those people that did help overthrow the Government would not have any civil rights whatsoever, no voting rights, or anything; they would be dished out to them according to the way they felt, way they fell in with the Communist office by the dictatorship.

Q. Now, Mr. Duran, what, if anything, did Mr. Moreau teach you in this school about the role that would be played by the Communist Party during this period of revolution when the Government would be overthrown by force and violence?

A. The role of the Communist Party, and specifically within the Communist Party, the Bolsheviks was to play a vanguard role, a leading role; that is explained scientifically in that so that first we teach the people the desirability of overthrowing them and teach them the, it could only be done through the Proletarian Revolution, and then when the time is ripe we could stampede them against the capitalist class.

Duran also testified to what he had been taught by Art Berry, District Organizer for seven States, in a Colorado school in 1952:

. . . we were discussing the scientific application of Marx and Lenin to the transition period between capitalism and socialism, and he demonstrated this with the kettle of water, that you could put a quantitative amount of water in a kettle and set it somewhere, nothing would happen, just like the masses, nothing does happen.

. . . [he] said, however, if you get that same amount, same kettle with the same amount of water in it, and put fire underneath it, then you begin to get quantitative changes, and eventually it reaches a nodule point to where it has a qualitative and abrupt transition into steam. He continued, same applied to the development of the revolution in this sense, the American people will not and cannot make a successful change over from capitalism to socialism by themselves, like the fire underneath the water, the Communist Party teaches and leads them to where when the society reaches that nodule point, the Communist people teaches the people before and then leads them to make that abrupt change into the society of socialism. . . .

Substantially, within the same explanation of violent overthrow of the Government . . . he stated that not only would it be that, but that we would have to set up barricades, establish a central point from where we would participate from; he stated that "we" literally speaking "we," would have to have a central point because during the revolution it may become necessary to ebb, retreat in certain battles, and we would have to learn to retreat in an organizational way and a correct way. It was essential to learn to ebb as it was to flow on the revolution.

In the ebbing we were to see that we ebb before the enemy wiped everybody out. Ebbing to the central point that had been barricaded, reorganization, and then at the correct time start flowing forward in the revolution.

The witness Obadiah Jones testified concerning a Party Training School in St. Louis which he attended in 1947. Jones was taught "that the only way the national problem could be solved would be in connection with the Proletariat Revolution." Jones was also instructed as to the nature of a Communist army:

A. He said general staff of an army was different from the Communist Party . . . general staff of an army operated from a safe spot from behind the line and led the army from a far distance, and that the Communist Party went forth and fought with the workers.

Q. Did he say anything with reference to the techniques?

A. Yes, he said that you couldn't be a good leader without knowing all the techniques of fighting.

Q. Did he say anything with respect to carrying out instructions?

A. Yes, sir.

Q. What did he say in that connection?

A. He said that capitalists in the army did not carry out the instructions in full, but the Communists did, irregardless of what the cost would be, they would carry out instructions completely.

At the final session, the students were required by the instructor to take a pledge:

The pledge was each of us are Communists or members of the Party and each of us have a responsibility and we must carry out our responsibility and work for the interests of the Party and its recipients and carry out the full will of the Party even though it meant to fight and to kill, we must carry out the demands of the Party and all of them.

The witnesses Clontz, Childs, and Reavis testified primarily as to their dealings with petitioner, Scales. We regard this testimony, which finds no counterpart in the *Yates* record with respect to any of the defendants whose acquittal was directed, as being of special importance in two ways: it supplies some of the strongest and most unequivocal evidence against the Party based on the statements and activities of a man whose words and deeds, by virtue of his high Party position, carry special weight in determining the character of the Party from the standpoint of the Smith Act; and it appears clearly dispositive as to the quality of petitioner's Party membership, and his knowledge and intent, when we come to consider him not as a Party official but as the defendant in this case.

In 1948 Ralph C. Clontz, Jr., then a student at Duke Law School, undertook to furnish the F.B.I. with information he had gained about

Communist Party activities in North Carolina, and to volunteer his services in attempting to penetrate the Party to acquire further information. As a result, in September of that year, Clontz sent a postcard to petitioner, informing him that he was a law student and that he was interested in communism. Petitioner replied by sending Clontz "a large cardboard box filled with Communist literature." An accompanying letter, headed "Carolina District Communist Party U.S.A." with the notation "Junius Scales, Chairman," explained:

Under separate cover I have already sent you a rather varied sample of our literature. I hope you will give it close attention. If I can discuss any matter relating to my Party and its program with you in person, I will be glad to do so.

Several days later Clontz went to visit petitioner and thus began a relationship which was to bring him into intimate contact with the Communist Party, its teachings, purposes and activities.

At an early meeting between the two, petitioner told Clontz that it was impossible for the Communist Party to succeed to power through educating the people in this country and gaining their votes at the polls, but that a forceful revolution would be necessary. At a later meeting, the discussion was not limited to the theoretical inevitability of revolution, but went beyond the theory itself to an explanation of "basic strategy" which the Communist Party was using to give concrete foundation to the theory, i.e., to bringing about the revolution:

The defendant [petitioner] explained that basically their strategy was bottomed on a concept that there were two classes of people in this country, that could be used by the Communist Party to foment a revolution.

The first class he termed the working class or Proletariat, working class, he said, had as its natural born leaders or vanguard, the Communist Party.

The second class, he described, in this country was what he termed the Negro nation. The Negro nation he described as a separate nation in what he termed the Black Belt, including thirteen Southern States, and the strategy of the Communist Party was to bring the working class, led by the Communist Party, and what he termed the Negro nation, together, to bring about a forceful overthrow of the Government.

Now Scales and the Communist Party taught that the basic strategy of the Communist Party would never change, but that tactics might be altered as the situation changed.

On petitioner's invitation, Clontz joined the Communist Party on January 17, 1950. He was not assigned to a particular group but became a member "at large," in order to continue his instruction under petitioner. In the course of this instruction, petitioner repeatedly told Clontz of the necessity for revolution to bring about the Dictatorship of the Proletariat. Scales analogized the situation in the United States to that in Russia prior to the 1917 Revolution. He pointed out that revolution would be "easier" in this country than it had been in Russia:

that while in the Soviet Union there had been no one to help the Soviet Party, that in this country when the revolution started, we would have the benefit of the help from the mother country, Russia, in bringing about our own revolution, because part of the purposes of the Communist Party in the Soviet Union was international in scope and that we naturally would continue to receive help in all circumstances from the Soviet Party when the revolution was started here in this country.

Petitioner explained that the Soviet Union could not be expected to land troops to start a revolution here. A similar procedure had been unsuccessful in China. Rather, he said "that we Communists in this country would have to start the revolution, and we would have to continue fighting it," but that the Soviet Union would aid the Communist Party in this endeavor by furnishing it "with experienced revolutionaries from Russia." He added that "if the United States declared war on the Communists in their revolution, then the Soviet Union would land troops, and he said that would be a bloody time for all." When asked by Clontz when all this would occur, Scales noted that a "depression would greatly accelerate the coming of the revolution" if the Communists used it properly to prepare the masses of the people.

Petitioner arranged for Clontz to be awarded a scholarship to study in New York at the Jefferson School of Social Science, an official Communist Party School, during the month of August 1950. Because Clontz arrived at a time when few scheduled courses were being offered, the bulk of his training at the school was received in private instruction from Doxey A. Wilkerson, the teacher with whom petitioner had communicated in arranging Clontz's scholarship. Wilkerson like petitioner, told Clontz, "that the Communist Party recognized and expressed to themselves that the only kind of means would be proper means, which would be forceful means, that no longer was there any even pretense among intelligent Communists that any voting system or any people's election could bring this government." He also stated, as Scales had, that "the revolution basically would come about by combining the forces of what had been already identified as the Negro nation and the working class as the vanguard."

In line with this strategy, Wilkerson advised Clontz that he should not let his membership in the Communist Party become known, that by remaining "under cover" he "would be much more helpful to the Party

when the Revolution came." As part of his undercover activity, Clontz
was directed to attempt to infiltrate various organizations of the working class in order to achieve "a background of respectability" and to be
able to lead such organizations "toward the goal of the Communist
Party, . . . the undermining of the Government and overthrowing of
the Government, bringing communism in the United States." But Clontz
was not to lose contact with the Party, for if he "got isolated without
Party direction . . . [his] efforts would be pretty largely wasted." In
connection with these instructions, Wilkerson mentioned "one of the
things that frightened the United States leaders was they knew that
not only did they have to contend with China and the other Communist-
dominated countries, but that also in every capitalist country the working class party, the Communists, would be working from within."

When Clontz returned to North Carolina, he reported to petitioner on
his activities at the Jefferson School. He also informed petitioner, under
instructions from the F.B.I., that he wished to move to New York. Petitioner arranged for Clontz to remain under his direction and to pay dues
to him, while in New York, rather than effecting a formal transfer.
Clontz moved to New York in March of 1951. While there Scales
directed him to "get in with the A.C.L.U. organization to report on what
value they might have in the coming struggle. . . ." Clontz had also
been advised by an associate of petitioner to "infiltrate . . . the Civilian Defense setup."

The witnesses Childs and Reavis also testified to their relationship
with Scales, who among other things arranged for their attendance at
Party schools where their instruction followed much the same pattern
as that described by Clontz. In 1952 Childs attended a "Party Training
School" of which petitioner was a director. The school was given "for
outstanding cadres in North and South Carolina and Virginia Districts
of the Communist Party." It was held on a farm and strict security measures were taken. The District Organizer of Virginia instructed at the
school. He told the students that "the role of the Communist Party is to
lead the working masses to the overthrow of the capitalist government."
With respect to the preliminary task of gaining the "broad coalition"
necessary to achieve this task, he stated that,

. . . the Communist Party has a program of industrial concentration in
which they try to get people, that is, people who are Communist Party
members, into key shops or key industries which the Party has determined
or designated to be industrial concentration industries or plants. This is so
that the Communist Party members in a particular plant will be able to
have a cell, or a Communist Party group in which they will be able to
more effectively plan for such things as attempting to control the union in
that particular plant.

And, in a compulsory recreation period, this same instructor gave a demonstration of jujitsu and, explaining that the students "might be able to use this on a picket line," how to kill a person with a pencil. According to Childs' testimony "what he showed us to do was to take our pencil, . . . just take the pencil and place it simply in the palm of your hand so that the back will rest against the base of the thumb, and then we were to take it, and the person, and give a quick jab so that it would penetrate through here [demonstrating], and enter the heart, and then if we could not do that, we just take it and grab it at the base of the throat."

Reavis attended the Party's New York Jefferson School in 1942. In a course on "Negro History" the students, drawn primarily from the South, were taught that ". . . the Negro people was the only revolutionary group within the United States that we could align themselves [sic] with, and hope to reach their [sic] gains through the avenue of force and violence, by overthrow of the Government, by Proletariat faction. . . ." Reavis was later advised to seek employment at the Western Electric Plant in Winston Salem. He stated:

I bumped into Mr. Scales at Harvey's home and I—the report said . . . the advice I'd been getting was confirmed by him. I advanced the question on what I should do in case I did get employment there at Western Electric, and I knew it was a, Government work, what I should do in case I was asked to sign certain papers, and I was told to do the same, that they had when signing a Taft-Hartley affidavit, to go ahead and sign them, that before they did, the defendant asked me if I had signed any papers that might be used as proof that I was in the Party, and I didn't remember any.

We conclude that this evidence sufficed to make a case for the jury on the issue of illegal Party advocacy. *Dennis* and *Yates* have definitely laid at rest any doubt but that present advocacy of *future* action for violent overthrow satisfies statutory and constitutional requirements equally with advocacy of *immediate* action to that end. 341 U.S., at 509; 354 U.S., at 321. Hence this record cannot be considered deficient because it contains no evidence of advocacy for immediate overthrow.

Since the evidence amply showed that Party leaders were continuously preaching during the indictment period the inevitability of eventual forcible overthrow, the first and basic question is a narrow one: whether the jury could permissibly infer that such preaching, in whole or in part, "was aimed at building up a seditious group and maintaining it in readiness for action at a propitious time . . . the kind of indoctrination preparatory to action which was condemned in *Dennis.*" *Yates, supra*, at 321–322. On this score, we think that the jury, under

instructions which fully satisfied the requirements of *Yates* * was entitled
to infer from this systematic preaching that where the explicitness and
concreteness, of the sort described previously, seemed necessary and
prudent the doctrine of violent revolution—elsewhere more a theory
of historical predictability than a rule of conduct—was put forward as
a guide to future action, in whatever tone, be it emotional or calculating,
that the audience and occasion required; in short, that "advocacy of
action" was engaged in.

* The trial court charged: "Moreover, the teaching in the abstract or teaching
objectively, that is, teaching, discussing, explaining, or expounding what is meant
by the aim or purpose of any author, group, or society of overthrowing the Government by force and violence is not criminal. For example, study and discussion by
the Communist Party or by any other group in classrooms, or in study groups, or
public or private meetings with the object of informing the participants or the
audience of the aims and purposes of the doctrines of Marx, Lenin, Stalin, or the
Communist Party is entirely lawful. Furthermore, without being criminal, the
Communist Party could privately or publicly endeavor to persuade its members
that they should adopt and espouse the belief that the Government of the United
States should be overthrown by force and violence as speedily as circumstances will
permit. This is no more than advocating an idea, and advocating an idea is no
crime. Moreover, without transgressing the Smith Act, the Party might even instruct its members that it would be for their good and benefit, if this belief or idea
were carried into effect.

"All of this is permissible because such utterances are protected by the First
Amendment of the Federal Constitution, guaranteeing freedom of speech.

"However, if the Party went further, and with the intention of overthrowing the
Government by force and violence, it taught, or advocated a rule or principle of
action which both, one, called on its members to take forcible and concrete action
at some advantageous time thereafter to overthrow the Government by force and
violence, and, two, expressed that call in such written or oral words as would
reasonably and ordinarily be calculated to incite its members to take concrete and
forcible action for such overthrow; then, if the Communist Party did that, the
Party became such a society or group, as was outlawed by the Smith Act.

"To be criminal the teaching or advocacy, or the call to action just described
need not be for immediate action, that is, for action today, tomorrow, next month,
or next year. It is criminal, nonetheless, if the action is to be at an unnamed time
in the future, to be fixed by the circumstances or on signal from the Party.

"It is criminal if it is a call upon the members to be ready or to stand in readiness
for action, or for a summons to action at a favorable, or opportune time in the
future, or as speedily as circumstances will permit, provided always that the urging
of such readiness be by words which would reasonably and ordinarily be calculated
to spur a person to ready himself for, and to take action towards, the overthrow of
the Government. But those to whom the advocacy or urging is addressed must be
urged to do something now or in the future, rather than merely to believe in something. In other words, the advocacy must be of concrete action, and not merely a
belief in abstract doctrine. However, the immediate concrete action urged should
be intended to lead towards the forcible overthrow, and be so understood by those
to whom the advocacy is addressed."

The only other question on this phase of the case is whether such advocacy was sufficiently broadly based to permit its attribution to the Party. We think it was. The advocacy of action was not "sporadic" the instances of it being neither infrequent, remote in time nor casual. It cannot be said that the jury could not have found the criminal advocacy was fully authorized and condoned by the Party. We regard the testimony of the witnesses, whose credibility, of course, is not for us, as indicating a sufficiently systematic and substantial course of utterances and conduct on the part of those high in the councils of the Party, including the petitioner himself, to entitle the jury to infer that such activities reflected tenets of the Party. The testimony described activities in various States, including the teaching at some seven schools, among them the national Party school. The witnesses told of advocacy by high Party officials, including that of leaders of the Party in nine States. Further, there was testimony that the Party followed the principle of "democratic-centralism" whereby a position once adopted by the Party must be unquestionably adhered to by the whole membership. The conformity of the views expressed and the terms employed in advocating violent overthrow in such States as Washington, North Carolina, Missouri, Colorado and Virginia could reasonably be taken by the jury as a practical manifestation of "democratic-centralism." Another concrete illustration of this principle could have been found in the circumstance that in almost every instance where a speaker engaged in advocacy of violent overthrow, he not only advocated violence to his audience but urged others to go out and do likewise. All of these factors combine to justify the inference that the illegal individual advocacy as to which testimony was adduced was in truth the expression of Party policy and purpose.

The requirement of Party imputability is adequately met in the record. . . .

The sufficiency of the evidence as to other elements of the crime requires no exposition. Scales' "active" membership in the Party is indisputable, and that issue was properly submitted to the jury under instructions that were entirely adequate. The elements of petitioner's "knowledge" and "specific intent" require no further discussion of the evidence beyond that already given as to Scales' utterances and activities. . . . They bear little resemblance to the fragmentary and equivocal utterances and conduct which were found insufficient in *Nowak* v. *United States*, 356 U.S. 660, and in *Maisenberg* v. *United States*, 356 U.S. 670.

We hold that this prosecution does not fail for insufficiency of the proof. . . .

The judgment of the Court of Appeals must be affirmed.

Mr. Justice Black, dissenting:

Petitioner was convicted for violation of the "membership clause" of the Smith Act which imposes a penalty of up to twenty years' imprisonment together with a fine of $20,000 upon anyone who "becomes or is a member of, or affiliates with, any . . . society, group or assembly of persons [who teach, advocate or encourage the overthrow of the existing government by force or violence], knowing the purposes thereof. . . ." Rejecting numerous contentions urged for reversal, the Court upholds a six-year sentence imposed upon petitioner under the authority of its prior decisions in *Dennis* v. *United States* and *Yates* v. *United States.* My reasons for dissenting from this decision are primarily those set out by Mr. Justice Brennan—that § 4 (f) of the Subversive Activities Control Act bars prosecutions under the membership clause of the Smith Act—and Mr. Justice Douglas—that the First Amendment absolutely forbids Congress to outlaw membership in a political party or similar association merely because one of the philosophical tenets of that group is that the existing government should be overthrown by force at some distant time in the future when circumstances may permit. There are, however, two additional points that I think should also be mentioned.

In an attempt to bring the issue of the constitutionality of the membership clause of the Smith Act within the authority of the *Dennis* and *Yates* cases, the Court has practically rewritten the statute under which petitioner stands convicted by treating the requirements of "activity" and "specific intent" as implicit in words that plainly do not include them. Petitioner's conviction is upheld just as though the membership clause had always contained these requirements. It seems clear to me that neither petitioner nor anyone else could ever have guessed that this law would be held to mean what this Court now holds it does mean. For that reason, it appears that petitioner has been convicted under a law that is, at best, unconstitutionally vague and, at worst, *ex post facto.* He has therefore been deprived of his right to be tried under a clearly defined, pre-existing "law of the land" as guaranteed by the Due Process Clause and I think his conviction should be reversed on that ground.

Secondly, I think it is important to point out the manner in which this case re-emphasizes the freedom-destroying nature of the "balancing test" presently in use by the Court to justify its refusal to apply specific constitutional protections of the Bill of Rights. In some of the recent cases in which it has "balanced" away the protections of the First Amendment, the Court has suggested that it was justified in the application of this "test" because no direct abridgment of First Amendment freedoms was involved, the abridgment in each of these cases being, in the Court's opinion, nothing more than "an incident of the informed exercise of a valid governmental function." A possible implication of that suggestion was that if the Court were confronted with what it would call a direct abridgment of speech, it would not apply the "balancing test" but would enforce the protections of the First Amendment according to its own terms. This case causes me to doubt that such an implication is justified. Petitioner is being sent to jail for the express reason that he has associated with people who have entertained unlawful ideas and said unlawful things, and that of course is a *direct* abridgment of his freedoms of speech and assembly—under any definition that has ever been used for that term. Nevertheless, even as to his admittedly direct abridgment, the Court relies upon its prior decisions to the effect that the Government has power to abridge speech and assembly if its interest in doing so is sufficient to outweigh the interest in protecting these First Amendment freedoms.

This, I think, demonstrates the unlimited breadth and danger of the "balancing test" as it is currently being applied by a majority of this Court. Under that "test," the question in every case in which a First Amendment right is asserted is not whether there has been an abridgment of that right, not whether the abridgment of that right was intentional on the part of the Government, and not whether there is any other way in which the Government could accomplish a lawful aim without an invasion of the constitutionally guaranteed rights of the people. It is, rather, simply whether the Government has an interest in abridging the rights involved and, if so, whether that interest is of sufficient importance, in the opinion of a majority of this Court, to justify the Government's action in doing so. This doctrine, to say the very least, is capable of being used to justify almost any action Government may wish to take to suppress First Amendment freedoms.

Mr. Justice Douglas, dissenting:

When we allow petitioner to be sentenced to prison for six years for being a "member" of the Communist Party, we make a sharp break with traditional concepts of First Amendment rights and make serious Mark Twain's lighthearted comment that "It is by the goodness of God that in our country we have those three unspeakably precious things: freedom of speech, freedom of conscience, and the prudence never to practice either of them."

Even the Alien and Sedition Laws—shameful reminders of an early chapter in intolerance—never went so far as we go today. They were aimed at conspiracy and advocacy of insurrection and at the publication of "false, scandalous, and malicious" writing against the Government. . . . The Government then sought control over the press "in order to strike at one of the chief sources of disaffection and sedition. . . ." There is here no charge of conspiracy, no charge of any overt act to overthrow the Government by force and violence, no charge of any other criminal act. The charge is being a "member" of the Communist Party, "well-knowing" that it advocated the overthrow of the Government by force and violence, "said defendant intending to bring about such overthrow by force and violence as speedily as circumstances would permit." That falls far short of a charge of conspiracy. Conspiracy rests not in intention alone but in an agreement with one or more others to promote an unlawful project. . . . No charge of any kind or sort of agreement hitherto embraced in the concept of a conspiracy is made here.

We legalize today guilt by association, sending a man to prison when he committed no unlawful act. Today's break with tradition is a serious one. It borrows from the totalitarian philosophy. . . .

The case is not saved by showing that petitioner was an active member. None of the activity constitutes a crime. The record contains evidence that Scales was the Chairman of the North and South Carolina Districts of the Communist Party. He recruited new members into the Party, and promoted the advanced education of selected young Party members in the theory of communism to be undertaken at secret schools. He was a director of one such school. He explained the principles of the Party to an FBI agent who posed as someone interested in joining the Party, and furnished him literature, including articles which criticized in vivid language the American "aggression" in Korea and described American "atrocities" committed on Korean citizens. He once remarked that the Party was setting up underground means of communication, and in 1951 he himself "went underground." At the school of which Scales was director, students were told (by someone else) that one of the Party's weaknesses was in failing to place people in key industrial positions. One witness told of a meeting arranged by Scales at which the staff of the school urged him to remain in his position in an industrial plant rather than return to college. In Scales' presence, students at the school were once shown how to kill a person with a pencil, a device which, it was said, might come in handy on a picket line. Other evidence showed Scales to have made several statements or distributed literature containing implicating messages. Among them were comments to the effect that the Party line was that the Negroes in the South and the working classes should be used to foment a violent revolution; that a Communist government could not be voted into power in this country because the Government controlled communication media, newspapers, the military, and the educational systems, and that force was the only way to achieve the revolution; that if a depression were to come the Communist America would be closer at hand than predicted by William Z. Foster; that the revolution would come within a generation; that it would be easier in the United States than in Russia to effectuate the revolution because of assistance and advice from Russian Communists. Petitioner at different times said or distributed literature which said that the goals of communism could only be achieved by violent revolution that would have to start internally with the working classes.

Not one single illegal act is charged to petitioner. That is why the essence of the crime covered by the indictment is merely belief—belief in the proletarian revolution, belief in Communist creed.

Spinoza summed up in a sentence much of the history of the struggle of man to think and speak what he believes:

> Laws which decree what every one must believe, and forbid utter-
> ance against this or that opinion, have too often been enacted to con-

firm or enlarge the power of those who dared not suffer free inquiry to be made, and have by a perversion of authority turned the superstition of the mob into violence against opponents. *Tractatus Theorlogico-Politicus* (London 1862) p. 349.

"The thought of man shall not be tried, for the devil himself knoweth not the thought of man," said Chief Justice Brian in Y. B. Pasch, 17 Edw. IV, f. 2, pl. 2. The crime of belief—presently prosecuted—is a carryback to the old law of treason where men were punished for compassing the death of the King. That law which had been employed for "suppression of political opposition or the expression of ideas or beliefs distasteful to those in power," Hurst, Historic Background of the Treason Clause, 6 *Fed. B.J.* 305, 307, was rejected here, and the treason clause of our Constitution was "most praised for the reason that it prevented the use of treason trials as an instrument of political faction." *Id.*, 307. Sedition or treason in the realm of politics and heresy in the ecclesiastical field had long centered on *beliefs* as the abhorrent criminal act. The struggle on this side of the Atlantic was to get rid of that concept and to punish men not for what they thought but for overt acts against the peace of the Nation. . . . Montesquieu, who was a force in the thinking of those times, proclaimed against punishing thoughts or words:

> There was a law passed in England under Henry VIII, by which whoever predicted the king's death was declared guilty of high treason. This law was extremely vague; the terror of despotic power is so great that it recoils upon those who exercise it. In the king's last illness, the physicians would not venture to say he was in danger; and surely they acted very right. . . . Marsyas dreamed that he had cut Dionysius's throat. Dionysius put him to death, pretending that he would never have dreamed of such a thing by night if he had not thought of it by day. This was a most tyrannical action: for though it had been the subject of his thoughts, yet he had made no attempt towards it. The laws do not take upon them to punish any other than overt acts. *The Spirit of Laws* (1949), pp. 192–193.
>
> Words do not constitute an overt act; they remain only in idea. *Id.*, 193.

These were the notions that led to the restrictive definition of treason, presently contained in Art. III, § 3, of the Constitution, which requires overt acts. . . . Our long and painful experience with the law of treason, wholly apart from the First Amendment, should be enough warning that we as a free people should not venture again into the field of prosecuting beliefs. . . .

Nothing but beliefs are on trial in this case. They are unpopular and to most of us revolting. But they are nonetheless ideas or dogma or faith within the broad framework of the First Amendment. . . . The creed truer to our faith was stated by the Bar Committee headed by Charles E. Hughes which in 1920 protested the refusal of New York Assembly to seat five members of the Socialist Party:

. . . it is of the essence of the institutions of liberty that it be recognized that guilt is personal and cannot be attributed to the holding of opinion or to mere intent in the absence of overt acts. . . .

Belief in the principle of revolution is deep in our traditions. The Declaration of Independence proclaims it:

whenever any Form of Government becomes destructive of these ends, it is the Right of the People to alter or abolish it, and to institute new Government, laying its foundation on such principles and organizing its powers in such form, as to them shall seem most likely to effect their Safety and Happiness.

This right of revolution has been and is a part of the fabric of our institutions. Last century when Russia invaded Hungary and subdued her, Louis Kossuth came here to enlist American support. On January 8, 1852, Lincoln spoke in sympathy of the Hungarian cause and was a member of a committee which on January 9, 1852, submitted Resolutions in Behalf of Hungarian Freedom. Among these resolutions was one that read:

That it is the right of any people, sufficiently numerous for natural independence, to throw off, to revolutionize, their existing form of government, and to establish such other in its stead as they may choose. Basler, Vol. II, *The Collected Works of Abraham Lincoln* (1953), p. 115.

On January 12, 1848, Lincoln in an address before the United States House of Representatives stated: "Any people anywhere, being inclined and having the power, have the right to rise up, and shake off the existing government, and form a new one that suits them better. This is a most valuable, —a most sacred right—a right, which we hope and believe, is to liberate the world." *Id.,* Vol. I, p. 438.

Of course, government can move against those who take up arms against it. Of course, the constituted authority has the right of self-preservation. But we deal in this prosecution of Scales only with the legality of ideas and beliefs, not with overt acts. The Court speaks of the prevention of "dangerous behavior" by punishing those "who work to bring about that behavior." That formula returns man to the dark days when government determined what behavior was "dangerous" and then policed the dissidents for tell-tale signs of advocacy. What is "dangerous behavior" that must be suppressed in its talk-stage has had a vivid history even on this continent. The British colonial philosophy was summed up by Sir William Berkeley who served from 1641 to 1677 as Virginia's Governor: ". . . I thank God, there are no free schools, nor printing, and I hope we shall not have these hundred years; for learning has brought disobedience and heresy, and sects into the world, and printing has divulged them, and libels against the best government. God keep us from both!" . . . The history is familiar; much of it is reviewed in Chafee, *The Blessings of Liberty* (1956). He states in one paragraph what I think is the Jeffersonian conception of the First Amendment rights involved in the present case:

> We must choose between freedom and fear—we cannot have both. If the citizens of the United States persist in being afraid, the real rulers of this country will be fanatics fired with a zeal to save grown men from objectionable ideas by putting them under the care of official nursemaids. *Id.*, 156.

In recent years we have been departing, I think, from the theory of government expressed in the First Amendment. We have too often been "balancing" the right of speech and association against other values in society to see if we, the judges, feel that a particular need is more important than those guaranteed by the Bill of Rights. . . . This approach, which treats the commands of the First Amendment as "no more than admonitions of moderation" (see Hand, *The Spirit of Liberty* (2d ed. 1954), p. 278), runs counter to our prior decisions. . . .

It also runs counter to Madison's views of the First Amendment as we are advised by his eminent biographer, Irving Brant:

> When Madison wrote, "Congress shall make no law" infringing these rights, he did not expect the Supreme Court to decide, on balance, whether Congress could or could not make a law infringing them. It was true, he observed in presenting his proposals, that state legislative bodies had violated many of the most valuable articles in bills of rights. But that furnished no basis for judging the effectiveness of the proposed amendments:
> "If they are incorporated into the Constitution, independent tribunals of justice will consider themselves in a peculiar manner the guardians of those rights; they will be an impenetrable bulwark against every assumption of power in the Legislative or Executive; they will be naturally led to resist every encroachment upon rights expressly stipulated for in the Constitution by the declaration of rights."
> This statement by Madison, along with all the rest of his speech, is so devastating to the "balance theory" that efforts have been and are being made to discredit its authenticity. The *Annals of Congress*, it is said, is not an official document, but a compilation of stenographic reports (by a shorthand reporter admitted to the floor for that purpose) published in the press and containing numerous errors. That is true, although the chief complaint was that partially caught sentences were meaningless. In general, that which was clearly reported was truly reported. In the case of this all-important speech, Madison spoke from notes, and the notes in his handwriting are in the Library of Congress. They parallel the speech from end to end, scantily, but leaving no doubt of the fundamental faithfulness of the report. The Madison Heritage, 35 *N.Y.U.L. Rev.* 882, 899–900.

Brant goes on to relate how Madison opposed a resolution of censure against societies creating the political turmoil that was behind the Whiskey

Rebellion. *Id.*, p. 900. He expressed in the House the view that opinions are not objects of legislation. "If we advert to the nature of Republican Government, we shall find that the censorial power is the people over the Government, and not in the Government over the people." *Id.*, p. 900.

The trend of history, as Jefferson noted, has been against the rights of man. He wrote that "The natural progress of things is for liberty to yield and government to gain ground." The formula he prepared for a society where ideas flourished was not punishment of the unorthodox but education and enlightenment of the masses. Jefferson wrote to Madison on December 20, 1787:

> "I own, I am not a friend to a very energetic government. It is always oppressive. It places the governors indeed more at their ease, at the expense of the people. The late rebellion in Massachusetts has given more alarm, than I think it should have done. Calculate that one rebellion in thirteen States in the course of eleven years, is but one for each State in a century and a half. No country should be so long without one. Nor will any degree of power in the hands of government, prevent insurrections. In England, where the hand of power is heavier than with us, there are seldom half a dozen years without an insurrection. In France, where it is still heavier, but less despotic, as Montesquieu supposes, than in some other countries, and where there are always two or three hundred thousand men ready to crush insurrections, there have been three in the course of the three years I have been here, in every one of which greater numbers were engaged than in Massachusetts, and a great deal more blood was spilt. In Turkey, where the sole nod of the despot is death, insurrections are the events of every day. Compare again the ferocious depredations of their insurgents, with the order, the moderation and the almost self-extinguishment of ours. And say, finally, whether peace is best preserved by giving energy to the government, or information to the people. This last is the most certain, and the most legitimate engine of government. Educate and inform the whole mass of the people. Enable them to see that it is their interest to preserve peace and order, and they will preserve them. And it requires no very high degree of education to convince them of this. They are the only sure reliance for the preservation of our liberty."

This is the only philosophy consistent with the First Amendment. When belief in an idea is punished as it is today, we sacrifice those ideals and substitute an alien, totalitarian philosophy in their stead.*

* Gellhorn, *American Rights* (1960) in commenting on *Dennis* v. *United States,* 341 U.S. 494 and *Yates* v. *United States,* 354 U.S. 298 states:

"The aftermath of the *Yates* case is interesting. By the end of 1956 convictions of Communist leaders under the Smith Act had numbered 114. Many of these cases were still pending in the appellate courts when the *Yates* decision was announced in June of 1957. On one ground or another, convictions were set aside and new trials were granted to many of these defendants. The Department of

"The most indifferent arguments," Bismark said, "are good when one has a majority of bayonets." That is also true when one has the votes.

What we lose by majority vote today may be reclaimed at a future time when the fear of advocacy, dissent, and non-conformity no longer cast a shadow over us.

The constitutions of 15 States have, at one time or another, made specific provision for the right of revolution by reserving to the people the right to "alter, reform or abolish" the existing frame of government. . . . The older constitutions often add a clause which shows the roots of these provisions in the right of revolution. "The doctrine of non-resistance against arbitrary power, and oppression, is absurd, slavish, and destructive of the good and happiness of mankind," the New Hampshire Const., Pt. I, Art. 10, recites. The same language may be found in Maryland Const., Dec. of Rights, Art. VI; Tennessee Const., Art. I, § 2. . . .

This does not mean the helplessness of the established government in the face of armed resistance, for that government has the duty of maintaining existing institutions. . . . But it does mean that the right of revolution is ultimately reserved to the people themselves, whatever formal, but useless remedies the existing government may offer. This is shown in the history of our own revolution. Legislatures and governments have the right to protect

---

Justice itself dropped the prosecution of a considerable number, on the ground that they could not properly be convicted on the basis of the evidence now available. Most significantly of all, the cases against the nine remaining defendants in *Yates*, as to whom the Supreme Court had refused to dismiss the charges, were abandoned by the prosecution because there was insufficient evidence that they had advocated action as distinct from opinion. After all the clamor, after all the expressed alarm about the peril into which the United States was being plunged by this handful of misguided fanatics, the prosecution felt itself unable to show persuasively that the Communist spokesmen had engaged in the forbidden incitements to illegality.

"This should stimulate a sober second look at the surface attractions of programs of suppression and coercion. Occasionally the supporters of these programs are scoundrels who falsely parade themselves as upholders of democracy; but more often they are good and sincere men. Men genuinely devoted to worthy ends sometimes endorse efforts to force unanimity of sentiment, not because they consciously espouse authoritarianism, but because they hope thus to assure maximum support for the nation and its people. No matter how well intentioned they may be, however, those efforts themselves create a graver danger than they overcome. The perils sought to be suppressed are regularly overestimated. History shows in one example after another how excessive have been the fears of earlier generations, who shuddered at menaces that, with the benefit of hindsight, we now know were mere shadows. This in itself should induce the modern generation to view with prudent skepticism the recurrent alarms about the fatal potentialities of dissent. In any event, in a world torn between the merits of freedom and the blandishments of totalitarian power, the lovers of freedom cannot afford to sacrifice their moral superiority by adopting totalitarian methods in order to create a self-deluding sense of security. Suppression, once accepted as a way of life, is likely to spread. It reinforces the herd urge toward orthodoxies of all kinds—religious, economic, and moral as well as political." Pp. 82, 83.

themselves. They may judge as to the appropriate means of meeting force
directed against them, but as to the propriety of the exercise of the ultimate
right of revolution, there, as John Locke says, "the people shall be judge."
Second Treatise on Civil Government, § 240. To forbid the teaching of the
propriety of revolution, even where the teacher believes his own lesson, is
to hinder the people in the free exercise of this great sovereign right. . . .

Lincoln's full statement, made in 1848 and already referred to, reads:

> Any people anywhere, being inclined and having the power, have
> the *right* to rise up, and shake off the existing government, and form a
> new one that suits them better. This is a most valuable,—a most
> sacred right—a right, which we hope and believe, is to liberate the
> world. Nor is this right confined to cases in which the whole people
> of an existing government, may choose to exercise it. Any portion of
> such people that *can, may* revolutionize, and make their *own*, of so
> much of the territory as they inhabit. More than this, a *majority* of
> any portion of such people may revolutionize, putting down a *minority*,
> intermingled with, or near about them, who may oppose their move-
> ment. Such minority, was precisely the case, of the tories of our own
> revolution. It is quality of revolutions not to go by *old* lines or *old*
> laws; but to break up both, and make new ones. I Basler, *The Col-
> lected Works of Abraham Lincoln* (1953), pp. 438–439.

*Mr. Justice Brennan with whom The Chief Justice and Mr. Justice Doug-
las join, dissenting:*

I think that in § 4 (f) of the Internal Security Act Congress legislated
immunity from prosecution under the membership clause of the Smith Act.
The first sentence of § 4 (f) is: "Neither the holding of office nor membership in any Communist organization by any person shall constitute per se a
violation of subsection (a) or subsection (c) of this section or of any other
criminal statute." The immunity granted by that sentence is not in my view
restricted, as the Court holds, to *mere* membership, that is to membership
which is nominal, passive or theoretical. The immunity also extends to
"active and purposive membership, purposive that is as to the organization's
criminal ends," which is the character of membership to which the Court
today restricts the application of the membership clause of the Smith Act.

In its approach to the relation of the first sentence of § 4 (f) to the membership clause of the Smith Act, I think the Court asks the wrong question.
The question is not whether the Congress meant in § 4 (f) to "repeal" the
membership clause of the Smith Act. The "repeal" of a statute connotes its
erasure from the statute books. The grant of immunity from prosecution
under a criminal statute merely suspends prosecution under the statute so
long as the immunity is not withdrawn. . . .

The Congress was faced with a dilemma in legislating the policy of compulsory registration of Communists into the Internal Security Act. This
statute represented, in the words of the late John W. Davis, a policy of

"ventilation rather than prohibition." Communists were to be forced to expose themselves to public view in order that the menace they present might be dealt with more effectively. The registration provisions of the Act are the very vitals of that measure. But compulsory disclosure of membership would compel admission of a crime, or provide a link to proof of a crime. Communists then could invoke their constitutional right to silence and the registration provisions would be wrecked on the rock of the Self-Incrimination Clause of the Fifth Amendment. It is no disparagement of the Congress to say that their deliberations reflect great uncertainty how to resolve the dilemma. Congress wrote the Internal Security Act knowing that the privilege against self-incrimination was a solid barrier against compulsory self-incrimination by congressional fiat. The legislative history of § 4 (f) is murky but I think there clearly emerges a congressional decision to extend immunity from prosecution for any membership in a Communist organization in order to safeguard against constitutional frustration the policy of disclosure embodied in the registration provisions.

The purpose of the first sentence of § 4 (f) seems clear in the setting of the Act. In § 2 Congress describes the Communist Party as a group bent on overthrowing the Government by force and violence, such as is described in the Smith Act, and establishing a totalitarian dictatorship in the United States. Section 4 (a) makes it a crime to conspire to that end. Sections 7 and 8 provide for compulsory registration of Communist organizations and members. Penalties for not registering are imposed. If members were required to register under the 1950 Act and if membership were a crime under the 1940 Act, then self-incrimination in violation of the Fifth Amendment might be required by the registration requirements of the 1950 Act. Plainly it was with that problem that Congress dealt in § 4 (f).

The bills introduced in the Eighty-first Congress provided for compulsory registration of members of the Communist Party, but afforded no immunity for registering. When the House Committee reported out its bill, a provision was included which forbade receipt in evidence of the fact of registration under the Internal Security Act. When the bill reached the floor, Congressman Celler pointed out that the immunity provision was constitutionally insufficient. In the first place, that bill only provided that the fact of registration under the Act should not be received in evidence against the registrant in prosecutions under the Act. Congressman Celler pointed out that there were other criminal statutes, including the Smith Act, for which no immunity was granted. He secondly pointed out that the immunity to be constitutionally protective must be complete; and he discussed *Counselman* v. *Hitchcock*, 142 U.S. 547, in support of that thesis. During these debates and in response to the challenge made by Congressman Celler, the manager of the bill, Congressman Wood, offered an amendment extending the same protection against prosecutions "for any alleged violation of any other criminal statute." It was adopted without discussion and the bill passed the House.

At that juncture it seems obvious that restricting the immunity to use of the fact of registration in any criminal prosecutions did not satisfy the constitutional requirements. Such a limited immunity was granted by statute in *Counselman* v. *Hitchcock, supra.* Yet as the Court stated in that case, p. 564:

> This, of course, protected him against the use of his testimony against him or his property in any prosecution against him or his property, in any criminal proceeding, in a court of the United States. But it had only that effect. It could not, and would not, prevent the use of his testimony to search out other testimony to be used in evidence against him or his property, in a criminal proceeding in such court. It could not prevent the obtaining and the use of witnesses and evidence which should be attributable directly to the testimony he might give under compulsion, and on which he might be convicted, when otherwise, and if he had refused to answer, he could not possibly have been convicted.

Meanwhile the Senate bill was reported out. The late John W. Davis had stated in a letter to the Senate Committee that compulsory registration might make a member "involuntarily incriminate himself." The Senate bill accordingly provided that neither holding office nor membership in the Communist Party should constitute a violation of certain provisions of the bill; and it also provided that the fact of registration should not be received in evidence against the registrant in prosecutions under those provisions. Senator Kilgore in a minority report made the same point that Congressman Celler had made in the House—that this immunity provision did not even purport to avoid self-incrimination in relation to the membership clause of the Smith Act and did not provide that complete immunity which *Counselman* v. *Hitchcock, supra,* held essential.

Senator Lehman spoke to the same effect when the bill reached the floor. . . .

But no change in the bill was made in this respect before it passed the Senate. The important changes in § 4 (f)—the ones that are critical here—took place in Conferences. No contemporary statement of the intended sweep of the revised § 4 (f) is in the legislative record. But I have set out enough history to indicate that the motivation was clearly the fear that the immunity granted under the earlier versions of the bill was not constitutionally sufficient to compel registration, since it did not extend to prosecutions under the membership clause of the Smith Act.

When the bill came back from the Conference Committee Congressman Multer referred to § 4 (f) in its new form and predicted it would "vitiate one of the most important parts of the Smith law." No reply was made to his comments. And only brief reference was made to § 4 (f) in the Senate. Senator Kefauver said, "There is nothing in the bill which provides that when a person registers that fact shall not be used in evidence against him in connection with the Smith Act." But that statement is irrelevant to our problem because the Senator apparently did not realize that the bill had been amended in Conference to include the words "or any other criminal statute." Senator Kilgore stated that the Conference bill differed from the one approved by the Judiciary Committee over his dissent, since it nullified the Smith Act. No one challenged the statement.

From this legislative history it seems tolerably clear that one purpose of § 4 (f) was to protect registrants from prosecution under the membership clause of the Smith Act.

The Court holds, however, that the first sentence of § 4 (f) is simply "a mandate to the courts charged with the construction of subsections (a) and (c) 'or . . . any other criminal statute' that neither those two named criminal provisions nor any other shall be *construed* so as to make 'membership . . . per se a violation.' " If the phraseology were that immunity is extended only to "*membership per se*," there might be support for the argument that the immunity granted by § 4 (f) extends only to nominal membership, excluding the type of active membership which we have here. But the statute does not say "membership *per se*." It provides that "neither the holding of office nor membership in any Communist organization shall constitute *per se* a violation of subsection (a) or subsection (c) of this section or of any other criminal statute." The kind of membership given immunity is not restricted. It may be nominal, short-term, long-term, dues-paying, non-dues-paying, inactive, or active membership. Every type of membership is included. What the Congress is saying is that no type of membership shall violate alone or by itself (that is to say, *per se*) any criminal statute. When Congress said that membership "shall not constitute *per se*" a violation of any criminal statute, it meant that additional conduct besides membership, whatever its nature, is necessary to constitute a violation. Only by transposing *per se* in § 4 (f) and making it modify "membership" can the Court's argument be made plausible. That entails a substantial revision of the Act and a drastic dilution of rights of immunity which have been granted by it.

If the Court is correct in its view, the constitutionality of registration provisions of the 1950 Act are called into question. True, today's decision in *Communist Party of America* v. *Subversive Activities Control Board*, . . . puts off to another day the constitutionality of the registration provisions in their conflict with the Fifth Amendment; I have noted my dissent as to the provision of the registration requirements that designated officials of the Party must complete, sign, and file the Party's registration statement. But if "active membership" remains as a crime under the Smith Act, there would be a serious question whether any Communist—active or nominal—could constitutionally be compelled to register under the 1950 Act. For it could be urged that the act of registering would supply one link that might complete the chain of evidence against him under the Smith Act. It is no answer to that contention that mere membership would not support a conviction. As we said in *Blau* v. *United States*, 340 U.S. 159:

> Whether such admissions by themselves would support a conviction under a criminal statute is immaterial. Answers to the questions asked by the grand jury would have furnished a link in the chain of evidence needed in a prosecution of petitioner for violation of (or conspiracy

to violate) the Smith Act. Prior decisions of this Court have clearly established that under such circumstances, the Constitution gives a witness the privilege of remaining silent. The attempt by the courts below to compel petitioner to testify runs counter to the Fifth Amendment as it has been interpreted from the beginning.

This principle had been an established one ever since *Counselman* v. *Hitchcock*, was decided.

The registration provisions of the 1950 Act were the very heart of that law. Disclosure of who the Communists were was the provision from which all other controls stemmed. As the Senate Report stated, the registration requirement is the "central provision" of the Act, the purpose being "(a) to expose the Communist movement and protect the public against innocent and unwitting colaboration with it; (b) to expose, and protect the public against, certain acts which are declared unlawful."

A fair and literal reading of § 4 (f) can save the 1950 Act against this Fifth Amendment objection. By reading § 4 (f) to provide that being a member of the Communist Party shall not "constitute *per se*" a crime, immunity from prosecution under the membership clause of the Smith Act is effected. And that is in full harmony with the purpose to make something more than "membership" necessary for conviction. That something more can be some kind of unlawful activity. After the 1950 Act was passed, membership without other activity was no longer sufficient for Smith Act prosecutions. That seems to me to be the only fair way to read § 4 (f). That conclusion necessarily results in a dismissal of this indictment.

NOTO *v.* UNITED STATES

367 US 290 (1961)

[This case, like its companion case *Scales* v. *United States, supra,* involved the constitutionality of the membership clause of the Smith Act. In this case, however, the Court unanimously reversed the judgment of conviction. Five of the Justices rested on the ground that the evidence at the trial was insufficient to show that the Communist Party, of which Noto was a member, engaged in advocacy of the doctrine of forcible overthrow of the government and in advocacy of action to that end (as distinguished from advocacy of mere abstract doctrine).

[Justice Brennan and Chief Justice Warren would have directed dismissal of the indictment on the ground that the prosecution was barred by Sec. 4 (f) of the Internal Security Act, providing that neither the holding of office nor membership in any Communist organization shall constitute *per se* a violation of any criminal statute.

[Justices Black and Douglas, in separate concurring opinions, expressed the view that the conviction was invalid under the First Amendment.]

Mr. Justice Harlan delivered the opinion of the Court:

This case, like *Scales* v. *United States,* was brought here to test the validity of a prosecution under the membership clause of the Smith Act. The case comes to us from the Court of Appeals for the Second Circuit which affirmed petitioner's conviction in the District Court for the Western District of New York, after a jury trial.

The only one of petitioner's points we need consider is his attack on the sufficiency of the evidence, since his statutory and constitutional challenges to the conviction are disposed of by our opinion in *Scales;* and consideration of his other contentions is rendered unnecessary by the view we take on his evidentiary challenge.

In considering that challenge we start from the premise that Smith Act offenses require rigorous standards of proof. . . . We find that the record in this case, which was tried before our opinion issued in *Yates* v. *United States,* 354 U.S. 298, bears much of the infirmity that we found in the *Yates* record, and requires us to conclude that the evidence of illegal Party advocacy was insufficient to support his conviction.

A large part of the evidence adduced by the Government on that issue came from the witness Lautner, and the reading of copious excerpts from the "communist classics." This evidence, to be sure, plentifully shows the Party's teaching of abstract doctrine that revolution is an inevitable product of the "proletarian" effort to achieve communism in a capitalist society, but testimony as to happenings which might have lent that evidence to an inference of "advocacy of action" to accomplish that end during the period of indictment, 1946–1954, or itself supported such an inference, is sparse indeed. Moreover, such testimony as there is of that nature was not broadly based, but was limited almost exclusively to Party doings in western New York, more especially in the cities of Rochester and Buffalo, the scene of petitioner's principal Party activities. Further, the showing of illegal Party advocacy lacked the compelling quality which in *Scales* was supplied by the petitioner's own utterances and systematic course of conduct as a high Party official. We proceed to a summary of this testimony.

The witness Dietch described mainly episodes from his indoctrination as a member of the Rochester Young Communist League during the years 1935–1938. In that time he knew petitioner, with whom he had gone to high school, and testified that petitioner, then a youth, was an active and convinced member of the League. Apart from those early years, Dietch's testimony as to the Party and the petitioner referred to one other possibly relevant episode, when, in 1951, he obtained for the Party at petitioner's request two pieces of special printing equipment for which petitioner paid $100 and $200. However, this episode is deprived of significance when it appears from the witness' testimony that petitioner explained to him at the time that pressure brought to bear on the Party had made it difficult for it to get its printing done by conventional commercial means.

The witness Geraldine Hicks had joined the Party in 1943 at the request of the F.B.I. and continued to be involved with it until 1953. She knew petitioner in connection with his work as Chairman of the Erie County Communist Party from 1946 until 1950. Her testimony related to classes and meetings which she attended in the Buffalo area, where the "communist classics" were used for teaching purposes. Extensive passages from these works were read into evidence. She also testified as to the importance attributed by the local Party to its "industrial concentration" work and to its recruitment of workers in those industries as well as to the importance attributed to the recruitment of Negroes.

The witness Chatley, who was a bus driver during the period of his Communist Party membership from 1949 onwards, testified to his contacts with petitioner and other Party members in the Buffalo area. He testified to Party teachings as to the importance of receiving solid support from the labor unions. He was given various items of literature such as the *History of the Russian Revolution* and *The Proletarian Revolution and the Renegade Kautsky*, which latter dealt with an early Communist who had been singled out for condemnation because of his views that communism could be achieved ultimately by peaceful means. He was told by petitioner that "if I would reread the book[s], most of my questions would be answered. He said if there were any points I did not understand he would be happy to clear them up at a later visit." Perhaps the most significant item of Chatley's testimony dealt with an interview with petitioner, at which Chatley was requested to hide out a Party member who was fleeing the F.B.I. in connection with "what the newspapers called this Atom Spy Ring business." So far as the record reveals, the plans never progressed beyond this request. The petitioner had also told Chatley that the Federal Government was building concentration camps. . . .

Certainly the most damaging testimony came from the witness Regan, who as a government agent and Party member from 1947 in the Buffalo-Rochester area gathered considerable information on the Party's "industrial concentration" program in that area. Regan, at the request of petitioner, attended a Party meeting in New York City on creating a Party commission in the United Auto Workers. The conference concerned the penetration of the United Auto Workers, and plans were made for getting people into various shops in automobile plants in the State, who could later assume positions of leadership in the union. At a later date petitioner also discussed the penetration of an automobile plant in the area by Party members sent up from New York City. Regan also received a pamphlet, but not from the petitioner, dealing with the concentration program in the steel industry. The pamphlet stated at one point:

1. Three basic industries, steel, railroad and mining. These are basis [sic] to the National Economy, that is if any one or all three are shut down by strike our economy is paralyzed. It is necessary for a Marxist revolutionary party to be rooted in these industries.

In 1949 Regan attended a conference in Rochester at which the petitioner spoke: "He discussed concentration work, and he said the task of the Party was to build the Party within the shop in Buffalo . . . he specifically mentioned both steel and Westinghouse electric." Another speaker said that "steel was a basic industry, by basic he said the entire section of industry within the country depended on steel." Regan also attended a conference in New York City at which petitioner spoke:

. . . He said a Lenin method of work within the shop was to decide upon the particular dependent within the shop, that the shop as a rule depended upon, to suspend production, it was the job of every communist to know the people, executives and product of the company, if possible to direct his attention on the key department, better still to get a job in the key department.

Several other passages in Regan's testimony should be adverted to for their bearing on the tone of the record before us. Speaking of the war in Korea, Regan testified that the petitioner had said at the conference of the Upstate District of the Party in 1950:

. . . the war . . . was caused by an aggressive action of the United States, American troops would follow Wall Street policy. He said it is possible for this to break out in other parts of the world. He mentioned the Near East.
   Q. Is that all?
   A. Yes.

No effort was made to link up this conference with particularly trusted Party members, but it does appear that it was at this conference that plans were laid for building a Communist Party club "on the railroad."
   Regan also testified to a remark made at another Party conference by a lecturer that a "social democrat was an evolutionist who waited for socialism where the Communist Party would achieve socialism through revolutions." At this same meeting the lecturer recounted an incident that had occurred at a class she had once taught in New Rochelle, New York, at an unspecified time:

. . . She said a person at this class, they were discussing the Soviet Union, asked her if it would be possible for him to own twenty pairs of shoes in the Soviet Union. She made the statement he was the kind of guy they hoped to shoot some day.

The witness recalled a similar intemperate remark by the petitioner, during a meeting in 1947:

Lumpkin [a Party member] was talking about a visit to his home by a local newspaper reporter. He said the reporter came to his home. They let him in and answered a lot of question[s]. . . . John Noto said Lumpkin should never let the reporter into his house. Should not have answered any questions. He said "Sometime I will see the time we can stand a person like this S.O.B. against the wall and shoot him.

The witness Greenberg testified largely about the Party program in the upstate area as to setting up printing and mimeographing equipment in case commercial channels were cut off or the Party was forced underground; and three other witnesses testified briefly to the effect that they had known petitioner when he had moved to Newark, New Jersey, and obtained a job under an assumed name as a helper or stockkeeper in the Goodyear Rubber Products Corporation factory, in connection with which he used a false Social Security number.

Finally, there was testimony through the witness Lautner as to the Party's underground organization in northern New York, including petitioner's participation therein as one of the three Party members in charge.

We must consider this evidence in the light most favorable to the Government to see whether it would support the conclusion that the Party engaged in the advocacy "not of . . . mere abstract doctrine of forcible overthrow, but of action to that end, by the use of language reasonably and ordinarily calculated to incite persons to . . . action" immediately or in the future. *Yates* v. *United States*. . . .

We held in *Yates,* and we reiterate now, that the mere abstract teaching of Communist theory, including the teaching of the moral propriety or even moral necessity for a resort to force and violence is not the same as preparing a group for violent action and steeling it to such action. There must be some substantial direct or circumstantial evidence of a call to violence now or in the future which is both sufficiently strong and sufficiently pervasive to lend color to the otherwise ambiguous theoretical material regarding Communist Party teaching, and to justify the inference that such a call to violence may fairly be imputed to the Party as a whole, and not merely to some narrow segment of it.

Surely the off-hand remarks that certain individuals hostile to the Party would one day be shot cannot demonstrate more than the venomous or spiteful attitude of the Party towards its enemies, and might indicate what could be expected from the Party if it should ever succeed to power. The "industrial concentration" program, as to which the witness Regan testified in some detail, does indeed come closer to the kind of concrete and particular program on which a criminal conviction in this sort of case must be based. But in examining that evidence it appears to us that, in the context of this record, this too fails to establish that the Communist Party was an organization which presently advocated violent overthrow of the Government now or in the future, for that is what must be proven. The most that can be said is that the evidence as to that program might justify an inference that the leadership of the Party was preparing the way for a situation in which future acts of sabotage might be facilitated, but there is no evidence that such acts of sabotage were presently advocated; and it is *present* advocacy, and not an intent to advocate in the future or a conspiracy to advocate in the future once a groundwork had been laid, which is an element of the crime under the membership clause. To permit an inference of present advocacy from evidence showing at best only a purpose or conspiracy to advocate in the future would be to allow the jury to blur the lines of distinction between the various offenses punishable under the Smith Act.

The kind of evidence which we found in *Scales* sufficient to support the jury's verdict of present illegal Party advocacy is lacking here in any adequately substantial degree. It need hardly be said that it is upon the particular evidence in a particular record that a particular defendant must be judged, and not upon evidence in some other record or upon what may be supposed to be the tenets of the Communist Party. . . .

Although our conclusion renders unnecessary consideration of the evidence as to petitioner's personal criminal purpose to bring about the overthrow of the Government by force and violence, a further word may be desirable. While evidence of the industrial concentration program, in which petitioner was active, does not alone justify an inference of the Party's present advocacy of violent overthrow, it may very well tend to show the quite different element of the petitioner's own purpose. Even though it is not enough to sustain a conviction that the party has engaged in "mere doctrinal justification of forcible overthrow . . . [even] with intent to accomplish overthrow," *Yates, supra,* at 321, it would seem that such a showing might be of weight in meeting the requirement that the particular defendant in a membership clause prosecution had the requisite criminal intent. But it should also be said that this element of the membership crime, like its others, must be judged *strictissimi juris,* for otherwise there is a danger that one in sympathy with the legitimate aims of such an organization, but not specifically intending to accomplish them by resort to violence, might be punished for his adherence to lawful and constitutionally protected purposes, because of other and unprotected purposes which he does not necessarily share.

In view of our conclusion as to the insufficiency of the evidence as to illegal Party advocacy, the judgment of the Court of Appeal must be reversed.

Mr. Justice Black, concurring:

In 1799, the English Parliament passed a law outlawing certain named societies on the ground that they were engaged in "a tratorous Conspiracy . . . in conjunction with the Persons from Time to Time exercising the Powers of Government in *France*. . . ." One of the many strong arguments made by those who opposed the enactment of this law was stated by a member of that body, Mr. Tierney:

> The remedy proposed goes to the putting an end to all these societies together. I object to the system, of which this is only a branch; for the right hon. gentleman has told us he intends to propose laws from time to time upon this subject, as cases may arise to require them. I say these attempts lead to consequences of the most horrible kind. I see that government are acting thus. Those whom they cannot prove to be guilty, they will punish for their suspicion. To support this system, we must have a swarm of spies and informers. They are the very pillars of such a system of government.

The decision in this case, in my judgment, dramatically illustrates the continuing vitality of this observation.

The conviction of the petitioner here is being reversed because the Government has failed to produce evidence the Court believes sufficient to prove that the Communist Party presently advocates the overthrow of the Government by force. The Government is being told, in effect, that if it wishes to get convictions under the Smith Act, it must maintain a permanent staff of informers who are prepared to give up-to-date information with respect to the present policies of the Communist Party. Given the fact that such prosecutions are to be permitted at all, I do not disagree with the wisdom of the Court's decision to compel the Government to come forward with evidence to prove its charges in each particular case. But I think that it is also important to realize the overriding pre-eminence that such a system of laws gives to the perpetuation and encouragement of the practice of informing—a practice which, I think it is fair to say, has not always been considered the sort of system to which a wise government would entrust the security of a Nation. I have always thought, as I still do think, that this Government was built upon a foundation strong enough to assure its endurance without resort to practices which most of us think of as being associated only with totalitarian governments.

I cannot join an opinion which implies that the existence of liberty is dependent upon the efficiency of the Government's informers. I prefer to rest my concurrence in the judgment reversing petitioner's conviction on what I regard as the more solid ground that the First Amendment forbids the Government to abridge the rights of freedom of speech, press and assembly.

COMMUNIST PARTY v. SUBVERSIVE ACTIVITIES CONTROL BOARD

367 US 1 (1961)

[The Subversive Activities Control Board ordered the Communist Party of the United States to register as a Communist-action organization under Sec. 7 of the Subversive Activities Control Act. By a vote of 5 to 4 the Supreme Court upheld the order.

[The Court construed the statute as a regulatory, rather than a prohibitory, measure; it also construed the statute as applying to an organization which, though not inciting the present use of force, has been found to operate to advance the establishment of a Communist totalitarian dictatorship and the overthrow of existing governments by any available means. The Court limited constitutional review to Sec. 7 as applied to the Communist Party—the section requires a Communist-action organization to register and to file a registration statement.

[Chief Justice Warren and Justices Black, Douglas, and Brennan dissented. The reasons for the dissents are various, including the view that the registration requirements of the act violated the constitutional privilege against self-incrimination; that the statute constituted a bill of attainder; that it violated the freedoms of expression and association protected by the First Amendment; that it violated the Due Process Clause by Congress' predetermination of the facts upon which the application of the registration requirements to the Communist Party depended.

[Since the opinions involve many important constitutional questions, and since the opinions deal with important congressional findings as to the nature of the Communist movement and the organizations that cluster about it, the opinions, in the abridgment published below, are given in substantial length in order to preserve their considerable constitutional significance. The dissenting opinion of Chief Justice Warren, concerned with nonconstitutional issues, is omitted.]

Mr. Justice Frankfurter delivered the opinion of the Court:

This is a proceeding pursuant to § 14 (a) of the Subversive Activities Control Act of 1950 to review an order of the Subversive Activities Control Board requiring the Communist Party of the United States to register as a Communist-action organization under § 7 of the Act. The

Court of Appeals for the District of Columbia has affirmed the Board's registration order. Because important questions of construction and constitutionality of the statute were raised by the Party's petition for certiorari, we brought the case here.

The Subversive Activities Control Act is Title I of the Internal Security Act of 1950, 64 Stat. 987, 50 U.S.C. § 781 *et seq.* It has been amended, principally by the Communist Control Act of 1954, 68 Stat. 775, and certain of its provisions have been carried forward in sections of the Immigration and Nationality Act adopted in 1952, 66 Stat. 163, 8 U.S.C. §§ 1182, 1251, 1424, 1451. A brief outline of its structure, in pertinent part, will frame the issues for decision.

Section 2 of the Act recites legislative findings based upon evidence adduced before various congressional committees. The first of these is:

> There exists a world Communist movement which, in its origins, its development, and its present practice, is a world-wide revolutionary movement whose purpose it is, by treachery, deceit, infiltration into other groups (governmental and otherwise), espionage, sabotage, terrorism, and any other means deemed necessary, to establish a Communist totalitarian dictatorship in the countries throughout the world through the medium of a world-wide Communist organization.

The characteristics of a "totalitarian dictatorship," as set forth in subsections (2) and (3) are the existence of a single, dictatorial political party substantially identified with the government of the country in which it exists, the suppression of all opposition to the party in power, the subordination of the rights of the individual to the state, and the denial of fundamental rights and liberties characteristic of a representative form of government. Subsection (4) finds that the direction and control of the "world Communist movement" is vested in and exercised by the Communist dictatorship of a foreign country; and subsection (5), that the Communist dictatorship of this foreign country, in furthering the purposes of the world Communist movement, establishes and utilizes in various countries action organizations which are not free and independent organizations, but are sections of a world-wide Communist organization and are controlled, directed, and subject to the discipline of the Communist dictatorship of the same foreign country. Subsection (6) sets forth that

> The Communist action organizations so established and utilized in various countries, acting under such control, direction, and discipline, endeavor to carry out the objectives of the world Communist movement by bringing about the overthrow of existing governments by any available means, including force if necessary, and setting up Communist totalitarian dictatorships which will be subservient to the most powerful existing Communist

totalitarian dictatorship. Although such organizations usually designate themselves as political parties, they are in fact constituent elements of the world-wide Communist movement and promote the objectives of such movement by conspiratorial and coercive tactics, instead of through the democratic processes of a free elective system or through the freedom-preserving means employed by a political party which operates as an agency by which people govern themselves.

In subsection (7) it is found that the Communist organizations thus described are organized on a secret conspiratorial basis and operate to a substantial extent through "Communist-front" organizations, in most instances created or used so as to conceal their true character and purpose, with the result that the "fronts" are able to obtain support from persons who would not extend their support if they knew the nature of the organizations with which they dealt. Congress makes other findings: that the most powerful existing Communist dictatorship has caused the establishment in numerous foreign countries of Communist totalitarian dictatorships, and threatens to establish such dictatorships in still other countries (10); that Communist agents have devised ruthless espionage and sabotage tactics successfully carried out in evasion of existing law (11); that the Communist network in the United States is inspired and controlled in large part by foreign agents who are sent in under various guises (12); that international travel is prerequisite for the carrying on of activities in furtherance of the Communist movement's purposes (8); that Communists have infiltrated the United States by procuring naturalization for disloyal aliens (14); that under our present immigration laws, many deportable aliens of the subversive, criminal or immoral classes are free to roam the country without supervision or control (13). Subsection (9) finds that in the United States individuals who knowingly participate in the world Communist movement in effect transfer their allegiance to the foreign country in which is vested the direction and control of the world Communist movement. Finally, in § 2 (15), Congress concludes that

The Communist movement in the United States is an organization numbering thousands of adherents, rigidly and ruthlessly disciplined. Awaiting and seeking to advance a moment when the United States may be so far extended by foreign engagements, so far divided in counsel, or so far in industrial or financial straits, that overthrow of the Government of the United States by force and violence may seem possible of achievement, it seeks converts far and wide by an extensive system of schooling and indoctrination. Such preparations by Communist organizations in other countries have aided in supplanting existing governments. The Communist organization in the United States, pursuing its stated objectives, the recent successes of Communist methods in other countries, and the nature and control of the world Communist movement itself, present a clear and present danger to the security of the United States and to the existence of free American institutions, and make it necessary that Congress, in order to provide for the common defense, to preserve the sovereignty of the United States as an independent nation, and to guarantee to each State a republican form of government, enact appropriate legislation recognizing the existence of such world-wide conspiracy and designed to prevent it from accomplishing its purpose in the United States.

Pursuant to these findings, § 7 (a) of the Act requires the registration with the Attorney General, on a form prescribed by him by regulations, of all Communist-action organizations. A Communist-action organization is defined by § 3 (3) as

(a) any organization in the United States (other than a diplomatic representative or mission of a foreign government accredited as such by the Department of State) which (i) is substantially directed, dominated, or controlled by the foreign government or foreign organization controllnig the world Communist movement referred to in section 2 of this title, and (ii) operates primarily to advance the objectives of such world Communist movement as referred to in section 2 of this title; and

(b) any section, branch, fraction, or cell of any organization defined in subparagraph (a) of this paragraph which has not complied with the registration requirements of this title.

Registration must be made within thirty days after the enactment of the Act, or, in the case of an organization which becomes a Communist-action organization after enactment, within thirty days of the date upon which it becomes such an organization; in the case of an organization which is ordered to register by the Subversive Activities Control Board, registration must take place within thirty days of the date upon which the Board's order becomes final. § 7 (c). Registration is to be accompanied by a registration statement, which must contain the name of the organization and the address of its principal office; the names and addresses of its present officers and of individuals who have been its officers within the past twelve months, with a designation of the office held by each and a brief statement of the functions and duties of each; an accounting of all moneys received and expended by the organization during the past twelve months, including the sources from which the moneys were received and the purposes for which they were expended; the name and address of each individual who was a member during the past twelve months; in the case of any officer or member required to be listed and who uses or has used more than one name, each name by which he is or has been known; and a listing of all printing presses and machines and all printing devices which are in the possession, custody, ownership, or control of the organization or its officers, members, affiliates, associates, or groups in which it or its officers or members have an interest. § 7 (d). Once an organization has registered, it must file an annual report containing the same information as is required in the registration statement. § 7 (e). A registered Communist-action organization must keep accurate records and accounts of all moneys received and expended, and of the names and addresses of its members and of persons who actively participate in its activities. § 7 (f).

Section 7 (b) requires the registration of Communist-front organizations, defined as those substantially directed, dominated, or controlled by a Communist-action organization and primarily operated for the purpose of giving aid and support to a Communist-action organization, a Communist foreign government, or the world Communist movement. § 3 (4). The procedures and requirements of registration for Communist fronts are identical with those for Communist-action organizations, except that fronts need not list their non-officer members.* In case of the failure of any organization to register, or to file a registration statement or annual report as required by the Act, it becomes the duty of the executive officer, the secretary, and such other officers of the organization as the Attorney General by regulations prescribes, to register for the organization or to file the statement or report. § 7 (h). Any individual who is or becomes a member of a registered Communist-action organization which he knows to be registered as such but to have failed to list his name as a member is required to register himself within sixty days after he obtains such knowledge; and any individual who is or

---

* By the Communist Control Act of 1954, 68 Stat. 775, the Subversive Activities Control Board is given jurisdiction to determine, in proper proceedings, whether any organization is a Communist-infiltrated organization, defined as (a) an organization substantially directed, dominated, or controlled by an individual or individuals who are, or who within three years have been actively engaged in, giving aid or support to a Communist-action organization, a Communist foreign government, or the world Communist movement, (b) which organization is serving or within three years has served as a means for giving aid or support to any such organization, government or movement, or for the impairment of the military strength of the United States or its industrial capacity to furnish logistical or other material support required by its armed forces. Evidentiary matters relevant to this determination are prescribed for the consideration of the Board. Communist-infiltrated organizations are not required to register with the Attorney General, but are required to label their publications mailed or transmitted through instrumentalities of interstate or foreign commerce, and their communications broadcasts, and are deprived of federal income-tax exemption, of certain benefits under the National Labor Relations Act as amended, etc.

Under § 13A (h), added to the Subversive Activities Control Act of 1950 by the Communist Control Act of 1954, 68 Stat. 775, 779, the provisions depriving labor organizations of National Labor Relations Act labor-union benefits apply to labor organizations determined by the Board to be Communist-action or Communist-front, as well as Communist-infiltrated, organizations. 50 U.S.C. § 792a (h).

becomes a member of an organization concerning which there is in effect a final order of the Subversive Activities Control Board requiring that it register as a Communist-action organization, but which has not so registered although more than thirty days have elapsed since the order became final, is required to register himself within thirty days of becoming a member or within sixty days after the registration order becomes final, whichever is later. § 8. Criminal penalties are imposed upon organizations, officers and individuals who fail to register or to file statements as required: fine of not more than $10,000 for each offense by an organization; fine of not more than $10,000 or imprisonment for not more than five years or both for each offense by an officer or individual; each day of failure to register constituting a separate offense. Individuals who in a registration statement or annual report willfully make any false statement, or willfully omit any fact required to be stated or which is necessary to make any information given not misleading, are subject to a like penalty. § 15.

The Attorney General is required by § 9 to keep in the Department of Justice separate registers of Communist-action and Communist-front organizations, containing the names and addresses of such organizations, their registration statements and annual reports, and, in the case of Communist-action organizations, the registration statements of individual members. These registers are to be open for public inspection. The Attorney General must submit a yearly report to the President and to Congress including the names and addresses of registered organizations and their listed members. He is required to publish in the Federal Register the fact that any organization has registered as a Communist-action or Communist-front organization, and such publication constitutes notice to all members of the registration of the organization.

Whenever the Attorney General has reason to believe that any organization which has not registered is an organization of a kind required to register, or that any individual who has not registered is required to register, he shall petition the Subversive Activities Control Board for an order that the organization or individual register in the manner provided by the Act. §§ 12, 13 (a). Any organization or any individual registered, or any individual listed in any registration statement who denies that he holds office or membership in the registered organization and whom the Attorney General, upon proper request, has failed to strike from the register, may, pursuant to designated procedures, file with the Subversive Activities Control Board a petition for cancellation of registration or other appropriate relief. § 13 (b).

The Board, whose organization and procedure are prescribed, §§ 12, 13 (d), 16, is empowered to hold hearings (which shall be public), to examine witnesses and receive evidence, and to compel the attendance and testimony of witnesses and the production of documents relevant to the matter under inquiry. § 13 (c), (d). If after hearing the Board determines that an organization is a Communist-action or a Communist-front organization or that an individual is a member of a Communist-action organization, it shall make a report in writing and shall issue an order requiring the organization or individual to register or denying its or his petition for relief. § 13 (g), (j). If the Board determines that an organization is not a Communist-action or a Communist-front organization or that an individual is not a member of a Communist-action organization, it shall make a report in writing and issue an order denying the Attorney General's petition for a registration order, or canceling the registration of the organization or the individual, or striking the name of the individual from a registration statement or annual report, as appropriate. § 13 (h), (i).

The party aggrieved by any such order of the Board may obtain review by filing in the Court of Appeals for the District of Columbia a petition praying that the order be set aside. The findings of the Board as to the facts, if supported by the preponderance of the evidence, shall be conclusive. If either party shall apply to the court for leave to adduce additional evidence and shall show to the satisfaction of the court that such additional evidence is material, the court may order such additional evidence to be taken before the Board, and the Board may modify its findings as to the facts, and shall file such modified or new findings, which, if supported by the preponderance of the evidence, shall be conclusive. The court may enter appropriate orders. Its judgment and decree shall be final, except that they may be reviewed in this Court on writ of certiorari. § 14 (a). When an order of the Board requiring the registration of a Communist organization has become final upon the termination of proceedings for judicial review or upon the expiration of the time allowed for institution of such proceedings, the Board shall publish in the Federal Register the fact that its order has become final, and that publication shall constitute notice to all members of the organization that the order has become final. §§ 13 (k), 14 (b).

Section 13 (e) of the Act provides that

In determining whether any organization is a "Communist-action organization," the Board shall take into consideration—

(1) the extent to which its policies are formulated and carried out and its activities performed, pursuant to directives or to effectuate the policies of the foreign government or foreign organization in which is vested, or under the domination or control of which is exercised, the direction and control of the world Communist movement referred to in section 2 of this title; and

(2) the extent to which its views and policies do not deviate from those of such foreign government or foreign organization; and

(3) the extent to which it receives financial or other aid, directly or indirectly, from or at the direction of such foreign government or foreign organization; and

(4) the extent to which it sends members or representatives to any foreign country for instruction or training in the principles, policies, strategy, or tactics of such world Communist movement; and

(5) the extent to which it reports to such foreign government or foreign organization or to its representatives; and

(6) the extent to which its principal leaders or a substantial number of its members are subject to or recognize the disciplinary power of such foreign government or foreign organization or its representatives; and

(7) the extent to which, for the purpose of concealing foreign direction, domination, or control, or of expediting or promoting its objectives, (i) it fails to disclose, or resists efforts to obtain information as to, its membership (by keeping membership lists in code, by instructing members to refuse to acknowledge membership, or by any other method); (ii) its members refuse to acknowledge membership therein; (iii) it fails to disclose, or resists efforts to obtain information as to, records other than membership lists; (iv) its meetings are secret; and (v) it otherwise operates on a secret basis; and

(8) the extent to which its principal leaders or a substantial number of its members consider the allegiance they owe to the United States as subordinate to their obligations to such foreign government or foreign organization.

Similarly, § 13 (f) enumerates a set of evidentiary considerations to guide the inquiry and judgment of the Board in determining whether a given organization is or is not a Communist-front organization.

When an organization is registered under the Act, or when there is in effect with respect to it a final order of the Board requiring it to register, § 10 (1) prohibits it, or any person acting in behalf of it, from transmitting through the mails or by any means or instrumentality of interstate or foreign commerce any publication which is intended to be, or which it may be reasonably believed is intended to be, circulated or disseminated among two or more persons, unless that publication, and its envelope, wrapper or container, bear the writing: "Disseminated by [the name of the organization], a Communist organization." Section 10 (2) prohibits the organization, or any person acting in its behalf, from broadcasting or causing to be broadcast any matter over any radio or television station unless the matter is preceded by the statement: "The following program is sponsored by [the name of the organization], a Communist organization." Under § 11 of the Act, the organization is not entitled to exemption from federal income tax under § 101 of the

1939 Internal Revenue Code, and no deduction for federal income-tax purposes is allowed in the case of a contribution to it. It is unlawful for any officer or employee of the United States, or of any department or agency of the United States, or of any corporation whose stock is owned in a major part by the United States, to communicate to any other person whom such officer or employee knows or has reason to believe is an officer or member of a Communist organization, any information classified by the President as affecting the security of the United States, knowing or having reason to know that such information has been classified. § 4 (b). It is unlawful for any officer or member of a Communist organization knowingly to obtain or receive, or attempt to obtain or receive, any classified information from any such government officer or employee. § 4 (c). When a Communist organization is registered or when there is in effect with respect to it a final registration order of the Subversive Activities Control Board, it is unlawful for any member of the organization, knowing or having notice that the organization is registered or the order final, to hold non-elective office or employment under the United States or to conceal or fail to disclose that he is a member of the organization in seeking, accepting, or holding such office or employment; and it is unlawful for him to conceal or fail to disclose that he is a member of the organization in seeking, accepting or holding employment in any defense facility,* or, if the organization is a Communist-action organization, to engage in any employment in any defense facility. It is unlawful for such a member to hold office or employment with any labor organization, as that term is defined in § 2 (5) of the National Labor Relations Act, as amended, 29 U.S.C. § 152, or to represent any employer in any matter or proceeding arising or pending under that Act. § 5 (a) (1). It is unlawful for any officer or employee of the United States or of a defense facility, knowing or having notice that the organization is registered or a registration order concerning it final, to advise or urge a member of the organization, with knowledge or notice that he is a member, to engage in conduct which constitutes any of the above violations of the act, or for such an officer or employee to contribute funds or services to the organization. § 5 (a) (2). When a Communist organization is registered or when there is in effect with respect to it a final registration order of the Subversive Activities Control Board, it is unlawful for a member of the organization, with knowledge or notice that it is registered or the order final, to apply for a passport, or the renewal of a passport, issued under

* Under § 5 (b) the Secretary of Defense is authorized and directed to designate and proclaim a list of facilities with respect to the operation of which he finds that the security of the United States requires the application of the controls prescribed by the Act.

the authority of the United States, or to use or to attempt to use a United States passport; and, in the case of a Communist-action organization, it is unlawful for any officer or employee of the United States to issue or renew a passport for any individual, knowing or having reason to believe that he is a member of the organization. § 6. Aliens who are members or affiliates of any organization during the time it is registered or required to be registered, unless they establish that they did not have knowledge or reason to believe that it was a Communist organization, are ineligible to receive visas, are excluded from admission to the United States, and, if in the United States, are subject to deportation upon the order of the Attorney General. . . . No person shall be naturalized as a citizen of the United States who is or, with certain exceptions, has within ten years immediately preceding filing of his naturalization petition been, a member or affiliate of any Communist-action organization during the time it is registered or is required to be registered, or a member or affiliate of any Communist-front organization during the time it is registered or required to be registered unless he establishes that he did not have knowledge or reason to believe that it was a Communist-front organization. . . . If any person naturalized after the effective date of the Act becomes within five years following his naturalization a member or affiliate of any organization, membership in which or affiliation with which at the time of naturalization would have precluded his having been naturalized, it shall be considered prima facie evidence that such person was not attached to the principles of the Constitution and was not well disposed to the good order and happiness of the United States at the time of naturalization, and in the absence of countervailing evidence, this shall suffice to authorize the revocation of naturalization. . . . Service in the employ of any organization then registered or in connection with which a final registration order is then in effect is not "employment" for purposes of the Social Security Act, . . . if performed after June 30, 1956.

Section 4 (f) of the Subversive Activities Control Act of 1950 provides that neither the holding of office nor membership in any Communist organization by any person shall constitute *per se* a violation of penal provisions of the Act or of any other criminal statute, and the fact of registration of any person as an officer or member of such an organization shall not be received in evidence against the person in any prosecution for violations of penal provisions of the Act or any other criminal statute. Section 32 provides:

If any provision of this title, or the application thereof to any person or circumstances, is held invalid, the remaining provisions of this title, or the application of such provision to other persons or circumstances, shall not be affected thereby.

I.

This litigation has a long history. On November 22, 1950, the Attorney General petitioned the Subversive Activities Control Board for an order to require that the Communist Party register as a Communist-action organization. The Party thereupon brought suit in the District Court for the District of Columbia, seeking to have the proceedings of the Board enjoined. A statutory three-judge court denied preliminary relief, *Communist Party of the United States* v. *McGrath*, 96 F. Supp. 47, but stayed answer and hearings before the Board pending appeal. After this Court denied a petition for extension of the stay, the Party abandoned the suit. Hearings began on April 23, 1951, and ended on July 1, 1952. Twenty-two witnesses for the Attorney General and three for the Party presented oral testimony; 507 exhibits, many of book length, were received; the stenographic record, exclusive of these exhibits, amounted to more than 14,000 pages. On April 20, 1953, the Board issued its 137-page report concluding that the Party was a Communist-action organization within the meaning of the Subversive Activities Control Act, and its order requiring that the Party register in the manner prescribed by § 7. Pending disposition in the Court of Appeals for the District of Columbia of the Party's petition for review of the registration order, the Party moved in that court, pursuant to § 14 (a), for leave to adduce additional evidence which it alleged would show that three witnesses for the Attorney General, Crouch, Johnson, and Matusow, had testified perjuriously before the Board. The Court of Appeals denied the motion and affirmed the order of the Board, one judge dissenting. *Communist Party of the United States* v. *Subversive Activities Control Board*, 223 F. 2d 531. Finding that the Party's allegations of perjury had not been denied by the Attorney General, and concluding that the registration order based on a record impugned by a charge of perjurious testimony on the part of three witnesses whose evidence constituted a not insubstantial portion of the Government's case could not stand, this Court remanded to the Board "to make certain that [it] bases its findings upon untainted evidence."

On remand the Party filed several motions with the Board seeking to reopen the record for the introduction of additional evidence. These were denied. A motion in the Court of Appeals for leave to adduce additional evidence was similarly denied, except that the Board was granted permission to entertain a motion concerning the Party's offer to show that another of the Attorney General's witnesses, Mrs. Markward, had committed perjury with regard to a specified aspect of her testimony. The Board granted the Party's motion; hearings were reopened; Mrs. Markward was cross-examined. Motions by the Party for orders requiring the Government to produce certain documents relevant to the matter of her testimony were denied. On December 18, 1956, the Board issued its 240-page Modified Report. It found that Mrs. Markward was a credible witness, made new findings of fact, and, having expunged the testimony of Crouch, Johnson and Matusow, reaffirmed its conclusion that the Party was a Communist-action organization and recommended that the Court of Appeals affirm its registration order. That court, while affirming the Board's actions in other regards, held that the Party was entitled to production of several documents relating to Mrs. Markward's testimony, and remanded. *Communist Party of the United States* v. *Subversive Activities Control Board*, 254 F. 2d 314. The scope of this remand was enlarged by subsequent orders requiring the production of recorded statements made to the F.B.I. by the Attorney General's witness Budenz, the existence of these recordings having become known to government counsel and to the Board only at this time. These statements related to Budenz's testimony at the original hearings concerning the "Starobin letter" and the "Childs-Weiner conversation." Motions pursuant to § 14 (a) seeking the production of other government-held documents—memoranda furnished to the Government by the Attorney General's witness Gitlow, and recordings made by the F.B.I. of interviews with Budenz—were denied.

On second remand, the documents specified by the orders of the Court of Appeals were made available to the Party. The hearing was reopened before a member of the Board sitting as an examiner. When the illness of Budenz made impossible his recall for cross-examination in connection with the documents produced, the examiner denied the Party's motion to strike all of Budenz's testimony, but did strike so much as related to the Starobin and Childs-Weiner matters. After re-evaluating the credibility of Budenz and Markward, and affirming the action of its examiner in striking only that portion of Budenz's testimony which concerned the Starobin letter and the Childs-Weiner conversation, the Board re-examined the record as a whole and issued its Modified Report on Second Remand—its findings of fact consisting principally of the findings contained in its first Modified Report, with a few deletions—again concluding that the Communist Party of the United States was a Communist-action organization, and again recommending that its order to register be affirmed. The same panel of the Court of Appeals affirmed the order, at the same time denying the Party's motion under § 14 (a) for an order requiring production of all statements made by government witnesses and now in the possession of the Government, the dissenting judge again dissenting in part. It is this decision which is now before us for review. . . .

III.

We come to the Communist Party's contentions that the Board and the Court of Appeals erred in their construction of the Act and in their application of it, on the facts of this record, to the Party. It is argued that both elements of the statutory definition of a Communist-action organization in § 3 (3) of the Act—what have come in the course of this litigation to be known as the "control" and "objectives" components— were misinterpreted below; that the Board misconceived the nature of each of the eight evidentiary considerations directed to its attention by § 13 (e) as pertinent to its determination whether an organization is or is not a Communist-action organization; that the Board misapplied the phrase "world Communist movement" in § 2; and that the Board erred in taking account, as relevant to that determination, of conduct of the Party prior to the date of the Act. The Court of Appeals is said to have erred in failing to remand to the Board after striking one of its subsidiary findings as unsupported by the evidence. Finally, it is contended, the record as a whole does not support by the preponderance of the evidence, as required by § 14 (a), the conclusion that the Party is a Communist-action organization within the correct meaning of that phrase.

A. *The "Control Component."* Under § 3 (3) of the Act an organization cannot be found to be a Communist-action organization unless it is "substantially directed, dominated, or controlled by the foreign government or foreign organization controlling the world Communist movement. . . ." The Party asserts that this requirement is not satisfied by any lesser demonstration than that the foreign government or foreign organization controlling the world Communist movement exercises over the organization an enforceable, coercive power to exact compliance with its demands. The Court of Appeals disagreed, holding that in the circumstances of this record a consistent, undeviating dedication, over an extended period of time, to carrying out the programs of the foreign government or foreign organization, despite significant variations in direction of those programs, was sufficient. The Subversive Activities Control Board has not, in its reports, articulated any other understanding of the standard, and since its final factual determination was made after the Court of Appeals had put this definitive gloss on § 3 (3), we must attribute to it acceptance of the court's interpretation.

We agree that substantial direction, domination, or control of one entity by another may exist without the latter's having power, in the event of non-compliance, effectively to enforce obedience to its will. The issue which the Communist Party tenders as one of construction of statutory language is more sharply drawn in the abstract sphere of words than in the realm of fact. It is true that the Court of Appeals compendiously expressed its understanding of the Party's conduct over a course of thirty years, as revealed by this record and as found by the Board, in terms of "voluntary compliance." Opposing this phrase, the Party insists that the statute demands "enforceable control." But neither of these verbalisms was used by Congress, and neither has an invariant content. Nor has the language of the statute: "substantially directed, dominated, or controlled." Each of these notions carries meaning only as a situation in human relationships which arises and takes shape in different modes and patterns in the context of different circumstances. . . .

. . . Manifestly, the various relationships among nations, organizations, movements and individuals of which the Act speaks will take a multiplicity of forms. A foreign government "dominates" or "controls" the "direction" of the world Communist movement through very different means and in very different ways than one organization "dominates" or "controls" another, or than an individual "dominates" or "controls" an organization. These differences do not deprive the concepts "domination" and "control" of ample meaning. Throughout various manifestations these concepts denote a relationship in which one entity so much holds ascendancy over another that it is predictably certain that the latter will comply with the directions expressed by the former solely by virtue of that relationship, and without reference to the nature and content of the directions. This is the sense we find in the opinions expounding the decisions of the Court of Appeals. The reports of the Board evidence a similar understanding. . . .

The subjection to foreign direction, domination, or control of which § 3 (3) speaks is a disposition unerringly to follow the dictates of a designated foreign country or foreign organization, not by the exercise of independent judgment on the intrinsic appeal that those dictates carry, but for the reason that they emanate from that country or organization. No more apt term than domination or control could be used to describe such a relationship. The nature of the circumstances which bind an organization to unwavering compliance may be diverse. They may consist, of course, of the sort of enforceable power over the organization's members which an employer has over an employee—the power to compel obedience by threat of discharge. But they may also consist of other incidents which assure that the organization will unquestioningly adhere to the line of conduct appointed for it. Some of these incidents are suggested by the evidentiary considerations which Congress has enumerated in § 13 (e) of the Act—foreign financial or other aid whose menaced withdrawal may serve as an instrument of influence, § 13 (e) (3); subjection to, or recognition of, personal disciplinary power of the designated foreign organs by the leaders or a substantial number of the members of an organization, § 13 (e) (6); obligations in the nature of allegiance owed to those foreign organs by an organization's leaders or a substantial number of its members. § 13 (e) (8). Other incidents may involve other forces felt by individuals or groups to be compelling: a recognition of mastery, for example, which makes criticism itself a severe sanction. The existence of direction, domination, or control in each instance is an issue of particular fact. The question whether in the case of a given organization such a compulsion or impulsion arises from the complex of ties which link it to a foreign government or organization that it will, because of those ties alone, adhere in its conduct to decisions made for it abroad, is one which Congress has committed, in the first instance, to an expert trier of fact. Since the determination that an organization is or is not a Communist-action organization is largely a matter of the working out of legislative policy in multiform situations of potentially great variety, the "construction" of the statute which ensues from its application to particular circumstances by the administrative agency charged with its enforcement is to be given weight by a reviewing court. . . .

While under § 14 (a) of the Subversive Activities Control Act, providing that the findings of the Board as to facts shall be conclusive if supported by the preponderance of the evidence, a stricter standard of re-examination is set than that to which administrative findings are ordinarily subject, we cannot in this case say that the Board—and, in affirming its order, the Court of Appeals—have misapplied the Act. Neither its written report nor the opinion of the court below support the Party's interpretation of them. They do not hold, as the Party suggests, that conformity which stems from nothing more than ideological agreement satisfies the reguirements of § 3 (3). What they do hold is that "the definition of a Communist-action organization was not intended by the Congress to be restricted to organizations which are subject to enforceable demands of the Soviet Union. . . . An organization or a person may be substantially under the direction or domination of another person or organization by voluntary compliance as well as through compulsion. This is especially true if voluntary compliance is simultaneous in time with the direction and is undeviating over a period of time and under variations of direction. If the Soviet Union directs a line of policy and an organization voluntarily follows the direction, the terms of this statutory definition would be met." 254 F. 2d 314, 319.

This must be read in the context of the facts of record in this proceeding. . . .

It is on the basis of these detailed findings that the Board and the court below predicated their conclusion that the Communist Party was substantially directed, dominated, or controlled by the Soviet Union. We cannot hold that they erred in the construction of the statute and in finding that the facts shown bring the Party within it.

B. *The "Objectives Component."* Section 3 (3), defining a Communist-action organization, requires a finding that the organization "operates primarily to advance the objectives of [the] . . . world Communist movement as referred to in section 2 of this title." Although asserting that the reference to § 2 is unclear, the Party offered in the Court of Appeals a construction of this requirement which defines the objectives of the world Communist movement as (a) overthrow of existing government by any means necessary, including force and violence, (b) establishment of a Communist totalitarian dictatorship, (c) which will be subservient to the Soviet Union. . . . We need not now determine whether this interpretation, insofar as it implies that an organization must operate to advance all of these objectives in order to come within the Act, is correct. Certainly, the elements which the Party has isolated are, singly or collectively, the major "objectives" described in § 2. The Court of Appeals accepted the Party's analysis *arguendo,* and its judgment affirming the order of the Board rests on its conclusion that the Party operates to advance all three of these objectives. This conclusion is supported by the findings of the Board. It adopts the interpretation most favorable to the Party.

Within the framework of these definitions, the Court of Appeals held sufficient to demonstrate the Communist Party's objective to overthrow existing government the finding of the Board that the Party advocates the overthrow of the Government of the United States by force and violence if necessary. The Party argues that this finding is inadequate to satisfy the conception of overthrow embodied in § 2 (1) and (6); that under the compulsion of the First Amendment the Act must be read as reaching only organizations whose purpose to overthrow existing government is expressed in illegal action or incitement to illegal action; that advocacy of the use of violence "if necessary" amounts at most to the promulgation of abstract doctrine, not incitement. Section 2 (1) recites that the purpose of the world Communist movement is "by treachery, deceit, infiltration. . . , espionage, sabotage, terrorism, and any other means deemed necessary, to establish a Communist totalitarian dictatorship in the countries throughout the world through the medium of a world-wide Communist organization." Section 2 (6) recites that Communist-action organizations "endeavor to carry out the objective of the world Communist movement by bringing about the overthrow of existing governments by any available means, including force if necessary. . . ." We think that an organization may be found to operate to advance objectives so defined although it does not incite the present use of force. Nor does the First Amendment compel any other construction. The Subversive Activities Control Act is a regulatory, not a prohibitory statute. It does not make unlawful pursuit of the objectives which § 2 defines. . . .

C. *The Evidentiary Considerations of Section 13 (e); the Striking by the Court of Appeals of a Subsidiary Finding Under Section 13 (e) (7).* Section 13 (e) prescribes that in determining whether any organization is a Communist-action organization, the Board shall take into consideration the extent of its conduct in eight enumerated dimensions. Accordingly, the Board made basic findings of fact in each, and on them based conclusions. The Party attacks each conclusion as based upon a misinterpretation or misapplication of the statutory considerations. . . .

. . . The Board, directed by Congress to consider "the extent to which" an organization engages in certain classes of conduct, was not, of course, obligated to make findings in each dimension which would be conclusive of the ultimate issues before it. It was required only to consider each of these dimensions—this it has painstakingly done—and, on the whole record before it, to appraise the probative force of the evidence in each dimension. . . . The Board has explained in detail the factors which urged it to take the view it has taken of the evidence concerning financial aid, foreign training and reporting. We cannot say that on the basis of all its findings it accorded inadmissible weight to these considerations.

By § 13 (e) (2), the Board is directed to consider, in determining whether a given organization is a Communist-action organization, "the extent to which its views and policies do not deviate from those of [the] . . . foreign government or foreign organization" directing the world Communist movement. In connection with this consideration, Dr. Philip Mosely, Professor of International Relations at Columbia University and Director of the University's Russian Institute, appeared as an expert witness for the Attorney General. He enumerated some forty-five major international issues during thirty years with respect to which, his testimony indicated, there had been no substantial difference between the announced positions of the Soviet Union and the Communist Party.* As to each issue, documents representative of the respective views of the Soviet and the Party were identified by Dr. Mosely and put into the

---

* Among these were the League of Nations; the Russo-Finnish War, 1939; the Hitler-Stalin non-aggression pact, 1939; attitude toward World War II before and after the German attack on the Soviet Union; dissolution of the Communist International, 1943; West Germany; the Italian election of 1948; North Atlantic Pact; control of atomic energy; election of Yugoslavia to the United Nations Security Council, 1949; Cardinal Mindszenty case, 1949; United Nations action in Korea; Communist China's intervention in Korea, 1950; seating of Communist China in the United Nations; Peace Treaty with Japan, 1951; peace in Korea.

record as exhibits. Both the Board and the Court of Appeals credited Dr. Mosely's testimony and placed significant reliance on it in concluding that the Communist Party is substantially dominated by the Soviet Union.

The Party urges two contentions relating to this aspect of the case. The first is that the Mosely evidence has no tendency to prove non-deviation, within the meaning of § 13 (e) (2), and no rational relevance to the ultimate issue of Soviet domination of the Party, because Dr. Mosely did not establish that as to each of the international issues concerning which Soviet Union and Party views coincided, the announced Soviet position antedated that of the Party, nor did Dr. Mosely testify that the coincidence of views evidenced parroting of the Soviet position by the Party—indeed, he expressly declined, as a matter of expert judgment, to draw any inference from the coincidence alone with respect to the reasoning processes by which the Party arrived at its views. The Party contends that under § 13 (e) (2) the Board was not authorized to consider evidence merely of sameness of policy, but that sameness would become relevant only after the Attorney General had shown that the Party took its position subsequent to, and not independently of, the announced policy of the Soviet. Second, the Party argues that the Board erred in refusing to let it show, both by cross-examination of Dr. Mosely and by proffered original evidence, that many other, assertedly non-Communist groups and individuals also expressed, contemporaneously with the Soviet Union and the Party, views identical to those in which the two concurred—and, further, that the views were correct.

We do not agree that the Board was not entitled to consider and evaluate evidence of a consistent identity of policies of an organization and the Soviet Union until the Government had shown the temporal antecedence of the Soviet's position and negatived the possibility that independent reasoning processes brought about the identity. Here the Board found that the coincidence of policies extended over a vast area of subject matter, was absolutely invariant during more than thirty years—the entire life of the Party—and was unbroken even in the face of sharp reversals in the Soviet's views. Section 13 (e) (2), directing the Board to consider the extent of non-deviation, does not purport to establish a litmus test of domination or control, requiring some fixed minimum level of policy-parroting. This requirement is satisfied by consideration of whatever is logically relevant in this regard. Of course, the Government would have established a stronger case had it shown not only identity of views on more than forty issues, but also that the Soviet's view had always led and the Party's always followed, and that the similarity could not conceivably be the result of autonomous application of similar basic philosophical principles. But this is no reason to say that the Board could not consider, and form its judgment on, the showing that the Government did make in the present proceeding. Certainly, if the Act contained no § 13 (e), Dr. Mosely's testimony would be both relevant and significantly probative with respect to the issue of Soviet domination of the Party. To hold that § 13 (e) (2) makes it a condition precedent to Board consideration of this long-continued, totally unwavering identity of policy lines, that the Attorney General also establish such elusive determinants as the dates of birth of the policies and the ratiocinative processes by which they came into being, we would have to find that by § 13 (e) (2) Congress meant to limit, and severely limit, the evidences of Soviet domination of which the Board could take account. The structure of § 13 (e) will not bear that construction.

With respect to the rulings precluding the Party from showing certain facts which would have tended to establish that the views in which it paralleled the Soviet Union were correct views, or were reached independently, or were also held by other persons, we do not think that the Board abused its discretion. . . .

The Party also argues that it should have been permitted to demonstrate, by cross-examination of Dr. Mosely and by original evidence, that many other persons than the Soviet and the Party held views similar to those on which the two agreed. We cannot hold that the Board erred in excluding these showings. They took two forms. First, with respect to some twenty-five international issues, the question was put to Dr. Mosely whether many non-Communist commentators did not also support the view expounded by the Party. A similar question was asked of a witness for the Party concerning one more issue. Second, with respect to somewhat more than thirty issues, the Party offered to establish, by questioning Dr. Mosely and by documents proffered in evidence, that particular named individuals and groups had concurred in the views of the Party on each individual issue. The most that the Party could have proved, had it been allowed to make the offered showings, was that on the subject of each specific, isolated one among the forty-five international issues enumerated, a considerable number of persons not Soviet-dominated took positions parallel to those of the Soviet and the Party. This is only to be expected in the case of issues of this character. The Party never offered to show, despite wide latitude allowed by the hearing panel in making proffers after similar proffers had been previously disallowed, that a continuing, substantial body of independent groups and persons concurred with the Party on a significant aggregate number of policies among the forty-five. Of the particular sources mentioned in the Party's separate questions and offers of proof, the greatest number of issues with reference to which a single source recurs—the *New York Times,* or individuals writing in the *Times*—is ten or less, and in most cases the agreement shown is with only a portion of the Party's position. No other source occurs more than roughly half a dozen times; most, two or three times. On the basis of these proffers, the Board's rulings did not amount to an abuse of the discretion which it must be allowed in the conduct of its hearings to avoid opening the sluices to litigation of the views of a multitude of third parties. . . .

D. *The Board Findings as to the World Communist Movement; Evidence of Past Practices; the Preponderance of the Evidence.* Under the Act an organization may be found to be a Communist-action organization only if the relations specified in the "control" and "objectives" components of § 3 (3) exist between it and the "world Communist movement referred to in section 2. . . ." In the present proceeding, the Board, after recognizing that "in section 2 of the Act Congress has found the existence of a world Communist movement and has described its characteristics," set forth its own description, based on the evidence presented in this record, of contemporary Communist institutions in their international aspect, and particularly of the role of the Soviet Union in those institutions. The Party argues that because this description does not duplicate in all details that of § 2 of the Act, the world Communist movement to which the Board found that the Communist Party bore the required statutory relationship is not the world Communist movement referred to in § 2.

But the attributes of the world Communist movement which are detailed in the legislative findings are not in the nature of a requisite category of characteristics comprising a definition of an entity whose existence *vel non* must be established, by proving those characteristics, in each administrative proceeding under the Act. Congress has itself found that that movement exists. The legislative description of its nature is not made a subject of litigation for the purpose of ascertaining the status of a particular organization under the Act. The Attorney General need not prove, in the case of each organization against whom a petition for a registration order is filed, that the international institutions to which the organization can be shown to be related fit the picture in every precise detail set forth in § 2. The only question, once an organization is found to have certain international relations, is one of statutory interpretation—of identifying the statutory referent. Are the institutions involved in those relations the "world Communist movement" to which Congress referred? We are satisfied from the Board's report that the "world Communist movement" to which its findings related the Communist Party was the same "world Communist movement" meant by Congress.

The Party contends that the Board and the Court below erred in relying on evidence of conduct in which it engaged prior to the enactment of the Act to support their conclusion that it is presently a Communist-action organization. This must be rejected. Where the current character of an organization and the nature of its connections with others is at issue, of course past conduct is pertinent. Institutions, like other organisms, are predominantly what their past has made them. History provides the illuminating context within which the implications of present conduct may be known.

Finally, the Party asks that we re-examine the evidence adduced before the Board and review the Board's findings of fact. The Court of Appeals, made thoroughly familiar with this record by three such re-examinations, has held that the Board's conclusions, as expressed in its Modified Report on Second Remand, are supported by a preponderance of the evidence. We see no reason why still another court should independently reappraise the record. We have declined to do this in the case of other agencies as to whom reviewing power on the facts has been vested in the Courts of Appeals, and we find no purpose to be served in departing now from this settled policy of appellate review. . . .

IV.

The Party's constitutional attack on the Subversive Activities Control Act of 1950 assails virtually every provision of this extended and intricate regulatory statute. The registration requirement of § 7, by demanding self-subjection to what may be deemed a defamatory characterization and, in addition, disclosure of the identity of all rank-and-file members, is said to abridge the First Amendment rights of free expression and association of the Communist Party and its adherents. . . . The Party's officers, it is asserted, who by filing a registration statement in its behalf evidence their status as active members of the Party, are required to incriminate themselves in violation of the Fifth Amendment, as are the individual members who must register themselves under § 8 if the Party fails to register or fails to list them. . . . The provision that Communist organizations label their publications is attacked as a prior restraint on, and such sanctions as denial of tax exemption are attacked as a penalty on the exercise of, the Party's constitutionally protected freedom of speech. . . . The various consequences of the Party's registration for its individual members—prohibition of application for and use of passports, disqualification from government or defense-facility employment, disqualification from naturalization, subjection to denaturalization, proscription of officership or employment in labor organizations—are said to deny those members due process of law by, in effect, attainting them by association, . . . and by subjecting them to potential criminal procedings in which the nature of the organization, membership in which is an element of various offenses, may not be judicially tried. Many of the statute's provisions are challenged as unconstitutionally vague, and it is said that the establishment of an agency, the Subversive Activities Control Board, whose continued existence depends upon its finding the Communist Party a Communist-action organization within the meaning of the Act, necessarily biases the agency and deprives the Party of a fair hearing. In fact, the Party asserts, the statute as written so particularly designates the Communist Party as the organization at which it is aimed, that it constitutes an abolition of the Party by legislative fiat, in the nature of a bill of attainder. The provisions must be read as a whole, it is said; and when so read, they are seen to envisage not the registration and regulation of the Party, but the imposition of impossible requirements whose only purpose is to lay a foundation for criminal prosecution of the Party and its officers and members, in effect "outlawing" the Party.

Many of these questions are prematurely raised in this litigation. Merely potential impairment of constitutional rights under a statute does not of itself create a justiciable controversy in which the nature and extent of those rights may be litigated. . . . Even where some of the provisions of a comprehensive legislative enactment are ripe for adjudication, portions of the enactment not immediately involved are not thereby thrown open for a judicial determination of constitutionality. "Passing upon the possible significance of the manifold provisions of a broad statute in advance of efforts to apply the separate provisions is analogous to rendering an advisory opinion upon a staute or a declaratory judgment upon a hypothetical case." . . . No rule of practice of this Court is better settled than "never to anticipate a question of constitutional law in advance of the necessity of deciding it." . . . In part, this principle is based upon the realization that, by the very nature of the judicial process, courts can most wisely determine issues precisely defined by the confining circumstances of particular situations. . . . In part it represents a conception of the role of the judiciary in a government premise upon a separation of powers, a role which precludes interference by courts with legislative and executive functions which have not yet proceeded so far as to affect individual interests adversely. . . . These considerations, crucial as they are to this Court's power and obligation in constitutional cases, require that we delimit at the outset the issues which are properly before us in the present litigation.

This proceeding was brought by the Attorney General under § 13 (a) of the Subversive Activities Control Act, seeking an order of the

Board that the Communist Party register as a Communist-action organization pursuant to § 7. The Board has issued such an order, in accordance with § 13 (g) (1), which is here reviewed, under § 14 (a). The effect of that order is to require the Party to register and to file a registration statement within thirty days after the order becomes final, § 7 (c) (3), upon pain of fine up to $10,000 for each day of failure to register. When the order becomes final, other consequences also ensue, for the Party, for its members and for other persons. Certain acts of the Party—distributing its publications through the mails or through the instrumentalities of interstate or foreign commerce, or causing matter to be broadcast by radio or television, without the required identification—are prohibited, § 10, and tax exemption is denied it, § 11. Specified acts of its members—*e.g.*, applying for or using a United States passport, holding government or defense-facility employment, holding labor-union office or employment—are forbidden, §§ 5, 6, and those members are definitively subject to certain disqualifications —if aliens, they may not enter the United States, may be deported, may not be naturalized, may in some circumstances be denaturalized, with qualifications. . . . Employment by the Party is not "employment" for purposes of the Social Security Act, as amended . . . ; contributions to the Party are not tax deductible, . . . Acts by third parties with regard to the Party or its members—the contributing of funds or services to the Party by government or defense-facility personnel, issuance of passports to Party members—are, under specified circumstances, prohibited, . . . All of these consequences depend upon action taken subsequent to the time when the registration order becomes final. Some depend upon action which is, at best, highly contingent. The question is which, if any, of these consequences are now before us for constitutional adjudication, as necessarily involved in the determination of the constitutionality of the Board's registration order.

A closely similar issue was presented to this Court in *Electric Bond & Share Co.* v. *Securities & Exchange Comm'n*, 303 U.S. 419. That was a statutory suit brought by the Securities and Exchange Commission to enforce against certain utility holding companies the provisions of §§ 4 (a) and 5 of the Public Utility Holding Company Act of 1935, 49 Stat. 803. The Act, like the Subversive Activities Control Act, was a statute of many intricate and interlocking sections, with a severability clause. Its fifth section provided that holding companies, as defined, might register with the Commission and file a registration statement containing specified information: unless such a company registered within the time fixed, § 4 (a) subjected it to what the Court referred to as the "penalty for failure to register": criminal liability for engaging in business in interstate commerce; or for selling, transporting, owning or operating utility assets for the transportation of gas or electricity in interstate commerce; or for using the mails or instrumentalities of interstate commerce to distribute or acquire utility securities, or to negotiate, make, or take any step in performing, service, sales or construction contracts for public utility or holding companies; or for owning, controlling or holding voting stock in any subsidiary engaging in any of these activities. . . .

The decision in *Electric Bond & Share* controls the present case. This Act, like the one involved there, has a section directing that if any of its provisions, or any of its applications, is held invalid, the remaining provisions and other possible applications shall not be affected. The authoritative legislative history clearly demonstrates that a major purpose of the enactment was to regulate Communist-action organizations by means of the public disclosure effected by registration, apart from the other regulatory provisions of the Act. Such is, of course, the very purpose of the severability clause. This being so, our consideration of any other provisions than those of § 7, requiring Communist-action organizations to register and file a registration statement, could in no way affect our decision in the present case. Were every portion of the Act purporting to regulate or prohibit the conduct of registered organizations (or organizations ordered to register) and of their members, as such, unconstitutional, we would still have to affirm the judgment below. Expatiation on the validity of those portions would remain mere pronouncements, addressed to future and hypothetical controversies. This is true with regard to those sections of the Act which prescribe consequences legally enforceable against the Communist Party once a final registration order is in effect against it—the "labeling" and tax-exemption denial provisions of §§ 10 and 11. These are analogous to the proscription of specified credit transactions, or specified security sales, or specified political contributions, by the Public Utility Holding Company Act considered in *Electric Bond & Share*. Although they become operative as soon as a registration order is made final, their application remains in a very real sense problematical. We cannot now foresee what effect, if any, upon the Party the denial of tax exemption will have. We do not know whether the Party now has, or whether it will have at any time after a Board order goes into effect, any taxable income, or, indeed, any income whatever. We do not know that, after such an order is in effect, the Party will wish to utilize the mails or any instrumentality of interstate commerce for the circulation of its publications. We cannot guess the nature of whatever publications it may wish to circulate, or their relation to the purposes and functions of the Party. These circumstances may be critical for constitutional determination. It will not do to discount their significance by saying, now, that no difference in circumstances will effect a different constitutional result—that the principles relevant to a determination of the validity of these statutory provisions do not depend upon the variations in circumstances in which they are potentially applicable. For this analysis presupposes that we now understand what are the relevant constitutional principles, whereas the reason of postponing decision until a constitutional issue is more clearly focused by, and receives the impact from, occurrence in particular circumstances is precisely that those circumstances may reveal relevancies that abstract, prospective supposition may not see or adequately assess.

These considerations are equally appropriate in the case of those sections of the Act which proscribe specified conduct by members of an organization concerning which a final registration order is in effect, or which impose obligations upon them, or which subject them to described disabilities under certain circumstances. It is wholly speculative now to foreshadow whether, or under what conditions, a member of the Party may in the future apply for a passport, or seek government or defense-facility or labor-union employment, or, being an alien, become a party to a naturalization or a denaturalization proceeding. None of these things may happen. If they do, appropriate administrative and judicial procedures will be available to test the constitutionality of applications of particular sections of the Act to particular persons in particular situations. Nothing justifies previsioning those issues now.

But the Party argues that the threat, however indefinite, of future application of these provisions to penalize individuals who are or become its members, affiliates or contributors, will effectively deter persons from associating with it or from aiding and supporting it. Thus, the provisions exercise a present effect upon the Party sufficiently prejudicial to justify its challenging them in this proceeding. In support of this contention, the Party cites cases in which we have held that litigants had "standing" to attack a statute or regulation which operated to coerce other persons to withdraw from profitable relations or associations with the litigants. . . . But these cases purported only to discuss what issues a litigant might raise, not when he might raise them. That a proper party is before the court is no answer to the objection that he is there prematurely. . . .

The present proceeding differs from all of these. The record here does not show that any present members, affiliates, or contributors of the Party have withdrawn because of the threatened consequences to them of its registration under the Subversive Activities Control Act, or that any prospective members, affiliates, or contributors have been deterred from joining the Party or giving it their support. We cannot know how many, if any, members or prospective members of the Party are also employees or prospective employees of the Government or of defense facilities or labor unions, or how many, if any, contributors to the Party hold government or defense-facility employment. It is thus impossible to say now what effect the provisions of the Act affecting members of a registered organization will have on the Party. . . . To pass upon the validity of those provisions would be to make abstract assertions of possible future injury, indefinite in nature and degree, the occasion for constitutional decision. If we did so, we would be straying beyond our judicial bounds. Of course, the Party may now assert those rights of its members, such as that of anonymity, which are allegedly infringed by the very act of its filing a registration statement, and which could not be otherwise asserted than by raising them here. . . . But the rights of its members, as potentially affected by the Act, to receive and use passports, seek and hold certain employment, be naturalized and preserve their citizenship once naturalized, are not of this category. We limit our consideration to the constitutionality of § 7 as applied in this proceeding.

V.

The constitutional contentions raised by the Party with respect to the registration requirement of § 7 are (A) that that requirement, in the context of the Act, in effect "outlaws" the Party and is in the nature of a bill of attainder; (B) that compelling organizations to register and to list their members on a showing merely that they are foreign-dominated and operate primarily to advance the objectives of the world Communist movement constitutes a restraint on freedom of expression and association in violation of the First Amendment; (C) that requiring Party officers to file registration statements for the Party subjects them to self-incrimination forbidden by the Fifth Amendment; (D) that the Act violates due process by legislative predetermination of facts essential to bring the Communist Party within the definition of a Communist-action organization, and that the evidentiary elements prescribed for consideration by the Board bear no rational relation to that definition; (E) that in several aspects the Act is unconstitutionally vague; and (F) that the Subversive Activities Control Board is so necessarily biased against the Communist Party as to deprive it of a fair hearing.

A. *"Outlawry" and Attainder.* Our determination that in the present proceeding all questions are premature which regard only the constitutionality of the various particular consequences of a registration order to a registered organization and its members, does not foreclose the Party from arguing—and it does argue—that in light of the cumulative effect of those consequences the registration provisions of § 7 are not what they seem, but represent a legislative attempt, by devious means, to "outlaw" the Party. The registration requirement, the Party contends, was designed not with the purpose of having Communist-action organizations register, but with a purpose to make it impossible to register, because of the onerous consequences of registration, and thus to establish a pretext for criminal prosecution of the organization and its members. The Act is said to be aimed particularly at the Communist Party as an identifiable entity, intending to punish it, and in this aspect to constitute a bill of attainder prohibited by Art. I, § 9, cl. 3 of the Constitution.

Of course, "only the clearest proof could suffice to establish the unconstitutionality of a statute on such a ground." . . . No such proof is offered here. The Act on its face gives no indication that the registration provisions were not intended to be complied with. None of the consequences which attach to registration, whatever may be their validity when weighed separately in the constitutional balance, is so devoid of rational relation to the purposes of the Act as expressed in its second section that it appears a mere pressuring device meant to catch an organization between two fires. Section 2 recites that the world Communist movement, whose purpose is to employ deceit, secrecy, infiltration, and sabotage as means to establish a Communist totalitarian dictatorship, establishes and utilizes action organizations. The Act requires such organizations to register and to label their communications, and prohibits their members from government, defense-facility and certain labor-organization employment. Section 2 sets forth that Communist-action organizations are sections of a world-wide Communist movement and that international travel of its members and agents facilitates the purposes of the movement. The Act restricts the ingress and access to United States citizenship of alien members of Communist-action organizations and deprives all members of the use of United States passports. Section 2 finds that Communist-action organizations purpose to overthrow the Government of the United States by any available, necessary means. The Act forbids government and defense-facility employees to support such organizations, and withdraws from the organizations and their contributors certain tax exemptions. None of this is so lacking in consonance as to suggest a clandestine purpose behind the registration provisions. Nor does the legislative history contain any such suggestion. Rather, the Committee reports on the bills from which the Act derived express an object "to require the Communist movement in the United States to operate in the open rather than underground," and "to expose the Communist movement and protect the public against innocent and unwitting collaboration with it."

It is true, as the Party asserts, that bills had been introduced in Congress that would have applied to the Communist Party by name, and it is no doubt also true that the form which the Subversive Activities Control Act finally took was dictated in part by constitutional scruples against outlawing of the Party by "legislative fiat." It is probable, too, that the legislators who voted for the Act in its final form expected that the Communist Party, if it continued to engage in the activities which had been reported to Congress as characterizing its past conduct, would be required to register under § 7. From this the Party would have us conclude that the Act is only an instrument serving to abolish the Communist Party by indirection. But such an analysis ignores our duty of respect for the exercise of the legislative power of Congress, and, more specifically, ignores the crucial constitutional significance of what Congress did when it rejected the approach of outlawing the Party by name and accepted instead a statutory program regulating not enumerated organizations but designated activities. We would be indulging in a revisory power over enactments as they come from Congress—a power which the Framers of the Constitution withheld from this Court—if we so interpreted what Congress refused to do and what in fact Congress did; that is, if we treated this Act as merely a ruse by Congress to evade constitutional safeguards. Congress deemed it an attempt to achieve its legislative purpose consistently with constitutional safeguards. Whether it has done so—the issue which is now before us—is to be determined by the manner in which the enactment works in its practical application. "So long as Congress acts in pursuance of its constitutional power, the Judiciary lacks authority to intervene on the basis of the motives which spurred the exercise of that power." . . . The true and sole question before us is whether the effects of the statute as it was passed and as it operates are constitutionally permissible.

The Act is not a bill of attainder. It attaches not to specified organizations but to described activities in which an organization may or may not engage. The singling out of an individual for legislatively prescribed punishment constitutes an attainder whether the individual is called by name or described in terms of conduct which, because it is past conduct, operates only as a designation of particular persons. . . . The Subversive Activities Control Act is not of that kind. It requires the registration only of organizations which, after the date of the Act, are found to be under the direction, domination, or control of certain foreign powers and to operate primarily to advance certain objectives. This finding must be made after full administrative hearing, subject to judicial review which opens the record for the reviewing court's determination whether the administrative findings as to fact are supported by the preponderance of the evidence. Present activity constitutes an operative element to which the statute attaches legal consequences, not merely a point of reference for the ascertainment of particular persons ineluctably designated by the legislature.

The fact that activity engaged in prior to the enactment of the legislation may be regarded administratively and judicially as relevant to a determination that an organization is presently foreign-controlled and presently works to advance the objectives of the world Communist movement, does not alter the operative structure of the Act. The incidents which it reaches are nonetheless present incidents. The past is pertinent only as probative of these. In this proceeding the Board has found, and the Court of Appeals has sustained its conclusion, that the Communist Party, by virtue of the activities in which it now engages, comes within the terms of the Act. If the Party should at any time choose to abandon these activities, after it is once registered pursuant to § 7, the Act provides adequate means of relief. As often as once a year it may apply to the Attorney General for cancellation of registration, and in the event of his refusal to remove it from the register and to relieve it from the duty of filing annual statements, it may petition the Board for a redetermination of its amenability to the registration requirements of the Act, pursuant to a hearing which, again, is subject to judicial review. §§ 13 (b), (i), (j), 14 (a). Far from attaching to the past and ineradicable actions of an organization, the application of the registration section is made to turn upon continuingly contemporaneous fact; its obligations arise only because, and endure only so long as, an organization presently conducts operations of a described character.

Nor is the statute made an act of "outlawry" or of attainder by the fact that the conduct which it regulates is described with such particularity that, in probability, few organizations will come within the statutory terms. Legislatures may act to curb behavior which they regard as harmful to the public welfare, whether that conduct is found to be engaged in by many persons or by one. So long as the incidence of legislation is such that the persons who engage in the regulated conduct, be they many or few, can escape regulation merely by altering the course of their own present activities, there can be no complaint of an attainder. It would be ingenuous to refuse to recognize that the Subversive Activities Control Act of 1950 was designed to reach the Communist Party's operations as then reported to Congress—operations in which, the Board has found, the Party persists. But to base a determination of constitutionality on this design would be to confuse the occasion of legislation with its operative effect and consequently to mistake decisive constitutional determinants. No doubt, the activity whose regulation the Act seeks to achieve is activity historically associated with the Communist Party. From its legislative study of the Communist Party, Congress concluded that that kind of activity was potentially dangerous to the national interest and that it must be subjected to control. But whatever the source from which the legislative experience and instruction derived, the Act applies to a class of activity only, not to the Communist Party as such. Nothing in this offends the constitutional prohibition of attainder.

B. *The Freedoms of Expression and Association Protected by the First Amendment.* The Communist Party would have us hold that the First Amendment prohibits Congress from requiring the registration and filing of information, including membership lists, by organizations substantially dominated or controlled by the foreign powers controlling the world Communist movement and which operate primarily to advance the objectives of that movement: the overthrow of existing government by any means necessary and the establishment in its place of a Communist totalitarian dictatorship (§§ 3 (3), 2 (1) and (6)). We cannot find such a prohibition in the First Amendment. So to find would make a travesty of that Amendment and the great ends for the well-being of our democracy that it serves.

No doubt, a governmental regulation which requires registration as a condition upon the exercise of speech may in some circumstances affront the constitutional guarantee of free expression. . . . The present statute does not, of course, attach the registration requirement to the incident of speech, but to the incidents of foreign domination and of operation to advance the objectives of the world Communist movement—operation which, the Board has found here, includes extensive, long-continuing organizational, as well as "speech" activity. . . .

Similarly, we agree that compulsory disclosure of the names of an organization's members may in certain instances infringe constitutionally protected right of association. . . . But to say this much is only to recognize one of the points of reference from which analysis must begin. To state that individual liberties may be affected is to establish the condition for, not to arrive at the conclusion of, constitutional decision. Against the impediments which particular governmental regulation causes to entire freedom of individual action, there must be weighed the value to the public of the ends which the regulation may achieve. . . .

The present case differs from *Thomas* v. *Collins* and from *N.A.A.C.P.*, *Bates,* and *Shelton* in the magnitude of the public interests which the registration and disclosure provisions are designed to protect and in the pertinence which registration and disclosure bear to the protection of those interests. Congress itself has expressed in § 2 of the Act both what those interests are and what, in its view, threatens them. On the basis of its detailed investigations Congress has found that there exists a world Communist movement, foreign-controlled, whose purpose it is by whatever means necessary to establish Communist totalitarian dictatorship in the countries throughout the world, and which has already succeeded in supplanting governments in other countries. Congress has found that in furthering these purposes, the foreign government controlling the world Communist movement establishes in various countries action organizations which, dominated from abroad, endeavor to bring about the overthrow of existing governments, by force if need be, and to establish totalitarian dictatorships subservient to that foreign government. And Congress has found that these action organizations employ methods of infiltration and secretive and coercive tactics; that by operating in concealment and through Communist-front organizations they are able to obtain the support of persons who would not extend such support knowing of their true nature; that a Communist network exists in the United States; and that the agents of communism have devised methods of sabotage and espionage carried out in successful evasion of existing law. The purpose of the Subversive Activities Control Act is said to be to prevent the world-wide Communist conspiracy from accomplishing its purpose in this country.

It is not for the courts to re-examine the validity of these legislative findings and reject them. . . . They are the product of extensive investigation by Committees of Congress over more than a decade and a half. . . . We certainly cannot dismiss them as unfounded or irrational imaginings. . . . And if we accept them, as we must, as a not unentertainable appraisal by Congress of the threat which Communist orgánizations pose not only to existing government in the United States, but to the United States as a sovereign, independent nation—if we accept as not wholly unsupportable the conclusion that those organizations "are not free and independent organizations, but are sections of world-wide Communist organization and are controlled, directed, and subject to the discipline of the Communist dictatorship of [a] . . . foreign country," § 2 (5)—we must recognize that the power of Congress to regulate Communist organizations of this nature is extensive. "Security against foreign danger is one of the primitive objects of civil society," James Madison wrote in *The Federalist* (No. 41). "It is an avowed and essential object of the American Union. The Powers requisite for attaining it must be effectually confided to the federal councils." *The Federalist* (Wright ed. 1961) 295. See also *The Federalist* (Nos. 2–5), *id.*, at 93 *et seq.* Means for effective resistance against foreign incursion—whether in the form of organizations which function, in some technical sense, as "agents" of a foreign power, or in the form of organizations which, by complete dedication and obedience to foreign directives, make themselves the instruments of a foreign power—may not be denied to the national legislature. "To preserve its independence, and give security against foreign aggression and encroachment, is the highest duty of every nation, and to attain these ends nearly all other considerations are to be subordinated. It matters not in what form such aggression and encroachment come. . . ."

Of course, congressional power in this sphere, as in all spheres, is limited by the First Amendment. Individual liberties fundamental to American institutions are not to be destroyed under pretext of preserving those institutions, even from the gravest external dangers. But where the problems of accommodating the exigencies of self-preservation and the values of liberty and as complex and intricate as they are in the situation described in the findings of § 2 of the Subversive Activities Control Act—when existing government is menaced by a worldwide integrated movement which employs every combination of possible means, peaceful and violent, domestic and foreign, overt and clandestine, to destroy the government itself—the legislative judgment as to how that threat may best be met consistently with the safeguarding of personal freedom is not to be set aside merely because the judgment of judges would, in the first instance, have chosen other methods. Especially where Congress, in seeking to reconcile competing and urgently demanding values within our social institutions, legislates not to prohibit individuals from organizing for the effectuation of ends found to be menacing to the very existence of those institutions, but only to prescribe the conditions under which such organization is permitted, the legislative determination must be respected. . . .

In a number of situations in which secrecy or the concealment of associations has been regarded as a threat to public safety and to the effective, free functioning of our national institutions Congress has met the threat by requiring registration or disclosure.* The Federal Cor-

* Compare 18 U.S.C. § 612 (prohibiting the publication or distribution of written statements concerning candidates for designated national elective offices unless such statements contain the names of the persons or associations responsible for the publication or distribution and, in the case of associations, the names of their officers); 37 Stat. 553, as amended, 39 U.S.C. §§ 233–234 (prescribing the withdrawal of second-class mailing privileges from publications which do not file with the Postmaster General, and publish in the second issue of the publication printed after filing a statement setting forth the names of the publication's editors, publishers, managers and owners, and, if the owners are corporations, the names of stockholders and other security holders; and prohibiting the printing, by publications enjoying second-class privileges, of paid advertisements not marked as such), sustained against First Amendment challenge in *Lewis Publishing Co.* v. *Morgan*, 229 U.S. 288; Communications Act of 1934, § 317, 48 Stat. 1089, 47 U.S.C. § 317 (requiring, in the case of all matter broadcast by radio for which a valuable con-

rupt Practices Act, enacted in 1925, 2 U.S.C. §§ 241–245, requires all political committees (organizations accepting contributions or making expenditures to influence the election of candidates for designated national offices in two or more States, or branches of national committees) to have a chairman and a treasurer, and makes it the duty of the treasurer to keep detailed financial accounts and to file with the Clerk of the House of Representatives periodic statements containing, *inter alia*, the names and addresses of all persons contributing more than $100 to the committee during any year. *Burroughs* v. *United States*, 290 U.S. 534, sustained that statute against the claim that Congress lacked constitutional power to regulate such political organizations; the Court found ample authority in congressional power "to preserve the departments and institutions of the general government from impairment or destruction, whether threatened by force or by corruption." The Federal Regulation of Lobbying Act, 2 U.S.C. §§ 261–270, applies to any person who solicits or receives money or anything of value to be used principally, or if the person's principal purpose is, to influence the passage or defeat of legislation by Congress. It requires any person receiving any contributions or expending any money for the purposes of influencing the passage or defeat of legislation to file with the Clerk of the House quarterly statements which set out the names and addresses of each person who has made a contribution of $500 or more not mentioned in the preceding report. It also requires that any person who engages himself for pay for the purpose of attempting to influence the passage or defeat of legislation, before doing anything in furtherance of that objective, register with the Clerk of the House and the Secretary of the Senate, and state in writing, *inter alia*, his name and address and the name and address of the person by whom he is employed, and in whose interest he works. These paid lobbyists must file quarterly reports of all money received and expended in carrying on their work, to whom paid, for what purposes, the names of publications in which they have caused any articles to be published, and the proposed legislation they are employed to support or oppose; this information is to be printed in the Congressional Record. In *United States* v. *Harriss*, 347 U.S. 612, we held that the First Amendment did not prohibit the prosecution of criminal informations charging violation of the registration and reporting provisions of the Act. . . . The Foreign Agents Registration Act, first enacted in 1938, and since several times amended, provides, as now set forth in 22 U.S.C. §§ 611–621, that agents of foreign principals must register with the Attorney General and file periodic registration statements (which are to be held by the

---

sideration is paid by any person, an announcement that the matter has been paid for by such person).

Attorney General open to public inspection) containing, among other information, the registrant's name, a comprehensive statement of the nature of the registrant's business, a complete list of the registrant's employees and a statement of the nature of the work of each (unless this requirement is waived by the Attorney General), the name and address of the registrant's foreign principals, with further information as to the principals' character, ownership and control, the names and addresses of all persons other than a registrant's foreign principal who contribute to the registrant in connection with specified activities of the registrant, and detailed financial accounts. Such agents must also file with the Attorney General and the Librarian of Congress, and must label as emanating from a registered agent of a foreign principal, and mark with the name of the agent and the principal, any political propaganda transmitted in the United States mails or through any instrumentality of interstate or foreign commerce. In addition, Title 18 U.S.C. § 2386, derived from the so-called Voorhis Act of 1940, 54 Stat. 1201, requires the registration with the Attorney General of organizations subject to foreign control which engage in political or civilian military activity (as those terms are defined in the section), organizations which engage in both political and civilian military activity (as defined), and organizations whose purpose is the overthrow of government by the use or threat of force or violence or military measures. Organizations required to register must report, *inter alia*, the names and addresses of their officers, branch officers and contributors, a detailed description of their activities, and a detailed statement of assets, and must file copies of publications which they issue or distribute; registration statements must be kept up to date and are to be open for public examination. Committee reports pertinent to the Subversive Activities Control Act of 1950 state that the necessity for the legislation derived in part from the difficulty of enforcing the Foreign Agents Registration and Voorhis Acts against Communist organizations "due in part to the skill and deceit which the Communists have used in concealing their foreign ties."

Certainly, as the *Burroughs* and *Harriss* cases abundantly recognize, secrecy of associations and organizations, even among groups concerned exclusively with political processes, may under some circumstances constitute a danger which legislatures do not lack constitutional power to curb. In *New York ex rel. Bryant* v. *Zimmerman*, 278 U.S. 63, this Court held that the Due Process Clause of the Fourteenth Amendment was not offended by a state statute requiring filing with the Secretary of State of the constitution and by-laws, rules and regulations, membership oath, roster of members and list of officers of every association of twenty or more members having as a condition of membership an oath. The statute made it unlawful to become or remain a member of such an association with knowledge that it had failed to comply with the filing requirement. Exceptions for labor unions and benevolent orders indicated that the measure was directed primarily at the Ku Klux Klan. Compelling disclosure of membership lists and other information by organizations of the character of the Klan, the Court found, was reasonable both as a means for providing the government of the State with knowledge of the activities of those organizations within its borders, and because "requiring this information to be supplied for the public files will operate as an effective or substantial deterrent from the violations of public and private right to which the association might be tempted if such a disclosure were not required." It was the nature of the organization regulated, and hence the danger involved in its covert operation, which justified the statute and caused us to distinguish the *Bryant* case in *N.A.A.C.P.* v. *Alabama, supra,* 357 U.S., at 465. In *N.A.A.C.P.* and *Bates* v. *Little Rock,* as we have said, there was no showing of any danger inherent in concealment, no showing that the State, in seeking disclosure, was attempting to cope with any perceived danger. Nor was this kind of danger—arising when secrecy itself is made an active instrument of public harm—put forth to justify the statute which was held invalid in *Shelton* v. *Tucker, supra.*

Congress, when it enacted the Subversive Activities Control Act, did attempt to cope with precisely such a danger. In light of its legislative findings, based on voluminous evidence collected during years of investigation, we cannot say that that danger is chimerical, or that the registration requirement of § 7 is an ill-adjusted means of dealing with it. In saying this, we are not insensitive to the fact that the public opprobrium and obloquy which may attach to an individual listed with the Attorney General as a member of a Communist-action organization is no less considerable than that with which members of the National Association for the Advancement of Colored People were threatened in *N.A.A.C.P.* and *Bates.* But while an angry public opinion, and the evils which it may spawn, are relevant considerations in adjudging, in light of the totality of relevant considerations, the validity of legislation that, in effecting disclosure, may thereby entail some restraints on speech and association, the existence of an ugly public temper does not, as such and without more, incapacitate government to require publicity demanded by rational interests high in the scale of national concern. Where the mask of anonymity which an organization's members wear serves the double purpose of protecting them from popular prejudice and of enabling them to cover over a foreign-directed conspiracy, infiltrate into other groups, and enlist the support of persons who would not, if the truth were revealed, lend their support, see § 2 (1), (6), (7), it would be a distortion of the First Amendment to hold that it prohibits Congress from removing the mask.

These considerations lead us to sustain the registration provisions of § 7, as not repugnant to the First Amendment, insofar as they require Communist-action organizations to file a registration statement containing the names and addresses of its present officers and members. The requirement that persons who were officers or members at any time during the year preceding registration must be listed, see § 7 (d) (2), (4), is a reasonable means of assuring that the obligation to list present members and officers will not be evaded. For reasons which do not require elaboration, the requirement that a registered organization list the aliases of officers and members, see § 7 (d) (5), must also be sustained. Nor do we find that § 7 (d) (3), requiring a financial accounting, or § 7 (d) (6), requiring a listing of all printing presses in the possession or control of the organization or its members violate First Amendment rights. Disclosure both of the financial transactions of a Communist-action organization and of the identity of the organs of publication which it controls might not unreasonably have been regarded by Congress as necessary to the objective which the Act seeks to achieve: to bring foreign-dominated organizations out into the open where the public can evaluate their activities informedly against the revealed background of their character, nature, and connections. Of course, printing presses may not be regulated like guns. That generalization gets us nowhere. On the concrete, specific issue before us, we hold that the obligation to give information identifying presses, without more and as applied to foreign-dominated organizations, does not fetter constitutionally protected free expression. No other kind of regulation is involved here. As to the penalties for failure to register, see § 15 (a), which the Party attacks as exorbitant and oppressive, these are not now before us. They have not yet been imposed on the Party and may never be. . . .

It is argued that if Congress may constitutionally enact legislation requiring the Communist Party to register, to list its members, to file financial statements, and to identify its printing presses, Congress may impose similar requirements upon any group which pursues unpopular political objectives or which expresses an unpopular political ideology. Nothing which we decide here remotely carries such an implication. The Subversive Activities Control Act applies only to foreign-dominated organizations which work primarily to advance the objectives of a world movement controlled by the government of a *foreign* country. See §§ 3 (3), 2 (4). It applies only to organizations directed, dominated, or controlled by a *particular* foreign country, the leader of a movement which, Congress has found, is "in its origins, its development, and its present practice, . . . a world-wide revolutionary movement whose purpose it is, by treachery, deceit, infiltration into other groups . . . , espionage, sabotage, terrorism, and any other means deemed necessary, to establish a Communist totalitarian dictatorship in the countries throughout the world through the medium of a world-wide Communist organization." § 2 (1). This is the full purported reach of the statute, and its fullest effect. There is no attempt here to impose stifling obligations upon the proponents of a particular political creed as such, or even to check the importation of particular political ideas from abroad for propagation here. The Act compels the registration of organized groups which have been made the instruments of a long-continued, systematic, disciplined activity directed by a foreign power and purposing to overthrow existing government in this country. Organizations are subject to it only when shown, after administrative hearing subject to judicial review, to be dominated by the foreign power or its organs and to operate primarily to advance its purposes. That a portion of the evidence upon which such a showing is made may consist in the expression of political views by the organization does not alter the character of the Act or of the incidents to which it attaches. Such expressions are relevant only as probative of foreign control and of the purposes to which the organization's actions are directed. The Board, in the present proceeding, so understood the Act. The registration requirement of § 7, on its face and as here applied, does not violate the First Amendment.

C. *Self-Incrimination of the Party's Officers.* Section 7 (a) and (c) requires that organizations determined to be Communist-action organizations by the Subversive Activities Control Board register within thirty days after the Board's registration order becomes final. Registration is to be accompanied by a registration statement, prepared in such manner and form as the Attorney General, by regulations, prescribes. § 7 (d). The form which, pursuant to this authority, the Attorney General has prescribed requires that registration statements "shall be signed by the partners, officers, and directors, including the members of the governing body of the organization." . . . If the organization fails to register or to file a registration statement, it is the duty of the executive officer, the secretary, the president or chairman, the vice-president or vice-chairman, the treasurer, and the members of the governing board, council, or body, to register the organization by filing a registration statement for it within ten days after the expiration of the thirty-day registration period allowed the organization. . . . The Party contends that these requirements cannot be imposed and exacted consistently with the Self-Incrimination Clause of the Fifth Amendment. Officers of the Party, it is argued, are compelled, in the very act of filing a signed registration statement, to admit that they *are* Party officers—an admission which we have held incriminating. *Blau* v. *United States,* 340 U.S. 159; cf. *Quinn* v. *United States,* 349 U.S. 155. What is required is said to be not merely the production of documents kept in an official capacity for the Party, . . . but individual action by the officers which, by establishing a connection between the officers and the documents, in effect convicts the officers out of their own mouths. . . .

Manifestly, insofar as this contention is directed against the provisions of § 7 (h) and 28 CFR § 11.205, requiring that designated officers file registration statements in default of registration by an organization, it is prematurely raised in the present proceedings. The duties imposed by those provisions will not arise until and unless the Party fails to register. At this time their application is wholly contingent and conjectural. . . .

We find that the self-incrimination challenge to § 7 (a) and (d), as implemented by the Attorney General's regulations and forms, is also premature at this time. The privilege against self-incrimination is one which normally must be claimed by the individual who seeks to avail himself of its protection. . . . We cannot know now that the Party's officers will ever claim the privilege. There is no indication that in the past its high-ranking officials have sought to conceal their identity, and no reason to believe that in the future they will decline to file a registration statement whose whole effect, in this regard, is further to evidence a fact which, traditionally, has been one of public notice. Within thirty days after the Board's registration order becomes final, the Party's officers may file signed registration statements in the form required by Form ISA-1. Or they may file statements claiming the privilege in lieu of furnishing the required information. If a claim of privilege is made, it may or may not be honored by the Attorney General. We cannot, on the basis of supposition that privilege will be claimed and not honored, proceed now to adjudicate the constitutionality under the Fifth Amendment of the registration provisions. Whatever proceeding may be taken after and if the privilege is claimed will provide an adequate forum for litigation of that issue.

The Party contends, however, that under the Subversive Activities Control Act there will be no opportunity for its officers to claim the Fifth Amendment privilege without, at the same time, giving up all the protection which the Fifth Amendment secures them. Persons who come forward to make the claim, it is said, will as much reveal themselves to the Attorney General as officers of the Party as if they had in fact filed a registration statement. But it is always true that one who is required to assert the privilege against self-incrimination may thereby arouse the suspicions of prosecuting authorities. Nevertheless, it is not and has never been the law that the privilege disallows the asking of potentially incriminatory questions or authorizes the person of whom they are asked to evade them without expressly asserting that his answers may tend to incriminate him. . . . In *United States* v. *Sullivan,* 274 U.S. 259, this Court sustained a conviction for failure to file an income tax return, despite the defendant's objection that answers called for on the return would have incriminated him. Mr. Justice Holmes, for a unanimous Court, wrote that "If the form of return provided called for answers that the defendant was privileged from making he could have raised the objection in the return, but could not on that account refuse to make any return at all. . . . [I]f the defendant desired to test that or any other point he should have tested it in the return so that it could be passed upon. He could not draw a conjurer's circle around the whole matter by his own declaration that to write any word upon the government blank would bring him into danger of the law." This would, of course, be the normal rule. Perhaps *Sullivan* is distinguishable, however, from the situation of registration under the Subversive Activities Control Act. Tax returns must be filed generally, and answers to tax return questions may involve any of a wide variety of activities, whereas the obligation to file a registration statement compels a few particular individuals to come forward, to identify themselves, and to suggest, at least, their connection with a relatively limited potential sphere of criminal conduct. Then, too, in *Sullivan,* Mr. Justice Holmes assumed that some, at least, of the answers to the questions on the tax return would not have been incriminating, whereas in the case of the registration statement, any claim of the privilege would involve the withholding of all information; thus, there is, presumably, a greater governmental interest in having the privilege claimed specifically on the form in the tax-return circumstances. To suggest these possible distinctions is to recognize that the applicability of the *Sullivan* principle here may raise novel and difficult questions as to the reach of the Fifth Amendment—questions which should not be discussed in advance of the necessity of deciding them. . . . The stage at which that decision will become necessary, if at all, is the stage at which *Sullivan* itself was decided: when enforcement proceedings for failure to register are instituted against the Party or against its officers. . . .

In arguing that the issue is not now premature, the Party cites *Boyd* v. *United States,* 116 U.S. 616, for the proposition that, where a statute compelling the production of potentially incriminating information allows the exercise of the Fifth Amendment privilege only under circumstances which effectively nullify the Amendment's protection, the statute may be held "unconstitutional and void," not merely unenforceable in cases in which a proper claim of privilege is made. Assuming *arguendo* that this proposition is correct, the most that can be drawn from it of pertinence to the present case is that, in a prosecution of the Party for failure to register, or in a prosecution of its officers for failure to register the Party, the Court would have to determine whether the Subversive Activities Control Act is a statute which, like the statute in *Boyd*, unconstitutionally circumscribes the effectual exercise of the privilege. Obviously, such a determination would never have to be made if an enforcement proceeding were never brought—either because Party officials registered pursuant to § 7 (a) and (d) without complaint, or because they did choose to assert the privilege in some form in which it could be recognized. The *Boyd* case involved a statute providing that in proceedings other than criminal arising under the revenue laws, the Government could secure an order of the court requiring the production by an opposing claimant or defendant of any documents under his control which, the Government asserted, might tend to prove any of the Government's allegations. If production were not made, the allegations were to be taken as confessed. On the Government's motion, the District Court had entered such an order, requiring the claimants in a forfeiture proceeding to produce a specified invoice. Although the claimants objected that the order was improper and the statute unconstitutional in coercing self-incriminatory disclosures and permitting unreasonable searches and seizures, they did, under protest, produce the invoice, which was, again over their constitutional objection, admitted into evidence. This Court held that on such a record a judgment for the United States could not stand, and that the statute was invalid as repugnant to the Fourth and Fifth Amendments. In *Boyd*, production had been ordered, objected to, and, the Court held, unconstitutionally compelled. There is nothing in the case which justifies advisory adjudication of self-incrimination questions prior to the time when a demand for information has been, at the least, made and resisted.

D. *Legislative Predetermination of Adjudicative Fact.* It is next asserted that the Act offends the Due Process Clause of the Fifth Amendment by predetermining legislative facts upon which the application of the registration provisions to the Communist Party depends. Two arguments are made in this regard. The first is that although § 3 (3), defining a "Communist-action organization," purports to require findings that an organization is controlled by "the foreign government for foreign organization controlling the world Communist movement referred to in section 2 ... ." and operates primarily to advance the objectives "of such world Communist movement as referred to in section 2 . . . ," the existence of a world Communist movement, its direction by the government of a foreign country, and the nature of its objectives are "found" by Congress in § 2, and may not be litigated in proceedings before the Board. Thus, an organization is precluded from showing operative facts which would take it out of § 3 (3): *viz.*, that there is no world Communist movement, or that, if there is, it is not controlled by a foreign government, or that it does not have the objectives attributed to it by § 2. The second agrument is that the Board was in effect foreclosed from finding that the Party was not a Communist-action organization by the declarations, in § 2 (9), (12), and (15), that there are in the United States individuals who knowingly and willfully participate in the world Communist movement, that there is a Communist network in the United States, and that the "Communist movement in the United States is an organization. . . ." Given these "facts," it is asserted, nothing is left to the Board but to supply the name of the organization—a name which, the Party contends, is obvious. Further, it is pointed out, Congress in 1954, prior to the Board's final determination in this proceeding, enacted the Communist Control Act, 50 U.S.C. § 841 *et seq.*, which declares in its second section:

> The Congress hereby finds and declares that the Communist Party of the United States, although purportedly a political party, is in fact an instrumentality of a conspiracy to overthrow the Government of the United States. . . . [T]he policies and programs of the Communist Party are secretly prescribed for it by the foreign leaders of the world Communist movement. . . . [I]ts role as the agency of a hostile foreign power renders its existence a clear present and continuing danger to the security of the United States. . . .

The Board could not, therefore, the Party argues, find that the Communist Party was not a Communist-action organization without contradicting Congress.

First: We have held, *supra,* that the congressional findings that there exists a world Communist movement, that it is directed by the Communist dictatorship of a foreign country, and that it has certain designated objectives, *inter alia,* the establishment of a Communist totalitarian dictatorship throughout the world through the medium of a world-wide Communist organization, § 2 (1), (4), are not open to reexamination by the Board. We find that nothing in this violates due process. Under § 3 (3) of the Act, an organization may not be found to be a Communist-action organization unless it is shown to be, first, "substantially directed, dominated, or controlled by the foreign government or foreign organization controlling the world Communist movement referred to in section 2. . . ." The only operative function of § 2 in this respect is to designate what Congress meant by "world Communist movement," "the foreign government," etc. The characteristics of the movement and the source of its control are not to be established by the Attorney General in procedings before the Board, nor may they be disproved. But this is because they are merely defining terms whose truth, as such, is irrelevant to the issues in such proceedings. They are referrents which identify "*the* foreign government" to which § 3 (3) adverts. The Board, construing the statute, concluded that that foreign government was the Soviet Union. We affirm that construction. The statute, then, defines a Communist-action organization in terms of substantial direction, domination, or control by the Soviet Union. The Government offered evidence to show that the Soviet Union substantially directed, dominated, or controlled the Communist Party. The Party had an opportunity to rebut this showing, and it attempted to do so. The Board found that the Government's showing was persuasive; it issued a 240-page report so concluding; and the Court of Appeals affirmed. None of the operative facts were "predetermined," except in the sense in which any statute, as construed, designates the nature of the facts pertinent to issues which may be litigated under it. If, in future years, in a future world situation, the Soviet Union is no longer the foreign country to which § 2 (1) and (4), fairly read in their context, refer—so that substantial domination by the Soviet Union would not bring an organization within the terms of § 3 (3)—that, too, will be a matter of statutory construction which no "findings" in the statute foreclose. The Board or a reviewing court will be able to say that the "world Communist movement," as Congress meant the term in 1950 (and whether or not there really existed, in 1950, a movement having all the characteristics described in § 2), no longer exists, or that Country X or Y, not the Soviet Union, now directs it. A similar process of adjudication is required under § 3 (3) (a) (ii), the "objectives" component of the definition of a Communist-action organization. It provides that, in order to be found a Communist-action organization, an organization must be shown to operate "primarily to advance the objectives of such world Communist movement as referred to in section 2. . . ." What those objectives are is made clear by the terms of § 2 itself. They are there described in detail. Whether they are in fact the objectives of some "world Communist movement" which in fact exists may not be litigated, because the question is irrelevant. Whether the particular organization against whom the Attorney General files a petition for a registration order operates primarily to advance those objectives is the pertinent issue under the statute, and this issue may be litigated. That is all that due process requires. . . .

Second: We do not find that the congressional assertions in § 2 (9), (12) and (15), that there exist in the United States individuals dedicated to communism, a "Communist network," a "Communist movement," and a Communist "organization," deprive the Party of the fair hearing which due process of law requires. Fairly read, these findings neither compel nor suggest the outcome in any particular litigation before the Board. They do not create the impression that there is a single Communist-action organization in the United States, still less that the Communist Party is "it." Nor can we hold that the findings of § 2 of the Communist Control Act of 1954 unconstitutionally prejudice the Party. It is not suggested that these were enacted with a purpose to influence the then-pending proceedings in the present case. Rather, they are a portion of legislation deemed necessary by Congress pursuant to its continuing duty to protect the national welfare. Nowhere in the extensive modified reports of the Board nor in the opinions of the Court of Appeals are the 1954 legislative findings considered. While we must, of course, assume that the Board was aware of them, we cannot say that their very annunciation by Congress—in the absence of any showing that the Board took them into acount—foreclosed or impaired a fair administrative determination.

The other constitutional questions raised by the Party have been carefully considered, but do not call for detailed discussion. And we must decline, of course, to enter into discussion of the wisdom of this legislation. The Constitution does not probihit the requirement that the Communist Party register with the Attorney General as a Communist-action organization pursuant to § 7.

The judgment of the Court of Appeals is affirmed.

Mr. Justice Black, dissenting:

I do not believe that it can be too often repeated that the freedoms of speech, press, petition and assembly guaranteed by the First Amendment must be accorded to the ideas we hate or sooner or later they will be denied to the ideas we cherish. The first banning of an association because it advocates hated ideas—whether that association be called a political party or not—marks a fateful moment in the history of a free country. That moment seems to have arrived for this country.

The Subversive Activities Control Act of 1950 here involved defines "Communist action" organizations and requires them to register with the Attorney General giving much information of every kind with regard to their property, income, activities and members. The Communist Party has been ordered to register under that Act by the Subversive Activities Control Board and has challenged the validity of that order on the ground, among others, that the Act is unconstitutional in that it amounts to a complete outlawry of the Communist Party. The contention is that this Act, considered as a whole and in its relation to existing laws which affect members of the Party, imposes such overhanging threats of disgrace, humiliation, fines, forfeitures and lengthy imprisonments upon registered organizations and their members, most of which burdens become effective automatically upon registration, that it will be impossible for the Party to continue to function if the registration order is upheld.

The Court's opinion is devoted chiefly to the task of explaining why it will not decide any of the substantial issues raised by this attack upon the constitutionality of the Act as it is actually written and will actually operate and why it must decide the case just as though none of these other burdens existed and we were dealing with an Act that required nothing more than the registration of an organization. I cannot agree to decide the case on any such hypothetical basis. If registration were the only issue in the case, I would agree at once that Congress has power to require every "person" acting as an agent of a foreign principal to file registration statements comprehensively showing his agency activities as is required, for example, by the Foreign Agents Registration Act. That Act requires the registration of any "person"—including an individual, partnership, association, corporation, organization, or other combination of individuals—"who acts or agrees to act, within the United States, as . . . a public-relations counsel, publicity agent, information-service employee, servant, agent, representative, or attorney for a foreign principal. . . ." Referring to that Act, I said in *Viereck* v. *United States* [318 US 236, 251]:

> Resting on the fundamental constitutional principle that our people, adequately informed, may be trusted to distinguish between the true and the false, the bill is intended to label information of foreign origin so that hearers and readers may not be deceived by the belief that the information comes from a disinterested source. Such legislation implements rather than detracts from the prized freedoms guaranteed by the First Amendment.

The Act before us now, however, unlike the Foreign Agents Registration Act involved in the *Viereck* case, is not based on the principle that "our people, adequately informed, may be trusted to distinguish between the true and the false." Instead, the present Act, like many other pieces of current legislation, is based on the precisely contrary principle that "our people [even when] adequately informed may [not] be trusted to distinguish between the true and the false." In this regard, the principle upon which Congress acted in passing the Subversive Activities Control Act is identical to that upon which it acted in making membership in the Communist Party a crime in the Smith Act, a provision under which the Court has today sustained the conviction and imprisonment for six years of a person for being a mere member of the Communist Party with knowledge of its purposes. Statutes based upon such a principle, which really amounts to nothing more than the idea that the Government must act as a paternal guardian to protect American voters from hearing public policies discussed, do not implement "the prized freedoms guaranteed by the First Amendment"—they are designed to and do directly detract from those freedoms.

The difference between the Subversive Activities Control Act and the Foreign Agents Registration Act is strikingly illustrated by the reasons Congress has itself given for the enactment of the statute now before us. When Viereck registered under the earlier and genuine registration statute, he was not thereby branded as being engaged in an evil, despicable undertaking bent on destroying this Nation. But that is precisely the effect of the present Act. Registration as a "Communist action organization" under the Subversive Activities Control Act means, according to the express provisions of the Act, that the Party and its members who register are under the control of a foreign dictatorship, that they have devised "clever and ruthless espionage and sabotage tactics," and that they are a part of a "world-wide revolutionary movement whose purpose it is, by treachery, deceit, infiltration . . . terrorism and any other means deemed necessary to establish a Communist totalitarian dictatorship in the countries throughout the world." A registrant organization is declared, by a finding of Congress, to be "an organization numbering thousands of adherents, rigidly and ruthlessly disciplined," merely awaiting a chance to overthrow this Government by force. And the members of such an organization are declared by the Act to have "repudiate[d] their allegiance to the United States, and in effect transfer[red] their allegiance to the foreign country in which is vested the direction and control of the world Communist movement."

This difference standing alone would be sufficient to establish the essential dissimilarity of the Subversive Activities Control Act from genuine registration statutes such as the Foreign Agents Registration Act. For the need of Government to provide means by which the people can obtain useful information—the basis of every genuine registration statute—can certainly be accomplished without resort to official legislative pronouncements as to the treasonable nature of those compelled to register. But this difference does not stand alone in the case of the Subversive Activities Control Act—indeed, there are so many other differences of so much greater magnitude that the recitals of the Act branding those who register under it pale almost into insignificance.

The plan of the Act is to make it impossible for an organization to continue to function once a registration order is issued against it. To this end, the Act first provides crushing penalties to insure complete compliance with the disclosure requirements of registration. Thus, if the Party or its members fail to register within the time required by the Act, or if they fail to make annual reports as required, or to keep records as required, each individual guilty of such failure can be punished by a fine of $10,000, by imprisonment for five years, or both, for each offense—and each offense means "each day of failure to register" or "each listing of the name or address of any one individual" either by the organization or by an individual. Thus, for a delay of thirty days in filing required reports, a fine of $300,000 and imprisonment for 150 years could be imposed by a trial judge.

Having thus made it mandatory that Communist organizations and individual Communists make a full disclosure of their identities and activities, the Act then proceeds to heap burden after burden upon those so exposed.

Certain tax deductions allowed to others are denied to a registered organization. Mail matter must be stamped before the organization sends it out to show that it was disseminated by a "Communist action" organization, with all the treasonable connotations given that term by the recitals of "fact" in the Act. Members of a registered organization cannot hold certain jobs with the Government, or any jobs with private businesses engaged in doing certain work for the Government. Members cannot use or attempt to use a passport and cannot even make application for a passport without being subject to a penalty of five years in the penitentiary. The Act thus makes it extremely difficult for a member of the Communist Party to live in this country and, at the same time, makes it a crime for him to try to get a passport to get out.

In addition to these burdens imposed directly by the Act itself, the registration requirement must also be considered in the context of the other laws now existing which affect the Communist Party. The Act requires that the information obtained upon registration be given wide publicity thus insuring that those identified as members of the Party will be subjected to all the civil disabilities, criminal prosecutions and public harassments that have become common in recent years. I agree with Mr. Justice Douglas that this aspect of the Act is alone sufficient to establish its invalidity under the self-incrimination provision of the Fifth Amendment. But I think the interrelationship between the present Act and these other laws goes deeper than that, for I think that interrelationship establishes all but conclusively that the present Act cannot be upheld as a mere registration statute. The information elicited by the Act must be considered, not, as in the *Viereck* case, an aid to the exercise of individual judgment by the people, but rather a part of a pattern of suppression by the Government, for that is certainly the inevitable effect of any system that requires registration on the one hand and imposes pains and penalties upon those registering on the other.

All of these enormous burdens, which are necessarily imposed upon the Party and its members by the act of registration, are dismissed by the Court on the basis of an alleged conflict with the Court-created rule that constitutional questions should be avoided whenever possible. Thus, the Court engages in extended discussions as to whether the people involved will ever want to do the things the Act says they cannot do and whether they will ever object to doing the things the Act says they must do, suggesting, among other things, that the members of the Communist Party may never object to providing the evidence needed to send them to prison for violating the Smith Act; that they may never protest because they are forced to give up the tax deductions that other people receive; that they may be willing to stamp all the Party's mail as coming from an evil organization; that they may never want to hold the jobs from which the Act disqualifies them; and that they may never want to get a passport to get out of the country. On the basis of all these "uncertainties" the Court seems to consider its hands tied because, it says, these are as yet only potential impairments of constitutional rights. In its view, there is no "justiciable" issue at all between the United States and the Communist Party except the bare requirement of registration.

In the context of this case, I can find no justification for the Court's refusal to pass upon the serious constitutional questions raised. The Court of Appeals met its responsibility by deciding the questions. The Government has not asked that the Court refrain from giving a full decision on these important matters. Assuming that the Act is wholly valid aside from registration and that Congress does have power to outlaw groups advocating dangerous ideas, it seems to me unfair to Congress for this Court to refuse to decide whether its Act can be fully enforced. And assuming that the Act is not wholly valid because of some limitation upon that power, it seems to me that we should say so now. By refusing to do so, the Court in effect allows this serious question to be decided by default. For the Party can no more continue to function with all of these tremendous burdens of undetermined constitutional validity overhanging it and its members than it could if the burdens were considered and upheld. The only sense in which the Court has avoided a constitutional issue is by permitting the destruction of a group seeking to raise the issue of the constitutionality of its destruction.

This whole Act, with its pains and penalties, embarks this country, for the first time, on the dangerous adventure of outlawing groups that preach doctrines nearly all Americans detest. When the practice of outlawing parties and various public groups begin, no one can say where it will end. In most countries such a practice once begun ends with a one-party government. There is something of tragic irony in the fact that this Act, expressly designed to protect this Nation from becoming a "totalitarian dictatorship" with "a single political party," has adopted to achieve its laudable purpose the policy of outlawing a party—a policy indispensable to totalitarian dictatorships. I think we should meet and decide this whole question now in the administration of a sound judicial policy that carries out our responsibilities both to Congress and to the American people.

In my judgment, the Act here under consideration is unconstitutional on at least three grounds in addition to its direct conflict with the self-incrimination provisions of the Fifth Amendment. It is, in the first instance, a classical bill of attainder which our Constitution in two places prohibits, for it is a legislative act that inflicts pains, penalties and punishments in a number of ways without a judicial trial. The legislative fact-findings as to Communist activities, which the Court—despite the constitutional command for trial of such facts by a court and jury—accepts as facts, supply practically all of the proof needed to bring the Communist Party within the proscriptions of the Act. The Act points unerringly to the members of that Party as guilty people who must be penalized as the Act provides. At the same time, these legislative fact-findings fall little short of being adequate in themselves to justify a finding of guilt against any person who can be identified, however faintly, by any informer, as ever having been a member of the Communist Party. Most of whatever is lacking in the legislative fact-findings is later supplied by administrative fact-findings of an agency which is not a court, which is not manned by independent judges, and which does not have to observe the constitutional right to trial by jury and other trial safeguards unequivocally commanded by the Bill of Rights. Yet, after this agency has made its findings and its conclusions, neither its findings of fact nor the findings of fact of the legislative body can subsequently be challenged in court by any individual who may later be brought up on a charge that he failed to register as required by the Act and the Board. The Act thus not only is a legislative bill of attainder but also violates due process by short-cutting practically all of the Bill of Rights, leaving no hope for anyone entangled in this legislative-administrative web except what has proved in this case to be one of the most truncated judicial reviews that the history of this Court can afford.

I think also that this outlawry of the Communist Party and imprisonment of its members violates the First Amendment. The question under that Amendment is whether Congress has power to outlaw an association, group or party either on the ground that it advocates a policy of violent overthrow of the existing government at some time in the distant future or on the ground that it is ideologically subservient to some foreign country. In my judgment, neither of these factors justifies an invasion of rights protected by the First Amendment. Talk about the desirability of revolution has a long and honorable history, not only in other parts of the world, but in our own country. This kind of talk, like any other, can be used at the wrong time and for the wrong purpose. But, under our system of Government, the remedy for this danger must be the same remedy that is applied to the danger that comes from any other erroneous talk—education and contrary argument. If that remedy is not sufficient, the only meaning of free speech must be that the revolutionary ideas will be allowed to prevail.*

This conclusion is not affected by the fact that those advocating a policy of revolution are in sympathy with a foreign government. If there is one thing certain about the First Amendment it is that this Amendment was designed to guarantee the freest interchange of ideas about all public matters and that, of course, means the interchange of *all* ideas, however such ideas may be viewed in other countries and whatever change in the existing structure of government it may be hoped that these ideas will bring about. Now, when this country is trying to spread the high ideals of democracy all over the world—ideals that are revolutionary in many countries—seems to be a particularly inappropriate time to stifle First Amendment freedoms in this country. The same arguments that are used to justify the outlawry of Communist ideas here could be used to justify an outlawry of the ideas of democracy in other countries.

The freedom to advocate ideas about public matters through associations of the nature of political parties and societies was contemplated and protected by the First Amendment. The existence of such groups is now, and for centuries has been, a necessary part of any effective promulgation of beliefs about governmental policies. And the destruction of such groups is now and always has been one of the first steps totalitarian governments take. Within recent months we have learned of such practices in other countries.

* Cf. *Gitlow* v. *New York*, 268 U.S. 652, 673: "If in the long run the beliefs expressed in proletarian dictatorship are destined to be accepted by the dominant forces of the community, the only meaning of free speech is that they should be given their chance and have their way." (Holmes, J., dissenting.)

Only a few weeks ago an executive edict outlawing all parties, groups and associations all the way down through Rotary Clubs was issued in a country where the government is largely in the hands of a single man. Indeed, our own ancestors were not unfamiliar with this practice. Men and women belonging to dissenting religious, political or social groups in England before the colonization of this country were sometimes imprisoned, mutilated, degraded by humiliating pillories, exiled and even killed for their views.

A typical example of the type of legislation under which this sort of persecution was carried on is provided by a statute enacted in 1593 to destroy dissenting religious sects and force all the people of England to become regular attendants at the established church. The basic premise upon which its commands rested was not at all unlike that upon which the Act here proceeds:

> For the better discovering and avoiding of such traiterous and most dangerous Conspiracies and Attempts, as are daily devised and practised against our most gracious Sovereign Lady the Queen's Majesty and the happy Estate of this common Weal, by sundry wicked and seditious Persons, who terming themselves Catholicks, and being indeed Spies and Intelligencers, not only for her Majesty's foreign Enemies, but also for rebellious and traiterous Subjects born within her Highness Realms and Dominions, and hiding their most detestable and devilish Purposes under a false Pretext of Religion and Conscience, do secretly wander and shift from Place to Place within this Realm, to corrupt and seduce her Majesty's Subjects, and to stir them to Sedition and Rebellion. . . .

These attainted Catholics were not permitted to go "above five Miles" from their homes. For violation of this command they could be sentenced to prison and have all their goods, lands and other possessions forfeited "to the Queen's Majesty." One has only to read this statute to see how thoroughgoing government can be in making life miserable for groups whose beliefs have fallen into disfavor.

That statute also has peculiar relevance to the consideration of the Subversive Activities Control Act because it too used disclosure as a lever to secure effective enforcement of its provisions. Thus, one section of the statute provided:

> And be it further enacted and ordained by the Authority aforesaid, That if any Person which shall be *suspected* to be a Jesuit, Seminary or Massing Priest, being examined by any Person having lawful Authority in that Behalf to examine such Person which shall be *so suspected*, shall refuse to answer directly and truly whether he be a Jesuit, or a Seminary or Massing Priest, as is aforesaid, every such Person so refusing to answer shall, for his Disobedience and Contempt in that Behalf, be committed to Prison by such as shall examine him as is aforesaid, and thereupon shall remain and continue in Prison without Bail or Mainprise, until he shall make direct and true Answer to

the said Questions whereupon he shall be so examined. (Emphasis supplied.)

One cannot help but wonder whether this Court, were it called upon to consider the constitutionality of a provision of that kind in this country, would pass it off as involving nothing more than potential impairments of religious freedoms and a right to travel which the attainted persons might never want to exercise.

There were many other statutes of this kind passed in England before our Revolutionary War. By no means all of them were aimed at the Catholics. Indeed, during the times when the Catholics were themselves in power, almost identical repressive measures were adopted in an attempt to curb the rise of Protestantism. And the persecution of Puritans in England, dramatized by some of the most famous writers of the time, is a story that is, I hope, familiar to most Americans. It is a matter of history that not one of these laws achieved its purpose. Many men died, suffered and were driven from their country. And, in a sense, it might be said that our own country profited from these laws because it was largely founded by refugees from English oppression. But England itself gained little if any profit from its policies of repression. The outlawed groups were not destroyed. Many people have thought that these repressive measures were more effective to bring about revolutions than to stop them. Be that as it may, it cannot be denied that the most tranquil period of English history, from an internal standpoint, has been the period since England abandoned these practices of trying to inculcate belief by oaths and force.

Even after the American Revolution, England continued to pass statutes outlawing groups and punishing their members. One that is of particular interest here because of the many similarities between it and the Act involved in this case was passed in 1799 under the title "An Act for the more effectual Suppression of Societies established for Seditious and Treasonable Purposes; and for better preventing Treasonable and Seditious practices." The premise upon which this Act was passed was also similar to that used here—"a traitorous Conspiracy has long been carried on, in conjunction with the Persons from Time to Time exercising the Powers of Government in *France,* to overturn the Laws, Constitution, and Government, and every existing Establishment, Civil and Ecclesiastical, both in *Great Britain* and Ireland. . . ." The Act broadly provided for the suppression and prohibition "as unlawful Combinations and Confederacies," of all such societies "particularly . . . *Societies of United Englishmen, United Scotsmen, United Britons, United Irishmen,* and *The London Corresponding Society.* . . ." This 1799 English Act, like the Subversive Activities Control Act here, comprehensively provided for fines, forfeitures, penalties and imprisonments. It went on to outlaw places where debates could take place or lectures be given or books be gathered and read unless, under very restrictive standards, licenses had been granted by Justices of the Peace. Great emphasis was laid upon the fact that unlicensed gatherings should be treated as nuisances and disorderly houses. Following the course that such repressive measures always must, and indeed precisely the course that is here being followed by our own Government with respect to the Communist Party, the English Act placed printing presses, type and everything else useful for publishing discussion of public matters under strict regulations.

The parliamentary debates underlying the enactment of this 1799 English statute indicate plainly the close parallel between it and the Act here under consideration. The chief fear of the English rulers that brought on the 1799 Act was that the people of England would be seduced away from their loyalty to their government if societies were left free to discuss public matters and if the common people were left free to read and hear arguments. William Pitt, the Younger, in offering the bill which provided the basis for the Act, expressed his fear that debating societies and other such manifestations of liberty of press and speech might call "the attention of the lower orders of the people to objects of discussion of the most mischievous tendency, objects which are not calculated for their understandings, and which are of all others the most liable to be attended with dreadful effects." He thought these "dreadful effects" could be averted, in large part, by making individual authors sign everything they wrote. But he then went on to urge that "in order to make the measure effectual, and prevent the press from becoming an engine of corruption and innovation in the hands of factions who are ready to circulate cheap publications, adapted to inflame and pervert the public mind, it will be necessary to keep a general register, not only of the presses used by printers, but of those in the possession of private persons." All of this, Mr. Pitt explained, was necessary in order to render "more effectual" an Act passed at the previous session of Parliament entitled "an Act to empower his majesty to secure and detain such persons as his majesty shall suspect are conspiring against his person and government."

The debates on the English statute also show the true nature of the "revolutionary" principles advocated by the various societies named which were being used to justify their outlawry. These principles were chiefly parliamentary reform providing for annual sessions of Parliament, universal suffrage and fair parliamentary representation, and repeal of the right of the King to veto measures passed by Parliament. It is, of course, true that Congress has no power to outlaw political parties advocating such measures in this country. But I wonder how this Court could ever reach the question in view of its holding today. And if the Court is, as it holds, truly bound by legislative findings as to the nature of political parties and their involvement with foreign powers, how could it strike down the very statute I have just described? For that statute purported to establish, as a matter of fact, that the named societies were a part of a "traitorous Conspiracy" acting "in conjunction with the Persons from Time to Time exercising the Powers of Government in *France.*"

At the very time England was going through its era of terror about the "Jacobins," a heated political struggle involving many of the same issues was going on in this country between the two chief political parties. One of those parties, the Federalists, wanted to outlaw the party of Jefferson on the ground that they too were "Jacobins" and therefore a threat to our security.

The Jeffersonians quite naturally opposed such outlawry and in fact opposed any measure which would restrict the freedoms of speech, press, petition and assembly. The difference between the two parties was expressed by Jefferson in this way: "Both of our political parties, at least the honest part of them, agree conscientiously in the same object, the public good. . . . One fears most the ignorance of the people; the other, the selfishness of rulers independent of them. Which is right, time and experience will prove." This conflict of ideals and policies was temporarily resolved in favor of the Federalist and the result was the infamous era of the Alien and Sedition Acts. These laws, passed over vigorous Jeffersonian opposition, declared that it was necessary in order to protect the security of the Nation to give the President the broadest of powers over aliens and to make substantial inroads upon the freedoms of speech, press and assembly.

The enforcement of these statutes, particularly the Sedition Act, constitutes one of the greatest blots on our country's record of freedom. Publishers were sent to jail for writing their own views and for publishing the views of others. The slightest criticism of government or policies of government officials was enough to cause biased federal prosecutors to put the machinery of government to work to crush and imprison the critic. Rumors which filled the air pointed the finger of suspicion at good men and bad men alike, sometimes causing the social ostracism of people who loved their free country with a deathless devotion. Members of the Jeffersonian Party were picked out as special targets so that they could be illustrious examples of what could happen to people who failed to sing paeons of praise for current federal officials and their policies. Matthew Lyon, a Congressman of the Jeffersonian Party, was prosecuted, convicted and forced to serve a prison sentence in a disreputable jailhouse because of criticisms he made of governmental officials and their activities. This was a particularly egregious example of the repressive nature of the Sedition Act for Lyon's conviction could not possibly have been upheld under even the most niggardly interpretation of the First Amendment. Lyon was but one of many who had to go to jail, be fined, or otherwise be made to suffer for the expression of his public views. Carpenters, preachers, lawyers, and many others furnished grist for the prosecutor's biased political activities in the "administration of justice." Unfortunately, our federal courts did not emerge from this fever of hysteria with the kind of reputations that shed lustre on the business of judging. Although the Founders had provided for federal judges to be appointed for life, thus intending to give them the independence necessary for the higher responsibility they had, some federal judges, even including members of the highest courts, presided over grand juries and trials in a way that is sad to be recalled even at this late date.

All the governmental activities set out above designed to suppress the freedom of American citizens to think their own views and speak their own thoughts and read their own selections, and even more, occurred under the 1798 Sedition Act. And all these things happened despite the fact that the promoters of that legislation were unable to make it as strong as their philosophical and political brethren in England had made their Act for the Complete suppression of all kinds of societies. But even this comparatively less repressive law and its enforcement was too much of an infringement upon personal liberty to stand the test of public opinion among the plain, sturdy pioneers of America. In the very next election following its enactment, Jefferson was elected President on a platform which contained, as its principal plank, a promise to abandon the Sedition Act and the policy of repression behind it. Members of Congress and the Senate were elected to help him carry out his pledge. The pledge was carried out, and in order to try to make amends to those who had suffered under this obnoxious law, Congress was busy for many years indemnifying those who had been prosecuted under its provisions and even their descendants. The superior judgment of the people over that of their legislators who passed the Act in the first place was graphically illustrated when Matthew Lyon, who had been sent to jail for refusing to refrain from criticizing Federalist office holders, was triumphantly re-elected by the people of Vermont while still in jail.

I regret, exceedingly regret, that I feel impelled to recount this history of the Federalist Sedition Act because, in all truth, it must be pointed out that this law—which has since been almost universally condemned as unconstitutional—did not go as far in suppressing the First Amendment freedoms of Americans as do the Smith Act and the Subversive Activities Control Act. All the fervor and all the eloquence and all the emotionalism and all the prejudice and all the parades of horrors about letting the people hear arguments for themselves were not sufficient in 1798 to persuade the members of Congress to pass a law which would directly and unequivocally outlaw the party of Jefferson, at which the law was undoubtedly aimed. The same arguments were made then about the "Jacobins," meaning the Jeffersonians, with regard to their alleged subservience to France, that are made today about the Communists with regard to their subservience to Russia. Even the language of the charges that were hurled was substantially the same as that used in the charges made today. The Jacobins were "trained, officered, regimented, and formed to subordination, in a manner that our militia have never yet equalled;" and "it is as certain as any future event can be, that they [the Jeffersonians] will take arms against the laws as soon as they dare. . . ."

These charges expressed fears that were echoed time and time again during the congressional debate on the Alien and Sedition Acts. The very same fears are again being voiced today as a justification for curtailing the liberties of the people of America. Thus, § 2 (15) of the Subversive Activities Control Act under consideration says that "[t]he Communist movement in the United States is an organization numbering thousands of adherents, rigidly and ruthlessly disciplined" only awaiting "a moment when . . . overthrow of the Government of the United States by force and violence may seem possible of achievement. . . ."

This excuse for repression is, of course, not a distinctively American creation. It is the same excuse that was used for the 1799 English Act described above. Thus, Charles Abbot, a member of Parliament, urged as one of the justifications for outlawing the societies named in that Act: "The malignancy of their character is distinguishable by the restless spirit which it infuses into the lowest orders of the people, encouraging them to take up arms, and teaching them that they have great and powerful partisans and leaders *who are secretly prepared to seize the favorable moment* for showing themselves openly at their head, when they can hope to do so with impunity."

The truth is that this statutory outlawry of the Communist Party is not at all novel when considered in the perspective of history. Quite the contrary, it represents nothing more than the adoption by this country, in part at least, of one of the two conflicting views that have emerged from a long-standing and widespread dispute among political philosophers as to what kind of Government will best serve the welfare of the people. That view is that Governments should have almost unlimited powers. The other view is that governmental power should be very strictly limited. Both the Smith Act and the Subversive Activities Control Act are based upon the view that officials of the Government should have power to suppress and crush by force critics and criticisms of governmental officials and their policies. The contrary view, which Congress necessarily rejected in passing these laws, is that current public officials should never be granted power to use governmental force to keep people from hearing, speaking or publishing such criticisms of Government or from assembling together to petition their Government to make changes in governmental policies, however basic the majority may deem these policies to be.

It is my belief that our Constitution with its Bill of Rights was expressly intended to make our Government one of strictly limited powers. The Founders were intimately familiar with the restrictions upon liberty which inevitably flow from a Government of unlimited powers. By and large, they had found this experience a painful one. Many of them were descended from families that had left England and had come to this country in order to escape laws that could send them to jail or penalize them in various ways for criticizing laws and policies which they thought bore too heavily and unfairly upon them. Others had personally felt the brunt of such repressive measures. Only after they won the Revolutionary War did these people have an opportunity to set up a Government to their liking. To that end they finally settled upon the Constitution, which very clearly adopted the policy of limiting the powers of the Federal Government. Even then the people of this country were not completely satisfied. They demanded more precise and unequivocal limitations upon the powers of Government and obtained the Bill of Rights, the central provisions of which were the First Amendment guarantees of complete religious and political freedom.

In the very face of the provisions of the First Amendment, however, the Court today upholds laws which ignore the wisdom of the Founders' decision to set up a limited Government and adopt the policy of force to crush views about public matters entertained by a small minority in this country. This, to me, marks a major break in the wall designed by the First Amendment to keep this country free by leaving the people free to talk about any kind of change in basic governmental policies they desire to talk about. I see no possible way to escape the fateful consequences of a return to the era in which all governmental critics had to face the probability of being sent to jail except for this Court to abandon what I consider to be the dangerous constitutional doctrine of "balancing" to which the Court is at present adhering. That doctrine is not a new one. In fact, history shows that it has been the excuse for practically every repressive measure that Government has ever seen fit to adopt. Mr. Pitt proved, in 1799, that he was a master of the concept and language of "balancing" in his speech urging the passage of laws to muzzle the press of England in order to prevent the dissemination of the "revolutionary" ideas that England should have parliamentary reform:

> We cannot too highly prize that sacred liberty [of the press] when we consider that it has been instrumental in bringing our Constitution to that envied perfection which it possesses. Yet it must also be admitted that when abused, the most fatal consequences have ever resulted from it. It has been the great principle of the Constitution that the liberty of the press should flourish, but it is also clear from the nature of the principle itself, and for the security of the press, that the author or publisher of every work should be amenable to the laws of his country.

And there certainly was no shortage of "balancers" in our own Congress when the Alien and Sedition and Sedition Acts of 1798 were passed.

The "balancing test" of First Amendment freedoms is said to justify laws aimed at the advocacy of overthrow of the Government "as speedily as circumstances would permit." Thus, the "test" being used here is identical to the arguments used to justify the Alien and Sedition Acts of 1798 in this country and the 1799 Sedition Act in England. The unprecedented incorporation into our constitutional law of this time-worn justification for tyranny has been used to break down even the minimal protections of the First Amendment forged by Mr. Justice Holmes and Mr. Justice Brandeis which would bar prosecution for speech or writings in all cases except those in which the words used "so imminently threaten immediate interference with the lawful and pressing purposes of the law that an immediate check is required to save the country."

I realize that these laws are aimed only at the Communist Party. No one need console himself, however, that the policy of using governmental force to crush dissident groups upon which they are based can or will be stopped at that point. The weakening of constitutional safeguards in order to suppress one obnoxious group is a technique too easily available for the suppression of other obnoxious groups to expect its abandonment when the next generally hated group appears. Only eleven years ago, this Court upheld a governmental penalty directed at Communists on the ground that "only a relative handful" would be affected by the penalty involved in that case. Today, it upholds statutes which I think totally outlaw that Party, claiming nonetheless that "[n]othing which we decide here remotely carries . . . [the] implication . . . [that] Congress may impose similar requirements upon any group which pursues unpopular political objectives or which expresses an unpopular political ideology." I am very much afraid that we will see the day when the very implication which the Court now denies is found.

I am ready to admit that strong arguments can be made for saying that Governments in general should have power to suppress speech and press. These arguments are particularly strong in countries where the existing Government does not represent the will of the people because history shows that people have a way of not being willing to bear oppressive grievances without protest. Such protests, when bottomed upon facts, lead almost inevitably to an irresistible popular demand for either a redress of those grievances or a change in the Government. It is plain that there are Governments in the world today that desperately need to suppress such protests for they probably could not survive a week or even a day if they were deprived of the power to use their informers to intimidate, their jails to imprison and their firing squads to shoot their critics. In countries of that kind, repressive measures like the Smith Act and the Subversive Activities Control Act are absolutely necessary to protect the ruling tyrants from the spread of information about their misdeeds. But in a democracy like ours, such laws are not only unnecessary but also constitute a baseless insult to the patriotism of our people.

I believe with the Framers of the First Amendment that the internal security of a nation like ours does not and cannot be made to depend upon the use of force by Government to make all the beliefs and opinions of the people fit into a common mold on any single subject. Such enforced conformity of thought would tend only to deprive our people of the bold spirit of adventure and progress which has brought this Nation to its present greatness. The creation of public opinion by groups, organizations, societies, clubs, and parties, has been and is a necessary part of our democratic society. Such groups, like the Sons of Liberty and the American Corresponding Societies, played a large part in creating sentiment in this country that led the people of the Colonies to want a nation of their own. The Father of the Constitution—James Madison—said, in speaking of the Sedition Act aimed at crushing the Jeffersonian Party, that had that law been in effect during the period before the Revolution, the United States might well have continued to be "miserable colonies, groaning under a foreign yoke."

In my judgment, this country's internal security can better be served by depending upon the affection of the people than by attempting to instill them with fear and dread of the power of Government. The Communist Party has never been more than a small group in this country. And its numbers had been dwindling even before the Government began its campaign to destroy the Party by force of law. This was because a vast majority of the American people were against the Party's policies and overwhelmingly rejected its candidates year after year. That is the true American way of securing this Nation against dangerous ideas. Of course that is not the way to protect the Nation against *actions* of violence and treason. The Founders drew a distinction in our Constitution which we would be wise to follow. They gave the Government the fullest power to prosecute overt actions in violation of valid laws but withheld any power to punish people for nothing more than advocacy of their views.

I am compelled to say in closing that I fear that all the arguments and urgings the Communists and their sympathizers can use in trying to convert Americans to an ideology wholly foreign to our habits and our instincts are far less dangerous to the security of this Nation than laws which embark us upon a policy of repression by the outlawry of minority parties because they advocate radical changes in the structure of Government. This widespread program for punishing ideas on the ground that they might impair the internal security of the Nation not only sadly fails to protect that security but also diverts our energies and thoughts from the many far more important problems that face us as a Nation in this troubled world.

I would reverse this case and leave the Communists free to advocate their beliefs in proletarian dictatorship publicly and openly among the people of this country with full confidence that the people will remain loyal to any democratic Government truly dedicated to freedom and justice—the kind of Government which some of us still think of as being "the last best hope of earth."

Mr. Justice Douglas, dissenting:

I.

The Subversive Activities Control Board found, and the Court of Appeals sustained the finding, that petitioner, the Communist Party of the United States, is "a disciplined organization" operating in this nation "under Soviet Union control" to install "a Soviet style dictatorship in the United States." Those findings are based, I think, on facts; and I would not disturb them.

The other objections made are not of the character of those which led us to reverse and remand for additional hearings five years ago. There we had a record tainted by perjury. *Communist Party* v. *Control Board*, 351 U.S. 115, 124–125. No one—no matter how venal—could suffer penalties under our regime of law where perjury tainted the record. The present errors that are urged are not of that character.

Had they appeared in a normal administrative hearing and timely claimed, they might give us pause. If we had before us the question whether a particular organization was, to use the statutory words a "Communist-front organization," . . . or a "Communist-infiltrated organization," . . . the errors urged might loom large. For then the decision might turn on intangibles to be closely appraised. The present problem, however, is in a somewhat different posture. We are in a field where Congress has found and declared that the Communist Party is "in fact an instrumentality of a conspiracy to overthrow the government of the United States," that its "policies and programs" are "secretly prescribed for it by the foreign leaders of the world communist movement," that it is "the agency of a hostile foreign power." These congressional findings amount to no more than facts of which some Justices have already taken judicial notice. . . . This does not mean that anything goes and that the hearings are *pro forma*. It does suggest, however, that where, as here, the case does not turn on nice nuances which in closer contests might have to be carefully weighed, we should not prolong the administrative hearings which already have extended a decade. With this as a starting point, I agree with Mr. Justice Frankfurter that the Court of Appeals did not err in overruling the objections based on procedural errors.

May then the Communist Party, under control of a foreign power, be required to register?

The vices of registration may be not unlike those of licensing. Despite *Times Film Corp.* v. *Chicago*, 365 U.S. 43, I think licensing is an impermissible form of regulation when it vests discretion in the authorities to grant or withhold the exercise of First Amendment rights or to permit them to be exercised only on condition. . . . Licensing, like a tax payable on the exercise of a First Amendment right . . . is therefore unconstitutional. . . . Yet registration, like licensing, may have aspects of harassment and burden. That is why we said in *Thomas* v. *Collins* [323 US 516]:

> If the exercise of the rights of free speech and free assembly cannot be made a crime, we do not think this can be accomplished by the device of requiring previous registration as a condition for exercising them and making such a condition the foundation for restraining in advance their exercise and for imposing a penalty for violating such a restraining order. So long as no more is involved than exercise of the rights of free speech and free assembly, it is immune to such a restriction. If one who solicits support for the cause of labor may be required to register as a condition to the exercise of his right to make a public speech, so may he who seeks to rally support for any social, business, religious or political cause. We think a requirement that one must register before he undertakes to make a public speech to enlist support for a lawful movement is quite incompatible with the requirements of the First Amendment.

Freedom of association is included in the bundle of First Amendment rights. . . . So if we had only the question whether those who band together to espouse a political, educational, literary, civic, or ideological cause could be made to register, I would protest. The late Zachariah Chafee spoke of the danger in limiting our freedoms under political pressures. "Universities," he wrote, "should not be transformed, as in Nazi Germany, into loudspeakers for the men who wield political power." *The Blessings of Liberty* (1956) 241. There have been attempts here to interfere by law in a myriad of ways with the shaping of public opinion through many groups, attacked because they were non-conformists of one kind or another. As we said recently, the identification of members of groups and fear of reprisal "might deter peaceful discussions of public matters of importance." . . . There is, in my view, a disability on the part of government to probe the intimacies of relationships in the myriad of lawful societies and groups in this country. . . . From . . . precedents I would hopefully deduce two principles. First, no individual may be required to register before he makes a speech, for the First Amendment rights are not subject to any prior restraint. Second, a group engaged in lawful conduct may not be required to file with the Government a list of its members, no matter how unpopular it may be. For the disclosure of membership lists may cause harassment of the members and seriously hamper their exercise of First Amendment rights. The more unpopular the group, the greater the likelihood of harassment. In logic then it might seem that the Communist Party, being at the low tide of popularity, might better make out a case of harassment than almost any other group on the contemporary scene.

We have, however, as I have said, findings that the Communist Party of the United States is "a disciplined organization" operating in this Nation "under Soviet Union control" with the aim of installing "a Soviet style dictatorship" here. These findings establish that more than debate, discourse, argumentation, propaganda, and other aspects of free speech and association are involved. An additional element enters, viz., espionage, business activities, and the formation of cells for subversion, as well as the use of speech, press, and association by a foreign power to produce on this continent a Soviet satellite.

Picketing is free speech plus . . . and hence can be restricted in all instances and banned in some. Registration of those who disseminate propaganda of foreign origin . . . has been thought to fall in the same category as barring speech in places that will create traffic conditions . . . or provoke breaches of the peace. . . . Though the activities themselves are under the First Amendment, the manner of their exercise or their collateral aspects fall without it.

Like reasons underlie our decisions which sustain laws that require various groups to register before engaging in specified activities. Thus lobbyists who receive fees for attempting to influence the passage or defeat of legislation in Congress may be required to register. . . . Criminal sanctions for failure to report and to disclose all contributions made to political parties are permitted. . . . Publishers of newspapers, desiring reduced postal rates, have long been required to file with the Postmaster General and with the local post-office certain data concerning ownership and circulation; and those disclosure requirements have been sustained. . . . In short, the exercise of First Amendment rights often involves business or commercial implications which Congress in its wisdom may desire to be disclosed, just as it did in strictly financial matters under the Public Utility Holding Company Act of 1935. . . .

If lobbyists can be required to register, if political parties can be required to make disclosure of the sources of their funds, if the owners of newspapers and periodicals must disclose their affiliates, so may a group operating under the control of a foreign power.

The Bill of Rights was designed to give fullest play to the exchange and dissemination of ideas that touch the politics, culture, and other aspects of our life. When an organization is used by a foreign power to make advances here, questions of security are raised beyond the ken of disputation and debate between the people resident here. Espionage, business activities, formation of cells for subversion, as well as the exercise of First Amendment rights, are then used to pry open our society and make intrusion of a foreign power easy. These machinations of a foreign power add additional elements to free speech just as marching up and down adds something to picketing that goes beyond free speech.

These are the reasons why, in my view, the bare requirement that the Communist Party register and disclose the names of its officers and directors is in line with the most exacting adjudications touching First Amendment activities.

II.

While the Act is pregnant with constitutional questions, I deal now with only one, *viz.*, whether § 7 of the Act is unconstitutional and void as conflicting with the provision against self-incrimination accorded by the Fifth Amendment.

The registration statement prepared by the Attorney General pursuant to § 7 (a) and (b) of the Act asks in Item 2 the name, address, position, and functions of any individual "who at any time during the twelve months preceding the execution of the statement was an officer, director, or person performing the functions of an officer or director" of the Communist Party. Item 3 requires a statement of any alias of any person listed in Item 2. Item 11 asks for the name, alias, and address of each individual "who was a member of the organization at any time during the period" of twelve months prior to the filing of the registration statement. The statement must be signed by the partners, officers, directors, and members of the governing body. 28 CFR § 11.200, Form ISA-1.

Those provisions are not conditional. The Government with all the authority it possesses has ordered the Party to register.

The duty to disclose the names of the officers, directors, and members is explicit. The duty is to make the disclosure here and now. The individuals who must make the disclosure are definitely described. There is no uncertainty as to what must be done. The question is whether the command made is constitutional under the Fifth Amendment.

If the requirement of Form ISA-1 that the statement be signed "by the partners, officers, and directors" were deleted and the statement was allowed to be filed by "any agent," the act of signing that implicates the partner, officer, or director would be eliminated. If the Court, sensitive to the high role performed by the Fifth Amendment, also deleted the compulsory disclosure of the others whose association with the Party is required to be disclosed without immunity, the problems presented by those disclosures would disappear. But the Court does none of these things. It requires officers and directors to sign; it requires that the names of officers, directors, and members within the 12-month period be disclosed. Thus the question of self-incrimination of each of those individuals is squarely presented.

III.

First as to the *officers, directors, and others who must sign the registration statement.* These individuals, who could be prosecuted as "active" Communist agents under *Yates* v. *United States*, 354, U.S. 298, and *Scales* v. *United States*, . . . cannot, in my view, be compelled to sign a registration statement. A compulsory admission of that ingredient of a crime would plainly violate the Fifth Amendment.

If a person who was on the witness stand in a courtroom or appearing before a Congressional Committee were asked whether he was an officer or director of the Communist Party, our decisions in *Blau* v. *United States*, 340 U.S. 159, 161, and *Quinn* v. *United States*, 349 U.S. 155, would protect him from self-incrimination. Under our system federal officials who desire to establish guilt must use the grand jury to get an indictment and a petit jury to obtain conviction. They cannot require the accused to "do their job for them." . . .

The clause of the Fifth Amendment with which we are here concerned provides that "No person . . . shall be compelled in any criminal case to be a witness against himself." The clause has been hospitably construed. . . .

How then can the Government ask a person to sign a registration statement which makes admissions that would not survive challenge under the Fifth Amendment if asked orally of the individuals that the disclosure implicates?

United States v. *White*, 322 U.S. 694, held that the privilege does not excuse an officer of an organization from producing its records on the grounds that the contents of the records will or may incriminate him. As to the officer or director, it is plain that he incriminates himself not merely by producing records but by signing and filing the registration statement. The preparation of the registration statement and its execution are in the same category as the giving of testimony in the *Blau* and *Quinn* cases, if the Fifth Amendment is to have continuing vitality. Part of what is today required is the furnishing of statements and admissions from the pens of men and women whose very signature may start them on the way to prison. We made clear in *Curcio* v. *United States*, 354 U.S. 118, that the ruling in the *White* case was restricted to the production of books and record. We there upheld the custodian's privilege against testifying as to the "whereabouts of books and records" where that testimony might incriminate him. We said ". . . he cannot lawfully be compelled, in the absence of a grant of adequate immunity from prosecution, to condemn himself by his own oral testimony."

It would seem to follow *a fortiori* that a custodian who need not testify concerning the whereabouts of records, if that testimony would tend to incriminate him, need not put into writing the admission that he is an officer or director of the Communist Party. What more incriminating admission could be compelled? This was the position of Judge Bazelon in the Court of Appeals, 223 F. 2d 531, 579, and it seems to me unassailable. . . .

Electric Bond & Share Co. v. *Securities & Exchange Comm'n, supra*, is irrelevant to our present problem under the Fifth Amendment. No claim was made in that case that the preparation and filing of a registration statement might implicate an officer or director and that the Fifth Amendment therefore protected him against signing unless immunity was granted. The problem in the present case is quite different. It raises the following kind of question: Can Congress, which has made embezzlement of national bank funds a criminal offense, require embezzlers to register without granting them the full immunity (cf. *Ullmann* v. *United States*, 350 U.S. 422) to which they are entitled? That is the closest analogy to the present case.

The compiling, the signing, and the filing of the registration statement required of officers, directors, and others by the registration form is a form of elicited testimony, not the surrender of pre-existing records. Where, as here, such disclosure will reveal knowledge of and relations with the Communist Party, I do not see how it can be demanded, unless immunity is granted.

The Bill of Rights does not go so far as to forbid all interrogation under threat of punishment. It does not prevent the breaking of myriad bonds of secrecy at the command of the Government. It protects only the individual who has himself become the object of the Government's punitive powers. From him it removes the humiliating presence of the questioner. The power of the Government is limited, so that it cannot punish either the silence or the passive hostility of one who claims the privilege, whether he be a criminal or a prophet or merely a bewildered citizen suddenly caught in the sinister web of suspicion.

The privilege is often criticized as a shield for wrongdoing. But not every hostile silence which greets official interrogation has its beginning in wrongdoing. In a nation such as ours the Government must often meet with hostility; we are not constrained to admire its activities; we are free to detest them. That freedom could not long remain if the Government were free to require us to recount all our doings. The Government may still threaten silence with prison, but its power to do so stops short when information sought is incriminating. Even so ardent an advocate of the totalitarian state as Thomas Hobbes respected this core of privacy:

> A covenant not to defend myself from force, by force, is always void. For (as I have shown before) no man can transfer or lay down his right to save himself from death, wounds, and imprisonment, the avoiding whereof is the only end of laying down any right. . . . A covenant to accuse oneself, without assurance of pardon, is likewise invalid. For in the condition of nature, where every man is judge, there is no place for accusation: and in the civil state the accusation is followed with punishment, which, being force, a man is not obliged not to resist. *Leviathan, 23 Great Books* 90.

The cases dealing with the duty to keep records . . . can be put to one side. Under the Smith Act, 18 U.S.C. § 2385, the very subject matter under regulation is interwoven with criminal activity. Where individuals compile and sign the registration statement, as they must, it is the very making of the registration statement that will incriminate them, not the underlying documents.

Signing as an officer or director of the Communist Party—an ingredient of an offense that results in punishment—must be done under the mandate of law. That is compulsory incrimination of those individuals and, in my view, a plain violation of the Fifth Amendment.

IV.

The compulsory disclosure of those who have been *officers, directors, or members* of the Party during the last 12 months is equally objectionable under the Fifth Amendment. Membership in the Party is, by virtue of federal statutes, the start of every prosecution whether it be for active "membership" as in *Scales* v. *United States,* or for conspiracy to teach the doctrine, as in *Dennis* v. *United States,* 341 U.S. 494. Membership is a "link in the chain of evidence" needed for such prosecution, as we held in *Blau* v. *United States; Quain* v. *United States.* It is therefore in the class of disclosure which we have held since the time of Chief Justice Marshall . . . could not be demanded by reason of the Fifth Amendment. The compulsory disclosure of membership in the Communist Party, which the *Blau* and *Quinn* cases have put within the protection of the Fifth Amendment, is the necessary and immediate effect of filing as a public record the registration statement required by § 7. As in case of officers and directors who must sign the registration statement, this is, in my view, compulsory incrimination of the members and a plain violation of the Fifth Amendment.

If Congress can through use of the registration device compel disclosure of people's activities that violate federal laws, the Fifth Amendment would be cast into a limbo.

As I have said, each person required to be listed in the registration statement, were he to be brought before his interrogators, could not be compelled to admit what the statute here requires petitioner to set forth at length. The only difference that exists between compelling each member and officer and between compelling petitioner is the thin "veil" of petitioner's fictitious juridical personality.

Hale v. *Henkel,* 201 U.S. 43, held that a corporation could not claim a privilege against self-incrimination. That case—and others, such as *Wilson* v. *United States, supra,* and *United States* v. *White, supra,* which I have mentioned—have implemented a constitutional policy of publicity for associational activities which would be abhorrent if required of individuals and in matters that were less clearly within the realm of day-to-day administrative regulation.

The present requirement for the disclosure of membership lists is not a regulatory provision, but a device for trapping those who are involved in an activity which, under federal statutes, is interwoven with criminality. The primary effect of the required registration is not disclosure to the public but criminal prosecution. I do not see how the Government that has branded an organization as criminal through its judiciary, its legislature, and its executive, can demand that it submit the names of all its members— unless it grants immunity for the disclosure.

Prior to today, the nearest the Court ever came to allowing the registration device to be used as a mechanism for compulsory disclosure of criminal activities was *United States* v. *Kahriger*, 345 U.S. 22. . . . Gamblers were required to register with the Collector of Internal Revenue and to pay an occupational tax. The defense of the Fifth Amendment was rejected on grounds that seemed to some of us at the time to be specious. Registration could be required, the Court held, because it pertained only to "the business of wagering in the future." . . . The Fifth Amendment, the Court said, "has relation only to past acts, not to future acts that may or may not be committed." The sluice gates, opened a hair's width by that case, are now flung wide. I remain in agreement with what Mr. Justice Black said in *United States* v. *Kahriger:* "[W]e have a Bill of Rights that condemns coerced confessions, however refined or legalistic may be the technique of extortion."

V.

It is said that the Party has no standing to assert the rights of its officers, directors or members.

The privilege against self-incrimination is a personal one. It must be claimed; it may be waived. In ordinary circumstances, there is no Fifth Amendment privilege against incriminating another. . . . On the other hand, the intimate connection between associations and their members has long been recognized. . . .

In *N.A.A.C.P.* v. *Alabama*, the Association was allowed to assert its members' constitutional rights:

> If petitioner's rank-and-file members are constitutionally entitled to withhold their connection with the Association despite the production order, it is manifest that this right is properly assertable by the Association. To require that it be claimed by the members themselves would result in nullification of the right at the very moment of its assertion. Petitioner is the appropriate party to assert these rights, because it and its members are in every practical sense identical.

We dealt there with a Negro group asserting the First Amendment rights of its members. The members, it was argued, would be harassed if their names were disclosed and that harassment would abridge their First Amendment rights. We agreed with that view, and held that N.A.A.C.P. could not be forced to disclose to Alabama its membership lists. We did not, I assume, write a rule good for that day only. Nor did I think we wrote only for Negro groups.

Nor did I think we restricted the assertion by a group of the rights of its members to those asserting First Amendment rights. In *Anti-Facist Refugee Committee* v. *McGrath*, three groups, under circumstances somewhat similar to the present case, claimed the right to invoke their members' rights under both the First and the Fifth Amendments. They had been designated as "communist" by the Attorney General; and the impact of that classification on the status of the members as federal employees was striking and immediate. Could that classification be constitutionally made without a hearing? The consensus of opinion among those who reached the issue seemed clear—that the groups could raise objections that involved the constitutional rights of their members. . . .

This analysis has support in a long line of cases where the Court has allowed A to assert B's constitutional right in seeking redress or prevention of harm to himself. The root of this doctrine is found in equity. In *Truax* v. *Raich*, 239 U.S. 33, an injunction had been sought by an employee who was an alien, seeking to restrain enforcement of an Arizona statute. The right invoked was the employee's own right under the Fourteenth Amendment. But the statute imposed no penalty on the alien for working. It penalized his employer for hiring him. Nevertheless, the injunction issued. In *Pierce* v. *Society of Sisters*, 268 U.S. 510, the proprietors of a private school, to protect their monetary interest in preserving the school, were allowed to assert rights of parents in the education of their children. Similarly, a white vendor was allowed to assert his Negro vendee's rights in enforcing a contract to sell real property, subject to a restrictive city ordinance, in *Buchanan* v. *Warley*, 245 U.S. 60. . . .

Bryant v. *Zimmerman*, 278 U.S. 63, which sustained a *state* law requiring the Ku Klux Klan to file its membership lists with state officials was explained in *N.A.A.C.P.* v. *Alabama* as a case involving an organization whose acts were "unlawful intimidation and violence," not First Amendment activities. That explanation was adequate for that case as only First Amendment rights were being considered in *N.A.A.C.P.* v. *Alabama.* No Fifth Amendment question, was, however, raised in *Bryant* v. *Zimmerman.*

Petitioner, the Communist Party, seeks in this case to assert that the statute under which it is ordered to register is unconstitutional, because it will have the necessary effect of depriving members of their privilege against being compelled to reveal their connection with the Party. This is not a case, as the majority opinion admits, like *United States* v. *Sullivan,* 274 U.S. 259, where a taxpayer, because he claimed the privilege against self-incrimination with respect to the source of some of his income, argued that he was wholly excused from filing a tax return. Nor is this a case where "one who is required to assert the privilege against self-incrimination may thereby arouse the suspicions of prosecuting authorities." For here, if an individual were to attempt to claim the privilege against filing for the Party, he would admit an ingredient of a crime, namely, his connection with the Party.

Clearly, this is a situation in which only the Party can effectively assert the privilege of its officers, directors, and members. This is the teaching of *N.A.A.C.P.* v. *Alabama* and of the opinions of Mr. Justice Jackson, Mr. Justice Frankfurter and myself in *Joint Anti-Fascist Refugee Committee* v. *McGrath* and of the other cases discussed above. When we reject those precedents, we create a special rule for this day only.

The Party is the proper party to raise the objection, because no one else can raise it effectively. The community of interest between the Party and its members is indeed closely analogous to the community of interest between a corporation and its stockholders. . . . Since the command to register cannot be separated from the means of registration, an attack is properly made on the incriminating features of the statute by petitioner who is commanded to register. . . .

In *Boyd* v. *United States,* 116 U.S. 616, a court order to produce an invoice, claimed to be privileged under the Fifth Amendment, was held to be unconstitutional and void. One need not, I have assumed, obey an unconstitutional command and raise his constitutional objection only on compliance. Of course, defiance of a governmental command because it is unconstitutional is deep in our traditions. . . . Yet heretofore a person claiming that a disclosure would violate his Fifth Amendment rights need not first tender the information claimed to be privileged. A person asked whether he is a member of the Communist Party can invoke the Fifth Amendment and refuse to reply since under existing federal laws the answer would tend to incriminate him. . . . The answers now demanded by the registration form and the regulations require precisely the kind of answers we held protected against self-incrimination in the *Quinn* and *Blau* cases.

VI.

The fact that there may be other times when the issue may be raised—as for example if a registration statement is not filed and officers or members are prosecuted for that default under § 15 of the Act—seems immaterial. This case is not in the category of those challenges of a law made before it is known how and in what manner it will be enforced and applied. . . . A final order to register under the Act has been issued. The disclosure requirements are clear and specific. Now is the time to raise Fifth Amendment questions. To relegate the parties to another time and place in order to raise those constitutional objections is to fashion an extremely harsh rule to fit the Communist Party but no one else. Default means the risk of criminal prosecution. No person, I think, should be forced to wait until his default to raise his constitutional objection. The great injustice in what we do today lies in compelling the officials of the Party to violate this law before their constitutional claims can be heard and determined. Never before, I believe, have we forced that choice on a litigant. . . . The modern trend has indeed been to protect a person against prosecutions that may involve infringements of his constitutional rights. At times even equity has stepped in. . . . The prevention of peril and insecurity, involved in the sanctions of some laws, has led to a generous use of the declaratory judgment procedure so that a person need not run the gantlet of a criminal prosecution to get an adjudication of his rights. . . . The order requiring registration requires disclosure; the constitutionality of that disclosure requirement is before us here and now. This case presents the only effective opportunity to secure the benefits of the Fifth Amendment guarantee. Indeed, if the question were not raised now, the strict rule of *Rogers* v. *United States* might mean that the question had been waived.

VII.

My conclusion is that while the Communist Party can be compelled to register, no one acting for it can be compelled to sign a statement that he is an officer or director nor to disclose the names of its officers, directors, or members—unless the required immunity is granted. Why then, one may ask, do we have a registration law? Congress (past or present) is attempting to have its cake and eat it too. In my view Congress can require full disclosure of all the paraphernalia through which a foreign dominated and controlled organization spreads propaganda, engages in agitation, or promotes politics in this country. But the Fifth Amendment bars Congress from requiring full disclosure by one Act and by another Act making the facts admitted or disclosed *under compulsion* the ingredients of a crime.

There is a giving of evidence by the filing of a registration. Its filing is the equivalent of officials testifying in investigations conducted by the Executive or Legislative Branch. It is compulsory disclosure of evidence which links officers, directors, and members of the group with a crime. Force and compulsion are outlawed techniques for federal law enforcement. Coerced confessions are taboo because of the long bitter experience of minorities in trying to maintain their freedom under hostile regimes. Our Constitution protects all minorities, no matter how despised they are.

Accordingly, I dissent.

Mr. Justice Brennan with whom The Chief Justice joins, dissenting in part:

I agree with the Court and with Mr. Justice Douglas that the order requiring that the Party register and disclose its officers and members is not constitutionally invalid as an invasion of the rights of freedom of advocacy and association guaranteed by the First Amendment to Communists as well as to all others.

I also share the Court's view that we are not called upon in this case to decide the constitutionality of the various duties and sanctions attaching to the Party, and to individual members, once orders to register become final. We are required by this case to decide only the validity of the order requiring the petitioner to register in accordance with § 7 of the Act as implemented by the regulations and Form ISA-1 of the Attorney General. We should properly reach at this time only such constitutional questions as necessarily relate to the requirements governing registration.

The questions in addition to those under the First Amendment which seem to me most nearly within the sphere of permissible constitutional adjudication in this proceeding arise from the interaction of the registration requirements with the criminal statutes under which Communist Party membership is implicated. This interplay poses the question whether the registration requirements violate the Fifth Amendment privilege against self-incrimination.

I do not believe that all of the self-incrimination questions raised by the registration provisions are properly adjudicable now. Some may be better left for subsequent adjudication as the necessity arises. For example, we need not decide now, I think, the constitutionality of the provision of § 8 for the self-registration of individual members. That provision becomes operative only upon the failure of the petitioner, or its officials, to list members in effecting its registration, pursuant to a final order; the Government's brief observes that the criminal sanction against a member arising from nonregistration must be preceded by a final order of the Subversive Activities Control Board directing him to register. § 15 (a) (2). We cannot know at this time the posture in which the case will appear when a member comes under an enforceable duty to register, if he ever does. I also lay aside the requirements of § 7 (h), and its implementing regulation, 28 CFR § 11.205, that Party officials effect the registration of the organization if the organization fails to register itself within 30 days of a final order. That duty, enforceable by criminal sanctions against the officials, arises only in the contingency of nonregistration by petitioner in accordance with the present order. Here again the situation may not arise. I assume that the opportunity of the officials to raise the same objections is not irrevocably lost if we do not consider them now. Nor, finally, do I now concern myself with whether the Party may interpose the constitutional privilege of its members because of the nature of the information about them required to be supplied to complete the registration statement as described in the Attorney General's Form ISA-1. Section 7 (d) requires that the registration statement accompanying the registration shall provide such information as the names and addresses of members, and their past and present aliases, as well as information about the officers and activities of the organization. The Attorney General's regulations and Form ISA-1 implement this requirement.

But I do think we must reach one issue of self-incrimination, namely, whether the requirement of § 7 (d) as spelled out in the Attorney General's regulations and Form ISA-1 are void as necessarily conflicting with the Fifth Amendment privilege of the Party officials who are charged with the duties necessary to complete the Party's registration. The statute, the regulations and the Form together clearly require that the registration statement shall be completed, signed and filed by designated officials. These officials are the "partners, officers and directors, including the members of the governing body of the organization"; they are explicitly required by the Form to sign the completed statement and vouchsafe their familiarity with, and the accuracy of, its contents. Whether these officials, consistently with the Fifth Amendment privilege, can be required to complete, sign and file the statement is a serious constitutional question. These requirements are in effect an inquiry into the status of officership and knowledge of Party activities of the signatories. Under today's decision in *Scales* v. *United States*, the answers to such an inquiry might well implicate the officials in criminality in violation of several federal statutes.

I believe that the constitutional validity of the inquiry that I find implicit in these requirements is ripe for adjudication now. I read the Court's opinion as saying that there is no fatal bar to adjudicability of the question merely in the fact that the organization, and not an individual official of the organization, is asserting the privilege in this proceeding. The requirement of "standing"—that a litigant must show that he himself is affected by the operation of the action he challenges as it affects another—is involved here.

But as the cases cited by my Brother Douglas show, and the Court seems to concede, a party has been allowed to raise the constitutional rights of another person not before the Court as a named party in a variety of situations where the effect of the challenged state action on himself is derivative from the impact on the other person. Of course, this Court has indicated on a number of occasions that the privilege is a personal right which must normally be claimed by the individual seeking its protection. . . . These statements were made in the context of an issue of waiver—whether a later claim of privilege should be honored where it was contended that the party had an earlier opportunity to make the claim and had failed to do so. The present case presents quite the opposite situation—not whether the privilege is being claimed too late but too early, not waiver but premature assertion.

The issue of justiciability which confronts us is therefore not whether the petitioner may raise the Fifth Amendment question at all but whether it may do so now. I agree with the Court that the cases which have upheld standing in the first sense are not decisive of our problem. The following considerations, in my view, justify our adjudication now: (a) the order imposes a presently enforceable duty on the organization to complete and file Form ISA-1 and creates an incentive for both organization and officials to make the disclosure implicit in the completion, signing and filing of that Form; (b) the inquiry eliciting these disclosures of officership and knowledge is specific and not open to possibly varying answers; (c) the incriminating character of the information thus disclosed is plain; and (d) finally, if the question is not decided now the officials must run the risk of not being able to make an acceptable claim of privilege at a later time. There thus inheres in putting off decision the substantial possibility of erosion of the privilege. We may and should avoid that undesirable result by deciding the question now.

I think the reasons advanced by the Court in support of the contrary conclusion are overborne by the considerations I have suggested. The Court says that the officials may sign the statement and comply with the requirements, or may claim the privilege in such a form that it will be honored and thus avoid incrimination, and that in any event, a claim of privilege cannot be evaluated at this time because of the varying and presently unknowable circumstances which may determine whether it would have to be honored. The possibility of "voluntary compliance by the officials should not be a bar to a decision now. Given the structure of the statute, compliance cannot indisputably be assumed to be a voluntary waiver of the privilege. The organization is under a duty by virtue of the order now before us to file a statement in accordance with the Attorney General's requirements, on penalty of prosecution for not filing a registration statement; the failure of the officials to complete, sign or file Form ISA-1 might subject it to such prosecution. And if the organization should not register within the 30-day period specified in § 7 (c), the officials are duty-bound under § 7 (h) to effect its registration, also on penalty of criminal sanctions. Plainly enough, then, the order generates pressure on the officials to complete, sign and file to avoid the possibility of prosecution either of the organization or themselves. This pressure may be increased by the uncertainties which attend efforts to make an acceptable claim of the privilege. If we pass the opportunity for decision now officials may well comply out of fear that a later effort to make an acceptable claim of privilege will fail.

A claim of privilege on the registration form which names the official would be self-defeating. For if the admission of officership in the Communist Party is incriminating, then a claim of privilege by name would amount to the very same admission—the claimant would be asserting that he could not complete, sign or file the form because the admission of his officership would incriminate him. The Court suggests that a claim of the privilege is potentially always incriminating in that it may arouse the suspicions of the interrogators. However, this registration requirement seems to present a different case in important respects. Claiming the privilege there does more than attract suspicion to the claimant; it admits an element of his possible criminality. Moreover, registration is unique because of the initial burden it puts on the potential defendant to come forward and claim the privilege. He may thereby arouse suspicions that had not even previously existed and, indeed, virtually establish a prima facie case against himself. The usual situation in which the privilege is invoked is a judicial, legislative, or administrative proceeding in which the person claiming it appears because there is already some reason to think that he has information on the subject matter of the inquiry. His invocation of the privilege in such circumstances may confirm the suspicions of his interrogators, but is less likely to arouse them initially than in the case of a registration regulation which calls on all persons everywhere, known or unknown, who fall within a prescribed category, to come forward and identify themselves. At least in governmentally initiated inquiries, there are likely to be certain checks on self-accusation, either the explicit requirement of probable cause governing the maintenance of a criminal prosecution or institutional limitations on the exercise of the power of inquiry. Here there is no such initial burden on government, no requirement, for example, that it identify officials in a proceding for that purpose and then seek to elicit the desired information as to other officials and members from them. I think, therefore, that if the privilege does protect an official from disclosure of his officership and knowledge when an inquiry explicitly in those terms is made, it would also protect him from disclosure in the kind of "indirect" inquiry and response that seems to me implicit in the suggestion that a claim of the privilege by name may be an adequate alternative.

There remains consideration of the possibility that an anonymous claim of the privilege may be made and honored by the Attorney General. The organization might simply file a statement in which it asserted the privilege on behalf of its officials, listing their titles but not their names. However, on the Court's own reasoning the right to have a claim of privilege honored may depend on a variety of circumstances, including such factors as already-existing public knowledge of the information which the claimant seeks to conceal, and it is difficult to see how following this course would advance the attempt of the claimant to have his privilege honored. In a subsequent enforcement proceeding against the organization for failure to register in accordance with the regulations, or against officials for failing to register the organization, the defense of privilege could be met with the same objection that the Court raises here—that the privilege claim could not be evaluated unless the identity of the claimant were known. The possibility that the Attorney General might honor even an anonymous claim of the privilege would simply mean abandonment of one of the requirements in the Form. But I do not see how we can view this case as if that requirement did not exist, since the order under review is to register in accordance with the Attorney General's requirements as they now are. Certainly an official might be sufficiently dubious as to the efficacy of an anonymous claim of the privilege by the organization on his behalf that he would choose one of the alternatives of complying, claiming the privilege by name, or not making any claim, all dangerous courses for him. Therefore, I cannot believe that the Court's suggestion that a claim may be made in a form in which it could be honored presents an official of petitioner with a sufficiently realistic choice to require us to defer consideration of this question until it arises at some time after a choice among these alternatives is made. . . .

The inquiry implicit in the requirements of completing, signing and filing here is precise; it demands disclosure on matters of officership in, and knowledge of, the Communist Party. The incriminating nature of that inquiry seems plain on its face, since an admission of officership and knowledge would be not merely a possible link in the chain needed to convict under the Smith Act but would establish a main ingredient of the crime proscribed in the membership clause of the Act as this Court construes it today in *Scales* v. *United States*. . . .

Nor am I persuaded that this Fifth Amendment claim should not be adjudicated now because some of the officials may not be entitled to the privilege if the fact of their officership is already known. Even on the assumption that public notoriety or prior admission in these or other proceedings would make the privilege inapplicable to such officials, there is nothing in the record to indicate how many officials fall into this category. The Government contends that since the record does not establish that any officials are not publicly known as such, we should refrain from adjudicating the privilege claim now because no one may actually be entitled to invoke it. But since the record also leaves open the possibility that there may be officials entitled to assert the privilege, and since I see such difficulty in the way of effective assertion of the privilege now or later without disclosure of the information sought to be protected, I do not believe that these persons should be subjected to the risks and uncertainties of deciding on a course of conduct with a view to litigating this question in a subsequent proceeding. Where the danger of compulsory incrimination in violation of the Fifth Amendment thus appears on the face of the requirements it seems to me improper to force any who are affected to hazard the loss of their protection because some, or even all, have no protection at all. . . .

I do not regard this position on adjudicability as calling for the impermissible decision of a hypothetical case. Nor does it open the way to the invalidation of the requirements on their face despite valid applications simply because they might be invalidly applied in other circumstances. . . . If the requirements violate the Fifth Amendment, they do so for all subject to them because they require incrimination without an effective protection of the privilege. And it is because I discern no adequate procedural protection for the privilege that I believe the Court should adjudicate this particular question now.

As to the merits of the Fifth Amendment claim, I believe that officials cannot be compelled to complete, sign and file the registration statement without abridging their privilege against self-incrimination. I do not think that the doctrine of *United States* v. *White*, 322 U.S. 694, applies to an inquiry directed to the fact of officership, *qua* officership, and knowledge, *qua* knowledge, as opposed to the production of organizational records by an officer who is their custodian. It is the individual official's own status and knowledge that is the subject of the inquiry I find implicit in the requirement that an official complete, sign and file the statement. The principle that a custodian of organizational records may be required to produce them, even if their contents would incriminate him personally, is a recognition that an organization acts only through people, and that to recognize the privilege in the custodian of its records might be to immunize the organization's past acts. But these officials are not directed to produce records of their organization as its custodians, but to complete, sign and file as its officials, and thus to identify themselves as possible participants in a criminal conspiracy and as persons persumptively exhibiting the degree of knowledge and activity necessary for a conviction under the membership clause of the Smith Act. Nor are they called on, in fact, to produce records at all, but rather to complete, sign and file a statement which may or may not incorporate the records of the organization. And more than the incorporation of existing records is required in any event. All the information on Form ISA-1 must be supplied whether or not in existing records. In addition, the requirement of signatures does not involve mere authentication or identification of records, cf. *Curcio* v. *United States*, 354 U.S. 118, 125, because the officials are required to vouchsafe completeness and accuracy of the information supplied in the Form. Thus the requirements go far beyond the compulsory production approved in *White*. If the admission both of officership status and knowledge of Party activities cannot be compelled in oral testimony in a criminal proceeding, I do not see how compulsion in writing in a registration statement makes a difference for constitutional purposes. . . . Since the immunity granted under § 4 (f) of the statute is not complete, I do not think that the official's compliance with the requirements can be exacted consistently with the Fifth Amendment. And if the officials cannot be required to complete, sign and file Form ISA-1, I do not see how the present order can be upheld. The requirements patently do not contemplate the effectuation of registration by any except Party officials in the precise manner specified by the requirements. I would therefore hold the order invalid insofar as it directs the petitioner to register in accordance with the requirements.

★ V ★

Freedom of Speech and Press:

Problems of Loyalty and Security

1. Loyalty Regulations for Trade Union Officers

AMERICAN COMMUNICATIONS ASSN. v. DOUDS

339 US 382 (1950)

[The Taft-Hartley Act of 1947 provides that a union can use the facilities and opportunities of the act only if each officer has filed an affidavit (1) that he is not a member of or affiliated with the Communist Party and (2) that he does not believe in the overthrow of the Government and that he is not a member or supporter of any organization that believes in or teaches the overthrow of the Government. The constitutionality of this provision was before the Court in the present case. Justices Douglas, Clark, and Minton did not participate. Justice Black, dissenting, maintained that the entire provision was unconstitutional. The other five Justices held that the section was constitutional insofar as it required an affidavit to the effect that the union officer was not a member of or affiliated with the Communist Party. As to the other provision, that relating to his beliefs or to the beliefs of an organization, its constitutionality was sustained by a vote of 3 (Vinson, Reed, and Burton) against 3 (Frankfurter, Jackson, and Black).

[Communist leaders of unions may call strikes for political ends that serve the "party line" and thus misuse the power vested in them by acts of Congress by virtue of their union offices. Congress may protect the free flow of interstate and foreign commerce from the interference of politically inspired strikes. This is a constitutional objective. Its implementation through the non-Communist affidavit is only an indirect, conditional, partial, and small abridgment of speech. In such a case, said Chief Justice Vinson for the Court, the clear and present danger rule cannot be used mechanically—if at all.]

Mr. Chief Justice Vinson delivered the opinion of the Court:

These cases present for decision the constitutionality of § 9 (h) of the Labor Management Relations Act of 1947. This section, commonly referred to as the non-Communist affidavit provision, reads as follows: "No investigation shall be made by the National Labor Relations Board of any question affecting commerce concerning the representation of employees, raised by a labor organization under subsection (c) of this section, no petition under section 9 (e) (1) shall be entertained, and no complaint shall be issued pursuant to a charge made by a labor organization under subsection (b) of section 10 unless there is on file with the Board an affidavit executed contemporaneously or within the preceding twelve-month period by each officer of such labor organization and the officers of any national or international labor organization of which it is an affiliate or constituent unit that he is not a member of the Communist Party or affiliated with such party, and that he does not believe in, and is not a member of or supports any organization that believes in or teaches, the overthrow of the United States Government by force or by any illegal or unconstitutional methods. The provisions of section 35 A of the Criminal Code shall be applicable in respect to such affidavits."

In No. 10, the constitutional issue was raised by a suit to restrain the Board from holding a representation election in a bargaining unit in which appellant union was the employee representative, without permitting its name to appear on the ballot, and, should the election be held, to restrain the Board from announcing the results or certifying the victor, until a hearing was granted to appellant. A hearing had been denied because of the non-compliance with § 9 (h). The complaint alleged that this requirement was unconstitutional. . . .

No. 13 is the outcome of an unfair labor practice complaint filed with the Board by petitioner unions. The Board found that Inland Steel Company had violated the Labor Relations Act in refusing to bargain on the subject of pensions. But the Board postponed the effective date of its order compelling the company to bargain, pending the unions' compliance with § 9 (h). Both sides appealed: the company urged that the Act had been misinterpreted; the unions contended that § 9 (h) was unconstitutional and therefore an invalid condition of a Board order. . . .

I.

The constitutional justification for the National Labor Relations Act was the power of Congress to protect interstate commerce by removing obstructions to the free flow of commerce. . . . That Act was designed to remove obstructions caused by strikes and other forms of industrial unrest, which Congress found were attributable to the inequality of bargaining power between unorganized employees and their employers. It did so by strengthening employee groups, by restraining certain employer practices, and by encouraging the processses of collective bargaining.

When the Labor-Management Relations Act was passed twelve years later, it was the view of Congress that additional impediments to the free flow of commerce made amendment of the original Act desirable. It was stated in the findings and declaration of policy that:

Experience has further demonstrated that certain practices by some labor organizations, their officers, and members have the intent or the necessary effect of burdening or obstructing commerce by preventing the free flow of goods in such commerce through strikes and other forms of industrial unrest or through concerted activities which impair the interest of the public in the free flow of such commerce. The elimination of such practices is a necessary condition to the assurance of the rights herein granted.

One such obstruction, which it was the purpose of § 9 (h) of the Act to remove, was the so-called "political strike." Substantial amounts of evidence were presented to various committees of Congress, including the committees immediately concerned with labor legislation, that Communist leaders of labor unions had in the past and would continue in the future to subordinate legitimate trade union objectives to obstructive strikes when dictated by Party leaders, often in support of the policies of a foreign government. And other evidence supports the view that some union leaders who hold to a belief in violent overthrow of the Government for reasons other than loyalty to the Communist Party likewise regard strikes and other forms of direct action designed to serve ultimate revolutionary goals as the primary objectives of labor unions which they control. At the committee hearings, the incident most fully developed was a strike at the Milwaukee plant of the Allis-Chalmers Manufacturing Company in 1941, when the plant was producing vital materials for the national defense program. A full hearing was given not only to company officials, but also to leaders of the international and local unions involved. Congress heard testimony that the strike had been called solely in obedience to Party orders for the purpose of starting the "snowballing of strikes" in defense plants.

No useful purpose would be served by setting out at length the evidence before Congress relating to the problem of political strikes, nor can we attempt to assess the validity of each item of evidence. It is sufficient to say that Congress had a great mass of material before it which tended to show that Communists and others proscribed by the statute had infiltrated union organizations not to support and further trade union objectives, including the advocacy of change by democratic methods, but to make them a device by which commerce and industry might be disrupted when the dictates of political policy required such action.

II.

The unions contend that the necessary effect of § 9 (h) is to make it impossible for persons who cannot sign the oath to be officers of labor unions. They urge that such a statute violates fundamental rights guaranteed by the First Amendment: the right of union officers to hold what political views they choose and to associate with what political groups they will and the right of unions to choose their officers without interference from government. The Board has argued, on the other hand, that § 9 (h) presents no First Amendment problem because its sole sanction is the withdrawal from noncomplying unions of the "privilege" of using its facilities.

Neither contention states the problem with complete accuracy. It cannot be denied that the practical effect of denial of access to the Board and the denial of a place on the ballot in representation proceedings is not merely to withhold benefits granted by the Government but to impose upon noncomplying unions a number of restrictions which would not exist if the Board had not been established. The statute does not, however, specifically forbid persons who do not sign the affidavit from holding positions of union leadership nor require their discharge from office. The fact is that § 9 (h) may well make it difficult for unions to remain effective if their officers do not sign the affidavits. How difficult depends upon the circumstances of the industry, the strength of the union and its organizational discipline. We are, therefore, neither free to treat § 9 (h) as if it merely withdraws a privilege gratuitously granted by the Government, nor able to consider it a licensing statute prohibiting those persons who do not sign the affidavit from holding union office. The practicalities of the situation place the proscriptions of § 9 (h) somewhere between those two extremes. The difficult question that emerges is whether consistently with the First Amendment, Congress, by statute, may exert these pressures upon labor unions to deny positions of leadership to certain persons who are identified by particular beliefs and political affiliations.

III.

There can be no doubt that Congress may, under its constitutional power to regulate commerce among the several States, attempt to prevent political strikes and other kinds of direct action designed to burden and interrupt the free flow of commerce. We think it is clear, in addition, that the remedy provided by § 9 (h) bears reasonable relation to the evil which the statute was designed to reach. Congress could rationally find that the Communist Party is not like other political parties in its utilization of positions of union leadership as means by which to bring about strikes and other obstructions of commerce for purposes of political advantage, and that many persons who believe in overthrow of the Government by force and violence are also likely to resort to such tactics when, as officers, they formulate union policy.

The fact that the statute identifies persons by their political affiliations and beliefs, which are circumstances ordinarily irrelevant to permissable subjects of government action, does not lead to the conclusion that such circumstances are never relevant. . . . We have held that aliens may be barred from certain occupations because of a reasonable relation between that classification and the apprehended evil . . . , even though the Constitution forbids arbitrary banning of aliens from the pursuit of lawful occupations. . . . Even distinctions based solely on ancestry, which we declared "are by their very nature odious to a free people," have been upheld under the unusual circumstances of wartime. . . . If accidents of birth and ancestry under some circumstances justify an inference concerning future conduct, it can hardly be doubted that voluntary affiliations and beliefs justify a similar inference when drawn by the legislature on the basis of its investigations.

This principle may be illustrated by reference to statutes denying positions of public importance to groups of persons identified by their business affiliations. One federal statute, for example, provides that no partner or employee of a firm primarily engaged in underwriting securities may be a director of a national bank. This Court noted that the statute is directed "to the probability or likelihood based on the experience of the 1920's, that a bank director interested in the underwriting business may use his influence in the bank to involve it or its customers in securities which his underwriting firm has in its portfolio or has committed itself to take." . . . It was designed "to remove tempting opportunities from the management and personnel of member banks." There was no showing, nor was one required, that all employees of underwriting firms would engage in such conduct. Because of their business connections, carrying as they do certain loyalties, interests and disciplines those persons were thought to pose a continuing threat of participation in the harmful activities described above. Political affiliations of the kind here involved, no less than business affiliations, provide rational ground for the legislative judgment that those persons proscribed by § 9 (h) would be subject to "tempting opportunities" to commit acts deemed harmful to the national economy. In this respect, § 9 (h) is not unlike a host of other statutes which prohibit specified groups of persons from holding positions of power and public interest because, in the legislative judgment, they threaten to abuse the trust that is a necessary concomitant of the power of office.

If no more were involved than possible loss of position, the foregoing would dispose of the case. But the more difficult problem here arises because, in drawing lines on the basis of beliefs and political affiliations, though it may be granted that the proscriptions of the statute bear a reasonable relation to the apprehended evil, Congress has undeniably discouraged the lawful exercise of political freedoms as well. Stated otherwise, the problem is this: Communists, we may assume, carry on legitimate political activities. Beliefs are inviolate.
. . . Congress might reasonably find, however, that Communists, unlike members of other political parties, and persons who believe in overthrow of the Government by force, unlike persons of other beliefs, represent a continuing danger of disruptive political strikes when they hold positions of union leadership. By exerting pressures on unions to deny office to Communists and others identified therein, § 9 (h) undoubtedly lessens the threat to interstate commerce, but it has the further necessary effect of discouraging the exercise of political rights protected by the First Amendment. Men who hold union offices often have little choice but to renounce Communism or give up their offices. Unions which wish to do so are discouraged from electing Communists to office. To the grave and difficult problem thus presented we must now turn our attention.

IV.

The unions contend that once it is determined that this is a free speech case, the "clear and present danger" test must apply. . . . But they disagree as to how it should be applied. Appellant in No. 10 would require that joining the Communist Party or the expression of belief in overthrow of the Government by force be shown to be a clear and present danger of some substantive evil, since those are the doctrines affected by the statute. Petitioner in No. 13, on the other hand, would require a showing that political strikes, the substantive evil involved, are a clear and present danger to the security of the Nation or threaten widespread industrial unrest.

This confusion suggests that the attempt to apply the term, "clear and present danger," as a mechanical test in every case touching First Amendment freedoms, without regard to the context of its application, mistakes the form in which an idea was cast for the substance of the idea. The provisions of the Constitution, said Mr. Justice Holmes, "are not mathematical formulas having their essence in their form; they are organized living institutions transplanted from English soil. Their significance is vital and formal; it is to be gathered not simply by taking the words and a dictionary, but by considering their origin and the line of their growth." . . . Still less should this Court's interpretations of the Constitution be reduced to the status of mathematical formulas. It is the considerations that gave birth to the phrase "clear and present danger," not the phrase itself, that are vital in our decision of questions involving liberties protected by the First Amendment.

Although the First Amendment provides that Congress shall make no law abridging the freedom of speech, press or assembly, it has long been established that those freedoms themselves are dependent upon the power of constitutional government to survive. If it is to survive it must have power to protect itself against unlawful conduct and, under some circumstances, against incitements to commit unlawful acts. Freedom of speech thus does not comprehend the right to speak on any subject at any time. The important question that came to this Court immediately after the First World War was not whether, but how far, the First Amendment permits the suppression of speech which advocates conduct inimical to the public welfare. Some thought speech having a reasonable tendency to lead to such conduct might be punished. Justice Holmes and Brandeis took a different view. They thought that the greater danger to a democracy lies in the suppression of public discussion; that ideas and doctrines thought harmful or dangerous are best fought with words. Only, therefore, when force is very likely to follow an utterance before there is a chance for counter-argument to have effect may that utterance be punished or prevented. Thus, "the necessity which is essential to a valid restriction does not exist unless the speech would produce, or is intended to produce, a clear and imminent danger of some substantive evil which the State or Congress constitutionally may seek to prevent." . . . By this means they sought to convey the philosophy that under the First Amendment the public has a right to every man's views and every man the right to speak them. Government may cut him off only when his views are no longer merely views but threaten, clearly and imminently, to ripen into conduct against which the public has a right to protect itself.

But the question with which we are here faced is not the same one that Justices Holmes and Brandeis found convenient to consider in terms of clear and present danger. Government's interest here is not in preventing the dissemination of Communist doctrine or the holding of particular beliefs because it is feared that unlawful action will result therefrom if free speech is practiced. Its interest is in protecting the free flow of commerce from what Congress considers to be substantial evils of conduct that are not the products of speech at all. Section 9 (h), in other words, does not interfere with speech because Congress fears the consequences of speech; it regulates harmful conduct which Congress has determined is carried on by persons who may be identified by their political affiliations and beliefs. The Board does not contend that political strikes, the substantive evil at which § 9 (h) is aimed, are the present or impending products of advocacy of the doctrines of Communism or the expression of belief in overthrow of the Government by force. On the contrary, it points out that such strikes are called by persons who, so Congress has found, have the will and power to do so without advocacy or persuasion that seeks acceptance in the competition of the market. Speech may be fought with speech. Falsehoods and fallacies must be exposed, not suppressed, unless there is not sufficient time to avert the evil consequences of noxious doctrine by argument and education. That is the command of the First Amendment. But force may and must be met with force. Section 9 (h) is designed to protect the public not against what Communists and others identified therein advocate or believe, but against what Congress has concluded they have done and are likely to do again.

The contention of petitioner in No. 13 that this Court must find that political strikes create a clear and present danger to the security of the Nation or of widespread industrial strife in order to sustain § 9 (h) similarly misconceives the purpose that phrase was intended to serve. In that view, not the relative certainty that evil conduct will result from speech in the immediate future, but the extent and gravity of the substantive evil must be measured by the "test" laid down in the *Schenck Case.* But there the Court said that: "The question in every case is whether the *words* used are used in such circumstances and are of such a nature as to create a clear and present danger that they will bring about the substantive evils that Congress has a right to prevent." *Schenck* v. *United States,* 249 U.S. at 52. (Emphasis supplied.)

So far as the *Schenck Case* itself is concerned, imminent danger of any substantive evil that Congress may prevent justifies the restriction of speech. Since that time this Court has decided, that however great the likelihood that a substantive evil will result, restrictions on speech and press cannot be sustained unless the evil itself is "substantial" and "relatively serious" . . . or sometimes "extremely serious." . . . And it follows therefrom that even harmful conduct cannot justify restrictions upon speech unless substantial interests of society are at stake.

But in suggesting that the substantive evil must be serious and substantial, it was never the intention of this Court to lay down an absolutist test measured in terms of danger to the Nation. When the effect of a statute or ordinance upon the exercise of First Amendment freedoms is relatively small and the public interest to be protected is substantial, it is obvious that a rigid test requiring a showing of imminent danger to the security of the Nation is an absurdity. We recently dismissed for want of substantiality an appeal in which a church group contended that its First Amendment rights were violated by a municipal zoning ordinance preventing the building of churches in certain residential areas. *Church of Jesus Christ of Latter-Day Saints* v. *Porterville*, 338 U.S. 805 (1949). And recent cases in this Court involving contempt by publication likewise have no meaning if imminent danger of national peril is the criterion.

On the contrary, however, the right of the public to be protected from evils of conduct, even though First Amendment rights of persons or groups are thereby in some manner infringed, has received frequent and consistent recognition by this Court. We have noted that the blaring sound truck invades the privacy of the home and may drown out others who wish to be heard. . . . The unauthorized parade through city streets by a religious or political group disrupts traffic and may prevent the discharge of the most essential obligations of local government. . . . The exercise of particular First Amendment rights may fly in the face of the public interest in the health of children . . . or of the whole community . . . and it may be offensive to the moral standards of the community. . . . And Government's obligation to provide an efficient public service . . . and its interest in the character of members of the bar . . . sometimes admit of limitations upon rights set out in the First Amendment. . . . We have never held that such freedoms are absolute. The reason is plain. As Chief Justice Hughes put it, "Civil liberties, as guaranteed by the Constitution, imply the existence of an organized society maintaining public order without which liberty itself would be lost in the excesses of unrestrained abuses." . . .

When particular conduct is regulated in the interest of public order, and the regulation results in an indirect, conditional, partial abridgement of speech, the duty of the courts is to determine which of these two conflicting interests demands the greater protection under the particular circumstances presented. The high place in which the right to speak, think, and assemble as you will was held by the Framers of the Bill of Rights and is held today by those who value liberty both as a means and an end indicates the solicitude with which we must view any assertion of personal freedoms. We must recognize, moreover, that regulation of "conduct" has all too frequently been employed by public authority as a cloak to hide censorship of unpopular ideas. We have been reminded that "It is not often in this country that we now meet with direct and candid efforts to stop speaking or publication as such. Modern inroads on these rights come from associating the speaking with some other factor which the state may regulate so as to bring the whole within official control."

On the other hand, legitimate attempts to protect the public, not from the remote possible effects of noxious ideologies, but from present excesses of direct, active conduct are not presumptively bad because they interfere with and, in some of its manifestations, restrain the exercise of First Amendment rights. . . . In essence, the problem is one of weighing the probable effects of the statute upon the free exercise of the right of speech and assembly against the congressional determination that political strikes are evils of conduct which cause substantial harm to interstate commerce and that Communists and others identified by § 9 (h) pose continuing threats to that public interest when in position of union leadership. We must, therefore, undertake the "delicate and difficult task . . . to weigh the circumstances and to appraise the substantiality of the reasons advanced in support of the regulation of the free enjoyment of the rights."

V.

The "reasons advanced in support of the regulation" are of considerable weight, as even the opponents § 9 (h) agreed. They are far from being "mere legislative preferences or beliefs respecting matters of public convenience which may well support regulation directed at other personal activities, but be insufficient to justify such as diminishes the exercise of rights so vital to the maintenance of democratic institutions." It should be emphasized that Congress, not the courts, is primarily charged with determination of the need for regulation of activities affecting interstate commerce. This Court must, if such regulation unduly infringes personal freedoms, declare the statute invalid under the First Amendment's command that the opportunities for free public discussion be maintained. But insofar as the problem is one of drawing inferences concerning the need for regulation of particular forms of conduct from conflicting evidence, this Court is in no position to substitute its judgment as to the necessity or desirability of the statute for that of Congress. . . . Even restrictions on particular kinds of utterances, if enacted by a legislature after appraisal of the need, come to this Court "encased in the armor wrought by prior legislative determination." . . . The deference due legislative determination of the need for restriction upon particular forms of conduct has found repeated expression in this Court's opinions.

When compared with ordinances and regulations dealing with littering of the streets or disturbance of householders by itinerant preachers, the relative significance and complexity of the problem of political strikes and how to deal with their leaders becomes at once apparent. It must be remembered that § 9 (h) is not an isolated statute dealing with a subject divorced from the problems of labor peace generally. It is a part of some very complex machinery set up by the Federal Government for the purpose of encouraging the peaceful settlement of labor disputes. Under the statutory scheme, unions which become collective bargaining representatives for groups of employees often represent not only members of the union but nonunion workers or members of other unions as well. Because of the necessity to have strong unions to bargain on equal terms with strong employers, individual employees are required by law to sacrifice rights which, in some cases, are valuable to them. . . . The loss of individual rights for the greater benefit of the group results in a tremendous increase in the power of the representative of the group—the union. But power is never without responsibility. And when authority derives in part from Government's thumb on the scales, the exercise of that power by private persons becomes closely akin, in some respects, to its exercise by Government itself.

We do not suggest that labor unions which utilize the facilities of the National Labor Relations Board become Government agencies or may be regulated as such. But it is plain that when Congress clothes the bargaining representative "with powers comparable to those possessed by a legislative body both to create and restrict the rights of those whom it represents," the public interest in the good faith exercise of that power is very great.

What of the effects of § 9 (h) upon the rights of speech and assembly of those proscribed by its terms? The statute does not prevent or punish by criminal sanctions the making of a speech, the affiliation with any organization, or the holding of any belief. But as we have noted, the fact that no direct restraint or punishment is imposed upon speech or assembly does not determine the free speech question. Under some circumstances, indirect "discouragements" undoubtedly have the same coercive effect upon the exercise of First Amendment rights as imprisonment, fines, injunctions or taxes. A requirement that adherents of particular religious faiths or political parties wear identifying armbands, for example, is obviously of this nature.

But we have here no statute which is either frankly aimed at the suppression of dangerous ideas nor one which, although ostensibly aimed at the regulation of conduct, may actually "be made the instrument of the arbitrary suppression of views." . . . There are here involved none of the elements of censorship or prohibition of the dissemination of information that were present in the cases mainly relied upon by those attacking the statute. The "discouragements" of § 9 (h) proceed not against the groups or beliefs identified therein, but only against the combination of those affiliations or beliefs with occupancy of a position of great power over the economy of the country. Congress has concluded that substantial harm, in the form of direct, positive action, may be expected from that combination. In this legislation, Congress did not restrain the activities of the Communist Party as a political organization; nor did it attempt to stifle beliefs. . . . Section 9 (h) touches only a relative handful of persons, leaving the great majority of persons of the identified affiliations and beliefs completely free from restraint. And it leaves those few who are affected free to maintain their affiliations and beliefs subject only to possible loss of positions which Congress has concluded are being abused to the injury of the public by members of the described groups.

We have previously had occasion to consider other statutes and regulations in which the interests involved were, in large measure, like those now being considered. In *United Public Workers* v. *Mitchell*, we upheld a statute which provided that employees of the Federal Government could not participate in partisan political activities, concededly a First Amendment right, if they would retain their positions. The decision was not put upon the ground that government employment is a privilege to be conferred or withheld at will. For it was recognized that Congress may not "enact a regulation providing that no Republican, Jew or Negro shall be appointed to federal office, or that no federal employee shall attend Mass or take any active part in missionary work." 330 U.S. at 100. But the rational connection between the prohibitions of the statute and its objects, the limited scope of the abridgment of First Amendment rights, and the large public interest in the efficiency of government service, which Congress had found necessitated the statute, led us to the conclusion that the statute may stand consistently with the First Amendment.

Similarly, in *In re Summers*, 325 U.S. 561, we upheld the refusal of a state supreme court to admit to membership of its bar an otherwise qualified person on the sole ground that he had conscientious scruples against war and would not use force to prevent wrong under any circumstances. Since he could not, so the justices of the state court found, swear in good faith to uphold the state constitution, which requires service in the militia in time of war, we held that refusal to permit him to practice law did not violate the First Amendment, as its commands are incorporated in the Due Process Clause of the Fourteenth Amendment. Again, the relation between the obligations of membership in the bar and service required by the state in time of war, the limited effect of the state's holding upon speech and assembly, and the strong interest which every state court has in the persons who become officers of the court were thought sufficient to justify the state action. . . .

It is contended that the principle that statutes touching First Amendment freedoms must be narrowly drawn dictates that a statute aimed at political strikes should make the calling of such strikes unlawful but should not attempt to bring about the removal of union officers, with its attendant effect upon First Amendment rights. We think, however, that the legislative judgment that interstate commerce must be protected from a continuing threat of such strikes is a permissible one in this case. The fact that the injury to interstate commerce would be an accomplished fact before any sanctions could be applied, the possibility that a large number of such strikes might be called at a time of external or internal crisis, and the practical difficulties which would be encountered in detecting illegal activities of this kind are factors which are persuasive that Congress should not be powerless to remove the threat, not limited to punishing the act. . . .

VI.

Previous discussion has considered the constitutional questions raised by § 9 (h) as they apply alike to members of the Communist Party and affiliated organizations and to persons who believe in overthrow of the government by force. The breadth of the provision concerning belief in overthrow of the government by force would raise additional questions, however, if it were read very literally to include all persons who might under any conceivable circumstances, subscribe to that belief.

But we see no reason to construe the statute so broadly. It is within the power and is the duty of this Court to construe a statute so as to avoid the danger of unconstitutionality if it may be done in consonance with the legislative purpose. . . . In enacting § 9 (h), Congress had as its objective the protection of interstate commerce from direct interference, not any intent to disturb or proscribe beliefs as such. Its manifest purpose was to bring within the terms of the statute only those persons whose beliefs strongly indicate a will to engage in political strikes and other forms of direct action when, as officers, they direct union activities. The congressional purpose is therefore served if we construe the clause, "that he does not believe in, and is not a member of or supports any organization that believes in or teaches, the overthrow of the United States Government by force or by any illegal or unconstitutional methods," to apply to persons and organizations who believe in violent overthrow of the Government as it presently exists under the Constitution as an objective, not merely a prophecy. Congress might well find that such persons—those who believe that the present form of the Government of the United States should be changed by force or other illegal methods—would carry that objective into their conduct of union affairs by calling political strikes designed to weaken and divide the American people, whether they consider actual overthrow of the Government to be near or distant. It is to those persons that § 9 (h) is intended to apply, and only to them. We hold, therefore, that the belief identified in § 9 (h) is a belief in the objective of overthrow by force or by any illegal or unconstitutional methods of the Government of the United States as it now exists under the Constitution and laws thereof.

As thus construed, we think that the "belief" provision of the oath presents no different problem from that present in that part of the section having to do with membership in the Communist Party. Of course we agree that one may not be imprisoned or executed because he holds particular beliefs. But to attack the straw man of "thought control" is to ignore the fact that the sole effect of the statute upon one who believes in overthrow of the Government by force and violence—and does not deny his belief—is that he may be forced to relinquish his position as a union leader. That fact was crucial in our discussion of the statute as it relates to membership in the Communist Party. . . .

If the principle that one may under no circumstances be required to state his beliefs on any subject nor suffer the loss of any right or privilege because of his beliefs be a valid one, its application in other possible situations becomes relevant. Suppose, for example, that a federal statute provides that no person may become a member of the Secret Service force assigned to protect the President unless he swears that he does not believe in assassination of the President. Is this beyond the power of Congress, whatever the need revealed by its investigations? An affirmative answer hardly commends itself to reason unless, indeed, the Bill of Rights has been converted into a "suicide pact." . . . Yet the example chosen is far-fetched only because of the manifest absurdity of reliance upon an oath in such a situation. One can have no doubt that the screening process in the selection of persons to occupy such positions probes far deeper than mere oath-taking can possibly do.

To hold that such an oath is permissible, on the other hand, is to admit that the circumstances under which one is asked to state his belief and the consequences which flow from his refusal to do so or his disclosure of a particular belief make a difference. The reason for the difference has been pointed out at some length above. First, the loss of a particular position is not the loss of life or liberty. We have noted that the distinction is one of degree, and it is for this reason that the effect of the statute in proscribing beliefs—like its effect in restraining speech or freedom of association—must be carefully weighed by the courts in determining whether the balance struck by Congress comports with the dictates of the Constitution. But it is inaccurate to speak of § 9 (h) as "punishing" of "forbidding" the holding of beliefs, any more than it punishes or forbids membership in the Communist Party.

Second, the public interest at stake in ascertaining one's beliefs cannot automatically be assigned at zero without consideration of the circumstances of the inquiry. If it is admitted that beliefs are springs to action, it becomes highly relevant whether the person who is asked whether he believes in overthrow of the Government by force is a general with five hundred thousand men at his command or a village constable. To argue that because the latter may not be asked his beliefs the former must necessarily be exempt is to make a fetish of beliefs. The answer to the implication that if this statute is upheld "then the power of government over beliefs is as unlimited as its power over conduct and the way is open to force disclosure of attitudes on all manner of social, economic, moral and political issues," . . . is that that result does not follow "while this Court sits." The circumstances giving rise to the inquiry, then, are likewise factors to be weighed by the courts, giving due weight, of course, to the congressional judgment concerning the need. In short, the problem of balancing the conflicting individual and national interests involved is no different from the problem presented by proscriptions based upon political affiliations.

Insofar as a distinction between beliefs and political affiliations is based upon absence of any "overt act" in the former case, it is relevant, if at all, in connection with problems of proof. In proving that one swore falsely that he is not a Communist, the act of joining the Party is crucial. Proof that one lied in swearing that he does not believe in overthrow of the Government by force, on the other hand, must consist in proof of his mental state. To that extent they differ.

To state the difference, however, is but to recognize that while objective facts may be proved directly, the state of a man's mind must be inferred from the things he says or does. Of course we agree that the courts cannot "ascertain the thought that has had no outward manifestation." But courts and juries every day pass upon knowledge, belief and intent—the state of men's minds—having before them no more than evidence of their words and conduct, from which, in ordinary human experience, mental condition may be inferred. . . . False swearing in signing the affidavit must, as in other cases where mental state is in issue, be proved by the outward manifestations of state of mind. In the absence of such manifestations, which are as much "overt acts" as the act of joining the Communist Party, there can be no successful prosecution for false swearing.

Considering the circumstances surrounding the problem—the deference due the congressional judgment concerning the need for regulation of conduct affecting interstate commerce and the effect of the statute upon rights of speech, assembly and belief—we conclude that § 9 (h) of the Labor-Management Relations Act does not unduly infringe freedoms protected by the First Amendment. Those who, so Congress has found, would subvert the public interest cannot escape all regulations because, at the same time, they carry on legitimate political activities. . . . To encourage unions to displace them from positions of great power over the national economy, while at the same time leaving free the outlets by which they may pursue legitimate political activities of persuasion and advocacy, does not seem to us to contravene the purposes of the First Amendment. That Amendment requires that one be permitted to believe what he will. It requires that one be permitted to advocate what he will unless there is a clear and present danger that a substantial public evil will result therefrom. It does not require that he be permitted to be the keeper of the arsenal.

VII.

There remain two contentions which merit discussion. One is that § 9 (h) is unconstitutionally vague. The other is that it violates the mandate of Art. 1, § 9 of the Constitution, that "No bill of attainder or ex-post-facto law shall be passed."

The argument as to vagueness stresses the breadth of such terms as "affiliated," "supports" and "illegal or unconstitutional methods." There is little doubt that imagination can conjure hypothetical cases in which the meaning of these terms will be in nice question. The applicable standard, however, is not one of wholly consistent academic definition of abstract terms. It is, rather, the practical criterion of fair notice to those to whom the statute is directed. The particular context is all important.

The only criminal punishment specified is the application of § 35A of the Criminal Code, 18 U.S.C. § 1001, which covers only those false statements made "knowingly and willfully." The question in any criminal prosecution involving a non-Communist affidavit must therefore be whether the affiant acted in good faith or knowingly lied concerning his affiliations, beliefs, support of organizations, etc. And since the constitutional vice in a vague or indefinite statute is the injustice to the accused in placing him on trial for an offense, the nature of which he is given no fair warning, the fact that punishment is restricted to acts done with knowledge that they contravene the statute makes this objection untenable. As this Court pointed out . . . "A mind intent upon willful evasion is inconsistent with surprised innocence." . . . Without considering, therefore, whether in other circumstances the words used in § 9 (h) would render a statute unconstitutionally vague and indefinite, we think that the fact that under § 35A of the Criminal Code no honest, untainted interpretation of those words is punishable removes the possibility of constitutional infirmity.

The unions' argument as to bill of attainder cites the familiar cases, *United States* v. *Lovett*, 328 U.S. 303 (1946); *Ex parte Garland*, 4 Wall. 333 (1866); *Cummings* v. *Missouri*, 4 Wall. 277 (1866). Those cases and this also, according to the argument, involve the proscription of certain occupations to a group classified according to belief and loyalty. But there is a decisive distinction: in the previous decisions the individuals involved were in fact being punished for *past* actions; whereas in this case they are subject to possible loss of position only because there is substantial ground for the congressional judgment that their beliefs and loyalties will be transformed into *future* conduct. Of course, the history of the past conduct is the foundation for the judgment as to what the future conduct is likely to be; but that does not alter the conclusion that § 9 (h) is intended to prevent future actions rather than to punish past action.

This distinction is emphasized by the fact that members of those groups identified in § 9 (h) are free to serve as union officers if at any time they renounce the allegiances which constituted a bar to signing the affidavit in the past. Past conduct, actual or threatened by their previous adherence to affiliations and beliefs mentioned in § 9 (h), is not a bar to resumption of the position. In the cases relied upon by the unions on the other hand, this Court has emphasized that, since the basis of disqualification was past action or loyalty, nothing that those persons proscribed by its terms could ever do would change the result. . . . Here the intention is to forestall future dangerous acts; there is no one who may not, by a voluntary alteration of the loyalties which impel him to action, become eligible to sign the affidavit. We cannot conclude that this section is a bill of attainder.

In their argument on this point, the unions seek some advantage from references to English history pertinent to a religious test oath. The experience is written into our Constitution in the following provision of Article VI: "The Senators and Representatives before mentioned, and the Members of the several State Legislatures, and all executive and judicial Officers, both of the United States and of the several States, shall be bound by Oath or Affirmation, to support this

Constitution; but no religious Test shall ever be required as a Qualification to any Office or public Trust under the United States." It is obvious that not all oaths were abolished; the mere fact that § 9 (h) is in oath form hardly rises to the stature of a constitutional objection. All that was forbidden was a "religious Test." We do not think that the oath here involved can rightly be taken as falling within that category.

Clearly the Constitution permits the requirement of oaths by office holders to uphold the Constitution itself. The obvious implication is that those unwilling to take such an oath are to be barred from public office. For the President, a specific oath was set forth in the Constitution itself, Art. II, § 1. And Congress has detailed an oath for other federal officers. Obviously, the Framers of the Constitution thought that the exaction of an affirmation of minimal loyalty to the Government was worth the price of whatever deprivation of individual freedom of conscience was involved. All that we need hold here is that the casting of § 9 (h) into the mold of an oath does not invalidate it, if it is otherwise constitutional.

We conclude that § 9 (h) of the Labor-Management Relations Act, as herein construed, is compatible with the Federal Constitution and may stand. . . .

Mr. Justice Black, dissenting:

We have said that "Freedom to think is absolute of its own nature; the most tyrannical government is powerless to control the inward workings of the mind." But people can be, and in less democratic countries have been, made to suffer for their admitted or conjectured thoughts. Blackstone recalls that Dionysius is "recorded to have executed a subject barely for dreaming that he had killed him; which was held sufficient proof that he had thought thereof in his waking hours." Such a result, while too barbaric to be tolerated in our nation, is not illogical if a government can tamper in the realm of thought and penalize "belief" on the ground that it might lead to illegal conduct. Individual freedom and governmental thought-probing cannot live together. As the Court admits even today, under the First Amendment "Beliefs are inviolate."

Today's decision rejects that fundamental principle. The Court admits, as it must, that the "proscriptions" of § 9 (h) of the Taft Hartley Act rest on "beliefs and political affiliations," and that "Congress has undeniably discouraged the lawful exercise of political freedoms" which are "protected by the First Amendment." These inescapable facts should compel a holding that § 9 (h) conflicts with the First Amendment.

Crucial to the Court's contrary holding is the premise that congressional power to regulate trade and traffic includes power to proscribe "beliefs and political affiliations." No case cited by the Court provides the least vestige of support for thus holding that the Commerce Clause restricts the right to think. On the contrary, the First Amendment was added after adoption of the Constitution for the express purpose of barring Congress from using previously granted powers to abridge belief or its expression. Freedom to think is inevitably abridged when beliefs are penalized by imposition of civil disabilities.

Since § 9 (h) was passed to exclude certain beliefs from one arena of the national economy, it was quite natural to utilize the test oath as a weapon. History attests the efficacy of that instrument for inflicting penalties and disabilities on obnoxious minorities. It was one of the major devices used against the Huguenots in France, and against "heretics" during the Spanish Inquisition. It helped English rulers identify and outlaw Catholics, Quakers, Baptists, and Congregationalists—groups considered dangerous for political as well as religious reasons. And wherever the test oath was in vogue, spies and informers found rewards far more tempting than truth. Painful awareness of the evils of thought espionage made such oaths "an abomination to the founders of this nation," *In re Summers*, 325 U.S. 561, 576, dissenting opinion. Whether religious, political, or both, test oaths are implacable foes of free thought. By approving their imposition, this Court has injected compromise into a field where the First Amendment forbids compromise.

The Court assures us that today's encroachment on liberty is just a small one, that this particular statutory provision "touches only a handful of persons, leaving the great majority of persons of the identified affiliations and beliefs completely free from restraint." But not the least of the virtues of the First Amendment is its protection of each member of the smallest and most unorthodox minority. Centuries of experience testify that laws aimed at one political or religious group, however rational in their beginnings, generate hatreds and prejudices which rapidly spread beyond control. Too often it is fear which inspires such passions, and nothing is more reckless or contagious. In the resulting hysteria, popular indignation tars with the same brush all those who have ever been associated with any member of the group under attack or who hold a view which, though supported by revered Americans as essential to democracy, has been adopted by that group for its own purposes.

Under such circumstances, restrictions imposed on proscribed groups are seldom static, even though the rate of expansion may not move in geometric progression from discrimination to arm-band to ghetto and worse. Thus I cannot regard the Court's holding as one which merely bars Communists from holding union office and nothing more. For its reasoning would apply just as forcibly to statutes barring Communists and their suspected sympathizers from election to political office, mere membership in unions, and in fact from getting or holding any jobs whereby they could earn a living.

The Court finds comfort in its assurance that we need not fear too much legislative restriction of political belief or association "while this Court sits." That expression, while felicitous, has no validity in this particular constitutional field. For it springs from the assumption that individual mental freedom can be constitutionally abridged whenever any majority of this

Court finds a satisfactory legislative reason. Never before has this Court held that the Government could for any reason attaint persons for their potical beliefs or affiliations. It does so today.

Today the "political affiliation" happens to be the Communist Party: testimony of an ex-Communist that some Communist union officers had called "political strikes" is held sufficient to uphold a law coercing union members not to elect any Communist as an officer. Under this reasoning, affiliations with other political parties could be proscribed just as validly. Of course there is no practical possibility that either major political party would turn this weapon on the other, even though members of one party were accused of "political lockouts" a few years ago and members of the other are now charged with fostering a "welfare state" alien to our system. But with minor parties the possibility is not wholly fanciful. One, for instance, advocates socialism; another allegedly follows the Communist "line"; still another is repeatedly charged with a desire and purpose to deprive Negroes of equal job opportunities. Under today's opinion Congress could validly bar all members of these parties from officership in unions or industrial corporations; the only showing required would be testimony that some members in such positions had, by attempts to further their party's purposes, unjustifiably fostered industrial strife which hampered interstate commerce.

It is indicated, although the opinion is not thus limited and is based on threats to commerce rather than to national security, that members of the Communist Party or its "affiliates" can be individually attainted without danger to others because there is some evidence that as a group they act in obedience to the commands of a foreign power. This was the precise reason given in Sixteenth-Century England for attainting all Catholics unless they subscribed to test oaths wholly incompatible with their religion. Yet in the hour of crisis, an overwhelming majority of the English Catholics thus persecuted rallied loyally to defend their homeland against Spain and its Catholic troops. And in our own country Jefferson and his followers were earnestly accused of subversive allegiance to France. At the time, imposition of civil disability on all members of his political party must have seemed at least as desirable as does § 9 (h) today. For at stake, so many believed, was the survival of a newly-founded nation, not merely a few potential interruptions of commerce by strikes "political" rather than economic in origin.

These experiences underline the wisdom of the basic constitutional precept that penalties should be imposed only for a person's own conduct, not for his beliefs or for the conduct of others with whom he may associate. Guilt should not be imputed solely from association or affiliation with political parties or any other organization, however much we abhor the ideas which they advocate. *Schneiderman* v. *United States*, 320 U.S. 118, 136–139.

Like anyone else, individual Communists who commit overt acts in violation of valid laws can and should be punished. But the postulate of the First Amendment is that our free institutions can be maintained without proscribing or penalizing political belief, speech, assembly, or party affiliation. This is a far bolder philosophy than despotic rulers can afford to follow. It is the heart of the system on which our freedom depends.

Fears of alien ideologies have frequently agitated the nation and inspired legislation aimed at suppressing advocacy of those ideologies. At such times the fog of public excitement obscures the ancient landmarks set up in our Bill of Rights. Yet then, of all times, should this Court adhere most closely to the course they mark. . . .

2. Loyalty or Security Regulations for Government Employees

a. Loyalty Review Boards

BAILEY v. RICHARDSON

182 F. 2d 46 (1950)

[This case was decided by the United States Court of Appeals for the District of Columbia Circuit. The decision was affirmed by an equally divided Supreme Court, without an opinion. 341 US 918 (1951).

[Loyalty investigations of Government employees were started by the House Un-American Activities Committee. In 1938 the chairman of the Committee, Congressman Dies, warned against "crackpots" and "internationalists" and Communists on the Government payroll. Spurred on by Dies and the Committee, Congress in 1939 enacted Section 9A of the Hatch Act, making it unlawful for any federal employee to have membership in any organization which advocates overthrow of the Government. Since 1941 appropriation bills of Congress have carried a rider that no part of the funds is to be used to pay the salary of a person who is a member of an organization that advocates overthrow of the Government.

[The Attorney General and the President, starting in 1942, appointed executive bodies to implement these provisions of law. In 1947 President Truman issued Order 9835, which provided for formal loyalty investigation procedures. It provided for the dismissal of an employee from the service of the Federal Government if "on all the evidence, reasonable grounds exist for the belief that the person involved is disloyal to the Government of the United States." It was under this provision that Dorothy Bailey was dismissed from her position.

[On April 28, 1951, President Truman amended the 1947 order to require dismissal if on the whole record there was "reasonable doubt" of the employee's loyalty. Under this amendment, it was thought, dismissal would be easier.

[On April 27, 1953, President Eisenhower issued an executive order which did away with "loyalty" as a test and substituted in its place "security." The order provided that an employee is to be dismissed if his employment "may not be clearly consistent with the interest of the national security." This order was to cover all security risks for whatever ground, e.g., suspected disloyalty, drunkenness, immorality. It also abolished the Loyalty Review Board, leaving the execution of the order to the various executive agencies and departments.

[In the *Bailey Case* a majority of the court in effect held that, in a loyalty case involving a Government employee, the courts have no function to perform. Judge Edgerton's dissenting opinion points up the weaknesses in the loyalty proceedings and the dangers in denying judicial review and relief.]

Prettyman, Circuit Judge:

This is a civil action brought in the United States District Court for the District of Columbia for a declaratory judgment and for an order directing plaintiff-appellant's reinstatement in Government employ. The defendants-appellees are the Administrator of the Federal Security Agency, the members of the Civil Service Commission, members of its Loyalty Review Board, and members of its Loyalty Board of the Fourth Civil Service Region. Answer to the complaint was made by the defendants-appellees, and affidavits were filed. Both plaintiff and defendants made motions for summary judgment. The District Court granted the motion of the defendants. This appeal followed. . . .

Appellant Bailey was employed in the classified civil service of the United States Government from August 19, 1939, to June 28, 1947. Upon the latter date she was separated from the service due to reduction in force. On March 25, 1948, she was given a temporary appointment, and on May 28, 1948, she was reinstated under circumstances to be related.

The regulations of the Civil Service Commission in effect at the time of appellant's reinstatement made reinstatements subject to the condition that removal might be ordered by the Commission if investigation of the individual's qualifications, made within eighteen months, disclosed disqualification. The regulations listed as a disqualification: "(7) On all the evidence, reasonable grounds exist for belief that the person involved is disloyal to the Government of the United States."

On July 31, 1948, two months after her reinstatement, Miss Bailey received from the Regional Loyalty Board of the Commission a letter and an enclosed interrogatory. The letter said in part:

During the course of an investigation of your suitability for appointment, information was received which the Commission believes you should be given an opportunity to clarify. Consequently, there are inclosed an original and copy of an interrogatory to be answered by you under affirmation or oath. . . .

Your cooperation in this matter will be appreciated.

The interrogatory said in part:

As part of the process of determining your suitability for Federal Employment, an investigation of you has been conducted under the provisions of Executive Order 9835, which established the Federal Employees Loyalty Program. This investigation disclosed information which, it is believed, you should have an opportunity to explain or refute.

The questions in the attached Interrogatory are based on the information received, and are to be answered in writing in sufficient detail to present fairly your explanation or answers thereto. . . .

You are further advised that you have the right, upon request, to an administrative hearing on the issues in the case before the Regional Loyalty Board. You may appear personally before the Board and be represented by counsel or representative of your own choice; and you may present evidence in your behalf. Such evidence may be presented by witnesses or by affidavit. . . .

The Commission has received information to the effect that you are or have been a member of the Communist Party or the Communist Political Association; that you have attended meetings of the Communist Party, and have associated on numerous occasions with known Communist Party members. . . .

The Commission has received information to the effect that you are or have been a member of the American League for Peace and Democracy, an organization which has been declared by the Attorney General to come within the purview of Executive Order 9835. . . .

The Commission has received information to the effect that you are or have been a member of the Washington Committee for Democratic Action, an organization which has been declared by the Attorney General to come within the purview of Executive Order 9835. . . .

Are you now, or have ever been, a member of, or in any manner affiliated with, the Nazi or Fascist movements or with any organization or political party whose objective is now, or has ever been, the overthrow of the Constitutional Government of the United States?

Miss Bailey answered the interrogatories directly and specifically, denying each item of information recited therein as having been received by the Commission, except that she admitted past membership for a short time in the American League for Peace and Democracy. She vigorously asserted her loyalty to the United States. She requested an administrative hearing. A hearing was held before the Regional Board. She appeared and testified and presented other witnesses and numerous affidavits. No person other than those presented by her testified.

On November 1, 1948, the Regional Board advised the Federal Security Agency, in which Miss Bailey was employed, that:

As a result of such investigation and after a hearing before this Board, it was found that, on all the evidence, reasonable grounds exist for belief that Miss Bailey is disloyal to the Government of the United States.

Therefore she has been rated ineligible for Federal employment; she has been barred from competing in civil service examinations for a period of three years, and your office is instructed to separate her from the service.

On the same day, a letter was sent by the Board to Miss Bailey, reading in part:

As shown in the attached copy of a letter to your employing agency, it has been found that, on all the evidence, reasonable grounds exist for belief that you are disloyal to the Government of the United States.

Your application for or eligibility from each of the examinations mentioned below has been cancelled and you have been barred from civil service examinations in the Federal service for a period of three years from October 29, 1948. When the period of debarment has expired the Commission will, upon request, consider the removal of the bar.

If you wish to appeal the Board's decision, the Loyalty Review Board, U. S. Civil Service Commission, Washington 25, D.C., should be notified within 20 days from the date of receipt by you of this letter.

Miss Bailey appealed to the Loyalty Review Board and requested a hearing. Hearing was held before a panel of that Board. Miss Bailey appeared, testified, and presented affidavits. No person other than Miss Bailey testified, and no affidavits other than hers were presented on the record.

On February 9, 1949, the Chairman of the Loyalty Review Board advised the Federal Security Agency that the finding of the Regional Board was sustained, and he requested that the Agency remove Miss Bailey's name from the rolls. Notice to that effect was sent to counsel for Miss Bailey on the same day. The full Board subsequently declined to review the conclusions of its panel.

Miss Bailey's position from May 28, 1948, to November 3, 1948, was that of a training officer (general fields) CAF-13.

The rights claimed by and for appellant must be discovered accurately and defined precisely. The events with which we are concerned were not accidental, thoughtless or mere petty tyrannies of subordinate officials. They were the deliberate design of the executive branch of the Government, knowingly supported by the Congress.

The case presented for Miss Bailey is undoubtedly appealing. She was denied reinstatement in her former employment because Government officials found reasonable ground to believe her disloyal. She was not given a trial in any sense of the word, and she does not know who informed upon her. Thus viewed, her situation appeals powerfully to our sense of the fair and the just. But the case must be placed in context and in perspective.

The Constitution placed upon the President and the Congress, and upon them alone, responsibility for the welfare of this country in the arena of world affairs. It so happens that we are presently in an adversary position to a government whose most successful recent method of contest is the infiltration of the government service by its sympathizers. This is the context of Miss Bailey's question.

The essence of her complaint is not that she was denied reinstatement; the complaint is that she was denied reinstatement without revelation by the Government of the names of those who informed against her and of the method by which her alleged activities were detected. So the question actually posed by the case is whether the President is faced with an inescapable dilemma, either to continue in Government employment a person whose loyalty he reasonably suspects or else to reveal publicly the methods by which he detects disloyalty and the names of any persons who may venture to assist him.

Even in normal times and as a matter of ordinary internal operation, the ability, integrity and loyalty of purely executive employees is exclusively for the executive branch of Government to determine, except in so far as the Congress has a constitutional voice in the matter. All such employees hold office at the pleasure of the appointing authority; again except only for statutory limitations. Never in our history . . . has a Government employee been entitled as of right to the sort of hearing Miss Bailey demands in respect to dismissal from office. These well-established principles give perspective to the present problem.

The presentation of appellant's contentions is impressive. Each detail of the trial which she unquestionably did not get is depicted separately, in a mounting cumulation into analogies to the Dreyfus case and the Nazi judicial process. Thus, a picture of a simple black-and-white fact—that appellant did not get a trial in the judicial sense—is drawn in bold and appealing colors. But the question is not whether she had a trial. The question is whether she should have had one.

If the whole of this case were as appellant pictures it, if we had only to decide the question which she states and as she states it, our task would indeed be simple and attractively pleasant. But it is not so. We are dealing with a major clash between individual and public interests. We must ascertain with precision whether individual rights are involved, and we must then weigh the sum of those rights, if there be any, against the inexorable necessities of the Government. We must examine not only one side of the controversy but both sides.

Appellant next says that the order of the Board which barred her from the federal service for three years, was constitutionally invalid under the decision of the Supreme Court in the *Lovett Case* [328 US 303]. We agree with that contention. The Court in that case clearly held that permanent proscription from Government service is "punishment" and that punishment can be inflicted only upon compliance with the Sixth Amendment. The difference between permanent and limited proscription is merely one of degree and not one of principle. So far as this record shows, this proscription of employment was not pursuant to a general regulation. It was not required by a general classification by Congress or by general regulation of the Civil Service Commission or of the Loyalty Board. No reference to proscription appears in the Executive Order, the Attorney General's orders, or the statements of the Loyalty Board. . . . The bar in the present proceeding appears on the record to be one imposed by the Board upon this particular individual in this particular case as a matter of individual adjudication. We hold that the portions of the orders and directions of the defendants-appellees which purported to bar Miss Bailey from federal employ for three years, are invalid.

We did not understand appellant to urge the unconstitutionality of her dismissal apart from the three-year bar. But there is a difference of opinion among us in that respect, and we, therefore, state our views upon the point. First we consider the contentions respecting the constitutionality of the procedure pursued, and then we consider the constitutionality of the condition imposed upon the reinstatement. For the first purpose, we must assume that Miss Bailey was in the classified service without condition at the time of her removal from the rolls and that she was, therefore, dismissed from employment and not merely denied appointment; although, as we have indicated we do not agree with that view of her status. If her status was merely that of an applicant for appointment, as we think it was, her nonappointment involved no procedural constitutional rights. Obviously, an applicant for office has no constitutional right to a hearing or a specification of the reasons why he is not appointed. We, therefore, consider the constitutionality of the procedure followed in this case upon the assumption that a Government employee in the classified service is being dismissed because her superiors have grounds, which to them are reasonable, to believe that she is disloyal.

Our first inquiry is whether the Sixth Amendment applies to a dismissal from Government service. That Amendment provides:

In all criminal prosecutions, the accused shall enjoy the right to a speedy and public trial, by an impartial jury of the State and district wherein the crime shall have been committed, which district shall have been previously ascertained by law, and to be informed of the nature and cause of the accusation; to be confronted with the witnesses against him; to have compulsory process for obtaining witnesses in his favor, and to have the assistance of counsel for his defense.

The Amendment in terms applies to criminal prosecutions, and requires not only confrontation by witnesses but also trial by jury. The process is a judicial process.

The Supreme Court held in the *Lovett Case* that "punishment" can be inflicted lawfully only upon compliance with the Sixth Amendment. The decision in that case is one of the keys to the contention presented on behalf of appellant. The Court held permanent proscription from Government service to be such "punishment," but it did not, as we read the case, hold mere dismissal from Government service to be punishment in that sense. . . . Throughout the entire opinion in the *Lovett Case*, it was meticulously explicit in limiting its discussion to the proscriptive feature of the statute before it. . . .

In the last place, even if there were no decided cases upon the point, we would not think that the Constitution meant that the President could not dismiss a subordinate executive employee without the judicial procedure required by the Sixth Amendment. The fundamental concept of the division of powers, and so of responsibilities, does not, in our opinion, permit the conclusion that the President cannot remove an employee in the executive branch without referring the matter to the judicial branch. And the long history of the controversy concerning removal from public office, beginning with the First Congress, cannot be read so as to permit that conclusion.

We are of the opinion that compliance with the Sixth Amendment is not a prerequisite to the dismissal of an employee from the Federal Government classified civil service. It is apparently admitted on behalf of appellant that this conclusion is true generally speaking but it is said that dismissal for suspicion of disloyalty is an exception and that an employee cannot be dismissed for that one particular reason without a jury trial, confrontation by witnesses, etc., in a judicial proceeding. We shall discuss that claim of exception in a moment.

It is next said on behalf of appellant that the due process clause of the Fifth Amendment requires that she be afforded a hearing of the quasi-judicial type before being dismissed. The due process clause provides: "No person shall . . . be deprived of life, liberty or property, without due process of law. . . ." It has been held repeatedly and consistently that Government employ is not "property" and that in this particular it is not a contract. We are unable to perceive how it could be held to be "liberty." Certainly it is not "life." So much that is clear would seem to dispose of the point. In terms the due process clause does not apply to the holding of a Government office.

Other considerations lead to the same conclusion. Never in our history has a Government administrative employee been entitled to a hearing of the quasi-judicial type upon his dismissal from Government service. That record of a hundred and sixty years of Government administration is the sort of history which speaks with great force. . . .

In the absence of statute or ancient custom to the contrary, executive offices are held at the will of the appointing authority, not for life or for fixed terms. If removal be at will, of what purpose would process be? To hold office at the will of a superior and to be removable therefrom only by constitutional due process of law are opposite and inherently conflicting ideas. Due process of law is not applicable unless one is being deprived of something to which he has a right.

Constitutionally, the criterion for retention or removal of subordinate employees is the confidence of superior executive officials. Confidence is not controllable by process. What may be required by acts of the Congress is another matter, but there is no requirement in the Constitution that the executive branch rely upon the services of persons in whom it lacks confidence. . . .

We hold that the due process of law clause of the Fifth Amendment does not restrict the President's discretion or the prescriptive power of Congress in respect to executive personnel.

We do not reach the question whether, if the due process of law clause does apply, it requires more than this appellant was given. Miss Bailey was not summarily cut off the rolls. She was advised in writing that information concerning her qualifications for Government employ had been received; she was asked specific questions; and she was told that those questions reflected the information received. The questions revealed the nature of the alleged activities giving rise to the inquiry and the names of the organizations in which she was alleged to have been active. Everything that she wished to present was received; all affidavits offered by her were accepted, and all witnesses presented by her testified. She was twice heard orally. She was represented at all stages by competent counsel. Her case was considered by two separate groups of executive officials. On the other hand, she was not told the names of the informants against her. She was not permitted to face or to cross-examine those informants. She was not given the dates or places at which she was alleged to have been active in the named alleged subversive organizations. So the claim in her behalf necessarily goes farther than an abstract claim for due process of law. The claim must be that the due process clause requires, in dismissals of subordinate Government employees, specificity in charges equivalent to that of valid criminal charges, confrontation by witnesses, cross examination of them, and hearing upon evidence openly submitted. Even if the due process clause applies, we would think it does not require so much.

Here again it is apparently conceded on behalf of appellant that our conclusions in respect to the Fifth Amendment are sound generally speaking, but an exception is claimed in the cases of those dismissed for suspicion of disloyalty. As we have said, we shall discuss that claimed exception in a moment.

It is next said that appellant's dismissal impinged upon the rights of free speech and assembly protected by the First Amendment, since the dismissal was premised upon alleged political activity. This suggestion goes not to the procedure but to the ultimate validity of the dismissal itself. But the plain hard fact is that so far as the Constitution is concerned there is no prohibition against the dismissal of Government employees because of their political beliefs, activities or affiliations. That document, standing alone, does not prevent Republican Presidents from dismissing Democrats or Democratic Presidents from dismissing Republicans. From the beginning, such has been the practice, with variations in scope. The reason that it has not continued to so great an extent is because the people became convinced that it was not good government and the Congress and the President wrote that view into statutes and regulations. They, not the Constitution, give Government employees such protection as they have against dismissal for political reasons. . . .

The situation of the Government employee is not different in this respect from that of private employees. A newspaper editor has a constitutional right to speak and write as he pleases. But the Constitution does not guarantee him a place in the columns of a publisher with whose political views he does not agree.

Government employment is subject to many restrictions upon otherwise unrestricted individual rights in respect to activities, property ownership, etc., as the Supreme Court long ago pointed out. . . .

It is said that the loyalty program as applied in this particular case went beyond the power of Congress and of the President to regulate the conduct of Government employees.

We must at this point be careful to note the precise ground upon which appellant was dismissed. It was that in the judgment of authorized executive officials, "reasonable grounds exist for belief that Miss Bailey is disloyal to the Government of the United States." So far as we have been able to ascertain, it is nowhere disputed that employees in fact disloyal to the Government may and should be removed. A classification of loyal and disloyal is undoubtedly a proper one descriptive of qualification and disqualification for public office. Appellant says: "We are of course not suggesting that a government employee who is reinstated in his job is immune from inquiry into his loyalty." So the points made in behalf of appellant must be these: (1) That mere belief on the part of executive officials of disloyalty, even though supported by grounds reasonable to them, is not a sufficient basis for valid removal. (2) That if the power to remove be limited, some authority other than executive or legislative must be able to determine whether the limitation be transgressed, and so the grounds for executive belief must be fully revealed. (3) That the information concerning appellant, as reflected in the interrogatory sent to her, does not, even if true, constitute reasonable ground for belief in her disloyalty.

The first proposition is in effect that reasonable ground for belief of disloyalty is not sufficient prerequisite to dismissal. But we can perceive no basis for holding that the executive departments must retain in the service those whose loyalty is reasonably doubtful. Reasonably grounded suspicion of disloyalty indicates a risk, and no concept of the Constitution requires the executive to endure recognizable and preventable risks in the administration of the law. He may decide to do so, but we see no basis for saying that he must. The Constitution does not require the President to continue to use in the training of Government personnel, the work performed by this appellant, a person whose loyalty to the Government he suspects. There is no reason in the Constitution why the President should not limit the training staff to persons whose loyalty is beyond the faintest shadow of suspicion.

The clear and present danger rule does not help us in this matter, because Government employ, with which we are here dealing, is not a right. The argument that the rule does apply confuses the subject matter of the controversy. No one denies Miss Bailey the right to any political activity or affiliation she may choose. What is denied her is Government employ. . . .

The second proposition concerns the mode of determining the sufficiency of a doubt of loyalty. If reasonable grounds for belief of disloyalty suffice for dismissal, in whose mind must such reasonable grounds be established?

Much argument at this point is premised upon the possibility of abuse of the removal power. It is said that if executive officers have power to remove without compliance with restrictive measures they may by terror destroy free thought and action in the Government service and so establish a tyranny. This fear is not new. It was held by some members of the First Congress and urged by them in the debate upon the removal power. But under our system of government the courts cannot assume a possible abuse of constitutional power as a reason for denying that power. Almost every power, constitutional, statutory, regulatory, contractual or whatnot, is susceptible of abuse. The Constitution bestows the several powers of government with such

checks and balances as the makers of the Government deemed necessary and adequate. All executive power, with the stated limitations,
was vested by the Constitution in the executive branch, and no part
of it was vested in the judicial branch. The judicial branch can no
more assume to limit executive power because of a possible abuse by
executive officials than can executive officials limit judicial power because of possible abuse by judicial officers. Abuse of power is, of
course, forbidden, but the mere potentiality of abuse does not constitute invalidity of power. We cannot declare an act unconstitutional
merely because under it there is a possibility of abuse. . . .

This brings us to the third proposition upon this subject, which is
that the revealed information in this particular case is insufficient
ground for suspicion of disloyalty. It is said that the interrogatory
showed that the basis for Miss Bailey's dismissal was an alleged
membership in the Communist Party and other allegedly "subversive"
organizations, and that this is an invalid discrimination.

It is perfectly true, as the Supreme Court said in the *United Public
Workers Case* [330 US 75], that Congress could not legislate that
"no Republican, Jew or Negro shall be appointed to federal office."
But if a Democratic President were to appoint few, if any, Republicans
to office, or vice versa, he would not be violating any provision of the
Constitution. Vigorous as the condemnation of the practice has been,
even in recent years, nowhere, so far as we are aware, has it been
responsibly asserted that such selection is invalid. In blunt terms, the
President can discriminate for political reasons. We do not think the
Supreme Court meant, by the quoted sentence, that if the President
or his authorized aides exercised the prerogative of selecting employees by selecting no Republicans, the choices would be constitutionally void. Some astonishing results would ensue from any such
holding. The Court was referring to permanent, blanket proscription
by the Congress. Of more importance, the classifications named in the
quoted suggestion have no discernible bearing upon qualification for
office. Such a statute would be purely arbitrary and capricious in the
most obnoxious meaning of those words.

Our conclusion upon this phase of the case, therefore, is that the
loyalty program established by the President's Order and applied to
this appellant is not, for any of the reasons thus far discussed, invalid.

Thus the controversy develops, step by step, to its ultimate crisis. It
is urged upon us that dismissal from Government employ for suspicion
of disloyalty is an exception to the established doctrines and rules
generally applicable to Government employees and their dismissal
from service.

It is said on behalf of appellant that disloyalty is akin to treason and that dismissal is akin to conviction. Forthwith it is asserted that Miss Bailey has been convicted of disloyalty. As we have seen, nothing resembling a conviction from the legal standpoint has been visited upon her. She was merely refused Government employment for reasons satisfactory to the appointing authorities.

But it is said that the public does not distinguish, that she has been stigmatized and her chance of making a living seriously impaired. The position implicit in that assertion dissolves into two contentions. One is that even if executive authorities had power to dismiss Miss Bailey without a judicial hearing, they had no power to hurt her while doing so; that is, they had no power to call her disloyal even if they had power to dismiss her for that reason. But it has long been established that if the Government, in the exercise of a governmental power, injures an individual, that individual has no redress. Official action beyond the scope of official authority can be prevented or nullified by the courts, and so official action which violates a constitutional right of an individual can be rectified. But if no constitutional right of the individual is being impinged and officials are acting within the scope of official authority, the fact that the individual concerned is injured in the process neither invalidates the official act nor gives the individual a right to redress. So in the present case if Miss Bailey had no constitutional right to her office and the executive officers had power to dismiss her, the fact that she was injured in the process of dismissal neither invalidates her dismissal nor gives her right to redress; this under a rule of law established long ago. . . .

The line of cases in which this court has said that courts will not review the action of executive officials in dismissing executive employees except to insure compliance with statutory requirements, is unvaried. . . .

The rule is applied even when the charges involve offenses of serious moral turpitude. . . .

It should be remarked parenthetically that, in so far as the case before us is concerned, any publicity which it received was not pursuant to but in flat contradiction of the Executive Order, the Attorney General's instructions, and the Loyalty Board's rules, all of which forbid publicity. Moreover, Miss Bailey accepted voluntarily the conditional reappointment which was premised upon her successful passage of the loyalty test laid down in the Executive Order.

The other contention implicit in the assertion, that Miss Bailey has been stigmatized and injured, is that disloyalty is a thing apart, suspicion of which gives rise to constitutional rights not applicable to suspicion of criminal offenses. It seems to us that in so far as suspicion of disloyalty has peculiarities which distinguish it from suspicions of bribery, seduction and other offenses they are adverse to appellant's conclusions. We must look not only at appellant's but also at the public side of this controversy. From that point of view, the retention in the Government service of one suspected of theft or a similar offense would not be of great importance, and the revelation of the method of detection and the names of informants would probably not affect the public interest. But disloyalty in the Government service under present circumstances is a matter of great public concern, and revelation of the methods of detecting it and of the names of witnesses involve public considerations of compelling importance.

We cannot ignore the world situation in which not merely two ideologies but two potentially adverse forces presently exist, and certainly we cannot require that the President and the Congress ignore it. Infiltration of government service is now a recognized technique for the overthrow of government. We do not think that the individual rights guaranteed by the Constitution necessarily mean that a government dedicated to those rights cannot preserve itself in the world as it is. This case presents a small segment of that momentous question. In the light of all that is well known, much of which is recited in opinions of the Supreme Court, we cannot say that a policy of caution in respect to members of the Communist Party in the Government service under current circumstances is forbidden by any restriction in the Constitution. The risks are for the President to estimate, and the assumption of risk is for him to decide. If he thinks that under present circumstances only those whose loyalty is beyond suspicion should be employed by this Government, the policy is his to make. The responsibility in this field is his, and the power to meet it must also be his. The judiciary cannot dictate that he must either retain in Government service those whom he reasonably suspects or else reveal publicly the means and methods by which he detects disloyalty.

Upon the contention that suspicion of disloyalty has characteristics distinguishing it from suspicion of other offenses, we conclude that the differences tend to solidify rather than to weaken the application of the doctrine that the President and the Congress are responsible for the qualifications, ability, judgment and loyalty of Government employees and that removal from Government employment is within their discretion.

It is our clear opinion that the President, absent congressional restriction, may remove from Government service any person of whose loyalty he is not completely convinced. He may do so without assigning any reason and without giving the employee any explanatory notice. If, as a matter of policy, he chooses to give the employee a general description of the information which concerns him and to hear what the employee has to say, he does not thereby strip himself of any portion of his constitutional power to choose and to remove.

We conclude that the Executive Order before us and the proceedings under it violated no congressional limitation upon the executive power of removal; that no constitutional right was involved in this non-appointment or dismissal; and that, in so far as the circumstances imposed hardship upon the individual, the exigencies of government in the public interest under current conditions must prevail, as they always must when a similar clash arises.

Able pleas are made based upon the American passion for fair play and upon the sincere fears of patriotic men that unqueried and unrestricted power of removal in the President may lead to tyranny. Such pleas are to be neither ignored nor belittled, but their forum is the Congress and the President's Office. "The problem," as the executive director of the National Civil Service League has written, is "not so much a matter of the legal issues involved as it is practical application of the President's loyalty review order and its administration."

Finding constitutional power for the procedure here followed, and no violation of congressional mandate, our function is exhausted. We have no concern with executive or legislative policy or with the processes by which those branches of the Government fulfill their constitutional responsibilities.

The case will be remanded to the District Court with instructions to enter a decree holding invalid those sections of the orders of the Loyalty Boards and the Federal Security Agency which would bar Miss Bailey from employment for three years, and holding valid those sections which accomplished her removal from the rolls and from office in the classified civil service.

Edgerton, Circuit Judge, dissenting:

Without trial by jury, without evidence, and without even being allowed to confront her accusers or know their identity, a citizen of the United States has been found disloyal to the government of the United States.

For her supposed disloyal thoughts she has been punished by dismissal from a wholly nonsensitive position in which her efficiency rating was high. The case received nation-wide publicity. Ostracism inevitably followed. A finding of disloyalty is closely akin to a finding of treason. The public hardly distinguishes between the two.

No charges were served on appellant. The chairman of the Regional Board said "Nobody has presented any charges." The Board told appellant it was inquiring whether there were reasonable grounds for believing she was disloyal to the government of the United States. The Federal Bureau of Investigation had reported that informants believed to be reliable had made general statements purporting to connect her with the Communist Party. These reports were not disclosed to the appellant and have not been disclosed in court. The informants were not identified to the appellant or even to the Board. Their statements were admittedly not made under oath. The appellant denied under oath any membership in and any relationship or sympathy with the Communist Party, any activities connected with it or with communism, and affiliation with any organization that advocated overthrow of the government of the United States. She asserted her loyalty to the government of the United States. She admitted attending one Communist meeting in 1932 in connection with a seminar study of the platforms of the various parties while she was a student at Bryn Mawr.

Appellant had no power to subpoena witnesses. Though it takes courage to appear as a voluntary defense witness in a loyalty case, four appeared. One was the pastor of the Methodist Church of which appellant is an active member. He testified: "When this charge or information came to me I was not only surprised, I was dumbfounded. . . . People in our community and in our church think of her and her family in the highest terms." Three officials of appellant's government agency, the United States Employment Service, who had known appellant professionally and socially for years, testified respectively that they were "extremely shocked" by the suggestion of her being disloyal, that it was "inconceivable" and "out of reason." Persons prominent in business, government and education who knew appellant but could not be present submitted affidavits.

No witness offered evidence, even hearsay evidence, against appellant. No affidavits were introduced against her. The record consists entirely of evidence in her favor. Yet the Board purported to find "on all the evidence" that there were reasonable grounds for believing she was disloyal to the government of the United States. Appellees admit the Board made this finding "after considering all the evidence, including the confidential reports of the Federal Bureau of Investigation." . . .

Appellant appeared and testified before a panel of the Loyalty Review Board. She submitted her own affidavit and the affidavits of some 70 persons who knew her, including bankers, corporate officials, federal and state officials, union members, and others. Again no one testified against her. She proved she had publicly and to the knowledge of a number of the affiants taken positions inconsistent with Communist sympathies. She showed not only by her own testimony but by that of other persons that she favored the Marshall Plan, which the Communist Party notoriously opposed, and that in 1940, during the Nazi-Soviet Pact, she favored Lend-Lease and was very critical of the Soviet position. In her union she urged its officers to execute non-communist affidavits, opposed a foreign policy resolution widely publicized as pro-Russian, and favored what was then the official CIO resolution on foreign policy.

Against all this, there were only the unsworn reports in the secret files to the effect that unsworn statements of a general sort, purporting to connect appellant with Communism, had been made by unnamed persons. Some if not all of these statements did not purport to be based on knowledge, but only on belief. Appellant sought to learn the names of the informants, or, if their names were confidential, then at least whether they had been active in appellant's union, in which there were factional quarrels. The Board did not furnish or even have this information. Chairman Richardson said: "I haven't the slightest knowledge as to who they were or how active they have been in anything." All that the Board knew or we know about the informants is that unidentified members of the Federal Bureau of Investigation, who did not appear before the Board, believed them to be reliable. . . .

Appellant's dismissal violates both the Constitution and the Executive Order. However respectable her anonymous accusers may have been, if her dismissal is sustained the livelihood and reputation of any civil servant today and perhaps of any American tomorrow are at the mercy not only of an innocently mistaken informer but also of a malicious or demented one unless his defect is apparent to the agent who interviews him. . . .

Dismissal for disloyalty is punishment and requires all the safeguards of a judicial trial. Most dismissals, including dismissals for colorless or undisclosed reasons and dismissals for incompetence, are plainly not punitive. They do not require a judicial trial or even a full administrative hearing. They are within the authority of the executive. Likewise most tax laws are within the authority of the legislature. It does not follow that all legislative taxation is constitutional or that all executive dismissals are constitutional.

Punishment is infliction of harm, usually for wrong conduct but in appellant's case for wrong views. Dismissals to provide jobs for persons of certain affiliations, whatever else may be said of such dismissals, are not punitive. But dismissals for disloyal views are punitive. This is what the Supreme Court squarely held in the *Lovett Case*. It overruled no cases in so holding. The earlier decisions of the Supreme Court on which this court relies are irrelevant because they involved dismissals for undisclosed reasons, not for disloyal views.

The question whether the rule of the *Lovett Case* extends to dismissals of "disloyal" persons from sensitive positions in which their presence might threaten substantial harm to the government does not arise in the present case and I express no opinion on it. Appellant was dismissed from a nonsensitive position. . . .

The distinction this court draws between dismissal as punishment and ineligibility as punishment not only contradicts the *Lovett Case* but has no basis in reason. Dismissal is more certainly damaging than ineligibility, for the necessary combination of vacancies, qualifications, and desire for public appointment may never occur again. A person dismissed as disloyal can obtain no normal employment, public or private. The President's Committee on Civil Rights said in 1947: "It is a severe punishment to be discharged from the Government for disloyalty, as the Supreme Court pointed out in 1946 in *United States* v. *Lovett*. . . . Loss of job and inability to obtain another one is a severe punishment to impose on any man." It makes no present or probable future difference to the appellant and it should make no difference to a court whether the appellant is told that she is separated from the civil service for life, for three years, or only for the moment. Whatever she is told, if her dismissal is sustained she will not be reemployed while the present climate of opinion continues.

Since dismissal from government service for disloyalty is punishment, due process of law requires that the accused employee be given all the safeguards of a judicial trial before it is imposed. . . .

Not only the basic right to judicial trial but every one of these basic safeguards . . . was violated here. (1) The appellant was not tried by a jury. (2) She was not clearly informed of the charge against her. This is true not only because there was no formal charge and, according to the Chairman of the Regional Board, no charge at all, but also because of the vagueness of the term "disloyal." It is so indefinite that neither the Executive Order nor, as far as appears, the Loyalty Review Board has attempted to define it. . . . (3) The appellant violated no law. (4) Even the Executive Order was issued after the activities from which her disloyalty is inferred took place, if they took place at all. (5) She was not confronted with any witnesses against her. (6) Forced idleness may well be considered a cruel as well as unusual punishment. It has been considered more severe than forced labor. . . .

Appellant's dismissal abridges freedom of speech and assembly. Mr. Justice Holmes' famous statement, made in 1892 when he was a member of the Supreme Judicial Court of Massachusetts, that "the petitioner may have a constitutional right to talk politics, but he has no constitutional right to be a policeman" is greatly over-simplified. "As pointed out in *Frost Trucking Co.* v. *Railroad Comm.*, 271 U.S. 583, even in the granting of a privilege the state 'may not impose conditions which require the relinquishment of constitutional rights . . .'" including the rights of free speech, press, and assembly. In the *Esquire Case* the Supreme Court said: "We may assume that Congress . . . need not open second-class mail to publications of all types. . . . But grave constitutional questions are immediately raised once it is said that the use of the mails is a privilege which may be extended or withheld on any grounds whatsoever. . . . Under that view the second-class rate could be granted on condition that certain economic or political ideas not be disseminated." Similarly, the premise that government employment is a privilege does not support the conclusion that it may be granted on condition that certain economic or political ideas not be entertained. Though members of minority parties have often been dismissed, in the past, to make room for members of a party in power, any comprehensive practice of that sort would today be unthinkable as well as illegal, and the Supreme Court has plainly indicated it would also be unconstitutional. The Court pointed out in the *Mitchell Case* that Congress could not "'enact a regulation providing that no Republican, Jew or Negro shall be appointed to federal office, or that no federal employee shall attend Mass or take any active part in missionary work.'"

The dismissal which the Court upheld in the *Mitchell Case* was not based on views but on conduct. . . .

"In loyalty hearings the following questions have been asked of employees against whom charges have been brought. . . . 'Do you read a good many books?' 'What books do you read?' 'What magazines do you read?' 'What newspapers do you buy or subscribe to?' 'Do you think that Russian Communism is likely to succeed?' 'How do you explain the fact that you have an album of Paul Robeson records in your home?' 'Do you ever entertain Negroes in your home?' . . . 'Is it not true . . . that you lived next door to and therefore were closely associated with a member of the I.W.W.?' " "Too often the line of questioning has revolved around conformity and prevailing mores in personal habits and personal opinion. . . . A woman employee was accused of disloyalty because, at the time of siege of Stalingrad, she collected money for Russian war relief (she also collected money for British and French relief)." A record filed in this court shows that an accused employee was taken to task for membership in Consumers Union and for favoring legislation against racial discrimination. The record in the present case contains the following colloquy between a member of the Regional Board and the present appellant: "Mr. Blair: Did you ever write a letter to the Red Cross about the segregation of blood? Miss Bailey: I do not recall. Mr. Blair: What was your personal position about that? Miss Bailey: Well, the medical—. Mr. Blair: I am asking yours."

No doubt some boards are quite aware that unconventional views and conduct have no tendency to indicate disloyalty. But the fact remains that some boards imagine the contrary. This fact is too well known. It puts government employees under economic and social pressure to protect their jobs and reputations by expressing in words and conduct only the most orthodox opinions on political, economic and social questions.

A regulation that restrains constitutionally protected speech along with other speech cannot be enforced against either. Legislation is unconstitutional as a whole if it "does not aim specifically at evils within the allowable area of state control but . . . sweeps within its ambit other activities that in ordinary circumstances constitute an exercise of freedom of speech or of the press. The existence of such a statute . . . results in a continuous and pervasive restraint on all freedom of discussion that might reasonably be regarded as within its purview. . . . An accused . . . under such a statute, does not have to sustain the burden of demonstrating that the State could not constitutionally have written a different and specific statute covering his activities as disclosed by the charge and the evidence introduced against him. . . . Where regulations of the liberty of free discussion are concerned, there are special reasons for observing the rule that it is the statute, and not the accusation or the evidence under it, which prescribes the limits of permissible conduct and warns against transgression." . . .

Freedoms that may not be abridged by law may not be abridged by executive order. Executive power to control public employment stands on no higher constitutional ground than legislative power to tax. The taxing power does not extend to sales of propaganda not made for profit; license taxes, though imposed for the legitimate purpose of raising revenue are unconstitutional in their application to such sales. Such taxes, even if they are too small to be a "substantial clog" on the circulation of propaganda, are "on their face . . . a restriction of the free exercise of those freedoms which are protected by the First Amendment." The loss of employment, reputation, and earning power here involved is on its face a very substantial clog on the free exercise of those protected freedoms. It is therefore more clearly unconstitutional than the taxes.

Appellant's dismissal abridges not only freedom of speech but freedom of thought. Whatever loyalty means in the present connection, it is not speech but a state of mind. The appellant was dismissed for thinking prohibited thoughts. A constitution that forbids speech control does not permit thought control.

Appellant's dismissal attributes guilt by association, and thereby denies both the freedom of assembly guaranteed by the First Amendment and the due process of law guaranteed by the Fifth. The appellant was dismissed as disloyal because she was believed to be a member or associate of the Communist Party. Undoubtedly many such persons are disloyal in every sense to the government of the United States. But the Supreme Court has held that a particular member of the Communist Party may be "attached to the principles of the Constitution" within the meaning of those words in a naturalization act: "As Justice Holmes said, 'Surely it cannot show lack of attachment to the principles of the Constitution that . . . [one] thinks it can be improved. . . . If there is any principle of the Constitution that more imperatively calls for attachment than any other it is the principle of free thought—not free thought for those who agree with us, but freedom for the thought that we hate.' . . . Under our traditions beliefs are personal and not a matter of mere association, and . . . men in adhering to a political party or other organization notoriously do not subscribe unqualifiedly to all of its platforms or asserted principles." As was said more recently, "To condemn or to interdict all members of a named political party is an abridgement of free speech, press and assembly. The Communist Party in this country is recognized as a political party." *Schneiderman* v. *U.S.*, 320 U.S. 118.

The court thinks Miss Bailey's interest and the public interest conflict. I think they coincide. On this record we have no sufficient reason to doubt either Miss Bailey's patriotism or the value of her services to the government, or to suppose that an unpatriotic person could do substantial harm in her sort of job. Even if her services were on the whole undesirable, to oust her as disloyal on rumor and without trial is to pay too much for protection against such harm as she could do in such a job. The cost is too great in morale and efficiency of government workers, in appeal of government employment to independent and inquiring minds, and in public confidence in democracy. But even if such dismissals strengthened the government instead of weakening it, they would still cost too much in constitutional rights. We cannot preserve our liberties by sacrificing them.

b. Retrospective Oaths and Affidavits

GARNER v. BOARD OF PUBLIC WORKS

341 US 716 (1951)

[Parallel with the loyalty or security requirements for federal employees are similar requirements imposed on state or municipal employees. There are often differences in the means used: the Federal Government relies heavily on investigations by the Federal Bureau of Investigation, while state and municipal governments use mainly oaths and affidavits.

[In *Gerende* v. *Board of Supervisors,* 341 US 56 (1951), the Court unanimously upheld a Maryland statute which required a candidate for public office to take an oath that he was not then engaged in an attempt to overthrow the Government by force or violence and that he was not at the time knowingly a member of an organization engaged in such an attempt.

[This oath, like the affidavit requirement considered in the *Douds Case,* above, was in the *present* tense; but many oath or affidavit provisions require an affirmation that denies *past* membership. The latter type offers substantial constitutional difficulties. In the *Garner Case* this type of requirement was upheld as constitutional by a vote of 5 to 4, with Justices Burton, Frankfurter, Douglas, and Black dissenting.]

Mr. Justice Clark delivered the opinion of the Court:

In 1941 the California Legislature amended the Charter of the City of Los Angeles to provide in part as follows:

. . . No person shall hold or retain or be eligible for any public office or employment in the service of the City of Los Angeles, in any office or department thereof, either elective or appointive, who has within five (5) years prior to the effective date of this section advised, advocated or taught, or who may, after this section becomes effective [April 28, 1941], advise, advocate or teach, or who is now or has been within five (5) years prior to the effective date of this section, or who may, after this section becomes effective, become a member of or affiliated with any group, society, association, organization or party which advises, advocates or teaches, or has, within said period of five (5) years, advised, advocated or taught the overthrow by force or violence of the government of the United States of America or of the State of California.

In so far as this section may be held by any court of competent jurisdiction not to be self-executing, the City Council is hereby given power and authority to adopt appropriate legislation for the purpose of effectuating the objects hereof.

Pursuant to the authority thus conferred the City of Los Angeles in 1948 passed ordinance No. 94,004 requiring every person who held an office or position in the service of the city to take an oath prior to January 6, 1949. In relevant part the oath was as follows:

I further swear (or affirm) that I do not advise, advocate or teach, and have not within the period beginning five (5) years prior to the effective date of the ordinance requiring the making of this oath or affirmation, advised, advocated or taught, the overthrow by force, violence or other unlawful means, of the Government of the United States of America or of the State of California and that I am not now and have not, within said period, been or become a member of or affiliated with any group, society, association, organization or party which advises, advocates or teaches, or has, within said period, advised, advocated or taught, the overthrow by force, violence or other unlawful means of the Government of the United States, or of the State of California. I further swear (or affirm) that I will not, while I am in the service of the City of Los Angeles, advise, advocate or teach, or be or become a member of or affiliated with any group, association, society, organization or party which advises, advocates or teaches, or has within said period, advised, advocated or taught, the overthrow by force, violence or other unlawful means, of the Government of the United States of America or of the State of California. . . .

The ordinance also required every employee to execute an affidavit "stating whether or not he is or ever was a member of the Communist Party of the United States of America or of the Communist Political Association, and if he is or was such a member, stating the dates when he became, and the periods during which he was, such a member. . . ."

On the final date for filing of the oath and affidavit petitioners were civil service employees of the City of Los Angeles. Petitioners Pacifico and Schwartz took the oath but refused to execute the affidavit. The remaining fifteen petitioners refused to do both. All were discharged for such cause, after administrative hearing, as of January 6, 1949. In this action they sue for reinstatement and unpaid salaries. The District Court of Appeal denied relief. . . .

Petitioners attack the ordinance as violative of the provision of Art. I, § 10 of the Federal Constitution that "No State shall . . . pass any Bill of Attainder, [or] ex post facto Law. . . ." They also contend that the ordinance deprives them of freedom of speech and assembly and of the right to petition for redress of grievances.

Petitioners have assumed that the oath and affidavit provisions of the ordinance present similar constitutional considerations and stand or fall together. We think, however, that separate disposition is indicated.

1. The affidavit raises the issue whether the City of Los Angeles is constitutionally forbidden to require that its employees disclose their

past or present membership in the Communist Party or the Communist Political Association. Not before us is the question whether the city may determine that an employee's disclosure of such political affiliation justifies his discharge.

We think that a municipal employer is not disabled because it is an agency of the State from inquiring of its employees as to matters that may prove relevant to their fitness and suitability for the public service. Past conduct may well relate to present fitness; past loyalty may have a reasonable relationship to present and future trust. Both are commonly inquired into in determining fitness for both high and low positions in private industry and are not less relevant in public employment. The affidavit requirement is valid.

2. In our view the validity of the oath turns upon the nature of the Charter amendment (1941) and the relation of the ordinance (1948) to this amendment. Immaterial here is any opinion we might have as to the Charter provision insofar as it purported to apply retrospectively for a five-year period prior to its effective date. We assume that under the Federal Constitution the Charter amendment is valid to the extent that it bars from the city's public service persons who, subsequent to its adoption in 1941, advise, advocate, or teach the violent overthrow of the Government or who are or become affiliated with any group doing so. The provisions operating thus prospectively were a reasonable regulation to protect the municipal service by establishing an employment qualification of loyalty to the State and the United States. . . . Likewise, as a regulation of political activity of municipal employees, the amendment was reasonably designed to protect the integrity and competency of the service. This Court has held that Congress may reasonably restrict the political activity of federal civil service employees for such a purpose, *United Public Workers* v. *Mitchell,* 1947, 330 U.S. 75, . . . and a State is not without power to do as much.

The Charter amendment defined standards of eligibility for employees and specifically denied city employment to those persons who thereafter should not comply with these standards. While the amendment deprived no one of employment with or without trial, yet from its effective date it terminated any privilege to work for the city in the case of persons who thereafter engaged in the activity proscribed.

The ordinance provided for administrative implementation of the provisions of the Charter amendment. The oath imposed by the ordinance proscribed to employees activity which had been denied them in identical terms and with identical sanctions in the Charter provision effective in 1941. The five-year period provided by the oath extended back only to 1943.

The ordinance would be *ex post facto* if it imposed punishment for past conduct lawful at the time it was engaged in. Passing for the moment the question whether separation of petitioners from their employment must be considered as punishment, the ordinance clearly is not *ex post facto*. The activity covered by the oath had been proscribed by the Charter in the same terms, for the same purpose, and to the same effect over seven years before, and two years prior to the period embraced in the oath. Not the law but the fact was posterior.

Bills of attainder are "legislative acts . . . that apply either to named individuals or to easily ascertainable members of a group in such a way as to inflict punishment on them without a judicial trial. . . ." *United States* v. *Lovett*, 1946, 328 U.S. 303. . . . Punishment is a prerequisite. . . . We are unable to conclude that punishment is imposed by a general regulation which merely provides standards of qualification and eligibility for employment. . . .

Nor are we impressed by the contention that the oath denies due process because its negation is not limited to affiliations with organizations known to the employee to be in the proscribed class. We have no reason to suppose that the oath is or will be construed by the City of Los Angeles or by California courts as affecting adversely those persons who during their affiliation with a proscribed organization were innocent of its purpose, or those who severed their relations with any such organization when its character became apparent, or those who were affiliated with organizations which at one time or another during the period covered by the ordinance were engaged in proscribed activity but not at the time of affiant's affiliation. We assume that scienter is implicit in each clause of the oath. As the city has done nothing to negative this interpretation, we take for granted that the ordinance will be so read to avoid raising difficult constitutional problems which any other application would present. . . .

Affirmed.

Mr. Justice Douglas, with whom Mr. Justice Black joins, dissenting:

. . . Petitioners were disqualified from office not for what they are today, not because of any program they currently espouse, . . . not because of standards related to fitness for the office, . . . but for what they once advocated. They are deprived of their livelihood by legislative act, not by judicial processes. We put the case in the aspect most invidious to petitioners. Whether they actually advocated the violent overthrow of Government does not appear. But here, as in the *Cummings Case* [*Cummings* v. *Missouri*, 4 Wall. 277], the vice is in the presumption of guilt which can only be removed by the expurgatory oath. That punishment, albeit conditional, violates here as it did in the *Cummings Case* the constitutional prohibition against bills of attainder. Whether the ordinance also amounts to an *ex post facto* law is a question we do not reach. . . .

c. The Feinberg Law

ADLER v. BOARD OF EDUCATION

342 US 485 (1952)

[The Civil Service Law of New York since 1940 has prohibited a person from teaching in any public school if he is a member of an organization that advocates the overthrow of the Government by force or violence. In 1949 the so-called Feinberg Law added the requirements that the Board of Regents proceed under rules to remove ineligible persons, to prepare a list of banned organizations, and to make membership in any listed organization prima-facie evidence of ineligibility.

[In a 6-to-3 decision the Court upheld these statutory provisions as constitutional. Justice Frankfurter dissented on jurisdictional grounds, while Justices Black and Douglas dissented on the merits, maintaining that the eligibility of a person for teaching should be determined solely by his overt acts within the school system. The majority held, however, that in addition to one's conduct, "one's associates, past and present," "may properly be considered in determining fitness and loyalty." There may be guilt by association, for "from time immemorial, one's reputation has been determined in part by the company he keeps." In determining the fitness and loyalty of teachers, the authorities may consider "the organizations and persons with whom they [the teachers] associate."

[Justices Black and Douglas argued that "what happens under this law is typical of what happens in a police state. . . . A pall is cast over the classrooms. There can be no real academic freedom in that environment."

[In a case decided in 1943, *Schneiderman* v. *United States*, 320 US 118, Justice Murphy, in his opinion for a majority of five Justices, rejected the theory of guilt by association. Under our traditions, he said, "beliefs are personal and not a matter of mere association"; for men in adhering to organizations are known not to subscribe unqualifiedly to all the platforms or asserted principles of said organizations. The Court condemned indiscriminate imputation of party dogma to a member. It must be shown that the member was aware of the proscribed character of the tenets of the organization and that he adopted them as his own.]

Mr. Justice Minton delivered the opinion of the Court:

. . . The preamble of the Feinberg Law, § 1, makes elaborate findings that members of subversive groups, particularly of the Communist Party and its affiliated organizations, have been infiltrating into public employment in the public schools of the State; that this has occurred and continues notwithstanding the existence of protective statutes designed to prevent the appointment to or retention in employment in public office, and particularly in the public schools, of members of any organizations which teach or advocate that the government of the United States or of any state or political subdivision thereof shall be overthrown by force or violence or by any other unlawful means. As a result, propaganda can be disseminated among the children by those who teach them and to whom they look for guidance, authority, and leadership. The Legislature further found that the members of such groups use their positions to advocate and teach their doctrines, and are frequently bound by oath, agreement, pledge, or understanding to follow, advocate and teach a prescribed party line or group dogma or doctrine without regard to truth or free inquiry. This propaganda, the Legislature declared, is sufficiently subtle to escape detection in the classroom; thus, the menace of such infiltration into the classroom is difficult to measure. Finally, to protect the children from such influence, it was thought essential that the laws prohibiting members of such groups, such as the Communist Party or its affiliated organizations, from obtaining or retaining employment in the public schools be rigorously enforced. It is the purpose of the Feinberg Law to provide for the disqualification and removal of superintendents of schools, teachers, and employees in the public schools in any city or school district of the State who advocate the overthrow of the Government by unlawful means or who are members of organizations which have a like purpose.

Section 3022 of the Education Law, added by the Feinberg Law, provides that the Board of Regents, which has charge of the public school system in the State of New York, shall, after full notice and hearing, make a listing of organizations which it finds advocate, advise, teach, or embrace the doctrine that the government should be overthrown by force or violence or any other unlawful means, and that such listing may be amended and revised from time to time.

It will be observed that the listings are made only after full notice and hearing. In addition, the Court of Appeals construed the statute in conjunction with Article 78 of the New York Civil Practice Act, . . . so as to provide listed organizations a right of review.

The Board of Regents is further authorized to provide in rules and regulations, and has so provided, that membership in any listed organization, after notice and hearing, "shall constitute prima facie evidence for disqualification for appointment to or retention in any office or position in the school system"; but before one who is an employee or seeks employment is severed from or denied employment, he likewise must be given a full hearing with the privilege of being represented by counsel and the right to judicial review. It is § 12-a of the Civil Service Law, as implemented by the Feinberg Law as above indicated, that is under attack here.

It is first argued that the Feinberg Law and the rules promulgated thereunder constitute an abridgment of the freedom of speech and assembly of persons employed or seeking employment in the public schools of the State of New York.

It is clear that such persons have the right under our law to assemble, speak, think and believe as they will. . . . It is equally clear that they have no right to work for the State in the school system on their own terms. . . . They may work for the school system upon the reasonable terms laid down by the proper authorities of New York. If they do not choose to work on such terms, they are at liberty to retain their beliefs and associations and go elsewhere. Has the State thus deprived them of any right to free speech or assembly? We think not. Such persons are or may be denied, under the statutes in question, the privilege of working for the school system of the State of New York because first, of their advocacy of the overthrow of the government by force or violence, or secondly, by unexplained membership in an organization found by the school authorities, after notice and hearing, to teach and advocate the overthrow of the government by force or violence, and known by such persons to have such purpose.

The constitutionality of the first proposition is not questioned here. . . .

As to the second, it is rather subtly suggested that we should not follow our recent decision in *Garner* v. *Los Angeles Board of Public Works*, 341 US 716. . . . We there said:

We think that a municipal employer is not disabled because it is an agency of the State from inquiring of its employees as to matters that may prove relevant to their fitness and suitability for the public service. Past conduct may well relate to present fitness; past loyalty may have a reasonable relationship to present and future trust. Both are commonly inquired into in determining fitness for both high and low positions in private industry and are not less relevant in public employment. . . .

We adhere to that case. A teacher works in a sensitive area in a schoolroom. There he shapes the attitude of young minds towards the society in which they live. In this, the state has a vital concern. It must preserve the integrity of the schools. That the school authorities have the right and the duty to screen the officials, teachers, and employees as to their fitness to maintain the integrity of the schools as a part of ordered society, cannot be doubted. One's associates, past and present, as well as one's conduct, may properly be considered in determining fitness and loyalty. From time immemorial, one's reputation has been determined in part by the company he keeps. In the employment of officials and teachers of the school system, the state may very properly inquire into the company they keep, and we know of no rule, constitutional or otherwise, that prevents the state, when determining the fitness and loyalty of such persons, from considering the organizations and persons with whom they associate.

If, under the procedure set up in the New York law, a person is found to be unfit and is disqualified from employment in the public school system because of membership in a listed organization, he is not thereby denied the right of free speech and assembly. His freedom of choice between membership in the organization and employment in the school system might be limited, but not his freedom of speech or assembly, except in the remote sense that limitation is inherent in every choice. Certainly such limitation is not one the state may not make in the exercise of its police power to protect the schools from pollution and thereby to defend its own existence.

It is next argued by appellants that the provision in § 3022 directing the Board of Regents to provide in rules and regulations that memberships in any organization listed by the Board after notice and hearing, with provision for review in accordance with the statute, shall constitute prima facie evidence of disqualification, denies due process, because the fact found bears no relation to the fact presumed. In other words, from the fact found that the organization was one that advocated the overthrow of government by unlawful means and that the person employed or to be employed was a member of the organization and knew of its purpose, to presume that such member is disqualified for employment is so unreasonable as to be a denial of due process of law. We do not agree. . . .

Membership in a listed organization found to be within the statute and known by the member to be within the statute is a legislative finding that the member by his membership supports the thing the organization stands for, namely, the overthrow of government by unlawful means. We cannot say that such a finding is contrary to fact or that "generality of experience" points to a different conclusion. Disqualification follows therefore as a reasonable presumption from such membership and support. Nor is there here a problem of procedural due process. The presumption is not conclusive but arises only in a hearing where the person against whom it may arise has full opportunity to rebut it. . . .

Where, as here, the relation between the fact found and the presumption is clear and direct and is not conclusive, the requirements of due process are satisfied. . . .

It is also suggested that the use of the word "subversive" is vague and indefinite. But the word is first used in § 1 of the Feinberg Law, which is the preamble to the Act, and not in a definitive part thereof. When used in subdivision 2 of § 3022, the word has a very definite meaning, namely, an organization that teaches and advocates the overthrow of government by force or violence.

We find no constitutional infirmity in § 12-a of the Civil Service Law of New York or in the Feinberg Law which implemented it, and the judgment is

Affirmed.

Mr. Justice Black, dissenting:

While I fully agree with the dissent of Mr. Justice Douglas, the importance of this holding prompts me to add these thoughts.

This is another of those rapidly multiplying legislative enactments which make it dangerous—this time for school teachers—to think or say anything except what a transient majority happen to approve at the moment. Basically these laws rest on the belief that government should supervise and limit the flow of ideas into the minds of men. The tendency of such governmental policy is to mould people into a common intellectual pattern. Quite a different governmental policy rests on the belief that government should leave the mind and spirit of man absolutely free. Such a governmental policy encourages varied intellectual outlooks in the belief that the best views will prevail. This policy of freedom is in my judgment embodied in the First Amendment and made applicable to the states by the Fourteenth. Because of this policy public officials cannot be constitutionally vested with powers to select the ideas people can think about, censor the public views they can express, or choose the persons or groups people can associate with. Public officials with such powers are not public servants; they are public masters.

I dissent from the Court's judgment sustaining this law which effectively penalizes school teachers for their thoughts and their associates.

Mr. Justice Douglas, with whom Mr. Justice Black concurs, dissenting:

I have not been able to accept the recent doctrine that a citizen who enters the public service can be forced to sacrifice his civil rights. I cannot for example find in our constitutional scheme the power of a state to place its employees in the category of second class citizens by denying them freedom of thought and expression. The Constitution guarantees freedom of thought and expression to everyone in our society. All are entitled to it; and none needs it more than the teacher.

The public school is in most respects the cradle of our democracy. The increasing role of the public school is seized upon by proponents of the type of legislation represented by New York's Feinberg law as proof of the importance and need for keeping the school free of "subversive influences." But that is to misconceive the effect of this type of legislation. Indeed the impact of this kind of censorship on the public school system illustrates the high purpose of the First Amendment in freeing speech and thought from censorship.

The present law proceeds on a principle repugnant to our society—guilt by association. A teacher is disqualified because of her membership in an organization found to be "subversive." The finding as to the "subversive" character of the organization is made in a proceeding to which the teacher is not a party and in which it is not clear that she may even be heard. To be sure she may have a hearing when charges of disloyalty are leveled against her. But in that hearing the finding as to the "subversive" character of the organization apparently may not be reopened in order to allow her to show the truth of the matter. The irrebuttable charge that the organization is "subversive" therefore hangs as an ominous cloud over her own hearing. The mere fact of membership in the organization raises a prima facie case of her own guilt. She may, it is said, show her innocence. But innocence in this case turns on knowledge; and when the witch hunt is on, one who must rely on ignorance leans on a feeble reed.

The very threat of such a procedure is certain to raise havoc with academic freedom. Youthful indiscretions, mistaken causes, misguided enthusiasms—all long forgotten—become the ghosts of a harrowing present. Any organization committed to a liberal cause, any group organized to revolt against an hysterical trend, any committee launched to sponsor an unpopular program becomes suspect. These are the organizations into which Communists often infiltrate. Their presence infects the whole, even though the project was not conceived in sin. A teacher caught in that mesh is almost certain to stand condemned. Fearing condemnation, she will tend to shrink from any association that stirs controversy. In that manner freedom of expression will be stifled.

But that is only part of it. Once a teacher's connection with a listed organization is shown, her views become subject to scrutiny to determine whether her membership in the organization is innocent or, if she was formerly a member, whether she has bona fide abandoned her membership.

The law inevitably turns the school system into a spying project. Regular loyalty reports on the teachers must be made out. The principals become detectives; the students, the parents, the community become informers. Ears are cocked for tell-tale signs of disloyalty. The prejudices of the community come into play in searching out the disloyal. This is not the usual type of supervision which checks a teacher's competency; it is a system which searches for hidden meanings in a teacher's utterances.

What was the significance of the reference of the art teacher to socialism?

Why was the history teacher so openly hostile to Franco Spain? Who heard overtones of revolution in the English teacher's discussion of the *Grapes of Wrath?* What was behind the praise of Soviet progress in metallurgy in the chemistry class? Was it not "subversive" for the teacher to cast doubt on the wisdom of the venture in Korea?

What happens under this law is typical of what happens in a police state. Teachers are under constant surveillance; their pasts are combed for signs of disloyalty; their utterances are watched for clues to dangerous thoughts. A pall is cast over the classrooms. There can be no real academic freedom in that environment. Where suspicion fills the air and holds scholars in line for fear of their jobs, there can be no exercise of the free intellect. Supineness and dogmatism take the place of inquiry. A "party line"—as dangerous as the "party line" of the Communists—lays hold. It is the "party line" of the orthodox view, of the conventional thought, of the accepted approach. A problem can no longer be pursued with impunity to its edges. Fear stalks the classroom. The teacher is no longer a stimulant to adventurous thinking; she becomes instead a pipe line for safe and sound information. A deadening dogma takes the place of free inquiry. Instruction tends to become sterile; pursuit of knowledge is discouraged; discussion often leaves off where it should begin.

This, I think, is what happens when a censor looks over a teacher's shoulder. This system of spying and surveillance with its accompanying reports and trials cannot go hand in hand with academic freedom. It produces standardized thought, not the pursuit of truth. Yet it was the pursuit of truth which the First Amendment was designed to protect. A system which directly or inevitably has that effect is alien to our system and should be struck down. Its survival is a real threat to our way of life. We need be bold and adventuresome in our thinking to survive. A school system producing students trained as robots threatens to rob a generation of the versatility that has been perhaps our greatest distinction. The Framers knew the danger of dogmatism; they also knew the strength that comes when the mind is free, when ideas may be pursued wherever they lead. We forget these teachings of the First Amendment when we sustain this law.

Of course the school systems of the country need not become cells for Communist activities; and the classrooms need not become forums for propagandizing the Marxist creed. But the guilt of the teacher should turn on overt acts. So long as she is a law abiding citizen, so long as her performance within the public school system meets professional standards, her private life, her political philosophy, her social creed should not be the cause of reprisals against her.

d. Test Oaths

WIEMAN v. UPDEGRAFF

344 US 183 (1952)

[In this case the Court (without Justice Jackson's participation) unanimously held that mere membership in a proscribed organization may not constitutionally serve as a basis for the conclusion that the person is disqualified from teaching in a state college; there must be proof of the teacher's knowledge of the nature and purpose of such organization at the time of his membership. This decision qualifies considerably the guilt by association doctrine that the Court approved in the *Garner Case*.

[Justice Frankfurter's concurring opinion is of special interest for what it says about the principles of academic freedom.]

Mr. Justice Clark delivered the opinion of the Court:

This is an appeal from a decision of the Supreme Court of Oklahoma, . . . upholding the validity of a loyalty oath prescribed by Oklahoma statute for all state officers and employees. . . . Appellants, employed by the state as members of the faculty and staff of Oklahoma Agricultural and Mechanical College, failed, within the thirty days permitted, to take the oath required by the Act. Appellee Updegraff, as a citizen and taxpayer, thereupon brought this suit in the District Court of Oklahoma County to enjoin the necessary state officials from paying further compensation to employees who had not subscribed to the oath. The appellants, who were permitted to intervene, attacked the validity of the Act on the grounds, among others, that it was a bill of attainder; an *ex post facto* law; impaired the obligation of their contracts with the State and violated the Due Process Clause of the Fourteenth Amendment. They also sought a mandatory injunction directing the state officers to pay their salaries regardless of their failure to take the oath. Their objections centered largely on the following clauses of the oath:

. . . That I am not affiliated directly or indirectly . . . with any foreign political agency, party, organization or Government, or with any agency, party, organization, association, or group whatever which has been officially determined by the United States Attorney General or other authorized agency of the United States to be a communist front or subversive organization; . . . that I will take up arms in the defense of the United States in time of War, or National Emergency, if necessary; that within the five (5) years immediately preceding the taking of this oath (or affirmation) I have not been a member of . . . any agency, party, organization, association, or group whatever which has been officially determined by the United States

Attorney General or other authorized public agency of the United States to be a communist front or subversive organization. . . .

The court upheld the Act and enjoined the state officers from making further salary payments to appellants. The Supreme Court of Oklahoma affirmed. . . .

The District Court of Oklahoma County in holding the Act valid concluded that the appellants were compelled to take the oath as written; that the appellants "and each of them, did not take and subscribe to the oath as provided in Section 2 of the Act and wilfully refused to take that oath and by reason thereof the Board of Regents is enjoined from paying them, and their employment is terminated." In affirming, the Supreme Court of Oklahoma held that the phrase of the oath "any foreign political agency, party, organization or Government, or with any agency, party, organization, association, or group whatever which has been officially determined by the United States Attorney General or other authorized agency of the United States to be a communist front or subversive organization" actually "refers to a list or lists of such organizations in existence at the time of the passage of the act which had been prepared by the Attorney General [of the United States] under Governmental directive. Such list or lists are in effect made a part of the oath by reference." On this point the opinion continues: "There is no requirement in the act that an oath be taken of non-membership in organizations not on the list of the Attorney General of the United States at the time of the passage of this act."

We read this part of the highest state court's decision as limiting the organizations proscribed by the Act to those designated on the list or lists of the Attorney General which had been issued prior to the effective date of the Act. . . .

The purpose of the Act, we are told, "was to make loyalty a qualification to hold public office or be employed by the state." . . . During periods of international stress, the extent of legislation with such objectives accentuates our traditional concern about the relation of government to the individual in a free society. The perennial problem of defining that relationship becomes acute when disloyalty is screened by ideological patterns and techniques of disguise that make it difficult to identify. Democratic government is not powerless to meet this threat, but it must do so without infringing the freedoms that are the ultimate values of all democratic living. In the adoption of such means as it believes effective, the legislature is therefore confronted with the problem of balancing its interest in national security with the often conflicting constitutional rights of the individual.

In a series of cases coming here in recent years, we have had occasion to consider legislation aimed at safeguarding the public service from disloyalty. *Garner v. Board of Public Works,* 1951, 341 U.S. 716 . . . ; *Adler v. Board of Education,* 1952, 342 U.S. 485 . . . ; *Gerende v. Board of Supervisors,* 1951, 341 U.S. 56. . . . It is in the context of these decisions that we determine the validity of the oath before us.

Garner involved a Los Angeles ordinance requiring all city employees to swear that they did not advocate the overthrow of the government by unlawful means or belong to organizations with such objectives. The ordinance implemented an earlier charter amendment which disqualified from municipal employment all persons unable to take such an oath truthfully. One of the attacks made on the oath in that case was that it violated due process because its negation was not limited to organizations known by the employee to be within the proscribed class. This argument was rejected because we felt justified in assuming that *scienter* was implicit in each clause of the oath.

Adler also indicated the importance of determining whether a rule of exclusion based on association applies to innocent as well as knowing activity. New York had sought to bar from employment in the public schools persons who advocate, or belong to organizations which advocate, the overthrow of the government by unlawful means. The Feinberg Law directed the New York Board of Regents to make a listing, after notice and hearing, of organizations of the type described. Under § 3022 of the statute, Education Law, McK. Consol. Laws, c. 16, the Regents provided by regulation that membership in a listed organization should be *prima facie* evidence of disqualification for office in the New York public schools. In upholding this legislation, we expressly noted that the New York courts had construed the statute to require knowledge of organizational purpose before the regulation could apply. . . .

The oath in *Gerende* was required of candidates for public office who sought places on a Maryland ballot. On oral argument in that case, the Maryland Attorney General assured us that he would advise the proper state authorities to accept, as complying with the statute, an affidavit stating that the affiant was not engaged in an attempt to overthrow the government by force or violence or knowingly a member of an organization engaged in such an attempt. Because we read an earlier Maryland Court of Appeals' decision as interpreting the statute so that such an affidavit would satisfy its requirements, we affirmed on the basis of this assurance.

We assumed in *Garner,* that if our interpretation of the oath as containing an implicit *scienter* requirement was correct, Los Angeles would give the petitioners who had refused to sign the oath an opportunity to take it as interpreted and resume their employment. But here, with our decision in *Garner* before it, the Oklahoma Supreme Court refused to extend to appellants an opportunity to take the oath. In addition, a petition for rehearing which urged that failure to permit appellants to take the oath as interpreted deprived them of due process was denied. This must be viewed as a holding that knowledge is not a factor under the Oklahoma statute. We are thus brought to the question touched on in *Garner, Adler,* and *Gerende:* whether the due process clause permits a state in attempting to bar disloyal individuals from its employ to exclude persons solely on the basis of organizational membership, regardless of their knowledge concerning the organizations to which they had belonged. For, under the statute before us, the fact of membership alone disqualifies. If the rule be expressed as a presumption of disloyalty, it is a conclusive one.

But membership may be innocent. A state servant may have joined a proscribed organization unaware of its activities and purposes. In recent years, many completely loyal persons have severed organizational ties after learning for the first time of the character of groups to which they had belonged. "They had joined, [but] did not know what it was; they were good, fine young men and women, loyal Americans, but they had been trapped into it—because one of the great weaknesses of all Americans, whether adult or youth, is to join something." At the time of affiliation, a group itself may be innocent, only later coming under the influence of those who would turn it toward illegitimate ends. Conversely, an organization formerly subversive and therefore designated as such may have subsequently freed itself from the influences which originally led to its listing.

There can be no dispute about the consequences visited upon a person excluded from public employment on disloyalty grounds. In the view of the community, the stain is a deep one; indeed, it has become a badge of infamy. Especially is this so in time of cold war and hot emotions when "each man begins to eye his neighbor as a possible enemy." Yet under the Oklahoma Act, the fact of association alone determines disloyalty and disqualification; it matters not whether association existed innocently or knowingly. To thus inhibit individual freedom of movement is to stifle the flow of democratic expression and controversy at one of its chief sources. We hold that the distinction observed between the case at bar and *Garner, Adler* and *Gerende* is decisive. Indiscriminate classification of innocent with knowing activity must fall as an assertion of arbitrary power. The oath offends due process.

But appellee insists that *Adler* and *United Public Workers* v. *Mitchell,* 1947, 330 U.S. 75, . . . are *contra.* We are referred to our statement in *Adler* that persons seeking employment in the New York public schools have "no right to work for the State in the school system

on their own terms. . . . They may work for the school system upon
the reasonable terms laid down by the proper authorities of New York."
. . . To draw from this language the facile generalization that there
is no constitutionally protected right to public employment is to obscure the issue. For, in *United Public Workers*, though we held that
the Federal Government through the Hatch Act could properly bar its
employees from certain types of political activity thought inimical to
the interests of the Civil Service, we cast this holding into perspective
by emphasizing that Congress could not "enact a regulation providing
that no Republican, Jew or Negro shall be appointed to federal office,
or that no federal employee shall attend Mass or take any active part
in missionary work." . . . We need not pause to consider whether an
abstract right to public employment exists. It is sufficient to say that
constitutional protection does extend to the public servant whose exclusion pursuant to a statute is patently arbitrary or discriminatory. . . .

Reversed.

Mr. Justice Black, concurring:

I concur in all the Court says in condemnation of Oklahoma's test oath.
I agree that the State Act prescribing that test oath is fatally offensive to the
due process guarantee of the United States Constitution.

History indicates that individual liberty is intermittently subjected to
extraordinary perils. Even countries dedicated to government by the people
are not free from such cyclical dangers. The first years of our Republic
marked such a period. Enforcement of the Alien and Sedition Laws by zealous patriots who feared ideas made it highly dangerous for people to think,
speak, or write critically about government, its agents, or its policies, either
foreign or domestic. Our constitutional liberties survived the ordeal of this
regrettable period because there were influential men and powerful organized groups bold enough to champion the undiluted right of individuals
to publish and argue for their beliefs however unorthodox or loathsome.
Today however, few individuals and organizations of power and influence
argue that unpopular advocacy has this same wholly unqualified immunity
from governmental interference. For this and other reasons the present period
of fear seems more ominously dangerous to speech and press than was that
of the Alien and Sedition Laws. Suppressive laws and practices are the
fashion. The Oklahoma oath statute is but one manifestation of a national
network of laws aimed at coercing and controlling the minds of men. Test
oaths are notorious tools of tyranny. When used to shackle the mind they
are, or at least they should be, unspeakably odious to a free people. Test oaths
are made still more dangerous when combined with bills of attainder which
like this Oklahoma statute impose pains and penalties for past lawful associations and utterances.

Governments need and have ample power to punish treasonable acts. But it does not follow that they must have a further power to punish thought and speech as distinguished from acts. Our own free society should never forget that laws which stigmatize and penalize thought and speech of the unorthodox have a way of reaching, ensnaring and silencing many more people than at first intended. We must have freedom of speech for all or we will in the long run have it for none but the cringing and the craven. And I cannot too often repeat my belief that the right to speak on matters of public concern must be wholly free or eventually be wholly lost.

It seems self-evident that all speech criticizing government rulers and challenging current beliefs may be dangerous to the *status quo*. With full knowledge of this danger the Framers rested our First Amendment on the premise that the slightest suppression of thought, speech, press, or public assembly is still more dangerous. This means that individuals are guaranteed an undiluted and unequivocal right to express themselves on questions of current public interest. It means that Americans discuss such questions as of right and not on sufferance of legislatures, courts or any other governmental agencies. It means that courts are without power to appraise and penalize utterances upon their notion that these utterances are dangerous. In my view this uncompromising interpretation of the Bill of Rights is the one that must prevail if its freedoms are to be saved. Tyrannical totalitarian governments cannot safely allow their people to speak with complete freedom. I believe with the Framers that our free Government can.

Mr. Justice Douglas concurs in this opinion.

Mr. Justice Frankfurter, whom Mr. Justice Douglas joins, concurring:

The times being what they are, it is appropriate to add a word by way of emphasis to the Court's opinion, which I join.

The case concerns the power of a State to exact from teachers in one of its colleges an oath that they are not, and for the five years immediately preceding the taking of the oath have not been, members of any organization listed by the Attorney General of the United States, prior to the passage of the statute, as "subversive" or "Communist-front." Since the affiliation which must thus be forsworn may well have been for reasons or for purposes as innocent as membership in a club of one of the established political parties, to require such an oath, on pain of a teacher's loss of his position in case of refusal to take the oath, penalizes a teacher for exercising a right of association peculiarly characteristic of our people. . . . Such joining is an exercise of the rights of free speech and free inquiry. By limiting the power of the States to interfere with freedom of speech and freedom of inquiry and freedom of association, the Fourteenth Amendment protects all persons, no matter what their calling. But, in view of the nature of the teacher's relation to the effective exercise of the rights which are safeguarded by the Bill of Rights and by the Fourteenth Amendment, inhibition of freedom of thought, and of action upon thought, in the case of teachers brings the safeguards of those amendments vividly into operation. Such unwarranted inhibition upon the free spirit of teachers affects not only those who, like the appellants, are immediately before the Court. It has an unmistakable tendency to chill that free play of the spirit which all teachers ought especially to cultivate and practice; it makes for caution and timidity in their associations by potential teachers.

The Constitution of the United States does not render the United States or the States impotent to guard their governments against destruction by enemies from within. It does not preclude measures of self-protection against anticipated overt acts of violence. Solid threats to our kind of government— manifestations of purposes that reject argument and the free ballot as the means for bringing about changes and promoting progress—may be met by preventive measures before such threats reach fruition. However, in considering the constitutionality of legislation like the statute before us it is necessary to keep steadfastly in mind what it is that is to be secured. Only thus will it be evident why the Court has found that the Oklahoma law violates those fundamental principles of liberty "which lie at the base of all our civil and political institutions" and as such are imbedded in the due process of law which no State may offend. . . .

That our democracy ultimately rests on public opinion is a platitude of speech but not a commonplace in action. Public opinion is the ultimate reliance of our society only if it be disciplined and responsible. It can be disciplined and responsible only if habits of open-mindedness and of critical inquiry are acquired in the formative years of our citizens. The process of education has naturally enough been the basis of hope for the perdurance of our democracy on the part of all our great leaders, from Thomas Jefferson onwards.

To regard teachers—in our entire educational system, from the primary grades to the university—as the priests of our democracy is therefore not to indulge in hyperbole. It is the special task of teachers to foster those habits of open-mindedness and critical inquiry which alone make for responsible citizens, who, in turn, make possible an enlightened and effective public opinion. Teachers must fulfill their function by precept and practice, by the very atmosphere which they generate; they must be exemplars of open-mindedness and free inquiry. They cannot carry out their noble task if the conditions for the practice of a responsible and critical mind are denied to them. They must have the freedom of responsible inquiry, by thought and action, into the meaning of social and economic ideas, into the checkered history of social and economic dogma. They must be free to sift evanescent doctrine, qualified by time and circumstance, from that restless, enduring process of extending the bounds of understanding and wisdom, to assure which the freedoms of thought, of speech, of inquiry, of worship are guaranteed by the Constitution of the United States against infraction by national or State government.

The functions of educational institutions in our national life and the conditions under which alone they can adequately perform them are at the

basis of these limitations upon State and national power. These functions
and the essential conditions for their effective discharge have been well
described by a leading educator:

Now, a university is a place that is established and will function for
the benefit of society, provided it is a center of independent thought.
It is a center of independent thought and criticism that is created in the
interest of the progress of society, and the one reason that we know
that every totalitarian government must fail is that no totalitarian government is prepared to face the consequences of creating free universities.

It is important for this purpose to attract into the institution men of
the greatest capacity, and to encourage them to exercise their independent judgment.

Education is a kind of continuing dialogue, and a dialogue assumes,
in the nature of the case, different points of view.

The civilization which I work and which, I am sure, every American
is working toward could be called a civilization of the dialogue, where,
instead of shooting one another when you differ, you reason things out
together.

In this dialogue, then, you cannot assume that you are going to have
everybody thinking the same way or feeling the same way. It would
be unprogressive if that happened. The hope of eventual development
would be gone. More than that, of course it would be very boring.

A university, then, is a kind of continuing Socratic conversation on
the highest level for the very best people you can think of, you can
bring together, about the most important questions, and the thing that
you must do to the uttermost possible limits is to guarantee those men
the freedom to think and to express themselves.

Now, the limits on this freedom, the limits on this freedom cannot
be merely prejudice, because although our prejudices might be perfectly satisfactory, the prejudices of our successors, or of those who
are in a position to bring pressure to bear on the institution, might be
subversive in the real sense, subverting the American doctrine of
free thought and free speech. [Statement of Robert M. Hutchins,
Associate Director of the Ford Foundation, November 25, 1952, in
Hearings before the House Select Committee to Investigate Tax-exempt
Foundations and Comparable Organizations, pursuant to H.Res. 561,
82d Cong., 2d Sess.]

SPEISER v. RANDALL

357 US 513 (1958)

[A California statute required anyone who claimed that his property
should be tax-exempt to sign a statement on his tax return that he
does not advocate the unlawful overthrow of government and that he
does not advocate the support of a foreign government against the
United States in event of hostilities. In his opinion for the Court,

Justice Brennan held that the statute denied freedom of speech without the procedural safeguards required by the Due Process Clause of the Fourteenth Amendment, since the statute placed the burden of proof on the taxpayer.

[Justice Black, with Justice Douglas concurring, said that the statute was an unconstitutional tax on belief and expression.

[Justice Douglas, in an opinion in which Justice Black concurred, stated that government has no constitutional right to ask a person questions about his beliefs, that it has a legitimate interest only in his actions, and that a person is constitutionally protected when he advocates ideas that others may despise.

[Justice Clark dissented; Justice Burton concurred in the result; Chief Justice Warren did not participate.

[In the instant case the constitutionality of the statute was challenged by veterans whose tax exemptions were affected by their refusal to file the required statement; in a companion case, *First Unitarian Church* v. *Los Angeles*, 357 US 545 (1958), the statute was challenged by several churches which refused to file the statements in order to secure tax exemption, and the Court applied the reasoning of *Speiser* v. *Randall* to the church case. Justice Douglas, joined by Justice Black, went further, however, and stated that the statute, as applied to churches, violated the freedom of religion guaranteed by the First Amendment.]

Mr. Justice Brennan delivered the opinion of the Court:

The appellants are honorably discharged veterans of World War II who claimed the veterans' property-tax exemption provided by Art. XIII, § 1¼, of the California Constitution. Under California law applicants for such exemption must annually complete a standard form of application and file it with the local assessor. The form was revised in 1954 to add an oath by the applicant: "I do not advocate the overthrow of the Government of the United States or of the State of California by force or violence or other unlawful means, nor advocate the support of a foreign Government against the United States in event of hostilities." Each refused to subscribe the oath and struck it from the form which he executed and filed for the tax year 1954–1955. Each contended that the exaction of the oath as a condition of obtaining a tax exemption was forbidden by the Federal Constitution. The respective assessors denied the exemption solely for the refusal to execute the oath. The Supreme Court of California sustained the assessors' actions against the appellants' claims of constitutional invalidity. We noted probable jurisdiction of the appeals. . . .

Article XX, § 19, of the California Constitution, adopted at the general election of November 4, 1952, provides as follows:

Notwithstanding any other provision of this Constitution, no person or organization which advocates the overthrow of the Government of the United States or the State by force or violence or other unlawful means or who advocates the support of a foreign government against the United States in the event of hostilities shall: . . .

(b) Receive any exemption from any tax imposed by this State or any county, city or county, city, district, political subdivision, authority, board, bureau, commission or other public agency of this State.

The Legislature shall enact such laws as may be necessary to enforce the provisions of this section.

To effectuate this constitutional amendment the California Legislature enacted § 32 of the Revenue and Taxation Code, which required the claimant, as a prerequisite to qualification for any property-tax exemption, to sign a statement on his tax return declaring that he does not engage in the activities described on the constitutional amendment. The California Supreme Court held that this declaration, like other statements required of those filing tax returns, was designed to relieve the tax assessor of "the burden . . . of ascertaining the facts with reference to tax exemption claimants." . . . The declaration, while intended to provide a means of determining whether a claimant qualifies for the exemption under the constitutional amendment, is not conclusive evidence of eligibility. The assessor has the duty of investigating the facts underlying all tax liabilities and is empowered by § 454 of the Code to subpoena taxpayers for the purpose of questioning them about statements they have furnished. If the assessor believes that the claimant is not qualified in any respect, he may deny the exemption and require the claimant, on judicial review, to prove the incorrectness of the determination. In other words, the factual determination whether the taxpayer is eligible for the exemption under the constitutional amendment is made in precisely the same manner as the determination of any other fact bearing on tax liability.

The appellants attack these provisions, *inter alia*, as denying them freedom of speech without the procedural safeguards required by the Due Process Clause of the Fourteenth Amendment.

I.

It cannot be gainsaid that a discriminatory denial of a tax exemption for engaging in speech is a limitation on free speech. The Supreme Court of California recognized that these provisions were limitations on speech but concluded that "by no standard can the infringement upon freedom of speech imposed by Section 19 of article XX be deemed a substantial one." . . . It is settled that speech can be effectively limited by the exercise of the taxing power. *Grosjean* v. *American Press Co.*, 297 US 233. To deny an exemption to claimants who engage in certain forms of speech is in effect to penalize them for such speech. Its deterrent effect is the same as if the State were to fine them for this speech. The appellees are plainly mistaken in their argument that, because a tax exemption is a "privilege" or "bounty," its denial may not infringe speech. This contention did not prevail before the California courts, which recognized that conditions imposed upon the granting of privileges or gratuities must be "reasonable." It has been said that Congress may not by withdrawal of mailing privileges place limitations upon the freedom of speech which if directly attempted would be unconstitutional. See *Hannegan* v. *Esquire, Inc.*, 327 US 146; cf. *Milwaukee Publishing Co.* v. *Burleson*, 255 US 407 (Brandeis, J., dissenting). This Court has similarly rejected the contention that speech was not abridged when the sole restraint on its exercise was withdrawal of the opportunity to invoke the facilities of the National Labor Relations Board, *American Communications Assn.* v. *Douds*, 339 US 382, or the opportunity for public employment, *Wieman* v. *Updegraff*, 344 US 183. So here, the denial of a tax exemption for engaging in certain speech necessarily will have the effect of coercing the claimants to refrain from the proscribed speech. The denial is "frankly aimed at the suppression of dangerous ideas." . . .

II.

But the question remains whether California has chosen a fair method for determining when a claimant is a member of that class to which the California court has said the constitutional and statutory provisions extend. When we deal with the complex of strands in the web of freedoms which make up free speech, the operation and effect of the method by which speech is sought to be restrained must be subjected to close analysis and critical judgment in the light of the particular circumstances to which it is applied. . . .

To experienced lawyers it is commonplace that the outcome of a lawsuit—and hence the vindication of legal rights—depends more often on how the fact-finder appraises the facts than on a disputed construction of a statute or interpretation of a line of precedents. Thus the procedures by which the facts of the case are determined assume an importance fully as great as the validity of the substantive rule of law to be applied. And the more important the rights at stake the more important must be the procedural safeguards surrounding those rights. . . . When the State undertakes to restrain unlawful advocacy it must provide procedures which are adequate to safeguard against infringement of constitutionally protected rights—rights which we value most highly and which are essential to the workings of a free society. Moreover, since only considerations of the greatest urgency can justify restrictions on speech, and since the validity of a restraint on speech in each case depends on careful analysis of the particular circumstances, . . . the procedures by which the facts of the case are adjudicated are of special importance and the validity of the restraint may turn on the safeguards which they afford. . . . It becomes essential, therefore, to scrutinize the procedures by which California has sought to restrain speech.

The principal feature of the California procedure, as the appellees themselves point out, is that the appellants, "as taxpayers under state law, have the affirmative burden of proof, in Court as well as before the Assessor. . . . [I]t is their burden to show that they are proper persons to qualify under the self-executing constitutional provision for the tax exemption in question—i.e., that they are not persons who advocate the overthrow of the government of the United States or the State by force or violence or other unlawful means or who advocate the support of a foreign government against the United States in the event of hostilities. . . . [T]he burden is on *them* to produce evidence justifying their claim of exemption." Not only does the initial burden of bringing forth proof of nonadvocacy rest on the taxpayer, but throughout the judicial and administrative proceedings the burden lies on the taxpayer of persuading the assessor, or the court, that he falls outside the class denied the tax exemption. The declaration required by § 32 is but a part of the probative process by which the State seeks to determine which taxpayers fall into the proscribed category. Thus the declaration cannot be regarded as having such independent significance that failure to sign it precludes review of the validity of the procedure of which it is a part. . . . The question for decision, therefore, is whether this allocation of the burden of proof, on an issue concerning freedom of speech, falls short of the requirements of due process.

It is of course within the power of the State to regulate procedures under which its laws are carried out, including the burden of producing evidence and the burden of persuasion, "unless in so doing it offends some principle of justice so rooted in the traditions and conscience of our people as to be ranked as fundamental." . . . "[O]f course the legislature may go a good way in raising . . . [presumptions] or in changing the burden of proof, but there are limits. . . . [I]t is not within the province of a legislature to declare an individual guilty or presumptively guilty of a crime." . . . The legislature cannot "place upon all defendants in criminal cases the burden of going forward with the evidence. . . . [It cannot] validly command that the finding of an indictment, or mere proof of the identity of the accused, should create a presumption of the existence of all the facts essential to guilt. This is not permissible." . . . Of course, the burden of going forward with the evidence at some stages of a criminal trial may be placed on the defendant, but only after the State has "proved enough to make it just for the defendant to be required to repel what has been proved with excuse or explanation, or at least that upon a balancing of convenience or of the opportunities for knowledge the shifting of the burden will be found to be an aid to the accuser without subjecting the accused to hardship or oppression." . . . In civil cases too this Court has struck down state statutes unfairly shifting the burden of proof. . . .

It is true that due process may not always compel the full formalities of a criminal prosecution before criminal advocacy can be suppressed or deterred, but it is clear that the State which attempts to do so must provide procedures amply adequate to safeguard against invasion speech which the Constitution protects. . . . It is, of course, familiar practice in the administration of a tax program for the taxpayer to carry the burden of introducing evidence to rebut the determination of the collector. . . . But while the fairness of placing the burden of proof on the taxpayer in most circumstances is recognized, this Court has not hesitated to declare a summary tax-collection procedure a violation of due process when the purported tax was shown to be in reality a penalty for a crime. . . . The underlying rationale of these cases is that where a person is to suffer a penalty for a crime he is entitled to greater procedural safeguards than when only the amount of his tax liability is in issue. Similarly it does not follow that because only a tax liability is here involved, the ordinary tax assessment procedures are adequate when applied to penalize speech.

It is true that in the present case the appellees purport to do no more than compute the amount of the taxpayer's liability in accordance with the usual procedures, but in fact they have undertaken to determine whether certain speech falls within a class which constitutionally may be curtailed. As cases decided in this Court have abundantly demonstrated, the line between speech unconditionally guaranteed and speech which may legitimately be regulated, suppressed, or punished is finely drawn. . . . The separation of legitimate from illegitimate speech calls for more sensitive tools than California has supplied. In all kinds of litigation it is plain that where the burden of proof lies may be decisive of the outcome. . . . There is always in litigation a margin of error, representing error in factfinding, which both parties must take into account. Where one party has at stake an interest of transcending value—as a criminal defendant his liberty—this margin of error is reduced as to him by the process of placing on the other party the burden of producing a sufficiency of proof in the first instance, and of persuading the factfinder at the conclusion of the trial of his guilt beyond a reasonable doubt. Due process commands that no man shall lose his liberty unless the Government has borne the burden of producing the evidence and convincing the factfinder of his guilt. . . . Where the transcendent value of speech is involved, due process certainly requires in the circumstances of this case that the State bear the burden of persuasion to show that the appellants engaged in criminal speech. . . .

The vice of the present procedure is that, where particular speech falls close to the line separating the lawful and the unlawful, the possibility of mistaken factfinding—inherent in all litigation—will create the danger that the legitimate utterance will be penalized. The man who knows that he must bring forth proof and persuade another of the lawfulness of his conduct necessarily must steer far wider of the unlawful zone, than if the State must bear these burdens. This is especially to be feared when the complexity of the proofs and the generality of the standards applied . . . provide but shifting sands on which the litigant must maintain his position. How can a claimant whose declaration is rejected possibly sustain the burden of proving the negative of these complex factual elements? In practical operation, therefore, this procedural advice must necessarily produce a result which the State could not command directly. It can only result in a deterrence of speech which the Constitution makes free. "It is apparent that a constitutional prohibition cannot be transgressed indirectly by the creation of a statutory presumption any more than it can be violated by direct enactment. The power to create presumptions is not a means of escape from constitutional restrictions." *Bailey* v. *Alabama,* 219 US 219.

The appellees, in controverting this position, rely on cases in which this Court has sustained the validity of loyalty oaths required of public employees, *Garner* v. *Board of Public Works,* 341 US 716, candidates for public office, *Gerende* v. *Board of Supervisors,* 341 US 56, and officers of labor unions, *American Communications Assn.* v. *Douds, supra.* In these cases, however, there was no attempt directly to control speech but rather to protect, from an evil shown to be grave, some interest clearly within the sphere of governmental concern. The purpose of the legislation sustained in the *Douds* case, the Court found, was to minimize the danger of political strikes disruptive of interstate commerce by discouraging labor unions from electing Communist Party members to union office. While the Court recognized that the necessary effect of the legislation was to discourage the exercise of rights protected by the First Amendment, this consequence was said to be only indirect. The congressional purpose was to achieve an objective other than restraint on speech. Only the method of achieving this end touched on protected rights and that only tangentially. The evil at which Congress had attempted to strike in that case was thought sufficiently grave to justify limited infringement of political rights. Similar considerations governed the other cases. Each case concerned a limited class of persons in or aspiring to public positions by virtue of which they could, if evilly motivated, create serious danger to the public safety. The principal aim of those statutes was not to penalize political beliefs but to deny positions to persons supposed to be dangerous because the position might be misused to the detriment of the public. The present legislation, however, can have no such justification. It purports to deal directly with speech and the expression of political ideas. "Encouragement to loyalty to our institutions . . . [is a doctrine] which the State has plainly promulgated and intends to foster." 48 Cal. 2d, at 439, 311 P. 2d, at 520. The State argues that veterans as a class occupy a position of special trust and influence in the community, and therefore any veteran who engages in the proscribed advocacy constitutes a special danger to the State. But while a union official or public employee may be deprived of his position and thereby removed from the place of special danger, the State is powerless to erase the service which the veteran has rendered his country; though he be denied a tax exemption, he remains a veteran. The State, consequently, can act against the veteran only as it can act against any other citizen, by imposing penalties to deter the unlawful conduct.

Moreover, the oaths required in those cases performed a very different function from the declaration in issue here. In the earlier cases it appears that the loyalty oath, once signed, became conclusive evidence of the facts attested so far as the right to office was concerned. If the person took the oath he retained his position. The oath was not part of a device to shift to the officeholder the burden of proving his right to retain his position. The signer, of course, could be prosecuted for perjury, but only in accordance with the strict procedural safeguards surrounding such criminal prosecutions. In the present case, however, it is clear that the declaration may be accepted or rejected on the basis of incompetent information or no information at all. It is only a step in a process throughout which the taxpayer must bear the burden of proof.

Believing that the principles of those cases have no application here, we hold that when the constitutional right to speak is sought to be deterred by a State's general taxing program due process demands that the speech be unencumbered until the State comes forward with sufficient proof to justify its inhibition. The State clearly has no such compelling interest at stake as to justify a short-cut procedure which must inevitably result in suppressing protected speech. Accordingly, though the validity of § 19 of Art. XX of the State Constitution be conceded *arguendo,* its enforcement through procedures which place the burdens of proof and persuasion on the taxpayer is a violation of due process. It follows from this that appellants could not be required to execute the declaration as a condition for obtaining a tax exemption or as a condition for the assessor proceeding further in determining whether they were entitled to such an exemption. Since the entire statutory procedure, by placing the burden of proof on the claimants, violated the requirements of due process, appellants were not obliged to take the first step in such a procedure.

The judgments are reversed and the causes are remanded for further proceedings not inconsistent with this opinion.

KONIGSBERG *v.* STATE BAR OF CALIFORNIA
366 US 36 (1961)

[Petitioner was excluded from practice of the law in California because he repeatedly refused to answer questions as to his membership in the Communist Party put to him by a bar committee investigating his qualifications for admission to the state bar. His exclusion by the state was upheld by a 5-to-4 vote in the Supreme Court.

[Justice Black (with Chief Justice Warren and Justice Douglas joining) dissented, saying that the denial of Konigsberg's admission to the bar violated his rights of free speech and association, and that the decision of the majority was inconsistent with *Speiser* v. *Randall, supra.* Justice Brennan, with Chief Justice Warren joining, dissented solely in reliance on the *Speiser Case.*]

Mr. Justice Harlan delivered the opinion of the Court:

This case, involving California's second rejection of petitioner's application for admission to the state bar, is a sequel to *Konigsberg* v. *State Bar of California,* 353 U.S. 252, in which this Court reversed the State's initial refusal of his application.

Under California law the State Supreme Court may admit to the practice of law any applicant whose qualifications have been certified to it by the California Committee of Bar Examiners. . . . To qualify for certification an applicant must, among other things, be of "good moral character," and no person may be certified "who advocates the overthrow of the Government of the United States or of this State by force, violence, or other unconstitutional means. . . ." The Committee is empowered and required to ascertain the qualifications of all candidates. Under rules prescribed by the Board of Governors of the State Bar, an applicant before the Committee has "the burden of proving that he is possessed of good moral character, of removing any and all reasonable suspicion of moral unfitness, and that he is entitled to the high regard and confidence of the public." Any applicant denied certification may have the Committee's action reviewed by the State Supreme Court.

In 1953 petitioner, having successfully passed the California bar examinations, applied for certification for bar membership. The Committee, after interrogating Konigsberg and receiving considerable evidence as to his qualifications, declined to certify him on the ground that he had failed to meet the burden of proving his eligibility under the two statutory requirements relating to good moral character and non-advocacy of violent overthrow. That determination centered largely around Konigsberg's repeated refusals to answer Committee questions as to his present or past membership in the Communist Party. The California Supreme Court denied review without opinion. . . .

On certiorari this Court, after reviewing the record, held the state determination to have been without rational support in the evidence and therefore offensive to the Due Process Clause of the Fourteenth Amendment. . . . At the same time the Court declined to decide whether Konigsberg's refusals to answer could constitutionally afford "an independent ground for exclusion from the Bar," considering that such an issue was not before it. The case was remanded to the State Supreme Court "for further proceedings not inconsistent with this opinion."

On remand petitioner moved the California Supreme Court for immediate admission to the bar. The Court vacated its previous order denying review and referred the matter to the Bar Committee for further consideration. At the ensuing Committee hearings Konigsberg introduced further evidence as to his good moral character (none of which was rebutted), reiterated unequivocally his disbelief in violent overthrow, and stated that he had never knowingly been a member of any organization which advocated such action. He persisted, however, in his refusals to answer any questions relating to his membership in the Communist Party. The Committee again declined to certify him, this time on the ground that his refusals to answer had obstructed a full investigation into his qualifications. The California Supreme Court, by a divided vote, refused review, and also denied Konigsberg's motion for direct admission to practice. We again brought the case here.

Petitioner's contentions in this Court in support of reversal of the California Supreme Court's order are reducible to three propositions: (1) the State's action was inconsistent with this Court's decision in the earlier *Konigsberg* case; (2) assuming the Committee's inquiries into Konigsberg's possible Communist Party membership were permissible, it was unconstitutionally arbitrary for the State to deny him admission because of his refusals to answer; and (3) in any event, Konigsberg was constitutionally justified in refusing to answer these questions.

I.

Consideration of petitioner's contentions as to the effect of this Court's decision in the former *Konigsberg* case requires that there be kept clearly in mind what is entailed in California's rule, comparable to that in many States, that an applicant for admission to the bar bears the burden of proof of "good moral character"—a requirement whose validity is not, nor could well be, drawn in question here.

Under such a rule an applicant must initially furnish enough evidence of good character to make a prima facie case. The examining Committee then has the opportunity to rebut that showing with evidence of bad character. Such evidence may result from the Committee's own independent investigation, from an applicant's responses to questions on his application form, or from Committee interrogation of the applicant himself. This interrogation may well be of decisive importance for, as all familiar with bar admission proceedings know, exclusion of unworthy candidates frequently depends upon the thoroughness of the Committee's questioning, revealing as it may infirmities in an otherwise satisfactory showing on his part. This is especially so where a bar committee, as is not infrequently the case, has no means of conducting an independent investigation of its own into an applicant's qualifications. If at the conclusion of the proceedings the evidence of good character and that of bad character are found in even balance, the State may refuse admission to the applicant, just as in an ordinary suit a plaintiff may fail in his case because he has not met his burden of proof.

In the first *Konigsberg* case this Court was concerned solely with the question whether the balance between the favorable and unfavorable evidence as to Konigsberg's qualifications had been struck in accordance with the requirements of due process. It was there held, first, that

Konigsberg had made out a prima facie case of good character and of nonadvocacy of violent overthrow, and, second, that the other evidence in the record could not, even with the aid of all reasonable inferences flowing therefrom, cast such doubts upon petitioner's prima facie case as to justify any finding other than that these two California qualification requirements had been satisfied. In assessing the significance of Konigsberg's refusal to answer questions as to Communist Party membership, the Court dealt only with the fact that this refusal could not provide any reasonable indication of a character not meeting these two standards for admission. The Court did not consider, but reserved for later decision, all questions as to the permissibility of the State treating Konigsberg's refusal to answer as a ground for exclusion, not because it was evidence from which substantive conclusions might be drawn, but because the refusal had thwarted a full investigation into his qualifications. The State now asserts that ground for exclusion, an issue that is not foreclosed by anything in this Court's earlier opinion which decided a quite different question.

It is equally clear that the State's ordering of the rehearing which led to petitioner's exclusion manifested no disrespect of the effect of the mandate in that case, which expressly left the matter open for further state proceedings "not inconsistent with" the Court's opinion. There is no basis for any suggestion that the State in so proceeding has adopted unusual or discriminatory procedures to avoid the normal consequences of this Court's earlier determination. In its earlier proceeding, the California Bar Committee may have found further investigation and questioning of petitioner unnecessary when, in its view, the applicant's prima facie case of qualifications had been sufficiently rebutted by evidence already in the record. While in its former opinion this Court held that the State could not constitutionally so conclude, it did not undertake to preclude the state agency from asking any questions or from conducting any investigation that it might have thought necessary had it known that the basis of its then decision would be overturned. In recalling Konigsberg for further testimony, the Committee did only what this Court has consistently held that federal administrative tribunals may do on remand after a reviewing court has set aside agency orders as unsupported by requisite findings of fact. . . .

In the absence of the slightest indication of any purpose on the part of the State to evade the Court's prior decision, principles of finality protecting the parties to this state litigation are, within broad limits of fundamental fairness, solely the concern of California law. Such limits are broad even in a criminal case, . . . In this instance they certainly have not been transgressed by the State merely taking further action in this essentially administrative type of proceeding.

II.

We think it clear that the Fourteenth Amendment's protection against arbitrary state action does not forbid a State from denying admission to a bar applicant so long as he refuses to provide unprivileged answers to questions having a substantial relevance to his qualifications. An investigation of this character, like a civil suit, requires procedural as well as substantive rules. It is surely not doubtful that a State could validly adopt an administrative rule analogous to Rule 37(b) of the Federal Rules of Civil Procedure, 28 U.S.C.A., which provides that refusal, after due warning, to answer relevant questions may result in "the matters regarding which the questions were asked" being considered for the purposes of the proceeding to be answered in a way unfavorable to the refusing party, or even that such refusal may result in "dismissing the action or proceeding" of the party asking affirmative relief.

The state procedural rule involved here is a less broad one, for all that California has in effect said is that in cases where, on matters material to an applicant's qualifications, there are gaps in the evidence presented by him which the agency charged with certification considers should be filled in the appropriate exercise of its responsibilities, an applicant will not be admitted to practice unless and until he co-operates with the agency's efforts to fill those gaps. The fact that this rule finds its source in the supervisory powers of the California Supreme Court over admissions to the bar, rather than in legislation, is not constitutionally significant. . . . Nor in the absence of a showing of arbitrary or discriminatory application in a particular case, is it a matter of federal concern whether such a rule requires the rejection of all applicants refusing to answer material questions, or only in instances where the examining committee deems that a refusal has materially obstructed its investigation. . . .

In the context of the entire record of these proceedings, the application of the California rule in this instance cannot be said to be arbitrary or discriminatory. In the first *Konigsberg* case this Court held that neither the somewhat weak, but uncontradicted testimony, that petitioner had been a Communist Party member in 1941, nor his refusal to answer questions relating to Party membership, could rationally support any substantive adverse inferences as to petitioner's character qualifications. That was not to say, however, that these factors, singly or together, could not be regarded as leaving the investigatory record in sufficient uncertainty as constitutionally to permit application of the procedural rule which the State has now invoked, provided that Konigsberg had been first given due warning of the consequences of his continuing refusal to respond to the Committee's questions.

It is no answer to say that petitioner has made out a prima facie case of qualifications, for this is precisely the posture of a proceeding in which the Committee's right to examine and cross-examine becomes significant. Assuming, as we do for the moment, that there is no privilege here to refuse to answer, petitioner could no more insist that his prima facie case makes improper further questioning of him than he could insist that such circumstance made improper the introduction of other forms of rebutting evidence.

We likewise regard as untenable petitioner's contentions that the questions as to Communist Party membership were made irrelevant either by the fact that bare, innocent membership is not a ground of disqualification or by petitioner's willingness to answer such ultimate questions as whether he himself believed in violent overthrow or knowingly belonged to an organization advocating violent overthrow. The Committee Chairman's answer to the former contention was entirely correct:

If you answered the question, for example, that you had been a member of the Communist Party during some period since 1951 or that you were presently a member of the Communist Party, the Committee would then be in a position to ask you what acts you engaged in to carry out the functions and purposes of that party, what the aims and purposes of the party were, to your knowledge, and questions of that type. You see by failing to answer the initial question there certainly is no basis and no opportunity for us to investigate with respect to the other matters to which the initial question might very well be considered preliminary.

And the explanation given to petitioner's counsel by another Committee member as to why Konigsberg's testimony about ultimate facts was not dispositive was also sound:

Mr. Mosk, you realize that if Mr. Konigsberg had answered the question that he refused to answer, an entirely new area of investigation might be opened up, and this Committee might be able to ascertain from Mr. Konigsberg that perhaps he is now and for many years past has been an active member of the Communist Party, and from finding out who his associates were in that enterprise we might discover that he does advocate the overthrow of this government by force and violence. I am not saying that he would do that, but it is a possibility, and we don't have to take any witness' testimony as precluding us from trying to discover if he is telling the truth. That is the point.

There remains the question as to whether Konigsberg was adequately warned of the consequences of his refusal to answer. At the outset of the renewed hearings the Chairman of the Committee stated:

As a result of our two-fold purpose [to investigate and reach determinations], particularly our function of investigation, we believe it will be necessary for you, Mr. Konigsberg, to answer our material questions or our investigation will be obstructed. We would not then as a result be able to certify you for admission.

After petitioner had refused to answer questions on Communist Party membership, the Chairman asked:

Mr. Konigsberg, I think you will recall that I initially advised you a failure to answer our material questions would obstruct our investigation and result in our failure to certify you. With this in mind do you wish to answer any of the questions which you heretofore up to now have refused to answer?

At the conclusion of the proceeding another Committee member stated:

I would like to make this statement so that there will be no misunderstanding on the part of any court that may review this record in the future, that I feel that as a member of the Committee that the failure of Mr. Konigsberg to answer the question as to whether or not he is now a member of the Communist Party is an obstruction of the function of this Committee, not a frustration if that word has been used. I think it would be an obstruction. There are phases of his moral character that we haven't been able to investigate simply because we have been stopped at this point, and I for one could not certify to the Supreme Court that he was a proper person to be admitted to practice law in this State until he answers the question about his Communist affiliation.

The record thus leaves no room for doubt on the score of "warning," and petitioner does not indeed contend to the contrary.

III.

Finally, petitioner argues that, in any event, he was privileged not to respond to questions dealing with Communist Party membership because they unconstitutionally impinged upon rights of free speech and association protected by the Fourteenth Amendment.

At the outset we reject the view that freedom of speech and association . . . as protected by the First and Fourteenth Amendments, are "absolutes," not only in the undoubted sense that where the constitutional protection exists it must prevail, but also in the sense that the scope of that protection must be gathered solely from a literal reading of the First Amendment. Throughout its history this Court has consistently recognized at least two ways in which constitutionally protected freedom of speech is narrower than an unlimited license to talk. On the one hand certain forms of speech, or speech in certain contexts, have been considered outside the scope of constitutional protection. . . . On the other hand, general regulatory statutes, not intended to control the content of speech but incidentally limiting its unfettered exercise, have not been regarded as the type of law the First or Fourteenth Amendments forbade Congress or the States to pass, when they have been found justified by subordinating valid governmental interests, a prerequisite to constitutionality which has necessarily involved a weighing of the governmental interest involved. . . . Whenever, in such a context, these constitutional protections are asserted against the exercise of valid governmental powers a reconciliation must be effected, and that perforce requires an appropriate weighing of the respective interests involved. . . . With more particular reference to the present context of a state decision as to character qualifications, it is difficult, indeed, to imagine a view of the constitutional protections of speech and association which would automatically and without consideration of the extent of the deterrence of speech and association and of the importance of the state function, exclude all reference to prior speech or association on such issues as character, purpose, credibility, or intent. On the basis of these considerations we now judge petitioner's contentions in the present case.

Petitioner does not challenge the constitutionality of § 6064.1 of the California Business and Professions Code forbidding certification for admission to practice of those advocating the violent overthrow of government. It would indeed be difficult to argue that a belief, firm enough to be carried over into advocacy, in the use of illegal means to change the form of the State or Federal Government is an unimportant consideration in determining the fitness of applicants for membership in a profession in whose hands so largely lies the safekeeping of this country's legal and political institutions. . . . Nor is the state interest in this respect insubstantially related to the right which California claims to inquire about Communist Party membership. This Court has long since recognized the legitimacy of a statutory finding that membership in the Communist Party is not unrelated to the danger of use for such illegal ends of powers given for limited purposes. . . .

As regards the questioning of public employees relative to Communist Party membership it has already been held that the interest in not subjecting speech and association to the deterrence of subsequent disclosure is outweighed by the State's interest in ascertaining the fitness of the employee for the post he holds, and hence that such questioning does not infringe constitutional protections. . . . With respect to this same question of Communist Party membership, we regard the State's interest in having lawyers who are devoted to the law in its broadest sense, including not only its substantive provisions, but also its procedures for orderly change, as clearly sufficient to outweigh the minimal effect upon free association occasioned by compulsory disclosure in the circumstances here presented.

There is here no likelihood that deterrence of association may result from foreseeable private action, . . . for bar committee interrogations such as this are conducted in private. . . . Nor is there the possibility that the State may be afforded the opportunity for imposing undetectable arbitrary consequences upon protected association, . . . for a bar applicant's exclusion by reason of Communist Party membership is subject to judicial review, including ultimate review by this Court, should it appear that such exclusion has rested on substantive or procedural factors that do not comport with the Federal constitution. . . . In these circumstances it is difficult indeed to perceive any solid basis for a claim of unconstitutional intrusion into rights assured by the Fourteenth Amendment.

If this were all there was to petitioner's claim of a privilege to refuse to answer, we would regard the *Beilan* [v. *Bd. of Public Education*, 357 U.S. 399] case as controlling. There is, however, a further aspect of the matter. In *Speiser* v. *Randall*, 357 U.S. 513, we held unconstitutional a state procedural rule that in order to obtain an exemption a taxpayer must bear the burden of proof, including both the burdens of establishing a prima facie case and of ultimate persuasion, that he did not advocate the violent overthrow of government. We said:

> The vice of the present procedure is that, where particular speech falls close to the line separating the lawful and the unlawful, the possibility of mistaken factfinding—inherent in all litigation—will create the danger that the legitimate utterance will be penalized. The man who knows that he must bring forth proof and persuade another of the lawfulness of his conduct necessarily must steer far wider of the unlawful zone than if the State must bear these burdens. This is especially to be feared when the complexity of the proofs and the generality of the standards applied, cf. *Dennis* v. *United States, supra,* provide but shifting sands on which the litigant must maintain his position. How can a claimant whose declaration is rejected possibly sustain the burden of proving the negative of these complex factual elements? In practical operation, therefore, this procedural device must necessarily produce a result which the State could not command directly. It can only result in a deterrence of speech which the Constitution makes free.

It would be a sufficient answer to any suggestion of the applicability of that holding to the present proceeding to observe that *Speiser* was explicitly limited so as not to reach cases where, as here, there is no showing of an intent to penalize political beliefs. . . .

But there are also additional factors making the rationale of *Speiser* inapplicable to the case before us. There is no unequivocal indication that California in this proceeding has placed upon petitioner the burden of proof of nonadvocacy of violent overthrow, as distinguished from its other requirement of "good moral character." All it has presently required is an applicant's cooperation with the Committee's search for evidence of forbidden advocacy. Petitioner has been denied admission to the California bar for obstructing the Committee in the performance of its necessary functions of examination and cross-examination, a ruling which indeed presupposes that the burden of producing substantial evidence on the issue of advocacy was not upon petitioner but upon the Committee. Requiring a defendant in a civil proceeding to testify or to submit to discovery has never been thought to shift the burden of proof to him. Moreover, when this Court has allowed a State to comment upon a criminal defendant's failure to testify it has been careful to note that this does not result in placing upon him the burden of proving his innocence. . . .

In contrast to our knowledge with respect to the burden of establishing a prima facie case, we do not now know where under California law, would rest the ultimate burden of persuasion on the issue of advocacy of violent overthrow. But it is for the Supreme Court of California first to decide this question. Only if and when that burden is placed by the State upon a bar applicant can there be drawn in question the distinction made in the *Speiser* case between penalizing statutes and those merely denying access to positions where unfitness may lead to the abuse of state-given powers or privileges. The issue is not now before us.

Thus as matters now stand, there is nothing involved here which is contrary to the reasoning of *Speiser,* for despite compelled testimony the prospective bar applicant need not "steer far wider of the unlawful zone" for fear of mistaken judgment or fact finding declaring unlawful speech which is in fact protected by the Constitution. This is so as to the ultimate burden of persuasion for, notwithstanding his duty to testify, the loss resulting from a failure of proof may, for all we now know, still fall upon the State. It is likewise so as to the initial burden of production, for there is no indication in the proceeding on rehearing of petitioner's application that the Bar Committee expected petitioner to "sustain the burden of proving the negative" of those complex factual elements which amount to forbidden advocacy of violent overthrow. To the contrary it is clear that the Committee had assumed the burden of proving the affirmative of those elements, but was prevented from attempting to discharge that burden by petitioner's refusal to answer relevant questions.

The judgment of the Supreme Court of California is affirmed.

CRAMP v. BOARD OF PUBLIC INSTRUCTION
368 US 278 (1961)

[A Florida statute required each public employee to execute an oath that he has never lent his "aid, support, advice, counsel or influence" to the Communist Party. Failure to subscribe to the oath was to result in immediate discharge. The Supreme Court unanimously held the statute unconstitutional because its terms were so vague that to prescribe a penalty for their violation would constitute a denial of due process of law.]

Mr. Justice Stewart delivered the opinion of the Court:

A Florida statute requires each employee of the State or its subdivisions to execute a written oath in which he must swear that, among other things, he has never lent his "aid, support, advice, counsel or influence to the Communist Party." Failure to subscribe to this oath results under the law in the employee's immediate discharge.

After the appellant had been employed for more than nine years as a public school teacher in Orange County, Florida, it was discovered in 1959 that he had never been required to execute this statutory oath. When requested to do so he refused. He then brought an action in the state circuit court asking for a judgment declaring the oath requirement unconstitutional, and for an injunction forbidding the appellee, the Orange County Board of Public Instruction, from requiring him to execute the oath and from discharging him for his failure to do so. The circuit court held the statute valid and denied the prayer for an injunction. The Supreme Court of Florida affirmed, and this is an appeal from the judgment of affirmance. Having doubt as to the jurisdiction of this Court, we postponed decision of that preliminary question until the hearing of the appeal on the merits. . . .

The Florida Supreme Court first considered the provisions of this legislative oath in *State* v. *Diez*, 97 So. 2d 105, a case involving the validity of an indictment for perjury. There the court upheld the constitutionality of the legislation only upon finding it ". . . inherent in the law that when one takes the oath that he has not lent aid, advice, counsel and the like to the Communist Party, he is representing under oath that he has not done so knowingly." In the present case the Florida court adhered to this construction of the statute, characterizing what has been said in *Diez* as a ruling that "the element of scienter was implicit in each of the requirements of the statute." We accept without question this view of the statute's meaning, as of course we must. This authoritative interpretation by the Florida Supreme Court "puts these words in the statute as definitely as if it had been so amended by the legislature." . . .

The issue to be decided, then, is whether a State can constitutionally compel those in its service to swear that they have never "knowingly lent their aid, support, advice, counsel, or influence to the Communist Party." More precisely, can Florida consistently with the Due Process Clause of the Fourteenth Amendment force an employee either to take such an oath, at the risk of subsequent prosecution for perjury, or face immediate dismissal from public service?

The provision of the oath here in question, it is to be noted, says nothing of advocacy of violent overthrow of state or federal government. It says nothing of membership or affiliation with the Communist Party, past or present. The provision is completely lacking in these or any other terms susceptible of objective measurement. Those who take this oath must swear, rather, that they have not in the unending past ever knowingly lent their "aid," or "support," or "advice," or "counsel" or "influence" to the Communist Party. What do these phrases mean? In the not too distant past Communist Party candidates appeared regularly and legally on the ballot in many state and local elections. Elsewhere the Communist Party has on occasion endorsed or supported candidates nominated by others. Could one who had ever cast his vote for such a candidate safely subscribe to this legislative oath? Could a lawyer who had ever represented the Communist Party or its members swear with either confidence or honesty that he had never knowingly lent his "counsel" to the Party? Could a journalist who had ever defended the constitutional rights of the Communist Party conscientiously take an oath that he had never lent the Party his "support?" Indeed, could anyone honestly subscribe to this oath who had ever supported any cause with contemporaneous knowledge that the Communist Party also supported it?

The very absurdity of these possibilities brings into focus the extraordinary ambiguity of the statutory language. With such vagaries in mind, it is not unrealistic to suggest that the compulsion of this oath provision might weigh most heavily upon those whose conscientious scruples were the most sensitive. While it is perhaps fanciful to suppose that a perjury prosecution would ever be instituted for past conduct of the kind suggested, it requires no strain of the imagination to envision the possibility of prosecution for other types of equally guiltless knowing behaviour. It would be blinking reality not to acknowledge that there are some among us always ready to affix a Communist label upon those whose ideas they violently oppose. And experience teaches that prosecutors too are human.

We think this case demonstrably falls within the compass of those decisions of the Court which hold that ". . . a statute which either forbids or requires the doing of an act in terms so vague that men of common intelligence must necessarily guess at its meaning and differ as to its application, violates the first essential of due process of law." *Connally* v. *General Construction Co.,* 269 U.S. 385. "No one may be required at peril of life, liberty or property to speculate as to the meaning of penal statutes. All are entitled to be informed as to what the State commands or forbids." *Lanzetta* v. *New Jersey,* 306 U.S. 451. "Words which are vague and fluid . . . may be as much of a trap for the innocent as the ancient laws of Caligula." *United States* v. *Cardiff,* 344 U.S. 174. "In the light of our decisions, it appears upon a mere inspection that these general words and phrases are so vague and indefinite that any penalty prescribed for their violation constitutes a denial of due process of law. It is not the penalty itself that is invalid but the exaction of obedience to a rule or standard that is so vague and indefinite as to be really no rule or standard at all." *Champlin Refining Co.* v. *Corporation Commission of Oklahoma,* 286 U.S. 210.

The vice of unconstitutional vagueness is further aggravated where, as here, the statute in question operates to inhibit the exercise of individual freedoms affirmatively protected by the Constitution. As we said in *Smith* v. *California,* ". . . stricter standards of permissible statutory vagueness may be applied to a statute having a potentially inhibiting effect on speech; a man may the less be required to act at his peril here, because the free dissemination of ideas may be the loser." 361 U.S. 147. "The maintenance of the opportunity for free political discussion to the end that government may be responsive to the will of the people and that changes may be obtained by lawful means, an opportunity essential to the security of the Republic, is a fundamental principle of our constitutional system. A statute which upon its face, and as authoritatively construed, is so vague and indefinite as to permit the punishment of the fair use of this opportunity is repugnant to the guaranty of liberty contained in the Fourteenth Amendment." *Stromberg* v. *California,* 283 U.S. 359. . . .

As in *Wieman* v. *Updegraff,* we are not concerned here with the question "whether an abstract right to public employment exists." 344 U.S. 183. Nor do we question the power of a State to safeguard the public service from disloyalty. Cf. *Slochower* v. *Board of Education,* 350 U.S. 551; *Adler* v. *Board of Education,* 342 U.S. 485. It is enough for the present case to reaffirm "that constitutional protection does extend to the public servant whose exclusion pursuant to a statute is patently arbitrary or discriminatory." *Wieman* v. *Updegraff, supra.* "The fact . . . that a person is not compelled to hold public office cannot possibly be an excuse for barring him from office by state-imposed criteria forbidden by the Constitution." *Torcaso* v. *Watkins,* 367 U.S. 488.

Reversed.

e. Inquisitorial Hearing

VITARELLI v. SEATON

359 US 535 (1959)

[By a 5-to-4 vote the Court held in this case that a former government employee should be reinstated, for the proceedings which led to his discharge fell short of departmental regulations in that the hearing was a wide-ranging inquisition into the employee's political and other beliefs, without regard to the relevancy, competency, or materiality of the questions.

[In his dissenting opinion (with which Justices Clark, Stewart, and Whittaker agreed), Justice Frankfurter, while agreeing with the majority that an executive agency "must be rigorously held to the standards by which it professes its action to be judged," argued that the Secretary of the Interior had "untrammelled right to dismiss Vitarelli out of hand," for the employee in question had no protected employment rights, and that this "untrammelled right" was in fact exercised.]

Mr. Justice Harlan delivered the opinion of the Court:

This case concerned the legality of petitioner's discharge as an employee of the Department of the Interior. Vitarelli, an educator holding a doctor's degree from Columbia University, was appointed in 1952 by the Department of the Interior as an Education and Training Specialist in the Education Department of the Trust Territory of the Pacific Islands, at Koror in the Palau District, a mandated area for which this country has responsibility.

By a letter dated March 30, 1954, respondent Secretary's predecessor in office notified petitioner of his suspension from duty without pay, effective April 2, 1954, assigning as ground therefor various charges. Essentially, the charges were that petitioner from 1941 to 1945 had been in "sympathetic association" with three named persons alleged to have been members of or in sympathetic association with the Communist Party, and had concealed from the Government the true extent of these associations at the time of a previous inquiry into them; that he had registered as a supporter of the American Labor Party in New York City in 1945, had subscribed to the *USSR Information Bulletin*, and had purchased copies of the *Daily Worker* and *New Masses*; and that because such associations and activities tended to show that petitioner was "not reliable or trustworthy" his continued employment might be "contrary to the best interests of national security."

Petitioner filed a written answer to the statement of charges, and appeared before a security hearing board on June 22 and July 1, 1954. At this hearing no evidence was adduced by the Department in support of the charges, nor did any witness testify against petitioner. Petitioner testified at length, and presented four witnesses, and he and the witnesses were extensively cross-examined by the security officer and the members of the hearing board. On September 2, 1954, a notice of dismissal effective September 10, 1954, was sent petitioner over the signature of the Secretary, reciting that the dismissal was "in the interest of national security for the reasons specifically set forth in the letter of charges dated March 30, 1954." This was followed on September 21, 1954, with the filing of a "Notification of Personnel Action" setting forth the Secretary's action. The record does not show that a copy of this document was ever sent to petitioner.

After having failed to obtain reinstatement by a demand upon the Secretary, petitioner filed suit in the United States District Court for the District of Columbia seeking a declaration that his dismissal had been illegal and ineffective and an injunction requiring his reinstatement. On October 10, 1956, while the case was pending in the District Court, a copy of a new "Notification of Personnel Action," dated September 21, 1954, and reciting that it was "a revision of and replaces the original bearing the same date," was filed in the District Court, and another copy of this document was delivered to petitioner shortly thereafter. This notification was identical with the one already mentioned, except that it omitted any reference to the reason for petitioner's discharge and to the authority under which it was carried out. Thereafter the District Court granted summary judgment for the respondent. That judgment was affirmed by the Court of Appeals, one judge dissenting. . . . We granted certiorari to consider the validity of petitioner's discharge. . . .

The Secretary's letter of March 30, 1954, and notice of dismissal of September 2, 1954, both relied upon Exec. Order No. 10450, 18 Fed. Reg. 2489 (1953), the Act of August 26, 1950, 5 U.S.C. § 22–1 et seq., and Department of the Interior Order No. 2738, all relating to discharges of government employees on security or loyalty grounds, as the authority for petitioner's dismissal. In *Cole* v. *Young*, 351 US 536, this Court held that the statute referred to did not apply to government employees in positions not designated as "sensitive." Respondent takes the position that since petitioner's position in government service has at no time been designated as sensitive the effect of *Cole*, which was decided after the 1954 dismissal of petitioner, was to render also inapplicable to petitioner Department of the Interior Order No. 2738, under which the proceedings relating to petitioner's dismissal were had. It is urged that in this state of affairs petitioner, who concededly was at no time within the protection of the Civil Service Act, Veteran's Preference Act, or any other statute relating to employment rights of government employees, and who, as a "Schedule A" employee, could have been summarily discharged by the Secretary at any time without the giving of a reason, under no circumstances could be entitled to more than that which he has already received—namely, an "expunging" from the record of his 1954 discharge of any reference to the authority or reasons therefor.

Respondent misconceives the effect of our decision in *Cole*. It is true that the Act of August 26, 1950, and the Executive Order did not alter the power of the Secretary to discharge summarily an employee in petitioner's status, without the giving of any reason. Nor did the Department's own regulations preclude such a course. Since, however, the Secretary gratuitously decided to give a reason, and that reason was national security, he was obligated to conform to the procedural standards he had formulated in Order No. 2738 for the dismissal of employees on security grounds. . . . That Order on its face applies to *all* security discharges in the Department of the Interior, including such discharges of Schedule A employees. *Cole v. Young* established that the Act of August 26, 1950, did not permit the discharge of nonsensitive employees pursuant to procedures authorized by that Act if those procedures were more summary than those to which the employee would have been entitled by virtue of any pre-existing statute or regulation. That decision cannot, however, justify noncompliance by the Secretary with regulations promulgated by him in the departmental Order, which as to petitioner afford greater procedural protections in the case of a dismissal stated to be for security reasons than in the case of dismissal without any statement of reasons. Having chosen to proceed against petitioner on security grounds, the Secretary . . . was bound by the regulations which he himself had promulgated for dealing with such cases, even though without such regulations he could have discharged petitioner summarily.

Petitioner makes various contentions as to the constitutional invalidity of the procedures provided by Order No. 2738. He further urges that even assuming the validity of the governing procedures, his dismissal cannot stand because the notice of suspension and hearing given him did not comply with the Order. We find it unnecessary to reach the constitutional issues, for we think that petitioner's second position is well taken and must be sustained.

Preliminarily, it should be said that departures from departmental regulations in matters of this kind involve more than mere consideration of procedural irregularities. For in proceedings of this nature, in which the ordinary rules of evidence do not apply, in which matters involving the disclosure of confidential information are withheld, and where it must be recognized that counsel is under practical constraints in the making of objections and in the tactical handling of his case which would not obtain in a cause being tried in a court of law before trained judges, scrupulous observance of departmental procedural safeguards is clearly of particular importance. In this instance an examination of the record, and of the transcript of the hearing before the departmental security board, discloses that petitioner's procedural rights under the applicable regulations were violated in at least three material respects in the proceedings which terminated in the final notice of his dismissal.

First, § 15 (a) of Order No. 2738 requires that the statement of charges served upon an employee at the time of his suspension on security grounds "shall be as specific and detailed as security considerations, including the need for protection of confidential sources of information, permit . . . and shall be subject to amendment within 30 days of issuance." Although the statement of charges furnished petitioner appears on its face to be reasonably specific, the transcript of hearing establishes that the statement, which was never amended, cannot conceivably be said in fact to be as specific and detailed as "security considerations . . . permit." For petitioner was questioned by the security officer and by the hearing board in great detail concerning his association with and knowledge of various persons and organizations nowhere mentioned in the statement of charges, and at length concerning his activities in Bucks County, Pennsylvania, and elsewhere after 1945, activities as to which the charges are also completely silent. These questions were presumably asked because they were deemed relevant to the inquiry before the board, and the very fact that they were asked and thus spread on the record is conclusive indication that "security considerations" could not have justified the omission of any statement concerning them in the charges furnished petitioner.

Second, §§ 21 (a) and (e) require that hearings before security hearing boards shall be "orderly" and that "reasonable restrictions shall be imposed as to relevancy, competency, and materiality of matters considered." The material set forth in the margin, taken from the transcript, and illustrative rather than exhaustive, shows that these indispensable indicia of a meaningful hearing were not observed.* It is not an overcharacterization to say that as the hearing

---

    * "MR. ARMSTRONG: [the departmental security officer, inquiring about petitioner's activities as a teacher in a Georgia college] Were these activities designed to be put into effect by both the white and the colored races? . . . What were your feelings at that time concerning race equality? . . . How about civil rights?

proceeded it developed into a wide-ranging inquisition into this man's educational, social, and political beliefs, encompassing even a question as to whether he was "a religious man."

Third, § 21 (c) (4) gives the employee the right "to cross-examine any witness offered in support of the charges." It is apparent from an

---

Did that enter into a discussion in your seminar groups?"

"Mr. Armstrong: Do I interpret your statement correctly that maybe Negroes and Jews are denied some of their constitutional rights at present?"

"Mr. Vitarelli: Yes.

"Mr. Armstrong: In what way?"

"Mr. Vitarelli: I saw it in the South where certain jobs were open to white people and not open to Negroes because they were Negroes. . . . In our own university, there was a quota at Columbia College for the medical students. Because they were Jewish, they would permit only so many. I thought that was wrong.

"Chairman Towson: Doctor, isn't it also true that Columbia College had quotas by states and other classifications as well?

"Mr. Vitarelli: I don't remember that. It may be true.

"Mr. Armstrong: In other words, wasn't there a quota on Gentiles as well as Jews?

"Mr. Vitarelli: . . . I had remembered that some Jews seemed to feel, and I felt, too, at the time, that they were being persecuted somewhat.

"Chairman Towson: Did you ever take the trouble to investigate whether or not they were or did you just accept their word?

"Mr. Vitarelli: No, I didn't investigate it.

"Chairman Towson: You accepted their word for it.

"Mr. Vitarelli: I accepted the general opinion of the group of professors with whom I associated and was taught. . . .

"Chairman Towson: I am simply asking you to verify the vague impression I have that Columbia College puts a severe quota on residents of New York City, whatever their race, creed or color may be.

"Mr. Vitarelli: I think that is true. . . .

"Chairman Towson: Otherwise there would be no students at Columbia College except residents of New York City.

"Mr. Vitarelli: There may be a few others, but mostly New York City.

"Chairman Towson: Isn't it true that the quota system is designed by the college in order to make it available to persons other than live in New York City?

"Mr. Vitarelli: I believe that is the reason.

"Chairman Towson: And any exclusion of a resident of New York City would be for that reason, rather than the race, creed or color?

"Mr. Vitarelli: I think that is the way the policy is stated.

"Chairman Towson: Is it not a fact?

"Mr. Vitarelli: I don't think so. . . .

"Chairman Towson: Excuse me, Mr. Armstrong.

"Mr. Armstrong: I went to Columbia Law School for two years and certainly there was not any quota system there at that time, and that is a long time ago. All right, we are getting afield."

Petitioner was also asked the following questions by the security officer during the course of the hearing:

"Mr. Armstrong: I think you indicated in an answer or a reply to an interrogatory that you at times voted for and sponsored the principles of Franklin

over-all reading of the regulations that it was not contemplated that this provision should require the Department to call witnesses to testify in support of any or all of the charges, because it was expected that charges might rest on information gathered from or by "confidential informants." We think, however, that § 21 (c) (4) did contemplate the calling by the Department of any informant not properly classifiable as "confidential," if information furnished by that informant was to be used by the board in assessing an employee's status. The transcript shows that this provision was violated on at least one occasion at petitioner's hearing, for the security officer identified by name a person who had given information apparently considered detrimental to petitioner, thus negating any possible inference that that person was considered a "confidential informant" whose identity it was necessary to keep secret, and questioned petitioner at some length concerning the information supplied from this source without calling the informant and affording petitioner the right to cross-examine.

Because the proceedings attendant upon petitioner's dismissal from government service on grounds of national security fell substantially short of the requirements of the applicable departmental regulations, we hold that such dismissal was illegal and of no effect. . . .

It follows from what we have said that petitioner is entitled to the reinstatement which he seeks, subject, of course to any lawful exercise of the Secretary's authority hereafter to dismiss him from employment in the Department of the Interior.

Reversed.

Delano Roosevelt, Norman A. Thomas, and Henry Wallace? . . . How many times did you vote for . . . [Thomas] if you care to say? . . . How about Henry Wallace? . . . How about Norman Thomas? Did his platform coincide more nearly with your ideas of democracy? . . . At one time, or two, you were a strong advocate of the United Nations. Are you still? . . . The file indicates, too, that you were quite hepped up over the one world idea at one time; is that right?"

Witnesses presented by petitioner were asked by the security officer and board members such questions as:

"The Doctor indicated that he was acquainted with and talked to Norman Thomas on occasions. Did you know about that? . . . How about Dr. Vitarelli? Is he scholarly? . . . A good administrator? . . . Was he careless with his language around the students or careful? . . . Did you consider Dr. Vitarelli as a religious man? . . . Was he an extremist on equality of races? . . . In connection with the activities that Dr. Vitarelli worked on that you know about, either in the form of projects or in connection with the educational activities that you have mentioned, did they extend to the Negro population of the country? In other words, were they contacts with Negro groups, with Negro instructors, with Negro students, and so on?"

It is not apparent how any of the above matters could be material to a consideration of the question whether petitioner's retention in government service would be consistent with national security.

3. *The Attorney General's List*

JOINT ANTI-FASCIST REFUGEE COMMITTEE *v.* McGRATH

341 US 123 (1951)

[President Truman's Executive Order 9835, which provided procedures for loyalty investigations of Federal Government employees—see *Bailey* v. *Richardson,* above—directed the Attorney General to promulgate a list of subversive organizations. Early in 1948 the first Attorney General's list was made public; it contained 82 organizations; early in 1953 the number had grown to over 250. (The House Committee on Un-American Activities also has published a list, with over 600 names.)

[The Attorney General's list has been used in the loyalty and security programs. The tax exemption of organizations on the list has been canceled. The list has been used against aliens applying for admission into the United States. Some states and cities, as well as some private employers, have made use of it. The importance of the list can hardly be exaggerated.

[In the present case the Court was concerned with the procedures for listing. In a 5-to-3 decision (Justice Clark not participating) the Court held that the three organizations that had brought the suit against the Attorney General had been improperly listed. The President's order provided for listing "after appropriate investigation and determination" by the Attorney General; this provision had not been followed; he thus acted arbitrarily. Justices Frankfurter and Jackson thought that an organization is entitled to due process—notice and a hearing. Justices Black and Douglas agreed with this but maintained that fundamental constitutional freedoms were also violated by administrative loyalty trials and the listing of organizations as a step in these trials. Chief Justice Vinson and Justices Reed and Minton dissented.

[Justice Frankfurter's observations on the significance of procedural due process are worthy of special note.]

Mr. Justice Burton announced the judgment of the Court and delivered the following opinion . . . :

In each of these cases the same issue is raised by the dismissal of a complaint for its failure to state a claim upon which relief can be granted. That issue is whether . . . the Attorney General of the United States has authority to include the complaining organization in a list of organizations designated by him as Communist and furnished by him to the Loyalty Review Board of the United States Civil Service Commission. He claims to derive authority to do this from the following provisions in Part III, § 3, of Executive Order No. 9835, issued by the President, March 21, 1947, 5 U.S.C.A. § 631 note:

Part III—Responsibilities of Civil Service Commission

3. The Loyalty Review Board shall currently be furnished by the Department of Justice the name of each foreign or domestic organization, association, movement, group or combination of persons which the Attorney General, after appropriate investigation and determination, designates as totalitarian, fascist, communist or subversive, or as having adopted a policy of advocating or approving the commission of acts of force or violence to deny others their rights under the Constitution of the United States, or as seeking to alter the form of government of the United States by unconstitutional means.

a. The Loyalty Review Board shall disseminate such information to all departments and agencies.

. . . At least since 1939, increasing concern has been expressed, in and out of Congress, as to the possible presence in the employ of the Government of persons disloyal to it. This is reflected in the legislation, reports and executive orders culminating in Executive Order No. 9835. That order announced the President's Employees Loyalty Program in the Executive Branch of the Government. It states that both "maximum protection must be afforded the United States against infiltration of disloyal persons into the ranks of its employees, and equal protection from unfounded accusations of disloyalty must be afforded the loyal employees of the Government: . . ." It provides for the Loyalty Review Board and sets up a standard for refusals of and removals from employment on grounds relating to loyalty. It outlines the use to be made in that connection of the list of organizations to be furnished by the Attorney General. The organizations to be designated on that list are not limited to those having federal employees in their memberships. They may even exclude such employees from membership. Accordingly, the impact of the Attorney General's list is by no means limited to persons who are subject to the Employees Loyalty Program.

The Attorney General included each of the complaining organizations in the list he furnished to the Loyalty Review Board November 24, 1947. That list was disseminated by the Board to all departments and agencies of the United States December 4, 1947. The complaints allege that such action resulted in nationwide publicity and caused the injuries to the complaining organizations which are detailed later. September 17, 1948, during the pendency of the instant cases but before action upon the appeals in any of them, "the Attorney General furnished the Loyalty Review Board with a consolidated list containing the names of all of the organizations previously designated by him as within Executive Order 9835, segregated according to the classifications enumerated in section 3, Part III, on the basis of dominant characteristics." He enumerated six classifications and classified the three complaining organizations as "Communist." . . .

The Refugee Committee Case

The complainant is the Joint Anti-Fascist Refugee Committee, an unincorporated association in the City and State of New York. . . .

The following statement, based on the allegations of the complaint, summarizes the situation before us: The complainant is "a charitable organization engaged in relief work" which carried on its relief activities from 1942 to 1946 under a license from the President's War Relief Control Board. Thereafter, it voluntarily submitted its program, budgets and audits for inspection by the Advisory Committee on Voluntary Foreign Aid of the United States Government. Since its inception, it has, through voluntary contributions, raised and disbursed funds for the benefit of anti-Fascist refugees who assisted the Government of Spain against its overthrow by force and violence. The organization's aims and purposes "are to raise, administer and distribute funds for the relief and rehabilitation of Spanish Republicans in exile and other anti-fascist refugees who fought in the war against Franco."

It has disbursed $1,011,448 in cash, and $217,903 in kind, for the relief of anti-Fascist refugees and their families. This relief has included money, food, shelter, educational facilities, medical treatment and supplies, and clothing to recipients in 11 countries including the United States. The acts of the Attorney General and the Loyalty Review Board, purporting to be taken by them under authority of the Executive Order, have seriously and irreparably impaired, and will continue to so impair, the reputation of the organization and the moral support and good will of the American people necessary for the continuance of its charitable activities. Upon information and belief, these acts have caused many contributors, especially present and prospective civil servants, to reduce or discontinue their contributions to the organization; members and participants in its activities have been "vilified and subjected to public shame, disgrace, ridicule and obloquy . . ." thereby inflicting upon it economic injury and discouraging participation in its activities; it has been hampered in securing meeting places; and many people have refused to take part in its fund-raising activities.

This complaint does not contain an express denial that the complaining organization is within the classifications named in Part III, § 3, of Executive Order No. 9835. It does, however, state that the actions of the Attorney General and the Loyalty Review Board which are complained of are unauthorized and without warrant in law and amount to a deprivation of the complainant's rights in violation of the Constitution; that Executive Order No. 9835, on its face and as construed and applied, violates the First, Fifth, Ninth and Tenth Amendments to the Constitution of the United States and that § 9A of the Hatch Act, 53 Stat. 1148, 5 U.S.C. (1946 ed., Supp. III) § 118j, insofar as it purports to authorize the instant application of the order, is void. It asks for declaratory and injunctive relief, alleging that the complaining organization is suffering irreparable loss and that no adequate remedy is available to it except through the equity powers of the District Court. That court granted a motion to dismiss the complaint for its failure to state a claim upon which relief could be granted and denied the complainant's motion for a preliminary injunction. The Court of Appeals affirmed, one judge dissenting. . . .

The National Council Case

In this case the court below relied upon its decision in the Refugee Committee case and reached the same result. . . . Except as indicated below in our summary of the facts alleged, this case, for our purposes, is like the first. The complainants, who are the petitioners here, are the National Council of American-Soviet Friendship, Inc., a New York nonprofit membership corporation, organized in 1943; the Denver Council of American-Soviet Friendship, a Colorado unincorporated association and local affiliate of the National Council; and six individual officers and directors of one or the other of these organizations. The purpose of the National Council "is to strengthen friendly relations between the United States and the Union of Soviet Socialist Republics by disseminating to the American people educational material regarding the Soviet Union, by developing cultural relations between the peoples of the two nations, and by combatting anti-Soviet propaganda designed to disrupt friendly relations between the people of these nations and to divide the United Nations." The complaint alleges that all of the complainants are seriously and irreparably injured in their capacity to conduct the National Council's educational, cultural and fund-raising program; and that the individual complainants have suffered personal losses such as the removal of one from an assistant rectorship of a church, the loss by another of a teaching position, and numerous cancellations of lecturing and professional engagements. The complaint expressly states that—"In all its activities the National Council has sought to further the best interests of the American people by lawful, peaceful and constitutional means. It has never in any way engaged in any conduct or activity which provides any basis for it to be designated as 'totalitarian, fascist, communist or subversive, or as having adopted a policy of advocating or approving the commission of acts of force or violence to deny others their rights under the Constitution of the United States, or as seeking to alter the form of government of the United States by unconstitutional means.' "

The International Workers Case

The complaining organization, which is the petitioner here, is a fraternal benefit society, organized in 1930 as a corporation under the Insurance Law of the State of New York, . . . operating for the mutual benefit of its members and their beneficiaries and not for profit. It is licensed and operates in the District of Columbia and several states; its purposes are comparable to those of fraternal benefit societies in general; it operates under a lodge system and has a representative form of government; at the time of the promulgation of the Department of Justice list it had 185,000 members, including employees of the Federal Government and of various states and municipalities; it provided life insurance protection for its membership exceeding $120,-000,000; its activities have been the subject of administrative and judicial proceedings in addition to those before the insurance departments of the states in which it functions, and, as a result of such proceedings, "the purposes and activities of the order have been held to be free from any illegal or improper taint. . . ." Among the allegations of damage, made upon information and belief, the complaint states that, solely as a result of the respondents' acts, there have been instituted against the order and its members a multiplicity of administrative proceedings, including those to rescind licenses, franchises, or tax exemptions, or to impede the naturalization of its members. Because of respondents' acts, many such members, especially present and prospective civil servants, have resigned or withdrawn from membership in the order, and many potential members have declined to join it. . . .

If, upon the allegations in any of these complaints, it had appeared that the acts of the respondents, from which relief was sought, were authorized by the President under his Executive Order No. 9835, the case would have bristled with constitutional issues. On that basis the complaint would have raised questions as to the justiciability and merit of claims based upon the First, Fifth, Ninth and Tenth Amendments to the Constitution. It is our obligation, however, not to reach those issues unless the allegations before us squarely present them. . . .

The Executive Order contains no express or implied attempt to confer power on anyone to act arbitrarily or capriciously—even assuming a constitutional power to do so. The order includes in the purposes of the President's program not only the protection of the United States against disloyal employees but the "equal protection" of loyal employees against unfounded accusations of disloyalty. . . . The standards stated for refusal of and removal from employment require that "on all the evidence, reasonable grounds [shall] exist for belief that the person involved is disloyal. . . ." . . . Obviously it would be contrary to the purpose of that order to place on a list to be disseminated under the Loyalty Program any designation of an organization that was patently arbitrary and contrary to the uncontroverted material facts. The order contains the express requirement that each designation of an organization by the Attorney General on such a list shall be made only after an "appropriate . . . determination" as prescribed in Part III, § 3. An "appropriate" governmental "determination" must be the result of a process of reasoning. It cannot be an arbitrary fiat contrary to the known facts. This is inherent in the meaning of "determination." It is implicit in a government of laws and not of men. Where an act of an official plainly falls outside of the scope of his authority, he does not make that act legal by doing it and then invoking the doctrine of administrative construction to cover it.

It remains, therefore, for us to decide whether, *on the face of these complaints,* the Attorney General is acting within his authority in furnishing the Loyalty Review Board with a designation of the complaining organizations either as "Communist" or as within any other classification of Part III, § 3, of the order. In the National Council and International Workers cases, the complaining organization is alleged not only to be a civic or insurance organization, apparently above reproach from the point of view of loyalty to the United States, but it is also declared to be one that is not within any classification listed in Part III, § 3, of the order. In the Refugee Committee case, the negative allegations are omitted but the affirmative allegations are incompatible with the inclusion of the complaining organization within any of the designated classifications. The inclusion of any of the complaining organizations in the designated list solely on the facts alleged in the respective complaints, which must be the basis for our decision here, is therefore an arbitrary and unauthorized act. In the two cases where the complaint specifically alleges the factual absence of any basis for the designation, and the respondents' motion admits that allegation, the designation is necessarily contrary to the record. The situation is comparable to one which would be created if the Attorney General, under like circumstances, were to designate the American National Red Cross as a Communist organization. Accepting as common knowledge the charitable and loyal status of that organization, there is no doubt that, in the absence of any contrary claim asserted against it, the Executive Order does not authorize its inclusion by the Attorney General as a "Communist" organization or as coming within any of the other classifications named in Part III, § 3, of the order.

Since we find that the conduct ascribed to the Attorney General by the complaints is patently arbitrary, the deference ordinarily due administrative construction of an administrative order is not sufficient to bring his alleged conduct within the authority conferred by Executive Order No. 9835. The doctrine of administrative construction never has been carried so far as to permit administrative discretion to run riot. If applied to this case and compounded with the assumption that the President's Executive Order was drafted for him by his Attorney General, the conclusion would rest upon the premise that the Attorney General has attempted to delegate to himself the power to act arbitrarily. We cannot impute such an attempt to the Nation's highest law enforcement officer any more than we can to its President.

In thus emphasizing an outer limit to what can be considered an authorized designation of an organization under the order, the instant cases serve a valuable purpose. They demonstrate that the order does not authorize, much less direct, the exercise of any such absolute power as would permit the inclusion in the Attorney General's list of a designation that is patently arbitrary or contrary to fact.

When the acts of the Attorney General and of the members of the Loyalty Review Board are stripped of the Presidential authorization claimed for them by the respondents, they stand, on the face of these complaints, as unauthorized publications of admittedly unfounded designations of the complaining organizations as "Communist." Their effect is to cripple the functioning and damage the reputation of those organizations in their respective communities and in the nation. The complaints, on that basis, sufficiently charge that such acts violate each complaining organization's common-law right to be free from defamation. "A communication is defamatory if it tends so to harm the reputation of another as to lower him in the estimation of the community or to deter third persons from associating or dealing with him." . . .

Nothing we have said purports to adjudicate the truth of petitioners' allegations that they are not in fact communistic. We have assumed that the designations made by the Attorney General are arbitrary because we are compelled to make that assumption by his motions to dismiss the complaints. Whether the complaining organizations are in fact communistic or whether the Attorney General possesses information from which he could reasonably find them to be so must await determination by the District Court upon remand.

For these reasons, we find it necessary to reverse the judgments of the Court of Appeals in the respective cases and to remand each case to the District Court with instructions to deny the respondents' motion that the complaint be dismissed for failure to state a claim upon which relief can be granted.

Reversed and remanded.

Mr. Justice Black, concurring:
Without notice or hearing and under color of the President's Executive

Order No. 9835, the Attorney General found petitioners guilty of harboring treasonable opinions and designs, officially branded them as Communists, and promulgated his findings and conclusions for particular use as evidence against government employees suspected of disloyalty. In the present climate of public opinion it appears certain that the Attorney General's much publicized findings, regardless of their truth or falsity, are the practical equivalents of confiscation and death sentences for any blacklisted organization not possessing extraordinary financial, political, or religious prestige and influence. The Government not only defends the power of the Attorney General to pronounce such deadly edicts but also argues that individuals or groups so condemned have no standing to seek redress in the courts, even though a fair judicial hearing might conclusively demonstrate their loyalty. . . .

More fundamentally, however, in my judgment the executive has no constitutional authority, with or without a hearing, officially to prepare and publish the lists challenged by petitioners. In the first place, the system adopted effectively punishes many organizations and their members merely because of their political beliefs and utterances, and to this extent smacks of a most evil type of censorship. This cannot be reconciled with the First Amendment as I interpret it. . . . Moreover, officially prepared and proclaimed governmental blacklists possess almost every quality of bills of attainder, the use of which was from the beginning forbidden to both national and state governments. U.S. Const. Art I, §§ 9, 10. It is true that the classic bill of attainder was a condemnation by the legislature following investigation by that body, see *United States* v. *Lovett*, 328 U.S. 303 (1946) . . . , while in the present case the Attorney General performed the official tasks. But I cannot believe that the authors of the Constitution, who outlawed the bill of attainder, inadvertently endowed the executive with power to engage in the same tyrannical practices that had made the bill such an odious institution.

There is argument that executive power to issue these pseudo-bills of attainder can be implied from the undoubted power of the Government to hire and discharge employees and to protect itself against treasonable individuals or organizations. Our basic law, however, wisely withheld authority for resort to executive investigations, condemnations and blacklists as a substitute for imposition of legal types of penalties by courts following trial and conviction in accordance with procedural safeguards of the Bill of Rights.

In this day when prejudice, hate and fear are constantly invoked to justify irresponsible smears and persecution of persons even faintly suspected of entertaining unpopular views, it may be futile to suggest that the cause of internal security would be fostered, not hurt, by faithful adherence to our constitutional guarantees of individual liberty. Nevertheless, since prejudice manifests itself in much the same way in every age and country and since what has happened before can happen again, it surely should not be amiss to call attention to what has occurred when dominant governmental groups have been left free to give uncontrolled rein to their prejudices against unorthodox minorities. . . .

Mr. Justice Frankfurter, concurring: . . .

In November, 1947, each of these organizations was included in the list of groups designated by the Attorney General as within the provisions of Executive Order No. 9835, the President's Loyalty Order. The list was disseminated to all departments and agencies of the Government. Six months later, each was with more particularity labeled "communist." Each alleges substantial injury as a consequence. Publicity and meeting places have become difficult for the Refugee Committee and the Council to obtain. The federal tax exemptions of all three organizations have been revoked; licenses necessary to solicitation of funds have been denied the Refugee Committee; and the New York Superintendent of Insurance has begun proceedings, in which a representative of the Attorney General of the United States has appeared, for dissolution of the Order. Most important, each of the organizations asserts that it has lost supporters and members, especially from present or prospective federal employees. Claiming that the injury is irreparable, each asks for relief by way of a declaratory judgment and an injunction. . . .

This controversy is . . . amenable to the judicial process. Its justiciability does not depend solely on the fact that the action challenged is defamatory. Not every injury inflicted by a defamatory statement of a government officer can be redressed in court. On the balance of all considerations, the exercise here of judicial power accords with traditional canons for access to courts without inroads on the effective conduct of government. . . .

Fairness of procedure is "due process in the primary sense." . . . It is ingrained in our national traditions and is designed to maintain them. In a variety of situations the Court has enforced this requirement by checking attempts of executives, legislatures, and lower courts to disregard the deep-rooted demands of fair play enshrined in the Constitution. "[T]his court has never held, nor must we now be understood as holding, that administrative officers, when executing the provisions of a statute involving the liberty of persons, may disregard the fundamental principles that inhere in 'due process of law' as understood at the time of the adoption of the Constitution. One of these principles is that no person shall be deprived of his liberty without opportunity, at some time, to be heard. . . ." "[B]y 'due process' is meant one which, following the forms of law, is appropriate to the case, and just to the parties to be affected. It must be pursued in the ordinary mode prescribed by the law; it must be adapted to the end to be attained; and wherever it is necessary for the protection of the parties, it must give them an opportunity to be heard respecting the justice of the judgment sought." . . . "Before its property can be taken under the edict of an administrative officer, the appellant is entitled to a fair hearing upon the fundamental facts." . . . "Whether acting through its judiciary or through its Legislature, a state may not deprive a person of all existing remedies for the enforcement of a right, which the state has no power to destroy, unless there is, or was, afforded to him some real opportunity to protect it." . . .

The requirement of "due process" is not a fair-weather or timid assurance. It must be respected in periods of calm and in times of trouble; it protects aliens as well as citizens. But "due process," unlike some legal rules, is not a technical conception with a fixed content unrelated to time, place and circumstances. Expressing as it does in its ultimate analysis respect enforced by law for that feeling of just treatment which has been evolved through centuries of Anglo-American constitutional history and civilization, "due process" cannot be imprisoned within the treacherous limits of any formula. Representing a profound attitude of fairness between man and man, and more particularly between the individual and government, "due process" is compounded of history, reason, the past course of decisions, and stout confidence in the strength of the democratic faith which we profess. Due process is not a mechanical instrument. It is not a yardstick. It is a process. It is a delicate process of adjustment inescapably involving the exercise of judgment by those whom the Constitution entrusted with the unfolding of the process.

Fully aware of the enormous powers thus given to the judiciary and especially to its Supreme Court, those who founded this Nation put their trust in a judiciary truly independent—in judges not subject to the fears or allurements of a limited tenure and by the very nature of their function detached from passing and partisan influences. . . .

Achievements of our civilization as precious as they were hard won were summarized by Mr. Justice Brandeis when he wrote that "in the development of our liberty insistence upon procedural regularity has been a large factor." . . . It is noteworthy that procedural safeguards constitute the major portion of our Bill of Rights. And so, no one now doubts that in the criminal law a "person's right to reasonable notice of a charge against him, and an opportunity to be heard in his defense—a right to his day in court—are basic in our system of jurisprudence." . . . "The hearing, moreover, must be a real one, not a sham or a pretense." . . . Nor is there doubt that notice and hearing are prerequisite to due process in civil proceedings, . . . Only the narrowest exceptions, justified by history become part of the habits of our people or by obvious necessity, are tolerated. . . .

The construction placed by this Court upon legislation conferring administrative powers shows consistent respect for a requirement of fair procedure before men are denied or deprived of rights. From a great mass of cases, running the full gamut of control over property and liberty, there emerges the principle that statutes should be interpreted, if explicit language does not preclude, so as to observe due process in its basic meaning. . . .

This Court is not alone in recognizing that the right to be heard before being condemned to suffer grievous loss of any kind, even though it may not involve the stigma and hardships of a criminal conviction, is a principle basic to our society. Regard for this principle has guided Congress and the Executive. Congress has often entrusted, as it may, protection of interests which it has created to administrative agencies rather than to the courts. But rarely has it authorized such agencies to act without those essential safeguards for fair judgment which in the course of centuries have come to be associated with due process. . . .

The heart of the matter is that democracy implies respect for the elementary rights of men, however suspect or unworthy; a democratic government must therefore practice fairness; and fairness can rarely be obtained by secret, one-sided determination of facts decisive of rights.

An opportunity to be heard may not seem vital when an issue relates only to technical questions susceptible of demonstrable proof on which evidence is not likely to be overlooked and argument on the meaning and worth of conflicting and cloudy data not apt to be helpful. But in other situations an admonition of Mr. Justice Holmes becomes relevant. "One has to remember that when one's interest is keenly excited evidence gathers from all sides around the magnetic point. . . ." It should be particularly heeded at times of agitation and anxiety, when fear and suspicion impregnate the air we breathe. . . . "The plea that evidence of guilt must be secret is abhorrent to free men, because it provides a cloak for the malevolent, the misinformed, the meddlesome, and the corrupt to play the role of informer undetected and uncorrected." . . . Appearances in the dark are apt to look different in the light of day.

Man being what he is cannot safely be trusted with complete immunity from outward responsibility in depriving others of their rights. At least such is the conviction underlying our Bill of Rights. That a conclusion satisfies one's private conscience does not attest its reliability. The validity and moral authority of a conclusion largely depend on the mode by which it was reached. Secrecy is not congenial to truth-seeking and self-righteousness gives too slender an assurance of rightness. No better instrument has been devised for arriving at truth than to give a person in jeopardy of serious loss notice of the case against him and opportunity to meet it. Nor has a better way been found for generating the feeling, so important to a popular government, that justice has been done. . . .

Nothing in the Loyalty Order requires him to deny organizations opportunity to present their case. The Executive Order, defining his powers, directs only that designation shall be made "after appropriate investigation and determination." This surely does not preclude an administrative procedure, however informal, which would incorporate the essentials of due process. Nothing has been presented to the Court to indicate that it will be impractical or prejudicial to a concrete public interest to disclose to organizations the nature of the case against them and to permit them to meet it if they can. Indeed, such a contention could hardly be made inasmuch as the Loyalty Order itself requires partial disclosure and hearing in proceedings against a Government employee who is a member of a proscribed organization. Whether such procedure sufficiently protects the rights of the employee is a different story. Such as it is, it affords evidence that the wholly summary process for the organizations is inadequate. And we have controlling proof that Congress did not think that the Attorney General's procedure was indispensable for the protection of the public interest. The McCarran Act, passed under circumstances certainly not more serene than when the Loyalty Order was issued, grants organizations a full administrative hearing, subject to judicial review, before they are required to register as "Communist-action" or "Communist-front." . . .

The Attorney General is certainly not immune from the historic requirements of fairness merely because he acts, however conscientiously, in the
name of security. Nor does he obtain immunity on the ground that designation is not an "adjudication" or a "regulation" in the conventional use of
those terms. Due process is not confined in its scope to the particular forms
in which rights have heretofore been found to have been curtailed for want
of procedural fairness. Due process is perhaps the most majestic concept
in our whole constitutional system. While it contains the garnered wisdom
of the past in assuring fundamental justice, it is also a living principle not
confined to past instances.

Therefore the petitioners did set forth causes of action which the District
Court should have entertained.

Mr. Justice Douglas, concurring:

. . . The requirements for fair trials under our system of government
need no elaboration. A party is entitled to know the charge against him;
he is also entitled to notice and opportunity to be heard. Those principles
were, in my opinion, violated here.

The charge that these organizations are "subversive" could be clearly
defined. But how can anyone in the context of the Executive Order say what
it means? It apparently does not necessarily mean "totalitarian," "facist" or
"communist" because they are separately listed. Does it mean an organization
with socialist ideas? There are some who lump Socialists and Communists
together. Does it mean an organization that thinks the lot of some peasants
has been improved under Soviet auspices? Does it include an organization
that is against the action of the United Nations in Korea? Does it embrace
a group which on some issues of international policy aligns itself with the
Soviet viewpoint? Does it mean a group which has unwittingly become the
tool for Soviet propaganda? Does it mean one into whose membership some
Communists have infiltrated? Or does it describe only an organization which
under the guise of honorable activities serves as a front for Communist activities?

No one can tell from the Executive Order what meaning is intended. No
one can tell from the records of the cases which one the Attorney General
applied. The charge is flexible; it will mean one thing to one officer, another
to someone else. It will be given meaning according to the predilections of
the prosecutor: "subversive" to some will be synonymous with "radical";
"subversive" to others will be synonymous with "communist." It can be expanded to include those who depart from the orthodox party line—to those
whose words and actions (though completely loyal) do not conform to the
orthodox view on foreign or domestic policy. These flexible standards, which
vary with the mood or political philosophy of the prosecutor, are weapons
which can be made as sharp or as blunt as the occasion requires. Since they
are subject to grave abuse, they have no place in our system of law. When
we employ them, we plant within our body politic the virus of the totalitarian
ideology which we oppose.

It is not enough to know that the men applying the standard are honorable and devoted men. This is a government of *laws* not of *men*. The powers being used are the powers of government over the reputations and fortunes of citizens. In situations far less severe or important than these a party is told the nature of the charge against him. Thus when a defendant is summoned before a federal court to answer to a claim for damages or to a demand for an injunction against him, there must be a "plain statement of the claim showing that the pleader is entitled to relief." If that is necessary for even the most minor claim asserted against a defendant, we should require no less when it comes to determinations that may well destroy the group against whom the charge of being "subversive" is directed. When the Government becomes the moving party and levels its great powers against the citizen, it should be held to the same standards of fair dealing as we prescribe for other legal contests. To let the Government adopt such lesser ones as suits the convenience of its officers is to start down the totalitarian path.

The trend in that direction is only emphasized by the failure to give notice and hearing on the charges in these cases. . . .

Notice and opportunity to be heard are fundamental to due process of law. We would reverse these cases out of hand if they were suits of a civil nature to establish a claim against petitioners. Notice and opportunity to be heard are indispensable to a fair trial whether the case be criminal or civil. . . . The gravity of the present charges is proof enough of the need for notice and hearing before the United States officially brands these organizations as "subversive." No more critical governmental ruling can be made against an organization these days. It condemns without trial. It destroys without opportunity to be heard. The condemnation may in each case be wholly justified. But government in this country cannot by edict condemn or place beyond the pale. The rudiments of justice, as we know it, call for notice and hearing— an opportunity to appear and to rebut the charge.

The system used to condemn these organizations is bad enough. The evil is only compounded when a government employee is charged with being disloyal. Association with or membership in an organization found to be "subversive" weighs heavily against the accused. He is not allowed to prove that the charge against the organization is false. That case is closed; that line of defense is taken away. The technique is one of guilt by association— one of the most odious institutions of history. The fact that the technique of guilt by association was used in the prosecutions at Nüremberg does not make it congenial to our constitutional scheme. Guilt under our system of government is personal. When we make guilt vicarious we borrow from systems alien to ours and ape our enemies. Those short-cuts may at times seem to serve noble aims; but we depreciate ourselves by indulging in them. When we deny even the most degraded person the rudiments of a fair trial, we endanger the liberties of everyone. We set a pattern of conduct that is dangerously expansive and is adaptable to the needs of any majority bent on suppressing opposition or dissension.

It is not without significance that most of the provisions of the Bill of Rights are procedural. It is procedure that spells much of the difference

between rule by law and rule by whim or caprice. Steadfast adherence to
strict procedural safeguards is our main assurance that there will be equal
justice under law. The case of Dorothy Bailey [*Bailey* v. *Richardson,* 182 F. 2d
46 (1950)] is an excellent illustration of how dangerous a departure from
our constitutional standards can be. She was charged with being a Communist and with being active in a Communist "front organization." The Review Board stated that the case against her was based on reports, some of
which came from "informants certified to us by the Federal Bureau of
Investigation as experienced and entirely reliable."

Counsel for Dorothy Bailey asked that their names be disclosed. That was
refused.

Counsel for Dorothy Bailey asked if these informants had been active in
a certain union. The chairman replied, "I haven't the slightest knowledge
as to who they were or how active they have been in anything."

Counsel for Dorothy Bailey asked if those statements of the informants
were under oath. The chairman answered, "I don't think so."

The Loyalty Board convicts on evidence which it cannot even appraise.
The critical evidence may be the word of an unknown witness who is "a
paragon of veracity, a knave, or the village idiot." His name, his reputation,
his prejudices, his animosities, his trustworthiness are unknown both to
the judge and to the accused. The accused has no opportunity to show that
the witness lied or was prejudiced or venal. Without knowing who her accusers are she has no way of defending. She has nothing to offer except her own
word and the character testimony of her friends.

Dorothy Bailey was not, to be sure, faced with a criminal charge and
hence not technically entitled under the Sixth Amendment to be confronted
with the witnesses against her. But she was on trial for her reputation, her
job, her professional standing. A disloyalty trial is the most crucial event in
the life of a public servant. If condemned, he is branded for life as a person
unworthy of trust or confidence. To make that condemnation without meticu-
lous regard for the decencies of a fair trial is abhorrent to fundamental
justice.

I do not mean to imply that but for these irregularities the system of
loyalty trials is constitutional. I do not see how the constitutionality of this
dragnet system of loyalty trials which has been entrusted to the administrative agencies of government can be sustained. Every government employee
must take an oath of loyalty. If he swears falsely, he commits perjury and
can be tried in court. In such a trial he gets the full protection of the Bill
of Rights, including trial by jury and the presumption of innocence. I am
inclined to the view that when a disloyalty charge is substituted for perjury
and an administrative board substituted for the court "the spirit and the letter
of the Bill of Rights" are offended.

The problem of security is real; and the Government need not be paralyzed
in handling it. The security problem, however, relates only to those sensitive
areas where secrets are or may be available, where critical policies are being
formulated, or where sabotage can be committed. The department heads
must have leeway in handling their personnel problems in these sensitive

areas. The question is one of the fitness or qualifications of an individual for a particular position. One can be transferred from those areas even when there is no more than a suspicion as to his loyalty. We meet constitutional difficulties when the Government undertakes to punish by proclaiming the disloyalty of an employee and making him ineligible for any government post. The British have avoided those difficulties by applying the loyalty procedure only in sensitive areas and in using it to test the qualifications of an employee for a particular post, not to condemn him for all public employment. When we go beyond that procedure and adopt the dragnet system now in force, we trench upon the civil rights of our people. We condemn by administrative edict, rather than by jury trial. Of course, no one has a constitutional right to a government job. But every citizen has a right to a fair trial when his government seeks to deprive him of the privileges of first class citizenship.

The evil of these cases is only emphasized by the procedure employed in Dorothy Bailey's case. Together they illustrate how deprivation of our citizens of fair trials is subversion from within.

Mr. Justice Jackson, concurring:

. . . But the real target of all this procedure is the government employee who is a member of, or sympathetic to, one or more accused organizations. He not only may be discharged, but disqualified from employment, upon no other ground than such membership or sympathetic affiliation. And he cannot attack the correctness of the Attorney General's designation in any loyalty proceeding.

Ordinary dismissals from government service which violate no fixed tenure concern only the Executive branch, and courts will not review such discretionary action. However, these are not discretionary discharges but discharges pursuant to an order having force of law. Administrative machinery is publicly set up to comb the whole government service to discharge persons or to declare them ineligible for employment upon an incontestable finding, made without hearing, that some organization is subversive. To be deprived not only of present government employment but of future opportunity for it certainly is no small injury when government employment so dominates the field of opportunity.

The fact that one may not have a legal right to get or keep a government post does not mean that he can be adjudged ineligible illegally. . . .

Unless a hearing is provided in which the organization can present evidence as to its character, a presumption of disloyalty is entered against its every member-employee, and because of it, he may be branded disloyal, discharged, and rendered ineligible for government service. I would reverse the decisions for lack of due process in denying a hearing at any stage.

Mr. Justice Reed, with whom the Chief Justice [Vinson] and Mr. Justice Minton join, dissenting:

. . . No objection is or could reasonably be made in the records or briefs to an examination by the Government into the loyalty of its employees. Although the Founders of this Republic rebelled against their established government of England and won our freedom, the ,creation of our own constitutional government endowed that new government, the United States of America, with the right and duty to protect its existence against any force that seeks its overthrow or changes in its structure by other than constitutional means. Tolerant as we are of all political efforts by argument or persuasion to change the basis of our social, economic or political life, the line is drawn sharply and clearly at any act or incitement to act in violation of our constitutional processes. Surely the Government need not await an employee's conviction of a crime involving disloyalty before separating him from public service. Governments cannot be indifferent to manifestations of subversion. As soon as these are significant enough reasonably to cause concern as to the likelihood of action, the duty to protect the state compels the exertion of governmental power. Not to move would brand a government with a dangerous weakness of will. The determination of the time for action rests with the executive and legislative arms. An objection to consideration of an employee's sympathetic association with an admitted totalitarian, fascist, communist or subversive group, as bearing upon the propriety of his retention or employment as a government employee would have no better standing. The Order gives conclusive indication of the type of organization that is meant by the four word-labels. . . .

This Court, throughout the years, has maintained the protection of the First Amendment as a major safeguard to the maintenance of a free republic. This Nation has never suffered from an enforced conformity of expression or a limitation of criticism. But neither are we compelled to endure espionage and sedition. Wide as are the freedoms of the First Amendment, this Court has never hesitated to deny the individual's right to use the privileges for the overturn of law and order. Reasonable restraints for the fair protection of the Government against incitement to sedition cannot properly be said to be "undemocratic" or contrary to the guarantees of free speech. Otherwise the guarantee of civil rights would be mockery. Even when this Court spoke out most strongly against previous restraints, it was careful to recognize that "The security of the community life may be protected against incitements to acts of violence and the overthrow by force of orderly government." *Near* v. *State of Minnesota*, 283 U.S. 697 (1930).

Recognizing that the designation, rightly or wrongly, of petitioner organizations as communist impairs their ability to carry forward successfully whatever legitimate objects they seek to accomplish, we do not accept their argument that such interference is an abridgment of First Amendment guarantees. They are in the position of every proponent of unpopular views. Heresy induces strong expressions of opposition. So long as petitioners are permitted to voice their political ideas, free from suggestions for the opportune use of force to accomplish their social and economic aims, it is hard to understand how any advocate of freedom of expression can assert their right has been unconstitutionally abridged. As nothing in the orders or regulations concerning this list limits the teachings or support of these organizations, we do not believe that any right of theirs under the First Amendment is abridged by publication of the list. . . .

Does due process require notice and hearing for the Department of Justice investigation under Executive Order No. 9835, Part III, § 3, . . . preliminary to listing? As a standard for due process one cannot do better than to accept as a measure that no one may be deprived of liberty or property without such reasonable notice and hearing as fairness requires. This is my understanding of the meaning of the opinions upon due process cited in the concurring opinions. We are not here concerned with the rightfulness of the extent of participation in the investigations that might be claimed by petitioners. They were given no chance to take part. Their claim is that the listing resulted in a deprivation of liberty or property contrary to the procedure required by the Fifth Amendment.

The contention can be answered summarily by saying that there is no deprivation of any property or liberty of any listed organization by the Attorney General's designation. It may be assumed that the listing is hurtful to their prestige, reputation and earning power. It may be such an injury as would entitle organizations to damages in a tort action against persons not protected by privilege. . . . This designation, however, does not prohibit any business of the organizations, subject them to any punishment or deprive them of liberty of speech or other freedom. . . .

These petitioners are not ordered to do anything and are not punished for anything. Their position may be analogized to that of persons under grand jury investigation. Such persons have no right to notice by and hearing before a grand jury; only a right to defend the charge at trial. . . .

To allow petitioners entry into the investigation would amount to interference with the Executive's discretion, contrary to the ordinary operations of Government. . . .

The Executive has authority to gather information concerning the loyalty of its employees as congressional committees have power to investigate matters of legislative interest. A public statement of legislative conclusions on information that later may be found erroneous may damage those investigated but it is not a civil judgment or a criminal conviction. Due process does not apply. Questions of propriety of political action are not for the courts. Information that an employee associates with or belongs to organizations considered communistic may be deemed by the Executive a sound reason for making inquiries into the desirability of the employment of that employee. That is not "guilt by association." It is a warning to investigate the conduct of the employee and his opportunity for harm. . . .

4. Limits on Powers of Congressional Committees

McGRAIN v. DAUGHERTY

273 US 135 (1927)

[Since 1792 Congress has asserted and exercised the power of investigation through committees and has empowered such committees to summon witnesses, records, and papers. One of the principal subjects of congressional investigations has been the conduct of executive agencies and departments, including possible violations of criminal laws; but there may be no such investigation of a matter pending before a judicial tribunal. *Kilbourn* v. *Thompson,* 103 US 168 (1881). There is no power, moreover, to investigate "into the private affairs of the citizen." *Interstate Commerce Commission* v. *Brinson,* 154 US 447 (1894). But the Senate or the House does not, when it sets up an investigating committee, declare beforehand what that body "meditated doing when the investigation was concluded." *In re Chapman,* 166 US 661 (1897). The Court presumes that the investigation is undertaken in good faith to aid the legislative process, even though the information elicited may be useful, as a by-product, in criminal prosecutions. *Sinclair* v. *United States,* 279 US 263 (1929).

[In the present case the Court unanimously sustained the power of a Senate committee to investigate the Department of Justice, for this is a matter with respect to which it could legislate, even though the information exacted from witnesses may possibly disclose crime. "The only legitimate object the Senate could have in ordering the investigation was to aid it in legislating; and we think the subject-matter was such that the presumption should be indulged that this was the real object. An express avowal of the object would have been better; but . . . was not indispensable." This is a broad power, and the Court recognized that it "may be abusively and oppressively exercised." In rare cases there are "admissible measures of relief."

[If the powers of the committee are exceeded or if the questions are not pertinent to the matter under inquiry, the witness may refuse to answer. The committee may then request the House to which it is responsible to cite the witness as in contempt. If the House votes accordingly, the Attorney General then presents the evidence to a federal grand jury. If the witness is indicted, he is entitled to a trial as in any other criminal prosecution, and this trial will settle the question as to whether the witness had the right to refuse to answer the questions. Another sanction against a witness may be an indictment and conviction for perjury. A recent case involving prosecution for perjury was *Christoffel* v. *United States,* 338 US 84 (1949); recent contempt cases were *United States* v. *Bryan*, 339 US 323 (1950), and *United States* v. *Fleischman*, 339 US 349 (1950).]

Mr. Justice Van Devanter delivered the opinion of the Court:

This is an appeal from the final order in a proceeding in *habeas corpus* discharging a recusant witness held in custody under process of attachment issued from the United States Senate in the course of an investigation which it was making of the administration of the Department of Justice. A full statement of the case is necessary.

The Department of Justice is one of the great executive departments established by congressional enactment and has charge, among other things, of the initiation and prosecution of all suits, civil and criminal, which may be brought in the right and name of the United States to compel obedience or punish disobedience to its laws, to recover property obtained from it by unlawful or fraudulent means, or to safeguard its rights in other respects; and also of the assertion and protection of its interests when it or its officers are sued by others. The Attorney General is the head of the department, and its functions are all to be exercised under his supervision and direction.

Harry M. Daugherty became the Attorney General March 5, 1921, and held that office until March 28, 1924, when he resigned. Late in that period various charges of misfeasance and nonfeasance in the Department of Justice after he became its supervising head were brought to the attention of the Senate by individual senators and made the basis of an insistent demand that the department be investigated to the end that the practices and deficiencies which, according to the charges, were operating to prevent or impair its right administration might be definitely ascertained and that appropriate and effective measures might be taken to remedy or eliminate the evil. The Senate regarded the charges as grave and requiring legislative attention and action. Accordingly it formulated, passed, and invited the House of Representatives to pass (and that body did pass) two measures taking important litigation then in immediate contemplation out of the control of the Department of Justice and placing the same in charge of special counsel to be appointed by the President; and also adopted a resolution authorizing and directing a select committee of five senators—

to investigate circumstances and facts, and report the same to the Senate, concerning the alleged failure of Harry M. Daugherty, Attorney General of the United States, to prosecute properly violators of the Sherman Antitrust Act and the Clayton Act against monopolies and unlawful restraint of trade; the alleged neglect and failure of the said Harry M. Daugherty, Attorney General of the United States, to arrest and prosecute Albert B. Fall, Harry F. Sinclair, E. L. Doheny, C. R. Forbes, and their co-conspirators in defrauding the Government, as well as the alleged neglect and failure of the said Attorney General to arrest and prosecute many others for violations of Federal statutes, and his alleged failure to prosecute properly, efficiently, and promptly, and to defend, all manner of civil and criminal actions wherein the Government of the United States is interested as a party plaintiff or defendant. And said committee is further directed to inquire into, investigate, and report to the Senate the activities of the said Harry M. Daugherty, Attorney General, and any of his assistants in the Department of Justice which would in any manner tend to impair their efficiency or influence as representatives of the Government of the United States.

The resolution also authorized the committee to send for books and papers, to subpoena witnesses, to administer oaths, and to sit at such times and places as it might deem advisable.

In the course of the investigation the committee issued and caused to be duly served on Mally S. Daugherty—who was a brother of Harry M. Daugherty and president of the Midland National Bank of Washington Court House, Ohio—a subpoena commanding him to appear before the committee for the purpose of giving testimony bearing on the subject under investigation, and to bring with him the "deposit ledgers of the Midland National Bank since November 1, 1920; also note files and transcript of owners of every safety vault; also records of income drafts; also records of any individual account or accounts showing withdrawals of amounts of $25,000 or over during above period." The witness failed to appear.

A little later in the course of the investigation the committee issued and caused to be duly served on the same witness another subpoena commanding him to appear before it for the purpose of giving testimony relating to the subject under consideration—nothing being said in this subpoena about bringing records, books, or papers. The witness again failed to appear; and no excuse was offered by him for either failure.

The committee then made a report to the Senate stating that the subpoenas had been issued, that according to the officer's returns—copies of which accompanied the report—the witness was personally served; and that he had failed and refused to appear. After a reading of the report, the Senate adopted a resolution reciting these facts and proceeding as follows:

Whereas the appearance and testimony of the said M. S. Daugherty is material and necessary in order that the committee may properly execute the functions imposed upon it and may obtain information necessary as a basis for such legislative and other action as the Senate may deem necessary and proper: Therefore be it

Resolved, That the President of the Senate pro tempore issue his warrant commanding the Sergeant at Arms or his deputy to take into custody the body of the said M. S. Daugherty wherever found, and to bring the said M. S. Daugherty before the bar of the Senate, then and there to answer such questions pertinent to the matter under inquiry as the Senate may order the President of the Senate pro tempore to propound; and to keep the said M. S. Daugherty in custody to await the further order of the Senate.

It will be observed from the terms of the resolution that the warrant was to be issued in furtherance of the effort to obtain the personal testimony of the witness and, like the second subpoena, was not intended to exact from him the production of the various records, books, and papers named in the first subpoena.

The warrant was issued agreeably to the resolution and was addressed simply to the Sergeant at Arms. That officer on receiving the warrant indorsed thereon a direction that it be executed by John J. McGrain, already his deputy, and delivered it to him for execution.

The deputy, proceeding under the warrant, took the witness into custody at Cincinnati, Ohio, with the purpose of bringing him before the bar of the Senate as commanded; whereupon the witness petitioned the federal district court in Cincinnati for a writ of *habeas corpus.* The writ was granted and the deputy made due return setting forth the warrant and the cause of the detention. After a hearing the court held the attachment and detention unlawful and discharged the witness, the decision being put on the ground that the Senate in directing the investigation and in ordering the attachment exceeded its powers under the Constitution. The deputy prayed and was allowed a direct appeal to this Court. . . .

We have given the case earnest and prolonged consideration because the principal questions involved are of unusual importance and delicacy. They are (a) whether the Senate—or the House of Representatives, both being on the same plane in this regard—has power, through its own process, to compel a private individual to appear before it or one of its committees and give testimony needed to enable it efficiently to exercise a legislative function belonging to it under the Constitution, and (b) whether it sufficiently appears that the process was being employed in this instance to obtain testimony for that purpose. . . .

In approaching the principal questions, which remain to be considered, two observations are in order. One is that we are not now concerned with the direction in the first subpoena that the witness produce various records, books, and papers of the Midland National Bank. That direction was not repeated in the second subpoena; and is not sought to be enforced by the attachment. . . . The other is that we are not now concerned with the right of the Senate to propound or the duty of the witness to answer specific questions, for as yet no questions have been propounded to him. He is asserting—and is standing on his assertion—that the Senate is without power to interrogate him, even if the questions propounded be pertinent and otherwise legitimate—which for present purposes must be assumed.

The first of the principal questions—the one which the witness particularly presses on our attention—is, as before shown, whether the Senate—or the House of Representatives, both being on the same plane in this regard—has power, through its own process, to compel a private individual to appear before it or one of its committees and give testimony needed to enable it efficiently to exercise a legislative function belonging to it under the Constitution.

The Constitution provides for a Congress consisting of a Senate and House of Representatives and invests it with "all legislative powers" granted to the United States, and with power "to make all laws which shall be necessary and proper" for carrying into execution these powers and "all other powers" vested by the Constitution in the United States or in any department or officer thereof. Art. I, secs. 1, 8. Other provisions show that, while bills can become laws only after being considered and passed by both houses of Congress, each house is to be distinct from the other, to have its own officers and rules, and to exercise its legislative function independently. Art. I, secs. 2, 3, 5, 7. But there is no provision expressly investing either house with power to make investigations and exact testimony to the end that it may exercise its legislative function advisedly and effectively. So the question arises whether this power is so far incidental to the legislative function as to be implied.

In actual legislative practice power to secure needed information by such means has long been treated as an attribute of the power to legislate. It was so regarded in the British Parliament and in the Colonial legislatures before the American Revolution; and a like view has prevailed and been carried into effect in both houses of Congress and in most of the state legislatures.

This power was both asserted and exerted by the House of Representatives in 1792, when it appointed a select committee to inquire into the St. Clair expedition and authorized the committee to send for necessary persons, papers and records. Mr. Madison, who had taken an important part in framing the Constitution only five years before, and four of his associates in that work, were members of the House of Representatives at the time, and all voted for the inquiry. 3 Cong. Ann. 494. Other exertions of the power by the House of Representatives, as also by the Senate, are shown in the citations. . . . Among those by the Senate, the inquiry ordered in 1859 respecting the raid by John Brown and his adherents on the armory and arsenal of the United States at Harper's Ferry is of special significance. The resolution directing the inquiry authorized the committee to send for persons and papers, to inquire into the facts pertaining to the raid and the means by which it was organized and supported, and to report what legislation, if any, was necessary to preserve the peace of the country and protect the public property. The resolution was briefly discussed and adopted without opposition. Later on the committee reported that Thaddeus Hyatt, although subpoenaed to appear as a witness, had refused to do so; whereupon the Senate ordered that he be attached and brought before it to answer for his refusal. When he was brought in he answered by challenging the power of the Senate to direct the inquiry and exact testimony to aid it in exercising its legislative function. The question of power thus presented was thoroughly discussed by several senators—Mr. Sumner of Massachusetts taking the lead in denying the power and Mr. Fessenden of Maine in supporting it. Sectional and party lines were put aside and the question was debated and determined with special regard to principle and precedent. The vote was taken on a resolution pronouncing the witness's answer insufficient and directing that he be committed until he should signify that he was ready and willing to testify. The resolution was adopted—44 senators voting for it and 10 against. . . .

The deliberate solution of the question on that occasion has been accepted and followed on other occasions by both houses of Congress, and never has been rejected or questioned by either.

The state courts quite generally have held that the power to legislate carries with it by necessary implication ample authority to obtain information needed in the rightful exercise of that power and to employ compulsory process for the purpose. . . .

We have referred to the practice of the two houses of Congress; and we now shall notice some significant congressional enactments. . . . January 24, 1857, ch. 19, 11 Stat. 155, it [Congress] passed "An Act more effectually to enforce the attendance of witnesses on the summons of either house of Congress, and to compel them to discover testimony." This act provided, first, that any person summoned as a witness to give testimony or produce papers in any matter under inquiry before either house of Congress, or any committee of either house, who should wilfully make default, or, if appearing, should refuse to answer any question pertinent to the inquiry, should, in addition to the pains and penalties then existing, be deemed guilty of a misdemeanor and be subject to indictment and punishment as there prescribed; and, secondly, that no person should be excused from giving evidence in such an inquiry on the ground that it might tend to incriminate or disgrace him, nor be held to answer criminally, or be subjected to any penalty or forfeiture, for any fact or act as to which he was required to testify, excepting that he might be subjected to prosecution for perjury committed while so testifying. January 24, 1862, ch. 11, 12 Stat. 333, Congress modified the immunity provision in particulars not material here. These enactments are now embodied in Sections 101–4 and 859 of Revised Statutes. They show very plainly that Congress intended thereby (a) to recognize the power of either house to institute inquiries and exact evidence touching subjects within its jurisdiction and on which it was disposed to act; (b) to recognize that such inquiries may be conducted through committees; (c) to subject defaulting and contumacious witnesses to indictment and punishment in the courts, and thereby to enable either house to exert the power of inquiry "more effectually"; and (d) to open the way for obtaining evidence in such an inquiry, which otherwise could not be obtained, by exempting witnesses required to give evidence therein from criminal and penal prosecutions in respect of matters disclosed by their evidence.

Four decisions of this Court are cited and more or less relied on, and we now turn to them.

The first decision was in *Anderson* v. *Dunn,* 6 Wheat. 204. The question there was whether, under the Constitution, the House of Representatives has power to attach and punish a person other than a member for contempt of its authority—in fact, an attempt to bribe one of its members. The Court regarded the power as essential to the effective exertion of other powers expressly granted, and therefore as implied. The argument advanced to the contrary was that as the Constitution expressly grants to each house power to punish or expel its own members and says nothing about punishing others, the implication or inference, if any, is that power to punish one who is not a member is neither given nor intended. The Court answered this by saying:

. . . This argument proves too much; for its direct application would lead to the annihilation of almost every power of Congress. To enforce its laws upon any subject without the sanction of punishment, is obviously impossible. Yet there is an express grant of power to punish in one class of cases and one only, and all the punishing power exercised by Congress, in any cases, except those which relate to piracy and offenses against the laws of nations, is derived from implication. Nor did the idea ever occur to any one, that the express grant in one class of cases repelled the assumption of the punishing power in any other. The truth is, that the exercise of the powers given over their own members, was of such a delicate nature, that a constitutional provision became necessary to assert or communicate it. Constituted, as that body is, of the delegates of confederated States, some such provision was necessary to guard against their mutual jealousy, since every proceeding against a representative would indirectly affect the honor or interests of the state which sent him.

The next decision was in *Kilbourn* v. *Thompson,* 103 U.S. 168. The question there was whether the House of Representatives had exceeded its power in directing one of its committees to make a particular investigation. The decision was that it had. The principles announced and applied in the case are—that neither house of Congress possesses a "general power of making inquiry into the private affairs of the citizen"; that the power actually possessed is limited to inquiries relating to matters of which the particular house "has jurisdiction" and in respect of which it rightfully may take other action; that if the inquiry relates to "a matter wherein relief or redress could be had only by a judicial proceeding" it is not within the range of this power, but must be left to the courts, conformably to the constitutional separation of governmental powers; and that for the purpose of determining the essential character of the inquiry recourse may be had to the resolution or order under which it is made. The court examined the resolution which was the basis of the particular inquiry, and ascertained therefrom that the inquiry related to a private real-estate pool or partnership in the District of Columbia. Jay Cooke & Co. had had an interest in the pool, but had become bankrupts, and their estate was in course of administration in a federal bankruptcy court in Pennsylvania. The United States was one of their creditors. The trustee in the bankruptcy proceeding had effected a settlement of the bankrupts' interest in the pool, and of course his action was subject to examination and approval or disapproval by the bankruptcy court. Some of the creditors, including the United States, were dissatisfied with the settlement. In these circumstances, disclosed in the preamble, the resolution directed the committee "to inquire into the matter and history of said real-estate pool and the character of said settlement, with the amount of property involved in which Jay Cooke & Co. were interested, and the amount paid or to be paid in said settlement, with power to send for persons and papers and report to the House." The Court pointed out that the resolution contained no suggestion of contemplated legislation; that the matter was one in respect to which no valid legislation could be had; that the bankrupts' estate and the trustee's settlement were still pending in the bankruptcy court; and that the United States and other creditors were free to press their claims in that proceeding. And on these grounds the Court held that in undertaking the investigation "the House of Representatives not only exceeded the limit of its own authority but assumed a power which could only be properly exercised by another branch of the government, because it was in its nature clearly judicial."

The case has been cited at times, and is cited to us now, as strongly intimating, if not holding, that neither house of Congress has power to make inquiries and exact evidence in aid of contemplated legislation. There are expressions in the opinion which, separately considered, might bear such an interpretation; but that this was not intended is shown by the immediately succeeding statement that "This latter proposition is one which we do not propose to decide in the present case because we are able to decide the case without passing upon the existence or non-existence of such a power in aid of the legislative function."

Next in order is *In re Chapman*, 166 U.S. 661. The inquiry there in question was conducted under a resolution of the Senate and related to charges, published in the press, that senators were yielding to corrupt influences in considering a tariff bill then before the Senate and were speculating in stocks the value of which would be affected by pending amendments to the bill. Chapman appeared before the committee in response to a subpoena, but refused to answer questions pertinent to the inquiry, and was indicted and convicted under the act of 1857 for his refusal. The Court sustained the constitutional validity of the act of 1857, and, after referring to the constitutional provision empowering either house to punish its members for disorderly behavior and by a vote of two-thirds to expel a member, held that the inquiry related to the integrity and fidelity of senators in the discharge of their duties, and therefore to a matter "within the range of the constitutional powers of the Senate" and in respect of which it could compel witnesses to appear and testify. . . .

The case is relied on here as fully sustaining the power of either house to conduct investigations and exact testimony from witnesses for legislative purposes. In the course of the opinion it is said that disclosures by witnesses may be compelled constitutionally "to enable the respective bodies to discharge their legitimate functions, and that it was to effect this that the act of 1857 was passed"; and also "We grant that Congress could not divest itself or either of its houses of the essential and inherent power to punish for contempt, in cases to which the power of either house properly extended; but, because Congress, by the act of 1857, sought to aid each of the houses in the discharge of its constitutional functions, it does not follow that any delegation of the power in each to punish for contempt was involved." The terms "legitimate functions" and "constitutional functions" are broad and might well be regarded as including the legislative function, but as the case in hand did not call for any expression respecting that function, it hardly can be said that these terms were purposely used as including it.

The latest case is *Marshall* v. *Gordon,* 243 U.S. 521. The question there was whether the House of Representatives exceeded its power in punishing, as for a contempt of its authority, a person—not a member—who had written, published, and sent to the chairman of one of its committees an ill-tempered and irritating letter respecting the action and purposes of the committee. Power to make inquiries and obtain evidence by compulsory process was not involved. The Court recognized distinctly that the House of Representatives has implied power to punish a person not a member for contempt, as was ruled in *Anderson* v. *Dunn, supra,* but held that its action in this instance was without constitutional justification. The decision was put on the ground that the letter, while offensive and vexatious, was not calculated or likely to affect the House in any of its proceedings or in the exercise of any of its functions—in short, that the act which was punished as a contempt was not of such a character as to bring it within the rule that an express power draws after it others which are necessary and appropriate to give effect to it.

While these cases are not decisive of the question we are considering, they definitely settle two propositions which we recognize as entirely sound and having a bearing on its solution: One, that the two houses of Congress, in their separate relations, possess not only such powers as are expressly granted to them by the Constitution, but such auxiliary powers as are necessary and appropriate to make the express powers effective; and, the other, that neither house is invested with "general" power to inquire into private affairs and compel disclosures but only with such limited power of inquiry as is shown to exist when the rule of constitutional interpretation just stated is rightly applied. . . .

With this review of the legislative practice, congressional enactments, and court decisions, we proceed to a statement of our conclusions on the question.

We are of opinion that the power of inquiry—with process to enforce it—is an essential and appropriate auxiliary to the legislative function. . . .

We are further of opinion that the provisions of the Constitution are not of doubtful meaning, but, as was held by this Court in the cases we have reviewed, are intended to be effectively exercised, and therefore to carry with them such auxiliary powers as are necessary and appropriate to that end. While the power to exact information in aid of the legislative function was not involved in those cases, the rule of interpretation applied there is applicable here. A legislative body cannot legislate wisely or effectively in the absence of information respecting the conditions which the legislation is intended to affect or change; and where the legislative body does not itself possess the requisite information—which not infrequently is true—recourse must be had to others who do possess it. Experience has taught that mere requests for such information often are unavailing, and also that information which is volunteered is not always accurate or complete; so some means of compulsion are essential to obtain what is needed. All this was true before and when the Constitution was framed and adopted. In that period the power of inquiry—with enforcing process —was regarded and employed as a necessary and appropriate attribute of the power to legislate—indeed, was treated as inhering in it. Thus there is ample warrant for thinking, as we do, that the constitutional provisions which commit the legislative function to the two houses are intended to include this attribute to the end that the function may be effectively exercised.

The contention is earnestly made on behalf of the witness that this power of inquiry, if sustained, may be abusively and oppressively exerted. If this be so, it affords no ground for denying the power. The same contention might be directed against the power to legislate and, of course, would be unavailing. We must assume, for present purposes, that neither house will be disposed to exert the power beyond its proper bounds, or without due regard to the rights of witnesses. But if, contrary to this assumption, controlling limitations or restrictions are disregarded, the decisions in *Kilbourn* v. *Thompson* and *Marshall* v. *Gordon* point to admissible measures of relief. And it is a necessary deduction from the decisions in *Kilbourn* v. *Thompson* and *In re Chapman* that a witness rightfully may refuse to answer where the bounds of the power are exceeded or the questions are not pertinent to the matter under inquiry.

We come now to the question whether it sufficiently appears that the purpose for which the witness's testimony was sought was to obtain information in aid of the legislative function. The court below answered the question in the negative and put its decision largely on this ground. . . .

We are of opinion that the court's ruling on this question was wrong, and that it sufficiently appears, when the proceedings are rightly interpreted, that the object of the investigation and of the effort to secure the witness's testimony was to obtain information for legislative purposes.

It is quite true that the resolution directing the investigation does not in terms avow that it is intended to be in aid of legislation; but it does show that the subject to be investigated was the administration of the Department of Justice—whether its functions were being properly discharged or were being neglected or misdirected, and particularly whether the Attorney General and his assistants were performing or neglecting their duties in respect of the institution and prosecution of proceedings to punish crimes and enforce appropriate remedies against the wrongdoers—specific instances of alleged neglect being recited. Plainly the subject was one on which legislation could be had and would be materially aided by the information which the investigation was calculated to elicit. This becomes manifest when it is reflected that the functions of the Department of Justice, the powers and duties of the Attorney General and the duties of his assistants are all subject to regulation by congressional legislation, and that the department is maintained and its activities are carried on under such appropriations as in the judgment of Congress are needed from year to year.

The only legitimate object the Senate could have in ordering the investigation was to aid it in legislating; and we think the subject-matter was such that the presumption should be indulged that this was the real object. An express avowal of the object would have been better; but in view of the particular subject-matter was not indispensable. . . .

The second resolution—the one directing that the witness be attached—declares that his testimony is sought with the purpose of obtaining "information necessary as a basis for such legislative and other action as the Senate may deem necessary and proper." This avowal of contemplated legislation is in accord with what we think is the right interpretation of the earlier resolution directing the investigation. The suggested possibility of "other action" if deemed "necessary or proper" is of course open to criticism in that there is no other action in the matter which would be within the power of the Senate. But we do not assent to the view that this indefinite and untenable suggestion invalidates the entire proceeding. The right view in our opinion is that it takes nothing from the lawful object avowed in the same resolution and rightly inferable from the earlier one. It is not as if an inadmissible or unlawful object were affirmatively and definitely avowed.

We conclude that the investigation was ordered for a legitimate object; that the witness wrongfully refused to appear and testify before the committee and was lawfully attached; that the Senate is entitled to have him give testimony pertinent to the inquiry, either at its bar or before the committee; and that the district court erred in discharging him from custody under the attachment. . . .

UNITED STATES v. RUMELY

345 US 41 (1953)

[The House of Representatives set up a committee to investigate lobbying activities. Rumely, as secretary of an organization known as the Committee for Constitutional Government, refused to disclose to the House committee the names of those who made bulk purchases of certain political books for further distribution. He was convicted of contempt. By a 5-to-2 decision (Justices Burton and Minton not participating) the Court set aside the conviction, on the ground that the resolution that created the House committee limited the investigation to activities that involved only direct lobbying of Congress, and not activities that involved efforts to influence the thinking of the community generally. The majority placed this narrow construction upon the resolution in order to avoid the constitutional issue, for an inquiry into the efforts of private citizens to influence public opinion through publications would raise doubts of constitutionality under the First Amendment. The dissenting Justices (Douglas and Black), however, maintained that the resolution was intended to vest broad powers and was unconstitutional.

[The case is significant as illustrating the area of possible conflict between the investigatory power of Congress and the personal rights guaranteed by the First Amendment.]

Mr. Justice Frankfurter delivered the opinion of the Court:

The respondent Rumely was Secretary of an organization known as the Committee for Constitutional Government, which, among other things, engaged in the sale of books of a particular political tendentiousness. He refused to disclose to the House Select Committee on Lobbying Activities the names of those who made bulk purchases of these books for further distribution, and was convicted under 2 U.S.C.A. § 192, which provides penalties for refusal to give testimony or to produce relevant papers "upon any matter" under congressional inquiry. The Court of Appeals reversed, one judge dissenting. It held that the committee before which Rumely refused to furnish this information had no authority to compel its production. . . . This issue —whether the committee had power to exact the information which the witness withheld—must first be settled before we may consider whether Congress had the power to confer upon the committee the authority which it claimed.

Although we are here dealing with a resolution of the House of Representatives, the problem is much the same as that which confronts the Court when called upon to construe a statute that carries the seeds of constitutional controversy. The potential constitutional questions have far-reaching import. We are asked to recognize the penetrating and pervasive scope of the investigative power of Congress. The reach that may be claimed for that power is indicated by Woodrow Wilson's characterization of it:

It is the proper duty of a representative body to look diligently into every affair of government and to talk much about what it sees. It is meant to be the eyes and the voice, and to embody the wisdom and will of its constituents. Unless Congress have and use every means of acquainting itself with the acts and the disposition of the administrative agents of the government, the country must be helpless to learn how it is being served; and unless Congress both scrutinize these things and sift them by every form of discussion, the country must remain in embarrassing, crippling ignorance of the very affairs which it is most important that it should understand and direct. The informing function of Congress should be preferred even to its legislative function. Wilson, *Congressional Government*, 303.

Although the indispensable "informing function of Congress" is not to be minimized, determination of the "rights" which this function implies illustrates the common juristic situation thus defined for the Court by Mr. Justice Holmes:

All rights tend to declare themselves absolute to their logical extreme. Yet all in fact are limited by the neighborhood of principles of policy which are other than those on which the particular right is founded, and which become strong enough to hold their own when a certain point is reached. *Hudson County Water Co.* v. *McCarter*, 209 U.S. 349.

. . . President Wilson did not write in light of the history of events since he wrote; more particularly he did not write of the investigative power of Congress in the context of the First Amendment. And so, we would have to be that "blind" Court, against which Mr. Chief Justice Taft admonished . . . that does not see what "[a]ll others can see and understand" not to know that there is wide concern, both in and out of Congress, over some aspects of the exercise of the congressional power of investigation.

Accommodation of these contending principles—the one underlying the power of Congress to investigate, the other at the basis of the limitation imposed by the First Amendment—is not called for until after we have construed the scope of the authority which the House of Representatives gave to the Select Committee on Lobbying Activities. The pertinent portion of the resolution of August 12, 1949, reads:

The Committee is authorized and directed to conduct a study and investigation of (1) all lobbying activities intended to influence, encourage, promote, or retard legislation; and (2) all activities of agencies of the Federal Government intended to influence, encourage, promote, or retard legislation. H. Res. 298, 81st Cong., 1st Sess.

This is the controlling charter of the committee's powers. Its right to exact testimony and to call for the production of documents must be found in this language. The resolution must speak for itself, since Congress put no gloss upon it at the time of its passage. Nor is any help to be had from the fact that the purpose of the Buchanan Committee, as the Select Committee was known, was to try to "find out how well [the Federal Regulation of Lobbying Act of 1946] worked." . . . That statute had a section of definitions, but Congress did not define the terms "lobbying" or "lobbying activities" in that Act, for it did not use them. Accordingly, the phrase "lobbying activities" in the resolution must be given the meaning that may fairly be attributed to it, having special regard for the principle of constitutional adjudication which makes it decisive in the choice of fair alternatives that one construction may raise serious constitutional questions avoided by another. In a long series of decisions we have acted on this principle. . . . As phrased by Mr. Chief Justice Hughes, "If a serious doubt of constitutionality is raised, it is a cardinal principle that this Court will first ascertain whether a construction of the statute is fairly possible by which the question may be avoided." . . .

Surely it cannot be denied that giving the scope to the resolution for which the Government contends, that is, deriving from it the power to inquire into all efforts of private individuals to influence public opinion through books and periodicals, however remote the radiations of influence which they may exert upon the ultimate legislative process, raises doubts of constitutionality in view of the prohibition of the First Amendment. In light of the opinion of Prettyman, J., below and of some of the views expressed here, it would not be seemly to maintain that these doubts are fanciful or factitious. Indeed, adjudication here, if it were necessary, would affect not an evanescent policy of Congress, but its power to inform itself, which underlies its policy-making function. Whenever constitutional limits upon the investigative power of Congress have to be drawn by this Court, it ought only to be done after Congress has demonstrated its full awareness of what is at stake by unequivocally authorizing an inquiry of dubious limits. . . .

Choice is left. As a matter of English, the phrase "lobbying activities" readily lends itself to the construction placed upon it below, namely, "lobbying in its commonly accepted sense," that is, "representations made directly to the Congress, its members, or its committees," . . . and does not reach what was in Chairman Buchanan's mind, attempts "to saturate the thinking of the community." . . . Certainly it does no violence to the phrase "lobbying activities" to give it a more restricted scope. To give such meaning is not barred by intellectual honesty. So to interpret is in the candid service of avoiding a serious constitutional doubt. . . .

Only a word need be said about the debate in Congress after the committee reported that Rumely had refused to produce the information which he had a right to refuse under the restricted meaning of the phrase "lobbying activities." The view taken at that time by the committee and by the Congress that the committee was authorized to ask Rumely for the information he withheld is not legislative history defining the scope of a congressional measure. What was said in the debate on August 30, 1950, after the controversy had arisen regarding the scope of the resolution of August 12, 1949, had the usual infirmity of *post litem motam*, self-serving declarations. In any event, Rumely's duty to answer must be judged as of the time of his refusal. The scope of the resolution defining that duty is therefore to be ascertained as of that time and cannot be enlarged by subsequent action of Congress.

Grave constitutional questions are matters properly to be decided by this Court but only when they inescapably come before us for adjudication. Until then it is our duty to abstain from marking the boundaries of congressional power or delimiting the protection guaranteed by the First Amendment. Only by such self-restraint will we avoid the mischief which has followed occasional departures from the principles which we profess.

The judgment below should be affirmed. . . .

Mr. Justice Douglas, with whom Mr. Justice Black concurs, concurring:

. . . I come then to the constitutional questions. Respondent represents a segment of the American press. Some may like what his group publishes; others may disapprove. These tracts may be the essence of wisdom to some; to others their point of view and philosophy may be anathema. To some ears their words may be harsh and repulsive; to others they may carry the hope of the future. We have here a publisher who through books and pamphlets seeks to reach the minds and hearts of the American people. He is different in some respects from other publishers. But the differences are minor. Like the publishers of newspapers, magazines, or books, this publisher bids for the minds of men in the market place of ideas. The aim of the historic struggle for a free press was "to establish and preserve the right of the English people to full information in respect to the doings or misdoings of their government." *Grosjean* v. *American Press Co.*, 297 U.S. 233. . . . That is the tradition behind the First Amendment. Censorship or previous restraint is banned. *Near* v. *Minnesota*, 283 U.S. 697. . . . Discriminatory taxation is outlawed. *Grosjean* v. *American Press Co., supra.* The privilege of pamphleteering, as well as the more orthodox types of publications, may neither be licensed, *Lovell* v. *City of Griffin,* 303 U.S. 444, . . . nor taxed. *Murdock* v. *Pennsylvania,* 319 U.S. 105. . . . These are illustrative of the preferred position granted speech and the press by the First Amendment. The command that "Congress shall make no law . . . abridging the freedom of speech, or of the press" has behind it a long history. It expresses the confidence that the safety of society depends on the tolerance of government for hostile as well as friendly criticism, that in a community where men's minds are free, there must be room for the unorthodox as well as the orthodox views.

If the present inquiry were sanctioned the press would be subjected to harassment that in practical effect might be as serious as censorship. A publisher, compelled to register with the federal government, would be subjected to vexatious inquiries. A requirement that a publisher disclose the identity of those who buy his books, pamphlets, or papers is indeed the beginning of surveillance of the press. True, no legal sanction is involved here. Congress has imposed no tax, established no board of censors, instituted no licensing system. But the potential restraint is equally severe. The finger of government leveled against the press is ominous. Once the government can demand of a publisher the names of the purchasers of his publications, the free press as we know it disappears. Then the spectre of a government agent will look over the shoulder of everyone who reads. The purchase of a book or pamphlet today may result in a subpoena tomorrow. Fear of criticism goes with every person into the bookstall. The subtle, imponderable pressures of the orthodox lay hold. Some will fear to read what is unpopular, what the powers-that-be dislike. When the light of publicity may reach any student, any teacher, inquiry will be discouraged. The books and pamphlets that are critical of the administration, that preach an unpopular policy in domestic or foreign affairs, that are in disrepute in the orthodox school of thought will be suspect and subject to investigation. The press and its readers will pay a heavy price in harassment. But that will be minor in comparison with the menace of the shadow which government will cast over literature that does not follow the dominant party line. If the lady from Toledo can be required to disclose what she read yesterday and what she will read tomorrow, fear will take the place of freedom in the libraries, bookstores, and homes of the land. Through the harassment of hearings, investigations, reports, and subpoenas government will hold a club over speech and over the press. Congress could not do this by law. The power of investigation is also limited. Inquiry into personal and private affairs is precluded. . . . And so is any matter in respect to which no valid legislation could be had. . . . Since Congress could not by law require of respondent what the House demanded, it may not take the first step in an inquiry ending in fine or imprisonment.

WATKINS v. UNITED STATES
354 US 178 (1957)

[A union officer, appearing as a witness before a congressional committee, refused to answer questions as to past Communist Party membership of certain persons. His conviction for contempt was set aside by six Justices of the Supreme Court (Justice Clark dissented, and Justices Burton and Whittaker did not participate).

[In his opinion for the Court, Chief Justice Warren set forth broad constitutional principles that place limits on legislative investigations; but the decision itself may be limited to the proposition that the conviction was set aside because the committee did not state the subject under inquiry and did not show the pertinence of the questions to the investigation. *Barenblatt* v. *United States, post,* decided two years later, should be read along with the instant case.

[The concurring opinion of Justice Frankfurter emphasizes the assimilation of the statutory crime of contempt to the criminal law generally and its subjection to specific provisions of the Constitution. The dissenting opinion of Justice Clark gives broad sweep to the informing function of Congress exercised through its committees.]

Mr. Chief Justice Warren delivered the opinion of the Court:

This is a review by certiorari of a conviction under 2 U.S.C. § 192, 2 U.S.C.A. § 192 for "contempt of Congress." The misdemeanor is alleged to have been committed during a hearing before a congressional investigating committee. It is not the case of a truculent or contumacious witness who refuses to answer all questions or who, by boisterous or discourteous conduct, disturbs the decorum of the committee room. Petitioner was prosecuted for refusing to make certain disclosures which he asserted to be beyond the authority of the committee to demand. The controversy thus rests upon fundamental principles of the power of the Congress and the limitations upon that power. We approach the questions presented with conscious awareness of the far-reaching ramifications that can follow from a decision of this nature.

On April 29, 1954, petitioner appeared as a witness in compliance with a subpoena issued by a Subcommittee of the Committee on Un-American Activities of the House of Representatives. The Subcommittee elicited from petitioner a description of his background in labor union activities. He had been an employee of the International Harvester Company between 1935 and 1953. During the last eleven of those years, he had been on leave of absence to serve as an official of the Farm Equipment Workers International Union, later merged into the United Electrical, Radio and Machine Workers. He rose to the position of President of District No. 2 of the Farm Equipment Workers, a district defined geographically to include generally Canton and Rock Falls, Illinois, and Dubuque, Iowa. In 1953, petitioner joined the United Auto Workers International Union as a labor organizer.

Petitioner's name had been mentioned by two witnesses who testified before the Committee at prior hearings. In September 1952, one Donald O. Spencer admitted having been a Communist from 1943 to 1946. He declared that he had been recruited into the Party with the endorsement and prior approval of petitioner, whom he identified as the then District Vice-President of the Farm Equipment Workers. Spencer also mentioned that petitioner had attended meetings at which only card-carrying Communists were admitted. A month before petitioner testified, one Walter Rumsey stated that he had been recruited into the Party by petitioner. Rumsey added that he had paid Party dues to and later collected dues from petitioner, who had assumed the name, Sam Brown. Rumsey told the Committee that he left the Party in 1944.

Petitioner answered these allegations freely and without reservation. His attitude toward the inquiry is clearly revealed from the statement he made when the questioning turned to the subject of his past conduct, associations and predilections:

I am not now nor have I ever been a card-carrying member of the Communist Party. Rumsey was wrong when he said I had recruited him into the party, that I had received his dues, that I paid dues to him, and that I had used the alias Sam Brown.

Spencer was wrong when he termed any meetings which I attended as closed Communist Party meetings.

I would like to make it clear that for a period of time from approximately 1942 to 1947 I cooperated with the Communist Party and participated in Communist activities to such a degree that some persons may honestly believe that I was a member of the party.

I have made contributions upon occasions to Communist causes. I have signed petitions for Communist causes. I attended caucuses at an FE convention at which Communist Party officials were present.

Since I freely cooperated with the Communist Party I have no motive for making the distinction between cooperation and membership except the simple fact that it is the truth. I never carried a Communist Party card. I never accepted discipline and indeed on several occasions I opposed their position.

In a special convention held in the summer of 1947 I led the fight for compliance with the Taft-Hartley Act by the FE-CIO International Union. This fight became so bitter that it ended any possibility of future cooperation.

The character of petitioner's testimony on these matters can perhaps best be summarized by the Government's own appraisal in its brief:

A more complete and candid statement of his past political associations and activities (treating the Communist Party for present purposes as a mere political party) can hardly be imagined. Petitioner certainly was not attempting to conceal or withhold from the Committee his own past political associations, predilections, and preferences. Furthermore, petitioner told the Committee that he was entirely willing to identify for the Committee, and answer any questions it might have concerning, "those persons whom I knew to be members of the Communist Party," provided that, "to [his] best knowledge and belief," they still were members of the Party. . . .

The Subcommittee, too, was apparently satisfied with petitioner's disclosures. After some further discussion elaborating on the statement, counsel for the Committee turned to another aspect of Rumsey's testimony. Rumsey had identified a group of persons whom he had known as members of the Communist Party, and counsel began to read this list of names to petitioner. Petitioner stated that he did not know several of the persons. Of those whom he did know, he refused to tell whether he knew them to have been members of the Communist Party. He explained to the Subcommittee why he took such a position:

I am not going to plead the fifth amendment, but I refuse to answer certain questions that I believe are outside the proper scope of your committee's activities. I will answer any questions which this committee puts to me about myself. I will also answer questions about those persons whom I knew to be members of the Communist Party and whom I believe still are. I will not, however, answer any questions with respect to others with whom I associated in the past. I do not believe that any law in this country requires me to testify about persons who may in the past have been Communist Party members or otherwise engaged in Communist Party activity but who to my best knowledge and belief have long since removed themselves from the Communist movement.

I do not believe that such questions are relevant to the work of this committee nor do I believe that this committee has the right to undertake the public exposure of persons because of their past activities. I may be wrong, and the committee may have this power, but until and unless a court of law so holds and directs me to answer, I most firmly refuse to discuss the political activities of my past associates.

The Chairman of the Committee submitted a report of petitioner's refusal to answer questions to the House of Representatives. . . . The House directed the Speaker to certify the Committee's report to the United States Attorney for initiation of criminal prosecution. . . . A seven-count indictment was returned. Petitioner waived his right to jury trial and was found guilty on all counts by the court. The sentence, a fine of $100 and one year in prison, was suspended, and petitioner was placed on probation.

An appeal was taken to the Court of Appeals for the District of Columbia. The conviction was reversed by a three-judge panel, one member dissenting. Upon rehearing *en banc,* the full bench affirmed the conviction with the judges of the original majority in dissent. We granted certiorari because of the very important questions of constitutional law presented. . . .

We start with several basic premises on which there is general agreement. The power of the Congress to conduct investigations is inherent in the legislative process. That power is broad. It encompasses inquiries concerning the administration of existing laws as well as proposed or possibly needed statutes. It includes surveys of defects in our social, economic or political system for the purpose of enabling the Congress to remedy them. It comprehends probes into departments of the Federal Government to expose corruption, inefficiency or waste. But broad as is this power of inquiry, it is not unlimited. There is no general authority to expose the private affairs of individuals without justification in terms of the functions of the Congress. This was freely conceded by the Solicitor General in his argument of this case. Nor is the Congress a law enforcement or trial agency. These are functions of the executive and judicial departments of government. No inquiry is an end in itself; it must be related to and in furtherance of a legitimate task of the Congress. Investigations conducted solely for the personal aggrandizement of the investigators or to "punish" those investigated are indefensible.

It is unquestionably the duty of all citizens to co-operate with the Congress in its efforts to obtain the facts needed for intelligent legislative action. It is their unremitting obligation to respond to subpoenas, to respect the dignity of the Congress and its committees and to testify fully with respect to matters within the province of proper investigation. This, of course, assumes that the constitutional rights of witnesses will be respected by the Congress as they are in a court of justice. The Bill of Rights is applicable to investigations as to all forms of governmental action. Witnesses cannot be compelled to give evidence against themselves. They cannot be subjected to unreasonable search and seizure. Nor can the First Amendment freedoms of speech, press, religion, or political belief and association be abridged.

The rudiments of the power to punish for "contempt of Congress" come to us from the pages of English history. The origin of privileges and contempts extends back into the period of the emergence of Parliament. The establishment of a legislative body which could challenge the absolute power of the monarch is a long and bitter story. In that struggle, Parliament made broad and varied use of the contempt power. Almost from the beginning both the House of Commons and the House of Lords claimed absolute and plenary authority over their privileges. This was an independent body of law, described by Coke as *lex parliamenti.* Only Parliament could declare what those privileges were or what new privileges were occasioned, and only Parliament could judge what conduct constituted a breach of privilege.

In particular, this exclusion of *lex parliamenti* from the *lex terrae,* or law of the land, precluded judicial review of the exercise of the contempt power or the assertion of privilege. Parliament declared that no court had jurisdiction to consider such questions. In the latter part of the seventeenth century, an action for false imprisonment was brought by one Jay who had been held in contempt. The defendant, the Serjeant-at-Arms of the House of Commons, demurred that he had taken the plaintiff into custody for breach of privilege. The Chief Justice, Pemberton, overruled the demurrer. Summoned to the bar of the House, the Chief Justice explained that he believed that the assertion of privilege went to the merits of the action and did not preclude jurisdiction. For his audacity, the Chief Justice was dispatched to Newgate prison.

It seems inevitable that the power claimed by Parliament would have been abused. Unquestionably it was. A few examples illustrate the way in which individual rights were infringed. During the seventeenth century, there was a violent upheaval, both religious and political. This was the time of the Reformation and the establishment of the Church of England. It was also the period when the Stuarts proclaimed that the royal prerogative was absolute. Ultimately there were two revolutions, one protracted and bloody, the second without bloodshed. Critical commentary of all kinds was treated as contempt of parliament in these troubled days. Even clergymen were imprisoned for remarks made in their sermons. Perhaps the outstanding case arose from the private conversation of one Floyd, a Catholic, in which he expressed pleasure over the misfortune of the King's Protestant son-in-law and his wife. Floyd was not a member of Parliament. None of the persons concerned was in any way connected with the House of Commons. Nevertheless, that body imposed an humiliating and cruel sentence upon Floyd for contempt. The House of Lords intervened, rebuking the Commons for their extension of the privilege. The Commons acceded and transferred the record of the case to the Lords, who imposed substantially the same penalty.

Later in that century, during the reign of Charles II, there was great unrest over the fact that the heir apparent, James, had embraced Catholicism. Anti-Catholic feeling ran high, spilling over a few years later when the infamous rogue, Titus Oates, inflamed the country with rumors of a "Popish Plot" to murder the King. A committee of Parliament was appointed to learn the sources of certain pamphlets that had been appearing. One was entitled: The Grand Question Concerning the Prorogation of this Parliament for a Year and Three Months Stated and Discussed. A Doctor Carey admitted to the committee that he knew the author, but refused to divulge his name. Brought to the bar of the House of Lords, he persisted in this stand. The House imposed a fine of £1,000 and committed the witness to the Tower.

A hundred years later, George III had managed to gain control of Parliament through his ministers. The King could not silence the opposition, however, and one of the most vocal was John Wilkes. This precipitated a struggle that lasted for several years until Wilkes finally prevailed. One writer sums up the case thus:

He had won a victory for freedom of the press. He had directed popular attention to the royally-controlled House of Commons, and pointed out its unrepresentative character, and had shown how easily a claim of privilege might be used to sanction the arbitrary proceedings of ministers and Parliament, even when a fundamental right of the subject was concerned. It is one of life's little ironies that work of such magnitude had been reserved for one of the worst libertines and demagogues of all times.

Even as late as 1835, the House of Commons appointed a select committee to inquire into ". . . the origin, nature, extent and tendency of the Orange Institutions." This was a political-religious organization, vehemently Protestant in religion and strongly in favor of the growth of the British Empire. The committee summoned the Deputy Grand Secretary and demanded that he produce all the records of the organization. The witness refused to turn over a letter-book, which he admitted contained his answers to many communications upon Orange business. But it also contained, he said, records of private communications with respect to Orangeism. Summoned to the bar of the House of Commons, he remained adamant and was committed to Newgate prison.

Modern times have seen a remarkable restraint in the use by Parliament of its contempt power. Important investigations, like those conducted in America by congressional committees, are made by Royal Commissions of Inquiry. These commissions are comprised of experts in the problem to be studied. They are removed from the turbulent forces of politics and partisan considerations. Seldom, if ever, have these commissions been given the authority to compel the testimony of witnesses or the production of documents. Their success in fulfilling their fact-finding missions without resort to coercive tactics is a tribute to the fairness of the processes to the witnesses and their close adherence to the subject matter committed to them.

The history of contempt of the legislature in this country is notably different from that of England. In the early days of the United States, there lingered the direct knowledge of the evil effects of absolute power. Most of the instances of use of compulsory process by the first Congresses concerned matters affecting the qualification or integrity of their members or came about in inquiries dealing with suspected corruption or mismanagement of government officials. Unlike the English practice, from the very outset the use of contempt power by the legislature was deemed subject to judicial review.

There was very little use of the power of compulsory process in early years to enable the Congress to obtain facts pertinent to the enactment of new statutes or the administration of existing laws. The first occasion for such an investigation arose in 1827 when the House of Representatives was considering a revision of the tariff laws. In the Senate, there was no use of a fact-finding investigation in aid of legislation until 1859. In the Legislative Reorganization Act, the Committee on Un-American Activities is the only standing committee of the House of Representatives that was given the power to compel disclosures.

It is not surprising, from the fact that the Houses of Congress so sparingly employed the power to conduct investigations, that there have been few cases requiring judicial review of the power. The nation was almost one hundred years old before the first case reached this Court to challenge the use of compulsory process as a legislative device, rather than in inquiries concerning the elections or privileges of Congressmen. In *Kilbourn* v. *Thompson,* 103 US 168, decided in 1881, an investigation had been authorized by the House of Representatives to learn the circumstances surrounding the bankruptcy of Jay Cooke & Company, in which the United States had deposited funds. The committee became particularly interested in a private real estate pool that was a part of the financial structure. The Court found that the subject matter of the inquiry was "in its nature clearly judicial and therefore one in respect to which no valid legislation could be enacted." The House had thereby exceeded the limits of its own authority.

Subsequent to the decision in *Kilbourn,* until recent times, there were very few cases dealing with the investigative power. The matter came to the fore again when the Senate undertook to study the corruption in handling of oil leases in the 1920's. In *McGrain* v. *Daugherty,*

273 US 135, and *Sinclair* v. *United States*, 279 US 263, the Court applied the precepts of *Kilbourn* to uphold the authority of the Congress to conduct the challenged investigations. The Court recognized the danger of effective and honest conduct of the Government if the legislature's power to probe corruption in the executive branch were unduly hampered.

Following these important decisions, there was another lull in judicial review of investigations. The absence of challenge, however, was not indicative of the absence of inquiries. To the contrary, there was vigorous use of the investigative process by a Congress bent upon harnessing and directing the vast economic and social forces of the times. Only one case came before this Court, and the authority of the Congress was affirmed.

In the decade following World War II, there appeared a new kind of congressional inquiry unknown in prior periods of American history. Principally this was the result of the various investigations into the threat of subversion of the United States Government, but other subjects of congressional interest also contributed to the changed scene. This new phase of legislative inquiry involved a broad-scale intrusion into the lives and affairs of private citizens. It brought before the courts novel questions of the appropriate limits of congressional inquiry. Prior cases, like *Kilbourn*, *McGrain* and *Sinclair*, had defined the scope of investigative power in terms of the inherent limitations of the sources of that power. In the more recent cases, the emphasis shifted to problems of accommodating the interest of the Government with the rights and privileges of individuals. The central theme was the application of the Bill of Rights as a restraint upon the assertion of governmental power in this form.

It was during this period that the Fifth Amendment privilege against self-incrimination was frequently invoked and recognized as a legal limit upon the authority of a committee to require that a witness answer its questions. Some early doubts as to the applicability of that privilege before a legislative committee never matured. When the matter reached this Court, the Government did not challenge in any way that the Fifth Amendment protection was available to the witness, and such a challenge could not have prevailed. It confined its argument to the character of the answers sought and to the adequacy of the claim of privilege. *Quinn* v. *United States*, 349 US 155, *Emspak* v. *United States*, 349, US 190, *Bart* v. *United States*, 349 US 219.

A far more difficult task evolved from the claim by witnesses that the committees' interrogations were infringements upon the freedoms of the First Amendment. Clearly, an investigation is subject to the command that the Congress shall make no law abridging freedom of speech or press or assembly. While it is true that there is no statute to be reviewed, and that an investigation is not a law, nevertheless an investigation is part of lawmaking. It is justified solely as an adjunct to the legislative process. The First Amendment may be invoked against infringement of the protected freedoms by law or by lawmaking.

Abuses of the investigative process may imperceptibly lead to abridgment of protected freedoms. The mere summoning of a witness and compelling him to testify against his will, about his beliefs, expressions or associations is a measure of governmental interference. And when those forced revelations concern matters that are unorthodox, unpopular, or even hateful to the general public, the reaction in the life of the witness may be disastrous. This effect is even more harsh when it is past beliefs, expressions or associations that are disclosed and judged by current standards rather than those contemporary with the matters exposed. Nor does the witness alone suffer the consequences. Those who are identified by witnesses and thereby placed in the same glare of publicity are equally subject to public stigma, scorn and obloquy. Beyond that, there is the more subtle and immeasurable effect upon those who tend to adhere to the most orthodox and uncontroversial views and associations in order to avoid a similar fate at some future time. That this impact is partly the result of non-governmental activity by private persons cannot relieve the investigators of their responsibility for initiating the reaction.

The Court recognized the restraints of the Bill of Rights upon congressional investigations in *United States* v. *Rumely,* 345 US 41. The magnitude and complexity of the problem of applying the First Amendment to that case led the Court to construe narrowly the resolution describing the committee's authority. It was concluded that, when First Amendment rights are threatened, the delegation of power to the committee must be clearly revealed in its charter.

Accommodation of the congressional need for particular information with the individual and personal interest in privacy is an arduous and delicate task for any court. We do not underestimate the difficulties that would attend such an undertaking. It is manifest that despite the adverse effects which follow upon compelled disclosure of private matters, not all such inquiries are barred. *Kilbourn* v. *Thompson* teaches that such an investigation into individual affairs is invalid if unrelated to any legislative purpose. That is beyond the powers conferred upon the Congress in the Constitution. *United States* v. *Rumely* makes it plain that the mere semblance of legislative purpose would not justify an inquiry in the face of the Bill of Rights. The critical element is the existence of, and the weight to be ascribed to, the interest of the Congress in demanding disclosures from an unwilling witness. We cannot simply assume, however, that every congressional investigation is justified by a public need that overbalances any private rights affected. To do so would be to abdicate the responsibility placed by the Constitution upon the judiciary to insure that the Congress does not unjustifiably encroach upon an individual's right to privacy nor abridge his liberty of speech, press, religion or assembly.

Petitioner has earnestly suggested that the difficult question of protecting these rights from infringement by legislative inquiries can be surmounted in this case because there was no public purpose served in his interrogation. His conclusion is based upon the thesis that the Subcommittee was engaged in a program of exposure for the sake of exposure. The sole purpose of the inquiry, he contends, was to bring down upon himself and others the violence of public reaction because of their past beliefs, expressions and associations. In support of this argument, petitioner has marshalled an impressive array of evidence that some Congressmen have believed that such was their duty, or part of it.

We have no doubt that there is no congressional power to expose for the sake of exposure. The public is, of course, entitled to be informed concerning the workings of its government. That cannot be inflated into a general power to expose where the predominant result can only be an invasion of the private rights of individuals. But a solution to our problem is not to be found in testing the motives of committee members for this purpose. Such is not our function. Their motives alone would not vitiate an investigation which had been instituted by a House of Congress if that assembly's legislative purpose is being served.

Petitioner's contentions do point to a situation of particular significance from the standpoint of the constitutional limitations upon congressional investigations. The theory of a committee inquiry is that the committee members are serving as the representatives of the parent assembly in collecting information for a legislative purpose. Their function is to act as the eyes and ears of the Congress in obtaining facts upon which the full legislature can act. To carry out this mission, committees and subcommittees, sometimes one Congressman, are endowed with the full power of the Congress to compel testimony. In this case, only two men exercised that authority in demanding information over petitioner's protest.

An essential premise in this situation is that the House or Senate shall have instructed the committee members on what they are to do with the power delegated to them. It is the responsibility of the Congress, in the first instance, to insure that compulsory process is used only in furtherance of a legislative purpose. That requires that the instructions to an investigating committee spell out that group's jurisdiction and purpose with sufficient particularity. Those instructions are embodied in the authorizing resolution. That document is the committee's charter. Broadly drafted and loosely worded, however, such resolutions can leave tremendous latitude to the discretion of the investigators. The more vague the committee's charter is, the greater becomes the possibility that the committee's specific actions are not in conformity with the will of the parent House of Congress.

The authorizing resolution of the Un-American Activities Committee was adopted in 1938 when a select committee, under the chairmanship of Representative Dies, was created. Several years later, the Committee was made a standing organ of the House with the same mandate. It defines the Committee's authority as follows:

The Committee on Un-American Activities, as a whole or by subcommittee, is authorized to make from time to time investigations of (i) the extent, character, and objects of un-American propaganda activities in the United States, (ii) the diffusion within the United States of subversive and un-American propaganda that is instigated from foreign countries or of a domestic origin and attacks the principle of the form of government, as guaranteed by our Constitution, and (iii) all other questions in relation thereto that would aid Congress in any necessary remedial legislation.

It would be difficult to imagine a less explicit authorizing resolution. Who could define the meaning of "un-American"? What is that single, solitary "principle of the form of government as guaranteed by our Constitution"? There is no need to dwell upon the language, however. At one time, perhaps, the resolution might have been read narrowly to confine the Committee to the subject of propaganda. The events that have transpired in the fifteen years before the interrogation of petitioner make such a construction impossible at this date.

The members of the Committee have clearly demonstrated that they did not feel themselves restricted in any way to propaganda in the narrow sense of the word. Unquestionably the Committee conceived of its task in the grand view of its name. Un-American activities were its target, no matter how or where manifested. Notwithstanding the broad purview of the Committee's experience, the House of Representatives repeatedly approved its continuation. Five times it extended the life of the special committee. Then it made the group a standing committee of the House. A year later, the Committee's charter was embodied in the Legislative Reorganization Act. On five occasions, at the beginning of sessions of Congress, it has made the authorizing resolution part of the rules of the House. On innumerable occasions, it has passed appropriation bills to allow the Committee to continue its efforts.

Combining the language of the resolution with the construction it has been given, it is evident that the preliminary control of the Committee exercised by the House of Representatives is slight or nonexistent. No one could reasonably deduce from the charter the kind of investigation that the Committee was directed to make. As a result, we are asked to engage in a process of retroactive rationalization. Looking backward from the events that transpired, we are asked to uphold the Committees' actions unless it appears that they were clearly not authorized by the charter. As a corollary to this inverse approach, the Government urges that we must view the matter hospitably to the power of the Congress—that if there is any legislative purpose which might have been furthered by the kind of disclosure sought, the witness must be punished for withholding it. No doubt every reasonable indulgence of legality must be accorded to the actions of a coordinate branch of our Government. But such deference cannot yield to an unnecessary and unreasonable dissipation of precious constitutional freedoms.

The Government contends that the public interest at the core of the investigations of the Un-American Activities Committee is the need by the Congress to be informed of efforts to overthrow the Government by force and violence so that adequate legislative safeguards can be erected. From this core, however, the Committee can radiate outward infinitely to any topic thought to be related in some way to armed insurrection. The outer reaches of this domain are known only by the content of "un-American activities." Remoteness of subject can be aggravated by a probe for a depth of detail even farther removed from any basis of legislative action. A third dimension is added when the investigators turn their attention to the past to collect minutiae on remote topics, on the hypothesis that the past may reflect upon the present.

The consequences that flow from this situation are manifold. In the first place, a reviewing court is unable to make the kind of judgment made by the Court in *United States* v. *Rumely, supra*. The Committee is allowed, in essence, to define its own authority, to choose the direction and focus of its activities. In deciding what to do with the power that has been conferred upon them, members of the Committee may act pursuant to motives that seem to them to be the highest. Their decisions, nevertheless, can lead to ruthless exposure of private lives in order to gather data that is neither desired by the Congress nor useful to it. Yet it is impossible in this circumstance, with constitutional freedoms in jeopardy, to declare that the Committee has ranged beyond the area committed to it by its parent assembly because the boundaries are so nebulous.

More important and more fundamental than that, however, it

insulates the House that has authorized the investigation from the witnesses who are subjected to the sanctions of compulsory process. There is a wide gulf between the responsibility for the use of investigative power and the actual exercise of that power. This is an especially vital consideration in assuring respect for constitutional liberties. Protected freedoms should not be placed in danger in the absence of a clear determination by the House or the Senate that a particular inquiry is justified by a specific legislative need.

It is, of course, not the function of this Court to prescribe rigid rules for the Congress to follow in drafting resolutions establishing investigating committees. That is a matter peculiarly within the realm of the legislature, and its decisions will be accepted by the courts up to the point where their own duty to enforce the constitutionally protected rights of individuals is affected. An excessively broad charter, like that of the House Un-American Activities Committee, places the courts in an untenable position if they are to strike a balance between the public need for a particular interrogation and the right of citizens to carry on their affairs free from unnecessary governmental interference. It is impossible in such a situation to ascertain whether any legislative purpose justifies the disclosures sought and, if so, the importance of that information to the Congress in furtherance of its legislative function. The reason no court can make this critical judgment is that the House of Representatives itself has never made it. Only the legislative assembly initiating an investigation can assay the relative necessity of specific disclosures.

Absence of the qualitative consideration of petitioner's questioning by the House of Representatives aggravates a serious problem revealed in this case, in the relationship of congressional investigating committees and the witnesses who appear before them. Plainly these committees are restricted to the missions delegated to them, i.e., to acquire certain data to be used by the House or the Senate in coping with a problem that falls within its legislative sphere. No witness can be compelled to make disclosures on matters outside that area. This is a jurisdictional concept of pertinency drawn from the nature of a congressional committee's source of authority. It is not wholly different from nor unrelated to the element of pertinency embodied in the criminal statute under which petitioner was prosecuted. When the definition of jurisdictional pertinency is as uncertain and wavering as in the case of the Un-American Activities Committee, it becomes extemely difficult for the Committee to limit its inquiries to statutory pertinency.

Since World War II, the Congress has practically abandoned its original practice of utilizing the coercive sanction of contempt proceedings at the bar of the House. The sanction there imposed is imprisonment by the House until the recalcitrant witness agrees to testify or disclose the matters sought, provided that the incarceration does not extend beyond adjournment. The Congress has instead invoked the aid of the federal judicial system in protecting itself against contumacious conduct. It has become customary to refer these matters to the United States Attorneys for prosecution under criminal law.

The appropriate statute is found in 2 U.S.C. § 192. It provides:

Every person who having been summoned as a witness by the authority of either House of Congress to give testimony or to produce papers upon any matter under inquiry before either House, or any joint committee established by a joint or concurrent resolution of the two Houses of Congress, or any committee of either House of Congress, willfully makes default, or who, having appeared, refuses to answer any question pertinent to the question under inquiry, shall be deemed guilty of a misdemeanor, punishable by a fine of not more than $1,000 nor less than $100 and imprisonment in a common jail for not less than one month nor more than twelve months.

In fulfillment of their obligation under this statute, the courts must accord to the defendants every right which is guaranteed to defendants in all other criminal cases. Among these is the right to have available, through a sufficiently precise statute, information revealing the standard of criminality before the commission of the alleged offense. Applied to persons prosecuted under § 192, this raises a special problem in that the statute defines the crime as refusal to answer "any question pertinent to the question under inquiry." Part of the standard of criminality, therefore, is the pertinency of the questions propounded to the witness.

The problem attains proportion when viewed from the standpoint of the witness who appears before a congressional committee. He must decide at the time the questions are propounded whether or not to answer. As the Court said in *Sinclair* v. *United States*, the witness acts at his peril. He is ". . . bound rightly to construe the statute." An erroneous determination on his part, even if made in the utmost good faith, does not exculpate him if the court should later rule that the questions were pertinent to the question under inquiry.

It is obvious that a person compelled to make this choice is entitled to have knowledge of the subject to which the interrogation is deemed pertinent. That knowledge must be available with the same degree of explicitness and clarity that the Due Process Clause requires in the expression of any element of a criminal offense. The "vice of vagueness" must be avoided here as in all other crimes. There are several sources that can outline the "question under inquiry" in such a way that the rules against vagueness are satisfied. The authorizing resolution, the remarks of the chairman or members of the committee, or even the nature of the proceedings themselves might sometimes make the topic clear. This case demonstrates, however, that these sources often leave the matter in grave doubt.

The first possibility is that the authorizing resolution itself will so clearly declare the "question under inquiry" that a witness can understand the pertinency of questions asked him. The Government does not contend that the authorizing resolution of the Un-American Activities Committee could serve such a purpose. Its confusing breadth is amply illustrated by the innumerable and diverse questions into which the Committee has inquired under this charter since 1938. If the "question under inquiry" were stated with such sweeping and uncertain scope we doubt that it would withstand an attack on the ground of vagueness.

That issue is not before us, however, in light of the Government's position that the immediate subject under inquiry before the Subcommittee interviewing petitioner was only one aspect of the Committee's authority to investigate un-American activities. Distilling that single topic from the broad field is an extremely difficult task upon the record before us. There was an opening statement by the Committee Chairman at the outset of the hearing, but this gives us no guidance. In this statement, the Chairman did no more than paraphrase the authorizing resolution and give a very general sketch of the past efforts of the Committee.

No aid is given as to the "question under inquiry" in the action of the full Committee that authorized the creation of the Subcommittee before which petitioner appeared. The Committee adopted a formal resolution giving the Chairman the power to appoint subcommittees ". . . for the purpose of performing any and all acts which the Committee as a whole is authorized to do." In effect, this was a device to enable the investigations to proceed with a quorum of one or two members and sheds no light on the relevancy of the questions asked of petitioner.

The Government believes that the topic of inquiry before the Subcommittee concerned Communist infiltration in labor. In his introductory remarks the Chairman made reference to a bill, then pending before the Committee, which would have penalized labor unions controlled or dominated by persons who were, or had been, members of a "Communist-action" organization, as defined in the Internal Security Act of 1950. The Subcommittee, it is contended, might have been endeavoring to determine the extent of such a problem. This view is corroborated somewhat by the witnesses who preceded and followed petitioner before the Subcommittee. Looking at the entire hearings, however, there is strong reason to doubt that the subject revolved about labor matters. The published transcript is entitled: *Investigation of Communist Activities in the Chicago Area,* and six of the nine witnesses had no connection with labor at all.

The most serious doubts as to the Subcommittee's "question under inquiry," however, stem from the precise questions that petitioner has been charged with refusing to answer. Under the terms of the statute, after all, it is these which must be proved pertinent. Petitioner is charged with refusing to tell the Subcommittee whether or not he knew that certain named persons had been members of the Communist Party in the past. The Subcommittee's counsel read the list from the testimony of a previous witness who had identified them as Communists. Although this former witness was identified with labor, he had not stated that the persons he named were involved in union affairs. Of the thirty names propounded to petitioner, seven were completely unconnected with organized labor. One operated a beauty parlor. Another was a watchmaker. Several were identified as "just citizens" or "only Communists." When almost a quarter of the persons on the list are not labor people, the inference becomes strong that the subject before the Subcommittee was not defined in terms of Communism in labor.

The final source of evidence as to the "question under inquiry" is the Chairman's response when petitioner objected to the questions on the grounds of lack of pertinency. The Chairman then announced that the Subcommittee was investigating "subversion and subversive propaganda." This is a subject at least as broad and indefinite as the authorizing resolution of the Committee, if not more so.

Having exhausted the several possible indicia of the "question under inquiry," we remain unenlightened as to the subject to which the questions asked petitioner were pertinent. Certainly, if the point is that obscure after trial and appeal, it was not adequately revealed to petitioner when he had to decide at his peril whether or not to answer. Fundamental fairness demands that no witness be compelled to make such a determination with so little guidance. Unless the subject matter has been made to appear with undisputable clarity, it is the duty of the investigative body, upon objection of the witness on grounds of pertinency, to state for the record the subject under inquiry at that time and the manner in which the propounded questions are pertinent thereto. To be meaningful, the explanation must describe what the topic under inquiry is and the connective reasoning whereby the precise questions asked relate to it. The statement of the Committee Chairman in this case, in response to petitioner's protest, was woefully inadequate to convey sufficient information as to the pertinency of the questions to the subject under inquiry. Petitioner was thus not accorded a fair opportunity to determine whether he was within his rights in refusing to answer, and his conviction is necessarily invalid under the Due Process Clause of the Fifth Amendment.

We are mindful of the complexities of modern government and the ample scope that must be left to the Congress as the sole constitutional depository of legislative power. Equally mindful are we of the indispensable function, in the exercise of that power, of congressional investigations. The conclusions we have reached in this case will not prevent the Congress, through its committees, from obtaining any information it needs for the proper fulfillment of its role in our scheme of government. The legislature is free to determine the kinds of data that should be collected. It is only those investigations that are conducted by use of compulsory process that give rise to a need to protect the rights of individuals against illegal encroachment. That protection can be readily achieved through procedures which prevent the separation of power from responsibility and which provide the constitutional requisites of fairness for witnesses. A measure of added care on the part of the House and the Senate in authorizing the use of compulsory process and by their committees in exercising that power would suffice. That is a small price to pay if it serves to uphold the principles of limited, constitutional government without constricting the power of the Congress to inform itself.

The judgment of the Court of Appeals is reversed, and the case is remanded to the District Court with instructions to dismiss the indictment.

It is so ordered.

BARENBLATT v. UNITED STATES
360 US 109 (1959)

[Testifying before a congressional committee, Barenblatt refused to answer questions regarding alleged membership in the Communist Party. He pleaded the First Amendment freedoms as protecting his silence. The Court by a 5-to-4 vote upheld his contempt conviction. The case should be read along with *Watkins* v. *United States*, 354 US 178 (1957). Justices Black, Douglas, and Brennan and Chief Justice Warren dissented.]

Mr. Justice Harlan delivered the opinion of the Court:

Once more the Court is required to resolve the conflicting constitutional claims of congressional power and of an individual's right to resist its exercise. The congressional power in question concerns the internal process of Congress in moving within its legislative domain; it involves the utilization of its committees to secure "testimony needed to enable it efficiently to exercise a legislative function belonging to it under the Constitution." . . . The power of inquiry has been employed by Congress throughout our history, over the whole range of the national interests concerning which Congress might legislate or decide upon due investigation not to legislate; it has similarly been utilized in determining what to appropriate from the national purse, or whether to appropriate. The scope of the power of inquiry, in short, is as penetrating and far-reaching as the potential power to enact and appropriate under the Constitution.

Broad as it is, the power is not, however, without limitations. Since Congress may only investigate into those areas in which it may potentially legislate or appropriate, it cannot inquire into matters which are within the exclusive province of one or the other branch of the Government. Lacking the judicial power given to the Judiciary, it cannot inquire into matters that are exclusively the concern of the Judiciary. Neither can it supplant the Executive in what exclusively belongs to the Executive. And the Congress, in common with all branches of the Government, must exercise its powers subject to the limitations placed by the Constitution on governmental action, more particularly in the context of this case the relevant limitations of the Bill of Rights.

The congressional power of inquiry, its range and scope, and an individual's duty in relation to it, must be viewed in proper perspective. . . . The power and the right of resistance to it are to be judged in the concrete, not on the basis of abstractions. In the present case congressional efforts to learn the extent of a nation-wide, indeed worldwide, problem have brought one of its investigating committees into the field of education. Of course, broadly viewed, inquiries cannot be made into the teaching that is pursued in any of our educational institutions. When academic teaching-freedom and its corollary learning-freedom, so essential to the well-being of the Nation, are claimed, this Court will always be on the alert against intrusion by Congress into this constitutionally protected domain. But this does not mean that the Congress is precluded from interrogating a witness merely because he is a teacher. An educational institution is not a constitutional sanctuary from inquiry into matters that may otherwise be within the constitutional legislative domain merely for the reason that inquiry is made of someone within its walls.

In the setting of this framework of constitutional history, practice and legal precedents, we turn to the particularities of this case.

We here review petitioner's conviction under 2 U.S.C. § 192, for contempt of Congress, arising from his refusal to answer certain questions put to him by a Subcommittee of the House Committee on Un-American Activities during the course of an inquiry concerning alleged Communist infiltration into the field of education.

The case is before us for the second time. Petitioner's conviction was originally affirmed in 1957 by a unanimous panel of the Court of Appeals. This Court granted certiorari, vacated the judgment of the Court of Appeals, and remanded the case to that court for further consideration in light of *Watkins* v. *United States*, 354 US 178, which had reversed a contempt of Congress conviction, and which was decided after the Court of Appeals' decision here had issued. Thereafter the Court of Appeals, sitting *en banc*, reaffirmed the conviction by a divided court. We again granted certiorari, to consider petitioner's statutory and constitutional challenges to his conviction, and particularly his claim that the judgment below cannot stand under our decision in the *Watkins* case.

Pursuant to a subpoena, and accompanied by counsel, petitioner on June 28, 1954, appeared as a witness before this congressional Subcommittee. After answering a few preliminary questions and testifying that he had been a graduate student and teaching fellow at the University of Michigan from 1947 to 1950 and an instructor in psychology at Vassar College from 1950 to shortly before his appearance before the Subcommittee, petitioner objected generally to the right of the Subcommittee to inquire into his "political" and "religious" beliefs or any "other personal and private affairs" or "associational activities," upon grounds set forth in a previously prepared memorandum which he was allowed to file with the Subcommittee. Thereafter petitioner specifically declined to answer each of the following five questions:

Are you now a member of the Communist Party? (Count One.)

Have you ever been a member of the Communist Party? (Count Two.)

Now, you have stated that you knew Francis Crowley. Did you know Francis Crowley as a member of the Communist Party? (Count Three.)

Were you ever a member of the Haldane Club of the Communist Party while at the University of Michigan? (Count Four.)

Were you a member while a student of the University of Michigan Council of Arts, Sciences, and Professions? (Count Five.)

In each instance the grounds of refusal were those set forth in the prepared statement. Petitioner expressly disclaimed reliance upon "the Fifth Amendment."

Following receipt of the Subcommittee's report of these occurrences the House duly certified the matter to the District of Columbia United

States Attorney for contempt proceedings. An indictment in five Counts, each embracing one of petitioner's several refusals to answer, ensued. With the consent of both sides the case was tried to the court without a jury, and upon conviction under all Counts a general sentence of six months' imprisonment and a fine of $250 was imposed.

Since this sentence was less than the maximum punishment authorized by the statute for conviction under any one Count, the judgment below must be upheld if the conviction upon any of the Counts is sustainable. . . . As we conceive the ultimate issue in this case to be whether petitioner could properly be convicted of contempt for refusing to answer questions relating to his participation in or knowledge of alleged Communist Party activities at educational institutions in this country, we find it unnecessary to consider the validity of his conviction under the Third and Fifth Counts, the only ones involving questions which on their face do not directly relate to such participation or knowledge.

Petitioner's various contentions resolve themselves into three propositions: First, the compelling of testimony by the Subcommittee was neither legislatively authorized nor constitutionally permissible because of the vagueness of Rule XI of the House of Representatives, Eighty-third Congress, the charter of authority of the parent Committee. Second, petitioner was not adequately apprised of the pertinency of the Subcommittee's questions to the subject matter of the inquiry. Third, the questions petitioner refused to answer infringed rights protected by the First Amendment.

Subcommittee's Authority to Compel Testimony.

At the outset it should be noted that Rule XI authorized this Subcommittee to compel testimony within the framework of the investigative authority conferred on the Un-American Activities Committee. Petitioner contends that *Watkins* v. *United States, supra,* nevertheless held the grant of this power in all circumstances ineffective because of the vagueness of Rule XI in delineating the Committee jurisdiction to which its exercise was to be appurtenant. This view of *Watkins* was accepted by two of the dissenting judges below.

The *Watkins* case cannot properly be read as standing for such a proposition. A principal contention in *Watkins* was that the refusals to answer were justified because the requirement of 2 U.S.C. § 192 that the questions asked be "pertinent to the questions under inquiry" had not been satisfied. This Court reversed the conviction solely on that ground, holding that Watkins had not been adequately apprised of the subject matter of the Subcommittee's investigation or the pertinency thereto of the questions he refused to answer. In so deciding the Court drew upon Rule XI only as one of the facets in the total *mise en scène* in its search for the "question under inquiry" in that particular investigation. The Court, in other words, was not dealing with Rule XI at large, and indeed in effect stated that no such issue was before it. That the vagueness of Rule XI was not alone determinative is also shown by the Court's further statement that aside from the Rule "the remarks of the chairman or members of the committee, or even the nature of the proceedings themselves, might sometimes make the topic [under inquiry] clear." In short, while *Watkins* was critical of Rule XI, it did not involve the broad and inflexible holding petitioner now attributes to it.

Petitioner also contends, independently of *Watkins*, that the vagueness of Rule XI deprived the Subcommittee of the right to compel testimony in this investigation into Communist activity. We cannot agree with this contention which in its furthest reach would mean that the House Un-American Activities Committee under its existing authority has no right to compel testimony in any circumstances. Granting the vagueness of the Rule, we may not read it in isolation from its long history in the House of Representatives. Just as legislation is often given meaning by the gloss of legislative reports, administrative interpretation, and long usage, so the proper meaning of an authorization to a congressional committee is not to be derived alone from its abstract terms unrelated to the definite content furnished them by the course of congressional actions. The Rule comes to us with a "persuasive gloss of legislative history," . . . which shows beyond doubt that in pursuance of its legislative concerns in the domain of "national security" the House has clothed the Un-American Activities Committee with pervasive authority to investigate Communist activities in this country.

The essence of that history can be briefly stated. The Un-American Activities Committee, originally known as the Dies Committee, was first established by the House in 1938. The Committee was principally a consequence of concern over the activities of the German-American Bund, whose members were suspected of allegiance to Hitler Germany, and of the Communist Party, supposed by many to be under the domination of the Soviet Union. From the beginning, without interruption to the present time, and with the undoubted knowledge and approval of the House, the Committee has devoted a major part of its energies to the investigation of Communist activities. More particularly, in 1947 the Committee announced a wide-range program in this field, pursuant to which during the years 1948 to 1952 it conducted diverse inquiries into such alleged Communist activities as espionage; efforts to learn atom bomb secrets; infiltration into labor, farmer, veteran, professional, youth, and motion picture groups; and in addition held a number of hearings upon various legislative proposals to curb Communist activities.

In the context of these unremitting pursuits, the House has steadily continued the life of the Committee at the commencement of each new Congress; it has never narrowed the powers of the Committee, whose authority has remained throughout identical with that contained in Rule XI; and it has continuingly supported the Committee's activities with substantial appropriations. Beyond this, the Committee was raised to the level of a standing committee of the House in 1945, it having been but a special committee prior to that time.

In light of this long and illuminating history it can hardly be seriously argued that the investigation of Communist activities generally, and the attendant use of compulsory process, was beyond the purview of the Committee's intended authority under Rule XI.

We are urged, however, to construe Rule XI so as at least to exclude the field of education from the Committee's compulsory authority. Two of the four dissenting judges below relied entirely, the other two alternatively, on this ground. The contention is premised on the course we took in *United States* v. *Rumely,* 345 US 41, where in order to avoid constitutional issues we construed narrowly the authority of the congressional committee there involved. We cannot follow that route here for this is not a case where Rule XI has to "speak for itself, since Congress put no gloss upon it at the time of its passage," nor one where the subsequent history of the Rule has the "infirmity of *post litem motam,* self-serving declarations."

To the contrary, the legislative gloss on Rule XI is again compelling. Not only is there no indication that the House ever viewed the field of education as being outside the Committee's authority under Rule XI, but the legislative history affirmatively evinces House approval of this phase of the Committee's work. During the first year of its activities, 1938, the Committee heard testimony on alleged Communist activities at Brooklyn College, N.Y. The following year it conducted similar hearings relating to the American Student Union and the Teachers Union. The field of "Communist influences in education" was one of the items contained in the Committee's 1947 program. Other investigations including education took place in 1952 and 1953. And in 1953, after the Committee had instituted the investigation involved in this case, the desirability of investigating Communism in education was specifically discussed during consideration of its appropriation for that year, which after controversial debate was approved.[*]

In this framework of the Committee's history we must conclude that its legislative authority to conduct the inquiry presently under consideration is unassailable, and that independently of whatever bearing the broad scope of Rule XI may have on the issue of "pertinency" in a given investigation into Communist activities, as in *Watkins*, the Rule cannot be said to be constitutionally infirm on the score of vagueness. The constitutional permissibility of that authority otherwise is a matter to be discussed later.

Pertinency Claim.

Undeniably a conviction for contempt under 2 U.S.C. § 192 cannot stand unless the questions asked are pertinent to the subject matter of the investigation. But the factors which led us to rest decision on this ground in *Watkins* were very different from those involved here.

In *Watkins* the petitioner had made specific objection to the Subcommittee's questions on the ground of pertinency; the question under inquiry had not been disclosed in any illuminating manner; and the questions asked the petitioner were not only amorphous on their face, but in some instances clearly foreign to the alleged subject matter of the investigation—"Communism in labor."

In contrast, petitioner in the case before us raised no objections on the ground of pertinency at the time any of the questions were put to him. It is true that the memorandum which petitioner brought with him to the Subcommittee hearing contained the statement, "to ask me whether I am or have been a member of the Communist Party may have dire consequences. I might wish to . . . challenge the pertinency of the question to the investigation," and at another point quoted from this Court's opinion in *Jones* v. *Securities & Exchange Comm.*, 298 US 1, language relating to a witness' right to

[*] In the course of that debate a member of the Un-American Activities Committee, Representative Jackson, commented: "So far as education is concerned, if the American educators, and if the gentlemen who are objecting to the investigation of communism and Communists in education, will recognize a valid distinction, I want to point out this is not a blunderbuss approach to the problem of communism in education. We are not interested in textbooks. We are not interested in the classroom operations of the universities. We are interested instead in finding out who the Communists are and what they are doing to further the Communist conspiracy. I may say in that connection that we have sworn testimony identifying individuals presently on the campuses of this country, men who have been identified under oath as one-time members of the Communist Party. Is there any Member of this body who would say we should not investigate this situation?" 83d Cong., 1st Sess., 99 *Cong.Rec.* 1360.

be informed of the pertinency of questions asked him by an administrative agency. These statements cannot, however, be accepted as the equivalent of a pertinency objection. At best they constituted but a contemplated objection to questions still unasked, and buried as they were in the context of petitioner's general challenge to the power of the Subcommittee they can hardly be considered adequate, within the meaning of what was said in *Watkins,* to trigger what would have been the Subcommittee's reciprocal obligation had it been faced with a pertinency objection.

We need not, however, rest decision on petitioner's failure to object on this score, for here "pertinency" was made to appear "with undisputable clarity." First of all, it goes without saying that the scope of the Committee's authority was for the House, not a witness, to determine, subject to the ultimate reviewing responsibility of this Court. What we deal with here is whether petitioner was sufficiently apprised of "the topic under inquiry" thus authorized "and the connective reasoning whereby the precise questions asked relate[d] to it." In light of his prepared memorandum of constitutional objections there can be no doubt that this petitioner was well aware of the Subcommittee's authority and purpose to question him as it did. In addition the other sources of this information which we recognized in *Watkins,* leave no room for a "pertinency" objection on this record. The subject matter of the inquiry had been identified at the commencement of the investigation as Communist infiltration into the field of education. Just prior to petitioner's appearance before the Subcommittee, the scope of the day's hearings had been announced as "in the main communism in education and the experiences and background in the party by Francis X. T. Crowley. It will deal with activities in Michigan, Boston, and in some small degree, New York." Petitioner had heard the Subcommittee interrogate the witness Crowley along the same lines as he, petitioner, was evidently to be questioned, and had listened to Crowley's testimony identifying him as a former member of an alleged Communist student organization at the University of Michigan while they both were in attendance there. Further, petitioner had stood mute in the face of the Chairman's statement as to why he had been called as a witness by the Subcommittee. And, lastly, unlike *Watkins,* petitioner refused to answer questions as to his own Communist Party affiliations, whose pertinency of course was clear beyond doubt.

Petitioner's contentions on this aspect of the case cannot be sustained.

Constitutional Contentions.

Our function, at this point, is purely one of constitutional adjudication in the particular case and upon the particular record before us, not to pass judgment upon the general wisdom or efficacy of the activities of this Committee in a vexing and complicated field.

The precise constitutional issue confronting us is whether the Subcommittee's inquiry into petitioner's past or present membership in the Communist Party transgressed the provisions of the First Amendment, which of course reach and limit congressional investigations. *Watkins, supra.*

The Court's past cases establish sure guides to decision. Undeniably, the First Amendment in some circumstances protects an individual from being compelled to disclose his associational relationships. However, the protections of the First Amendment, unlike a proper claim of the privilege against self-incrimination under the Fifth Amendment, do not afford a witness the right to resist inquiry in all circumstances. Where First Amendment rights are asserted to bar governmental interrogation resolution of the issue always involves a balancing by the courts of the competing private and public interests at stake in the particular circumstances shown. These principles were recognized in the *Watkins* case, where, in speaking of the First Amendment in relation to congressional inquiries, we said: "It is manifest that despite the adverse effects which follow upon compelled disclosure of private matters, not all such inquiries are barred. . . . The critical element is the existence of, and the weight to be ascribed to, the interest of the Congress in demanding disclosures from an unwilling witness." . . . More recently in *National Association for Advancement of Colored People* v. *State of Alabama,* 357 US 449, we applied the same principles in judging state action claimed to infringe rights of association assured by the Due Process Clause of the Fourteenth Amendment, and stated that the " 'subordinating interest of the State must be compelling' " in order to overcome the individual constitutional rights at stake. In light of these principles we now consider petitioner's First Amendment claims.

The first question is whether this investigation was related to a valid legislative purpose, for Congress may not constitutionally require an individual to disclose his political relationships or other private affairs except in relation to such a purpose. . . .

That Congress has wide power to legislate in the field of Communist activity in this Country, and to conduct appropriate investigations in aid thereof, is hardly debatable. The existence of such power has never been questioned by this Court, and it is sufficient to say, without particularization, that Congress has enacted or considered in this field a wide range of legislative measures, not a few of which have stemmed from recommendations of the very Committee whose actions have been drawn in question here. In the last analysis this power rests on the right of self-preservation, "the ultimate value of any society," *Dennis* v. *United States*, 341 US 494. Justification for its exercise in turn rests on the long and widely accepted view that the tenets of the Communist Party include the ultimate overthrow of the Government of the United States by force and violence, a view which has been given formal expression by the Congress.

On these premises, this Court in its constitutional adjudications has consistently refused to view the Communist Party as an ordinary political party, and has upheld federal legislation aimed at the Communist problem which in a different context would certainly have raised constitutional issues of the gravest character. See, e.g., *Carlson* v. *Landon*, 342 US 524; *Galvan* v. *Press*, 347 US 522. On the same premises this Court has upheld under the Fourteenth Amendment state legislation requiring those occupying or seeking public office to disclaim knowing membership in any organization advocating overthrow of the Government by force and violence, which legislation none can avoid seeing was aimed at membership in the Communist Party. . . . Similarly, in other areas, this Court has recognized the close nexus between the Communist Party and violent overthrow of government. . . . To suggest that because the Communist Party may also sponsor peaceable political reforms the constitutional issues before us should now be judged as if that Party were just an ordinary political party from the standpoint of national security, is to ask this Court to blind itself to world affairs which have determined the whole course of our national policy since the close of World War II, affairs to which Judge Learned Hand gave vivid expression in his opinion in *United States* v. *Dennis*, 2 Cir., 183 F.2d 201, 213, and to the vast burdens which these conditions have entailed for the entire Nation.

We think that investigatory power in this domain is not to be denied Congress solely because the field of education is involved. Nothing in the prevailing opinions in *Sweezy* v. *State of New Hampshire, supra,* stands for a contrary view. The vice existing there was that the questioning of Sweezy, who had not been shown ever to have been connected with the Communist Party, as to the contents of a lecture he had given at the University of New Hampshire, and as to his connections with the Progressive Party, then on the ballot as a normal political party in some 26 States, was too far removed from the premises on which the constitutionality of the State's investigation had to depend to withstand attack under the Fourteenth Amendment. . . . This is a very different thing from inquiring into the extent to which the Communist Party has succeeded in infiltrating into our universities, or elsewhere, persons and groups committed to furthering the objective of overthrow. . . . Indeed we do not understand petitioner here to suggest that Congress in no circumstances may inquire into Communist activity in the field of education.* Rather, his position is in effect that this particular investigation was aimed not at the revolutionary aspects but at the theoretical classroom discussion of communism.

In our opinion this position rests on a too constricted view of the nature of the investigatory process, and is not supported by a fair assessment of the record before us. An investigation of advocacy of or preparation for overthrow certainly embraces the right to identify a witness as a member of the Communist Party, . . . and to inquire into the various manifestations of the Party's tenets. The strict requirements of a prosecution under the Smith Act . . . are not the measure of the permissible scope of a congressional investigation into "overthrow," for of necessity the investigatory process must proceed step by step. Nor can it fairly be concluded that this investigation was directed at controlling what is being taught at our universities rather than at overthrow. The statement of the Subcommittee Chairman at the opening of the investigation evinces no such intention, and so far as this record reveals nothing thereafter transpired which would justify our holding that the thrust of the investigation later changed. The record discloses considerable testimony concerning the foreign domination and revolutionary purposes and efforts of the Communist Party. That there was also testimony on the abstract philosophical level does not detract from the dominant theme of this investigation—Communist infiltration furthering the alleged ultimate purpose of overthrow. And certainly the conclusion would not be justified that the questioning of petitioner would have exceeded permissible bounds had he not shut off the Subcommittee at the threshold.

Nor can we accept the further contention that this investigation should not be deemed to have been in furtherance of a legislative

* The *amicus* brief of the American Association of University Professors states at page 24: "The claims of academic freedom cannot be asserted unqualifiedly. The social interest it embodies is but one of a larger set, within which the interest in national self-preservation and in enlightened and well-informed law-making also prominently appear. When two major interests collide, as they do in the present case, neither the one nor the other can claim *a priori* supremacy. But it is in the nature of our system of laws that there must be demonstrable justification for an action by the Government which endangers or denies a freedom guaranteed by the Constitution."

purpose because the true objective of the Committee and of the Congress was purely "exposure." So long as Congress acts in pursuance of its constitutional power, the judiciary lacks authority to intervene on the basis of the motives which spurred the exercise of that power. . . . "It is, of course, true," as was said in *McCray* v. *United States*, 195 US 27, "that if there be no authority in the judiciary to restrain a lawful exercise of power by another department of the government, where a wrong motive or purpose has impelled to the exertion of the power, that abuses of a power conferred may be temporarily effectual. The remedy for this, however, lies, not in the abuse by the judicial authority of its functions, but in the people, upon whom, after all, under our institutions, reliance must be placed for the correction of abuses committed in the exercise of a lawful power." These principles of course apply as well to committee investigations into the need for legislation as to the enactments which such investigations may produce. . . . Thus, in stating in the *Watkins* case that "there is no congressional power to expose for the sake of exposure," we at the same time declined to inquire into the "motives of committee members," and recognized that their "motives alone would not vitiate an investigation which had been instituted by a House of Congress if that assembly's legislative purpose is being served." Having scrutinized this record we cannot say that the unanimous panel of the Court of Appeals which first considered this case was wrong in concluding that "the primary purposes of the inquiry were in aid of legislative processes." Certainly this is not a case like *Kilbourn* v. *Thompson*, 103 US 168, where "The House of Representatives not only exceeded the limit of its own authority, but assumed a power which could only be properly exercised by another branch of the government, because it was in its nature clearly judicial." . . . The constitutional legislative power of Congress in this instance is beyond question.

Finally, the record is barren of other factors which in themselves might sometimes lead to the conclusion that the individual interests at stake were not subordinate to those of the state. There is no indication in this record that the Subcommittee was attempting to pillory witnesses. Nor did petitioner's appearance as a witness follow from indiscriminate dragnet procedures, lacking in probable cause for belief that he possessed information which might be helpful to the Subcommittee. And the relevancy of the questions put to him by the Subcommittee is not open to doubt.

We conclude that the balance between the individual and the governmental interests here at stake must be struck in favor of the latter, and that therefore the provisions of the First Amendment have not been offended.

We hold that petitioner's conviction for contempt of Congress discloses no infirmity, and that the judgment of the Court of Appeals must be affirmed.

Affirmed.

Mr. Justice Black, with whom the Chief Justice, and Mr. Justice Douglas concur, dissenting:

On May 28, 1954, petitioner Lloyd Barenblatt, then 31 years old, and a teacher of psychology at Vassar College, was summoned to appear before a Subcommittee of the House Committee on Un-American Activities. After service of the summons, but before Barenblatt appeared on June 28, his four-year contract with Vassar expired and was not renewed. He, therefore, came to the Committee as a private citizen without a job. Earlier that day, the Committee's interest in Barenblatt had been aroused by the testimony of an ex-Communist named Crowley. When Crowley had first appeared before the Un-American Activities Committee he had steadfastly refused to admit or deny Communist affilations or to identify others as Communists. After the House reported this refusal to the United States Attorney for prosecution, Crowley "voluntarily" returned and asked to testify. He was sworn in and interrogated, but not before he was made aware by various Committee members of Committee policy to "make an appropriate recommendation" to protect any witness who "fully cooperates with the committee." He then talked at length, identifying by name, address and occupation, whenever possible, people he claimed had been Communists. One of these was Barenblatt, who, according to Crowley, had been a Communist during 1947–1950 while a graduate student and teaching fellow at the University of Michigan. Though Crowley testified in great detail about the small group of Communists who had been at Michigan at that time and though the Committee was very satisfied with his testimony, it sought repetition of much of the information from Barenblatt. Barenblatt, however, refused to answer their questions and filed a long statement outlining his constitutional objections. He asserted that the Committee was violating the Constitution by abridging freedom of speech, thought, press, and association, and by conducting legislative trials of known or suspected Communists which trespassed on the exclusive power of the judiciary. He argued that however he answered questions relating to membership in the Communist Party his position in society and his ability to earn a living would be seriously jeopardized; that he would, in effect, be subjected to a bill of attainder despite the twice-expressed constitutional mandate against such legislative punishments. This would occur, he pointed out, even if he did no more than invoke the protection of clearly applicable provisions of the Bill of Rights as a reason for refusing to answer.

He repeated these, and other objections, in the District Court as a reason for dismissing an indictment for contempt of Congress. His position, however, was rejected at the trial and in the Court of Appeals for the District of Columbia Circuit over the strong dissents of Chief Judge Edgerton and Judges Bazelon, Fahy and Washington. The Court today affirms, and thereby sanctions the use of the contempt power to enforce questioning by congressional committees in the realm of speech and association. I cannot agree with this disposition of the case for I believe that the resolution establishing the House Un-American Activities Committee and the questions that Committee asked Barenblatt violate the Constitution in several respects. (1) Rule XI creating the Committee authorizes such a sweeping, unlimited, all-inclusive and undiscriminating compulsory examination of witnesses in the field of speech, press, petition and assembly that it violates 'the procedural requirements of the Due Process Clause of the Fifth Amendment. (2) Compelling an answer to the questions asked Barenblatt abridges freedom of speech and association in contravention of the First Amendment. (3) The Committee proceedings were part of a legislative program to stigmatize and punish by public identification and exposure all witnesses considered by the Committee to be guilty of Communist affilations, as well as all witnesses who refused to answer Committee questions on constitutional grounds; the Committee was thus improperly seeking to try, convict, and punish suspects, a task which the Constitution expressly denies to Congress and grants exclusively to the courts, to be exercised by them only after indictment and in full compliance with all the safeguards provided by the Bill of Rights.

I

It goes without saying that a law to be valid must be clear enough to make its commands understandable. For obvious reasons, the standard of certainty required in criminal statutes is more exacting than in noncriminal statutes. This is simply because it would be unthinkable to convict a man for violating a law he could not understand. This Court has recognized that the stricter standard is as much required in criminal contempt cases as in all other criminal cases, and has emphasized that the "vice of vagueness" is especially pernicious where legislative power over an area involving speech, press, petition and assembly is involved. In this area the statement that a statute is void if it "attempts to cover so much that it effectively covers nothing" . . . takes on double significance. For a statute broad enough to support infringement of speech, writings, thought and public assemblies, against the unequivocal command of the First Amendment necessarily leaves all persons to guess just what the law really means to cover, and fear of a wrong guess inevitably leads people to forego the very rights the Constitution sought to protect above all others. Vagueness becomes even more intolerable in this area if one accepts, as the Court today does, a balancing test to decide if First Amendment rights shall be protected. It is difficult at best to make a man guess—at the penalty of imprisonment—whether a court will consider the State's need for certain information superior to society's interest in unfettered freedom. It is unconscionable to make him choose between the right to keep silent and the need to speak when the statute supposedly establishing the "state's interest" is too vague to give him guidance. . . .

Measured by the foregoing standards, Rule XI cannot support any conviction for refusal to testify. In substance it authorizes the Committee to compel witnesses to give evidence about all "un-American propaganda" whether instigated in this country or abroad. The word "propaganda" seems to mean anything that people say, write, think or associate together about. The term "un-American" is equally vague. As was said in *Watkins* v. *United States,* "Who can define [its] meaning . . . ? What is that single, solitary 'principle of the form of government as guaranteed by our Constitution' ?" I think it clear that the boundaries of the Committee are, to say the least, "nebulous." Indeed, "It would be difficult to imagine a less explicit authorizing resolution."

The Court—while not denying the vagueness of Rule XI—nevertheless defends its application here because the questions asked concerned communism, a subject of investigation which had been reported to the House by the Committee on numerous occasions. If the issue were merely whether Congress intended to allow an investigation of communism, or even of communism in education, it may well be that we could hold the data cited by the Court sufficient to support a finding of intent. But that is expressly not the issue. On the Court's own test, the issue is whether Barenblatt can know with sufficient certainty, at the time of his interrogation, that there is so compelling a need for his replies that infringement of his rights of free association is justified. The record does not disclose where Barenblatt can find what that need is. There is certainly no clear congressional statement of it in Rule XI. Perhaps if Barenblatt had had time to read all the reports of the Committee to the House, and in addition had examined the appropriations made to the Committee he, like the Court, could have discerned an intent by Congress to allow an investigation of communism in education. Even so he would be hard put to decide what the need for this investigation is since Congress expressed it neither when it enacted Rule XI nor when it acquiesced in the Committee's assertions of power. Yet it is knowledge of this need—what is wanted from him and why it is wanted—that a witness must have if he is to be in a position to comply with the Court's rule that he balance individual rights against the requirements of the State. I cannot see how that knowledge can exist under Rule XI.

But even if Barenblatt could evaluate the importance to the Government of the information sought, Rule XI would still be too broad to support his conviction. For we are dealing here with governmental procedures which the Court itself admits reach to the very fringes of congressional power. In such cases more is required of legislatures than a vague delegation to be filled in later by mute acquiescence. If Congress wants ideas investigated, if it even wants them investigated in the field of education, it must be prepared to say so expressly and unequivocally. And it is not enough that a court through exhaustive research can establish, even conclusively, that Congress wished to allow the investigation. I can find no such unequivocal statement here.

For all these reasons, I would hold that Rule XI is too broad to be meaningful and cannot support petitioner's conviction.

II

The First Amendment says in no equivocal language that Congress shall pass no law abridging freedom of speech, press, assembly or petition. The activities of this Committee, authorized by Congress, do precisely that, through exposure, obloquy and public scorn. . . . The Court does not really deny this fact but relies on a combination of three reasons for permitting the infringement: (A) The notion that despite the First Amendment's command Congress can abridge speech and association if this Court decides that the governmental interest in abridging speech is greater than an individual's interest in exercising that freedom, (B) the Government's right to "preserve itself," (C) the fact that the Committee is only after Communists or suspected Communists in this investigation.

(A) I do not agree that laws directly abridging First Amendment freedoms can be justified by a congressional or judicial balancing process. There are, of course, cases suggesting that a law which primarily regulates conduct but which might also indirectly affect speech can be upheld if the effect on speech is minor in relation to the need for control of the conduct. With these cases I agree. Typical of them are *Cantwell* v. *State of Connecticut*, 310 US 296 and, *Schneider* v. *State of New Jersey, Town of Irvington*, 308 US 147. Both of these involved the right of a city to control its streets. In *Cantwell*, a man had been convicted of breach of the peace for playing a phonograph on the street. He defended on the ground that he was disseminating religious views and could not, therefore, be stopped. We upheld his defense, but in so doing we pointed out that the city did have substantial power over conduct on the streets even where this power might to some extent affect speech. A State, we said, might "by general and non-discriminatory legislation regulate the times, the places, and the manner of soliciting upon its streets, and holding meetings thereon." But even such laws governing conduct, we emphasized, must be tested, though only by a balancing process, if they indirectly affect ideas. On one side of the balance, we pointed out, is the interest of the United States in seeing that its fundamental law protecting freedom of communication is not abridged; on the other the obvious interest of the State to regulate conduct within its boundaries. In *Cantwell* we held that the need to control the streets could not justify the restriction made on speech. We stressed the fact that where a man had a right to be on a street, "he had a right peacefully to impart his views to others." Similar views were expressed in *Schneider*, which concerned ordinances prohibiting the distribution of handbills to prevent littering. We forbade application of such ordinances when they affected literature designed to spread ideas. There were other ways, we said, to protect the city from littering which would not sacrifice the right of the people to be informed. In so holding, we, of course, found it necessary to "weigh the circumstances." But we did not in *Schneider*, any more than in *Cantwell*, even remotely suggest that a law directly aimed at curtailing speech and political persuasion could be saved through a balancing process. Neither these cases, nor any others, can be read as allowing legislative bodies to pass laws abridging freedom of speech, press and association merely because of hostility to views peacefully expressed in a place where the speaker had a right to be. Rule XI, on its face and as here applied, since it attempts inquiry into beliefs, not action—ideas and associations, not conduct, does just that.

To apply the Court's balancing test under such circumstances is to read the First Amendment to say "Congress shall pass no law abridging freedom of speech, press, assembly and petition, unless Congress and the Supreme Court reach the joint conclusion that on balance the interests of the Government in stifling these freedoms is greater than the interest of the people in having them exercised." This is closely akin to the notion that neither the First Amendment nor any other provision of the Bill of Rights should be enforced unless the Court believes it is *reasonable* to do so. Not only does this violate the genius of our *written* Constitution, but it runs expressly counter to the injunction to Court and Congress made by Madison when he introduced the Bill of Rights. "If they [the first ten amendments] are incorporated into the Constitution, independent tribunals of justice will consider themselves in a peculiar manner the guardians of those rights; they will be an impenetrable bulwark against *every* assumption of power in the Legislative or Executive; they will be naturally led to resist *every* encroachment upon rights expressly stipulated for in the Constitution by the declaration of rights." Unless we return to this view of our judicial function, unless we once again accept the notion that the Bill of Rights means what it says and that this Court must enforce that meaning, I am of the opinion that our great charter of liberty will be more honored in the breach than in the observance.

But even assuming what I cannot assume, that some balancing is proper in this case, I feel that the Court after stating the test ignores it completely. At most it balances the right of the Government to preserve itself, against Barenblatt's right to refrain from revealing Communist affiliations. Such a balance, however, mistakes the factors to be weighed. In the first place, it completely leaves out the real interest in Barenblatt's silence, the interest of the people as a whole in being able to join organizations, advocate causes and make political "mistakes" without later being subjected to governmental penalties for having dared to think for themselves. It is this right, the right to err politically, which keeps us strong as a Nation. For no number of laws against communism can have as much effect as the personal conviction which comes from having heard its arguments and rejected them, or from having once accepted its tenets and later recognized their worthlessness. Instead, the obloquy which results from investigations such as this not only stifles "mistakes" but prevents all but the most courageous from hazarding any views which might at some later time become disfavored. This result, whose importance cannot be overestimated, is doubly crucial when it affects the universities, on which we must largely rely for the experimentation and development of new ideas essential to our country's welfare. It is these interests of society, rather than Barenblatt's own right to silence, which I think the Court should put on the balance against the demands of the Government, if any balancing process is to be tolerated. Instead they are not mentioned, while on the other side the demands of the Government are vastly overstated and called "self preservation." It is admitted that this

Committee can only seek information for the purpose of suggesting laws, and that Congress' power to make laws in the realm of speech and association is quite limited, even on the Court's test. Its interest in making such laws in the field of education, primarily a state function, is clearly narrower still. Yet the Court styles this attenuated interest self-preservation and allows it to overcome the need our country has to let us all think, speak, and associate politically as we like and without fear of reprisal. Such a result reduces "balancing" to a mere play on words and is completely inconsistent with the rules this Court has previously given for applying a "balancing test," where it is proper: "[T]he courts should be *astute* to examine the *effect* of the challenged legislation. Mere *legislative preferences or beliefs* . . . may well support regulation directed at other personal activities, but be insufficient to justify such as diminishes the exercise of rights so vital to the maintenance of democratic institutions." *Schneider* v. *State of New Jersey.* (Italics supplied.)

(B) Moreover, I cannot agree with the Court's notion that First Amendment freedoms must be abridged in order to "preserve" our country. That notion rests on the unarticulated premise that this Nation's security hangs upon its power to punish people because of what they think, speak or write about, or because of those with whom they associate for political purposes. The Government, in its brief, virtually admits this position when it speaks of the "communication of unlawful ideas." I challenge this premise, and deny that ideas can be proscribed under our Constitution. I agree that despotic governments cannot exist without stifling the voice of opposition to their oppressive practices. The First Amendment means to me, however, that the only constitutional way our Government can preserve itself is to leave its people the fullest possible freedom to praise, criticize or discuss, as they see fit, all governmental policies and to suggest, if they desire, that even its most fundamental postulates are bad and should be changed; "Therein lies the security of the Republic, the very foundation of constitutional government." On that premise this land was created, and on that premise it has grown to greatness. Our Constitution assumes that the common sense of the people and their attachment to our country will enable them, after free discussion, to withstand ideas that are wrong. To say that our patriotism must be protected against false ideas by means other than these is, I think, to make a baseless charge. Unless we can rely on these qualities—if, in short, we begin to punish speech—we cannot honestly proclaim ourselves to be a free Nation and we have lost what the Founders of this land risked their lives and their sacred honors to defend.

(C) The Court implies, however, that the ordinary rules and requirements of the Constitution do not apply because the Committee is merely after Communists and they do not constitute a political party but only a criminal gang. "[T]he long and widely accepted view," the Court says, is "that the tenets of the Communist Party include the ultimate overthrow of the Government of the United States by force and violence." This justifies the investigation undertaken. By accepting this charge and allowing it to support treatment of the Communist Party and its members which would violate the Constitution if applied to other groups, the Court, in effect, declares that Party outlawed. It has been only a few years since there was a practically unanimous feeling throughout the country and in our courts that this could not be done in our free land. Of course it has always been recognized that members of the Party who, either individually or in combination, commit acts in violation of valid laws can be prosecuted. But the Party as a whole and innocent members of it could not be attainted merely because it had some illegal aims and because some of its members were lawbreakers. Thus in *De Jonge v. State of Oregon*, 299 US 353, on stipulated facts that the Communist Party advocated criminal syndicalism—"crime, physical violence, sabotage, or any unlawful acts or methods as a means of accomplishing or effecting industrial or political change or revolution"—a unanimous Court, speaking through Chief Justice Hughes, held that a Communist addressing a Communist rally could be found guilty of no offense so long as no violence or crime was urged at the meeting. The Court absolutely refused to concede that either De Jonge or the Communist Party forfeited the protections of the First and Fourteenth Amendments because one of the Party's purposes was to effect a violent change of government. See also *Herndon v. Lowry*, 301 US 242.

Later, in 1948, when various bills were proposed in the House and Senate to handicap or outlaw the Communist Party, leaders of the Bar who had been asked to give their views rose up to contest the constitutionality of the measures. The late Charles Evans Hughes, Jr., questioned the validity under both the First and Fifth Amendments of one of these bills, which in effect outlawed the Party. The late John W. Davis attacked it as lacking an ascertainable standard of guilt under many of this Court's cases. And the Attorney General of the United States not only indicated that such a measure would be unconstitutional but declared it to be unwise even if valid. He buttressed his position by citing a statement by J. Edgar Hoover, Director of the Federal Bureau of Investigation, and the declaration of this court in *West Virginia State Board of Education v. Barnette*, 319 US 624, that:

> If there is any fixed star in our constitutional constellation, it is that no official, high or petty, can prescribe what shall be orthodox in politics, nationalism, religion or other matters of opinion or force citizens to confess by word or act their faith therein.

Even the proponent of the bill disclaimed any aim to outlaw the Communist Party and pointed out the "disadvantages" of such a move by stating that "the Communist Party was illegal and outlawed in Russia when it took over control of the Soviet Union."* Again, when the Attorney General testified

* Hearings, Subcommittee on Legislation of the Committee on Un-American Activities on H.R. 4422, H.R. 4581, 80th Cong., 2d Sess. 13. This statement was relied on by the Honorable Thomas E. Dewey, then a candidate for the presidency of the United States, in a speech given in Portland, Oregon, in May, 1948. Mr. Dewey went on to say, in opposing outlawry of the Communist Party:

"I am against it because it is a violation of the Constitution of the United

on a proposal to bar the Communist Party from the ballot he said, "an organized group, whether you call it political or not, could hardly be barred from the ballot without jeopardizing the constitutional guarantees of all other political groups and parties."

All these statements indicate quite clearly that no matter how often or how quickly we repeat the claim that the Communist Party is not a political party, we cannot outlaw it, as a group, without endangering the liberty of all of us. The reason is not hard to find, for mixed among those aims of communism which are illegal are perfectly normal political and social goals. And muddled with its revolutionary tenets is a drive to achieve power through the ballot, if it can be done. These things necessarily make it a political party whatever other, illegal, aims it may have. . . . Significantly until recently the Communist Party was on the ballot in many States. When that was so, many Communists undoubtedly hoped to accomplish its lawful goals through support of Communist candidates. Even now some such may still remain. To attribute to them, and to those who have left the Party, the taint of the group is to ignore both our traditions that guilt like belief is "personal and not a matter of mere association" and the obvious fact that "men adhering to a political party or other organization notoriously do not subscribe unqualifiedly to all of its platforms or asserted principles." *Schneiderman* v. *United States,* 320 US 118.

The fact is that once we allow any group which has some political aims or ideas to be driven from the ballot and from the battle for men's minds because some of its members are bad and some of its tenets are illegal, no group is safe. Today we deal with Communists or suspected Communists. In 1920, instead, the New York Assembly suspended duly elected legislators on the ground that, being Socialists, they were disloyal to the country's principles.* In the 1830's the Masons were hunted as outlaws and subversives, and abolitionists were considered revolutionaries of the most dangerous kind in both North and South.† Earlier still, at the time of the universally unlamented alien

States and of the Bill of Rights, and clearly so. I am against it because it is immoral and nothing but totalitarianism itself. I am against it because I know from a great many years' experience in the enforcement of the law that the proposal wouldn't work, and instead it would rapidly advance the cause of communism in the United States and all over the world. . . .

"There is an American way to do this job, a perfectly simple American way . . . outlawing every conceivable *act* of subversion against the United States. . . .

"Now, times are too grave to try any expedients and fail. This expedient has failed, this expedient of outlawing has failed in Russia. It failed in Europe, it failed in Italy, it failed in Canada. . . .

"Let us not make such a terrific blunder in the United States. . . . Let us go forward as Free Americans. Let us have the courage to be free." XIV Vital Speeches of the Day, 486–487. (Italics supplied.)

* See O'Brian, Loyalty Tests and Guilt by Association, 61 Harv.L.Rev. 592, 593. Significantly the action of the New York Assembly was strongly condemned by Charles Evans Hughes, then a former Associate Justice of this Court, and later its Chief Justice.

† See generally, McCarthy, The Antimasonic Party: A Study of Political An-

and sedition laws, Thomas Jefferson's party was attacked and its members were derisively called "Jacobins." Fisher Ames described the party as a "French faction" guilty of "subversion" and "officered, regimented and formed to subordination." Its members, he claimed, intended to "take arms against the laws as soon as they dare." History should teach us then, that in times of high emotional excitement minority parties and groups which advocate extremely unpopular social or governmental innovations will always be typed as criminal gangs and attempts will always be made to drive them out. It was knowledge of this fact, and of its great dangers, that caused the Founders of our land to enact the First Amendment as a guarantee that neither Congress nor the people would do anything to hinder or destroy the capacity of individuals and groups to seek converts and votes for any cause, however radical or unpalatable their principles might seem under the accepted notions of the time. Whatever the States were left free to do, the First Amendment sought to leave Congress devoid of any kind or quality of power to direct any type of national laws against the freedom of individuals to think what they please, advocate whatever policy they choose, and join with others to bring about the social, religious, political and governmental changes which seem best to them. Today's holding, in my judgment, marks another major step in the progressively increasing retreat from the safeguards of the First Amendment.

It is, sadly, no answer to say that this Court will not allow the trend to overwhelm us; that today's holding will be strictly confined to "Communists," as the Court's language implies. This decision can no more be contained than could the holding in *American Communications Ass'n, C. I. O. v. Douds,* 339 US 382. In that case the Court sustained as an exercise of the commerce power an Act which required labor union officials to take an oath that they were not members of the Communist Party. The Court rejected the idea that the *Douds* holding meant that the Party and all its members could be attainted because of their Communist beliefs. It went to great lengths to explain that the Act held valid "touches only a relative handful of persons, leaving the great majority of persons of the identified affiliations and beliefs completely free from restraint." "[W]hile this Court sits," the Court proclaimed, no wholesale proscription of Communists or their Party can occur. I dissented and said:

> Under such circumstances, restrictions imposed on proscribed groups are seldom static, even though the rate of expansion may not move in geometric progression from discrimination to arm-band to ghetto and worse. Thus I cannot regard the Court's holding as one which merely bars Communists from holding union office and nothing more. For its reasoning would apply just as forcibly to statutes barring Communists and their suspected sympathizers from election to political office,

timasonry in the United States, 1827–1840. H.R.Doc. No. 461, 57th Cong., 2d Sess. 365. Nye, William Lloyd Garrison, 88–105; Korngold, Two Friends of Man. 82–104. Cf. St. George Tucker, Appendix, 1 Blackstone (Tucker ed. 1803) 315, discussing English laws "for suppressing assemblies of free-masons" and pointing out that similar laws cannot be enacted under our Constitution.

mere membership in unions, and in fact from getting or holding any job whereby they could earn a living.

My prediction was all too accurate. Today, Communists or suspected Communists have been denied an opportunity to work as government employees, lawyers, doctors, teachers, pharmacists, veterinarians, subway conductors, industrial workers and in just about any other job. . . . In today's holding they are singled out and, as a class, are subjected to inquisitions which the Court suggests would be unconstitutional but for the fact of "Communism." Nevertheless, this Court still sits!*

III

Finally, I think Barenblatt's conviction violates the Constitution because the chief aim, purpose and practice of the House Un-American Activities Committee, as disclosed by its many reports, is to try witnesses and punish them because they are or have been Communists or because they refuse to admit or deny Communist affiliations. The punishment imposed is generally punishment by humiliation and public shame. There is nothing strange or novel about this kind of punishment. It is in fact one of the oldest forms of governmental punishment known to mankind; branding, the pillory, ostracism and subjection to public hatred being but a few examples of it. Nor is there anything strange about a court's reviewing the power of a congressional committee to inflict punishment. In 1880 this Court nullified the action of the House of Representatives in sentencing a witness to jail for failing to answer questions of a congressional committee. *Kilbourn* v. *Thompson*, 103 US 168. The Court held that the Committee in its investigation of the Jay Cooke bankruptcy was seeking to exercise judical power, and this, it emphatically said, no committee could do. It seems to me that the proof that the Un-American Activities Committee is here undertaking a purely judicial function is overwhelming, far stronger, in fact, than it was in the Jay Cooke investigation which, moreover, concerned only business transactions, not freedom of association.

The Un-American Activities Committee was created in 1938. It immediately conceived of its function on a grand scale as one of ferreting out "subversives" and especially of having them removed from government jobs. It made many reports to the House urging removal of such employees. Finally, at the instigation of the Committee, the House put a rider on an appropriation bill to bar three government workers from collecting their salary. The House action was based on Committee findings that each of the three employees was a member of, or associated with, organizations deemed

* The record in this very case indicates how easily such restrictions spread. During the testimony of one witness an organization known as the Americans for Democratic Action was mentioned. Despite testimony that this organization did not admit Communists, one member of the Committee insisted that it was a Communist front because "it followed a party line, almost identical in many particulars with the Communist Party line." Presumably if this accusation were repeated frequently and loudly enough that organization, or any other, would also be called a "criminal gang. . . ."

undesirable and that the "views and philosophies" of these workers "as expressed in various statements and writings constitute subversive activity within the definition adopted by your committee, and that [they are], therefore, unfit for the present to continue in Government employment." The Senate and the President agreed to the rider, though not without protest. We held that statute void as a bill of attainder in *United States* v. *Lovett*, 1946, 328 US 303, stating that its "effect was to inflict punishment without the safeguards of a judicial trial" and that this "cannot be done either by a state or by the United States."

Even after our *Lovett* holding, however, the Committee continued to view itself as the "only agency of government that has the power of exposure," and to work unceasingly and sincerely to identify and expose all suspected Communists and "subversives" in order to eliminate them from virtually all fields of employment. How well it has succeeded in its declared program of "pitiless publicity and exposure" is a matter of public record. It is enough to cite the experience of a man who masqueraded as a Communist for the F. B. I. and who reported to this same Committee that since 1952 when his "membership" became known he has been unable to hold any job. To accomplish this kind of result, the Committee has called witnesses who are suspected of Communist affiliation, has subjected them to severe questioning and has insisted that each tell the name of every person he has ever known at any time to have been a Communist, and, if possible, to give the addresses and occupations of the people named. These names are then indexed, published, and reported to Congress, and often to the press. The same technique is employed to cripple the job opportunities of those who strongly criticize the Committee or take other actions it deems undesirable. Thus, in 1949, the Committee reported that it had indexed and printed some 335,000 names of people who had signed "Communist" petitions of one kind or another. All this the Committee did and does to punish by exposure the many phases of "un-American" activities that it reports cannot be reached by legislation, by administrative action, or by any other agency of Government, which, of course, includes the courts.

The same intent to expose and punish is manifest in the Committee's investigation which led to Barenblatt's conviction. The declared purpose of the investigation was to identify to the people of Michigan the individuals responsible for the, alleged, Communist success there. The Committee claimed that its investigation "uncovered" members of the Communist Party holding positions in the school systems in Michigan; that most of the teachers subpoenaed before the Committee refused to answer questions on the ground that to do so might result in self-incrimination, and that most of these teachers had lost their jobs. It then stated that "the Committee on Un-American Activities approves of this action. . . ." Similarly, as a result of its Michigan investigation, the Committee called upon American labor unions to amend their constitutions, if necessary, in order to deny membership to any Communist Party member. This would, of course, prevent many workers from getting or holding the only kind of jobs their particular skills qualified them for. The Court, today, barely mentions these statements, which, especially when read in the context of past reports by the Committee, show unmistakably what the Committee was doing. I cannot understand why these reports are deemed relevant to a determination of a congressional intent to investigate communism in education, but irrelevant to any finding of congressional intent to bring about exposure for its own sake or for the purpose of punishment.

I do not question the Committee's patriotism and sincerity in doing all this. I merely feel that it cannot be done by Congress under our Constitution. For, even assuming that the Federal Government can compel witnesses to testify as to Communist affiliations in order to subject them to ridicule and social and economic retaliation, I cannot agree that this is a legislative function. Such publicity is clearly punishment, and the Constitution allows only one way in which people can be convicted and punished. As we said in *Lovett*, "Those who wrote our Constitution well knew the danger inherent in special legislative acts which take away the life, liberty, or property of particular named persons, because the legislature thinks them guilty of conduct which deserves punishment. *They intended to safeguard the people of this country from punishment without trial by duly constituted courts.*" (Italics added.) Thus if communism is to be made a crime, and communists are to be subjected to "pains and penalties," I would still hold this conviction bad, for the crime of communism, like all others, can be punished only by court and jury after a trial with all judicial safeguards.

It is no answer to all this to suggest that legislative committees should be allowed to punish if they grant the accused some rules of courtesy or allow him counsel. For the Constitution proscribes *all* bills of attainder by State or Nation, not merely those which lack counsel or courtesy. It does this because the Founders believed that punishment was too serious a matter to be entrusted to any group other than an independent judiciary and a jury of twelve men acting on previously passed, unambiguous laws, with all the procedural safeguards they put in the Constitution as essential to a fair trial—safeguards which included the right to counsel, compulsory process for witnesses, specific indictments, confrontation of accusers, as well as protection against self-incrimination, double jeopardy and cruel and unusual punishment—in short, due process of law. . . . They believed this because not long before worthy men had been deprived of their liberties, and indeed their lives, through parliamentary trials without these safeguards. The memory of one of these, John Lilburne—banished and disgraced by a parliamentary committee on penalty of death if he returned to his country—was particularly vivid when our Constitution was written. His attack on trials by such committees and his warning that "what is done unto any one, may be done unto every one" * was part of the history of the times which moved

* "For certainly it cannot be denied, but if he be really an offender, he is such by the breach of some law, made and published before the fact, and ought by due process of law, and verdict of 12 men, to be thereof convict, and found guilty of such crime; unto which the law also hath prescribed such a punishment agreeable to that our fundamental liberty; which enjoineth than no freeman of England should be adjudged of life, limb, liberty, or estate, but by

those who wrote our Constitution to determine that no such arbitrary punishments should ever occur here. It is the protection from arbitrary punishments through the right to a judicial trial with all these safeguards which over the years has distinguished America from lands where drum-head courts and other similar "tribunals" deprive the weak and the unorthodox of life, liberty and property without due process of law. It is this same right which is denied to Barenblatt, because the Court today fails to see what is here for all to see—that exposure and punishment is the aim of this Committee and the reason for its existence. To deny this aim is to ignore the Committee's own claims and the reports it has issued ever since it was established. I cannot believe that the nature of our judicial office requires us to be so blind, and must conclude that the Un-American Activities Committee's "identification" and "exposure" of Communists and suspected Communists, like the activities of the Committee in *Kilbourn* v. *Thompson*, amount to an encroachment on the judiciary which bodes ill for the liberties of the people of this land.

Ultimately all the questions in this case really boil down to one—whether we as a people will try fearfully and futilely to preserve Democracy by

---

Juries; a freedom which parliaments in all ages contended to preserve from violation; as the birthright and chief inheritance of the people, as may appear most remarkably in the Petition of Right, which you have stiled that most excellent law.

"And therefore we trust upon second thoughts, being the parliament of England, you will be so far from bereaving us, who have never forfeited our right, of this our native right, and way of Trials by Juries, (for what is done unto any one, may be done unto every one), that you will preserve them entire to us, and to posterity, from the encroachments of any that would innovate upon them. . . .

"And it is believed, that . . . had [the cause] at any time either at first or last been admitted to a trial at law, and had passed any way by verdict of twelve sworn men: all the trouble and inconveniences arising thereupon had been prevented: the way of determination by major votes of committees, being neither so certain nor so satisfactory in any case as by way of Juries, the benefit of challenges and exceptions, and unanimous consent, being all essential privileges in the latter; whereas committees are tied to no such rules, but are at liberty to be present or absent at pleasure. Besides, Juries being birthright, and the other but new and temporary, men do not, nor, as we humbly conceive, ever will acquiesce in the one as in the other; from whence it is not altogether so much to be wondered at, if upon dissatisfactions, there have been such frequent printing of men's cases, and dealings of Committees, as there have been; and such harsh and inordinate heats and expressions between parties interested, such sudden and importunate appeals to your authority, being indeed all alike out of the true English road, and leading into nothing but trouble and perplexity, breeding hatred and enmities between worthy families, affronts and disgust between worthy persons of the same public affection and interest, and to the rejoicing of none but public adversaries. All which, and many more inconveniences, can only be avoided, by referring all such cases to the usual Trials and final determinations of law." 5 Howell's *State Trials* 411–412, Statement of John Lilburne (1653).

adopting totalitarian methods, or whether in accordance with our traditions and our Constitution we will have the confidence and courage to be free.

I would reverse this conviction.

APPENDIX.

Random Selection of Statements by the House Un-American Activities Committee on Exposure and Punishment of "Subversives."

"[T]o inform the American people of the activities of any such organizations . . . is the real purpose of the House Committee"; "The purpose of this committee is the task of protecting our constitutional democracy by turning the light of pitiless publicity on [these] organizations." H.R. Rep. No. 1476, 76th Cong., 3d Sess. 1–2, 24.

"The very first exposure which our committee undertook in the summer of 1938 was that of the German-American Bund"; "Other organizations . . . have been greatly crippled . . . as a result of our exposures. The American Youth Congress once enjoyed a very considerable prestige. . . . Today many of its distinguished former sponsors refuse to be found in its company. . . . We kept the spotlight of publicity focused upon the American Youth Congress, and today it is clear to all that, in spite of a degree of participation in its activities by many fine young people, it was never at its core anything less than a tool of Moscow"; "This committee is the only agency of Government that has the power of exposure. . . . There are many phases of un-American activities that cannot be reached by legislation or administrative action. We believe that the Committee has shown that fearless exposure . . . is the . . . answer." H.R. Rep. No. 1, 77th Cong., 1st Sess. 21–22, 24.

"Our investigation has shown that a steady barrage against Congress comes . . . from the *New Republic,* one of whose editors . . . was recently forced out of an $8,000 Government job by the exposure of his Communist activities." H.R. Rep. No. 2277, 77th Cong., 2d Sess. 3. . . .

"Early in 1947 the committee adopted the following eight point program. . . .

"1. To expose and ferret out the Communists and Communist sympathizers in the Federal Government.

"2. To spotlight the spectacle of . . . Communists . . . in American labor."

"In a sense the storm of opposition to the activities of the committee is a tribute to its achievements in the field of exposure." Report of the Committee on Un-American Activities to the United States House of Representatives, 80th Cong., 2d Sess., Dec. 31, 1948, 2, 3 (Committee print).

"The committee would like to remind the Congress that its work is part of an 11-year continuity of effort that began . . . in August 1938. The committee would also like to recall that at no time in those 11 years has it ever wavered from a relentless pursuit and exposure"; "In the course of its investigations . . . the committee has made available a large, completely indexed, and readily accessible reference collection of lists of signers of Communist Party election petitions." H.R. Rep. No. 1950, 81st Cong., 2d Sess. 15, 19.

"To conduct the exposé . . . it was necessary for the investigative staff to interview over 100 persons. . . .

"The same tedious investigation of details was necessary prior to the successful exposure . . . in the Territory of Hawaii"; "As a result of the investigation and hearings held by the committee, Dolivet's contract with the United Nations has not been renewed, and it is the Committee's understanding that he was removed from editorship of the *United Nations World.*" H.R. Rep. No. 3249, 81st Cong., 2d Sess. 4, 5. . . .

"The focal point of the investigation into the general area of education was to the individual who had been identified"; "The question has been asked as to what purpose is served by the disclosure of the names of individuals who may long ago have left the conspiracy"; "The committee has no way of knowing the status of his membership at present until he is placed under oath and the information is sought to be elicited." H.R. No. 1192, 83d Cong., 2d Sess. 1, 7.

Mr. Justice Brennan, dissenting:

I would reverse this conviction. It is sufficient that I state my complete agreement with my Brother Black that no purpose for the investigation of Barenblatt is revealed by the record except exposure purely for the sake of exposure. This is not a purpose to which Barenblatt's rights under the First Amendment can validly be subordinated. An investigation in which the processes of law-making and law-evaluating are submerged entirely in exposure of individual behavior—in adjudication, of a sort, through the exposure process—is outside the constitutional pale of congressional inquiry. . . .

SWEEZY *v.* NEW HAMPSHIRE
354 US 234 (1957)

[The Attorney General of New Hampshire, conducting a one-man investigation, authorized by the state legislature, put questions to Sweezy concerning some lectures he delivered at the state university and concerning his political interests and activities. Sweezy refused to answer the questions on the ground that they violated his freedoms under the Constitution of the United States. His conviction for contempt was set aside by the Court on the ground that the authorizing resolution of the state legislature did not authorize the questions put to the witness. But the opinion of Chief Justice Warren (joined by Justices Black, Douglas, and Brennan) reaches broadly into constitutional considerations, especially as they spell out or affect academic freedom in colleges and universities. The opinions in *Uphaus*

v. *Wyman, post,* decided two years later, should, however, be read in connection with the instant case.

[Justices Clark and Burton dissented; Justice Whittaker did not participate.

[Justice Frankfurter (joined by Justice Harlan) concurred, stating that the questions infringed upon academic and political freedoms protected by the Constitution. In this connection Justice Frankfurter's concurring opinion in *Wieman* v. *Updegraff,* 344 US 183 (1952), should be considered.]

Mr. Chief Justice Warren announced the judgment of the Court and delivered an opinion, in which Mr. Justice Black, Mr. Justice Douglas, and Mr. Justice Brennan join:

This case, like *Watkins* v. *United States,* 354 US 178, brings before us a question concerning the constitutional limits of legislative inquiry. The investigation here was conducted under the aegis of a state legislature, rather than a House of Congress. This places the controversy in a slightly different setting from that in Watkins. The ultimate question here is whether the investigation deprived Sweezy of due process of law under the Fourteenth Amendment. For the reasons to be set out in this opinion, we conclude that the record in this case does not sustain the power of the State to compel the disclosures that the witness refused to make. . . .

The investigation in which petitioner was summoned to testify had its origins in a statute passed by the New Hampshire legislature in 1951. It was a comprehensive scheme of regulation of subversive activities. There was a section defining criminal conduct in the nature of sedition. "Subversive organizations" were declared unlawful and ordered dissolved. "Subversive persons" were made ineligible for employment by the state government. Included in the disability were those employed as teachers or in other capacities by any public educational institution. A loyalty program was instituted to eliminate "subversive persons" among government personnel. All present employees, as well as candidates for elective office in the future, were required to make sworn statements that they were not "subversive persons."

In 1953, the legislature adopted a "Joint Resolution Relating to the Investigation of Subversive Activities." It was resolved:

That the attorney general is hereby authorized and directed to make full and complete investigation with respect to violations of the subversive activities act of 1951 and to determine whether subversive persons as defined in said act are presently located within this state. The attorney general is authorized to act upon his own motion and upon such information as in his judgment may be reasonable or reliable. . . .

The attorney general is directed to proceed with criminal prosecutions under the subversive activities act whenever evidence presented to him in the course of the investigation indicates violation thereof, and he shall report to the 1955 session on the first day of its regular session the results of his investigation, together with his recommendations, if any, for necessary legislation.

Under state law, this was construed to constitute the Attorney General as a one-man legislative committee. He was given the authority to delegate any part of the investigation to any member of his staff. The legislature conferred upon the Attorney General the further authority to subpoena witnesses or documents. He did not have power to hold witnesses in contempt, however. In the event that coercive or punitive sanctions were needed, the Attorney General could invoke the aid of a State Superior Court which could find recalcitrant witnesses in contempt of court.

Petitioner was summoned to appear before the Attorney General on two separate occasions. On January 5, 1954, petitioner testified at length upon his past conduct and associations. He denied that he had ever been a member of the Communist Party or that he had ever been part of any program to overthrow the government by force or violence. The interrogation ranged over many matters, from petitioner's World War II military service with the Office of Strategic Services to his sponsorship, in 1949, of the Scientific and Cultural Conference for World Peace, at which he spoke.

During the course of the inquiry, petitioner declined to answer several questions. His reasons for doing so were given in a statement he read to the Committee at the outset of the hearing. He declared he would not answer those questions which were not pertinent to the subject under inquiry as well as those which transgress the limitations of the First Amendment. In keeping with this stand, he refused to disclose his knowledge of the Progressive Party in New Hampshire or of persons with whom he was acquainted in that organization. No action was taken by the Attorney General to compel answers to these questions.

The Attorney General again summoned petitioner to testify on June 3, 1954. There was more interrogation about the witness' prior contacts with Communists. The Attorney General lays great stress upon an article which petitioner had coauthored. It deplored the use of violence by the United States and other capitalist countries in attempting to preserve a social order which the writers thought must inevitably fall. This resistance, the article continued, will be met by violence from the oncoming socialism, violence which is to be less condemned morally than that of capitalism since its purpose is to create a "truly human society." Petitioner affirmed that he styled himself a "classical Marxist" and a "socialist" and that the article expressed his continuing opinion.

Again, at the second hearing, the Attorney General asked, and petitioner refused to answer, questions concerning the Progressive Party, and its predecessor, the Progressive Citizens of America. Those were:

Was she, Nancy Sweezy, your wife, active in the formation of the Progressive Citizens of America?

Was Nancy Sweezy then working with individuals who were then members of the Communist Party?

Was Charles Beebe active in forming the Progressive Citizens of America?

Was Charles Beebe active in the Progressive Party in New Hampshire?

Did he work with your present wife—Did Charles Beebe work with your present wife in 1947?

Did it [a meeting at the home of Abraham Walenko in Weare during 1948] have anything to do with the Progressive Party?

The Attorney General also turned to a subject which had not yet occurred at the time of the first hearing. On March 22, 1954, petitioner had delivered a lecture to a class of 100 students in the humanities course at the University of New Hampshire. This talk was given at the invitation of the faculty teaching that course. Petitioner had addressed the class upon such invitations in the two preceding years as well. He declined to answer the following questions:

What was the subject of your lecture?

Didn't you tell the class at the University of New Hampshire on Monday, March 22, 1954, that Socialism was inevitable in this country?

Did you advocate Marxism at that time?

Did you express the opinion, or did you make the statement at that time that Socialism was inevitable in America?

Did you in this last lecture on March 22 or in any of the former lectures espouse the theory of dialectical materialism?

Distinct from the categories of questions about the Progressive Party and the lectures was one question about petitioner's opinions. He was asked: "Do you believe in Communism?" He had already testified that he had never been a member of the Communist Party, but he refused to answer this or any other question concerning opinion or belief.

Petitioner adhered in this second proceeding to the same reasons for not answering he had given in his statement at the first hearing. He maintained that the questions were not pertinent to the matter under inquiry and that they infringed upon an area protected under the First Amendment.

Following the hearings, the Attorney General petitioned the Superior Court of Merrimack County, New Hampshire, setting forth the circumstances of petitioner's appearance before the Committee and his refusal to answer certain questions. The petition prayed that the court propound the questions to the witness. After hearing argument, the court ruled that the questions set out above were pertinent. Petitioner was called as a witness by the court and persisted in his refusal to answer for constitutional reasons. The court adjudged him in contempt and ordered him committed to the county jail until purged of the contempt. . . .

There is no doubt that legislative investigations, whether on a federal or state level, are capable of encroaching upon the constitutional liberties of individuals. It is particularly important that the exercise of the power of compulsory process be carefully circumscribed when the investigative process tends to impinge upon such highly sensitive areas as freedom of speech or press, freedom of political association, and freedom of communication of ideas, particularly in the academic community. Responsibility for the proper conduct of investigations rests, of course, upon the legislature itself. If that assembly chooses to authorize inquiries on its behalf by a legislatively created committee, that basic responsibility carries forward to include the duty of adequate supervision of the actions of the committee. This safeguard can be nullified when a committee is invested with a broad and ill-defined jurisdiction. The authorizing resolution thus becomes especially significant in that it reveals the amount of discretion that has been conferred upon the committee.

In this case, the investigation is governed by provisions in the New Hampshire Subversive Activities Act of 1951. The Attorney General was instructed by the legislature to look into violations of that Act. In addition, he was given the far more sweeping mandate to find out if there were subversive persons, as defined in that Act, present in New Hampshire. That statute, therefore, measures the breadth and scope of the investigation before us.

"Subversive persons" are defined in many gradations of conduct. Our interest is in the minimal requirements of that definition since they will outline its reach. According to the statute, a person is a "subversive person" if he, by any means, aids in the commission of any act intended to assist in the alteration of the constitutional form of government by force or violence. The possible remoteness from armed insurrection of conduct that could satisfy these criteria is obvious from the language. The statute goes well beyond those who are engaged in efforts designed to alter the form of government by force or violence. The statute declares, in effect, that the assistant of an assistant is caught up in the definition. This chain of conduct attains increased significance in light of the lack of a necessary element of guilty knowledge in either stage of assistants. The State Supreme Court has held that the definition encompasses persons engaged in the specified conduct ". . . whether or not done 'knowingly and willfully'. . . ." The potential sweep of this definition extends to conduct which is only remotely related to actual subversion and which is done completely free of any conscious intent to be a part of such activity.

The statute's definition of "subversive organizations" is also broad. An association is said to be any group of persons, whether temporarily or permanently associated together, for joint action or advancement of views on any subject. An organization is deemed subversive if it has a purpose to abet, advise or teach activities intended to assist in the alteration of the constitutional form of government by force or violence.

The situation before us is in many respects analogous to that in *Wieman* v. *Updegraff,* 344 US 183. The Court held there that a loyalty oath prescribed by the State of Oklahoma for all its officers and employees violated the requirements of the Due Process Clause because it entailed sanctions for membership in subversive organizations without scienter. A State cannot, in attempting to bar disloyal individuals from it employ, exclude persons solely on the basis of organizational membership, regardless of their knowledge concerning the organizations to which they belonged. The Court said:

There can be no dispute about the consequences visited upon a person excluded from public employment on disloyalty grounds. In the view of the community, the stain is a deep one; indeed, it has become a badge of infamy. Especially is this so in time of cold war and hot emotions when "each man begins to eye his neighbor as a possible enemy." Yet under the Oklahoma Act, the fact of association alone determines disloyalty and disqualification; it matters not whether association existed innocently or knowingly. To thus inhibit individual freedom of movement is to stifle the flow of democratic expression and controversy at one of its chief sources. . . .

The sanction emanating from legislative investigations is of a different kind than loss of employment. But the stain of the stamp of disloyalty is just as deep. The inhibiting effect in the flow of democratic expression and controversy upon those directly affected and those touched more subtly is equally grave. Yet here, as in *Wieman,* the program for the rooting out of subversion is drawn without regard to the presence or absence of guilty knowledge in those affected.

The nature of the investigation which the Attorney General was authorized to conduct is revealed by this case. He delved minutely into the past conduct of petitioner, thereby making his private life a matter of public record. The questioning indicates that the investigators had thoroughly prepared for the interview and were not acquiring new information as much as corroborating data already in their possession. On the great majority of questions, the witness was cooperative, even though he made clear his opinion that the interrogation was unjustified and unconstitutional. Two subjects arose upon which petitioner refused to answer: his lectures at the University of New Hampshire, and his knowledge of the Progressive Party and its adherents.

The state courts upheld the attempt to investigate the academic subject on the ground that it might indicate whether petitioner was a "subversive person." What he taught the class at a state university was found relevant to the character of the teacher. The State Supreme Court carefully excluded the possibility that the inquiry was sustainable because of the state interest in the state university. There was no warrant in the authorizing resolution for that. . . . The sole basis for the inquiry was to scrutinize the teacher as a person, and the inquiry must stand or fall on that basis.

The interrogation on the subject of the Progressive Party was deemed to come within the Attorney General's mandate because that party might have been shown to be a "subversive organization." The State Supreme Court held that the ". . . questions called for answers concerning the membership or participation of named persons in the Progressive Party which, if given, would aid the Attorney General in determining whether that party and its predecessor are or were subversive organizations." . . .

The New Hampshire court concluded that the ". . . right to lecture and the right to associate with others for a common purpose, be it political or otherwise, are individual liberties guaranteed to every citizen by the State and Federal Constitutions but are not absolute rights. . . . The inquiries authorized by the Legislature in connection with this investigation concerning the contents of the lecture and the membership, purposes and activities of the Progressive Party undoubtedly interfered with the defendant's free exercise of those liberties."

The State Supreme Court thus conceded without extended discussion that petitioner's right to lecture and his right to associate with others were constitutionally protected freedoms which had been abridged through this investigation. These conclusions could not be seriously debated. Merely to summon a witness and compel him, against his will, to disclose the nature of his past expressions and associations is a measure of governmental interference in these matters.

These are rights which are safeguarded by the Bill of Rights and the Fourteenth Amendment. We believe that there unquestionably was an invasion of petitioner's liberties in the areas of academic freedom and political expression—areas in which government should be extremely reticent to tread.

The essentiality of freedom in the community of American universities is almost self-evident. No one should underestimate the vital role in a democracy that is played by those who guide and train our youth. To impose any strait jacket upon the intellectual leaders in our colleges and universities would imperil the future of our nation. No field of education is so thoroughly comprehended by man that new discoveries cannot yet be made. Particularly is that true in the social sciences, where few, if any, principles are accepted as absolutes. Scholarship cannot flourish in an atmosphere of suspicion and distrust. Teachers and students must always remain free to inquire, to study and to evaluate, to gain new maturity and understanding; otherwise our civilization will stagnate and die.

Equally manifest as a fundamental principle of a democratic society is political freedom of the individual. Our form of government is built on the premise that every citizen shall have the right to engage in political expression and association. This right was enshrined in the First Amendment of the Bill of Rights. Exercise of these basic freedoms in America has traditionally been through the media of political associations. Any interference with the freedom of a party is simultaneously an interference with the freedom of its adherents. All political ideas cannot and should not be channeled into the programs of our two major parties. History has amply proved the virtue of political activity by minority, dissident groups, who innumerable times have been in the vanguard of democratic thought and whose programs were ultimately accepted. Mere unorthodoxy or dissent from the prevailing mores is not to be condemned. The absence of such voices would be a symptom of grave illness in our society.

Notwithstanding the undeniable importance of freedom in the areas, the Supreme Court of New Hampshire did not consider that the abridgement of petitioner's rights under the Constitution vitiated the investigation. In the view of that court, "the answer lies in a determination of whether the object of the legislative investigation under consideration is such as to justify the restriction thereby imposed upon the defendant's liberties." . . . It found such justification in the legislature's judgment, expressed by its authorizing resolution, that there exists a potential menace from those who would overthrow the government by force and violence. That court concluded that the need for the legislature to be informed on so elemental a subject as the self-preservation of government outweighed the deprivation of constitutional rights that occurred in the process.

We do not now conceive of any circumstance wherein a state interest would justify infringement of rights in these fields. But we do not need to reach such fundamental questions of state power to decide this case. The State Supreme Court itself recognized that there was a weakness in its conclusion that the menace of forcible overthrow of the government justified sacrificing constitutional rights. There was a missing link in the chain of reasoning. The syllogism was not complete. There was nothing to connect the questioning of petitioner with this fundamental interest of the State. Petitioner had been interrogated by a one-man legislative committee, not by the legislature itself. The relationship of the committee to the full assembly is vital, therefore, as revealing the relationship of the questioning to the state interest.

In light of this, the state court emphasized a factor in the authorizing resolution which confined the inquiries which the Attorney General might undertake to the object of the investigation. That limitation was thought to stem from the authorizing resolution's condition precedent to the institution of any inquiry. The New Hampshire legislature specified that the Attorney General should act only when he had information which ". . . in his judgment may be reasonable or reliable." The state court construed this to mean that the Attorney General must have something like probable cause for conducting a particular investigation. It is not likely that this device would prove an adequate safeguard against unwarranted inquiries. The legislature has specified that the determination of the necessity for inquiry shall be left in the judgment of the investigator. In this case, the record does not reveal what reasonable or reliable information led the Attorney General to question petitioner. The state court relied upon the Attorney General's description of prior information that had come into his possession.

The respective roles of the legislature and the investigator thus revealed are of considerable significance to the issue before us. It is eminently clear that the basic discretion of determining the direction of the legislative inquiry has been turned over to the investigative agency. The Attorney General has been given such a sweeping and uncertain mandate that it is his decision which picks out the subjects that will be pursued, what witnesses will be summoned and what questions will be asked. In this circumstance, it cannot be stated authoritatively that the legislature asked the Attorney General to gather the kind of facts comprised in the subjects upon which petitioner was interrogated.

Instead of making known the nature of the date it desired, the legislature has insulated itself from those witnesses whose rights may be vitally affected by the investigation. Incorporating by reference provisions from its subversive activities act, it has told the Attorney General, in effect to screen the citizenry of New Hampshire to bring to light anyone who fits into the expansive definitions.

Within the very broad area thus committed to the discretion of the Attorney General there may be many facts which the legislature might find useful. There would also be a great deal of data which that assembly would not want or need. In the classes of information that the legislature might deem it desirable to have, there will be some which it could not validly acquire because of the effect upon the constitutional rights of individual citizens. Separating the wheat from the chaff, from the standpoint of the legislature's object, is the legislature's responsibility because it alone can make that judgment. In this case, the New Hampshire legislature has delegated that task to the Attorney General.

As a result neither we nor the state courts have any assurance that the questions petitioner refused to answer fall into a category of matters upon which the legislature wanted to be informed when it initiated this inquiry. The judiciary are thus placed in an untenable position. Lacking even the elementary fact that the legislature wants certain questions answered and recognizing that petitioner's constitutional rights are in jeopardy, we are asked to approve or disapprove his incarceration for contempt.

In our view, the answer is clear. No one would deny that the infringement of constitutional rights of individuals would violate the guarantee of due process where no state interest underlies the state action. Thus, if the Attorney General's interrogation of petitioner were in fact wholly unrelated to the object of the legislature in authorizing the inquiry, the Due Process Clause would preclude the endangering of constitutional liberties. We believe that an equivalent situation is presented in this case. The lack of any indications that the legislature wanted the information the Attorney General attempted to elicit from petitioner must be treated as the absence of authority. It follows that the use of the contempt power, notwithstanding the interference with constitutional rights, was not in accordance with the due process requirements of the Fourteenth Amendment.

The conclusion that we have reached in this case is not grounded upon the doctrine of separation of powers. In the Federal Government, it is clear that the Constitution has conferred the powers of government upon three major branches: the Executive, the Legislative and the Judicial. No contention has been made by petitioner that the New

Hampshire legislature, by this investigation, arrogated to itself executive or judicial powers. We accept the finding of the State Supreme Court that the employment of the Attorney General as the investigating committee does not alter the legislative nature of the proceedings. Moreover, this Court has held that the concept of separation of powers embodied in the United States Constitution is not mandatory in state governments. . . . Our conclusion does rest upon a separation of the power of a state legislature to conduct investigations from the responsibility to direct the use of that power insofar as that separation causes a deprivation of the constitutional rights of individuals and a denial of due process of law.

The judgment of the Supreme Court of New Hampshire is reversed.

Mr. Justice Frankfurter, whom Mr. Justice Harlan joins, concurring in the result:

For me this is a very different case from *Watkins* v. *United States* . . . . This case comes to us solely through the limited power to review the action of the States conferred upon the Court by the Fourteenth Amendment. Petitioner claims that respect for liberties guaranteed by the Due Process Clause of that Amendment precludes the State of New Hampshire from compelling him to answer certain questions put to him by the investigating arm of its legislature. Ours is the narrowly circumscribed but exceedingly difficult task of making the final judicial accommodation between the competing weighty claims that underlie all such questions of due process.

In assessing the claim of the State of New Hampshire to the information denied it by petitioner, we cannot concern ourselves with the fact that New Hampshire chose to make its Attorney General in effect a standing Committee of its legislature for the purpose of investigating the extent of "subversive" activities within its bounds. The case must be judged as though the whole body of the legislature had demanded the information of petitioner. It would make the deepest inroads upon our federal system for this Court now to hold that it can determine the appropriate distribution of powers and their delegation within the forty-eight States. . . .

Whether the state legislature should operate largely by committees, as does the Congress, or whether committees should be the exception, as is true of the House of Commons, whether the legislature should have two chambers or only one, as in Nebraska, whether the State's chief executive should have the pardoning power, whether the State's judicial branch must provide trial by jury, are all matters beyond the reviewing powers of this Court. Similarly, whether the Attorney General of New Hampshire acted within the scope of the authority given him by the state legislature is a matter for the decision of the courts of that State, as it is for the federal courts to determine whether an agency to which Congress has delegated power has acted within the confines of its mandate. . . .

Petitioner answered most . . . questions, making it very plain that he had never been a Communist, never taught violent overthrow of the Government, never knowingly associated with Communists in the State, but was a socialist believer in peaceful change who had at one time belonged to certain organizations on the list of the United States Attorney General (which did not include the Progressive Party) or cited by the House Un-American Activities Committee. He declined to answer as irrelevant or violative of free speech guaranties certain questions about the Progressive Party and whether he knew particular persons. He stated repeatedly, however, that he had no knowledge of Communists or of Communist influence in the Progressive Party, and he testified that he had been a candidate for that Party, signing the required loyalty oath, and that he did not know whether an alleged Communist leader was active in the Progressive Party.

Despite the exhaustive scope of this inquiry, the Attorney General again subpoenaed petitioner to testify on June 3, 1954, and the interrogation was similarly sweeping. Petitioner again answered virtually all questions . . . He refused, however, to answer certain questions regarding (1) a lecture given by him at the University of New Hampshire, (2) activities of himself and others in the Progressive political organization, and (3) "opinions and beliefs," invoking the constitutional guarantees of free speech.

The Attorney General then petitioned the Superior Court to order petitioner to answer questions in these categories. The court ruled that petitioner had to answer those questions pertaining to the lectures and to the Progressive Party and its predecessor but not those otherwise pertaining to "opinions and beliefs." Upon petitioner's refusal to answer the questions sanctioned by the court, he was found in contempt of court and ordered committed to the county jail until purged of contempt.

The Supreme Court of New Hampshire affirmed the order of the Superior Court. It held that the questions at issue were relevant and that no constitutional provision permitted petitioner to frustrate the State's demands. . . .

The questions that petitioner refused to answer regarding the university lecture, the third given by him in three years at the invitation of the faculty for humanities, were:

> What was the subject of your lecture?
>
> Didn't you tell the class at the University of New Hampshire on Monday, March 22, 1954, that Socialism was inevitable in this country?
>
> Did you advocate Marxism at that time?
>
> Did you express the opinion, or did you make the statement at that time that Socialism was inevitable in America?
>
> Did you in this last lecture on March 22 or in any of the former lectures espouse the theory of dialectical materialism?
>
> I have in the file here a statement from a person who attended your class, and I will read it in part because I don't want you to think I am just fishing. "His talk this time was on the inevitability of the Socialist program. It was glossed-over interpretation of the materialist dialectic." Now, again I ask you the original question.

In response to the first question of this series, petitioner had said at the hearing:

> I would like to say one thing in this connection, Mr. Wyman. I stated under oath at my last appearance that, and I now repeat it, that I do not advocate or in any way further the aim of overthrowing constitutional government by force and violence. I did not so advocate in the lecture I gave at the University of New Hampshire. In fact I have never at any time so advocated in a lecture anywhere. Aside from that I have nothing I want to say about the lecture in question.

The New Hampshire Supreme Court, although recognizing that such inquiries . . . "undoubtedly interfered with the defendant's free exercise" of his constitutionally guaranteed right to lecture, justified the interference on the ground that it would occur "in a limited area in which the legislative committee may reasonably believe that the overthrow of existing government by force and violence is being or has been taught, advocated or planned, an area in which the interest of the State justifies this intrusion upon civil liberties." According to the court, the facts that made reasonable the committee's belief that petitioner had taught violent overthrow in his lecture were that he was a Socialist with a record of affiliation with groups cited by the Attorney General of the United States or the House Un-American Activities Committee and that he was co-editor of an article stating that, although the authors hated violence, it was less to be deplored when used by the Soviet Union than by capitalist countries.

When weighed against the grave harm resulting from governmental intrusion into the intellectual life of a university, such justification for compelling a witness to discuss the contents of his lecture appears grossly inadequate. Particularly is this so where the witness has sworn that neither in the lecture nor at any other time did he ever advocate overthrowing the Government by force and violence.

Progress in the natural sciences is not remotely confined to findings made in the laboratory. Insights into the mysteries of nature are born of hypothesis and speculation. The more so is this true in the pursuit of understanding in the groping endeavors of what are called the social sciences, the concern of which is man and society. The problems that are the respective preoccupation of anthropology, economics, law, psychology, sociology and related areas of scholarship are merely departmentalized dealing, by way of manageable division of analysis, with interpenetrating aspects of holistic perplexities. For society's good—if understanding be an essential need of society—inquiries into these problems, speculations about them, stimulation in others of reflection upon them, must be left as unfettered as possible. Political power must abstain from intrusion into this activity of freedom, pursued in the interest of wise government and the people's well-being, except for reasons that are exigent and obviously compelling.

These pages need not be burdened with proof, based on the testimony of a cloud of impressive witnesses, of the dependence of a free society on free universities. This means the exclusion of governmental intervention in the intellectual life of a university. It matters little whether such intervention occurs avowedly or through action that inevitably tends to check the ardor and fearlessness of scholars, qualities at once so fragile and so indispensable for fruitful academic labor. . . . Suffice it to quote the latest expression on this subject. It is also perhaps the most poignant because its plea on behalf of continuing the free spirit of the open universities of South Africa has gone unheeded.

In a university knowledge is its own end, not merely a means to an end. A university ceases to be true to its own nature if it becomes the tool of Church or State or any sectional interest. A university is characterized by the spirit of free inquiry, its ideal being the ideal of Socrates—"to follow the argument where it leads." This implies the right to examine, question, modify or reject traditional ideas and beliefs. Dogma and hypothesis are incompatible, and the concept of an immutable doctrine is repugnant to the spirit of a university. The concern of its scholars is not merely to add and revise facts in relation to an accepted framework, but to be ever examining and modifying the framework itself. . . .

Freedom to reason and freedom for disputation on the basis of observation and experiment are the necessary conditions for the advancement of scientific knowledge. A sense of freedom is also necessary for creative work in the arts which, equally with scientific research, is the concern of the university. . . .

It is the business of a university to provide that atmosphere which is most conducive to speculation, experiment and creation. It is an atmosphere in which there prevail "the four essential freedoms" of a university—to determine for itself on academic grounds who may teach, what may be taught, how it shall be taught, and who may be admitted to study. *The Open Universities in South Africa*, 10–12. (A statement of a conference of senior scholars from the University of Cape Town and the University of Witwatersrand, including A. v. d. S. Centlivres and Richard Feetham, as Chancellors of the respective universities.)

I do not suggest that what New Hampshire has here sanctioned bears any resemblance to the policy against which this South African remonstrance was directed. I do say that in these matters of the spirit inroads on legitimacy must be resisted at their incipiency. This kind of evil grows by what it is allowed to feed on. The admonition of this Court in another context is applicable here. "It may be that it is the obnoxious thing in its mildest and least repulsive form; but illegitimate and unconstitutional practices get their first footing in that way, namely, by silent approaches and slight deviations from legal modes of procedure." *Boyd* v. *United States*, 116 US 616.

Petitioner stated, in response to questions at the hearing, that he did not know of any Communist interest in connection with, influence over, activity in, or manipulation of the Progressive Party. He refused to answer, despite court order, the following questions on the ground that, by inquiring into the activities of a lawful political organization, they infringed upon the inviolability of the right to privacy in his political thoughts, actions and associations:

> Was she, Nancy Sweezy, your wife, active in the formation of the Progressive Citizens of America?
>
> Was Nancy Sweezy then working with individuals who were then members of the Communist Party?
>
> Was Charles Beebe active in forming the Progressive Citizens of America?
>
> Did he work with your present wife—Did Charles Beebe work with your present wife in 1947?
>
> Did it [a meeting at the home of one Abraham Walenko] have anything to do with the Progressive Party?

The Supreme Court of New Hampshire justified this intrusion upon his freedom on the same basis that it upheld questioning about the university lecture, namely, that the restriction was limited to situations where the Committee had reason to believe that violent overthrow of the Government was being advocated or planned. . . . But the inviolability of privacy belonging to a citizen's political loyalties has so overwhelming an importance to the well-being of our kind of society that it cannot be constitutionally encroached upon on the basis of so meagre a countervailing interest of the State as may be argumentatively found in the remote, shadowy threat to the security of New Hampshire allegedly presented in the origins and contributing elements of the Progressive Party and in petitioner's relations to these.

In the political realm, as in the academic, thought and action are presumptively immune from inquisition by political authority. It cannot require argument that inquiry would be barred to ascertain whether a citizen had voted for one or the other of the two major parties either in a state or national election. Until recently, no difference would have been entertained in regard to inquiries about a voter's affiliations with one of the various so-called third parties that have had their day, or longer, in our political history. This is so, even though adequate protection of secrecy by way of the Australian ballot did not come into use till 1888. The implications of the United States Constitution for national elections and "the concept of ordered liberty" implicit in the Due Process Clause of the Fourteenth Amendment as against the States, . . . were not frozen as of 1789 or 1868, respectively. While the language of the Constitution does not change, the changing circumstances of a progressive society for which it was designed yield new and fuller import to its meaning. . . . Whatever, on the basis of massive proof and in the light of history, of which this Court may well take judicial notice, be the justification for not regarding the Communist Party as a conventional political party, no such justification has been afforded in regard to the Progressive Party. A foundation in fact and reason would have to be established far weightier than the intimations that appear in the record to warrant such a view of the Progressive Party. This precludes the questioning that petitioner resisted in regard to that Party.

To be sure, this is a conclusion based on a judicial judgment in balancing two contending principles—the right of a citizen to political privacy, as protected by the Fourteenth Amendment, and the right of the State to self-protection. And striking the balance implies the exercise of judgment. This is the inescapable judicial task in giving substantive content, legally enforced, to the Due Process Clause, and it is a task ultimately committed to this Court. It must not be an exercise of whim or will. It must be an over-riding judgment founded on something much deeper and more justifiable than personal preference. As far as it lies within human limitations, it must be an impersonal judgment. It must rest on fundamental presuppositions rooted in history to which widespread acceptance may fairly be attributed. Such a judgment must be arrived at in a spirit of humility when it counters the judgment of the State's highest court. But, in the end, judgment cannot be escaped—the judgment of this Court. . . .

And so I am compelled to conclude that the judgment of the New Hampshire court must be reversed.

UPHAUS v. WYMAN

360 US 72 (1959)

[This case, decided two years after *Sweezy* v. *New Hampshire*, 354 US 234 (1957), is to be read along with that case. The Attorney General of New Hampshire, constituted by statute a one-man investigating committee, sought to determine whether there were subversive persons or organizations in that state. Uphaus, executive director of World Fellowship, was asked to produce records of a summer camp conducted by the organization, including the lists of guests. Uphaus refused and thereupon was held in contempt. The Supreme Court by a 5-to-4 vote upheld the contempt conviction. Justices Brennan, Black, and Douglas, and Chief Justice Warren dissented.]

Mr. Justice Clark delivered the opinion of the Court:

This case is here again on appeal from a judgment of civil contempt entered against appellant by the Merrimack County Court and affirmed by the Supreme Court of New Hampshire. It arises out of appellant's refusal to produce certain documents before a New Hampshire legislative investigating committee which was authorized and directed to determine, *inter alia*, whether there were subversive persons or organizations present in the State of New Hampshire. Upon the first appeal from the New Hampshire court, we vacated the judgment, and remanded the case to it for consideration in the light of *Sweezy* v. *State of New Hampshire*, 1957, 354 US 234. That court reaffirmed its former decision, deeming *Sweezy* not to control the issues in the instant case. For reasons which will appear, we agree with the Supreme Court of New Hampshire.

As in *Sweezy*, the Attorney General of New Hampshire, who had been constituted a one-man legislative investigating committee by Joint Resolution of the Legislature, was conducting a probe of subversive activities in the State. In the course of his investigation the Attorney General called appellant, Executive Director of World Fellowship, Inc., a voluntary corporation organized under the laws of New Hampshire and maintaining a summer camp in the State. Appellant testified concerning his own activities, but refused to comply with two subpoenas *duces tecum* which called for the production of certain corporate records for the years 1954 and 1955. The information sought consisted of: (1) a list of the names of all the camp's nonprofessional employees for those two summer seasons; (2) the correspondence which appellant had carried on with and concerning those persons who came to the camp as speakers; and (3) the names of all persons who attended the camp during the same periods of time. Met with appellant's refusal, the Attorney General, in accordance with state procedure, petitioned the Merrimack County Court to call appellant before it and require compliance with the subpoenas.

In court, appellant again refused to produce the information. He claimed that by the Smith Act, as construed by this Court in *Com. of Pennsylvania* v. *Nelson*, 1956, 350 US 497, Congress had so completely occupied the field of subversive activities that the States were without power to investigate in that area. Additionally, he contended that the Due Process Clause precluded enforcement of the subpoenas, first, because the resolution under which the Attorney General was authorized to operate was vague and, second, because the documents sought were not relevant to the inquiry. Finally, appellant argued that enforcement would violate his rights of free speech and association.

The Merrimack County Court sustained appellant's objection to the production of the names of the nonprofessional employees. The Attorney General took no appeal from that ruling, and it is not before us. Appellant's objections to the production of the names of the camp's guests were overruled, and he was ordered to produce them. Upon his refusal, he was adjudged in contempt of court and ordered committed to jail until he should have complied with the court order. On the demand for the correspondence and the objection thereto, the trial court made no ruling but transferred the question to the Supreme Court of New Hampshire. That court affirmed the trial court's action in regard to the guest list. Concerning the requested production of the correspondence, the Supreme Court entered no order, but directed that on remand the trial court "may exercise its discretion with respect to the entry of an order to enforce the command of the subpoena for the production of correspondence." No remand having yet been effected, the trial court has not acted upon this phase of the case, and there is no final judgment requiring the appellant to produce the letters. We therefore do not treat with that question. . . . We now pass to a consideration of the sole question before us, namely, the validity of the order of contempt for refusal to produce the list of guests at World Fellowship, Inc., during the summer seasons of 1954 and 1955. In addition to the arguments appellant made to the trial court, he urges here that the "indefinite sentence" imposed upon him constitutes such cruel and unusual punishment as to be a denial of due process.

Appellant vigorously contends that the New Hampshire Subversive Activities Act of 1951 and the resolution creating the committee have been superseded by the Smith Act, as amended. In support of this position appellant cites *Com. of Pennsylvania v. Nelson, supra.* The argument is that *Nelson,* which involved a prosecution under a state sedition law, held that "Congress has intended to occupy the field of sedition." This rule of decision, it is contended, should embrace legislative investigations made pursuant to an effort by the Legislature to inform itself of the presence of subversives within the State and possibly to enact laws in the subversive field. The appellant's argument sweeps too broad. In *Nelson* itself we said that the "precise holding of the court . . . is that the Smith Act . . . which prohibits the knowing advocacy of the overthrow of the Government of the United States by force and violence, supersedes the enforceability of the Pennsylvania Sedition Act which proscribes the *same conduct.*" (Italics supplied.) The basis of *Nelson* thus rejects the notion that it stripped the States of the right to protect themselves. All the opinion proscribed was a race between federal and state prosecutors to the courthouse door. The opinion made clear that a State could proceed with prosecutions for sedition against the State itself; that it can legitimately investigate in this area follows *a fortiori.* In *Sweezy v. State of New Hampshire, supra,* where the same contention was made as to the identical state Act, it was denied *sub silentio.* Nor did our opinion in *Nelson* hold that the Smith Act had proscribed state activity in protection of itself either from actual or threatened "sabotage or attempted violence of all kinds." In footnote 8 of the opinion it is pointed out that the State had full power to deal with internal civil disturbances. Thus registration statutes, *quo warranto* proceedings as to subversive corporations, the subversive instigation of riots and a host of other subjects directly affecting state security furnish grist for the State's legislative mill. Moreover, the right of the State to require the production of corporate papers of a state-chartered corporation in an inquiry to determine whether corporate activity is violative of state policy is, of course, not touched upon in *Nelson* and today stands unimpaired, either by the Smith Act or the *Nelson* opinion.

Appellant's other objections can be capsuled into the single question of whether New Hampshire, under the facts here, is precluded from compelling the production of the documents by the Due Process Clause of the Fourteenth Amendment. Let us first clear away some of the underbrush necessarily surrounding the case because of its setting.

First, the academic and political freedoms discussed in *Sweezy* v. *State of New Hampshire, supra,* are not present here in the same degree, since World Fellowship in neither a university nor a political party. Next, since questions concerning the authority of the committee to act as it did are questions of state law, . . . we accept as controlling the New Hampshire Supreme Court's conclusion that "[t]he legislative history makes it clear beyond a reasonable doubt that it [the Legislature] did and does desire an answer to these questions." Finally, we assume, without deciding, that Uphaus had sufficient standing to assert any rights of the guests whose identity the committee seeks to determine. . . . The interest of the guests at World Fellowship in their associational privacy having been asserted, we have for decision the federal question of whether the public interests overbalance these conflicting private ones. Whether there was "justification" for the production order turns on the "substantiality" of New Hampshire's interests in obtaining the identity of the guests when weighed against the individual interests which the appellant asserts.

What was the interest of the State? The Attorney General was commissioned to determine if there were any subversive persons within New Hampshire. The obvious starting point of such an inquiry was to learn what persons were within the State. It is therefore clear that the requests relate directly to the Legislature's area of interest, i.e., the presence of subversives in the State, as announced in its resolution. Nor was the demand of the subpoena burdensome; as to time, only a few months of each of the two years were involved; as to place, only the camp conducted by the Corporation; nor as to the lists of names, which included about 300 each year.

Moreover, the Attorney General had valid reason to believe that the speakers and guests at World Fellowship might be subversive persons within the meaning of the New Hampshire Act. The Supreme Court of New Hampshire found Uphaus' contrary position "unrelated to reality." Although the evidence as to the nexus between World Fellowship and subversive activities may not be conclusive, we believe it sufficiently relevant to support the Attorney General's action.

The New Hampshire definition of subversive persons was born of the legislative determination that the Communist movement posed a serious threat to the security of the State. The record reveals that appellant had participated in "Communist front" activities and that "[n]ot less than nineteen speakers invited by Uphaus to talk at World Fellowship had either been members of the Communist Party or had connections or affiliations with it or with one or more of the organizations cited as subversive or Communist controlled in the United States Attorney General's list." While the Attorney General's list is designed for the limited purpose of determining fitness for federal employment, *Wieman* v. *Updegraff*, 1952, 344 US, and guilt by association remains a thoroughly discredited doctrine, it is with a legislative investigation—not a criminal prosecution— that we deal here. Certainly the investigatory power of the State need not be constricted until sufficient evidence of subversion is gathered to justify the institution of criminal proceedings.

The nexus between World Fellowship and subversive activities disclosed by the record furnished adequate justification for the investigation we here review. The Attorney General sought to learn if subversive persons were in the State because of the legislative determination that such persons, statutorily defined with a view toward the Communist Party, posed a serious threat to the security of the State. The investigation was, therefore, undertaken in the interest of self-preservation, "the ultimate value of any society," *Dennis* v. *United States*, 1951, 341 US 494. This governmental interest out- weighs individual rights in an associational privacy which, however real in other circumstances, . . . were here tenuous at best. The camp was operating as a public one, furnishing both board and lodging to persons applying therefor. As to them, New Hampshire law requires that World Fellowship, Inc., maintain a register, open to inspection of sheriffs and police officers. It is contended that the list might be "circulated throughout the States and the Attorney Generals through- out the States have cross-indexed files, so that any guest whose name is mentioned in that kind of proceeding immediately becomes suspect, even in his own place of residence." The record before us, however, only reveals a report to the Legislature of New Hampshire made by the Attorney General in accordance with the requirements of the resolution. We 'recognize, of course, that compliance with the sub- poena will result in exposing the fact that the persons therein named were guests at World Fellowship. But so long as a committee must report to its legislative parent, exposure—in the sense of disclosure— is an inescapable incident of an investigation into the presence of subversive persons within a State. And the governmental interest in self-preservation is sufficiently compelling to subordinate the interest in associational privacy of persons who, at least to the extent of the guest registration statute, made public at the inception the association they now wish to keep private. In the light of such a record we conclude that the State's interest has not been "pressed, in this instance, to a point where it has come into fatal collision with the overriding" constitutionally protected rights of appellant and those he may represent. . . .

We now reach the question of the validity of the sentence. The judgment of contempt orders the appellant confined until he produces the documents called for in the subpoenas. He himself admitted to the court that although they were at hand, not only had he failed to bring them with him to court, but that, further, he had no intention of producing them. In view of appellant's unjustified refusal we think the order a proper one. As was said in *Green* v. *United States*, 1958, 356 US 165 (dissenting opinion):

Before going any further, perhaps it should be emphasized that we are not at all concerned with the power of courts to impose conditional imprisonment for the purpose of compelling a person to obey a valid order. Such coercion, where the defendant carries the keys to freedom in his willingness to comply with the court's directive, is essentially a civil remedy designed for the benefit of other parties and has quite properly been exercised for centuries to secure compliance with judicial decrees.

We have concluded that the committee's demand for the documents was a legitimate one; it follows that the judgment of contempt for refusal to produce them is valid. We do not impugn appellant's good faith in the assertion of what he believed to be his rights. But three courts have disagreed with him in interpreting those rights. If appellant chooses to abide by the result of the adjudication and obey the order of New Hampshire's courts, he need not face jail. If, however, he continues to disobey, we find on this record no constitutional objection to the exercise of the traditional remedy of contempt to secure compliance.

Affirmed.

Mr. Justice Brennan, with whom the Chief Justice, Mr. Justice Black and Mr. Justice Douglas join, dissenting:

The Court holds today that the constitutionally protected rights of speech and assembly of appellant and those whom he may represent are to be subordinated to New Hampshire's legislative investigation because, as applied in the demands made on him, the investigation is rationally connected with a discernible legislative purpose. With due respect for my Brothers' views, I do not agree that a showing of any requisite legislative purpose or other state interest that constitutionally can subordinate appellant's rights is to be found in his record. Exposure purely for the sake of exposure is not such a valid subordinating purpose. . . . This record, I think, not only fails to reveal any interest of the State sufficient to subordinate appellant's constitutionally protected rights, but affirmatively shows that the investigatory objective was the impermissible one of exposure for exposure's sake. I therefore dissent from the judgment of the Court.

I fully appreciate the delicacy of the judicial task of questioning the workings of a legislative investigation. A proper regard for the primacy of the legislative function in its own field, and for the broad scope of the investigatory power to achieve legislative ends, necessarily should constrain the judiciary to indulge every reasonable intendment in favor of the validity of legislative inquiry. However, our frame of government also imposes another inescapable duty upon the judiciary, that of protecting the constitutional rights of freedom of speech and assembly from improper invasion, whether by the national or the state legislatures. . . . Where that invasion is as clear as I think this record discloses, the appellant is entitled to our judgment of reversal.

Judicial consideration of the collision of the investigatory function with constitutionally protected rights of speech and assembly is a recent development in our constitutional law. The Court has often examined the validity under the Federal Constitution of federal and state statutes and executive action imposing criminal and other traditional sanctions on conduct alleged to be protected by the guarantees of freedom of speech and of assembly. The role of the state-imposed sanctions of imprisonment, fines and prohibitory injunctions directed against association or speech and their limitations under the First and Fourteenth Amendments has been canvassed quite fully, beginning as early as *Gitlow* v. *People of State of New York*, 268 US 652; and *Near* v. *State of Minnesota*, 283 US 697. And other state action, such as deprivation of public employment and the denial of admission to a profession, has also been recognized as being subject to the restraints of the Constitution. . . .

But only recently has the Court been required to begin a full exploration of the impact of the governmental investigatory function on these freedoms. Here is introduced the weighty consideration that the power of investigation, whether exercised in aid of the governmental legislative power, . . . or in aid of the governmental power to adjudicate disputes, . . . is vital to the functioning of free governments and is therefore necessarily broad. But where the exercise of the investigatory power collides with constitutionally guaranteed freedoms, that power too has inevitable limitations, and the delicate and always difficult accommodation of the two with minimum sacrifice of either is the hard task of the judiciary and ultimately of this Court.

It was logical that the adverse effects of unwanted publicity—of exposure —as concomitants of the exercise of the investigatory power, should come to be recognized, in certain circumstances, as invading protected freedoms and offending constitutional inhibitions upon governmental actions. For in an era of mass communications and mass opinion, and of international tensions and domestic anxiety, exposure and group identification by the state of those holding unpopular and dissident views are fraught with such serious consequences for the individual as inevitably to inhibit seriously the expression of views which the Constitution intended to make free. . . .

Of course, the considerations entering into the weighing of the interests concerned is different where the problem is one of state exposure in the area of assembly and expression from where the problem is that of evaluating a state criminal or regulatory statute in these areas. Government must have freedom to make an appropriate investigation where there appears a rational connection with the lawmaking process, the processes of adjudication, or other essential governmental functions. In the investigatory stage of the legislative process, for example, the specific interest of the state and the final legislative means to be chosen to implement it are almost by definition not precisely defined at the start of the inquiry, and due allowance must accordingly be made. Also, when exposure is evaluated judicially as a governmental sanction, there should be taken into account the differences between it and the more traditional state-inflicted pains and penalties. True it is, therefore, that any line other than a universal subordination of free expression and association to the asserted interests of the state in investigation and exposure will be difficult of definition; but this Court has rightly turned its back on the alternative of universal subordination of protected interests, and we must define rights in this area the best we can. The problem is one in its nature calling for traditional case-by-case development of principles in the various permutations of circumstances where the conflict may appear. But guide lines must be marked out by the courts. "This is the inescapable judicial task in giving substantive content, legally enforced, to the Due Process Clause, and it is a task ultimately committed to this Court." *Sweezy v. State of New Hampshire* (concurring opinion). On the facts of this case I think that New Hampshire's investigation, as applied to the appellant, was demonstrably and clearly outside the wide limits of the power which must be conceded to the State even though it be attended by some exposure. In demonstration of this I turn to the detailed examination of the facts which this case requires.

The appellant, Uphaus, is Executive Director of a group called World Fellowship which runs a discussion program at a summer camp in New Hampshire, at which the public is invited to stay. Various speakers come to the camp primarily for discussion of political, economic and social matters. The appellee reports that Uphaus and some of the speakers have been said by third persons to have a history of association with "Communist front" movements, to have followed the "Communist line," signed amnesty petitions and *amicus curiae* briefs, and carried on similar activities of a sort which have recently been viewed hostilely and suspiciously by many Americans. A strain of pacifism runs through the appellant's thinking, and the appellee apparently would seek to determine whether there should be drawn therefrom an inference of harm for our institutions; he conjectures, officially, whether "the advocacy of this so-called peace crusade is for the purpose of achieving a quicker and a cheaper occupation by the Soviet Union and Communism." There is no evidence that any activity of a sort that violates the law of New

Hampshire or could in fact be constitutionally punished went on at the camp. What is clear was that there was some sort of assemblage at the camp that was oriented toward the discussion of political and other public matters. The activities going on were those of private citizens. The views expounded obviously were minority views. But the assemblage was, on its face, for purposes to which the First and Fourteenth Amendments give constitutional protection against incursion by the powers of government. . . .

The investigation with which this case is concerned was undertaken under authority of a 1953 Resolution of the New Hampshire General Court and extended by an enactment in 1955. The Resolution directed the Attorney General of the State (appellee here) to make a "full and complete investigation" of "violations of the subversive activities act of 1951" and to determine whether "subversive persons as defined in said act are presently located within the state." Under New Hampshire law, this constituted the Attorney General (who is ordinarily the chief law-enforcement official of the State) a one-man legislative committee. The sanctions of prosecution of individuals and dissolution of organizations for violation of the 1951 law seem to have been discarded, with the passage of the Resolution, in favor of the sanction of exposure. A provision of the 1951 Act providing for confidential treatment of material reflecting on individuals' loyalty was made inapplicable to the investigation the Attorney General was directed to conduct, and the Attorney General was authorized in sweeping terms to give publicity to the details of his investigation. A report to the Legislature of the fruits of the investigation was to be made on the first day of the 1955 legislative session; the 1955 extension called* for a similar report to the 1957 session. Efforts to obtain from the appellant the disclosures relative to World Fellowship in controversy here began during the period covered by the 1953 Resolution, but his final refusal and the proceeding for contempt under review here occurred during the extension.

The fruits of the first two years of the investigation were delivered to the Legislature in a comprehensive volume on January 5, 1955. The Attorney General urges this report on our consideration as extremely relevant to a consideration of the investigation as it relates to appellant. I think that this is quite the case; the report is an official indication of the nature of the investigation and is, in fact, the stated objective of the duty assigned by the Resolution to the Attorney General. It was with this report before it that the Legislature renewed the investigation, and it must be taken as characterizing the nature of the investigation before us. The report proper is divided into numerous sections. First is a series of general and introductory essays by various authors entitled "Pertinent Aspects of World Communism Today." Essays discuss "The Nature of the Russian Threat"; "The Role of the Communist Front Organizations"; "Some Important Aspects of Marxism and Marxism-Leninism"; "The Test of a Front Organization"; and "Communism vs. Religion." General descriptive matter on the Communist Party in New Hampshire follows. It hardly needs to be said that this introductory material would focus attention on the whole report in terms of "Communism" regardless of what was said about the individuals later named. Next comes a general section titled "Communist Influence in a Field of Education" which is replete with names and biographical material of individuals; a similar section on "Communist Influence in the Field of Labor"; and one more generically captioned "Organizations," in which various details as to the appellant, his organization, and others associated in it are presented. Last comes a section entitled "Individuals" in which biographical sketches of 23 persons are presented.

The introductory matter in the volume, to put the matter mildly, showed consciousness of the practical effect of the change of policy from judicial prosecution to exposure by the Attorney General of persons reported to be connected with groups charged to be "subversive" or "substantially Communist-influenced." Virtually the entire "Letter of Transmittal" of the Attorney General addressed itself to discussing the policy used in the report in disclosing the names of individuals. The Attorney General drew a significant distinction as to the names he would disclose: "Persons with past membership of affiliation with the Communist Party or substantially Communist-influenced groups have not been disclosed in this report where those persons have provided assistance to the investigation. It is felt that no good reasons exist requiring a listing of names of cooperative witnesses in these categories." A "Foreword" declared that "[t]his report deals with a controversial subject," and, concentrating on the fact that the report contained an extensive list of persons, their addresses, and miscellaneous activities and associations attributed to them, made several disclaimers. The report was not to be considered an indictment of any individual, the Attorney General suitably pointing out that a grand jury was the only authority in New Hampshire having the formal power of indictment. Nor was it "the result of an inquisition. No witness in this investigation has ever, at any time, been treated other than courteously." Finally, the Attorney General stressed that "[t]he reporting of facts herein does NOT (nor should it be taken to by any reader) constitute a charge against any witness." He observed that "facts are facts. . . . Conclusions of opprobrium relative to any individual, while within the privilege of personal opinion, are neither recommended nor intended to be encouraged by any phraseology of this report." In fact, the listing of names might well contain the names of many innocent people, implied the Attorney General. This was permissible, he believed, because, as interpreted in the courts of New Hampshire, "the scope of relevant questioning in the investigation goes far beyond the requirements of individual felonious intention. In fact, the General Court has directed that inquiry be made to determine the extent of innocent or ignorant membership, affiliation or support of subversive organizations. . . ."

The report certainly is one that would be suggested by the quoted parts of the foreword. No opinion was, as a matter of course, expressed by the Attorney General as to whether any person named therein was in fact a "subversive person" within the meaning of the statute. The report did not disclose whether any indictments under the 1951 Act would be sought against any person. Its sole recommendations for legislation were for a broad evidentiary statute to be applied in trials of persons under the State Act as "subversive," which cannot really be said to have been the fruit of the investigation, being copied from a then recent Act of Congress, and which made apparently no change in the 1951 law's standard of guilt, and for an immunity measure calculated to facilitate future investigations. The report, once the introductory material on Communism is done with, contains primarily an assorted list of names with descriptions of what had been said about the named persons. In most cases, the caveat of the Attorney General that the information should not be understood as indicating a violation of the New Hampshire Subversive Activities Act was, to say the least, well-taken, in the light of the conduct ascribed to them. Many of the biographical summaries would strike a discerning analyst as very mild stuff indeed. In many cases, a positive diligence was demonstrated in efforts to add the names of individuals to a list and then render a Scotch verdict of "not proven" in regard to them. The most vivid example of this is the material relating to the appellant's group, World Fellowship. After some introductory pages, there comes extensive biographical material relating to the reported memberships, associations, advocacies, and signings of open letters on the part of certain speakers at the World Fellowship camp. A very few had admitted membership in the Communist Party, or had been "identified" as being members by third persons generally not named. Others were said to be or to have been members of "Communist influenced," "front," or "officially cited" groups. Some were said to have signed open letters and petitions against deportations, to have criticized the Federal Bureau of Investigation, to have given free medical treatment to Communist Party officials, and the like. Finally the report addresses itself to the remainder of the speakers: "Information easily available to this office does *not* indicate records of affiliation with or support of Communist causes on the part of these people. However, due to the burden of work imposed on the staff of the House Committee on Un-American Activities by thousands of such requests from all over the country, it has not been possible to check each of these persons thoroughly. Inasmuch as no committee or public agency can hope to have all the information in its files concerning all subversive activity all over this country, it is not possible for this office to guarantee that the following individuals do not have such activities in their backgrounds. Therefore, it is necessary to report their identities to the General Court, with the explanation that based upon what information we have been able to assemble, the following individuals would appear at this time to be the usual contingent of 'dupes' and unsuspecting persons that surround almost every venture that is instigated or propelled by the 'perennials' and articulate apologists for Communists and Soviet chicanery, but of this fact we are not certain. This list does not include the many persons who were merely guests. . . ." The names of 36 persons with their addresses then followed.

The emphasis of the entire report is on individual guilt, individual near-guilt, and individual questionable behavior. Its flavor and tone, regardless of its introductory disclaimers, cannot help but stimulate readers to attach a "badge of infamy," . . . to the persons named in it. The authorizing Resolution requested that the Attorney General address himself to ascertaining whether there were "subversive persons" in New Hampshire, and the report indicates that this was interpreted as the making of lists of persons who were either classifiable in this amorphous category, or almost so, and the presenting of the result, as a public, official document, to the Legislature, and to the public generally. The main thrust of the Resolution itself was in terms of individual behavior—violation of the 1951 Act and the presence, in the State, of "subversive persons," were the objects of investigation. The collection of such data, and of data having some peripheral reference to it, with explicit detail as to names and places, was what the Attorney General set himself to doing in response to it. As the report itself stated, "A very considerable amount of questioning is absolutely essential to separate the wheat from the chaff in applying the legislative formula to individual conduct which involves that part of the spectrum very close to the line of subversive conduct. Only through such questioning is it possible to be able to report to the Legislature whether the activity of a given individual has been subversive or not subversive; whether or not intentionally so or knowingly so on his part." One must feel, on reading the report, that the first sentence—"A very considerable amount of questioning is absolutely essential . . . in applying the legislative formula to individual conduct which involves that part of the spectrum very close to the line of subversive conduct"—is a serious overstatement, because in the usual citation of a person in the report no expression of his innocence or guilt, or his precise coloration in the Attorney General's spectrum was given. But still the report was made in terms of the activity of named individuals. Of course, if the Attorney General had information relating to guilt under the statute, he was empowered to seek indictment and conviction of the offenders in criminal proceedings, in which of course the normal rights afforded criminal defendants and the normal limitations on state prosecution for conduct related to political association and expression, under the Constitution, would apply. The citation of names in the book does not appear to have any relation to the possibility of an orthodox or traditional criminal prosecution, and the Attorney General seems to acknowledge this. The investigation in question here was not one ancillary to a prosecution—to grand jury or trial procedure. If it had been, if a definite prosecution were undertaken, we would have that narrowed context in which to relate the State's demand for exposure. . . . This process of relation is part and parcel of examining the "substantiality" of the State's interest in the concrete context in which it is alleged. But here we are without the aid of such a precise issue and our task requires that we look further to ascertain whether this legislative investigation, as applied in the demands made upon the appellant, is connected rationally with a discernible general legislative end to which the rights of the appellant and those whom he may represent can constitutionally be subordinated.

The Legislature, upon receiving the report, extended the investigation for a further two years. It was during this period that the refusals of the appellant to furnish information with which we are now concerned took place. The Attorney General had already published the names of speakers at the World Fellowship camp. Now he wanted the correspondence between Uphaus and the speakers. The Attorney General admitted that it was unlikely that the correspondence between Uphaus and the speakers was going to contain a damning admission of a purpose to advocate the overthrow of the government (presumably of New Hampshire) by force and violence. He said that it might indicate a sinister purpose behind the advocacy of pacifism—"the purpose of achieving a quicker and a cheaper occupation by the Soviet Union and Communism." The guest list, the nonavailability of which to the Attorney General was commented on in the passage from the 1955 report quoted above, was also desired. Appellant's counsel, at the hearing in court giving rise to the contempt finding under review, protested that appellant did not want to allow the Attorney General to have the names to expose them. The Attorney General also wished the names of the nonprofessional help at the camp—the cooks and dishwashers and the like. It was objected that the cooks and dishwashers were hired from the local labor pool and that if such employment were attended by a trip to the Attorney General's office and the possibility of public exposure, help might become hard to find at the camp. This last objection was sustained in the trial court, but the other two inquiries were allowed and appellant's failure to respond to the one relating to the guest list was found contemptuous.

First. The Court seems to experience difficulty in discerning that appellant has any standing to plead the rights of free speech and association he does because the material he seeks to withhold may technically belong to World Fellowship, Inc., a corporation, and may relate to the protected activities of other persons, rather than those of himself. In *N. A. A. C. P.* v. *State of Alabama,* 357 US 449, a corporation was permitted to represent its membership in pleading their rights to freedom of association for public purposes. Here appellant, as a corporate officer if one will, seeks to protect a list of those who have assembled together for public discussion on the corporation's premises. Of course this is not technically a membership list, but to distinguish *N. A. A. C. P.* v. *State of Alabama* on this ground is to miss its point. The point is that if the members of the assemblage could only plead their assembly rights themselves, the very interest being safeguarded by the Constitution here could never be protected meaningfully, since to require that the guests claim this right themselves would "result in nullification of the right at the very moment of its assertion." . . . I do not think it likely that anyone would deny the right of a bookseller (including a corporate bookseller) to decline to produce the names of those who had purchased his books. *Cf. United States* v. *Rumely,* 345 US 41, 57 (concurring opinion). . . .

Second. In examining the right of the State to obtain this information from the appellant by compulsory process, we must recollect what we so recently said in *N. A. A. C. P.* v. *State of Alabama:*

> Effective advocacy of both public and private points of view, particularly controversial ones, is undeniably enhanced by group association, as this Court has more than once recognized by remarking upon the close nexus between the freedoms of speech and assembly. . . .
> It is beyond debate that freedom to engage in association for the advancement of beliefs and ideas is an inseparable aspect of the "liberty"

assured by the Due Process Clause of the Fourteenth Amendment which embraces freedom of speech. . . . Of course, it is immaterial whether the beliefs sought to be advanced by association pertain to political, economic, religious or cultural matters, and state action which may have the effect of curtailing the freedom to associate is subject to the closest scrutiny. . . .

And in examining the State's interest in carrying out a legislative investigation, as was said in a similar context in *United States* v. *Rumely, supra,* we must strive not to be "that 'blind' Court, against which Mr. Chief Justice Taft admonished in a famous passage . . . that does not see what '[a]ll others can see and understand.'" The problem of protecting the citizen's constitutional rights from legislative investigation and exposure is a practical one, and we must take a practical, realistic approach to it.

Most legislative investigations unavoidably involve exposure of some sort or another. But it is quite clear that exposure was the very core, and deliberately and purposefully so, of the legislative investigation we are concerned with here. The Legislature had passed a broad and comprehensive statute, which included criminal sanctions. That statute was, to say the least, readily susceptible of many applications in which it might enter a constitutional danger zone. . . . And it could not be applied at all insofar as it amounted to a sanction for behavior directed against the United States. *Com. of Pennsylvania* v. *Nelson,* 350 US 497. Therefore, indictment would be fraught with constitutional and evidentiary problems of an obvious and hardly subtle nature. This may suggest the reason why the pattern of application of the Subversive Activities statute in New Hampshire was not through the processes of indictment. The Resolution was cast in terms of an investigation of conduct restricted by this existing statute. The Resolution and the Attorney General's implementation of it reveal the making of a choice. The choice was to reach the end of exposure through the process of investigation, backed with the contempt power and the making of reports to the Legislature, of persons and groups thought to be somehow related to offenses under the statute or, further, to an uncertain penumbra of conduct about the proscribed area of the statute. And, as was said of the same investigation in *Sweezy* v. *State of New Hampshire,* by *Wyman, supra:* "The program for the rooting out of subversion . . . [was] drawn without regard to the presence or absence of guilty knowledge in those affected." The sanction of exposure was applied much more widely than anyone could remotely suggest that even traditional judicial sanctions might be applied in this area.

One may accept the Court's truism that preservation of the state's existence is undoubtedly a proper purpose for legislation. But, in descending from this peak of abstraction to the facts of this case, one must ask the question: What relation did this investigation of individual conduct have to legislative ends here? If bills of attainder were still a legitimate legislative end, it is clear that the investigations and reports might naturally have furnished the starting point (though only that) for a legislative adjudication of guilt under the 1951 Act. But what other legislative purpose was actually being fulfilled by the course taken by this investigation, with its overwhelming emphasis on individual associations and conduct?

The investigation, as revealed by the report, was overwhelmingly and predominantly a roving, self-contained investigation of individual and group behavior, and behavior in a constitutionally protected area. Its whole approach was to name names, disclose information about those named, and observe that "facts are facts." The New Hampshire Supreme Court has upheld the investigation as being a proper legislative inquiry, it is true. In *Nelson* v. *Wyman*, 99 N.H. 33, it said: "No sound basis can exist for denying to the Legislature the power to so investigate the effectiveness of its 1951 act even though, as an incident to that general investigation, it may be necessary to inquire as to whether a particular person has violated the act. . . . When the investigation provided for is a general one, the discovery of a specific, individual violation of law is collateral and subordinate to the main object of the inquiry." In evaluating this, it must be admitted that maintenance of the separation of powers in the States is not, in and of itself, a concern of the Federal Constitution. . . . But for an investigation in the field of the constitutionally protected freedoms of speech and assemblage to be upheld by the broad standards of relevance permissible in a legislative inquiry, some relevance to a valid legislative purpose must be shown, and certainly the ruling made below, that under the state law the Legislature has authorized the inquiry, . . . does not conclude the issue here. The bare fact that the Legislature has authorized the inquiry does not mean that the inquiry is for a valid legislative end when viewed in the light of the federal constitutional test we must apply. Nor, while it is entitled to weight, is the determination by a state court that the inquiry relates to a valid legislative end conclusive. It is the task of this Court, as the Court recognizes in theory today, to evaluate the facts to determine if there actually has been demonstrated a valid legislative end to which the inquiry is related. With all due respect, the quoted observations of the New Hampshire Supreme Court in the case of *Nelson* v. *Wyman* bear little relationship to the course of the inquiry, as revealed by the report published after that decision. The report discloses an investigation in which the processes of law-making and law-evaluating were submerged entirely in exposure of individual behavior—in adjudication, of a sort, however much disclaimed, through the exposure process. If an investigation or trial, conducted by any organ of the State, which is aimed at the application of sanctions to individual behavior is to be upheld, it must meet the traditional standards that the common law in this country has established for the application of sanctions to the individual, or a constitutionally permissible modification of them. . . . As a bare minimum there must be general standards of conduct, substantively constitutionally proper, applied to the individual in a fair proceeding with defined issues resulting in a binding, final determination. I had not supposed that a legislative investigation of the sort practiced here provided such a framework under the Constitution.

It is not enough to say, as the Court's position I fear may amount to, that what was taking place was an investigation and until the Attorney General and the Legislature had in all the data, the precise shape of the legislative action to be taken was necessarily unknown. Investigation and exposure, in the area which we are here concerned with, are not recognized as self-contained legislative powers in themselves. . . . Since this is so, it hardly fulfills the responsibility with which this Court is charged, of protecting the constitutional rights of freedom of speech and assembly, to admit that an investigation going on indefinitely in time, roving in subject matter, and cumulative in detail in this area can be in aid of a valid legislative end, on the theory that some day it may come to some point. Even the most abusive investigation, the one most totally committed to the constitutionally impermissible end of individual adjudication through publication, could pass such a test. At the stage of this investigation that we are concerned with, it continued to be a cumulative, broad inquiry into the specific details of past individual and associational behavior in the political area. It appears to have been a classic example of "a fruitless investigation into the personal affairs of individuals." . . . Investigation appears to have been a satisfactory end product for the State, but it cannot be so for us in this case as we evaluate the demands of the Constitution. Nor can we accept the legislative renewal of the investigation, or the taking of other legislative measures to facilitate the investigation, as being themselves the legislative justification of the inquiry. The report indicates that it so viewed them; in requesting legislation renewing the investigation and an investigation immunity statute, the Attorney General significantly stated that if the renewal legislation or some investigatory substitute were not passed, it "would mean no further investigation, no continuing check upon Communist activities. . . ." This is just to admit the continuing existence of the investigation as a self-contained justification for the inquiry. However much the State may be content to rely on the investigation as its own sanction, I think it perfectly plain that it cannot be regarded as a justification here. Nor can the faint possibility that an already questionably broad criminal statute might be further broadened, if constitutionally permissible, be considered the subordinating legislative purpose here, particularly in the light of what the investigation was in fact as revealed by its report. Of course, after further investigation and further reports, legislation of some sort might eventuate, or at least be considered. Perhaps it might be rejected because of serious doubts as to its constitutionality—which would, I think, underline the point I am making. But on such airy speculation, I do not see how we can say that the State has made any showing that this investigation, which on its surface has an overwhelming appearance of a simple wide-ranging exposure campaign, presents an implementation of a subordinating law-making interest that, as the Court concedes, the State must be shown to have.

This Court's approach to a very similar problem in *N. A. A. C. P. v. State of Alabama, supra,* should furnish a guide to the proper course of decision here. There the State demonstrated a definite purpose which was admittedly within its competence. That purpose was the ascertainment whether a foreign corporation was unlawfully carrying on local activities within Alabama's borders, because not qualified to do business in the manner required by state law. In a judicial proceeding having this as its express stated purpose, the State sought to obtain the membership list of the corporation. This Court carefully recognized the curbing of associational freedom that the disclosure called for by this inquiry would entail. It then analyzed the relationship between the inquiry and this purpose, and concluding that there was no rational connection, it held the inquiry constitutionally impermissible. Here the situation is even more extreme; there is no demonstration at all of what the legislative purpose is, outside of the investigation of violations, suspicions of violations, and conduct raising some question of violation of an existing statute. It is anomalous to say, as I fear the Court says today, that the vaguer the State's interest is, the more laxly will the Court view the matter and indulge a presumption of the existence of a valid subordinating state interest. In effect, a roving investigation and exposure of past associations and expressions in the political field is upheld because it might lead to some sort of legislation which might be sustained as constitutional, and the entire process is said to become the more defensible rather than the less because of the vagueness of the issues. The Court says that the appellant cannot argue against the exposure because this is an investigation and the exposure may make the investigation lead somewhere, possibly to legislative action. But this is just to say that an investigation, once under state law it is classified as "legislative," needs no showing of purpose beyond its own existence. A start must be made somewhere, and if the principles this Court has announced, and to which the Court today makes some deference, are to have any meaning, it must be up to the State to make some at least plausible disclosure of its law-making interest so that the relevance of its inquiries to it may be tested. Then the courts could begin to evaluate the justification for the impact on the individual's rights of freedom of speech and assembly. But here not only has the State failed to begin to elucidate such an interest; it has positively demonstrated, it appears to me, through its Resolution, the Attorney General's and the state courts' interpretation of it, and the Resolution's re-enactment, that what it is interested in is exposure, in lieu of prosecution, and nothing definable else.

The precise details of the inquiry we are concerned with here underlines this. The Attorney General had World Fellowship's speaker list and had already made publication of it in the fashion to which I have alluded. He had considerable other data about World Fellowship, Inc., which he had already published. What reason has been demonstrated, in terms of a legislative inquiry, for going into the matter in further depth? Outside of the fact that it might afford some further evidence as to the existence of "subversive persons" within the State, which I have endeavored to show was not in itself a matter related to any legislative function except self-contained investigation and exposure themselves, the relevance of further detail is not demonstrated. But its damaging effect on the persons to be named in the guest list is obvious. And since the only discernible purpose of the investigation on this record is revealed to be investigation and exposure *per se*, and the relevance of the names to that purpose alone is quite apparent, this discloses the constitutional infirmity in the inquiry which requires us to strike down the adjudication of contempt in question here.

The Court describes the inquiry we must make in this matter as a balancing of interests. I think I have indicated that there has been no valid legislative interest of the State actually defined and shown in the investigation as it operated, so that there is really nothing against which the appellant's rights of association and expression can be balanced. But if some proper legislative end of the inquiry can be surmised, through what must be a process of speculation, I think it is patent that there is really no subordinating interest in it demonstrated on the part of the State. The evidence inquired about was simply an effort to get further details about an activity as to which there already were considerable details in the hands of the Attorney General. I can see no serious and substantial relationship between the furnishing of these further minutiae about what was going on at the World Fellowship camp and the process of legislation, and it is the process of legislation, the consideration of the enactment of laws, with which ultimately we are concerned. We have a detailed inquiry into an assemblage the general contours of which were already known on the one hand, and on the other the remote and speculative possibility of some sort of legislation—albeit legislation in a field where there are serious constitutional limitations. We have this in the context of an inquiry which was in practice being conducted in its overwhelming thrust as a vehicle of exposure, and where the practice had been followed of publishing names on the basis of a "not proven" verdict. We are not asked to hold that the State cannot carry on such fact-finding at all, with or without compulsory process. Nor are we asked to hold that as a general matter compulsory process cannot be used to amass facts whose initial relevance to an ultimate legislative interest may be remote. . . . We deal with a narrow and more subtle problem. We deal here with inquiries into the areas of free speech and assemblage where the process of compulsory disclosure itself tends to have a repressive effect. . . . We deal only with the power of the State to *compel* such a disclosure. We are asked, in this narrow context, only to give meaning to our statement in *Watkins* v. *United States,* supra, "that the mere semblance of a legislative purpose would not justify an inquiry in the face of the Bill of Rights." Here we must demand some initial showing by the State sufficient to counterbalance the interest in privacy as it relates to freedom of speech and assembly. On any basis that has practical meaning, New Hampshire has not made such a showing here. I would reverse the judgment of the New Hampshire Supreme Court.

Mr. Justice Black, and Mr. Justice Douglas would decide this case on the ground that appellant is being deprived of rights under the First and Fourteenth Amendments, for the reasons developed in *Adler* v. *Board of Education of City of New York,* 342 US 485 (dissenting opinion); *Beauharnais* v. *People of State of Illinois,* 343 US 250 (dissenting opinions). But they join Mr. Justice Brennan's dissent because he makes clear to them that New Hampshire's legislative program resulting in the incarceration of appellant for contempt violates Art. I, § 10 of the Constitution which provides that "No state shall . . . pass any bill of attainder." See *United States* v. *Lovett,* 328 US 303, and cases cited; *Joint Anti-Fascist Refugee Committee* v. *McGrath,* 341 US 123 (concurring opinion).

UPHAUS *v.* WYMAN
364 US 388 (1960)

[Following the preceding case, *Uphaus* v. *Wyman*, New Hampshire enacted another statute which omitted the provision in the earlier act directing the state Attorney General to determine whether subversive persons were presently in the State of New Hampshire, and limited the authority of the Attorney General to making investigations of violations of law. Despite this statutory change, an order committing Uphaus until he purged himself of his contempt was affirmed by the state Supreme Court on the ground that the legislature had not intended that the earlier statute should terminate pending proceedings. Uphaus appealed from this last judgment, and the United States Supreme Court dismissed his appeal. The decision was 5 to 4, with Chief Justice Warren and Justices Black, Douglas, and Brennan dissenting.]

PER CURIAM.

In view of the Court's decision in *Uphaus* v. *Wyman*, 360 U.S. 72, re-hearing denied, the motion to dismiss is granted and the appeal herein is dismissed for want of jurisdiction, in that the judgment sought to be reviewed is based on a non-federal ground.

Mr. Justice Brennan:

The New Hampshire Supreme Court has held in this proceeding that the New Hampshire Legislature still wanted Dr. Uphaus' answers on December 14, 1959, notwithstanding the omission from Laws 1957, c. 178, of the provision of Laws 1955, cc. 340 and 197, authorizing the Attorney General "to determine whether subversive persons . . . are presently located within this state," *Wyman* v. *Uphaus*, 102 N.H. 461; . . . . We are bound by the highest state court's construction of the pertinent New Hampshire statutes. We must therefore consider the substantiality of the federal constitutional questions presented on this appeal on the basis of that construction and not upon the premise urged by Dr. Uphaus that the 1957 statute shows that the legislature on December 14, 1959 no longer wanted him to produce the list of names. In consequence, while I remain of the view that the Court in *Uphaus* v. *Wyman*, 360 U.S. 72, incorrectly sustained the previous order of civil contempt made against Dr. Uphaus, see dissent at page 82, that hold-ing, while it stands, also sustains the order challenged on this appeal. Solely under compulsion of that decision, I think that the appeal must be dismissed as not presenting a substantial federal question.

Mr. Justice Black, with whom The Chief Justice and Mr. Justice Douglas concur, dissenting:

I concur in the dissent of Mr. Justice Douglas and agree with him that since the New Hampshire law upheld by this Court in *Uphaus* v. *Wyman*, 360 U.S. 72, has now been changed, a new federal question is presented which cannot be dismissed as involving only the correctness of a ruling on local law, and that we consequently should not dismiss this appeal but should note jurisdiction, grant bail and hear arguments. The recent amendment withdrew the power, involved in the previous appeal, which authorized the Attorney General of New Hampshire "to determine whether subversive persons . . . are presently located within" the State, and thus took away the very power under which the Attorney General was acting when he demanded the names of guests at the summer camp in New Hampshire managed by the appellant, Dr. Willard Uphaus. Notwithstanding that fact, the New Hampshire courts have held that the State still has an interest in those names sufficient to justify the continued imprisonment of Dr. Uphaus for his refusal to comply with the demand to produce them. This appeal therefore raises federal questions as to whether this latter holding violates the Federal Constitution. I think that the Court's action today in treating those federal questions as insubstantial is wrong in at least two different respects.

First, I think this action is inconsistent with the Court's own test as set forth in its opinion on the prior appeal and there used to square . the imprisonment of Dr. Uphaus with the First Amendment. That test was stated in these terms: "The interest of the guests at World Fellowship in their associational privacy having been asserted, we have for decision the federal question of whether the public interests overbalance these conflicting private ones." This required the Court to weigh the interest of those guests against the interest of the State, as broadly expressed by its legislature, in knowing "whether subversive persons . . . are presently located within" the State, a balancing process which there resulted in the conclusion that the state interest must prevail. Now, however, it is clear that the interest of the State so weighed no longer exists and a new balance must be made if the invasion of "associational privacy" previously sanctioned is to be permitted to continue. But this the Court refuses to do, apparently on the theory that the present appeal is controlled by the previous disposition. It seems to me that "balancing" which refuses to take note of such an important change in the interest of the State is little balancing at all—a mere illusion, in fact.

Secondly, it seems to me that the record as it now stands before this Court requires a reappraisal of the question whether the actions of the State of New Hampshire constitute a bill of attainder in violation of Art. I, § 10, of the Constitution. On the prior appeal, the majority of this Court held that the record as it then stood would not justify such a conclusion. The present record, however, presents new facts relevant to that issue. For here we are confronted with a situation in which the courts of New Hampshire have stated that it was the intention of the legislature of that State to permit the Attorney General to single out Dr. Uphaus and any others (if, indeed, there are any others) against whom investigative proceedings had already been commenced and to pursue those proceedings, not in furtherance of any general aim of the State—that general aim, if it ever existed, has been abandoned by the amendment—but apparently for the sole purpose of setting these people off for special treatment. What this special treatment is to be is clearly shown by the brief filed before this Court in this appeal by the State Attorney General himself, who administers the Act. That brief states unequivocally that "[t]hose who voluntarily and knowingly appear with, consult with, confer with, attend functions with and otherwise act in concert with Communists or former Communists in America cannot possibly have any reasonable right of privacy in regard to such activities. . . ." In the light of all these new facts, the decision upon the former appeal is not and cannot properly be held to be dispositive of the question whether this record shows that New Hampshire is unconstitutionally imposing a bill of attainder upon Dr. Uphaus.

I think the summary dismissal of this appeal without even so much as the benefit of oral argument, when the abridgment of the rights of free speech and assembly is so obvious, is a sad indication of just how far this Court has already departed from the protections of the Bill of Rights and an omen of things yet to come. Such retrogression, of course, follows naturally from the Court's recent trend toward substituting for the plain language of the commands of the Bill of Rights elastic concepts which permit the Court to uphold direct abridgments of liberty unless the Court views those abridgments as "arbitrary," "unreasonable," "offensive to decency" or "unjustified on balance," for these concepts reduce the absolute commands of the Constitution to mere admonitions. I think it is time for all who cherish the liberties guaranteed by the Bill of Rights to look closely at the disastrous consequences upon those liberties which have resulted from the Court's use of such concepts. In my mind, the present case graphically illustrates those consequences when it is stripped of the ambiguous legal formulations which have been imposed upon it and considered in the context in which it actually arose—the conduct of Dr. Uphaus as an individual.

He is a citizen of this country by birth. Throughout the nearly seventy years of his life, evidently from early boyhood, he has been a deeply religious person. The record shows his active membership in an official service for various Methodist churches in the communities where he has lived. The value of that membership and those services is attested by affidavits filed by the pastors of those churches. The record further indicates, without dispute, that he is a man whose life has been dedicated to the principles of his religion. He holds a degree as a Doctor of Theology. He taught religious education at Yale University and was associated with the Religion and Labor Foundation for a number of years. Over the years, his religious faith manifested itself in an increasing opposition to war. It was this belief which led him, in 1952, to become the Director of World Fellowship, Inc., a summer camp operated, he says, in the interest of promoting the ideas of pacifism.

Almost immediately upon his arrival at World Fellowship, Dr. Uphaus came under the fire of an investigation being conducted by the Attorney General of New Hampshire, apparently on the theory that World Fellowship was frequented by "subversive" persons. Eventually, as the Director of World Fellowship, he was called before the Attorney General to testify. At the very outset of the hearing before the Attorney General, he expressed a complete willingness to answer any question concerning himself, including any views he might hold or any actions he might have taken with regard to any subject. In addition, he expressed a willingness to give the Attorney General any information which might be wanted in regard to the subject matter of any speeches made at World Fellowship. But he absolutely refused to give the Attorney General: (1) a list of the nonprofessional employees of the camp; (2) a list of all the guests who had stayed at the camp; and (3) his personal correspondence with the speakers who had appeared at the camp. Upon being met with this refusal, the Attorney General sought a court order requiring Dr. Uphaus to produce these items. At the resulting hearing, the court, apparently viewing the request of the Attorney General for the names of the camp's dishwashers and floor sweepers as totally unreasonable and being uncertain as to the legal amenability to subpoena of the correspondence, ordered Dr. Uphaus to produce only the names of the guests. This, Dr. Uphaus persisted, he could not do, resting his refusal upon the following reasons, to which he has adhered throughout this long ordeal: (1) because "by the direct teachings of the Bible . . . it is wrong to bear false witness against my brother; and inasmuch as I have no reason to believe that any of these persons whose names have been called for have in any sense hurt this state or our country, I have reason to believe that they should not be in the possession of the Attorney General"; (2) because "the social teachings of the Methodist Church . . . condemn guilt by association"; * and (3) because "I love this document [the Bill of Rights] and I propose to uphold it with the full strength and power of my spirit and intelligence."

Nonetheless, the order to produce was upheld and Dr. Uphaus was imprisoned for his failure to comply with it. As a result, he has been in jail since last December 14 under a judgment which sentenced him to imprisonment for one year or until such time as he would comply with the order to produce. His plight, however, is even worse than would normally be indicated by that sentence in that there can be no assurance at all that he will be released at the end of the year specified. The Attorney General of New

* At the hearing upon remand of these proceedings to the New Hampshire courts following this Court's affirmance of the first contempt order, Dr. Uphaus expanded this second reason to encompass the teachings of all religions. Relying upon a recent article by a Professor of Church History at Harvard University, Williams, Reluctance to Inform, 14 *Theology Today* 229, Dr. Uphaus argued that his position with respect to informing against his friends is required by the historic traditions of all religions. That article pointed to the indisputable truth that religious groups have time and again resorted to a refusal to inform as a shield against persecution.

Hampshire insists, notwithstanding the recent legislation reducing his powers, that he has a right to continue all investigations presently pending, and the Supreme Court of New Hampshire apparently agrees with him. This Court, by its action today, necessarily takes the position that this serious abridgment of the rights of free speech and peaceable assembly does not even raise a substantial federal question. As a result, it is entirely possible that Dr. Uphaus will be subjected to new questioning and forced into a new "contempt" as soon as he serves out this year's imprisonment. The brief filed by the Attorney General of New Hampshire makes it appear that he has every intention of doing just that. Thus, a distinct possibility exists that this man who, at least so far as these records show, has never committed a single crime, nor even so much as an immoral act, faces imprisonment for the rest of his life. This simply because he has refused to violate his religious principles and sacrifice his constitutional rights by disclosing the names of those with whom he has peaceably assembled to discuss public affairs in this country.

In this respect, the predicament of Dr. Uphaus may be likened to that of the defendant in the famous *Sheriff's Case* before the House of Lords in 1767. There the City of London sought to prosecute a religious dissenter for refusing to serve in the office of sheriff as required by its by-laws. The defense was that the Corporation Act would have made it a crime for a dissenter to serve in that office for it required an oath from all office-holders that they had taken the sacraments of the Church of England within the year. The dilemma of the dissenter was vividly described by Lord Mansfield in stating his views on the case:

> Make a law to render them incapable of office; make another, to punish them for not serving. . . . If they accept, punish them; if they refuse, punish them; if they say, yes, punish them; if they say, no, punish them. My Lords, this is a most exquisite dilemma, from which there is no escaping; it is a trap a man cannot get out of; it is as bad persecution as the bed of Procrustes: If they are too short, stretch them; if they are too long, lop them.

This technique of putting unorthodox groups into a position where their only real choice is between various alternative punishments (a technique the prevalence of which today extends far beyond the borders of New Hampshire) is strikingly similar to that being utilized here against Dr. Uphaus. If he testifies, his friends will suffer; if he refuses to testify, he goes to jail. The dilemma is truly one "from which there is no escaping" for a man who, like Dr. Uphaus or like the religious dissenter in the *Sheriff's Case*, cannot bring himself to sacrifice either his religious principles or his legal rights.

That case also serves to highlight a most unfortunate aspect of the decision in this case. For there, nearly two hundred years ago and in England where there was no Bill of Rights, the House of Lords refused to countenance the use of that technique. They held it to be inconsistent with the Toleration Act by which Parliament had guaranteed religious freedom even though the terms of that guarantee were far less sweeping and more limited in application than the absolute commands of our First Amendment. In my view, the marjority's disposition of this case, reducing as it does those absolute commands to mere admonitions, means that our First Amendment amounts to something less as a charter of freedom than England's Toleration Act was held to be. This in the very face of the indisputable historical fact that one of the primary reasons for the establishment of this country was the desire of early settlers to escape religious persecution.

I do not suggest, of course, that this imprisonment of Dr. Uphaus is without precedent in history. Indeed, I am painfully aware that there are a multitude of such precedents extending from many centuries back in the past and continuing forward in an almost unbroken line to the present day. There is, for example, the case of the Puritan minister John Udall in 1590, a case which bears a strong similarity to that of Dr. Uphaus. Udall was called before a court in connection with the investigation of the authorship of certain religious tracts which, in the words of one of the judges, "tend[ed] to the overthrowing of the State, and the moving of Rebellion." That court sought to force Udall to disclose the identity of other Puritans so that it might question them as to the authorship of the tracts. In refusing to divulge the demanded names, Udall gave his reasons in a statement not unlike that of Dr. Uphaus before the New Hampshire court. "I will take an oath of allegiance to her majesty, wherein I will acknowledge her supremacy according to statute, and promise my obedience as becometh a subject; but to swear to accuse myself or others, I think you have no law for it." Udall, like Dr. Uphaus, was sentenced to jail for civil contempt under a judgment which ordered his imprisonment until such time as he would consent to testify. But such coercion was as ineffective in that case as it has been to date in this. Udall's dauntless spirit was never broken even though his body was. He died in prison within a few years.

It would not be difficult to point out many other cases such as that of Udall, but I will content myself with one other. Some seventy years after John Udall's experiences, there was a dissenting preacher in England named John Bunyan. He was arrested for preaching and efforts were made to get him to agree not to preach any more. He refused to be coerced into silence. The result was that he was put through a kind of trial and sentenced to prison for holding "several unlawful [religious] meetings . . . to the great disturbance and distraction of the good subjects of this kingdom. . . ." In Bunyan's case the imprisonment lasted 12 years, and it was during those 12 years that he gave to the world *The Pilgrim's Progress*. One of the judges who acquiesced in the imprisonment of Bunyan was Sir Matthew Hale, later Lord Chief Justice Hale, a man described by Lord Campbell as "one of the most pure, the most pious, the most independent, and the most learned" Chief Justices England ever had. That this description is not entirely unjustified, despite the fact that his record was also marred by the part he took in the conviction and sentencing to death of two unfortunate women as witches is, I think, a tragic commentary upon the record of the judiciary, throughout the centuries, in discharging its duty to protect civil liberties. It is perhaps one of the ironies of history that the name of John Bunyan, a

poor tinker and preacher, is at least as well known and respected today as
that of the great Chief Justice of England who permitted him to languish
in jail.

My guess is that history will look with no more favor upon the imprisonment of Willard Uphaus than it has upon that of Udall, Bunyan or the many
others like them. For this is another of that ever-lengthening line of cases
where people have been sent to prison and kept there for long periods of
their lives because their beliefs were inconsistent with the prevailing views
of the moment. I believe the First and Fourteenth Amendments were intended to prevent any such imprisonments in this country. The grounds
urged by the Attorney General of New Hampshire here are, as shown by
the cases of Udall and Bunyan, precisely those that have always been urged
for throwing dissenters in jail, namely, that they are a menace to the community and it is dangerous to leave them free. It may be true, as the
Attorney General of New Hampshire suspects, that Dr. Uphaus has at some
time been in the company of Communists, or that the people who have been
in his camp have been in the company of Communists. But even if it is true
and those associates are as bad as they are suspected to be, it is my belief
that our Constitution with its Bill of Rights absolutely forbids the imposition
of pains and penalties upon him for peaceably assembling with them. That
great charter was drafted by men who were well aware of the constant
danger to individual liberty in a country where public officials are permitted
to harass and punish people on nothing more than charges that they associate with others labeled by the Government as publicans and sinners.

*Mr. Justice Douglas, with whom The Chief Justice and Mr. Justice Black
concur, dissenting:*

I would note jurisdiction in this case. . . .

Recently when Alabama asked the National Association for the Advancement of Colored People to disclose its membership list, we held that disclosure was not required because if compelled it might well abridge the
rights of members to engage in lawful association in support of their common beliefs. We said in *N.A.A.C.P.* v. *Alabama,* 357 U.S. 449:

> It is hardly a novel perception that compelled disclosure of affilia-
> tion with groups engaged in advocacy may constitute as effective a
> restraint on freedom of association as the forms of governmental action
> in the cases above were thought likely to produce upon the particular
> constitutional rights there involved. This Court has recognized the
> vital relationship between freedom to associate and privacy in one's
> associations. When referring to the varied forms of governmental
> action which might interfere with freedom of assembly, it said in
> *American Communications Assn.* v. *Douds,* 339 U.S. 382; "A require-
> ment that adherents of particular religious faiths or political parties
> wear identifying armbands, for example, is obviously of this nature."
> Compelled disclosure of membership in an organization engaged in

advocacy of particular beliefs is of the same order. Inviolability of privacy in group association may in many circumstances be indispensable to preservation of freedom of association, particularly where a group espouses dissident beliefs. Cf. *United States* v. *Rumely,* 345 U.S. 41 (concurring opinion).

What we there said was not designed, as I understood it, as a rule for Negroes only. The Constitution favors no racial group, no political or social group. The group, with which Dr. Uphaus was associated and whose membership list he refused to disclose, is entitled under the First Amendment to the same protection as the N.A.A.C.P. No groundwork whatever was laid in any of the records before us that World Fellowship, Inc. was at any time engaged in any conduct that could be called unlawful.

We had *N.A.A.C.P.* v. *Alabama,* before us when the *Uphaus* case was decided. It involved rights of the organization itself to defy those who wanted its membership lists. Not until later, however, did we have the case where an *individual* who possessed membership lists challenged the right of government to demand their production. In *Bates* v. *Little Rock,* 361 U.S. 516, decided after we handed down our decision in the *Uphaus* case, we reversed a state conviction of custodians of the records of local branches of N.A.A.C.P. for refusing to disclose its membership lists to city officials. We said:

> On this record it sufficiently appears that compulsory disclosure of the membership lists of the local branches of the National Association for the Advancement of Colored People would work a significant interference with the freedom of association of their members. There was substantial uncontroverted evidence that public identification of persons in the community as members of the organizations had been followed by harassment and threats of bodily harm. There was also evidence that fear of community hostility and economic reprisals that would follow public disclosure of the membership lists had discouraged new members from joining the organizations and induced former members to withdraw. This repressive effect, while in part the result of private attitudes and pressures, was brought to bear only after the exercise of governmental power had threatened to force disclosure of the members' names. *N.A.A.C.P.* v. *Alabama.* . . . Thus, the threat of substantial government encroachment upon important and traditional aspects of individual freedom is neither speculative nor remote.

Can there be any doubt that harassment of members of World Fellowship, Inc., in the climate prevailing among New Hampshire's law-enforcement officials will not likewise be severe? Can there be any doubt that its members will be as closely pursued as might be members of N.A.A.C.P. in some communities? If either N.A.A.C.P. or World Fellowship were engaged in criminal activity, we would have a different problem. But neither is shown to be. World Fellowship, so far as this record shows, is as law-abiding as N.A.A.C.P.

The members of one are entitled to the same freedom of speech, of press, of assembly, and of association as the members of the other. These rights extend even to Communists, as a unanimous Court held in *De Jonge* v. *Oregon*, 299 U.S. 353.

What is an unconstitutional invasion of freedom of association in Alabama or in Arkansas should be unconstitutional in New Hampshire. All groups— white or colored—engaged in lawful conduct are entitled to the same protection against harassment as the N.A.A.C.P. enjoys. Since we allowed in the *Bates* case the protection we deny here and since Bates was decided after we decided Uphaus' case, we should reconsider our earlier decision in this case. The *Bates* case and the Uphaus case put into focus for the first time the responsibility of an *individual* to make disclosure of membership lists. We cannot administer justice with an even hand if we allow Bates to go free and Uphaus to languish in prison.

For these reasons, as well as those advanced by Mr. Justice Black which I wholly share, I would note probable jurisdiction of this appeal. And Dr. Uphaus should, of course, be released on bail pending resolution of the questions by the Court.

WILKINSON v. UNITED STATES

365 US 399 (1961)

[Defendant, an outspoken opponent of the House Un-American Activities Committee, was summoned before a subcommittee investigating Communist propaganda in the South. He refused to answer the question whether he was a member of the Communist Party, claiming that the inquiry violated his liberties under the First Amendment. He was convicted of contempt of Congress. The Supreme Court, by a 5-to-4 vote, affirmed. Chief Justice Warren and Justices Black, Douglas, and Brennan dissented.]

Mr. Justice Stewart delivered the opinion of the Court:

The petitioner was convicted for having unlawfully refused to answer a question pertinent to a matter under inquiry before a subcommittee of the House Committee on Un-American Activities at a hearing in Atlanta, Georgia, on July 30, 1958. His conviction was affirmed by the Court of Appeals, which held that our decision in *Barenblatt* v. *United States*, 360 U.S. 109, was "controlling." We granted certiorari, to consider the petitioner's claim that the Court of Appeals had misconceived the meaning of the Barenblatt decision. For the reasons that follow, we are of the view that the Court of Appeals .was correct, and that its judgment must be affirmed.

I.

The following circumstances were established by uncontroverted evidence at the petitioner's trial:

The Committee on Un-American Activities is a standing committee of the House of Representatives, elected at the commencement of each Congress. The Committee, or any subcommittee thereof, is authorized to investigate "(i) the extent, character, and objects of un-American propaganda activities in the United States, (ii) the diffusion within the United States of subversive and un-American propaganda that is instigated from foreign countries or of a domestic origin and that attacks the principle of the form of government as guaranteed by our Constitution, and (iii) all other questions in relation thereto that would aid Congress in any necessary remedial legislation."

In the spring of 1958 the Committee passed a resolution providing for a subcommittee hearing to be held in Atlanta, Georgia, "relating to the following subjects and having the legislative purposes indicated:

1. The extent, character and objects of Communist colonization and infiltration in the textile and other basic industries located in the South, and Communist Party propaganda activities in the South, the legislative purpose being:

(a) To obtain additional information for use by the Committee in its consideration of Section 16 of H.R. 9352, relating to the proposed amendment of Section 4 of the Communist Control Act of 1954, prescribing a penalty for knowingly and wilfully becoming or remaining a member of the Communist Party with knowledge of the purposes or objectives thereof; and

(b) To obtain additional information, adding to the Committee's overall knowledge on the subject so that Congress may be kept informed and thus prepared to enact remedial legislation in the National Defense, and for internal security, when and if the exigencies of the situation require it.

2. Entry and dissemination within the United States of foreign Communist Party propaganda, the legislative purpose being to determine the necessity for, and advisability of, amendments to the Foreign Agents Registration Act designed more effectively to counteract the Communist schemes and devices now used in avoiding the prohibitions of the Act.

3. Any other matter within the jurisdiction of the Committee which it, or any subcommittee thereof, appointed to conduct this hearing, may designate.

The subcommittee which was appointed pursuant to this resolution convened in Atlanta on July 29, 1958. At the opening of the proceedings on that day, the Chairman of the Committee orally summarized the purposes of the hearings. The petitioner was present and heard the Chairman's statement.

The first witness to appear was Amando Penha, who testified that he had been a member of the Communist Party from 1950 to 1958, having joined the Party at the request of the Federal Bureau of Investigation. He stated that he had served as a member of the National Textile Commission of the Party, which, he said, was set up to control and supervise the infiltration and colonization of the textile industry, particularly in the South. He described the "colonizer" system, which, he said, involves sending hard-core Party members into plants in jobs where they have close contact with rank and file workers. Penha described in some detail his trips throughout the South in compliance with the instructions of the National Textile Commission, and identified a number of individuals as "colonizers." Another witness, a Deputy Collector of Customs, described the influx of Communist propaganda sent from abroad into the United States and particularly into the South. Several other witnesses were then interrogated, some as to their activities as alleged Communist colonizers, others as to their connection with certain allegedly Communist-controlled publications. A number of these witnesses declined to answer most of the questions put to them.

On the following day the first witness before the subcommittee was Carl Braden. Although interrogated at length he declined to answer questions relating to alleged Communist activity. The next witness was the petitioner. After being sworn and stating his name he declined to give his residence address, stating that, "As a matter of conscience and personal responsibility, I refuse to answer any questions of this committee." When asked his occupation, he made the same response. He was then asked the question which was to become the subject of the present indictment and conviction: "Mr. Wilkinson, are you now a member of the Communist Party?" He declined to answer the question, giving the same response as before.

The Committee's Staff Director then addressed the petitioner at length, in explanation "of the reasons, the pertinency, and the relevancy of that question and certain other questions which I propose to propound to you."

In response the petitioner stated "I am refusing to answer any questions of this committee." He was then directed by the Subcommittee Chairman to answer the question as to his Communist Party membership. This time he responded as follows:

I challenge, in the most fundamental sense, the legality of the House Committee on Un-American Activities. It is my opinion that this committee stands in direct violation by its mandate and by its practices of the first amendment to the United States Constitution. It is my belief that Congress had no authority to establish this committee in the first instance, nor to instruct it with the mandate which it has.

I have the utmost respect for the broad powers which the Congress of the

United States must have to carry on its investigations for legislative purposes. However, the United States Supreme Court has held, that, broad as these powers may be, the Congress cannot investigate into an area where it cannot legislate, and this committee tends, by its mandate and by its practices, to investigate into precisely those areas of free speech, religion, peaceful association and assembly, and the press, wherein it cannot legislate and therefore it cannot investigate.

The hearing continued. The Staff Director read part of the record of an earlier hearing in California, where a witness had testified to knowing the petitioner as a Communist. The petitioner was then asked whether this testimony was true. He refused to answer this and several further questions addressed to him. There was introduced into the record a reproduction of the petitioner's registration at an Atlanta hotel a week earlier, in which he had indicated that his business firm association was the "Emergency Civil Liberties Committee."

The subsequent indictment and conviction of the petitioner were based upon his refusal, in the foregoing context, to answer the single question "Are you now a member of the Communist Party?"

II.

The judgment affirming the petitioner's conviction is attacked here from several different directions. It is contended that the subcommittee was without authority to interrogate him, because its purpose in doing so was to investigate public opposition to the Committee itself and to harass and expose him. It is argued that the petitioner was wrongly convicted because the question which he refused to answer was not pertinent to a question under inquiry by the subcommittee, so that a basic element of the statutory offense was lacking. It is said that in any event the pertinency of the question was not made clear to the petitioner at the time he was directed to answer it, so that he was denied due process. Finally, it is urged that the action of the subcommittee in subpoenaing and questioning him violated his rights under the First Amendment to the Constitution.

In considering these contentions the starting point must be to determine the subject matter of the subcommittee's inquiry. House Rule XI, which confers investigative authority upon the Committee and its subcommittees, is quoted above. Because of the breadth and generailty of its language, Rule XI cannot be said to state with adequate precision the subject under inquiry by a subcommittee at any given hearing. This the Court had occasion to point out in *Watkins* v. *United States*, 354 U.S. 178. See also *Barenblatt* v. *United States*, 360 U.S. 109. But, as the *Watkins* opinion recognized, Rule XI is only one of several possible points of reference. The Court in that case said that "[t]he authorizing resolution, the remarks of the chairman or members of the committee, or even the nature of the proceedings themselves" might reveal the subject under inquiry. Here, as in *Barenblatt*, other sources do supply the requisite concreteness.

The resolution authorizing the subcommittee hearing in Atlanta was explicit. It clearly set forth three concrete areas of investigation: Communist infiltration into basic industry in the South, Communist Party propaganda in the South, and foreign Communist Party propaganda in the United States. The pattern of interrogation of the witnesses who appeared on the first day of the hearing confirms that the subcommittee was pursuing those three subjects of investigation. The Staff Director's statement to the petitioner explicitly referred to the second of the three subjects—Communist Party propaganda in the South. We think that the record thus clearly establishes that the subcommittee at the time of the petitioner's interrogation was pursuing at least two related and specific subjects of investigation: Communist infiltration into basic southern industry, and Communist Party propaganda activities in that area of the country.

If these, then, were the two subjects of the subcommittee's inquiry, the questions that must be answered in considering the petitioner's contentions are several. First, was the subcommittee's investigation of these subjects, through interrogation of the petitioner, authorized by Congress? Second, was the subcommittee pursuing a valid legislative purpose? Third, was the question asked the petitioner pertinent to the subject matter of the investigation? Fourth, was he contemporaneously apprised of the pertinency of the question? Fifth, did the subcommittee's interrogation violate his First Amendment rights of free association and free speech?

The question of basic congressional authorization was clearly decided in *Barenblatt* v. *United States*. There we said, after reviewing the genesis and subsequent history of Rule XI, that "[I]t can hardly be seriously argued that the investigation of Communist activities generally, and the attendant use of compulsory process, was beyond the purview of the Committee's intended authority under Rule XI." The subjects under inquiry here surely fall within "the investigation of Communist activities generally."

The petitioner argues, however, that the subcommittee was inspired to interrogate him by reason of his opposition to the existence of the Un-American Activities Committee itself, and that its purpose was unauthorized harassment and exposure. He points to the Chairman's opening statement which mentioned activity against the Committee, to the fact that he was subpoenaed to appear before the subcommittee soon after he arrived in Atlanta to stir up opposition to the Committee's activities, and to the statement of the Staff Director indicating the sub-committee's awareness of his efforts to develop a "hostile sentiment" to the Committee and to "bring pressure upon the United States Congress to preclude these particular hearings."

But, just as in *Barenblatt*, we could find nothing in Rule XI to ex-clude the field of education from the Committee's compulsory author-ity, we can find nothing to indicate that it was the intent of Congress to immunize from interrogation all those (and there are many) who are opposed to the existence of the Un-American Activities Committee.

Nor can we say on this record that the subcommittee was not pur-suing a valid legislative purpose. The Committee resolution authorizing the Atlanta hearing, quoted above, expressly referred to two legislative proposals, an amendment to § 4 of the Communist Control Act and amendments to the Foreign Agents Registration Act. A number of other sources also indicate the presence of a legislative purpose. The Chair-man's statement at the opening of the hearings contained a lengthy discussion of legislation. The Staff Director's statement to the petitioner also discussed legislation which the Committee had under considera-tion. All these sources indicate the existence of a legislative purpose. And the determination that purposes of the kind referred to are un-assailably valid was a cornerstone of our decision in *Barenblatt*: "That Congress has wide power to legislate in the field of Communist activity in this Country, and to conduct appropriate investigations in aid thereof, is hardly debatable. The existence of such power has never been questioned by this Court, and it is sufficient to say, without par-ticularization, that Congress has enacted or considered in this field a wide range of legislative measures, not a few of which have stemmed from recommendations of the very Committee whose actions have been drawn in question here. In the last analysis this power rests on the right of self-preservation. . . ."

The petitioner's contention that, while the hearing generally may have been pursuant to a valid legislative purpose, the sole reason for interrogating him was to expose him to public censure because of his activities against the Committee is not persuasive. It is true that the Staff Director's statement reveals the subcommittee's awareness of the petitioner's opposition to the hearings and indicates that the petitioner was not summoned to appear until after he had arrived in Atlanta as the representative of a group carrying on a public campaign to abolish the House Committee. These circumstances, however, do not neces-sarily lead to the conclusion that the subcommittee's intent was per-sonal persecution of the petitioner. As we have noted, a prime purpose of the hearings was to investigate Communist propaganda activities in the South. It therefore was entirely logical for the subcommittee to subpoena the petitioner after he had arrived at the site of the hearings, had registered as a member of a group which the subcommittee believed to be Communist dominated and had conducted a public campaign against the subcommittee. The fact that the petitioner might not have been summoned to appear had he not come to Atlanta illustrates the very point, for in that event he might not have been thought to have been connected with a subject under inquiry—Communist Party propaganda activities in that area of the country.

Moreover, it is not for us to speculate as to the motivations that may have prompted the decision of individual members of the subcommittee to summon the petitioner. As was said in *Watkins*, "a solution to our problem is not to be found in testing the motives of committee members for this purpose. Such is not our function. Their motives alone would not vitiate an investigation which had been instituted by a House of Congress if that assembly's legislative purpose is being served." . . .

It is to be emphasized that the petitioner was not summoned to appear as the result of an indiscriminate dragnet procedure, lacking in probable cause for belief that he possessed information which might be helpful to the subcommittee. As was made clear by the testimony of the Committee's Staff Director at the trial, the subcommittee had reason to believe at the time it summoned the petitioner that he was an active Communist leader engaged primarily in propaganda activities. This is borne out by the record of the subcommittee hearings, including the content of the Staff Director's statement to the petitioner and evidence that at a prior hearing the petitioner had been identified as a Communist Party member.

The petitioner's claim that the question he refused to answer was not pertinent to a subject under inquiry merits no extended discussion. Indeed, it is difficult to imagine a preliminary question more pertinent to the topics under investigation than whether petitioner was in fact a member of the Communist Party. As was said in *Barenblatt*, "petitioner refused to answer questions as to his own Communist Party affiliations, whose pertinency of course was clear beyond doubt." The contention that the pertinency of the question was not made clear to the petitioner at the time he was directed to answer it is equally without foundation. After the Staff Director gave a detailed explanation of the question's pertinency, the petitioner said nothing to indicate that he entertained any doubt on this score.

We come finally to the claim that the subcommittee's interrogation of the petitioner violated his rights under the First Amendment. The basic issues which this contention raises were thoroughly canvassed by us in *Barenblatt*. Substantially all that was said there is equally applicable here, and it would serve no purpose to enlarge this opinion with a paraphrased repetition of what was in that opinion thoughtfully considered and carefully expressed.

It is sought to differentiate this case upon the basis that "the activities in which petitioner was believed to be participating consisted of public criticism of the Committee and attempts to influence public opinion to petition Congress for redress—to abolish the Committee." But we cannot say that, simply because the petitioner at the moment may have been engaged in lawful conduct, his Communist activities in connection therewith could not be investigated. The subcommittee had reasonable ground to suppose that the petitioner was an active Communist Party member, and that as such he possesed information that would substantially aid it in its legislative investigation. As the *Barenblatt* opinion makes clear, it is the nature of the Communist activity involved, whether the momentary conduct is legitimate or illegitimate politically, that establishes the Government's overbalancing interests. "To suggest that because the Communist Party may also sponsor peaceable political reforms the constitutional issues before us should now be judged as if that Party were just an ordinary political party from the standpoint of national security, is to ask this Court to blind itself to world affairs which have determined the whole course of our national policy since the close of World War II. . . ."

The subcommittee's legitimate legislative interest was not the activity in which the petitioner might have happened at the time to be engaged, but in the manipulation and infiltration of activities and organizations by persons advocating overthrow of the Government. "The strict requirements of a prosecution under the Smith Act . . . are not the measure of the permissible scope of a congressional investigation into 'overthrow,' for of necessity the investigatory process must proceed step by step."

We conclude that the First Amendment claims pressed here are indistinguishable from those considered in *Barenblatt*, and that upon the reasoning and the authority of that case they cannot prevail.

Affirmed.

Mr. Justice Black, with whom The Chief Justice and Mr. Justice Douglas concur, dissenting:

In July 1958 the House Un-American Activities Committee announced its intention to conduct a series of hearings in Atlanta, Georgia, ostensibly to obtain information in aid of the legislative function of the House of Representatives. Petitioner, a long-time opponent of the Committee, decided to go to Atlanta for the purpose of lending his support to those who were fighting against the hearings. He arrived in Atlanta and registered in a hotel there on July 23 as a representative of the Emergency Civil Liberties Committee, a New York organization which was working for the abolition of the Un-American Activities Committee. Within an hour of his registration, petitioner was served with a subpoena requiring his appearance before the Committee. When he appeared in response to this subpoena, petitioner was told that he had been subpoenaed because the Committee was informed that "you were sent to this area by the Communist Party for the purpose of developing a hostile sentiment to this Committee and to its work for the purpose of undertaking to bring pressure upon the United States Congress to preclude these particular hearings." A number of questions were then put to petitioner all of which related to his personal beliefs and associations, but petitioner refused to answer any of these questions on the ground that they violated his rights under the First Amendment. For this, he was convicted under 2 U.S.C. § 192 and sentenced to jail for 12 months.

On these facts, which are undisputed in the record, the majority upholds petitioner's conviction as "indistinguishable" from that upheld in *Barenblat* v. *United States*. On this point, I find myself only partially in disagreement with the majority. I think this case could and should be distinguished from Barenblatt on the ground urged by Mr. Justice Douglas—that the resolution authorizing the Un-American Activities Committee does not authorize that Committee to interrogate a person for criticizing it. I therefore join in the dissent filed by Mr. Justice Douglas on that ground. On the other hand, I must agree with the majority that so far as petitioner's constitutional claims are concerned, *Barenblatt* is "indistinguishable." Unlike the majority, however, I regard this recognition of the unlimited sweep of the decision in the *Barenblatt* case a compelling reason, not to reaffirm that case, but to overrule it.

In my view, the majority by its decision today places the stamp of constitutional approval upon a practice as clearly inconsistent with the Constitution, and indeed with every ideal of individual freedom for which this country has so long stood, as any that has ever come before this Court. For, like Mr. Justice Douglas, I think it clear that this case involves nothing more nor less than an attempt by the Un-American Activities Committee to use the contempt power of the House of Representatives as a weapon against those who dare to criticize it. The majority does not and, in reason, could not deny this for the conclusion is all but inescapable for anyone who will take the time to read the record. They say instead that it makes no difference whether the Committee was harassing petitioner solely by reason of his opposition to it or not because "it is not for us to speculate as to the motivations that may have prompted the decision of individual members of the subcommittee to summon the petitioner." The clear thrust of this sweeping abdication of judicial power is that the Committee may continue to harass its opponents with absolute impunity so long as the "protections" of *Barenblatt* are observed. Since this is to be the rule under which the Committee will be permitted to operate, I think it necessary in the interest of fairness to those who may in the future wish to exercise their constitutional right to criticize the Committee that the true nature of those "protections" be clearly set forth.

The first such "protection" relates to the question of whom the Committee may call before it. Is there any limitation upon the power of the Committee to subpoena and compel testimony from anyone who attacks it? On this point, the majority, relying upon the fact that at a previous hearing the Committee was told by a paid informant that petitioner was a Communist and upon statements by the Committee's counsel to the effect that the Committee had information that petitioner had been sent to Atlanta by the Communist Party, says simply: "It is to be emphasized that the petitioner was not summoned to appear as the result of an indiscriminate dragnet procedure, lacking in probable cause for belief that he possessed information which might be helpful to the subcommittee." Significantly, the majority does not say just how much its "emphasis" on this point is worth, if anything. Thus, for all that appears in the majority opinion, there is no assurance that the Committee will be required to produce any information at all as a prerequisite to the exercise of its subpoena and contempt powers. Assuming for the sake of argument, however, that such a requirement will be imposed, it then becomes relevant to inquire as to just how much this requirement will mean in terms of genuine protection for those who in good faith wish to criticize the Committee.

That inquiry is, to my mind, satisfactorily settled by a look at the facts of this case. So far as appears from this record, the only information the Committee had with regard to petitioner was the testimony of a paid informant at a previous Committee hearing. The only evidence to the effect that petitioner was in fact a member of the Communist Party that emerges from that testimony is a flat conclusory statement by the informant that it was so. No testimony as to particular happenings upon which such a conclusion could rationally be based was given at that hearing. When this fact is considered in conjunction with the fact that petitioner was not accorded the opportunity to cross-examine the informant or the protection of the statute permitting inspection of statements given to the F.B.I. by paid informants, it seems obvious to me that such testimony is almost totally worthless for the purpose of establishing probable cause. For all we know, the informant may have had no basis at all for her conclusion and, indeed, the possibility of perjury cannot, in view of its frequent recurrence in these sorts of cases, be entirely discounted. Thus, in my view, the "protection" afforded by a requirement of some sort of probable cause, even if imposed, is almost totally worthless. In the atmosphere existing in this country today, the charge that someone is a Communist is so common that hardly anyone active in public life escapes it. Every member of this Court has, on one occasion or another, been so designated. And a vast majority of the members of the other two branches of Government have fared no better. If the mere fact that someone has been called a Communist is to be permitted to satisfy a requirement of probable cause, I think it plain that such a requirement is wholly without value. To impose it would only give apparent respectability to a practice which is inherently in conflict with our concepts of justice and due process.

The other such "protection" afforded to critics of the Un-American Activities Committee under these decisions is included in the majority's so-called balancing test. Under that test, we are told, this Court will permit only those abridgments of personal beliefs and associations by Committee inquiry that the Court believes so important in terms of the need of the Committee for information that such need outweighs the First Amendment rights of the witness and the public. For my part, I need look no further than this very case to see how little protection this high-sounding slogan really affords. For in this case the majority is holding that the interest of the Committee in the information sought outweighs that of the witness and the public in free discussion while, at the same time, it disclaims any power to determine whether the Committee is in fact interested in the information at all. The truth of the matter is that the balancing test, at least as applied to date, means that the Committee may engage in *any* inquiry a majority of this Court happens to think could possibly be for a legitimate purpose whether that "purpose" be the true reason for the inquiry or not. And under the tests of legitimacy that are used in this area, any first-year law school student worth his salt could construct a rationalization to justify almost any question put to any witness at any time.

Thus, in my view, the conclusion is inescapable that the only real limitation upon the Committee's power to harass its opponents is the Committee's own self-restraint, a characteristic which probably has not been predominant in the Committee's work over the past few years. The result of all this is that from now on anyone who takes a public position contrary to that being urged by the House Un-American Activities Committee should realize that he runs the risk of being subpoenaed to appear at a hearing in some far off place, of being questioned with regard to every minute detail of his past life, of being asked to repeat all the gossip he may have heard about any of his friends and acquaintances, of being accused by the Committee of membership in the Communist Party, of being held up to the public as a subversive and a traitor, of being jailed for contempt if he refuses to co-operate with the Committee in its probe of his mind and associations, and of being branded by his neighbors, employer and erstwhile friends as a menace to society *regardless of the outcome of that hearing*. With such a powerful weapon in its hands, it seems quite likely that the Committee will weather all criticism, even though justifiable, that may be directed toward it. For there are not many people in our society who will have the courage to speak out against such a formidable opponent. . . . If the present trend continues, this already small number will necessarily dwindle as their ranks are thinned by the jails. Government by consent will disappear to be replaced by government by intimidation because some people are afraid that this country cannot survive unless Congress has the power to set aside the freedoms of the First Amendment at will.

I can only reiterate my firm conviction that these people are tragically wrong. This country was not built by men who were afraid and it cannot be preserved by such men.* Our Constitution, in unequivocal terms, gives the right to each of us to say what we think without fear of the power of the Government. That principle has served us so well for so long that I cannot believe it necessary to allow any governmental group to reject it in order to preserve its own existence. Least of all do I believe that such a privilege should be accorded the House Un-American Activities Committee. For I believe that true Americanism is to be protected, not by committees that persecute unorthodox minorities, but by strict adherence to basic principles of freedom that are responsible for this Nation's greatness. Those principles are embodied for all who care to see in our Bill of Rights. They were put there for the specific purpose of preventing just the sort of governmental suppression of criticism that the majority upholds here. Their ineffectiveness to that end stems, not from any lack of precision in the statement of the principles, but from the refusal of the majority to apply those principles as precisely stated. For the principles of the First Amendment are stated in precise and mandatory terms and unless they are applied in those terms, the freedoms of religion, speech, press, assembly and petition will have no effective protection. Where these freedoms are left to depend upon a balance to be struck by this Court in each particular case, liberty cannot survive. For under such a rule, there are no constitutional rights that cannot be "balanced" away.

Mr. Justice Douglas, with whom The Chief Justice and Mr. Justice Black concur, dissenting:

When petitioner was summoned before a subcommittee of the House Committee on Un-American Activities in Atlanta, Georgia, the Staff Director for the Committee made the following statement to him:

> It is the information of the committee or the suggestion of the committee that in anticipation of the hearings here in Atlanta, Georgia, you were sent to this area by the Communist Party for the purpose of developing a hostile sentiment to this committee and to its work for the purpose of undertaking to bring pressure upon the United States Congress to preclude these particular hearings. Indeed it is the fact that you were not even subpoenaed for these particular hearings until we

---

* Mr. Justice Brandeis made this very point in his concurring opinion in *Whitney* v. *California*, where he said: "Those who won our independence believed that the final end of the State was to make men free to develop their faculties; and that in its government the deliberative forces should prevail over the arbitrary. They valued liberty both as an end and as a means. They believed liberty to be the secret of happiness and courage to be the secret of liberty." 274 U.S. 357, 375. Mr. Justice Brandeis doubtless had in mind, and indeed made specific reference to, the famous words in Thomas Jefferson's first inaugural address: "If there be any among us who would wish to dissolve this union or change its republican form, let them stand undisturbed as monuments of the safety with which error of opinion may be tolerated where reason is left free to combat it."

learned that you were in town for that very purpose and that you were not subpoenaed to appear before this committee until you had actually registered in the hotel here in Atlanta.

Now, sir, if you will tell this committee whether or not, while you are under oath, you are now a Communist, we intend to pursue that area of inquiry and undertake to solicit from you information respecting your activities as a Communist on behalf of the Communist Party, which is tied up directly with the Kremlin; your activities from the standpoint of propaganda; your activities from the standpoint of undertaking to destroy the Federal Bureau of Investigation and the Committee on Un-American Activities, because indeed this committee issued a report entitled "Operation Abolition," in which we told something, the information we then possessed, respecting the efforts of the Emergency Civil Liberties Committee, of which you are the guiding light, to destroy the F.B.I. and discredit the director of the F.B.I. and to undertake to hamstring the work of this Committee on Un-American Activities.

So if you will answer that principal question, I intend to pursue the other questions with you to solicit information which would be of interest—which will be of vital necessity, indeed—to this committee in undertaking to develop legislation to protect the United States of America under whose flag you, sir, have protection.

Now please answer the question: "Are you now a member of the Communist Party?"

Petitioner answered, "I am refusing to answer any questions of this committee."

After a further explanation he was directed to answer. He replied:

I have the utmost respect for the broad powers which the Congress of the United States must have to carry on its investigations for legislative purposes. However, the United States Supreme Court has held that, broad as these powers may be, the Congress cannot investigate into an area where it cannot legislate, and this committee tends, by its mandate and by its practices, to investigate into precisely those areas of free speech, religion, peaceful association and assembly, and the press, wherein it cannot legislate and therefore it cannot investigate.

The Committee is authorized by the Resolution governing it to make investigations of "the extent, character, and objects of un-American propaganda activities in the United States."

If it is "un-American" to criticize, impeach, and berate the Committee and to seek to have it abolished, then the Committee acted within the scope of its authority in asking the questions. But we take a dangerous leap when we reach the conclusion that criticism of the Committee was within the scope of the Resolution.

Criticism of government finds sanctuary in several portions of the First Amendment. It is part of the right of free speech. It embraces freedom of the press. Can editors be summoned before the Committee and be made to account for their editorials denouncing the Committee, its tactics, its practices, its policies? If petitioner can be questioned concerning his opposition to the Committee, then I see no reason why editors are immune. The list of editors will be long as evident from the editorial protests against the Committee's activities, including its recent film, Operation Abolition.

The First Amendment rights involved here are more than freedom of speech and press. Bringing people together in peaceable assemblies is in the same category. *De Jonge* v. *Oregon*, 299 U.S. 353. "The right of peaceable assembly is a right cognate to those of free speech and free press and is equally fundamental." *Id.*, at 364. The right to petition "for a redress of grievances" is also part of the First Amendment; it too is fundamental to "the very idea of a government, republican in form." *United States* v. *Cruikshank*, 92 U.S. 542. Chief Justice Hughes, speaking for the Court in the *De Jonge* case involving communist activities no more nor less lawful than those charged here, said:

> The greater the importance of safeguarding the community from incitements to the overthrow of our institutions by force and violence, the more imperative is the need to preserve inviolate the constitutional rights of free speech, free press and free assembly in order to maintain the opportunity for free political discussion, to the end that government may be responsive to the will of the people and that changes, if desired, may be obtained by peaceful means. Therein lies the security of the Republic, the very foundation of constitutional government.

These are reasons why I would construe the Resolution narrowly so as to exclude criticism of the Committee. We have customarily done just that, insisting that if "an inquiry of dubious limits" is to be found in an Act or Resolution, Congress should unequivocally authorize it. . . .

The indictment charged only the failure to answer the one question, "Are you now a member of the Communist Party?" That question in other contexts might well have been appropriate. We have here, however, an investigation whose central aim was finding out what criticism a citizen was making of the government. That was the gist of the case presented to the jury.

We cannot allow this man to go to prison for 12 months unless we hold that an investigation of those who criticize the Un-American Activities Committee was both authorized and constitutional. I cannot read the Resolution as authorizing that kind of investigation without assuming that the Congress intended to flout the First Amendment.

Mr. Justice Brennan, with whom Mr. Justice Douglas joins, dissenting:

For the reasons stated in my Brother Douglas' dissenting opinion in *Braden* v. *United States,* which I joined, I believe that the Committee failed to lay an adequate foundation at the hearing for questions which, it was claimed, concerned the exercise of rights protected by the First Amendment.

I also dissent because on these facts the inference is inescapable that the dominant purpose of these questions was not to gather information in aid of law-making or law-evaluation but rather to harass the petitioner and expose him for the sake of exposure. A scant 19 months before the hearing in question petitioner was summoned before this very Committee and refused to answer questions on substantially the same grounds as those he claimed in this instance. Nor did his conduct in the interim afford any basis for a hope that he might have repented. . . . For petitioner continued to proclaim his hostility to the Committee and his belief that it had no power to probe areas of free expression. He was not even called to testify at these hearings in Atlanta until the Committee learned that he was to be present in Atlanta to express his opposition to the Committee's work, as, of course, he had a right to do. In fact, the Committee's Staff Director came perilously close to admitting, on cross-examination by petitioner's counsel, that petitioner was called to the stand only because of his opposition to the Committee's activities.

It is particularly important that congressional committees confine themselves to the function of gathering information when their investigation begins to touch the realm of speech and opinion: On this record, I cannot help concluding that the Committee had no reasonable prospect that petitioner would answer its questions, and accordingly that the Committee's purpose could not have been the legitimate one of fact-gathering. I am forced to the view that the questions asked of petitioner were therefore not within the Committee's power. . . .

BRADEN v. UNITED STATES

365 US 431 (1961)

[This is a companion case to the *Wilkinson Case, supra.* Braden refused to answer questions put to him by a subcommittee of the House Un-American Activities Committee regarding his associations, including a question whether he was a member of the Communist Party when he signed a letter urging opposition to certain bills before Congress. He was convicted of contempt of Congress. The Supreme Court, by a 5-to-4 vote, upheld the conviction. Chief Justice Warren and Justices Black, Douglas, and Brennan dissented.]

Mr. Justice Stewart delivered the opinion of the Court:

This case is a companion to *Wilkinson* v. *United States*, decided today. The petitioner was the witness immediately preceding Wilkinson at the hearing of a subcommittee of the House Un-American Activites Committee, in Atlanta, Georgia, on July 30, 1958. He refused to answer many of the questions directed to him, basing his refusal upon the grounds that the questions were not pertinent to a question under inquiry by the subcommittee, and that the interrogation invaded his First Amendment rights. He was subsequently indicted and, after a jury trial, convicted for having violated 2 U.S.C. § 192, in refusing to answer six specific questions which had been put to him by the sub-committee. The Court of Appeals affirmed, relying on *Barenblatt* v. *United States*, 360 U.S. 109, and we granted certiorari.

The principal issues raised by the petitioner are substantially iden-tical to those considered in Wilkinson, and extended discussion is not required in resolving them. Based upon the same record that was brought here in Wilkinson, we conclude for the reasons stated there that the subjects under subcommittee investigation at the time the petitioner was interrogated were Communist infiltration into basic southern industry and Communist Party propaganda activities in the southern part of the United States. We conclude for the same reasons that the subcommittee's investigation of these subjects was authorized by Congress, that the interrogation was pertinent to a question under subcommittee inquiry, and that the petitioner was fully apprised of its pertinency.

In asserting a violation of his First Amendment rights, the petitioner here points out that he was asked, not simply whether he was or had been a Communist Party member, as in *Wilkinson* and *Barenblatt*, but whether he was a member "the instant you affixed your signature to that letter." The letter in question, which had admittedly been signed by the petitioner and his wife, urged opposition to certain bills in Congress. The petitioner emphasizes that the writing of such a letter is not only legitimate but constitutionally protected activity, and points to other evidence in the record to indicate that he had been active in other completely legitimate causes. Based upon these circumstances, he argues that the subcommittee did not have a proper legislative pur-pose in calling him before it, but that it was bent rather on persecuting him for publicly opppposing the subcommittee's activities. He contends that under such circumstances an inquiry into his personal and associa-tional conduct violated his First Amendment freedoms. On these grounds, the petitioner would differentiate the constitutional issues here from those that were before the Court in *Barenblatt, supra*.

But *Barenblatt* did not confine Congressional Committee investiga-tion to overt criminal activity, nor did that case determine that Con-gress can only investigate the Communist Party itself. Rather, the decision upheld an investigation of Communist activity in education. Education, too, is legitimate and protected activity. Communist in-filtration and propaganda in a given area of the country, which were the subjects of the subcommittee investigation here, are surely as much within its pervasive authority as Communist activity in educational institutions. The subcommittee had reason to believe that the petitioner was a member of the Communist Party, and that he had been actively engaged in propaganda efforts. It was making a legislative inquiry into Communist Party propaganda activities in the southern States. Information as to the extent to which the Communist Party was utilizing legitimate organizations and causes in its propaganda efforts in that region was surely not constitutionally beyond the reach of the subcommittee's inquiry. Upon the reasoning and authority of *Barenblatt*, we hold that the judgment is not to be set aside on First Amendment grounds.

The petitioner in this case raises two additional issues that were not considered either in *Barenblatt*, or in *Wilkinson*. First, he says that it was error for the trial court not to leave it for the jury to determine whether the questions asked by the subcommittee were pertinent to the subject under inquiry. Secondly, he asserts that he could not properly be convicted, because in refusing to answer the subcommittee's questions he relied upon his understanding of the meaning of previous decisions of this Court. We think that both of these contentions have been foreclosed by *Sinclair* v. *United States*, 279 U.S. 263.

At the trial the district judge determined as a matter of law that the questions were pertinent to a matter under inquiry by the subcommittee, leaving to the jury the question whether the pertinence of the questions had been brought home to the petitioner. It is to be noted that counsel made no timely objection to this procedure and, indeed, affirmatively acquiesced in it. But we need not base rejection of the petitioner's contention here on that ground, for in any event, it was proper for the court to determine the question as a matter of law. This is precisely what was held in *Sinclair* v. *United States*, where the Court said at 279 U.S. 299: "The reasons for holding relevancy and materiality to be questions of law . . . apply with equal force to the determination of pertinency arising under § 102 [the predecessor of 2 U.S.C. § 192]. The matter for determination in this case was whether the facts called for by the question were so related to the subjects covered by the Senate's resolutions that such facts reasonably could be said to be 'pertinent to the question under inquiry.' It would be incongruous and contrary to well-established principles to leave the determination of such a matter to a jury."

During his interrogation the petitioner was asked: "Now do I understand that you have refused to answer the question as to whether or not you are now a member of the Communist Party solely upon the invocation of the provisions of the first amendment, but that you have not invoked the protection of the fifth amendment to the Constitution. Is that correct?" He gave the following answer: "That is right, sir. I am standing on the *Watkins, Sweezy, Konigsberg,* and other decisions of the United States Supreme Court which protect my right, and the

Constitution as they interpret the Constitution of the United States, protecting my right to private belief and association."

It is now argued that because he relied upon his understanding of this Court's previous decisions he could not be convicted under the statute for failing to answer the questions. An almost identical contention was also rejected in *Sinclair* v. *United States, supra:* "There is no merit in appellant's contention that he is entitled to a new trial because the court excluded evidence that in refusing to answer he acted in good faith on the advice of competent counsel. The gist of the offense is refusal to answer pertinent questions. No moral turpitude is involved. Intentional violation is sufficient to constitute guilt. There was no misapprehension as to what was called for. The refusal to answer was deliberate. The facts sought were pertinent as a matter of law, and § 102 made it appellant's duty to answer. He was bound rightly to construe the statute. His mistaken view of law is no defense."

Here, as in *Sinclair,* the refusal to answer was deliberate and intentional.

Affirmed.

Mr. Justice Black, with whom The Chief Justice and Mr. Justice Douglas concur, dissenting:

The petitioner in this case, as is shown by the facts set forth in the dissenting opinion of Mr. Justice Douglas, in which I concur, has for some time been at odds with strong sentiment favoring racial segregation in his home State of Kentucky. A white man himself, the petitioner has nonetheless spoken out strongly against that sentiment. This activity, which once before resulted in his being charged with a serious crime, seems also to have been the primary reason for his being called before the Un-American Activities Committee. For the occasion of that Committee's compelling petitioner to go from Rhode Island, where he was vacationing, to Atlanta for questioning appears from the record to have been the circulation of two letters, both in the nature of petitions to Congress, urging that certain legislative action be taken which, in the view of the signers of the petitions, would help those working against segregation. One of these petitions, signed by petitioner and his wife, asked those who read it to urge their representatives in Congress to vote against proposed legislation which would have empowered the States to enact antisedition statutes because, in the view of the signers, those statutes could too readily be used against citizens working for integration. The other petition, bearing the signature of 200 southern Negroes, was sent directly to the House of Representatives and requested that body not to allow the Un-American Activities Committee to conduct hearings in the South because, so the petition charged, "all of its [the Committee's] activities in recent years suggest that it is much more interested in harassing and labeling as 'subversive' any citizen who is inclined to be liberal or an independent thinker." The record shows that the Committee apparently believed that petitioner had drafted both of these petitions and that he had circulated them, not—as would appear from the face of the petitions—for the purpose of furthering the cause of integration, but for the purpose of furthering the interests of the Communist Party, of which the Committee claimed to have information that he was a member, by fomenting racial strife and interfering with the investigations of the Un-American Activities Committee.

When petitioner appeared in response to this subpoena, he was asked a number of questions regarding his personal beliefs and associations, culminating in the question of whether he was a member of the Communist Party at "the instant" he affixed his signature to the petition urging defeat of the statute authorizing state antisedition laws. Petitioner refused to answer these questions on the grounds, first, that the Committee had no power to ask the questions it put to him, and, secondly, that he could properly refuse to answer such questions under the First Amendment. For this refusal to answer he, like Frank Wilkinson who followed him on the witness stand at the Atlanta hearing, was convicted under 2 U.S.C. § 192 and sentenced to 12 months in jail. And, as was the case with the conviction of Wilkinson, the majority here affirms petitioner's conviction "[u]pon the reasoning and authority" of *Barenblatt* v. *United States*.

Again I must agree with the majority that insofar as the conviction is attacked on constitutional grounds, the decision in *Barenblatt* constitutes ample authority for its action, even though it cannot be denied that the Committee's conduct constitutes a direct abridgment of the right of petition. Indeed, I thing the majority might well have, with equal justification, relied upon a much earlier decision of this Court, that in *Beauharnais* v. *Illinois*. For it was there that a majority of this Court first applied to the right of petition the flexible constitutional rule upon which the decision in this case is based—the rule that the right of petition, though guaranteed in precise and mandatory terms by the First Amendment, may be abandoned at any time Government can offer a reason for doing so that a majority of this Court finds sufficiently compelling. Ironically, the need there asserted by the State of Illinois and accepted by a majority of this Court as sufficiently compelling to warrant abridgment of the right of petition was the need to protect Negroes against what was subsequently labeled "libel . . . of a racial group," although it was actually nothing more than the circulation of a petition seeking governmental and public support for a program of racial segregation. Thus, the decision in *Beauharnais* had all the outward appearances of being one which would aid the underprivileged Negro minority. This decision, however, is a dramatic illustration of the shortsightedness of such an interpretation of that case. For the very constitutional philosophy that gave birth to *Beauharnais* today gives birth to a decision which may well strip the Negro of the aid of many of the white people who have been willing to speak up in his behalf. If the House Un-American Activities Committee is to have the power to interrogate everyone who is called a Communist, there is one thing certain beyond the peradventure of a doubt—no legislative committee, state or federal, will have trouble finding cause to subpoena all persons anywhere who take a public stand for or against segregation. The lesson to be learned from these two cases is, to my mind, clear. Liberty, to be secure for any, must be secure for all—even for the most miserable merchants of hated and unpopular ideas.

Both *Barenblatt* and *Beauharnais* are offspring of a constitutional doctrine that is steadily sacrificing individual freedom of religion, speech, press, assembly and petition to governmental control. There have been many other such decisions and the indications are that this number will continue to grow at an alarming rate. For the presently prevailing constitutional doctrine, which treats the First Amendment as a mere admonition, leaves the liberty-giving freedoms which were intended to be protected by that Amendment completely at the mercy of Congress and this Court whenever a majority of this Court concludes, on the basis of any of the several judicially created "tests" now in vogue, that abridgment of these freedoms is more desirable than freedom itself. Only a few days ago, the application of this constitutional doctrine wiped out the rule forbidding prior censorship of movies in an opinion that leaves the door wide open, if indeed it does not actually invite, prior censorship of other means of publication. And the Blackstonian condemnation of prior censorship had long been thought, even by those whose idea of First Amendment liberties have been most restricted, to be the absolute minimum of the protection demanded by that Amendment.

I once more deny, as I have found it repeatedly necessary to do in other cases, that this Nation's ability to preserve itself depends upon suppression of the freedoms of religion, speech, press, assembly and petition. But I do believe that the noble-sounding slogan of "self-preservation" rests upon a premise that can itself destroy any democratic nation by a slow process of eating away at the liberties that are indispensable to its healthy growth. The very foundation of a true democracy and the foundation upon which this Nation was built is the fact that government is responsive to the views of its citizens, and no nation can continue to exist on such a foundation unless its citizens are wholly free to speak out fearlessly for or against their officials and their laws. When it begins to send its dissenters, such as Barenblatt, Uphaus, Wilkinson, and now Braden, to jail, the liberties indispensable to its existence must be fast disappearing. If self-preservation is to be the issue that decides these cases, I firmly believe they must be decided the other way. Only by a dedicated preservation of the freedoms of the First Amendment can we hope to preserve our Nation and its traditional way of life.

It is already past the time when people who recognize and cherish the life-giving and life-preserving qualities of the freedoms protected by the Bill of Rights can afford to sit complacently by while those freedoms are being destroyed by sophistry and dialectics. For at least 11 years, since the decision of this Court in *American Communications Assn.* v. *Douds*, the forces of destruction have been hard at work. Much damage has already been done. If this dangerous trend is not stopped now, it may be an impossible task to stop it at all. The area set off for individual freedom by the Bill of Rights was marked by boundaries precisely defined. It is my belief that the area so set off provides an adequate minimum protection for the freedoms indispensable to individual liberty. Thus we have only to observe faithfully the boundaries already marked for us. For the present, however, the two cases decided by this Court today and the many others like them that have been decided in the past 11 years have all but obliterated those boundaries. There are now no limits to congressional encroachment in this field except such as a majority of this Court may choose to set by a value-weighing process on a case-by-case basis.

I cannot accept such a process. As I understand it, this Court's duty to guard constitutional liberties is to guard those liberties the Constitution defined, not those that may be defined from case to case on the basis of this Court's judgment as to the relative importance of individual liberty and governmental power. The majority's approach makes the First Amendment, not the rigid protection of liberty its language imports, but a poor flexible imitation. This weak substitute for the First Amendment is, to my mind, totally unacceptable for I believe that Amendment forbids, among other things, any agency of the federal government—be it legislative, executive or judicial—to harass or punish people for their beliefs, or for their speech about, or public criticism of, laws and public officials. The Founders of this Nation were not then willing to trust the definition of First Amendment freedoms to Congress or this Court, nor am I now. History and the affairs of the present day show that the Founders were right. There are grim reminders all around this world that the distance between individual liberty and firing squads is not always as far as it seems. I would overrule *Barenblatt*, its forerunners and its progeny, and return to the language of the Bill of Rights. The new and different course the Court is following is too dangerous.

Mr. Justice Douglas, with whom The Chief Justice, Mr. Justice Black and Mr. Justice Brennan concur, dissenting:

At the bottom of this case are this Court's decisions in *Pennsylvania* v. *Nelson*, 350 U.S. 497, holding that Congress did not entrust to the States protection of the Federal Government against sedition, and *Brown* v. *Board of Education*, 347 U.S. 483, holding that racial segregation of students in public schools is unconstitutional. I had supposed until today that one could agree or disagree with those decisions without being hounded for his belief and sent to jail for concluding that his belief was beyond the reach of government.

On June 17, 1957, we decided *Watkins* v. *United States*, 354 U.S. 178, defining and curtailing the authority of Congressional Committees who sought the aid of the courts in holding witnesses in contempt. We said in a six-to-one decision that "when First Amendment rights are threatened, the delegation of power to the committee must be clearly revealed in its charter"; that "there is no Congressional power to expose for the sake of exposure"; that the meaning of "un-American" in the Resolution defining the Committee's authority is so vague that it is "difficult to imagine a less explicit authorizing resolution"; that before a witness chooses between answering or not answering he is entitled "to have knowledge of the subject to which the interrogation is deemed pertinent"; that in that case the Resolution and the statement of the Committee's chairman was "woefully inadequate to convey sufficient information as to the pertinency of the questions to the subject under inquiry."

Sweezy v. *New Hampshire*, 354 U.S. 234, decided the same day as the *Watkins* case reversed a conviction arising out of a state investigation into "subversive activities" where a teacher was asked questions concerning his relation to Marxism. The Chief Justice in his opinion stated:

> Equally manifest as a fundamental principle of a democratic society is political freedom of the individual. Our form of government 'is built on the premise that every citizen shall have the right to engage in political expression and association. This right was enshrined in the First Amendment of the Bill of Rights. Exercise of these basic freedoms in America has traditionally been through the media of political associations. Any interference with the freedom of a party is simultaneously an interference with the freedom of its adherents. All political ideas cannot and should not be channeled into the programs of our two major parties. History has amply proved the virtue of political activity by minority, dissident groups, who innumerable times have been in the vanguard of democratic thought and whose programs were ultimately accepted. Mere unorthodoxy or dissent from the prevailing mores is not to be condemned. The absence of such voices would be a symptom of grave illness in our society.

The concurring opinion stated:

> Progress in the natural sciences is not remotely confined to findings made in the laboratory. Insights into the mysteries of nature are born of hypothesis and speculation. The more so is this true in the pursuit of understanding in the groping endeavors of what are called the social sciences, the concern of which is man and society. The problems that are the respective preoccupations of anthropology, economics, law, psychology, sociology and related areas of scholarship are merely departmentalized dealing, by way of manageable division of analysis, with interpenetrating aspects of holistic perplexities. For society's good —if understanding be an essential need of society—inquiries into these problems, speculations about them, stimulation in others of reflection upon them, must be left as unfettered as possible. Political power must abstain from intrusion into this activity of freedom, pursued in the interest of wise government and the people's well-being, except for reasons that are exigent and obviously compelling.

On June 8, 1959—two years after the *Watkins* and *Sweezy* decisions—we decided *Barenblatt* v. *United States*, 360 U.S. 109, where a divided Court gave only slight consideration to the type of pertinency claim that was raised in *Watkins*, *Sweezy* and the present case, in part because it could rely on the petitioner's failure to raise that objection before the Committee.

Petitioner, who was called as a witness by the Committee in July 1958, which was even before *Barenblatt* was decided, refused to answer, relying on the *Watkins* and *Sweezy* decisions "as they interpret the Constitution of the United States, protecting my right to private belief and association."

I think he was entitled to rely on them. The Act under which he stands convicted states that a witness is guilty if he "wilfully makes default, or who having appeared, refuses to answer any question pertinent to the question under inquiry." 2 U.S.C. § 192. A refusal to answer was held in *Sinclair* v. *United States*, 279 U.S. 263, not to be justified because one acted in good faith, the Court saying, "His mistaken view of the law is no defense." Yet no issue concerning the First Amendment was involved in the *Sinclair* case. When it is involved, as it is here, the propriety of the question in terms of pertinency should be narrowly resolved.

The Resolution under which the Committee on Un-American Activities acted in this case is precisely the same as the one involved in *Watkins* v. *United States*. We said concerning it, "It would be difficult to imagine a less explicit authorizing resolution. Who can define the meaning of 'un-American'? What is that single, solitary 'principle of the form of government as guaranteed by our Constitution'? . . . At one time, perhaps, the resolution might have been read narrowly to confine the Committee to the subject of propaganda. The events that have transpired in the fifteen years before the interrogation of petitioner make such a construction impossible at this date."

We emphasized the need, when First Amendment rights were implicated, to lay a foundation before probing that area. The authority of the Committee must then "be clearly revealed in its charter." The "specific legislative need" must be disclosed. The pertinency of the questions and the subject matter under inquiry must be made known "with the same degree of explicitness and clarity that the Due Process Clause requires in the expression of any element of a criminal offense."

After *Watkins* anyone was entitled to rely on those propositions for protection of his First Amendment rights. The conditions and circumstances under which the questions were asked petitioner plainly did not satisfy the requirements specified in *Watkins*.

The setting of the six questions which were asked petitioner and which he refused to answer show nothing more than an exercise by him of First Amendment rights of speech and press and of petition to Congress. It was not shown that they were part of a matrix for the overthrow of government. It was not shown—unless the bare word of the Committee is taken as gospel —that these constitutional activities had any relation whatever to communism, subversion, or illegal activity of any sort or kind. It was not shown where and how the Committee was ever granted the right to investigate those who petition Congress for redress of grievances.

Petitioner and his wife were field secretaries of an organization known as the Southern Conference Educational Fund. Prior to the committee hearing at Atlanta, Georgia, they wrote a letter on the letterhead of the Southern Conference urging people to write their Congressmen and Senators to oppose three bills pending before the Congress which would, to use their words, "nullify" a decision of this Court "declaring state sedition laws inoperative." They added "We are especially concerned about this because we know from our own experience how such laws can be used against people working to bring about integration in the South. Most of these state statutes are broad and loosely worded, and to the officials of many of our Southern states integration is sedition. You can imagine what may happen if every little prosecutor in the South is turned loose with the state sedition law."

Also prior to the Committee hearing in Atlanta, a group of Negroes petitioned Congress against the proposed Atlanta investigation of the House Committee on Un-American Activities. That petition stated:

We are informed that the Committee on Un-American Activities of the House of Representatives is planning to hold hearings in Atlanta, Georgia, at an early date.

As Negroes residing in Southern states and the District of Columbia, all deeply involved in the struggle to secure full and equal rights for our people, we are very much concerned by this development.

We are acutely aware of the fact that there is at the present time a shocking amount of un-American activity in our Southern states. To cite only a few examples, there are the bombings of the homes, schools, and houses of worship of not only Negroes but also of our Jewish citizens; the terror against Negroes in Dawson, Ga.; the continued refusal of boards of registrars in many Southern communities to allow Negroes to register and vote; and the activities of White Citizens Councils encouraging open defiance of the United States Supreme Court.

However, there is nothing in the record of the House Committee on Un-American Activities to indicate that, if it comes South, it will investigate these things. On the contrary, all of its activities in recent years suggest that it is much more interested in harassing and labeling as 'subversive' any citizen who is inclined to be liberal or an independent thinker.

For this reason, we are alarmed at the prospect of this committee coming South to follow the lead of Senator Eastland, as well as several state investigating committees, in trying to attach the 'subversive' label to any liberal white Southerner who dares to raise his voice in support of our democratic ideals.

It was recently pointed out by four Negro leaders who met with President Eisenhower that one of our great needs in the South is to build lines of communication between Negro and white Southerners. Many people in the South are seeking to do this. But if white people who support integration are labeled 'subversive' by congressional committees, terror is spread among our white citizens and it becomes increasingly difficult to find white people who are willing to support our efforts for full citizenship. Southerners, white and Negro, who strive today for full democracy must work at best against tremendous odds. They need the support of every agency of our Federal Government. It is unthinkable that they should instead be harassed by committees of the United States Congress.

We therefore urge you to use your influence to see that the House

Committee on Un-American Activities stays out of the South—unless it can be persuaded to come to our region to help defend us against those subversives who oppose our Supreme Court, our Federal policy of civil rights for all, and our American ideals of equality and brotherhood.

Petitioner was charged by the Committee with preparing that petition; counsel for the Committee later stated that the purpose of the petition was "precluding or attempting to preclude or softening the very hearings which we proposed to have here." The Committee said that it was not concerned with integration. It said that "A number of names on that letter were names of those who had been closely associated with the Communist Party. Their interest and major part does not lie with honest integration. Their interest lies with the purposes of the Communist Party. And that is what we are looking into. . . ."

Two of the questions which petitioner refused to answer pertained to the Southern Conference, the first one being "Did you participate in a meeting here at that time?" And the second one was "Who solicited quarters to be made available to the Southern Conference Educational Fund?"

Two other questions which petitioner refused to answer related to the Emergency Civil Liberties Committee. The first of these was "Are you connected with the Emergency Civil Liberties Committee?" The second one was "Did you and Harvey O'Connor in the course of your conferences there in Rhode Island develop plans and strategy outlining work schedules for the Emergency Civil Liberties Committee?" The Committee counsel charged that Mr. O'Connor was "a hard-core member of the communist conspiracy, head of the Emergency Civil Liberties Committee."

A fifth question which petitioner refused to answer related to the letter I have previously mentioned which he and his wife sent to the people urging them to write their Senators and Congressmen opposing three bills that would reinstate state sedition laws. The question relating to this letter was "Were you a member of the Communist Party the instant you affixed your signature to that letter?"

The sixth and final question which petitioner refused to answer concerned the Southern Newsletter. Counsel asked if petitioner had "anything to do" with that letter. Petitioner replied "I think you are now invading freedom of the press. . . . I object to your invasion of the freedom of the press, and I also decline to answer the questions on the same grounds. You are not only attacking integrationists, you are attacking the press."

There is nothing in the record to show that the Southern Conference or the Emergency Civil Liberties Committee or the Southern Newsletter had the remotest connection with the Communist Party. There is only the charge of the Committee that there was such a connection. That charge amounts to little more than innuendo. This is particularly clear with respect to the question relating to petitioner's membership in the Communist Party. Having drawn petitioner's attention to the letter he had written, counsel for the Committee demanded to know if petitioner was a Communist "the instant you affixed your signature to that letter." No foundation at all had been laid for that question, and from the record no purpose for it appears, save the hope of the Committee to link communism with that letter which supported this Court's decision in *Pennsylvania* v. *Nelson, supra.* This Court, passing on the pertinency issue in *Barenblatt* v. *United States,* was careful to emphasize that Barenblatt "had heard the Subcommittee interrogate the witness Crowley along the same lines as he, petitioner, was evidently to be questioned, *and had listened to Crowley's testimony identifying him as a former member of an alleged Communist student orgainzation. . . .*" (Emphasis added.) No such foundation was ever laid here.

One would be wholly warranted, I think, in light of the *Watkins* and *Sweezy* decisions that a Committee's undisclosed information or unsupported surmise would not justify an investigation into matters that on their face seemed well within the First Amendment. If *Watkins* and *Sweezy* decided anything, they decided that before inroads in the First Amendment domain may be made, some demonstrable connection with communism must first be established and the matter be plainly shown to be within the scope of the Committee's authority. Otherwise the Committee may roam at will, requiring any individual to disclose his association with any group or with any publication which is unpopular with the Committee and which it can discredit by calling it communistic.

DEUTCH v. UNITED STATES
367 US 456 (1961)

[Defendant was convicted for refusing to answer questions put to him by a congressional subcommittee. By a 5-to-4 vote, the Supreme Court reversed, holding that the government had failed at the trial to carry the burden of proving the pertinancy of the questions put to the defendant. The subcommittee was supposed to be investigating Communist infiltration in the Albany, New York, area, particularly in the field of labor, whereas the questions put to Deutch related to Communist infiltration at a university located 165 miles from Albany—entirely different economic and geographic areas. Justice Harlan wrote a dissenting opinion, in which Justice Frankfurter joined, and Justice Whittaker wrote a dissenting opinion, in which Justice Clark joined.]

Mr. Justice Stewart delivered the opinion of the Court:

Once again we are called upon to review a criminal conviction for refusal to answer questions before a subcommittee of the Committee on Un-American Activities of the House of Representatives. . . . The petitioner was brought to trial in the District Court for the District of Columbia upon an indictment which charged that he had violated 2 U.S.C. § 192 by refusing to answer five questions "which were pertinent to the question then under inquiry" by the subcommittee. He waived a jury and was convicted upon four of the five counts of the indictment. The judgment was affirmed by the Court of Appeals, and we brought the case here because of doubt as to the validity of the conviction in the light of our previous decisions. A careful review of the trial record convinces us that the District Court should have ordered an acquittal.

At the trial the Government's case consisted largely of documentary evidence. That evidence showed that a subcommittee of the House Committee on Un-American Activities conducted hearings in Albany, New York, in July of 1953, and again in early April of 1954. The petitioner was not present on either occasion. He was subpoenaed to appear before the subcommittee in Albany on April 9, 1954, but, at the request of his counsel, it was agreed that he should appear instead before the subcommittee three days later in the Old House Office Building in Washington, D.C.

He appeared there on the appointed day, accompanied by counsel, and without further ado his interrogation began. The petitioner freely answered all preliminary questions, revealing that he was then twenty-four years old and a graduate student at the University of Pennsylvania. He stated that his early education had been in the public schools of Brooklyn, New York, from where he had gone to Cornell University in 1947 for four years as an undergraduate and two additional years as a graduate student.

The subcommittee's counsel then made the following statement:

Mr. Deutch, during hearings at Albany last week, the committee heard testimony regarding the existence of a Communist Party group or cell operating among undergraduates at Cornell University, among certain graduates at Cornell and in the city of Ithaca.

In connection with that testimony, the committee was informed that you were a member of one or more of those groups. If so, I would like to ask you certain matters relating to your activity there.

Were you a member of a group of the Communist Party at Cornell?

The petitioner answered, "under protest," that he had indeed been a member of the Communist Party while at Cornell. He then testified freely and without further objection as to his own activities and associations. He stated that "from the age of 13 or 14 I had read many books on Marxism and at that time was very much impressed with trying to solve certain of the injustices we have nowadays." He said that when he got to college "I felt if I had ideas I shouldn't be half pregnant about them, so when I came to college I was approached and joined." He stated that the approach to join the Party had been made by a student.

As to the general nature of his Communist Party acitvities at Cornell he said "about all that happened were bull sessions on Marxism, and some activities like giving out a leaflet or two. The people I met didn't advocate the overthrowing of the Government by force and violence, and if they had, I wouldn't have allowed it." He testified that he had known one faculty member at Cornell who was a Communist, but that this person had quit the Party. He stated that he had once received from "a personal friend," who was not connected with the Cornell faculty, a $100 contribution to give to the Party. He stated that he had been the only graduate student at Cornell who was a Communist, and that, as the "head" (and lone member) of the "graduate group," he had attended meetings in a private house where a "maximum of 4 or 5" people were present. Many of his answers indicated a lack of awareness of the details of Communist activities at Cornell.* The petitioner testified that as of the time of the hearings he was no longer a member of the Communist Party, but he volunteered the information that "[t]o a great extent it is only fair to say I am a Marxist today—I don't want to deny that."

While the petitioner's answers to the many questions put to him about his own activities and conduct were thus fully responsive, he refused to answer five questions he was asked concerning other people. He declined to give the names of the faculty member who had been a

* The following colloquies are typical:

"Mr. Doyle: Who published the leaflets?

"Mr. Deutch: I believe the Communist Party published them.

"Mr. Doyle: What Communist Party? Where did you get the leaflets? From the national headquarters?

"Mr. Deutch: I don't believe so. It was a local branch.

"Mr. Doyle: Where was the office of the local branch from which you got these leaflets?

"Mr. Deutch: I didn't know where it was. I was just asked to distribute them." . . .

"Mr. Tavenner: Were you ever a member of the Downtown Club of the Communist Party in Ithaca?

"Mr. Deutch: I don't believe so.

"Mr. Tavenner: Did you attend meetings of that group?

"Mr. Deutch: No. That is, I don't believe so. The reason I wonder is because that organization became defunct so that there was really no organization. Downtown was Uptown, and there were so few people that I just want to qualify that statement." . . .

"Mr. Scherer: Let me ask you this question. You knew where the meetings were held?

"Mr. Deutch: I don't believe I know exactly where they were. This is because— since Mr. Richardson drove me there." [Mr. Richardson was a law student at Cornell who had joined the Communist Party at the behest of the Federal Bureau of Investigation.]

Communist, of the friend who had made the $100 contribution, of the student who had originally approached him about joining the Communist Party, and of the owners of the house where the meetings had been held. He also declined to say whether he was acquainted with one Homer Owen. For his refusal to answer these questions he was indicted, tried, and convicted.

The reason which the petitioner gave the subcommittee for his refusal to answer these questions can best be put in his own words:

Sir, I am perfectly willing to tell about my own activities, but do you feel I should trade my moral scruples by informing on someone else? . . . . I can only say that whereas I do not want to be in contempt of the committee, I do not believe I can answer questions about other people, but only about myself. . . . I happen to have been a graduate student—the only one there, and the organization is completely defunct, and the individual you are interested in wasn't even a professor. The magnitude of this is really beyond reason.

The chairman of the subcommittee ruled that it was the petitioner's duty nevertheless to answer the questions:

That decision does not rest with you as to whether or not the scope of this inquiry—as to whether or not certain individuals are important now or not. That is the responsibility of we Representatives to determine. That determination cannot rest with you. It may be very true that the individual to whom you have referred is no longer a member of the Communist Party. However, that is a supposition on your part—and a supposition which the committee cannot accept. . . . I think that it is only fair to advise the witness—again advise the witness—that any scruples he may have due to a desire to protect friends and acquaintances, is not a legal reason for declining to answer the questions which are now being put to you, and which will be put to you by counsel.

In an effort to prove the pertinence of the questions which the petitioner had refused to answer, the Government offered at the trial the transcripts of the opening statements of Subcommittee Chairman Kearney at the Albany hearings in 1953 and 1954 and of Subcommittee Chairman Velde at a hearing in Chicago in 1954, as well as an additional portion of the transcript of the 1954 Albany hearing. One witness, the counsel for the Committee on Un-American Activities, testified. A review of this evidence convinces us that the Government failed to prove the charge in the indictment that the questions which the petitioner refused to answer were "pertinent to the question then under inquiry" by the subcommittee before which he appeared.

The Chairman's opening statement at the Albany hearing in 1953 consisted largely of a paraphrase of the Committee's authorizing resolution and a general summary of the Committee's past activities.* The only statement of a specific purpose was as follows:

The committee, in its course of investigation, came into possession of reliable information indicating Communist Party activities within the Albany area. The committee decided that this information was of such a character as to merit an investigation to determine its nature, extent, character, and objects.

At the opening of the Albany hearings in 1954 the Chairman stated that the subcommittee would "resume this morning the investigation of Communist Party activities within the capital area." He made clear that the hearings were "a continuation of the open hearings which were conducted in Albany" in 1953. He pointed out that testimony at the 1953 hearings had "related to the efforts of the Communist Party to infiltrate industry and other segments of society in the capital area." "This committee," he said, ". . . is investigating communism within the field of labor where it has substantial evidence that it exists."

The opening statement of the Chairman of the subcommittee which held hearings in Chicago in 1954 is the same statement that was before this Court in *Watkins* v. *United States*, 354 U.S. 178, 210. As was pointed out in the *Watkins* opinion, Mr. Velde "did no more than paraphrase

* "The committee is charged by the Congress of the United States with the responsibility of investigating the extent, character and objects of un-American propaganda activities in the United States, the diffusion within the United States of subversive and un-American propaganda that is instigated from foreign countries, or of a domestic origin, and attacks the principles of the form of government as guaranteed by our Constitution and all other questions in relation thereto that will aid Congress in any necessary remedial legislation.

"It has been fully established by testimony before this and other congressional committees and before the courts of our land that the Communist Party of the United States is part of an international conspiracy, which is being used as a tool or a weapon by a foreign power to promote its own foreign policy and which has for its objective the overthrow of the governments of all non-Communist countries, resorting to the use of force and violence if necessary. This organization cannot live and expand within the United States except by the promulgation and diffusion of subversive and un-American propaganda designed to win adherence to its cause.

"The first witness in this hearing will testify regarding certain aspects of the worldwide Communist conspiracy, which should demonstrate what a serious matter it is to permit individuals who are subject to the directives and discipline of the Communist Party to be placed in positions of leadership in any functional organization.

"The committee, in its course of investigation, came into possession of reliable information indicating Communist Party activities within the Albany area. The committee decided that this information was of such a character as to merit an investigation to determine its nature, extent, character, and objects.

"Many witnesses have appeared before this committee, sitting in various places throughout the United States, and have revealed their experiences as former Com-the authorizing resolution and. give a very general sketch of the past efforts of the Committee." Moreover, the statement indicated that that subcommittee hearing was directed primarily towards investigation of activities in the Chicago area: "We are here in Chicago, Ill., realizing that this is the center of the great midwestern area of the United States. It cannot be said that subversive infiltration has had a greater, nor a lesser success in infiltrating this important area. The hearings today are the culmination of an investigation that has been conducted by the committee's competent staff and is a part of the committee's intention for holding hearings in various parts of the country."

The transcript of part of the testimony of two witnesses at the 1954 Albany hearings, John Marqusee and Emmanuel Richardson, was also introduced at the petitioner's trial. These transcripts showed that Marqusee's testimony had related primarily to Communist infiltration of a labor union in Schenectady for which he had worked during a summer vacation in 1948. At that time he had been a student at the New York State School of Industrial and Labor Relations which, he had testified, was a part of Cornell University. He had told the subcommittee that he had never had any contact with the Communist Party before taking the

---

munist Party members. Such testimony has added immeasurably to the sum total of the knowledge, character, extent, and objects of Communist activities in this country.

"Witnesses from Hollywood, labor unions, the legal profession, medical profession, and other groups have made a great contribution to the defense of our country by disclosing to this committee facts within their knowledge.

"In the view of this committee, such testimony should not be held against an individual where it has that character of trustworthiness which convinces one that the witness had completely and finally terminated Communist Party membership and that such testimony has been given in all good faith.

"The committee is not concerned with the political beliefs or opinions of any witness who has been called before it. It is concerned only with the facts showing the extent, character, and objects of the Communist Party activities.

"In keeping with the long-standing policy of this committee, any individual or organization whose name is mentioned during the course of the hearings in such a manner as to adversely affect them shall have an opportunity to appear before the committee for the purpose of making a denial or explanation of any adverse references.

"I would also like at this time, before the beginning of these hearings, to make this announcement to the public: We are here at the discretion of the Congress of the United States, trying to discharge a duty and obligation that has been placed upon us. The public is here by permission of the committee and not by any compulsion. Any attempt or effort on the part of anyone to make a demonstration or audible comment in this hearing room, either favorably or unfavorably, toward the committee's undertaking, or to what any witness may have to say, will not be countenanced by the committee. If such conduct should occur, the officers on duty will be requested to eject the offenders from the hearing room."

labor union job. The transcript showed that he had explained that he had taken the job in accordance with the school's requirement "that every student should put forth his efforts in securing a job during the summer, during the intervening summers of his 4-year program, 1 summer with a labor union, 1 with a management group, if possible, and 1 summer with a neutral agency, such as a mediation agency or arbitration service." There was not mention of the Cornell Graduate School, nor of the petitioner, in the transcript of Marqusee's testimony.

The transcript of Richardson's testimony showed that he had testified that as a student at the Cornell Law School in 1950 he had joined the Communist Party at the request of the Federal Bureau of Investigation. He had named several people he had known as Communists on the Cornell campus, including the petitioner and Homer Owens. He had stated that the petitioner had known a member of the Cornell faculty who was a Communist Party member, and that he had once received through the petitioner a contribution to the Party from someone else of "one hundred and some dollars." The transcript showed that Richardson had also testified at length concerning Communist infiltration into a labor union in a plant in Syracuse where he had worked during the summers of 1951 and 1952.

After these transcripts had been introduced at the petitioner's trial, the Government called its only witness, Frank S. Tavenner, Jr., who had been the "interrogating attorney" at the Albany hearings and at the petitioner's hearing before the subcommittee in Washington. Mr. Tavenner emphasized that the hearing in Washington was a continuation of the Albany hearings, which he characterized as "a general investigation of Communist Party activities in what was referred to as the 'Capital Area.'" Under interrogation of government counsel, the witness expressly disclaimed that the purpose of the Washington hearing had been to investigate Communist activities in educational institutions. He was asked what "connection was there between [the subject of the petitioner's testimony] and the investigations entitled 'Albany, New York'?" This question was never answered.

On this record the District Court found the subject under inquiry to be "the infiltration of Communism into educational and labor fields." The Court of Appeals never stated what it thought the subject under inquiry by the subcommittee was.

As our cases make clear, two quite different issues regarding pertinency may be involved in a prosecution under 2 U.S.C. § 192. One issue reflects the requirement of the Due Process Clause of the Fifth Amendment that the pertinency of the interrogation to the topic under the congressional committee's inquiry must be brought home to the witness at the time the questions are put to him. "Unless the subject matter has been made to appear with undisputable clarity, it is the duty of the investigative body, upon objection of the witness on grounds of pertinency, to state for the record the subject under inquiry at that time and the manner in which the propounded questions are pertinent thereto." *Watkins* v. *United States,* 354 U.S., at 214–215. See *Barenblatt* v. *United States,* 360 U.S., at 123–124. The other and different pertinency issue stems from the prosecution's duty at the trial to prove that the questions propounded by the congressional committee were in fact "pertinent to the question under inquiry" by the committee. "Undeniably a conviction for contempt under 2 U.S.C. § 192 cannot stand unless the questions asked are pertinent to the subject matter of the investigation." *Barenblatt, supra,* at 123, "[T]he statute defines the crime as refusal to answer 'any question pertinent to the question under inquiry.' Part of the standard of criminality, therefore, is the pertinency of the questions propounded to the witness." *Watkins, supra,* at 208. . . . These two basically different issues must not be blurred by treating them as a single question of "pertinency."

With regard to the first issue, it is evident that the petitioner was not made aware at the time he was questioned of the question then under inquiry nor of how the questions which were asked related to such a subject. The chairman made no opening statement, and the petitioner heard no other witnesses testify. The resolution creating the subcommittee revealed nothing. It was merely a general resolution authorizing the creation of a subcommittee to act for the Committee. Committee counsel simply advised the petitioner that the committee had previously heard evidence regarding Communist activity at Cornell, and that he proposed to ask the petitioner "certain matters relating to your activity there." As to his own activity there the petitioner freely testified. When the petitioner declined to give the names of other people, no clear explanation of the topic under inquiry was forthcoming.

It is also evident, however, that the thoughts which the petitioner voiced in refusing to answer the questions about other people can hardly be considered as the equivalent of an objection upon the grounds of pertinency. Although he did indicate doubt as to the importance of the questions, the petitioner's main concern was clearly his own conscientious unwillingness to act as an informer. It can hardly be considered, therefore, that the objections which the petitioner made at the time were "adequate, within the meaning of what was said in *Watkins, supra,* at 214–215, to trigger what would have been the Subcommittee's reciprocal obligation had it been faced with a pertinency objection." *Barenblatt, supra,* at 124.

We need not pursue the matter, however, because, in any event, it is clear that the Government at the trial failed to carry its burden of proving the pertinence of the questions. . . . The first step in proving that component of the offense was to show the subject of the subcommittee's inquiry. . . . As related above the Government offered documentary evidence of statements made by the chairman of the subcommittees at two hearings in Albany which tended to show that those subcommittees were investigating Communist infiltration in the Albany or "capital" area, particularly in the field of labor. The Government presented one witness who testified that the petitioner's hearing was a continuation of the Albany hearings, and that the subject of those hearings was Communist infiltration in the Albany area. He disavowed any implication that the topic under inquiry was Communism either at Cornell or in educational institutions generally.

Yet the questions which the petitioner was convicted of refusing to answer obviously had nothing to do with the Albany area or with Communist infiltration into labor unions. It can hardly be seriously contended that Cornell University is in the Albany area. Indeed, we may take judicial notice of the fact that Ithaca is more than one hundred and sixty-five miles from Albany, and in an entirely different economic and geographic area of New York. The petitioner was asked nothing about Albany or the Albany area. So far as the record shows, he knew nothing about that subject. He was asked nothing about labor or labor unions. So far as the record shows, he knew nothing about them. He was asked nothing about any possible connection between Cornell or its graduate school and Communist infiltration in Albany. Yet the petitioner was basically a cooperative witness, and there is nothing in the record to indicate that, except for giving the names of others, he would not have freely answered any inquiry the subcommittee wished to pursue with respect to these subjects. It is true that the transcript of the testimony of two witnesses at the Albany hearings established that, in addition to testifying about Communist infiltration into labor unions in the Albany area, they had been willingly led into some testimony about Communist activities by the petitioner and others at Cornell. But that excursion can hardly justify a disregard of the Government's careful proof at the petitioner's trial of what the subject under inquiry actually was. The pertinence of the interrogation of those two witnesses is not before us. The pertinence of the petitioner's interrogation is.

In enacting 2 U.S.C. § 192, the Congress invoked the aid of the federal judicial system to protect itself from contumacious conduct. *Watkins, supra,* at 207. "In fulfillment of their obligation under this statute, the courts must accord to the defendants every right which is guaranteed to defendants in all other criminal cases." *Id.,* at 208. "One of the rightful boasts of Western civilization is that the [prosecution] has the burden of establishing guilt solely on the basis of evidence produced in court and under circumstances assuring an accused all the safeguards of a fair procedure." . . . Among these is the presumption of the defendant's innocence. . . . It was incumbent upon the prosecution in this case to prove that the petitioner had committed the offense for which he was indicted. One element of that offense was the pertinence to the subject matter under inquiry of the questions the petitioner refused to answer. We hold, as a matter of law, that there was a failure of such proof in this case. . . .

We do not decide today any question respecting the power or legislative purpose of this subcommittee of the House Un-American Activities Committee. Nor do we reach the large issues stirred by the petitioner's First Amendment claims. Our decision is made within the conventional framework of the federal criminal law, and in accord with its traditional concepts. In a word, we hold only that the Government failed to prove its case.*

Reversed.

Mr. Justice Harlan, whom Mr. Justice Frankfurter joins, dissenting:

There is, of course, no doubt that a showing of "pertinency" is an essential part of the Government's burden in a prosecution under 2 U.S.C. § 192. But the nature of this burden may differ, dependent upon what transpired at the Congressional inquiry giving rise to the prosecution.

In a case where the prosecution involves the defendant's refusal to answer a question whose pertinency was explained to him by the Congressional Committee before which he appeared as a witness—following his appropriate objection that the question was not pertinent to the matter "under inquiry," . . . the Government must stand or fall upon that explanation. For it would be obviously unfair to allow the Government at trial to prove pertinency on a different theory than was given to the defendant at the time he testified, and on the basis of which he presumably determined that he need not answer the question put.

---

* For a Court opinion specifically to join issue with what is written in dissent is a practice ordinarily to be avoided. One of the dissenting opinions in this case, however, is largely based upon what are asserted to be "the undisputed relevant facts in the record." Since every litigant is entitled to have his case reviewed on the facts in the record, it is appropriate to state explicitly that:

(1) The record affirmatively shows that neither Marqusee nor Richardson testified, directly or indirectly, to "passing out handbills at strike scenes" or to any "plan of using the prestige and innocent aid of the university's placement service in getting summer jobs with labor unions in upper New York," or anywhere else.

(2) The record affirmatively shows that at no time did the subcommittee, or anyone on its behalf, "advise" the petitioner, or anyone else, that the subcommittee was investigating the infiltration of communism into the "educational and labor fields."

Where, however, the defendant made no "pertinency" objection as a witness before the Congressional Committee, the Government at trial is left free to satisfy the requirement of pertinency in any way it may chose. The present case is such a one, for, as the Court's opinion recognizes, the petitioner here made no adequate pertinency objection before the House Un-American Activities Subcommittee.

I dissent because in my opinion the Court's holding that the Government failed to establish "pertinency" rests on a too niggardly view of both the issue and the record. Pertinency, which in the context of an investigatory proceeding is of course a term of wider import than "relevancy" in the context of a trial, is to be judged not in terms of the immediate probative significance of a particular question to the matter under authorized inquiry, but in light of its tendency to elicit information which might be a useful link in the investigatory chain. An investigation must proceed "step by step."

Pertinency is found lacking here because (1) the inquiry as to affairs relating to petitioner's student days at Cornell University, situated at Ithaca, N.Y., it is said, was not germane to the Subcommittee's investigation as to Communist activities in the "the Albany area;" and (2) in any event, such investigation, the Court finds, related only to alleged Communist infiltration into labor unions and not as well to infiltration "at Cornell or in educational institutions generally." I can agree with neither facet of this holding.

It is quite true, as the Court says, that Ithaca is some 165 miles away from Albany, but it seems to me much too refined to say, as a matter of law, that the trial court could not reasonably determine that Ithaca was within the Subcommittee's terms of reference. Indeed, I think it fair to suggest that in common usage, at least among New Yorkers, "Albany area" would be regarded as aptly descriptive of "upstate" New York. In relation to "pertinency" the matter should not be judged as if it were one of technical jurisdiction or venue.

The other aspect of the Court's holding seems to me equally infirm. Accepting, as I shall, the Court's view that the trial record shows that the Subcommittee, at the relevant time, was investigating only alleged Communist "labor union," and not "educational," infiltration, it seems to me abundantly clear that the lower courts were justified in concluding that all of the questions with respect to which the petitioner was convicted were pertinent to that matter.

Only shortly before it examined petitioner, the Subcommittee had interrogated two witnesses, Marqusee and Richardson, with respect to their Communist affiliations, their summer work with two labor unions in Schenectady and in Syracuse, and Communist infiltration into such unions, all while they were both students at Cornell. One of these witnesses, Richardson, had testified that during this period he had known the petitioner, and one Homer Owen . . . as Communists on the Cornell campus. I do not see why it should now be deemed either that the Subcommittee's interest in petitioner's testimony was confined to "educational infiltration," or that its preliminary questioning of him might not have led to developing information bearing on "labor union infiltration," possibly stemming from student Communist activity on the Cornell campus, had further inquiry not been blocked by petitioner's refusal to answer.

I cannot agree that the decision of this case has been made "within the conventional framework of the federal criminal law." For surely in judging the pertinency of a question put in the course of an otherwise valid Congressional inquiry, as this one is recognized to have been, we should not insist that the inquiring committee follow stricter rules than the courts themselves apply in determining, for example, the sufficiency of a plea of self-incrimination under the "link in the chain" rule . . . or in judging "materiality" in a perjury case. . . . In reversing this conviction, I think the Court has strayed from the even course of decision.

I would affirm.

RUSSELL v. UNITED STATES

369 US 749 (1962)

[Six witnesses before a congressional subcommittee were convicted of contempt of Congress for refusal to answer quesitons. The Supreme Court by a 5-to-2 vote, with Justices Frankfurter and White not participating, reversed, holding that the indictments charging refusal to answer certain questions were insufficient because the indictments did not identify the subject under inquiry at the time of the refusals to answer. Justices Harlan and Clark dissented.]

Mr. Justice Stewart delivered the opinion of the Court:

In these six cases we review judgments of the Court of Appeals for the District of Columbia, which affirmed convictions obtained in the District Court under 2 U.S.C. § 192. Each of the petitioners was convicted for refusing to answer certain questions when summoned before a congressional subcommittee. The cases were separately briefed and argued here, and many issues were presented. We decide each case upon a single ground common to all, and we therefore reach no other questions.

In each case the indictment returned by the grand jury failed to identify the subject under congressional subcommittee inquiry at the time the witness was interrogated. The indictments were practically identical in this respect, stating only that the questions to which answers were refused "were pertinent to the question then under inquiry" by the subcommittee. In each case a motion was filed to quash the indictment before trial upon the ground that the indictment failed to state the subject under investigation at the time of the subcommittee's interrogation of the defendant. In each case the motion was denied. In each case the issue thus raised was preserved on appeal, in the petition for writ of certiorari, and in brief and argument here.

Congress has expressly provided that no one can be prosecuted under 2 U.S.C. § 192 except upon indictment by a grand jury. This Court has never decided whether the indictment must identify the subject which was under inquiry at the time of the defendant's alleged default or refusal to answer. For the reasons that follow, we hold that the indictment must contain such an averment, and we accordingly reverse the judgments before us.

In enacting the criminal statute under which these petitioners were convicted Congress invoked the aid of the federal judicial system in protecting itself against contumacious conduct. . . . The obvious consequence, as the Court has repeatedly emphasized, was to confer upon the federal courts the duty to accord a person prosecuted for this statutory offense every safeguard which the law accords in all other federal criminal cases. . . .

Recognizing this elementary concept, the *Sinclair* case established several propositions which provide a relevant starting point here. First, there can be criminality under the statute only if the question which the witness refused to answer pertained to a subject then under investigation by the congressional body which summoned him. "[A] witness rightfully may refuse to answer where . . . the questions asked are not pertinent to the matter under inquiry." *Sinclair* v. *United States*, 279 U.S. 263. Secondly, because the defendant is presumed to be innocent, it is "incumbent upon the United States to plead and show that the question [he refused to answer] pertained to some matter under investigation." Finally, *Sinclair* held that the question of pertinency is one for determination by the court as a matter of law.

In that case the Court had before it an indictment which set out in specific and lengthy detail the subject under investigation by the Senate Committee which had summoned Sinclair. The Court was thereby enabled to make an enlightened and precise determination that the question he had refused to answer was pertinent to that subject. *Id.*, at 285–289, 296–298.

That the making of such a determination would be a vital function of the federal judiciary in a prosecution brought under 2 U.S.C. § 192 was clearly foreseen by the Congress which originally enacted the law in 1857. Congress not only provided that a person could be prosecuted only upon an indictment by a grand jury, but, as the record of the legislative debates shows, Congress was expressly aware that pertinency to the subject under inquiry was the basic preliminary question which the federal courts were going to have to decide in determining whether a criminal offense had been alleged or proved. The principal spokesman for the bill, Senator Bayard, repeatedly made this very point:

The bill provides for punishing a witness who shall refuse to answer any question 'pertinent' to the matter of inquiry under consideration before the House or its committee. If he refuses to answer an irrelevant question, he is not subject to the penalties of the bill. The question must be pertinent to the subject-matter, and that will have to be decided by the courts of justice on the indictment. That power is not given to Congress; it is given appropriately to the judiciary. . . .

This law does not propose to give to this miscellaneous political body the power of punishment; but one of its greatest recommendations is, that it transfers that power of punishment to a court of justice after judicial inquiry. All that is to be done in the case of a refusal to testify is to certify the fact to the district attorney, who is to lay it before the grand jury, and if the party is indicted he is bound to answer according to the terms of the law, as any other person would for an offense against the laws of the land. . . . I am aware that legislative bodies have transcended their powers—that under the influence of passion and political excitement they have very often invaded the rights of individuals, and may have invaded the rights of co-ordinate branches of the Government; but if our institutions are to last, there can be no greater safeguard than will result from transferring that which now stands on an indefinite power (the punishment as well as the offense resting in the breast of either House) from Congress to the courts of justice. When a case of this kind comes before a court, will not the first inquiry be, have Congress jurisdiction of the subject-matter?—has the House which undertakes to inquire, jurisdiction of the subject? If they have not, the whole proceedings are *coram non judice* and void, and the party cannot be held liable under indictment. The Court would quash the indictment if this fact appeared on its face; and if it appeared on the trial they would direct the jury to acquit. . . .

The law prescribes that, in case of such refusal, the House shall certify the fact to the district attorney, and he shall bring the matter before the grand jury. When that comes up by indictment before the court, must not the court decide whether the question put was pertinent to the inquiry? Of course they must; and they cannot hold the party guilty without doing it. . . .

These forecasts of the office which the federal courts would be called upon to perform under 2 U.S.C. § 192 have been amply borne out by the cases which have arisen under the statute. The crucial importance of determining the issue of pertinency is reflected in many cases which have come here since *Sinclair, supra. Watkins* v. *United States*, 354 U.S. 178; *Sacher* v. *United States*, 356 U.S. 576; *Barenblatt* v. *United States*, 360 U.S. 109; *Wilkinson* v. *United States*, 365 U.S. 399; *Braden* v. *United States*, 365 U.S. 431; *Deutch* v. *United States*, 367 U.S. 456. Our decisions have pointed out that the obvious first step in determining whether the questions asked were pertinent to the subject under inquiry is to ascertain what that subject was. . . . Identification of the subject under inquiry is also an essential preliminary to the determination of a host of other issues which typically arise in prosecutions under the statute. . . .

Where, as in the *Sinclair* case, the subject under inquiry has been identified in the indictment, this essential first step has presented no problem. Where, as in the more recent cases, the indictment has not identified the topic under inquiry, the Court has often found it difficult or impossible to ascertain what the subject was. The difficulty of such a determination in the absence of an allegation in the indictment is illustrated by *Deutch* v. *United States, supra.* In that case the members of this Court were in sharp disagreement as to what the subject under subcommittee inquiry had been. Moreover, all of us disagreed with the District Court's theory, and the Court of Appeals had not even ventured a view on the question. In *Watkins* v. *United States, supra,* the Court found it not merely difficult, but actually impossible, to determine what the topic under subcommittee inquiry had been at the time the petitioner had refused to answer the questions addressed to him. "Having exhausted the several possible indicia of the 'question under inquiry,' we remain unenlightened as to the subject to which the questions asked petitioner were pertinent."

To be sure, the fact that difficulties and doubts have beset the federal courts in trying to ascertain the subject under inquiry in cases arising under 2 U.S.C. § 192, could hardly justify, in the abstract, a requirement that indictments under the statute contain averments which would simplify the courts' task. Difficult and doubtful questions are inherent in the judicial process, particularly under a system of criminal law which places heavy emphasis upon the protection of the rights and liberties of the individual. Courts sit to resolve just such questions, and rules of law are not to be made merely to suit judicial convenience. But a proliferation of doubtful issues which not only burden the judiciary, but, because of uncertainties inherent in their resolution, work a hardship upon both the prosecution and the defense in criminal cases, is hardly a desideratum. And the repeated appearance in prosecutions under a particular criminal statute of the same critical and difficult question, which could be obviated by a simple averment in the indictment, invites inquiry into the purposes and functions which a grand jury indictment is intended to serve. The cases we have discussed, therefore, furnish an appropriate background for the inquiry to which we now turn.

Any discussion of the purpose served by a grand jury indictment in the administration of federal criminal law must begin with the Fifth and Sixth Amendments to the Constitution. The Fifth Amendment provides that "No person shall be held to answer for a capital, or otherwise infamous crime, unless on a presentment or indictment of a Grand Jury, except in cases arising in the land or naval forces, or in the Militia, when in actual service in time of War or public danger." We need not pause to consider whether an offense under 2 U.S.C. § 192 is an "infamous crime," *Duke* v. *United States*, 301 U.S. 492, since Congress has from the beginning explicitly conferred upon those prosecuted under the statute the protection which the Fifth Amendment confers, by providing that no one can be prosecuted for this offense except upon an indictment by a grand jury. This specific guaranty, as well as the Fifth Amendment's Due Process Clause, are, therefore, both brought to bear here. Of like relevance is the guaranty of the Sixth Amendment that "In all criminal prosecutions, the accused shall enjoy the right . . . to be informed of the nature and cause of the accusation; . . ."

The constitutional provision that a trial may be held in a serious federal criminal case only if a grand jury has first intervened reflects centuries of antecedent development of common law, going back to the Assize of Clarendon in 1166. "The grand jury is an English institution, brought to this country by the early colonists and incorporated in the Constitution by the Founders. There is every reason to believe that our constitutional grand jury was intended to operate substantially like its English progenitor. The basic purpose of the English grand jury was to provide a fair method for instituting criminal proceedings against persons believed to have committed crimes." *Costello* v. *United States*, 350 U.S. 359. . . .

For many years the federal courts were guided in their judgments concerning the construction and sufficiency of grand jury indictments by the common law alone. Not until 1872 did Congress enact general legislation touching upon the subject. In that year a statute was enacted which reflected the drift of the law away from the rules of technical and formalized pleading which had characterized an earlier era. The 1872 statute provided that "no indictment found and presented by a grand jury in any district or circuit or other court of the United States shall be deemed insufficient, nor shall the trial, judgment, or other proceeding thereon be affected by reason of any defect or imperfection in matter of form only, which shall not tend to the prejudice of the defendant." . . . This legislation has now been repealed, but its substance is preserved in the more generalized provision of Rule 52 (a) of the Federal Rules of Criminal Procedure, which states that "Any error, defect, irregularity or variance which does not affect substantial rights shall be disregarded."

There was apparently no other legislation dealing with the subject of indictments generally until the promulgation of Rule 7 (c), Fed. Rules Crim. Proc., in 1946. The Rule provides:

The indictment or the information shall be a plain, concise and definite written statement of the essential facts constituting the offense charged. It shall be signed by the attorney for the government. It need not contain a formal commencement, a formal conclusion or any other matter not necessary to such statement. Allegations made in one count may be incorporated by reference in another count. It may be alleged in a single count that the means by which the defendant committed the offense are unknown or that he committed it by one or more specified means. The indictment or information shall state for each count the official or customary citation of the statute, rule, regulation or other provision of law which the defendant is alleged therein to have violated. Error in the citation or its omission shall not be ground for dismissal of the indictment or information or for reversal of a conviction if the error or omission did not mislead the defendant to his prejudice.

As we have elsewhere noted, "This Court has, in recent years, upheld many convictions in the face of questions concerning the sufficiency of the charging papers. Convictions are no longer reversed because of minor and technical deficiences which did not prejudice the accused. . . . This has been a salutary development in the criminal law." *Smith* v. *United States*, 360 U.S. 1. "But," as the Smith opinion went on to point out, "the substantial safeguards to those charged with serious crimes cannot be eradicated under the guise of technical departures from the rules." Resolution of the issue presented in the cases before us thus ultimately depends upon the nature of "the substantial safeguards" to a criminal defendant which an indictment is designed to provide. Stated concretely, does the omission from an indictment under 2 U.S.C. § 192 of the subject under congressional committee inquiry amount to no more than a technical deficiency of no prejudice to the defendant? Or does such an omission deprive the defendant of one of the significant protections which the guaranty of a grand jury indictment was intended to confer?

In a number of cases the Court has emphasized two of the protections which an indictment is intended to guarantee, reflected by two of the criteria by which the sufficiency of an indictment is to be measured. These criteria are first, whether the indictment "contains the elements of the offense intended to be charged, 'and sufficiently apprises the defendant of what he must be prepared to meet,'" and, secondly, "'in case any other proceedings are taken against him for a similar offence, whether the record shows with accuracy to what extent he may plead a former acquittal or conviction.'" . . .

Without doubt the second of these preliminary criteria was sufficiently met by the indictments in these cases. Since the indictments set out not only the times and places of the hearings at which the petitioners refused to testify, but also specified the precise questions which they then and there refused to answer, it can hardly be doubted that the petitioners would be fully protected from again being put in jeopardy for the same offense, particularly when it is remembered that they could rely upon other parts of the present record in the event that future proceedings should be taken against them. . . . The vice of these indictments, rather, is that they failed to satisfy the first essential criterion by which the sufficiency of an indictment is to be tested, *i.e.*, that they failed to sufficiently apprise the defendant "of what he must be prepared to meet."

As has been pointed out, the very core of criminality under 2 U.S.C. § 192 is pertinency to the subject under inquiry of the questions which the defendant refused to answer. What the subject actually was, therefore, is central to every prosecution under the statute. Where guilt depends so crucially upon such a specific identification of fact, our cases have uniformly held that an indictment must do more than simply repeat the language of the criminal statute.

"It is an elementary principle of criminal pleading, that where the definition of an offence, whether it be at common law or by statute, 'includes generic terms, it is not sufficient that the indictment shall charge the offence in the same generic terms as in the definition; but it must state the species,—it must descend to particulars.'" . . . An indictment not framed to apprise the defendant "with reasonable certainty, of the nature of the accusation against him . . . is defective, although it may follow the language of the statute." . . . "In an indictment upon a statute, it is not sufficient to set forth the offence in the words of the statute, unless those words of themselves fully, directly, and expressly, without any uncertainty or ambiguity, set forth all the elements necessary to constitute the offence intended to be punished." . . . "Undoubtedly the language of the statute may be used in the general description of an offence, but it must be accompanied with such a statement of the facts and circumstances as will inform the accused of the specific offence, coming under the general description, with which he is charged." . . . That these basic principles of fundamental fairness retain their full vitality under modern concepts of pleading, and specifically under Rule 7 (c) of the Federal Rules of Criminal Procedure, is illustrated by many recent federal decisions.

The vice which inheres in the failure of an indictment under 2 U.S.C. § 192 to identify the subject under inquiry is thus the violation of the basic principle "that the accused must be apprised by the indictment, with reasonable certainty, of the nature of the accusation against him." . . . A cryptic form of indictment in cases of this kind requires the defendant to go to trial with the chief issue undefined. It enables his conviction to rest on one point and the affirmance of the conviction to rest on another. It gives the prosecution free hand on appeal to fill in the gaps of proof by surmise or conjecture. The Court has had occasion before now to condemn just such a practice in a quite different factual setting. . . . And the unfairness and uncertainty which have characteristically infected criminal proceedings under this statute which were based upon indictments which failed to specify the subject under inquiry are illustrated by the cases in this Court we have already discussed. The same uncertainty and unfairness are underscored by the records of the cases now before us. A single example will suffice to illustrate the point.

In No. 12, *Price* v. *United States,* the petitioner refused to answer a number of questions put to him by the Internal Security Subcommittee of the Senate Judiciary Committee. At the beginning of the hearing in question, the Chairman and other subcommittee members made widely meandering statements purporting to identify the subject under inquiry. It was said that the hearings were "not . . . an attack upon the free press," that the investigation was of "such attempt as may be disclosed on the part of the Communist Party . . . to influence or to subvert the American press." It was also said that "We are simply investigating communism wherever we find it." In dealing with a witness who testified shortly before Price, counsel for the subcommittee emphatically denied that it was the subcommittee's purpose "to investigate Communist infiltration of the press and other forms of communication." But when Price was called to testify before the subcommittee no one offered even to attempt to inform him of what subject the subcommittee did have under inquiry. At the trial the Government took the position that the subject under inquiry had been Communist activities generally. The district judge before whom the case was tried found that "the questions put were pertinent to the matter under inquiry" without indicating what he thought the subject under inquiry was. The Court of Appeals, in affirming the conviction, likewise omitted to state what it thought the subject under inquiry had been. In this Court the Government contends that the subject under inquiry at the time the petitioner was called to testify was "Communist activity in news media."

It is difficult to imagine a case in which an indictment's insufficiency resulted so clearly in the indictment's failure to fulfill its primary office —to inform the defendant of the nature of the accusation against him. Price refused to answer some questions of a Senate subcommittee. He was not told at the time what subject the subcommittee was investigating. The prior record of the subcommittee hearings, with which Price may or may not have been familiar, gave a completely confused and inconsistent account of what, if anything, that subject was. Price was put to trial and convicted upon an indictment which did not even purport to inform him in any way of the identity of the topic under subcommittee inquiry. At every stage in the ensuing criminal proceeding Price was met with a different theory, or by no theory at all, as to what the topic had been. Far from informing Price of the nature of the accusation against him, the indictment instead left the prosecution free to roam at large—to shift its theory of criminality so as to take advantage of each passing vicissitude of the trial and appeal. Yet Price could be guilty of no criminal offense unless the questions he refused to answer were in fact pertinent to a specific topic under subcommittee inquiry at the time he was interrogated. . . .

It has long been recognized that there is an important corollary purpose to be served by the requirement that an indictment set out "the specific offence coming under the general description," with which the defendant is charged. This purpose, as defined in *United States* v. *Cruikshank*, 92 U.S. 542, is "to inform the court of the facts alleged, so that it may decide whether they are sufficient in law to support a conviction, if one should be had." This criterion is of the greatest relevance here, in the light of the difficulties and uncertainties with which the federal trial and reviewing courts have had to deal in cases arising under 2 U.S.C. § 192, to which reference has already been made. . . . Viewed in this context, the rule is designed not alone for the protection of the defendant, but for the benefit of the prosecution as well, by making it possible for courts called upon to pass on the validity of convictions under the statute to bring an enlightened judgment to that task. . . .

For these reasons we conclude that an indictment under 2 U.S.C. § 192 must state the question under congressional committee inquiry as found by the grand jury. Only then can the federal courts responsibly carry out the duty which Congress imposed upon them more than a century ago:

The question must be pertinent to the subject-matter, and that will have to be decided by the courts of justice on the indictment.

Reversed.

GIBSON v. FLORIDA LEGISLATIVE INVESTIGATION COMMITTEE

372 US 539 (1963)

[This case could have been placed with the cases on freedom of association, but it belongs more significantly with *Uphaus, Barenblatt, Wilkinson,* and similar cases, though in this instance the Supreme

Court, by a 5-to-4 vote, reversed the judgment of conviction for contempt. Justices Black and Douglas wrote separate concurring opinions. Justice Harlan wrote a dissenting opinion, in which he was joined by Justices Clark, Stewart, and White. The latter also wrote a separate dissenting opinion. The dissenting opinions rejected the notion that the Court should distinguish between an investigation of Communist activity *by* an organization, like the Communist Party, and an investigation of Communist infiltration *of* organizations, including a legitimate organization like the NAACP.]

Mr. Justice Goldberg delivered the opinion of the Court:

This case is the culmination of protracted litigation involving legislative investigating committees of the State of Florida and the Miami branch of the National Association for the Advancement of Colored People.

The origins of the controversy date from 1956, when a committee of the Florida Legislature commenced an investigation of the N.A.A.C.P. Upon expiration of this committee's authority, a new committee was established to pursue the inquiry. The new committee, created in 1957, held hearings and sought by subpoena to obtain the entire membership list of the Miami branch of the N.A.A.C.P.; production was refused and the committee obtained a court order requiring that the list be submitted. On appeal, the Florida Supreme Court held that the committee could not require production and disclosure of the entire membership list of the organization, but that it could compel the custodian of the records to bring them to the hearings and to refer to them to determine whether specific individuals, otherwise identified as, or "suspected of being," Communists, were N.A.A.C.P. members.

Because of the impending expiration of the authority of the 1957 committee, the Florida Legislature in 1959 established the respondent Legislative Investigation Committee to resume the investigation of the N.A.A.C.P. The authorizing statute, c. 59–207, Fla. Laws 1959, defining the purpose and operations of the respondent, declared:

It shall be the duty of the committee to make as complete an investigation as time permits of all organizations whose principles or activities include a course of conduct on the part of any person or group which would constitute violence, or a violation of the laws of the state, or would be inimical to the well-being and orderly pursuit of their personal and business activities by the majority of the citizens of this state. . . .

The petitioner, then president of the Miami branch of the N.A.A.C.P., was ordered to appear before the respondent Committee on November 4, 1959, and, in accordance with the prior decision of the Florida

Supreme Court, to bring with him records of the association which were in his possession or custody and which pertained to the identity of members of, and contributors to, the Miami and state N.A.A.C.P. organizations. Prior to interrogation of any witnesses the Committee chairman read the text of the statute creating the Committee and declared that the hearings would be "concerned with the activities of various organizations which have been or are presently operating in this State in the fields of, first, race relations; second, the coercive reform of social and educational practices and mores by litigation and pressured administrative action; third, of labor; fourth, of education; fifth, and other vital phases of life in this State." The chairman also stated that the inquiry would be directed to Communists and Communist activities, including infiltration of Communists into organizations operating in the described fields.

Upon being called to the stand, the petitioner admitted that he was custodian of his organization's membership records and testified that the local group had about 1,000 members, that individual membership was renewed annually, and that the only membership lists maintained were those for the then current year.

The petitioner told the Committee that he had not brought these records with him to the hearing and announced that he would not produce them for the purpose of answering questions concerning membership in the N.A.A.C.P. He did, however, volunteer to answer such questions on the basis of his own personal knowledge; when given the names and shown photographs of 14 persons previously identified as Communists or members of Communist front or affiliated organizations, the petitioner said that he could associate none of them with the N.A.A.C.P.

The petitioner's refusal to produce his organization's membership lists was based on the ground that to bring the lists to the hearing and to utilize them as the basis of his testimony would interfere with the free exercise of Fourteenth Amendment associational rights of members and prospective members of the N.A.A.C.P.

In accordance with Florida procedure, the petitioner was brought before a state court and, after a hearing, was adjudged in contempt, and sentenced to six months' imprisonment and fined $1,200, or in default in payment thereof, sentenced to an additional six months' imprisonment. The Florida Supreme Court sustained the judgment below, and this Court granted certiorari; the case was argued last Term and restored to the calendar for reargument this Term.

I.

We are here called upon once again to resolve a conflict between individual rights of free speech and association and governmental interest in conducting legislative investigations. Prior decisions illumine the contending principles.

This Court has repeatedly held that rights of association are within the ambit of the constitutional protections afforded by the First and Fourteenth Amendments. *NAACP* v. *Alabama,* 357 U.S. 449; *Bates* v. *Little Rock,* 361 U.S. 516; *Shelton* v. *Tucker,* 364 U.S. 479; *NAACP* v. *Button* [9 L. ed. 2d 405 (US) (1963)]. The respondent Committee does not contend otherwise, nor could it, for, as was said in *NAACP* v. *Alabama, supra,* "It is beyond debate that freedom to engage in association for the advancement of beliefs and ideas is an inseparable aspect of the 'liberty' assured by the Due Process Clause of the Fourteenth Amendment, which embraces freedom of speech." And it is equally clear that the guarantee encompasses protection of privacy of association in organizations such as that of which the petitioner is president; indeed, in both the *Bates* and *Alabama* cases, *supra,* this Court held N.A.A.C.P. membership lists of the very type here in question to be beyond the States' power of discovery in the circumstances there presented.

The First and Fourteenth Amendment rights of free speech and free association are fundamental and highly prized, and "need breathing space to survive." . . . "Freedoms such as these are protected not only against heavy-handed frontal attack, but also from being stifled by more subtle governmental interference." . . . And, as declared in *NAACP* v. *Alabama, supra,* "It is hardly a novel perception that compelled disclosure of affiliation with groups engaged in advocacy may constitute [an] . . . effective restraint on freedom of association. . . . This Court has recognized the vital relationship between freedom to associate and privacy in one's associations. . . . Inviolability of privacy in group association may in many circumstances be indispensable to preservation of freedom of association, particularly where a group espouses dissident beliefs." So it is here.

At the same time, however, this Court's prior holdings demonstrate that there can be no question but that the State has power adequately to inform itself—through legislative investigation, if it so desires— in order to act and protect its legitimate and vital interests. As this Court said in considering the propriety of the congressional inquiry challenged in *Watkins* v. *United States,* 354 U.S. 178: "The power . . . to conduct investigations is inherent in the legislative process. That power is broad. It encompasses inquiries concerning the administration of existing laws as well as proposed or possibly needed statutes. It includes surveys of defects in our social, economic or political system for the purpose of enabling the Congress to remedy them." And, more recently, it was declared that "The scope of the power of inquiry, in short, is as penetrating and far-reaching as the

potential power to enact and appropriate under the Constitution."
Barenblatt v. *United States,* 360 U.S. 109, 111. It is no less obvious,
however, that the legislative power to investigate, broad as it may
be, is not without limit. The fact that the general scope of the inquiry is authorized and permissible does not compel the conclusion
that the investigatory body is free to inquire into or demand all forms
of information. Validation of the broad subject matter under investigation does not necessarily carry with it automatic and wholesale
validation of all individual questions, subpoenas, and documentary
demands. See, *e.g., Watkins* v. *United States, supra.* See also *Barenblatt*
v. *United States, supra.* When, as in this case, the claim is made that
particular legislative inquiries and demands infringe substantially
upon First and Fourteenth Amendment associational rights of individuals, the courts are called upon to, and must, determine the
permissibility of the challenged actions, *Watkins* v. *United States,*
supra; "[T]he delicate and difficult task falls upon the courts to weigh
the circumstances and to appraise the substantiality of the reasons
advanced in support of the regulation of the free enjoyment of the
rights," *Schneider* v. *State,* 308 U.S. 147. The interests here at stake
are of significant magnitude, and neither their resolution nor impact
is limited to, or dependent upon, the particular parties here involved.
Freedom and viable government are both, for this purpose, indivisible
concepts; whatever affects the rights of the parties here, affects all.

II.

Significantly, the parties are in substantial agreement as to the
proper test to be applied to reconcile the competing claims of government and individual and to determine the propriety of the Committee's demands. As declared by the respondent Committee in its brief
to this Court, "Basically, this case hinges entirely on the question of
whether the evidence before the Committee [was] . . . sufficient to
show probable cause or nexus between the N.A.A.C.P. Miami Branch,
and Communist activities." We understand this to mean—regardless
of the label applied, be it "nexus," "foundation," or whatever—that
it is an essential prerequisite to the validity of an investigation which
intrudes into the area of constitutionally protected rights of speech,
press, association and petition that the State convincingly show a
substantial relation between the information sought and a subject of
overriding and compelling state interest. Absent such a relation between the N.A.A.C.P. and conduct in which the State may have a
compelling regulatory concern, the Committee has not "demonstrated
so cogent an interest in obtaining and making public" the membership information sought to be obtained as to "justify the substantial

abridgement of associational freedoms which such disclosure will effect." *Bates* v. *Little Rock, supra*. "Where there is a significant encroachment upon personal liberty, the State may prevail only upon showing a subordinating interest which is compelling." *Ibid.*

Applying these principles to the facts of this case, the respondent Committee contends that the prior decisions of this Court in *Uphaus* v. *Wyman,* 360 U.S. 72; *Barenblatt* v. *United States,* 360 U.S. 109; *Wilkinson* v. *United States,* 365 U.S. 399; and *Braden* v. *United States,* 365 U.S. 431, compel a result here upholding the legislative right of inquiry. In *Barenblatt, Wilkinson,* and *Braden,* however, it was a refusal to answer a question or questions concerning the witness' *own* past or present membership *in the Communist Party* which supported his conviction. It is apparent that the necessary preponderating governmental interest and, in fact, the very result in those cases was founded on the holding that the Communist Party is not an ordinary or legitimate political party, as known in this country, and that, because of its particular nature, membership therein is *itself* a permissible subject of regulation and legislative scrutiny. Assuming the correctness of the premises on which those cases were decided, no further demonstration of compelling governmental interest was deemed necessary, since the direct object of the challenged questions there was discovery of membership in the Communist Party, a matter held pertinent to a proper subject then under inquiry.

Here, however, it is not alleged Communists who are the witnesses before the Committee and it is not discovery of their membership in that party which is the object of the challenged inquiries. Rather, it is the N.A.A.C.P. itself which is the subject of the investigation, and it is its local president, the petitioner, who was called before the Committee and held in contempt because he refused to divulge the contents of its membership records. There is no suggestion that the Miami branch of the N.A.A.C.P. or the national organization with which it is affiliated were, or are, themselves subversive organizations. Nor is there any indication that the activities or policies of the N.A.A.C.P. were either Communist-dominated or influenced. In fact, this very record indicates that the association was and is against communism and has voluntarily taken steps to keep Communists from being members. Each year since 1950, the N.A.A.C.P. has adopted resolutions barring Communists from membership in the organization. Moreover, the petitioner testified that all prospective officers of the local organization are thoroughly investigated for Communist or subversive connections and, though subversive activities constitute grounds for termination of association membership, no such expulsions from the branch occurred during the five years preceding the investigation.

Thus, unlike the situation in *Barenblatt, Wilkinson* and *Braden, supra,* the Committee was not here seeking from the petitioner or the records of which he was custodian any information as to whether he, himself, or even other persons were members of the Communist Party, Communist front or affiliated organizations, or other allegedly subversive groups; instead, the entire thrust of the demands on the petitioner was that he disclose whether other persons were members of the N.A.A.C.P., itself a concededly legitimate and nonsubversive organization. Compelling such an organization, engaged in the exercise of First and Fourteenth Amendment rights, to disclose its membership presents, under our cases, a question wholly different from compelling the Communist Party to disclose its own membership. Moreover, even to say, as in *Barenblatt, supra,* that it is permissible to inquire into the subject of Communist infiltration of educational or other organizations does not mean that it is permissible to demand or require from such other groups disclosure of their membership by inquiry into their records when such disclosure will seriously inhibit or impair the exercise of constitutional rights and has not itself been demonstrated to bear a crucial relation to a proper governmental interest or to be essential to fulfillment of a proper governmental purpose. The prior holdings that governmental interest in controlling subversion and the particular character of the Communist Party and its objectives outweigh the right of individual Communists to conceal party membership or affiliations by no means require the wholly different conclusion that other groups— concededly legitimate—automatically forfeit their rights to privacy of association simply because the general subject matter of the legislative inquiry is Communist subversion or infiltration. The fact that governmental interest was deemed compelling in *Barenblatt, Wilkinson,* and *Braden* and held to support the inquiries there made into membership in the Communist Party does not resolve the issues here, where the challenged questions go to membership in an admittedly lawful organization.

Respondent's reliance on *Uphaus* v. *Wyman, supra,* as controlling is similarly misplaced. There, this Court upheld the right of the State of New Hampshire, in connection with an investigation of whether "subversive" persons were within the State, to obtain a list of guests who attended a World Fellowship summer camp located in the State. In *Uphaus* this Court found that there was demonstrated a sufficient connection between subversive activity—held there to be a proper subject of governmental concern—and the World Fellowship, itself, to justify discovery of the guest list; no semblance of such a nexus between the N.A.A.C.P. and subversive *activities* has been shown here. Moreover, contrary to the facts in this case, the claim to associational privacy in *Uphaus* was held to be "tenuous at best," since the disputed list was already a matter of public record by virtue of a generally applicable New Hampshire law requiring that places of accommodation, including the camp in question, maintain a guest register open to public authorities. Thus, this Court noted that the registration statute "made public at the inception the association they [the guests] now wish to keep private." Finally, in *Uphaus*, the State was investigating whether subversive persons were within its boundaries and whether their presence constituted a threat to the State. No such purpose or need is evident here. The Florida Committee is not seeking to identify subversives by questioning the petitioner; apparently it is satisfied that it already knows who they are.

III.

In the absence of directly determinative authority, we turn, then, to consideration of the facts now before us. Obviously, if the respondent were still seeking discovery of the entire membership list, we could readily dispose of this case on the authority of *Bates* v. *Little Rock*, and *N.A.A.C.P.* v. *Alabama, supra;* a like result would follow if it were merely attempting to do piecemeal what could not be done in a single step. Though there are indications that the respondent Committee intended to inquire broadly into the N.A.A.C.P. membership records, there is no need to base our decision today upon a prediction as to the course which the Committee might have pursued if initially unopposed by the petitioner. Instead, we rest our result on the fact that the record in this case is insufficient to show a substantial connection between the Miami branch of the N.A.A.C.P. and Communist *activities* which the respondent Committee itself concedes is an essential prerequisite to demonstrating the immediate, substantial, and subordinating state interest necessary to sustain its right of inquiry into the membership lists of the association.

Basically, the evidence relied upon by the respondent to demonstrate the necessary foundation consists of the testimony of R. J. Strickland, an investigator for the Committee and its predecessors, and Arlington Sands, a former association official.

Strickland identified by name some 14 persons whom he said either were or had been Communists or members of Communist "front" or "affiliated" organizations. His description of their connection with the association was simply that "each of them has been a member of and/or participated in the meetings and other affairs of the N.A.A.C.P. in Dade County, Florida." In addition, one of the group was identified as having made, at an unspecified time, a contribution of unspecified amount to the local organization.

We do not know from this ambiguous testimony how many of the 14 were supposed to have been N.A.A.C.P. members. For all that appears, and there is no indicated reason to entertain a contrary belief, each or all of the named persons may have attended no more than one or two wholly public meetings of the N.A.A.C.P., and such attendance, like their membership, to the extent it existed, in the association, may have been wholly peripheral and begun and ended many years prior even to commencement of the present investigation in 1956. In addition, it is not clear whether the asserted Communist affiliations and the association with the N.A.A.C.P., however slight, coincided in time. Moreover, except for passing reference to participation in annual elections, there is no indication that membership carried with it any right to control over policy or activities, much less that any was sought. The reasoning which would find support for the challenged inquiries in Communist attendance at meetings from which no member of the public appears to have been barred is even more attenuated, since the only prerogative seemingly attaching to such attendance was the right to listen to the scheduled speaker or program. Mere presence at a public meeting or bare membership—without more—is not infiltration of the sponsoring organization.

It also appears that a number of the 14 persons named by Strickland were no longer even residents of Florida; as to these people, it is difficult to see any basis for supposing that they would be current—much less influential—members of the Miami branch of the N.A.A.C.P., and no other pertinent reason for the inquiry as to them could be found because, as the petitioner testified, the only membership records available related to the then current year.

Strickland did refer to one informant as having been instructed to infiltrate the N.A.A.C.P. and "other organizations." But any persuasive impact this recitation might otherwise have had is neutralized by the same informant's disclosure that his response to this command was simply to attend N.A.A.C.P. meetings "on occasions" and by the absence of any other substantial indication of infiltration. This is not a case in which, after a proper foundation has been laid, a Communist is himself interrogated about his own alleged subversive activities or those of the Communist Party, all as part of an inquiry related to what this Court has held to be a legitimate legislative purpose to investigate the activities of the party or its knowing members.

The testimony of Sands, the other assertedly important witness, added not even a semblance of anything more convincing with regard to the existence of a connection between subversion and the N.A.A.C.P. Sands, whose officership in the association predated 1950 and who admitted that he was uncertain even as to his then current membership in the N.A.A.C.P., merely corroborated to some extent certain of Strickland's references to attendance at N.A.A.C.P. meetings by a few of the persons identified as Communists. However, this too must have related to some time in the unspecified past, since Sands admitted that he had not even been to an N.A.A.C.P. meeting in two years. Sands also noted that one of the asserted Communists, a lawyer, had represented the association in a "murder case," but there is no explanation as to how this fact might indicate or support a conclusion of Communist influence.

Nor does the fact that the N.A.A.C.P. has demonstrated its antipathy to communism and an awareness of its threat by passage of annual antisubversion resolutions carry with it any permissible inference that it has, in fact, been infiltrated, influenced, or in any way dominated or used by Communists. Indeed, given the gross improbability of a Communist dominated or influenced organization denouncing communism, the more reasonable inference would seem to be to the contrary.

Finally, the Committee can find no support for its inquiry into the membership list from Strickland's suggestion that Sands had once uncertainly told him (Strickland) that one or possibly two of the group of 14 may have "made a talk" to the local N.A.A.C.P. chapter, again at some unspecified time in the past. There is no indication that the subject of the "talks" was in any way improper and, in any event, such isolated incidents cannot be made to do the work of substantial evidence of subversive influence or infiltration. The same is true of the few additional vague and somewhat inspecific references to other minor, and nondirective participation in the affairs of the local group.

This summary of the evidence discloses the utter failure to demonstrate the existence of any substantial relationship between the N.A.A.C.P. and subversive or Communist activities. In essence, there is here merely indirect, less than unequivocal, and mostly hearsay testimony that in years past some 14 people who were asserted to be, or to have been, Communists or members of Communist front or "affiliated organizations" attended occasional meetings of the Miami branch of the N.A.A.C.P. "and/or" were members of that branch, which had a total membership of about 1,000.

On the other hand, there was no claim made at the hearings, or since, that the N.A.A.C.P. or its Miami branch was engaged in any subversive activities or that its legitimate activities have been dominated or influenced by Communists. Without any indication of present subversive infiltration in, or influence on, the Miami branch of the N.A.A.C.P., and without any reasonable, demonstrated factual basis to believe that such infiltration or influence existed in the past, or was actively attempted or sought in the present—in short without any showing of a meaningful relationship between the N.A.A.C.P., Miami branch, and subversives or surversive or other illegal activities—we are asked to find the compelling and subordinating state interest which must exist if essential freedoms are to be curtailed or inhibited. This we cannot do. The respondent Committee has laid no adequate foundation for its direct demands upon the officers and records of a wholly legitimate organization for disclosure of its membership; the Committee has neither demonstrated nor pointed out any threat to the State by virtue of the existence of the N.A.A.C.P. or the pursuit of its activities or the minimal associational ties of the 14 asserted Communists. The strong associational interest in maintaining the privacy of membership lists of groups engaged in the constitutionally protected free trade in ideas and beliefs may not be substantially infringed upon such a slender showing as here made by the respondent. While, of course, all legitimate organizations are the benficiaries of these protections, they are all the more essential here, where the challenged privacy is that of persons espousing beliefs already unpopular with their neighbors and the deterrent and "chilling" effect on the free exercise of constitutionally enshrined rights of free speech, expression, and association are consequently the more immediate and substantial. What we recently said in *NAACP* v. *Button, supra,* with respect to the State of Virginia is, as appears from the record, equally applicable here: "We cannot close our eyes to the fact that the militant Negro civil rights movement has engendered the intense resentment and opposition of the politically dominant white community. . . ."

Of course, a legislative investigation—as any investigation—must proceed "step by step," *Barenblatt* v. *United States, supra,* but step by step or in totality, an adequate foundation for inquiry must be laid before proceeding in such a manner as will substantially intrude upon and severely curtail or inhibit constitutionally protected activities or seriously interfere with similarly protected associational rights. No such foundation has been laid here. The respondent Committee has failed to demonstrate the compelling and subordinating governmental interest essential to support direct inquiry into the membership records of the N.A.A.C.P.

Nothing we say here impairs or denies the existence of the underlying legislative right to investigate or legislate with respect to subversive activities by Communists or anyone else; our decision today deals only with the manner in which such power may be exercised and we hold simply that groups which themselves are neither engaged in subversive or other illegal or improper activities, nor demonstrated to have any substantial connections with such activities, are to be protected in their rights of free and private association. As declared in *Sweezy* v. *New Hampshire,* 354 U.S. 234, . . . "It is particularly important that the exercise of the power of compulsory process be carefully circumscribed when the investigative process tends to impinge upon such highly sensitive areas as freedom of speech or press, freedom of political association, and freedom of communication of ideas. . . ."

To permit legislative inquiry to proceed on less than an adequate foundation would be to sanction unjustified and unwarranted intrusions into the very heart of the constitutional privilege to be secure in associations in legitimate organizations engaged in the exercise of First and Fourteenth Amendment rights; to impose a lesser standard than we here do would be inconsistent with the maintenance of those essential conditions basic to the preservation of our democracy.

The judgment below must be and is reversed.

5. Aliens and Loyalty

HARISIADES v. SHAUGHNESSY

342 US 580 (1952)

[In this case three aliens were ordered deported under the Alien Registration Act of 1940. Each had been a member of the Communist Party of the United States, but his or her membership had terminated before the 1940 act was adopted. They contended that they could not be deported under the provisions of the act without violation of basic constitutional freedoms. The Court, by a 6-to-2 vote, upheld the deportation orders. Justice Clark did not participate, and Justices Douglas and Black dissented.

[The American residence of an alien is held, said the Court, by a "precarious tenure." To remain here "is not his right, but is a matter of permission and tolerance." In the present state of the world, said the Court, "it would be rash and irresponsible to reinterpret our fundamental law to deny or qualify the Government's power of deportation." Neither freedom of speech nor due process, the Court held, was violated by the deportations.

[It seems that all the Justices felt that the statutory deportation provisions were offensive to American ideals, but the majority held that "the place to resist unwise or cruel legislation touching aliens is the Congress, not this Court" (concurring opinion by Justice Frankfurter). Cf. *Galvan v. Press,* 74 S. Ct. 737 (1954).

[The Immigration and Nationality Act of 1952 (the McCarran-Walter Act) has imposed even more severe restrictions on aliens. See Milton R. Konvitz, *Civil Rights in Immigration* (Ithaca, N.Y.: Cornell University Press, 1953).]

Mr. Justice Jackson delivered the opinion of the Court:

The ultimate question in these three cases is whether the United States constitutionally may deport a legally resident alien because of membership in the Communist Party which terminated before enactment of the Alien Registration Act of 1940.

Harisiades, a Greek national, accompanied his father to the United States in 1916, when thirteen years of age, and has resided here since. He has taken a wife and sired two children, all citizens. He joined the Communist Party in 1925, when it was known as the Workers Party, and served as an organizer, Branch Executive Committeeman, secretary of its Greek Bureau, and editor of its paper *Empros.* The party discontinued his membership, along with that of other aliens, in 1939, but he has continued association with members. He was familiar with the principles and philosophy of the Communist Party and says he still believes in them. He disclaims personal belief in use of force and violence and asserts that the party favored their use only in defense. A warrant for his deportation because of his membership was issued in 1930 but was not served until 1946. The delay was due to inability to locate him because of his use of a number of aliases. After hearings, he was ordered deported on the grounds that after entry he had been a member of an organization which advocates overthrow of the Government by force and violence and distributes printed matter so advocating. He sought release by habeas corpus, which was denied by the District Court. The Court of Appeals for the Second Circuit affirmed.

Mascitti, a citizen of Italy, came to this country in 1920, at the age of sixteen. He married a resident alien and has one American-born child. He was a member of the Young Workers Party, the Workers Party and the Communist Party between 1923 and 1929. His testimony was that he knew the party advocated a proletarian dictatorship, to be established by force and violence if the capitalist class resisted. He heard some speakers advocate violence, in which he says he did not personally believe, and he was not clear as to the party policy. He resigned in 1929, apparently because he lost sympathy with or interest in the party. A warrant for his deportation issued and was served in 1946. After the usual administrative hearings he was ordered deported on the same grounds as Harisiades. He sought relief by declaratory judgment, which was denied without opinion by a three-judge District Court of the District of Columbia. His case comes to this Court by direct appeal.

Mrs. Coleman, a native of Russia, was admitted to the United States in 1914, when thirteen years of age. She married an American citizen and has three children, citizens by birth. She admits being a member of the Communist Party for about a year, beginning in 1919, and again from 1928 to 1930, and again from 1936 to 1937 or 1938. She held no office and her activities were not significant. She disavowed much knowledge of party principles and program, claiming she joined each time because of some injustice the party was then fighting. The reasons she gives for leaving the party are her health and the party's discontinuance of alien memberships. She has been ordered deported because after entry she became a member of an organization advocating overthrow of the Government by force and violence. She sought an injunction on constitutional grounds, among others. Relief was denied, without opinion, by a three-judge District Court of the District of Columbia and her case also comes here by direct appeal.

Validity of the hearing procedures are questioned for noncompliance with the Administrative Procedure Act, which we think is here inapplicable. Admittedly, each of these deportations is authorized and required by the letter, spirit and intention of the statute. But the Act is assailed on three grounds: (1) that it deprives the aliens of liberty without due process of law in violation of the Fifth Amendment; (2) that it abridges their freedoms of speech and assembly in contravention of the First Amendment; and, (3) that it is an *ex post facto* law which Congress is forbidden to pass by Art. I, § 9, cl. 3 of the Constitution.

We have in each case a finding, approved by the court below, that the Communist Party during the period of the alien's membership taught and advocated overthrow of the Government of the United States by force and violence. Those findings are not questioned here.

These aliens ask us to forbid their expulsion by a departure from the long-accepted application to such cases of the Fifth Amendment provision that no person shall be deprived of life, liberty or property without due process of law. Their basic contention is that admission for permanent residence confers a "vested right" on the alien, equal to that of the citizen, to remain within the country, and that the alien is entitled to constitutional protection in that matter to the same extent as the citizen. Their second line of defense is that if any power to deport domiciled aliens exists it is so dispersed that the judiciary must concur in the grounds for its exercise to the extent of finding them reasonable. The argument goes on to the contention that the grounds prescribed by the Act of 1940 bear no reasonable relation to protection of legitimate interests of the United States and concludes that the Act should be declared invalid. Admittedly these propositions are not founded in precedents of this Court.

For over thirty years each of these aliens has enjoyed such advantages as accrue from residence here without renouncing his foreign allegiance or formally acknowledging adherence to the Constitution he now invokes. Each was admitted to the United States, upon passing formidable exclusionary hurdles, in the hope that, after what may be called a probationary period, he would desire and be found desirable for citizenship. Each has been offered naturalization, with all of the rights and privileges of citizenship, conditioned only upon open and honest assumption to undivided allegiance to our government. But acceptance was and is not compulsory. Each has been permitted to prolong his original nationality indefinitely.

So long as one thus perpetuates a dual status as an American inhabitant but foreign citizen, he may derive advantages from two sources of law—American and international. He may claim protection against our Government unavailable to the citizen. As an alien he retains a claim upon the state of his citizenship to diplomatic intervention on his behalf, a patronage often of considerable value. The state of origin of each of these aliens could presently enter diplomatic remonstrance against these deportations if they were inconsistent with international law, the prevailing custom among nations or their own practices.

The alien retains immunities from burdens which the citizen must shoulder. By withholding his allegiance from the United States, he leaves outstanding a foreign call on his loyalties which international law not only permits our Government to recognize but commands it to respect. In deference to it certain dispensations from conscription for any military service have been granted foreign nationals. They can not, consistently with our international commitments, be compelled "to take part in the operations of war directed against their own country." In addition to such general immunities they may enjoy particular treaty privileges.

Under our law, the alien in several respects stands on an equal footing with citizens, but in others has never been conceded legal parity with the citizen. Most importantly, to protract this ambiguous status within the country is not his right but is a matter of permission and tolerance. The Government's power to terminate its hospitality has been asserted and sustained by this Court since the question first arose.

War, of course, is the most usual occasion for extensive resort to the power. Though the resident alien may be personally loyal to the United States, if his nation becomes our enemy his allegiance prevails over his personal preference and makes him also our enemy, liable to expulsion or internment, and his property becomes subject to seizure and perhaps confiscation. But it does not require war to bring the power of deportation into existence or to authorize its exercise. Congressional apprehension of foreign or internal dangers short of war may lead to its use. So long as the alien elects to continue the ambiguity of his allegiance his domicile here is held by a precarious tenure.

That aliens remain vulnerable to expulsion after long residence is a practice that bristles with severities. But it is a weapon of defense and reprisal confirmed by international law as a power inherent in every sovereign state. Such is the traditional power of the Nation over the alien and we leave the law on the subject as we find it.

This brings us to the alternative defense under the Due Process Clause—that, granting the power, it is so unreasonably and harshly exercised by this enactment that it should be held unconstitutional.

In historical context the Act before us stands out as an extreme application of the expulsion power. There is no denying that as world convulsions have driven us toward a closed society the expulsion power has been exercised with increasing severity, manifest in multiplication of grounds for deportation, in expanding the subject classes from illegal entrants to legal residents, and in greatly lengthening the period of residence after which one may be expelled. This is said to have reached a point where it is the duty of this Court to call a halt upon the political branches of the Government.

It is pertinent to observe that any policy toward aliens is vitally and intricately interwoven with contemporaneous policies in regard to the conduct of foreign relations, the war power, and the maintenance of a republican form of government. Such matters are so exclusively entrusted to the political branches of government as to be largely immune from judicial inquiry or interference.

These restraints upon the judiciary, occasioned by different events, do not control today's decision but they are pertinent. It is not necessary and probably not possible to delineate a fixed and precise line of separation in these matters between political and judicial power under the Constitution. Certainly, however, nothing in the structure of our Government or the text of our Constitution would warrant judicial review by standards which would require us to equate our political judgment with that of Congress.

Under the conditions which produced this Act can we declare that congressional alarm about a coalition of Communist power without and Communist conspiracy within the United States is either a fantasy or a pretense? This Act was approved by President Roosevelt June 28, 1940, when a world war was threatening to involve us, as soon it did. Communists in the United States were exerting every effort to defeat and delay our preparations. Certainly no responsible American would say that there were then or are now no possible grounds on which Congress might believe that Communists in our midst are inimical to our security.

Congress received evidence that the Communist movement here has been heavily laden with aliens and that Soviet control of the American Communist Party has been largely through alien Communists. It would be easy for those of us who do not have security responsibility to say that those who do are taking Communism too seriously and overestimating its danger. But we have an Act of one Congress which, for a decade, subsequent Congresses have never repealed but have strengthened and extended. We, in our private opinions, need not concur in Congress' policies to hold its enactments constitutional. Judicially we must tolerate what personally we may regard as a legislative mistake.

We are urged, because the policy inflicts severe and undoubted hardship on affected individuals, to find a restraint in the Due Process

Clause. But the Due Process Clause does not shield the citizen from conscription and the consequent calamity of being separated from family, friends, home and business while he is transported to foreign lands to stem the tide of Communism. If Communist aggression creates such hardships for loyal citizens, it is hard to find justification for holding that the Constitution requires that its hardships must be spared the Communist alien. When citizens raised the Constitution as a shield against expulsion from their homes and places of business, the Court refused to find hardship a cause for judicial intervention.

We think that, in the present state of the world, it would be rash and irresponsible to reinterpret our fundamental law to deny or qualify the Government's power of deportation. However desirable worldwide amelioration of the lot of aliens, we think it is peculiarly a subject for international diplomacy. It should not be initiated by judicial decision which can only deprive our own Government of a power of defense and reprisal without obtaining for American citizens abroad any reciprocal privileges or immunities. Reform in this field must be entrusted to the branches of the Government in control of our international relations and treaty-making powers.

We hold that the Act is not invalid under the Due Process Clause. These aliens are not entitled to judicial relief unless some other constitutional limitation has been transgressed, to which inquiry we turn.

The First Amendment is invoked as a barrier against this enactment. The claim is that in joining an organization advocating overthrow of government by force and violence the alien has merely exercised freedoms of speech, press and assembly which that Amendment guarantees to him.

The assumption is that the First Amendment allows Congress to make no distinction between advocating change in the existing order by lawful elective processes and advocating change by force and violence, that freedom for the one includes freedom for the other, and that when teaching of violence is denied so is freedom of speech.

Our Constitution sought to leave no excuse for violent attack on the status quo by providing a legal alternative—attack by ballot. To arm all men for orderly change, the Constitution put in their hands a right to influence the electorate by press, speech and assembly. This means freedom to advocate or promote Communism by means of the ballot box, but it does not include the practice or incitement of violence.

True, it often is difficult to determine whether ambiguous speech is advocacy of political methods or subtly shades into a methodical but prudent incitement to violence. Communist governments avoid the inquiry by suppressing everything distasteful. Some would have us avoid the difficulty by going to the opposite extreme of permitting incitement to violent overthrow at least unless it seems certain to succeed immediately. We apprehend that the Constitution enjoins upon us the duty, however difficult, of distinguishing between the two. Different formulae have been applied in different situations and the test applicable to the Communist Party has been stated too recently to make further discussion at this time profitable. We think the First Amendment does not prevent the deportation of these aliens.

The remaining claim is that this Act conflicts with Art. I, § 9, of the Constitution forbidding *ex post facto* enactments. An impression of retroactivity results from reading as a new and isolated enactment what is actually a continuation of prior legislation.

During all the years since 1920 Congress has maintained a standing admonition to aliens, on pain of deportation, not to become members of any organization that advocates overthrow of the United States by force and violence, a category repeatedly held to include the Communist Party. These aliens violated that prohibition and incurred liability to deportation. They were not caught unawares by a change of law. There can be no contention that they were not adequately forewarned both that their conduct was prohibited and of its consequences.

In 1939, this Court decided *Kessler* v. *Strecker,* 307 U.S. 22, . . . in which it was held that Congress, in the statute as it then stood, had not clearly expressed an intent that Communist Party membership remained cause for deportation after it ceased. The Court concluded that in the absence of such expression only contemporaneous membership would authorize deportation.

The reaction of the Communist Party was to drop aliens from membership, at least in form, in order to immunize them from the consequences of their party membership.

The reaction of Congress was that the Court had misunderstood its legislation. In the Act here before us it supplied unmistakable language that past violators of its prohibitions continued to be deportable in spite of resignation or expulsion from the party. It regarded the fact that an alien defied our laws to join the Communist Party as an indication that he had developed little comprehension of the principles or practice of representative government or else was unwilling to abide by them.

However, even if the Act were found to be retroactive, to strike it down would require us to overrule the construction of the *ex post facto* provision which has been followed by this Court from earliest times. It always has been considered that that which it forbids is penal legislation which imposes or increases criminal punishment for conduct lawful previous to its enactment. Deportation, however severe its consequences, has been consistently classified as a civil rather than a criminal procedure. Both of these doctrines as original proposals might be debatable, but both have been considered closed for many years and a body of statute and decisional law has been built upon them. In *Bugajewitz* v. *Adams*, 228 U.S. 585, Mr. Justice Holmes, for the Court, said:

It is thoroughly established that Congress has power to order the deportation of aliens whose presence in the country it deems hurtful. The determination by facts that might constitute a crime under local law is not a conviction of crime, nor is the deportation a punishment; it is simply a refusal by the government to harbor persons whom it does not want. The coincidence of the local penal law with the policy of Congress is an accident. . . . The prohibition of *ex post facto* laws in article 1, § 9, has no application . . . and with regard to the petitioner, it is not necessary to construe the statute as having any retrospective effect.

Later, the Court said,

It is well settled that deportation, while it may be burdensome and severe for the alien, is not a punishment. . . . The inhibition against the passage of an *ex post facto* law by Congress in section 9 of article 1 of the Constitution applies only to criminal laws . . . and not to a deportation act like this. . . .

It is contended that this policy allows no escape by reformation. We are urged to apply some doctrine of atonement and redemption. Congress might well have done so, but it is not for the judiciary to usurp the function of granting absolution or pardon. We can not do so for deportable ex-convicts, even though they have served a term of imprisonment calculated to bring about their reformation.

When the Communist Party as a matter of party strategy formally expelled alien members en masse, it destroyed any significance that discontinued membership might otherwise have as indication of change of heart by the individual. Congress may have believed that the party tactics threw upon the Government an almost impossible burden if it attempted to separate those who sincerely renounced Communist principles of force and violence from those who left the party the better to serve it. Congress, exercising the wide discretion that it alone has in these matters, declined to accept that as the Government's burden.

We find none of the constitutional objections to the Act well founded. The judgments accordingly are affirmed.

Mr. Justice Douglas, with whom Mr. Justice Black concurs, dissenting:
There are two possible bases for sustaining this Act:
(1) A person who was once a Communist is tainted for all time and forever dangerous to our society; or
(2) Punishment through banishment from the country may be placed

upon an alien not for what he did, but for what his political views once were or are.

Each of these is foreign to our philosophy. We repudiate our traditions of tolerance and our articles of faith based upon the Bill of Rights when we bow to them by sustaining an Act of Congress which has them as a foundation.

The view that the power of Congress to deport aliens is absolute and may be exercised for any reason which Congress deems appropriate rests on *Fong Yue Ting* v. *United States,* 149 U.S. 698, decided in 1893 by a six to three vote. That decision seems to me to be inconsistent with the philosophy of constitutional law which we have developed for the protection of resident aliens. We have long held that a resident alien is a "person" within the meaning of the Fifth and the Fourteenth Amendments. He therefore may not be deprived either by the national government or by any state of life, liberty, or property without due process of law. Nor may he be denied the equal protection of the laws. A state was not allowed to exclude an alien from the laundry business because he was a Chinese, nor discharge him from employment because he was not a citizen, nor deprive him of the right to fish because he was a Japanese ineligible to citizenship. An alien's property (provided he is not an enemy alien) may not be taken without just compensation. He is entitled to habeas corpus to test the legality of his restraint, to the protection of the Fifth and Sixth Amendments in criminal trials, and to the right of free speech as guaranteed by the First Amendment.

An alien, who is assimilated in our society, is treated as a citizen so far as his property and his liberty are concerned. He can live and work here and raise a family, secure in the personal guarantees every resident has and safe from discriminations that might be leveled against him because he was born abroad. Those guarantees of liberty and livelihood are the essence of the freedom which this country from the beginning has offered the people of all lands. If those rights, great as they are, have constitutional protection, I think the more important one—the right to remain here—has a like dignity.

The power of Congress to exclude, admit, or deport aliens flows from sovereignty itself and from the power "To establish an uniform Rule of Naturalization." U.S. Const., Art. I, § 8, cl. 4. The power of deportation is therefore an *implied* one. The right to life and liberty is an *express* one. Why this *implied* power should be given priority over the *express* guarantee of the Fifth Amendment has never been satisfactorily answered. Mr. Justice Brewer's dissent in *Fong Yue Ting* v. *United States, . . .* grows in power with the passing years:

It is said that the power here asserted is inherent in sovereignty. This doctrine of powers inherent in sovereignty is one both indefinite and dangerous. Where are the limits to such powers to be found, and by whom are they to be pronounced? Is it within legislative capacity to declare the limits? If so, then the mere assertion of an inherent power creates it, and despotism exists. May the courts establish the boundaries? Whence do they obtain the authority for this? Shall they look to the practices of other nations to ascertain the limits? The governments of other nations have elastic powers. Ours are fixed and bounded by a written constitution. The expulsion of a race may be within the inherent powers of a despotism. History, before the adoption of this constitution, was not destitute of examples of the exercise of such a power; and its framers were familiar with history and wisely, as it seems to me, they gave to this government no general power to banish. Banishment may be resorted to as punishment for crime; but among the powers reserved to the people, and not delegated to the government, is that of determining whether whole classes in our midst shall, for no crime but that of their race and birthplace, be driven from our territory.

The right to be immune from arbitrary decrees of banishment certainly may be more important to "liberty" than the civil rights which all aliens enjoy when they reside here. Unless they are free from arbitrary banishment, the "liberty" they enjoy while they live here is indeed illusory. Banishment is punishment in the practical sense. It may deprive a man and his family of all that makes life worth while. Those who have their roots here have an important stake in this country. Their plans for themselves and their hopes for their children all depend on their right to stay. If they are uprooted and sent to lands no longer known to them, no longer hospitable, they become displaced, homeless people condemned to bitterness and despair.

This drastic step may at times be necessary in order to protect the national interest. There may be occasion when the continued presence of an alien, no matter how long he may have been here, would be hostile to the safety or welfare of the nation due to the nature of his conduct. But unless such condition is shown, I would stay the hand of the government and let those to whom we have extended our hospitality and who have become members of our communities remain here and enjoy the life and liberty which the Constitution guarantees.

Congress has not proceeded by that standard. It has ordered these aliens deported not for what they are but for what they once were. Perhaps a hearing would show that they continue to be people dangerous and hostile to us. But the principle of forgiveness and the doctrine of redemption are too deep in our philosophy to admit that there is no return for those who have once erred.

Freedom of Speech and Press:

Censorship and Contempt

by Publication

1. *Indecent and Obscene Literature*

a. Post Office Control

HANNEGAN *v.* ESQUIRE, INC.

327 US 146 (1946)

[The second-class-mail privilege is a valuable asset to a periodical; for, if this privilege were denied, a periodical would have to pay substantially higher postage rates, which would subject it to a serious competitive disadvantage. If the Postmaster General were given wide discretionary powers in awarding or denying the second-class-mail privilege, he could "make" or "break" a publication; the privilege could be used to impose political, economic, religious, literary, or aesthetic orthodoxy on the press.

[The Court has held that Congress need not open second-class mail "to publications of all types." The furthest the Court ever went in sustaining a revocation of the privilege was in the *Milwaukee Leader Case*, 255 US 407 (1921). The Court (Justices Holmes and Brandeis dissented) upheld the order of the Postmaster General revoking the privilege on the ground that the newspaper had systematically published matter that was banned by the Espionage Act of 1917. The newspaper was thus not merely punished for its *past* misdeeds but was subjected to penalties as to the *future.*

[In the present case the Postmaster General attempted to accomplish the same result with respect to *Esquire,* a monthly magazine, because its contents seemed to him, by reason of vulgarity or poor taste, not to "contribute to the public good and the public welfare." The Court unanimously decided in favor of the publication. The ends of the legislation that provides for the second-class privilege, said the Court, "can be served only by uncensored distribution of literature." A requirement "that literature or art conform to some norm prescribed by an official smacks of an ideology foreign to our system." If the Postmaster General could withdraw the privilege from *Esquire,* he might try to do the same thing tomorrow respecting a periodical "whose social or economic views seemed harmful." It is doubtful, in the light of this decision and opinion, whether the *Milwaukee Leader Case* is still good law; in the *Esquire Case,* it should be noted, the Court cited only the dissents of Holmes and Brandeis in the earlier case.]

Mr. Justice Douglas delivered the opinion of the Court:

Congress has made obscene material nonmailable (18 USCA § 334), and has applied criminal sanctions for the enforcement of that policy. It has divided mailable matter into four classes, periodical publications constituting the second-class. . . . And it has specified four conditions upon which a publication shall be admitted to the second-class. . . . The Fourth condition, which is the only one relevant here, provides:

Except as otherwise provided by law, the conditions upon which a publication shall be admitted to the second class are as follows . . . Fourth. It must be originated and published for the dissemination of information of a public character, or devoted to literature, the sciences, arts, or some special industry, and having a legitimate list of subscribers. Nothing herein contained shall be so construed as to admit to the second-class rate regular publications designed primarily for advertising purposes, or for free circulation, or for circulation at nominal rates.

Respondent is the publisher of *Esquire Magazine,* a monthly periodical which was granted a second-class permit in 1933. In 1943, pursuant to 39 USCA § 232, a citation was issued to respondent by the then Postmaster General (for whom the present Postmaster General has now been substituted as petitioner) to show cause why that permit should not be suspended or revoked. A hearing was held before a board designated by the then Postmaster General. The board recommended that the permit not be revoked. Petitioner's predecessor took a different view. He did not find that *Esquire Magazine* contained obscene material and therefore was nonmailable. He revoked its second-class permit because he found that it did not comply with the Fourth condition. The gist of his holding is contained in the following excerpt from his opinion:

The plain language of this statute does not assume that a publication must in fact be "obscene" within the intendment of the postal obscenity statutes before it can be found not to be "originated and published for the dissemination of information of a public character, or devoted to literature, the sciences, arts, or some special industry."

Writings and pictures may be indecent, vulgar, and risque and still not be obscene in a technical sense. Such writings and pictures may be in that obscure and treacherous borderland zone where the average person hesitates to find them technically obscene, but still may see ample proof that they are morally improper and not for the public welfare and the public good. When such writings or pictures occur in isolated instances their dangerous tendencies and malignant qualities may be considered of lesser importance.

When, however, they become a dominant and systematic feature they most certainly cannot be said to be for the public good, and a publication which uses them in that manner is not making the "special contribution to the public welfare" which Congress intended by the Fourth condition.

A publication to enjoy these unique mail privileges and special preferences is bound to do more than refrain from disseminating material which is obscene or bordering on the obscene. It is under a positive duty to contribute to the public good and the public welfare. . . .

The issues of *Esquire Magazine* under attack are those for January to November inclusive of 1943. The material complained of embraces in bulk only a small percentage of those issues. Regular features of the magazine (called "The Magazine for Men") include articles on topics of current interest, short stories, sports articles or stories, short articles by men prominent in various fields of activities, articles about men prominent in the news, a book review department headed by the late William Lyon Phelps, a theatrical department headed by George Jean Nathan, . . . [a department on] lively arts by Gilbert Seldes, . . . pictorial features, including war action paintings, color photographs of game birds and reproductions of famous paintings, prints and drawings. There was very little in these features which was challenged. But petitioner's predecessor found that the objectionable items, though a small percentage of the total bulk, were regular recurrent features which gave the magazine its dominant tone or characteristic. These include jokes, cartoons, pictures, articles, and poems. They were said to reflect the smoking-room type of humor, featuring, in the main, sex. Some witnesses found the challenged items highly objectionable, calling them salacious and indecent. Others thought they were only racy and risque. Some condemned them as being merely in poor taste. Other witnesses could find no objection to them.

An examination of the items makes plain, we think, that the controversy is not whether the magazine publishes "information of a public character" or is devoted to "literature" or to the "arts." It is whether the contents are "good" or "bad." To uphold the order of revocation would, therefore, grant the Postmaster General a power of censorship. Such a power is so abhorrent to our traditions that a purpose to grant it should not be easily inferred. . . .

If the Fourth condition is read in that way, it is plain that Congress made no radical or basic change in the type of regulation which it adopted for second-class mail in 1879. The inauguration of even a limited type of censorship would have been such a startling change as to have left some traces in the legislative history. But we find none. . . .

We may assume that Congress has a broad power of classification and need not open second-class mail to publications of all types. The categories of publications entitled to that classification have indeed varied through the years. And the Court held in *Ex parte Jackson,* 96 US 727, that Congress could constitutionally make it a crime to send fraudulent or obscene material through the mails. But grave constitutional questions are immediately raised once it is said that the use of the mails is a privilege which may be extended or withheld on any grounds whatsoever. . . . Under that view the second-class rate could be granted on condition that certain economic or political ideas not be disseminated. The provisions of the Fourth condition would have to be far more explicit for us to assume that Congress made such a radical departure from our traditions and undertook to clothe the Postmaster General with the power to supervise the tastes of the reading public of the country.

. . . Under our system of government there is an accommodation for the widest varieties of tastes and ideas. What is good literature, what has educational value, what is refined public information, what is good art, varies with individuals as it does from one generation to another. There doubtless would be a contrariety of views concerning Cervantes' *Don Quixote,* Shakespeare's *Venus and Adonis,* or Zola's *Nana.* But a requirement that literature or art conform to some norm prescribed by an official smacks of an ideology foreign to our system. The basic values implicit in the requirements of the Fourth condition can be served only by uncensored distribution of literature. From the multitude of competing offerings the public will pick and choose. What seems to one to be trash may have for others fleeting or even enduring values. But to withdraw the second-class rate from this publication today because its contents seemed to one official not good for the public would sanction withdrawal of the second-class rate tomorrow from another periodical whose social or economic views seemed harmful to another official. The validity of the obscenity laws is recognition that the mails may not be used to satisfy all tastes, no matter how perverted. But Congress has left the Postmaster General with no power to prescribe standards for the literature or the art which a mailable periodical disseminates. . . .

Affirmed. [The order of the Postmaster General may be enjoined.]

GROVE PRESS v. CHRISTENBERRY

276 F. 2d 433 (1960)

[Soon after Grove Press announced that it would publish the unexpurgated *Lady Chatterley's Lover* by D. H. Lawrence, the Postmaster General formally barred the book from the mails. Judge Bryan, of the Federal District Court, issued an order permanently restraining the Post Office, and this judgment was affirmed by the Court of Appeals, Second Circuit. The opinion of Judge Clark for the latter court is published below. The Post Office, on the advice of the Solicitor General of the United States, did not appeal to the United States Supreme Court.]

Clark, Circuit Judge:

D. H. Lawrence completed the third manuscript version of his novel "Lady Chatterley's Lover" in Italy in 1928, and it was then published in Florence for private distribution. It is this version which has now been published by the plaintiff Grove Press, Inc., in a sumptuous edition selling for $6.00, with a prefatory letter of commendation by Archibald MacLeish, poet, playwright, and Boylston Professor of Rhetoric and Oratory at Harvard University, and with an extensive Introduction and a concluding Bibliographical Note by Mark Schorer, Professor of English Literature at the University of California and a Lawrence scholar.* The book (together with circulars showing its availability by Readers' Subscription, Inc., the second plaintiff) has been detained as unmailable by the New York Postmaster and, after a hearing before the Judicial Officer of the Post Office Department and reference to the Postmaster General for final departmental decision, was held by the latter to be "obscene and non-mailable pursuant to 18 U.S. Code § 1461." The Postmaster General wrote a substantial decision, of which these are salient paragraphs:

---

* This edition has never before been legally published in this country or in England, although it has been frequently pirated here; and an abridged edition was published by Knopf in 1930. The complete version, however, has been published in some continental countries in English and in most in translation. It is not protected here by copyright, and various paperback editions—we are told—are now appearing. . . .

The contemporary community standards are not such that this book should be allowed to be transmitted in the mails.

The book is replete with descriptions in minute detail of sexual acts engaged in or discussed by the book's principal characters. These descriptions utilize filthy, offensive and degrading words and terms. Any literary merit the book may have is far outweighed by the pornographic and smutty passages and words, so that the book, taken as a whole, is an obscene and filthy work.

The plaintiffs then sought a declaratory judgment and an injunction from the court below to reverse this decision. On cross motions for summary judgment, Judge Bryan gave a declaration that the Grove Edition here involved "is neither obscene, lewd, lascivious, indecent nor filthy in content or character, and is not nonmailable matter within the meaning of Title 18, Section 1461 of the United States Code." He also held that the bar order of the Postmaster General "is illegal and void and violates plaintiffs' rights in contravention of the Constitution," and entered an order permanently enjoining its enforcement. His complete and reasoned opinion, with which we are in accord, gives further background, and reference is therefore made to it.

The important question on the merits is whether this now famous book is obscene within the meaning of 18 U.S.C. § 1461. This is a lengthy statute going back to 1876 and 1873 and amended as recently as 1958, which in portions here pertinent provides: "Every obscene, lewd, lascivious, indecent, filthy or vile article . . . is declared to be nonmailable matter and shall not be conveyed in the mails or delivered from any post office or by any letter carrier. Whoever knowingly uses the mails for the mailing, carriage in the mails, or delivery of anything declared by this section to be nonmailable . . . shall be fined not more than $5,000 or imprisoned not more than five years, or both, for the first such offense, and shall be fined not more than $10,000 or imprisoned not more than ten years, or both, for each such offense thereafter."

But before we reach the merits, we must consider the procedural aspects of the issue involved, since the government on this appeal has directed much the greater force of its argument to a reliance upon the principle of administrative law that an agency action supported by substantial evidence is beyond judicial review. Its major contention is that the statute obligates the Post Office Department to prevent the conveyance of obscene matter through the mails and that, since the Postmaster General has made a finding of obscenity based upon substantial evidence, the district court erred in reviewing it. The district court rejected this contention of agency finality, and so do we.

Preliminarily we should note the query whether the statute, being one defining a crime with criminal penalties, may afford justification for the acts of seizure by the Postmaster General in any event, or whether its sanction is not limited to criminal prosecution for crimes already committed. This is an issue which divided the court in *Sunshine Book Co. v. Summerfield*, F. 2d 114, summarily reversed in 355 U.S. 372. It is one of serious difficulty; but we shall not attempt to resolve it here, since we think the result is clear on other grounds.

Judge Bryan ruled that the issue was one of law fully reviewable by a court of law, since there was no dispute in matters of evidence and hence there was no occasion or the application of the substantial evidence rule. Although this conclusion is vigorously attacked by the government, it is difficult to see why it is not sound, particularly as reinforced by the constitutional overtones implicit in the issue. There can be no doubt that in large areas of postal activity involving the delivery of the mail the Post Office Department exercies discretion not to be controlled by courts. But to determine whether a work of art or literature is obscene has little, if anything, to do with the expedition or efficiency with which the mails are dispatched. And here it is clear that no question of evidence was involved. In fact the Departmental officials considered only the novel itself against the background of the statute and declined to consider the expert opinion proffered by the plaintiffs. The question was thus one starkly of law. Moreover, the plaintiffs raised the constitutional issue of freedom of expression, Judge Bryan ruled upon it below, and it can hardly be escaped in this class of cases. . . . Even factual matters must be reviewed on appeal against a claim of denial of a constitutional right. . . . Both legally and practically the claim of final censorship powers here made for the Postmaster General is extreme. Indeed it has received an incisive answer in the public press thus: "And courts, not post offices, are the proper places for a determination of what is and is not protected by the Constitution."

Passing then to the merits we must of course be cognizant of the risk run by judges in enforcing obscenity statutes such as this and thus perchance condemning what become classics of our intellectual heritage. Some of the present Justices of the Supreme Court revolt against all this supervision as violative of constitutional precepts. But since the statute has been upheld by majority vote, . . . it remains the duty of those of us who sit in inferior courts to enforce it as best we may. And we need have no illusions but that a large business is done in exploiting "hard core pornography" for money's sake. In general this trash is easily recognized, with its repetitive emphasis (usually illustrated) upon purely physical action without character or plot development; and even if its direct connection with crime or incitement to juvenile or other delinquency is not proven—as many now assert—it cannot arouse sympathy because of its essentially repulsive, as well as fraudulent, character. It is when we come to more genuine works of literature that troublesome issues arise.

At the outset we may well recall the classic warning by a great American judge in probably the leading case on the subject prior to the recent utterances of the Supreme Court, Judge Augustus N. Hand in *United States* v. *One Book Entitled Ulysses by James Joyce:* "The foolish judgments of Lord Eldon about one hundred years ago, proscribing the works of Byron and Southey, and the finding by the jury under a charge by Lord Denman that the publication of Shelley's 'Queen Mab' was an indictable offense are a warning to all who have to determine the limits of the field within which authors may exercise themselves." And he went on to this judgment upon a then disputed book now recognized as classic: "We think that Ulysses is a book of originality and sincerity of treatment and that it has not the effect of promoting lust." Here we have one advantage over our predecessors in that the time which has elapsed since the writing and original publication of this book has been sufficient for the crystallization of at least a literary judgment upon it. And it seems clear without dissent from the expert evaluations presented both in the record and in the introductory material to this edition, as well as in the contemporary literature, that this is a major and a distinguished novel, and Lawrence one of the great writers of the era.°

For present purposes our test must be based upon that prescribed by the majority in *Roth* v. *United States,* 354 U.S. 476. Justice Brennan said:

> However, sex and obscenity are not synonymous. Obscene material is material which deals with sex in a manner appealing to prurient interest. The portrayal of sex, e.g., in art, literature and scientific works, is not itself sufficient reason to deny material the consitutional protection of freedom of speech and press. Sex, a great and mysterious motive force in human life, has indisputably been a subject of absorbing interest to mankind through the ages; it is one of the vital problems of human interest and public concern.

° This judgment of Messrs. MacLeish, Schorer, Malcolm Cowley, Alfred Kazin, and other competent critics appearing in the record or offered at the departmental hearing seems to be rather regularly and continuously confirmed in literary journals. For example, the reviewer for the Saturday Review, Granville Hicks, in an article entitled, D. H. Lawrence Reconsidered, Saturday Review, Dec. 19, 1959, p. 31, quotes the distinguished English scholar John Middleton Murry as saying shortly before his death in 1957 that "since the end of the Second World War, there has emerged a growing consensus of opinion that he [Lawrence] is the most significant writer of his time." So Professor Harry T. Moore, Lawrence biographer, reviewing

And he gave support to the definition in the A.L.I. Model Penal Code thus:

We perceive no significant difference between the meaning of obscenity developed in the case law and the definition of the A.L.I., Model Penal Code, § 207.10 (2) (Tent. Draft No. 6, 1957), viz.:
'. . . A thing is obscene if, considered as a whole, its predominant appeal is to prurient interest, i.e., a shameful or morbid interest in nudity, sex, or excretion, and if it goes substantially beyond customary limits of candor in description or representation of such matters. . . .'

Examined with care and "considered as a whole," the predominant appeal of "Lady Chatterley's Lover" in our judgment is demonstrably not to "prurient interest," as thus defined. By now the story of the novel is well known. It is thus succinctly summarized in Professor Schorer's Introduction: "Constance Chatterly, the frustrated wife of an aristocratic mine owner who has been wounded in the war and left paralyzed and impotent, is drawn to his game-keeper, the misanthropic son of a miner, becomes pregnant by him, and hopes at the end of the book to be able to divorce her husband and leave her class for a life with the other man." But of course the story is a small part of the work. Actually the book is a polemic against three things which Lawrence hated: the crass industrialization of the English Midlands, the British caste system, and inhibited sex relations between man and woman. We may not see the close relation he did between the three as instruments of repression of the natural man, but we can understand his plea for greater freedom and naturalness even if we may not share his conviction of the all-inclusive nature of his remedy. Lawrence grew up in the English coal regions as the son of a miner who had married a teacher, and the theme of a relationship between a man of a low social status with a woman of a higher level is one he has used in previous works. The rationale he seeks to establish is thus one surely arguable and open to a writer. And if the aristocratic, but frustrated, heroine is to be taught naturalness in self-expression by her husband's servant, the plot line is rather clearly indicated. It is hardly surprising, therefore, that we find descriptions of increasingly more intimate scenes between the two protagonists and an increasingly greater use of "natural" language as the man's demonstration of naturalness to his feminine partner is stepped up to the author's climax.

What has apparently given surprise over the years—probably less so now than formerly in view of the changing climate of opinion—is the

---

this book for the N.Y. Times Book Review Section, May 3, 1959, terms it "our time's most significant romance."

degree or extent to which the author has carried his plan. Undoubtedly to these critics of morals a little description of sex goes a long way; and judging by other examples, classical and modern, less directness would have left the work unchallenged. Obviously a writer can employ various means to achieve the effect he has in mind, and so probably Lawrence could have omitted some of the passages found "smutty" by the Postmaster General and yet have produced an effective work of literature. But clearly it would not have been the book he planned, because for what he had in mind his selection was most effective, as the agitation and success of the book over the years have proven.* In these sex descriptions showing how his aristocratic, but frustrated, lady achieved fulfillment and naturalness in her life, he also writes with power and indeed with a moving tenderness which is compelling, once our age-long inhibitions against sex revelations in print have been passed. In actuality his thesis here is only that pressed continuously in the modern marriage-counseling and doctors' books written with apparently quite worthy objectives and advertised steadily in our most sober journals and magazines. Of course it is old in literature; one may recall, for instance, the passionate love scenes between the young tutor and his employer's wife in Stendhal's classic, *Le Rouge et Noir* (The Red and the Black), published in 1830. Actually in present-day literature such descriptions of physical relations appear as regular staples of literary diet and quite without Lawrence's straightforward and somewhat refreshing candor.†

The same is true of the so-called four-letter words found particularly objectionable by the Postmaster General. These appear in the latter portion of the book in the mouth of the game-keeper in his tutelage of the lady in naturalness and are accepted by her as such. Again this

---

* The defense complains that Lawrence need not "so vividly" have portrayed his scenes of sex and objects to the "Constant repetition of such intimate scenes." But that was at least one way of arousing reader interest, as the careful textual examination by the distinguished government counsel and associate counsel demonstrates. Compare the comment in a somewhat analogous situation of the New York Times Scandinavian reporter Werner Wiskari upon the presently popular Swedish motion picture director Ingmar Bergman, in the Sunday Times Magazine, Dec. 20, 1959, § 6, p. 20: "Why does Bergman insist on such brutality? Because he cannot abide the merely indifferent presence of a popcorn-chewing audience. In creating scenes that are almost physically felt in the midsection, he aims to involve the onlooker in the action so as to win active understanding of the motivations of his characters."

† As in a recent book of wide popularity in respected book circles, said to have had a sale of nearly three million copies, a tale of continuous seduction of or by a twelve-year-old girl by or with a middle-aged lover; or another, locally nominated for the Nobel prize, depicting in detail the sexual activities, marital and extramarital, of a middle-aged Pennsylvania lawyer.

could be taken as an object lesson at least in directness as compared to the smirk of much contemporary usage, which (perhaps strangely) does not seem to have offended our mailmen. In short, all these passages to which the Postmaster General takes exception—in bulk only a portion of the book—are subordinate, but highly useful, elements to the development of the author's central purpose. And that is not prurient. Should a court in reading meaning into the word "obscene"—which proves far from self-defining—make it so all-inclusive as to prohibit a writer from making use of normal and no longer unusual descriptions and parts of English speech to accomplish a worthy objective? And should a mature and sophisticated reading public be kept in blinders because a government official thinks reading certain works of power and literary value is not good for it? We agree with the court below in believing and holding that definitions of obscenity consistent with modern intellectual standards and morals neither require nor permit such a restriction.

Judgment affirmed.

MANUAL ENTERPRISES *v.* DAY

370 US 478(1962)

[The Post Office barred from the mails certain magazines published primarily for homosexuals. The Supreme Court held that the magazines were not subject to repression as legally obscene. Justices Frankfurter and White did not participate in the case. Justice Black concurred in the result. Justice Brennan wrote a concurring opinion, in which Chief Justice Warren and Justice Douglas joined. Justice Clark dissented.]

Mr. Justice Harlan announced the judgment of the Court and an opinion in which Mr. Justice Stewart joins:

This case draws in question a ruling of the Post Office Department, sustained both by the District Court and the Court of Appeals, . . . barring from the mails a shipment of petitioners' magazines. That ruling was based on alternative determinations that the magazines were (1) themselves "obscene," and (2) gave information where obscene matter could be obtained, thus rendering them nonmailable under two separate provisions of 18 U.S.C. § 1461, known as the Comstock Act.*

---

* Section 1461 of 18 U.S.C. provides in part:

"Every obscene, lewd, lascivious, indecent, filthy or vile article, matter, thing, device, or substance; and— . . .

"Every written or printed card, letter, circular, book, phamphlet, advertisement, or notice of any kind giving information, directly or indirectly, where, or how, or

Certiorari was granted to consider the claim that this ruling was inconsistent with the proper interpretation and application of § 1461, and with principles established in two of this Court's prior decisions, *Roth* v. *United States*, 354 U.S. 476; *Smith* v. *California*, 361 U.S. 147.

Petitioners are three corporations respectively engaged in publishing magazines titled *MANual*, *Trim*, and *Grecian Guild Pictorial*. They have offices at the same address in Washington, D.C., and a common president, one Herman L. Womack. The magazines consist largely of photographs of nude, or near-nude, male models and give the names of each model and the photographer, together with the address of the latter. They also contain a number of advertisements by independent photographers offering nudist photographs for sale.

On March 25, 1960, six parcels containing an aggregate of 405 copies of the three magazines, destined from Alexandria, Virginia, to Chicago, Illinois, were detained by the Alexandria postmaster, pending a ruling by his superiors at Washington as to whether the magazines were "nonmailable." Following an evidentiary hearing before the Judicial Officer of the Post Office Department there ensued the administrative and court decisions now under review.

I.

On the issue of obscenity, as distinguished from unlawful advertising, the case comes to us with the following administrative findings, which are supported by substantial evidence and which we, and indeed the parties, for the most part, themselves, accept: (1) the magazines are not, as initially asserted by petitioners, physical culture or "body-building" publications, but are composed primarily, if not exclusively, for homosexuals, and have no literary, scientific or other merit; (2) they would appeal to the "prurient interest" of such sexual deviates, but would not have any interest for sexually normal individuals; and (3) the magazines are read almost entirely by homo-

---

from whom, or by what means any of such mentioned matters, articles, or things may be obtained or made, . . .

"Is declared to be nonmailable matter and shall not be conveyed in the mails or delivered from any post office or by any letter carrier.

"Whoever knowingly uses the mails for the mailing, carriage in the mails, or delivery of anything declared by this section to be nonmailable, or knowingly causes to be delivered by mail according to the direction thereon, or at the place at which it is directed to be delivered by the person to whom it is addressed, or knowingly takes any such thing from the mails for the purpose of circulating or disposing thereof, or of aiding in the circulation or disposition thereof, shall be fined not more than $5,000 or imprisoned not more than five years. . . ."

sexuals, and possibly a few adolescent males; the ordinary male adult would not normally buy them.

On these premises, the question whether these magazines are "obscene," as it was decided below and argued before us, was thought to depend solely on a determination as to the relevant "audience" in terms of which their "prurient interest" appeal should be judged. This view of the obscenity issue evidently stemmed from the belief that in *Roth* v. *United States*, this Court established the following *single* test for determining whether challenged material is obscene: "whether to the average person, applying contemporary community standards, the dominant theme of the material taken as a whole appeals to prurient interest." . . . On this basis the Court of Appeals, rejecting the petitioners' contention that the "prurient interest" appeal of the magazines should be judged in terms of their likely impact on the "average person," even though not a likely recipient of the magazines, held that the administrative finding respecting their impact on the "average homosexual" sufficed to establish the Government's case as to their obscenity.

We do not reach the question thus thought below to be dispositive on this aspect of the case. For we find lacking in these magazines an element which, no less than "prurient interest," is essential to a valid determination of obscenity under § 1461, and to which neither the Post Office Department nor the Court of Appeals addressed itself at all: These magazines cannot be deemed so offensive on their face as to affront current community standards of decency—a quality that we shall hereafter refer to as "patent offensiveness" or "indecency." Lacking that quality, the magazines cannot be deemed legally "obscene," and we need not consider the question of the proper "audience" by which their "prurient interest" appeal should be judged.

The words of § 1461, "obscene, lewd, lascivious, indecent, filthy or vile" connote something that is portrayed in a manner so offensive as to make it unacceptable under current community *mores*. While in common usage the words have different shades of meaning, the statute since its inception has always been taken as aimed at obnoxiously debasing portrayals of sex. Although the statute condemns such material, irrespective of the *effect* it may have upon those into whose hands it falls, the early case of *United States* v. *Bennett,* 24 Fed. Cas. 1093 (No. 14571), put a limiting gloss upon the statutory language: the statute reaches only indecent material which, as now expressed in *Roth* v. *United States, supra,* "taken as a whole appeals to prurient interest." This "effect" element, originally cast in somewhat different language from that of *Roth* . . . , was taken into federal obscenity law from the leading English case of *Regina* v. *Hicklin,* [1868] L.R. 3 Q.B.

360, of which a distinguished Australian judge has given the following illuminating analysis:

As soon as one reflects that the word 'obscene,' as an ordinary English word, has nothing to do with corrupting or depraving susceptible people, and that it is used to describe things which are offensive to current standards of decency and not things which may induce to sinful thoughts, it becomes plain, I think, that Cockburn, C. J., in . . . R. v. *Hicklin* . . . was not propounding a logical definition of the word 'obscene,' but was merely explaining that particular characteristic which was necessary to bring an obscene publication within the law relating to obscene libel. . . . The tendency to deprave is not the characteristic which makes a publication obscene but is the characteristic which makes an obscene publication criminal. It is at once an essential element in the crime and the justification for the intervention of the common law. But it is not the whole and sole test of what constitutes an obscene libel. There is not obscene libel unless what is published is *both* offensive according to current standards of decency *and* calculated or likely to have the effect described in *R. v. Hicklin.* . . .

The thoughtful studies of the American Law Institute reflect the same twofold concept of obscenity. Its earlier draft of a Model Penal Code contains the following definition of "obscene": "A thing is obscene if, considered as a whole, its predominant appeal is to prurient interest . . . *and* if it goes substantially beyond customary limits of candor in description or representation of such matters." A.L.I., Model Penal Code, Tent. Draft No. 6 (1957), § 207.10 (2). (Emphasis added.) The same organization's currently proposed definition reads: "Material is obscene if, considered as a whole, its predominant appeal is to prurient interest . . . and if *in addition* it goes substantially beyond customary limits of candor in describing or representing such matters." A.L.I., Model Penal Code, Proposed Official Draft (May 4, 1962), § 251.4 (1). (Emphasis added.) *

Obscenity under the federal statute thus requires proof of two distinct elements: (1) patent offensiveness; and (2) "prurient interest" appeal. Both must conjoin before challenged material can be found "obscene" under § 1461. In most obscenity cases, to be sure, the two elements tend to coalesce, for that which is patently offensive will also usually carry the requisite "prurient interest" appeal. It is only in the unusual instance where, as here, the "prurient interest" appeal of the material is found limited to a particular class of persons that occasion arises for a truly independent inquiry into the question whether or not the material is patently offensive.

* This definition was approved by the Institute, as part of the "Proposed Official Draft," at its annual meeting in Washington, D.C., in May 1962.

The Court of Appeals was mistaken in considering that *Roth* made "prurient interest" appeal the sole test of obscenity. Reading that case as dispensing with the requisite of patently offensive portrayal would be not only inconsistent with § 1461 and its common-law background, but out of keeping with *Roth's* evident purpose to tighten obscenity standards. The Court there both rejected the "isolated excerpt" and "particularly susceptible persons" tests of the *Hicklin* case, . . . and was at pains to point out that not all portrayals of sex could be reached by obscenity laws but only those treating that subject "in a manner appealing to prurient interest." . . . That, of course, was but a compendious way of embracing in the obscenity standard *both* the concept of patent offensivenes, manifested by the terms of § 1461 itself, and the element of the likely corruptive effect of the challenged material, brought into federal law via *Regina* v. *Hicklin*.

To consider that the "obscenity" exception in "the area of constitutionally protected speech or press," *Roth*, at 485, does not require any determination as to the patent offensiveness *vel non* of the material itself might well put the American public in jeopardy of being denied access to many worthwhile works in literature, science, or art. For one would not have to travel far even among the acknowledged masterpieces in any of these fields to find works whose "dominant theme" might, not beyond reason, be claimed to appeal to the "prurient interest" of the reader or observer. We decline to attribute to Congress any such quixotic and deadening purpose as would bar from the mails all material, not patently offensive, which stimulates impure desires relating to sex. Indeed such a construction of § 1461 would doubtless encounter constitutional barriers. *Roth,* at 487–489. Consequently we consider the power exercised by Congress in enacting § 1461 as no more embracing than the interdiction of "obscenity" as it had theretofore been understood. It is only material whose indecency is self-demonstrating *and* which, from the standpoint of its effect, may be said predominantly to appeal to the prurient interest that Congress has chosen to bar from the mails by the force of § 1461.

We come then to what we consider the dispositive question on this phase of the case. Are these magazines offensive on their face? Whether this question be deemed one of fact or of mixed fact and law, . . . we see no need of remanding the case for initial consideration by the Post Office Department or the Court of Appeals of this missing factor in their determinations. That issue, involving factual matters entangled in a constitutional claim, see *Grove Press, Inc.,* v. *Christenberry,* 276 F. 2d 433, is ultimately one for this Court. The relevant materials being before us, we determine the issue for ourselves.

There must first be decided the relevant "community" in terms of whose standards of decency the issue must be judged. We think that the proper test under this federal statute, reaching as it does to all parts of the United States whose population reflects many different ethnic and cultural backgrounds, is a national standard of decency. We need not decide whether Congress could constitutionally prescribe a lesser geographical framework for judging this issue which would not have the intolerable consequence of denying some sections of the country access to material, there deemed acceptable, which in others might be considered offensive to prevailing community standards of decency. . . .

As regards the standard for judging the element of "indecency," the *Roth* case gives little guidance beyond indicating that the standard is a constitutional one which, as with "prurient interest," requires taking the challenged material "as a whole." . . . Being ultimately concerned only with the question whether the First and Fourteenth Amendments protect material that is admittedly obscene, the Court there had no occasion to explore the application of a particular obscenity standard. At least one important state court and some authoritative commentators have considered *Roth* and subsequent cases to indicate that only "hard-core" pornography can constitutionally be reached under this or similar state obscenity statutes. . . . Whether "hard-core" pornography, or something less, be the proper test, we need go no further in the present case than to hold that the magazines in question, taken as a whole, cannot, under any permissible constitutional standard, be deemed to be beyond the pale of contemporary notions of rudimentary decency.

We cannot accept in full the Government's description of these magazines which, contrary to *Roth*, tends to emphasize and in some respects overdraw certain features in several of the photographs, at the expense of what the magazines fairly taken as a whole depict. Our own independent examination of the magazines leads us to conclude that the most that can be said of them is that they are dismally unpleasant, uncouth, and tawdry. But this is not enough to make them "obscene." Divorced from their "prurient interest" appeal to the unfortunate persons whose patronage they were aimed at capturing (a separate issue), these portrayals of the male nude cannot fairly be regarded as more objectionable than many portrayals of the female nude that society tolerates. Of course not every portrayal of male or female nudity is obscene. . . . Were we to hold that these magazines, although they do not transcend the prevailing bounds of decency, may be denied access to the mails by such undifferentiated legislation as that before us, we would be ignoring the admonition that "the door . . . into this area [the First Amendment] cannot be left ajar; it must be kept tightly closed and opened only the slightest crack necessary to prevent encroachment upon more important interests." . . . *Roth*, at 488.*

We conclude that the administrative ruling respecting nonmailability is improvident insofar as it depends on a determination that these magazines are obscene.

II.

There remains the question of the advertising. It is not contended that the petitioners held themselves out as purveyors of obscene material, or that the advertisements, as distinguished from the other contents of the magazines, were obscene on their own account. The advertisements were all by independent third-party photographers. And, neither with respect to the advertisements nor the magazines themselves, do we understand the Government to suggest that the "advertising" provisions of § 1461 are violated if the mailed material merely "gives the leer that promises the customer some obscene pictures." . . . Such an approach to the statute could not withstand the underlying precepts of *Roth*. . . . The claim on this branch of the case rests, then, on the fact that some of the third-party advertisers were found in possession of what undoubtedly may be regarded as "hard-core" photographs, and that postal officials, although not obtaining the names of the advertisers from the lists in petitioners' magazines, received somewhat less offensive material through the mails from certain studios which were advertising in petitioner's magazines.

A question of law must first be dealt with. Should the "obscene-advertising" proscription of § 1461 be construed as not requiring proof that the publisher *knew* that at least some of his advertisers were offering to sell obscene material? In other words, although the criminal provisions of § 1461 do require *scienter* . . . can the Post Office Department in civil proceedings under that section escape with a lesser burden of proof? We are constrained to a negative answer. *First,* Congress has required *scienter* in respect of one indicted for mailing material proscribed by the statute. In the constitutional climate in which this statute finds itself, we should hesitate to attribute to Congress a purpose to render a publisher civilly responsible for the innocuous advertisements of the materials of others, in the absence of any show-

---

* Since Congress has sought to bar from the mails only material that is "obscene, lewd, lascivious, indecent, filthy, or vile," and it is within this statutory framework that we must judge the materials before us, we need not consider whether these magazines could constitutionally be reached under "a statute narrowly drawn to define and punish specific conduct as constituting a clear and present danger." *Cantwell* v. *Connecticut*, 310 U.S. 296.

ing that he knew that the character of such materials was offensive. And with no express grant of authority to the Post Office Department to keep obscene matter from the mail . . . we should be slow to accept the suggestion that an element of proof expressly required in a criminal proceeding may be omitted in an altogether parallel civil proceeding. *Second*, this Court's ground of decision in *Smith* v. *California*, 361 U.S. 147, indicates that a substantial constitutional question would arise were we to construe § 1461 as not requiring proof of *scienter* in civil proceedings. For the power of the Post Office to bar a magazine from the mails, if exercised without proof of the publisher's knowledge of the character of the advertisements included in the magazine, would as effectively "impose a severe limitation on the public's access to constitutionally protected matter," . . . as would a state obscenity statute which makes criminal the possession of obscene material without proof of *scienter*. Since publisher cannot practicably be expected to investigate each of their advertisers, and since the economic consequences of an order barring even a single issue of a periodical from the mails might entail heavy financial sacrifice, a magazine publisher might refrain from accepting advertisements from those whose own materials could conceivably be deemed objectionable by the Post Office Department. This would deprive such materials, which might otherwise be entitled to constitutional protection, of a legitimate and recognized avenue of access to the public. To be sure, the Court found it unnecessary in *Smith* to delineate the scope of *scienter* which would satisfy the Fourteenth Amendment. Yet it may safely be said that a federal statute which, as we construe it, requires the presence of that element is not satisfied, as the Government suggests it might be, merely by showing that a defendant did not make a "good faith effort" to ascertain the character of his advertiser's materals.

On these premises we turn to the record in this case. Although postal officials had informed petitioners' president, Womack, that their Department was *prosecuting* several of his advertisers for sending obscene matter through the mails, there is no evidence that any of this material was shown to him. He thus was afforded no opportunity to judge for himself as to its alleged obscenity. Contrariwise, one of the government witnesses at the administrative hearing admitted that the petitioners had deleted the advertisements of several photographic studios after being informed by the Post Office that the proprietors had been *convicted* of mailing obscene material. The record reveals that none of the postal officials who received allegedly obscene matter from some of the advertisers obtained their names from petitioners' magazines; this material was received as a result of independent test checks. Nor on the record before us can petitioners be linked with the material seized by the police. . . . The only such asserted connection—that "hard-core" matter was seized at the studio of one of petitioners' advertisers—falls short of an adequate showing that petitioners knew that the advertiser was offering for sale obscene matter. Womack's own conviction for sending obscene material through the mails, *Womack* v. *United States*, 294 F. 2d 204, is remote from proof or like conduct on the part of the advertisers. At that time he was acting as president of another studio; the vendee of the material, while an advertiser in petitioners' magazines, had closed his own studio before the present issues were published. Finally, the general testimony by one postal inspector to the effect that in his experience advertisers of this character, after first leading their customers on with borderline material, usually followed up with "hard-core" matter, can hardly be deemed of probative significance on the issue at hand.

At best the Government's proof showed no more than that petitioners were chargeable with knowledge that these advertisers were offering photographs of the same character, and with the same purposes, as those reflected in their own magazines. This is not enough to satisfy the Government's burden of proof on this score.

In conclusion, nothing in this opinion of course remotely implies approval of the type of magazines published by these petitioners, still less of the sordid motives which prompted their publication. All we decide is that on this record these particular magazines are not subject to repression under § 1461.

Reversed.

b. Customs Control

UNITED STATES *v.* ONE BOOK CALLED "ULYSSES"

5 F. Supp. 182 (1933)

[A form of censorship that might have a serious effect on American culture could be achieved by customs officials if they stopped at the border books that they considered objectionable. Literary, aesthetic, or political isolationism could be strengthened in this way.

[Until the law was changed by Congress in 1930 customs officials prevented the entry of such classics as Rousseau's *Confessions*, Casanova's *Memoirs*, the *Golden Ass* of Apuleius, all of Rabelais, Boccaccio's *Decameron*, *The Arabian Nights*, Voltaire's *Candide*, and modern books like *The Enormous Room* by E. E. Cummings and *Psychopathia Sexualis* by Krafft-Ebing. Many of these books had already been published in the United States, but this fact did not impress the customs officials; they seized and confiscated the books, and the citizen was quite helpless. Congress in 1930 amended the Tariff Act to authorize the Secretary of the Treasury to admit classics and books of recognized scientific or literary merit when imported for noncommercial purposes. The act provided also that, when a book was seized, the collector was to notify the federal district attorney, who was to institute proceedings in the Federal District Court for the forfeiture of the book. Any party in interest could demand a trial by jury.

[In 1933 an attempt was made to keep out a copy of *Ulysses* by James Joyce. In a notable decision, Judge Woolsey of the Federal District Court ruled that the book was not "obscene" within the meaning of the act and so was not subject to seizure and confiscation. His decision was affirmed by the Court of Appeals. 72 F. 2d 705 (1934). The 1930 statute and Judge Woolsey's decision have, on the whole, emancipated books from customs censorship; but see *Besig* v. *United States*, 208 F. 2d 142 (1953).]

On cross motions for a decree in a libel of confiscation, supplemented by a stipulation—hereinafter described—brought by the United States against the book "Ulysses" by James Joyce, under Section 305 of the Tariff Act of 1930, Title 19 United States Code, Section 1305, on the ground that the book is obscene within the meaning of that Section, and, hence, is not importable into the United States, but is subject to seizure, forfeiture and confiscation and destruction.

Judge Woolsey:

The motion for a decree dismissing the libel herein is granted, and, consequently, of course, the Government's motion for a decree of forfeiture and destruction is denied.

Accordingly a decree dismissing the libel without costs may be entered herein.

I. The practice followed in this case is in accordance with the suggestion made by me in the case of *United States* v. *One Book Entitled "Contraception,"* 51 F. (2d) 525, and is as follows:

After issue was joined by the filing of the claimant's answer to the libel for forfeiture against "Ulysses," a stipulation was made between the United States Attorney's office and the attorneys for the claimant providing:

1. That the book "Ulysses" should be deemed to have been annexed to and to have become part of the libel just as if it had been incorporated in its entirety therein.

2. That the parties waived their right to a trial by jury.

3. That each party agreed to move for decree in its favor.

4. That on such cross motions the Court might decide all the questions of law and fact involved and render a general finding thereon.

5. That on the decision of such motions the decree of the Court might be entered as if it were a decree after trial.

It seems to me that a procedure of this kind is highly appropriate in libels for the confiscation of books such as this. It is an especially advantageous procedure in the instant case because on account of the length of "Ulysses" and the difficulty of reading it, a jury trial would have been an extremely unsatisfactory, if not an almost impossible, method of dealing with it.

II. I have read "Ulysses" once in its entirety and I have read those passages of which the Government particularly complains several times. In fact, for many weeks, my spare time has been devoted to the consideration of the decision which my duty would require me to make in this matter.

"Ulysses" is not an easy book to read or to understand. But there has been much written about it, and in order properly to approach the consideration of it, it is advisable to read a number of other books which have now become its satellites. The study of "Ulysses" is, therefore, a heavy task.

III. The reputation of "Ulysses" in the literary world, however, warranted my taking such time as was necessary to enable me to satisfy myself as to the intent with which the book was written, for, of course, in any case where a book is claimed to be obscene it must first be determined, whether the intent with which it was written was what is called, according to the usual phrase, pornographic,—that is, written for the purpose of exploiting obscenity.

If the conclusion is that the book is pornographic that is the end of the inquiry and forfeiture must follow.

But in "Ulysses," in spite of its unusual frankness, I do not detect anywhere the leer of the sensualist. I hold, therefore, that it is not pornographic.

IV. In writing "Ulysses," Joyce sought to make a serious experiment in a new, if not wholly novel, literary genre. He takes persons of the lower middle class living in Dublin in 1904 and seeks not only to describe what they did on a certain day early in June of that year as they went about the City bent on their usual occupations, but also to tell what many of them thought about the while.

Joyce has attempted—it seems to me, with astonishing success—to show how the screen of consciousness with its ever-shifting kaleidoscopic impressions carries, as it were on a plastic palimpsest, not only what is in the focus of each man's observation of the actual things about him, but also in a penumbral zone residua of past impressions, some recent and some drawn up by association from the domain of the subconscious. He shows how each of these impressions affects the life and behavior of the character which he is describing.

What he seeks to get is not unlike the result of a double or, if that is possible, a multiple exposure on a cinema film which would give a clear foreground with a background visible but somewhat blurred and out of focus in varying degrees.

To convey by words an effect which obviously lends itself more appropriately to a graphic technique, accounts, it seems to me, for much of the obscurity which meets a reader of "Ulysses." And it also explains another aspect of the book, which I have further to consider, namely, Joyce's sincerity and his honest effort to show exactly how the minds of his characters operate.

If Joyce did not attempt to be honest in developing the technique which he has adopted in "Ulysses" the result would be psychologically misleading and thus unfaithful to his chosen technique. Such an attitude would be artistically inexcusable.

It is because Joyce has been loyal to his technique and has not funked its necessary implications, but has honestly attempted to tell fully what his characters think about, that he has been the subject of so many attacks and that his purpose has been so often misunderstood and misrepresented. For his attempt sincerely and honestly to realize his objective has required him incidentally to use certain words which are generally considered dirty words and has led at times to what many think is a too poignant preoccupation with sex in the thoughts of his characters.

The words which are criticized as dirty are old Saxon words known to almost all men and, I venture, to many women, and are such words as would be naturally and habitually used, I believe, by the types of folk whose life, physical and mental, Joyce is seeking to describe. In respect of the recurrent emergence of the theme of sex in the minds of his characters, it must always be remembered that his locale was Celtic and his season Spring.

Whether or not one enjoys such a technique as Joyce uses is a matter of taste on which disagreement or argument is futile, but to subject that technique to the standards of some other technique seems to me to be little short of absurd.

Accordingly, I hold that "Ulysses" is a sincere and honest book and I think that the criticisms of it are entirely disposed of by its rationale.

V. Furthermore, "Ulysses" is an amazing *tour de force* when one considers the success which has been in the main achieved with such a difficult objective as Joyce set for himself. As I have stated, "Ulysses" is not an easy book to read. It is brilliant and dull, intelligible and obscure by turns. In many places it seems to me to be disgusting, but although it contains, as I have mentioned above, many words usually considered dirty, I have not found anything that I consider to be dirt for dirt's sake. Each word of the book contributes like a bit of mosaic to the detail of the picture which Joyce is seeking to construct for his readers.

If one does not wish to associate with such folk as Joyce describes, that is one's own choice. In order to avoid indirect contact with them one may not wish to read "Ulysses"; that is quite understandable. But when such a real artist in words, as Joyce undoubtedly is, seeks to draw a true picture of the lower middle class in a European city, ought it to be impossible for the American public legally to see that picture?

To answer this question it is not sufficient merely to find, as I have found above, that Joyce did not write "Ulysses" with what is commonly called pornographic intent, I must endeavor to apply a more objective standard to his book in order to determine its effect in the result, irrespective of the intent with which it was written.

VI. The statute under which the libel is filed only denounces, in so far as we are here concerned, the importation into the United States from any foreign country of "any obscene book." Section 305 of the Tariff Act of 1930, Title 19 United States Code, Section 1305. It does not marshal against books the spectrum of condemnatory adjectives found, commonly, in laws dealing with matters of this kind. I am, therefore, only required to determine whether "Ulysses" is obscene within the legal definition of that word.

The meaning of the word "obscene" as legally defined by the Courts is: tending to stir the sex impulses or to lead to sexually impure and lustful thoughts. . . .

Whether a particular book would tend to excite such impulses and thoughts must be tested by the Court's opinion as to its effect on a person with average sex instincts—what the French would call l'homme moyen sensuel—who plays, in this branch of legal inquiry, the same role of hypothetical reagent as does the "reasonable man" in the law of torts and "the man learned in the art" on questions of invention in patent law.

The risk involved in the use of such a reagent arises from the inherent tendency of the trier of facts, however fair he may intend to be, to make his reagent too much subservient to his own idiosyncrasies. Here, I have attempted to avoid this, if possible, and to make my reagent herein more objective than he might otherwise be, by adopting the following course:

After I had made my decision in regard to the aspect of "Uylsses," now under consideration, I checked my impressions with two friends of mine who in my opinion answered to the above stated requirement for my reagent.

These literary assessors—as I might properly describe them—were called on separately, and neither knew that I was consulting the other. They are men whose opinion on literature and on life I value most highly. They had both read "Ulysses," and, of course, were wholly unconnected with this cause.

Without letting either of my assessors know what my decision was, I gave to each of them the legal definition of obscene and asked each whether in his opinion "Ulysses" was obscene within that definition.

I was interested to find that they both agreed with my opinion: that reading "Ulysses" in its entirety, as a book must be read on such a test as this, did not tend to excite sexual impulses or lustful thoughts but that its net effect on them was only that of a somewhat tragic and very powerful commentary on the inner lives of men and women.

It is only with the normal person that the law is concerned. Such a test as I have described, therefore, is the only proper test of obscenity in the case of a book like "Ulysses" which is a sincere and serious attempt to devise a new literary method for the observation and description of mankind.

I am quite aware that owing to some of its scenes "Ulysses" is a rather strong draught to ask some sensitive, though normal, persons to take. But my considered opinion, after long reflection, is that whilst in many places the effect of "Ulysses" on the reader undoubtedly is somewhat emetic, nowhere does it tend to be an aphrodisiac.

"Ulysses" may, therefore, be admitted into the United States.

c. Police Control

COMMONWEALTH v. GORDON

66 D. & C. 101 (1949)

[Books are molested by the Post Office and by the customs relatively seldom, as we have seen, but they continue to be subject to considerable harassment under state criminal statutes and from local police authorities. About 1870 Anthony Comstock began to cause trouble for authors, books, and book dealers when he found a book that in his judgment was obscene. Books by D. H. Lawrence, Sherwood Anderson, Bertrand Russell, and Theodore Dreiser—to name only a few—have been in the courts. The highest courts. of Massachusetts and New York, for instance, have upheld police bans on books by Theodore Dreiser, Arthur Schnitzler, and Edmund Wilson. The courts differ on the definition of "obscenity," on the test to be used—the effect on youth or on the normal adult—and on other essential matters.

[The opinion by Judge Bok of the Court of Quarter Sessions in Philadelphia summarizes the conflict of authorities. His decision conforms with that of Judge Woolsey in the *Ulysses Case*, but it has not had the effect on state and local police authorities that the Woolsey decision has had on customs officers.

[Judge Bok's decision was affirmed by the Pennsylvania Superior and Supreme Courts. 166 Pa. Super. Ct. 120 (1950). The latter court, however, refused to approve the clear and present danger test as it was applied by Judge Bok. *Cf. Chaplinsky* v. *New Hampshire,* 315 US 568 (1942).]

Judge Bok:

. . . The evidence consists of nine books and an oral stipulation at bar that defendants are booksellers and that they possessed the books with the intent to sell them on the dates and at the time and places set forth in the indictments. This constituted in full the Commonwealth's evidence, to which defendants have demurred.

I have read the books with thoughtful care and find that they are not obscene, as alleged. The demurrers are therefore sustained.

The Statute

The indictments are drawn under section 524 of The Penal Code of June 24, 1939, which reads as follows:

Whoever sells, lends, distributes, exhibits, gives away or shows or offers to sell, lend, distribute, exhibit, or give away or show, or has in his possession with intent to sell, lend, distribute or give away or to show, or knowingly advertise in any manner, any obscene, lewd, lascivious, filthy, indecent or disgusting book, magazine, pamphlet, newspaper, storypaper, paper, writing, drawing, photograph, figure or image, or any written or printed matter of an indecent character, or any article or instrument of indecent or immoral use or purporting to be for indecent or immoral use or purpose, or whoever designs, copies, draws, photographs, prints, utters, publishes, or in any manner manufactures or prepares any such book, picture, drawing, magazine, pamphlet, newspaper, storypaper, paper, writing, figure, image, matter, article or thing, or whoever writes, prints, publishes, or utters, or causes to be printed, published or uttered, any advertisement or notice of any kind giving information, directly or indirectly, stating or purporting to do so, where, how, of whom, or by what means any, or what purports to be, any obscene, lewd, lascivious, filthy, disgusting or indecent book, picture, writing, paper, figure, image, matter, article or thing named in this section can be purchased, obtained or had, or whoever prints, utters, publishes, sells, lends, gives away, or shows, or has in his possession with intent to sell, lend, give away, or show, or otherwise offers for sale, loan or gift, or distribution, any pamphlet, magazine, newspaper or other printed paper devoted to the publication and principally made up of criminal news, police reports or accounts of criminal deeds, or pictures of stories of deeds of bloodshed, lust or crime, or whoever hires, employes, uses or permits any minor or child to do so or assist in doing any act or thing mentioned in this section, is guilty of a misdemeanor, and upon conviction, shall be sentenced to imprisonment not exceeding one (1) year, or to pay a fine not exceeding five hundred dollars ($500), or both.

The particular and only charge in the indictments is that defendants possessed some or all of the books with the intent to sell them. . . .

It should be noted at once that the wording of section 524 requires consideration of the indicted material as a whole; it does not proscribe articles or publications that merely contain obscene matter. This is now true in all jurisdictions that have dealt with the subject: [in] the Federal courts, . . . also . . . in Pennsylvania. . . .

Section 524, for all its verbiage, is very bare. The full weight of the legislative prohibition dangles from the word "obscene" and its synonyms. Nowhere are these words defined; nowhere is the danger to be expected of them stated; nowhere is a standard of judgment set forth. I assume that "obscenity" is expected to have a familiar and inherent meaning, both as to what it is and as to what it does.

It is my purpose to show that it has no such inherent meaning; that different meanings given to it at different times are not constant, either historically or legally; and that it is not constitutionally indictable unless it takes the form of sexual impurity, i.e., "dirt for dirt's sake" and can be traced to actual criminal behavior, either actual or demonstrably imminent.

Résumé of the Books

1, 2 and 3. The Studs Lonigan trilogy ("Young Lonigan," "The Young Manhood of Studs Lonigan," "Judgment Day"), by James T. Farrell; Vanguard Press, 1932–1935.

This is the story of the moral and physical disintegration of a young man living in Chicago between the years 1916 and 1932. Nothing that he attempted ever quite came off, and his failures became more and more incisive. He left school to hang around the streets with others of his kind; he was too young to enlist for war service; he loved Lucy since they were in school together, but avoided her for four years and finally alienated her by making drunken advances to her; he worked for his father as a painter, but, on a casual tip, invested his savings in a dubious stock, which failed; he fell half-heartedly in love with Catherine, and they were engaged to be married, but she became pregnant by him before the ceremony; looking for a job on a stormy day a few weeks before the wedding, he caught cold and died of pneumonia and a weakened heart.

The background of the semi-slum district in which Lonigan was born and lived was the outward counter-part of his own nature, and both together were too much for such decency of soul as he had. His drift downhill was relentless and inevitable. On the theory that no literature is vital that cannot be vulgarized, this trilogy may rank as an epic, for our criminal courts and prisons and many of our streets are peopled by Studs Lonigans. The characters in these books act and speak the kind of life that bred them, and Mr. Farrell has brought to the surface the groundswell of thought and inclination that move more people than, if they were honest, would admit to them.

It is not a pleasant story, nor are the characters gentle and refined. There is rape and dissipation and lust in these books, expressed in matching language, but they do not strike me as being out of proportion. The books as a whole create a sustained arc of a man's life and era, and the obvious effort of the author is to be faithful to the scene he depicts.

No one would want to be Studs Lonigan.

4. "A World I Never Made," by James T. Farrell; The Vanguard Press, New York, 1936.

This book could well be the beginning of another series, for it takes a minor character from the Lonigan books, Danny O'Neill, and shows him as a child. The milieu is the same—Chicago in 1911—but there is a discernible effort to show Danny's struggle uphill against the same factors that pushed Lonigan down.

This is the one book of the nine that does not end tragically; it merely stops in midstream, but the people who surround Danny do and say the same things that appear in the Lonigan series. Unlike the latter, this book is plastered with the short Saxon words of common vulgarity; they are consistent with the characters who use them and with the quality of the lives and actions that are the subject of the author's scrutiny.

I am not of mind, nor do I have the authority, to require an author to write about one kind of people and not about another, nor do I object to his effort to paint a complete picture of those whom he has chosen. Certainly I will not say that it is not a good thing to look deeply into life and people, regardless of the shadows that are to be found there.

5. "Sanctuary," by William Faulkner; Random House, 1931.

This is a powerful and dreadful story about a gay but virginal girl of 17 who accidentally falls into the hands of a sadistic man called Popeye, who is sexually impotent. He kills a half-witted boy who is informally guarding the girl, and ravishes her with a corncob. He then keeps her imprisoned in a house of prostitution and takes pleasure in watching her have intercourse with a man whom he kills when she tries to escape with him. Terrified of Popeye, she testifies that another man committed the murder, and is taken from court by her father, who has finally been able to locate her. Popeye is later apprehended on another charge of murder and is convicted.

There are no vulgar Saxon words in the book, but the situations are stark and unrelieved. It makes one shudder to think of what can happen by misadventure.

6. "Wild Palms," by William Faulkner; Random House, 1939.

This book concerns a wife who left her husband and children to seek integrity of experience, in terms of vitality, with her lover; "hunger is in the heart," she says, when the next meal seems uncertain, "not in the stomach." They wander about the country together, living as they must or as they wish, and she finally becomes pregnant. Her lover, a former doctor, attempts to abort her but mishandles it and she dies. He pleads guilty and is sentenced to 50 years in prison. He refuses a gift of cyanide from the woman's husband, saying: "Between grief and nothing I will take grief."

The redeeming feature of this tale is that an acid loneliness comes through, the awful loneliness that pervades lost people, even in company. No one could envy these two miserable creatures.

7. "God's Little Acre," by Erskine Caldwell; Random House, 1933.

An able companion to the same author's "Tobacco Road," it is the story of a poor and illiterate farmer's family in Georgia. The central figure is the father, who for 15 years has dug holes in his farm in search of gold. God's Little Acre is a part of the farm which he mentally moves about in order to keep it from getting in the way of his search for treasure; his idea is to give all that comes from it to the church, but he never works it. His daughters and sons and their wives get variously tangled up in sexual affairs which are taken as being in the nature of things. One brother kills another over his wife. The final and despairing cry of the father, who has always tried to keep peace, is, "Blood on my land!"

It is a frank and turbulent story, but it is an obvious effort to be faithful to the locality and its people.   •

8. "End As a Man," by Calder Willingham; The Vanguard Press, 1947.

Life in a southern military academy. A drinking party and crooked poker game finally result in the expulsion of several cadets, including the wily and unmoral ringleader. The retired general in charge of the academy is the stereotype of military martinet, whose conception of the narrow and rigid discipline necessary to produce "a man" is set in bold relief against the energy of growing boys. The result is a fair picture of the frustration inherent in an overdose of discipline and in the license and disobedience that is largely engendered by it.

No one would care to send his son to such an institution.

This is perhaps the foulest book of the lot, so far as language is concerned, but it is the language of vulgarity and not of erotic allurement.

9. "Never Love a Stranger," by Harold Robbins; Knopf, 1948.

The story of a boy brought up in an orphanage who finds that he has an uncle and is Jewish. After losing touch with his uncle he has various experiences and is finally down and out because he can find no work. He then becomes head of New York City's gambling racket, which he ultimately leaves in order to marry a childhood friend. She dies in childbirth and he is killed in the war; his friends take over the child, who will presumably have a better chance in life than he had.

It is a swift story that covers a great deal of ground, its point being to portray a hard and lonely man who could not fully trust or give himself to anyone. Its last and least convincing part is also the least open to attack for obscenity; the rest, particularly the section dealing with New York City during the depression of the early 1930's, is very moving, not because there are sexual incidents but because the lines of the story are deep and authentic.

General Comment

Three of these books [4, 7, and 8] have already been judicially cleared in New York City. . . .

After clearance by the magistrates, these books could have been brought before the grand jury, but no such indictments were attempted.

As I have indicated above, all but one of these books are profoundly tragic, and that one has its normal quota of frustration and despair. No one could envy or wish to emulate the characters that move so desolately through these pages. Far from inciting to lewd or lecherous desires, which are sensorially pleasurable, these books leave one either with a sense of horror or a pity for the degradation of mankind. The effect upon the normal reader, "l'homme moyen sensuel" (there is no such deft precision in English), would be anything but what the vice hunters fear it might be. We are so fearful for other people's morals; they so seldom have the courage of our own convictions.

It will be asked whether one would care to have one's young daughter read these books. I suppose that by the time she is old enough to wish to read them she will have learned the biologic facts of life and the words that go with them. There is something seriously wrong at home if those facts have not been met and faced and sorted by then; it is not children so much as parents that should receive our concern about this. I should prefer that my own three daughters meet the facts of life and the literature of the world in my library than behind a neighbor's barn, for I can face the adversary there directly. If the young ladies are appalled by what they read, they can close the book at the bottom of page one; if they read further, they will learn what is in the world and in its people, and no parents who have been discerning with their children need fear the outcome. Nor can they hold it back, for life is a series of little battles and minor issues, and the burden of choice is on us all, every day, young and old. Our daughters must live in the world and decide what sort of women they are to be, and we should be willing to prefer their deliberate and informed choice of decency rather than an innocence that continues to spring from ignorance. If that choice be made in the open sunlight, it is more apt than when made in shadow to fall on the side of honorable behavior.

The lesson to be learned from such books as these is not so facile as that the wages of sin is death, or, in Hollywood's more modern version, that the penalty of sinning is suffering. That is not enough to save a book from proper censorship. The tragedy of these books is not in death but in the texture of the slope that leads to death—in the inner suffering that comes at times from crimes against oneself as much as from crimes against society. That has been the green pastures of story-tellers ever since the Greek dramatists, especially when the pressures on a character are not, as they are not always, of his own making or within his control. Sin is too apt a word to take in the full reach of cir-cumstance, and I venture to say that in human experience suffering does not automatically follow sinning. Our laws have a good deal to do with that guarded notion. It is necessary to know what our laws are up to, and it is my conviction that, outside the police power, the laws of Anglo-Saxon countries are made less as absolute mandates than as clinical experiments. Democratic nations prefer checks and balances to absolute authority, and it is worthy of notice that the jury system exists only in those countries where the law is not considered to have been drawn, as Cicero put it, from the forehead of the gods, but rather from the will of the people, who wish to keep an eye on it. The eight-eenth amendment to the Constitution is a case in point.

Such sumptuary laws, and some economic ones, differ from obscenity statutes only in the degree of danger to society inherent in the appetite in question. The need for decency is as old as the appetites, but it is not expressed in uniform law or custom. The ancient Hebrews had a rigid moral code which, for example, excluded bastards from the con-gregation up to the tenth generation, for the combined reasons of preserving their ancient tradition of tribe and family and of increasing the number of effective warriors. The Greeks, more cosmopolitan in the country whose sterile soil could not support many people comfort-ably, approved pederasty and a restricted form of concubinage in order to keep the population down. Standards of sexual behavior, as well as of the need to censor it, have shifted from age to age, from country to country, and from economy to economy. The State of New Mexico has no obscenity statute. South Carolina had no divorce law until a few months ago.

Censorship, which is the policeman of decency, whether religious, patriotic, or moral, has had distinct fashions, depending on which great questions were agitating society at the time. During the Middle Ages, when the church was supreme, the focus of suppression was upon heresy and blasphemy. When the State became uppermost, the focus of suppression was upon treason and sedition. The advent of tech-nology made Queen Victoria realize, perhaps subconsciously, that loose morals would threaten the peace of mind necessary to the devel-opment of invention and big business; the focus moved to sexual morality. We are now emerging into an era of social ideology and psychology, and the focus is turning to these. The right to speak out and to act freely is always at a minimum in the area of the fighting faiths.

The censorship of books did not become a broad public issue until after the invention of printing in the fifteenth century. The earliest real example of it was the first Index Librorium Prohibitorum of the Catholic Church in 1559, and the church was broadly tolerant of sexual impurity in the books that it considered; its main object was the suppression of heresy. I think it is a fair general statement that from ancient times until the Comstockian laws of 1873 the only form of written obscenity that was censored was "dirt for dirt's sake."

I do not regard the above as apart from the decisional purpose of this case. The words of the statute—"obscene, lewd, lascivious, filthy, indecent, or disgusting"—restrict rather than broaden the meaning of a highly penal statute. The effect of this plethora of epithets is to merge them into one prevailing meaning—that of sexual impurity alone, and this has been universally held. . . .

The statute is therefore directed only at sexual impurity and not at blasphemy or coarse and vulgar behavior of any kind. The word in common use for the purpose of such a statute is "obscenity." The great point of this case is to find out what that word means.

Nowhere in the statute is there a definition of it or a formula given for determining when it exists. Its derivation, *ob* and *scena,* suggests that anything done offstage, furtively, or lefthandedly, is obscene. The act does not penalize anyone who seeks to change the prevailing moral or sexual code, nor does it state that the writing must be such as to corrupt the morals of the public or of youth; it merely proscribes books that *are* obscene and leaves it to the authorities to decide whether or not they are. This cannot be done without regard to the nature and history of obscenity. It is unlike the fundamental laws of property, of crimes like murder, rape, and theft, or even of negligence, whose meaning has remained relatively constant. That of obscenity has frequently changed, almost from decade to decade within the past century; "Ulysses" was condemned by the State courts in New York just 10 years before it was cleared by Judge Woolsey in the District Court for the Southern District of New York. I must determine what this elusive word means now.

Something might be said at the outset about the familiar four-letter words that are so often associated with sexual impurity. These are, almost without exception, of honest Anglo-Saxon ancestry, and were not invented for purely scatological effect. The one, for example, that is used to denote the sexual act is an old agricultural word meaning "to plant," and was at one time a wholly respectable member of the English vocabulary. The distinction between a word of decent etymological history and one of smut alone is important; it shows that fashions in language change as expectably as do the concepts of what language connotes. It is the old business of semantics again, the difference between word and concept.

But there is another distinction. The decisions that I shall cite have sliced off vulgarity from obscenity. This has had the effect of making a clear division between the words of the bathroom and those of the bedroom: the former can no longer be regarded as obscene, since they have no erotic allurement, and the latter may be so regarded, depending on the circumstances of their use. This reduces the number of potentially offensive words sharply.

With such changes as these, the question is whether the legal mace should fall upon words or upon concepts—language or ideas.

Obscenity is not like sedition, blasphemy, or open lewdness, against which there are also criminal statutes. These offenses not only have acquired precise meaning but are defined specifically in the act. . . .

No such definition of standard or legislative intention occurs in section 524, and I am convinced that without a declaration of the legislature's intention as to what obscenity means or of what the law makers sought to prevent, there is no constant or reliable indication of it to be found in human experience.

The argument is often made that anyone can tell by instinct what is obscene and what is not, even if it is hard to put the difference into words. The same might be said of sedition, blasphemy, and open lewdness, but the legislature was careful to specify. With regard to obscenity, however, the argument does not hold water. When he was an editor, Walter Hines Page deleted the word "chaste" because it was suggestive, and the play "Sappho" was banned in New York City because a man carried a leading lady up a flight of stairs. A librarian once charged Mark Twain's "Tom Sawyer" and "Huckleberry Finn" with corrupting the morals of children. In 1907 Richard Strauss's "Salome" was banned in Boston. Charlotte Brontë's "Jane Eyre," when first published, was called "too immoral to be ranked as decent literature." Hawthorne's "Scarlet Letter" was referred to as "a brokerage of lust." George Eliot's "Adam Bede" was called "the vile outpourings of a lewd woman's mind." Others to suffer similarly were Elizabeth Barrett Browning's "Aurora Leigh," Hardy's "Tess" and "Jude," Du-Maurier's "Trilby," and Shaw's "Mrs. Warren's Profession." Walt Whitman lost his job in the United States Department of the Interior because of "Leaves of Grass."

It is presumed that Mr. Page and the others who attacked this imposing array of classics could tell by instinct what was decent and what was not. The idea that instinct can be resorted to as a process of moral *stare decisis* reduces to absurdity.

It is a far cry from the examples just cited to what society accepts as innocuous now. The stage, literature, painting, sculpture, photography, fashions of dress, and even the still pudibund screen tolerate things that would have made Anthony Comstock burn blue. In its issue of April 11, 1938, *Life* magazine ran a series of factual and dignified pictures called "The Birth of a Baby." It was attacked in the courts but was exonerated. Dr. Kinsey's report on the sexual behavior of men is now current. Truth and error, as Milton urged in his "Areopagitica," are being allowed to grapple, and we are the better for it.

In addition to the books whose banning is the subject of cases cited later in this opinion, I suggest a short list of modern books that have not been banned, so far as I can find out. All of these books contain sexual material, and all of them can be found in the Boston Public Library. I defy anyone to provide a rational basis for the distinction between these two sets of books. My list includes: Fanny Hurst's "Back Street"; Arthur Koestler's "Arrival and Departure"; Erich Maria Remarque's "All Quiet on the Western Front" and "Arch of Triumph"; Eugene O'Neill's "Anna Christie" and "Hairy Ape"; John Dos Passos's "U.S.A."; Ernest Hemingway's "For Whom the Bell Tolls"; Somerset Maugham's "Of Human Bondage"; Charles Morgan's "The Fountain" and "The Voyage"; Richard Wright's "Black Boy."

It is no answer to say that if my point about the books just listed be sound, then by analogy the law against murder is useless because all murderers are not caught. The inherent evil of murder is apparent, but by what apparent, inherent standard of evil is obscenity to be judged, from book to book? It is my purpose to provide such a standard, but it will reduce to a minimum the operation of any norm of indefinite interpretation.

Before leaving this point, research discloses a curious but complete confusion between the post office and the customs over what constitutes obscenity. No unanimity of opinion unites these two governmental services in a common standard. Books have cleared the port only to find the mails closed to them: others, printed here, have circulated freely while foreign copies were stopped at the ports. One would expect greater uniformity than this if obscenity could be unmistakably detected. . . .

It is my conclusion that the books before me are obvious efforts to show life as it is. I cannot be convinced that the deep drives and appetites of life are very much different from what they have always been, or that censorship has ever had any effect on them, except as the law's police power to preserve the peace in censorship. I believe that the consensus of preference today is for disclosure and not stealth, for frankness and not hypocrisy, and for public and not secret distribution. That in itself is a moral code.

It is my opinion that frank disclosure cannot legally be censored, even as an exercise of the police power, unless it is sexually impure and pornographic, as I shall define those words. They furnish the only possible test for obscenity and its effect.

These books are not, in my view, sexually impure and pornographic. . . .

The English Cases

Regina v. *Hicklin* [1868] is an example of judge-made law quite at variance with the parliamentary intent behind the act on which it was based. Lord Campbell's act provided for search and seizure warrants that would enable the police to take and destroy obscene publications. The reports of the debates in Hansard show the lords' difficulties in deciding what an obscene publication might be. Lord Campbell, who was lord chief justice at the time, explained that the act was to apply exclusively to works written for the purpose of corrupting the morals of youth and of a nature calculated to shock the common feelings of decency in any well regulated mind. He was ready to make whatever was then indictable a test of obscenity in his new act. He made it clear that any work that even pretended to be literature or art, classic or modern, had little to fear.

All of this was nullified by Lord Chief Justice Cockburn in the *Hicklin Case*, where the subject matter was a pamphlet entitled "The Confessional Unmasked," and containing a diatribe against the Catholic Church; its purpose was to show the depravity of the priesthood and the character of the questions put to women in the confessional. This is now the famous rule of the case: "I think that the test of obscenity is this, whether the tendency of the matter charged as obscenity is to deprave and corrupt those whose minds are open to such immoral influences, and into whose hands a publication of this sort may fall."

Strictly applied, this rule renders any book unsafe, since a moron could pervert to some sexual fantasy to which his mind is open the listings in a seed catalogue. Not even the Bible would be exempt; Annie Besant once compiled a list of 150 passages in Scripture that might fairly be considered obscene—it is enough to cite the story of Lot and his daughters, Genesis 19, 30–38. Portions of Shakespeare would also be offensive, and of Chaucer, to say nothing of Aristophanes, Juvenal, Ovid, Swift, Defoe, Fielding, Smollett, Rousseau, Maupassant, Voltaire, Balzac, Baudelaire, Rabelais, Swinburne, Shelley, Byron, Boccaccio, Marguerite de Navarre, Hardy, Shaw, Whitman, and a host more.

As will be seen later, the classics—whatever that may mean precisely—are considered exempt from censorship, but many of them were hounded in England, despite Lord Campbell's assurances, as a result of the rule of the *Hicklin Case.* . . .

The lower court case of *Regina* v. *Thompson* (1900), in which the jury found defendant not guilty in an issue of whether or not the "Heptameron," by Queen Margaret of Navarre, was obscene, is interesting because of the charge of Bosanquet. . . . It is the first mention that I have found in the English reports of the idea that fashions in obscenity change. After mentioning that in the Middle Ages things were discussed which would not be tolerated now, if given general publicity, Sergeant Bosanquet left it to the jury to say "whether the book is a fit book to put into people's hands in these days at the end of the nineteenth century." The jury felt that it was. . . .

This exhausts the reported English cases that are in point. They show continued adherence to the *Hicklin* rule, but the paucity of authority is noteworthy. It is as if the English public does not want to risk the severity of the common law, and it is clear proof to me of the clinical nature of the laws that are made to cover social situations. While the higher English courts were kept relatively idle on the question, private censorship in England has been very active; the most effective censor of the Victorian era was Mudie's circulating library. It was the time of the three-decker novel—ponderous, dull, and pure as the driven snow. When Mudie's power was finally broken, smaller circulating libraries continued to wield the same sort of influence and to reflect the general desire of the public for no disturbing material of an emotional nature. England was the pioneer in the advance of the Industrial Age, and the nation of shopkeepers was unwilling to be diverted from making money by sidetrips into erotica; what individuals did in the dark was their affair, but bad morals could not profitably become a matter of public concern.

The rule of *Regina* v. *Hicklin* suited the English, and presumably still does—not as a satisfying standard but as an effective policeman to take over and tone down the situation when the social experiment threatens to get out of hand.

Censorship should be the proper activity of the community rather than of the law, and the community has never been lazy upholding what it believes to be inherently decent at the moment. With a legal policeman handy, the market place is the best crucible in which to distil an instinctive morality. We have the evidence of Milton that there is no authoritative example of the suppression of a book in ancient times solely because of obscenity, but this does not mean that private criticism was not alert. Plato thought that Homer should be expurgated before Greek children should be allowed to read him. In Plutarch's opinion the comedies of Aristophanes were coarse and vulgar.

This is healthy, for it is the struggle of free opinion: it is not suppression by law. In the English community the people argue and *Hicklin* stands guard in case of trouble. The American method is different: the rule has been modernized.

The American Cases

1. The Federal Courts. There are two important opinions involving James Joyce's "Ulysses." Judge Woolsey's, in the district court, is reported as *United States* v. *One Book entitled "Ulysses,"* 5 F. Supp. 182 (S.D.N.Y., 1933), and Judge Hand's affirming Judge Woolsey is reported in 72 F. (2d) 705 (C.C.A. 2d, 1934).

Judge Woolsey's decision may well be considered the keystone of the modern American rule, as it brings out clearly that indictable obscenity must be "dirt for dirt's sake." . . .

In affirming Judge Woolsey, Judge Hand said, in the circuit court of appeals:

That numerous long passages in Ulysses contain matter that is obscene under any fair definition of the word cannot be gainsaid; yet they are relevant to the purpose of depicting the thoughts of the characters and are introduced to give meaning to the whole, rather than to promote lust or portray filth for its own sake. The net effect even of portions most open to attack, such as the closing monologue of the wife of Leopold Bloom, is pitiful and tragic, rather than lustful. The book depicts the souls of men and women that are by turns bewildered and keenly apprehensive, sordid and aspiring, ugly and beautiful, hateful and loving. In the end one feels, more than anything else, pity and sorrow for the confusion, misery, and degradation of humanity. . . . The book as a whole is not pornographic, and while in not a few spots it is coarse, blasphemous, and obscene, it does not, in our opinion, tend to promote lust. The erotic passages are submerged in the book as a whole and have little resultant effect. . . .

It is quite clear that the harsh rule of *Regina* v. *Hicklin* has been supplanted by the modern test of obscenity, namely, whether the matter in question has a substantial tendency to deprave or corrupt by inciting lascivious thoughts or arousing lustful desire in the ordinary reader. This has been stated in various ways.

It has been said that the matter charged, to be obscene, must "suggest impure or libidinous thoughts," must "invite to lewd and lascivious practices and conduct," must "be offensive to chastity," must "incite dissolute acts," must "create a desire for gratification of animal passions," must "encourage unlawful indulgences of lust," must "attempt to satisfy the morbid appetite of the salacious," must "pander to the prurient taste." . . .

In *Walker* v. *Popenoe*, 149 F. (2d) 511 (1945), it was held: "The effect of a publication on the ordinary reader is what counts. The Statute does not intend that we shall 'reduce our treatment of sex to the standard of a child's library in the supposed interest of a salacious few.'"

This test, however, should not be left to stand alone, for there is another element of equal importance—the tenor of the times and the change in social acceptance of what is inherently decent. This element is clearly set forth in *United States* v. *Kennerley,* 209 Fed. 119 (D.C., N.Y., 1913), where Judge [Learned] Hand said:

If there be no abstract definition, such as I have suggested, should not the word "obscene" be allowed to indicate the present critical point in the compromise between candor and shame at which the community may have arrived here and now? . . . Nor is it an objection, I think, that such an interpretation gives to the words of the statute a varying meaning from time to time. Such words as these do not embalm the precise morals of an age or place; while they presuppose that some things will always be shocking to the public taste, the vague subject matter is left to the gradual development of general notions about what is decent. . . .

The New York Courts. The modern test was applied in *People* v. *Wendling,* 258 N.Y. 451 (1932), which involved the dramatization of the song "Frankie and Johnnie." In holding that the courts are not censors of morals and manners, Judge Pound said:

The language of the play is coarse, vulgar and profane; the plot cheap and tawdry. As a dramatic composition it serves to degrade the stage where vice is thought by some to lose "half its evil by losing all its grossness." That it is "indecent" from every consideration of propriety is entirely clear, but the court is not a censor of plays and does not attempt to regulate manners. One may call a spade a spade without offending decency, although modesty may be shocked thereby. The question is not whether the scene is laid in a low dive where refined people are not found or whether the language is that of the bar room rather than the parlor. The question is whether the tendency of the play is to excite lustful and lecherous desire. . . .

Since the New York cases are generally in line with the modern Federal rule above stated, it is necessary only to cite the principal one[s]: *Halsey* v. *N.Y. Society for the Suppression of Vice,* 234 N.Y. 1 (1922), which involved Theophile Gautier's "Mademoiselle de Maupin"; *People* v. *Brainard,* 192 App. Div. (N.Y.) 816 (1920), where the subject was "Madeleine," the anonymous autobiography of a prostitute.

The Massachusetts Courts. Boston has long been the center of book suppression in this country. Before 1930 the Massachusetts obscenity statute forbade the sale of any book "containing obscene, indecent language." The Supreme Court upheld convictions for the sale of

Dreiser's "An American Tragedy" and D. H. Lawrence's "Lady Chatterley's Lover." After a general wave of censorship that swept over Boston in 1929 and resulted in the suppression of 68 books, the law was changed to proscribe the sale of "a book which is obscene, indecent," etc.

The result was the modern rule, but the Massachusetts courts were still severe with individual books. *Commonwealth* v. *Isenstadt*, 318 Mass. 543 (1945), upheld a conviction for the sale of "Strange Fruit," and while it announced the modern rule to great extent, it refused to sanction the idea that sincerity of purpose and artistic merit would necessarily dispel obscenity. But it clearly held that the time and custom of the community are important elements. . . .

The Modern Test of Obscenity

From all of these cases the modern rule is that obscenity is measured by the erotic allurement upon the average modern reader; that the erotic allurement of a book is measured by whether it is sexually impure—i.e., pornographic, "dirt for dirt's sake," a calculated incitement to sexual desire—or whether it reveals an effort to reflect life, including its dirt, with reasonable accuracy and balance; and that mere coarseness or vulgarity is not obscenity.

Forging such a rule from the precedents does not fully reach the heart of the matter, for I am sure that the books before me could be declared obscene or not obscene under either the *Hicklin* or the modern rule. Current standards create both the book and the judgment of it.

The evil of an indefinite statute like our section 524, however, is that it is also too loose. Current standards of what is obscene can swing to extremes if the entire question is left open, and even in the domestic laboratories of the States such freedom cannot safely be allowed. It is no longer possible that free speech be guaranteed Federally and denied locally; under modern methods of instantaneous communication such a discrepancy makes no sense. If speech is to be free anywhere, it must be free everywhere, and a law that can be used as a spigot that allows speech to flow freely or to be checked altogether is a general threat to free opinion and enlightened solution. What is said in Pennsylvania may clarify an issue in California, and what is suppressed in California may leave us the worse in Pennsylvania. Unless a restriction on free speech be of national validity, it can no longer have any local validity whatever. Some danger to us all must appear before any of us can be muzzled.

In the field of written obscenity this principle has met oblique acceptance with regard to what is called "the classics," which are now exempt from legal censorship. Just how old a work must be before it can enjoy this immunity is uncertain, but what we know as classics are the books by remarkable people that have withstood the test of time and are accepted as having lasting value; they have become historical samples, which itself is important. This importance could not be as great if the screening process were not free.

Current literature, good, bad, or indifferent, goes into the hopper without any background for judgment; it is in the idiom of the moment and is keyed to the tempo of modern life. I do not believe that such considerations should result in removing any of the output from the hopper before the process of screening can begin. What is pure dirt to some may be another's sincere effort to make clear a point, and there is not much difference, from the historical angle, between censoring books before publication and suppressing them afterwards, before there has been a reasonable chance to judge them. Blackstone's neat distinction may satisfy an exact legal mind, but it has no meaning for history. The unworthy books will die soon enough, but the great work of genius has a hard enough time to make its way even in the free market of thought. James Joyce, whose work is difficult to understand, even after years of study, has evolved a new form of communication, by his method of using words, that will some day be a shorthand for complexity. The public was deprived for years of this work of genius because someone found objectionable passages in it.

I can find no universally valid restriction on free expression to be drawn from the behavior of "l'homme moyen sensuel," who is the average modern reader. It is impossible to say just what his reactions to a book actually are. "Moyen" means, generally, average, and average means a median between extremes. If he reads an obscene book when his sensuality is low, he will yawn over it or find that its suggestibility leads him off on quite different paths. If he reads the Mechanics' Lien Act while his sensuality is high, things will stand between him and the page that have no business there. How can anyone say that he will infallibly be affected one way or another by one book or another? When, where, how, and why are questions that cannot be answered clearly in this field. The professional answer that is suggested is the one general compromise—that the appetite of sex is old, universal, and unpredictable, and that the best we can do to keep it within reasonable bounds is to be our brother's keeper and censor, because we never know when his sensuality may be high. This does not satisfy me, for in a field where even reasonable precision is utterly impossible, I trust people more than I do the law. Had legal censorship been as constant throughout the centuries as the law of murder, rape, theft, and negligence, a case for the compromise could be made out; as it is, legal censorship is not old, it is not popular, and it has failed to strengthen the private censor in each individual that has kept the race as decent as it has been for several thousand years. I regard legal censorship as an experiment of more than dubious value.

I am well aware that the law is not ready to discard censorship altogether. The English keep their policeman handy, just in case, and the modern rule is a more efficient policeman. Its scope, however, must be defined with regard to the universal right of free speech, as limited only by some universally valid restriction required by a clear and present danger. For this we must consider the Constitution and the cases lately decided under it.

Constitutional Questions

The fourteenth amendment to the Federal Constitution prohibits any State from encroaching upon freedom of speech and freedom of the press to the same extent that the first amendment prevents the Federal Congress from doing so. . . .

These guarantees occupy a preferred position under our law to such an extent that the courts, when considering whether legislation infringes upon them, neutralizes the presumption usually indulged in favor of constitutionality. . . .

And article 1, sec. 7 of the Pennsylvania Constitution states that: "The free communication of thoughts and opinions is one of the invaluable rights of man, and every citizen may freely speak, write and print on any subject, being responsible for the abuse of that liberty." When the first amendment came before the Supreme Court for interpretation in *Reynolds* v. *United States,* 98 U.S. 145 (1878), the court declared that government had no authority whatsoever in the field of thought or opinion: only in the area of conduct or action could it step in. Chief Justice Waite said: "Congress was deprived of all legislative power over mere opinion, but was left free to reach actions which were in violation of social duties or subversive of good order." Quoting from Jefferson's bill for establishing religious freedom, the Chief Justice stated:

"That to suffer the Civil magistrate to intrude his powers into the field of opinion, and to restrain the profession or propagation of principles on supposition of their *ill tendency* is a dangerous fallacy which at once destroys all religious liberty." . . . "It is time enough for the rightful purposes of civil government for its officers to interfere *when principles break out into overt acts against peace and good order." In these two sentences is found the true distinction between what properly belongs to the Church and what to the State.* (Italics supplied.)

The now familiar "clear and present danger" rule, first stated by Mr. Justice Holmes in *Schenck* v. *United States*, 249 U.S. 47 (1918), represents a compromise between the ideas of Jefferson and those of the judges, who had in the meantime departed from the forthright views of the great statesman. Under that rule the publisher of a writing may be punished if the publication in question creates a clear and present danger that there will result from it some substantive evil which the legislature has a right to proscribe and punish.

The famous illustration in the *Schenck Case* was: "The most stringent protection of free speech would not protect a man in falsely shouting fire in a theatre and causing a panic. It does not even protect a man from an injunction against uttering words that may have all the effect of force."

Mr. Justice Brandeis added, in *Whitney* v. *California*, 274 U.S. 357 (1927), the idea that free speech may not be curbed where the community has the chance to answer back. He said:

Those who won our independence by revolution were not cowards. They did not fear political change. They did not exalt order at the cost of liberty. To courageous, self-reliant men, with confidence in the power of free and fearless reasoning applied through the processes of popular government, *no danger flowing from speech can be deemed clear and present, unless the incidence of the evil apprehended is so imminent that it may befall before there is opportunity for full discussion.* If there be time to expose through discussion the falsehood and fallacies, to avert the evil by the processes of education, the remedy to be applied is more speech, not enforced silence. *Only an emergency can justify repression.* Such must be the rule if authority is to be reconciled with freedom. Such, in my opinion, is the command of the Constitution. It is therefore always open to Americans to challenge a law abridging free speech and assembly by showing that there was no emergency justifying it.

Moreover, even imminent danger cannot justify resort to prohibition of these functions essential to effective democracy, unless the evil apprehended is relatively serious. Prohibition of free speech and assembly is a measure so stringent that it would be inappropriate as the means for averting a relatively trivial harm to society. A police measure may be unconstitutional merely because the remedy, although effective as means of protection, is unduly harsh or oppressive. Thus, a State might, in the exercise of its police power, make any trespass upon the land of another a crime, regardless of the results or of the intent or purpose of the trespasser. It might, also punish an attempt, a conspiracy, or an incitement to commit the trespass. But it is hardly conceivable that this Court would hold constitutional a statute which punished as a felony the mere voluntary assembly with a society formed to teach that pedestrians had the moral right to cross unenclosed, unposted, waste lands and to advocate their doing so, even if there was imminent danger that advocacy would lead to a trespass. The fact that speech is likely to result in some violence or in destruction of property is not enough to justify its suppression. There must be the probability of serious injury to the State. Among free men, the deterrents ordinarily to be applied to prevent crime are education and punishment for violations of the law, not abridgment of the rights of free speech and assembly. . . .

The history of the Supreme Court, since its decision in *Gitlow* v. *New York,* 268 U.S. 652 (1925), has been marked by gradual progress along the path staked out by Justices Holmes and Brandeis, culminating finally in the complete acceptance of their views. . . .

The nature of the evil which the legislature has the power to guard against by enacting an obscenity statute is not clearly defined. As Jefferson saw it, the legislature was restricted to punishing criminal acts and not publications. To Holmes and Brandeis the bookseller could be punished if his relation to the criminal act was such that he could be said to have incited it. In neither view could the bookseller be punished if his books merely "tended" to result in illegal acts and much less if his books "tended" to lower the moral standards of the community. A much closer relationship was required. The legislature may validly prevent criminal acts and legislate to protect the moral standards of the community. But the threat must in either case be more than a mere tendency. The older cases which upheld obscenity statutes on the "tendency" theory would appear to be invalid in the light of the more recent expressions of the Supreme Court. . . .

These principles have not been applied specifically to an obscenity statute by any recent opinion of the United States Supreme Court, but as Mr. Justice Rutledge said orally when the "Hecate County" case, *Doubleday & Co., Inc.* v. *New York,* 335 U.S. 848 (an obscenity case), was recently argued before the court:

Before we get to the question of clear and present danger, we've got to have something which the State can forbid as dangerous. We are talking in a vacuum until we can establish that there is some occasion for the exercise of the State's power.

Yes, you must first ascertain the substantive evil at which the statute is aimed, and then determine whether the publication of this book constitutes a clear and present danger.

It is up to the State to demonstrate that there was a danger, and until they demonstrate that, plus the clarity and imminence of the danger, the constitutional prohibition would seem to apply. (Italics supplied.) (Quoted in 17 U.S. Law Week [Supreme Court Sections 3118]).*

---

* [*Doubleday & Co.* v. *New York,* 71 N.Y. Supp. 2d 736 (1947), conviction affirmed by App. Div. without opinion; affirmed without opinion by Court of Appeals, 297 N.Y. 687 (1947); affirmed by equally divided court, 335 U.S. 848 (1948).]

This appears to me much closer to a correct solution of obscenity cases than several general dicta by the Supreme Court to the effect that obscenity is indictable just because it is obscenity. . . .

It seems impossible, in view of the late decisions under the first amendment, that the word "obscene" can no longer stand alone, lighted up only by a vague and mystic sense of impurity, unless it is interpreted by other solid factors such as clear and present danger, pornography, and divorcement from mere coarseness of vulgarity. . . .

It is not clear to me, nor, I venture to assert, would it be to the Supreme Court, if faced directly by an appropriate case of literary obscenity, what words inflict injury by their very utterance or how such injury is inflicted. As for the notion of an obscene book tending to incite to an immediate breach of the peace, the proper point of emphasis is the breach of the peace. That is different from saying that obscenity automatically tends to a breach of the peace, for the idea is unreal. . . .

The difficulty here is that insofar as they apply to literature, obscenity and its imposing string of synonymns do *not* have a fixed meaning through long use in the criminal law—or put it the other way, that they have a very narrow and restricted meaning quite at variance with the assumption that obscenity debauches public morals by a mysterious and self-executing process that can be feared but not proved.

Certainly the books before me do not command, or urge, or incite, or even encourage persons to commit sexual misconduct of a nature that the legislature has the right to prevent or punish. Nor are they an imminent threat to the morality of the community as a whole. The conduct described in them is at most offensive. It does not incite to unlawfulness of any kind. . . .

Short of books that are sexually impure and pornographic, I can see no rational legal catalyst that can detect or define a clear and present danger inherent in a writing or that can demonstrate what result ensues from reading it. All that is relied upon, in a prosecution, is an indefinable fear for other people's moral standards—a fear that I regard as a democratic anomaly. . . .

I am clear that the books before me are within the protection of the first and fourteenth amendments of the Federal Constitution, and of article 1, sec. 7 of the Pennsylvania Constitution. They bear obvious internal evidence of an effort to portray certain segments of American life, including parts that more refined people than the characters may deplore, but which we know exist. The vulgarity and obscenity in them are inherent in the characters themselves and are obviously not set forth as erotic allurements or as an excuse for selling the volumes. Nor can it be said that they have the effect of inciting to lewdness, or of inciting to any sexual crime, or that they are sexually impure and pornographic, i.e., "dirt for dirt's sake."

Definition of Obscenity as Sexual Impurity

Sexual impurity in literature (pornography, as some of the cases call it) I define as any writing whose dominant purpose and effect is erotic allurement—that is to say, a calculated and effective incitement to sexual desire. It is the effect that counts, more than the purpose, and no indictment can stand unless it can be shown. This definition is in accord with the cases that have restricted the meaning of obscenity and its synonyms to that of sexual impurity, and with those cases that have made erotic allurement the test of its effect.

This excludes from pornography medical or educational writings, whether in technical or layman's language, and whether used only in schools or generally distributed, whose dominant purpose and effect is exegetical and instructional rather than enticing. It leaves room for interpretation of individual books, for as long as censorship is considered necessary it is as impossible as it is inadvisable to find a self-executing formula.

Sex education has been before the courts in many cases. In *United States* v. *"Married Love,"* 48 F. (2d) 821 (1931), Judge Woolsey said:

It makes also some apparently justified criticisms of the inopportune exercise by the man in the marriage relation of what are often referred to as his conjugal or marital rights, and it pleads with seriousness, and not without some eloquence, for a better understanding by husbands of the physical and emotional side of the sex life of their wives. I do not find anything exceptionable anywhere in the book, and I cannot imagine a normal mind to which this book would seem to be obscene or immoral within the proper definition of these words, or whose sex impulses would be stirred by reading it.

Judge Woolsey held similarly in *United States* v. *"Contraception,"* 51 F. (2d) 525 (1941). Both of the above books were by Dr. Marie C. Stopes.

The case of *United States* v. *Dennett,* 39 F. (2d) 564 (C.C.A. 2d, 1930), involved a pamphlet written by a woman for the education of her children. Sections of it appear in the reporter's summary of the case, and show that it gave full and frank information, together with the view that the sexual impulse is not a base passion but is a great joy when accompanied by love between two human beings. In reversing a conviction, Judge [Augustus] Hand said:

It also may reasonably be thought that accurate information, rather than mystery and curiosity, is better in the long run and is less likely to occasion lascivious thoughts than ignorance and anxiety. Perhaps instruction other than that which the defendant suggests would be better. That is a matter as to which there is bound to be a wide difference of opinion, but, irrespective of this, we hold that an accurate exposition of the relevant facts of the sex side of life in decent language and in manifestly serious and disinterested spirit cannot ordinarily be regarded as obscene. Any incidental tendency to arouse sex impulses which such a pamphlet may perhaps have, is apart from and subordinate to its main effect. The tendency can only exist in so far as it is inherent in any sex instruction, and it would seem to be outweighed by the elimination of ignorance, curiosity, and morbid fear. The direct aim and the net result is to promote understanding and self-control.

The definition of sexual impurity given above brings literary obscenity into workable analogy with sedition, blasphemy, open lewdness, and the other examples set forth earlier, as those terms are used in our Penal Code, except for one remaining point. Sedition, blasphemy, and open lewdness, by definition, carry their own threat of danger to the public peace. The deep and peculiar nature of religious faith is such that people are entitled to protection against those who call their gods in vain; religion has too recently and for too long been one of the greatest of the fighting faiths to assume that disorder will not follow from public irreverence. He who is publicly lewd is in himself an open and immediate invitation to morally criminal behavior. The pressing danger inherent in sedition speaks for itself.

A book, however sexually impure and pornographic, is in a different case. It cannot be a present danger unless its reader closes it, lays it aside, and transmutes its erotic allurement into overt action. That such action must inevitably follow as a direct consequence of reading the book does not bear analysis, nor is it borne out by general human experience; too much can intervene and too many diversions take place. It must be constantly borne in mind that section 524 does not include the element of debauching public morals or of seeking to alter the prevailing moral code. It only proscribes what *is* obscene, and that term is meaningless unless activated by precise dangers within legal limits. Since section 524 provides no standard, the danger and the limits must be found elsewhere, and the only clear and discernible ones are those having to do with the police power and the preservation of the peace.

The Clear and Present Danger

I have pointed out above that any test of the effect of obscenity is bound to be elusive. Section 524 is therefore vague, indefinite, and unconstitutional unless some exact definition can be found for the "clear and present danger" to be prevented that will satisfy the constitutional protection of free speech. There are various types of cases in which definition is clear because the need is clear. The police power operates in pure food cases because people can sicken and die from eating bad food; in traffic cases because people can be injured or killed unless there is regulation; in weights and measures cases because of the ease with which the consumer can be cheated; and in conventional crimes because of the threat to persons and property. The list could be extended.

Mr. Justice Holmes's example in *Schenck* v. *United States* is no test for the case before me; the public does not read a book and simultaneously rush by the hundreds into the streets to engage in orgiastic riots. Mr. Justice Brandeis's discussion in *Whitney* v. *California* is a better yardstick, for in the field of the printed word the community has full opportunity to answer back. How can it be said that there is a "clear and present danger"—granted that anyone can say what it is—when there is both time and means for ample discussion?

These words of Jefferson should not be forgotten:

> I deplore . . . the putrid state into which our newspapers have passed, and the malignity, the vulgarity, and the mendacious spirit of those who write them. . . . These ordures are rapidly depraving the public taste.
>
> It is, however, an evil for which there is no remedy: our liberty depends on the freedom of the press and that cannot be limited without being lost.

Who can define the clear and present danger to the community that arises from reading a book? If we say it is that the reader is young and inexperienced and incapable of resisting the sexual temptations that the book may present to him, we put the entire reading public at the mercy of the adolescent mind and of those adolescents who do not have the expected advantages of home influence, school training, or religious teaching. Nor can we say into how many such hands the book may come. Adults, or even a gifted minor, may be capable of challenging the book in public and thus of forwarding the education and enlightenment of us all by free discussion and correction. If the argument be applied to the general public, the situation becomes absurd, for then no publication is safe. How is it possible to say that reading a certain book is bound to make people behave in a way that is socially undesirable? And beyond a reasonable doubt, since we are dealing with a penal statute?

We might remember the words of Macaulay: "We find it difficult to believe that in a world so full of temptations as this, any gentleman, whose life would have been virtuous if he had not read Aristophanes and Juvenal, will be made vicious by reading them."

Substitute the names of the books before me for "Aristophanes and Juvenal," and the analogy is exact.

The only clear and present danger to be prevented by section 524 that will satisfy both the Constitution and the current customs of our era is the commission or the imminence of the commission of criminal behavior resulting from the reading of a book. Publication alone can have no such automatic effect.

The Rule of Decision

Thus limited, the constitutional operation of section 524 of our act rests on narrow ground.

The modern test of obscenity, as I have stated it above, furnishes a means of determining whether a book, taken as a whole, is sexually impure, as I have defined that term.

I hold that section 524 may not constitutionally be applied to any writing unless it is sexually impure and pornographic. It may then be applied, as an exercise of the police power, only where there is a reasonable and demonstrable cause to believe that a crime or misdemeanor has been committed or is about to be committed as the perceptible result of the publication and distribution of the writing in question: the opinion of anyone that a tendency thereto exists or that such a result is self-evident is insufficient and irrelevant. The causal connection between the book and the criminal behavior must appear beyond a reasonable doubt. The criminal law is not, in my opinion, "the *custos morum* of the King's subjects," as *Regina* v. *Hicklin* states; it is only the custodian of the peace and good order that free men and women need for the shaping of their common destiny.

There is no such proof in the instant case.

For that reason, and also because of the character of the books themselves, I hold that the books before me are not sexually impure and pornographic, and are therefore not obscene, lewd, lascivious, filthy, indecent, or disgusting. . . .

ROTH v. UNITED STATES
ALBERTS v. CALIFORNIA
354 US 476 (1957)

[In these cases, decided together, the Court held broadly that state and federal obscenity statutes may be enforced without a showing that the obscene material mailed or produced will create a clear and present danger of antisocial conduct, for obscene matter is not constitutionally protected. In one case the Court upheld a conviction for mailing obscene literature, in the other case for keeping for sale obscene books and publishing an obscene advertisement of them.

[In the majority opinion, however, Justice Brennan stated that, while obscenity is not within the area of constitutionally protected speech or press, it is vital that the standards for judging obscenity shall "safeguard the protection of freedom of speech and press for material which does not treat sex in a manner appealing to prurient interests." Accordingly, he rejected the *Hicklin* test as unconstitutionally restrictive of speech and press insofar as it permits judgment on the basis of the effect of isolated passages on the most susceptible persons. The publication must be judged as a whole, and only the effect on the average or normal person should be considered.

[Chief Justice Warren wrote a short concurring opinion; Justice Harlan concurred in the state case but dissented in the federal case; Justices Douglas and Black dissented in both cases.]

Mr. Justice Brennan delivered the opinion of the Court:

The constitutionality of a criminal obscenity statute is the question in each of these cases. In *Roth,* the primary constitutional question is whether the federal obscenity statute violates the provision of the First Amendment that "Congress shall make no law . . . abridging the freedom of speech, or of the press. . . ." In *Alberts,* the primary constitutional question is whether the obscenity provisions of the California Penal Code invade the freedoms of speech and press as they may be incorporated in the liberty protected from state action by the Due Process Clause of the Fourteenth Amendment.

Other constitutional questions are: whether these statutes violate due process, because too vague to support conviction for crime; whether power to punish speech and press offensive to decency and morality is in the states alone, so that the federal obscenity statute violates the Ninth and Tenth Amendments (raised in *Roth*); and whether Congress, by enacting the federal obscenity statute, under the power delegated by Art. I, § 8, cl. 7, to establish post offices and post roads, pre-empted the regulation of the subject matter (raised in *Alberts*).

Roth conducted a business in New York in the publication and sale of books, photographs and magazines. He used circulars and advertising matter to solicit sales. He was convicted by a jury in the District Court for the Southern District of New York upon 4 counts of a 26-count indictment charging him with mailing obscene circulars and advertising, and an obscene book, in violation of the federal obscenity statute. His conviction was affirmed by the Court of Appeals for the Second Circuit. We granted certiorari.

Alberts conducted a mail-order business from Los Angeles. He was convicted by the Judge of the Municipal Court of the Beverly Hills Judicial District (having waived a jury trial) under a misdemeanor complaint which charged him with lewdly keeping for sale obscene and indecent books, and with writing, composing and publishing an obscene advertisement of them, in violation of the California Penal Code. The conviction was affirmed by the Appellate Department of the Superior Court of the State of California in and for the County of Los Angeles. We noted probable jurisdiction.

The dispositive question is whether obscenity is utterance within the area of protected speech and press. Although this is the first time the question has been squarely presented to this Court, either under the First Amendment or under the Fourteenth Amendment, expressions found in numerous opinions indicate that this Court has always assumed that obscenity is not protected by the freedoms of speech and press. . . .

The guaranties of freedom of expression in effect in 10 of the 14 States which by 1792 had ratified the Constitution, gave no absolute protection for every utterance. Thirteen of the 14 States provided for the prosecution of libel, and all of those states made either blasphemy or profanity, or both, statutory crimes. As early as 1712, Massachusetts made it criminal to publish "any filthy, obscene, or profane song, pamphlet, libel or mock sermon" in imitation or mimicking of religious services. . . . Thus, profanity and obscenity were related offenses.

In light of this history, it is apparent that the unconditional phrasing of the First Amendment was not intended to protect every utterance. This phrasing did not prevent this Court from concluding that libelous utterances are not within the area of constitutionally protected speech. *Beauharnais* v. *Illinois,* 343 US 250. At the time of the adoption of the First Amendment, obscenity law was not as fully developed as libel law, but there is sufficiently contemporaneous evidence to show that obscenity, too, was outside the protection intended for speech and press.

The protection given speech and press was fashioned to assure unfettered interchange of ideas for the bringing about of political and social changes desired by the people. This objective was made explicit as early as 1774 in a letter of the Continental Congress to the inhabitants of Quebec:

The last right we shall mention, regards the freedom of the press. The importance of this consists, besides the advancement of truth, science, morality, and arts in general, in its diffusion of liberal sentiments on the administration of Government, its ready communication of thoughts between subjects, and its consequential promotion of union among them, whereby oppressive officers are shamed or intimidated, into more honourable and just modes of conducting affairs. 1 *Journals of the Continental Congress* 108 (1774).

All ideas having even the slightest redeeming social importance—unorthodox ideas, controversial ideas, even ideas hateful to the prevailing climate of opinion—have the full protection of the guaranties, unless excludable because they encroach upon the limited area of more important interests. But implicit in the history of the First Amendment is the rejection of obscenity as utterly without redeeming social importance. This rejection for that reason is mirrored in the universal judgment that obscenity should be restrained, reflected in the international agreement of over 50 nations, in the obscenity laws of all of the 48 States, and in the 20 obscenity laws enacted by the Congress from 1842 to 1956. . . . We hold that obscenity is not within the area of constitutionally protected speech or press.

It is strenuously urged that these obscenity statutes offend the constitutional guaranties because they punish incitation to impure sexual *thoughts,* not shown to be related to any overt antisocial conduct which is or may be incited in the persons stimulated to such *thoughts.* In *Roth,* the trial judge instructed the jury: "The words 'obscene, lewd and lascivious' as used in the law, signify that form of immorality which has relation to sexual impurity and has a tendency to excite lustful *thoughts.*" (Emphasis added.) In *Alberts,* the trial judge applied the test . . . namely, whether the material has "a substantial tendency to deprave or corrupt its readers by inciting lascivious *thoughts* or arousing lustful desires." (Emphasis added.) It is insisted that the constitutional guaranties are violated because convictions may be had without proof either that obscene material will perceptibly create a clear and present danger of antisocial conduct, or will probably induce its recipients to such conduct. But, in light of our holding that obscenity is not protected speech, the complete answer to this argument is in the holding of this Court in *Beauharnais* v. *Illinois, supra,* at 266:

> Libelous utterances not being within the area of constitutionally protected speech, it is unnecessary, either for us or for the State courts, to consider the issues behind the phrase "clear and present danger." Certainly no one would contend that obscene speech, for example, may be punished only upon a showing of such circumstances. Libel, as we have seen, is in the same class.

However, sex and obscenity are not synonymous. Obscene material is material which deals with sex in a manner appealing to prurient interest. The portrayal of sex, e.g., in art, literature and scientific works, is not itself sufficient reason to deny material the constitutional protection of freedom of speech and press. Sex, a great and mysterious motive force in human life, has indisputably been a subject of absorbing interest to mankind through the ages; it is one of the vital problems of human interest and public concern. As to all such problems, this Court said in *Thornhill* v. *Alabama*, 310 US 88:

> The freedom of speech and of the press guaranteed by the Constitution embraces at the least the liberty to discuss publicly and truthfully *all matters of public concern* without previous restraint or fear of subsequent punishment. The exigencies of the colonial period and the efforts to secure freedom from oppressive administration developed a broadened conception of these liberties as adequate to supply the public need for *information and education with respect to the significant issues of the times.* . . . Freedom of discussion, if it would fulfill its historic function in this nation, must embrace *all issues about which information is needed or appropriate to enable the members of society to cope with the exigencies of their period.* [Emphasis added.]

The fundamental freedoms of speech and press have contributed greatly to the development and well-being of our free society and are indispensable to its continued growth. Ceaseless vigilance is the watchword to prevent their erosion by Congress or by the states. The door barring federal and state intrusion into this area cannot be left ajar; it must be kept tightly closed and opened only the slightest crack necessary to prevent encroachment upon more important interests. It is therefore vital that the standards for judging obscenity safeguard the protection of freedom of speech and press for material which does not treat sex in a manner appealing to prurient interest.

The early leading standard of obscenity allowed material to be judged merely by the effect of an isolated excerpt upon particularly susceptible persons. *Regina* v. *Hicklin*, [1868] L.R. 3 Q.B. 360. Some American courts adopted this standard but later decisions have rejected it and substituted this test: whether to the average person, applying contemporary community standards, the dominant theme of the material taken as a whole appeals to prurient interest. The *Hicklin* test, judging obscenity by the effect of isolated passages upon the most susceptible persons, might well encompass material legitimately treating with sex, and so it must be rejected as unconstitutionally restrictive of the freedoms of speech and press. On the other hand, the substituted standard provides safeguards adequate to withstand the charge of constitutional infirmity.

Both trial courts below sufficiently followed the proper standard. Both courts used the proper definition of obscenity. In addition, in the *Alberts* case, in ruling on a motion to dismiss, the trial judge indicated that, as the trier of facts, he was judging each item as a whole as it would affect the normal person, and in *Roth*, the trial judge instructed the jury as follows:

. . . The test is not whether it would arouse sexual desires or sexual impure thoughts in those comprising a particular segment of the community, the young, the immature or the highly prudish or would leave another segment, the scientific or highly educated or the so-called worldly-wise and sophisticated indifferent and unmoved. . . .

The test in each case is the effect of the book, picture or publication considered as a whole, not upon any particular class, but upon all those whom it is likely to reach. In other words, you determine its impact upon the average person in the community. The books, pictures and circulars must be judged as a whole, in their entire context, and you are not to consider detached or separate portions in reaching a conclusion. You judge the circulars, pictures and publications which have been put in evidence by present-day standards of the community. You may ask yourselves does it offend the common conscience of the community by present-day standards. . . .

In this case, ladies and gentlemen of the jury, you and you alone are the exclusive judges of what the common conscience of the community is, and in determining that conscience you are to consider the community as a whole, young and old, educated and uneducated, the religious and the irreligious—men, women and children.

It is argued that the statutes do not provide reasonably ascertainable standards of guilt and therefore violate the constitutional requirements of due process. *Winters* v. *New York*, 333 US 507. The federal obscenity statute makes punishable the mailing of material that is "obscene, lewd, lascivious, or filthy . . . or other publication of an indecent character." The California statute makes punishable, *inter alia*, the keeping for sale or advertising material that is "obscene or indecent." The thrust of the argument is that these words are not sufficiently precise because they do not mean the same thing to all people, all the time, everywhere.

Many decisions have recognized that these terms of obscenity statutes are not precise. This Court, however, has consistently held that lack of precision is not itself offensive to the requirements of due process. ". . . [T]he Constitution does not require impossible standards"; all that is required is that the language "conveys sufficiently definite warning as to the proscribed conduct when measured by common understanding and practices. . . ." . . . These words, applied according to the proper standard for judging obscenity, already discussed, give adequate warning of the conduct proscribed and mark ". . . boundaries sufficiently distinct for judges and juries fairly to administer the law." . . .

In summary, then, we hold that these statutes, applied according to the proper standard for judging obscenity, do not offend constitutional safeguards against convictions based upon protected material, or fail to give men in acting adequate notice of what is prohibited.

Roth's argument that the federal obscenity statute unconstitutionally encroaches upon the powers reserved by the Ninth and Tenth Amendments to the states and to the people to punish speech and press where offensive to decency and morality is hinged upon his contention that obscenity is expression not excepted from the sweep of the provision of the First Amendment that "*Congress* shall make *no law* . . . abridging the freedom of speech, or of the press. . . ." (Emphasis added.) That argument falls in light of our holding that obscenity is not expression protected by the First Amendment. We therefore hold that the federal obscenity statute punishing the use of the mails for obscene material is a proper exercise of the postal power delegated to Congress by Art. I, § 8, cl. 7. . . .

Alberts argues that because his was a mail-order business, the California statute is repugnant to Art. I, § 8, cl. 7, under which the Congress allegedly pre-empted the regulatory field by enacting the federal obscenity statute punishing the mailing or advertising by mail of obscene material. The federal statute deals only with actual mailing; it does not eliminate the power of the state to punish "keeping for sale" or "advertising" obscene material. The state statute in no way imposes a burden or interferes with the federal postal functions. . . .

The judgments are affirmed.

Mr. Justice Harlan, concurring in the result in Alberts v. California, *and dissenting in* Roth v. United States:

I regret not to be able to join the Court's opinion. I cannot do so because I find lurking beneath its disarming generalizations a number of problems which not only leave me with serious misgivings as to the future effect of today's decisions, but which also, in my view, call for different results in these two cases.

I.

My basic difficulties with the Court's opinion are three-fold. First, the opinion paints with such a broad brush that I fear it may result in a loosening of the tight reins which state and federal courts should hold upon the enforcement of obscenity statutes. Second, the Court fails to discriminate between the different factors which, in my opinion, are involved in the constitutional adjudication of state and federal obscenity cases. Third, relevant distinctions between the two obscenity statutes here involved, and the Court's own definition of "obscenity," are ignored.

In final analysis, the problem presented by these cases is how far, and on what terms, the state and federal governments have power to punish individuals for disseminating books considered to be undesirable because of their nature or supposed deleterious effect upon human conduct. Proceeding from the premise that "no issue is presented in either case, concerning the obscenity of the material involved," the Court finds the "dispositive question" to be "whether obscenity is utterance within the area of protected speech and press," and then holds that "obscenity" is not so protected because it is "utterly without redeeming social importance." This sweeping formula appears to me to beg the very question before us. The Court seems to assume that "obscenity" is a peculiar *genus* of "speech ànd press," which is as distinct, recognizable, and classifiable as poison ivy is among other plants. On this basis the *constitutional* question before us simply becomes, as the Court says, whether "obscenity," as an abstraction, is protected by the First and Fourteenth Amendments, and the question whether a *particular* book may be suppressed becomes a mere matter of classification, of "fact," to be entrusted to a fact-finder and insulated from independent constitutional judgment. But surely the problem cannot be solved in such a generalized fashion. Every communication has an individuality and "value" of its own. The suppression of a particular writing or other tangible form of expression is, therefore, an *individual* matter, and in the nature of things every such suppression raises an individual constitutional problem in which a reviewing court must determine for *itself* whether the attacked expression is suppressible within constitutional standards. Since those standards do not readily lend themselves to generalized definitions, the constitutional problem in the last analysis becomes one of particularized judgments which appellate courts must make for themselves.

I do not think that reviewing courts can escape this responsibility by saying that the trier of the facts, be it a jury or a judge, has labeled the questioned matter as "obscene," for, if "obscenity" is to be suppressed, the question whether a particular work is of that character involves not really an issue of fact but a question of constitutional *judgment* of the most sensitive and delicate kind. Many juries might find that Joyce's *Ulysses* or Boccaccio's *Decameron* was obscene, and yet the conviction of a defendant for selling either book would raise, for me, the gravest constitutional problems, for no such verdict could convince me, without more, that these books are "utterly without redeeming social importance." In short, I do not understand how the Court can resolve the constitutional problems now before it without making its own independent judgment upon the character of the material upon which these convictions were based. I am very much afraid that the broad manner in which the Court has decided these cases will tend to obscure the peculiar responsibilities resting on state and federal courts in this field and encourage them to rely on easy labeling and jury verdicts as a substitute for facing up to the tough individual problems of constitutional judgment involved in every obscenity case.

My second reason for dissatisfaction with the Court's opinion is that the broad strides with which the Court has proceeded has led it to brush aside with perfunctory ease the vital constitutional considerations which, in my opinion, differentiate these two cases. It does not seem to matter to the Court that in one case we balance the power of a State in this field against the restrictions of the Fourteenth Amendment, and in the other the power of the Federal Government against the limitations of the First Amendment. I deal with this subject more particularly later.

Thirdly, the Court has not been bothered by the fact that the two cases involve different statutes. In California the book must have a "tendency to deprave or corrupt readers"; under the federal statute it must tend "to stir sexual impulses and lead to sexually impure thoughts." The two statutes do not seem to me to present the same problems. Yet the Court compounds confusion when it super-imposes on these two statutory definitions a third, drawn from the American Law Institute's Model Penal Code, Tentative Draft No. 6: "A thing is obscene if, considered as a whole, its predominant appeal is to prurient interest." The bland assurance that this definition is the same as the ones with which we deal flies in the face of the authors' express rejection of the "deprave and corrupt" and "sexual thoughts" test:

> Obscenity [in the Tentative Draft] is defined in terms of material which appeals predominantly to prurient interest in sexual matters and which goes beyond customary freedom of expression in these matters. We reject the prevailing test of tendency to arouse lustful thoughts or desires because it is unrealistically broad for a society that plainly tolerates a great deal of erotic interest in literature, advertising, and art, and because regulation of thought or desire, unconnected with overt misbehavior, raises the most acute constitutional as well as practical difficulties. We likewise reject the common definition of obscene as that which "tends to corrupt or debase." If this means anything different from tendency to arouse lustful thought and desire, it suggests that change of character or actual misbehavior follows from contact with obscenity. Evidence of such consequences is lacking. . . . On the other hand, "appeal to prurient interest" refers to qualities of the material itself: the capacity to attract individuals eager for a forbidden look. . . .

As this passage makes clear, there is a significant distinction between the definitions used in the prosecutions before us, and the American Law Institute formula. If, therefore, the latter is the correct standard, as my Brother Brennan elsewhere intimates, then these convictions should surely be reversed. Instead, the Court merely assimilates the various tests into one indiscriminate potpourri.

I now pass to the consideration of the two cases before us.

II.

I concur in the judgment of the Court in . . . *Alberts* v. *California*.

The question in this case is whether the defendant was deprived of liberty without due process of law when he was convicted for selling certain materials found by the judge to be obscene because they would have a "tendency to deprave or corrupt readers by exciting lascivious thoughts or arousing lustful desire."

In judging the constitutionality of this conviction, we should remember that our function in reviewing state judgments under the Fourteenth Amendment is a narrow one. We do not decide whether the policy of the State is wise, or whether it is based on assumptions scientifically substantiated. We can inquire only whether the state action so subverts the fundamental liberties implicit in the Due Process Clause that it cannot be sustained as a rational exercise of power. . . . The States' power to make printed words criminal is, of course, confined by the Fourteenth Amendment, but only insofar as such power is inconsistent with our concepts of "ordered liberty." *Palko* v. *Connecticut*, 302 US 319.

What, then, is the purpose of this California statute? Clearly the state legislature has made the judgment that printed words *can* "deprave or corrupt" the reader—that words can incite to anti-social or immoral action. The assumption seems to be that the distribution of certain types of literature will induce criminal or immoral sexual conduct. It is well known, of course, that the validity of this assumption is a matter of dispute among critics, sociologists, psychiatrists, and penologists. There is a large school of thought, particularly in the scientific community, which denies any causal connection between the reading of pornography and immorality, crime, or delinquency. Others disagree. Clearly it is not our function to decide this question. That function belongs to the state legislature. Nothing in the Constitution requires California to accept as truth the most advanced and sophisticated psychiatric opinion. It seems to me clear that it is not irrational, in our present state of knowledge, to consider that pornography can induce to a type of sexual conduct which a State may deem obnoxious to the moral fabric of society. In fact the very division of opinion on the subject counsels us to respect the choice made by the State.

Furthermore, even assuming that pornography cannot be deemed ever to cause, in an immediate sense, criminal sexual conduct, other interests within the proper cognizance of the States may be protected by the prohibition placed on such materials. The State can reasonably draw the inference that over a long period of time the indiscriminate dissemination of materials, the essential character of which is to degrade sex, will have an eroding effect on moral standards. And the State has a legitimate interest in protecting the privacy of the home against invasion of unsolicited obscenity.

Above all stands the realization that we deal here with an area where knowledge is small, data is insufficient, and experts are divided. Since the domain of sexual morality is pre-eminently a matter of state concern, this Court should be slow to interfere with state legislation calculated to protect that morality. It seems to me that nothing in the broad and flexible command of the Due Process Clause forbids California to prosecute one who sells books whose dominant tendency might be to "deprave or corrupt a reader." I agree with the Court, of course, that the books must be judged as a whole and in relation to the normal adult reader.

What has been said, however, does not dispose of the case. It still remains for us to decide whether the state court's determination that this material should be suppressed is consistent with the Fourteenth Amendment; and that, of course, presents a federal question as to which we, and not the state court, have the ultimate responsibility. And so, in the final analysis, I concur in the judgment because, upon an independent perusal of the material involved, and in light of the considerations discussed above, I cannot say that its suppression would so interfere with the communication of "ideas" in any proper sense of that term that it would offend the Due Process Clause. I therefore agree with the Court that appellant's conviction must be affirmed.

III.

I dissent in . . . *Roth* v. *United States.*

We are faced here with the question whether the federal obscenity statute, as construed and applied in this case, violates the First Amendment to the Constitution. To me, this question is of quite a different order than one where we are dealing with state legislation under the Fourteenth Amendment. I do not think it follows that state and federal powers in this area are the same, and that just because the State may suppress a particular utterance, it is automatically permissible for the Federal Government to do the same. I agree with Mr. Justice Jackson that the historical evidence does not bear out the claim that the Fourteenth Amendment "incorporates" the First in any literal sense. . . . But laying aside any consequences which might flow from that conclusion, . . . I prefer to rest my views about this case on broader and less abstract grounds.

The Constitution differentiates between those areas of human conduct subject to the regulation of the States and those subject to the powers of the Federal Government. The substantive powers of the two governments, in many instances, are distinct. And in every case where we are called upon to balance the interest in free expression against other interests, it seems to me important that we should keep in the forefront the question of whether those other interests are state or federal. Since under our constitutional scheme the two are not necessarily equivalent, the balancing process must needs often produce different results. Whether a particular limitation on speech or press is to be upheld because it subserves a paramount governmental interest must, to a large extent, I think, depend on whether that government has, under the Constitution, a direct substantive interest, that is, the power to act, in the particular area involved.

The Federal Government has, for example, power to restrict seditious speech directed against it, because that Government certainly has the substantive authority to protect itself against revolution. . . . But in dealing with obscenity we are faced with the converse situation, for the interests which obscenity statutes purportedly protect are primarily entrusted to the care, not of the Federal Government, but of the States. Congress has no substantive power over sexual morality. Such powers as the Federal Government has in this field are but incidental to its other powers, here the postal power, and are not of the same nature as those possessed by the States, which bear direct responsibility for the protection of the local moral fabric. What Mr. Justice Jackson said in *Beauharnais* about criminal libel is equally true of obscenity:

> The inappropriateness of a single standard for restricting State and Nation is indicated by the disparity between their functions and duties in relation to those freedoms. Criminality of defamation is predicated upon power either to protect the private right to enjoy integrity of reputation or the public right to tranquillity. Neither of these are objects of federal cognizance except when necessary to the accomplishment of some delegated power. . . . When the Federal Government puts liberty of press in one scale, it has a very limited duty to personal reputation or local tranquillity to weigh against it in the other. But state action affecting speech or press can and should be weighed against and reconciled with these conflicting social interests.

Not only is the federal interest in protecting the Nation against pornography attenuated, but the dangers of federal censorship in this field are far greater than anything the States may do. It has often been said that one of the great strengths of our federal system is that we have, in the forty-eight States, forty-eight experimental social laboratories. "State statutory law reflects predominantly this capacity of a legislature to introduce novel techniques of social control. The federal system has the immense advantage of providing forty-eight separate centers for such experimentation." Different States will have different attitudes toward the same work of literature. The same book which is freely read in one State might be classed as obscene in another. And it seems to me that no overwhelming danger to our freedom to experiment and to gratify our tastes in literature is likely to result from the suppression of a borderline book in one of the States, so long as there is no uniform nation-wide suppression of the book, and so long as other States are free to experiment with the same or bolder books.

Quite a different situation is presented, however, where the Federal Government imposes the ban. The danger is perhaps not great if the people of one State, through their legislature, decide that *Lady Chatterley's Lover* goes so far beyond the acceptable standards of candor that it will be deemed offensive and nonsellable, for the State next door is still free to make its own choice. At least we do not have one uniform standard. But the dangers to free thought and expression are truly great if the Federal Government imposes a blanket ban over the Nation on such a book. The prerogative of the States to differ on their ideas of morality will be destroyed, the ability of States to experiment will be stunted. The fact that the people of one State cannot read some of the works of D. H. Lawrence seems to me, if not wise or desirable, at least acceptable. But that no person in the United States should be allowed to do so seems to me to be intolerable, and violative of both the letter and spirit of the First Amendment.

I judge this case, then, in view of what I think is the attenuated federal interest in this field, in view of the very real danger of a deadening uniformity which can result from nation-wide federal censorship, and in view of the fact that the constitutionality of this conviction must be weighed against the First and not the Fourteenth Amendment. So viewed, I do not think that this conviction can be upheld. The petitioner was convicted under a statute which, under the judge's charge, makes it criminal to sell any book which "tends to stir sexual impulses and lead to sexually impure thoughts." I cannot agree that any book which "tends to stir sexual impulses and lead to sexually impure thoughts" necessarily is "utterly without redeeming social importance." Not only did this charge fail to measure up to the standards which I understand the Court to approve, but as far as I can see, much of the great literature of the world could lead to conviction under such a view of the statute. Moreover, in no event do I think that the limited federal interest in this area can extend to mere "thoughts." The Federal Government has no business, whether under the postal or commerce power, to bar the sale of books because they might lead to any kind of "thoughts."

It is no answer to say, as the Court does, that obscenity is not protected speech. The point is that this statute, as here construed, defines obscenity so widely that it encompasses matters which might very well be protected speech. I do not think that the federal statute can be constitutionally construed to reach other than what the Government has termed as "hard-core" pornography. Nor do I think the statute can fairly be read as directed only at *persons* who are engaged in the business of catering to the prurient minded, even though their wares fall short of hard-core pornography. Such a statute would raise constitutional questions of a different order. That being so, and since in my opinion the material here involved cannot be said to be hard-core pornography, I would reverse this case with instructions to dismiss the indictment.

Mr. Justice Douglas, with whom Mr. Justice Black concurs, dissenting:

When we sustain these convictions, we make the legality of a publication turn on the purity of thought which a book or tract instills in the mind of the reader. I do not think we can approve that standard and be faithful to the command of the First Amendment which by its terms is a restraint on Congress and which by the Fourteenth is a restraint on the states.

In the *Roth* case the trial judge charged the jury that the statutory words "obscene, lewd and lascivious" describe "that form of immorality which has relation to sexual impurity and has a tendency to excite lustful thoughts." He stated that the term "filthy" in the statute pertains "to that sort of treatment of sexual matters in such a vulgar and indecent way, so that it tends to arouse a feeling of disgust and revulsion." He went on to say that the material "must be calculated to corrupt and debauch the minds and morals" of "the average person in the community," not those of any particular class. "You judge the circulars, pictures and publications which have been put in evidence by present-day standards of the community. You may ask yourselves does it offend the common conscience of the community by present-day standards."

The trial judge who, sitting without a jury, heard the *Alberts* case and the appellate court that sustained the judgment of conviction, took California's definition of "obscenity" from *People* v. *Wepplo*, 78 Cal. App. 2d Supp. 959. That case held that a book is obscene "if it has a substantial tendency to deprave or corrupt its readers by inciting lascivious thoughts or arousing lustful desire."

By these standards punishment is inflicted for thoughts provoked, not for overt acts nor anti-social conduct. This test cannot be squared with our decisions under the First Amendment. Even the ill-starred *Dennis* case conceded that speech to be punishable must have some relation to action which could be penalized by government. *Dennis* v. *United States,* 341 US 494. . . . This issue cannot be avoided by saying that obscenity is not protected by the First Amendment. The question remains, what is the constitutional test of obscenity?

The tests by which these convictions were obtained require only the arousing of sexual thoughts. Yet the arousing of sexual thoughts and desires happens every day in normal life in dozens of ways. Nearly 30 years ago a questionnaire sent to college and normal school women graduates asked what things were most stimulating sexually. Of 409 replies, 9 said "music"; 18 said "pictures"; 29 said "dancing"; 40 said "drama"; 95 said "books"; and 218 said "man." . . .

The test of obscenity the Court endorses today gives the censor free range over a vast domain. To allow the state to step in and punish mere speech or publication that the judge or the jury thinks has an *undesirable* impact on thoughts but that is not shown to be a part of unlawful action is drastically to curtail the First Amendment. . . .

If we were certain that impurity of sexual thoughts impelled to action, we would be on less dangerous ground in punishing the distributors of this sex literature. But it is by no means clear that obscene literature, as so defined, is a significant factor in influencing substantial deviations from the community standards.

There are a number of reasons for real and substantial doubts as to the soundness of that hypothesis. (1) Scientific studies of juvenile delinquency demonstrate that those who get into trouble, and are the greatest concern of the advocates of censorship, are far less inclined to read than those who do not become delinquent. The delinquents are generally the adventurous type, who have little use for reading and other non-active entertainment. Thus, even assuming that reading sometimes has an adverse effect upon moral conduct, the effect is not likely to be substantial, for those who are susceptible seldom read. (2) Sheldon and Eleanor Glueck, who are among the country's leading authorities on the treatment and causes of juvenile delinquency, have recently published the results of a ten year study of its causes. They exhaustively studied approximately 90 factors and influences that might lead to or explain juvenile delinquency, but the Gluecks gave no consideration to the type of reading material, if any, read by the delinquents. This is, of course, consistent with their finding that delinquents read very little. When those who know so much about the problem of delinquency among youth—the very group about whom the advocates of censorship are most concerned—conclude that what delinquents read has so little effect upon their conduct that it is not worth investigating in an exhaustive study of causes, there is good reason for serious doubt concerning the basic hypothesis on which obscenity censorship is defended. (3) The many other influences in society that stimulate sexual desire are so much more frequent in their influence, and so much more potent in their effect, that the influence of reading is likely, at most, to be relatively insignificant in the composite of forces that lead an individual into conduct deviating from the community sex standards. The Kinsey studies show the minor degree to which literature serves as a potent sexual stimulant. And the studies demonstrating that sex knowledge seldom results from reading indicates the relative unimportance of literature in sex thoughts as compared with other factors in society. Lockhart and McClure [38 *Minn. L. Rev.* 295].

The absence of dependable information on the effect of obscene literature on human conduct should make us wary. It should put us on the side of protecting society's interest in literature, except and unless it can be said that the particular publication has an impact on action that the government can control.

As noted, the trial judge in the *Roth* case charged the jury in the alternative that the federal obscenity statute outlaws literature dealing with sex which offends "the common conscience of the community." That standard is, in my view, more inimical still to freedom of expression.

The standard of what offends "the common conscience of the community" conflicts, in my judgment, with the command of the First Amendment that "Congress shall make no law . . . abridging the freedom of speech, or of the press." Certainly that standard would not be an acceptable one if religion, economics, politics or philosophy were involved. How does it become a constitutional standard when literature treating with sex is concerned?

Any test that turns on what is offensive to the community's standards is too loose, too capricious, too destructive of freedom of expression to be squared with the First Amendment. Under that test, juries can censor, suppress, and punish what they don't like, provided the matter relates to "sexual impurity" or has a tendency "to excite lustful thoughts." This is community censorship in one of its worst forms. It creates a regime where in the battle between the literati and the Philistines, the Philistines are certain to win. If experience in this field teaches anything, it is that "censorship of obscenity has almost always been both irrational and indiscriminate." . . . The test adopted here accentuates that trend.

I assume there is nothing in the Constitution which forbids Congress from using its power over the mails to proscribe *conduct* on the grounds of good morals. No one would suggest that the First Amendment permits nudity in public places, adultery, and other phases of sexual misconduct.

I can understand (and at times even sympathize) with programs of civic groups and church groups to protect and defend the existing moral standards of the community. I can understand the motives of the Anthony Comstocks who would impose Victorian standards on the community. When speech alone is involved, I do not think that government, consistently with the First Amendment, can become the sponsor of any of these movements. I do not think that government, consistently with the First Amendment, can throw its weight behind one school or another. Government should be concerned with anti-social conduct, not with utterances. Thus if the First Amendment guarantee of freedom of speech and press is to mean anything in this field, it must allow protests even against the moral code that the standard of the day sets for the community. In other words, literature should not be suppressed merely because it offends the moral code of the censor.

The legality of a publication in this country should never be allowed to turn either on the purity of thought which it instills in the mind of the reader or on the degree to which it offends the community conscience. By either test the role of the censor is exalted, and society's values in literary freedom are sacrificed.

The Court today suggests a third standard. It defines obscene material as that "which deals with sex in a manner appealing to prurient interest." Like the standards applied by the trial judges below, that standard does not require any nexus between the literature which is prohibited and action which the legislature can regulate or prohibit. Under the First Amendment, that standard is no more valid than those which the courts below adopted.

I do not think that the problem can be resolved by the Court's statement that "obscenity is not expression protected by the First Amendment." With the exception of *Beauharnais* v. *Illinois*, none of our cases have resolved problems of free speech and free press by placing any form of expression beyond the pale of the absolute prohibition of the First Amendment. Unlike the law of libel, wrongfully relied on in *Beauharnais*, there is no special historical evidence that literature dealing with sex was intended to be treated in a special manner by those who drafted the First Amendment. In fact, the first reported court decision in this country involving obscene literature was in 1821. . . . I reject too the implication that problems of freedom of speech and of the press are to be resolved by weighing against the values of free expression, the judgment of the Court that a particular form of that expression has "no redeeming social importance." The First Amendment, its prohibition in terms absolute, was designed to preclude courts as well as legislatures from weighing the values of speech against silence. The First Amendment puts free speech in the preferred position.

Freedom of expression can be suppressed if, and to the extent that, it is so closely brigaded with illegal action as to be an inseparable part of it. . . . As a people, we cannot afford to relax that standard. For the test that suppresses a cheap tract today can suppress a literary gem tomorrow. All it need do is to incite a lascivious thought or arouse a lustful desire. The list of books that judges or juries can place in that category is endless.

I would give the broad sweep of the First Amendment full support. I have the same confidence in the ability of our people to reject noxious literature as I have in their capacity to sort out the true from the false in theology, economics, politics, or any other field.

KINGSLEY BOOKS, INC. *v.* BROWN
354 US 436 (1957)

[A New York statute authorizes a designated municipal officer to seek an injunction to prevent the sale or distribution of obscene publications. By a 5-to-4 decision the Court upheld the statute as constitutional, regarding it as a valid regulation of obscenity that places a restraint upon writings after publication and a finding of obscenity. Writing for the majority, Justice Frankfurter pointed out that *Near* v. *Minnesota, supra,* stated that "the protection even as to previous restraint is not absolutely unlimited."

[Dissenting, Chief Justice Warren stated that the statute imposed an unconstitutional prior restraint on publications. Justices Douglas and Black said that the statute made the state a censor and that the procedure for restraining the distribution of condemned literature violated the First Amendment. Justice Brennan condemned the statute for failing to provide a trial by jury.]

Mr. Justice Frankfurter delivered the opinion of the Court:

This is a proceeding under § 22-a of the New York Code of Criminal Procedure (L. 1941, c. 925), as amended in 1954 (L. 1954, c. 702). This section supplements the existing conventional criminal provision dealing with pornography by authorizing the chief executive, or legal officer, of a municipality to invoke a "limited injunctive remedy," under closely defined procedural safeguards, against the sale and distribution of written and printed matter found after due trial to be obscene, and to obtain an order for the seizure, in default of surrender, of the condemned publications.

A complaint dated September 10, 1954, charged appellants with displaying for sale paper-covered obscene booklets, fourteen of which were annexed, under the general title of *Nights of Horror*. The complaint prayed that appellants be enjoined from further distribution of the booklets, that they be required to surrender to the sheriff for destruction all copies in their possession, and, upon failure to do so, that the sheriff be commanded to seize and destroy those copies. The same day the appellants were ordered to show cause within four days why they should not be enjoined *pendente lite* from distributing the booklets. Appellants consented to the granting of an injunction *pendente lite* and did not bring the matter to issue promptly, as was their right under sub-division 2 of the challenged section, which provides that the persons sought to be enjoined "shall be entitled to a trial of the issues within one day after joinder of issue and a decision shall be rendered by the court within two days of the conclusion of the trial." After the case came to trial, the judge, sitting in equity, found that the booklets annexed to the complaint and introduced in evidence were clearly obscene—were "dirt for dirt's sake"; he enjoined their further distribution and ordered their destruction. He refused to enjoin "the sale and distribution of later issues" on the ground that "to rule against a volume not offered in evidence would . . . impose an unreasonable prior restraint upon freedom of the press." . . .

Not challenging the construction of the statute or the finding of obscenity, appellants took a direct appeal to the New York Court of Appeals, a proceeding in which the constitutionality of the statute was the sole question open to them. That court (one judge not sitting) found no constitutional infirmity: three judges supported the unanimous conclusion by detailed discussion, the other three deemed a brief disposition justified by "ample authority." . . . A claim under the Due Process Clause of the Fourteenth Amendment made throughout the state litigation brought the case here on appeal. . . .

Neither in the New York Court of Appeals, nor here, did appellants assail the legislation insofar as it outlaws obscenity. The claim they make lies within a very narrow compass. Their attack is upon the power of New York to employ the remedial scheme of § 22-a. Authorization of an injunction *pendente lite,* as part of this scheme, during the period within which the issue of obscenity must be promptly tried and adjudicated in an adversary proceeding for which "[a]dequate notice, judicial hearing, [and] fair determination" are assured, . . . is a safeguard against frustration of the public interest in effectuating judicial condemnation of obscene matter. It is a brake on the temptation to exploit a filthy business offered by the limited hazards of piecemeal prosecutions, sale by sale, of a publication already condemned as obscene. New York enacted this procedure on the basis of study by a joint legislative committee. Resort to this injunctive remedy, it is claimed, is beyond the constitutional power of New York in that it amounts to a prior censorship of literary product and as such is violative of that "freedom of thought, and speech" which has been "withdrawn by the Fourteenth Amendment from encroachment by the states." . . . Reliance is particularly placed upon *Near* v. *Minnesota,* 283 US 697.

In an unbroken series of cases extending over a long stretch of this Court's history, it has been accepted as a postulate that "the primary requirements of decency may be enforced against obscene publication." . . . And so our starting point is that New York can constitutionally convict appellants of keeping for sale the booklets incontestably found to be obscene. *Alberts* v. *California*, [354 US 476] decided this day. The immediate problem then is whether New York can adopt as an auxiliary means of dealing with such obscene merchandising the procedure of § 22-a.

We need not linger over the suggestion that something can be drawn out of the Due Process Clause of the Fourteenth Amendment that restricts New York to the criminal process in seeking to protect its people against the dissemination of pornography. It is not for this Court thus to limit the State in resorting to various weapons in the armory of the law. Whether proscribed conduct is to be visited by a criminal prosecution or by a *qui tam* action or by an injunction or by some or all of these remedies in combination, is a matter within the legislature's range of choice. . . . If New York chooses to subject persons who disseminate obscene "literature" to criminal prosecution and also to deal with such books as deodands of old, or both, with due regard, of course, to appropriate opportunities for the trial of the underlying issue, it is not for us to gainsay its selection of remedies. Just as *Near* v. *Minnesota, supra,* one of the landmark opinions in shaping the constitutional protection of freedom of speech and of the press, left no doubts that "Liberty of speech, and of the press, is also not an absolute right," . . . it likewise made clear that "the protection even as to previous restraint is not absolutely unlimited." . . . To be sure, the limitation is the exception; it is to be closely confined so as to preclude what may fairly be deemed licensing or censorship.

The judicial angle of vision in testing the validity of a statute like § 22-a is "the operation and effect of the statute in substance." . . . The phrase "prior restraint" is not a self-wielding sword. Nor can it serve as a talismanic test. The duty of closer analysis and critical judgment in applying the thought behind the phrase has thus been authoritatively put by one who brings weighty learning to his support of constitutionally protected liberties: "What is needed," writes Professor Paul Freund, "is a pragmatic assessment of its operation in the particular circumstances. The generalization that prior restraint is particularly obnoxious in civil liberties cases must yield to more particularistic analysis." *The Supreme Court and Civil Liberties,* 4 *Vand. L. Rev.* 533, 539.

Wherein does § 22-a differ in its effective operation from the type of statute upheld in *Alberts?* Section 311 of California's Penal Code provides that "Every person who wilfully and lewdly . . . keeps for sale . . . any obscene book . . . is guilty of a misdemeanor. . . ." Section 1141 of New York's Penal Law is similar. One would be bold to assert that the *in terrorem* effect of such statutes less restrains booksellers in the period before the law strikes than does § 22-a. Instead of requiring the bookseller to dread that the offer for sale of a book may without prior warning subject him to a criminal prosecution with the hazard of imprisonment, the civil procedure assures him that such consequences cannot follow unless he ignores a court order specifically directed to him for a prompt and carefully circumscribed determination of the issue of obscenity. Until then, he may keep the book for sale and sell it on his own judgment rather than "steer . . . nervously among the treacherous shoals." . . .

Criminal enforcement and the proceeding under § 22-a interfere with a book's solicitation of the public precisely at the same stage. In each situation the law moves after publication; the book need not in either case have yet passed into the hands of the public. The *Alberts* record does not show that the matter there found to be obscene had reached the public at the time that the criminal charge of keeping such matter for sale was lodged, while here as a matter of fact copies of the booklets whose distribution was enjoined had been on sale for several weeks when process was served. In each case the bookseller is put on notice by the complaint that sale of the publication charged with obscenity in the period before trial may subject him to penal consequences. In the one case he may suffer fine and imprisonment for violation of the criminal statute, in the other, for disobedience of the temporary injunction. The bookseller may of course stand his ground and confidently believe that in any judicial proceeding the book could not be condemned as obscene, but both modes of procedure provide an effective deterrent against distribution prior to adjudication of the book's content—the threat of subsequent penalization.

The method devised by New York in § 22-a for determining whether a publication is obscene does not differ in essential procedural safeguards from that provided under many state statutes making the distribution of obscene publications a misdemeanor. For example, while the New York criminal provision brings the State's criminal procedure into operation, a defendant is not thereby entitled to a jury trial. In each case a judge is the conventional trier of fact; in each, a jury may as a matter of discretion be summoned. . . . (Appellants, as a matter of fact, did not request a jury trial, they did not attack the statute in the courts below for failure to require a jury, and they did not bring that issue to this Court.) Of course, the Due Process

Clause does not subject the States to the necessity of having trial by jury in misdemeanor prosecutions.

Nor are the consequences of a judicial condemnation for obscenity under § 22-a more restrictive of freedom of expression than the result of conviction for a misdemeanor. In *Alberts*, the defendant was fined $500, sentenced to sixty days in prison, and put on probation for two years on condition that he not violate the obscenity statute. Not only was he completely separated from society for two months but he was also seriously restrained from trafficking in all obscene publications for a considerable time. Appellants, on the other hand, were enjoined from displaying for sale or distributing only the particular booklets theretofore published and adjudged to be obscene. Thus, the restraint upon appellants as merchants in obscenity was narrower than that imposed on *Alberts*.

Section 22-a's provision for the seizure and destruction of the instruments of ascertained wrongdoing expresses resort to a legal remedy sanctioned by the long history of Anglo-American law. . . . It is worth noting that although the *Alberts* record does not reveal whether the publications found to be obscene were destroyed, provision is made for that by §§ 313 and 314 of the California Penal Code. Similarly, § 1144 of New York's Penal Law provides for destruction of obscene matter following conviction for its dissemination.

It only remains to say that the difference between *Near* v. *Minnesota, supra,* and this case is glaring in fact. The two cases are no less glaringly different when judged by the appropriate criteria of constitutional law. Minnesota empowered its courts to enjoin the dissemination of future issues of a publication because its past issues had been found offensive. In the language of Mr. Chief Justice Hughes, "This is of the essence of censorship." . . . As such, it was found unconstitutional. This was enough to condemn the statute wholly apart from the fact that the proceeding in *Near* involved not obscenity but matters deemed to be derogatory to a public officer. Unlike *Near*, § 22-a is concerned solely with obscenity and, as authoritatively construed, it studiously withholds restraint upon matters not already published and not yet found to be offensive.

The judgment is affirmed.

Mr. Chief Justice Warren, dissenting:

My views on the right of a State to protect its people against the purveyance of obscenity were expressed in *Alberts* v. *California*, also decided today. Here we have an entirely different situation.

This is not a criminal obscenity case. Nor is it a case ordering the destruction of materials disseminated by a person who has been convicted of an offense for doing so, as would be authorized under provisions in the laws of New York and other States. It is a case wherein the New York police, under a different state statute, summarily seized books which, in their opinion, were unfit for public use because of obscenity and then obtained a court order for their condemnation and destruction.

The majority opinion sanctions this proceeding. I would not. Unlike the criminal cases decided today, this New York law places the book on trial. There is totally lacking any standard in the statute for judging the book in context. The personal element basic to the criminal laws is entirely absent. In my judgment, the same object may have wholly different impact depending upon the setting in which it is placed. Under this statute, the setting is irrelevant.

It is the manner of use that should determine obscenity. It is the conduct of the individual that should be judged, not the quality of art or literature. To do otherwise is to impose a prior restraint and hence to violate the Constitution. Certainly in the absence of a prior judicial determination of illegal use, books, pictures and other objects of expression should not be destroyed. It savors too much of book burning.

I would reverse.

Mr. Justice Douglas, with whom Mr. Justice Black concurs, dissenting:

There are two reasons why I think this restraining order should be dissolved.

First, the provision for an injunction *pendente lite* gives the State the paralyzing power of a censor. A decree can issue *ex parte*—without a hearing and without any ruling or finding on the issue of obscenity. This provision is defended on the ground that it is only a little encroachment, that a hearing must be promptly given and a finding of obscenity promptly made. But every publisher knows what awful effect a decree issued in secret can have. We tread here on First Amendment grounds. And nothing is more devastating to the rights that it guarantees than the power to restrain publication before even a hearing is held. This is prior restraint and censorship at its worst.

Second, the procedure for restraining by equity decree the distribution of all the condemned literature does violence to the First Amendment. The judge or jury which finds the publisher guilty in New York City acts on evidence that may be quite different from evidence before the judge or jury that finds the publisher not guilty in Rochester. In New York City the publisher may have been selling his tracts to juveniles, while in Rochester he may have sold to professional people. The nature of the group among whom the tracts are distributed may have an important bearing on the issue of guilt in any obscenity prosecution. Yet the present statute makes one criminal conviction conclusive and authorizes a statewide decree that subjects the distributor to the contempt power. I think every publication is a separate offense which entitles the accused to a separate trial. Juries or judges may differ in their opinions, community by community, case by case. The publisher is entitled to that leeway under our constitutional system. One is entitled to defend every utterance on its merits and not to suffer today for what he uttered yesterday. Free speech is not to be regulated like diseased cattle and impure butter. The audience (in this case the judge or the jury) that hissed yesterday may applaud today, even for the same performance.

The regime approved by the Court goes far toward making the censor supreme. It also substitutes punishment by contempt for punishment by jury trial. In both respects it transgresses constitutional guarantees.

I would reverse this judgment and direct the restraining order to be dissolved.

Mr. Justice Brennan, dissenting:

I believe the absence in this New York obscenity statute of a right to jury trial is a fatal defect. Provision for jury trials in equity causes is made by § 430 of the New York Civil Practice Act, but only for discretionary jury trials, and advisory verdicts, to be followed or rejected by the trial judge as he deems fit and proper.

In *Alberts* v. *California* and *Roth* v. *United States*, decided today, . . . the Court held to be constitutional the following standard for judging obscenity—whether to the average person, applying contemporary community standards, the dominant theme of the material taken as a whole appeals to prurient interest. The statutes there involved allowed a jury trial of right, and we did not reach the question whether the safeguards necessary for securing the freedoms of speech and press for material not obscene included a jury determination of obscenity.

The jury represents a cross-section of the community and has a special aptitude for reflecting the view of the average person. Jury trial of obscenity therefore provides a peculiarly competent application of the standard for judging obscenity which, by its definition, calls for an appraisal of material according to the average person's application of contemporary community standards. A statute which does not afford the defendant, of right, a jury determination of obscenity falls short, in my view, of giving proper effect to the standard fashioned as the necessary safeguard demanded by the freedoms of speech and press for material which is not obscene. Of course, as with jury questions generally, the trial judge must initially determine that there is a jury question, i.e., that reasonable men may differ whether the material is obscene.

I would reverse the judgment and direct the restraining order to be dissolved.

BUTLER v. MICHIGAN

352 US 380 (1957)

[A Michigan statute made it a crime to make available for the general reading public a book "tending to incite minors to violent or depraved or immoral acts, manifestly tending to the corruption of the morals of youth." The Court unanimously held that the statute was unconstitutional. In his opinion for the Court, Justice Frankfurter pointed out that the effect of the statute was to set for the general, adult reading public a standard that reduced the adult to the level of the immature. The decision is significant for emancipating adult literature from police tests that might be appropriate for children's books. Justice Black concurred in the result.]

Mr. Justice Frankfurter delivered the opinion of the Court:

This appeal from a judgment of conviction entered by the Recorder's Court of the City of Detroit, Michigan, challenges the constitutionality of the following provision, § 343, of the Michigan Penal Code:

Any person who shall import, print, publish, sell, possess with the intent to sell, design, prepare, loan, give away, distribute or offer for sale, any book, magazine, newspaper, writing, pamphlet, ballad, printed paper, print, picture, drawing, photograph, publication or other thing, including any recordings, containing obscene, immoral, lewd or lascivious language, or obscene, immoral, lewd or lascivious prints, pictures, figures or descriptions, tending to incite minors to violent or depraved or immoral acts, manifestly tending to corruption of the morals of youth, or shall introduce into any family, school or place of education or shall buy, procure, receive or have in his possession, any such book, pamphlet, magazine, newspaper, writing, ballad, printed paper, print, picture, drawing, photograph, publication or other thing, either for the purpose of sale, exhibition, loan or circulation, or with intent to introduce the same into any family, school or place of education, shall be guilty of a misdemeanor.

Appellant was charged with its violation for selling to a police officer what the trial judge characterized as "a book containing obscene, immoral, lewd, lascivious language, or descriptions, tending to incite minors to violent or depraved or immoral acts, manifestly tending to the corruption of the morals of youth." Appellant moved to dismiss the proceeding on the claim that application of § 343 unduly restricted freedom of speech as protected by the Due Process Clause of the Fourteenth Amendment in that the statute (1) prohibited distribution of a book to the general public on the basis of the undesirable influence it may have upon youth; (2) damned a book and proscribed its sale merely because of some isolated passages that appeared objectionable when divorced from the book as a whole; and (3) failed to provide a sufficiently definite standard of guilt. After hearing the evidence, the trial judge denied the motion, and, in an oral opinion, held that ". . . the defendant is guilty because he sold a book in the City of Detroit containing this language [the passages deemed offensive], and also because the Court feels that even viewing the book as a whole, it [the objectionable language] was not necessary to the proper development of the theme of the book nor of the conflict expressed therein." Appellant was fined $100.

Pressing his federal claims, appellant applied for leave to appeal to the Supreme Court of Michigan. Although the State consented to the granting of the application "because the issues involved in this case are of great public interest, and because it appears that further clarification of the language of . . . [the statute] is necessary," leave to appeal was denied. In view of this denial, the appeal is here from the Recorder's Court of Detroit. . . .

Appellant's argument here took a wide sweep. We need not follow him. Thus, it is unnecessary to dissect the remarks of the trial judge in order to determine whether he construed § 343 to ban the distribution of books merely because certain of their passages, when viewed in isolation, were deemed objectionable. Likewise, we are free to put aside the claim that the Michigan law falls within the doctrine whereby a New York obscenity statute was found invalid in *Winters* v. *New York,* 333 US 507.

It is clear on the record that appellant was convicted because Michigan, by § 343, made it an offense for him to make available for the general reading public (and he in fact sold to a police officer) a book that the trial judge found to have a potentially deleterious influence upon youth. The State insists that, by thus quarantining the general reading public against books not too rugged for grown men and women in order to shield juvenile innocence, it is exercising its power to promote the general welfare. Surely, this is to burn the house to roast the pig. Indeed, the Solicitor General of Michigan has, with characteristic candor, advised the Court that Michigan has a statute specifically designed to protect its children against obscene matter "tending to the corruption of the morals of youth." But the appellant was not convicted for violating this statute.

We have before us legislation not reasonably restricted to the evil with which it is said to deal. The incidence of this enactment is to reduce the adult population of Michigan to reading only what is fit for children. It thereby arbitrarily curtails one of those liberties of the individual, now enshrined in the Due Process Clause of the

Fourteenth Amendment, that history has attested as the indispensable conditions for the maintenance and progress of a free society. We are constrained to reverse this conviction.

Reversed.

SMITH v. CALIFORNIA

361 US 147 (1959)

[The proprietor of a bookstore in Los Angeles was convicted for possessing in his store a book found to be obscene by the Los Angeles municipal court. At his trial there was no evidence that the defendant had knowledge of the obscene character of the book. The Supreme Court reversed the judgment of conviction. In his opinion for the Court, Justice Brennan held that the ordinance, by dispensing with the element of scienter, or knowledge by the bookseller of the contents of the book, and imposing a strict criminal liability on a bookseller possessing obscene publications, had an unconstitutional tendency to inhibit the freedom of expression protected by the First and Fourteenth Amendments.

[In a concurring opinion, Justice Black said that a burden on freedom of expression is imposed even when the law requires knowledge of the contents of books. The First Amendment, he said, is an absolute bar on legislation abridging such freedom. Furthermore, he objected to making the Supreme Court a "Supreme Board of Censors," required to read books and observe television programs to judge if they adversely affect the morals of the people in communities throughout the country. Justice Frankfurter, in a concurring opinion, said that the Court's requirement of scienter in obscenity cases should not be left vague and undefined; the standard of awareness or knowledge should be stated in such a way that the state's interest in the prohibition of traffic in obscene literature may not be nullified. He also said that in obscenity prosecutions the defendant should have the right to submit testimony of qualified experts, for literary, psychological, and moral standards change; but the final determination of what is obscene rests with the judge or jury. Justice Douglas, in a concurring opinion, contended that obscene publications were not intended to be excluded from the protection of the First Amendment; and he shared the feeling of Justice Black against making the Supreme Court a censor of publications. Justice Harlan concurred in part and dissented in part.]

Mr. Justice Brennan delivered the opinion of the Court:

Appellant, the proprietor of a bookstore, was convicted in a California Municipal Court under a Los Angeles City ordinance which makes it unlawful "for any person to have in his possession any obscene or indecent writing, [or] book . . . in any place of business where . . . books . . . are sold or kept for sale." The offense was defined by the Municipal Court, and by the Appellate Department of the Superior Court, which affirmed the Municipal Court judgment imposing a jail sentence on appellant, as consisting solely of the possession, in the appellant's bookstore, of a certain book found upon judicial investigation to be obscene. The definition included no element of scienter—knowledge by appellant of the contents of the book—and thus the ordinance was construed as imposing a "strict" or "absolute" criminal liability. The appellant made timely objection below that if the ordinance were so construed it would be in conflict with the Constitution of the United States. This contention, together with other contentions based on the Constitution, was rejected, and the case comes here on appeal. . . .

Almost 30 years ago, Chief Justice Hughes declared for this Court: "It is no longer open to doubt that the liberty of the press, and of speech, is within the liberty safeguarded by the due process clause of the Fourteenth Amendment from invasion by state action. It was found impossible to conclude that this essential personal liberty of the citizen was left unprotected by the general guaranty of fundamental rights of person and property. . . ." *Near* v. *Minnesota*, 283 US 697. It is too familiar for citation that such has been the doctrine of this Court, in respect of these freedoms, ever since. And it also requires no elaboration that the free publication and dissemination of books and other forms of the printed word furnish very familiar applications of these constitutionally protected freedoms. It is of course no matter that the dissemination takes place under commercial auspices. See *Joseph Burstyn, Inc.,* v. *Wilson,* 343 US 495; *Grosjean* v. *American Press Co.,* 297 US 233. Certainly a retail bookseller plays a most significant role in the process of the distribution of books.

California here imposed a strict or absolute criminal responsibility on appellant not to have obscene books in his shop. "The existence of a *mens rea* is the rule of, rather than the exception to, the principles of Anglo-American criminal jurisprudence." *Dennis* v. *United States,* 341 US 494. Still, it is doubtless competent for the States to create strict criminal liabilities by defining criminal offenses without any element of scienter—though even where no freedom-of-expression question is involved, there is precedent in this Court that this power is not without limitations. See *Lambert* v. *California,* 355 US 225. But the question here is as to the validity of this ordinance's elimination of the scienter requirement—an elimination which may tend to work a substantial restriction on freedom of speech. Our decisions furnish examples of legal devices and doctrines, in most applications consistent with the Constitution, which cannot be applied in settings where they have the collateral effect of inhibiting the freedom of expression, by making the individual the more reluctant to exercise it. The States generally may regulate the allocation of the burden of proof in their courts, and it is a common procedural device to impose on a taxpayer the burden of proving his entitlement to exemptions from taxation, but where we conceived that this device was being applied in a manner tending to cause even a self-imposed restriction of free expression, we struck down its application. *Speiser* v. *Randall*, 357 US 513. See *Near* v. *Minnesota, supra,* at 712–713. It has been stated here that the usual doctrines as to the separability of constitutional and unconstitutional applications of statutes may not apply where their effect is to leave standing a statute patently capable of many unconstitutional applications, threatening those who validly exercise their rights of free expression with the expense and inconvenience of criminal prosecution. *Thornhill* v. *Alabama*, 310 US 88. Cf. *Staub* v. *City of Baxley*, 355 US 313. And this Court has intimated that stricter standards of permissible statutory vagueness may be applied to a statute having a potentially inhibiting effect on speech; a man may the less be required to act at his peril here, because the free dissemination of ideas may be the loser. *Winters* v. *New York*, 333 US 507. Very much to the point here, where the question is the elimination of the mental element in an offense, is this Court's holding in *Wieman* v. *Updegraff*, 344 US 183. . . .

These principles guide us to our decision here. We have held that obscene speech and writings are not protected by the constitutional guarantees of freedom of speech and the press. *Roth* v. *United States*, 354 US 476. The ordinance here in question, to be sure, only imposes criminal sanctions on a bookseller if there in fact is to be found in his shop an obscene book. But our holding in *Roth* does not recognize any state power to restrict the dissemination of books which are not obscene; and we think this ordinance's strict liability feature would tend seriously to have that effect, by penalizing booksellers, even though they had not the slightest notice of the character of the books they sold. The appellee and the court below analogize this strict-liability penal ordinance to familiar forms of penal statutes which dispense with any element of knowledge on the part of the person charged, food and drug legislation being a principal example. We find the analogy instructive in our examination of the question before us. The usual rationale for such statutes is that the public interest in the purity of its food is so great as to warrant the imposition of the highest standard of care on distributors—in fact an absolute standard which will not hear the distributor's plea as to the amount of care he has used. . . .

His ignorance of the character of the food is irrelevant. There is no specific constitutional inhibition against making the distributors of food the strictest censors of their merchandise, but the constitutional guarantees of the freedom of speech and of the press stand in the way of imposing a similar requirement on the bookseller. By dispensing with any requirement of knowledge of the contents of the book on the part of the seller, the ordinance tends to impose a severe limitation on the public's access to constitutionally-protected matter. For if the bookseller is criminally liable without knowledge of the contents, and the ordinance fulfills its purpose, he will tend to restrict the books he sells to those he has inspected; and thus the State will have imposed a restriction upon the distribution of constitutionally protected as well as obscene literature. It has been well observed of a statute construed as dispensing with any requirement of scienter that: "Every bookseller would be placed under an obligation to make himself aware of the contents of every book in his shop. It would be altogether unreasonable to demand so near an approach to omniscience." . . . And the bookseller's burden would become the public's burden, for by restricting him the public's access to reading matter would be restricted. If the contents of bookshops and periodical stands were restricted to material of which their proprietors had made an inspection, they might be depleted indeed. The bookseller's limitation in the amount of reading material with which he could familiarize himself, and his timidity in the face of his absolute criminal liability, thus would tend to restrict the public's access to forms of the printed word which the State could not constitutionally suppress directly. The bookseller's self-censorship, compelled by the State, would be a censorship affecting the whole public, hardly less virulent for being privately administered. Through it, the distribution of all books, both obscene and not obscene, would be impeded.

It is argued that unless the scienter requirement is dispensed with, regulation of the distribution of obscene material will be ineffective, as booksellers will falsely disclaim knowledge of their books' contents or falsely deny reason to suspect their obscenity. We might observe that it has been some time now since the law viewed itself as impotent to explore the actual state of a man's mind. . . . Eyewitness testimony of a bookseller's perusal of a book hardly need be a necessary element in proving his awareness of its contents. The circumstances may warrant the inference that he was aware of what a book contained, despite his denial.

We need not and most definitely do not pass today on what sort of mental element is requisite to a constitutionally permissible prosecution of a bookseller for carrying an obscene book in stock; whether honest mistake as to whether its contents in fact constituted obscenity need be an excuse; whether there might be circumstances under which the State constitutionally might require that a bookseller investigate further, or might put on him the burden of explaining why he did not, and what such circumstances might be. Doubtless any form of criminal obscenity statute applicable to a bookseller will induce some tendency to self-censorship and have some inhibitory effect on the dissemination of material not obscene, but we consider today only one which goes to the extent of eliminating all mental elements from the crime.

We have said: "The fundamental freedoms of speech and press have contributed greatly to the development and well-being of our free society and are indispensable to its continued growth. Ceaseless vigilance is the watchword to prevent their erosion by Congress or by the States. The door barring federal and state intrusion into this area cannot be left ajar; it must be kept tightly closed and opened only the slightest crack necessary to prevent encroachment upon more important interests." . . . This ordinance opens that door too far. The existence of the State's power to prevent the distribution of obscene matter does not mean that there can be no constitutional barrier to any form of practical exercise of that power. . . . It is plain to us that the ordinance in question, though aimed at obscene matter, has such a tendency to inhibit constitutionally protected expression that it cannot stand under the Constitution.

Reversed.

ATTORNEY GENERAL *v.* THE BOOK NAMED
"TROPIC OF CANCER"

184 N.E. 2d 328 (Mass., 1962)

[Soon after Grove Press published *Tropic of Cancer* by Henry Miller, the Attorney General of Massachusetts started a proceeding against the book. The Supreme Judicial Court of Massachusetts, in a 4-to-3 decision, held that the book was not obscene and was entitled to protection under the First Amendment.]

Cutter, Justice:

The Attorney General proceeds under G.L. c. 272, §§ 28C–28G (inserted by St. 1945, c. 278, § 1 *), against a book by Henry Miller, "Tropic

* Section 28C reads in part, "Whenever there is reasonable cause to believe that a book which is being . . . distributed . . . is obscene, indecent or impure, the attorney general . . . shall bring an information . . . in equity in the superior

of Cancer" (Tropic), published by Grove Press, Inc. (Grove). Answers were filed by Grove, Miller, and other interveners, alleging that c. 272, § § 28C through 28H, "as applied herein . . . violate rights of the intervenor[s] guaranteed . . . by the . . . Constitution of the United States," under the First Amendment, "as embraced in the Fourteenth Amendment," and under the Constitution of the Commonwealth, Part I, arts. 10, 12, and 16. The case was heard by a judge of the Superior Court, who made a report of material facts. A final decree was entered adjudging Tropic to be "obscene." The interveners appealed. The evidence is reported. The trial judge made the findings summarized below.

"The book was first published in Paris in 1934. The first publication in the United States was on June 24, 1961." Its distribution in Massachusetts was enjoined on July 24, 1961. "There is no connected plot. . . . It is largely a tale of the sex experiences of an American . . . [who went to] Paris . . . in the hope of becoming a writer, and who, except on a few occasions, lived the life of a down-and-outer, sponging on friends. . . . It graphically describes sex episodes with almost minute detail. It is in many respects filthy, disgusting, nauseating and offensive to good taste. As one favorable review, which was introduced in evidence, put it, 'Now it must be granted that parts of "Tropic of Cancer" will hammer away at some of the strongest of stomachs.'" *

The book, several book reviews, and some advertising were in evidence. "Persons who qualified as literary experts testified." The trial judge stated that he was "irresistibly led to the conclusion that the book is obscene, indecent and impure."

1. The opinion testimony is significant principally in that it discloses that competent critics entertain (and, in some cases, have entertained since 1934) the view that Tropic has great literary merit despite its repulsive features. Because the only important evidence is documentary, we are in essentially the same position as the trial judge, and

court directed against said book by name." Then follow provisions for isuing an order of notice to interested persons and for interlocutory action. Section 28E provides for an adjudication against the book, in the event of default, "if the court finds that the book is obscene, indecent or impure. . . ." Section 28F provides for a similar adjudication in the event of a contested hearing, at which "the court may receive the testimony of experts and may receive evidence as to the literary, cultural or educational character of said book and as to the manner and form of its publication, advertisement, and distribution."

* The findings also state, "Of the 318 pages of the book, there are sex episodes on 85 pages, some of which are described on two or more pages, and all of which are described with precise physical detail and four-letter words. The author's descriptive powers are truly impressive and he rises to great literary heights when he describes Paris. And suddenly he descends into the filthy gutter. The literary experts testified that the book depicts a type of life in the thirties in a portion of Paris and that it has great literary merit."

"may draw our own inferences . . . from the basic facts . . . without deference to any inferences . . . drawn by the trial judge." . . .

2. The issue "is whether the" material can "reasonably and constitutionally be found to be obscene." . . . The interveners "concede that the statute covers all material that is obscene in the constitutional sense."

In *Roth* v. *United States*, 354 U.S. 476, the majority rejected the test of obscenity in *Regina* v. *Hicklin*, L.R. 3 Q.B. 360 (1868), and pointed out that later decisions have sought to determine "whether to the average person, applying contemporary community standards, the dominant theme of the material taken as a whole appeals to prurient interest." Material "appealing to prurient interest" was defined as "material having a tendency to excite lustful thoughts" and was equated by him to the definition of obscenity in A.L.I., Model Penal Code, § 207.10(2) (Tent. Draft No. 6, 1957). The *Roth* case recognized that there is constitutional protection for works containing "ideas having even the slightest redeeming social importance—unorthodox ideas, controversial ideas, even ideas hateful to the prevailing climate of opinion—[which] have the full protection of the [First Amendment] guaranties, unless excludable because they encroach upon the limited area of more important interests." The court, however, stated that "implicit in the history of the First Amendment is the rejection of obscenity as utterly without redeeming social importance" and that "obscenity is not within the area of constitutionally protected speech or press."

The *Roth* opinions discuss "obscenity" on a highly theoretical basis. Indeed the court said, "No issue is presented . . . concerning the obscenity of the material." . . . At least the Chief Justice thought that he was dealing with "the commercial exploitation of the morbid and shameful craving for materials with prurient effect."

Some principles have been established by the *Roth* case, as applied in the *Moniz* case, 338 Mass. 442. (1) Hard core, commercial pornography, "utterly without redeeming social importance" (see 354 U.S. 476, 484–485, 77 S. Ct. 1304, 1309), is not within the protection of the First Amendment. (2) "The portrayal of sex, e.g., in art, literature and scientific works, is not itself sufficient reason to deny material the constitutional protection of freedom of speech and press." (3) "[W]hether a particular work is . . . [obscene] involves not . . . an issue of fact but a question of constitutional *judgment* of the most sensitive . . . kind." . . . (4) Material must be judged by its effect upon the "*average* person" (not susceptible persons or youths) and by whether the "*dominant theme* of the material *taken as a whole* appeals to prurient interest" (emphasis supplied). (5) "[A] work may not be adjudged obscene only because" objectionable "to many citizens as violative of accepted standards of propriety." . . . Apart from these principles, what the Supreme Court means by "obscenity" must be determined by what it has done in other cases.

(a) In *Kingsley Books, Inc.* v. *Brown*, 354 U.S. 436, the New York courts were sustained in enjoining distribution of fourteen booklets, "Nights of Horror," clearly hard core pornography. The Supreme Court assumed that the books were obscene and that only the issue of the constitutionality of the testing statute was before it.

(b) In four per curiam decisions (October term, 1957) the Supreme Court reversed decisions of Federal courts of appeal which had treated several different types of material as obscene. See *Times Film Corp.* v. *Chicago*, 355 U.S. 35 (on a film dealing with the seduction of a sixteen year old boy by an older woman, and other "illicit sexual intimacies and acts"); *Mounce* v. *United States*, 355 U.S. 180 (nudist publications; see *United States* v. *4200 Copies International Journal*, 134 F. Supp. 490 [E.D., Wash.]); *One, Inc.* v. *Olesen*, 355 U.S. 371 (dealing with a post office order in respect of "One—The Homosexual Magazine"); *Sunshine Book Co.* v. *Summerfield*, 355 U.S. 372 (nudist material). . . .

(c) In *Kingsley International Pictures Corp.* v. *Regents of Univ. of N.Y.*, 360 U.S. 684, a New York decision was reversed which has sustained the denial of a license to show the film "Lady Chatterley's Lover." The majority did not consider whether the film was obscene, but said, "What New York has done . . . is to prevent the exhibition of a motion picture because that picture advocates an idea—that adultery under certain circumstances may be proper behavior. . . . [The First Amendment's] guarantee is not confined to the expression of ideas that are conventional or shared by a majority. It protects advocacy of the opinion that adultery may sometimes be proper, no less than advocacy of socialism or the single tax."

(d) *Manual Enterprises, Inc.* v. *Day*, 82 S. Ct. 1432, dealt with a ruling of the Post Office Department barring from the mails magazines ("titled MANual, Trim, and Grecian Guild Pictorial") consisting "largely of photographs of nude, or near-nude, male models"; and containing "advertisements . . . offering nudist photographs for sale." Mr. Justice Harlan's opinion accepts findings that "(1) the magazines . . . are composed primarily, if not exclusively, for homosexuals, and have no literary, scientific or other merit; [and] (2) they would appeal to the 'prurient interest' of such sexual deviates, but would not have any interest for sexually normal individuals." The Supreme Court on a diversity of grounds reversed the Court of Appeals decision which had sustained the post office order. . . .

The New York Court of Appeals has interpreted § 1141 of the New York Penal Law dealing with obscenity, as applying "only to . . . 'hard-core pornography.'" . . .

The issue is where to draw the line between what the First Amendment protects and what is obscene in the constitutional sense. . . . The Supreme Court of the United States thus far, as Mr. Justice Harlan's opinion in the *Manual Enterprises* case indicates, has not drawn that line with precision. We, however, are confronted with litigation which should be decided under the law as it now stands, and it is our duty to draw that line as well as we can according to our best judgment of the dictates of the authoritative decisions. A majority of the court feels that we cannot properly evade that duty, even though (as the dissenting opinion points out) the *Roth* case in some respects is a "dim . . . beacon."

Referring to the three general categories of allegedly obscene material, it appears that the Supreme Court already has treated some "borderline entertainment" material and works "of serious . . . intent" as not obscene. Hard core pornography (which involves a "kind of 'pandering'" or "commerce in the obscene," see Model Penal Code, Tent. Draft No. 6, pp. 13–17) is clearly obscene. The most difficult area is that of works which some persons reasonably believe to have literary merit but which, equally reasonably, may be even more objectional to others than "Lady Chatterley's Lover."

We think, in the light of the decisions reviewed above, that the First Amendment protects material which has value because of ideas, news, or artistic, literary, or scientific attributes. If the appeal of material (taken as a whole) to adults is not predominantly prurient, adults cannot be denied the material. When the public risks of suppressing ideas are weighed against the risks of permitting their circulation, the guaranties of the First Amendment must be given controlling effect. The dangers of subjective judgments in the matter of censorship lead to a strong presupposition against suppression. We conclude, therefore, as in effect the New York court did in the Richmond County News case, that, with respect to material designed for general circulation, only predominantly "hard core" pornography, without redeeming social significance, is obscene in the constitutional sense.

The Attorney General relies largely on earlier Massachusetts decisions. *Commonwealth v. Isenstadt*, 318 Mass. 543 (conviction for the sale of a book called "Strange Fruit," under G.L. c. 272, § 28, prior to its amendment by St. 1945, c. 278, § 1). *Attorney General v. "God's Little Acre,"* 326 Mass. 281. These cases were decided, respectively, in 1945 and 1950, each several years before the decision in the *Roth* case. Compare *Attorney General v. "Forever Amber,"* 323 Mass. 302; *Attorney General v. "Serenade,"* 326 Mass. 324, also decided in 1950. The later Supreme Court cases, to the extent inconsistent with our earlier decisions, are controlling, of course, on constitutional issues.

3. Whether Tropic is "obscene" in the constitutional sense thus depends upon whether the appeal (if any) of Tropic (taken as a whole) to the normal adult is predominantly prurient. It is not relevant that we think that the book at many places is repulsive, vulgar, and grossly offensive in the use of four letter words, and in the detailed and coarse statement of sexual episodes. That a serious work uses four letter words and has a grossly offensive tone does not mean that the work is not entitled to constitutional protection. Much in modern art, literature, and music is likely to seem ugly and thoroughly objectionable to those who have different standards of taste. It is not the function of judges to serve as arbiters of taste or to say that an author must regard vulgarity as unnecessary to his portrayal of particular scenes or characters or to establish particular ideas. Within broad limits each writer, attempting to be a literary artist, is entitled to determine such matters for himself, even if the result is as dull, dreary, and offensive as the writer of this opinion finds almost all of Topic.

Competent critics assert, and we conclude, that Tropic has serious purpose * even if many will find that purpose obscure. There can be no doubt that a significant segment of the literary world has long regarded the book as of literary importance. A majority of the court are of opinion that the predominant effect and purpose of the book as a whole is not prurient. If under the *Roth* case it be a relevant consideration, a majority of the court are of opinion that Tropic is more likely to discourage than "to excite lustful thoughts." We think that the book must be accepted as a conscious effort to create a work of literary art and as having significance, which prevents treating it as hard core pornography. In reaching this conclusion, we have carefully considered all the

* Professor Levin of Harvard testified that he thought the author's attitude was "one of disgust with sex" and "the mood . . . one of sexual revulsion. Although a good deal of sex is presented, the author, as it were, is backing away from it and even admonishing against it. It doesn't seem . . . [that] it would be a book to incite lustful thoughts. . . . [I]t . . . [seems] designed to show up western culture at a late stage by dealing with the most ignoble sides of it. . . . [I]t also has passages of some critical and philosophic purport in which the author endeavors to take a more positive view. . . . [S]ome interpreters . . . end by thinking . . . that it is a very healthy book. In my opinion, it is a somewhat morbid book, but a serious one. . . . I think the author is saying, in effect, 'All this is morbid. I am fed up with it.'" More favorable appraisals of the merits of the book were given by other qualified expert witnesses, who expressed, or referred to, opinions that the book contains substantial areas showing literary power. These witnesses included Research Professor Harry T. Moore, Southern Illinois University; Professor Mark Schorer, Chairman of the Department of English, University of California (Berkeley); Professor Morton Bloomfield, English Department, Harvard.

aspects of the book upon which the dissenting justices and the trial judge have commented.

This is not the first time that Tropic has run into censorship. In *Besig* v. *United States,* 208 F.2d 142, the court sustained a customs prohibition of its importation, relying, however, upon something very close to the discredited Hicklin test of obscenity. A customs libel of the book by the United States, however, was recently withdrawn. See order of the United States District Court, Eastern District, New York, dated August 15, 1961, in evidence. Compare the discussion by Judge Murphy in *Upham* v. *Dill,* 195 F. Supp. 5, decided June 27, 1961. An unreported case (*Haiman* v. *Morris,* Illinois Superior Court, Cook County, February 21, 1962) has held the book not to be obscene. The Pennsylvania Court of Common Pleas reached a contrary conclusion in *Commonwealth* v. *Robin,* 30 U.S. L. Week 2551 (dec. April 17, 1962).

We hold that Tropic is not "obscene" in the constitutional sense. It cannot constitutionally be held to be obscene under G.L. c. 272, §§ 28C, 28E, and 28F. We rest our decision squarely on the First Amendment, so that, if review of our decision is sought, there may be no doubt that this case has been decided solely upon the Federal issue.

4. We are not confronted with any question arising under G.L. c. 272, § 28, as amended through St. 1948, c. 328, providing for prosecution for a sale to "a person under the age of eighteen years [of] a book . . . which is obscene . . . *or manifestly tends to corrupt* the morals of youth" (emphasis supplied). See *Butler* v. *Michigan,* 352 U.S. 380. . . .

5. The final decree is reversed. A new decree is to be entered that the book "Tropic of Cancer" is entitled to the protection of the First Amendment and cannot be held to be obscene under G.L. c. 272, §§ 28C, 28E, and 28F.

So ordered.

BANTAM BOOKS *v.* SULLIVAN
372 US 58 (1963)

[The Rhode Island legislature created a commission with the duty to educate the public concerning obscene literature or material manifestly tending to corrupt the youth. The commission notified distributors that certain publications were considered objectionable for youths under eighteen years of age, and the notices in fact stopped circulation of books on the commission's list. The Supreme Court, in an 8-to-1 decision, held that the activities and practices of the commission abridged First Amendment liberties. Justice Douglas wrote a concurring opinion.

Justice Clark concurred in the result and wrote a separate opinion. Justice Harlan wrote a dissenting opinion.]

Mr. Justice Brennan delivered the opinion of the Court:

The Rhode Island Legislature created the "Rhode Island Commission to Encourage Morality in Youth," whose members and Executive Secretary are the appellees herein, and gave the Commission *inter alia* ". . . the duty . . . to educate the public concerning any book, picture, pamphlet, ballad, printed paper or other thing containing obscene, indecent or impure language, or manifestly tending to the corruption of the youth as defined in sections 13, 47, 48 and 49 of chapter 610 of the general laws, as amended, and to investigate and recommend the prosecution of all violations of said sections. . . ." The appellants brought this action in the Superior Court of Rhode Island (1) to declare the law creating the Commission in violation of the First and Fourteenth Amendments, and (2) to declare unconstitutional and enjoin the acts and practices of the appellees thereunder. The Superior Court declined to declare the law creating the Commission unconstitutional on its face but granted the appellants an injunction against the acts and practices of the appellees in performance of their duties. The Supreme Court of Rhode Island affirmed the Superior Court with respect to appellants' first prayer but reversed the grant of injunctive relief. . . . Appellants brought this appeal and we noted probable jurisdiction. . . .

Appellants are four New York publishers of paperback books which have for sometime been widely distributed in Rhode Island. Max Silverstein & Sons is the exclusive wholesale distributor of appellants publications throughout most of the State. The Commission's practice has been to notify a distributor on official Commission stationery that certain designated books or magazines distributed by him had been reviewed by the Commission and had been declared by a majority of its members to be objectionable for sale, distribution or display to youths under 18 years of age. Silverstein had received at least 35 such notices at the time this suit was brought. Among the paperback books listed by the Commission as "objectionable" were one published by appellant Dell Publishing Co., Inc., and another published by appellant Bantam Books, Inc.*

---

* Peyton Place, by Grace Metalious, published (in paperback edition) by appellant Dell Publishing Co., Inc.; The Bramble Bush, by Charles Mergendahl, published (in paperback edition) by appellant Bantam Books, Inc. Most of the other 106 publications which, as of January 1960, had been listed as objectionable by the Commission were issues of such magazines as "Playboy," "Rogue," "Frolic,"

The typical notice to Silverstein either solicited or thanked Silverstein, in advance, for his "cooperation" with the Commission, usually reminding Silverstein of the Commission's duty to recommend to the Attorney General prosecution of purveyors of obscenity. Copies of the lists of "objectionable" publications were circulated to local police departments, and Silverstein was so informed in the notices.

Silverstein's reaction on receipt of a notice was to take steps to stop further circulation of copies of the listed publications. He would not fill pending orders for such publications and would refuse new orders. He instructed his field men to visit his retailers and to pick up all unsold copies, and would then promptly return them to the publishers. A local police officer usually visited Silverstein shortly after Silverstein's receipt of a notice to learn what action he had taken. Silverstein was usually able to inform the officer that a specified number of the total of copies received from a publisher had been returned. According to the testimony, Silverstein acted as he did on receipt of the notice "rather than face the possibility of some sort of a court action against ourselves, as well as the people that we supply." His "cooperation" was given to avoid becoming involved in a "court proceeding" with a "duly authorized organization."

The Superior Court made fact findings and the following two, supported by the evidence and not rejected by the Supreme Court of Rhode Island, are particularly relevant:

"8. The effect of the said notices [those received by Silverstein, including the two listing publications of appellants] was clearly to intimidate the various book and magazine wholesale distributors and retailers and to cause them, by reason of such intimidation and threat of prosecution, (a) to refuse to take new orders for the proscribed publications, (b) to cease selling any of the copies on hand, (c) to withdraw from retailers all unsold copies, and (d) to return all unsold copies to the publishers.

"9. The activities of the respondents [appellees here] have resulted in the suppression of the sale and circulation of the books listed in said notices. . . ."

In addition to these findings it should be noted that the Attorney General of Rhode Island conceded on oral argument in this Court that the books listed in the notices included several that were not obscene within this Court's definition of the term.

Appellants argue that the Commission's activities under Resolution 73, as amended, amount to a scheme of governmental censorship de-

---

and so forth. The Attorney General of Rhode Island described some of the 106 publications as "horror" comics which he said were not obscene as this Court has defined the term.

void of the constitutionally required safeguards for state regulation of obscenity, and thus abridge First Amendment liberties, protected by the Fourteenth Amendment from infringement by the States. We agree that the activities of the Commission are unconstitutional and therefore reverse the Rhode Island Supreme Court's judgment and remand the case for further proceedings not inconsistent with this opinion.

We held in *Alberts* v. *State of California,* decided with *Roth* v. *United States,* 354 U.S. 476, 485, that "obscenity is not within the area of constitutionally protected speech or press" and may therefore be regulated by the States. But this principle cannot be stated without an important qualification:

> . . . [I]n Roth itself we expressly recognized the complexity of the test of obscenity fashioned in that case and the vital necessity of its application of safeguards to prevent denial of 'the protection of freedom of speech and press for material which does not treat sex in a manner appealing to prurient interest.' [354 U.S. at 488, 77 S.Ct. at 1311] . . . It follows that, under the Fourteenth Amendment, a State is not free to adopt whatever procedures it pleases for dealing with obscenity . . . without regard to the possible consequences for constitutionally protected speech." . . .

Thus, the Fourteenth Amendment requires that regulation by the States of obscenity conform to procedures that will ensure against the curtailment of constitutionally protected expression, which is often separated from obscenity only by a dim and uncertain line. It is characteristic of the freedoms of expression in general that they are vulnerable to gravely damaging yet barely visible encroachments. Our insistence that regulations of obscenity scrupulously embody the most rigorous procedural safeguards, . . . *Marcus* v. *Search Warrant; supra,* is therefore but a special instance of the larger principle that the freedoms of expression must be ringed about with adequate bulwarks. . . . "[T]he line between speech unconditionally guaranteed and speech which may legitimately be regulated . . . is finely drawn. . . . The separation of legitimate from illegitimate speech calls for . . . sensitive tools. . . ." *Speiser* v. *Randall,* 357 U.S. 513.

But is it contended, these salutary principles have no application to the activities of the Rhode Island Commission because it does not regulate or suppress obscenity but simply exhorts booksellers and advises them of their legal rights. This contention, premised on the Commission's want of power to apply formal legal sanctions, is untenable. It is true that appellants' books have not been seized or banned by the State, and that no one has been prosecuted for their possession or sale. But though the Commission is limited to informal sanctions—the threat of invoking legal sanctions and other means of coercion, persuasion, and intimidation—the record amply demonstrates that the Commission deliberately set about to achieve the suppression of publications deemed "objectionable" and succeeded in its aim. We are not the first court to look through forms to the substance and recognize that informal censorship may sufficiently inhibit the circulation of publications to warrant injunctive relief.

It is not as if this were not regulation by the State of Rhode Island. The acts and practices of the members and Executive Secretary of the Commission disclosed on this record were performed under color of state law and so constituted acts of the State within the meaning of the Fourteenth Amendment. . . . These acts and practices directly and designedly stopped the circulation of publications in many parts of Rhode Island. It is true, as noted by the Supreme Court of Rhode Island, that Silverstein was "free" to ignore the Commission's notices, in the sense that his refusal to "cooperate" would have violated no law. But it was found as a fact—and the finding, being amply supported by the record, binds us—that Silverstein's compliance with the Commission's directives was not voluntary. People do not lightly disregard public officers' thinly veiled threats to institute criminal proceedings against them if they do not come around, and Silverstein's reaction, according to uncontroverted testimony, was no exception to this general rule. The Commission's notices, phrased virtually as orders, reasonably understood to be such by the distributor, invariably followed up by police visitations, in fact stopped the circulation of the listed publications *ex proprio vigore*. It would be naive to credit the State's assertion that these blacklists are in the nature of mere legal advice, when they plainly serve as instruments of regulation independent of the laws against obscenity. . . .

Herein lies the vice of the system. The Commission's operation is a form of effective state regulation superimposed upon the State's criminal regulation of obscenity and making such regulation largely unnecessary. In thus obviating the need to employ criminal sanctions, the State has at the same time eliminated the safeguards of the criminal process. Criminal sanctions may be applied only after a determination of obscenity has been made in a criminal trial hedged about with the procedural safeguards of the criminal process. The Commission's practice is in striking contrast, in that it provides no safeguards whatever against the suppression of nonobscene, and therefore constitutionally protected, matter. It is a form of regulation that creates hazards to protected freedoms markedly greater than those that attend reliance upon the criminal law.

What Rhode Island has done, in fact, has been to subject the distribution of publications to a system of prior administrative restraints, since the Commission is not a judicial body and its decisions to list particular publications as objectionable do not follow judicial determinations that such publications may lawfully be banned. Any system of prior restraints of expression comes to this Court bearing a heavy presumption against its constitutional validity. . . . We have tolerated such a system only where it operated under judicial superintendence and assured an almost immediate judicial determination of the validity of the restraint. . . . The system at bar includes no such saving features. On the contrary, its capacity for suppression of constitutionally protected publications is far in excess of that of the typical licensing scheme held constitutionally invalid by this Court. There is no provision whatever for judicial superintendence before notices issue or even for judicial review of the Commission's determinations of objectionableness. The publisher or distributor is not even entitled to notice and hearing before his publications are listed by the Commission as objectionable. Moreover, the Commission's statutory mandate is vague and uninformative, and the Commission has done nothing to make it more precise. Publications are listed as "objectionable" without further elucidation. The distributor is left to speculate whether the Commission considers his publication obscene or simply harmful to juvenile morality. For the Commission's domain is the whole of youthful morals. Finally, we note that although the Commission's supposed concern is limited to youthful readers, the "cooperation" it seeks from distributors invariably entails the complete suppression of the listed publications; adult readers are equally deprived of the opportunity to purchase the publications in the State. . . .

The procedures of the Commission are radically deficient. They fall far short of the constitutional requirements of governmental regulation of obscenity. We hold that the system of informal censorship disclosed by this record violates the Fourteenth Amendment.

In holding that the activities disclosed on this record are constitutionally proscribed, we do not mean to suggest that private consultation between law enforcement officers and distributors prior to the institution of a judicial proceeding can never be constitutionally permissible. We do not hold that law enforcement officers must renounce all informal contacts with persons suspected of violating valid laws prohibiting obscenity. Where such consultation is genuinely undertaken with the purpose of aiding the distributor to comply with such laws and avoid prosecution under them, it need not retard the full enjoyment of First Amendment freedoms. But that is not this case. The appellees are not law enforcement officers; they do not pretend that they are qualified to give or that they attempt to give distributors only fair legal advice. Their conduct as disclosed by this record shows plainly that they went far beyond advising the distributors of their legal rights and liabilities. Their operation was in fact a scheme of state censorship effectuated by extra-legal sanctions; they acted as an agency not to advise but to suppress.

Reversed and remanded.

2. Movie Censorship

BURSTYN, INC. v. WILSON

343 US 495 (1952)

[The Supreme Court in 1915 excluded the movies from the protection of the First Amendment. It held that movies are purely business undertakings, conducted for profit, and in no sense part of the press of the country. *Mutual Film Corp.* v. *Ohio Industrial Comm.*, 236 US 230 (1915). This meant that movies were subject to state and local licensing or censorship.

[In the present case, commonly referred to as the *Miracle Case*, the Court overruled the principle of the *Mutual Film Case*. Six members of the Court, in an opinion by Justice Clark, held that the basic principles of freedom of speech and press applied to motion pictures. The Court did not, however, outlaw movie censorship if exercised within narrowly defined rules; it left this question open. The decision was limited to the holding that the guaranty of free speech and press prevents a state from banning a film on a finding by a censor that it is "sacrilegious." Justice Frankfurter, with the concurrence of Justices Jackson and Burton, held that the term "sacrilegious" as used in the New York statute was unconstitutionally vague.

[Early in 1953 the Court unanimously held that New York could not ban the French film "La Ronde" on the ground that it was "immoral" and that Ohio could not ban the American picture "M" as "tending to promote crime." The Court cited their decision in the *Miracle Case* as the basis for their decision regarding these two films. The decision with respect to these films has not completely outlawed all movie censorship, for Justice Douglas found it necessary to write a concurring opinion, with which Justice Black agreed, to say that he found any form of governmental movie censorship unacceptable under the First and Fourteenth Amendments. *Superior Films* v. *Department of Education*, 346 US 587 (1954). Cf. *Gelling* v. *Texas*, 343 US 960 (1952).

[Preceding Justice Clark's opinion for the Court, we present the following statement of facts from Justice Frankfurter's concurring opinion:

[A practised hand has thus summarized the story of "The Miracle":

[A poor, simple-minded girl is tending a herd of goats on a mountainside one day, when a bearded stranger passes. Suddenly it strikes her fancy that he is St. Joseph, her favorite saint, and that he has come to take her to heaven, where she will be happy and free. While she pleads with him to transport her, the stranger gently plies the girl with wine, and when she is in a state of tumult, he apparently ravishes her. (This incident in the story is only briefly and discreetly implied.)

[The girl awakens later, finds the stranger gone, and climbs down the mountain not knowing whether he was real or a dream. She meets an old priest who tells her that it is quite possible that she did see a saint, but a younger priest scoffs at the notion. "Materialist!" the old priest says.

[There follows now a brief sequence—intended to be symbolic, obviously—in which the girl is reverently sitting with other villagers in church. Moved by a whim of appetite, she snitches an apple from the basket of a woman next to her. When she leaves the church, a cackling beggar tries to make her share the apple with him, but she chases him away as by habit and munches the fruit contentedly.

[Then, one day, while tending the village youngsters as their mothers work at the vines, the girl faints and the women discover that she is going to have a child. Frightened and bewildered, she suddenly murmurs, "It is the grace of God!" and she runs to the church in great excitement, looks for the statue of St. Joseph, and then prostrates herself on the floor.

[Thereafter she meekly refuses to do any menial work and the housewives humor her gently but the young people are not so kind. In a scene of brutal torment, they first flatter and laughingly mock her, then they cruelly shove and hit her and clamp a basin as a halo on her head. Even abused by the beggars, the poor girl gathers together her pitiful rags and sadly departs from the village to live alone in a cave.

[When she feels her time coming upon her, she starts towards the village. But then she sees the crowds in the streets; dark memories haunt her; so she turns towards a church on a high hill and instinctively struggles towards it, crying desperately to God. A goat is her sole companion. She drinks water dripping from a rock. And when she comes to the church and finds the door locked, the goat attracts her to a small side door. Inside the church, the poor girl braces herself for her labor pains. There is a dissolve, and when we next see her sad face, in close-up, it is full of a tender light. There is the cry of an unseen baby. The girl reaches towards it and murmurs, "My son! My love! My flesh!"

["The Miracle"—a film lasting forty minutes—was produced in Italy by Roberto Rosselini. Anna Magnani played the lead as the demented goat-tender. It was first shown at the Venice Film Festival in August, 1948, combined with another moving picture, "L'Umano Voce," into a diptych called "Amore." According to an affidavit, from the Director of that Festival, if the motion picture had been "blasphemous" it would have been barred by the Festival Committee. In a review of the film in *L'Osservatore Romano*, the organ of the Vatican, its film critic, Piero Regnoli, wrote: "Opinions may vary and questions may arise—even serious ones—of a religious nature (not to be diminished by the fact that the woman portrayed is mad [because] the author who attributed madness to her is not mad). . . . While acknowledging that there were "passages of undoubted cinematic distinction," Regnoli criticized the film as being "on such a pretentiously cerebral plane that it reminds one of the early d'Annunzio." The Vatican newspaper's critic concluded: "We continue to believe in Rosselini's art and we look forward to his next achievement." In October, 1948, a month after the Rome premiere of "The Miracle," the Vatican's censorship agency, the Catholic Cinematographic Centre, declared that the picture "constitutes in effect an abominable profanation from religious and moral viewpoints." By the Lateran agreements and the Italian Constitution the Italian Government is bound to bar whatever may offend the Catholic religion. However, the Catholic Cinematographic Centre did not invoke any governmental sanction thereby afforded. The Italian Government's censorship agency gave "The Miracle" the regular *nulla osta* clearance. The film was freely shown throughout Italy, but was not a great success. Italian movie critics divided in opinion. The critic for *Il Popolo*, speaking for the Christian Democratic Party, the Catholic party, profusely praised the picture as "a beautiful thing, humanly felt, alive, true and without religious profanation as someone has said, because in our opinion the meaning of the characters is clear and there is no possibility of misunderstanding." Regnoli again reviewed "The Miracle" for *L'Osservatore Romano*. After criticising the film for technical faults, he found "the most courageous and interesting passage of Rosselini's work" in contrasting portrayals in the film; he added: "Unfortunately, concerning morals, it is necessary to note some slight defects." He objected to its "carnality" and to the representation of illegitimate motherhood. But he did not suggest that the picture was "sacrilegious." The tone of Regnoli's critique was one of respect for Rosselini, "the illustrious Italian producer."

[On March 2, 1949, "The Miracle" was licensed in New York State for showing without English titles. However, it was never exhibited until after a second license was issued on November 30, 1950, for the trilogy, "Ways of Love," combining "The Miracle" with two French films, Jean Renoir's "A Day in the Country" and Marcel Pagnol's "Jofroi." All had English subtitles. Both licenses were issued in the usual course after viewings of the picture by the Motion Picture Division of the New York State Education Department. . . . The trilogy opened on December 12, 1950, at the Paris Theatre on 58th Street in Manhattan. It was promptly attacked as "a sacrilegious and blasphemous mockery of Christian religious truth" by the National Legion of Decency, a private Catholic organization for film censorship, whose objectives have intermittently been approved by various non-Catholic church and social groups since its formation in 1933. However, the National Board of Review (a non-industry lay organization devoted to raising the level of motion pictures by mobilizing public opinion, under the slogan "Selection Not Censorship") recommended the picture as "especially worth seeing." New York critics on the whole praised "The Miracle"; those who dispraised did not suggest sacrilege. On December 27 the critics selected the "Ways of Love" as the best foreign language film in 1950. Meanwhile on December 23, Edward T. McCaffrey, Commissioner of Licenses for New York City, declared the film "officially and personally blasphemous" and ordered it withdrawn at the risk of suspension of the license to operate the Paris Theatre. A week later the program was restored at the theatre upon the decision by the New York Supreme Court that the City License Commissioner had exceeded his authority in that he was without powers of movie censorship.

[Upon the failure of the License Commissioner's effort to cut off showings of "The Miracle," the controversy took a new turn. On Sunday, January 7, 1951, a statement of His Eminence, Francis Cardinal Spellman, condemning the picture and calling on "all right thinking citizens" to unite to tighten censorship laws, was read at all masses in St. Patrick's Cathedral.

[The views of Cardinal Spellman aroused dissent among other devout Christians. Protestant clergymen, representing various denominations, after seeing the picture, found in it nothing "sacrilegious or immoral to the views held by Christian men and women," and with a few exceptions agreed that the film was "unquestionably one of unusual artistic merit."

[In this estimate some Catholic laymen concurred. Their opinion is represented by the comment by Otto L. Spaeth, Director of the American Federation of Arts and prominent in Catholic lay activities:

[At the outbreak of the controversy, I immediately arranged for a private showing of the film. I invited a group of Catholics, competent and respected for their writings on both religious and cultural subjects. The essential approval of the film was unanimous.

[There was indeed "blasphemy" in the picture—but it was the blasphemy of the villagers, who stopped at nothing, not even the mock singing of a hymn to the Virgin, in their brutal badgering of the tragic woman. The scathing indictment of their evil behaviour, implicit in the film, was seemingly overlooked by its critics.

[William C. Clancy, a teacher at the University of Notre Dame, wrote in *The Commonweal*, the well-known Catholic weekly, that "the film is not *obviously* blasphemous or obscene, either in its intention or execution." *The Commonweal* itself questioned the wisdom of transforming Church dogma which Catholics may obey as "a free act" into state-enforced censorship for all. Allen Tate, the well-known Catholic poet and critic, wrote: "The picture seems to me to be superior in acting and photography but inferior dramatically. . . . In the long run what Cardinal Spellman will have succeeded in doing is insulting the intelligence and faith of American Catholics with the assumption that a second-rate motion picture could in any way undermine their morals or shake their faith."

[At the time "The Miracle" was filmed, all the persons having significant positions in the production—producer, director, and cast—were Catholics. Roberto Rosselini, who had Vatican approval in 1949 for filming a life of St. Francis, using in the cast members of the Franciscan Order, cabled Cardinal Spellman protesting against boycott of "The Miracle":

[In "The Miracle" men are still without pity because they still have not come back to God, but God is already in the faith, however confused, of that poor, persecuted woman; and since God is wherever a human being suffers and is misunderstood, "The Miracle" occurs when at the birth of the child the poor, demented woman regains sanity in her eternal love.

[In view of the controversy thus aroused by the picture, the Chairman of the Board of Regents appointed a committee of three Board members to review the action of the Motion Picture Division in granting the two licenses. After viewing the picture on Jan. 15, 1951, the committee declared it "sacrilegious." The Board four days later issued an order to the licensees to show cause why the licenses should not be cancelled in that the picture was "sacrilegious." The Board of Regents rescinded the licenses on Feb. 16, 1951, saying that the "mockery or profaning of these beliefs that are sacred to any portion of our citizenship is abhorrent to the laws of this great State." On review the Appellate Division upheld the Board of Regents, holding that the banning of any motion picture "that may fairly be deemed sacrilegious to the adherents of any religious group . . . is directly related to public peace and order" and is not a denial of religious freedom, and that there was "substantial evidence upon which the Regents could act."

[The New York Court of Appeals, with one judge concurring in a separate opinion and two others dissenting, affirmed the order of the Appellate Division. . . .]

Mr. Justice Clark delivered the opinion of the Court:

The issue here is the constitutionality, under the First and Fourteenth Amendments, of a New York statute which permits the banning of motion picture films on the ground that they are "sacrilegious." That statute makes it unlawful "to exhibit, or to sell, lease or lend for exhibition at any place of amusement for pay or in connection with any business in the state of New York, any motion picture film or reel [with specified exceptions not relevant here], unless there is at the time in full force and effect a valid license or permit therefor of the education department. . . ." The statute further provides:

The director of the [motion picture] division [of the education department] or, when authorized by the regents, the officers of a local office or bureau shall cause to be promptly examined every motion picture film submitted to them as herein required, and unless such film or a part thereof is obscene, indecent, immoral, inhuman, sacrilegious, or is of such a character that its exhibition would tend to corrupt morals or incite to crime, shall issue a license therefor. If such director or, when so authorized, such officer shall not license any film submitted, he shall furnish to the applicant therefor a written report of the reasons for his refusal and a description of each rejected part of a film not rejected in toto. . . .

Appellant brought the present action in the New York courts to review the determination of the Regents. Among the claims advanced by appellant were (1) that the statute violates the Fourteenth Amendment as a prior restraint upon freedom of speech and of the press; (2) that it is invalid under the same Amendment as a violation of the guaranty of separate church and state and as a prohibition of the free exercise of religion; and, (3) that the term "sacrilegious" is so vague and indefinite as to offend due process. . . . The case is here on appeal. . . .

As we view the case, we need consider only appellant's contention that the New York statute is an unconstitutional abridgment of free speech and a free press. In *Mutual Film Corp.* v. *Industrial Comm. of Ohio*, 236 U.S. 230 (1915), . . . this Court stated:

It cannot be put out of view that the exhibition of moving pictures is a business, pure and simple, originated and conducted for profit, like other spectacles, not to be regarded, nor intended to be regarded by the Ohio Constitution, we think, as part of the press of the country, or as organs of public opinion.

In a series of decisions beginning with *Gitlow* v. *People of State of New York*, 268 U.S. 652 (1925), this Court held that the liberty of speech and of the press which the First Amendment guarantees against abridgment by the federal government is within the liberty safeguarded by the Due Process Clause of the Fourteenth Amendment from invasion by state action. That principle has been followed and reaffirmed to the present day. Since this series of decisions came after the *Mutual* decision, the present case is the first to present squarely to us the question whether motion pictures are within the ambit of protection which the First Amendment, through the Fourteenth, secures to any form of "speech" or "the press."

It cannot be doubted that motion pictures are a significant medium for the communication of ideas. They may affect public attitudes and behaviors in a variety of ways, ranging from direct espousal of a political or social doctrine to the subtle shaping of thought which characterizes all artistic expression. The importance of motion pictures as an organ of public opinion is not lessened by the fact that they are designed to entertain as well as to inform. As was said in *Winters* v. *People of State of New York*, 333 U.S. 507 (1948), "The line between the informing and the entertaining is too elusive for the protection of that basic right [a free press]. Everyone is familiar with instances of propaganda through fiction. What is one man's amusement, teaches another's doctrine."

It is urged that motion pictures do not fall within the First Amendment's aegis because their production, distribution, and exhibition is a large-scale business conducted for private profit. We cannot agree. That books, newspapers, and magazines are published and sold for profit does not prevent them from being a form of expression whose liberty is safeguarded by the First Amendment. We fail to see why operation for profit should have any different effect in the case of motion pictures.

It is further urged that motion pictures possess a greater capacity for evil, particularly among the youth of a community, than other modes of expression. Even if one were to accept this hypothesis, it does not follow that motion pictures should be disqualified from First Amendment protection. If there be capacity for evil it may be relevant in determining the permissible scope of community control, but it does not authorize substantially unbridled censorship such as we have here.

For the foregoing reasons, we conclude that expression by means of motion pictures is included within the free speech and free press guaranty of the First and Fourteenth Amendments. To the extent that language in the opinion in *Mutual Film Corp.* v. *Industrial Comm.,* *supra,* is out of harmony with the views here set forth, we no longer adhere to it.

To hold that liberty of expression by means of motion pictures is guaranteed by the First and Fourteenth Amendments, however, is not the end of our problem. It does not follow that the Constitution requires absolute freedom to exhibit every motion picture of every kind at all times and all places. That much is evident from the series of decisions of this Court with respect to other media of communication of ideas. Nor does it follow that motion pictures are necessarily subject to the precise rules governing any other particular method of expression. Each method tends to present its own peculiar problems. But the basic principles of freedom of speech and the press, like the First Amendment's command, do not vary. Those principles, as they have frequently been enunciated by this Court, make freedom of expression the rule. There is no justification in this case for making an exception to that rule.

The statute involved here does not seek to punish, as a past offense, speech or writing falling within the permissible scope of subsequent punishment. On the contrary, New York requires that permission to communicate ideas be obtained in advance from state officials who judge the content of the words and pictures sought to be communicated. This Court recognized many years ago that such a previous restraint is a form of infringement upon freedom of expression to be especially condemned. *Near* v. *State of Minnesota* ex rel. *Olson,* 283 U.S. 697 (1931). . . .

New York's highest court says there is "nothing mysterious" about the statutory provision applied in this case: "It is simply this: that no religion, as that word is understood by the ordinary, reasonable person, shall be treated with contempt, mockery, scorn and ridicule. . . ." This is far from the kind of narrow exception to freedom of expression which a state may carve out to satisfy the adverse demands of other interests of society. In seeking to apply the broad and all-inclusive definition of "sacrilegious" given by the New York courts, the censor is set adrift upon a boundless sea amid a myriad of conflicting currents of religious views, with no charts but those provided by the most vocal and powerful orthodoxies. New York cannot vest such unlimited restraining control over motion pictures in a censor. . . . Under such a standard the most careful and tolerant censor would find it virtually impossible to avoid favoring one religion over another, and he would be subject to an inevitable tendency to ban the expression of unpopular sentiments sacred to a religious minority. Application of the "sacrilegious" test, in these or other respects, might raise substantial questions under the First Amendment's guaranty of separate church and state with freedom of worship for all. However, from the standpoint of freedom of speech and the press, it is enough to point out that the state has no legitimate interest in protecting any or all religions from views distasteful to them which is sufficient to justify prior restraints upon the expression of those views. It is not the business of government in our nation to suppress real or imagined attacks upon a particular religious doctrine, whether they appear in publications, speeches, or motion pictures.

Since the term "sacrilegious" is the sole standard under attack here, it is not necessary for us to decide, for example, whether a state may censor motion pictures under a clearly-drawn statute designed and applied to prevent the showing of obscene films. That is a very different question from the one now before us. We hold only that under the First and Fourteenth Amendments a state may not ban a film on the basis of a censor's conclusion that it is "sacrilegious."

Reversed.

KINGSLEY INTERNATIONAL PICTURES CORP. v. REGENTS OF UNIVERSITY OF STATE OF NEW YORK

360 US 684 (1959)

[The film "Lady Chatterley's Lover," based on the novel by D. H. Lawrence, was banned in the State of New York. The ban was unanimously upset by the United States Supreme Court. The New York statute required the denial of a license to motion pictures "which are immoral in that they portray 'acts of sexual immorality . . .

as desirable, acceptable, or proper patterns of behavior.'" The New York authorities held that this language required the denial of a license to the film "because its subject matter is adultery presented as being right and desirable for certain people under certain circumstances." The United States Supreme Court held that the ban on the film violated the First Amendment guarantee of the freedom to advocate ideas. The Constitution "protects advocacy of the opinion that adultery may sometimes be proper, no less than advocacy of socialism or the single tax."]

Mr. Justice Stewart delivered the opinion of the Court:

Once again the Court is required to consider the impact of New York's motion picture licensing law upon First Amendment liberties, protected by the Fourteenth Amendment from infringement by the States. . . .

The New York statute makes it unlawful "to exhibit, or to sell, lease or lend for exhibition at any place of amusement for pay or in connection with any business in the state of New York, any motion picture film or reel [with certain exceptions not relevant here], unless there is at the time in full force and effect a valid license or permit therefor of the education department. . . ." The law provides that a license shall issue "unless such film or a part thereof is obscene, indecent, immoral, inhuman, sacrilegious, or is of such a character that its exhibition would tend to corrupt morals or incite to crime. . . ." A recent statutory amendment provides that, "the term 'immoral' and the phrase 'of such a character that its exhibition would tend to corrupt morals' shall denote a motion picture film or part thereof, the dominant purpose or effect of which is erotic or pornographic; or which portrays acts of sexual immorality, perversion, or lewdness, or which expressly or impliedly presents such acts as desirable, acceptable or proper patterns of behavior."

As the distributor of a motion picture entitled "Lady Chatterley's Lover," the appellant Kingsley submitted that film to the Motion Picture Division of the New York Education Department for a license. Finding three isolated scenes in the film " 'immoral' within the intent of our Law," the Division refused to issue a license until the scenes in question were deleted. The distributor petitioned the Regents of the State of New York for a review of that ruling. The Regents upheld the denial of a license, but on the broader ground that "the whole theme of this motion picture is immoral under said law, for that theme is the presentation of adultery as a desirable, acceptable and proper pattern of behavior."

Kingsley sought judicial review of the Regents' determination. The Appellate Division unanimously annulled the action of the Regents and directed that a license be issued. . . . A sharply divided Court of Appeals, however, reversed the Appellate Division and upheld the Regents' refusal to license the film for exhibition. . . .

The Court of Appeals unanimously and explicitly rejected any notion that the film is obscene. . . . Rather, the court found that the picture as a whole "alluringly portrays adultery as proper behavior." As Chief Judge Conway's prevailing opinion emphasized, therefore, the only portion of the statute involved in this case is that part of §§ 122 and 122 (a) of the Education Law requiring the denial of a license to motion pictures "which are immoral in that they portray 'acts of sexual immorality . . . as desirable, acceptable, or proper patterns of behavior.'" A majority of the Court of Appeals ascribed to that language a precise purpose of the New York Legislature to require the denial of a license to a motion picture "because its subject matter is adultery presented as being right and desirable for certain people under certain circumstances."

We accept the premise that the motion picture here in question can be so characterized. We accept too, as we must, the construction of the New York Legislature's language which the Court of Appeals has put upon it. . . . That construction, we emphasize, gives to the term "sexual immorality" a concept entirely different from the concept embraced in words like "obscenity" or "pornography." Moreover, it is not suggested that the film would itself operate as an incitement to illegal action. Rather, the New York Court of Appeals tells us that the relevant portion of the New York Education Law requires the denial of a license to any motion picture which approvingly portrays an adulterous relationship, quite without reference to the manner of its portrayal.

What New York has done, therefore, is to prevent the exhibition of a motion picture because that picture advocates an idea—that adultery under certain circumstances may be proper behavior. Yet the First Amendment's basic guarantee is of freedom to advocate ideas. The State, quite simply, has thus struck at the very heart of constitutionally protected liberty.

It is contended that the State's action was justified because the motion picture attractively portrays a relationship which is contrary to the moral standards, the religious precepts, and the legal code of its citizenry. This argument misconceives what it is that the Constitution protects. Its guarantee is not confined to the expression of ideas that are conventional or shared by a majority. It protects advocacy of the opinion that adultery may sometimes be proper, no less than advocacy of socialism or the single tax. And in the realm of ideas it protects expression which is eloquent no less than that which is unconvincing.

Advocacy of conduct proscribed by law is not, as Mr. Justice

Brandeis long ago pointed out, "a justification for denying free speech where the advocacy falls short of incitement and there is nothing to indicate that the advocacy would be immediately acted on." *Whitney v. California*, 274 US 357, at 376 (concurring opinion). "Among free men, the deterrents ordinarily to be applied to prevent crime are education and punishment for violations of the law, not abridgment of the rights of free speech. . . ." *Id.*, at 378.*

The inflexible command which the New York Court of Appeals has attributed to the State Legislature thus cuts so close to the core of constitutional freedom as to make it quite needless in this case to examine the periphery. Specifically, there is no occasion to consider the appellant's contention that the State is entirely without power to require films of any kind to be licensed prior to their exhibition. Nor need we here determine whether, despite problems peculiar to motion pictures, the controls which a State may impose upon this medium of expression are precisely coextensive with those allowable for newspapers, books, or individual speech. It is enough for the present case to reaffirm that motion pictures are within the First and Fourteenth Amendments' basic protection. *Joseph Burstyn, Inc.*, v. *Wilson*, 343 US 495.

Reversed.

Mr. Justice Black, concurring:

I concur in the Court's opinion and judgment but add a few words because of concurring opinions by several Justices who rely on their appraisal of the movie Lady Chatterley's Lover for holding that New York cannot constitutionally bar it. Unlike them, I have not seen the picture. My view is that stated by Mr. Justice Douglas, that prior censorship of moving pictures like prior censorship of newspapers and books violates the First and Fourteenth Amendments. If despite the Constitution, however, this Nation is to embark on the dangerous road of censorship, my belief is that this Court is about the most inappropriate Supreme Board of Censors that could be found. So far as I know, judges possess no special expertise providing exceptional competency to set standards and to supervise the private morals of the Nation. In addition, the Justices of this Court seem especially unsuited to make the kind of value judgments—as to what movies are good or bad for local communities—which the concurring opinions appear to require. We are told that the only way we can decide whether a State or municipality can constitutionally bar movies is for this Court to view and appraise each movie on a case-by-case basis. Under these circumstances, every member of the Court must exercise his own judgment as to how bad a picture is, a judgment which is ultimately based at least in large part on his own standard of what

* Thomas Jefferson wrote more than a hundred and fifty years ago, "But we have nothing to fear from the demoralizing reasonings of some, if others are left free to demonstrate their errors. And especially when the law stands ready to

is immoral. The end result of such decisions seems to me to be a purely personal determination by individual Justices as to whether a particular picture viewed is too bad to allow it to be seen by the public. Such an individualized determination cannot be guided by reasonably fixed and certain standards. Accordingly, neither States nor moving picture makers can possibly know in advance, with any fair degree of certainty, what can or cannot be done in the field of movie making and exhibiting. This uncertainty cannot easily be reconciled with the rule of law which our Constitution envisages.

The different standards which different people may use to decide about the badness of pictures are well illustrated by the contrasting standards mentioned in the opinion of the New York Court of Appeals and the concurring opinion of Mr. Justice Frankfurter here. As I read the New York court's opinion this movie was held immoral and banned because it makes adultery too alluring. Mr. Justice Frankfurter quotes Mr. Lawrence, author of the book from which the movie was made, as believing censorship should be applied only to publications that make sex look ugly, that is, as I understand it, less alluring.

In my judgment, this Court should not permit itself to get into the very center of such policy controversies, which have so little in common with lawsuits.

Mr. Justice Frankfurter, concurring in the result:

As one whose taste in art and literature hardly qualifies him for the *avant-garde,* I am more than surprised, after viewing the picture, that the New York authorities should have banned "Lady Chatterley's Lover." To assume that this motion picture would have offended Victorian moral sensibilities is to rely only on the stuffiest of Victorian conventions. Whatever one's personal preferences may be about such matters, the refusal to license the exhibition of this picture, on the basis of the 1954 amendment to the New York State Education Law, can only mean that that enactment forbids the public showing of any film that deals with adultery except by way of sermonizing condemnation or depicts any physical manifestation of an illicit amorous relation. Since the denial of a license by the Board of Regents was confirmed by the highest court of the State, I have no choice but to agree with this Court's judgment in holding that the State exceeded the bounds of free expression protected by the "liberty" of the Fourteenth Amendment. But I also believe that the Court's opinion takes ground that exceeds the appropriate limits for decision. By way of reinforcing my brother Harlan's objections to the scope of the Court's opinion, I add the following.

Even the author of "Lady Chatterley's Lover" did not altogether rule out censorship, nor was his passionate zeal on behalf of society's profound interest in the endeavors of true artists so doctrinaire as to be unmindful of the facts

---

punish the first criminal *act* produced by the false reasoning. These are safer correctives than the conscience of a judge." Letter of Thomas Jefferson to Elijah Boardman, July 3, 1801, Jefferson Papers, Library of Congress, Vol. 115, folio 19761.

of life regarding the sordid exploitation of man's nature and impulses. He knew there was such a thing as pornography, dirt for dirt's sake, or, to be more accurate, dirt for money's sake. This is what D. H. Lawrence wrote:

> But even I would censor genuine pornography, rigorously. It would not be very difficult. In the first place, genuine pornography is almost always underworld, it doesn't come into the open. In the second, you can recognize it by the insult it offers invariably, to sex, and to the human spirit.
>
> Pornography is the attempt to insult sex, to do dirt on it. This is unpardonable. Take the very lowest instance, the picture post-card sold underhand, by the underworld, in most cities. What I have seen of them have been of an ugliness to make you cry. The insult to the human body, the insult to a vital human relationship! Ugly and cheap they make the human nudity, ugly and degraded they make the sexual act, trivial and cheap and nasty. (D. H. Lawrence, *Pornography and Obscenity*, p. 13.)

This traffic has not lessened since Lawrence wrote. Apparently it is on the increase. In the course of the recent debate in both Houses of Parliament on the Obscene Publications Bill, now on its way to passage, designed to free British authors from the hazards of too rigorous application in our day of Lord Cockburn's ruling, in 1868, in *Regina* v. *Hicklin*, L. R. 3 Q. B. 360, weighty experience was adduced regarding the extensive dissemination of pornographic materials. . . . Nor is there any reason to believe that on this side of the ocean there has been a diminution in the pornographic business which years ago sought a flourishing market in some of the leading secondary schools for boys, who presumably had more means than boys in the public high schools.

It is not surprising, therefore, that the pertinacious, eloquent and free-spirited promoters of the liberalizing legislation in Great Britain did not conceive the needs of a civilized society, in assuring the utmost freedom to those who make literature and art possible—authors, artists, publishers, producers, book sellers—easily attainable by sounding abstract and unqualified dogmas about freedom. They had a keen awareness that freedom of expression is no more an absolute than any other freedom, an awareness that is reflected in the opinions of Mr. Justice Holmes and Mr. Justice Brandeis, to whom we predominantly owe the present constitutional safeguards on behalf of freedom of expression. . . .

In short, there is an evil against which a State may constitutionally protect itself, whatever we may think about the questions of policy involved. The real problem is the formulation of constitutionally allowable safeguards which society may take against evil without impinging upon the necessary dependence of a free society upon the fullest scope of free expression. One cannot read the debates in the House of Commons and the House of Lords and not realize the difficulty of reconciling these conflicting interests, in the framing of legislation on the ends of which there was agreement, even for those who most generously espouse that freedom of expression without which all freedom gradually withers.

It is not our province to meet these recalcitrant problems of legislative drafting. Ours is the vital but very limited task of scrutinizing the work of the draftsmen in order to determine whether they have kept within the narrow limits of the kind of censorship which even D. H. Lawrence deemed necessary. The legislation must not be so vague, the language so loose, as to leave to those who have to apply it too wide a discretion for sweeping within its condemnation what is permissible expression as well as what society may permissibly prohibit. Always remembering that the widest scope of freedom is to be given to the adventurous and imaginative exercise of the human spirit, we have struck down legislation phrased in language intrinsically vague, unless it be responsive to the common understanding of men even though not susceptible of explicit definition. The ultimate reason for invalidating such laws is that they lead to timidity and inertia and thereby discourage the boldness of expression indispensable for a progressive society.

The New York legislation of 1954 was the product of careful lawyers who sought to meet decisions of this Court which had left no doubt that a motion-picture licensing law is not inherently outside the scope of the regulatory powers of a State under the Fourteenth Amendment. The Court does not strike the law down because of vagueness, as we struck down prior New York legislation. Nor does it reverse the judgment of the New York Court of Appeals, as I would, because in applying the New York law to "Lady Chatterley's Lover" it applied it to a picture to which it cannot constitutionally be applied without invading the area of constitutionally free expression. The difficulty which the Court finds seems to derive from some expressions culled here and there from the opinion of the Chief Judge of the New York Court of Appeals. This leads the Court to give the phrase "acts of sexual immorality . . . as desirable, acceptable or proper patterns of behavior" an innocent content, meaning, in effect, an allowable subject-matter for discussion. But, surely, to attribute that result to the decision of the Court of Appeals, on the basis of a few detached phrases of Chief Judge Conway, is to break a faggot into pieces, is to forget that the meaning of language is to be felt and its phrases not to be treated disjointedly. "Sexual immorality" is not a new phrase in this branch of law and its implications dominate the context. I hardly conceive it possible that the Court would strike down as unconstitutional the federal statute against mailing lewd, obscene and lascivious matter, which has been the law of the land for nearly a hundred years, . . . whatever specific instances may be found not within its allowable prohibition. In sustaining this legislation this Court gave the words "lewd, obscene and lascivious" concreteness by saying that they concern "sexual immorality."

Unless I misread the opinion of the Court, it strikes down the New York legislation in order to escape the task of deciding whether a particular picture is entitled to the protection of expression under the Fourteenth Amendment. Such an exercise of the judicial function, however onerous or ungrateful, inheres in the very nature of the judicial enforcement of the Due Process Clause. We cannot escape such instance-by-instance, case-by-case application of that clause in all the variety of situations that come before this Court. It would be comfortable if, by a comprehensive formula, we could decide when a confession is coerced so as to vitiate a state conviction. There is no such talismanic formula. Every Term we have to examine the particular circumstances of a particular case in order to apply generalities which no one disputes. It would be equally comfortable if a general formula could determine the unfairness of a state trial for want of counsel. But, except in capital cases, we have to thread our way, Term after Term, through the particular circumstances of a particular case in relation to a particular defendant in order to ascertain whether due process was denied in the unique situation before us. We are constantly called upon to consider the alleged misconduct of a prosecutor as vitiating the fairness of a particular trial or the inflamed state of public opinion in a particular case as undermining the constitutional right to due process. Again, in the series of cases coming here from the state courts, in which Due Process was invoked to enforce separation of church and state, decision certainly turned on the particularities of the specific situations before the Court. It is needless to multiply instances. It is the nature of the concept of Due Process, and, I venture to believe, its high serviceability in our constitutional system, that the judicial enforcement of the Due Process Clause is the very antithesis of a Procrustean rule. This was recognized in the first full-dress discussion of the Due Process Clause of the Fourteenth Amendment, when the Court defined the nature of the problem as a "gradual process of judicial inclusion and exclusion, as the cases presented for decision shall require, with the reasons on which such decision may be founded." . . . The task is onerous and exacting, demanding as it does the utmost discipline in objectivity, the severest control of personal predilections. But it cannot be escaped, not even by disavowing that such is the nature of our task.

Mr. Justice Douglas, with whom Mr. Justice Black joins, concurring:

While I join in the opinion of the Court, I adhere to the views I expressed in *Superior Films* v. *Department of Education*, 346 US 587, that censorship of movies is unconstitutional, since it is a form of "previous restraint" that is as much at war with the First Amendment, made applicable to the States through the Fourteenth, as the censorship struck down in *Near* v. *Minnesota*, 283 US 697. If a particular movie violates a valid law, the exhibitor can be prosecuted in the usual way. I can find in the First Amendment no room for any censor whether he is scanning an editorial, reading a news broadcast, editing a novel or a play, or previewing a movie.

Reference is made to British law and British practice. But they have little relevance to our problem, since we live under a written Constitution. What is entrusted to the keeping of the legislature in England is protected from legislative interference or regulation here. As we stated in *Bridges* v. *California*, 314 US 252, 265, "No purpose in ratifying the Bill of Rights was clearer than that of securing for the people of the United States much greater freedom of religion, expression, assembly, and petition than the people of Great Britain had ever enjoyed." If we had a provision in our Constitution for "reasonable" regulation of the press such as India has included in hers, there would be room for argument that censorship in the interests of morality would be permissible. Judges sometimes try to read the word "reasonable" into the First Amendment or make the rights it grants subject to reasonable regulation . . . or apply to the States a watered-down version of the First Amendment. . . . But its language, in terms that are absolute, is utterly at war with censorship. Different questions may arise as to censorship of some news when the Nation is actually at war. But any possible exceptions are extremely limited. That is why the tradition represented by *Near* v. *Minnesota, supra,* represents our constitutional ideal.

Happily government censorship has put down few roots in this country. The American tradition is represented by *Near* v. *Minnesota, supra.* . . . We have in the United States no counterpart of the Lord Chamberlain who is censor over England's stage. As late as 1941 only six States had systems of censorship for movies. . . . That number has now been reduced to four— Kansas, Maryland, New York, and Virginia—plus a few cities. Even in these areas, censorship of movies shown on television gives way by reason of the Federal Communications Act. . . . And from what information is available, movie censors do not seem to be very active. Deletion of the residual part of censorship that remains would constitute the elimination of an institution that intrudes on First Amendment rights.

Mr. Justice Clark, concurring in the result:

I can take the words of the majority of the New York Court of Appeals only in their clear, unsophisticated and common meaning. They say that §§ 122 and 122-a of New York's Education Law "require the denial of a license to motion pictures which are immoral in that they portray 'acts of sexual immorality . . . as desirable, acceptable or proper patterns of behavior.'" That court states the issue in the case in this language:

> Moving pictures are our only concern and, what is more to the point, only those motion pictures which alluringly present acts of sexual immorality as proper behavior.

Moreover, it is significant to note that in its 14-page opinion that court says again and again, in fact 15 times, that the picture "Lady Chatterley's Lover" is proscribed because of its "espousal" of sexual immorality as "desirable" or as "proper conduct for the people of our State."

The minority of my brothers here, however, twist this holding into one that New York's Act requires "obscenity or incitement, not just abstract expressions of opinion." But I cannot so obliterate the repeated declarations above-mentioned that were made not only 15 times by the Court of Appeals but which were the basis of the Board of Regent's decision as well. Such a construction would raise many problems, not the least of which would be our failure to accept New York's interpretation of the scope of its own Act. I feel, as does the majority here, bound by their holding.

In this context, the Act comes within the ban of *Burstyn* v. *Wilson,* 343 US 495 (1952). We held there that "expression by means of motion pictures is included within the free speech and free press guaranty of the First and Fourteenth Amendments." Referring to *Near* v. *Minnesota*, 283 US 697 (1931), we said that while "a major purpose of the First Amendment guaranty of a free press was to prevent prior restraints upon publication" such protection was not unlimited but did place on the State "a heavy burden to demonstrate that the limitation challenged" was exceptional. The standard applied there was the word "sacrilegious" and we found it set the censor "adrift upon a boundless sea amid a myriad of conflicting currents of religious views. . . ." We struck it down.

Here the standard is the portrayal of "acts of sexual immorality . . . as desirable, acceptable or proper patterns of behavior." Motion picture plays invariably have a hero, a villain, supporting characters, a location, a plot, a diversion from the main theme and usually a moral. As we said in *Burstyn:* "They may affect public attitudes and behavior in a variety of ways, ranging from direct espousal of a political or social doctrine to the subtle shaping of thought which characterizes all artistic expression." What may be to one viewer the glorification of an idea as being "desirable, acceptable or proper" may to the notions of another be entirely devoid of such a teaching. The only limits on the censor's discretion is his understanding of what is included within the term "desirable, acceptable or proper." This is nothing less than a roving commission in which individual impressions become the yardstick of action, and results in regulation in accordance with the beliefs of the individual censor rather than regulation by law. Even here three of my brothers "cannot regard this film as depicting anything more than a somewhat unusual, and rather pathetic, 'love triangle.' " At least three—perhaps four—of the members of New York's highest court thought otherwise. I need only say that the obscurity of the standard presents such a choice of difficulties that even the most experienced find themselves at dagger's point.

It may be, as Chief Judge Conway said, "that our public morality, possibly more than ever before, needs every protection government can give." And, as my Brother Harlan points out, "each time such a statute is struck down, the State is left in more confusion." This is true where broad grounds are employed leaving no indication as to what may be necessary to meet the requirements of due process. I see no grounds for confusion, however, were a statute to ban "pornographic" films, or those that "portray *acts* of sexual immorality, perversion or lewdness." If New York's statute had been so construed by its highest court I believe it would have met the requirements of due process. Instead, it placed more emphasis on what the film teaches than on what it depicts. There is where the confusion enters. For this reason, I would reverse on the authority of *Burstyn*.

Mr. Justice Harlan, whom Mr. Justice Frankfurter and Mr. Justice Whittaker join, concurring in the result:

I think the Court has moved too swiftly in striking down a statute which is the product of a deliberate and conscientious effort on the part of New

York to meet constitutional objections raised by this Court's decisions respecting predecessor statutes in this field. But although I disagree with the Court that the parts of §§ 122 and 122-a of the New York Education Law, here particularly involved are unconstitutional on their face, I believe that in their application to this film constitutional bounds were exceeded.

I.

Section 122-a of the State Education Law was passed in 1954 to meet this Court's decision in *Commercial Pictures Corp.* v. *Regents,* 346 US 587, which overturned the New York Court of Appeals' holding . . . that the film *La Ronde* could be banned as "immoral" and as "tend[ing] to corrupt morals" under § 122. The Court's decision in *Commercial Pictures* was but a one line *per curiam* with a citation to *Joseph Burstyn, Inc.* v. *Wilson,* which in turn had held for naught not the word "immoral" but the term "sacrilegious" in the statute.

New York, nevertheless, set about repairing its statute. This it did by enacting § 122-a which in the respects emphasized in the present opinion of Chief Judge Conway as pertinent here defines an "immoral" motion picture film as one which portrays " 'acts of sexual immorality . . . as desirable, acceptable or proper patterns of behavior.' " The Court now holds this part of New York's effort unconstitutional on its face under the Fourteenth Amendment. I cannot agree.

The Court does not suggest that these provisions are bad for vagueness. Any such suggestion appears to me untenable in view of the long-standing usage in this Court of the concept "sexual immorality" to explain in part the meaning of "obscenity." Instead, the Court finds a constitutional vice in these provisions in that they require, so it is said, neither "obscenity" nor incitement to "sexual immorality," but strike of their own force at the mere advocacy of "an idea—that adultery under certain circumstances may be proper behavior"; expressions of "opinion that adultery may sometimes be proper. . . ." I think this characterization of these provisions misconceives the construction put upon them by the prevailing opinions in the Court of Appeals. Granting that the abstract public discussion or advocacy of adultery, unaccompanied by obscene portrayal or actual incitement to such behavior, may not constitutionally be proscribed by the State, I do not read those opinions to hold that the statute on its face undertakes any such proscription. Chief Judge Conway's opinion, which was joined by two others of the seven judges of the Court of Appeals, and in the thrust of which one more concurred, to be sure with some doubt, states:

> It should first be emphasized that the scope of section 122-a is not mere expression of opinion in the form, for example, of a filmed lecture whose subject matter is the espousal of adultery. We reiterate that this case involves the espousal of sexually immoral acts (here adultery) *plus* actual scenes of a suggestive and obscene nature. [Emphasis in original.]

The opinion elsewhere, as indeed is also the case with §§ 122 and 122-a themselves when independently read in their entirety, is instinct with the notion that mere abstract expressions of opinion regarding the desirability of sexual immorality, unaccompanied by obscenity or incitement, are not proscribed. . . . It is the corruption of public morals, occasioned by the inciting effect of a particular portrayal or by what New York has deemed the necessary effect of obscenity, at which the statute is aimed. In the words of Chief Judge Conway, "There is no difference in substance between motion pictures which are corruptive of the public morals, and sexually suggestive, because of a predominance of suggestive scenes, and those which achieve precisely the same effect by presenting only several such scenes in a clearly approbatory manner throughout the course of the film. *The law is concerned with effect, not merely with but one means of producing it . . . the objection lies in the corrosive effect upon the public sense of sexual morality."* . . . [Emphasis in original.]

I do not understand that the Court would question the constitutionality of the particular portions of the statute with which we are here concerned if the Court read, as I do, the majority opinions in the Court of Appeals as construing these provisions to require obscenity or incitement, not just mere abstract expressions of opinion. It is difficult to understand why the Court should strain to read those opinions as it has. Our usual course in constitutional adjudication is precisely the opposite.

II.

The application of the statute to this film is quite a different matter. I have heretofore ventured the view that in this field the States have wider constitutional latitude than the Federal Government. . . .

Giving descriptive expression to what in matters of this kind are in the last analysis bound to be but individual subjective impressions, objectively as one may try to discharge his duty as a judge, is not apt to be repaying. I shall therefore content myself with saying that, according full respect to, and with, I hope, sympathetic consideration for, the views and characterizations expressed by others, I cannot regard this film as depicting anything more than a somewhat unusual, and rather pathetic, "love triangle," lacking in anything that could properly be termed obscene or corruptive of the public morals by inciting the commission of adultery. I therefore think that in banning this film New York has exceeded constitutional limits.

I conclude with one further observation. It is sometimes said that this Court should shun considering the particularities of individual cases in this difficult field lest the Court become a final "board of censorship." But I cannot understand why it should be thought that the process of constitutional judgment in this realm somehow stands apart from that involved in other fields, particularly those presenting questions of due process. Nor can I see, short of holding that all state "censorship" laws are constitutionally impermissible, a course from which the Court is carefully abstaining, how the Court can hope ultimately to spare itself the necessity for individualized adjudication. In the very nature of things the problems in this area are ones of individual cases, . . . for a "censorship" statute can hardly be contrived that would in effect be self-executing. And, lastly, each time such a statute is struck down, the State is left in more confusion, as witness New York's experience with its statute.

Because I believe the New York statute was unconstitutionally applied in this instance I concur in the judgment of the Court.

TIMES FILM CORPORATION *v.* CHICAGO

365 US 43 (1961)

[An ordinance of the city of Chicago required the submission of moving pictures to a censor as a prerequisite to a public showing. Petitioner applied for a permit to show "Don Juan" but refused to submit the film for examination. The permit was refused. Petitioner applied for an injunction ordering the issuance of the permit without prior submission of the film, on the ground that the ordinance on its face was unconstitutional as a prior restraint. The injunction was denied. The Supreme Court affirmed the judgments below, holding that the ordinance was not void on its face. Chief Justice Warren dissented, joined by Justices Black, Douglas, and Brennan. Justice Douglas also wrote a dissenting opinion, in which he was joined by Chief Justice Warren and Justice Black.]

Mr. Justice Clark delivered the opinion of the Court:

Petitioner challenges on constitutional grounds the validity on its face of that portion of § 155-4 of the Municipal Code of the City of Chicago which requires submission of all motion pictures for examination prior to their public exhibition. Petitioner is a New York corporation owning the exclusive right to publicly exhibit in Chicago the film known as "Don Juan." It applied for a permit as Chicago's ordinance required, and tendered the license fee but refused to submit the film for examination. The appropriate city official refused to issue the permit and his order was made final on appeal to the Mayor. The sole ground for denial was petitioner's refusal to submit the film for examination as required. Petitioner then brought this suit seeking injunctive relief ordering the issuance of the permit without submission of the film and restraining the city officials from interfering with the exhibition of the picture. Its sole ground is that the provision of the ordinance requiring submission of the film constitutes, on its face, a prior restraint within the prohibition of the First and Fourteenth Amendments. The District Court dismissed the complaint on the grounds, *inter alia,* that neither a substantial federal question nor even a justiciable controversy was presented. The Court of Appeals affirmed, finding that the case presented merely an abstract question of law since neither the film nor evidence of its content was submitted. The precise question at issue here never having been specifically decided by this Court, we granted certiorari.

We are satisfied that a justiciable controversy exists. The section of Chicago's ordinance in controversy specifically provides that a permit for the public exhibition of a motion picture must be obtained; that such "permit shall be granted only after the motion picture film for which said permit is requested has been produced at the office of the commissioner of police for examination"; that the Commissioner shall refuse the permit if the picture does not meet certain standards; and that in the event of such refusal the applicant may appeal to the Mayor for a *de novo* hearing and his action shall be final. Violation of the ordinance carries certain punishments. The petitioner complied with the requirements of the ordinance, save for the production of the film for examination. The claim is that this concrete and specific statutory requirement, the production of the film at the office of the Commissioner for examination, is invalid as a previous restraint on freedom of speech. In *Joseph Burstyn, Inc.,* v. *Wilson,* 343 U.S. 495 (1952), we held that motion pictures are included "within the free speech and free press guaranty of the First and Fourteenth Amendments." Admittedly, the challenged section of the ordinance imposes a previous restraint, and the broad justiciable issue is therefore present as to whether the ambit of constitutional protection includes complete and absolute freedom to exhibit, at least once, any and every kind of motion picture. It is that question alone which we decide. We have concluded that § 155-4 of Chicago's ordinance requiring the submission of films prior to their public exhibition is not, on the grounds set forth, void on its face.

Petitioner's narrow attack upon the ordinance does not require that any consideration be given to the validity of the standards set out therein. They are not challenged and are not before us. Prior motion picture censorship cases which reached this Court involved questions of standards. The films had all been submitted to the authorities and permits for their exhibition were refused because of their content. Obviously, whether a particular statute is "clearly drawn," or "vague," or "indefinite," or whether a clear standard is in fact met by a film are different questions involving other constitutional challenges to be tested by considerations not here involved.

Moreover, there is not a word in the record as to the nature and content of "Don Juan." We are left entirely in the dark in this regard, as were the city officials and the other reviewing courts. Petitioner claims that the nature of the film is irrelevant, and that even if this film contains the basest type of pornography, or incitement to riot, or forceful overthrow of orderly government, it may nonetheless be shown without prior submission for examination. The challenge here is to the censor's basic authority; it does not go to any statutory standards employed by the censor or procedural requirements as to the submission of the film.

In this perspective we consider the prior decisions of this Court touching on the problem. Beginning over a third of a century ago in *Gitlow* v. *New York*, 268 U.S. 652 (1925), they have consistently reserved for future decision possible situations in which the claimed First Amendment privilege might have to give way to the necessities of the public welfare. It has never been held that liberty of speech is absolute. Nor has it been suggested that all previous restraints on speech are invalid. On the contrary, in *Near* v. *Minnesota*, 283 U.S. 697 (1931), Chief Justice Hughes, in discussing the classic legal statements concerning the immunity of the press from censorship, observed that the principle forbidding previous restraint "is stated too broadly, if every such restraint is deemed to be prohibited. . . . [T]he protection even as to previous restraint is not absolutely unlimited. But the limitation has been recognized only in exceptional cases." These included, the Chief Justice found, utterances creating "a hindrance" to the Government's war effort, and "actual obstruction to its recruiting service or the publication of the sailing dates of transports or the number and location of troops." In addition, the Court said that "the primary requirements of decency may be enforced against obscene publications" and the "security of the community life may be protected against incitements to acts of violence and the overthrow by force of orderly government." Some years later a unanimous Court, speaking through Mr. Justice Murphy, in *Chaplinsky* v. *New Hampshire*, 315 U.S. 568 (1942), held that there were "certain well-defined and narrowly limited classes of speech, the prevention and punishment of which have never been thought to raise any Constitutional problem. These include the lewd and obscence, the profane, the libelous, and the insulting or 'fighting' words—those which by their very utterance inflict injury or tend to incite an immediate breach of the peace." Thereafter, as we have mentioned, in *Joseph Burstyn, Inc.*, v. *Wilson, supra,* we found motion pictures to be within the guarantees of the First and Fourteenth Amendments, but we added that this was "not the end of our problem. It does not follow that the Constitution requires absolute freedom to exhibit every motion picture of every kind at all times and all places." Five years later, in *Roth* v. *United States*, 354 U.S. 476 (1957), we held that "in light of . . . history it is apparent that the unconditional phrasing of the First Amendment was not intended to protect every utterance." Even those in dissent found that "freedom of expression can be suppressed if, and to the extent that, it is so closely brigaded with illegal action as to be an inseparable part of it." And, during the same Term, in *Kingsley Books, Inc.,* v. *Brown,* 354 U.S. 436 (1957), after characterizing *Near v. Minnesota, supra,* as "one of the landmark opinions" in its area, we took notice that *Near* "left no doubts that 'Liberty of speech, and of the press, is also not an absolute right . . . the protection even as to previous restraint is not absolutely unlimited.' . . . The judicial angle of vision," we said there, "in testing the validity of a statute like § 22-a [New York's injunctive remedy against certain forms of obscenity] is 'the operation and effect of the statute in substance.'" And as if to emphasize the point involved here, we added that "The phrase 'prior restraint' is not a self-wielding sword. Nor can it serve as a talismanic test." Even as recently as our last Term we again observed the principle, albeit in an allied area, that the State possesses some measure of power "to prevent the distribution of obscene matter." *Smith* v. *California,* 361 U.S. 147 (1959).

Petitioner would have us hold that the public exhibition of motion pictures must be allowed under any circumstances. The State's sole remedy, it says, is the invocation of criminal process under the Illinois pornography statute, . . . and then only after a transgression. But this position, as we have seen, is founded upon the claim of absolute privilege against prior restraint under the First Amendment—a claim without sanction in our cases. To illustrate its fallacy we need only point to one of the "exceptional cases" which Chief Justice Hughes enumerated in *Near* v. *Minnesota, supra,* namely, "the primary requirements of decency [that] may be enforced against obscene publications." Moreover, we later held specifically "that obscenity is not within the area of constitutionally protected speech or press." *Roth* v. *United States.* . . . Chicago emphasizes here its duty to protect its people against the dangers of obscenity in the public exhibition of motion pictures. To this argument petitioner's only answer is that regardless of the capacity for, or extent of such an evil, previous restraint cannot be justified. With this we cannot agree. We recognized in *Burstyn, supra,* that "capacity for evil . . . may be relevant in determining the permissible scope of community control," and that motion pictures were not "necessarily subject to the precise rules governing any other particular method of expression. Each method," we said, "tends to present its own peculiar problems." Certainly petitioner's broadside attack does not warrant, nor could it justify on the record here, our saying that—aside from any consideration of the other "exceptional cases" mentioned in our decisions—the State is stripped of all constitutional power to prevent, in the most effective fashion, the utterance of this class of speech. It is not for this Court to limit the State in its selection of the remedy it deems most effective to cope with such a problem, absent, of course, a showing of unreasonable strictures on individual liberty resulting from its application in particular circumstances. . . . We, of course, are not holding that city officials may be granted the power to prevent the showing of any motion picture they deem unworthy of a license. . . .

As to what may be decided when a concrete case involving a specific standard provided by this ordinance is present, we intimate no opinion. The petitioner has not challenged all—or for that matter any—of the ordinance's standards. Naturally we could not say that every one of the standards, including those which Illinois' highest court has found sufficient, is so vague on its face that the entire ordinance is void. At this time we say no more than this—that we are dealing only with motion pictures and, even as to them, only in the context of the broadside attack presented on this record.

Affirmed.

Mr. Chief Justice Warren, with whom Mr. Justice Black, Mr. Justice Douglas and Mr. Justice Brennan join, dissenting:

I cannot agree with either the conclusion reached by the Court or with the reasons advanced for its support. To me, this case clearly presents the question of our approval of unlimited censorship of motion pictures before exhibition through a system of administrative licensing. Moreover, the decision presents a real danger of eventual censorship for every form of communication be it newspapers, journals, books, magazines, television, radio or public speeches. The Court purports to leave these questions for another day, but I am aware of no constitutional principle which permits us to hold that the communication of ideas through one medium may be censored while other media are immune. Of course each medium presents its own peculiar problems, but they are not of the kind which would authorize the censorship of one form of communication and not the others. I submit that in arriving at its decision the Court has interpreted our cases contrary to the intention at the time of their rendition and, in exalting the censor of motion pictures, has endangered the First and Fourteenth Amendment rights of all others engaged in the dissemination of ideas.

Near v. *Minnesota*, 283 U.S. 697, was a landmark opinion in this area. It was there that Chief Justice Hughes said for the Court "that liberty of the press, historically considered and taken up by the Federal Constitution, has meant, principally although not exclusively, immunity from previous restraints or censorship." The sole dissenter in *Near* sought to uphold the Minnesota statute, struck down by the Court, on the ground that the statute did "not authorize administrative control in advance such as was formerly exercised by the licensers and censors. . . ." Thus, three decades ago, the Constitution's abhorrence of licensing or censorship was first clearly articulated by this Court.

This was not a tenet seldom considered or soon forgotten. Five years later, a unanimous Court observed:

> As early as 1644, John Milton, in an 'Appeal for the Liberty of Unlicensed Printing,' assailed an act of Parliament which had just been passed providing for censorship of the press previous to publication. He vigorously defended the right of every man to make public his honest views 'without previous censure'; and declared the impossibility of finding any man base enough to accept the office of censor and at the same time good enough to be allowed to perform its duties. *Grosjean* v. *American Press Co.*, 297 U.S. 233.

Shortly thereafter, a unanimous Court once more recalled that the "struggle for the freedom of the press was primarily directed against the power of the licensor." *Lovell* v. *Griffin*, 303 U.S. 444. And two years after this, the Court firmly announced in *Schneider* v. *State*, 308 U.S. 147:

> [T]he ordinance imposes censorship, abuse of which engendered the struggle in England which eventuated in the establishment of the doctrine of the freedom of the press embodied in our Constitution. To require a censorship through license which makes impossible the free and unhampered distribution of pamphlets strikes at the very heart of the constitutional guarantees.

Just twenty years ago, in the oft-cited case of *Cantwell* v. *Connecticut*, 310 U.S. 296, the Court, again without dissent, decided:

> [T]he availability of a judicial remedy for abuses in the system of licensing still leaves that system one of previous restraint which, in the field of free speech and press, we have held inadmissible. A statute authorizing previous restraint upon the exercise of the guaranteed freedom by judicial decision after trial is as obnoxious to the Constitution as one providing for like restraint by administrative action.

This doctrine, which was fully explored and was the focus of this Court's attention on numerous occasions, had become an established principle of constitutional law. It is not to be disputed that this Court has stated that the protection afforded First Amendment liberties from previous restraint is not absolutely unlimited. . . . But, licensing or censorship was not, at any point, considered within the "exceptional cases" discussed in the opinion in *Near*. And, only a few Terms ago, the Court, speaking through Mr. Justice Frankfurter, in *Kingsley Books, Inc.,* v. *Brown*, 354 U.S. 436, reaffirmed that "the limitation is the exception; it is to be closely confined so as to preclude what may fairly be deemed *licensing* or *censorship.*" (Emphasis added.)

The vice of censorship through licensing and, more generally, the particular evil of previous restraint on the right of free speech have many times been recognized when this Court has carefully distinguished between laws establishing sundry systems of previous restraint on the right of free speech and penal laws imposing subsequent punishment on utterances and activities not within the ambit of the First Amendment's protection. . . .

Examination of the background and circumstances leading to the adoption of the First Amendment reveal the basis for the Court's steadfast observance of the proscription of licensing, censorship and previous restraint of speech. Such inquiry often begins with Blackstone's assertion: "The liberty of the press is indeed essential to the nature of a free state; but this consists in laying no previous restraints upon publications, and not in freedom from censure for criminal matter when published." 4 Bl. Comm. 151. Blackstone probably here referred to the common law's definition of freedom of the press; he probably spoke of the situation existing in England after the disappearance of the licensing systems but during the existence of the law of crown libels. There has been general criticism of the theory that Blackstone's statement was embodied in the First Amendment, the objection being " 'that the mere exemption from previous restraints cannot be all that is secured by the constitutional provisions'; and that 'the liberty of the press might be rendered a mockery and a delusion, and the phrase itself a by-word if, while every man was at liberty to publish what he pleased, the public authorities might nevertheless punish him for harmless publications.' " The objection has been that Blackstone's definition is too narrow; it had been generally conceded that the protection of the First Amendment extends *at least* to the interdiction of licensing and censorship and to the previous restraint of free speech.

On June 24, 1957, in *Kingsley Books, Inc.,* v. *Brown, supra,* the Court turned a corner from the landmark opinion in *Near* and from one of the bases of the First Amendment. Today it falls into full retreat.

I hesitate to disagree with the Court's formulation of the issue before us, but, with all deference, I must insist that the question presented in this case is *not* whether a motion picture exhibitor has a constitutionally protected, "complete and absolute freedom to exhibit, at least once, any and every kind of motion picture." Surely, the Court is not bound by the petitioner's conception of the issue or by the more extreme positions that petitioner may have argued at one time in the case. The question here presented is whether the City of Chicago—or, for that matter, any city, any State or the Federal Government—may require all motion picture exhibitors to submit all films to a police chief, mayor or other administrative official, for licensing and censorship prior to public exhibition within the jurisdiction.

The Court does not even have before it an attempt by the city to restrain the exhibition of an allegedly "obscene" film, ... Nor does the city contend that it is seeking to prohibit the showing of a film which will impair the "security of community life" because it acts as an incitement to "violence and the overthrow by force of orderly government." . . . The problem before us is not whether the city may forbid the exhibition of a motion picture, which, by its very showing, might in some way "inflict injury or tend to incite an immediate breach of the peace." . . .

Let it be completely clear what the Court's decision does. It gives official license to the censor, approving a grant of power to city officials to prevent the showing of any moving picture these officials deem unworthy of a license. It thus gives formal sanction to censorship in its purest and most far-reaching form, to a classical plan of licensing that, in our country, most closely approaches the English licensing laws of the seventeenth century which were commonly used to suppress dissent in the mother country and in the colonies. . . . The Court treats motion pictures, food for the mind, held to be within the shield of the First Amendment, *Joseph Burstyn, Inc.,* v. *Wilson,* . . . little differently than it would treat edibles. Only a few days ago, the Court, speaking through Mr. Justice Stewart, noted in *Shelton* v. *Tucker:*

> In a series of decisions this Court has held that, even though the governmental purpose be legitimate and substantial, that purpose cannot be pursued by means that broadly stifle fundamental personal liberties when the end can be more narrowly achieved. The breadth of legislative abridgment must be viewed in the light of less drastic means for achieving the same basic purpose.

Here, the Court ignores this considered principle and indiscriminately casts the net of control too broadly. . . . By its decision, the Court gives its assent to unlimited censorship of moving pictures through a licensing system, despite the fact that Chicago has chosen this most objectionable course to attain its goals without any apparent attempt to devise other means so as not to intrude on the constitutionally protected liberties of speech and press.

Perhaps the most striking demonstration of how far the Court departs from its holdings in *Near* and subsequent cases may be made by examining the various schemes that it has previously determined to be violative of the First and Fourteenth Amendments' guaranty.

A remarkable parallel to the censorship plan now before the Court, although one less offensive to the First Amendment, is found in the *Near* case itself. The Minnesota statute there under attack did not require that *all* publications need to be approved before distribution. That statute only provided that a person may be enjoined by a court from publishing a newspaper which was "malicious, scandalous or defamatory." The injunction in that case was issued only after Near had allegedly published nine such newspapers. The statute permitted issuance of an injunction only on proof that, within the prior three months, such an offensive newspaper had already been published. Near was not prevented "from operating a newspaper in harmony with the public welfare." If the state court found that Near's subsequent publication conformed to this standard, Near would not have been held in contempt. But, the Court there found that this system of censorship by a state court, used only after it had already been determined that the publisher had previously violated the standard, had to fall before the First and the Fourteenth Amendments. It would seem that, *a fortiori,* the present system must also fall.

The case of *Grosjean* v. *American Press Co., supra,* provides another forceful illustration. The Court held there that a license tax of two percent of the gross receipts from advertising of newspapers and periodicals having a circulation of over 20,000 a week was a form of prior restraint and therefore invalid. Certainly this would seem much less an infringement on the liberties of speech and press protected by the First and Fourteenth Amendments than the classic system of censorship we now have before us. It was held, in *Grosjean*, that the imposition of the tax would curtail the amount of revenue realized from advertising and therefore operate as a restraint on publication. The license tax in *Grosjean* is analogous to the license fee in the case at bar, a fee to which petitioner raises no objection. It was also held, in *Grosjean*, that the tax had a "direct *tendency* to restrict circulation," (emphasis added), because it was imposed only on publications with a weekly circulation of 20,000 or more; that "if it were increased to a high degree . . . it *might well result* in destroying both advertising and circulation." (Emphasis added.) These were the evils calling for reversal in *Grosjean*. I should think that these evils are of minor import in comparison to the evils consequent to the licensing system which the Court here approves.

In *Hague* v. *C.I.O.*, 307 U.S. 496, a city ordinance required that a permit be obtained for public parades or public assembly. The permit could "only be refused for the purpose of preventing riots, disturbances or disorderly assemblage." Mr. Justice Roberts' opinion said of the ordinance:

> It enables the Director of Safety to refuse a permit on his mere opinion that such refusal will prevent 'riots, disturbances or disorderly assemblage.' It can thus, as the record discloses, be made the instrument of arbitrary suppression of free expression of views on national affairs, for the prohibition of all speaking will undoubtedly "prevent" such eventualities.

May anything less be said of Chicago's movie censorship plan?

The question before the Court in *Schneider* v. *State, supra*, concerned the constitutional validity of a town ordinance requiring a license for the distribution of circulars. The police chief was permitted to refuse the license if the application for it or further investigation showed "that the canvasser is not of good character or is canvassing for a project not free from fraud. . . ." The Court said of that ordinance:

> It bans unlicensed communication of any views or the advocacy of any cause from door to door, and permits canvassing only subject to the power of a police officer to determine, as a censor, what literature may be distributed from house to house and who may distribute it. The applicant must submit to that officer's judgment evidence as to his good character and as to the absence of fraud in the "project" he proposes to promote or the literature he intends to distribute, and must undergo a burdensome and inquisitorial examination, including photographing and fingerprinting. In the end, his liberty to communicate with the residents of the town at their homes depends upon the exercise of the officer's discretion.

I believe that the licensing plan at bar is fatally defective because of this precise objection.

A study of the opinion in *Cantwell* v. *Connecticut, supra,* further reveals the Court's sharp divergence today from seriously deliberated precedent. The statute in *Cantwell* forbade solicitation for any alleged religious, charitable or philanthropic cause unless the secretary of the public welfare council determined that the "cause [was] a religious one or [was] a bona fide object of charity or philanthropy and conform[ed] to reasonable standards of efficiency and integrity. . . ." Speaking of the secretary of the public welfare council, the Court held:

> If he finds that the cause is not that of religion, to solicit for it becomes a crime. He is not to issue a certificate as a matter of course. His decision to issue or refuse it involves appraisal of facts, the exercise of judgment, and the formation of an opinion. He is authorized to withhold his approval if he determines that the cause is not a religious one. Such a censorship of religion as the means of determining its right to survive is a denial of liberty protected by the First Amendment and included in the liberty which is within the protection of the Fourteenth.

Does the Court today wish to distinguish between the protection accorded to religion by the First and Fourteenth Amendments and the protection accorded to speech by those same provisions? I cannot perceive the distinction between this case and *Cantwell*. Chicago says that it faces a problem —obscene and incendious films. Connecticut faced the problem of fraudulent solicitation. Constitutionally, is there a difference? . . .

In *Thomas* v. *Collins,* 323 U.S. 516, this Court held that a state statute requiring a labor union organizer to obtain an organizer's card was incompatible with the free speech and free assembly mandates of the First and Fourteenth Amendments. The statute demanded nothing more than that the labor union organizer register, stating his name, his union affiliations and describing his credentials. This information having been filed, the issuance of the organizer's card was subject to no further conditions. The State's obvious interest in acquiring this pertinent information was felt not to constitute an exceptional circumstance to justify the restraint imposed by the statute. It seems clear to me that the Chicago ordinance in his case presents a greater danger of stifling speech.

The two sound truck cases are further poignant examples of what had been this Court's steadfast adherence to the opposition of previous restraints on First Amendment liberties. In *Saia* v. *New York,* 334 U.S. 558, it was held that a city ordinance which forbade the use of sound amplification devices in public places without the permission of the Chief of Police was unconstitutionally void on its face since it imposed a previous restraint on public speech. Two years later, the Court upheld a different city's ordinance making unlawful the use of "any instrument[of any kind or character which emits therefrom loud and raucous noises and is attached to and upon any

vehicle operated or standing upon . . . streets or public places. . . ."
Kovacs v. *Cooper*, 336 U.S. 77. One of the grounds by which the opinion
of Mr. Justice Reed distinguished *Saia* was that the *Kovacs* ordinance imposed no previous restraint. Mr. Justice Jackson chose to differentiate sound
trucks from the "*moving picture screen,* the radio, the newspaper, the handbill . . . and the street corner orator. . . ." (Emphasis added.) He further stated that "no violation of the Due Process Clause of the Fourteenth
Amendment by reason of infringement of free speech arises unless such
regulation or prohibition undertakes to censor the contents of the broadcasting." Needless to repeat, this is the violation the Court sanctions today.

Another extremely similar, but again less objectionable, situation was
brought to the Court in *Kunz* v. *New York,* 340 U.S. 290. There, a city
ordinance proscribed the right of citizens to speak on religious matters in
the city streets without an annual permit. Kunz had previously had his permit revoked because "he had ridiculed and denounced other religious beliefs
in his meetings." Kunz was arrested for subsequently speaking in the city
streets without a permit. The Court reversed Kunz' conviction holding:

> We have here, then, an ordinance which gives an administrative
> official discretionary power to control in advance the right of citizens
> to speak on religious matters on the streets of New York. As such, the
> ordinance is clearly invalid as a prior restraint on the exercise of First
> Amendment rights.

The Chicago censorship and licensing plan is effectively no different. The
only meaningful distinction between *Kunz* and the case at bar appears to be
in the disposition of them by the Court.

The ordinance before us in *Staub* v. *City of Baxley,* 355 U.S. 313, made
unlawful the solicitation, without a permit, of members for an organization
which requires the payment of membership dues. The ordinance stated that
"in passing upon such application the Mayor and Council shall consider the
character of the applicant, the nature of the business of the organization for
which members are desired to be solicited, and its effects upon the general
welfare of citizens of the City of Baxley." Mr. Justice Whittaker, speaking
for the Court, stated "that the ordinance is invalid on its face because it
makes enjoyment of the constitutionally guaranteed freedom of speech
contingent upon the will of the Mayor and Council of the City and thereby
constitutes a prior restraint upon, and abridges, that freedom." In *Staub,*
the ordinance required a permit for solicitation; in the case decided today,
the ordinance requires a permit for the exhibition of movies. If this is a valid
distinction, it has not been so revealed. In Staub, the permit was to be
granted on the basis of certain indefinite standards; in the case decided
today, nothing different may be said.

As the Court recalls, in *Joseph Burstyn, Inc.,* v. *Wilson,* . . . it was held
that motion pictures come "within the free speech and free press guaranty
of the First and Fourteenth Amendments." Although the Court found it
unnecessary to decide "whether a state may censor motion pictures under

a clearly drawn statute designed and applied to prevent the showing of obscene films," Mr. Justice Clark stated, in the Court's opinion, quite accurately:

> But the basic principles of freedom of speech and the press, like the First Amendment's command, do not vary. Those principles, as they have frequently been enunciated by this Court, make freedom of expression the rule. There is no justification in this case for making an exception to that rule.
>
> The statute involved here does not seek to punish, as a past offense, speech or writing falling within the permissible scope of subsequent punishment. On the contrary, New York requires that permission to communicate ideas be obtained in advance from state officials who judge the content of the words and picture sought to be communicated. This Court recognized many years ago that such a previous restraint is a form of infringement upon freedom of expression to be especially condemned. *Near* v. *Minnesota, ex rel Olson,* . . . . The Court there recounted the history which indicates that a major purpose of the First Amendment guaranty of a free press was to prevent prior restraints upon publication, although it was carefully pointed out that the liberty of the press is not limited to that protection. It was further stated that "the protection even as to previous restraint is not absolutely unlimited. But the limitation has been recognized only in exceptional cases." In the light of the First Amendment's history and of the *Near* decision, the State has a heavy burden to demonstrate that the limitation challenged here presents such an exceptional case.

Here, once more, the Court recognized that the First Amendment's rejection of prior censorship through licensing and previous restraint is an inherent and basic principle of freedom of speech and the press. Now, the Court strays from that principle; it strikes down that tenet without requiring any demonstration that this is an "exceptional case," whatever that might be, and without any indication that Chicago has sustained the "heavy burden" which was supposed to have been placed upon it. Clearly, this is neither an exceptional case nor has Chicago sustained *any* burden.

Perhaps today's surrender was forecast by *Kingsley Books, Inc.,* v. *Brown, supra.* But, that was obviously not this case, and accepting *arguendo* the correctness of that decision, I believe that it leads to a result contrary to that reached today. The statute in *Kingsley* authorized "the chief executive, or legal officer, of a municipality to invoke a 'limited injunctive remedy,' under closely defined procedural safeguards, against the sale and distribution of written and printed matter found after due trial [by a court] to be obscene. . . ." The Chicago scheme has no procedural safeguards; there is no trial of the issue before the blanket injunction against exhibition becomes effective. In *Kingsley,* the grounds for the restraint were that the written or printed matter was "obscene, lewd, lascivious, filthy, indecent, or disgusting . . . or immoral. . . ." The Chicago objective is to capture much more. The *Kingsley* statute required the existence of some cause to believe that the publication was obscene before the publication was put on trial. The Chicago ordinance requires no such showing.

The booklets enjoined from distribution in *Kingsley* were concededly obscene. There is no indication that this is true of the moving picture here. This was treated as a particularly crucial distinction. Thus, the Court has suggested that, in times of national emergency, the Government might impose a prior restraint upon "the publication of the sailing dates of transports or the number and location of troops." . . . But, surely this is not to suggest that the Government might require that all newspapers be submitted to a censor in order to assist it in preventing such information from reaching print. Yet in this case the Court gives its blessing to the censorship of all motion pictures in order to prevent the exhibition of those it feels to be constitutionally unprotected.

The statute in *Kingsley* specified that the person sought to be enjoined was to be entitled to a trial of the issues within one day after joinder and a decision was to be rendered by the court within two days of the conclusion of the trial. The Chicago plan makes no provision for prompt judicial determination. In *Kingsley*, the person enjoined had available the defense that the written or printed matter was not obscene if an attempt was made to punish him for disobedience of the injunction. The Chicago ordinance admits no defense in a prosecution for failure to procure a license other than that the motion picture was submitted to the censor and a license was obtained.

Finally, the Court in *Kingsley* painstakingly attempted to establish that that statute, in its effective operation, was no more a previous restraint on, or interference with, the liberty of speech and press than a statute imposing criminal punishment for the publication of pornography. In each situation, it contended, the publication may have passed into the hands of the public. Of course, this argument is inadmissible in this case and the Court does not purport to advance it.

It would seem idle to suppose that the Court today is unaware of the evils of the censor's basic authority, of the mischief of the system against which so many great men have waged stubborn and often precarious warfare for centuries, . . . of the scheme that impedes all communication by hanging threateningly over creative thought. But the Court dismisses all of this simply by opining that "the phrase 'prior restraint' is not a self-wielding sword. Nor can it serve as a talismanic test." I must insist that "a pragmatic assessment of its operation," . . . lucidly portrays that the system that the Court sanctions today is inherently bad. One need not disagree with the Court that Chicago has chosen the most effective means of suppressing obscenity. Censorship has been so recognized for centuries. But, this is not to say that the Chicago plan, the old, abhorrent English system of censorship through licensing, is a permissible *form* of prohibiting unprotected speech. The inquiry, as stated by the Court but never resolved, is whether this form of prohibition results in "unreasonable strictures on individual liberty;" whether licensing, as a prerequisite to exhibition, is barred by the First and Fourteenth Amendments.

A most distinguished antagonist of censorship, in "a plea for unlicensed printing," has said:

> If he [the censor] be of such worth as behoovs him, there cannot be a more tedious and unpleasing Journey-work, a greater loss of time levied upon his head, then to be made the perpetuall reader of unchosen books and pamphlets . . . we may easily forsee what kind of licensers we are to expect hereafter, either ignorant, imperious, and remisse or basely pecuniary. *Areopagitica,* in the *Complete Poetry and Selected Prose of John Milton* (Modern Library Ed. 1950), 677, at 700.

There is no sign that Milton's fear of the censor would be dispelled in twentieth century America. The censor is beholden to those who sponsored the creation of his office, to those who are most radically preoccupied with the suppression of communication. The censor's function is to restrict and to restrain; his decisions are insulated from the pressures that might be brought to bear by public sentiment if the public were given an opportunity to see that which the censor has curbed.

The censor performs free from all of the procedural safeguards afforded litigants in a court of law. . . . The likelihood of a fair and impartial trial disappears when the censor is both prosecutor and judge. There is a complete absence of rules of evidence; the fact is that there is usually no evidence at all as the system at bar vividly illustrates. How different from a judicial proceeding where a full case is presented by the litigants. The inexistence of a jury to determine contemporary community standards is a vital flaw. . . .

A revelation of the extent to which censorship has recently been used in this country is indeed astonishing. The Chicago licensors have banned newsreel films of Chicago policemen shooting at labor pickets and have ordered the deletion of a scene depicting the birth of a buffalo in Walt Disney's *Vanishing Prairie.* . . . Before World War II, the Chicago censor denied licenses to a number of films portraying and criticizing life in Nazi Germany including the March of Time's *Inside Nazi Germany.* . . . Recently, Chicago refused to issue a permit for the exhibition of the motion picture *Anatomy of a Murder* based upon the best-selling novel of the same title, because it found the use of words "rape" and "contraceptive" to be objectionable. . . . The Chicago censor bureau excised a scene in *Street With No Name* in which a girl was slapped because this was thought to be a "too violent" episode. . . . *It Happened in Europe* was severely cut by the Ohio censors who deleted scenes of war orphans resorting to violence. The moral theme of the picture was that such children could even then be saved by love, affection and satisfaction of their basic needs for food. . . . The Memphis censors banned *The Southerner* which dealt with poverty among tenant farmers because "it reflects on the south." *Brewster's Millions,* an innocuous comedy of fifty years ago, was recently forbidden in Memphis because the radio and film character Rochester, a Negro, was deemed "too familiar." . . . Maryland censors restricted a Polish documentary film on the basis that it failed to present a true picture of modern Poland. . . . *No Way Out,* the story of a Negro doctor's struggle against race prejudice, was banned by the Chicago censor on the ground that "there's a possibility it could cause trouble." The principal objection to the film was that the conclusion showed no reconciliation between blacks and whites. The ban was lifted after a storm of protest and later deletion of a scene showing Negroes and whites arming for a gang fight. . . . Memphis banned *Curley* because it contained scenes of white and Negro children in school together. . . . Atlanta barred *Lost Boundaries,* the story of a Negro physician and his family who "passed" for white, on the ground that the exhibition of said picture "will adversely affect the peace, morals and good order" in the city. . . . *Witchcraft,* a study of superstition through the ages, was suppressed for years because it depicted the devil as a genial rake with amorous leanings, and because it was feared that certain historical scenes, portraying the excesses of religious fanatics, might offend religion. *Scarface,* thought by some as the best of the gangster films, was held up for months; then it was so badly mutilated that retakes costing a hundred thousand dollars were required to preserve continuity. The New York censors banned *Damaged Lives,* a film dealing with venereal disease, although it treated a difficult theme with dignity and had the sponsorship of the American Social Hygiene Society. The picture of Lenin's tomb bearing the Inscription "Religion is the opiate of the people" was excised from *Potemkin.* From *Joan of Arc* the Maryland board eliminated Joan's exclamation as she stood at the stake: "Oh, God, why hast thou forsaken me?" and from *Idiot's Delight,* the sentence: "We, the workers of the world, will take care of that." *Professor Mamlock* was produced in Russia and portrayed the persecution of the Jews by Nazis. The Ohio censors condemned it as "harmful" and calculated to "stir up hatred and ill will and gain nothing." It was released only after substantial deletions were made. The police refused to permit its showing in Providence, Rhode Island, on the ground that it was communistic propaganda. *Millions of Us,* a strong union propaganda film, encountered trouble in a number of jurisdictions. *Spanish Earth,* a pro-Loyalist documentary picture, was banned by the board in Pennsylvania. . . . During the year ending June 30, 1938, the New York board censored, in one way or another, over five percent of the moving pictures it reviewed. Charlie Chaplain's satire on Hitler, *The Great Dictator,* was banned in Chicago, apparently out of deference to its large German population. . . . Ohio and Kansas banned newsreels considered pro labor. Kansas ordered a speech by Senator Wheeler opposing the bill for enlarging the Supreme Court to be cut from the *March of Time* as "partisan and biased." An early version of *Carmen* was condemned on several different grounds. The Ohio censor objected because cigarette-girls smoked cigarettes in public. The Pennsylvania censor disapproved the duration of a kiss. The New York censors forbade the discussion in films of pregnancy, venereal disease, eugenics, birth control, abortion, illegitimacy, prostitution, miscegenation and divorce. . . . A member of the Chicago censor board explained that she rejected a film because "it was immoral, corrupt, indecent, against my . . . religious principles." . . . A police sergeant attached to the censor board explained, "Coarse language or anything that would be derogatory to the government—propaganda" is ruled out of foreign films. "Nothing pink or red is allowed," he added. . . . The police sergeant in charge of the censor unit has said: "Children should be allowed to see any movie that plays in Chicago. If a picture is objectionable for a child, it is objectionable period." . . . And this is but a smattering produced from limited research. Perhaps the most powerful indictment of Chicago's licensing device is found in the fact that between the Court's decision in 1952 in *Joseph Burstyn, Inc.,* v. *Wilson, supra,* and the filing of the petition for certiorari in 1960 in the present case, not once have the state courts upheld the censor when the exhibitor elected to appeal. . . .

This is the regimen to which the Court holds that all films must be submitted. It officially unleashes the censor and permits him to roam at will, limited only by an ordinance which contains some standards that, although concededly not before us in this case, are patently imprecise. The Chicago ordinance commands the censor to reject films that are "immoral," . . . or those that portray "depravity, criminality, or lack of virtue of a class of citizens of any race, color, creed, or religion and exposes them to contempt, derision, or obloquy, or tends to produce a breach of the peace or riots, or [purports] to represent any hanging, lynching, or burning of a human being." May it not be said that almost every censored motion picture that was cited above could also be rejected, under the ordinance, by the Chicago censors. It does not require an active imagination to conceive of the quantum of ideas that will surely be suppressed.

If the censor denies rights protected by the First and Fourteenth Amendments, the courts might be called upon to correct the abuse if the exhibitor decides to pursue judicial remedies. But, this is not a satisfactory answer as emphasized by this very case. The delays in adjudication may well result in irreparable damage, both to the litigants and to the public. Vindication by the courts of *The Miracle* was not had until five years after the Chicago censor refused to license it. And then the picture was never shown in Chicago. . . . The instant litigation has now consumed almost three years. This is the delay occasioned by the censor; this is the injury done to the free communication of ideas. This damage is not inflicted by the ordinary criminal penalties. The threat of these penalties, intelligently applied, will ordinarily be sufficient to deter the exhibition of obscenity. However, if the exhibitor believes that his film is constitutionally protected, he will show the film, and, if prosecuted under criminal statute, will have ready that defense. The perniciousness of a system of censorship is that the exhibitor's belief that his film is constitutionally protected is irrelevant. Once the censor has made his estimation that the film is "bad" and has refused to issue a permit, there is ordinarily no defense to a prosecution for showing the film without a license. Thus, the film is not shown, perhaps not for years and sometimes not ever. Simply a talismanic test or self-wielding sword? I think not.

Moreover, more likely than not, the exhibitor will not pursue judicial remedies. . . . His inclination may well be simply to capitulate rather than initiate a lengthy and costly litigation. In such case, the liberty of speech and press and the public, which benefits from the shielding of that liberty, are in effect, at the mercy of the censor's whim. This powerful tendency to restrict the free dissemination of ideas calls for reversal. . . .

Freedom of speech and freedom of the press are further endangered by this "most effective" means for confinement of ideas. It is axiomatic that the stroke of the censor's pen or the cut of his scissors will be a less contemplated decision than will be the prosecutor's determination to prepare a criminal indictment. The standards of proof, the judicial safeguards afforded a criminal defendant and the consequences of bringing such charges will all provoke the mature deliberation of the prosecutor. None of these hinder the quick judgment of the censor, the speedy determination to suppress. Finally, the fear of the censor by the composer of ideas acts as a substantial deterrent to the creation of new thoughts. . . . This is especially true of motion pictures due to the large financial burden that must be assumed by their producers. The censor's sword pierces deeply into the heart of free expression.

It seems to me that the Court's opinion comes perilously close to holding that not only may motion pictures be censored but that a licensing scheme may also be applied to newspapers, books and periodicals, radio, television, public speeches, and every other medium of expression. The Court suggests that its decision today is limited to motion pictures by asserting that they are "not necessarily subject to the precise rules governing any other particular method of expression. Each method tends to present its own peculiar problems." But this, I believe, is the invocation of a talismanic phrase. The Court, in no way, explains why moving pictures should be treated differently than any other form of expression, why moving pictures should be denied the protection against censorship—"a form of infringement upon freedom of expression to be *especially* condemned." *Joseph Burstyn, Inc.,* v. *Wilson, supra,* at p. 503. (Emphasis added.) When pressed during oral argument, counsel for the city could make no meaningful distinction between the censorship of newspapers and motion pictures. In fact, the percentage of motion pictures dealing with social and political issues is steadily rising. The Chicago ordinance makes no exception for newsreels, documentaries, instructional and educational films or the like. All must undergo the censor's inquisition. Nor may it be suggested that motion pictures may be treated differently from newspapers because many movies are produced essentially for purposes of entertainment. As the Court said in *Winters* v. *New York,* 333 U.S. 507:

> We do not accede to appellee's suggestion that the constitutional protection for a free press applies only to the exposition of ideas. The line between the informing and the entertaining is too elusive for the protection of that basic right. Everyone is familiar with instances of propaganda through fiction. What is one man's amusement, teaches another's doctrine.

The contention may be advanced that the impact of motion pictures is such that a licensing system of prior censorship is permissible. There are several answers to this, the first of which I think is the Constitution itself. Although it is an open question whether the impact of motion pictures is greater or less than that of other media, there is not much doubt that the exposure of television far exceeds that of the motion picture. . . . But, even if the impact of the motion picture is greater than that of some other media, that fact constitutes no basis for the argument that motion pictures should be subject to greater suppression. This is the traditional argument made in the censor's behalf; this is the argument advanced against newspapers at the time of the invention of the printing press. The argument was ultimately rejected in England, and has consistently been held to be contrary to our Constitution. No compelling reason has been predicated for accepting the contention now.

It is true that "each method [of expression] tends to present its own peculiar problems." . . . The Court has addressed itself on several occasions to these problems. In *Schneider* v. *State, supra,* the Court stated, in reference to speaking in public, that "a person could not exercise this liberty by taking his stand in the middle of a crowded street, contrary to traffic regulations, and maintain his position to the stoppage of all traffic; a group of distributors could not insist upon a constitutional right to form a cordon across the street and to allow no pedestrian to pass who did not accept a tendered leaflet; nor does the guarantee of freedom of speech or of the press deprive a municipality of power to enact regulations against throwing literature broadcast in the streets." The Court recognized that sound trucks call for particularized consideration when it said in *Saia* v. *New York, supra,* "Noise can be regulated by regulating decibels. The hours and place of public discussion can be controlled. . . . Any abuses which loud-speakers create can be controlled by narrowly drawn statutes." But, the Court's decision today does not follow from this. Our prior decisions do not deal with the *content* of the speech; they deal only with the conditions surrounding its delivery. *These* conditions "tend to present the problems peculiar to each method of expression." Here the Court uses this magical phrase to cripple a basic principle of the Constitution.

The Court, not the petitioner, makes the "broadside attack." I would reverse the decision below.

Mr. Justice Douglas, with whom The Chief Justice and Mr. Justice Black concur, dissenting:

. . . While the problem of movie censorship is relatively new, the censorship device is an ancient one. It was recently stated, "There is a law of action and reaction in the decline and resurgence of censorship and control. Whenever liberty is in the ascendant, a social group will begin to resist it; and when the reverse is true, a similar resistance in favor of liberty will occur." . . .

Whether or not that statement of history is accurate, censorship has had many champions throughout time.

Socrates: "And shall we just carelessly allow children to hear any casual tales which may be devised by casual persons, and to receive into their minds ideas for the most part the very opposite of those which we should wish them to have when they are grown up?"

Glaucon: "We cannot."

Socrates: "Then the first thing will be to establish a censorship of the writers of fiction, and let the censors receive any tale of fiction which is good, and reject the bad; and we will desire mothers and nurses to tell their children the authorised ones only. Let them fashion the mind with such tales, even more fondly than they mould the body with their hands; but most of those which are now in use must be discarded." Plato, *Republic*, Bk. II.

Hobbes was the censor's proponent: ". . . it is annexed to the sovereignty, to be judge of what opinions and doctrines are averse, and what conducing to peace; and consequently, on what occasions, how far, and what men are to be trusted withal, in speaking to multitudes of people; and who shall examine the doctrines of all books before they be published. For the actions of men proceed from their opinions; and in the well-governing of opinions, consisteth the well-governing of men's actions, in order to their peace, and concord." *Leviathan* (Oakeshott ed. 1947), p. 116.

Regimes of censorship are common in the world today. Every dictator has one; every Communist regime finds it indispensable. One shield against world opinion that colonial powers have used was the censor, as dramatized by France in North Africa. Even England has a vestige of censorship in the Lord Chamberlain . . . who presides over the stage—a system that in origin was concerned with the barbs of political satire. But the concern with political satire shifted to a concern with atheism and with sexual morality— the last being the concern evident in Chicago's system now before us.

The problems of the wayward mind concern the clerics, the psychiatrists, and the philosophers. Few groups have hesitated to create the political pressures that translate into secular law their notions of morality. . . . No more powerful weapon for sectarian control can be imagined than governmental censorship. Yet in this country the state is not the secular arm of any religious school of thought, as in some nations; nor is the church an instrument of the state. Whether—as here—city officials or—as in Russia—a political party lays claim to the power of governmental censorship, whether the pressures are for a conformist moral code or for a conformist political ideology, no such regime is permitted by the First Amendment.

The forces that build up demands for censorship are heterogeneous.

The comstocks are not merely people with intellectual theories who might be convinced by more persuasive theories; nor are they pragmatists who will be guided by the balance of power among pressure groups. Many of them are so emotionally involved in the condemnation of what they find objectionable that they find rational arguments irrelevant. They *must* suppress what is offensive in order to stabilize their own tremulous values and consciences. Panic rules them, and they cannot be calmed by discussions of legal rights, literary integrity or artistic merit. . . .

Yet as long as the First Amendment survives, the censor, no matter how respectable his cause, cannot have the support of government. It is not for government to pick and choose according to the standards of any religious, political, or philosophical group. It is not permissible, as I read the Constitution, for government to release one movie and refuse to release another because of an official's concept of the prevailing need or the public good. The Court in *Near* v. *Minnesota* . . . said that the "chief purpose" of the First Amendment's guarantee of freedom of press was "to prevent previous restraints upon publication."

A noted Jesuit has recently stated one reason against government censorship:

> The freedom toward which the American people are fundamentally orientated is a freedom under God, a freedom that knows itself to be bound by the imperatives of the moral law. Antecedently it is presumed that a man will make morally and socially responsible use of his freedom of expression; hence there is to be no prior restraint on it. However, if his use of freedom is irresponsible, he is summoned after the fact to responsibility before the judgment of the law. There are indeed other reasons why prior restraint on communications in outlawed; but none are more fundamental than this. Murray, *We Hold These Truths* (1960), pp. 164–165.

Experience shows other evils of "prior restraint." The regime of the censor is deadening. One who writes cannot afford entanglements with the man whose pencil can keep his production from the market. The result is a pattern of conformity. Milton made the point long ago: "For though a licenser should happen to be judicious more than ordinarily, which will be a great jeopardy of the next succession, yet his very office, and his commission enjoins him to let pass nothing but what is vulgarily received already." . . .

Another evil of censorship is the ease with which the censor can erode liberty of expression. One stroke of the pen is all that is needed. Under a censor's regime the weights are cast against freedom.° If, however, government must proceed against an illegal publication in a prosecution, then the advantages are on the other side. All the protections of the Bill of Rights come into play. The presumption of innocence, the right to jury trial, proof of guilt beyond a reasonable doubt—these become barriers in the path of officials who want to impose their standard of morality on the author or producer. The advantage a censor enjoys while working as a supreme bureaucracy disappear. The public trial to which a person is entitled who

° John Galsworthy wrote in opposition to the British censorship of plays: "In this country the tongue and pen are subject to the law; so may it ever be! But in

violates the law gives a hearing on the merits, airs the grievance, and brings the community judgment to bear upon it. If a court sits in review of a censor's ruling, its function is limited. There is leeway left the censor, who like any agency and its *expertise,* is given a presumption of being correct. That advantage disappears when the government must wait until a publication is made and then prove its case in the accepted manner before a jury in a public trial. All of this is anathema to the censor who prefers to work in secret, perhaps because as Milton said, he is "either ignorant, imperious, and remiss, or basely pecuniary." . . .

The First Amendment was designed to enlarge, not to limit, freedom in literature and in the arts as well as in politics, economics, law, and other fields. . . . Its aim was to unlock all ideas for argument, debate, and dissemination. No more potent force in defeat of that freedom could be designed than censorship. It is a weapon that no minority or majority group, acting through government, should be allowed to wield over any of us. *

---

this country neither tongue nor pen are in any other instance subject to the despotic judgments of a single man. The protest is not aimed at the single man who holds this office. He may be the wisest man in England, the best fitted for his despotic office. It is not he; it is the office that offends. It offends the decent pride and self-respect of an entire profession. To those who are surprised that dramatic authors should take themselves so seriously we say, What workman worthy of his tools does not believe in the honour of his craft? In this appeal for common justice we dramatists, one little branch of the sacred tree of letters, appeal to our brother branches. We appeal to the whole knighthood of the pen—scientists, historians, novelists, journalists. The history of the health of nations is the history of the freedom—not the licence—of the tongue and pen. We are claiming the freedom—not the licence—of our pens. Let those hold back in helping us who would tamely suffer their own pens to be warped and split as ours are before we take them up." *London Times,* Nov. 1, 1907, p. 7. And see the testimony of George Bernard Shaw in Report, Joint Select Committee of the House of Lords and the House of Commons on the Stage Plays (Censorship) (1909), p. 46 *et seq.* Shaw, three of whose plays had been suppressed, caused a contemporary sensation by asking, and being refused, permission to file with the Committee an attack on censorship that he had prepared. Shaw's version of the story and the rejected statement can be found as his preface to *The Shewing-Up of Blanco Posnet.* He says in his statement: "Any journalist may publish an article, any demagogue may deliver a speech without giving notice to the government or obtaining its license. The risk of such freedom is great; but as it is the price of our political liberty, we think it worth paying. We may abrogate it in emergencies . . . just as we stop the traffic in a street during a fire or shoot thieves on sight after an earthquake. But when the emergency is past, liberty is restored everywhere except in the theatre. [Censorship is] a permanent proclamation of martial law with a single official substituted for a court martial." *The Shewing-Up of Blanco Posnet* (Brentano's, 1913), p. 36.

* First, within the larger pluralist society each minority group has the right to censor for its own members, if it so chooses, the content of the various media of communication, and to protect them, by means of its own choosing, from materials considered harmful according to its own standards.

"Second, in a pluralist society no minority group has the right to demand

3. *Contempt by Publication*

BRIDGES *v.* CALIFORNIA

314 US 252 (1941)

[There is obviously a strong public interest that "the calm course of justice" in a courtroom be assured, in order that the minds of judges and jurors may not become "distorted by extrajudicial considerations." Newspaper reports and editorials on pending trials may have an inflammatory effect and thus obstruct the administration of justice. On the other hand, there is an equally strong public interest that the press be and remain untrammeled and that the public be told by the press what goes on in the courts, in order that "the public may judge whether our system of criminal justice is fair and right." A defendant is entitled to a fair trial by court; he does not want a trial by newspaper; but news reporting of trials is in itself an aid toward achievement of a fair trial by court. This conflict of competing values has led to the problem of contempt by publication.

[In 1907 the Supreme Court, with Justices Harlan and Brewer dissenting, refused to review a decision of a Colorado court holding a publisher in contempt for publishing articles and a cartoon which reflected upon the motives and conduct of the court in pending cases. In his opinion for the Court, Justice Holmes said that even if what the articles said was true, the publisher might none the less be guilty of contempt if a judge finds that the publication *tends* toward an interference with the administration of justice.

[In *Bridges* v. *California* the Court moved away from this position. The clear and present danger, and not the bad tendency, test is applied to comments on pending cases. Each case must be decided on its own facts. Four Justices dissented: Frankfurter, Roberts, Byrnes, and Chief Justice Stone. The majority decision was followed in *Craig* v. *Harney,*

---

that government should impose a general censorship, affecting all the citizenry, upon any medium of communication, with a view to punishing the communication of materials that are judged to be harmful according to the special standards held within one group.

"Third, any minority group has the right to work toward the elevation of standards of public morality in the pluralist society, through the use of the methods of persuasion and pacific argument.

"Fourth, in a pluralist society no minority group has the right to impose its own religious or moral views on other groups, through the use of the methods of force, coercion, or violence." Murray, *We Hold These Truths* (1960), p. 168.

331 US 367 (1947), with only Justices Frankfurter and Jackson dissenting. Cf. the concurring opinion of Justice Jackson in *Shepard* v. *Florida*, 341 US 50 (1951).]

Mr. Justice Black delivered the opinion of the Court:

These two cases [*Bridges* v. *California* and *Times-Mirror Co.* v. *Superior Court*], while growing out of different circumstances and concerning different parties, both relate to the scope of our national constitutional policy safeguarding free speech and a free press. All of the petitioners were adjudged guilty and fined for contempt of court by the Superior Court of Los Angeles County. Their conviction rested upon comments pertaining to pending litigation which were published in newspapers. In the Superior Court and later in the California Supreme Court, petitioners challenged the state's action as an abridgment, prohibited by the Federal Constitution, of freedom of speech and of the press, but the Superior Court overruled this contention, and the [California] Supreme Court affirmed. . . .

In brief, the state courts asserted and exercised a power to punish petitioners for publishing their views concerning cases not in all respects finally determined, upon the following chain of reasoning: California is invested with the power and duty to provide an adequate administration of justice; by virtue of this power and duty, it can take appropriate measures for providing fair judicial trials free from coercion or intimidation; included among such appropriate measures is the common law procedure of punishing certain interferences and obstructions through contempt proceedings; this particular measure, devolving upon the courts of California by reason of their creation as courts, includes the power to punish for publications made outside the court room if they tend to interfere with the fair and orderly administration of justice in a pending case; the trial court having found that the publications had such a tendency, and there being substantial evidence to support the finding, the punishments here imposed were an appropriate exercise of the state's power; in so far as these punishments constitute a restriction on liberty of expression, the public interest in that liberty was properly subordinated to the public interest in judicial impartiality and decorum.

If the inference of conflict raised by the last clause be correct, the issue before us is of the very gravest moment. For free speech and fair trials are two of the most cherished policies of our civilization, and it would be a trying task to choose between them. But even if such a conflict is not actually raised by the question before us, we are still confronted with the delicate problems entailed in passing upon the deliberations of the highest court of a state. This is not, however, solely an issue between state and nation, as it would be if we were called upon to mediate in one of those troublous situations where each claims to be the repository of a particular sovereign power. To be sure, the exercise of power here in question was by a state judge. But in deciding whether or not the sweeping constitutional mandate against any law "abridging the freedom of speech or of the press" forbids it, we are necessarily measuring a power of all American courts, both state and federal, including this one.

I. It is to be noted at once that we have no direction by the legislature of California that publications outside the court room which comment upon a pending case in a specified manner should be punishable. As we said in *Cantwell* v. *Connecticut,* 310 US 296, such a "declaration of the State's policy would weigh heavily in any challenge of the law as infringing constitutional limitations." But as we also said there, the problem is different where "the judgment is based on a common law concept of the most general and undefined nature." . . . The judgments below, therefore, do not come to us encased in the armor wrought by prior legislative deliberation. Under such circumstances, this Court has said that "it must necessarily be found, as an original question" that the specified publications involved created "such likelihood of bringing about the substantive evil as to deprive [them] of the constitutional protection." *Gitlow* v. *New York,* 268 US 652.

How much "likelihood" is another question, "a question of proximity and degree" that cannot be completely captured in a formula. In *Schenck* v. *United States,* 249 US 47, however, this Court said that there must be a determination of whether or not "the words used are used in such circumstances and are of such a nature as to create a clear and present danger that they will bring about the substantive evils." We recognize that this statement, however helpful, does not comprehend the whole problem. As Mr. Justice Brandeis said in his concurring opinion in *Whitney* v. *California,* 274 US 357: "This Court has not yet fixed the standard by which to determine when a danger shall be deemed clear; how remote the danger may be and yet be deemed present."

Nevertheless, the "clear and present danger" language of the *Schenck Case* has afforded practical guidance in a great variety of cases in which the scope of constitutional protections of freedom of expression was in issue. It has been utilized by either a majority or minority of this Court in passing upon the constitutionality of convictions under espionage acts . . . ; under a criminal syndicalism act . . . ; under an "anti-insurrection" act . . . ; and for breach of the peace at common law. . . . And very recently we have also suggested that "clear and present danger" is an appropriate guide in determining the constitutionality of restrictions upon expression where the substantive evil sought to be prevented by the restriction is "destruction of life or property, or invasion of the right of privacy." *Thornhill* v. *Alabama,* 310 US 88.

Moreover, the likelihood, however great, that a substantive evil will result cannot alone justify a restriction upon freedom of speech or the press. The evil itself must be "substantial," Brandeis, J., concurring in *Whitney* v. *California;* it must be "serious." And even the expression of "legislative preferences or beliefs" cannot transform minor matters of public inconvenience or annoyance into substantive evils of sufficient weight to warrant the curtailment of liberty of expression. *Schneider* v. *Irvington,* 308 US 147.

What finally emerges from the "clear and present danger" cases is a working principle that the substantive evil must be extremely serious and the degree of imminence extremely high before utterances can be punished. Those cases do not purport to mark the furthermost constitutional boundaries of protected expression, nor do we here. They do no more than recognize a minimum compulsion of the Bill of Rights. For the First Amendment does not speak equivocally. It prohibits any law "abridging the freedom of speech or of the press." It must be taken as a command of the broadest scope that explicit language, read in the context of a liberty-loving society, will allow.

II. Before analyzing the punished utterances and the circumstances surrounding their publication, we must consider an argument which, if valid, would destroy the relevance of the foregoing discussion to this case. In brief, this argument is that the publications here in question belong to a special category marked off by history, a category to which the criteria of constitutional immunity from punishment used where other types of utterances are concerned are not applicable. For, the argument runs, the power of judges to punish by contempt out-of-court publications tending to obstruct the orderly and fair administration of justice in a pending case was deeply rooted in English common law at the time the Constitution was adopted. That this historical contention is dubious has been persuasively argued elsewhere. . . . In any event it need not detain us, for to assume that English common law in this field became ours is to deny the generally accepted historical belief that "one of the objects of the Revolution was to get rid of the English common law on liberty of speech and of the press." . . .

More specifically, it is to forget the environment in which the First Amendment was ratified. In presenting the proposals which were later embodied in the Bill of Rights, James Madison, the leader in the preparation of the First Amendment, said:

Although I know whenever the great rights, the trial by jury, freedom of the press, or liberty of conscience, come in question in that body [Parliament], the invasion of them is resisted by able advocates, yet their Magna Charta does not contain any one provision for the security of those rights, respecting which the people of America are most alarmed. The freedom of the press and the rights of conscience, those choicest privileges of the people, are unguarded in the British Constitution. [1 *Annals of Congress* 1789–1790, 434.]

And Madison elsewhere wrote that "the state of the press . . . under the common law, cannot . . . be the standard of its freedom in the United States." VI *Writings of James Madison 1790–1802,* 387.

There are no contrary implications in any part of the history of the period in which the First Amendment was framed and adopted. No purpose in ratifying the Bill of Rights was clearer than that of securing for the people of the United States much greater freedom of religion, expression, assembly, and petition than the people of Great Britain had ever enjoyed. It cannot be denied, for example, that the religious test oath or the restrictions upon assembly then prevalent in England would have been regarded as measures which the Constitution prohibited the American Congress from passing. And since the same unequivocal language is used with respect to freedom of the press, it signifies a similar enlargement of that concept as well. Ratified as it was while the memory of many oppressive English restrictions on the enumerated liberties was still fresh, the First Amendment cannot reasonably be taken as approving prevalent English practices. On the contrary, the only conclusion supported by history is that the unqualified prohibitions laid down by the framers were intended to give to liberty of the press, as to the other liberties, the broadest scope that could be countenanced in an orderly society.

The implications of subsequent American history confirm such a construction of the First Amendment. To be sure, it occurred no more to the people who lived in the decades following Ratification than it would to us now that the power of courts to protect themselves from disturbances and disorder in the court room by use of contempt proceedings could seriously be challenged as conflicting with constitutionally secured guarantees of liberty. In both state and federal courts, this power has been universally recognized. . . . But attempts to expand it in the post-Ratification years evoked popular reactions that bespeak a feeling of jealous solicitude for freedom of the press. In Pennsylvania and New York, for example, heated controversies arose over alleged abuses in the exercise of the contempt power, which in both places culminated in legislation practically forbidding summary punishment for publications. . . .

In the federal courts, there was the celebrated case of Judge Peck, recently referred to by this Court in *Nye* v. *United States*, 313 US 33. The impeachment proceedings against him, it should be noted, and the strong feelings they engendered, were set in motion by his summary punishment of a lawyer for publishing comment on a case which was on appeal at the time of publication and which raised the identical issue of several other cases then pending before him. Here again legislation was the outcome, Congress proclaiming in a statute expressly captioned "An Act *declaratory* of the law concerning contempts of court," that the power of federal courts to inflict summary punishment for contempt "shall not be construed to extend to any cases except the misbehaviour of . . . persons in the presence of the said courts, or so near thereto as to obstruct the administration of justice." . . .

We are aware that although some states have by statute or decision expressly repudiated the power of judges to punish publications as contempts on a finding of mere tendency to interfere with the orderly administration of justice in a pending case, other states have sanctioned the exercise of such a power. . . . But state power in this field was not tested in this Court for more than a century. Not until 1925, with the decision in *Gitlow* v. *New York*, 268 US 652, did this Court recognize in the Fourteenth Amendment the application to the states of the same standards of freedom of expression as, under the First Amendment, are applicable to the federal government. And this is the first time since 1925 that we have been called upon to determine the constitutionality of a state's exercise of the contempt power in this kind of situation. Now that such a case is before us, we cannot allow the mere existence of other untested state decisions to destroy the historic constitutional meaning of freedom of speech and of the press.

History affords no support for the contention that the criteria applicable under the Constitution to other types of utterances are not applicable, in contempt proceedings, to out-of-court publications pertaining to a pending case.

III. We may appropriately begin our discussion of the judgments below by considering how much, as a practical matter, they would affect liberty of expression. It must be recognized that public interest is much more likely to be kindled by a controversial event of the day than by a generalization, however penetrating, of the historian or scientist. Since they punish utterances made during the pendency of a case, the judgments below therefore produce their restrictive results at the precise time when public interest in the matters discussed would naturally be at its height. Moreover, the ban is likely to fall not only at a crucial time but upon the most important topics of discussion. Here, for example, labor controversies were the topics of some of the publications. Experience shows that the more acute labor controversies are, the more likely it is that in some aspect they will get into court. It is therefore the controversies that command most interest that the decisions below would remove from the arena of public discussion.

No suggestion can be found in the Constitution that the freedom there guaranteed for speech and the press bears an inverse ratio to the timeliness and importance of the ideas seeking expression. Yet, it would follow as a practical result of the decisions below that anyone who might wish to give public expression to his views on a pending case involving no matter what problem of public interest, just at the time his audience would be most receptive, would be as effectively discouraged as if a deliberate statutory scheme of censorship had been adopted. Indeed, perhaps more so, because under a legislative specification of the particular kinds of expressions prohibited and the circumstances under which the prohibitions are to operate, the speaker or publisher might at least have an authoritative guide to the permissible scope of comment, instead of being compelled to act at the peril that judges might find in the utterance a "reasonable tendency" to obstruct justice in a pending case.

This unfocussed threat is, to be sure, limited in time, terminating as it does upon final disposition of the case. But this does not change its censorial quality. An endless series of moratoria on public discussion, even if each were very short, could hardly be dismissed as an insignificant abridgment of freedom of expression. And to assume that each would be short is to overlook the fact that the "pendency" of a case is frequently a matter of months or even years rather than days or weeks.

For these reasons we are convinced that the judgments below result in a curtailment of expression that cannot be dismissed as insignificant. If they can be justified at all, it must be in terms of some serious substantive evil which they are designed to avert. The substantive evil here sought to be averted has been variously described below. It appears to be double: disrespect for the judiciary; and disorderly and unfair administration of justice. The assumption that respect for the judiciary can be won by shielding judges from published criticism wrongly appraises the character of American public opinion. For it is a prized American privilege to speak one's mind, although not always with perfect good taste, on all public institutions. And an enforced silence, however limited, solely in the name of preserving the dignity of the bench, would probably engender resentment, suspicion, and contempt much more than it would enhance respect.

The other evil feared, disorderly and unfair administration of justice, is more plausibly associated with restricting publications which touch upon pending litigation. The very word "trial" connotes decisions on the evidence and arguments properly advanced in open court. Legal trials are not like elections, to be won through the use of the meeting-hall, the radio, and the newspaper. But we cannot start with the assumption that publications of the kind here involved actually do threaten to change the nature of legal trials, and that to preserve judicial impartiality, it is necessary for judges to have a contempt power by which they can close all channels of public expression to all matters which touch upon pending cases. We must therefore turn to the particular utterances here in question and the circumstances of their publication to determine to what extent the substantive evil of unfair administration of justice was a likely consequence, and whether the degree of likelihood was sufficient to justify summary punishment.

The Los Angeles Times Editorials. The Times-Mirror Company, publisher of the *Los Angeles Times,* and L. D. Hotchkiss, its managing editor, were cited for contempt for the publication of three editorials. Both found by the trial court to be responsible for one of the editorials, the company and Hotchkiss were each fined $100. The company alone was held responsible for the other two, and was fined $100 more on account of one, and $300 more on account of the other.

The $300 fine presumably marks the most serious offense. The editorial thus distinguished was entitled "Probation for Gorillas?". After vigorously denouncing two members of a labor union who had previously been found guilty of assaulting nonunion truck drivers, it closes with the observation: "Judge A. A. Scott will make a serious mistake if he grants probation to Matthew Shannon and Kennan Holmes. This community needs the example of their assignment to the jute mill." Judge Scott had previously set a day (about a month after the publication) for passing upon the application of Shannon and Holmes for probation and for pronouncing sentence.

The basis for punishing the publication as contempt was by the trial court said to be its "inherent tendency" and by the Supreme Court its "reasonable tendency" to interfere with the orderly administration of justice in an action then before a court for consideration. In accordance with what we have said on the "clear and present danger" cases, neither "inherent tendency" nor "reasonable tendency" is enough to justify a restriction of free expression. But even if they were appropriate measures, we should find exaggeration in the use of those phrases to describe the facts here.

From the indications in the record of the position taken by the *Los Angeles Times* on labor controversies in the past, there could have been little doubt of its attitude toward the probation of Shannon and Holmes. In view of the paper's long-continued militancy in this field, it is inconceivable that any judge in Los Angeles would expect anything but adverse criticism from it in the event probation were granted. Yet such criticism after final disposition of the proceedings would clearly have been privileged. Hence, this editorial, given the most intimidating construction it will bear, did no more than threaten future adverse criticism which was reasonably to be expected anyway in the event of a lenient disposition of the pending case. To regard it, therefore, as in itself of substantial influence upon the course of justice would be to impute to judges a lack of firmness, wisdom, or honor, which we cannot accept as a major premise. . . .

With respect to these [other] two editorials, there is no divergence of conclusions among the members of this Court. We are all of the opinion that, upon any fair construction, their possible influence on the course of justice can be dismissed as negligible, and that the Constitution compels us to set aside the convictions as unpermissible exercises of the state's power. In view of the foregoing discussion of "Probation for Gorillas?", analysis of these editorials and their setting is deemed unnecessary.

The Bridges Telegram. While a motion for a new trial was pending in a case involving a dispute between an A.F. of L. union and a C.I.O. union of which Bridges was an officer, he either caused to be published or acquiesced in the publication of a telegram which he had sent to the Secretary of Labor. The telegram referred to the judge's decision as "outrageous"; said that attempted enforcement of it would tie up the port of Los Angeles and involve the entire Pacific Coast; and concluded with the announcement that the C.I.O. union, representing some twelve thousand members, did "not intend to allow state courts to override the majority vote of members in choosing its officers and representatives and to override the National Labor Relations Board."

Apparently Bridges' conviction is not rested at all upon his use of the word "outrageous." The remainder of the telegram fairly construed appears to be a statement that if the court's decree should be enforced there would be a strike. It is not claimed that such a strike would have been in violation of the terms of the decree, nor that in any other way it would have run afoul of the law of California. On no construction, therefore, can the telegram be taken as a threat either by Bridges or the union to follow an illegal course of action. . . . [The words of Justice] Holmes, spoken in reference to very different facts, seem entirely applicable here: "I confess that I cannot find in all this or in the evidence in the case anything that would have affected a mind of reasonable fortitude, and still less can I find there anything that obstructed the administration of justice in any sense that I possibly can give to those words." . . .

Reversed.

4. Censorship on Advice as to
Use of Contraceptives

POE *v.* ULLMAN

367 US 497 (1961)

[Connecticut statutes prescribed criminal penalties for any person using a contraceptive drug or device. They also prescribed criminal penalties for any accessory to such use. The constitutionality of these statutes was challenged in declaratory judgment suits by married couples who, because of the statutes, were unable to obtain medical advice on the use of contraceptives from their physician. The statutes were also challenged by a physician who, because of the statutes, was unable to give such advice to his married patients. The Connecticut courts dismissed the actions. Appeals to the Supreme Court were dismissed. Although there was no opinion by a majority, five members of the Court agreed that the cases presented no justiciable controversy. The opinion on this point was written by Justice Frankfurter, with Chief Justice Warren and Justices Clark and Whittaker joining; and Justice Brennan wrote a concurring opinion on this point.

[Justices Douglas, Stewart, Harlan, and Black stated that the appeals presented a justiciable controversy. Justice Black stated that the constitutional issue should be reached and decided. Justice Douglas and Justice Harlan, in separate dissenting opinions, held that the statutes denied due process under the Fourteenth Amendment. The freedom of speech aspects of the cases were discussed by Justice Douglas.]

Mr. Justice Frankfurter announced the judgment of the Court in an opinion which The Chief Justice, Mr. Justice Clark and Mr. Justice Whittaker join:

These appeals challenge the constitutionality, under the Fourteenth Amendment, of Connecticut statutes which, as authoritatively construed by the Connecticut Supreme Court of Errors, prohibit the use of contraceptive devices and the giving of medical advice in the use of such devices. In proceedings seeking declarations of law, not on review of convictions for violation of the statutes, that court has ruled that these statutes would be applicable in the case of married couples and even under claim that conception would constitute a serious threat to the health or life of the female spouse.

No. 60 combines two actions brought in a Connecticut Superior Court for declaratory relief. The complaint in the first alleges that the plaintiffs Paul and Pauline Poe ° are a husband and wife, thirty and twenty-six years old respectively, who live together and have no children. Mrs. Poe has had three consecutive pregnancies terminating in infants with multiple congenital abnormalities from which each died shortly after birth. Plaintiffs have consulted Dr. Buxton, an obstetrician and gynecologist of eminence, and it is Dr. Buxton's opinion that the cause of the infants' abnormalities is genetic, although the underlying "mechanism" is unclear. In view of the great emotional stress already suffered by plaintiffs, the probable consequence of another pregnancy is psychological strain extremely disturbing to the physical and mental health of both husband and wife. Plaintiffs know that it is Dr. Buxton's opinion that the best and safest medical treatment which could be prescribed for their situtation is advice in methods of preventing conception. Dr. Buxton knows of drugs, medicinal articles and instruments which can be safely used to effect contraception. Medically, the use of these devices is indicated as the best and safest preventive measure necessary for the protection of plaintiffs' health. Plaintiffs, however, have been unable to obtain this information for the sole reason that its delivery and use may or will be claimed by the defendant State's attorney (appellee in this Court) to constitute offenses at Connecticut law. The State's attorney intends to prosecute offenses against the State's laws, and claims that the giving of conrtaceptive advice and the use of contraceptive devices would be offenses forbidden by Conn. Gen. Stat. Rev., 1958, §§ 53-32 and 54-196.† Alleging irreparable injury and a substantial uncertainty of legal relations (a local procedural

° Plaintiffs in the two cases composing No. 60 sue under fictitious names. The Supreme Court of Errors of Connecticut approved this procedure in the special circumstances of the cases.

† As a matter of specific legislation, Connecticut outlaws only the use of contraceptive materials. Conn. Gen. Stat. Rev., 1958, § 53–32 provides:

"*Use of drugs or instruments to prevent conception.* Any person who uses any drug, medicinal article or instrument for the purpose of preventing conception shall be fined not less than fifty dollars or imprisoned not less than sixty days nor more than one year or be both fined and imprisoned."

There are no substantive provisions dealing with the sale or distribution of such devices, nor with the giving of information concerning their use. These activities

requisite for a declaration), plaintiffs ask a declaratory judgment that §§ 53-32 and 54-196 are unconstitutional, in that they deprive the plaintiffs of life and liberty without due process of law.

The second action in No. 60 is brought by Jane Doe, a twenty-five-year-old housewife. Mrs. Doe, it is alleged, lives with her husband, they have no children; Mrs. Doe recently underwent a pregnancy which induced in her a critical physical illness—two weeks' unconsciousness and a total of nine weeks' acute sickness which left her with partial paralysis, marked impairment of speech, and emotional instability. Another pregnancy would be exceedingly perilous to her life. She, too, has consulted Dr. Buxton, who believes that the best and safest treatment for her is contraceptive advice. The remaining allegations of Mrs. Doe's complaint, and the relief sought, are similar to those in the case of Mr. and Mrs. Poe.

In No. 61, also a declaratory judgment action, Dr. Buxton is the plaintiff. Setting forth facts identical to those alleged by Jane Doe, he asks that the Connecticut statutes prohibiting his giving of contraceptive advice to Mrs. Doe be adjudged unconstitutional, as depriving him of liberty and property without due process.

In all three actions, demurrers were advanced, *inter alia,* on the ground that the statutes attacked had been previously construed and sustained by the Supreme Court of Errors of Connecticut, and thus there did not exist the uncertainty of legal relations requisite to maintain suits for declaratory judgment. While the Connecticut Supreme Court of Errors in sustaining the demurrers referred to this local procedural ground, . . . we cannot say that its decision rested on it. . . . We noted probable jurisdiction.

Appellants' complaints in these declaratory proceedings do not clearly, and certainly do not in terms, allege that appellee Ullman threatens to prosecute them for use of, or for giving advice concerning, contraceptive devices. The allegations are merely that, in the course of his public duty, he intends to prosecute any offenses against Connecticut law, and that he claims that use of and advice concerning contraceptives would constitute offenses. The lack of immediacy of the threat described by these allegations might alone raise serious questions of nonjusticiability of appellants' claims. . . . But even were we to read the allegations to convey a clear threat of imminent prosecutions, we are not bound to accept as true all that is alleged on the face of the

---

are deemed to be involved in law solely because of the general criminal accessory enactment of Connecticut. This is Conn. Gen. Stat. Rev., 1958, § 54-196:

"*Accessories.* Any person who assists, abets, counsels, causes, hires or commands another to commit any offense may be prosecuted and punished as if he were the principal offender."

complaint and admitted, technically, by demurrer, any more than the Court is bound by stipulation of the parties. . . . Formal agreement between parties that collides with plausibility is too fragile a foundation for indulging in constitutional adjudication.

The Connecticut law prohibiting the use of contraceptives has been on the State's books since 1879. . . . During the more than three quarters of a century since its enactment, a prosecution for its violation seems never to have been initiated, save in *State* v. *Nelson*, 126 Conn. 412. The circumstances of that case, decided in 1940, only prove the abstract character of what is before us. There, a test case was brought to determine the constitutionality of the act as applied against two doctors and a nurse who had allegedly disseminated contraceptive information. After the Supreme Court of Errors sustained the legislation on appeal from a demurrer to the information, the State moved to dismiss the information. Neither counsel nor our own researches have discovered any other attempt to enforce the prohibition of distribution or use of contraceptive devices by criminal process.* The unreality of these law suits is illumined by another circumstance. We were advised by counsel for appellant that contraceptives are commonly and notoriously sold in Connecticut drug stores.† Yet no prosecutions are recorded; and certainly such ubiquitous, open, public sales would more quickly invite the attention of enforcement officials than the conduct in which the present appellants wish to engage—the giving of private medical advice by a doctor to his individual patients, and their private use of the devices prescribed. The undeviating policy of nullification by Connecticut of its anti-contraceptive laws throughout all the long years that they have been on the statute books bespeaks more than prosecutorial paralysis. What was said in another context is relevant here. "Deeply embedded traditional ways of carrying out state policy. . ."—or not carrying it out—"are often tougher and truer law than the dead words of the written text." . . .

The restriction of our jurisdiction to cases and controversies within the meaning of Article III of the Constitution . . . is not the sole limitation on the exercise of our appellate powers, especially in cases raising constitutional questions. The policy reflected in numerous cases and over a long period was thus summarized in the oft-quoted state-

---

* The assumption of prosecution of spouses for use of contraceptives is not only inherently bizarre, as was admitted by counsel, but is underscored in its implausibility by the disability of spouses, under Connecticut law, from being compelled to testify against one another.

† It is also worthy of note that the Supreme Court of Errors has held that contraceptive devices could not be seized and destroyed as nuisances under the State's seizure statutes. . . .

ment of Mr. Justice Brandeis: "The Court [has] developed, for its own governance in the cases confessedly within its jurisdiction, a series of rules under which it has avoided passing upon a large part of all the constitutional questions pressed upon it for decision." *Ashwander* v. *Tennessee Authority,* 297 U.S. 288 (concurring opinion). In part the rules summarized in the *Ashwander* opinion have derived from the historically defined, limited nature and function of courts and from the recognition that, within the framework of our adversary system, the adjudicatory process is most securely founded when it is exercised under the impact of a lively conflict between antagonistic demands, actively pressed, which make resolution of the controverted issue a practical necessity. . . . In part they derive from the fundamental federal and tripartite character of our national government and from the role—restricted by its very responsibility—of the federal courts, and particularly this Court, within that structure. . . .

These considerations press with special urgency in cases challenging legislative action or state judicial action as repugnant to the Constitution. "The best teaching of this Court's experience admonishes us not to entertain constitutional questions in advance of the strictest necessity." . . . The various doctrines of "standing," "ripeness," and "mootness," which this Court has evolved with particular, though not exclusive, reference to such cases are but several manifestations—each having its own "varied application"—of the primary conception that federal judicial power is to be exercised to strike down legislation, whether state or federal, only at the instance of one who is himself immediately harmed, or immediately threatened with harm, by the challenged action. . . . "This court can have no right to pronounce an abstract opinion upon the constitutionality of a state law. Such law must be brought into action or threatened operation, upon rights properly falling under judicial cognizance, or a remedy is not to be had here." . . . "The party who invokes the power [to annul legislation on grounds of its unconstitutionality] must be able to show not only that the statute is invalid but that he has sustained or is immediately in danger of sustaining some direct injury as the result of its enforcement." . . .

The requirement for adversity was classically expounded in *Chicago & Grand Trunk R. Co.* v. *Wellman,* 143 U.S. 339:

> . . . The theory upon which, apparently, this suit was brought is that parties have an appeal from the legislature to the courts; and that the latter are given an immediate and general supervision of the constitutionality of the acts of the former. Such is not true. Whenever, in pursuance of an honest and actual antagonistic assertion of rights by one individual against another, there is presented a question involving the validity of any act of any legislature, State or Federal, and the decision necessarily rests on the competency

of the legislature to so enact, the court must, in the exercise of its solemn duties, determine whether the act be constitutional or not; but such an exercise of power is the ultimate and supreme function of courts. It is legitimate only in the last resort, and as a necessity in the determination of real, earnest and vital controversy between individuals. It never was the thought that, by means of a friendly suit, a party beaten in the legislature could transfer to the courts an inquiry as to the constitutionality of the legislative act.

What was said in the *Wellman* case found ready application in proceedings brought under modern declaratory judgment procedures. For just as the declaratory judgment device does not "purport to alter the character of the controversies which are the subject of the judicial power under the Constitution," . . . it does not permit litigants to invoke the power of this Court to obtain constitutional rulings in advance of necessity. . . . The Court has been on the alert against use of the declaratory judgment device for avoiding the rigorous insistence on exigent adversity as a condition for evoking Court adjudication. . . .

Insofar as appellants seek to justify the exercise of our declaratory power by the threat of prosecution, facts which they can no more negative by complaint and demurrer than they could by stipulation preclude our determining their appeals on the merits. . . . It is clear that the mere existence of a state penal statute would constitute insufficient grounds to support a federal court's adjudication of its constitutionality in proceedings brought against the State's prosecuting officials if real threat of enforcement is wanting. . . . If the prosecutor expressly agrees not to prosecute, a suit against him for declaratory and injunctive relief is not such an adversary case as will be reviewed here. . . . Eighty years of Connecticut history demonstrate a similar, albeit tacit agreement. The fact that Conneticut has not chosen to press the enforcement of this statute deprives these controversies of the immediacy which is an indispensable condition of constitutional abjudication. This Court cannot be umpire to debates concerning harmless, empty shadows. To find it necessary to pass on these statutes now, in order to protect appellants from the hazards of prosecution, would be to close our eyes to reality.

Nor does the allegation by appellants Poe and Doe that they are unable to obtain information concerning contraceptive devices from Dr. Buxton "for the sole reason that the delivery and use of such information and advice may or will be claimed by the defendant State's Attorney to constitute offenses," disclose a necessity for present constitutional decision. It is true that this Court has several times passed upon criminal statutes challenged by persons who claimed that the effects of the statutes were to deter others from maintaining profitable or advantageous relations with the complainants. See, e.g., *Truax* v. *Raich*, 239 U.S. 33; *Pierce* v. *Society of Sisters*, 268 U.S. 510. But in these cases the deterrent effect complained of was one which was grounded in a realistic fear of prosecution. We cannot agree that if Dr. Buxton's compliance with these statutes is uncoerced by the risk of their enforcement, his patients are entitled to a declaratory judgment concerning the statutes' validity. And, with due regard to Dr. Buxton's standing as a physician and to his personal sensitiveness, we cannot accept, as the basis of constitutional adjudication, other than as chimerical the fear of enforcement of provisions that have during so many years gone uniformly and without exception unenforced.

Justiciability is of course not a legal concept with a fixed content or susceptible of scientific verification. Its utilization is the resultant of many subtle pressures, including the appropriateness of the issues for decision by this Court and the actual hardship to the litigants of denying them the relief sought. Both these factors justify withholding adjudication of the constitutional issue raised under the circumstances and in the manner in which they are now before the Court.

Dismissed.

Mr. Justice Douglas, dissenting:

I.

These cases are dismissed because a majority of the members of this Court conclude, for varying reasons, that this controversy does not present a justiciable question. That conclusion is too transparent to require an extended reply. The device of the declaratory judgment is an honored one. Its use in the federal system is restricted to "cases" or "controversies" within the meaning of Article III. The question must be "appropriate for judicial determination," not hypothetical, abstract, academic or moot. . . . It must touch "the legal relations of parties having adverse legal interests." It must be "real and substantial" and admit of "specific relief through a decree of a conclusive character." The fact that damages are not awarded or an injunction does not issue, the fact that there are no allegations of irreparable injury are irrelevant. This is hornbook law. . . .

If there is a case where the need for this remedy in the shadow of a criminal prosecution is shown, it is this one, as Mr. Justice Harlan demonstrates. Plaintiffs in No. 60 are two sets of husband and wife. One wife is pathetically ill, having delivered a stillborn fetus. If she becomes pregnant again, her life will be gravely jeopardized. This couple have been unable to get medical advice concerning the "best and safest" means to avoid pregnancy from their physician, plaintiff in No. 61, because if he gave it he would commit a crime. The use of contraceptive devices would also constitute a crime. And it is alleged—and admitted by the State—that the State's

Attorney intends to enforce the law by prosecuting offenses under the laws.

A public clinic dispensing birth control information has indeed been closed by the State. Doctors and a nurse working in that clinic were arrested by the police and charged with advising married women on the use of contraceptives. That litigation produced *State* v. *Nelson*, 126 Conn. 412, which upheld these statutes. That same police raid on the clinic resulted in the seizure of a quantity of the clinic's contraception literature and medical equipment and supplies. The legality of that seizure was in question in *State* v. *Certain Contraceptive Materials*, 126 Conn. 428.

The Court refers to the *Nelson* prosecution as a "test case" and implies that it had little impact. Yet its impact was described differently by a contemporary observer who concluded his comment with this sentence: "This serious setback to the birth control movement [the *Nelson* case] led to the closing of all the clinics in the state, just as they had been previously closed in the state of Massachusetts." At oral argument, counsel for appellants confirmed that the clinics are still closed. In response to a question from the bench he affirmed that "no public or private clinic" has dared give birth control advise since the decision in the *Nelson* case.

These, then, are the circumstances in which the Court feels that it can, contrary to every principle of American or English common laws, go outside the record to conclude that there exists a "tacit agreement" that these statutes will not be enforced. No lawyer, I think, would advise his client to rely on that "tacit agreement." No police official, I think, would feel himself bound by that "tacit agreement." After our national experience during the prohibition era, it would be absurd to pretend that all criminal statutes are adequately enforced. But that does not mean that bootlegging was the less a crime. . . . In fact, an arbitrary administrative pattern of non-enforcement may increase the hardships of those subjects to the law. . . .

When the Court goes outside the record to determine that Connecticut has adopted "an undeviating policy of nullification . . . of its anti-contraceptive laws," it selects a particularly poor case in which to exercise such a novel power. This is not a law which is a dead-letter. Twice since 1940, Connecticut has re-enacted these laws as part of general statutory revisions. Consistently, bills to remove the statutes from the books have been rejected by the legislature. In short, the statutes—far from being the accidental left-overs of another era are the center of a continuing controversy in the State. . . .

Again, the Court relies on the inability of counsel to show any attempts, other than the *Nelson* case, "to enforce the prohibition of distribution or use of contraceptive devices by criminal processes." Yet, on oral argument, counsel for the appellee stated on his own knowledge that several proprietors had been prosecuted in the "minor police courts of Connecticut" after they had been "picked up" for selling contraceptives. The enforcement of criminal laws in minor courts have just as much impact as in those cases where appellate courts are resorted to. The need of the protection of constiutional guarantees, and the right to them, are not less because the matter is small or the court lowly. . . . Nor is the need lacking because the dispensing of birth-control information is by a single doctor rather than by birth-control clinics. The nature of the controversy would not be changed one iota had a dozen doctors, representing a dozen birth-control clinics, sued for remedial relief.

What are these people—doctor and patients—to do? Flout the law and go to prison? Violate the law surreptitiously and hope they will not get caught? By today's decision we leave them no other alternatives. It is not the choice they need have under the regime of the declaratory judgment and our constitutional system. It is not the choice worthy of a civilized society. A sick wife, a concerned husband, a conscientious doctor seek a dignified, discrete, orderly answer to the critical problem confronting them. We should not turn them away and make them flout the law and get arrested to have their constitutional rights determined. . . . They are entitled to an answer to their predicament here and now.

II.

The right of the doctor to advise his patients according to his best lights seems so obviously within First Amendment rights as to need no extended discussion. The leading cases on freedom of expression are generally framed with reference to public debate and discourse. But as Chafee said, "the First Amendment and other parts of the law erect a fence inside which men can talk. The law-makers, legislators and officials stay on the outside of that fence. But what the men inside the fence say when they are let alone is no concern of the law." *The Blessings of Liberty* (1956), p. 108.

The teacher (*Sweezy* v. *New Hampshire*, 354 U.S. 234) as well as the public speaker (*Thomas* v. *Collins*, 323 U.S. 516) are included. The actor on stage or screen, the artist whose creation is in oil or clay or marble, the poet whose reading public may be practically nonexistent, the musician and his musical scores, the counselor whether priest, parent or teacher no matter how small his audience—these too are beneficiaries of freedom of expression. The remark by President James A. Garfield that his ideal of a college was a log in the woods with a student at one end and Mark Hopkins at another . . . puts the present problem in proper First Amendment dimensions. Of course a physician can talk freely and fully with his patient without threat of retaliation by the State. The contrary thought—the one endorsed *sub silentio* by the courts below—has the cast regimentation about it, a cast at war with the philosophy and presuppositions of this free society.

We should say with Kant that "It is absurd to expect to be enlightened by Reason, and at the same time to prescribe to her what side of the question she must adopt." Leveling the discourse of medical men to the morality of a particular community is a deadening influence. Mill spoke of the pressures of intolerant groups that produce "either mere conformers to commonplace or time-servers for truth." We witness in this case a sealing of the lips of a doctor because he desires to observe the law, obnoxious as the law may be. The State has no power to put any sanctions of any kind on him for any views or beliefs that he has or for any advice he renders. These are his professional domains into which the State may not intrude. The chronciles are filled with sad attempts of government to stomp out ideas, to ban thoughts because they are heretical or obnoxious. As Mill stated, "Our merely social intolerance kills no one, roots out no opinions, but induces men to disguise them, or to abstain from any active effort for their diffusion." When that happens society suffers. Freedom working underground, freedom bootlegged around the law is freedom crippled. A society that tells its doctors under pain of criminal penalty what they may not tell their patients is not a free society. Only free exchange of views and information is consistent with "a civilization of the dialogue," to borrow a phrase from Dr. Robert M. Hutchins. See *Wieman* v. *Updegraff*, 344 U.S. 183 (concurring opinion).

III.

I am also clear that this Connecticut law as applied to this married couple deprives them of "liberty" without due process of law, as that concept is used in the Fourteenth Amendment.

The first eight Amendments to the Constitution have been made applicable to the States only in part. My view has been that when the Fourteenth Amendment was adopted, its Due Process Clause incorporated all of those Amendments. See *Adamson* v. *California*, 332 U.S. 46, 68 (dissenting opinion). Although the history of the Fourteenth Amendment may not be conclusive, the words "due process" acquired specific meaning from Anglo-American experience.* As Mr. Justice Brennan recently stated, "The Bill of Rights is the primary source of expressed information as to what is meant by constitutional liberty. The safeguards enshrined in it are deeply etched in the foundations of American's freedoms." . . . When the Framers wrote the Bill of Rights they enshrined in the form of constitutional guarantees those rights—in part substantive, in part procedural—which experience indicated were indispensable to a free society. Some would disagree as to their importance; the debate concerning them did indeed start before their adoption and has continued to this day. Yet the constitutional conception of "due process" must in my view include them all until and unless there are amendments that remove them. That has indeed been the view of a full court of nine Justices, though the members who make up that court unfortunately did not sit at the same time.†

Though I believe that "due process" as used in the Fourteenth Amendment

---

* See Konvitz, *Fundamental Liberties of a Free People* (1957), pp. 37–39; Green, "The Bill of Rights, the Fourteenth Amendment and the Supreme Court," 46 *Mich. L. Rev.* 869, 904 *et seq.* (1948); Holmes, "The Fourteenth Amendment and the Bill of Rights," 7 *S. C. L. Rev.* 596 (1955).

And see Mr. Justice Rutledge (concurring) in *In re Oliver*, 333 U.S. 257, 280–281.

† I start with Justices Bradley, Swayne, Field, Clifford and Harlan. To this number, Mr. Justice Brewer can probably be joined on the basis of his agreement "in the main" with Mr. Justice Harlan in *O'Neill* v. *Vermont*, 144 U.S. 323, 371. See the Apendix to Mr. Justice Black's dissent in *Adamson* v. *California*, 332 U.S. 46, 120, 123. To these I add Mr. Justice Black, Mr. Justice Murphy, Mr. Justice Rutledge and myself (*Adamson* v. *California*, supra, 68, 123).

includes all of the first eight Amendments, I do not think it is restricted and confined to them. We recently held that the undefined "liberty" in the Due Process Clause of the Fifth Amendment includes freedom to travel. *Kent* v. *Dulles,* 357 U.S. 116. Cf. *Edwards* v. *California,* 314 U.S. 160, 177, 178 (concurring opinion). The right "to marry, establish a home and bring up children" was said in *Meyer* v. *Nebraska,* 262 U.S. 390, 399, to come within the "liberty" of the person protected by the Due Process Clause of the Fourteenth Amendment. As I indicated in my dissent in *Public Utilities Comm'n* v. *Pollak,* 343 U.S. 451, 467, "liberty" within the purview of the Fifth Amendment includes the right of "privacy," a right I thought infringed in that case because a member of a "captive audience" was forced to listen to a government-sponsored radio program. "Liberty" is a conception that sometimes gains content from the emanations of other specific guarantees (*N.A.A.C.P.* v. *Alabama,* 357 U.S. 449, 460) or from experience with the requirements of a free society.

For years the Court struck down social legislation when a particular law did not fit the notions of a majority of Justices as to legislation appropriate for a free enterprise system. Mr. Justice Holmes, dissenting, rightly said that "a Constitution is not intended to embody a particular economic theory, whether of paternalism and the organic relation of the citizen to the State or of *laissez faire.* It is made for people of fundamentally differing views, and the accident of our finding certain opinions natural and familiar, or novel, and even shocking, ought not to conclude our judgment upon the question whether statutes embodying them conflict with the Constitution of the United States." *Lochner* v. *New York,* 198 U.S. 45.

The error of the old Court, as I see it, was not in entertaining inquiries concerning the constitutionality of social legislation but in applying the standards that it did. . . . Social legislation dealing with business and economic matters touches no particularized prohibition of the Constitution, unless it be the provision of the Fifth Amendment that private property should not be taken for public use without just compensation. If it is free of the latter guarantee, it has a wide scope for application. Some go so far as to suggest that whatever the majority in the legislature says goes . . . that there is no other standard of constitutionality. That reduces the legislative power to sheer voting strength and the judicial function to a matter of statistics. As Robert M. Hutchins has said, "It is obviously impossible to raise questions of freedom and justice if the sole duty of the court is to decide whether the case at bar falls within the scope of the duly issued command of a duly constituted sovereign." . . . While the legislative judgment on economic and business matters is "well-nigh conclusive" . . . , it is not beyond judicial inquiry.

The regime of a free society needs room for vast experimentation. Crises, emergencies, experience at the individual and community levels produce new insights; problems emerge in new dimensions; needs, once never imagined, appear. To stop experimentation and the testing of new decrees and controls, is to deprive society of a needed versatility. Yet to say that a legislature may do anything not within a specific guarantee of the Constitution may be as crippling to a free society as to allow it to override specific guarantees so long as what it does fails to shock the sensibilities of a majority of the Court.

The present legislation is an excellent example. If a State banned completely the sale of contraceptives in drug stores, the case would be quite different. It might seem to some or to all judges an unreasonable restriction. Yet it might not be irrational to conclude that a better way of dispensing those articles is through physicians. The same might be said of a state law banning the manufacture of contraceptives. Health, religious, and moral arguments might be marshalled *pro* and *con*. Yet it is not for judges to weigh the evidence. Where either the sale or the manufacture are put under regulation, the structures are on business and commercial dealings that have had a long history with the police power of the States.

The present law, however, deals not with sale, not with manufacture but with *use*. It provides:

> Any person who uses any drug, medicinal article or instrument for the purpose of preventing conception shall be fined not less than fifty dollars or imprisoned not less than sixty days nor more than one year or be both fined and imprisoned. . . .

The regulation as applied in this case touches the relationship between man and wife. It reaches into the intimacies of the marriage relationship. If we imagine a regime of full enforcement of the law in the manner of an Anthony Comstock,° we would reach the point where search warrants issued and officers appeared in bedrooms to find out what went on. It is said that this is not that case. And so it is not. But when the State makes "use" a

---

° Anthony Comstock (1844–1915)—the Congregationalist who inspired the foundation of the New York Society for the Suppression of Vice in 1873 and the Watch and Ward Society of Boston in 1876 and who inspired George Bernard Shaw to use the approbious word "comstockery" in *Mrs. Warren's Profession*—was responsible for the passage in 1879 of this Connecticut law.

"Anthony Comstock had moral earnestness and it can't be faked. His concern was with Puritan theology rather than Puritan ethics. Righteousness seemed to him less important than salvation and consequently tricks which seemed shabby to neutrals left him without shame. A man who fights for the safety of his immortal soul can hardly be expected to live up to the best Queensberry traditions in the clinches. To grant the major premises of Comstock's religious and social philosophy is to acquit him of any lack of logic. Obscenity was to Anthony poison to soul and body, and anything remotely touching upon sex was to his mind obscene. He seems to have believed implicitly in medical theories which have since his time been discarded. Even in his day beliefs were changing, but Comstock was loyal to the old-line ideas. It was his notion that idiocy, epilepsy and locomotor-ataxia were among the ailments for which auto-eroticism was responsible. Since death and damnation might be, according to his belief, the portion of the girl or boy who read a ribald story, it is easy to understand why he was so impatient with those who advanced the claims of art. Even those who love beauty would hardly be prepared to burn in hell forever in its service. Comstock's decision was even easier, for he did not know, understand or care anything about beauty." Broun and Leech, *Anthony Comstock* (1927), pp. 265–266.

crime and applies the criminal sanction to man and wife, the State has entered the innermost sanctum of the home. If it can make this law, it can enforce it. And proof of its violation necessarily involves an inquiry into the relations between man and wife.

That is an invasion of the privacy that is implicit in a free society. A noted theologian who conceives of the use of a contraceptive as a "sin" nonetheless admits that a "use" statute such as this enters a forbidden domain.

> . . . the Connecticut statute confuses the moral and legal, in that it transposes without further ado a private sin into a public crime. The criminal act here is the private use of contraceptives. The real area where the coercions of law might, and ought to, be applied, at least to control an evil—namely, the contraceptive industry—is quite overlooked. As it stands, the statute is, of course, unenforceable without police invasion of the bedroom, and is therefore indefensible as a piece of legal draughtmanship. Murray, *We Hold These Truths* (1960), pp. 157–158.

This notion of privacy is not drawn from the blue. It emanates from the totality of the constitutional scheme under which we live.

> One of the earmarks of the totalitarian understanding of society is that it seeks to make all subcommittees,—family, school, business, press, church—completely subject to control by the State. The State then is not one vital institution among others: a policeman, a referee, and a source of initiative for the common good. Instead, it seeks to be coextensive with family and school, press, business community, and the Church, so that all of these component interest groups are, in principal, reduced to organs and agencies of the State. In a democratic political order, this megatherian concept is expressly rejected as out of accord with the democratic understanding of social good, and with the actual make-up of the human community. Calhoun, "Democracy and Natural Law," 5 *Nat. Law Forum*, 31, 36 (1960).

Can there be any doubt that a Bill of Rights that in time of peace bars soldiers from being quartered in a home "without the consent of the owner" should also bar the police from investigating the intimacies of the marriage relation? The ideal of allowing the State that leeway is congenial only to a totalitarian regime.

I dissent from a dismissal of these cases and our refusal to strike down this law.

Mr. Justice Harlan, dissenting:

I am compelled, with all respect, to dissent from the dismissal of these appeals. In my view the course which the Court has taken does violence to established concepts of "justiciability," and unjustifiably leaves these appellants under the threat of unconstitutional prosecution. Regrettably, an adequate exposition of my views calls for a dissenting opinion of unusual length. . . .

In my view of these cases a present determination of the Constitutional issues is the only course which will advance justice, and I can find no sound reason born of considerations as to the possible inadequacy or ineffectiveness of the judgment that might be rendered which justifies the Court's contrary disposition. While ordinarily I would not deem it appropriate to deal, in dissent, with Constitutional issues which the Court has not reached, I shall do so here because such issues, as I see things, are entangled with the Court's conclusion as to the nonjusticiability of these appeals. . . .

Part One. Justiciability.

·   ·   ·   ·   ·

As far as the record is concerned, I think it is pure conjecture, and indeed conjecture which to me seems contrary to realities, that an open violation of the statute by a doctor (or more obviously still by a birth control clinic) would not result in a substantial threat of prosecution. Crucial to the opposite conclusion is the description of the 1940 prosecution instituted in *State* v. *Nelson*, . . . as a "test case" which, as it is viewed, scarcely even punctuates the uniform State practice of nonenforcement of this statute. I read the history of Connecticut enforcement in a very different light. The *Nelson* case, as appears from the state court's opinion, was a prosecution of two doctors and a nurse for aiding and abetting violations of this statute by married women in prescribing and advising in the use of contraceptive materials by them. It is true that there is evidence of a customary unwillingness to enforce the statute prior to *Nelson*, for in that case the prosecutor stated to the trial court in a later motion to discontinue the prosecutions that "when this Waterbury clinic [operated by the defendants] was opened there were in operation elsewhere in the State at least eight other contraceptive clinics which had been in existence for a long period of time and no question as to their right to operate had been raised. . . ."

What must also be noted is that the prosecutor followed this statement with an explanation that the primary purpose of the prosecution was to provide clear warning to all those who, like Nelson, might rely on this practice of nonenforcement. He stated that the purpose of the prosecution was:

> the establishment of the constitutional validity and efficacy of the statutes under which these accused are informed against. Henceforth any person, whether a physician or layman, who violates the provisions of these statutes, must expect to be prosecuted and punished in accordance with the literal provisions of the law.

Thus the respect in which *Nelson* was a test case is only that it was brought for the purpose of making entirely clear the State's power and willingness to enforce against "*any* person, whether physician or layman" (emphasis supplied), the statute and to eliminate from future cases the very doubt about the existence of these elements which had resulted in eight open birth control clinics, and which would have made unfair the conviction of Nelson.

The plurality opinion now finds, and the concurring opinion must assume, that the only explanation of the absence of recorded prosecutions subsequent to the *Nelson* case is that Connecticut has renounced that intention to prosecute and punish "*any* person . . . in accordance with the literal provisions of the law" which it announced in *Nelson*. But if renunciation of the purposes of the Nelson prosecution is consistent with a lack of subsequent prosecutions, success of that purpose is no less consistent with this lack. I find it difficult to believe that doctors generally—and not just those operating specialized clinics—would continue openly to disseminate advice about contraceptives after *Nelson* in reliance on the State's supposed unwillingness to prosecute, or to consider that high-minded members of the profession would in consequence of such inaction deem themselves warranted in disrespecting this law so long as it is on the books. Nor can I regard as "chimerical" the fear of enforcement of these provisions that seems to have caused the disappearance of at least nine birth control clinics. In short, I fear that the Court has indulged in a bit of sleight-of-hand to be rid of this case. It has treated the significance of the absence of prosecutions during the twenty years since *Nelson* as identical with that of the absence of prosecutions during the years before *Nelson*. It has ignored the fact that the very purpose of the *Nelson* prosecution was to change defiance into compliance. It has ignored the very possibility that this purpose may have been successful. The result is to postulate a security from prosecution for open defiance of the statute which I do not believe the record supports.

These considerations alone serve to bring appellants so squarely within the rule of *Pierce* v. *Society of Sisters*, 268 U.S. 510, and *Truax* v. *Raich*, 239 U.S. 33, that further demonstration would be pointless. . . .

Part Two. *Constitutionality*.

I consider that this Connecticut legislation, as construed to apply to these appellants, violates the Fourteenth Amendment. I believe that a statute making it a criminal offense for *married couples* to use contraceptives is an intolerable and unjustifiable invasion of privacy in the conduct of the most intimate concerns of an individual's personal life. I reach this conclusion, even though I find it difficult and unnecessary at this juncture to accept appellants' other argument that the judgment of policy behind the statute, so applied, is so arbitrary and unreasonable as to render the enactment invalid for that reason alone. Since both the contentions draw their basis in no explicit language of the Constitution, and have yet to find expression in any decision of this Court, I feel it desirable at the outset to state the framework of Constitutional principles in which I think the issue must be judged.

I.

In reviewing state legislation, whether considered to be in the exercise of the State's police powers, or in provision for the health, safety, morals or welfare of its people, it is clear that what is concerned are "the powers of government inherent in every sovereignty." . . . Only to the extent that the Constitution so requires may this Court interfere with the exercise of this plenary power of government. . . . But precisely because it is the Constitution alone which warrants judicial interference in sovereign operations of the State, the basis of judgment as to the Constitutionality of state action must be a rational one, approaching the text which is the only commission for our power not in a literalistic way, as if we had a tax statute before us, but as the basic charter of our society, setting out in spare but meaningful terms the principles of government. . . . But as inescapable as is the rational process in Constitutional adjudication in general, nowhere is it more so than in giving meaning to the prohibitions of the Fourteenth Amendment and, where the Federal Government is involved, the Fifth Amendment, against the deprivation of life, liberty or property without due process of law.

It is but a truism to say that this provision of both Amendments is not self-explanatory. As to the Fourteenth, which is involved here, the history of the Amendment also sheds little light on the meaning of the provision. . . . It is important to note, however, that two views of the Amendment have not been accepted by this Court as delineating its scope. One view, which was ably and insistently argued in response to what were felt to be abuses by this Court of its reviewing power, sought to limit the provision to a guarantee of procedural fairness. . . . The other view which has been rejected would have it that the Fourteenth Amendment, whether by way of the Privileges and Immunities Clause or the Due Process Clause, applied against the States only and precisely those restraints which had prior to the Amendment been applicable merely to federal action. However, "due process" in the consistent view of this Court has ever been a broader concept than the first view and more flexible than the second.

Were due process merely a procedural safeguard it would fail to reach those situations where the deprivation of life, liberty or property was accomplished by legislation which by operating in the future could, given even the fairest possible procedure in application to individuals, nevertheless destroy the enjoyment of all three. . . . Thus the guaranties of due process, though having their roots in Magna Carta's *per legem terrae* and considered as procedural safeguards "against executive usurpation and tyranny," have in this country "become bulwarks also against arbitrary legislation." . . .

However it is not the particular enumeration of rights in the first eight Amendments which spells out the reach of Fourteenth Amendment due process, but rather, as was suggested in another context long before the adoption of that Amendment, those concepts which are considered to embrace the "fundamental rights of free men" *Corfield* v. *Corryell*, 4 Wash. 380, 386, for "the purpose [of securing] which men enter into society," *Calder* v. *Bull*, 3 Dall. 386, 388. Again and again this Court has resisted the notion that the Fourteenth Amendment is no more than a short-hand reference to what is explicitly set out elsewhere in the Bill of Rights. . . . Indeed the fact that an identical provision limiting federal action is found among the first eight Amendments, applying to the Federal Government, suggests that due process is a discrete concept which subsists as an independent guaranty of liberty and procedural fairness more general and inclusive than the specific prohibitions. . . .

Due process has not been reduced to any formula; its content cannot be determined by reference to any code. The best that can be said is that through the course of this Court's decisions it has represented the balance which our Nation, built upon postulates of respect for the liberty of the individual, has struck between that liberty and the demands of organized society. If the supplying of content to this Constitutional concept has of necessity been a rational process, it certainly has not been one where judges have felt free to roam where unguided speculation might take them. The balance of which I speak is the balance struck by this country, having regard to what history teaches are the traditions from which it developed as well as the traditions from which it broke. That tradition is a living thing. A decision of this Court which radically departs from it could not long survive, while a decision which builds on what has survived is likely to be sound. No formula could serve as a substitute, in this area, for judgment and restraint.

It is this outlook which has led the Court continuingly to perceive distinctions in the imperative character of Constitutional provisions, since that character must be discerned from a particular provision's larger context. And inasmuch as this context is one not of words, but of history and purposes, the full scope of the liberty guaranteed by the Due Process Clause cannot be found in or limited by the precise terms of the specific guarantees elsewhere provided in the Constitution. This "liberty" is not a series of isolated points pricked out in terms of the taking of property, the freedom of speech, press, and religion; the right to keep and bear arms; the freedom from unreasonable searches and seizures; and so on. It is a rational continuum which, broadly speaking, includes a freedom from all substantial arbitrary impositions and purposeless restraints, . . . and which also recognizes, what a reasonable and sensitive judgment must, that certain interests require particularly careful scrutiny of the state needs asserted to justify their abridgment. . . .

As was said in *Meyer* v. *Nebraska*, 262 U.S., at 399, "this Court has not attempted to define with exactness the liberty thus guaranteed . . . without doubt it denotes not merely freedom from bodily restraint. . . ." Thus, for instance, when in that case and in *Pierce* v. *Society of Sisters*, 268 U.S. 530, the Court struck down laws which sought not to require what children must learn in schools, but to prescribe, in the first case, what they must *not* learn, and in the second, *where* they must learn it, I do not think it was wrong to put those decisions on "the right of the individual to . . . establish a home and bring up children," . . . or on the basis that "The fundamental theory of liberty upon which all governments in this union repose excludes any general power of the State to standardize the children by forcing them to accept instruction from public teachers only," . . . . I consider this so, even though today those decisions would probably have gone by reference to the concepts of freedom of expression and conscience assured against state action by the Fourteenth Amendment, concepts that are derived from the explicit guarantees of the First Amendment against federal encroachment

upon freedom of speech and belief. . . . For it is the purpose of those
guarantees and not their text, the reasons for their statement by the Framers
and not the statement itself, . . . which have led to their present status in
the compendious notion of "liberty" embraced in the Fourteenth Amendment.

Each new claim to Constitutional protection must be considered against
a background of Constitutional purposes, as they have been rationally perceived and historically developed. Though we exercise limited and sharply
restrained judgment, yet there is no "mechanical yardstick," no "mechanical
answer." The decision of an apparently novel claim must depend on grounds
which follow closely on well-accepted principles and criteria. The new
decision must take "its place in relation to what went before and further
[cut] a channel for what is to come." The matter was well put in *Rochin* v.
California, 342 U.S. 165:

> The vague contours of the Due Process Clause do not leave judges at
> large. We may not draw on our merely personal and private notions
> and disregard the limits that bind judges in their judicial function.
> Even though the concept of due process of law is not final and fixed,
> these limits are derived from considerations that are fused in the whole
> nature of our judicial process. . . . These are considerations rooted in
> reason and in the compelling traditions of the legal profession. . . .

On these premises I turn to the particular Constitutional claim in this case.

II.

Appellants contend that the Connecticut statute deprives them, as it unquestionably does, of a substantial measure of liberty in carrying on the most
intimate of all personal relationships, and that it does so arbitrarily and without any rational, justifying purpose. The State, on the other hand, asserts
that it is acting to protect the moral welfare of its citizenry, both directly,
in that it considers the practice of contraception immoral in itself, and in-
strumentally, in that the availability of contraceptive materials tends to
minimize "the disastrous consequence of dissolute action," that is fornication
and adultery.

It is argued by appellants that the judgment, implicit in this statute—
that the use of contraceptives by married couples is immoral—is an irrational
one, that in effect it subjects them in a very important matter to the arbitrary whim of the legislature, and that it does so for no good purpose. Where,
as here, we are dealing with what must be considered "a basic liberty," . . .
"there are limits to which the presumption of constitutionality can be
pressed," . . . and the mere assertion that the action of the State finds
justification in the controversial realm of morals cannot justify alone any and
every restriction it imposes. . . .

Yet the very inclusion of the category of morality among state concerns
indicates that society is not limited in its objects only to the physical well-
being of the community, but has traditionally concerned itself with the moral

soundness of its people as well. Indeed to attempt a line between public behavior, and that which is purely consensual or solitary, would be to withdraw from community concern a range of subjects with which every society in civilized times has found it necessary to deal. The laws regarding marriage which provide both when the sexual powers may be used and the legal and societal context in which children are born and brought up, as well as laws forbidding adultery, fornication and homosexual practices which express the negative of the proposition, confining sexuality to lawful marriage, form a pattern so deeply pressed into the substance of our social life that any Constitutional doctrine in this area must build upon that basis. . . .

It is in this area of sexual morality, which contains many proscriptions of consensual behavior having little or no direct impact on others, that the State of Connecticut has expressed its moral judgment that all use of contraceptives is improper. Appellants cite an impressive list of authorities who, from a great variety of points of view, commend the considered use of contraceptives by married couples. What they do not emphasize is that not too long ago the current of opinion was very probably quite the opposite, and that even today the issue is not free of controversy. Certainly, Connecticut's judgment is no more demonstrably correct or incorrect than are the varieties of judgment, expressed in law, on marriage and divorce, on adult consensual homosexuality, abortion, and sterilization, or euthanasia and suicide. If we had a case before us which required us to decide simply, and in abstraction, whether the moral judgment implicit in the application of the present statute to married couples was a sound one, the very controversial nature of these questions would, I think, require us to hesitate long before concluding that the Constitution precluded Connecticut from choosing as it has among these various views. . . .

But, as might be expected, we are not presented simply with this moral judgment to be passed on as an abstract proposition. The secular state is not an examiner of consciences: it must operate in the realm of behavior, of overt actions, and where it does so operate, not only the underlying, moral purpose of its operations, but the *choice of means* become relevant to any Constitutional judgment on what is done. The moral presupposition on which appellants ask us to pass judgment could form the basis of a variety of legal rules and administrative choices, each presenting a different issue for adjudication. For example, one practical expression of the moral view propounded here might be the rule that a marriage in which only contraceptive relations had taken place had never been consummated and could be annulled. . . . Again, the use of contraceptives might be made a ground for divorce, or perhaps tax benefits and subsidies could be provided for large families. Other examples also readily suggest themselves.

III.

Precisely what is involved here is this: The State is asserting the right to enforce its moral judgment by intruding upon the most intimate details of the marital relation with the full power of the criminal law. Potentially, this could allow the deployment of all the incidental machinery of the criminal law, arrests, searches and seizures; inevitably, it must mean at the very least the lodging of criminal charges, a public trial, and testimony as to the *corpus delicti*. Nor could any imaginable elaboration of presumption, testimonial privileges, or other safeguards, alleviate the necessity for testimony as to the mode and manner of the married couples' sexual relations, or at least the opportunity for the accused to make denial of the charges. In sum, the statute allows the State to enquire into, prove and punish married people for the private use of their marital intimacy.

This, then, is the precise character of the enactment whose Constitutional measure we must take. The statute must pass a more rigorous Constitutional test than that going merely to the plausibility of its underlying rationale. . . . This enactment involves what, by common understanding throughout the English-speaking world, must be granted to be a most fundamental aspect of "liberty," the privacy of the home in its most basic sense, and it is this which requires that the statute be subjected to "strict scrutiny." . . .

That aspect of liberty which embraces the concept of the privacy of the home receives explicit Constitutional protection at two places only. These are the Third Amendment, relating to the quartering of soldiers,° and the Fourth Amendment, prohibiting unreasonable searches and seizures.† While these Amendments reach only the Federal Government, this Court has held in the strongest terms, and today again confirms, that the concept of "privacy" embodied in the Fourth Amendment is part of the "ordered liberty" assured against state action by the Fourteenth Amendment. . . .

It is clear, of course, that this Connecticut statute does not invade the privacy of the home in the usual sense, since the invasion involved here may, and doubtless usually would, be accomplished without any physical intrusion whatever into the home. What the statute undertakes to do, however, is to create a crime which is grossly offensive to this privacy, while the Constitution refers only to methods of ferreting out substantive wrongs, and the procedure it requires presupposes that substantive offenses may be committed and sought out in the privacy of the home. But such an analysis forecloses any claim to Constitutional protection against this form of deprivation of privacy, only if due process in this respect is limited to what is explicitly provided in the Constitution, divorced from the rational purposes, historical roots, and subsequent developments of the relevant provisions.

Perhaps the most comprehensive statement of the principle of liberty underlying these aspects of the Constitution was given by Mr. Justice Brandeis, dissenting in *Olmstead* v. *United States*, 277 U.S. 438, at 478:

° "No soldier shall, in time of peace be quartered in any house, without the consent of the Owner, nor in time of war, but in a manner to be prescribed by law."

† "The right of the people to be secure in their persons, houses, papers, and effects, against unreasonable searches and seisures, shall not be violated, and no Warrants shall issue, but upon probable cause, supported by Oath or affirmation, and particularly describing the place to be searched, and the persons or things to be seized."

The protection guaranteed by the [Fourth and Fifth] Amendments is much broader in scope. The makers of our Constitution undertook to secure conditions favorable to the pursuit of happiness. They recognized the significance of man's spiritual nature, of his feelings and of his intellect. They knew that only a part of the pain, pleasure and satisfactions of life are to be found in material things. They sought to protect Americans in their beliefs, their thoughts, their emotions and their sensations. They conferred, as against the Government, the right to be let alone—the most comprehensive of rights and the right most valued by civilized men. To protect that right, every unjustifiable intrusion by the Government upon the privacy of the individual, whatever the means employed, must be deemed a violation of the Fourth Amendment. . . .

I think the sweep of the Court's decisions, under both the Fourth and Fourteenth Amendments amply shows that the Constitution protects the privacy of the home against all unreasonable intrusion of whatever character. "[These] principles . . . affect the very essence of constitutional liberty and security. They reach further [a] concrete case . . . before the court with its adventitious circumstances; they apply to all invasions on the part of the government and its employes of the sanctity of a man's home and the privacies of life." . . . "The security of one's privacy against arbitrary intrusion by the police—which is at the heart of the Fourth Amendment—is basic to a free society." . . .

It would surely be an extreme instance of sacrificing substance to form were it to be held that the Constitutional principle of privacy against arbitrary official intrusion comprehends only physical invasions by the police. To be sure, the times presented the Framers with two particular threats to that principle, the general warrant . . . and the quartering of soldiers in private homes. But though "legislation, both statutory and constitutional, is enacted, . . . from an experience of evils, . . . its general language should not, therefore, be necessarily confined to the form that evil had theretofore taken. . . . [A] principle to be vital must be capable of wider application than the mischief which gave it birth." . . .

Although the form of intrusion here—the enactment of a substantive offense—does not, in my opinion, preclude the making of a claim based on the right of privacy embraced in the "liberty" of the Due Process Clause, it must be acknowledged that there is another sense in which it could be argued that this intrusion on privacy differs from what the Fourth Amendment, and the similar concept of the Fourteenth, were intended to protect: here we have not an intrusion into the home so much as on the life which characteristically has its place in the home. But to my mind such a distinction is so insubstantial as to be captious: if the physical curtilage of the home is protected, it is surely as a result of solicitude to protect the privacies of the life within. Certainly the safeguarding of the home does not follow merely from the sanctity of property rights. The home derives its pre-eminence as the seat of family life. And the integrity of that life is something so fundamental that it has been found to draw to its protection the principles of more than one explicitly granted Constitutional right. Thus, Mr. Justice Brandeis, writing of a statute which made "it punishable to teach pacificism in any place [to] a single person . . . no matter what the relation of the parties may be," found such a "statute invades the privacy and freedom of the home. Father and mother may not follow the promptings of religious belief, of conscience or conviction, and teach son or daughter the doctrine of pacificism. If they do, any police officer may summarily arrest them." *Gilbert* v. *Minnesota*, 254 U.S. 325, 335–336 (dissenting opinion). This same principle is expressed in the *Pierce Case* and the *Meyer Case*, both *supra*. These decisions, as was said in *Prince* v. *Massachusetts*, 321 U.S. 158, at 166, "have respected the private realm of family life which the state cannot enter."

Of this whole "private realm of family life" it is difficult to imagine what is more private or more intimate than a husband and wife's marital relations. We would indeed be straining at a gnat and swallowing a camel were we to show concern for the niceties of property law involved in our recent decision, under the Fourth Amendment, in *Chapman* v. *United States*, 365 U.S. 610, and yet fail at least to see any substantial claim here.

Of course, just as the requirement of a warrant is not inflexible in carrying out searches and seizures, . . . so there are countervailing considerations at this more fundamental aspect of the right involved. "The family . . . is not beyond regulation," *Prince v. Massachusetts, supra*, and it would be an absurdity to suggest either that offenses may not be committed in the bosom of the family or that the home can be made a sanctuary for crime. The right of privacy most manifestly is not an absolute. Thus, I would not suggest that adultery, homosexuality, fornication or incest are immune from criminal enquiry, however privately practiced. So much has been explicitly recognized in acknowledging the State's rightful concern for its people's moral welfare. . . . But not to discriminate between what is involved in this case and either the traditional offenses against good morals or crimes which, though they may be committed anywhere, happen to have been committed or concealed in the home, would entirely misconceive the argument that is being made.

Adultery, homosexuality and the like are sexual intimacies which the State forbids altogether, but the intimacy of husband and wife is necessarily an essential and accepted feature of the institution of marriage, an institution which the State not only must allow, but which always and in every age it has fostered and protected. It is one thing when the State exerts its power either to forbid extra-marital sexuality altogether, or to say who may marry, but it is quite another when, having acknowledged a marriage and the intimacies inherent in it, it undertakes to regulate by means of the criminal law the details of that intimacy.

In sum, even though the State has determined that the use of contraceptives is as iniquitous as any act of extra-marital sexual immorality, the intrusion of the whole machinery of the criminal law into the very heart of marital privacy, requiring husband and wife to render account before a criminal tribunal of their uses of that intimacy, is surely a very different thing indeed from punishing those who establish intimacies which the law has always forbidden and which can have no claim to social protection.

In my view the appellants have presented a very pressing claim for Constitutional protection. Such difficulty as the claim presents lies only in evaluating it against the State's countervailing contention that it be allowed to enforce, by whatever means it deems appropriate, its judgment of the immorality of the practice this law condemns. In resolving this conflict a number of factors compel me to conclude that the decision here must most emphatically be for the appellants. Since, as it appears to me, the statute marks an abridgment of important fundamental liberties protected by the Fourteenth Amendment, it will not do to urge in justification of that abridgment simply that the statute is rationally related to the effectuation of a proper state purpose. A closer scrutiny and stronger justification than that are required. . . .

Though the State has argued the Constitutional permissibility of the moral judgment underlying this statute, neither its brief, nor its argument, nor anything in any of the opinions of its highest court in these or other cases even remotely suggests a justification for the obnoxiously intrusive means it has chosen to effectuate that policy. To me the very circumstance that Connecticut has not chosen to press the enforcement of this statute against individual users, while it nevertheless persists in asserting its right to do so at any time—in effect a right to hold this statute as an imminent threat to the privacy of the households of the State—conduces to the inference either that it does not consider the policy of the statute a very important one, or that it does not regard the means it has chosen for its effectuation as appropriate or necessary.

But conclusive, in my view, is the utter novelty of this enactment. Although the Federal Government and many States have at one time or other had on their books statutes forbidding or regulating the distribution of contraceptives, none, so far as I can find, has made the *use* of contraceptives a crime. Indeed, a diligent search has revealed that no nation, including several who quite evidently share Connecticut's moral policy, has seen fit to effectuate that policy by the means presented here.

Though undoubtedly the States are and should be left free to reflect a wide variety of policies, and should be allowed broad scope in experimenting with various means of promoting those policies, I must agree with Justice Jackson that "there are limits to the extent to which a legislatively represented majority may conduct . . . experiments at the expense of the dignity and personality" of the individual. . . . In this instance these limits are, in my view, reached and passed.

I would adjudicate these appeals and hold this statute unconstitutional, insofar as it purports to make criminal the conduct contemplated by these married women. It follows that if their conduct cannot be a crime, appellant Buxton cannot be an accomplice thereto. I would reverse the judgment in each of these cases.

Date Due